S0-BKI-331

THE OFFICIAL®
1999 PRICE GUIDE TO

BASKETBALL CARDS

BY
DR. JAMES BECKETT

EIGHTH EDITION

HOUSE OF COLLECTIBLES
THE BALLANTINE PUBLISHING GROUP • NEW YORK

Important Notice: All of the information, including valuations, in this book has been compiled from the most reliable sources, and every effort has been made to eliminate errors and questionable data. Nevertheless, the possibility of error in a work of such scope always exists. The publisher will not be held responsible for losses which may occur in the purchase, sale or other transaction of items because of information contained herein. Readers who feel they have discovered errors are invited to write and inform us, so that they may be corrected in subsequent editions. Those seeking further information on the topics covered in this book are advised to refer to the complete line of *Official Price Guides* published by the House of Collectibles.

© 1998 by James Beckett III

All rights reserved under International
and Pan-American Copyright Conventions.

 This is a registered trademark of Random House, Inc.

Published by:
House of Collectibles
The Ballantine Publishing Group
201 East 50th Street
New York, New York 10022

Distributed by The Ballantine Publishing Group,
a division of Random House, Inc.,
New York, and simultaneously in Canada by
Random House of Canada Limited, Toronto.

Manufactured in the United States of America

ISSN: 1062-6980

ISBN: 0-676-60147-2

Cover design by Min Choi

Cover photo © Rocky Widner/Active Images, Inc.

Eighth Edition: December 1998

10 9 8 7 6 5 4 3 2 1

Table of Contents

About the Author

Jim Beckett, the leading authority on sport card values in the United States, maintains a wide range of activities in the world of sports. He possesses one of the finest collections of sports cards and autographs in the world, has made numerous appearances on radio and television, and has been frequently cited in many national publications. He was awarded the first "Special Achievement Award" for Contributions to the Hobby by the National Sports Collectors Convention in 1980, the "Jock-Jaspersen Award" for Hobby Dedication in 1983, and the "Buck Barker, Spirit of the Hobby Award" in 1991.

Dr. Beckett is the author of *Beckett Baseball Card Price Guide, The Official Price Guide to Baseball Cards, The Sport Americana Price Guide to Baseball Collectibles, The Sport Americana Baseball Memorabilia and Autograph Price Guide, Beckett Football Card Price Guide, The Official Price Guide to Football Cards, Beckett Hockey Card Price Guide, The Official Price Guide to Hockey Cards, Beckett Basketball Card Price Guide, The Official Price Guide to Basketball Cards, and The Sport Americana Baseball Card Alphabetical Checklist*. In addition, he is the founder, publisher, and editor of *Beckett Baseball Card Monthly,*

Beckett Basketball Monthly, Beckett Football Card Monthly, Beckett Hockey Monthly, Beckett Sports Collectibles and Autographs, Beckett Racing Monthly magazines, and *Beckett Hot Toys*.

Jim Beckett received his Ph.D. in Statistics from Southern Methodist University in 1975. Prior to starting Beckett Publications in 1984, Dr. Beckett served as an Associate Professor of Statistics at Bowling Green State University and as a Vice President of a consulting firm in Dallas, Texas. He currently resides in Dallas with his wife, Patti, and their daughters, Christina, Rebecca, and Melissa.

How to Use This Book

Isn't it great? Every year this book gets bigger and bigger with all the new sets coming out. But even more exciting is that every year there are more attractive choices and, subsequently, more interest in the cards we love so much. This edition has been enhanced and expanded from the previous edition. The cards you collect — who appears on them, what they look like, where they are from, and (most important to most of you) what their current values are — are enumerated within. Many of the features contained in the other *Beckett Price Guides* have been incorporated into this volume since condition grading, terminology, and many other aspects of collecting are common to the card hobby in general. We hope you find the book both interesting and useful in your collecting pursuits.

The Beckett Guide has been successful where other attempts have failed because it is complete, current, and valid. This Price Guide contains not just one, but three prices by condition for all the basketball cards listed. These account for most of the basketball cards in existence. The prices were added to the card lists just prior to printing and reflect not the author's opinions or desires but the going retail prices for each card, based on the marketplace (sports memorabilia conventions and shows, sports card shops, hobby papers, current mail-order catalogs, local club meetings, auction results, and other firsthand reportings of actually realized prices).

What is the best price guide available on the market today? Of course card sellers will prefer the price guide with the highest prices, while card buyers will naturally prefer the one with the lowest prices. Accuracy, however, is the true test. Use the price guide used by more collectors and dealers than all the others combined. Look for the Beckett name. I won't put my name on anything I won't stake my reputation on. Not the lowest and not the highest — but the most accurate, with integrity.

To facilitate your use of this book, read the complete introductory section on the following pages before going to the pricing pages. Every collectible field has its own terminology; we've tried to capture most of these terms and definitions in our glossary. Please read carefully the section on grading and the condition of your cards, as you will not be able to determine which price column is appropriate for a given card without first knowing its condition.

Introduction

Welcome to the exciting world of sports card collecting, one of America's most popular avocations. You have made a good choice in buying this book, since it will open up to you the entire panorama of this field in the simplest, most concise way.

The growth of *Beckett Baseball Card Monthly, Beckett Basketball Monthly, Beckett Football Card Monthly, Beckett Hockey Monthly, Beckett*

Sports Collectibles and Autographs, Beckett Racing Monthly and *Beckett Hot Toys* is another indication of the unprecedented popularity of sports cards. Founded in 1984 by Dr. James Beckett, the author of this Price Guide, *Beckett Baseball Card Monthly* contains the most extensive and accepted monthly Price Guide, collectible glossy superstar covers, colorful feature articles, "Hot List," Convention Calendar, tips for beginners, "Readers Write" letters to and responses from the editor, information on errors and varieties, autograph collecting tips and profiles of the sport's Hottest stars. Published every month, *BBCM* is the hobby's largest paid circulation periodical. The other five magazines were built on the success of *BBCM*.

So collecting sports cards — while still pursued as a hobby with youthful exuberance by kids in the neighborhood — has also taken on the trappings of an industry, with thousands of full- and part-time card dealers, as well as vendors of supplies, clubs and conventions. In fact, each year since 1980 thousands of hobbyists have assembled for a National Sports Collectors Convention, at which hundreds of dealers have displayed their wares, seminars have been conducted, autographs penned by sports notables, and millions of cards changed hands.

The Beckett Guide is the best annual guide available to the exciting world of basketball cards. Read it and use it. May your enjoyment and your card collection increase in the coming months and years.

How to Collect

Each collection is personal and reflects the individuality of its owner. There are no set rules on how to collect cards. Since card collecting is a hobby or leisure pastime, what you collect, how much you collect, and how much time and money you spend collecting are entirely up to you. The funds you have available for collecting and your own personal taste should determine how you collect. The information and ideas presented here are intended to help you get the most enjoyment from this hobby.

It is impossible to collect every card ever produced. Therefore, beginners as well as intermediate and advanced collectors usually specialize in some way. One of the reasons this hobby is popular is that individual collectors can define and tailor their collecting methods to match their own tastes. To give you some ideas of the various approaches to collecting, we will list some of the more popular areas of specialization.

Many collectors select complete sets from particular years. For example, they may concentrate on assembling complete sets from all the years since their birth or since they became avid sports fans. They may try to collect a card for every player during that specified period of time. Many others wish to acquire only certain players. Usually such players are the superstars of the sport, but occasionally collectors will specialize in all the cards of players who attended a particular college or came from a certain town. Some collectors are only interested in the first cards or Rookie Cards of certain players.

Another fun way to collect cards is by team. Most fans have a favorite team, and it is natural for that loyalty to be translated into a desire for cards of the players on that favorite team. For most of the recent years, team sets (all the cards from a given team for that year) are readily available at a reasonable price. *The Sport Americana Team Football* and *Basketball Card Checklist* will open up this field to the collector.

Obtaining Cards

Several avenues are open to card collectors. Cards still can be purchased in the traditional way: by the pack at the local discount, grocery or convenience stores. But there are also thousands of card shops across the country that specialize in selling cards individually or by the pack, box, or set. Another alternative is the thousands of card shows held each month around the country, which feature anywhere from five to 800 tables of sports cards and memorabilia for sale.

For many years, it has been possible to purchase complete sets of cards through mail-order advertisers found in traditional sports media publications, such as *The Sporting News, Basketball Digest, Street & Smith* yearbooks, and others. These sets also are advertised in the card collecting periodicals. Many collectors will begin by subscribing to at least one of the hobby periodicals, all with good up-to-date information. In fact, subscription offers can be found in the advertising section of this book.

Most serious card collectors obtain old (and new) cards from one or more of several main sources: (1) trading or buying from other collectors or dealers; (2) responding to sale or auction ads in the hobby publications; (3) buying at a local hobby store; and/or (4) attending sports collectibles shows or conventions.

We advise that you try all four methods since each has its own distinct advantages: (1) trading is a great way to make new friends; (2) hobby periodicals help you keep up with what's going on in the hobby (including when and where the conventions are happening); (3) stores provide the opportunity to enjoy personalized service and consider a great diversity of material in a relaxed sports-oriented atmosphere; and (4) shows allow you to choose from multiple dealers and thousands of cards under one roof in a competitive situation.

Preserving Your Cards

Cards are fragile. They must be handled properly in order to retain their value. Careless handling can easily result in creased or bent cards. It is, however, not recommended that tweezers or tongs be used to pick up your cards since such utensils might mar or indent card surfaces and thus reduce those cards' conditions and values. In general, your cards should be handled directly as little as possible. This is sometimes easier to say than to do.

Although there are still many who use custom boxes, storage trays, or even shoe boxes, plastic sheets are the preferred method of many collectors for storing cards. A collection stored in plastic pages in a three-ring album allows you to view your collection at any time without the need to touch the card itself. Cards can also be kept in single holders (of various types and thickness) designed for the enjoyment of each card individually. For a large collection, some collectors may use a combination of the above methods. When purchasing plastic sheets for your cards, be sure that you find the pocket size that fits the cards snugly. Don't put your 1969-70 Topps in a sheet designed to fit 1992-93 Topps.

Most hobby and collectibles shops and virtually all collectors' conventions will have these plastic pages available in quantity for the various sizes offered, or you can purchase them directly from the advertisers in this book. Also, remember that pocket size isn't the only factor to consider when looking for plastic sheets. Other factors such as safety, economy, appearance, availability, or personal preference also may indicate which types of sheets a collector may want to buy.

Damp, sunny and/or hot conditions — no, this is not a weather forecast — are three elements to avoid in extremes if you are interested in preserving your collection. Too much (or too little) humidity can cause gradual deterioration of a card. Direct, bright sun (or fluorescent light) over time will bleach out the color of a card. Extreme heat accelerates the decomposition of the card. On the other hand, many cards have lasted more than 50 years without much scientific intervention. So be cautious, even if the above factors typically present a problem only when present in the extreme. It never hurts to be prudent.

Collecting vs. Investing

Collecting individual players and collecting complete sets are both popular vehicles for investment and speculation. Most investors and speculators stock up on complete sets or on quantities of players they think have good investment potential.

There is obviously no guarantee in this book, or anywhere else for that matter, that cards will outperform the stock market or other investment alternatives in the future. After all, basketball cards do not pay quarterly dividends and cards cannot be sold at their "current values" as easily as stocks or bonds.

Nevertheless, investors have noticed a favorable long-term trend in the past performance of sports collectibles, and certain cards and sets have outperformed just about any other investment in some years. Many hobbyists maintain that the best investment is and always will be the building of a collection, which traditionally has held up better than outright speculation.

Some of the obvious questions are: Which cards? When to buy? When to sell? The best investment you can make is in your own education. The more you know about your collection and the hobby, the more informed the decisions you will be able to make. We're not selling investment tips. We're selling information about the current value of basketball cards. It's up to you to use that information to your best advantage.

Glossary/Legend

Our glossary defines terms frequently used in the card collecting hobby. Many of these terms are also common to other types of sports memorabilia collecting. Some terms may have several meanings depending on use and context.

ABA - American Basketball Association.

ACC - Accomplishment.

ACO - Assistant Coach Card.

AL - Active Leader.

ART - All-Rookie Team.

AS - All-Star.

ASA - All-Star Advice.

ASW - All-Star Weekend.

AUTO - Autograph.

AW - Award Winner.

B - Bronze.

BC - Bonus Card.

BRICK - A group or "lot" or cards, usually 50 or more having common characteristics, that is intended to be bought, sold, or traded as a unit.

BT - Beam Team or Breakaway Threats.

CB - Collegiate Best.

CBA - Continental Basketball Association.

CL - Checklist card. A card that lists in order the cards and players in the set or series. Older checklist cards in Mint condition that have not been checked off are very desirable and command large premiums.

CO - Coach card.

COIN - A small disc of metal or plastic portraying a player in its center.

COLLECTOR - A person who engages in the hobby of collecting cards primarily for his own enjoyment, with any profit motive being secondary.

COMBINATION CARD - A single card depicting two or more players (not including team cards).

COMMON CARD - The typical card of any set; it has no premium value accruing from subject matter, numerical scarcity, popular demand, or anomaly.

CONVENTION ISSUE - A set produced in conjunction with a sports collectibles convention to commemorate or promote the show. Most recent convention issues could also be classified as promo sets.

COR - Corrected card. A version of an error card that was fixed by the manufacturer.

COUPON - See Tab.

CY - City Lights.

DEALER - A person who engages in buying, selling, and trading sports collectibles or supplies. A dealer may also be a collector, but as a dealer, he anticipates a profit.

DIE-CUT - A card with part of its stock partially cut for ornamental reasons.

DISC - A circular-shaped card.

DISPLAY SHEET - A clear, plastic page that is punched for insertion into a binder (with standard three-ring spacing) containing pockets for displaying cards. Many different styles of sheets exist with pockets of varying sizes to hold the many differing card formats. The vast majority of current cards measure 2 1/2 by 3 1/2 inches and fit in nine-pocket sheets.

DP - Double Print. A card that was printed in approximately double the quantity compared to other cards in the same series, or draft pick card.

ERR - Error card. A card with erroneous information, spelling, or depiction on either side of the card. Most errors are never corrected by the producing card company.

EXCH - An exchange card that is inserted into packs that can be redeemed for something else–usually a set or autograph.

FIN - Finals.

FLB - Flashback.

FPM - Future Playoff MVP's.

FSL - Future Scoring Leaders.

FULL SHEET - A complete sheet of cards that has not been cut into individual cards by the manufacturer. Also called an uncut sheet.

G - Gold.

GQ - Gentleman's Quarterly.

GRA - Grace.

HL - Highlight card.

HOF - Hall of Fame, or Hall of Famer (also abbreviated HOFer).

HOR - Horizontal pose on a card as opposed to the standard vertical orientation found on most cards.

IA - In Action card. A special type of card depicting a player in an action photo, such as the 1982 Topps cards.

INSERT - A card of a different type, e.g., a poster, or any other sports collectible contained and sold in the same package along with a card or cards of a major set.

IS - Inside Stuff.

ISSUE - Synonymous with set, but usually used in conjunction with a manufacturer, e.g., a Topps issue.

JWA - John Wooden Award.

KID - Kid Picture card.

LEGITIMATE ISSUE - A set produced to promote or boost sales of a product or service, e.g., bubble gum, cereal, cigarettes, etc. Most collector issues are not legitimate issues in this sense.

LID - A circular-shaped card (possibly with tab) that forms the top of the container for the product being promoted.

MAG - Magic of SkyBox cards.

MAJOR SET - A set produced by a national manufacturer of cards, containing a large number of cards. Usually 100 or more different cards comprise a major set.

MC - Members Choice.

MEM - Memorial.

MO - McDonald's Open.

MINI - A small card or stamp (the 1991-92 SkyBox Canadian set, for example).

MVP - Most Valuable Player.

NNO - No number on back.

NY - New York.

OBVERSE - The front, face, or pictured side of the card.

OLY - Olympic card.

PANEL - An extended card that is composed of multiple individual cards.

PC - Poster card.

PERIPHERAL SET - A loosely defined term that applies to any non-regular issue set. This term most often is used to describe food issue, giveaway, regional or sendaway sets that contain a fairly small number of cards and are not accepted by the hobby as major sets.

PF - Pacific Finest.

POY - Player of the Year.

PREMIUM - A card, sometimes on photographic stock, that is purchased or obtained in conjunction with (or redeemed for) another card or product. This term applies mainly to older products, as newer cards distributed in this manner are generally lumped together as peripheral sets.

PREMIUM CARDS - A class of products introduced recently, intended to have higher quality card stock and photography than regular cards, but more limited production and higher cost. Defining what is and isn't a premium card is somewhat subjective.

PROMOTIONAL SET - A set, usually containing a small number of cards, issued by a national card producer and distributed in limited quantities or to a select group of people, such as major show attendees or dealers with wholesale accounts. Presumably, the purpose of a promo set is to stir up demand for an upcoming set. Also called a preview, prototype, promo, or test set.

QP - Quadruple Print. A card that was printed in approximately four times the quantity compared to other cards in the same series.

RARE - A card or series of cards of very limited availability. Unfortunately, "rare" is a subjective term sometimes used indiscriminately. Using the strict definitions, rare cards are harder to obtain than scarce cards.

RC - Rookie Card. A player's first appearance on a regular issue card from one of the major card companies. Each company has only one regular issue set per season, and that is the widely available traditional set. With a few exceptions, each player has only one RC in any given set. A Rookie Card cannot be an All-Star, Highlight, In Action, League Leader, Super Action or Team Leader card. It can, however, be a coach card or draft pick card.

REGIONAL - A card issued and distributed only in a limited geographical area of the country. The producer may or may not be a major, national producer of trading cards. The key is whether the set was distributed nationally in any form or not.

REVERSE - The back or narrative side of the card.

REV NEG - Reversed or flopped photo side of the card. This is a common type of error card, but only some are corrected.

RIS - Rising Star.

ROY - Rookie of the Year.

S - Silver.

SA - Super Action card. Similar to an In Action card.

SAL - SkyBox Salutes.

SASE - Self-addressed, stamped envelope.

SCARCE - A card or series of cards of limited availability. This subjective term is sometimes used indiscriminately to promote or hype value. Using strict definitions, scarce cards are easier to obtain than rare cards.

SERIES - The entire set of cards issued by a particular producer in a particular year, e.g., the 1978-79 Topps series. Also, within a particular set, series can refer to a group of (consecutively numbered) cards printed at the same time, e.g., the first series of the 1972-73 Topps set (#1 through #132).

SET - One each of an entire run of cards of the same type, produced by a particular manufacturer during a single season. In other words, if you have a complete set of 1989-90 Fleer cards, then you have every card from #1 up to and including #132; i.e., all the different cards that were produced.

SHOOT - Shooting Star.

SHOW - A large gathering of dealers and collectors at a single location for the purpose of buying, selling, and trading sorts cards and memorabilia. Conventions are open to the public and sometimes also feature autograph guests, door prizes, films, contests, etc. (Or, Showcase, as in 1996–97 Flair Showcase).

SKED - Schedules.

SP - Single or Short Print. A card which was printed in lesser quantity compared to the other cards in the same series (also see DP). This term only can be used in a relative sense and in reference to one particular set. For instance, the 1989-90 Hoops Pistons Championship card (#353A) is less common than the other cards in that set, but it isn't necessarily scarcer than regular cards of any other set.

SPECIAL CARD - A card that portrays something other than a single player or team.

SS - Star Stats.

STANDARD SIZE - The standard size for sports cards is 2 1/2 by 3 1/2 inches. All exceptions, such as 1969-70 Topps, are noted in card descriptions.

STAR CARD - A card that portrays a player of some repute, usually determined by his ability, but sometimes referring to sheer popularity.

STAY - Stay in School.

STICKER - A card-like item with a removable layer that can be affixed to another surface. Example: 1986-87 through 1989-90 Fleer bonus cards.

STOCK - The cardboard or paper on which the card is printed.

STY - Style.

SUPERSTAR CARD - A card that portrays a superstar, e.g., a Hall of Fame member or a player whose current performance may eventually warrant serious Hall of Fame consideration.

SY - Schoolyard Stars.

TC - Team card or team checklist card.

TD - Triple Double. A term used for having double digit totals in three categories.

TEAM CARD - A card that depicts an entire team, notably the 1989-90 and 1990-91 NBA Hoops Detroit Pistons championship cards and the 1991-92 NBA Hoops subset.

TEST SET - A set, usually containing a small number of cards, issued by a national producer and distributed in a limited section of the country or to a select group of people. Presumably, the purpose of a test set is to measure market appeal for a particular type of card. Also called a promo or prototype set.

TFC - Team Fact card.

TL - Team Leader.

TO - Tip-off.

TR - Traded card.

TRIB - Tribune.

TRV - Trivia.

TT - Team Tickets card.

UER - Uncorrected Error card.

USA - Team USA.

VAR - Variation card. One of two or more cards from the same series, with the same card number (or player with identical pose, if the series is unnumbered) differing from one another in some aspect, from the printing, stock or other feature of the card. This is often caused when the manufacturer of the cards notices an error in a particular card, corrects the error and then resumes the print run. In this case there will be two versions or variations of the same card. Sometimes one of the variations is relatively scarce. Variations also can result from accidental or deliberate design changes, information updates, photo substitutions, etc.

VERT - Vertical pose on a card.

XRC - Extended Rookie Card. A player's first appearance on a card, but issued in a set that was not distributed nationally nor in packs. In basketball sets, this term only refers to the 1983, '84 and '85 Star Company sets.

YB - Yearbook.

20A - Twenty assist club.

50P - Fifty point club.

6M - Sixth Man.

! - Condition sensitive card or set *(see Grading Your Cards)*.

* - Multi-sport set.

Understanding Card Values

Determining Value

Why are some cards more valuable than others? Obviously, the economic laws of supply and demand are applicable to card collecting just as they are to any other field where a commodity is bought, sold or traded in a free, unregulated market.

Supply (the number of cards available on the market) is less than the total number of cards originally produced since attrition diminishes that original quantity. Each year a percentage of cards is typically thrown away, destroyed or otherwise lost to collectors. This percentage is much, much smaller today than it was in the past because more and more people have become increasingly aware of the value of their cards.

For those who collect only Mint condition cards, the supply of older cards can be quite small indeed. Until recently, collectors were not so conscious of the need to preserve the condition of their cards. For this reason, it is difficult to know exactly how many 1957-58 Topps are currently available, Mint or otherwise. It is generally accepted that there are fewer 1957-58 Topps available than 1969-70, 1979-80 or 1992-93 Topps cards. If demand were equal for each of these sets, the law of supply and demand would increase the price for the least available sets.

Demand, however, is never equal for all sets, so price correlations can be complicated. The demand for a card is influenced by many factors. These include: (1) the age of the card; (2) the number of cards printed; (3) the player(s) portrayed on the card; (4) the attractiveness and popularity of the set; and (5) the physical condition of the card.

In general, (1) the older the card, (2) the fewer the number of the cards printed, (3) the more famous, popular and talented the player, (4) the more attractive and popular the set, and (5) the better the condition of the card, the higher the value of the card will be. There are exceptions to all but one of these factors: the condition of the card. Given two cards similar in all respects except condition, the one in the best condition will always be valued higher.

While those guidelines help to establish the value of a card, the countless exceptions and peculiarities make any simple, direct mathematical formula to determine card values impossible.

Regional Variation

Since the market varies from region to region, card prices of local players may be higher. This is known as a regional premium. How significant the premium is — and if there is any premium at all — depends on the local popularity of the team and the player.

The largest regional premiums usually do not apply to superstars, who often are so well known nationwide that the prices of their key cards are too high for local dealers to realize a premium.

Lesser stars often command the strongest premiums. Their popularity is concentrated in their home region, creating local demand that greatly exceeds overall demand.

Regional premiums can apply to popular retired players and sometimes can be found in the areas where the players grew up or starred in college.

A regional discount is the converse of a regional premium. Regional discounts occur when a player has been so popular in his region for so long that local collectors and dealers have accumulated quantities of his cards. The abundant supply may make the cards available in that area at the lowest prices anywhere.

Set Prices

A somewhat paradoxical situation exists in the price of a complete set vs. the combined cost of the individual cards in the set. In nearly every case, the sum of the prices for the individual cards is higher than the cost for the complete set. This is prevalent especially in the cards of the past few years. The reasons for this apparent anomaly stem from the habits of collectors and from the carrying costs to dealers. Today, each card in a set normally is produced in the same quantity as all others in its set.

Many collectors pick up only stars, superstars and particular teams. As a result, the dealer is left with a shortage of certain player cards and an abundance of others. He therefore incurs an expense in simply "carrying" these less desirable cards in stock. On the other hand, if he sells a complete set, he gets rid of large numbers of cards at one time. For this reason, he generally is willing to receive less money for a complete set. By doing this, he recovers all of his costs and also makes a profit.

Set prices do not include rare card varieties, unless specifically stated. Of course, the prices for sets do include one example of each type for the given set, but this is the least expensive variety.

For some sets, a complete set price is not listed. This is due to sets currently not trading on the market in that form. Usually, the sets that have low serial number print runs do not have complete set prices.

Centering

Well-centered

Slightly off-centered

Off-centered

Badly off-centered

Miscut

Scarce Series

Only a select few basketball sets contain scarce series: 1948 Bowman, 1970-71 and 1972-73 Topps, 1983-84, 1984-85 and 1985-86 Star. The 1948 Bowman set was printed on two 36-card sheets, the second of which was issued in significantly lower quantities. The two Topps scarce series are only marginally tougher than the set as a whole. The Star Company scarcities relate to particular team sets that, to different extents, were less widely distributed.

We are always looking for information or photographs of printing sheets of cards for research. Each year, we try to update the hobby's knowledge of distribution anomalies. Please let us know at the address in this book if you have first-hand knowledge that would be helpful in this pursuit.

Grading Your Cards

Each hobby has its own grading terminology — stamps, coins, comic books, record collecting, etc. Collectors of sports cards are no exception. The one invariable criterion for determining the value of a card is its condition: the better the condition of the card, the more valuable it is. Condition grading, however, is subjective. Individual card dealers and collectors differ in the strictness of their grading, but the stated condition of a card should be determined without regard to whether it is being bought or sold.

No allowance is made for age. A 1961-62 Fleer card is judged by the same standards as a 1991-92 Fleer card. But there are specific sets and cards that are condition sensitive (marked with "!" in the Price Guide) because of their border color, consistently poor centering, etc. Such cards and sets sometimes command premiums above the listed percentages in Mint condition.

Centering

Current centering terminology uses numbers representing the percentage of border on either side of the main design. Obviously, centering is diminished in importance for borderless cards such as Stadium Club.

Slightly Off-Center (60/40): A slightly off-center card is one that upon close inspection is found to have one border bigger than the opposite border. This degree once was offensive to only purists, but now some hobbyists try to avoid cards that are anything other than perfectly centered.

Off-Center (70/30): An off-center card has one border that is noticeably more than twice as wide as the opposite border.

Badly Off-Center (80/20 or worse): A badly off-center card has virtually no border on one side of the card.

Miscut: A miscut card actually shows part of the adjacent card in its larger border and consequently a corresponding amount of its card is cut off.

Corner Wear

Corner wear is the most scrutinized grading criteria in the hobby. These are the major categories of corner wear:

Corner with a slight touch of wear: The corner still is sharp, but there is a slight touch of wear showing. On a dark-bordered card, this shows as a dot of white.

Fuzzy corner: The corner still comes to a point, but the point has just begun to fray. A slightly "dinged" corner is considered the same as a fuzzy corner.

Slightly rounded corner: The fraying of the corner has increased to where there is only a hint of a point. Mild layering may be evident. A "dinged" corner is considered the same as a slightly rounded corner.

Rounded corner: The point is completely gone. Some layering is noticeable.

Corner Wear

The partial cards here have been photographed at 300%. This was done in order to magnify each card's corner wear to such a degree that differences could be shown on a printed page.

This 1986-87 Fleer Mark Aguirre card has a touch of wear. Notice the extremely slight fraying on the corner.

This 1986-87 Fleer Isiah Thomas card has a fuzzy corner. Notice that there is no longer a sharp corner.

This 1986-87 Fleer Wayman Tisdale card has a slightly rounded corner evident by the lack of a sharp point and heavy wear on both edges.

This 1986-87 Fleer Herb Williams card displays a badly rounded corner. Notice a large portion of missing cardboard accompanied by heavy wear and excessive fraying.

This 1986-87 Fleer Maurice Cheeks card displays several creases of varying degrees. Light creases (middle of the card) may not break the card's surface, while heavy creases (right side) will.

Badly rounded corner: The corner is completely round and rough. Severe layering is evident.

Creases

A third common defect is the crease. The degree of creasing in a card is difficult to show in a drawing or picture. On giving the specific condition of an expensive card for sale, the seller should note any creases additionally. Creases can be categorized as to severity according to the following scale.

Light Crease: A light crease is a crease that is barely noticeable upon close inspection. In fact, when cards are in plastic sheets or holders, a light crease may not be seen (until the card is taken out of the holder). A light crease on the front is much more serious than a light crease on the card back only.

Medium Crease: A medium crease is noticeable when held and studied at arm's length by the naked eye, but does not overly detract from the appearance of the card. It is an obvious crease, but not one that breaks the picture surface of the card.

Heavy Crease: A heavy crease is one that has torn or broken through the card's picture surface, e.g., puts a tear in the photo surface.

Alterations

Deceptive Trimming: This occurs when someone alters the card in order (1) to shave off edge wear, (2) to improve the sharpness of the corners, or (3) to improve centering — obviously their objective is to falsely increase the perceived value of the card to an unsuspecting buyer. The shrinkage usually is evident only if the trimmed card is compared to an adjacent full-sized card or if the trimmed card is itself measured.

Obvious Trimming: Obvious trimming is noticeable and unfortunate. It is usually performed by non-collectors who give no thought to the present or future value of their cards.

Deceptively Retouched Borders: This occurs when the borders (especially on those cards with dark borders) are touched up on the edges and corners with magic marker or crayons of appropriate color in order to make the card appear to be Mint.

Categorization of Defects

Miscellaneous Flaws

The following are common minor flaws that, depending on severity, lower a card's condition by one to four grades and often render it no better than Excellent-Mint: bubbles (lumps in surface), gum and wax stains, diamond cutting (slanted borders), notching, off-centered backs, paper wrinkles, scratched-off cartoons or puzzles on back, rubber band marks, scratches, surface impressions and warping.

The following are common serious flaws that, depending on severity, lower a card's condition at least four grades and often render it no better than Good: chemical or sun fading, erasure marks, mildew, miscutting (severe off-centering), holes, bleached or retouched borders, tape marks, tears, trimming, water or coffee stains and writing.

Condition Guide

Grades

Mint (Mt) - A card with no flaws or wear. The card has four perfect corners, 55/45 or better centering from top to bottom and from left to right, original gloss, smooth edges and original color borders. A Mint card does not have print spots, color or focus imperfections.

Near Mint-Mint (NrMt-Mt) - A card with one minor flaw. Any one of the following would lower a Mint card to Near Mint-Mint: one corner with a slight touch of wear, barely noticeable print spots, color or focus imperfections. The card must have 60/40 or better centering in both directions, original gloss, smooth edges and original color borders.

Near Mint (NrMt) - A card with one minor flaw. Any one of the following would lower a Mint card to Near Mint: one fuzzy corner or two to four corners with slight touches of wear, 70/30 to 60/40 centering, slightly rough edges, minor print spots, color or focus imperfections. The card must have original gloss and original color borders.

Excellent-Mint (ExMt) - A card with two or three fuzzy, but not rounded, corners and centering no worse than 80/20. The card may have no more than two of the following: slightly rough edges, very slightly discolored borders, minor print spots, color or focus imperfections. The card must have original gloss.

Excellent (Ex) - A card with four fuzzy but definitely not rounded corners and centering no worse than 80/20. The card may have a small amount of original gloss lost, rough edges, slightly discolored borders and minor print spots, color or focus imperfections.

Very Good (Vg) - A card that has been handled but not abused: slightly rounded corners with slight layering, slight notching on edges, a significant amount of gloss lost from the surface but no scuffing and moderate discoloration of borders. The card may have a few light creases.

Good (G), Fair (F), Poor (P) - A well-worn, mishandled or abused card: badly rounded and layered corners, scuffing, most or all original gloss missing, seriously discolored borders, moderate or heavy creases, and one or more serious flaws. The grade of Good, Fair or Poor depends on the severity of wear and flaws. Good, Fair and Poor cards generally are used only as fillers.

The most widely used grades are defined above. Obviously, many cards will not perfectly fit one of the definitions.

Therefore, categories between the major grades known as in-between grades are used, such as Good to Very Good (G-Vg), Very Good to Excellent (VgEx), and Excellent-Mint to Near Mint (ExMt-NrMt). Such grades indicate a card with all qualities of the lower category but with at least a few qualities of the higher category.

This Price Guide book lists each card and set in three grades, with the middle grade valued at about 40-45% of the top grade, and the bottom grade valued at about 10-15% of the top grade.

The value of cards that fall between the listed columns can also be calculated using a percentage of the top grade. For example, a card that falls between the top and middle grades (Ex, ExMt or NrMt in most cases) will generally be valued at anywhere from 50% to 90% of the top grade.

Similarly, a card that falls between the middle and bottom grades (G-Vg, Vg or VgEx in most cases) will generally be valued at anywhere from 20% to 40% of the top grade.

There are also cases where cards are in better condition than the top grade or worse than the bottom grade. Cards that grade worse than the lowest grade are generally valued at 5-10% of the top grade.

When a card exceeds the top grade by one — such as NrMt-Mt when the top grade is NrMt, or Mint when the top grade is NrMt-Mt — a premium of up to 50% is possible, with 10-20% the usual norm.

When a card exceeds the top grade by two — such as Mint when the top grade is NrMt, or NrMt-Mt when the top grade is ExMt — a premium of 25-50% is the usual norm. But certain condition sensitive cards or sets, particularly those from the pre-war era, can bring premiums of up to 100% or even more.

Unopened packs, boxes and factory-collated sets are considered Mint in their unknown (and presumed perfect) state. Once opened, however, each card can be graded (and valued) in its own right by taking into account any defects that may be present in spite of the fact that the card has never been handled.

Selling Your Cards

Just about every collector sells cards or will sell cards eventually. Someday you may be interested in selling your duplicates or maybe even your whole collection. You may sell to other collectors, friends or dealers. You may even sell cards you purchased from a certain dealer back to that same dealer. In any event, it helps to know some of the mechanics of the typical transaction between buyer and seller.

Dealers will buy cards in order to resell them to other collectors who are interested in the cards. Dealers will always pay a higher percentage for items that (in their opinion) can be resold quickly, and a much lower percentage for those items that are perceived as having low demand and hence are slow moving. In either case, dealers must buy at a price that allows for the expense of doing business and a margin for profit.

If you have cards for sale, the best advice we can give is that you get several offers for your cards — either from card shops or at a card show — and take the best offer, all things considered. Note, the "best" offer may not be the one for the highest amount. And remember, if a dealer really wants your cards, he won't let you get away without making his best competitive offer. Another alternative is to place your cards in an auction as one or several lots.

Many people think nothing of going into a department store and paying $15 for an item of clothing for which the store paid $5. But if you were selling your $15 card to a dealer and he offered you $5 for it, you might think his mark-up unreasonable. To complete the analogy: most department stores (and card dealers) that consistently pay $10 for $15 items eventually go out of business. An exception is when the dealer has lined up a willing buyer for the item(s) you are attempting to sell, or if the cards are so Hot that it's likely he'll have to hold the cards for only a short period of time.

In those cases, an offer of up to 75 percent of book value still will allow the dealer to make a reasonable profit considering the short time he will need to hold the merchandise. In general, however, most cards and collections will bring offers in the range of 25 to 50 percent of retail price. Also consider that most material from the past five to 10 years is plentiful. If that's what you're selling, don't be surprised if your best offer is well below that range.

Interesting Notes

The first card numerically of an issue is the single card most likely to obtain excessive wear. Consequently, you typically will find the price on the #1 card (in NrMt or Mint condition) somewhat higher than might otherwise be the case. Similarly, but to a lesser extent (because normally the less important, reverse side of the card is the one exposed), the last card numerically in an issue also is prone to abnormal wear. This extra wear and tear occurs because the first and last cards are exposed to the elements (human element included) more than any other cards. They are generally end cards in any brick formations, rubber bandings, stackings on wet surfaces, and like activities.

Sports cards have no intrinsic value. The value of a card, like the value of other collectibles, can be determined only by you and your enjoyment in viewing and possessing these cardboard treasures.

Remember, the buyer ultimately determines the price of each card. You are the determining price factor because you have the ability to say "No" to the price of any card by not exchanging your hard-earned money for a given card. When the cost of a trading card exceeds the enjoyment you will receive from it, your answer should be "No." We assess and report the prices. You set them!

We are always interested in receiving the price input of collectors and dealers from around the country. We happily credit all contributors. We welcome your opinions, since your contributions assist us in ensuring a better guide each year. If you would like to join our survey list for the next editions of this book and others authored by Dr. Beckett, please send your name and address to Dr. James Beckett, 15850 Dallas Parkway, Dallas, Texas 75248.

History of Basketball Cards

The earliest basketball collectibles known are team postcards issued at the turn of the 20th century. Many of these postcards feature collegiate or high school teams of that day. Postcards were intermittently issued throughout the first half of the 20th century, with the bulk of them coming out in the 1920s and '30s. Unfortunately, the cataloging of these collectibles is sporadic at best. In addition, many collectors consider these postcards as memorabilia more so than trading cards, thus their exclusion from this book.

In 1910, College Athlete Felts (catalog number B-33) made their debut. Of a total of 270 felts, 20 featured basketball plays.

The first true basketball trading cards were issued by Murad cigarettes in 1911. The "College Series" cards depict a number of various sports and colleges, including four basketball cards (Luther, Northwestern, Williams and Xavier). In addition to these small (2-by-3 inch) cards, Murad issued a large (8-by-5 inch) basketball card featuring Williams college (catalog number T-6) as part of another multisport set.

The first basketball cards ever to be issued in gum packs were distributed in 1933 by Goudey in its multisport Sport Kings set, which was the first issue to list individual and professional players. Four cards from the complete 48-card set feature Original Celtics basketball players Nat Holman, Ed Wachter, Joe Lapchick and Eddie Burke.

The period of growth that the NBA experienced from 1948 to 1951 marked the first initial boom, both for that sport and the cards that chronicle it. In 1948, Bowman created the first trading card set exclusively devoted to basketball cards, ushering in the modern era of hoops collectibles. The 72-card Bowman set contains the Rookie Card of HOFer George Mikan, one of the most valuable, and important, basketball cards in the hobby. Mikan, pro basketball's first dominant big man, set the stage for Bill Russell, Wilt Chamberlain and all the other legendary centers who have played the game since.

In addition to the Bowman release, Topps included 11 basketball cards in its 252-card multisport 1948 Magic Photo set. Five of the cards feature individual players (including collegiate great "Easy" Ed Macauley), another five feature colleges, and one additional card highlights a Manhattan-Dartmouth game. These 11 cards represent Topps first effort to produce basketball trading cards. Kellogg's also created an 18-card multisport set of trading cards in 1948 that were inserted into boxes of Pep cereal. The only basketball card in the set features Mikan. Throughout 1948 and 1949, the Exhibit Supply Company of Chicago issued oversized thick-stock multisport trading cards in conjunction with the 1948 Olympic games. Six basketball players were featured, including HOFers Mikan and Joe Fulks, among others. The cards were distributed through penny arcade machines.

In 1950-51, Scott's Chips issued a 13-card set featuring the Minneapolis Lakers. The cards were issued in Scott's Potato and Cheese Potato Chip boxes. The cards are extremely scarce today due to the fact that many were redeemed back in 1950-51 in exchange for game tickets and signed team pictures. This set contains possibly the scarcest Mikan issue in existence. In 1951, a Philadelphia-based meat company called Berk Ross issued a four-series, 72-card multisport set. The set contains five different basketball players, including the first cards of HOFers Bob Cousy and Bill Sharman.

Wheaties issued an oversized six-card multisport set on the backs of its cereal boxes in 1951. The only basketball player featured in the set is Mikan.

In 1952, Wheaties expanded the cereal box set to 30 cards, including six issues featuring basketball players of that day. Of these six cards, two feature Mikan (a portrait and an action shot). The 1952 cards are significantly smaller than the previous year's issue. That same year, the 32-card Bread for Health set was issued. The set was one of the few trading card issues of that decade exclusively devoted to the sport of basketball. The cards are actually bread end labels and were probably meant to be housed in an album. To date, the only companies known to have issued this set are Fisher's Bread in the New Jersey, New York and Pennsylvania areas and NBC Bread in the Michigan area.

One must skip ahead to 1957-58 to find the next major basketball issue, again produced by Topps. Its 80-card basketball set from that year is recognized within the hobby as the second major modern basketball issue, including Rookie Cards of all-time greats such as Bill Russell, Bob Cousy and Bob Pettit.

In 1960, Post cereal created a nine-card multisport set by devoting most of the back of the actual cereal boxes to full color picture frames of the athletes. HOFers Cousy and Pettit are the two featured basketball players.

In 1961-62, Fleer issued the third major modern basketball set. The 66-card set contains the Rookie Cards of all-time greats such as Wilt Chamberlain, Oscar Robertson and Jerry West. That same year, Bell Brand Potato Chips inserted trading cards (one per bag) featuring the L.A. Lakers team of that year and including scarce, early issues of HOFers West and Elgin Baylor.

From 1963 to 1968 no major companies manufactured basketball cards. Kahn's (an Ohio-based meat company) issued small regional basketball sets from 1957-58 through 1965-66 (including the first cards of Jerry West and Oscar Robertson in its 1960-61 set). All the Kahn's sets feature members of the Cincinnati Royals, except for the few issues featuring the Lakers' West.

In 1968, Topps printed a very limited quantity of standard-size black-and-white test issue cards, preluding its 1969-70 nationwide return to the basketball card market.

The 1969-70 Topps set began a 13-year run of producing nationally distributed basketball card sets which ended in 1981-82. This was about the time the league's popularity bottomed out and was about to begin its ascent to the lofty level it's at today.

Topps' run included several sets that are troublesome for today's collectors. The 1969-70, 1970-71 and 1976-77 sets are larger than standard size, thus making them hard to store and preserve. The 1980-81 set consists of standard-size panels containing three cards each. Completing and cataloging the 1980-81 set (which features the classic Larry Bird RC/Magic Johnson RC/Julius Erving panel) is challenging, to say the least.

In 1983, this basketball card void was filled by the Star Company, a small company which issued three attractive sets of basketball cards, along with a plethora of peripheral sets. Star's 1983-84 premiere offering was issued in four groups, with the first series (cards 1-100) very difficult to obtain, as many of the early team subsets were miscut and destroyed before release. The 1984-85 and 1985-86 sets were more widely and evenly distributed. Even so, players' initial appearances on any of the three Star Company sets are considered Extended Rookie Cards, not regular Rookie Cards, because of the relatively limited distribution. Chief among these is Michael Jordan's 1984-85 Star XRC, the most valuable sports card issued in a 1980s major set.

Then, in 1986, Fleer took over the rights to produce cards for the NBA. Their 1986-87, 1987-88 and 1988-89 sets each contain 132 attractive, colorful cards depicting mostly stars and superstars. They were sold in the familiar wax pack format (12 cards and one sticker per pack). Fleer increased its set size to 168 in 1989-90, and was joined by NBA Hoops, which produced a 300-card first series (containing David Robinson's only Rookie Card) and a 52-card second series. The demand for all three Star Company sets, along with the first four Fleer sets and the premiere NBA Hoops set, skyrocketed during the early part of 1990.

The basketball card market stabilized somewhat in 1990-91, with both Fleer and Hoops stepping up production tremendously. A new major set, SkyBox, also made a splash in the market with its unique "high-tech" cards featuring computer-generated backgrounds. Because of overproduction, none of the three major 1990-91 sets have experienced significant price growth, although the increased competition has led to higher quality and more innovative products.

Another milestone in 1990-91 was the first-time inclusion of current rookies in update sets (NBA Hoops and SkyBox Series II, Fleer Update). The NBA Hoops and SkyBox issues contain just the 11 lottery picks, while Fleer's 100-card boxed set includes all rookies of any significance. A small company called "Star Pics" (not to be confused with Star Company) tried to fill this niche by printing a 70-card set in late 1990, but because the set was not licensed by the NBA, it is not considered a major set by the majority of collectors. It does, however, contain the first nationally distributed cards of 1990-91 rookies such as Derrick Coleman and Kendall Gill, among others.

In 1991-92, the draft pick set market that Star Pics opened in 1990-91 expanded to include several competitors. More significantly, that season brought with it the three established NBA card brands plus Upper Deck, known throughout the hobby for its high quality card stock and photography in other sports. Upper Deck's first basketball set probably captured NBA action better than any previous set. But its value — like all other major 1990-91 and 1991-92 NBA sets — declined because of overproduction.

On the bright side, the historic entrance of NBA players to Olympic competition kept interest in basketball cards going long after the Chicago Bulls won their second straight NBA championship. So for at least one year, the basketball card market — probably the most seasonal of the four major team sports — remained in the spotlight for an extended period of time.

The 1992-93 season will be remembered as the year of Shaq — the debut campaign of the most heralded rookie in many years. Shaquille O'Neal headlined the most promising rookie class in NBA history, sparking unprecedented interest in basketball cards. Among O'Neal's many talented rookie companions were Alonzo Mourning, Jim Jackson and Latrell Sprewell.

Classic Games, known primarily for producing draft picks and minor league baseball cards, signed O'Neal to an exclusive contract through 1992, thus postponing the appearances of O'Neal's NBA-licensed cards.

Shaquille's Classic and NBA cards, particularly the inserts, became some of the most sought-after collectibles in years. As a direct result of O'Neal and his fellow rookie standouts, the basketball card market achieved a new level of popularity in 1993.

The hobby rode that crest of popularity throughout the 1993-94 season. Michael Jordan may have retired, but his absence only spurred interest in some of his tougher inserts. Another strong rookie class followed Shaq, and Reggie Miller elevated its collectibility to a superstar level. Hakeem Olajuwon, by leading the Rockets to an NBA title, boosted his early cards to levels surpassed only by Jordan.

No new cardmakers came on board, but super premium Topps Finest raised the stakes, and the parallel set came into its own.

In 1994-95, the return of Michael Jordan, coupled with the high impact splash of Detroit Pistons rookie Grant Hill, kept collector interest high. In addition, the NBA granted all the licensed manufacturers the opportunity to create a fourth brand of basketball cards that year, allowing each company to create a selection of clearly defined niche products at different price points. The manufacturers also expanded the calendar release dates with 1994-95 cards being released on a consistent basis from August, 1994 all the way through June, 1995. The super-premium card market expanded greatly as the battle for the best selling five dollar (or more) pack reached epic levels by season's end. The key new super premium products included the premier of SP, Embossed and Emotion. This has continued through 1996 with the release of SPX, which contained only one card per pack.

The collecting year of 1996-97 brought even more to the table with a prominent motif of tough parallel sets and an influx of autographs available at lower ratio pulls. One of the greatest rookie classes in some time also carried the collecting season with players showing great promise: Allen Iverson, Kobe Bryant, Stephon Marbury, Antoine Walker and Shareef Abdur-Rahim. Topps Chrome was also introduced bringing about a rookie frenzy not seen since the 1986-87 Fleer set.

In 1997-98, Kobe Bryant was deemed the next Michael Jordan and his cards escalated throughout the year. In addition, a stronger than expected rookie class gave collector's some new blood to chase after, including Tim Duncan, Keith Van Horn, Ron Mercer and Tim Thomas. Autographs and serial-numbered inserts were the key inserts to chase featuring numbering as low as one of one.

Additional Reading

Each year Beckett Publications produces comprehensive annual price guides for each of the four major sports: *Beckett Baseball Card Price Guide, Beckett Football Card Price Guide, Beckett Basketball Card Price Guide,* and *Beckett Hockey Card Price Guide.* The aim of these annual guides is to provide information and accurate pricing on a wide array of sports cards, ranging from main issues by the major card manufacturers to various regional, promotional, and food issues. Also alphabetical checklists, such as *Beckett Basketball Card Alphabetical Checklist # 1,* are published to assist the collector in identifying all the cards of a particular player. The seasoned collector will find these tools valuable sources of information that will enable him to pursue his hobby interests.

In addition, abridged editions of the Beckett Price Guides have been published for each of the four major sports as part of the House of Collectible series: *The Official Price Guide to Baseball Cards, The Official Price Guide to Football Cards, The Official Price Guide to Basketball Cards,* and *The Official Price Guide to Hockey Cards*. Published in a convenient mass-market paper-back format, these price guides provide information and accurate pricing on all the main issues by the major card manufacturers.

Advertising

Within this Price Guide you will find advertisements for sports memorabilia material, mail order, and retail sports collectibles establishments. All advertisements were accepted in good faith based on the reputation of the advertiser; however, neither the author, the publisher, the distributors, nor the other advertisers in this Price Guide accept any responsibility for any particular advertiser not complying with the terms of his or her ad.

Readers also should be aware that prices in advertisements are subject to change over the annual period before a new edition of this volume is issued each spring. When replying to an advertisement late in the basketball year, the reader should take this into account, and contact the dealer by phone or in writing for up-to-date price information. Should you come into contact with any of the advertisers in this guide as a result of their advertisement herein, please mention this source as your contact.

Prices in This Guide

Prices found in this guide reflect current retail rates just prior to the printing of this book. They do not reflect the FOR SALE prices of the author, the publisher, the distributors, the advertisers, or any card dealers associated with this guide. No one is obligated in any way to buy, sell or trade his or her cards based on these prices. The price listings were compiled by the author from actual buy/sell transactions at sports conventions, sports card shops, buy/sell advertisements in the hobby papers, for sale prices from dealer catalogs and price lists, and discussions with leading hobbyists in the U.S. and Canada. All prices are in U.S. dollars.

Acknowledgments

A great deal of diligence, hard work, and dedicated effort went into this year's volume. The high standards to which we hold ourselves, however, could not have been met without the expert input and generous amount of time contributed by many people. Our sincere thanks are extended to each and every one of you.

A complete list of these invaluable contributors appears after the price guide.

1948 Bowman

The 1948 Bowman set of 72 cards was the company's only basketball issue. Five cards were issued in each pack. It was also the only major basketball issue until 1957-58 when Topps released a set. Cards in the set measure 2 1/16" by 2 1/2". The set is in color and features both player cards and diagram cards. The player cards in the second series are sometimes found without the red or blue printing on the card front, leaving only a gray background. These gray versions are more difficult to find, as they are printing errors where the printer apparently ran out of red or blue ink that was supposed to print on the player's uniform. The key Rookie Card in this set is George Mikan. Other Rookie Cards include Carl Braun, Joe Fulks, William Red Holzman, Jim Pollard, and Max Zaslofsky.

	EX-MT	VG-E
COMPLETE SET (72)	8000.00	3600.00
COMMON CARD (1-36)	60.00	27.00
COMMON CARD (37-72)	100.00	45.00
PLAY (5/11/17/23/29/35)	50.00	22.00
PLAY (41/47/53/59/65/71)	80.00	36.00
LO SEMISTARS (1-36)	80.00	36.00
HI SEMISTARS (37-72)	130.00	57.50
CARDS PRICED IN EX-MT CONDITION		
□ 1 Ernie Calverley	250.00	75.00
□ 2 Ralph Hamilton	60.00	27.00
□ 3 Gale Bishop	60.00	27.00
□ 4 Fred Lewis CO	70.00	32.00
□ 5 Basketball Play	50.00	22.00
Single cut off post		
□ 6 Bob Ferrick	70.00	32.00
□ 7 John Logan	60.00	27.00
□ 8 Mel Riebe	60.00	27.00
□ 9 Andy Phillip	160.00	70.00
□ 10 Bob Davies	175.00	80.00
□ 11 Basketball Play	50.00	22.00
Single cut with return pass to post		
□ 12 Kenny Sailors	70.00	32.00
□ 13 Paul Armstrong	60.00	27.00
□ 14 Howard Dallmar	70.00	32.00
□ 15 Bruce Hale	70.00	32.00
□ 16 Sid Hertzberg	80.00	36.00
□ 17 Basketball Play	50.00	22.00
Single cut		
□ 18 Red Rocha	60.00	27.00
□ 19 Eddie Ehlers	60.00	27.00

□ 20 Ellis(Gene) Vance	60.00	27.00
□ 21 Andrew(Fuzzy) Levane	70.00	32.00
□ 22 Earl Shannon	60.00	27.00
□ 23 Basketball Play	50.00	22.00
Double cut off post		
□ 24 Leo(Crystal) Klier	60.00	27.00
□ 25 George Senesky	60.00	27.00
□ 26 Price Brookfield	60.00	27.00
□ 27 John Norlander	60.00	27.00
□ 28 Don Putman	60.00	27.00
□ 29 Basketball Play	50.00	22.00
Double post		
□ 30 Jack Garfinkel	60.00	27.00
□ 31 Chuck Gilmur	60.00	27.00
□ 32 William Holzman	450.00	200.00
□ 33 Jack Smiley	60.00	27.00
□ 34 Joe Fulks	450.00	200.00
□ 35 Basketball Play	50.00	22.00
Screen play		
□ 36 Hal Tidrick	60.00	27.00
□ 37 Don(Swede) Carlson	100.00	45.00
□ 38 Buddy Jeanette CO	175.00	80.00
□ 39 Ray Kuka	100.00	45.00
□ 40 Stan Miasek	100.00	45.00
□ 41 Basketball Play	80.00	36.00
Double screen		
□ 42 George Nostrand	100.00	45.00
□ 43 Chuck Halbert	130.00	57.50
□ 44 Arnie Johnson	100.00	45.00
□ 45 Bob Doll	100.00	45.00
□ 46 Horace McKinney	150.00	70.00
□ 47 Basketball Play	80.00	36.00
Out of bounds		
□ 48 Ed Sadowski	125.00	55.00
□ 49 Bob Kinney	100.00	45.00
□ 50 Charles(Hawk) Black	100.00	45.00
□ 51 Jack Dwan	80.00	36.00
□ 52 Cornelius Simmons	130.00	57.50
□ 53 Basketball Play	80.00	36.00
Out of bounds		
□ 54 Bud Palmer	100.00	70.00
□ 55 Max Zaslofsky	325.00	145.00
□ 56 Lee Roy Robbins	100.00	45.00
□ 57 Arthur Spector	100.00	45.00
□ 58 Arnie Risen	175.00	80.00
□ 59 Basketball Play	80.00	36.00
Out of bounds play		
□ 60 Ariel Maughan	100.00	45.00
□ 61 Dick O'Keefe	100.00	45.00
□ 62 Herman Schaefer	100.00	45.00
□ 63 John Mahnken	100.00	45.00
□ 64 Tommy Byrnes	100.00	45.00
□ 65 Basketball Play	80.00	36.00
Held ball		
□ 66 Jim Pollard	450.00	200.00
□ 67 Lee Mogus	100.00	45.00
□ 68 Lee Knorek	100.00	45.00
□ 69 George Mikan	4500.00	2000.00
□ 70 Walter Budko	100.00	45.00
□ 71 Basketball Play	80.00	36.00
Guards Play		
□ 72 Carl Braun	500.00	150.00

1996-97 Bowman's Best

The premier edition of 1996-97 Bowman's Best set was issued in one series totalling 125 cards. The basic set consists of 80 veterans on a gold foil card background, 25 rookies on a silver foil card background and 20 throwback cards on a black and white card background. Each six-card pack had a suggested retail price of $3.99.

	MINT	NRMT
COMPLETE SET (125)	110.00	50.00
COMMON CARD (1-80/TB1-20)	.25	.11
COMMON CARD (R1-R25)	.75	.35
SEMISTARS	.40	.18
UNLISTED STARS	.60	.25
COMP REF.SET (125)	1200.00	550.00
COMMON REF (1-80/TB1-20)	2.00	.90
COMMON REF (R1-R25)	4.00	1.80
*REF.STARS: 6X TO 12X HI COLUMN		
*REF.RCs: 2.5X TO 5X HI COLUMN		
REF: STATED ODDS 1:12 HOB, 1:20 RET		
□ 1 Scottie Pippen	2.00	.90
□ 2 Glen Rice	.60	.25
□ 3 Bryant Stith	.25	.11
□ 4 Dino Radja	.25	.11
□ 5 Horace Grant	.40	.18
□ 6 M.Abdul-Rauf	.25	.11
□ 7 Mookie Blaylock	.40	.18
□ 8 Clifford Robinson	.25	.11
□ 9 Vin Baker	1.25	.55
□ 10 Grant Hill	4.00	1.80
□ 11 Terrell Brandon	.60	.25
□ 12 P.J. Brown	.25	.11
□ 13 Kendall Gill	.40	.18
□ 14 Brent Barry	.40	.18
□ 15 Hakeem Olajuwon	1.25	.55
□ 16 Allan Houston	.40	.18
□ 17 Elden Campbell	.40	.18
□ 18 Latrell Sprewell	.40	.18
□ 19 Jerry Stackhouse	.75	.35
□ 20 Robert Horry	.40	.18
□ 21 Mitch Richmond	.60	.25
□ 22 Gary Payton	1.00	.45
□ 23 Rik Smits	.40	.18
□ 24 Jim Jackson	.40	.18
□ 25 D.Stoudamire	1.50	.70
□ 26 Bobby Phills	.25	.11
□ 27 Chris Webber	1.50	.70
□ 28 Shawn Bradley	.25	.11
□ 29 Arvydas Sabonis	.40	.18
□ 30 John Stockton	.60	.25
□ 31 A.Hardaway	2.50	1.10
□ 32 Christian Laettner	.40	.18
□ 33 Juwan Howard	.75	.35
□ 34 Anthony Mason	.40	.18
□ 35 Tom Gugliotta	.60	.25
□ 36 Avery Johnson	.25	.11
□ 37 Cedric Ceballos	.25	.11
□ 38 Patrick Ewing	.60	.25
□ 39 Joe Smith	.75	.35
□ 40 Dennis Rodman	2.50	1.10
□ 41 Alonzo Mourning	.60	.25
□ 42 Kevin Garnett	4.00	1.80
□ 43 Antonio McDyess	1.00	.45
□ 44 Detlef Schrempf	.40	.18
□ 45 Reggie Miller	.60	.25
□ 46 Charles Barkley	1.00	.45
□ 47 Derrick Coleman	.40	.18
□ 48 Brian Grant	.25	.11
□ 49 Kenny Anderson	.40	.18
□ 50 Otis Thorpe	.40	.18
□ 51 Rod Strickland	.40	.18
□ 52 Eric Williams	.25	.11
□ 53 Rony Seikaly	.25	.11
□ 54 Danny Manning	.40	.18
□ 55 Karl Malone	1.00	.45

	MINT	NRMT
☐ 56 B.J. Armstrong	.25	.11
☐ 57 Greg Anthony	.25	.11
☐ 58 Larry Johnson	.40	.18
☐ 59 Loy Vaught	.40	.18
☐ 60 Sean Elliott	.25	.11
☐ 61 D.Mutombo	.40	.18
☐ 62 C.Weatherspoon	.25	.11
☐ 63 Jamal Mashburn	.40	.18
☐ 64 Bryant Reeves	.40	.18
☐ 65 Vlade Divac	.40	.18
☐ 66 Shawn Kemp	2.00	.90
☐ 67 LaPhonso Ellis	.25	.11
☐ 68 Tyrone Hill	.25	.11
☐ 69 David Robinson	1.00	.45
☐ 70 Shaquille O'Neal	2.50	1.10
☐ 71 Doug Christie	.25	.11
☐ 72 Jayson Williams	.40	.18
☐ 73 Michael Finley	.75	.35
☐ 74 Tim Hardaway	.75	.35
☐ 75 Clyde Drexler	.75	.35
☐ 76 Joe Dumars	.60	.25
☐ 77 Glenn Robinson	.60	.25
☐ 78 Dana Barros	.25	.11
☐ 79 Jason Kidd	1.25	.55
☐ 80 Michael Jordan	8.00	3.60
☐ R1 Allen Iverson	12.00	5.50
☐ R2 Stephon Marbury	12.00	5.50
☐ R3 S.Abdur-Rahim	8.00	3.60
☐ R4 Marcus Camby	4.00	1.80
☐ R5 Ray Allen	5.00	2.20
☐ R6 Antoine Walker	15.00	6.75
☐ R7 Lorenzen Wright	1.50	.70
☐ R8 Kerry Kittles	4.00	1.80
☐ R9 Samaki Walker	1.50	.70
☐ R10 Tony Delk	1.50	.70
☐ R11 Vitaly Potapenko	1.00	.45
☐ R12 Jerome Williams	1.00	.45
☐ R13 Todd Fuller	.75	.35
☐ R14 Erick Dampier	1.50	.70
☐ R15 Derek Fisher	1.50	.70
☐ R16 Donald Whiteside	.75	.35
☐ R17 John Wallace	2.00	.90
☐ R18 Steve Nash	2.50	1.10
☐ R19 Brian Evans	.75	.35
☐ R20 Jermaine O'Neal	2.50	1.10
☐ R21 Roy Rogers	.75	.35
☐ R22 Priest Lauderdale	.75	.35
☐ R23 Kobe Bryant	30.00	13.50
☐ R24 Martin Muursepp	.75	.35
☐ R25 Zydrunas Ilgauskas	6.00	2.70
☐ TB1 Avery Johnson RET.	.25	.11
☐ TB2 Chris Webber RET.	.75	.35
☐ TB3 Sean Elliott RET	.25	.11
☐ TB4 Joe Dumars RET.	.40	.18
☐ TB5 Grant Hill RET	2.00	.90
☐ TB6 Gary Payton RET.	.60	.25
☐ TB7 Shawn Kemp RET	1.00	.45
☐ TB8 Shaquille O'Neal	1.25	.55
☐ TB9 Eddie Jones RET.	.60	.25
☐ TB10 John Wallace RET.	.60	.25
☐ TB11 Patrick Ewing RET.	.40	.18
☐ TB12 Jerry Stackhouse RET	.60	.25
☐ TB13 Allen Iverson RET ..	3.00	1.35
☐ TB14 Latrell Sprewell RET	.25	.11
☐ TB15 Dino Radja RET	.25	.11
☐ TB16 David Wesley RET.	.25	.11
☐ TB17 Joe Smith RET	.60	.25
☐ TB18 D. Stoudamire RET	.75	.35
☐ TB19 Marcus Camby RET	.75	.35
☐ TB20 Juwan Howard RET.	.60	.25

	MINT	NRMT
COMPLETE SET (125)	3500.00	1600.00
COMMON CARD (1-80/TB1-20)	8.00	3.60
COMMON CARD (R1-R25)..	15.00	6.75
SEMISTARS	12.00	5.50
UNLISTED STARS	12.00	5.50
STATED ODDS 1:24 HOBBY, 1:40 RETAIL		
☐ 1 Scottie Pippen	60.00	27.00
☐ 2 Glen Rice	20.00	9.00
☐ 3 Bryant Stith	8.00	3.60
☐ 4 Dino Radja	8.00	3.60
☐ 5 Horace Grant	12.00	5.50
☐ 6 M.Abdul-Rauf	8.00	3.60
☐ 7 Mookie Blaylock	12.00	5.50
☐ 8 Clifford Robinson	8.00	3.60
☐ 9 Vin Baker	40.00	18.00
☐ 10 Grant Hill	120.00	55.00
☐ 11 Terrell Brandon	20.00	9.00
☐ 12 P.J. Brown	8.00	3.60
☐ 13 Kendall Gill	12.00	5.50
☐ 14 Brent Barry	8.00	3.60
☐ 15 Hakeem Olajuwon	40.00	18.00
☐ 16 Allan Houston	12.00	5.50
☐ 17 Elden Campbell	12.00	5.50
☐ 18 Latrell Sprewell	12.00	5.50
☐ 19 Jerry Stackhouse	25.00	11.00
☐ 20 Robert Horry	12.00	5.50
☐ 21 Mitch Richmond	20.00	9.00
☐ 22 Gary Payton	30.00	13.50
☐ 23 Rik Smits	12.00	5.50
☐ 24 Jim Jackson	12.00	5.50
☐ 25 D.Stoudamire	50.00	22.00
☐ 26 Bobby Phills	8.00	3.60
☐ 27 Chris Webber	50.00	22.00
☐ 28 Shawn Bradley	8.00	3.60
☐ 29 Arvydas Sabonis	12.00	5.50
☐ 30 John Stockton	20.00	9.00
☐ 31 A.Hardaway	80.00	36.00
☐ 32 Christian Laettner	12.00	5.50
☐ 33 Juwan Howard	25.00	11.00
☐ 34 Anthony Mason	12.00	5.50
☐ 35 Tom Gugliotta	20.00	9.00
☐ 36 Avery Johnson	8.00	3.60
☐ 37 Cedric Ceballos	8.00	3.60
☐ 38 Patrick Ewing	20.00	9.00
☐ 39 Joe Smith	25.00	11.00
☐ 40 Dennis Rodman	80.00	36.00
☐ 41 Alonzo Mourning	25.00	11.00
☐ 42 Kevin Garnett	120.00	55.00
☐ 43 Antonio McDyess	30.00	13.50
☐ 44 Detlef Schrempf	12.00	5.50
☐ 45 Reggie Miller	20.00	9.00
☐ 46 Charles Barkley	30.00	13.50
☐ 47 Derrick Coleman	12.00	5.50
☐ 48 Brian Grant	8.00	3.60
☐ 49 Kenny Anderson	12.00	5.50
☐ 50 Otis Thorpe	12.00	5.50
☐ 51 Rod Strickland	12.00	5.50
☐ 52 Eric Williams	8.00	3.60
☐ 53 Rony Seikaly	8.00	3.60
☐ 54 Danny Manning	12.00	5.50
☐ 55 Karl Malone	30.00	13.50
☐ 56 B.J. Armstrong	8.00	3.60
☐ 57 Greg Anthony	8.00	3.60
☐ 58 Larry Johnson	12.00	5.50
☐ 59 Loy Vaught	12.00	5.50
☐ 60 Sean Elliott	8.00	3.60

	MINT	NRMT
☐ 61 D.Mutombo	12.00	5.50
☐ 62 C.Weatherspoon	8.00	3.60
☐ 63 Jamal Mashburn	12.00	5.50
☐ 64 Bryant Reeves	12.00	5.50
☐ 65 Vlade Divac	12.00	5.50
☐ 66 Shawn Kemp	60.00	27.00
☐ 67 LaPhonso Ellis	8.00	3.60
☐ 68 Tyrone Hill	8.00	3.60
☐ 69 David Robinson	30.00	13.50
☐ 70 Shaquille O'Neal	80.00	36.00
☐ 71 Doug Christie	8.00	3.60
☐ 72 Jayson Williams	12.00	5.50
☐ 73 Michael Finley	25.00	11.00
☐ 74 Tim Hardaway	25.00	11.00
☐ 75 Clyde Drexler	25.00	11.00
☐ 76 Joe Dumars	20.00	9.00
☐ 77 Glenn Robinson	20.00	9.00
☐ 78 Dana Barros	8.00	3.60
☐ 79 Jason Kidd	40.00	18.00
☐ 80 Michael Jordan	240.00	110.00
☐ R1 Allen Iverson	200.00	90.00
☐ R2 Stephon Marbury	200.00	90.00
☐ R3 S. Abdur-Rahim	125.00	55.00
☐ R4 Marcus Camby	50.00	22.00
☐ R5 Ray Allen	60.00	27.00
☐ R6 Antoine Walker	200.00	.90.00
☐ R7 Lorenzen Wright	25.00	11.00
☐ R8 Kerry Kittles	50.00	22.00
☐ R9 Samaki Walker	25.00	11.00
☐ R10 Tony Delk	25.00	11.00
☐ R11 Vitaly Potapenko	20.00	9.00
☐ R12 Jerome Williams	20.00	9.00
☐ R13 Todd Fuller	15.00	6.75
☐ R14 Erick Dampier	25.00	11.00
☐ R15 Derek Fisher	25.00	11.00
☐ R16 Donald Whiteside	15.00	6.75
☐ R17 John Wallace	30.00	13.50
☐ R18 Steve Nash	30.00	13.50
☐ R19 Brian Evans	15.00	6.75
☐ R20 Jermaine O'Neal	30.00	13.50
☐ R21 Roy Rogers	15.00	6.75
☐ R22 Priest Lauderdale	15.00	6.75
☐ R23 Kobe Bryant	350.00	160.00
☐ R24 Martin Muursepp	15.00	6.75
☐ R25 Zydrunas Ilgauskas	50.00	22.00
☐ TB1 Avery Johnson RET.	8.00	3.60
☐ TB2 Chris Webber RET.	25.00	11.00
☐ TB3 Sean Elliott RET	8.00	3.60
☐ TB4 Joe Dumars RET	12.00	5.50
☐ TB5 Grant Hill RET	60.00	27.00
☐ TB6 Gary Payton RET	20.00	9.00
☐ TB7 Shawn Kemp RET	30.00	13.50
☐ TB8 Shaquille O'Neal RET	40.00	18.00
☐ TB9 Eddie Jones RET	20.00	9.00
☐ TB10 John Wallace RET	20.00	9.00
☐ TB11 Patrick Ewing RET	12.00	5.50
☐ TB12 Jerry Stackhouse RET	20.00	9.00
☐ TB13 Allen Iverson RET	100.00	45.00
☐ TB14 Latrell Sprewell RET	8.00	3.60
☐ TB15 Dino Radja RET	8.00	3.60
☐ TB16 David Wesley RET.	8.00	3.60
☐ TB17 Joe Smith RET	20.00	9.00
☐ TB18 D. Stoudamire RET	25.00	11.00
☐ TB19 Marcus Camby RET	25.00	11.00
☐ TB20 Juwan Howard RET	20.00	9.00

1996-97 Bowman's Best Atomic Refractors

Randomly inserted in packs at a rate of one in 24, this 80-card set parallels the Refractor insert. The only difference is the use of the "hyper-plaid" atomic refractor technology.

1996-97 Bowman's Best Cuts

Randomly inserted in packs at a rate of one in 24, this 20-card set features the best in the NBA against a die-cut chromium background. Each card front also contains a facsimile autograph of the player. Card backs are numbered with a "BC" prefix.

	MINT	NRMT
COMPLETE SET (20)	160.00	70.00
COMMON CARD (BC1-BC20)	3.00	1.35

STATED ODDS 1:24 HOBBY, 1:40 RETAIL
*REFRACTORS: 1X TO 2.5X HI COLUMN
REF: STATED ODDS 1:96 HOB, 1:160 RET
*ATOMIC REFRACTORS: 2X TO 4X HI
ATO: STATED ODDS 1:192 HOB, 1:320 RET

		MINT	NRMT
☐ BC1	Karl Malone	5.00	2.20
☐ BC2	Michael Jordan	40.00	18.00
☐ BC3	Juwan Howard	4.00	1.80
☐ BC4	Charles Barkley	5.00	2.20
☐ BC5	Jerry Stackhouse	4.00	1.80
☐ BC6	A.Hardaway	12.00	5.50
☐ BC7	Shaquille O'Neal	12.00	5.50
☐ BC8	Alonzo Mourning	3.00	1.35
☐ BC9	Shawn Kemp	10.00	4.50
☐ BC10	Scottie Pippen	10.00	4.50
☐ BC11	David Robinson	5.00	2.20
☐ BC12	Kevin Garnett	20.00	9.00
☐ BC13	Patrick Ewing	3.00	1.35
☐ BC14	Hakeem Olajuwon	6.00	2.70
☐ BC15	D.Stoudamire	8.00	3.60
☐ BC16	Grant Hill	20.00	9.00
☐ BC17	Dennis Rodman	12.00	5.50
☐ BC18	Chris Webber	8.00	3.60
☐ BC19	Gary Payton	5.00	2.20
☐ BC20	John Stockton	3.00	1.35

1996-97 Bowman's Best Honor Roll

Randomly inserted in packs at a rate of one in 48, this 10-card set showcases some of the top draft pick combos all the way back to 1984. Card backs are numbered with a "HR" prefix.

	MINT	NRMT
COMPLETE SET (10)	200.00	90.00
COMMON CARD (HR1-HR10)	8.00	3.60

STATED ODDS 1:48 HOBBY, 1:80 RETAIL
*REFRACTORS: 1.25X TO 3X HI COLUMN
REF: STATED ODDS 1:192 HOB, 1:320 RET
*ATOMIC REFRACTORS: 3X TO 6X HI
ATO: STATED ODDS 1:384 HOB, 1:640 RET

		MINT	NRMT
☐ HR1	Charles Barkley John Stockton	10.00	4.50
☐ HR2	Michael Jordan Hakeem Olajuwon	60.00	27.00
☐ HR3	Patrick Ewing Karl Malone	10.00	4.50
☐ HR4	Dennis Rodman Arvydas Sabonis	12.00	5.50
☐ HR5	Scottie Pippen David Robinson	20.00	9.00
☐ HR6	Glen Rice Shawn Kemp	15.00	6.75
☐ HR7	Shaquille O'Neal Alonzo Mourning	20.00	9.00
☐ HR8	A.Hardaway Chris Webber	25.00	11.00
☐ HR9	Grant Hill Juwan Howard	25.00	11.00
☐ HR10	Kevin Garnett Jerry Stackhouse	30.00	13.50

1996-97 Bowman's Best Picks

Randomly inserted in packs at a rate of one in 24, this 10-card set features some of the best players from the class of 1996. Card fronts also contain a fac-simile autograph of each player. Card backs are numbered with a "BP" prefix.

	MINT	NRMT
COMPLETE SET (10)	70.00	32.00
COMMON CARD (BP1-BP10)	1.25	.55
SEMISTARS	2.00	.90
UNLISTED STARS	3.00	1.35

STATED ODDS 1:24 HOBBY, 1:40 RETAIL
*REFRACTORS: 1X TO 2.5X HI COLUMN
REF: STATED ODDS 1:96 HOB, 1:160 RET
*ATOMIC REFRACTORS: 2.5X TO 5X HI
ATO: STATED ODDS 1:192 HOB, 1:320 RET

		MINT	NRMT
☐ BP1	Stephon Marbury	15.00	6.75
☐ BP2	Marcus Camby	4.00	1.80
☐ BP3	Lorenzen Wright	2.00	.90
☐ BP4	John Wallace	3.00	1.35
☐ BP5	Ray Allen	5.00	2.20
☐ BP6	Kerry Kittles	4.00	1.80
☐ BP7	S.Abdur-Rahim	10.00	4.50
☐ BP8	Todd Fuller	1.25	.55
☐ BP9	Allen Iverson	15.00	6.75
☐ BP10	Kobe Bryant	30.00	13.50

1996-97 Bowman's Best Shots

Randomly inserted in packs at a rate of one in 12, this 10-card set features some of the top NBA superstars on crystal clear chromium cards. Card backs are numbered with a "BS" prefix.

	MINT	NRMT
COMPLETE SET (10)	60.00	27.00
COMMON CARD (BS1-BS10)	2.50	1.10

STATED ODDS 1:12 HOBBY, 1:20 RETAIL
*REFRACTORS: 1X TO 2X HI COLUMN
REF: STATED ODDS 1:48 HOB, 1:80 RET
*ATOMIC REFRACTORS: 2X TO 4X HI
ATO: STATED ODDS 1:96 HOB, 1:160 RET

		MINT	NRMT
☐ BS1	Scottie Pippen	5.00	2.20
☐ BS2	Gary Payton	2.50	1.10
☐ BS3	Shaquille O'Neal	6.00	2.70
☐ BS4	Hakeem Olajuwon	3.00	1.35
☐ BS5	Kevin Garnett	10.00	4.50
☐ BS6	Michael Jordan	20.00	9.00
☐ BS7	A.Hardaway	6.00	2.70
☐ BS8	Grant Hill	10.00	4.50
☐ BS9	Shawn Kemp	5.00	2.20
☐ BS10	Dennis Rodman	6.00	2.70

1997-98 Bowman's Best

The 1997-98 Bowman's Best set was issued in one series totaling 125 cards. The basic set con-sists of 90 veterans, a 10 card Best Performances subset and 25 rookie cards. Each six-card pack had a suggested retail price of $3.99.

	MINT	NRMT
COMPLETE SET (125)	70.00	32.00
COMMON CARD (1-100)	.25	.11
COMMON CARD (101-125)	.75	.35
SEMISTARS	.30	.14
UNLISTED STARS	.50	.23
COMP.REF SET (125)	800.00	350.00
COMMON REF (1-125)	3.00	1.35
*REF.STARS: 5X TO 12X HI COLUMN		
*REF.RCs: 1.5X TO 4X HI		
REF: STATED ODDS 1:12 HOB, 1:20 RET		

		MINT	NRMT
☐ 1	Scottie Pippen	1.50	.70
☐ 2	Michael Finley	.50	.23
☐ 3	David Wesley	.25	.11
☐ 4	Brent Barry	.25	.11
☐ 5	Gary Payton	.75	.35
☐ 6	Christian Laettner	.25	.14
☐ 7	Grant Hill	3.00	1.35
☐ 8	Glenn Robinson	.50	.23
☐ 9	Reggie Miller	.50	.23
☐ 10	Tyus Edney	.25	.11
☐ 11	Jim Jackson	.30	.14
☐ 12	John Stockton	.50	.23
☐ 13	Karl Malone	.75	.35
☐ 14	Samaki Walker	.25	.11
☐ 15	Bryant Stith	.25	.11
☐ 16	Clyde Drexler	.60	.25
☐ 17	Danny Ferry	.25	.11
☐ 18	Shawn Bradley	.25	.11
☐ 19	Bryant Reeves	.30	.14
☐ 20	John Starks	.30	.14
☐ 21	Joe Dumars	.50	.23
☐ 22	Checklist	.25	.11
☐ 23	Antonio McDyess	.60	.25
☐ 24	Jeff Hornacek	.30	.14
☐ 25	Terrell Brandon	.50	.23
☐ 26	Kendall Gill	.30	.14
☐ 27	LaPhonso Ellis	.25	.11
☐ 28	Shaquille O'Neal	2.00	.90
☐ 29	M.Abdul-Rauf	.25	.11
☐ 30	Eric Williams	.25	.11
☐ 31	Lorenzen Wright	.25	.11
☐ 32	S.Abdur-Rahim	1.50	.70
☐ 33	Avery Johnson	.25	.11
☐ 34	Juwan Howard	.50	.23
☐ 35	Vin Baker	1.00	.45
☐ 36	D.Mutombo	.30	.14
☐ 37	Patrick Ewing	.50	.23
☐ 38	Allen Iverson	2.50	1.10
☐ 39	Alonzo Mourning	.50	.23
☐ 40	Travis Knight	.25	.11
☐ 41	Ray Allen	.60	.25
☐ 42	Detlef Schrempf	.30	.14
☐ 43	Kevin Johnson	.30	.14
☐ 44	David Robinson	.75	.35
☐ 45	Tim Hardaway	.60	.25
☐ 46	Shawn Kemp	1.50	.70
☐ 47	Marcus Camby	.50	.23
☐ 48	Rony Seikaly	.25	.11
☐ 49	Eddie Jones	1.00	.45
☐ 50	Rik Smits	.30	.14
☐ 51	Jayson Williams	.30	.14
☐ 52	Malik Sealy	.25	.11
☐ 53	Chris Mullin	.50	.23
☐ 54	Larry Johnson	.30	.14
☐ 55	Isaiah Rider	.30	.14
☐ 56	Dennis Rodman	2.00	.90
☐ 57	Bob Sura	.25	.11
☐ 58	Hakeem Olajuwon	1.00	.45
☐ 59	Steve Smith	.30	.14
☐ 60	Michael Jordan	6.00	2.70
☐ 61	Jerry Stackhouse	.50	.23
☐ 62	Joe Smith	.50	.23
☐ 63	Walt Williams	.25	.11
☐ 64	Anthony Peeler	.25	.11
☐ 65	Charles Barkley	.75	.35
☐ 66	Erick Dampier	.25	.11
☐ 67	Horace Grant	.30	.14
☐ 68	Anthony Mason	.30	.14
☐ 69	A.Hardaway	2.00	.90
☐ 70	Elden Campbell	.25	.11
☐ 71	Cedric Ceballos	.25	.11
☐ 72	Allan Houston	.30	.14
☐ 73	Kerry Kittles	.50	.23
☐ 74	Antoine Walker	2.50	1.10

		MINT	NRMT
☐ 75	Sean Elliott	.25	.11
☐ 76	Jamal Mashburn	.30	.14
☐ 77	Mitch Richmond	.50	.23
☐ 78	D.Stoudamire	1.00	.45
☐ 79	Tom Gugliotta	.50	.23
☐ 80	Jason Kidd	1.00	.45
☐ 81	Chris Webber	1.25	.55
☐ 82	Glen Rice	.50	.23
☐ 83	Loy Vaught	.30	.14
☐ 84	Olden Polynice	.25	.11
☐ 85	Kenny Anderson	.30	.14
☐ 86	Stephon Marbury	2.50	1.10
☐ 87	Calbert Cheaney	.25	.11
☐ 88	Kobe Bryant	4.00	1.80
☐ 89	Arvydas Sabonis	.30	.14
☐ 90	Kevin Garnett	3.00	1.35
☐ 91	Grant Hill BP	1.50	.70
☐ 92	Clyde Drexler BP	.50	.23
☐ 93	Patrick Ewing BP	.30	.14
☐ 94	Shawn Kemp BP	.75	.35
☐ 95	Shaquille O'Neal BP	1.00	.45
☐ 96	Michael Jordan BP	3.00	1.35
☐ 97	Karl Malone BP	.50	.23
☐ 98	Allen Iverson BP	1.25	.55
☐ 99	S.Abdur-Rahim BP	.75	.35
☐ 100	D.Mutombo BP	.25	.11
☐ 101	Bobby Jackson	2.50	1.10
☐ 102	Tony Battie	2.50	1.10
☐ 103	Keith Booth	.75	.35
☐ 104	Keith Van Horn	12.00	5.50
☐ 105	Paul Grant	.75	.35
☐ 106	Tim Duncan	15.00	6.75
☐ 107	Scot Pollard	.75	.35
☐ 108	Maurice Taylor	5.00	2.20
☐ 109	Antonio Daniels	3.00	1.35
☐ 110	Austin Croshere	1.50	.70
☐ 111	Tracy McGrady	8.00	3.60
☐ 112	Charles O'Bannon	.75	.35
☐ 113	Rodrick Rhodes	1.50	.70
☐ 114	Johnny Taylor	.75	.35
☐ 115	Danny Fortson	2.50	1.10
☐ 116	Chauncey Billups	5.00	2.20
☐ 117	Tim Thomas	8.00	3.60
☐ 118	Derek Anderson	5.00	2.20
☐ 119	Ed Gray	1.50	.70
☐ 120	Jacque Vaughn	2.00	.90
☐ 121	Kelvin Cato	1.50	.70
☐ 122	Tariq Abdul-Wahad	2.00	.90
☐ 123	Ron Mercer	10.00	4.50
☐ 124	Brevin Knight	5.00	2.20
☐ 125	Adonal Foyle	1.50	.70

1997-98 Bowman's Best Atomic Refractors

Randomly inserted into packs at a rate of one in 24, this 125-card set parallels the basic issue. The cards feature the "hyper-plaid" refractor pattern.

	MINT	NRMT
COMPLETE SET (125)	2500.00	1100.00
COMMON CARD (1-100)	5.00	2.20
COMMON CARD (101-125)	8.00	3.60
SEMISTARS	8.00	3.60
UNLISTED STARS	12.00	5.50
STATED ODDS 1:24 HOB, 1:40 RET		

		MINT	NRMT
☐ 1	Scottie Pippen	40.00	18.00
☐ 2	Michael Finley	12.00	5.50
☐ 3	David Wesley	5.00	2.20
☐ 4	Brent Barry	5.00	2.20
☐ 5	Gary Payton	20.00	9.00
☐ 6	Christian Laettner	8.00	3.60
☐ 7	Grant Hill	80.00	36.00
☐ 8	Glenn Robinson	12.00	5.50
☐ 9	Reggie Miller	12.00	5.50
☐ 10	Tyus Edney	5.00	2.20
☐ 11	Jim Jackson	8.00	3.60
☐ 12	John Stockton	12.00	5.50
☐ 13	Karl Malone	20.00	9.00
☐ 14	Samaki Walker	5.00	2.20
☐ 15	Bryant Stith	5.00	2.20
☐ 16	Clyde Drexler	15.00	6.75
☐ 17	Danny Ferry	5.00	2.20
☐ 18	Shawn Bradley	5.00	2.20
☐ 19	Bryant Reeves	5.00	2.20
☐ 20	John Starks	8.00	3.60
☐ 21	Joe Dumars	12.00	5.50
☐ 22	Checklist	5.00	2.20
☐ 23	Antonio McDyess	15.00	6.75
☐ 24	Jeff Hornacek	8.00	3.60
☐ 25	Terrell Brandon	12.00	5.50
☐ 26	Kendall Gill	8.00	3.60
☐ 27	LaPhonso Ellis	5.00	2.20
☐ 28	Shaquille O'Neal	50.00	22.00
☐ 29	M.Abdul-Rauf	5.00	2.20
☐ 30	Eric Williams	5.00	2.20
☐ 31	Lorenzen Wright	5.00	2.20
☐ 32	S.Abdur-Rahim	40.00	18.00
☐ 33	Avery Johnson	5.00	2.20
☐ 34	Juwan Howard	12.00	5.50
☐ 35	Vin Baker	25.00	11.00
☐ 36	D.Mutombo	8.00	3.60
☐ 37	Patrick Ewing	12.00	5.50
☐ 38	Allen Iverson	60.00	27.00
☐ 39	Alonzo Mourning	12.00	5.50
☐ 40	Travis Knight	5.00	2.20
☐ 41	Ray Allen	15.00	6.75
☐ 42	Detlef Schrempf	8.00	3.60
☐ 43	Kevin Johnson	8.00	3.60
☐ 44	David Robinson	20.00	9.00
☐ 45	Tim Hardaway	15.00	6.75
☐ 46	Shawn Kemp	40.00	18.00
☐ 47	Marcus Camby	12.00	5.50
☐ 48	Rony Seikaly	5.00	2.20
☐ 49	Eddie Jones	25.00	11.00
☐ 50	Rik Smits	8.00	3.60
☐ 51	Jayson Williams	8.00	3.60
☐ 52	Malik Sealy	5.00	2.20
☐ 53	Chris Mullin	12.00	5.50
☐ 54	Larry Johnson	8.00	3.60
☐ 55	Isaiah Rider	8.00	3.60
☐ 56	Dennis Rodman	50.00	22.00
☐ 57	Bob Sura	5.00	2.20
☐ 58	Hakeem Olajuwon	25.00	11.00
☐ 59	Steve Smith	8.00	3.60
☐ 60	Michael Jordan	150.00	70.00
☐ 61	Jerry Stackhouse	12.00	5.50
☐ 62	Joe Smith	12.00	5.50
☐ 63	Walt Williams	5.00	2.20
☐ 64	Anthony Peeler	5.00	2.20
☐ 65	Charles Barkley	20.00	9.00
☐ 66	Erick Dampier	5.00	2.20
☐ 67	Horace Grant	8.00	3.60
☐ 68	Anthony Mason	8.00	3.60
☐ 69	A.Hardaway	50.00	22.00
☐ 70	Elden Campbell	8.00	3.60
☐ 71	Cedric Ceballos	5.00	2.20
☐ 72	Allan Houston	8.00	3.60
☐ 73	Kerry Kittles	12.00	5.50
☐ 74	Antoine Walker	60.00	27.00

□ 75	Sean Elliott	5.00	2.20
□ 76	Jamal Mashburn	8.00	3.60
□ 77	Mitch Richmond	12.00	5.50
□ 78	D.Stoudamire	25.00	11.00
□ 79	Tom Gugliotta	12.00	5.50
□ 80	Jason Kidd	25.00	11.00
□ 81	Chris Webber	30.00	13.50
□ 82	Glen Rice	12.00	5.50
□ 83	Loy Vaught	8.00	3.60
□ 84	Olden Polynice	5.00	2.20
□ 85	Kenny Anderson	8.00	3.60
□ 86	Stephon Marbury	60.00	27.00
□ 87	Calbert Cheaney	5.00	2.20
□ 88	Kobe Bryant	100.00	45.00
□ 89	Arvydas Sabonis	8.00	3.60
□ 90	Kevin Garnett	80.00	36.00
□ 91	Grant Hill BP	40.00	18.00
□ 92	Clyde Drexler BP	12.00	5.50
□ 93	Patrick Ewing BP	8.00	3.60
□ 94	Shawn Kemp BP	20.00	9.00
□ 95	Shaquille O'Neal BP	25.00	11.00
□ 96	Michael Jordan BP	80.00	36.00
□ 97	Karl Malone BP	12.00	5.50
□ 98	Allen Iverson BP	30.00	13.50
□ 99	S. Abdur-Rahim BP	20.00	9.00
□ 100	D.Mutombo BP	5.00	2.20
□ 101	Bobby Jackson	25.00	11.00
□ 102	Tony Battie	25.00	11.00
□ 103	Keith Booth	8.00	3.60
□ 104	Keith Van Horn	125.00	55.00
□ 105	Paul Grant	8.00	3.60
□ 106	Tim Duncan	150.00	70.00
□ 107	Scot Pollard	8.00	3.60
□ 108	Maurice Taylor	40.00	18.00
□ 109	Antonio Daniels	30.00	13.50
□ 110	Austin Croshere	12.00	5.50
□ 111	Tracy McGrady	80.00	36.00
□ 112	Charles O'Bannon	8.00	3.60
□ 113	Rodrick Rhodes	12.00	5.50
□ 114	Johnny Taylor	8.00	3.60
□ 115	Danny Fortson	25.00	11.00
□ 116	Chauncey Billups	50.00	22.00
□ 117	Tim Thomas	80.00	36.00
□ 118	Derek Anderson	40.00	18.00
□ 119	Ed Gray	12.00	5.50
□ 120	Jacque Vaughn	20.00	9.00
□ 121	Kelvin Cato	12.00	5.50
□ 122	Tariq Abdul-Wahad	20.00	9.00
□ 123	Ron Mercer	100.00	45.00
□ 124	Brevin Knight	40.00	18.00
□ 125	Adonal Foyle	12.00	5.50

□ 8	Glenn Robinson	60.00	27.00
□ 13	Karl Malone	80.00	36.00
□ 36	D.Mutombo	30.00	13.50
□ 59	Steve Smith	30.00	13.50
□ 77	Mitch Richmond	60.00	27.00
□ 102	Tony Battie	60.00	27.00
□ 104	Keith Van Horn	200.00	90.00
□ 116	Chauncey Billups	80.00	36.00
□ 123	Ron Mercer	150.00	70.00
□ 125	Adonal Foyle	30.00	13.50
□ KM	Karl Malone MVP	100.00	45.00

1997-98 Bowman's Best Cuts

Randomly inserted into packs at one in 24, this 10-card laser cut set features ten of the hottest players in the game today. Card backs feature a "BC" prefix.

	MINT	NRMT
COMPLETE SET (10)	75.00	34.00
COMMON CARD (BC1-BC10)	3.00	1.35

STATED ODDS 1:24 HOB, 1:40 RET
*REFRACTORS: .6X to 1.5X HI COLUMN
REF: STATED ODDS 1:48 HOB, 1:80 RET
*ATOMIC REFRACTORS: 1.25X TO 3X HI
ATO: STATED ODDS 1:96 HOB, 1:160 RET

□ BC1	Vin Baker	6.00	2.70
□ BC2	Patrick Ewing	3.00	1.35
□ BC3	Scottie Pippen	10.00	4.50
□ BC4	Karl Malone	5.00	2.20
□ BC5	Kevin Garnett	20.00	9.00
□ BC6	A.Hardaway	12.00	5.50
□ BC7	Shawn Kemp	10.00	4.50
□ BC8	Charles Barkley	5.00	2.20
□ BC9	Stephon Marbury	15.00	6.75
□ BC10	Shaquille O'Neal	12.00	5.50

1997-98 Bowman's Best Autographs

Randomly inserted into packs at a rate of one in 373, this 11-card set features autographs on the regular player cards. The only exception is Karl Malone, who has a regular autograph and a special MVP card autograph. There is no special insertion rate for the MVP card.

	MINT	NRMT
COMPLETE SET (11)	800.00	350.00
COMMON CARD	30.00	13.50

STATED ODDS 1:373 HOB, 1:745 RET
*REFRACTORS: 1X TO 2X HI COLUMN
REF: STATED ODDS 1:1,987 H, 1:3,974 R
*ATOMIC REFRACTORS: 2X TO 3X HI
ATO: STATED ODDS 1:5,961 H, 1:11,922 R

1997-98 Bowman's Best Mirror Image

Randomly inserted into packs at a rate of one in 48, this 10-card set features two veterans and two rookies together on double-sided cards. The cards look similar to "playing cards". Card backs carry a "MI" prefix.

	MINT	NRMT
COMPLETE SET (10)	225.00	100.00
COMMON CARD (MI1-MI10)	6.00	2.70

STATED ODDS 1:48 HOB, 1:80 RET
*REFRACTORS: .6X TO 1.5X HI COLUMN
REF: STATED ODDS 1:96 HOB, 1:160 RET
*ATOMIC REFRACTORS: 1.25X TO 3X HI
ATO: STATED ODDS 1:192 HOB, 1:320 RET

□ MI1	Michael Jordan	50.00	22.00
	Ron Mercer		
	Stephon Marbury		
	Gary Payton		
□ MI2	Tim Thomas	20.00	9.00
	Chris Webber		
	Shaquille O'Neal		
	Adonal Foyle		
□ MI3	Tim Hardaway	20.00	9.00
	Allen Iverson		
	Bobby Jackson		
	Jason Kidd		
□ MI4	Scottie Pippen	40.00	18.00
	Keith Van Horn		
	Kobe Bryant		
	Cedric Ceballos		
□ MI5	Grant Hill	30.00	13.50
	Tracy McGrady		
	S.Abdur-Rahim		
	Kevin Garnett		
□ MI6	Shawn Kemp	40.00	18.00
	Marcus Camby		
	Tim Duncan		
	David Robinson		
□ MI7	Ray Allen	6.00	2.70
	Steve Smith		
	Shandon Anderson		
	Sean Elliott		
□ MI8	Chauncey Billups	10.00	4.50
	Terrell Brandon		
	Antonio Daniels		
	Kevin Johnson		
□ MI9	Kerry Kittles	15.00	6.75
	Reggie Miller		
	Tony Battie		
	Hakeem Olajuwon		
□ MI10	Larry Johnson	20.00	9.00
	Antoine Walker		
	Maurice Taylor		
	Vin Baker		

1997-98 Bowman's Best Picks

Randomly inserted into packs at a rate of one in 24, this 10-card set features some of the top rookies from the 1997 class. Card backs carry a "BP" prefix.

	MINT	NRMT
COMPLETE SET (10)	70.00	32.00
COMMON CARD (BP1-BP10)	2.00	.90
UNLISTED STARS	3.00	1.35

STATED ODDS 1:24 HOB, 1:40 RET

*REFRACTORS: .6X TO 1.5X HI COLUMN
REF: STATED ODDS 1:48 HOB, 1:80 RET
*ATOMIC REFRACTORS: 1.25X TO 3X HI
ATO: STATED ODDS 1:96 HOB, 1:160 RET

		MINT	NRMT
☐ BP1	Adonal Foyle	2.00	.90
☐ BP2	Maurice Taylor	5.00	2.20
☐ BP3	Austin Croshere	2.00	.90
☐ BP4	Tracy McGrady	10.00	4.50
☐ BP5	Antonio Daniels	4.00	1.80
☐ BP6	Tony Battie	3.00	1.35
☐ BP7	Chauncey Billups	6.00	2.70
☐ BP8	Tim Duncan	20.00	9.00
☐ BP9	Ron Mercer	12.00	5.50
☐ BP10	Keith Van Horn	15.00	6.75

1997-98 Bowman's Best Techniques

Randomly inserted into packs at a rate of one in 12, this 10-card set focuses on some of the NBA's top players at their positions. Card backs carry a "T" prefix.

		MINT	NRMT
COMPLETE SET (10)		50.00	22.00
COMMON CARD (T1-T10)		1.00	.45
UNLISTED STARS		1.50	.70

*STATED ODDS 1:12 HOB, 1:20 RET
*REFRACTORS: 1X TO 2.5X HI COLUMN
REF: STATED ODDS 1:48 HOB, 1:80 RET
*ATOMIC REFRACTORS: 2X TO 5X HI
ATO: STATED ODDS 1:96 HOB, 1:160 RET

		MINT	NRMT
☐ T1	D.Mutombo	1.00	.45
☐ T2	Michael Jordan	20.00	9.00
☐ T3	Grant Hill	10.00	4.50
☐ T4	Kobe Bryant	12.00	5.50
☐ T5	Gary Payton	2.50	1.10
☐ T6	Glen Rice	1.50	.70
☐ T7	Dennis Rodman	6.00	2.70
☐ T8	Hakeem Olajuwon	3.00	1.35
☐ T9	Allen Iverson	8.00	3.60
☐ T10	John Stockton	1.50	.70

1994-95 Collector's Choice

These 420 standard-size cards, issued in two separate series of 210-cards each, comprise Upper Deck's '94-95 Collector's Choice set. Cards were issued in 12-card hobby packs (suggested retail of ninety-nine cents), 13-card retail packs (suggested retail of $1.18), and 20-card retail jumbo packs. White bordered fronts feature color player action shots. The player's name, team, and position appear in a lower corner. The back carries another color player action shot at the top, with statistics and career highlights displayed below. The following subsets are included in this set: Tip-Off (166-192), All-Star Advice (193-198), NBA Profiles (199-206), Blueprints (372-398), Trivia (399-406), and Draft Class (407-416). Rookie Cards in this set include Grant Hill, Juwan Howard, Eddie Jones, Jason Kidd and Glenn Robinson.

	MINT	NRMT
COMPLETE SET (420)	30.00	13.50
COMPLETE SERIES 1 (210)	12.00	5.50
COMPLETE SERIES 2 (210)	18.00	8.00
COMMON CARD (1-420)	.05	.02
SEMISTARS	.10	.05
UNLISTED STARS	.20	.09
COMP.SILVER SET (420)	100.00	45.00
COMP.SILVER SER.1 (210)	40.00	18.00
COMP.SILVER SER.2 (210)	60.00	27.00
COMMON SILVER (1-420)	.10	.05

*SILVER STARS: 1.5X TO 3X HI COLUMN
*SILVER RCs: 1.25X TO 2.5X HI
ONE SILVER SIGNATURE PER PACK
THREE SILVER PER RETAIL JUMBO PACK

COMP.GOLD SET (420)	1000.00	450.00
COMP.GOLD SERIES 1 (210)	400.00	180.00
COMP.GOLD SERIES 2 (210)	600.00	275.00
COMMON GOLD (1-420)	1.50	.70

*GOLD STARS: 20X TO 40X HI COLUMN
*GOLD RCs: 15X TO 30X HI
GOLD: SER.1/2 STATED ODDS 1:35 HOB/RET

☐ 1	A.Hardaway	.75	.35
☐ 2	Mark Macon	.05	.02
☐ 3	Steve Smith	.10	.05
☐ 4	Chris Webber	.50	.23
☐ 5	Donald Royal	.05	.02
☐ 6	Avery Johnson	.05	.02
☐ 7	Kevin Johnson	.10	.05
☐ 8	Doug Christie	.05	.02
☐ 9	Derrick McKey	.05	.02
☐ 10	Dennis Rodman	.75	.35
☐ 11	Scott Skiles UER	.05	.02
	(Listed as playing with Cavaliers		
	instead of Pacers in '87-'88, '88-'89)		
☐ 12	Johnny Dawkins	.05	.02
☐ 13	Kendall Gill	.05	.02
☐ 14	Jeff Hornacek	.10	.05
☐ 15	Latrell Sprewell	.10	.05
☐ 16	Lucious Harris	.05	.02
☐ 17	Chris Mullin	.20	.09
☐ 18	John Williams	.05	.02
☐ 19	Tony Campbell	.05	.02
☐ 20	LaPhonso Ellis	.10	.05
☐ 21	Gerald Wilkins	.05	.02
☐ 22	Clyde Drexler	.25	.11
☐ 23	Michael Jordan	2.50	1.10
☐ 24	George Lynch	.05	.02
☐ 25	Mark Price	.05	.02
☐ 26	James Robinson	.05	.02
☐ 27	Elmore Spencer	.05	.02
☐ 28	Stacey King	.05	.02
☐ 29	Corie Blount	.05	.02
☐ 30	Dell Curry	.05	.02
☐ 31	Reggie Miller	.20	.09
☐ 32	Karl Malone	.30	.14
☐ 33	Scottie Pippen	.60	.25
☐ 34	Hakeem Olajuwon	.40	.18
☐ 35	C.Weatherspoon	.05	.02
☐ 36	Kevin Edwards	.05	.02
☐ 37	Pete Myers	.05	.02
☐ 38	Jeff Turner	.05	.02
☐ 39	Ennis Whatley	.05	.02
☐ 40	Calbert Cheaney	.10	.05
☐ 41	Glen Rice	.20	.09
☐ 42	Vin Baker	.50	.23
☐ 43	Grant Long	.05	.02
☐ 44	Derrick Coleman	.10	.05
☐ 45	Rik Smits	.10	.05
☐ 46	Chris Smith	.05	.02
☐ 47	Carl Herrera	.05	.02
☐ 48	Bob Martin	.05	.02
☐ 49	Terrell Brandon	.20	.09
☐ 50	David Robinson	.30	.14
☐ 51	Danny Ferry	.05	.02
☐ 52	Buck Williams	.10	.05
☐ 53	Josh Grant	.05	.02
☐ 54	Ed Pinckney	.05	.02
☐ 55	D.Mutombo	.20	.09
☐ 56	Clifford Robinson	.10	.05
☐ 57	Luther Wright	.05	.02
☐ 58	Scott Burrell	.05	.02
☐ 59	Stacey Augmon	.05	.02
☐ 60	Jeff Malone	.05	.02
☐ 61	Byron Houston	.05	.02
☐ 62	Anthony Peeler	.05	.02
☐ 63	Michael Adams	.05	.02
☐ 64	Negele Knight	.05	.02
☐ 65	Terry Cummings	.05	.02
☐ 66	Christian Laettner	.10	.05
☐ 67	Tracy Murray	.05	.02
☐ 68	Sedale Threatt	.05	.02
☐ 69	Dan Majerle	.10	.05
☐ 70	Frank Brickowski	.05	.02
☐ 71	Ken Norman	.05	.02
☐ 72	Charles Smith	.05	.02
☐ 73	Adam Keefe	.05	.02
☐ 74	P.J. Brown	.05	.02
☐ 75	Kevin Duckworth	.05	.02
☐ 76	Shawn Bradley UER	.10	.05
	Bradely on back		
☐ 77	Darnell Mee	.05	.02
☐ 78	Nick Anderson	.10	.05
☐ 79	Mark West	.05	.02
☐ 80	B.J. Armstrong	.05	.02
☐ 81	Dennis Scott	.05	.02
☐ 82	Lindsey Hunter	.10	.05
☐ 83	Derek Strong	.05	.02

84	Mike Brown	.05	.02
85	Antonio Harvey	.05	.02
86	Anthony Bonner	.05	.02
87	Sam Cassell	.20	.09
88	Harold Miner	.05	.02
89	Spud Webb	.10	.05
90	Mookie Blaylock	.10	.05
91	Greg Anthony	.05	.02
92	Richard Petruska	.05	.02
93	Sean Rooks	.05	.02
94	Ervin Johnson	.05	.02
95	Randy Brown	.05	.02
96	Orlando Woolridge	.05	.02
97	Charles Oakley	.10	.05
98	Craig Ehlo	.05	.02
99	Derek Harper	.05	.02
100	Doug Edwards	.05	.02
101	Muggsy Bogues	.10	.05
102	Mitch Richmond	.20	.09
103	M.Abdul-Rauf	.05	.02
104	Joe Dumars	.20	.09
105	Eric Riley	.05	.02
106	Terry Mills	.05	.02
107	Toni Kukoc	.20	.09
108	Jon Koncak	.05	.02
109	Haywoode Workman	.05	.02
110	Todd Day	.05	.02
111	Detlef Schrempf	.10	.05
112	David Wesley	.10	.05
113	Mark Jackson	.10	.05
114	Doug Overton	.05	.02
115	Vinny Del Negro	.05	.02
116	Loy Vaught	.05	.02
117	Mike Peplowski	.05	.02
118	Bimbo Coles	.05	.02
119	Rex Walters	.05	.02
120	Sherman Douglas	.05	.02
121	David Benoit	.05	.02
122	John Salley	.05	.02
123	Cedric Ceballos	.10	.05
124	Chris Mills	.10	.05
125	Robert Horry	.10	.05
126	Johnny Newman	.05	.02
127	Malcolm Mackey	.05	.02
128	Terry Dehere	.05	.02
129	Dino Radja	.05	.02
130	Tree Rollins	.05	.02
131	Xavier McDaniel	.05	.02
132	Bobby Hurley	.05	.02
133	Alonzo Mourning	.25	.11
134	Isaiah Rider	.10	.05
135	Antoine Carr	.05	.02
136	Robert Pack	.05	.02
137	Walt Williams	.05	.02
138	Tyrone Corbin	.05	.02
139	Popeye Jones	.05	.02
140	Shawn Kemp	.60	.25
141	Thurl Bailey	.05	.02
142	James Worthy	.20	.09
143	Scott Haskin	.05	.02
144	Hubert Davis	.05	.02
145	A.C. Green	.10	.05
146	Dale Davis	.05	.02
147	Nate McMillan	.05	.02
148	Chris Morris	.05	.02
149	Will Perdue	.05	.02
150	Felton Spencer	.05	.02
151	Rod Strickland	.10	.05
152	Blue Edwards	.05	.02
153	John Williams	.05	.02
154	Rodney Rogers	.05	.02
155	Acie Earl	.05	.02
156	Hersey Hawkins	.05	.02
157	Jamal Mashburn	.20	.09
158	Don MacLean	.05	.02
159	Micheal Williams	.05	.02
160	Kenny Gattison	.05	.02
161	Rich King	.05	.02
162	Allan Houston	.20	.09
163	Hoop-it-up	.05	.02
	Men's Champions		
164	Hoop-it-up	.05	.02
	Women's Champions		
	Lisa Harrison		
165	Hoop-it-up	.05	.02
	Slam-Dunk Champions		
	Corey Etheridge		
166	Danny Manning TO	.05	.02
167	Robert Parish TO	.05	.02
168	Alonzo Mourning TO	.20	.09
169	Scottie Pippen TO	.30	.14
170	Mark Price TO	.05	.02
171	Jamal Mashburn TO	.10	.05
172	D.Mutombo TO	.10	.05
173	Joe Dumars TO	.10	.05
174	Chris Webber TO	.25	.11
175	Hakeem Olajuwon TO	.20	.09
176	Reggie Miller TO	.10	.05
177	Ron Harper TO	.05	.02
178	Nick Van Exel TO	.10	.05
179	Steve Smith TO	.05	.02
180	Vin Baker TO	.25	.11
181	Isaiah Rider TO	.05	.02
182	Derrick Coleman TO	.05	.02
183	Patrick Ewing TO	.10	.05
184	Shaquille O'Neal TO	.40	.18
185	C. Weatherspoon TO	.05	.02
186	Charles Barkley TO	.20	.09
187	Clyde Drexler TO	.20	.09
188	Mitch Richmond TO	.10	.05
189	David Robinson TO	.20	.09
190	Shawn Kemp TO	.30	.14
191	Karl Malone TO	.20	.09
192	Tom Gugliotta TO	.10	.05
193	Kenny Anderson ASA	.05	.02
194	Alonzo Mourning ASA	.20	.09
195	Mark Price ASA	.05	.02
196	John Stockton ASA	.10	.05
197	Shaquille O'Neal ASA	.40	.18
198	Latrell Sprewell ASA	.05	.02
199	Charles Barkley PRO	.20	.09
200	Chris Webber PRO	.25	.11
201	Patrick Ewing PRO	.10	.05
202	Dennis Rodman PRO	.40	.18
203	Shawn Kemp PRO	.30	.14
204	Michael Jordan PRO	1.25	.55
205	Shaquille O'Neal PRO	.40	.18
206	Larry Johnson PRO	.05	.02
207	Tim Hardaway CL	.20	.09
208	John Stockton CL	.10	.05
209	Harold Miner CL	.05	.02
210	B.J. Armstrong CL	.05	.02
211	Vernon Maxwell	.05	.02
212	John Stockton	.20	.09
213	Luc Longley	.10	.05
214	Sam Perkins	.10	.05
215	Pooh Richardson	.05	.02
216	Tyrone Corbin	.05	.02
217	Mario Elie	.05	.02
218	Bobby Phills	.05	.02
219	Grant Hill	2.50	1.10
220	Gary Payton	.30	.14
221	Tom Hammonds	.05	.02
222	Danny Ainge	.10	.05
223	Gary Grant	.05	.02
224	Jim Jackson	.10	.05
225	Chris Gatling	.05	.02
226	Sergei Bazarevich	.05	.02
227	Tony Dumas	.05	.02
228	Andrew Lang	.05	.02
229	Wesley Person	.25	.11
230	Terry Porter	.05	.02
231	Duane Causwell	.05	.02
232	Shaquille O'Neal	.75	.35
233	Antonio Davis	.05	.02
234	Charles Barkley	.30	.14
235	Tony Massenburg	.05	.02
236	Ricky Pierce	.05	.02
237	Scott Skiles	.05	.02
238	Jalen Rose	.20	.09
239	Charlie Ward	.10	.05
240	Michael Jordan	1.25	.55
241	Elden Campbell	.10	.05
242	Bill Cartwright	.05	.02
243	Armon Gilliam	.05	.02
244	Rick Fox	.05	.02
245	Tim Breaux	.05	.02
246	Monty Williams	.05	.02
247	Dominique Wilkins	.20	.09
248	Robert Parish	.10	.05
249	Mark Jackson	.10	.05
250	Jason Kidd	1.50	.70
251	Andres Guibert	.05	.02
252	Matt Geiger	.05	.02
253	Stanley Roberts	.05	.02
254	Jack Haley	.05	.02
255	David Wingate	.05	.02
256	John Crotty	.05	.02
257	Brian Grant	.20	.09
258	Otis Thorpe	.10	.05
259	Clifford Rozier	.05	.02
260	Grant Long	.05	.02
261	Eric Mobley	.05	.02
262	Dickey Simpkins	.05	.02
263	J.R. Reid	.05	.02
264	Kevin Willis	.05	.02
265	Scott Brooks	.05	.02
266	Glenn Robinson	.75	.35
267	Dana Barros	.05	.02
268	Ken Norman	.05	.02
269	Herb Williams	.05	.02
270	Dee Brown	.05	.02
271	Steve Kerr	.10	.05
272	Jon Barry	.05	.02
273	Sean Elliott	.10	.05
274	Elliot Perry	.05	.02
275	Kenny Smith	.05	.02
276	Sean Rooks	.05	.02
277	Gheorghe Muresan	.10	.05
278	Juwan Howard	1.00	.45
279	Steve Smith	.10	.05
280	Anthony Bowie	.05	.02
281	Moses Malone	.20	.09
282	Olden Polynice	.05	.02
283	Jo Jo English	.05	.02
284	Marty Conlon	.05	.02
285	Sam Mitchell	.05	.02
286	Doug West	.05	.02
287	Cedric Ceballos	.10	.05
288	Lorenzo Williams	.05	.02
289	Harold Ellis	.05	.02
290	Doc Rivers	.10	.05
291	Keith Tower	.05	.02
292	Mark Bryant	.05	.02
293	Oliver Miller	.05	.02
294	Michael Adams	.05	.02
295	Tree Rollins	.05	.02
296	Eddie Jones	1.50	.70
297	Malik Sealy	.05	.02
298	Blue Edwards	.05	.02
299	Brooks Thompson	.05	.02
300	Benoit Benjamin	.05	.02
301	Avery Johnson	.05	.02
302	Larry Johnson	.10	.05
303	John Starks	.10	.05
304	Byron Scott	.05	.02
305	Eric Murdock	.05	.02
306	Jay Humphries	.05	.02
307	Kenny Anderson	.10	.05
308	Brian Williams	.05	.02
309	Nick Van Exel	.20	.09
310	Tim Hardaway	.25	.11
311	Lee Mayberry	.05	.02
312	Vlade Divac	.10	.05
313	Donyell Marshall	.25	.11
314	Anthony Mason	.10	.05
315	Danny Manning	.05	.02
316	Tyrone Hill	.05	.02
317	Vincent Askew	.05	.02
318	Khalid Reeves	.05	.02
319	Ron Harper	.10	.05
320	Brent Price	.05	.02
321	Byron Houston	.05	.02
322	Lamond Murray	.10	.05
323	Bryant Stith	.05	.02
324	Tom Gugliotta	.20	.09
325	Jerome Kersey	.05	.02
326	B.J. Tyler	.05	.02
327	Antonio Lang	.05	.02
328	Carlos Rogers	.05	.02
329	Wayman Tisdale	.05	.02
330	Kevin Gamble	.05	.02
331	Eric Piatkowski	.05	.02
332	Mitchell Butler	.05	.02
333	Patrick Ewing	.20	.09
334	Doug Smith	.05	.02
335	Joe Kleine	.05	.02
336	Keith Jennings	.05	.02

☐ 337 Bill Curley	.05	.02
☐ 338 Johnny Newman	.05	.02
☐ 339 Howard Eisley	.05	.02
☐ 340 Willie Anderson	.05	.02
☐ 341 Aaron McKie	.05	.02
☐ 342 Tom Chambers	.05	.02
☐ 343 Scott Williams	.05	.02
☐ 344 Harvey Grant	.05	.02
☐ 345 Billy Owens	.05	.02
☐ 346 Sharone Wright	.05	.02
☐ 347 Michael Cage	.05	.02
☐ 348 Vern Fleming	.05	.02
☐ 349 Darrin Hancock	.05	.02
☐ 350 Matt Fish	.05	.02
☐ 351 Rony Seikaly	.05	.02
☐ 352 Victor Alexander	.05	.02
☐ 353 Anthony Miller	.05	.02
☐ 354 Horace Grant	.10	.05
☐ 355 Jayson Williams	.05	.02
☐ 356 Dale Ellis	.05	.02
☐ 357 Sarunas Marciulionis	.05	.02
☐ 358 Anthony Avent	.05	.02
☐ 359 Rex Chapman	.05	.02
☐ 360 Askia Jones	.05	.02
☐ 361 Charles Outlaw	.05	.02
☐ 362 Chuck Person	.05	.02
☐ 363 Dan Schayes	.05	.02
☐ 364 Morlon Wiley	.05	.02
☐ 365 Dontonio Wingfield	.05	.02
☐ 366 Tony Smith	.05	.02
☐ 367 Bill Wennington	.05	.02
☐ 368 Bryon Russell	.10	.05
☐ 369 Geert Hammink	.05	.02
☐ 370 Eric Montross	.05	.02
☐ 371 Cliff Levingston	.05	.02
☐ 372 Stacey Augmon BP	.05	.02
☐ 373 Eric Montross BP	.05	.02
☐ 374 Alonzo Mourning BP	.20	.09
☐ 375 Scottie Pippen BP	.30	.14
☐ 376 Mark Price BP	.05	.02
☐ 377 Jason Kidd BP	.60	.25
☐ 378 Jalen Rose BP	.10	.05
☐ 379 Grant Hill BP	1.00	.45
☐ 380 Latrell Sprewell BP	.05	.09
☐ 381 Hakeem Olajuwon BP	.20	.09
☐ 382 Reggie Miller BP	.10	.05
☐ 383 Lamond Murray BP	.05	.02
☐ 384 Eddie Jones BP	.60	.02
☐ 385 Khalid Reeves BP	.05	.02
☐ 386 Glenn Robinson BP	.30	.14
☐ 387 Donyell Marshall BP	.10	.05
☐ 388 Derrick Coleman BP	.05	.02
☐ 389 Patrick Ewing BP	.10	.05
☐ 390 Shaquille O'Neal BP	.40	.18
☐ 391 Sharone Wright BP	.05	.02
☐ 392 Charles Barkley BP	.20	.09
☐ 393 Aaron McKie BP	.05	.02
☐ 394 Brian Grant BP	.10	.05
☐ 395 David Robinson BP	.20	.09
☐ 396 Shawn Kemp BP	.30	.14
☐ 397 Karl Malone BP	.20	.09
☐ 398 Tom Gugliotta BP	.10	.05
☐ 399 Hakeem Olajuwon TRIV	.20	.09
☐ 400 Shaquille O'Neal TRIV	.40	.18
☐ 401 Chris Webber TRIV	.25	.11
☐ 402 Michael Jordan TRIV	1.25	.55
☐ 403 David Robinson TRIV	.20	.09
☐ 404 Shawn Kemp TRIV	.30	.14
☐ 405 Patrick Ewing TRIV	.10	.05
☐ 406 Charles Barkley TRIV	.20	.09
☐ 407 Glenn Robinson DC	.30	.14
☐ 408 Jason Kidd DC	.60	.25
☐ 409 Grant Hill DC	1.00	.45
☐ 410 Donyell Marshall DC	.10	.05
☐ 411 Sharone Wright DC	.05	.02
☐ 412 Lamond Murray DC	.05	.02
☐ 413 Brian Grant DC	.10	.05
☐ 414 Eric Montross DC	.05	.02
☐ 415 Eddie Jones DC	.60	.02
☐ 416 Carlos Rogers DC	.05	.02
☐ 417 Shawn Kemp CL	.10	.05
☐ 418 Bobby Hurley CL	.05	.02
☐ 419 Shawn Bradley CL	.05	.02
☐ 420 Michael Jordan CL	.75	.35

1994-95 Collector's Choice Blow-Ups

One of these oversized (5" by 7") cards was inserted exclusively into each series 2 hobby box. Each Blow-Up is identical in design and numbering to their corresponding basic issue card. According to information provided by Upper Deck at least 3,000 of these cards were autographed and randomly seeded into boxes. There are far fewer autographed Michael Jordan Blow-Ups than the other four players featured.

	MINT	NRMT
COMPLETE SET (5)	10.00	4.50
COMMON CARD (40/76/132)	.50	.23
ONE PER SER.2 HOBBY BOX		
AU CARDS RANDOMLY INSERTED		

		MINT	NRMT
☐ 23 Michael Jordan BB		8.00	3.60
☐ 40 Calbert Cheaney		.75	.35
☐ 76 Shawn Bradley		.75	.35
☐ 132 Bobby Hurley		.50	.23
☐ 140 Shawn Kemp		2.00	.90
☐ A23 Michael Jordan AU	5000.00	2200.00
☐ A40 Calbert Cheaney AU	30.00	13.50
☐ A76 Shawn Bradley AU	30.00	13.50
☐ A132 Bobby Hurley AU	30.00	13.50
☐ A140 Shawn Kemp AU	150.00	70.00

1994-95 Collector's Choice Crash the Game Assists

These fifteen standard-size Crash the Game Assists cards were randomly inserted exclusively into first series retail packs at a rate of one in 20. Cards that featured players who tallied 750 or more assists during the 1994-95 campaign were redeemable for a 15-card parallel Crash the Game Assists Redemption set. Only John Stockton eclipsed the mark. The

fronts feature a color-action photo with the background of the game in black and white. The top has the player's name in a box the color of his team and the bottom has the words "You Crash The Game" in foil with the player's position behind it in his team's color. The back says 750 assists at the top below his name surrounded by the player's team color. There are instructions on how to redeem your cards if you win. The exchange deadline was June 16th, 1995. The redemption cards were delayed in shipping until late October, 1995.

	MINT	NRMT
COMPLETE SET (15)	12.00	5.50
COMMON CARD (A1-A15)	.50	.23
SEMISTARS	1.00	.45
UNLISTED STARS	1.50	.70
SER.1 STATED ODDS 1:20 RETAIL		
COMP.AST.RED.SET (15)	6.00	2.70
*ASSISTS RED.CARDS: 50% OF HI COLUMN		
ONE EXCH.SET PER WINNER CARD BY MAIL		

	MINT	NRMT
☐ A1 Michael Adams	.50	.23
☐ A2 Kenny Anderson	1.00	.45
☐ A3 Mookie Blaylock	1.00	.45
☐ A4 Muggsy Bogues	1.00	.45
☐ A5 Sherman Douglas	.50	.23
☐ A6 A.Hardaway	6.00	2.70
☐ A7 Tim Hardaway	2.00	.90
☐ A8 Lindsey Hunter	1.00	.45
☐ A9 Mark Jackson	1.00	.45
☐ A10 Kevin Johnson	1.00	.45
☐ A11 Eric Murdock	.50	.23
☐ A12 Mark Price	.50	.23
☐ A13 John Stockton	1.50	.70
☐ A14 Rod Strickland	1.00	.45
☐ A15 Micheal Williams	.50	.23

1994-95 Collector's Choice Crash the Game Rebounds

These fifteen standard-size Crash the Game Rebounds cards were randomly inserted exclusively into second series

retail packs at a rate of one in 20. Cards that featured players who grabbed 1,000 or more rebounds during the 1994-95 campaign were redeemable for a 15-card parallel Crash the Game Rebounds Redemption set. The card design is the same as the Assists set except on the back it says 1,000 Rebounds. Only D.Mutombo eclipsed the mark. The exchange deadline was June 30, 1995. The redemption cards were delayed in shipping until late October, 1995.

	MINT	NRMT
COMPLETE SET (15)	20.00	9.00
COMMON CARD (R1-R15)	.50	.23
SEMISTARS	.75	.35
UNLISTED STARS	1.25	.55
SER.2 STATED ODDS 1:20 RETAIL		
COMP.REB.RED.SET (15) ..	10.00	4.50
*REB.RED.CARDS: 50% OF HI COLUMN		
ONE EXCH.SET PER WINNER CARD BY MAIL		

		MINT	NRMT
☐ R1	Derrick Coleman	.75	.35
☐ R2	Patrick Ewing	1.25	.55
☐ R3	Horace Grant	.75	.35
☐ R4	Shawn Kemp	4.00	1.80
☐ R5	Karl Malone	2.00	.90
☐ R6	Alonzo Mourning	1.50	.70
☐ R7	D.Mutombo	1.25	.55
☐ R8	Charles Oakley	.75	.35
☐ R9	Hakeem Olajuwon	2.50	1.10
☐ R10	Shaquille O'Neal	5.00	2.20
☐ R11	Olden Polynice	.50	.23
☐ R12	David Robinson	2.00	.90
☐ R13	Dennis Rodman	5.00	2.20
☐ R14	Otis Thorpe	.75	.35
☐ R15	Kevin Willis	.50	.23

1994-95 Collector's Choice Crash the Game Rookie Scoring

These fifteen standard-size Crash the Game Rookie Scoring cards were randomly inserted exclusively into second series hobby packs at a rate of one in 20. Cards that featured rookies

who scored more than 1,250 points during the 1994-95 campaign were redeemable for a 15-card parallel Crash the Game Rookie Scoring Redemption set. The card design is the same as the Assists set except on the back it says 1,250 Points. Only Grant Hill and Glenn Robinson eclipsed the mark. The exchange deadline was June 30th, 1995. The redemption cards were delayed in shipping until late October, 1995.

	MINT	NRMT
COMPLETE SET (15)	15.00	6.75
COMMON CARD (S1-S15)	.40	.18
SEMISTARS	.50	.23
SER.2 STATED ODDS 1:20 HOBBY		
COMP.ROOK.RED.SET (15) ..	8.00	3.60
*ROOKIES RED.CARDS: 50% OF HI COLUMN		
ONE EXCH.SET PER WINNER CARD BY MAIL		

		MINT	NRMT
☐ S1	Tony Dumas	.40	.18
☐ S2	Brian Grant	.50	.23
☐ S3	Grant Hill	6.00	2.70
☐ S4	Juwan Howard	2.50	1.10
☐ S5	Eddie Jones	4.00	1.80
☐ S6	Jason Kidd	4.00	1.80
☐ S7	Donyell Marshall	.50	.23
☐ S8	Eric Montross	.40	.18
☐ S9	Lamond Murray	.50	.23
☐ S10	Khalid Reeves	.40	.18
☐ S11	Glenn Robinson	2.00	.90
☐ S12	Jalen Rose	.50	.23
☐ S13	Dickey Simpkins	.40	.18
☐ S14	Charlie Ward	.40	.18
☐ S15	Sharone Wright...........	.40	.18

1994-95 Collector's Choice Crash the Game Scoring

These fifteen standard-size Crash the Game Scoring cards were randomly inserted exclusively into first series hobby packs at a rate of one in 20. Cards that featured players who posted 2,000 or more points during the 1994-95 campaign were redeemable for a 15-card

parallel Crash the Game Scoring Redemption set. The card design is the same as the Assists set except on the back it says 2,000 Points. Karl Malone, Shaquille O'Neal, Hakeem Olajuwon and David Robinson all eclipsed the mark. The exchange deadline was June 30, 1995. The redemption cards were delayed in shipping until late October, 1995.

	MINT	NRMT
COMPLETE SET (15)	20.00	9.00
COMMON CARD (S1-S15)	.50	.23
SEMISTARS	.75	.35
UNLISTED STARS	1.25	.55
SER.1 STATED ODDS 1:20 HOBBY		
COMP.SCOR.RED.SET (15)	10.00	4.50
*SCORING RED.CARDS: 50% OF HI COLUMN		
ONE EXCH.SET PER WINNER CARD BY MAIL		

		MINT	NRMT
☐ S1	Charles Barkley	2.00	.90
☐ S2	Derrick Coleman	.50	.23
☐ S3	Joe Dumars	1.25	.55
☐ S4	Patrick Ewing	1.25	.55
☐ S5	Karl Malone	2.00	.90
☐ S6	Reggie Miller	1.25	.55
☐ S7	Shaquille O'Neal	3.00	1.35
☐ S8	Hakeem Olajuwon	2.50	1.10
☐ S9	Scottie Pippen	4.00	1.80
☐ S10	Glen Rice	1.25	.55
☐ S11	Mitch Richmond	1.25	.55
☐ S12	David Robinson	2.00	.90
☐ S13	Latrell Sprewell	.75	.35
☐ S14	Chris Webber	3.00	1.35
☐ S15	Dominique Wilkins	1.25	.55

1994-95 Collector's Choice Draft Trade

This 10-card set was available only by redeeming a Draft Trade card that was randomly seeded into one in every 36 first series Collector's Choice hobby or retail packs. The fronts have a color-action photo with the top-half having the background of the game in black and white. The bottom of the card has a white background. On the left side of the card are the words

"NBA Draft Lottery Picks" with the player's name above it. The backs have the player's name and information set against the colors of his team. The expiration date on the redemption was June 16th, 1995.

	MINT	NRMT
COMPLETE SET (10)	8.00	3.60
COMMON CARD (1-10)	.25	.11
SEMISTARS	.30	.14

ONE SET PER DRAFT TRADE CARD BY MAIL
DT CARD: SER.1 STATED ODDS 1:36

#	Name	MINT	NRMT
1	Glenn Robinson	1.25	.55
2	Jason Kidd	2.50	1.10
3	Grant Hill	4.00	1.80
4	Donyell Marshall	.30	.14
5	Juwan Howard	1.50	.70
6	Sharone Wright	.25	.11
7	Lamond Murray	.30	.14
8	Brian Grant	.30	.14
9	Eric Montross	.25	.11
10	Eddie Jones	2.50	1.10
NNO	Draft Trade Card	.25	.11

1995-96 Collector's Choice

These 410-standard size cards, issued in two separate series of 210 and 200 cards respectively, comprise Upper Deck's 1995-96 Collector's Choice set. Cards were primarily issued in 12-card hobby and retail packs (suggested retail price of ninety-nine cents) and five-card retail mini-packs. In addition, large retail chain stores received complete factory sets around the end of the season (SRP $29.97). Each factory set contains a basic 410 card set, four Collector's Choice Jordan Collection inserts, four Player's Club Platinum inserts and a special 5" by 7" Bulls Commemorative card celebrating their 70 win season. Regular issue cards feature white-bordered fronts with color player action shots. The backs have a color photo and statistics. The following subsets are included: Fun Facts (166-194), Professor Dunk (195-208), Scouting Report (321-349), Playoff Time (350-365), I Love this Team (366-394), Photo Gallery (395-403) and Shawn Kemp's Top 40 (404-408). Special Crash Packs containing only inserts (an assortion of Player's Club, Player's Club Platinum and Crash the Game cards) were randomly inserted into one in every 175 12-card packs. Rookie Cards of note include Michael Finley, Kevin Garnett, Joe Smith, Jerry Stackhouse and D.Stoudamire.

	MINT	NRMT
COMPLETE SET (410)	35.00	16.00
COMP.FACTORY SET (419)	35.00	16.00
COMPLETE SERIES 1 (210)	15.00	6.75
COMPLETE SERIES 2 (200)	20.00	9.00
COMMON CARD (1-410)	.05	.02
SEMISTARS	.10	.05
UNLISTED STARS	.20	.09
COMP.PLA.CLB.SET (410)	70.00	32.00
COMP.PLA.CLB.SER.1 (210)	30.00	13.50
COMP.PLA.CLB.SER.2 (200)	40.00	18.00
COMMON PLA.CLB. (1-410)	.15	.07

*PLA.CLB.STARS: 1.5X TO 3X HI CLMN
*PLA.CLB.RCs: 1.25X TO 2.5X HI
ONE PLAYER'S CLUB PER PACK

	MINT	NRMT
COMP.PLA.PLAT.SET (410)	800.00	350.00
COMP.PLA.PLAT.SER.1 (210)	300.00	135.00
COMP.PLA.PLAT.SER.2 (200)	500.00	220.00
COMMON PLA.PLAT (1-410)	1.50	.70

*PLA.PLAT.STARS: 15X TO 30X HI COLUMN
*PLA.PLAT.RCs: 10X TO 20X HI COLUMN
PLAT: SER.1/2 STATED ODDS 1:35

#	Name	MINT	NRMT
1	Rod Strickland	.10	.05
2	Larry Johnson	.10	.05
3	M.Abdul-Rauf	.05	.02
4	Joe Dumars	.20	.09
5	Jason Kidd	.50	.23
6	Avery Johnson	.05	.02
7	Dee Brown	.05	.02
8	Brian Williams	.05	.02
9	Nick Van Exel	.20	.09
10	Dennis Rodman	.75	.35
11	Rony Seikaly	.05	.02
12	Harvey Grant	.05	.02
13	Craig Ehlo	.05	.02
14	Derek Harper	.05	.02
15	Oliver Miller	.05	.02
	Drafted by the Raptors		
16	Dennis Scott	.05	.02
17	Ed Pinckney	.05	.02
	Drafted by the Raptors		
18	Eric Piatkowski	.05	.02
19	B.J. Armstrong	.05	.02
20	Tyrone Hill	.05	.02
21	Malik Sealy	.05	.02
22	Clyde Drexler	.25	.11
23	Aaron McKie	.05	.02
24	Harold Miner	.05	.02
25	Bobby Hurley	.05	.02
26	Dell Curry	.05	.02
27	Micheal Williams	.05	.02
28	Adam Keefe	.05	.02
29	Antonio Harvey	.05	.02
	Drafted by the Grizzlies		
30	Billy Owens	.05	.02
31	Nate McMillan	.05	.02
32	J.R. Reid	.05	.02
33	Grant Hill	1.25	.55
34	Charles Barkley	.30	.14
35	Tyrone Corbin	.05	.02
	Traded to the Kings		
36	Don MacLean	.05	.02
37	Kenny Smith	.05	.02
38	Juwan Howard	.30	.14
39	Charles Smith	.05	.02
40	Shawn Kemp	.60	.25
41	Dana Barros	.05	.02
42	Vin Baker	.40	.18
43	Armon Gilliam	.05	.02
44	Spud Webb	.10	.05
	Traded to the Hawks		
45	Michael Jordan	2.50	1.10
46	Scott Williams	.05	.02
47	Vlade Divac	.10	.05
48	Roy Tarpley	.05	.02
49	Bimbo Coles	.05	.02
50	David Robinson	.30	.14
51	Terry Dehere	.05	.02
52	Bobby Phills	.05	.02
53	Sherman Douglas	.05	.02
54	Rodney Rogers	.05	.02
	Traded to the Clippers		
55	Detlef Schrempf	.10	.05
56	Calbert Cheaney	.05	.02
57	Tom Gugliotta	.20	.09
58	Jeff Turner	.05	.02
59	Mookie Blaylock	.10	.05
60	Bill Curley	.05	.02
61	Chris Dudley	.05	.02
62	Popeye Jones	.05	.02
63	Scott Burrell	.05	.02
64	Dale Davis	.05	.02
65	Mitchell Butler	.05	.02
66	Pervis Ellison	.05	.02
67	Todd Day	.05	.02
68	Carl Herrera	.05	.02
69	Jeff Hornacek	.10	.05
70	Vincent Askew	.05	.02
71	A.C. Green	.10	.05
72	Kevin Gamble	.05	.02
73	Chris Gatling	.05	.02
74	Otis Thorpe	.10	.05
75	Michael Cage	.05	.02
76	Carlos Rogers	.05	.02
77	Gheorghe Muresan	.05	.02
78	Olden Polynice	.05	.02
79	Grant Long	.05	.02
80	Allan Houston	.10	.05
81	Charles Outlaw	.05	.02
82	C.Weatherspoon	.05	.02
83	Tony Dumas	.05	.02
84	Herb Williams	.05	.02
85	P.J. Brown	.05	.02
86	Robert Horry	.05	.02
87	Byron Scott	.05	.02
	Drafted by the Grizzlies		
88	Horace Grant	.10	.05
89	Dominique Wilkins	.20	.09
90	Doug West	.05	.02
91	Antoine Carr	.05	.02
92	Dickey Simpkins	.05	.02
	Washington Bulls		
93	Elden Campbell	.10	.05
94	Kevin Johnson	.10	.05
95	Rex Chapman	.05	.02
	Traded to the Heat		
96	John Williams	.05	.02
97	Tim Hardaway	.25	.11
98	Rik Smits	.10	.05
99	Rex Walters	.05	.02

☐ 100	Robert Parish	.10	.05
☐ 101	Isaiah Rider	.10	.05
☐ 102	Sarunas Marciulionis	.05	.02
☐ 103	Andrew Lang	.05	.02
☐ 104	Eric Mobley	.05	.02
☐ 105	Randy Brown	.05	.02
☐ 106	John Stockton	.20	.09
☐ 107	Lamond Murray	.05	.02
☐ 108	Will Perdue	.05	.02
☐ 109	Wayman Tisdale	.05	.02
☐ 110	John Starks	.10	.05
☐ 111	John Salley	.05	.02
☐ 112	Lucious Harris	.05	.02
☐ 113	Jeff Malone	.05	.02
☐ 114	Anthony Bowie	.05	.02
☐ 115	Vinny Del Negro	.05	.02
☐ 116	Michael Adams	.05	.02
☐ 117	Chris Mullin	.20	.09
☐ 118	Benoit Benjamin	.05	.02

Drafted by the Grizzlies

☐ 119	Byron Houston	.05	.02
☐ 120	LaPhonso Ellis	.10	.05
☐ 121	Doug Overton	.05	.02
☐ 122	Jerome Kersey	.05	.02

Drafted by the Grizzlies

☐ 123	Greg Minor	.05	.02
☐ 124	Christian Laettner	.10	.05
☐ 125	Mark Price	.05	.02
☐ 126	Kevin Willis	.05	.02
☐ 127	Kenny Anderson	.10	.05
☐ 128	Marty Conlon	.05	.02
☐ 129	Blue Edwards	.05	.02

Drafted by the Grizzlies

☐ 130	Dan Schayes	.05	.02
☐ 131	Duane Ferrell	.05	.02
☐ 132	Charles Oakley	.05	.02
☐ 133	Brian Grant	.10	.05
☐ 134	Reggie Williams	.05	.02
☐ 135	Steve Kerr	.10	.05
☐ 136	Khalid Reeves	.05	.02
☐ 137	David Benoit	.05	.02
☐ 138	Derrick Coleman	.10	.05
☐ 139	Anthony Peeler	.05	.02
☐ 140	Jim Jackson	.20	.09
☐ 141	Stacey Augmon	.05	.02
☐ 142	Sam Cassell	.05	.02
☐ 143	Derrick McKey	.05	.02
☐ 144	Danny Ferry	.05	.02
☐ 145	A.Hardaway	.75	.35
☐ 146	Clifford Robinson	.05	.02
☐ 147	B.J. Tyler	.05	.02

Drafted by the Raptors

☐ 148	Mark West	.05	.02
☐ 149	David Wingate	.05	.02

Traded to the Sonics

☐ 150	Willie Anderson	.05	.02

Drafted by the Raptors

☐ 151	Hersey Hawkins	.10	.05

Traded to the Sonics

☐ 152	Bryant Stith	.05	.02
☐ 153	Dan Majerle	.05	.02
☐ 154	Chris Smith	.05	.02
☐ 155	Donyell Marshall	.10	.05
☐ 156	Loy Vaught	.05	.02
☐ 157	Reggie Miller	.20	.09
☐ 158	Hubert Davis	.05	.02
☐ 159	Ron Harper	.10	.05
☐ 160	Lee Mayberry	.05	.02
☐ 161	Eddie Jones	.50	.23
☐ 162	Shawn Bradley	.10	.05
☐ 163	Nick Anderson	.05	.02
☐ 164	Ervin Johnson	.05	.02
☐ 165	Walt Williams	.05	.02
☐ 166	Steve Smith FF	.10	.05
☐ 167	Dino Radja FF	.05	.02
☐ 168	Alonzo Mourning FF	.20	.09
☐ 169	Michael Jordan FF	1.25	.55
☐ 170	Tyrone Hill FF	.05	.02
☐ 171	Jamal Mashburn FF	.05	.02
☐ 172	D.Mutombo FF	.05	.02
☐ 173	Grant Hill FF	.75	.35

with Michael Jordan

☐ 174	Latrell Sprewell FF	.05	.02
☐ 175	Hakeem Olajuwon FF	.20	.09
☐ 176	Reggie Miller FF	.10	.05
☐ 177	Pooh Richardson FF	.05	.02

☐ 178	Cedric Ceballos FF	.05	.02
☐ 179	Glen Rice FF	.10	.05
☐ 180	Glenn Robinson FF	.20	.09
☐ 181	Isaiah Rider FF	.05	.02
☐ 182	Derrick Coleman FF	.05	.02
☐ 183	Patrick Ewing FF	.10	.05
☐ 184	Shaquille O'Neal FF	.40	.18
☐ 185	Dana Barros FF	.05	.02
☐ 186	Dan Majerle FF	.05	.02
☐ 187	Clifford Robinson FF	.05	.02
☐ 188	Mitch Richmond FF	.10	.05
☐ 189	David Robinson FF	.20	.09
☐ 190	Gary Payton FF	.20	.09
☐ 191	Oliver Miller FF	.05	.02
☐ 192	Karl Malone FF	.20	.09
☐ 193	Kevin Pritchard FF	.05	.02
☐ 194	Chris Webber FF	.25	.11
☐ 195	Michael Jordan PD	1.25	.55
☐ 196	Hakeem Olajuwon PD	.20	.09
☐ 197	Vin Baker PD	.20	.09
☐ 198	Grant Hill PD	.60	.25
☐ 199	Clyde Drexler PD	.20	.09
☐ 200	Chris Webber PD	.25	.11
☐ 201	Shawn Kemp PD	.30	.14
☐ 202	Shaquille O'Neal PD	.40	.18
☐ 203	Stacey Augmon PD	.05	.02
☐ 204	David Benoit PD	.05	.02
☐ 205	Rodney Rogers PD	.05	.02
☐ 206	Latrell Sprewell PD	.05	.02
☐ 207	Brian Grant PD	.05	.02
☐ 208	Lamond Murray PD	.05	.02
☐ 209	Shawn Kemp CL	.10	.05
☐ 210	Michael Jordan CL	.60	.25
☐ 211	Cory Alexander	.05	.02
☐ 212	Vernon Maxwell	.05	.02
☐ 213	George Lynch	.05	.02
☐ 214	Terry Mills	.05	.02
☐ 215	Scottie Pippen	.60	.25
☐ 216	Donald Royal	.05	.02
☐ 217	Wesley Person	.10	.05
☐ 218	Antonio Davis	.05	.02
☐ 219	Glenn Robinson	.25	.11
☐ 220	Jerry Stackhouse	.75	.35
☐ 221	James Robinson	.05	.02
☐ 222	Chris Mills	.05	.02
☐ 223	Chuck Person	.05	.02
☐ 224	Duane Causwell	.05	.02
☐ 225	Gary Payton	.30	.14
☐ 226	Eric Montross	.05	.02
☐ 227	Felton Spencer	.05	.02
☐ 228	Scott Skiles	.05	.02
☐ 229	Latrell Sprewell	.10	.05
☐ 230	Sedale Threatt	.05	.02
☐ 231	Mark Bryant	.05	.02
☐ 232	Buck Williams	.05	.02
☐ 233	Brian Williams	.05	.02
☐ 234	Sharone Wright	.05	.02
☐ 235	Karl Malone	.30	.14
☐ 236	Kevin Edwards	.05	.02
☐ 237	Muggsy Bogues	.05	.02
☐ 238	Mario Elie	.05	.02
☐ 239	Rasheed Wallace	.50	.23
☐ 240	George Zidek	.05	.02
☐ 241	Cedric Ceballos	.05	.02
☐ 242	Alan Henderson	.20	.09
☐ 243	Joe Kleine	.05	.02
☐ 244	Patrick Ewing	.20	.09
☐ 245	Sasha Danilovic	.05	.02
☐ 246	Bill Wennington	.05	.02
☐ 247	Steve Smith	.10	.05
☐ 248	Bryant Stith	.05	.02
☐ 249	Dino Radja	.05	.02
☐ 250	Monty Williams	.05	.02
☐ 251	Andrew DeClercq	.05	.02
☐ 252	Sean Elliott	.05	.02
☐ 253	Rick Fox	.05	.02
☐ 254	Lionel Simmons	.05	.02
☐ 255	D.Mutombo	.10	.05
☐ 256	Lindsey Hunter	.05	.02
☐ 257	Terrell Brandon	.20	.09
☐ 258	Shawn Respert	.05	.02
☐ 259	Rodney Rogers	.05	.02
☐ 260	Bryon Russell	.05	.02
☐ 261	David Wesley	.05	.02
☐ 262	Ken Norman	.05	.02
☐ 263	Mitch Richmond	.20	.09

☐ 264	Sam Perkins	.10	.05
☐ 265	Hakeem Olajuwon	.40	.18
☐ 266	Brian Shaw	.05	.02
☐ 267	B.J. Armstrong	.05	.02
☐ 268	Jalen Rose	.10	.05
☐ 269	Bryant Reeves	.50	.23
☐ 270	Cherokee Parks	.05	.02
☐ 271	Dennis Rodman	1.25	.55
☐ 272	Kendall Gill	.10	.05
☐ 273	Elliot Perry	.05	.02
☐ 274	Anthony Mason	.10	.05
☐ 275	Kevin Garnett	2.50	1.10
☐ 276	D.Stoudamire	1.50	.70
☐ 277	Lawrence Moten	.05	.02
☐ 278	Ed O'Bannon	.05	.02
☐ 279	Toni Kukoc	.10	.05
☐ 280	Greg Ostertag	.05	.02
☐ 281	Tom Hammonds	.05	.02
☐ 282	Yinka Dare	.05	.02
☐ 283	Michael Smith	.05	.02
☐ 284	Clifford Rozier	.05	.02
☐ 285	Gary Trent	.05	.02
☐ 286	Shaquille O'Neal	.75	.35
☐ 287	Luc Longley	.10	.05
☐ 288	Bob Sura	.10	.05
☐ 289	Dana Barros	.05	.02
☐ 290	Lorenzo Williams	.05	.02
☐ 291	Haywoode Workman	.05	.02
☐ 292	Randolph Childress	.05	.02
☐ 293	Doc Rivers	.10	.05
☐ 294	Chris Webber	.50	.23
☐ 295	Kurt Thomas	.10	.05
☐ 296	Greg Anthony	.05	.02
☐ 297	Tyus Edney	.05	.02
☐ 298	Danny Manning	.10	.05
☐ 299	Brent Barry	.20	.09
☐ 300	Joe Smith	.75	.35
☐ 301	Pooh Richardson	.05	.02
☐ 302	Mark Jackson	.10	.05
☐ 303	Richard Dumas	.05	.02
☐ 304	Michael Finley	.75	.35
☐ 305	Theo Ratliff	.20	.09
☐ 306	Gary Grant	.05	.02
☐ 307	Jamal Mashburn	.10	.05
☐ 308	Corliss Williamson	.25	.11
☐ 309	Eric Williams	.10	.05
☐ 310	Zan Tabak	.05	.02
☐ 311	Eric Murdock	.05	.02
☐ 312	Sherrell Ford	.05	.02
☐ 313	Terry Davis	.05	.02
☐ 314	Vern Fleming	.05	.02
☐ 315	Jason Caffey	.20	.09
☐ 316	Mario Bennett	.05	.02
☐ 317	David Vaughn	.05	.02
☐ 318	Loren Meyer	.05	.02
☐ 319	Travis Best	.10	.05
☐ 320	Byron Scott	.05	.02
☐ 321	Mookie Blaylock SR	.05	.02
☐ 322	Dee Brown SR	.05	.02
☐ 323	Alonzo Mourning SR	.10	.05
☐ 324	Michael Jordan SR	1.25	.55
☐ 325	Terrell Brandon SR	.10	.05
☐ 326	Jim Jackson SR	.05	.02
☐ 327	D.Mutombo SR	.05	.02
☐ 328	Grant Hill SR	.60	.25
☐ 329	Joe Smith SR UER	.30	.14

Team stats say Seattle
Should be Golden State

☐ 330	Clyde Drexler SR	.20	.09
☐ 331	Reggie Miller SR	.10	.05
☐ 332	Lamond Murray SR	.05	.02
☐ 333	Nick Van Exel SR	.10	.05
☐ 334	Glen Rice SR	.10	.05
☐ 335	Glenn Robinson SR	.20	.09
☐ 336	Christian Laettner SR	.05	.02
☐ 337	Kenny Anderson SR	.10	.05
☐ 338	Patrick Ewing SR	.10	.05
☐ 339	Shaquille O'Neal SR	.40	.18
☐ 340	Jerry Stackhouse SR	.30	.14
☐ 341	Charles Barkley SR	.20	.09
☐ 342	Clifford Robinson SR	.05	.02
☐ 343	Brian Grant SR	.05	.02
☐ 344	David Robinson SR	.20	.09
☐ 345	Shawn Kemp SR	.30	.14
☐ 346	D.Stoudamire SR	.60	.25
☐ 347	Karl Malone SR	.20	.09

- ☐ 348 Bryant Reeves SR ..... .20 .... .09
- ☐ 349 Juwan Howard SR ..... .20 .... .09
- ☐ 350 Nick Anderson .... .05 .... .02
  Dee Brown PT
  Orlando vs. Boston East Conf.
  1st Round
- ☐ 351 Rik Smits PT .... .05 .... .02
  Indiana vs Atlanta East Conf.
  1st Round
- ☐ 352 Herb Williams .... .05 .... .02
  Greg Dreiling PT
  New York vs Cleveland East Conf.
  1st Round
- ☐ 353 Michael Jordan PT.... 1.25 .... .55
  Chicago vs Charlotte East Conf.
  1st Round
- ☐ 354 David Robinson PT .... .20 .... .09
  San Antonio vs Denver West Conf.
  1st Round
- ☐ 355 Terry Porter .... .10 .... .05
  Kevin Johnson PT
  Phoenix vs Portland West Conf.
  1st Round
- ☐ 356 Clyde Drexler PT ...... .20 .... .09
  Houston vs Utah West Conf.
  1st Round
- ☐ 357 Cedric Ceballos PT ... .05 .... .02
  L.A. Lakers vs Seattle West Conf.
  1st Round
- ☐ 358 Horace Grant .... .05 .... .02
  Group PT
  Orlando vs Chicago
  East Conf. Semifinals
- ☐ 359 Reggie Miller PT ..... .10 .... .05
  Indiana vs New York East Conf.
  Semifinals
- ☐ 360 Avery Johnson .... .10 .... .05
  Nick Van Exel PT
  SA vs L.A. Lakers West Conf.
  Semifinals
- ☐ 361 Hakeem Olajuwon ..... .20 .... .09
  Robert Horry PT
  Houston vs Phoenix West Conf.
  Semifinals
- ☐ 362 Rik Smits PT .... .05 .... .02
  Orlando vs Indiana East Conf.
  Finals
- ☐ 363 David Robinson .... .20 .... .09
  Hakeem Olajuwon PT
  Houston vs San Antonio West
  Conf. Finals
- ☐ 364 Robert Horry PT .... .05 .... .02
  Houston vs Orlando NBA Finals
- ☐ 365 Kenny Smith PT........ .05 .... .02
  Houston Rockets 1995 NBA
  Champs
- ☐ 366 Stacey Augmon LOVE .05 .... .02
- ☐ 367 S. Douglas LOVE ...... .05 .... .02
- ☐ 368 Larry Johnson LOVE .. .05 .... .02
- ☐ 369 Scottie Pippen LOVE .. .30 .... .14
- ☐ 370 Tyrone Hill LOVE ..... .05 .... .02
- ☐ 371 Jamal Mashburn LOVE .05 .... .02
- ☐ 372 M. Abdul-Rauf LOVE .. .05 .... .02
- ☐ 373 Grant Hill LOVE ...... .60 .... .25
- ☐ 374 Latrell Sprewell LOVE .05 .... .02
- ☐ 375 Sam Cassell LOVE .... .05 .... .02
- ☐ 376 Rik Smits LOVE....... .05 .... .02
- ☐ 377 Terry Dehere LOVE ... .05 .... .02
- ☐ 378 Eddie Jones LOVE .... .25 .... .11
- ☐ 379 Billy Owens LOVE .... .05 .... .02
- ☐ 380 Vin Baker LOVE ...... .20 .... .09
- ☐ 381 Isaiah Rider LOVE .... .05 .... .02
- ☐ 382 Kenny Anderson LOVE .05 .... .02
- ☐ 383 John Starks LOVE .... .05 .... .02
- ☐ 384 A. Hardaway LOVE ... .40 .... .18
- ☐ 385 Sharone Wright LOVE .05 .... .02
- ☐ 386 Charles Barkley LOVE .20 .... .09
- ☐ 387 C. Robinson LOVE .... .05 .... .02
- ☐ 388 Walt Williams LOVE... .05 .... .02
- ☐ 389 Sean Elliott LOVE..... .05 .... .02
- ☐ 390 Gary Payton LOVE ... .20 .... .09
- ☐ 391 Carlos Rogers LOVE .. .05 .... .02
- ☐ 392 John Stockton LOVE .. .10 .... .05
- ☐ 393 Greg Anthony LOVE .. .05 .... .02
- ☐ 394 Chris Webber LOVE .. .25 .... .11
- ☐ 395 Gary Payton PG .... .20 .... .09

- ☐ 396 Mookie Blaylock PG.... .05 .... .02
- ☐ 397 Charles Barkley PG ... .20 .... .09
- ☐ 398 Grant Hill PG .... .60 .... .25
- ☐ 399 A Hardaway PG ...... .40 .... .18
- ☐ 400 Kenny Anderson PG .. .05 .... .02
- ☐ 401 Mark Jackson PG ..... .05 .... .02
- ☐ 402 Karl Malone PG ...... .20 .... .09
- ☐ 403 Avery Johnson PG..... .05 .... .02
- ☐ 404 Larry Johnson 40 ..... .05 .... .02
  Top Scorers
- ☐ 405 Nick Van Exel 40 ..... .10 .... .05
  Top Shooters
- ☐ 406 Vin Baker 40 .... .20 .... .09
  Top Rebounders
- ☐ 407 Jason Kidd 40 .... .25 .... .11
  Top Passers
- ☐ 408 David Robinson 40 .... .20 .... .09
  Top Defenders
- ☐ 409 Shawn Kemp CL ...... .10 .... .05
- ☐ 410 Michael Jordan CL..... .60 .... .25
- ☐ NNO Bulls Commem. Card 6.00 .... 2.70
  Issued with Factory set

1995-96 Collector's Choice Crash the Game Assists/Rebounds

Issued randomly into one in every five second series 12-card packs, cards from this 90-card set feature three separate versions of thirty different player cards. Each player was given three separate specific game dates. If the player depicted on the card tallied 10 or more assists or rebounds on that date, the card was redeemable for a special 30-card Crash the Game Assists/Rebounds Silver Trade set. Losing cards are signified with an "L" and winning cards with a "W". The winning cards are actually in shorter supply than losing cards due to the fact that many of them were mailed in for redemption and then destroyed.

	MINT	NRMT
COMPLETE SILVER SET (90)	60.00	27.00
COMMON SILVER (C1-C30)	.25	.11
SEMISTARS	.40	.18
UNLISTED STARS	.60	.25
*GOLD CARDS: 2X TO 4X HI COLUMN		
EACH PLAYER HAS THREE		

DIFF.SILV.CARDS
EACH PLAYER HAS THREE DIFF.GOLD CARDS
SER.2 STATED ODDS 1:5
GOLD: SER.2 STATED ODDS 1:49
COMP.SILVER RED.SET (30) 8.00 .... 3.60
*SILVER RED.CARDS: 50% OF HI COLUMN
*GOLD RED: 2X TO 4X SILVER RED.
ONE RED.SET PER WINNER BY MAIL

- ☐ C1 Michael Jordan 1/30 L.... 8.00 3.60
- ☐ C1B Michael Jordan 2/22 L... 8.00 3.60
- ☐ C1C Michael Jordan 3/19 L... 8.00 3.60
- ☐ C2 Tim Hardaway 2/4 L ..... .75 .35
- ☐ C2B Tim Hardaway 3/12 L ... .75 .35
- ☐ C2C Tim Hardaway 4/11 W... .75 .35
- ☐ C3 Juwan Howard 2/2 L ..... 1.00 .45
- ☐ C3B Juwan Howard 3/21 L ... 1.00 .45
- ☐ C3C Juwan Howard 3/30 L ... 1.00 .45
- ☐ C4 Shawn Kemp 1/29 L ..... 2.00 .90
- ☐ C4B Shawn Kemp 3/15 W .... 2.00 .90
- ☐ C4C Shawn Kemp 4/3 L ..... 2.00 .90
- ☐ C5 Nick Van Exel 2/4 L ..... .60 .25
- ☐ C5B Nick Van Exel 2/21 L .... .60 .25
- ☐ C5C Nick Van Exel 4/14 L .... .60 .25
- ☐ C6 Mookie Blaylock 2/16 L ... .40 .18
- ☐ C6B Mookie Blaylock 3/8 L ... .40 .18
- ☐ C6C Mookie Blaylock 4/20 L .. .40 .18
- ☐ C7 John Stockton 2/13 W .... .60 .25
- ☐ C7B John Stockton 3/6 L ..... .60 .25
- ☐ C7C John Stockton 4/14 W ... .60 .25
- ☐ C8 Scottie Pippen 2/1 L ..... 2.00 .90
- ☐ C8B Scottie Pippen 3/15 L ... 2.00 .90
- ☐ C8C Scottie Pippen 4/11 L ... 2.00 .90
- ☐ C9 Vin Baker 2/3 L .... 1.25 .55
- ☐ C9B Vin Baker 3/4 W .... 1.25 .55
- ☐ C9C Vin Baker 4/5 W .... 1.25 .55
- ☐ C10 Lamond Murray 2/3 L ... .25 .11
- ☐ C10B Lamond Murray 2/17 L .. .25 .11
- ☐ C10C Lamond Murray 3/30 L .. .25 .11
- ☐ C11 David Robinson 2/15 W .. 1.00 .45
- ☐ C11B David Robinson 3/14 W .. 1.00 .45
- ☐ C11C David Robinson 4/13 W .. 1.00 .45
- ☐ C12 Jason Kidd 2/6 L .... 1.50 .70
- ☐ C12B Jason Kidd 3/19 L ..... 1.50 .70
- ☐ C12C Jason Kidd 4/13 W ..... 1.50 .70
- ☐ C13 Rod Strickland 2/15 L ... .40 .18
- ☐ C13B Rod Strickland 3/8 W ... .40 .18
- ☐ C13C Rod Strickland 4/5 L ... .40 .18
- ☐ C14 Glen Rice 1/29 L .... .60 .25
- ☐ C14B Glen Rice 2/28 L ...... .60 .25
- ☐ C14C Glen Rice 4/2 L .... .60 .25
- ☐ C15 A. Hardaway 2/4 W 2.50 1.10
- ☐ C15B A. Hardaway 3/31 L 2.50 1.10
- ☐ C15C A. Hardaway 4/21 W ... 2.50 1.10
- ☐ C16 H. Olajuwon 2/15 L ..... 1.25 .55
- ☐ C16B H. Olajuwon 3/8 L ..... 1.25 .55
- ☐ C16C H. Olajuwon 4/15 W ... 1.25 .55
- ☐ C17 K. Anderson 2/14 W ..... .40 .18
- ☐ C17B K. Anderson 3/29 W .... .40 .18
- ☐ C17C K. Anderson 4/29 L .... .40 .18
- ☐ C18 S. Wright 2/14 L .... .25 .11
- ☐ C18B S. Wright 3/22 L ...... .25 .11
- ☐ C18C S. Wright 4/17 L ...... .25 .11
- ☐ C19 D. Mutombo 2/16 L ..... .40 .18
- ☐ C19B D. Mutombo 3/2 W ..... .40 .18
- ☐ C19C D. Mutombo 4/5 W ..... .40 .18
- ☐ C20 M. Bogues 2/1 .... .40 .18
- ☐ C20B M. Bogues 2/21 L ..... .40 .18
- ☐ C20C M. Bogues 3/8 W ...... .40 .18
- ☐ C21 Reggie Miller 2/18 L .... .60 .25
- ☐ C21B Reggie Miller 3/8 L .... .60 .25
- ☐ C21C Reggie Miller 4/8 L .... .60 .25
- ☐ C22 D. Manning 2/6 L ...... .40 .18
- ☐ C22B D. Manning 3/3 L ..... .40 .18
- ☐ C22C D. Manning 4/16 L .... .40 .18
- ☐ C23 C. Laettner 2/5 L ...... .40 .18
- ☐ C23B C. Laettner 3/10 L ..... .40 .18
- ☐ C23C C. Laettner 3/27 W .... .40 .18
- ☐ C24 Eric Montross 2/14 L .... .25 .11
- ☐ C24B Eric Montross 3/8 L .... .25 .11
- ☐ C24C Eric Montross 3/31 L ... .25 .11
- ☐ C25 Patrick Ewing 2/1 L ..... .60 .25
- ☐ C25B Patrick Ewing 3/29 W ... .60 .25
- ☐ C25C Patrick Ewing 4/3 W .... .60 .25
- ☐ C26 D. Stoudamire 1/30 L ... 3.00 1.35

		MINT	NRMT
☐ C26B	D. Stoudamire 3/10 L	3.00	1.35
☐ C26C	D. Stoudamire 3/22 W	3.00	1.35
☐ C27	Bryant Reeves 2/28 L	1.00	.45
☐ C27B	Bryant Reeves 3/31 L	1.00	.45
☐ C27C	Bryant Reeves 4/9 L	1.00	.45
☐ C28	Joe Dumars 2/15 L	.60	.25
☐ C28B	Joe Dumars 3/22 L	.60	.25
☐ C28C	Joe Dumars 4/13 L	.60	.25
☐ C29	Tyrone Hill 2/6 L	.25	.11
☐ C29B	Tyrone Hill 3/10 L	.25	.11
☐ C29C	Tyrone Hill 4/20 L	.25	.11
☐ C30	Brian Grant 2/13 L	.40	.18
☐ C30B	Brian Grant 3/20 L	.40	.18
☐ C30C	Brian Grant 4/21 L	.40	.18

1995-96 Collector's Choice Crash the Game Scoring

Issued randomly into one in every five first series 12-card packs, cards from this 81-card set features three separate versions of twenty-seven different player cards. Each player is matched up against three different teams (two within their conference and one outside of their conference). If the player depicted on the card scored 30 or more points versus the team depicted on the card, the card was redeemable for a special 30-card Crash the Game Scoring Silver Trade set. Losing cards are signified with an "L" and winning cards are signified with a "W". The winning cards are actually in shorter supply than losing cards due to the fact that many of them were mailed in for redemption and then destroyed.

	MINT	NRMT
COMPLETE SILVER SET (81)	60.00	27.00
COMMON SILVER (C1-C27)	.25	.11
SEMISTARS	.40	.18
UNLISTED SER	.60	.25
*GOLD CARDS: 2X TO 4X HI COLUMN		
EACH PLAYER HAS THREE		
DIFF.SILV.CARDS		
EACH PLAYER HAS THREE DIFF.GOLD		
CARDS		
SER.1 STATED ODDS 1:5		
GOLD: SER.1 STATED ODDS 1:50		

COMP.SILVER RED.SET (30) 10.00   4.50
*SILVER RED.CARDS: 50% OF HI COLUMN
*GOLD RED: 2X TO 4X SILVER RED.
ONE RED.SET PER WINNER BY MAIL

		MINT	NRMT
☐ C1	M. Jordan HOU W	8.00	3.60
☐ C1B	M. Jordan NY W	8.00	3.60
☐ C1C	M. Jordan ORL W	8.00	3.60
☐ C2	K. Anderson CLE L	.40	.18
☐ C2B	K. Anderson LAC L	.40	.18
☐ C2C	K. Anderson MIA L	.40	.18
☐ C3	C. Barkley CLE L	1.00	.45
☐ C3B	C. Barkley GS W	1.00	.45
☐ C3C	C. Barkley SA W	1.00	.45
☐ C4	Dana Barros ATL L	.25	.11
☐ C4B	Dana Barros BOS W	.25	.11
☐ C4C	Dana Barros LAL L	.25	.11
☐ C5	A. Hardaway CHI W	2.50	1.10
☐ C5B	A. Hardaway SA W	2.50	1.10
☐ C5C	A. Hardaway MIL W	2.50	1.10
☐ C6	M. Blaylock DAL L	.40	.18
☐ C6B	M. Blaylock DET L	.40	.18
☐ C6C	M. Blaylock TOR L	.40	.18
☐ C7	L. Murray ATL L	.25	.11
☐ C7B	L. Murray MIN L	.25	.11
☐ C7C	L. Murray VAN L	.25	.11
☐ C8	K. Malone HOU L	1.00	.45
☐ C8B	K. Malone NY L	1.00	.45
☐ C8C	K. Malone POR W	1.00	.45
☐ C9	A. Mourning CHI L	.60	.25
☐ C9B	A. Mourning IND L	.60	.25
☐ C9C	A. Mourning WASH W	.60	.25
☐ C10	H. Olajuwon LAL W	1.25	.55
☐ C10B	H. Olajuwon ORL W	1.25	.55
☐ C10C	H. Olajuwon POR W	1.25	.55
☐ C11	Mark Price CHI L	.25	.11
☐ C11B	Mark Price NJ L	.25	.11
☐ C11C	Mark Price SEA L	.25	.11
☐ C12	Isaiah Rider BOS L	.40	.18
☐ C12B	Isaiah Rider PHO L	.40	.18
☐ C12C	Isaiah Rider SAC L	.40	.18
☐ C13	Glen Rice NJ W	.60	.25
☐ C13B	Glen Rice SAC W	.60	.25
☐ C13C	Glen Rice WASH W	.60	.25
☐ C14	M. Richmond LAL L	.60	.25
☐ C14B	M. Richmond MIN W	.60	.25
☐ C14C	M. Richmond NJ L	.60	.25
☐ C15	C. Webber GS W	1.50	.70
☐ C15B	C. Webber IND L	1.50	.70
☐ C15C	C. Webber PHI L	1.50	.70
☐ C16	N. Van Exel DAL L	.60	.25
☐ C16B	N. Van Exel MIL L	.60	.25
☐ C16C	N. Van Exel SAC L	.60	.25
☐ C17	M. Abdul-Rauf CHA L	.25	.11
☐ C17B	M. Abdul-Rauf PHO W	.25	.11
☐ C17C	M. Abdul-Rauf SEA	.25	.11
☐ C18	D. Wilkins PHI L	.60	.25
☐ C18B	D. Wilkins POR L	.60	.25
☐ C18C	D. Wilkins TOR L	.60	.25
☐ C19	Patrick Ewing BOS W	.60	.25
☐ C19B	Patrick Ewing CHA L	.60	.25
☐ C19C	Patrick Ewing PHO L	.60	.25
☐ C20	D. Robinson DEN L	1.00	.45
☐ C20B	D. Robinson SEA	1.00	.45
☐ C20C	D. Robinson WASH W	1.00	.45
☐ C21	S. Kemp DEN L	2.00	.90
☐ C21B	S. Kemp DET L	2.00	.90
☐ C21C	S. Kemp UTAH L	2.00	.90
☐ C22	Jason Kidd IND W	1.50	.70
☐ C22B	Jason Kidd LAC L	1.50	.70
☐ C22C	Jason Kidd SA L	1.50	.70
☐ C23	G. Robinson ATL W	.75	.35
☐ C23B	G. Robinson CHA L	.75	.35
☐ C23C	G. Robinson VAN L	.75	.35
☐ C24	Reggie Miller MIN L	.60	.25
☐ C24B	Reggie Miller NY L	.60	.25
☐ C24C	Reggie Miller ORL L	.60	.25
☐ C25	Joe Dumars CLE L	.60	.25
☐ C25B	Joe Dumars MIL L	.60	.25
☐ C25C	Joe Dumars UTAH L	.60	.25
☐ C26	L. Sprewell DAL L	.40	.18
☐ C26B	L. Sprewell HOU L	.40	.18
☐ C26C	L. Sprewell MIA L	.40	.18
☐ C27	C. Robinson LAC L	.40	.18
☐ C27B	C. Robinson PHI L	.40	.18
☐ C27C	C. Robinson UTAH W	.40	.18

		MINT	NRMT
☐ XC28	D. Stoudamire EXCH	2.00	.90
☐ XC29	Bryant Reeves EXCH	.60	.25
☐ XC30	Michael Jordan EXCH	4.00	1.80

1995-96 Collector's Choice Debut Trade

This 30-card set was only available by redeeming the Collector's Choice Debut Trade card, which was randomly seeded into second series 12-card packs at a rate of one in 30. The 30-card set primarily consists of a selection of player's traded during the 1995-96 season. The prices listed below are for the more common regular issue cards. The Debut Trade card program expired on May 8th, 1996. Collectors started receiving their cards around late June, 1996. It's interesting to note that rookies Antonio McDyess and Arvydas Sabonis were left out of the regular issue Collector's Choice set but included here in the Debut Trade set.

	MINT	NRMT
COMPLETE SET (30)	4.00	1.80
COMMON CARD (T1-T30)	.05	.02
SEMISTARS	.15	.07
UNLISTED STARS	.30	.14
COMP.PLAY.CLUB SET (30)	10.00	4.50
*PLAY.CLUB STARS: 1X TO 2X HI COLUMN		
*PLAY.CLUB RCs: .75X TO 1.5X HI		
COMP.PLAY.PLAT.SET (30)	40.00	18.00
*PLAY.PLAT.STARS: 10X TO 20X HI COL-		
UMN		
*PLAY.PLAT.RCs: 6X TO 12X HI		
ONE SET PER DEBUT TRADE CARD VIA		
MAIL		
TRADE: SER.2 STATED ODDS 1:30		
PC TRADE: SER.2 STATED ODDS 1:144		
PCP TRADE: SER.2 STATED ODDS 1:720		

		MINT	NRMT
☐ T1	Magic Johnson	1.00	.45
☐ T2	Arvydas Sabonis	.60	.25
☐ T3	Kenny Anderson	.15	.07
☐ T4	Antonio McDyess	1.50	.70
☐ T5	Sherman Douglas	.05	.02
☐ T6	Spud Webb	.15	.07
☐ T7	Glen Rice	.30	.14
☐ T8	Todd Day	.05	.02
☐ T9	John Williams	.05	.02
☐ T10	Chris Morris	.05	.02

			MINT	NRMT
☐	T11	Shawn Bradley	.15	.07
☐	T12	Dan Majerle	.05	.02
☐	T13	George McCloud	.05	.02
☐	T14	Derrick Coleman	.15	.02
☐	T15	Kendall Gill	.15	.07
☐	T16	Ricky Pierce	.05	.02
☐	T17	Robert Pack	.05	.02
☐	T18	Alonzo Mourning	.30	.14
☐	T19	Matt Geiger	.05	.02
☐	T20	Don MacLean	.05	.02
☐	T21	Willie Anderson	.05	.02
☐	T22	Oliver Miller	.05	.02
☐	T23	Tracy Murray	.05	.02
☐	T24	Ed Pinckney	.05	.02
☐	T25	Alvin Robertson	.05	.02
☐	T26	Anthony Avent	.05	.02
☐	T27	Blue Edwards	.05	.02
☐	T28	Kenny Gattison	.05	.02
☐	T29	Chris King	.05	.02
☐	T30	Eric Murdock	.05	.02

1995-96 Collector's Choice Draft Trade

This 10-card set was only available by redeeming a Collector's Choice Draft Trade card, which was randomly inserted into series one packs at a rate of one in 144 packs. The 10-card set consists of the top rookies from the 1995-96 season. Card fronts contain a photo with the player's name, draft pick number and position. Card backs contain biographical and statistical information from the player's college/high school year(s) and are numbered with a "D" prefix. The Draft Trade card program expired on June 7, 1996.

	MINT	NRMT
COMPLETE SET (10)	15.00	6.75
COMMON CARD (D1-D10)	.25	.11
SEMISTARS	.50	.23

ONE SET PER DRAFT TRADE CARD VIA MAIL
TRADE: SER.1 STATED ODDS 1:144

			MINT	NRMT
☐	D1	Joe Smith	2.00	.90
☐	D2	Antonio McDyess	2.50	1.10
☐	D3	Jerry Stackhouse	2.00	.90
☐	D4	Rasheed Wallace	1.25	.55
☐	D5	Kevin Garnett	6.00	2.70
☐	D6	Bryant Reeves	1.25	.55
☐	D7	D.Stoudamire	4.00	1.80
☐	D8	Shawn Respert	.25	.11
☐	D9	Ed O'Bannon	.25	.11
☐	D10	Kurt Thomas	.50	.23

1995-96 Collector's Choice Jordan He's Back

Inserted one per special retail pack, this five-card set commemorates Michael Jordan coming back in the 1994-95 season. Each card focuses on a particular moment/game.

	MINT	NRMT
COMPLETE SET (5)	6.00	2.70
COMMON JORDAN (M1-M5)	1.50	.70

ONE PER SPECIAL RETAIL PACK

			MINT	NRMT
☐	M1	Michael Jordan First Game Back	1.50	.70
☐	M2	Michael Jordan Buzzer beater versus Hawks	1.50	.70
☐	M3	Michael Jordan Versus Knicks	1.50	.70
☐	M4	Michael Jordan Playoffs versus Charlotte	1.50	.70
☐	M5	Michael Jordan Playoffs versus Orlando Switch to #23	1.50	.70

1996-97 Collector's Choice

These 400-standard size cards, comprise Upper Deck's 1996-97 Collector's Choice series one and two set. Cards were primarily issued in 12-card hobby and retail packs with a suggested retail price of ninety-nine cents. Regular issue cards feature white-bordered fronts with color player action shots. The backs have a color photo and statistics. A Factory Set was also issued in early May 1997. The set contained all the basic cards from both series, five Gold Mini-Cards (randomly inserted) and one of four commemorative cards (measuring 3 1/2" by 5") featuring either Shawn Kemp, Michael Jordan, A.Hardaway or a Jordan/Hardaway dual card. The set was issued as a 406-card factory set with a suggested retail price of $29.99. Also included as an insert in packs (1:4 packs) was a game piece for Upper Deck's Meet the Stars promotion. Each game piece was a multiple choice trivia card about basketball. The collector would scratch off the box next to the answer that they felt best matched the question to determine if they won. Instant win game pieces were also inserted one in 72 packs. Winning game pieces could be sent into Upper Deck for a prize drawing. The Grand Prize was a chance to meet Michael Jordan. Prizes for 2nd through 4th were for Upper Deck Authenticated shopping sprees. The 5th prize was two special Michael Jordan Meet the Stars cards. The blank back cards measure 5" by 7" and are titled Dynamic Debut and Magic Memories. These two cards are priced at the bottom of the base set.

	MINT	NRMT
COMPLETE SET (400)	30.00	13.50
COMP.FACT.SET (406)	35.00	16.00
COMPLETE SERIES 1 (200)	15.00	6.75
COMPLETE SERIES 2 (200)	15.00	6.75
COMMON CARD (1-400)	.05	.02
COMMON PENNY (113-117)	.40	.18
SEMISTARS	.10	.05
UNLISTED STARS	.20	.09
COMP.UPDATE SET (30)	12.00	5.50
COMMON UPDATE (401-430)	.40	.18
UPDATE SEMISTARS	.60	.25
UPDATE UNLISTED STARS	1.00	.45

ONE UPDATE SET VIA TRADE CARD
UPDATE TRADE: STATED ODDS 1:71
F1-F4: RANDOM INS.IN FACT.SETS

			MINT	NRMT
☐	1	Mookie Blaylock	.10	.05
☐	2	Grant Long	.05	.02
☐	3	Christian Laettner	.10	.05
☐	4	Craig Ehlo	.05	.02
☐	5	Ken Norman	.05	.02
☐	6	Stacey Augmon	.05	.02
☐	7	Dana Barros	.05	.02
☐	8	Dino Radja	.05	.02
☐	9	Rick Fox	.05	.02
☐	10	Eric Montross	.05	.02
☐	11	David Wesley	.05	.02
☐	12	Eric Williams	.05	.02
☐	13	Glen Rice	.20	.09
☐	14	Dell Curry	.05	.02
☐	15	Matt Geiger	.05	.02
☐	16	Scott Burrell	.05	.02
☐	17	George Zidek	.05	.02
☐	18	Muggsy Bogues	.05	.02
☐	19	Ron Harper	.10	.05
☐	20	Steve Kerr	.05	.02
☐	21	Toni Kukoc	.10	.05
☐	22	Dennis Rodman	.75	.35
☐	23	Michael Jordan	2.50	1.10
☐	24	Luc Longley	.10	.05
☐	25	Michael Jordan Vlade Divac VT	1.25	.55

□ 26	Michael Jordan Bulls VT	1.25	.55
□ 27	Luc Longley VT	.05	.02
□ 28	Scottie Pippen VT	.30	.14
□ 29	Toni Kukoc	.10	.05
	Juwan Howard VT		
□ 30	Terrell Brandon	.20	.09
□ 31	Bobby Phills	.05	.02
□ 32	Tyrone Hill	.05	.02
□ 33	Michael Cage	.05	.02
□ 34	Bob Sura	.05	.02
□ 35	Tony Dumas	.05	.02
□ 36	Jim Jackson	.10	.05
□ 37	Loren Meyer	.05	.02
□ 38	Cherokee Parks	.05	.02
□ 39	Jamal Mashburn	.10	.05
□ 40	Popeye Jones	.05	.02
□ 41	LaPhonso Ellis	.05	.02
□ 42	Jalen Rose	.05	.02
□ 43	Antonio McDyess	.30	.14
□ 44	Tom Hammonds	.05	.02
□ 45	M.Abdul-Rauf	.05	.02
□ 46	Dale Ellis	.05	.02
□ 47	Joe Dumars	.20	.09
□ 48	Theo Ratliff	.05	.02
□ 49	Lindsey Hunter	.05	.02
□ 50	Terry Mills	.05	.02
□ 51	Don Reid	.05	.02
□ 52	B.J. Armstrong	.05	.02
□ 53	Bimbo Coles	.05	.02
□ 54	Joe Smith	.25	.11
□ 55	Chris Mullin	.20	.09
□ 56	Rony Seikaly	.05	.02
□ 57	Donyell Marshall	.05	.02
□ 58	Hakeem Olajuwon	.40	.18
□ 59	Robert Horry	.10	.05
□ 60	Mario Elie	.05	.02
□ 61	Mark Bryant	.05	.02
□ 62	Chucky Brown	.05	.02
□ 63	Rik Smits	.10	.05
□ 64	Derrick McKey	.05	.02
□ 65	Eddie Johnson	.05	.02
□ 66	Mark Jackson	.05	.02
□ 67	Ricky Pierce	.05	.02
□ 68	Travis Best	.05	.02
□ 69	Rodney Rogers	.05	.02
□ 70	Brent Barry	.05	.02
□ 71	Lamond Murray	.05	.02
□ 72	Eric Piatkowski	.05	.02
□ 73	Pooh Richardson	.05	.02
□ 74	Cedric Ceballos	.05	.02
□ 75	Eddie Jones	.40	.18
□ 76	Anthony Peeler	.05	.02
□ 77	George Lynch	.05	.02
□ 78	Vlade Divac	.10	.05
□ 79	Rex Chapman	.05	.02
□ 80	Sasha Danilovic	.05	.02
□ 81	Kurt Thomas	.05	.02
□ 82	Keith Askins	.05	.02
□ 83	Walt Williams	.05	.02
□ 84	Vin Baker	.40	.18
□ 85	Shawn Respert	.05	.02
□ 86	Sherman Douglas	.05	.02
□ 87	Marty Conlon	.05	.02
□ 88	Johnny Newman	.05	.02
□ 89	Kevin Garnett	1.25	.55
□ 90	Andrew Lang	.05	.02
□ 91	Terry Porter	.05	.02
□ 92	Sam Mitchell	.05	.02
□ 93	Tom Gugliotta	.20	.09
□ 94	Spud Webb	.10	.05
□ 95	Kendall Gill	.10	.05
□ 96	Vern Fleming	.05	.02
□ 97	Shawn Bradley	.05	.02
□ 98	Yinka Dare	.05	.02
□ 99	Jayson Williams	.10	.05
□ 100	Kevin Edwards	.05	.02
□ 101	Charles Oakley	.05	.02
□ 102	Anthony Mason	.10	.05
□ 103	John Starks	.10	.05
□ 104	J.R. Reid	.05	.02
□ 105	Hubert Davis	.05	.02
□ 106	Gary Grant	.05	.02
□ 107	Nick Anderson	.05	.02
□ 108	Donald Royal	.05	.02
□ 109	Brian Shaw	.05	.02
□ 110	Brooks Thompson	.05	.02
□ 111	A.Hardaway	.75	.35
□ 112	Dennis Scott	.05	.02
□ 113	A. Hardaway PEN	.40	.18
□ 114	A. Hardaway PEN	.40	.18
□ 115	A. Hardaway PEN	.40	.18
□ 116	A. Hardaway PEN	.40	.18
□ 117	A. Hardaway PEN	.40	.18
□ 118	Derrick Coleman	.10	.05
□ 119	Rex Walters	.05	.02
□ 120	Sean Higgins	.05	.02
□ 121	C. Weatherspoon	.05	.02
□ 122	Jerry Stackhouse	.25	.11
□ 123	Elliot Perry	.05	.02
□ 124	Wayman Tisdale	.05	.02
□ 125	Wesley Person	.05	.02
□ 126	Charles Barkley	.30	.14
□ 127	A.C. Green	.05	.02
□ 128	Harvey Grant	.05	.02
□ 129	Arvydas Sabonis	.10	.05
□ 130	Aaron McKie	.05	.02
□ 131	Gary Trent	.05	.02
□ 132	Buck Williams	.05	.02
□ 133	Billy Owens	.05	.02
□ 134	Brian Grant	.05	.02
□ 135	Corliss Williamson	.10	.05
□ 136	Tyus Edney	.05	.02
□ 137	Olden Polynice	.05	.02
□ 138	Avery Johnson	.05	.02
□ 139	Vinny Del Negro	.05	.02
□ 140	Sean Elliott	.05	.02
□ 141	Chuck Person	.05	.02
□ 142	Will Perdue	.05	.02
□ 143	Nate McMillan	.05	.02
□ 144	Vincent Askew	.05	.02
□ 145	Detlef Schrempf	.10	.05
□ 146	Hersey Hawkins	.10	.05
□ 147	Sharone Wright	.05	.02
□ 148	Zan Tabak	.05	.02
□ 149	Oliver Miller	.05	.02
□ 150	Doug Christie	.05	.02
□ 151	D.Stoudamire	.50	.23
□ 152	Jeff Hornacek	.10	.05
□ 153	Chris Morris	.05	.02
□ 154	Antoine Carr	.05	.02
□ 155	Karl Malone	.30	.14
□ 156	Adam Keefe	.05	.02
□ 157	Greg Anthony	.05	.02
□ 158	Blue Edwards	.05	.02
□ 159	Bryant Reeves	.10	.05
□ 160	Anthony Avent	.05	.02
□ 161	Lawrence Moten	.05	.02
□ 162	Calbert Cheaney	.05	.02
□ 163	Chris Webber	.50	.23
□ 164	Tim Legler	.05	.02
□ 165	Gheorghe Muresan	.05	.02
□ 166	Stacey Augmon FUND	.05	.02
□ 167	Dee Brown FUND	.05	.02
□ 168	Glen Rice FUND	.10	.05
□ 169	Scottie Pippen FUND	.30	.14
□ 170	Danny Ferry FUND	.05	.02
□ 171	Jason Kidd FUND	.20	.09
□ 172	LaPhonso Ellis FUND	.05	.02
□ 173	Grant Hill FUND	.60	.25
□ 174	Chris Mullin FUND	.10	.05
□ 175	Clyde Drexler FUND	.20	.09
□ 176	Rik Smits FUND	.05	.02
□ 177	Loy Vaught FUND	.05	.02
□ 178	Nick Van Exel FUND	.10	.05
□ 179	Alonzo Mourning FUND	.10	.05
□ 180	Glenn Robinson FUND	.10	.05
□ 181	Isaiah Rider FUND	.05	.02
□ 182	Ed O'Bannon FUND	.05	.02
□ 183	Patrick Ewing FUND	.10	.05
□ 184	Shaquille O'Neal FUND	.40	.18
□ 185	Derrick Coleman FUND	.05	.02
□ 186	Danny Manning FUND	.05	.02
□ 187	C. Robinson FUND	.05	.02
□ 188	Mitch Richmond FUND	.10	.05
□ 189	David Robinson FUND	.20	.09
□ 190	Shawn Kemp FUND	.30	.14
□ 191	Oliver Miller FUND	.05	.02
□ 192	John Stockton FUND	.10	.05
□ 193	Greg Anthony FUND	.05	.02
□ 194	Rasheed Wallace FUND	.10	.05
□ 195	Michael Jordan FUND	1.25	.55
□ 196	Michael Jordan	.15	.07
	Matt Geiger CL		
□ 197	Eddie Jones	.05	.02
	Antonio McDyess CL		
□ 198	A.Hardaway	.20	.09
	Kevin Garnett CL		
□ 199	D.Stoudamire CL	.05	.02
	Avery Johnson CL		
□ 200	David Robinson CL	.05	.02
	Chris Mullin CL		
□ 201	Alan Henderson	.05	.02
□ 202	Steve Smith	.10	.05
□ 203	Donnie Boyce	.05	.02
□ 204	Priest Lauderdale	.05	.02
□ 205	D.Mutombo	.10	.05
□ 206	Dee Brown	.05	.02
□ 207	Junior Burrough	.05	.02
□ 208	Todd Day	.05	.02
□ 209	Pervis Ellison	.05	.02
□ 210	Greg Minor	.05	.02
□ 211	Antoine Walker	2.00	.90
□ 212	Rafael Addison	.05	.02
□ 213	Tony Delk	.25	.11
□ 214	Vlade Divac	.10	.05
□ 215	Anthony Goldwire	.05	.02
□ 216	Anthony Mason	.10	.05
□ 217	Dickey Simpkins	.05	.02
□ 218	Randy Brown	.05	.02
□ 219	Jud Buechler	.05	.02
□ 220	Jason Caffey	.05	.02
□ 221	Scottie Pippen	.60	.25
□ 222	Bill Wennington	.05	.02
□ 223	Danny Ferry	.05	.02
□ 224	Antonio Lang	.05	.02
□ 225	Chris Mills	.05	.02
□ 226	Vitaly Potapenko	.10	.05
□ 227	Terry Davis	.05	.02
□ 228	Chris Gatling	.05	.02
□ 229	Jason Kidd	.40	.18
□ 230	George McCloud	.05	.02
□ 231	Eric Montross	.05	.02
□ 232	Samaki Walker	.25	.11
□ 233	Mark Jackson	.05	.02
□ 234	Ervin Johnson	.05	.02
□ 235	Sarunas Marciulionis	.05	.02
□ 236	Eric Murdock	.05	.02
□ 237	Ricky Pierce	.05	.02
□ 238	Bryant Stith	.05	.02
□ 239	Stacey Augmon	.05	.02
□ 240	Grant Hill	1.25	.55
□ 241	Otis Thorpe	.10	.05
□ 242	Jerome Williams	.10	.05
□ 243	Andrew DeClercq	.05	.02
□ 244	Todd Fuller	.05	.02
□ 245	Mark Price	.05	.02
□ 246	Clifford Rozier	.05	.02
□ 247	Latrell Sprewell	.10	.05
□ 248	Charles Barkley	.30	.14
□ 249	Clyde Drexler	.25	.11
□ 250	Othella Harrington	.10	.05
□ 251	Sam Mack	.05	.02
□ 252	Kevin Willis	.05	.02
□ 253	Erick Dampier	.25	.11
□ 254	Antonio Davis	.05	.02
□ 255	Dale Davis	.05	.02
□ 256	Duane Ferrell	.05	.02
□ 257	Reggie Miller	.20	.09
□ 258	Jalen Rose	.05	.02
□ 259	Reggie Williams	.05	.02
□ 260	Terry Dehere	.05	.02
□ 261	Charles Outlaw	.05	.02
□ 262	Stanley Roberts	.05	.02
□ 263	Malik Sealy	.05	.02
□ 264	Loy Vaught	.10	.05
□ 265	Lorenzen Wright	.25	.11
□ 266	Corie Blount	.05	.02
□ 267	Kobe Bryant	4.00	1.80
□ 268	Elden Campbell	.10	.05
□ 269	Derek Fisher	.05	.02
□ 270	Shaquille O'Neal	.75	.35
□ 271	Nick Van Exel	.20	.09
□ 272	P.J. Brown	.05	.02
□ 273	Tim Hardaway	.25	.11
□ 274	Voshon Lenard	.10	.05
□ 275	Dan Majerle	.10	.05
□ 276	Alonzo Mourning	.20	.09
□ 277	Martin Muursepp	.05	.02

Card	MINT	NRMT
☐ 278 Ray Allen	.60	.25
☐ 279 Elliot Perry	.05	.02
☐ 280 Glenn Robinson	.20	.09
☐ 281 Stephon Marbury	2.00	.90
☐ 282 Cherokee Parks	.05	.02
☐ 283 Doug West	.05	.02
☐ 284 Micheal Williams	.05	.02
☐ 285 Kerry Kittles	.50	.23
☐ 286 Ed O'Bannon	.05	.02
☐ 287 Robert Pack	.05	.02
☐ 288 Khalid Reeves	.05	.02
☐ 289 David Benoit	.05	.02
☐ 290 Patrick Ewing	.20	.09
☐ 291 Allan Houston	.10	.05
☐ 292 Larry Johnson	.10	.05
☐ 293 Dontae' Jones	.05	.02
☐ 294 Walter McCarty	.10	.05
☐ 295 John Wallace	.30	.14
☐ 296 Charlie Ward	.05	.02
☐ 297 Brian Evans	.05	.02
☐ 298 Horace Grant	.10	.05
☐ 299 Jon Koncak	.05	.02
☐ 300 Felton Spencer	.05	.02
☐ 301 Allen Iverson	2.00	.90
☐ 302 Don MacLean	.05	.02
☐ 303 Scott Williams	.05	.02
☐ 304 Sam Cassell	.05	.02
☐ 305 Michael Finley	.25	.11
☐ 306 Robert Horry	.10	.05
☐ 307 Kevin Johnson	.10	.05
☐ 308 Joe Kleine	.05	.02
☐ 309 Danny Manning	.10	.05
☐ 310 Steve Nash	.30	.14
☐ 311 John Williams	.05	.02
☐ 312 Kenny Anderson	.10	.05
☐ 313 Randolph Childress	.05	.02
☐ 314 Chris Dudley	.05	.02
☐ 315 Jermaine O'Neal	.30	.14
☐ 316 Isaiah Rider	.10	.05
☐ 317 Clifford Robinson	.05	.02
☐ 318 Rasheed Wallace	.05	.02
☐ 319 M.Abdul-Rauf	.05	.02
☐ 320 Duane Causwell	.05	.02
☐ 321 Bobby Hurley	.05	.02
☐ 322 Mitch Richmond	.20	.09
☐ 323 Lionel Simmons	.05	.02
☐ 324 Michael Smith	.05	.02
☐ 325 Dominique Wilkins	.20	.09
☐ 326 Cory Alexander	.05	.02
☐ 327 Greg Anderson	.05	.02
☐ 328 Carl Herrera	.05	.02
☐ 329 David Robinson	.30	.14
☐ 330 Charles Smith	.05	.02
☐ 331 Craig Ehlo	.05	.02
☐ 332 Sherrell Ford	.05	.02
☐ 333 Shawn Kemp	.60	.25
☐ 334 Jim McIlvaine	.05	.02
☐ 335 Gary Payton	.30	.14
☐ 336 Sam Perkins	.10	.05
☐ 337 Eric Snow	.05	.02
☐ 338 David Wingate	.05	.02
☐ 339 Marcus Camby	.50	.23
☐ 340 Acie Earl	.05	.02
☐ 341 Carlos Rogers	.05	.02
☐ 342 Greg Ostertag	.05	.02
☐ 343 Bryon Russell	.05	.02
☐ 344 John Stockton	.20	.09
☐ 345 Jamie Watson	.05	.02
☐ 346 S.Abdur-Rahim	1.25	.55
☐ 347 Doug Edwards	.05	.02
☐ 348 George Lynch	.05	.02
☐ 349 Eric Mobley	.05	.02
☐ 350 Anthony Peeler	.05	.02
☐ 351 Roy Rogers	.05	.02
☐ 352 Juwan Howard	.25	.11
☐ 353 Harvey Grant	.05	.02
☐ 354 Tracy Murray	.05	.02
☐ 355 Rod Strickland	.10	.05
☐ 356 A.Hardaway	1.25	.55
Michael Jordan ONE		
☐ 357 Hakeem Olajuwon	.60	.25
Shaquille O'Neal ONE		
☐ 358 Joe Smith	.40	.18
Shawn Kemp ONE		
☐ 359 Detlef Schrempf	.10	.05
Toni Kukoc ONE		
☐ 360 Jim Jackson	.10	.05
Jerry Stackhouse ONE		
☐ 361 Kobe Bryant	1.25	.55
S.Abdur-Rahim ONE		
☐ 362 Nick Anderson	.75	.35
Michael Jordan AJ		
☐ 363 Joe Dumars	.75	.35
Michael Jordan AJ		
☐ 364 John Starks	.75	.35
Michael Jordan AJ		
☐ 365 Reggie Miller	1.00	.45
Michael Jordan AJ		
☐ 366 Gary Payton	1.00	.45
Michael Jordan AJ		
☐ 367 Mookie Blaylock PLAY	.05	.02
☐ 368 Dino Radja PLAY	.05	.02
Rick Fox		
David Wesley PLAY		
☐ 369 Glen Rice PLAY	.10	.05
☐ 370 Michael Jordan	1.25	.55
Scottie Pippen PLAY		
☐ 371 Terrell Brandon PLAY	.10	.05
☐ 372 Jason Kidd PLAY	.20	.09
☐ 373 A.McDyess PLAY	.20	.09
☐ 374 Grant Hill PLAY	.60	.25
☐ 375 Joe Smith PLAY	.20	.09
☐ 376 Charles Barkley	.75	.35
Hakeem Olajuwon		
Clyde Drexler PLAY		
☐ 377 Reggie Miller PLAY	.10	.05
☐ 378 L.A. Clippers PLAY	.05	.02
☐ 379 Nick Van Exel PLAY	.10	.05
☐ 380 Alonzo Mourning PLAY	.10	.05
☐ 381 Ray Allen PLAY	.30	.14
☐ 382 S.Marbury PLAY	1.00	.45
☐ 383 Shawn Bradley PLAY	.05	.02
☐ 384 Patrick Ewing PLAY	.10	.05
☐ 385 A.Hardaway PLAY	.40	.18
☐ 386 J.Stackhouse PLAY	.20	.09
☐ 387 Danny Manning PLAY	.05	.02
☐ 388 C.Robinson PLAY	.05	.02
☐ 389 Tyus Edney PLAY	.05	.02
☐ 390 S.Antonio Spurs PLAY	.05	.02
☐ 391 Shawn Kemp PLAY	.30	.14
☐ 392 Toronto Raptors PLAY	.05	.02
☐ 393 John Stockton PLAY	.10	.05
☐ 394 Greg Anthony PLAY	.05	.02
☐ 395 G.Muresan PLAY	.05	.02
☐ 396 Checklist	.05	.02
☐ 397 Checklist	.05	.02
☐ 398 Checklist	.05	.02
☐ 399 Checklist	.05	.02
☐ 400 Checklist	.05	.02
☐ 401 Henry James TRADE	.40	.18
☐ 402 Shawn Bradley TRADE	.40	.18
☐ 403 S.Danilovic TRADE	.40	.18
☐ 404 M.Finley TRADE	1.00	.45
☐ 405 A.C. Green TRADE	.60	.25
☐ 406 Derek Harper TRADE	.40	.18
☐ 407 Khalid Reeves TRADE	.40	.18
☐ 408 Aaron McKie TRADE	.40	.18
☐ 409 Matt Maloney TRADE	1.25	.55
☐ 410 Detrick Martin TRADE	.40	.18
☐ 411 Robert Horry TRADE	.60	.25
☐ 412 Travis Knight TRADE	.40	.18
☐ 413 Isaac Austin TRADE	.40	.18
☐ 414 J. Mashburn TRADE	.60	.25
☐ 415 Armon Gilliam TRADE	.40	.18
☐ 416 Chris Carr TRADE	.40	.18
☐ 417 Dean Garrett TRADE	.40	.18
☐ 418 Shane Heal TRADE	.40	.18
☐ 419 Sam Cassell TRADE	.60	.25
☐ 420 Chris Gatling TRADE	.40	.18
☐ 421 Jim Jackson TRADE	.60	.25
☐ 422 Chris Childs TRADE	.40	.18
☐ 423 Rony Seikaly TRADE	.40	.18
☐ 424 Gerald Wilkins TRADE	.40	.18
☐ 425 Cedric Ceballos TRADE	.40	.18
☐ 426 Tony Dumas TRADE	.40	.18
☐ 427 Jason Kidd TRADE	1.50	.70
☐ 428 Popeye Jones TRADE	.40	.18
☐ 429 Walt Williams TRADE	.40	.18
☐ 430 Jaren Jackson TRADE	.60	.25
☐ NNO M. Jordan 5x7 DD	5.00	2.20
☐ NNO M. Jordan 5x7 MM	5.00	2.20
☐ NNO Update Trade Card	1.00	.45

1996-97 Collector's Choice Crash the Game Scoring 1

Randomly inserted into first series packs at a rate of one in 5, this 60-card silver set features two separate versions of thirty different player cards. Each player is given two seperate weeks to score 30 points in any given game during that time period. If the player depicted on the card scores 30 or more points in the given week, the card can be redeemed for one premium quality silver card of the depicted player. The expiration date for the cards was May 9, 1997.

	MINT	NRMT
COMPLETE SILVER SET (60)	60.00	27.00
COMMON CARD (C1-C30)	.40	.18
SEMISTARS	.60	.25
UNLISTED STARS	1.00	.45
SER.1 STATED ODDS 1:5		
*GOLD CARDS: 3X TO 6X HI COLUMN		
GOLD: SER.1 STATED ODDS 1:49		
*SILVER RED.CARDS: .75X TO 1.25X HI		
*GOLD RED.CARDS: 3X TO 6X HI		
ONE RED.CARD PER WINNER BY MAIL		
EACH PLAYER HAS TWO DIFF.SILVER CARDS		
EACH PLAYER HAS TWO DIFF.GOLD CARDS		
☐ C1 M. Blaylock 11/4 L	.60	.25
☐ C1B M. Blaylock 12/16 L	.60	.25
☐ C2 Dino Radja 11/18 L	.40	.18
☐ C2B Dino Radja 1/6 L	.40	.18
☐ C3 Glen Rice 11/18 L	1.00	.45
☐ C3B Glen Rice 1/27 W	1.00	.45
☐ C4 Scottie Pippen 12/2 L	3.00	1.35
☐ C4B Scottie Pippen 1/13 L	3.00	1.35
☐ C5 Terrell Brandon 11/4 L	1.00	.45
☐ C5B T. Brandon 1/13 L	1.00	.45
☐ C6 Jason Kidd 12/9 L	2.00	.90
☐ C6B Jason Kidd 12/23 W	2.00	.90
☐ C7 A. McDyess 11/11 L	1.50	.70
☐ C7B A. McDyess 12/23	1.50	.70
☐ C8 Joe Dumars 12/9 L	1.00	.45
☐ C8B Joe Dumars 1/13 L	1.00	.45
☐ C9 Joe Smith 12/2 L	1.25	.55
☐ C9B Joe Smith 12/23 W	1.25	.55
☐ C10 H.Olajuwon 11/4 W	2.00	.90
☐ C10B H.Olajuwon 12/23 W	2.00	.90
☐ C11 R.Miller 12/9 L	1.00	.45
☐ C11B R.Miller 1/27 W	1.00	.45

□ C12 Loy Vaught 11/18 L .... .60 — .25
□ C12B Loy Vaught 1/6 L ..... .60 — .25
□ C13 Cedric Ceballos 12/2 L .40 — .18
□ C13B C. Ceballos 1/27 L .... .40 — .18
□ C14 A. Mourning 11/11 L 1.00 — .45
□ C14B A. Mourning 1/6 W 1.00 — .45
□ C15 Vin Baker 12/9 L ...... 2.00 — .90
□ C15B Vin Baker 1/27 L ..... 2.00 — .90
□ C16 K. Garnett 11/18 L ..... 6.00 — 2.70
□ C16B K. Garnett 1/13 L ..... 6.00 — 2.70
□ C17 Ed O'Bannon 12/2 L .... .40 — .18
□ C17B Ed O'Bannon 1/6 L ..... .40 — .18
□ C18 Patrick Ewing 11/4 W 1.00 — .45
□ C18B Patrick Ewing 1/13 L 1.00 — .45
□ C19 A. Hardaway 12/23 L 4.00 — 1.80
□ C19B A. Hardaway 1/27 W 4.00 — 1.80
□ C20 C.Weatherspoon 12/16 L .40 — .18
□ C20B C.Weatherspoon 1/13 W .40 — .18
□ C21 Kevin Johnson 11/11 L .60 — .25
□ C21B Kevin Johnson 1/27 L .60 — .25
□ C22 C. Robinson 12/16 L .... .40 — .18
□ C22B C. Robinson 1/6 L ..... .40 — .18
□ C23 M. Richmond 12/16 W 1.00 — .45
□ C23B M. Richmond 1/27 W 1.00 — .45
□ C24 Sean Elliott 11/4 L ...... .40 — .18
□ C24B Sean Elliott 1/6 L ..... .40 — .18
□ C25 Shawn Kemp 12/16 L 3.00 — 1.35
□ C25B Shawn Kemp 1/13 L 3.00 — 1.35
□ C26 D. Stoudamire 12/9 W 2.50 — 1.10
□ C26B D. Stoudamire 1/6 L 2.50 — 1.10
□ C27 J.Stockton 11/11 L ..... 1.00 — .45
□ C27B J.Stockton 12/23 L .... 1.00 — .45
□ C28 Bryant Reeves 12/2 L .60 — .25
□ C28B B.Reeves 1/27 W ..... .60 — .25
□ C29 R.Wallace 11/18 L ..... .60 — .25
□ C29B R.Wallace 1/13 L ..... .60 — .25
□ C30 M.Jordan 11/11 W 12.00 — 5.50
□ C30B M.Jordan 12/23 W 12.00 — 5.50

1996-97 Collector's Choice Crash the Game Scoring 2

Randomly inserted into second series packs at a rate of one in 5, this 60-card silver set features two separate versions of thirty different player cards. Each player is given two separate weeks to score 30 points in any given game during that time period. If the player depicted on the card scores 30 or more points in the given week, the card can be redeemed for one premium quality silver card of the depicted player. The expiration date for the cards was July 1, 1997.

	MINT	NRMT
COMPLETE SILVER SET (60)	60.00	27.00
COMMON CARD (C1-C30)	.40	.18
SEMISTARS	.60	.25
UNLISTED STARS	1.00	.45

SER.2 STATED ODDS 1:5
*GOLD CARDS: 3X TO 6X HI COLUMN
GOLD: SER.2 STATED ODDS 1:49
*SILVER RED.CARDS: .75X TO 1.25X HI
*GOLD RED.CARDS: 3X TO 6X HI
ONE RED.CARD PER WINNER BY MAIL
EACH PLAYER HAS TWO DIFF.SILVER CARDS
EACH PLAYER HAS TWO DIFF.GOLD CARDS

□ C1 Steve Smith 2/17 L .... .60 — .25
□ C1B Steve Smith 4/14 W .. .60 — .25
□ C2 Dana Barros 3/3 L ..... .40 — .18
□ C2B Dana Barros 3/31 L .. .40 — .18
□ C3 Tony Delk 2/24 L ...... 1.00 — .45
□ C3B Tony Delk 4/7 L ...... 1.00 — .45
□ C4 Toni Kukoc 3/10 L ..... .60 — .25
□ C4B Toni Kukoc 3/31 L .... .60 — .25
□ C5 Bobby Phills 2/24 L .... .40 — .18
□ C5B Bobby Phills 3/17 L ... .40 — .18
□ C6 J.Mashburn 3/3 L ...... .60 — .25
□ C6B J.Mashburn 3/31 L .... .60 — .25
□ C7 LaPhonso Ellis 2/24 W .40 — .18
□ C7B LaPhonso Ellis 3/31 L .40 — .18
□ C8 Jerome Williams 2/17 L .40 — .18
□ C8B Jerome Williams 4/7 L .60 — .25
□ C9 Latrell Sprewell 3/3 L .40 — .18
□ C9B Latrell Sprewell 4/7 L .40 — .18
□ C10 Clyde Drexler 2/24 L 1.25 — .55
□ C10B Clyde Drexler 4/7 L 1.25 — .55
□ C11 Dale Davis 3/3 L ..... .40 — .18
□ C11B Dale Davis 3/24 L ... .40 — .18
□ C12 Brent Barry 3/3 L .... .40 — .18
□ C12B Brent Barry 4/14 L .. .40 — .18
□ C13 Nick Van Exel 3/10 L 1.00 — .45
□ C13B Nick Van Exel 4/7 L 1.00 — .45
□ C14 S.Danilovic 2/17 L ... .40 — .18
□ C14B S.Danilovic 3/17 L .. .40 — .18
□ C15 G.Robinson 2/24 L 1.00 — .45
□ C15B G.Robinson 3/17 L 1.00 — .45
□ C16 S.Marbury 2/17 L .... 5.00 — 2.20
□ C16B S.Marbury 3/31 L ... 5.00 — 2.20
□ C17 S.Bradley 3/10 W .... .40 — .18
□ C17B S.Bradley 3/24 L .... .40 — .18
□ C18 J.Wallace 3/3 L ...... 1.00 — .45
□ C18B J.Wallace 4/14 L .... 1.00 — .45
□ C19 A.Hardaway 2/24 L 4.00 — 1.80
□ C19B A.Hardaway 4/14 L 4.00 — 1.80
□ C20 J.Stackhouse 3/10 W 1.25 — .55
□ C20B J.Stackhouse 3/31 W 1.25 — .55
□ C21 D.Manning 2/17 L .... .40 — .18
□ C21B D.Manning 3/24 L .... .40 — .18
□ C22 A.Sabonis 2/24 L ..... .40 — .18
□ C22B A.Sabonis 3/31 L .... .40 — .18
□ C23 B.Grant 3/3 L .... .40 — .18
□ C23B B.Grant 3/31 L ...... .40 — .18
□ C24 D.Robinson 2/24 L .. 1.50 — .70
□ C24B D.Robinson 3/24 L .. 1.50 — .70
□ C25 Gary Payton 3/3 L ... 1.50 — .70
□ C25B Gary Payton 4/14 L 1.50 — .70
□ C26 Marcus Camby 3/3 L 1.25 — .55
□ C26B Marcus Camby 4/7 L 1.25 — .55
□ C27 Karl Malone 3/3 L ... 1.50 — .70
□ C27B Karl Malone 4/14 W 1.50 — .70
□ C28 S.Abdur-Rahim 2/24 L 3.00 — 1.35
□ C28B S.Abdur-Rahim 3/17 L 3.00 — 1.35
□ C29 Juwan Howard 2/17 L 1.25 — .55
□ C29B Juwan Howard 4/7 L 1.25 — .55
□ C30 M.Jordan 3/3 W .... 12.00 — 5.50
□ C30B M.Jordan 4/14 W 12.00 — 5.50

1996-97 Collector's Choice Draft Trade

This 10-card set was available by exchanging a Draft Trade card, inserted at a rate of one in 144 in the series one set. The trade card expired May 9, 1997. Each card has a full portrait shot of the player and career information on the back. The cards are numbered with a "DR" prefix.

	MINT	NRMT
COMPLETE SET (10)	15.00	6.75
COMMON CARD (DR1-DR10)	.75	.35

ONE SET PER DRAFT TRADE CARD VIA MAIL
TRADE: SER.1 STATED ODDS 1:144

□ DR1 Allen Iverson ...... 4.00 — 1.80
□ DR2 Marcus Camby ..... 1.00 — .45
□ DR3 S.Abdur-Rahim ..... 2.50 — 1.10
□ DR4 Stephon Marbury ... 4.00 — 1.80
□ DR5 Ray Allen .... 1.25 — .55
□ DR6 Antoine Walker ..... 4.00 — 1.80
□ DR7 Lorenzen Wright .... .75 — .35
□ DR8 Kerry Kittles ...... 1.00 — .45
□ DR9 Samaki Walker ...... .75 — .35
□ DR10 Erick Dampier ..... .75 — .35
□ NNO Exp. Draft Trade Card 1.00 — .45

1996-97 Collector's Choice Game Face

Inserted one per special retail pack, this 10-card set is standard-sized with white bordered fronts and the logo "Game Face" in gold on the front. Card backs include an inset photo of the player with commentary. Cards are numbered with a "GF" prefix.

	MINT	NRMT
COMPLETE SET (10)	12.00	5.50
COMMON CARD (GF1-GF10)	.30	.14
SEMISTARS	.40	.18
UNLISTED STARS	.60	.25
ONE PER SPECIAL SER.1 RETAIL PACK		

☐ GF1	A.Hardaway	2.50	1.10
☐ GF2	Michael Jordan	8.00	3.60
☐ GF3	Shawn Kemp	2.00	.90
☐ GF4	Alonzo Mourning	.60	.25
☐ GF5	Cherokee Parks	.30	.14
☐ GF6	Avery Johnson	.30	.14
☐ GF7	LaPhonso Ellis	.30	.14
☐ GF8	Rasheed Wallace	.30	.14
☐ GF9	Jim Jackson	.30	.14
☐ GF10	Larry Johnson	.40	.18

1996-97 Collector's Choice Jordan A Cut Above

One of these ten Jordan ACA cards was inserted into every special Wal-Mart ninety-nine cent series one retail pack. This 10-card set focuses on Michael Jordan's career feats. Each card front is die cut at the top with the set name "A Cut Above" in gold foil. Card backs feature a head shot with a summary of each feat.

	MINT	NRMT
COMPLETE SET (10)	20.00	9.00
COM. JORDAN (CA1-CA10)	2.50	1.10
ONE PER SPECIAL SER.1 RETAIL PACK		

☐ CA1	Michael Jordan 1985 Rookie of the Year	2.50	1.10
☐ CA2	Michael Jordan 8-Time Scoring Leader	2.50	1.10
☐ CA3	Michael Jordan 8-Time All-NBA First Team	2.50	1.10
☐ CA4	Michael Jordan Defensive POY	2.50	1.10
☐ CA5	Michael Jordan 10-Time All-Star	2.50	1.10
☐ CA6	Michael Jordan 2-Time All-Star Game MVP	2.50	1.10
☐ CA7	Michael Jordan 4-Time MVP	2.50	1.10
☐ CA8	Michael Jordan 4-Time Champion	2.50	1.10
☐ CA9	Michael Jordan 4-Time Finals MVP	2.50	1.10
☐ CA10	Michael Jordan Continuing Excellence	2.50	1.10

1996-97 Collector's Choice Memorable Moments

Inserted one per special series two retail pack, this 10-card set features memorable moments from the 1996 NBA season. The cards have a die cut design on both the top and bottom of the card with gold foil running along each of those die cut borders. Card backs describe the moment.

	MINT	NRMT
COMPLETE SET (10)	15.00	6.75
COMMON CARD (1-10)	.50	.23
SEMISTARS	.60	.25
ONE PER SPECIAL SER.2 RETAIL PACK		

☐ 1	Michael Jordan	8.00	3.60
☐ 2	Nick Van Exel	.60	.25
☐ 3	Karl Malone	1.00	.45
☐ 4	Latrell Sprewell	.50	.23
☐ 5	A.Hardaway	2.50	1.10
☐ 6	Glenn Robinson	.60	.25
☐ 7	Shaquille O'Neal	2.50	1.10
☐ 8	D.Stoudamire	1.50	.70
☐ 9	Clyde Drexler	.75	.35
☐ 10	Shawn Kemp	2.00	.90

1996-97 Collector's Choice Mini-Cards

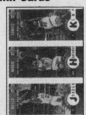

Inserted in both series at a rate of one per pack, this 60-card set

is comprised of 180 different "mini-cards". Three of these mini-cards form one standard-sized card and are issued in that form. Card fronts feature perforated panels of three players with silver foil. Card backs feature a brief commentary on each player. Each card contains it's own individual number, with an "M" prefix and is ordered below by the far left number on the card back. Also, card number M106 was never issued. Both Bob Sura and Bryant Stith were numbered M112.

	MINT	NRMT
COMPLETE SET (60)	20.00	9.00
COMPLETE SERIES 1 (30)	8.00	3.60
COMPLETE SERIES 2 (30)	12.00	5.50
COMMON CARD (1-60)	.10	.05
SEMISTARS	.20	.09
UNLISTED STARS	.30	.14
ONE PER BOTH SERIES PACKS		
TWO PER SPECIAL SER.1 RETAIL PACK		
*GOLD: 6X TO 12X HI COLUMN		
GOLD: SER.1/2 STATED ODDS 1:35		
ORDERED BY FAR LEFT NUMBER ON BACK		
NUMBER M106 NEVER ISSUED		
SURA AND STITH NUMBERED M112		
SKIP-NUMBERED SET		

☐ M2	Rex Walters Jeff Hornacek Mookie Blaylock	.20	.09
☐ M5	Detlef Schrempf Toni Kukoc Dino Radja	.20	.09
☐ M6	Ashraf Amaya Sharone Wright Eric Williams	.10	.05
☐ M10	Tyus Edney Ed O'Bannon George Zidek	.10	.05
☐ M13	Theo Ratliff Shawn Bradley Luc Longley	.20	.09
☐ M22	Bobby Phills Avery Johnson M.Abdul-Rauf	.10	.05
☐ M23	Popeye Jones Chris Morris Tom Hammonds	.10	.05
☐ M25	Bobby Hurley Christian Laettner Grant Hill	1.50	.70
☐ M28	Sherman Douglas Derrick Coleman Rony Seikaly	.10	.05
☐ M30	Nick Van Exel John Starks Sam Cassell	.30	.14
☐ M33	Matt Geiger Dennis Scott Travis Best	.10	.05
☐ M36	Cedric Ceballos Isaiah Rider Brent Barry	.20	.09
☐ M37	Jason Kidd Kevin Johnson Lamond Murray	.30	.14
☐ M38	Chris Mullin Jayson Williams Terry Dehere	.20	.09
☐ M39	Arvedas Sabonis Sasha Danilovic Vlade Divac	.20	.09
☐ M43	Tyrone Hill Brian Grant	.10	.05

Kurt Thomas
- M44 Derrick McKey .... .10 .05
  Robert Horry
  Keith Askins
- M46 Randolph Childress ... .40 .18
  David Robinson
  Shawn Respert
- M49 Todd Day .... .10 .05
  Oliver Miller
  Andrew Lang
- M56 Dell Curry .... .10 .05
  Bimbo Coles
  Charles Oakley
- M57 Rasheed Wallace ... .40 .18
  Jerry Stackhouse
  J.R. Reid
- M66 Joe Dumars .... .30 .14
  Clyde Drexler
  A.C. Green
- M67 Kendall Gill .... .20 .09
  Nick Anderson
  Aaron McKie
- M75 Danny Ferry .... .10 .05
  Mark Jackson
  Doc Rivers
- M78 Michael Jordan .. 5.00 2.20
  A.Hardaway
  Shawn Kemp
- M79 Jalen Rose .... .50 .23
  Chris Webber
  Jimmy King
- M83 Dennis Rodman ...... 2.00 .90
  Charles Barkley
  Karl Malone
- M85 Stacey Augmon ...... .20 .09
  Larry Johnson
  Greg Anthony
- M86 Nate McMillan .... .20 .09
  Tom Gugliotta
  Blue Edwards
- M90 Jim Jackson .... .30 .14
  Glenn Robinson
  Calbert Cheaney
- M92 Ken Norman............. .10 .05
  Doug West
  Kevin Edwards
- M93 Steve Smith .... .30 .14
  Tim Hardaway
  BJ Armstrong
- M99 Glen Rice .... .30 .14
  Danny Manning
  Sam Perkins
- M102 Steve Kerr .... .20 .09
  Reggie Miller
  Dana Barros
- M109 Samaki Walker .. .30 .14
  Lorenzen Wright
  Greg Minor
- M110 LaPhonso Ellis .... .10 .05
  Kevin Willis
  C.Weatherspoon
- M111 Antonio McDyess... .50 .23
  Latrell Sprewell
  Jason Caffey
- M112A Bryant Stith .... .10 .05
  Vinny Del Negro
  Kenny Anderson
- M112B Bob Sura .... .10 .05
  Rodney Rogers
  Olden Polynice
- M113 Lindsey Hunter .. .30 .14
  Eddie Jones
  Ron Harper
- M115 Otis Thorpe .... .30 .14
  John Stockton
  Antoine Carr
- M125 Rik Smits .... .75 .35
  Hakeem Olajuwon
  Gheorghe Muresan
- M129 Kobe Bryant .. 6.00 2.70
  Jermaine O'Neal
  Kevin Garnett
- M135 Alonzo Mourning .. .50 .23
  D.Mutombo
  Patrick Ewing
- M137 Vin Baker .... 1.50 .70

Jamal Mashburn
Scottie Pippen
- M140 Stephon Marbury .. 1.25 .55
  Darrin Hancock
  Wesley Person
- M146 Allan Houston..... .75 .35
  Marcus Camby
  Kerry Kittles
- M148 John Wallace .. 1.50 .70
  Walter McCarty
  Antoine Walker
- M149 Horace Grant .... .20 .09
  Elden Campbell
  Dale Davis
- M150 Donald Royal .... .10 .05
  Tim Legler
  Mario Elie
- M151 Brian Shaw .... .10 .05
  Antonio Davis
  P.J. Brown
- M152 Allen Iverson ... 4.00 1.80
  Joe Smith
  Shaquille O'Neal
- M159 Cliff Robinson .... .40 .18
  Scott Burrell
  Ray Allen
- M161 Mitch Richmond...... .30 .14
  Will Perdue
  Hersey Hawkins
- M167 Gary Payton .... .40 .18
  Terrell Brandon
  Sean Elliott
- M170 Doug Christie .... .10 .05
  Johnny Newman
  Tony Dumas
- M175 S.Abdur-Rahim .. .75 .35
  Chris Mills
  Khalid Reeves
- M176 Lawrence Moten..... .10 .05
  Michael Smith
  Bryon Russell
- M177 Bryant Reeves .... .60 .25
  Michael Finley
  D.Stoudamire
- M178 Juwan Howard .. .30 .14
  Loy Vaught
  Terry Mills

1996-97 Collector's Choice Stick-Ums 1

Randomly inserted into first series packs at a rate of one in 4, this 30-card set features separate removable stickers of the actual player, the player's name and the given statistical categories. Card backs are black and white and feature set information including the complete Stick-Um checklist. Card stock is

noticeably thin. Cards are numbered with an "S" prefix.

	MINT	NRMT
COMPLETE SET (30)	10.00	4.50
COMMON STICKER (S1-S30)	.15	.07
SEMISTARS	.20	.09
UNLISTED STARS	.30	.14
SER.1 STATED ODDS 1:4		

- S1 Mookie Blaylock .... .20 .09
- S2 Dana Barros .... .15 .07
- S3 Scott Burrell .... .15 .07
- S4 Dennis Rodman .... 1.25 .55
- S5 Terrell Brandon .... .30 .14
- S6 Jamal Mashburn .... .20 .09
- S7 LaPhonso Ellis .... .15 .07
- S8 Grant Hill .... 2.00 .90
- S9 Joe Smith .... .40 .18
- S10 Hakeem Olajuwon ...... .60 .25
- S11 Rik Smits .... .20 .09
- S12 Brent Barry .... .15 .07
- S13 Nick Van Exel .... .30 .14
- S14 Sasha Danilovic ...... .15 .07
- S15 Vin Baker .... .60 .25
- S16 Kevin Garnett .... 2.00 .90
- S17 Shawn Bradley .... .15 .07
- S18 Patrick Ewing .... .30 .14
- S19 A.Hardaway .... 1.25 .55
- S20 C. Weatherspoon ...... .15 .07
- S21 Charles Barkley .... .50 .23
- S22 Clifford Robinson ...... .15 .07
- S23 Mitch Richmond .... .30 .14
- S24 David Robinson .... .50 .23
- S25 Shawn Kemp .... 1.00 .45
- S26 D.Stoudamire .... .75 .35
- S27 Karl Malone .... .50 .23
- S28 Bryant Reeves .... .20 .09
- S29 Gheorghe Muresan ...... .15 .07
- S30 Michael Jordan 4.00 1.80

1996-97 Collector's Choice Stick-Ums 2

Randomly inserted into second series packs at a rate of one in 3, this 30-card set features separate removable stickers of the actual player, the player's name and the given statistical categories. Card backs are black and white and feature set information including the complete Stick-Um checklist. Card stock is noticeably thin. Cards are numbered with an "S" prefix.

	MINT	NRMT
COMPLETE SET (30)	8.00	3.60

	MINT	NRMT
COMMON STICKER (S1-S30)	.15	.07
SEMISTARS	.20	.09
UNLISTED STARS	.30	.14
SER.2 STATED ODDS 1:3		
COMPLETE BASE SET (30) ..	4.00	1.80
COMMON BASE (B1-B30)	.10	.05
*BASE STARS: 50% VALUE OF LISTED CARDS		
BASE: SER.2 STATED ODDS 1:4		
☐ S1 Steve Smith	.20	.09
☐ S2 Dino Radja	.15	.07
☐ S3 Glen Rice	.30	.14
☐ S4 Toni Kukoc	.20	.09
☐ S5 Bobby Phills	.15	.07
☐ S6 Jason Kidd	.60	.25
☐ S7 Antonio McDyess	.50	.23
☐ S8 Joe Dumars	.30	.14
☐ S9 Latrell Sprewell	.20	.09
☐ S10 Clyde Drexler	.40	.18
☐ S11 Reggie Miller	.30	.14
☐ S12 Loy Vaught	.20	.09
☐ S13 Eddie Jones	.60	.25
☐ S14 Alonzo Mourning	.30	.14
☐ S15 Glenn Robinson	.30	.14
☐ S16 Tom Gugliotta	.30	.14
☐ S17 Ed O'Bannon	.15	.07
☐ S18 John Starks	.20	.09
☐ S19 A.Hardaway	1.25	.55
☐ S20 Jerry Stackhouse	.40	.18
☐ S21 Kevin Johnson	.20	.09
☐ S22 Arvydas Sabonis	.15	.07
☐ S23 Brian Grant	.15	.07
☐ S24 Sean Elliott	.15	.07
☐ S25 Gary Payton	.50	.23
☐ S26 Zan Tabak	.15	.07
☐ S27 John Stockton	.30	.14
☐ S28 Greg Anthony	.15	.07
☐ S29 Juwan Howard	.40	.18
☐ S30 Michael Jordan	4.00	1.80

1997-98 Collector's Choice

The 1997-98 Collector's Choice issue totaled 400 cards with each series containing 200. Each pack contained 14 cards and carried a suggested retail price of $1.29. The set contains the topical subsets: Game Night (156-185), Catch 23 (186-195), Hot Properties (356-385) and Michael's Magic (386-395). The fronts feature color action player photos in a white border. The backs carry player information. Checklist cards 196-200 were Challenge cards which when filled in correctly could be redeemed for a set of the Top 10 Picks in the 1997 NBA Draft. A factory set was also released, which contained not only the 400 basic cards, but also five Miniatures, and 10 special StarQuest cards that were available only in the factory set.

	MINT	NRMT
COMPLETE SET (400)	30.00	13.50
COMP.FACTORY SET (415)	40.00	18.00
COMPLETE SERIES 1 (200)	15.00	6.75
COMPLETE SERIES 2 (200)	15.00	6.75
COMMON CARD (1-400)	.05	.02
COMMON MJ C23 (186-195)	1.00	.45
COM. MJ MAGIC (386-395)	1.00	.45
SEMISTARS	.10	.05
UNLISTED STARS	.20	.09
☐ 1 Mookie Blaylock	.10	.05
☐ 2 D.Mutombo	.10	.05
☐ 3 Eldridge Recasner	.05	.02
☐ 4 Christian Laettner	.10	.05
☐ 5 Tyrone Corbin	.05	.02
☐ 6 Antoine Walker	1.00	.45
☐ 7 Eric Williams	.05	.02
☐ 8 Dana Barros	.05	.02
☐ 9 David Wesley	.05	.02
☐ 10 Dino Radja	.10	.05
☐ 11 Vlade Divac	.10	.05
☐ 12 Dell Curry	.05	.02
☐ 13 Muggsy Bogues	.05	.02
☐ 14 Tony Smith	.05	.02
☐ 15 Glen Rice	.20	.09
☐ 16 Anthony Mason	.10	.05
☐ 17 Dennis Rodman	.75	.35
☐ 18 Brian Williams	.05	.02
☐ 19 Toni Kukoc	.10	.05
☐ 20 Jason Caffey	.05	.02
☐ 21 Steve Kerr	.05	.02
☐ 22 Luc Longley	.10	.05
☐ 23 Michael Jordan	2.50	1.10
☐ 24 Chris Mills	.05	.02
☐ 25 Tyrone Hill	.05	.02
☐ 26 Vitaly Potapenko	.05	.02
☐ 27 Bob Sura	.05	.02
☐ 28 Robert Pack	.05	.02
☐ 29 Ed O'Bannon	.05	.02
☐ 30 Michael Finley	.20	.09
☐ 31 Shawn Bradley	.05	.02
☐ 32 Khalid Reeves	.05	.02
☐ 33 Antonio McDyess	.25	.11
☐ 34 Ervin Johnson	.05	.02
☐ 35 Dale Ellis	.05	.02
☐ 36 Bryant Stith	.05	.02
☐ 37 Tom Hammonds	.05	.02
☐ 38 Otis Thorpe	.10	.05
☐ 39 Lindsey Hunter	.05	.02
☐ 40 Grant Long	.05	.02
☐ 41 Aaron McKie	.05	.02
☐ 42 Randolph Childress	.05	.02
☐ 43 Scott Burrell	.05	.02
☐ 44 Bimbo Coles	.05	.02
☐ 45 B.J. Armstrong	.05	.02
☐ 46 Mark Price	.05	.02
☐ 47 Latrell Sprewell	.10	.05
☐ 48 Felton Spencer	.05	.02
☐ 49 Charles Barkley	.30	.14
☐ 50 Mario Elie	.05	.02
☐ 51 Clyde Drexler	.25	.11
☐ 52 Kevin Willis	.05	.02
☐ 53 Antonio Davis	.05	.02
☐ 54 Reggie Miller	.20	.09
☐ 55 Dale Davis	.05	.02
☐ 56 Mark Jackson	.05	.02
☐ 57 Erick Dampier	.05	.02
☐ 58 Pooh Richardson	.05	.02
☐ 59 Terry Dehere	.05	.02
☐ 60 Brent Barry	.05	.02
☐ 61 Loy Vaught	.10	.05
☐ 62 Lorenzen Wright	.05	.02
☐ 63 Eddie Jones	.40	.18
☐ 64 Kobe Bryant	1.50	.70
☐ 65 Elden Campbell	.10	.05
☐ 66 Corie Blount	.05	.02
☐ 67 Shaquille O'Neal	.75	.35
☐ 68 Dan Majerle	.10	.05
☐ 69 P.J. Brown	.05	.02
☐ 70 Tim Hardaway	.25	.11
☐ 71 Isaac Austin	.05	.02
☐ 72 Jamal Mashburn	.10	.05
☐ 73 Ray Allen	.25	.11
☐ 74 Glenn Robinson	.20	.09
☐ 75 Armon Gilliam	.05	.02
☐ 76 Johnny Newman	.05	.02
☐ 77 Elliot Perry	.05	.02
☐ 78 Sherman Douglas	.05	.02
☐ 79 Doug West	.05	.02
☐ 80 Kevin Garnett	1.25	.55
☐ 81 Sam Mitchell	.05	.02
☐ 82 Tom Gugliotta	.20	.09
☐ 83 Terry Porter	.05	.02
☐ 84 Chris Carr	.05	.02
☐ 85 Kevin Edwards	.05	.02
☐ 86 Jayson Williams	.10	.05
☐ 87 Kendall Gill	.10	.05
☐ 88 Kerry Kittles	.20	.09
☐ 89 Chris Gatling	.05	.02
☐ 90 John Starks	.10	.05
☐ 91 Charlie Ward	.05	.02
☐ 92 Larry Johnson	.10	.05
☐ 93 Charles Oakley	.05	.02
☐ 94 Chris Childs	.05	.02
☐ 95 Allan Houston	.10	.05
☐ 96 Horace Grant	.10	.05
☐ 97 Darrell Armstrong	.05	.02
☐ 98 Rony Seikaly	.05	.02
☐ 99 Dennis Scott	.05	.02
☐ 100 A.Hardaway	.75	.35
☐ 101 Brian Shaw	.05	.02
☐ 102 Jerry Stackhouse	.20	.09
☐ 103 Rex Walters	.05	.02
☐ 104 Don MacLean	.05	.02
☐ 105 Derrick Coleman	.10	.05
☐ 106 Lucious Harris	.05	.02
☐ 107 C.Weatherspoon	.05	.02
☐ 108 Cedric Ceballos	.05	.02
☐ 109 Danny Manning	.05	.02
☐ 110 Jason Kidd	.40	.18
☐ 111 Loren Meyer	.05	.02
☐ 112 Wesley Person	.05	.02
☐ 113 Steve Nash	.10	.05
☐ 114 Isaiah Rider	.05	.02
☐ 115 Stacey Augmon	.05	.02
☐ 116 Arvydas Sabonis	.10	.05
☐ 117 Kenny Anderson	.10	.05
☐ 118 Jermaine O'Neal	.10	.05
☐ 119 Gary Trent	.05	.02
☐ 120 Michael Smith	.05	.02
☐ 121 Kevin Gamble	.05	.02
☐ 122 Olden Polynice	.05	.02
☐ 123 Billy Owens	.05	.02
☐ 124 Corliss Williamson	.10	.05
☐ 125 Cory Alexander	.05	.02
☐ 126 Vinny Del Negro	.05	.02
☐ 127 Sean Elliott	.05	.02
☐ 128 Will Perdue	.05	.02
☐ 129 Carl Herrera	.05	.02
☐ 130 Shawn Kemp	.60	.25
☐ 131 Hersey Hawkins	.10	.05
☐ 132 Nate McMillan	.05	.02
☐ 133 Craig Ehlo	.05	.02
☐ 134 Detlef Schrempf	.10	.05
☐ 135 Sam Perkins	.10	.05
☐ 136 Sharone Wright	.05	.02
☐ 137 Doug Christie	.05	.02
☐ 138 Popeye Jones	.05	.02
☐ 139 Shawn Respert	.05	.02
☐ 140 Marcus Camby	.20	.09
☐ 141 Adam Keefe	.05	.02
☐ 142 Karl Malone	.30	.14
☐ 143 John Stockton	.20	.09
☐ 144 Greg Ostertag	.05	.02
☐ 145 Chris Morris	.05	.02
☐ 146 S.Abdur-Rahim	.60	.25
☐ 147 Roy Rogers	.05	.02
☐ 148 George Lynch	.05	.02

☐ 149	Anthony Peeler	.05	.02
☐ 150	Lee Mayberry	.05	.02
☐ 151	Calbert Cheaney	.05	.02
☐ 152	Harvey Grant	.05	.02
☐ 153	Rod Strickland	.10	.05
☐ 154	Tracy Murray	.05	.02
☐ 155	Chris Webber	.50	.23
☐ 156	Atlanta Hawks GN	.05	.02
	Mookie Blaylock		
	Christian Laettner		
	D.Mutombo		
	Steve Smith		
☐ 157	Boston Celtics GN	.50	.23
	Antoine Walker		
	Dana Barros		
	David Wesley		
☐ 158	Charlotte Hornets GN	.10	.05
	Glen Rice		
	Anthony Mason		
	Tony Delk		
	Vlade Divac		
☐ 159	Chicago Bulls GN	1.25	.55
	Michael Jordan		
	Toni Kukoc		
	Scottie Pippen		
	Dennis Rodman		
☐ 160	Cleveland Cavaliers GN	.05	.02
	Tyrone Hill		
	Terrell Brandon		
	Bob Sura		
☐ 161	Dallas Mavericks GN	.05	.02
	Shawn Bradley		
	Michael Finley		
	Ed O'Bannon		
	Robert Pack		
☐ 162	Denver Nuggets GN	.20	.09
	Antoino McDyess		
	Ervin Johnson		
	Dale Ellis		
	LaPhonso Ellis		
☐ 163	Detroit Pistons GN	.60	.25
	Grant Hill		
	Joe Dumars		
	Theo Ratliff		
	Lindsey Hunter		
☐ 164	Gldn State Warriors GN	.05	.02
	Latrell Sprewell		
	Chris Mullin		
	Joe Smith		
☐ 165	Houston Rockets GN	.20	.09
	Hakeem Olajuwon		
	Clyde Drexler		
	Charles Barkley		
	Kevin Willis		
☐ 166	Indiana Pacers GN	.10	.05
	Reggie Miller		
	Antonio Davis		
	Dale Davis		
☐ 167	L.A. Clippers GN	.05	.02
	Loy Vaught		
	Terry Dehere		
	Pooh Richardson		
	Brent Barry		
☐ 168	L.A. Lakers GN	.20	.09
	Eddie Jones		
	Shaquille O'Neal		
	Kobe Bryant		
	Nick Van Exel		
☐ 169	Miami Heat GN	.20	.09
	Tim Hardaway		
	Alonzo Mourning		
	P.J. Brown		
	Jamal Mashburn		
☐ 170	Milwaukee Bucks GN	.20	.09
	Vin Baker		
	Ray Allen		
	Elliot Perry		
	Johnny Newman		
	Glenn Robinson		
☐ 171	Minnesota T'wolves	.60	.25
	Game Night		
	Kevin Garnett		
	Stephon Marbury		
	Terry Porter		
	Tom Gugliotta		
☐ 172	New Jersey Nets GN	.10	.05
	Kendall Gill		
	Jim Jackson		
	Chris Gatling		
	Jayson Williams		
☐ 173	New York Knicks GN	.10	.05
	Patrick Ewing		
	Allan Houston		
	Charles Oakley		
	Larry Johnson		
	Charlie Ward		
☐ 174	Orlando Magic GN	.40	.18
	A.Hardaway		
	Horace Grant		
	Brian Shaw		
	Rony Seikaly		
☐ 175	Philadelphia 76ers GN	.50	.23
	Allen Iverson		
	Jerry Stackhouse		
	Derrick Coleman		
	Rex Walters		
☐ 176	Phoenix Suns GN	.20	.09
	Jason Kidd		
	Danny Manning		
	Wesley Person		
	Kevin Johnson		
☐ 177	Portland Trail Blazers	.05	.02
	Game Night		
	Rasheed Wallace		
	Kenny Anderson		
	Isaiah Rider		
☐ 178	Sacramento Kings GN	.10	.05
	Mitch Richmond		
	Olden Polynice		
	Billy Owens		
	M.Abdul-Rauf		
☐ 179	San Antonio Spurs GN	.05	.02
	Sean Elliott		
	Avery Johnson		
	David Robinson		
	Cory Alexander		
☐ 180	Seattle Supersonics GN	.20	.09
	Gary Payton		
	Detlef Schrempf		
	Shawn Kemp		
	Hersey Hawkins		
☐ 181	Toronto Raptors GN	.20	.09
	D.Stoudamire		
	Marcus Camby		
	Zan Tabak		
	Doug Christie		
☐ 182	Utah Jazz Game Night	.20	.09
	Karl Malone		
	John Stockton		
	Jeff Hornacek		
☐ 183	Vancouver Grizzlies GN	.30	.14
	S.Abdur-Rahim		
	Roy Rogers		
	Anthony Peeler		
	Bryant Reeves		
☐ 184	Washgtn Wizards GN	.25	.11
	Chris Webber		
	Juwan Howard		
	Calbert Cheaney		
	Rod Strickland		
☐ 185	1997 NBA Finals GN	1.25	.55
	Michael Jordan		
	Karl Malone		
	Dennis Rodman		
	John Stockton		
☐ 186	Michael Jordan	1.00	.45
	Catch 23 Fast Break		
☐ 187	Michael Jordan	1.00	.45
	Catch 23 Finger Roll		
☐ 188	Michael Jordan	1.00	.45
	Catch 23 Favorite Pastimes		
☐ 189	Michael Jordan	1.00	.45
	Catch 23 Championship Drive		
☐ 190	Michael Jordan	1.00	.45
	Catch 23 Road Show		
☐ 191	Michael Jordan	1.00	.45
	Catch 23 Media Circus		
☐ 192	Michael Jordan	1.00	.45
	Catch 23 Jump Shot		
☐ 193	Michael Jordan	1.00	.45
	Catch 23 Shake and Bake		
☐ 194	Michael Jordan	1.00	.45
	Catch 23 Strong Finish		
☐ 195	Michael Jordan	1.00	.45
	Catch 23 Leader		
☐ 196	Checklist #1	.05	.02
☐ 197	Checklist #2	.05	.02
☐ 198	Checklist #3	.05	.02
☐ 199	Checklist #4	.05	.02
☐ 200	Checklist #5	.05	.02
☐ 201	Steve Smith	.10	.05
☐ 202	Chris Crawford	.05	.02
☐ 203	Ed Gray	.25	.11
☐ 204	Alan Henderson	.05	.02
☐ 205	Walter McCarty	.05	.02
☐ 206	Dee Brown	.05	.02
☐ 207	Chauncey Billups	.75	.35
☐ 208	Ron Mercer	1.50	.70
☐ 209	Travis Knight	.05	.02
☐ 210	Andrew DeClercq	.05	.02
☐ 211	Tyus Edney	.05	.02
☐ 212	Matt Geiger	.05	.02
☐ 213	Tony Delk	.05	.02
☐ 214	J.R. Reid	.05	.02
☐ 215	Bobby Phills	.05	.02
☐ 216	David Wesley	.05	.02
☐ 217	Ron Harper	.10	.05
☐ 218	Scottie Pippen	.60	.25
☐ 219	Scott Burrell	.05	.02
☐ 220	Keith Booth	.05	.02
☐ 221	Bill Wennington	.05	.02
☐ 222	Shawn Kemp	.60	.25
☐ 223	Zydrunas Ilgauskas	.10	.05
☐ 224	Brevin Knight	.60	.25
☐ 225	Danny Ferry	.05	.02
☐ 226	Derek Anderson	.60	.25
☐ 227	Wesley Person	.05	.02
☐ 228	A.C. Green	.10	.05
☐ 229	Samaki Walker	.05	.02
☐ 230	Hubert Davis	.05	.02
☐ 231	Erick Strickland	.10	.05
☐ 232	Dennis Scott	.05	.02
☐ 233	Tony Battie	.40	.18
☐ 234	LaPhonso Ellis	.05	.02
☐ 235	Eric Williams	.05	.02
☐ 236	Bobby Jackson	.40	.18
☐ 237	Anthony Goldwire	.05	.02
☐ 238	Danny Fortson	.40	.18
☐ 239	Joe Dumars	.20	.09
☐ 240	Grant Hill	1.25	.55
☐ 241	Malik Sealy	.05	.02
☐ 242	Brian Williams	.05	.02
☐ 243	Theo Ratliff	.05	.02
☐ 244	Scot Pollard	.05	.02
☐ 245	Erick Dampier	.05	.02
☐ 246	Duane Ferrell	.05	.02
☐ 247	Joe Smith	.20	.09
☐ 248	Todd Fuller	.05	.02
☐ 249	Adonal Foyle	.25	.11
☐ 250	Othella Harrington	.05	.02
☐ 251	Matt Maloney	.05	.02
☐ 252	Hakeem Olajuwon	.40	.18
☐ 253	Rodrick Rhodes	.25	.11
☐ 254	Eddie Johnson	.05	.02
☐ 255	Brent Price	.05	.02
☐ 256	Austin Croshere	.25	.11
☐ 257	Derrick McKey	.05	.02
☐ 258	Chris Mullin	.20	.09
☐ 259	Rik Smits	.10	.05
☐ 260	Jalen Rose	.05	.02
☐ 261	Darrick Martin	.05	.02
☐ 262	Lamond Murray	.05	.02
☐ 263	Maurice Taylor	.60	.25
☐ 264	Rodney Rogers	.05	.02
☐ 265	James Robinson	.05	.02
☐ 266	Rick Fox	.05	.02
☐ 267	Nick Van Exel	.20	.09
☐ 268	Sean Rooks	.05	.02
☐ 269	Derek Fisher	.05	.02
☐ 270	Jon Barry	.05	.02
☐ 271	Robert Horry	.10	.05
☐ 272	Terry Mills	.05	.02
☐ 273	Charles Smith	.05	.02
☐ 274	Alonzo Mourning	.20	.09
☐ 275	Voshon Lenard	.05	.02
☐ 276	Todd Day	.05	.02
☐ 277	Ervin Johnson	.05	.02

☐ 278 Terrell Brandon	.20	.09
☐ 279 Michael Curry	.05	.02
☐ 280 Andrew Lang	.05	.02
☐ 281 Tyrone Hill	.05	.02
☐ 282 Stephon Marbury	1.00	.45
☐ 283 Cherokee Parks	.05	.02
☐ 284 Stanley Roberts	.05	.02
☐ 285 Paul Grant	.05	.02
☐ 286 David Benoit	.05	.02
☐ 287 Lucious Harris	.05	.02
☐ 288 Don MacLean	.05	.02
☐ 289 Sam Cassell	.05	.02
☐ 290 Keith Van Horn	2.00	.90
☐ 291 Patrick Ewing	.20	.09
☐ 292 Walter McCarty	.05	.02
☐ 293 Chris Dudley	.05	.02
☐ 294 Chris Mills	.05	.02
☐ 295 Buck Williams	.05	.02
☐ 296 Nick Anderson	.05	.02
☐ 297 Derek Strong	.05	.02
☐ 298 Gerald Wilkins	.05	.02
☐ 299 Johnny Taylor	.05	.02
☐ 300 Derek Harper	.05	.02
☐ 301 Anthony Parker	.05	.02
☐ 302 Allen Iverson	1.00	.45
☐ 303 Jim Jackson	.10	.05
☐ 304 Eric Montross	.05	.02
☐ 305 Tim Thomas	1.25	.55
☐ 306 Kebu Stewart	.05	.02
☐ 307 Rex Chapman	.05	.02
☐ 308 Tom Chambers	.05	.02
☐ 309 Kevin Johnson	.10	.05
☐ 310 John Williams	.05	.02
☐ 311 Clifford Robinson	.05	.02
☐ 312 Antonio McDyess	.25	.11
☐ 313 Rasheed Wallace	.10	.05
☐ 314 Brian Grant	.05	.02
☐ 315 Dontonio Wingfield	.05	.02
☐ 316 Kelvin Cato	.25	.11
☐ 317 M.Abdul-Rauf	.05	.02
☐ 318 Lawrence Funderburke	.20	.09
☐ 319 Mitch Richmond	.20	.09
☐ 320 Tariq Abdul-Wahad	.30	.14
☐ 321 Terry Dehere	.05	.02
☐ 322 Michael Stewart	.20	.09
☐ 323 Tim Duncan	2.50	1.10
☐ 324 Avery Johnson	.05	.02
☐ 325 David Robinson	.30	.14
☐ 326 Charles Smith	.05	.02
☐ 327 Chuck Person	.05	.02
☐ 328 Monty Williams	.05	.02
☐ 329 Jim McIlvaine	.05	.02
☐ 330 Gary Payton	.30	.14
☐ 331 Eric Snow	.05	.02
☐ 332 Dale Ellis	.05	.02
☐ 333 Vin Baker	.40	.18
☐ 334 Walt Williams	.05	.02
☐ 335 Tracy McGrady	1.25	.55
☐ 336 D.Stoudamire	.40	.18
☐ 337 Carlos Rogers	.05	.02
☐ 338 John Wallace	.10	.05
☐ 339 Shandon Anderson	.05	.02
☐ 340 Jeff Hornacek	.10	.05
☐ 341 Howard Eisley	.05	.02
☐ 342 Jacque Vaughn	.30	.14
☐ 343 Bryon Russell	.05	.02
☐ 344 Antoine Carr	.05	.02
☐ 345 Antonio Daniels	.50	.23
☐ 346 Pete Chilcutt	.05	.02
☐ 347 Blue Edwards	.05	.02
☐ 348 Bryant Reeves	.10	.05
☐ 349 Chris Robinson	.05	.02
☐ 350 Otis Thorpe	.10	.05
☐ 351 Tim Legler	.05	.02
☐ 352 Juwan Howard	.20	.09
☐ 353 God Shammgod	.05	.02
☐ 354 Gheorghe Muresan	.05	.02
☐ 355 Chris Whitney	.05	.02
☐ 356 D.Mutombo HP	.05	.02
☐ 357 Antoine Walker HP	.50	.23
☐ 358 Glen Rice HP	.10	.05
☐ 359 Scottie Pippen HP	.30	.14
☐ 360 Derek Anderson HP	.20	.09
☐ 361 Michael Finley HP	.10	.05
☐ 362 LaPhonso Ellis HP	.05	.02
☐ 363 Grant Hill HP	.60	.25

☐ 364 Joe Smith HP	.10	.05
☐ 365 Charles Barkley HP	.20	.09
☐ 366 Reggie Miller HP	.10	.05
☐ 367 Loy Vaught HP	.05	.02
☐ 368 Shaquille O'Neal HP	.40	.18
☐ 369 Alonzo Mourning HP	.10	.05
☐ 370 Glenn Robinson HP	.10	.05
☐ 371 Kevin Garnett HP	.60	.25
☐ 372 Kendall Gill HP	.05	.02
☐ 373 Allan Houston HP	.05	.02
☐ 374 A.Hardaway HP	.40	.18
☐ 375 Tim Thomas HP	.60	.25
☐ 376 Jason Kidd HP	.20	.09
☐ 377 Kenny Anderson HP	.05	.02
☐ 378 Mitch Richmond HP	.10	.05
☐ 379 Tim Duncan HP	1.25	.55
☐ 380 Gary Payton HP	.20	.09
☐ 381 Marcus Camby HP	.10	.05
☐ 382 Karl Malone HP	.20	.09
☐ 383 S. Abdur-Rahim HP	.30	.14
☐ 384 Chris Webber HP	.25	.11
☐ 385 Michael Jordan HP	1.25	.55
☐ 386 Michael Jordan MM	1.00	.45
☐ 387 Michael Jordan MM	1.00	.45
☐ 388 Michael Jordan MM	1.00	.45
☐ 389 Michael Jordan MM	1.00	.45
☐ 390 Michael Jordan MM	1.00	.45
☐ 391 Michael Jordan MM	1.00	.45
☐ 392 Michael Jordan MM	1.00	.45
☐ 393 Michael Jordan MM	1.00	.45
☐ 394 Michael Jordan MM	1.00	.45
☐ 395 Michael Jordan MM	1.00	.45
☐ 396 Checklist #1	.05	.02
☐ 397 Checklist #2	.05	.02
☐ 398 Checklist #3	.05	.02
☐ 399 Checklist #4	.05	.02
☐ 400 Checklist #5	.05	.02

1997-98 Collector's Choice Crash the Game Scoring

Randomly inserted in series one packs at the rate of one in five, this 30-card set features color action player cards in white borders. If the player pictured on the card scored 30 or more points in the week they were designated, the card was a winner and could be redeemed for a complete 30-card redemption set. The expiration date for the game was July 1, 1998. Card backs are numbered with a "C" prefix.

	MINT	NRMT
COMPLETE SET (60)	80.00	36.00
COMMON CARD (C1-C30)	.40	.18
SEMISTARS	.50	.23
UNLISTED STARS	.75	.35
ONE WEEK PER CARD		
SER.1 STATED ODDS 1:5		
COMP.RED.SET (30)	15.00	6.75
COMMON RED.(R1-R30)	.20	.09
*RED.CARDS: 2X TO .5X HI COLUMN		
ONE RED.SET PER WINNER BY MAIL		
ONE RED.SET PER 15 NON-WIN BY MAIL		

☐ C1A D.Mutombo 11/17 L	.50	.23
☐ C1B D.Mutombo 1/12 L	.50	.23
☐ C2A Dana Barros 12/1 L	.40	.18
☐ C2B Dana Barros 12/22 L	.40	.18
☐ C3A Glen Rice 12/15 W	1.25	.55
☐ C3B Glen Rice 1/19 W	1.25	.55
☐ C4A S.Pippen 11/10 L	2.50	1.10
☐ C4B S.Pippen 1/5 L	2.50	1.10
☐ C5A T.Brandon 11/17 L	.75	.35
☐ C5B T.Brandon 1/5 L	.75	.35
☐ C6A S.Bradley 12/1 L	.40	.18
☐ C6B S.Bradley 12/22 L	.40	.18
☐ C7A A.McDyess 12/8 L	1.00	.45
☐ C7B A.McDyess 1/19 L	1.00	.45
☐ C8A L.Hunter 12/8 L	.40	.18
☐ C8B L.Hunter 12/22 L	.40	.18
☐ C9A J.Smith 11/17 L	.75	.35
☐ C9B J.Smith 1/19 W	1.25	.55
☐ C10A H.Olajuwon 11/17 L	1.50	.70
☐ C10B H.Olajuwon 1/5 L	1.50	.70
☐ C11A R.Miller 11/24 W	1.25	.55
☐ C11B R.Miller 12/29 L	.75	.35
☐ C12A R.Rogers 11/24 L	.40	.18
☐ C12B R.Rogers 1/19 L	.40	.18
☐ C13A N.Van Exel 12/1 L	.75	.35
☐ C13B N.Van Exel 1/5 L	.75	.35
☐ C14A T.Hardaway 12/8 L	.45	
☐ C14B T.Hardaway 12/29 L	1.00	.45
☐ C15A G.Robinson 11/17 L	.75	.35
☐ C15B G.Robinson 1/5 L	.75	.35
☐ C16A K.Garnett 11/10 L	5.00	2.20
☐ C16B K.Garnett 12/15 L	5.00	2.20
☐ C17A K.Kitles 11/24 L	.75	.35
☐ C17B K.Kitles 12/29 L	.75	.35
☐ C18A L.Johnson 12/1 L	.50	.23
☐ C18B L.Johnson 1/12 L	.50	.23
☐ C19A A.Hardaway 11/24 L	3.00	1.35
☐ C19B A.Hardaway 1/5 L	3.00	1.35
☐ C20A A.Iverson 12/1 L	4.00	1.80
☐ C20B A.Iverson 1/12 W	6.00	2.70
☐ C21A J.Kidd 11/24 L	1.50	.70
☐ C21B J.Kidd 12/29 L	1.50	.70
☐ C22A A.Sabonis 11/17 L	.50	.23
☐ C22B A.Sabonis 1/19 W	1.00	.45
☐ C23A M.Richmond 12/8 W	1.25	.55
☐ C23B M.Richmond 1/5 L	.75	.35
☐ C24A D.Robinson 11/10 W	2.00	.90
☐ C24B D.Robinson 12/29 L	1.25	.55
☐ C25A G.Payton 12/1 L	1.25	.55
☐ C25B G.Payton 12/22 L	1.25	.55
☐ C26A M.Camby 12/15 L	.75	.35
☐ C26B M.Camby 1/12 L	.75	.35
☐ C27A K.Malone 12/8 W	2.00	.90
☐ C27B K.Malone 1/19 W	2.00	.90
☐ C28A B.Reeves 11/17 L	.50	.23
☐ C28B B.Reeves 1/5 L	.50	.23
☐ C29A C.Webber 12/8 W	3.00	1.35
☐ C29B C.Webber 1/12 W	3.00	1.35
☐ C30A M.Jordan 11/24 W	15.00	6.75
☐ C30B M.Jordan 12/29 W	15.00	6.75

1997-98 Collector's Choice Draft Trade

Available only through the checklist challenge redemption from series one, this 10-card set

features the top picks from the 1997 Draft.

	MINT	NRMT
COMPLETE SET (10)	15.00	6.75
COMMON CARD (1-10)	.50	.23
UNLISTED STARS	.75	.35
RED.THROUGH CHECK.CHALLENGE		

		MINT	NRMT
☐ 1	Tim Duncan	5.00	2.20
☐ 2	Keith Van Horn	4.00	1.80
☐ 3	Chauncey Billups	1.50	.70
☐ 4	Antonio Daniels	1.00	.45
☐ 5	Tony Battie	.75	.35
☐ 6	Ron Mercer	3.00	1.35
☐ 7	Tim Thomas	2.50	1.10
☐ 8	Adonal Foyle	.50	.23
☐ 9	Tracy McGrady	2.50	1.10
☐ 10	Danny Fortson	.75	.35

1997-98 Collector's Choice Miniatures

Randomly inserted into series two packs at a rate of one in 3, this 30-card set features one player from all 29 teams on a mini-standee card. Each card is die cut. Each factory set also included five random cards from this set. Card backs carry a "M" prefix.

	MINT	NRMT
COMPLETE SET (30)	12.00	5.50
COMMON CARD (M1-M30)	.10	.05
SEMISTARS	.15	.07
UNLISTED STARS	.25	.11
SER.2 STATED ODDS 1:3		
FIVE PER FACTORY SET		

☐ M1	Mookie Blaylock	.15	.07
☐ M2	Chauncey Billups	.50	.23
☐ M3	Glen Rice	.25	.11
☐ M4	Scottie Pippen	.75	.35
☐ M5	Bob Sura	.10	.05
☐ M6	Erick Strickland	.15	.07
☐ M7	Tony Battie	.25	.11
☐ M8	Joe Dumars	.25	.11
☐ M9	Adonal Foyle	.25	.11
☐ M10	Charles Barkley	.40	.18
☐ M11	Dale Davis	.10	.05
☐ M12	Lamond Murray	.10	.05
☐ M13	Kobe Bryant	2.00	.90
☐ M14	Tim Hardaway	.30	.14
☐ M15	Glenn Robinson	.25	.11
☐ M16	Kevin Garnett	1.50	.70
☐ M17	Keith Van Horn	1.25	.55
☐ M18	Patrick Ewing	.25	.11
☐ M19	A. Hardaway	1.00	.45
☐ M20	Tim Thomas	.75	.35
☐ M21	Jason Kidd	.50	.23
☐ M22	Isaiah Rider	.15	.07
☐ M23	M. Abdul-Rauf	.10	.05
☐ M24	Tim Duncan	1.50	.70
☐ M25	Detlef Schrempf	.15	.07
☐ M26	D.Stoudamire	.50	.23
☐ M27	John Stockton	.25	.11
☐ M28	Bryant Reeves	.15	.07
☐ M29	Juwan Howard	.25	.11
☐ M30	Michael Jordan	3.00	1.35

1997-98 Collector's Choice MJ Bullseye

Randomly inserted into series two packs at a rate of one in 5, this 30-card set features a double Crash the Game theme focused solely on Michael Jordan. Each card had two ways to win, by either matching between the given range Jordan's total points from the 1997-98 season or by having Jordan score 100 points in the given week. Winning cards were redeemable for either individual cards from a 13-card Blow-up Jordan Rewind redemption set or the complete set. The game ended on June 1, 1998.

	MINT	NRMT
COMPLETE SET (30)	125.00	55.00
COMMON CARD (B1-B30)	4.00	1.80
ONE WEEK/TARGET PER CARD		
SER.2 STATED ODDS 1:5		

COMP.REW.RED.SET (13)	40.00	18.00
COMMON REW. (R1-R13)	4.00	1.80
REW.RED.PER WINNER BY MAIL		

☐ B1	M.Jordan2/9;1,750 W	6.00	2.70
☐ B2	M.Jordan2/9;2,000 W	6.00	2.70
☐ B3	M.Jordan2/16;1,750 L	4.00	1.80
☐ B4	M.Jordan2/23;1,750 L	4.00	1.80
☐ B5	M.Jordan2/16;2,000 L	4.00	1.80
☐ B6	M.Jordan2/9;2,250 W	6.00	2.70
☐ B7	M.Jordan2/16;2,250 W	6.00	2.70
☐ B8	M.Jordan2/23;2,000 L	4.00	1.80
☐ B9	M.Jordan2/23;2,250 W	6.00	2.70
☐ B10	M.Jordan2/9;2,500 W	6.00	2.70
☐ B11	M.Jordan3/9;1,750 L	4.00	1.80
☐ B12	M.Jordan3/9;2,000 L	4.00	1.80
☐ B13	M.Jordan3/16;1,750 W	6.00	2.70
☐ B14	M.Jordan3/23;1,750 W	6.00	2.70
☐ B15	M.Jordan3/16;2,000 W	6.00	2.70
☐ B16	M.Jordan3/23;2,500 W	6.00	2.70
☐ B17	M.Jordan3/16;2,250 W	6.00	2.70
☐ B18	M.Jordan3/23;2,000 W	6.00	2.70
☐ B19	M.Jordan3/23;2,250 W	6.00	2.70
☐ B20	M.Jordan3/9;2,500 L	4.00	1.80
☐ B21	M.Jordan3/30;1,750 W	6.00	2.70
☐ B22	M.Jordan4/6;1,750 L	4.00	1.80
☐ B23	M.Jordan4/13;1,750 W	6.00	2.70
☐ B24	M.Jordan3/30;2,000 W	6.00	2.70
☐ B25	M.Jordan4/6;2,000 L	4.00	1.80
☐ B26	M.Jordan4/13;2,000 W	6.00	2.70
☐ B27	M.Jordan3/30;2,250 W	6.00	2.70
☐ B28	M.Jordan4/6;2,250 W	6.00	2.70
☐ B29	M.Jordan4/13;2,250 W	6.00	2.70
☐ B30	M.Jordan3/30;2,500 W	6.00	2.70

1997-98 Collector's Choice Star Attractions

Inserted one per special Collector's Choice series one and two Anco pack, this 20-card set was divided up into two sets of ten cards. The cards feature a silver metallic background and the die cut front with the theme "Star Attractions" logo located at the top. Card backs were numbered with a "SA" prefix.

	MINT	NRMT
COMPLETE SET (20)	40.00	18.00
COMPLETE SERIES 1 (10)	20.00	9.00
COMPLETE SERIES 2 (10)	20.00	9.00
COMMON CARD (SA1-SA20)	.75	.35
ONE PER SPECIAL RETAIL PACK		
*GOLD: 2.5X TO 5X HI COLUMN		
GOLD: SER.1/2 STATED ODDS 1:20 SPEC.		

☐ SA1	Michael Jordan	12.00	5.50
☐ SA2	Joe Smith	.75	.35

		MINT	NRMT
☐ SA3	Karl Malone	1.25	.55
☐ SA4	Chauncey Billups	1.50	.70
☐ SA5	Charles Barkley	1.25	.55
☐ SA6	Shaquille O'Neal	3.00	1.35
☐ SA7	Jason Kidd	1.50	.70
☐ SA8	Chris Webber	2.00	.90
☐ SA9	Allen Iverson	4.00	1.80
☐ SA10	Patrick Ewing	.75	.35
☐ SA11	Tim Duncan	5.00	2.20
☐ SA12	Kevin Garnett	5.00	2.20
☐ SA13	Tony Battie	.75	.35
☐ SA14	Gary Payton	1.25	.55
☐ SA15	Hakeem Olajuwon	1.50	.70
☐ SA16	Antonio Daniels	1.00	.45
☐ SA17	Grant Hill	5.00	2.20
☐ SA18	A.Hardaway	3.00	1.35
☐ SA19	Scottie Pippen	2.50	1.10
☐ SA20	Keith Van Horn	4.00	1.80

1997-98 Collector's Choice StarQuest

Randomly inserted both series packs, this 180-card set features color action photos of the top players of the game. Both 90-card sets features tiering, containing bronze, silver, gold, and platinum levels. The bronze tier contains 90 players with an insertion rate of 1:1; silver has 40 players with an insertion rate of 1:21; gold contains 30 players with a 1:71 insertion rate; the top twenty stars in the platinum tier with a 1:145 insertion rate. Card backs are numbered with a "SQ" prefix.

		MINT	NRMT
COMPLETE SET (180)		1000.00	450.00
COMPLETE SERIES 1 (90)		500.00	220.00
COMPLETE SERIES 2 (90)		500.00	220.00
COMMON (1-45/91-135)		.15	.07
COMMON (46-65/136-155)		1.50	.70
COMMON (66-80/156-170)		5.00	2.20
COMMON (81-90/171-180)		6.00	2.70
SEMISTARS (1-45/91-135)		.20	.09
SEMISTARS (46-65/136-155)		2.00	.90
STARS (1-45/91-135)		.30	.14
STARS (46-65/136-155)		3.00	1.35
STARS (66-80/156-170)		5.00	2.20
STARS (81-90/171-180)		6.00	2.70

1-45/91-135 SER.1/2 STATED ODDS 1:1
46-65/136-155 SER.1/2 STATED ODDS 1:21
66-80/156-170 SER.1/2 STATED ODDS 1:71
81-90/171-180 SER.1/2 STATED ODDS 1:145
SQ PREFIX ON CARD NUMBERS

☐ 1	Dale Davis	.15	.07
☐ 2	Jamal Mashburn	.20	.09
☐ 3	Christian Laettner	.20	.09
☐ 4	Billy Owens	.15	.07
☐ 5	Vlade Divac	.20	.09
☐ 6	Sean Elliott	.15	.07
☐ 7	Marcus Camby	.30	.14
☐ 8	Dana Barros	.15	.07
☐ 9	Rod Strickland	.20	.09
☐ 10	Jim Jackson	.20	.09
☐ 11	Tyrone Hill	.15	.07
☐ 12	Ervin Johnson	.15	.07
☐ 13	Antoine Walker	1.50	.70
☐ 14	Lorenzen Wright	.15	.07
☐ 15	Shawn Bradley	.15	.07
☐ 16	John Starks	.20	.09
☐ 17	Corliss Williamson	.20	.09
☐ 18	Steve Smith	.20	.09
☐ 19	Chris Mills	.15	.07
☐ 20	Vinny Del Negro	.15	.07
☐ 21	Jayson Williams	.20	.09
☐ 22	Anthony Mason	.20	.09
☐ 23	Dennis Scott	.15	.07
☐ 24	Mark Jackson	.15	.07
☐ 25	Dino Radja	.15	.07
☐ 26	Greg Ostertag	.15	.07
☐ 27	Anthony Peeler	.15	.07
☐ 28	Toni Kukoc	.20	.09
☐ 29	Michael Finley	.30	.14
☐ 30	Brent Barry	.15	.07
☐ 31	Wesley Person	.15	.07
☐ 32	Horace Grant	.20	.09
☐ 33	Walt Williams	.15	.07
☐ 34	Bryant Stith	.15	.07
☐ 35	Ray Allen	.40	.18
☐ 36	Otis Thorpe	.20	.09
☐ 37	Rasheed Wallace	.20	.09
☐ 38	Charles Oakley	.15	.07
☐ 39	Robert Pack	.15	.07
☐ 40	Kendall Gill	.20	.09
☐ 41	Lindsey Hunter	.15	.07
☐ 42	Cedric Ceballos	.15	.07
☐ 43	Allan Houston	.20	.09
☐ 44	Bryant Reeves	.20	.09
☐ 45	Derrick Coleman	.20	.09
☐ 46	Isaiah Rider	2.00	.90
☐ 47	Detlef Schrempf	2.00	.90
☐ 48	Antonio McDyess	4.00	1.80
☐ 49	Glenn Robinson	3.00	1.35
☐ 50	D.Stoudamire	6.00	2.70
☐ 51	Terrell Brandon	3.00	1.35
☐ 52	Joe Smith	3.00	1.35
☐ 53	Tom Gugliotta	3.00	1.35
☐ 54	Loy Vaught	2.00	.90
☐ 55	Kenny Anderson	2.00	.90
☐ 56	D.Mutombo	2.00	.90
☐ 57	Tim Hardaway	4.00	1.80
☐ 58	Chris Webber	8.00	3.60
☐ 59	Nick Van Exel	3.00	1.35
☐ 60	Kerry Kittles	3.00	1.35
☐ 61	Chris Mullin	3.00	1.35
☐ 62	Stephon Marbury	15.00	6.75
☐ 63	Juwan Howard	3.00	1.35
☐ 64	Larry Johnson	2.00	.90
☐ 65	S.Abdur-Rahim	10.00	4.50
☐ 66	Dennis Rodman	20.00	9.00
☐ 67	Vin Baker	10.00	4.50
☐ 68	Clyde Drexler	6.00	2.70
☐ 69	Eddie Jones	10.00	4.50
☐ 70	Jerry Stackhouse	5.00	2.20
☐ 71	Karl Malone	8.00	3.60
☐ 72	Mitch Richmond	5.00	2.20
☐ 73	Glen Rice	5.00	2.20
☐ 74	Jason Kidd	5.00	2.20
☐ 75	Latrell Sprewell	5.00	2.20
☐ 76	David Robinson	8.00	3.60
☐ 77	Charles Barkley	8.00	3.60
☐ 78	Gary Payton	8.00	3.60
☐ 79	Scottie Pippen	15.00	6.75
☐ 80	Reggie Miller	.30	.14
☐ 81	Alonzo Mourning	6.00	2.70
☐ 82	Allen Iverson	30.00	13.50
☐ 83	Michael Jordan	80.00	36.00
☐ 84	Shawn Kemp	20.00	9.00
☐ 85	Kevin Garnett	40.00	18.00
☐ 86	Grant Hill	40.00	18.00

☐ 87	A.Hardaway	25.00	11.00
☐ 88	Shaquille O'Neal	25.00	11.00
☐ 89	John Stockton	6.00	2.70
☐ 90	Hakeem Olajuwon	12.00	5.50
☐ 91	Billy Owens	.15	.07
☐ 92	Derek Anderson	.50	.23
☐ 93	Hersey Hawkins	.20	.09
☐ 94	Bryon Russell	.15	.07
☐ 95	Rik Smits	.20	.09
☐ 96	Tracy McGrady	1.00	.45
☐ 97	Kendall Gill	.20	.09
☐ 98	Tim Thomas	1.00	.45
☐ 99	Robert Horry	.20	.09
☐ 100	Marcus Camby	.30	.14
☐ 101	Rodney Rogers	.15	.07
☐ 102	Danny Manning	.20	.09
☐ 103	John Starks	.20	.09
☐ 104	M.Abdul-Rauf	.15	.07
☐ 105	Chris Childs	.15	.07
☐ 106	Antonio Davis	.15	.07
☐ 107	Lamond Murray	.15	.07
☐ 108	Nick Anderson	.15	.07
☐ 109	Antoine Walker	1.50	.70
☐ 110	Christian Laettner	.20	.09
☐ 111	Gary Trent	.15	.07
☐ 112	Tony Battie	.30	.14
☐ 113	Vlade Divac	.20	.09
☐ 114	Kevin Johnson	.20	.09
☐ 115	Erick Strickland	.20	.09
☐ 116	Ray Allen	.40	.18
☐ 117	Antonio Daniels	.40	.18
☐ 118	Sean Elliott	.15	.07
☐ 119	Horace Grant	.20	.09
☐ 120	Walt Williams	.15	.07
☐ 121	Rony Seikaly	.15	.07
☐ 122	Allan Houston	.20	.09
☐ 123	Michael Finley	.30	.14
☐ 124	Rasheed Wallace	.20	.09
☐ 125	Doug Christie	.15	.07
☐ 126	Danny Ferry	.15	.07
☐ 127	Arvydas Sabonis	.20	.09
☐ 128	Shandon Anderson	.15	.07
☐ 129	Otis Thorpe	.20	.09
☐ 130	Adonal Foyle	.30	.14
☐ 131	Bryant Reeves	.20	.09
☐ 132	Theo Ratliff	.15	.07
☐ 133	Matt Maloney	.15	.07
☐ 134	Voshon Lenard	.15	.07
☐ 135	Danny Fortson	.30	.14
☐ 136	Joe Smith	3.00	1.35
☐ 137	Mookie Blaylock	2.00	.90
☐ 138	Loy Vaught	2.00	.90
☐ 139	Tom Gugliotta	3.00	1.35
☐ 140	D.Stoudamire	6.00	2.70
☐ 141	Antonio McDyess	4.00	1.80
☐ 142	Kobe Bryant	25.00	11.00
☐ 143	Juwan Howard	3.00	1.35
☐ 144	Tim Hardaway	4.00	1.80
☐ 145	Ron Mercer	12.00	5.50
☐ 146	Joe Dumars	3.00	1.35
☐ 147	Clyde Drexler	4.00	1.80
☐ 148	S.Abdur-Rahim	10.00	4.50
☐ 149	LaPhonso Ellis	1.50	.70
☐ 150	D.Mutombo	2.00	.90
☐ 151	Chauncey Billups	6.00	2.70
☐ 152	Chris Webber	8.00	3.60
☐ 153	Glenn Robinson	3.00	1.35
☐ 154	Patrick Ewing	3.00	1.35
☐ 155	Stephon Marbury	15.00	6.75
☐ 156	Keith Van Horn	25.00	11.00
☐ 157	Karl Malone	8.00	3.60
☐ 158	Terrell Brandon	5.00	2.20
☐ 159	Sam Cassell	5.00	2.20
☐ 160	Jerry Stackhouse	5.00	2.20
☐ 161	Vin Baker	10.00	4.50
☐ 162	Jason Kidd	10.00	4.50
☐ 163	Charles Barkley	8.00	3.60
☐ 164	Reggie Miller	5.00	2.20
☐ 165	Alonzo Mourning	5.00	2.20
☐ 166	Scottie Pippen	15.00	6.75
☐ 167	Glen Rice	5.00	2.20
☐ 168	Allen Iverson	25.00	11.00
☐ 169	David Robinson	8.00	3.60
☐ 170	Shawn Kemp	15.00	6.75
☐ 171	Michael Jordan	80.00	36.00
☐ 172	Tim Duncan	40.00	18.00

		MINT	NRMT
☐ 173	A.Hardaway	25.00	11.00
☐ 174	Shaquille O'Neal	25.00	11.00
☐ 175	John Stockton	6.00	2.70
☐ 176	Gary Payton	10.00	4.50
☐ 177	Mitch Richmond	6.00	2.70
☐ 178	Kevin Garnett	40.00	18.00
☐ 179	Hakeem Olajuwon	12.00	5.50
☐ 180	Grant Hill	40.00	18.00

1997-98 Collector's Choice Stick-Ums

Randomly inserted in series one packs at the rate of one in three, this 30-sticker set features color action images of a player from each NBA team in the middle of a dunk and can be stuck anywhere. Card backs carry a checklist for the set and are numbered with a "S" prefix.

	MINT	NRMT
COMPLETE SET (30)	12.00	5.50
COMMON CARD (S1-S30)	.10	.05
SEMISTARS	.15	.07
UNLISTED STARS	.25	.11
SER.1 STATED ODDS 1:3		

		MINT	NRMT
☐ S1	Steve Smith	.15	.07
☐ S2	Antoine Walker	1.25	.55
☐ S3	Anthony Mason	.15	.07
☐ S4	Dennis Rodman	1.00	.45
☐ S5	Terrell Brandon	.25	.11
☐ S6	Michael Finley	.25	.11
☐ S7	Antonio McDyess	.30	.14
☐ S8	Grant Hill	1.50	.70
☐ S9	Joe Smith	.25	.11
☐ S10	Hakeem Olajuwon	.50	.23
☐ S11	Reggie Miller	.25	.11
☐ S12	Loy Vaught	.10	.05
☐ S13	Shaquille O'Neal	1.00	.45
☐ S14	Alonzo Mourning	.25	.11
☐ S15	Vin Baker	.50	.23
☐ S16	Stephon Marbury	1.25	.55
☐ S17	Jim Jackson	.10	.05
☐ S18	John Starks	.10	.05
☐ S19	A.Hardaway	1.00	.45
☐ S20	Allen Iverson	1.25	.55
☐ S21	Jason Kidd	.50	.23
☐ S22	Kenny Anderson	.15	.07
☐ S23	Mitch Richmond	.25	.11
☐ S24	David Robinson	.40	.18
☐ S25	Shawn Kemp	.75	.35
☐ S26	D.Stoudamire	.50	.23
☐ S27	Karl Malone	.40	.18
☐ S28	Bryant Reeves	.15	.07
☐ S29	Juwan Howard	.25	.11
☐ S30	Michael Jordan	3.00	1.35

1997-98 Collector's Choice The Jordan Dynasty

Randomly inserted in series one packs, this five-card insert set features color player photos of Michael Jordan and celebrates the five NBA championships he and the Bulls have brought to Chicago. Each card contains a detailed summary of the highlights of each of the five seasons. Only 23,000 of each card was produced.

	MINT	NRMT
COMPLETE SET (5)	60.00	27.00
COMMON CARD (1-5)	15.00	6.75
RANDOM INSERTS IN SER.1 PACKS		
STATED PRINT RUN 23,000 EACH		

		MINT	NRMT
☐ 1	Michael Jordan	15.00	6.75
	1990-91 NBA Champs		
☐ 2	Michael Jordan	15.00	6.75
	1991-92 NBA Champs		
☐ 3	Michael Jordan	15.00	6.75
	1992-93 NBA Champs		
☐ 4	Michael Jordan	15.00	6.75
	1995-96 NBA Champs		
☐ 5	Michael Jordan	15.00	6.75
	1996-97 NBA Champs		

1994-95 Embossed

Featuring 121 double-sided, standard-size embossed cards, the 1994-95 Embossed set marks the premier of a new product for Topps. Each six-card pack contained five basic cards and one Golden Idols parallel gold foil card, with a suggested retail of 3.00 per pack. The fronts display a color embossed player photo framed by a textured pattern. The backs carry a second embossed player photo, biography, statistics, and a special "Did You Know" section containing unique information not found on other Topps cards. The cards are grouped alphabetically within teams. The set closes with a silver foil Draft Picks subset (101-120) followed by a Michael Jordan card that was added at the last minute. In addition to the Draft Picks, all of the Houston Rockets cards were given a foil background treatment. Rookie Cards of note in this set include Grant Hill, Juwan Howard, Jason Kidd and Glenn Robinson.

	MINT	NRMT
COMPLETE SET (121)	30.00	13.50
COMMON CARD (1-121)	.10	.05
SEMISTARS	.25	.11
UNLISTED STARS	.50	.23
COMP.GOLD SET (121)	80.00	36.00
COMMON GOLD (1-121)	.25	.11
GOLD SEMISTARS	.60	.25
*GOLD STARS: 1.25X TO 2.5X HI COLUMN		
*GOLD RCs: 1X TO 2X HI		
ONE GOLDEN IDOL PER PACK		

		MINT	NRMT
☐ 1	Stacey Augmon	.10	.05
☐ 2	Mookie Blaylock	.25	.11
☐ 3	Ken Norman	.10	.05
☐ 4	Steve Smith	.25	.11
☐ 5	Dee Brown	.10	.05
☐ 6	Blue Edwards	.10	.05
☐ 7	Dino Radja	.10	.05
☐ 8	Dominique Wilkins	.50	.23
☐ 9	Muggsy Bogues	.25	.11
☐ 10	Dell Curry	.10	.05
☐ 11	Larry Johnson	.25	.11
☐ 12	Alonzo Mourning	.60	.25
☐ 13	B.J. Armstrong	.10	.05
☐ 14	Ron Harper	.25	.11
☐ 15	Toni Kukoc	.50	.23
☐ 16	Scottie Pippen	1.50	.70
☐ 17	Tyrone Hill	.10	.05
☐ 18	Mark Price	.10	.05
☐ 19	John Williams	.10	.05
☐ 20	Jim Jackson	.25	.11
☐ 21	Popeye Jones	.10	.05
☐ 22	Jamal Mashburn	.50	.23
☐ 23	M.Abdul-Rauf	.10	.05
☐ 24	LaPhonso Ellis	.25	.11
☐ 25	D.Mutombo	.50	.23
☐ 26	Rodney Rogers	.10	.05
☐ 27	Joe Dumars	.50	.23
☐ 28	Lindsey Hunter	.25	.11
☐ 29	Oliver Miller	.10	.05
☐ 30	Terry Mills	.10	.05
☐ 31	Tom Gugliotta	.50	.23
☐ 32	Tim Hardaway	.60	.25
☐ 33	Chris Mullin	.50	.23
☐ 34	Latrell Sprewell	.25	.11
☐ 35	Sam Cassell FOIL	.50	.23
☐ 36	Robert Horry FOIL	.25	.11
☐ 37	Vernon Maxwell FOIL	.10	.05

		MINT	NRMT
☐ 38	Hakeem Olajuwon FOIL	1.00	.45
☐ 39	Otis Thorpe FOIL	.25	.11
☐ 40	Mark Jackson	.25	.11
☐ 41	Reggie Miller	.50	.23
☐ 42	Rik Smits	.25	.11
☐ 43	Terry Dehere	.10	.05
☐ 44	Stanley Roberts	.10	.05
☐ 45	Loy Vaught	.25	.11
☐ 46	Vlade Divac	.25	.11
☐ 47	George Lynch	.10	.05
☐ 48	Nick Van Exel	.50	.23
☐ 49	Billy Owens	.10	.05
☐ 50	Glen Rice	.50	.23
☐ 51	Kevin Willis	.10	.05
☐ 52	Vin Baker	1.25	.55
☐ 53	Todd Day	.10	.05
☐ 54	Eric Murdock	.10	.05
☐ 55	Christian Laettner	.25	.11
☐ 56	Isaiah Rider	.25	.11
☐ 57	Micheal Williams	.10	.05
☐ 58	Kenny Anderson	.25	.11
☐ 59	P.J. Brown	.10	.05
☐ 60	Derrick Coleman	.25	.11
☐ 61	Chris Morris	.10	.05
☐ 62	Patrick Ewing	.50	.23
☐ 63	Derek Harper	.25	.11
☐ 64	Anthony Mason	.25	.11
☐ 65	Charles Oakley	.25	.11
☐ 66	John Starks	.25	.11
☐ 67	Horace Grant	.25	.11
☐ 68	A.Hardaway	2.00	.90
☐ 69	Shaquille O'Neal	2.00	.90
☐ 70	Dennis Scott	.25	.11
☐ 71	Shawn Bradley	.10	.05
☐ 72	Jeff Malone	.10	.05
☐ 73	C.Weatherspoon	.10	.05
☐ 74	Charles Barkley	.75	.35
☐ 75	Kevin Johnson	.25	.11
☐ 76	Dan Majerle	.25	.11
☐ 77	Danny Manning	.10	.05
☐ 78	Wayman Tisdale	.10	.05
☐ 79	Clyde Drexler	.60	.25
☐ 80	Clifford Robinson	.25	.11
☐ 81	Rod Strickland	.25	.11
☐ 82	Bobby Hurley	.10	.05
☐ 83	Olden Polynice	.10	.05
☐ 84	Mitch Richmond	.50	.23
☐ 85	Spud Webb	.25	.11
☐ 86	Sean Elliott	.25	.11
☐ 87	Chuck Person	.10	.05
☐ 88	David Robinson	.75	.35
☐ 89	Dennis Rodman	2.00	.90
☐ 90	Kendall Gill	.25	.11
☐ 91	Shawn Kemp	1.50	.70
☐ 92	Sarunas Marciulionis	.10	.05
☐ 93	Gary Payton	.75	.35
☐ 94	Detlef Schrempf	.25	.11
☐ 95	Jeff Hornacek	.25	.11
☐ 96	Karl Malone	.75	.35
☐ 97	John Stockton	.50	.23
☐ 98	Don MacLean	.10	.05
☐ 99	Scott Skiles	.10	.05
☐ 100	Chris Webber	1.25	.55
☐ 101	Glenn Robinson FOIL	2.00	.90
☐ 102	Jason Kidd FOIL	4.00	1.80
☐ 103	Grant Hill FOIL	6.00	2.70
☐ 104	Donyell Marshall FOIL	.60	.25
☐ 105	Juwan Howard FOIL	2.50	1.10
☐ 106	Sharone Wright FOIL	.10	.05
☐ 107	Lamont Murray FOIL	.25	.11
☐ 108	Brian Grant FOIL	.50	.23
☐ 109	Eric Montross FOIL	.10	.05
☐ 110	Eddie Jones FOIL	4.00	1.80
☐ 111	Carlos Rogers FOIL	.10	.05
☐ 112	Khalid Reeves FOIL	.10	.05
☐ 113	Jalen Rose FOIL	.50	.23
☐ 114	Yinka Dare FOIL	.10	.05
☐ 115	Eric Piatkowski FOIL	.10	.05
☐ 116	Clifford Rozier FOIL	.10	.05
☐ 117	Aaron McKie FOIL	.10	.05
☐ 118	Eric Mobley FOIL	.10	.05
☐ 119	Tony Dumas FOIL	.10	.05
☐ 120	B.J. Tyler FOIL	.10	.05
☐ 121	Michael Jordan	10.00	4.50

1994-95 Emotion

The complete 1994-95 Emotion set (produced by SkyBox) consists of 121 standard size cards. The cards were issued in eight-card packs with 36 packs per box. Suggested retail price was $4.99 per pack. The fronts have full-bleed color photos. Predominantly placed in the middle is a one word description of the player. The backs have career statistics and player information against a two photo background. The cards are grouped alphabetically within teams. The set closes with two topical subsets: Rookies (101-110) and Masters (111-120). A Grant Hill SkyMotion card was offered to those who sent in two wrappers and a check or money order for 24.99 before December 31st, 1995. The card shows three seconds of a Hill dunk. Rookie Cards of note in this set include Grant Hill, Juwan Howard, Eddie Jones, Jason Kidd and Glenn Robinson.

		MINT	NRMT
COMPLETE SET (121)		50.00	22.00
COMMON CARD (1-121)		.15	.07
SEMISTARS		.30	.14
UNLISTED STARS		.60	.25
☐ 1	Stacey Augmon	.15	.07
☐ 2	Mookie Blaylock	.30	.14
☐ 3	Steve Smith	.30	.14
☐ 4	Greg Minor	.15	.07
☐ 5	Eric Montross	.15	.07
☐ 6	Dino Radja	.15	.07
☐ 7	Dominique Wilkins	.60	.25
☐ 8	Muggsy Bogues	.30	.14
☐ 9	Larry Johnson	.30	.14
☐ 10	Alonzo Mourning	.75	.35
☐ 11	B.J. Armstrong	.15	.07
☐ 12	Toni Kukoc	.60	.25
☐ 13	Scottie Pippen	2.00	.90
☐ 14	Dickey Simpkins	.15	.07
☐ 15	Tyrone Hill	.15	.07
☐ 16	Chris Mills	.30	.14
☐ 17	Mark Price	.15	.07
☐ 18	Tony Dumas	.15	.07
☐ 19	Jim Jackson	.30	.14
☐ 20	Jason Kidd	5.00	2.20
☐ 21	Jamal Mashburn	.60	.25
☐ 22	LaPhonso Ellis	.30	.14
☐ 23	D.Mutombo	.60	.25
☐ 24	Rodney Rogers	.15	.07
☐ 25	Jalen Rose	.60	.25
☐ 26	Bill Curley	.15	.07
☐ 27	Joe Dumars	.60	.25
☐ 28	Grant Hill	8.00	3.60
☐ 29	Tim Hardaway	.75	.35
☐ 30	Donyell Marshall	.75	.35
☐ 31	Chris Mullin	.60	.25
☐ 32	Carlos Rogers	.15	.07
☐ 33	Clifford Rozier	.15	.07
☐ 34	Latrell Sprewell	.30	.14
☐ 35	Sam Cassell	.60	.25
☐ 36	Clyde Drexler	2.50	1.10
☐ 37	Robert Horry	.30	.14
☐ 38	Hakeem Olajuwon	1.25	.55
☐ 39	Mark Jackson	.30	.14
☐ 40	Reggie Miller	.60	.25
☐ 41	Rik Smits	.30	.14
☐ 42	Lamond Murray	.30	.14
☐ 43	Eric Piatkowski	.15	.07
☐ 44	Loy Vaught	.30	.14
☐ 45	Cedric Ceballos	.30	.14
☐ 46	Eddie Jones	5.00	2.20
☐ 47	George Lynch	.15	.07
☐ 48	Nick Van Exel	.60	.25
☐ 49	Harold Miner	.15	.07
☐ 50	Khalid Reeves	.15	.07
☐ 51	Glen Rice	.60	.25
☐ 52	Kevin Willis	.15	.07
☐ 53	Vin Baker	1.50	.70
☐ 54	Eric Mobley	.15	.07
☐ 55	Eric Murdock	.15	.07
☐ 56	Glenn Robinson	2.50	1.10
☐ 57	Tom Gugliotta	.30	.14
☐ 58	Christian Laettner	.30	.14
☐ 59	Isaiah Rider	.30	.14
☐ 60	Kenny Anderson	.30	.14
☐ 61	Derrick Coleman	.30	.14
☐ 62	Yinka Dare	.15	.07
☐ 63	Patrick Ewing	.60	.25
☐ 64	John Starks	.30	.14
☐ 65	Charlie Ward	.30	.14
☐ 66	Monty Williams	.15	.07
☐ 67	Nick Anderson	.30	.14
☐ 68	Horace Grant	.30	.14
☐ 69	A.Hardaway	2.50	1.10
☐ 70	Shaquille O'Neal	2.50	1.10
☐ 71	Brooks Thompson	.15	.07
☐ 72	Dana Barros	.15	.07
☐ 73	Shawn Bradley	.30	.14
☐ 74	B.J. Tyler	.15	.07
☐ 75	C.Weatherspoon	.15	.07
☐ 76	Sharone Wright	.15	.07
☐ 77	Charles Barkley	1.00	.45
☐ 78	Kevin Johnson	.30	.14
☐ 79	Dan Majerle	.30	.14
☐ 80	Danny Manning	.15	.07
☐ 81	Wesley Person	.75	.35
☐ 82	Aaron McKie	.15	.07
☐ 83	Clifford Robinson	.30	.14
☐ 84	Rod Strickland	.30	.14
☐ 85	Brian Grant	.60	.25
☐ 86	Mookie Blaylock	.15	.07
☐ 87	Mitch Richmond	.60	.25
☐ 88	Sean Elliott	.30	.14
☐ 89	David Robinson	1.00	.45
☐ 90	Dennis Rodman	2.50	1.10
☐ 91	Shawn Kemp	2.00	.90
☐ 92	Gary Payton	1.00	.45
☐ 93	Dontonio Wingfield	.15	.07
☐ 94	Jeff Hornacek	.30	.14
☐ 95	Karl Malone	1.00	.45
☐ 96	John Stockton	.60	.25
☐ 97	Calbert Cheaney	.30	.14
☐ 98	Juwan Howard	3.00	1.35
☐ 99	Chris Webber	1.50	.70
☐ 100	Michael Jordan	12.00	5.50
☐ 101	Brian Grant ROO	.30	.14
☐ 102	Grant Hill ROO	3.00	1.35
☐ 103	Juwan Howard ROO	1.25	.55
☐ 104	Eddie Jones ROO	2.00	.90
☐ 105	Jason Kidd ROO	2.00	.90
☐ 106	Eric Montross ROO	.15	.07
☐ 107	Lamond Murray ROO	.15	.07

		MINT	NRMT
☐ 108	Wesley Person ROO ..	.30	.14
☐ 109	Glenn Robinson ROO	1.00	.45
☐ 110	Sharone Wright ROO...	.15	.07
☐ 111	A.Hardaway MAS	1.25	.55
☐ 112	Shawn Kemp MAS ...	1.00	.45
☐ 113	Karl Malone MAS	.60	.25
☐ 114	Alonzo Mourning MAS	.60	.25
☐ 115	Shaquille O'Neal MAS	1.25	.55
☐ 116	Hakeem Olajuwon MAS	.60	.25
☐ 117	Scottie Pippen MAS	1.00	.45
☐ 118	David Robinson MAS	.60	.25
☐ 119	Latrell Sprewell MAS...	.15	.07
☐ 120	Chris Webber MAS	.75	.35
☐ 121	Checklist	.15	.07
☐ NNO	Grant Hill SkyMotion	75.00	34.00
	Exchange		
☐ NNO	Grant Hill	5.00	2.20
	David Robinson Promo		

1994-95 Emotion N-Tense

Cards from this 10-card standard-size set were randomly inserted in Emotion packs at a rate of one in 18. The set contains a selection of some of the top players in the NBA. The fronts have full-bleed color photos and the player's name down the left in a hologram set against a sparkling gold background. The backs have two color action photos with the players name across the middle against a black background. The set is sequenced in alphabetical order.

	MINT	NRMT
COMPLETE SET (10)	100.00	45.00
COMMON CARD (N1-N10)....	4.00	1.80
STATED ODDS 1:18		
☐ N1 Charles Barkley	6.00	2.70
☐ N2 Patrick Ewing	4.00	1.80
☐ N3 Michael Jordan	50.00	22.00
☐ N4 Shawn Kemp	12.00	5.50
☐ N5 Karl Malone	6.00	2.70
☐ N6 Alonzo Mourning	5.00	2.20
☐ N7 Shaquille O'Neal	15.00	6.75
☐ N8 Hakeem Olajuwon	8.00	3.60
☐ N9 David Robinson	6.00	2.70
☐ N10 Glenn Robinson	6.00	2.70

1994-95 Emotion X-Cited

Cards from this 20-card standard-size set were randomly

inserted in Emotion packs at a rate of one in four. The set features a selection of the top guards and small forwards in the NBA. The fronts have full-bleed color photos and the player's last name across the top set against a sparkling background. The backs have two color action photos set against a black background. The set is sequenced in alphabetical order.

	MINT	NRMT
COMPLETE SET (2u)	60.00	27.00
COMMON CARD (X1-X20)......	.75	.35
SEMISTARS	1.50	.70
UNLISTED STARS	2.50	1.10
STATED ODDS 1:4		
☐ X1 Kenny Anderson	1.50	.70
☐ X2 A.Hardaway..........	10.00	4.50
☐ X3 Tim Hardaway........	3.00	1.35
☐ X4 Grant Hill	15.00	6.75
☐ X5 Jim Jackson	1.50	.70
☐ X6 Eddie Jones	10.00	4.50
☐ X7 Jason Kidd	10.00	4.50
☐ X8 Dan Majerle..........	1.50	.70
☐ X9 Jamal Mashburn	2.50	1.10
☐ X10 Lamond Murray	1.50	.70
☐ X11 Gary Payton	4.00	1.80
☐ X12 Wesley Person	2.50	1.10
☐ X13 Scottie Pippen......	8.00	3.60
☐ X14 Mark Price...........	.75	.35
☐ X15 Mitch Richmond	2.50	1.10
☐ X16 Isaiah Rider	1.50	.70
☐ X17 Latrell Sprewell	1.50	.70
☐ X18 John Stockton	2.50	1.10
☐ X19 Rod Strickland	1.50	.70
☐ X20 Nick Van Exel	2.50	1.10

1993-94 Finest

The premier edition of the 1993-94 Finest basketball set (produced by Topps) contains 220 standard-size cards. The set is comprised of 180 player cards and a 40-card subset of ten of the best players in each of the four divisions as follows: Atlantic (90-99), Central (100-109), Midwest (110-119), and Pacific (120-129). These subset cards are commonly referred to as "brick" cards due to their brick wall background design. The seven-card packs (24 per box)

included six player cards plus one subset card and had a suggested retail price of 3.99. Topps also issued a 14-card jumbo pack for 7.99, which included 11 regulars, two subsets, and a jumbo-only Main Attraction chase card. Packs hit the market upon release well above the aforementioned prices. The rainbow colored metallic front features a color action cutout on a metallic marble background. The white bordered back features a color player cutout on the left inset in a marble textured background. Rookie Cards of note include Vin Baker, A.Hardaway, Jamal Mashburn and Chris Webber.

	MINT	NRMT
COMPLETE SET (220)	130.00	57.50
COMMON CARD (1-220)	.30	.14
SEMISTARS	.60	.25
UNLISTED STARS	1.25	.55
☐ 1 Michael Jordan	20.00	9.00
☐ 2 Larry Bird	5.00	2.20
☐ 3 Shaquille O'Neal	5.00	2.20
☐ 4 Benoit Benjamin	.30	.14
☐ 5 Ricky Pierce	.30	.14
☐ 6 Ken Norman	.30	.14
☐ 7 Victor Alexander	.30	.14
☐ 8 Mark Jackson	.60	.25
☐ 9 Mark West...........	.30	.14
☐ 10 Don MacLean	.30	.14
☐ 11 Reggie Miller	1.25	.55
☐ 12 Sarunas Marciulionis...	.30	.14
☐ 13 Craig Ehlo	.30	.14
☐ 14 Toni Kukoc	4.00	1.80
☐ 15 Glen Rice	1.25	.55
☐ 16 Otis Thorpe	.60	.25
☐ 17 Reggie Williams	.30	.14
☐ 18 Charles Smith	.30	.14
☐ 19 Micheal Williams	.30	.14
☐ 20 Tom Chambers	.30	.14
☐ 21 David Robinson	2.00	.90
☐ 22 Jamal Mashburn	5.00	2.20
☐ 23 Clifford Robinson	.60	.25
☐ 24 Acie Earl	.30	.14
☐ 25 Danny Ferry..........	.30	.14
☐ 26 Bobby Hurley	.60	.25
☐ 27 Eddie Johnson.......	.30	.14
☐ 28 Detlef Schrempf	.60	.25
☐ 29 Mike Brown	.30	.14
☐ 30 Latrell Sprewell	1.25	.55
☐ 31 Derek Harper	.60	.25
☐ 32 Stacey Augmon	.30	.14
☐ 33 Pooh Richardson	.30	.14
☐ 34 Larry Krystkowiak	.30	.14

□ 35 Pervis Ellison	.30	.14
□ 36 Jeff Malone	.30	.14
□ 37 Sean Elliott	.30	.25
□ 38 John Paxson	.30	.14
□ 39 Robert Parish	.60	.25
□ 40 Mark Aguirre	.30	.14
□ 41 Danny Ainge	.60	.25
□ 42 Brian Shaw	.30	.14
□ 43 LaPhonso Ellis	.60	.25
□ 44 Carl Herrera	.30	.14
□ 45 Terry Cummings	.30	.14
□ 46 Chris Dudley	.30	.14
□ 47 Anthony Mason	.60	.25
□ 48 Chris Morris	.30	.14
□ 49 Todd Day	.30	.14
□ 50 Nick Van Exel	8.00	3.60
□ 51 Larry Nance	.60	.25
□ 52 Derrick McKey	.30	.14
□ 53 Muggsy Bogues	.60	.25
□ 54 Andrew Lang	.30	.14
□ 55 Chuck Person	.30	.14
□ 56 Michael Adams	.30	.14
□ 57 Spud Webb	.60	.25
□ 58 Scott Skiles	.30	.14
□ 59 A.C. Green	.60	.25
□ 60 Terry Mills	.30	.14
□ 61 Xavier McDaniel	.30	.14
□ 62 B.J. Armstrong	.30	.14
□ 63 Donald Hodge	.30	.14
□ 64 Gary Grant	.30	.14
□ 65 Billy Owens	.30	.14
□ 66 Greg Anthony	.30	.14
□ 67 Jay Humphries	.30	.14
□ 68 Lionel Simmons	.30	.14
□ 69 Dana Barros	.30	.14
□ 70 Steve Smith	.60	.25
□ 71 Ervin Johnson	.60	.25
□ 72 Sleepy Floyd	.30	.14
□ 73 Blue Edwards	.30	.14
□ 74 Clyde Drexler	1.50	.70
□ 75 Elden Campbell	.30	.25
□ 76 Hakeem Olajuwon	2.50	1.10
□ 77 C.Weatherspoon	.30	.14
□ 78 Kevin Willis	.30	.14
□ 79 Isaiah Rider	3.00	1.35
□ 80 Derrick Coleman	.60	.25
□ 81 Nick Anderson	.60	.25
□ 82 Bryant Stith	.30	.14
□ 83 Johnny Newman	.30	.14
□ 84 Calbert Cheaney	1.50	.70
□ 85 Oliver Miller	.30	.14
□ 86 Loy Vaught	.60	.25
□ 87 Isiah Thomas	1.25	.55
□ 88 Dee Brown	.30	.14
□ 89 Horace Grant	.60	.25
□ 90 Patrick Ewing AF	.60	.25
□ 91 C.Weatherspoon AF	.30	.14
□ 92 Rony Seikaly AF	.30	.14
□ 93 Dino Radja AF	.30	.14
□ 94 Kenny Anderson AF	.30	.14
□ 95 John Starks AF	.30	.14
□ 96 Tom Gugliotta AF	.60	.25
□ 97 Steve Smith AF	.30	.25
□ 98 Derrick Coleman AF	.30	.14
□ 99 Shaquille O'Neal AF	3.00	1.35
□ 100 Brad Daugherty CF	.30	.14
□ 101 Horace Grant CF	.30	.14
□ 102 Dominique Wilkins CF	.60	.25
□ 103 Joe Dumars CF	.30	.25
□ 104 Alonzo Mourning CF	1.25	.55
□ 105 Scottie Pippen CF	2.50	1.10
□ 106 Reggie Miller CF	.60	.25
□ 107 Mark Price CF	.30	.14
□ 108 Ken Norman CF	.30	.14
□ 109 Larry Johnson CF	.60	.25
□ 110 Jamal Mashburn MF	1.25	.55
□ 111 Christian Laettner MF	.60	.25
□ 112 Karl Malone MF	1.25	.55
□ 113 Dennis Rodman MF	3.00	1.35
□ 114 M.Abdul-Rauf MF	.30	.14
□ 115 Hakeem Olajuwon MF	1.25	.55
□ 116 Jim Jackson MF	.60	.25
□ 117 John Stockton MF	.60	.25
□ 118 David Robinson MF	1.25	.55
□ 119 D.Mutombo MF	.30	.14
□ 120 Vlade Divac PF	.30	.14

□ 121 Dan Majerle PF	.30	.14
□ 122 Chris Mullin PF	.30	.14
□ 123 Shawn Kemp PF	2.50	1.10
□ 124 Danny Manning PF	.30	.14
□ 125 Charles Barkley PF	.60	.25
□ 126 Mitch Richmond PF	.60	.25
□ 127 Tim Hardaway PF	1.25	.55
□ 128 Detlef Schrempf PF	.30	.14
□ 129 Clyde Drexler PF	1.25	.55
□ 130 Christian Laettner	1.25	.55
□ 131 Rodney Rogers	1.50	.70
□ 132 Rik Smits	.60	.25
□ 133 Chris Mills	2.00	.90
□ 134 Corie Blount	.30	.14
□ 135 Mookie Blaylock	.60	.25
□ 136 Jim Jackson	1.25	.55
□ 137 Tom Gugliotta	1.25	.55
□ 138 Dennis Scott	.30	.14
□ 139 Vin Baker	20.00	9.00
□ 140 Gary Payton	2.00	.90
□ 141 Sedale Threatt	.30	.14
□ 142 Orlando Woolridge	.30	.14
□ 143 Avery Johnson	.30	.14
□ 144 Charles Oakley	.60	.25
□ 145 Harvey Grant	.30	.14
□ 146 Bimbo Coles	.30	.14
□ 147 Vernon Maxwell	.30	.14
□ 148 Danny Manning	.30	.14
□ 149 Hersey Hawkins	.60	.25
□ 150 Kevin Gamble	.30	.14
□ 151 Johnny Dawkins	.30	.14
□ 152 Olden Polynice	.30	.14
□ 153 Kevin Edwards	.30	.14
□ 154 Willie Anderson	.30	.14
□ 155 Wayman Tisdale	.30	.14
□ 156 Popeye Jones	.30	.14
□ 157 Dan Majerle	.60	.25
□ 158 Rex Chapman	.30	.14
□ 159 Shawn Kemp	4.00	1.80
□ 160 Eric Murdock	.30	.14
□ 161 Randy White	.30	.14
□ 162 Larry Johnson	1.25	.55
□ 163 Dominique Wilkins	1.25	.55
□ 164 D.Mutombo	1.25	.55
□ 165 Patrick Ewing	1.25	.55
□ 166 Jerome Kersey	.30	.14
□ 167 Dale Davis	.30	.25
□ 168 Ron Harper	.60	.25
□ 169 Sam Cassell	4.00	1.80
□ 170 Bill Cartwright	.30	.14
□ 171 John Williams	.30	.14
□ 172 Dino Radja	.60	.25
□ 173 Dennis Rodman	5.00	2.20
□ 174 Kenny Anderson	.60	.25
□ 175 Robert Horry	.60	.25
□ 176 Chris Mullin	1.25	.55
□ 177 John Salley	.30	.14
□ 178 Scott Burrell	1.50	.70
□ 179 Mitch Richmond	1.25	.55
□ 180 Lee Mayberry	.30	.14
□ 181 James Worthy	1.25	.55
□ 182 Rick Fox	.30	.14
□ 183 Kevin Johnson	.60	.25
□ 184 Lindsey Hunter	2.00	.90
□ 185 Marlon Maxey	.30	.14
□ 186 Sam Perkins	.60	.25
□ 187 Kevin Duckworth	.30	.25
□ 188 Jeff Hornacek	.60	.25
□ 189 A.Hardaway	35.00	16.00
□ 190 Rex Walters	.30	.14
□ 191 M.Abdul-Rauf	.30	.14
□ 192 Terry Dehere	.30	.14
□ 193 Brad Daugherty	.30	.25
□ 194 Jon Starks	.60	.25
□ 195 Rod Strickland	.60	.25
□ 196 Luther Wright	.30	.14
□ 197 Vlade Divac	.60	.25
□ 198 Tim Hardaway	1.50	.70
□ 199 Joe Dumars	1.25	.55
□ 200 Charles Barkley	2.00	.90
□ 201 Alonzo Mourning	2.00	.90
□ 202 Doug West	.30	.14
□ 203 Anthony Avent	.30	.14
□ 204 Lloyd Daniels	.30	.14
□ 205 Mark Price	.30	.14
□ 206 Rumeal Robinson	.30	.14

□ 207 Kendall Gill	.60	.25
□ 208 Scottie Pippen	4.00	1.80
□ 209 Kenny Smith	.30	.14
□ 210 Walt Williams	.60	.25
□ 211 Hubert Davis	.30	.14
□ 212 Chris Webber	18.00	8.00
□ 213 Rony Seikaly	.30	.14
□ 214 Sam Bowie	.30	.14
□ 215 Karl Malone	2.00	.90
□ 216 Malik Sealy	.30	.14
□ 217 Dale Ellis	.30	.14
□ 218 Harold Miner	.30	.14
□ 219 John Stockton	1.25	.55
□ 220 Shawn Bradley	2.00	.90

1993-94 Finest Refractors

This set of Refractor cards parallels that of the 220-card Finest set. Information provided by Topps indicated the cards were randomly inserted at a rate of one in every nine seven-card packs and one in approximately four 14-card jumbo packs. However, widespread evidence indicates the cards were easier to obtain. In addition, a good amount of the cards were included in retail "re-packs" at chains like Wal-Mart and Sams. The only difference in design to the basic cards is refracting foil that creates a glossy shine to the card fronts when held under light. Cards with an asterisk next to their listing signify that it is currently perceived to be in shorter supply.

	MINT	NRMT
COMP.SET (220)	2300.00	1050.00
COMMON CARD (1-220)	4.00	1.80
SP (10/28/35/40/47/49/53)	8.00	3.60
SP (55/107/190/204/218)	8.00	3.60
SP (7/33/36/41/66/78/89)	12.00	5.50
SP (91/116/128/142/147)	12.00	5.50
SP (155/180/211/217)	12.00	5.50
SEMISTARS	10.00	4.50
UNLISTED STARS	15.00	6.75
STATED ODDS 1:9 HOBBY, 1:4 JUMBO		
ASTERISK CARDS: PERCEIVED SCARCITY		

□ 1 Michael Jordan	300.00	135.00
□ 2 Larry Bird	40.00	18.00
□ 3 Shaquille O'Neal	125.00	55.00
□ 4 Benoit Benjamin	4.00	1.80
□ 5 Ricky Pierce	4.00	1.80

6	Ken Norman	4.00	1.80
7	Victor Alexander *	12.00	5.50
8	Mark Jackson	10.00	4.50
9	Mark West	4.00	1.80
10	Don MacLean *	8.00	3.60
11	Reggie Miller	30.00	13.50
12	Sarunas Marciulionis *	30.00	13.50
13	Craig Ehlo	4.00	1.80
14	Toni Kukoc *	40.00	18.00
15	Glen Rice	25.00	11.00
16	Otis Thorpe	10.00	4.50
17	Reggie Williams	4.00	1.80
18	Charles Smith	4.00	1.80
19	Micheal Williams	4.00	1.80
20	Tom Chambers	4.00	1.80
21	David Robinson	30.00	13.50
22	Jamal Mashburn	40.00	18.00
23	Clifford Robinson	10.00	4.50
24	Acie Earl	4.00	1.80
25	Danny Ferry	4.00	1.80
26	Bobby Hurley	10.00	4.50
27	Eddie Johnson	4.00	1.80
28	Detlef Schrempf *	8.00	3.60
29	Mike Brown	4.00	1.80
30	Latrell Sprewell	20.00	9.00
31	Derek Harper	10.00	4.50
32	Stacey Augmon	4.00	1.80
33	Pooh Richardson	12.00	5.50
34	Larry Krystkowiak	4.00	1.80
35	Pervis Ellison	8.00	3.60
36	Jeff Malone	12.00	5.50
37	Sean Elliott	10.00	4.50
38	John Paxson	4.00	1.80
39	Robert Parish	10.00	4.50
40	Mark Aguirre *	8.00	3.60
41	Danny Ainge *	12.00	5.50
42	Brian Shaw	4.00	1.80
43	LaPhonso Ellis	10.00	4.50
44	Carl Herrera	4.00	1.80
45	Terry Cummings	4.00	1.80
46	Chris Dudley	4.00	1.80
47	Anthony Mason *	8.00	3.60
48	Chris Morris *	20.00	9.00
49	Todd Day	8.00	3.60
50	Nick Van Exel	60.00	27.00
51	Larry Nance	10.00	4.50
52	Derrick McKey	4.00	1.80
53	Muggsy Bogues *	8.00	3.60
54	Andrew Lang	4.00	1.80
55	Chuck Person	4.00	1.80
56	Michael Adams *	8.00	3.60
57	Spud Webb *	8.00	3.60
58	Scott Skiles	4.00	1.80
59	A.C. Green	10.00	4.50
60	Terry Mills	4.00	1.80
61	Xavier McDaniel	4.00	1.80
62	B.J. Armstrong *	8.00	3.60
63	Donald Hodge	4.00	1.80
64	Gary Grant *	30.00	13.50
65	Billy Owens	4.00	1.80
66	Greg Anthony *	12.00	5.50
67	Jay Humphries	4.00	1.80
68	Lionel Simmons	4.00	1.80
69	Dana Barros	4.00	1.80
70	Steve Smith	10.00	4.50
71	Ervin Johnson	10.00	4.50
72	Sleepy Floyd	4.00	1.80
73	Blue Edwards	4.00	1.80
74	Clyde Drexler *	35.00	16.00
75	Elden Campbell	10.00	4.50
76	Hakeem Olajuwon	40.00	18.00
77	C.Weatherspoon	4.00	1.80
78	Kevin Willis *	12.00	5.50
79	Isaiah Rider	20.00	9.00
80	Derrick Coleman	10.00	4.50
81	Nick Anderson	10.00	4.50
82	Bryant Stith	4.00	1.80
83	Johnny Newman	4.00	1.80
84	Calbert Cheaney *	40.00	18.00
85	Oliver Miller	4.00	1.80
86	Loy Vaught	10.00	4.50
87	Isiah Thomas	15.00	6.75
88	Dee Brown	4.00	1.80
89	Horace Grant *	12.00	5.50
90	Patrick Ewing AF	10.00	4.50
91	C.Weatherspoon	12.00	5.50

AF *

92	Rony Seikaly AF	4.00	1.80
93	Dino Radja AF	4.00	1.80
94	Kenny Anderson AF	4.00	1.80
95	John Starks AF	4.00	1.80
96	Tom Gugliotta AF	10.00	4.50
97	Steve Smith AF	10.00	4.50
98	Derrick Coleman AF	4.00	1.80
99	Shaquille O'Neal AF	50.00	22.00
100	Brad Daugherty CF	4.00	1.80
101	Horace Grant CF	4.00	1.80
102	Dominique Wilkins CF	10.00	4.50
103	Joe Dumars CF	10.00	4.50
104	Alonzo Mourning CF	20.00	9.00
105	Scottie Pippen CF *	50.00	22.00
106	Reggie Miller CF *	25.00	11.00
107	Mark Price CF *	8.00	3.60
108	Ken Norman CF	4.00	1.80
109	Larry Johnson CF	10.00	4.50
110	Jamal Mashburn MF *	15.00	6.75
111	Christian Laettner MF	10.00	4.50
112	Karl Malone MF	25.00	11.00
113	Dennis Rodman MF * !	60.00	27.00
114	M.Abdul-Rauf MF	4.00	1.80
115	Hakeem Olajuwon MF	30.00	13.50
116	Jim Jackson MF *	12.00	5.50
117	John Stockton MF	10.00	4.50
118	David Robinson MF *	25.00	11.00
119	D.Mutombo MF	4.00	1.80
120	Vlade Divac PF	4.00	1.80
121	Dan Majerle PF	4.00	1.80
122	Chris Mullin PF	4.00	1.80
123	Shawn Kemp PF	35.00	16.00
124	Danny Manning PF *	4.00	1.80
125	Charles Barkley PF	20.00	9.00
126	Mitch Richmond PF	15.00	6.75
127	Tim Hardaway PF	15.00	6.75
128	Detlef Schrempf PF *	12.00	5.50
129	Clyde Drexler PF	15.00	6.75
130	Christian Laettner *	15.00	6.75
131	Rodney Rogers	4.00	1.80
132	Rik Smits	10.00	4.50
133	Chris Mills *	60.00	27.00
134	Corie Blount	4.00	1.80
135	Mookie Blaylock	10.00	4.50
136	Jim Jackson	15.00	6.75
137	Tom Gugliotta	25.00	11.00
138	Dennis Scott	4.00	1.80
139	Vin Baker *	110.00	50.00
140	Gary Payton *	70.00	32.00
141	Sedale Threatt	4.00	1.80
142	Orlando Woolridge *	12.00	5.50
143	Avery Johnson	4.00	1.80
144	Charles Oakley	10.00	4.50
145	Harvey Grant	4.00	1.80
146	Bimbo Coles	4.00	1.80
147	Vernon Maxwell *	12.00	5.50
148	Danny Manning	4.00	1.80
149	Hersey Hawkins	10.00	4.50
150	Kevin Gamble	4.00	1.80
151	Johnny Dawkins	4.00	1.80
152	Olden Polynice	4.00	1.80
153	Kevin Edwards	4.00	1.80
154	Willie Anderson	4.00	1.80
155	Wayman Tisdale *	12.00	5.50
156	Popeye Jones	4.00	1.80
157	Dan Majerle	10.00	4.50
158	Rex Chapman	4.00	1.80
159	Shawn Kemp UER *	70.00	32.00
	(Misnumbered 136)		
160	Eric Murdock	4.00	1.80
161	Randy White	4.00	1.80
162	Larry Johnson	20.00	9.00
163	Dominique Wilkins	15.00	6.75
164	D.Mutombo	15.00	6.75
165	Patrick Ewing	30.00	13.50
166	Jerome Kersey	4.00	1.80
167	Dale Davis	4.00	1.80
168	Ron Harper	10.00	4.50
169	Sam Cassell	40.00	18.00
170	Bill Cartwright *	25.00	11.00
171	John Williams	4.00	1.80
172	Rony Radja	10.00	4.50
173	Dennis Rodman *	80.00	36.00
174	Kenny Anderson	10.00	4.50
175	Robert Horry	10.00	4.50

176	Chris Mullin	15.00	6.75
177	John Salley	4.00	1.80
178	Scott Burrell	15.00	6.75
179	Mitch Richmond	35.00	16.00
180	Lee Mayberry *	12.00	5.50
181	James Worthy	15.00	6.75
182	Rick Fox *	25.00	11.00
183	Kevin Johnson	10.00	4.50
184	Lindsey Hunter	20.00	9.00
185	Marlon Maxey	4.00	1.80
186	Sam Perkins	10.00	4.50
187	Kevin Duckworth	4.00	1.80
188	Jeff Hornacek	10.00	4.50
189	A.Hardaway	250.00	110.00
190	Rex Walters	8.00	3.60
191	M.Abdul-Rauf	4.00	1.80
192	Terry Dehere	4.00	1.80
193	Brad Daugherty	4.00	1.80
194	John Starks	10.00	4.50
195	Rod Strickland	15.00	6.75
196	Luther Wright	4.00	1.80
197	Vlade Divac	10.00	4.50
198	Tim Hardaway	30.00	13.50
199	Joe Dumars	15.00	6.75
200	Charles Barkley	40.00	18.00
201	Alonzo Mourning	40.00	18.00
202	Doug West	4.00	1.80
203	Anthony Avent	4.00	1.80
204	Lloyd Daniels	8.00	3.60
205	Mark Price	4.00	1.80
206	Rumeal Robinson	4.00	1.80
207	Kendall Gill	10.00	4.50
208	Scottie Pippen *	80.00	36.00
209	Kenny Smith	4.00	1.80
210	Walt Williams	10.00	4.50
211	Hubert Davis *	12.00	5.50
212	Chris Webber *	170.00	75.00
213	Rony Seikaly	4.00	1.80
214	Sam Bowie	4.00	1.80
215	Karl Malone	40.00	18.00
216	Malik Sealy	4.00	1.80
217	Dale Ellis *	12.00	5.50
218	Harold Miner *	8.00	3.60
219	John Stockton	25.00	11.00
220	Shawn Bradley	20.00	9.00

1993-94 Finest Main Attraction

Distributed one per 14-card jumbo pack, a player from each of the 27 NBA teams is represented in this standard size set. The rainbow colored metallic front features a semi-embossed color action cutout on textured metallic background. The brick textured bordered back features a color action shot with a gold border. Player's statistics and profile appear below the photo.

The cards are numbered on the back "X of 27."

	MINT	NRMT
COMPLETE SET (27)	75.00	34.00
COMMON CARD (1-27)	1.00	.45
SEMISTARS	1.50	.70
UNLISTED STARS	3.00	1.35
ONE PER JUMBO PACK		
☐ 1 Dominique Wilkins	3.00	1.35
☐ 2 Dino Radja	1.50	.70
☐ 3 Larry Johnson	3.00	1.35
☐ 4 Scottie Pippen	10.00	4.50
☐ 5 Mark Price	1.00	.45
☐ 6 Jamal Mashburn	6.00	2.70
☐ 7 M.Abdul-Raul	1.00	.45
☐ 8 Joe Dumars	3.00	1.35
☐ 9 Chris Webber	12.00	5.50
☐ 10 Hakeem Olajuwon	6.00	2.70
☐ 11 Reggie Miller	3.00	1.35
☐ 12 Danny Manning	1.00	.45
☐ 13 Doug Christie	1.00	.45
☐ 14 Steve Smith	1.50	.70
☐ 15 Eric Murdock	1.00	.45
☐ 16 Isaiah Rider	3.00	1.35
☐ 17 Derrick Coleman	1.50	.70
☐ 18 Patrick Ewing	3.00	1.35
☐ 19 Shaquille O'Neal	12.00	5.50
☐ 20 Shawn Bradley	3.00	1.35
☐ 21 Charles Barkley	5.00	2.20
☐ 22 Clyde Drexler	4.00	1.80
☐ 23 Mitch Richmond	3.00	1.35
☐ 24 David Robinson	5.00	2.20
☐ 25 Shawn Kemp	10.00	4.50
☐ 26 Karl Malone	5.00	2.20
☐ 27 Tom Gugliotta	3.00	1.35

1994-95 Finest

This 331-card standard size set was issued in two series of 165 and 166 cards each. Cards were distributed in seven-card packs carrying a suggested retail price of $5.00 each. Metallic silver fronts feature a color player photo against a prismatic background. The backs have a small photo, stats, bio and a "Finest Moment `93-94". The backs have blue borders with the player's name and position at the top. Topical subsets featured are City Legend-NYC (1-10), City Legend-Balt/DC (51-55), City Legend-Detroit (101-105), City Legend-Chicago (106-110), City Legend/LA (151-155), Finest's ACC's Best (201-209), Finest's Big East's Best (226-234), Finest's Big Ten's Best (250-259), and Finest's SEC's Best (275-284). Each card features a protective coating on front that was designed to protect the card from problems that may arise from handling. The coating can be removed by carefully peeling it from the card. Values provided below are for unpeeled cards. Peeled cards generally trade for about ten to twenty-five percent less. Rookie Cards of note include Grant Hill, Juwan Howard, Eddie Jones, Jason Kidd and Glenn Robinson.

	MINT	NRMT
COMPLETE SET (1-331)	330.00	150.00
COMP.SERIES 1 (165)	130.00	57.50
COMP.SERIES 2 (166)	200.00	90.00
COMMON CARD (1-165)	.30	.25
COMMON CARD (166-331)	.30	.14
SEMISTARS SER.1	1.25	.55
SEMISTARS SER.2	.60	.25
UNLISTED STARS SER.1	2.50	1.10
UNLISTED STARS SER.2	.60	.55

		MINT	NRMT
☐ 1	Chris Mullin CY	1.25	.25
☐ 2	Anthony Mason CY	.60	.25
☐ 3	John Salley CY	.60	.25
☐ 4	Jamal Mashburn CY	1.25	.55
☐ 5	Mark Jackson CY	.60	.25
☐ 6	Mario Elie CY	.60	.25
☐ 7	Kenny Anderson CY	.60	.25
☐ 8	Rod Strickland CY	.60	.25
☐ 9	Kenny Smith CY	.60	.25
☐ 10	Olden Polynice CY	.60	.25
☐ 11	Derek Harper	1.25	.25
☐ 12	Danny Ainge	1.25	.55
☐ 13	Dino Radja	.60	.25
☐ 14	Eric Murdock	.60	.25
☐ 15	Sean Rooks	.60	.25
☐ 16	Dell Curry	.60	.25
☐ 17	Victor Alexander	.60	.25
☐ 18	Rodney Rogers	.60	.25
☐ 19	John Salley	.60	.25
☐ 20	Brad Daugherty	.60	.25
☐ 21	Elmore Spencer	.60	.25
☐ 22	Mitch Richmond	2.50	1.10
☐ 23	Rex Walters	.60	.25
☐ 24	Antonio Davis	.60	.25
☐ 25	B.J. Armstrong	.60	.25
☐ 26	Andrew Lang	.60	.25
☐ 27	Carl Herrera	.60	.25
☐ 28	Kevin Edwards	.60	.25
☐ 29	Micheal Williams	.60	.25
☐ 30	Clyde Drexler	3.00	1.35
☐ 31	Dana Barros	.60	.25
☐ 32	Shaquille O'Neal	10.00	4.50
☐ 33	Patrick Ewing	2.50	1.10
☐ 34	Charles Barkley	4.00	1.80
☐ 35	J.R. Reid	.60	.25
☐ 36	Lindsey Hunter	1.25	.25
☐ 37	Jeff Malone	.60	.25
☐ 38	Rik Smits	1.25	.55
☐ 39	Brian Williams	.60	.25
☐ 40	Shawn Kemp	8.00	3.60
☐ 41	Terry Porter	.60	.25
☐ 42	James Worthy	2.50	1.10
☐ 43	Rex Chapman	.60	.25
☐ 44	Stanley Roberts	.60	.25
☐ 45	Chris Smith	.60	.25
☐ 46	Dee Brown	.60	.25
☐ 47	Chris Gatling	.60	.25
☐ 48	Donald Hodge	.60	.25
☐ 49	Bimbo Coles	.60	.25
☐ 50	Derrick Coleman	1.25	.55
☐ 51	Muggsy Bogues CY	.60	.25
☐ 52	Reggie Williams CY	.60	.25
☐ 53	David Wingate CY	.60	.25
☐ 54	Sam Cassell CY	.60	.25
☐ 55	Sherman Douglas CY	.60	.25
☐ 56	Keith Jennings	.60	.25
☐ 57	Kenny Gattison	.60	.25
☐ 58	Brent Price	.60	.25
☐ 59	Luc Longley	1.25	.55
☐ 60	Jamal Mashburn	2.50	1.10
☐ 61	Doug West	.60	.25
☐ 62	Walt Williams	.60	.25
☐ 63	Tracy Murray	.60	.25
☐ 64	Robert Pack	.60	.25
☐ 65	Johnny Dawkins	.60	.25
☐ 66	Vin Baker	6.00	2.70
☐ 67	Sam Cassell	2.50	1.10
☐ 68	Dale Davis	.60	.25
☐ 69	Terrell Brandon	2.50	1.10
☐ 70	Billy Owens	.60	.25
☐ 71	Ervin Johnson	.60	.25
☐ 72	Allan Houston	2.50	1.10
☐ 73	Craig Ehlo	.60	.25
☐ 74	Loy Vaught	1.25	.55
☐ 75	Scottie Pippen	8.00	3.60
☐ 76	Sam Bowie	.60	.25
☐ 77	Anthony Mason	1.25	.55
☐ 78	Felton Spencer	.60	.25
☐ 79	P.J. Brown	.60	.25
☐ 80	Christian Laettner	1.25	.55
☐ 81	Todd Day	.60	.25
☐ 82	Sean Elliott	1.25	.55
☐ 83	Grant Long	.60	.25
☐ 84	Xavier McDaniel	.60	.25
☐ 85	David Benoit	.60	.25
☐ 86	Larry Stewart	.60	.25
☐ 87	Donald Royal	.60	.25
☐ 88	Duane Causwell	.60	.25
☐ 89	Vlade Divac	1.25	.55
☐ 90	Derrick McKey	.60	.25
☐ 91	Kevin Johnson	1.25	.55
☐ 92	LaPhonso Ellis	1.25	.55
☐ 93	Jerome Kersey	.60	.25
☐ 94	Muggsy Bogues	1.25	.55
☐ 95	Tom Gugliotta	2.50	1.10
☐ 96	Jeff Hornacek	1.25	.55
☐ 97	Kevin Willis	.60	.25
☐ 98	Chris Mills	1.25	.55
☐ 99	Sam Perkins	1.25	.55
☐ 100	Alonzo Mourning	3.00	1.35
☐ 101	Derrick Coleman CY	.60	.25
☐ 102	Glen Rice CY	1.25	.55
☐ 103	Kevin Willis CY	.60	.25
☐ 104	Chris Webber CY	3.00	1.35
☐ 105	Terry Mills CY	.60	.25
☐ 106	Tim Hardaway CY	2.50	1.10
☐ 107	Nick Anderson CY	.60	.25
☐ 108	Terry Cummings CY	.60	.25
☐ 109	Hersey Hawkins CY	.60	.25
☐ 110	Ken Norman CY	.60	.25
☐ 111	Nick Anderson	1.25	.55
☐ 112	Tim Perry	.60	.25
☐ 113	Terry Dehere	.60	.25
☐ 114	Chris Morris	.60	.25
☐ 115	John Williams	.60	.25
☐ 116	Jon Barry	.60	.25
☐ 117	Rony Seikaly	.60	.25
☐ 118	Detlef Schrempt	1.25	.55
☐ 119	Terry Cummings	.60	.25
☐ 120	Chris Webber	6.00	2.70
☐ 121	David Wingate	.60	.25
☐ 122	Popeye Jones	.60	.25
☐ 123	Sherman Douglas	.60	.25
☐ 124	Greg Anthony	.60	.25
☐ 125	Mookie Blaylock	1.25	.55
☐ 126	Don MacLean	.60	.25
☐ 127	Lionel Simmons	.60	.25
☐ 128	Scott Brooks	.60	.25
☐ 129	Jeff Turner	.60	.25
☐ 130	Bryant Stith	.60	.25
☐ 131	Shawn Bradley	1.25	.55
☐ 132	Byron Scott	1.25	.55
☐ 133	Doug Christie	.60	.25
☐ 134	Dennis Rodman	10.00	4.50
☐ 135	Dan Majerle	1.25	.55
☐ 136	Gary Grant	.60	.25
☐ 137	Bryon Russell	1.25	.55

138	Will Perdue	.60	.25
139	Gheorghe Muresan	1.25	.55
140	Kendall Gill	1.25	.55
141	Isaiah Rider	1.25	.55
142	Terry Mills	.60	.25
143	Willie Anderson	.60	.25
144	Hubert Davis	.60	.25
145	Lucious Harris	.60	.25
146	Spud Webb	1.25	.55
147	Glen Rice	2.50	1.10
148	Dennis Scott	1.25	.55
149	Robert Horry	1.25	.55
150	John Stockton	2.50	1.10
151	Stacey Augmon CY	.60	.25
152	Chris Mills CY	.60	.25
153	Elden Campbell CY	.60	.25
154	Jay Humphries CY	.60	.25
155	Reggie Miller CY	1.25	.55
156	George Lynch	.60	.25
157	Tyrone Hill	.60	.25
158	Lee Mayberry	.60	.25
159	Jon Koncak	.60	.25
160	Joe Dumars	2.50	1.10
161	Vernon Maxwell	.60	.25
162	Joe Kleine	.60	.25
163	Acie Earl	.60	.25
164	Steve Kerr	1.25	.55
165	Rod Strickland	1.25	.55
166	Glenn Robinson	12.00	5.50
167	A.Hardaway	6.00	2.70
168	Latrell Sprewell	.60	.25
169	Sergei Bazarevich	.30	.14
170	Hakeem Olajuwon	2.50	1.10
171	Nick Van Exel	1.25	.55
172	Buck Williams	.60	.25
173	Antoine Carr	.30	.14
174	Corie Blount	.30	.14
175	Dominique Wilkins	.75	.35
176	Yinka Dare	.30	.14
177	Byron Houston	.30	.14
178	LaSalle Thompson	.30	.14
179	Doug Smith	.30	.14
180	David Robinson	2.00	.90
181	Eric Piatkowski	.30	.14
182	Scott Skiles	.30	.14
183	Scott Burrell	.30	.14
184	Mark West	.30	.14
185	Billy Owens	.30	.14
186	Brian Grant	5.00	2.20
187	Scott Williams	.30	.14
188	Gerald Madkins	.30	.14
189	Reggie Williams	.30	.14
190	Danny Manning	.30	.14
191	Mike Brown	.30	.14
192	Charles Smith	.30	.14
193	Elden Campbell	.60	.25
194	Ricky Pierce	.30	.14
195	Karl Malone	2.00	.90
196	Brooks Thompson	.30	.14
197	Alaa Abdelnaby	.30	.14
198	Tyrone Corbin	.30	.14
199	Johnny Newman	.30	.14
200	Grant Hill CB	10.00	4.50
201	Kenny Anderson CB	.30	.14
202	Olden Polynice CB	.30	.14
203	Horace Grant CB	.30	.14
204	Muggsy Bogues CB	.30	.14
205	Mark Price CB	.30	.14
206	Tom Gugliotta CB	.75	.35
207	Christian Laettner CB	.30	.14
208	Eric Montross CB	.30	.14
209	Sam Cassell CB	.60	.25
210	Charles Oakley	.30	.25
211	Harold Ellis	.30	.14
212	Nate McMillan	.30	.14
213	Chuck Person	.30	.14
214	Harold Miner	.30	.14
215	C.Weatherspoon	.30	.14
216	Robert Parish	.60	.25
217	Michael Cage	.30	.14
218	Kenny Smith	.30	.14
219	Larry Krystkowiak	.30	.14
220	D.Mutombo	.75	.35
221	Wayman Tisdale	.30	.14
222	Kevin Duckworth	.30	.14
223	Vern Fleming	.30	.14
224	Eric Mobley	.30	.14
225	Patrick Ewing CB	.75	.35
226	Clifford Robinson CB	.30	.14
227	Eric Murdock CB	.30	.14
228	Derrick Coleman CB	.60	.25
229	Otis Thorpe CB	.30	.14
230	Alonzo Mourning CB	.75	.35
231	Donyell Marshall CB	.30	.14
232	D.Mutombo CB	.60	.25
233	Rony Seikaly CB	.30	.14
234	Chris Mullin CB	.60	.25
235	Reggie Miller	1.25	.55
236	Benoit Benjamin	.30	.14
237	Sean Rooks	.30	.14
238	Terry Davis	.30	.14
239	Anthony Avent	.30	.14
240	Grant Hill	85.00	38.00
241	Randy Woods	.30	.14
242	Tom Chambers	.30	.14
243	Michael Adams	.30	.14
244	Monty Williams	.30	.14
245	Chris Mullin	1.25	.55
246	Bill Wennington	.30	.14
247	Mark Jackson	.60	.25
248	Blue Edwards	.30	.14
249	Jalen Rose	3.00	1.35
250	Glenn Robinson CB	2.00	.90
251	Kevin Willis CB	.30	.14
252	B.J. Armstrong CB	.30	.14
253	Jim Jackson CB	.30	.14
254	Steve Smith CB	.30	.14
255	Chris Webber CB	1.50	.70
256	Glen Rice CB	.75	.35
257	Derek Harper CB	.30	.14
258	Jalen Rose CB	.60	.25
259	Juwan Howard CB	2.00	.90
260	Kenny Anderson	.75	.35
261	Calbert Cheaney	.60	.25
262	Bill Cartwright	.30	.14
263	Mario Elie	.30	.14
264	Chris Dudley	.30	.14
265	Jim Jackson	.75	.35
266	Antonio Harvey	.30	.14
267	Bill Curley	.30	.14
268	Moses Malone	1.25	.55
269	A.C. Green	.60	.25
270	Larry Johnson	.75	.35
271	Marty Conlon	.30	.14
272	Greg Graham	.30	.14
273	Eric Montross	.30	.14
274	Stacey King	.30	.14
275	Charles Barkley CB	1.25	.55
276	Chris Morris CB	.30	.14
277	Robert Horry CB	.30	.14
278	Dominique Wilkins CB	.60	.25
279	Latrell Sprewell CB	.30	.14
280	Shaquille O'Neal CB	2.50	1.10
281	Wesley Person CB	.60	.25
282	M.Abdul-Rauf CB	.30	.14
283	Jamal Mashburn CB	.75	.35
284	Dale Ellis CB	.30	.14
285	Gary Payton	.30	.14
286	Jason Kidd	20.00	9.00
287	Ken Norman	.30	.14
288	Juwan Howard	12.00	5.50
289	Lamond Murray	2.00	.90
290	Clifford Robinson	.60	.25
291	Frank Brickowski	.30	.14
292	Adam Keefe	.30	.14
293	Ron Harper	.30	.25
294	Tom Hammonds	.30	.14
295	Otis Thorpe	.60	.25
296	Rick Mahorn	.30	.14
297	Alton Lister	.30	.14
298	Vinny Del Negro	.30	.14
299	Danny Ferry	.30	.14
300	John Starks	.60	.25
301	Duane Ferrell	.30	.14
302	Hersey Hawkins	.60	.25
303	Khalid Reeves	.30	.14
304	Anthony Peeler	.30	.14
305	Tim Hardaway	1.50	.70
306	Rick Fox	.30	.14
307	Jay Humphries	.30	.14
308	Brian Shaw	.30	.14
309	Dan Schayes	.30	.14
310	Stacey Augmon	.30	.14
311	Oliver Miller	.30	.14
312	Pooh Richardson	.30	.14
313	Donyell Marshall	5.00	2.20
314	Aaron McKie	.30	.14
315	Mark Price	.30	.14
316	B.J. Tyler	.30	.14
317	Olden Polynice	.30	.14
318	Avery Johnson	.30	.14
319	Derek Strong	.30	.14
320	Toni Kukoc	1.25	.55
321	Charlie Ward	2.50	1.10
322	Wesley Person	4.00	1.80
323	Eddie Jones	25.00	11.00
324	Horace Grant	.60	.25
325	M.Abdul-Rauf	.30	.14
326	Sharone Wright	.30	.14
327	Kevin Gamble	.30	.14
328	Sarunas Marciulionis	.30	.14
329	Harvey Grant	.30	.14
330	Bobby Hurley	.30	.14
331	Michael Jordan	25.00	11.00

1994-95 Finest Refractors

Parallel to the basic set, Refractors were randomly inserted in first and second packs at a rate of one in 12. Refractors are distinguished from the basic cards by their rainbow-like appearance that refracts more light. Just like regular issue Finest cards, each Refractor comes with a protective coating designed to protect the card from wear and tear. Values provided below are for unpeeled cards. Peeled cards trade for about twenty-five to fifty percent less. The set is condition sensitive. The cards marked with an asterisk are perceived to be more scare than the other singles.

	MINT	NRMT
COMP.SET (331)	5700.00	2600.00
COMP.SERIES 1 (165)	2500.00	1100.00
COMP.SERIES 2 (166)	3200.00	1450.00
COMMON CARD (1-331)	8.00	3.60
SP (39,138,143,156)	15.00	6.75
SP (2,135,149,164)	20.00	9.00
SP (4,27,38,140,162)	25.00	11.00
SP (1,18,139,153)	30.00	13.50
SEMISTARS	12.00	5.50
SER. 1/2 STATED ODDS 1:12		
CONDITION SENSITIVE SET		
ASTERISK CARDS: PERCEIVED SCARCITY		

#	Player	Price 1	Price 2
1	Chris Mullin CY *	30.00	13.50
2	Anthony Mason CY *..	20.00	9.00
3	John Salley CY	8.00	3.60
4	Jamal Mashburn CY *	25.00	11.00
5	Mark Jackson CY	8.00	3.60
6	Mario Elie CY	8.00	3.60
7	Kenny Anderson CY	8.00	3.60
8	Rod Strickland CY	12.00	5.50
9	Kenny Smith CY	8.00	3.60
10	Olden Polynice CY	8.00	3.60
11	Derek Harper	12.00	5.50
12	Danny Ainge	12.00	5.50
13	Dino Radja	8.00	3.60
14	Eric Murdock	8.00	3.60
15	Sean Rooks	8.00	3.60
16	Dell Curry	8.00	3.60
17	Victor Alexander	8.00	3.60
18	Rodney Rogers *	30.00	13.50
19	John Salley	8.00	3.60
20	Brad Daugherty	8.00	3.60
21	Elmore Spencer	8.00	3.60
22	Mitch Richmond	50.00	22.00
23	Rex Walters	8.00	3.60
24	Antonio Davis	8.00	3.60
25	B.J. Armstrong	8.00	3.60
26	Andrew Lang	8.00	3.60
27	Carl Herrera *	25.00	11.00
28	Kevin Edwards	8.00	3.60
29	Micheal Williams	8.00	3.60
30	Clyde Drexler	50.00	22.00
31	Dana Barros	8.00	3.60
32	Shaquille O'Neal	150.00	70.00
33	Patrick Ewing	40.00	18.00
34	Charles Barkley	70.00	32.00
35	J.R. Reid	8.00	3.60
36	Lindsey Hunter	12.00	5.50
37	Jeff Malone	8.00	3.60
38	Rik Smits *	25.00	11.00
39	Brian Williams *	15.00	6.75
40	Shawn Kemp	80.00	36.00
41	Terry Porter	8.00	3.60
42	James Worthy	15.00	6.75
43	Rex Chapman	8.00	3.60
44	Stanley Roberts	8.00	3.60
45	Chris Smith	8.00	3.60
46	Dee Brown	8.00	3.60
47	Chris Gatling	8.00	3.60
48	Donald Hodge	8.00	3.60
49	Bimbo Coles	8.00	3.60
50	Derrick Coleman	12.00	5.50
51	Muggsy Bogues CY	8.00	3.60
52	Reggie Williams CY	8.00	3.60
53	David Wingate CY	8.00	3.60
54	Sam Cassell CY	8.00	3.60
55	Sherman Douglas CY	8.00	3.60
56	Keith Jennings	8.00	3.60
57	Kenny Gattison	8.00	3.60
58	Brent Price	8.00	3.60
59	Luc Longley	12.00	5.50
60	Jamal Mashburn	40.00	18.00
61	Doug West	8.00	3.60
62	Walt Williams	8.00	3.60
63	Tracy Murray	8.00	3.60
64	Robert Pack	8.00	3.60
65	Johnny Dawkins	8.00	3.60
66	Vin Baker	80.00	36.00
67	Sam Cassell	15.00	6.75
68	Dale Davis	8.00	3.60
69	Terrell Brandon	30.00	13.50
70	Billy Owens	8.00	3.60
71	Ervin Johnson	8.00	3.60
72	Allan Houston	60.00	27.00
73	Craig Ehlo	8.00	3.60
74	Loy Vaught	12.00	5.50
75	Scottie Pippen	100.00	45.00
76	Sam Bowie	8.00	3.60
77	Anthony Mason	15.00	6.75
78	Felton Spencer	8.00	3.60
79	P.J. Brown	8.00	3.60
80	Christian Laettner	20.00	9.00
81	Todd Day	8.00	3.60
82	Sean Elliott	12.00	5.50
83	Grant Long	8.00	3.60
84	Xavier McDaniel	8.00	3.60
85	David Benoit	8.00	3.60
86	Larry Stewart	8.00	3.60
87	Donald Royal	8.00	3.60
88	Duane Causwell	8.00	3.60
89	Vlade Divac	12.00	5.50
90	Derrick McKey	8.00	3.60
91	Kevin Johnson	15.00	6.75
92	LaPhonso Ellis	12.00	5.50
93	Jerome Kersey	8.00	3.60
94	Muggsy Bogues	12.00	5.50
95	Tom Gugliotta	30.00	13.50
96	Jeff Hornacek	12.00	5.50
97	Kevin Willis	8.00	3.60
98	Chris Mills	12.00	5.50
99	Sam Perkins	12.00	5.50
100	Alonzo Mourning	50.00	22.00
101	Derrick Coleman CY	8.00	3.60
102	Glen Rice CY *	125.00	55.00
103	Kevin Willis CY	8.00	3.60
104	Chris Webber CY *	100.00	45.00
105	Terry Mills CY	8.00	3.60
106	Tim Hardaway CY *	30.00	13.50
107	Nick Anderson CY	8.00	3.60
108	Terry Cummings CY	8.00	3.60
109	Hersey Hawkins CY	8.00	3.60
110	Ken Norman CY	8.00	3.60
111	Nick Anderson	12.00	5.50
112	Tim Perry	8.00	3.60
113	Terry Dehere	8.00	3.60
114	Chris Morris	8.00	3.60
115	John Williams	8.00	3.60
116	Jon Barry	8.00	3.60
117	Rony Seikaly	8.00	3.60
118	Detlef Schrempf	12.00	5.50
119	Terry Cummings	8.00	3.60
120	Chris Webber *	200.00	90.00
121	David Wingate	8.00	3.60
122	Popeye Jones	8.00	3.60
123	Sherman Douglas	8.00	3.60
124	Greg Anthony	8.00	3.60
125	Mookie Blaylock	12.00	5.50
126	Don MacLean	8.00	3.60
127	Lionel Simmons	8.00	3.60
128	Scott Brooks	8.00	3.60
129	Jeff Turner	8.00	3.60
130	Bryant Stith	8.00	3.60
131	Shawn Bradley	12.00	5.50
132	Byron Scott	12.00	5.50
133	Doug Christie	8.00	3.60
134	Dennis Rodman	100.00	45.00
135	Dan Majerle *	20.00	9.00
136	Gary Grant	8.00	3.60
137	Bryon Russell	12.00	5.50
138	Will Perdue *	15.00	6.75
139	Gheorghe Muresan *	30.00	13.50
140	Kendall Gill *	25.00	11.00
141	Isaiah Rider	12.00	5.50
142	Terry Mills	8.00	3.60
143	Willie Anderson * ..	15.00	6.75
144	Hubert Davis	8.00	3.60
145	Lucious Harris	8.00	3.60
146	Spud Webb	12.00	5.50
147	Glen Rice	60.00	27.00
148	Dennis Scott	12.00	5.50
149	Robert Horry *	20.00	9.00
150	John Stockton *	70.00	32.00
151	Stacey Augmon CY *	8.00	3.60
152	Chris Mills CY	8.00	3.60
153	Elden Campbell CY *	30.00	13.50
154	Jay Humphries CY	8.00	3.60
155	Reggie Miller CY *..	50.00	22.00
156	George Lynch *	15.00	6.75
157	Tyrone Hill	8.00	3.60
158	Lee Mayberry	8.00	3.60
159	Jon Koncak	8.00	3.60
160	Joe Dumars	15.00	6.75
161	Vernon Maxwell	8.00	3.60
162	Joe Kleine *	25.00	11.00
163	Acie Earl	8.00	3.60
164	Steve Kerr *	20.00	9.00
165	Rod Strickland	20.00	9.00
166	Glenn Robinson	120.00	55.00
167	A.Hardaway	250.00	110.00
168	Latrell Sprewell	20.00	9.00
169	Sergei Bazarevich	8.00	3.60
170	Hakeem Olajuwon	50.00	22.00
171	Nick Van Exel	50.00	22.00
172	Buck Williams	12.00	5.50
173	Antoine Carr	8.00	3.60
174	Corie Blount	8.00	3.60
175	Dominique Wilkins	15.00	6.75
176	Yinka Dare	8.00	3.60
177	Byron Houston	8.00	3.60
178	LaSalle Thompson	8.00	3.60
179	Doug Smith	8.00	3.60
180	David Robinson	40.00	18.00
181	Eric Piatkowski	8.00	3.60
182	Scott Skiles	8.00	3.60
183	Scott Burrell	8.00	3.60
184	Mark West	8.00	3.60
185	Billy Owens	8.00	3.60
186	Brian Grant	25.00	11.00
187	Scott Williams	8.00	3.60
188	Gerald Madkins	8.00	3.60
189	Reggie Williams	8.00	3.60
190	Danny Manning	8.00	3.60
191	Mike Brown	8.00	3.60
192	Charles Smith	8.00	3.60
193	Elden Campbell	12.00	5.50
194	Ricky Pierce	8.00	3.60
195	Karl Malone	50.00	22.00
196	Brooks Thompson	8.00	3.60
197	Alaa Abdelnaby	8.00	3.60
198	Tyrone Corbin	8.00	3.60
199	Johnny Newman	8.00	3.60
200	Grant Hill CB *	150.00	70.00
201	Kenny Anderson CB	8.00	3.60
202	Olden Polynice CB	8.00	3.60
203	Horace Grant CB	8.00	3.60
204	Muggsy Bogues CB..	8.00	3.60
205	Mark Price CB	8.00	3.60
206	Tom Gugliotta CB	15.00	6.75
207	Christian Laettner CB	8.00	3.60
208	Eric Montross CB	8.00	3.60
209	Sam Cassell CB	8.00	3.60
210	Charles Oakley	12.00	5.50
211	Harold Ellis	8.00	3.60
212	Nate McMillan	8.00	3.60
213	Chuck Person	8.00	3.60
214	Harold Miner	8.00	3.60
215	C.Weatherspoon	8.00	3.60
216	Robert Parish	12.00	5.50
217	Michael Cage	8.00	3.60
218	Kenny Smith	8.00	3.60
219	Larry Krystkowiak	8.00	3.60
220	D.Mutombo	15.00	6.75
221	Wayman Tisdale	8.00	3.60
222	Kevin Duckworth	8.00	3.60
223	Vern Fleming	8.00	3.60
224	Eric Mobley	8.00	3.60
225	Patrick Ewing CB	15.00	6.75
226	Clifford Robinson CB	8.00	3.60
227	Eric Murdock CB	8.00	3.60
228	Derrick Coleman CB	8.00	3.60
229	Otis Thorpe CB	8.00	3.60
230	Alonzo Mourning CB	15.00	6.75
231	Donyell Marshall CB	12.00	5.50
232	D.Mutombo CB	12.00	5.50
233	Rony Seikaly CB	8.00	3.60
234	Chris Mullin CB	12.00	5.50
235	Reggie Miller	40.00	18.00
236	Benoit Benjamin	8.00	3.60
237	Sean Rooks	8.00	3.60
238	Terry Davis	8.00	3.60
239	Anthony Avent	8.00	3.60
240	Grant Hill	500.00	220.00
241	Randy Woods	8.00	3.60
242	Tom Chambers	8.00	3.60
243	Michael Adams	8.00	3.60
244	Monty Williams	8.00	3.60
245	Chris Mullin	15.00	6.75
246	Bill Wennington	8.00	3.60
247	Mark Jackson	12.00	5.50
248	Blue Edwards	8.00	3.60
249	Jalen Rose	20.00	9.00
250	Glenn Robinson	40.00	18.00
251	Kevin Willis CB	8.00	3.60
252	B.J. Armstrong CB ..	8.00	3.60
253	Jim Jackson CB	12.00	5.50
254	Steve Smith CB	8.00	3.60
255	Chris Webber CB	60.00	27.00
256	Glen Rice CB	25.00	11.00
257	Derek Harper CB	8.00	3.60
258	Jalen Rose CB	12.00	5.50

		MINT	NRMT
☐ 259	Juwan Howard CB... 40.00		18.00
☐ 260	Kenny Anderson 15.00		6.75
☐ 261	Calbert Cheaney 12.00		5.50
☐ 262	Bill Cartwright........ 8.00		3.60
☐ 263	Mario Elie 8.00		3.60
☐ 264	Chris Dudley........... 8.00		3.60
☐ 265	Jim Jackson 15.00		6.75
☐ 266	Antonio Harvey 8.00		3.60
☐ 267	Bill Curley............... 8.00		3.60
☐ 268	Moses Malone 15.00		6.75
☐ 269	A.C. Green 12.00		5.50
☐ 270	Larry Johnson 20.00		9.00
☐ 271	Marty Conlon.......... 8.00		3.60
☐ 272	Greg Graham........... 8.00		3.60
☐ 273	Eric Montross 8.00		3.60
☐ 274	Stacey King 8.00		3.60
☐ 275	Charles Barkley CB 20.00		9.00
☐ 276	Chris Morris CB....... 8.00		3.60
☐ 277	Robert Horry CB 8.00		3.60
☐ 278	Dominique Wilkins CB 12.00		5.50
☐ 279	Latrell Sprewell CB .. 8.00		3.60
☐ 280	Shaquille O'Neal CB 50.00		22.00
☐ 281	Wesley Person CB.. 12.00		5.50
☐ 282	M.Abdul-Rauf CB 8.00		3.60
☐ 283	Jamal Mashburn CB 15.00		6.75
☐ 284	Dale Ellis CB 8.00		3.60
☐ 285	Gary Payton.......... 80.00		36.00
☐ 286	Jason Kidd 160.00		70.00
☐ 287	Ken Norman 8.00		3.60
☐ 288	Juwan Howard 125.00		55.00
☐ 289	Lamond Murray...... 15.00		6.75
☐ 290	Clifford Robinson .. 12.00		5.50
☐ 291	Frank Brickowski..... 8.00		3.60
☐ 292	Adam Keefe 8.00		3.60
☐ 293	Ron Harper 12.00		5.50
☐ 294	Tom Hammonds 8.00		3.60
☐ 295	Otis Thorpe 12.00		5.50
☐ 296	Rick Mahorn 8.00		3.60
☐ 297	Alton Lister 8.00		3.60
☐ 298	Vinny Del Negro 8.00		3.60
☐ 299	Danny Ferry............ 8.00		3.60
☐ 300	John Starks 12.00		5.50
☐ 301	Duane Ferrell......... 8.00		3.60
☐ 302	Hersey Hawkins 12.00		5.50
☐ 303	Khalid Reeves 8.00		3.60
☐ 304	Anthony Peeler 8.00		3.60
☐ 305	Tim Hardaway........ 50.00		22.00
☐ 306	Rick Fox 8.00		3.60
☐ 307	Jay Humphries 8.00		3.60
☐ 308	Brian Shaw 8.00		3.60
☐ 309	Dan Schayes........... 8.00		3.60
☐ 310	Stacey Augmon....... 8.00		3.60
☐ 311	Oliver Miller............. 8.00		3.60
☐ 312	Pooh Richardson..... 8.00		3.60
☐ 313	Donyell Marshall.... 25.00		11.00
☐ 314	Aaron McKie 8.00		3.60
☐ 315	Mark Price............... 8.00		3.60
☐ 316	B.J. Tyler................. 8.00		3.60
☐ 317	Olden Polynice 8.00		3.60
☐ 318	Avery Johnson 8.00		3.60
☐ 319	Derek Strong 8.00		3.60
☐ 320	Toni Kukoc 50.00		22.00
☐ 321	Charlie Ward 15.00		6.75
☐ 322	Wesley Person 25.00		11.00
☐ 323	Eddie Jones 175.00		80.00
☐ 324	Horace Grant 12.00		5.50
☐ 325	M.Abdul-Rauf 8.00		3.60
☐ 326	Sharone Wright....... 8.00		3.60
☐ 327	Kevin Gamble 8.00		3.60
☐ 328	Sarunas Marciulionis 8.00		3.60
☐ 329	Harvey Grant 8.00		3.60
☐ 330	Bobby Hurley........... 8.00		3.60
☐ 331	Michael Jordan 400.00		180.00

1994-95 Finest Cornerstone

Randomly inserted in second series packs at a rate of one in every 24, cards from this 15-card standard-size set highlight

players who are foundations of their respective teams. The fronts have a color-action photo set against a multi-colored background. The backs have a color-photo and player information. Values provided below are for unpeeled cards. Peeled cards generally trade for ten to twenty-five percent less.

	MINT	NRMT
COMPLETE SET (15)	110.00	50.00
COMMON CARD (1-15)	4.00	1.80
SEMISTARS	5.00	2.20
UNLISTED STARS	6.00	2.70
SER.2 STATED ODDS 1:24		

		MINT	NRMT
☐ CS1	Shaquille O'Neal	25.00	11.00
☐ CS2	Alonzo Mourning	8.00	3.60
☐ CS3	Patrick Ewing	6.00	2.70
☐ CS4	Karl Malone...........	10.00	4.50
☐ CS5	Kenny Anderson	5.00	2.20
☐ CS6	Latrell Sprewell	4.00	1.80
☐ CS7	D.Mutombo..........	5.00	2.20
☐ CS8	Charles Barkley	10.00	4.50
☐ CS9	John Stockton	6.00	2.70
☐ CS10	Reggie Miller........	6.00	2.70
☐ CS11	Jamal Mashburn ...	5.00	2.20
☐ CS12	A.Hardaway.........	25.00	11.00
☐ CS13	Jim Jackson	4.00	1.80
☐ CS14	David Robinson	10.00	4.50
☐ CS15	Hakeem Olajuwon	12.00	5.50

1994-95 Finest Iron Men

Randomly inserted in first series packs at a rate of one in 24, cards from this 10-card standard-size set spotlight players who played at least 3,000 minutes during the 1993-94 NBA

season. These transparent cards have a front design much like the basic Finest cards with "Iron Man" at the top. The only design element on back is a small stat box at the bottom. Unlike most other 1994-95 Finest cards, Iron Men inserts have no protective coating.

	MINT	NRMT
COMPLETE SET (10)	40.00	18.00
COMMON CARD (1-10)	1.00	.45
SEMISTARS	2.00	.90
SER.1 STATED ODDS 1:24		

		MINT	NRMT
☐ 1	Shaquille O'Neal	12.00	5.50
☐ 2	Kenny Anderson	2.00	.90
☐ 3	Jim Jackson	2.00	.90
☐ 4	C.Weatherspoon	1.00	.45
☐ 5	Karl Malone	5.00	2.20
☐ 6	Dan Majerle	2.00	.90
☐ 7	A.Hardaway............	12.00	5.50
☐ 8	David Robinson	5.00	2.20
☐ 9	Latrell Sprewell	2.00	.90
☐ 10	Hakeem Olajuwon ...	6.00	2.70

1994-95 Finest Lottery Prize

Randomly inserted in second series packs at a rate of one in six, cards from this 22-card standard-size set showcase lottery picks who went on to become impact players. The fronts have a color-action photo with background having a large basketball surrounded by a variety of colors and stars. The backs have a color photo and player information with the words "Lottery Prize" set against a basketball. Values provided below are for unpeeled cards. Peeled cards generally trade for ten to twenty-five percent less.

	MINT	NRMT
COMPLETE SET (22)	50.00	22.00
COMMON CARD (1-22)	.75	.35
SEMISTARS	1.50	.70
UNLISTED STARS	2.50	1.10
SER.2 STATED ODDS 1:6		

		MINT	NRMT
☐ LP1	Patrick Ewing	2.50	1.10
☐ LP2	Chris Mullin.............	2.50	1.10
☐ LP3	David Robinson........	4.00	1.80

		MINT	NRMT
☐	LP4 Scottie Pippen......... 8.00	3.60
☐	LP5 Kevin Johnson 1.50	.70
☐	LP6 Danny Manning....... .75	.35
☐	LP7 Mitch Richmond 2.50	1.10
☐	LP8 Derrick Coleman 1.50	.70
☐	LP9 Gary Payton 4.00	1.80
☐	LP10 M.Abdul-Rauf .... .75	.35
☐	LP11 Larry Johnson....... 1.50	.70
☐	LP12 Kenny Anderson 1.50	.70
☐	LP13 D.Mutombo......... 2.50	1.10
☐	LP14 Stacey Augmon...... .75	.35
☐	LP15 Shaquille O'Neal .. 10.00	4.50
☐	LP16 Alonzo Mourning.... 3.00	1.35
☐	LP17 C.Weatherspoon ... .75	.35
☐	LP18 Robert Horry 1.50	.70
☐	LP19 Chris Webber 6.00	2.70
☐	LP20 A.Hardaway....... 10.00	4.50
☐	LP21 Jamal Mashburn ... 2.50	1.10
☐	LP22 Vin Baker............ 6.00	2.70

1994-95 Finest Marathon Men

Randomly inserted into first series packs at a rate of one in 12, cards from this 12-card standard-size set highlight players who played in all 82 games during the 1993-94 NBA season. These transparent cards have a design on front that is similar to the basic issue with the words "Marathon Man" at the top. The back contains a small stat box at the bottom. Unlike most other 1994-95 Finest cards, Marathon Men inserts have no protective coatings.

	MINT	NRMT
COMPLETE SET (20) 50.00	22.00
COMMON CARD (1-20) 1.25	.55
SEMISTARS 3.00	1.35
SER.1 STATED ODDS 1:12		

		MINT	NRMT
☐	1 Latrell Sprewell 3.00	1.35
☐	2 Gary Payton 8.00	3.60
☐	3 Kenny Anderson 3.00	1.35
☐	4 Jim Jackson 3.00	1.35
☐	5 Lindsey Hunter 3.00	1.35
☐	6 Rod Strickland 3.00	1.35
☐	7 Hersey Hawkins......... 3.00	1.35
☐	8 Gerald Wilkins 1.25	.55
☐	9 B.J. Armstrong 1.25	.55
☐	10 A.Hardaway............ 20.00	9.00
☐	11 Stacey Augmon 1.25	.55
☐	12 Eric Murdock........... 1.25	.55
☐	13 C.Weatherspoon 1.25	.55
☐	14 Karl Malone 8.00	3.60
☐	15 Charles Oakley......... 3.00	1.35
☐	16 Rick Fox 1.25	.55

		MINT	NRMT
☐	17 Otis Thorpe 3.00	1.35
☐	18 D.Mutombo............ 3.00	1.35
☐	19 Mike Brown............ 1.25	.55
☐	20 A.C. Green............ 3.00	1.35

1994-95 Finest Rack Pack

Randomly inserted in second series packs at a rate of one in every 72, cards from this seven-card standard-size set spotlight a selection of top performers from the 1994 NBA draft class. The fronts have a color-action photo with a basketball hoop and lights in the background. The words "Rack Pack" appear at the top in a red-foil. The backs have player information inside of a computer monitor. Like many of the Finest cards, these cards also came with a protective covering. The prices listed below are for peeled cards. Peeled cards generally trade for ten to twenty-five percent less.

	MINT	NRMT
COMPLETE SET (7) 120.00	55.00
COMMON CARD (1-7) 2.00	.90
SEMISTARS 5.00	2.20
SER.2 STATED ODDS 1:72		

		MINT	NRMT
☐	RP1 Grant Hill 60.00	27.00
☐	RP2 Wesley Person 5.00	2.20
☐	RP3 Juwan Howard 20.00	9.00
☐	RP4 Lamond Murray 2.00	.90
☐	RP5 Glenn Robinson 15.00	6.75
☐	RP6 Donyell Marshall..... 5.00	2.20
☐	RP7 Jason Kidd 30.00	13.50

1995-96 Finest

The 1995-96 Topps Finest set was issued in two separate series of 140 and 111 standard-size cards. Cards for both series were issued in 6-card packs (suggested retail price of $5.00). Each pack contained five basic cards and one Mystery insert card. Basic player cards feature blue-bordered metallic fronts and cut-out action shots set against a swirling court background. The Rookie subset cards (111-139) feature orange-bordered cards. Magic Johnson's card (#252) was added very late in the production schedule and unlike other player cards features a red border on front instead of blue. The checklist card (#111) has an uncorrected error - it should have been numbered 140 as the last card in the first series. Also, card #251, originally scheduled to be a checklist for the second series set, was never printed. Each card features an opaque coating that can be carefully peeled off designed to protect the card front from problems that may arise from handling. Values provided below are for unpeeled cards. Peeled cards generally trade for ten to twenty-five percent less. Noteworthy Rookie Cards include Michael Finley, Kevin Garnett, Joe Smith, Jerry Stackhouse and D.Stoudamire.

	MINT	NRMT
COMPLETE SET (251) 240.00	110.00
COMP.SERIES 1 (140) 200.00	90.00
COMP.SERIES 2 (111) 40.00	18.00
COMMON CARD (1-250/252).. .30	.14
SEMISTARS .... .60	.25
UNLISTED STARS 1.25	.55
UER CL 111 SHOULD BE NUMBERED 140		
NUMBER 251 NEVER ISSUED		

		MINT	NRMT
☐	1 Hakeem Olajuwon 2.50	1.10
☐	2 Stacey Augmon .... .30	.14
☐	3 John Starks .... .60	.25
☐	4 Sharone Wright .... .30	.14
☐	5 Jason Kidd 3.00	1.35
☐	6 Lamond Murray .... .30	.14
☐	7 Kenny Anderson .... .60	.25
☐	8 James Robinson .... .30	.14
☐	9 Wesley Person .... .60	.25
☐	10 Latrell Sprewell .... .60	.25
☐	11 Sean Elliott .... .30	.14
☐	12 Greg Anthony .... .30	.14
☐	13 Kendall Gill .... .60	.25
☐	14 Mark Jackson .... .60	.25
☐	15 John Stockton 1.25	.55
☐	16 Steve Smith........... .60	.25
☐	17 Bobby Hurley.......... .30	.14

☐ ☐ 18 Ervin Johnson	.30	.14	☐ 104 Christian Laettner	.60	.25	☐ 189 Glen Rice	1.25	.55
☐ 19 Elden Campbell	.60	.25	☐ 105 Horace Grant	.60	.25	☐ 190 Grant Hill	8.00	3.60
☐ 20 Vin Baker	2.50	1.10	☐ 106 Rony Seikaly	.30	.14	☐ 191 Michael Smith	.30	.14
☐ 21 Micheal Williams	.30	.14	☐ 107 Reggie Williams	.30	.14	☐ 192 Sean Rooks	.30	.14
☐ 22 Steve Kerr	.60	.25	☐ 108 Toni Kukoc	.60	.25	☐ 193 Clifford Rozier	.30	.14
☐ 23 Kevin Duckworth	.30	.14	☐ 109 Terrell Brandon	1.25	.55	☐ 194 Rik Smits	.60	.25
☐ 24 Willie Anderson	.30	.14	☐ 110 Clifford Robinson	.30	.14	☐ 195 Spud Webb	.60	.25
☐ 25 Joe Dumars	1.25	.55	☐ 111 Joe Smith	12.00	5.50	☐ 196 Aaron McKie	.30	.14
☐ 26 Dale Ellis	.30	.14	☐ 112 Antonio McDyess	18.00	8.00	☐ 197 Nate McMillan	.30	.14
☐ 27 Bimbo Coles	.30	.14	☐ 113 Jerry Stackhouse	12.00	5.50	☐ 198 Bobby Phills	.30	.14
☐ 28 Nick Anderson	.30	.14	☐ 114 Rasheed Wallace	12.00	5.50	☐ 199 Dennis Scott	.30	.14
☐ 29 Dee Brown	.30	.14	☐ 115 Kevin Garnett	85.00	38.00	☐ 200 Mark West	.30	.14
☐ 30 Tyrone Hill	.30	.14	☐ 116 Bryant Reeves	5.00	2.20	☐ 201 George McCloud	.30	.14
☐ 31 Reggie Miller	1.25	.55	☐ 117 D.Stoudamire	18.00	8.00	☐ 202 B.J. Tyler	.30	.14
☐ 32 Shaquille O'Neal	5.00	2.20	☐ 118 Shawn Respert	.30	.14	☐ 203 Lionel Simmons	.30	.14
☐ 33 Brian Grant	.60	.25	☐ 119 Ed O'Bannon	.30	.14	☐ 204 Loy Vaught	.30	.14
☐ 34 Charles Barkley	2.00	.90	☐ 120 Kurt Thomas	.60	.25	☐ 205 Kevin Edwards	.30	.14
☐ 35 Cedric Ceballos	.30	.14	☐ 121 Gary Trent	2.00	.90	☐ 206 Eric Montross	.30	.14
☐ 36 Rex Walters	.30	.14	☐ 122 Cherokee Parks	1.50	.70	☐ 207 Kenny Gattison	.30	.14
☐ 37 Kenny Smith	.30	.14	☐ 123 Corliss Williamson	8.00	3.60	☐ 208 Mario Elie	.30	.14
☐ 38 Popeye Jones	.30	.14	☐ 124 Eric Williams	2.50	1.10	☐ 209 Karl Malone	2.00	.90
☐ 39 Harvey Grant	.30	.14	☐ 125 Brent Barry	6.00	2.70	☐ 210 Ken Norman	.30	.14
☐ 40 Gary Payton	2.00	.90	☐ 126 Alan Henderson	5.00	2.20	☐ 211 Antonio Davis	.30	.14
☐ 41 John Williams	.30	.14	☐ 127 Bob Sura	3.00	1.35	☐ 212 Doc Rivers	.60	.25
☐ 42 Sherman Douglas	.30	.14	☐ 128 Theo Ratliff	3.00	1.35	☐ 213 Hubert Davis	.30	.14
☐ 43 Oliver Miller	.30	.14	☐ 129 Randolph Childress	.30	.14	☐ 214 Jamal Mashburn	.60	.25
☐ 44 Kevin Willis	.30	.14	☐ 130 Jason Caffey	4.00	1.80	☐ 215 Donyell Marshall	.60	.25
☐ 45 Isaiah Rider	.60	.25	☐ 131 Michael Finley	15.00	6.75	☐ 216 Sasha Danilovic	.30	.14
☐ 46 Gheorghe Muresan	.30	.14	☐ 132 George Zidek	.30	.14	☐ 217 Danny Manning	.60	.25
☐ 47 Blue Edwards	.30	.14	☐ 133 Travis Best	1.50	.70	☐ 218 Scott Burrell	.30	.14
☐ 48 Jeff Hornacek	.60	.25	☐ 134 Loren Meyer	.30	.14	☐ 219 Vlade Divac	.60	.25
☐ 49 J.R. Reid	.30	.14	☐ 135 David Vaughn	.30	.14	☐ 220 Marty Conlon	.30	.14
☐ 50 Glenn Robinson	1.50	.70	☐ 136 Sherrell Ford	.30	.14	☐ 221 C.Weatherspoon	.30	.14
☐ 51 Dell Curry	.30	.14	☐ 137 Mario Bennett	.30	.14	☐ 222 Terry Porter	.30	.14
☐ 52 Greg Graham	.30	.14	☐ 138 Greg Ostertag	.30	.14	☐ 223 Luc Longley	.60	.25
☐ 53 Ron Harper	.60	.25	☐ 139 Cory Alexander	2.00	.90	☐ 224 Juwan Howard	2.00	.90
☐ 54 Derek Harper	.60	.25	☐ 140 Checklist UER #111	.30	.14	☐ 225 Danny Ferry	.30	.14
☐ 55 D.Mutombo	.60	.25	☐ 141 Chucky Brown	.30	.14	☐ 226 Rod Strickland	.60	.25
☐ 56 Terry Mills	.30	.14	☐ 142 Eric Mobley	.30	.14	☐ 227 Bryant Stith	.30	.14
☐ 57 Victor Alexander	.30	.14	☐ 143 Tom Hammonds	.30	.14	☐ 228 Derrick McKey	.30	.14
☐ 58 Malik Sealy	.30	.14	☐ 144 Chris Webber	3.00	1.35	☐ 229 Michael Jordan	15.00	6.75
☐ 59 Vincent Askew	.30	.14	☐ 145 Carlos Rogers	.30	.14	☐ 230 Jamie Watson	.30	.14
☐ 60 Mitch Richmond	1.25	.55	☐ 146 Chuck Person	.30	.14	☐ 231 Rick Fox	.30	.14
☐ 61 Duane Ferrell	.30	.14	☐ 147 Brian Williams	.30	.14	☐ 232 Scott Williams	.30	.14
☐ 62 Dickey Simpkins	.30	.14	☐ 148 Kevin Gamble	.30	.14	☐ 233 Larry Johnson	.60	.25
☐ 63 Pooh Richardson	.30	.14	☐ 149 Dennis Rodman	8.00	3.60	☐ 234 A.Hardaway	5.00	2.20
☐ 64 Khalid Reeves	.30	.14	☐ 150 Pervis Ellison	.30	.14	☐ 235 Hersey Hawkins	.60	.25
☐ 65 Dino Radja	.30	.14	☐ 151 Jayson Williams	.60	.25	☐ 236 Robert Horry	.60	.25
☐ 66 Lee Mayberry	.30	.14	☐ 152 Buck Williams	.30	.14	☐ 237 Kevin Johnson	.60	.25
☐ 67 Kenny Gattison	.30	.14	☐ 153 Allan Houston	.60	.25	☐ 238 Rodney Rogers	.30	.14
☐ 68 Joe Kleine	.30	.14	☐ 154 Tom Gugliotta	1.25	.55	☐ 239 Detlef Schrempf	.60	.25
☐ 69 Tony Dumas	.30	.14	☐ 155 Charles Smith	.30	.14	☐ 240 Derrick Coleman	.60	.25
☐ 70 Nick Van Exel	1.25	.55	☐ 156 Chris Gatling	.30	.14	☐ 241 Walt Williams	.30	.14
☐ 71 Armon Gilliam	.30	.14	☐ 157 Darrin Hancock	.30	.14	☐ 242 LaPhonso Ellis	.60	.25
☐ 72 Craig Ehlo	.30	.14	☐ 158 Blue Edwards	.30	.14	☐ 243 Patrick Ewing	1.25	.55
☐ 73 Adam Keefe	.30	.14	☐ 159 Shawn Kemp	4.00	1.80	☐ 244 Grant Long	.30	.14
☐ 74 Chris Dudley	.30	.14	☐ 160 Michael Cage	.30	.14	☐ 245 David Robinson	2.00	.90
☐ 75 Clyde Drexler	1.50	.70	☐ 161 Sedale Threatt	.30	.14	☐ 246 Chris Mullin	1.25	.55
☐ 76 Jeff Turner	.30	.14	☐ 162 Byron Scott	.30	.14	☐ 247 Alonzo Mourning	1.25	.55
☐ 77 Calbert Cheaney	.30	.14	☐ 163 Elliot Perry	.30	.14	☐ 248 Dan Majerle	.30	.14
☐ 78 Vinny Del Negro	.30	.14	☐ 164 Jim Jackson	.60	.25	☐ 249 Johnny Newman	.30	.14
☐ 79 Tim Perry	.30	.14	☐ 165 Wayman Tisdale	.30	.14	☐ 250 Chris Morris	.30	.14
☐ 80 Tim Hardaway	1.50	.70	☐ 166 Vernon Maxwell	.30	.14	☐ 252 Magic Johnson	4.00	1.80
☐ 81 B.J. Armstrong	.30	.14	☐ 167 Brian Shaw	.30	.14			
☐ 82 Muggsy Bogues	.60	.25	☐ 168 Haywoode Workman	.30	.14			
☐ 83 Mark Macon	.30	.14	☐ 169 Mookie Blaylock	.60	.25			
☐ 84 Doug West	.30	.14	☐ 170 Donald Royal	.30	.14			
☐ 85 Jalen Rose	.60	.25	☐ 171 Lorenzo Williams	.30	.14			
☐ 86 Chris Mills	.30	.14	☐ 172 Eric Piatkowski UER	.30	.14			
☐ 87 Charles Oakley	.30	.14	Name spelled Paitkowski on back					
☐ 88 Andrew Lang	.30	.14	☐ 173 Sarunas Marciulionis	.30	.14			
☐ 89 Olden Polynice	.30	.14	☐ 174 Otis Thorpe	.60	.25			
☐ 90 Sam Cassell	.60	.25	☐ 175 Rex Chapman	.30	.14			
☐ 91 Todd Day	.30	.14	☐ 176 Felton Spencer	.30	.14			
☐ 92 P.J. Brown	.30	.14	☐ 177 John Salley	.30	.14			
☐ 93 Benoit Benjamin	.30	.14	☐ 178 Pete Chilcutt	.30	.14			
☐ 94 Sam Perkins	.30	.25	☐ 179 Scottie Pippen	4.00	1.80			
☐ 95 Eddie Jones	3.00	1.35	☐ 180 Robert Pack	.30	.14			
☐ 96 Robert Parish	.60	.25	☐ 181 Dana Barros	.30	.14			
☐ 97 Avery Johnson	.30	.14	☐ 182 M.Abdul-Rauf	.30	.14			
☐ 98 Lindsey Hunter	.30	.14	☐ 183 Eric Murdock	.30	.14			
☐ 99 Billy Owens	.30	.14	☐ 184 Anthony Mason	.60	.25			
☐ 100 Shawn Bradley	.30	.14	☐ 185 Will Perdue	.30	.14			
☐ 101 Dale Davis	.30	.14	☐ 186 Jeff Malone	.30	.14			
☐ 102 Terry Dehere	.30	.14	☐ 187 Anthony Peeler	.30	.14			
☐ 103 A.C. Green	.60	.25	☐ 188 Chris Childs	.30	.14			

1995-96 Finest Refractors

Parallel to cards 1-110, 141-250 and 252, Refractors were randomly inserted into first and second series packs at a rate of one in 12. For the first time ever, Topps decided to randomly seed entire 24-pack boxes full of Refractors into their cases. The insertion ratio of these Refractor "Hot Boxes" is one in every 450 boxes. None of the regular issue first series Rookie Cards (111-139) were given parallel

Refractor cards, thus the first series is complete at 110 cards. In addition, card #251 does not exist, thus the second series set is complete at 111 cards. The Magic Johnson card (#252) was inserted into one in every 216 packs, making it approximately six times easier to pull than other second series Refractors. Refractors are distinguished from the basic cards by their rainbow-like appearance that refracts more light. Just like regular issue cards, each Refractor comes with a protective coating to protect the card from wear and tear. Values provided below are for unpeeled cards. Peeled cards generally trade for ten to twenty-five percent less.

	MINT	NRMT
COMPLETE SET (221)	2000.00	900.00
COMP.SERIES 1 (110)	800.00	350.00
COMP.SERIES 2 (111)	1200.00	550.00
COMMON CARD	4.00	1.80
SEMISTARS	10.00	4.50
UNLISTED STARS	20.00	9.00
SER.1/2 STATED ODDS: 1:12 HOB, 1:18 RET		

#	Player	MINT	NRMT
1	Hakeem Olajuwon	40.00	18.00
2	Stacey Augmon	4.00	1.80
3	John Starks	10.00	4.50
4	Sharone Wright	4.00	1.80
5	Jason Kidd	50.00	22.00
6	Lamond Murray	4.00	1.80
7	Kenny Anderson	10.00	4.50
8	James Robinson	4.00	1.80
9	Wesley Person	10.00	4.50
10	Latrell Sprewell	10.00	4.50
11	Sean Elliott	4.00	1.80
12	Greg Anthony	4.00	1.80
13	Kendall Gill	10.00	4.50
14	Mark Jackson	4.00	1.80
15	John Stockton	20.00	9.00
16	Steve Smith	10.00	4.50
17	Bobby Hurley	4.00	1.80
18	Ervin Johnson	4.00	1.80
19	Elden Campbell	10.00	4.50
20	Vin Baker	40.00	18.00
21	Micheal Williams	4.00	1.80
22	Steve Kerr	10.00	4.50
23	Kevin Duckworth	4.00	1.80
24	Willie Anderson	4.00	1.80
25	Joe Dumars	20.00	9.00
26	Dale Ellis	4.00	1.80
27	Bimbo Coles	4.00	1.80
28	Nick Anderson	4.00	1.80
29	Dee Brown	4.00	1.80
30	Tyrone Hill	4.00	1.80
31	Reggie Miller	25.00	11.00
32	Shaquille O'Neal	75.00	34.00
33	Brian Grant	10.00	4.50
34	Charles Barkley	30.00	13.50
35	Cedric Ceballos	4.00	1.80
36	Rex Walters	4.00	1.80
37	Kenny Smith	4.00	1.80
38	Popeye Jones	4.00	1.80
39	Harvey Grant	4.00	1.80
40	Gary Payton	30.00	13.50
41	John Williams	4.00	1.80
42	Sherman Douglas	4.00	1.80
43	Oliver Miller	4.00	1.80
44	Kevin Willis	4.00	1.80
45	Isaiah Rider	10.00	4.50
46	Gheorghe Muresan	4.00	1.80
47	Blue Edwards	4.00	1.80
48	Jeff Hornacek	10.00	4.50
49	J.R. Reid	4.00	1.80
50	Glenn Robinson	25.00	11.00
51	Dell Curry	4.00	1.80
52	Greg Graham	4.00	1.80
53	Ron Harper	10.00	4.50
54	Derek Harper	10.00	4.50
55	D.Mutombo	10.00	4.50
56	Terry Mills	4.00	1.80
57	Victor Alexander	4.00	1.80
58	Malik Sealy	4.00	1.80
59	Vincent Askew	4.00	1.80
60	Mitch Richmond	25.00	11.00
61	Duane Ferrell	4.00	1.80
62	Dickey Simpkins	4.00	1.80
63	Pooh Richardson	4.00	1.80
64	Khalid Reeves	4.00	1.80
65	Dino Radja	4.00	1.80
66	Lee Mayberry	4.00	1.80
67	Kenny Gattison	4.00	1.80
68	Joe Kleine	4.00	1.80
69	Tony Dumas	4.00	1.80
70	Nick Van Exel	20.00	9.00
71	Armon Gilliam	4.00	1.80
72	Craig Ehlo	4.00	1.80
73	Adam Keefe	4.00	1.80
74	Chris Dudley	4.00	1.80
75	Clyde Drexler	25.00	11.00
76	Jeff Turner	4.00	1.80
77	Calbert Cheaney	4.00	1.80
78	Vinny Del Negro	4.00	1.80
79	Tim Perry	4.00	1.80
80	Tim Hardaway	25.00	11.00
81	B.J. Armstrong	4.00	1.80
82	Muggsy Bogues	10.00	4.50
83	Mark Macon	4.00	1.80
84	Doug West	4.00	1.80
85	Jalen Rose	10.00	4.50
86	Chris Mills	4.00	1.80
87	Charles Oakley	4.00	1.80
88	Andrew Lang	4.00	1.80
89	Olden Polynice	4.00	1.80
90	Sam Cassell	10.00	4.50
91	Todd Day	4.00	1.80
92	P.J. Brown	4.00	1.80
93	Benoit Benjamin	4.00	1.80
94	Sam Perkins	10.00	4.50
95	Eddie Jones	50.00	22.00
96	Robert Parish	10.00	4.50
97	Avery Johnson	4.00	1.80
98	Lindsey Hunter	4.00	1.80
99	Billy Owens	4.00	1.80
100	Shawn Bradley	10.00	4.50
101	Dale Davis	10.00	4.50
102	Terry Dehere	4.00	1.80
103	A.C. Green	10.00	4.50
104	Christian Laettner	10.00	4.50
105	Horace Grant	10.00	4.50
106	Rony Seikaly	4.00	1.80
107	Reggie Williams	4.00	1.80
108	Toni Kukoc	10.00	4.50
109	Terrell Brandon	20.00	9.00
110	Clifford Robinson	4.00	1.80
141	Charley Brown	4.00	1.80
142	Eric Mobley	4.00	1.80
143	Tom Hammonds	4.00	1.80
144	Chris Webber	50.00	22.00
145	Carlos Rogers	4.00	1.80
146	Chuck Person	4.00	1.80
147	Brian Williams	4.00	1.80
148	Kevin Gamble	4.00	1.80
149	Dennis Rodman	75.00	34.00
150	Pervis Ellison	4.00	1.80
151	Jayson Williams	10.00	4.50
152	Buck Williams	4.00	1.80
153	Allan Houston	10.00	4.50
154	Tom Gugliotta	20.00	9.00
155	Charles Smith	4.00	1.80
156	Chris Gatling	4.00	1.80
157	Darrin Hancock	4.00	1.80
158	Blue Edwards	4.00	1.80
159	Shawn Kemp	60.00	27.00
160	Michael Cage	4.00	1.80
161	Sedale Threatt	4.00	1.80
162	Byron Scott	10.00	4.50
163	Elliot Perry	4.00	1.80
164	Jim Jackson	12.00	5.50
165	Wayman Tisdale	4.00	1.80
166	Vernon Maxwell	4.00	1.80
167	Brian Shaw	4.00	1.80
168	Haywoode Workman	4.00	1.80
169	Mookie Blaylock	10.00	4.50
170	Donald Royal	4.00	1.80
171	Lorenzo Williams	4.00	1.80
172	Eric Piatkowski	4.00	1.80
173	Sarunas Marciulionis	4.00	1.80
174	Otis Thorpe	10.00	4.50
175	Rex Chapman	4.00	1.80
176	Felton Spencer	4.00	1.80
177	John Salley	4.00	1.80
178	Pete Chilcutt	4.00	1.80
179	Scottie Pippen	60.00	27.00
180	Robert Pack	4.00	1.80
181	Dana Barros	4.00	1.80
182	M.Abdul-Rauf	4.00	1.80
183	Eric Murdock	4.00	1.80
184	Anthony Mason	10.00	4.50
185	Will Perdue	4.00	1.80
186	Jeff Malone	4.00	1.80
187	Anthony Peeler	4.00	1.80
188	Chris Childs	4.00	1.80
189	Glen Rice	20.00	9.00
190	Grant Hill	125.00	55.00
191	Michael Smith	4.00	1.80
192	Sean Rooks	4.00	1.80
193	Clifford Rozier	4.00	1.80
194	Rik Smits	10.00	4.50
195	Spud Webb	4.00	1.80
196	Aaron McKie	4.00	1.80
197	Nate McMillan	4.00	1.80
198	Bobby Phills	4.00	1.80
199	Dennis Scott	4.00	1.80
200	Mark West	4.00	1.80
201	George McCloud	4.00	1.80
202	B.J. Tyler	4.00	1.80
203	Lionel Simmons	4.00	1.80
204	Loy Vaught	10.00	4.50
205	Kevin Edwards	4.00	1.80
206	Eric Montross	4.00	1.80
207	Kenny Gattison	4.00	1.80
208	Mario Elie	4.00	1.80
209	Karl Malone	30.00	13.50
210	Ken Norman	4.00	1.80
211	Antonio Davis	4.00	1.80
212	Doc Rivers	10.00	4.50
213	Hubert Davis	4.00	1.80
214	Jamal Mashburn	10.00	4.50
215	Donyell Marshall	4.00	1.80
216	Sasha Danilovic	4.00	1.80
217	Danny Manning	10.00	4.50
218	Scott Burrell	4.00	1.80
219	Vlade Divac	10.00	4.50
220	Marty Conlon	4.00	1.80
221	C.Weatherspoon	4.00	1.80
222	Terry Porter	4.00	1.80
223	Luc Longley	10.00	4.50
224	Juwan Howard	30.00	13.50
225	Danny Ferry	4.00	1.80
226	Rod Strickland	10.00	4.50
227	Bryant Stith	4.00	1.80
228	Derrick McKey	4.00	1.80
229	Michael Jordan	300.00	135.00
230	Jamie Watson	4.00	1.80
231	Rick Fox	4.00	1.80
232	Scott Williams	4.00	1.80

			MINT	NRMT
☐	233	Larry Johnson	10.00	4.50
☐	234	A.Hardaway	75.00	34.00
☐	235	Hersey Hawkins	10.00	4.50
☐	236	Robert Horry	4.00	1.80
☐	237	Kevin Johnson	10.00	4.50
☐	238	Rodney Rogers	4.00	1.80
☐	239	Detlef Schrempf	10.00	4.50
☐	240	Derrick Coleman	10.00	4.50
☐	241	Walt Williams	4.00	1.80
☐	242	LaPhonso Ellis	10.00	4.50
☐	243	Patrick Ewing	20.00	9.00
☐	244	Grant Long	4.00	1.80
☐	245	David Robinson	30.00	13.50
☐	246	Chris Mullin	12.00	5.50
☐	247	Alonzo Mourning	20.00	9.00
☐	248	Dan Majerle	4.00	1.80
☐	249	Johnny Newman	4.00	1.80
☐	250	Chris Morris	4.00	1.80
☐	251	Checklist	4.00	1.80
☐	252	Magic Johnson 6P	25.00	11.00

1995-96 Finest Dish and Swish

Randomly inserted into first series packs at a rate of one in 24, cards from this dual-sided, 29-card standard-size set feature combinations of two key players from each NBA team. Each side features one of the two players in game action, with the words "Dish" or "Swish" along the bottom. Values provided below are for unpeeled cards. Peeled cards generally trade for ten to twenty-five percent less. The set is sequenced in alphabetical order by team.

	MINT	NRMT
COMPLETE SET (29)	400.00	180.00
COMMON CARD (DS1-DS29)	3.00	1.35
SEMISTARS	5.00	2.20
UNLISTED STARS	8.00	3.60
SER.1 STATED ODDS 1:24		

			MINT	NRMT
☐	DS1	Mookie Blaylock	3.00	1.35
		Steve Smith		
☐	DS2	Sherman Douglas	3.00	1.35
		Dino Radja		
☐	DS3	Muggsy Bogues	5.00	2.20
		Larry Johnson		
☐	DS4	Scottie Pippen	100.00	45.00
		Michael Jordan		
☐	DS5	Mark Price	3.00	1.35

			MINT	NRMT
		Chris Mills		
☐	DS6	Jason Kidd	20.00	9.00
		Jamal Mashburn		
☐	DS7	M.Abdul-Rauf	3.00	1.35
		D.Mutombo		
☐	DS8	Grant Hill	50.00	22.00
		Joe Dumars		
☐	DS9	Tim Hardaway	10.00	4.50
		Chris Mullin		
☐	DS10	Clyde Drexler	25.00	11.00
		Hakeem Olajuwon		
☐	DS11	Mark Jackson	8.00	3.60
		Reggie Miller		
☐	DS12	Pooh Richardson	3.00	1.35
		Lamond Murray		
☐	DS13	Nick Van Exel	8.00	3.60
		Cedric Ceballos		
☐	DS14	Glen Rice	8.00	3.60
		Khalid Reeves		
☐	DS15	Glenn Robinson	10.00	4.50
		Eric Murdock		
☐	DS16	Tom Gugliotta	6.00	2.70
		Christian Laettner		
☐	DS17	Kenny Anderson	5.00	2.20
		Derrick Coleman		
☐	DS18	Patrick Ewing	8.00	3.60
		Derek Harper		
☐	DS19	A.Hardaway	60.00	27.00
		Shaquille O'Neal		
☐	DS20	Dana Barros	3.00	1.35
		C.Weatherspoon		
☐	DS21	Kevin Johnson	12.00	5.50
		Charles Barkley		
☐	DS22	Rod Strickland	5.00	2.20
		Clifford Robinson		
☐	DS23	Mitch Richmond	8.00	3.60
		Walt Williams		
☐	DS24	Avery Johnson	12.00	5.50
		David Robinson		
☐	DS25	Gary Payton	30.00	13.50
		Shawn Kemp		
☐	DS26	B.J.Armstrong	3.00	1.35
		Oliver Miller		
☐	DS27	John Stockton	20.00	9.00
		Karl Malone		
☐	DS28	Greg Anthony	3.00	1.35
		Byron Scott		
☐	DS29	Juwan Howard	30.00	13.50
		Chris Webber		

1995-96 Finest Hot Stuff

Randomly inserted into first series packs at a rate of one in nine, cards from this 15-card standard-size set highlight some of the NBA's top stars in slam-dunk action. Orange-bordered

fronts feature game action shots. The words "Hot Stuff" run down the left hand side of the card front. Values provided below are for unpeeled cards. Peeled cards generally trade for ten to twenty-five percent less.

	MINT	NRMT
COMPLETE SET (15)	60.00	27.00
COMMON CARD (HS1-HS15)	1.00	.45
SEMISTARS	1.25	.55
SER.1 STATED ODDS 1:9		

			MINT	NRMT
☐	HS1	Michael Jordan	25.00	11.00
☐	HS2	Grant Hill	12.00	5.50
☐	HS3	Clyde Drexler	2.50	1.10
☐	HS4	A.Hardaway	8.00	3.60
☐	HS5	Sean Elliott	1.00	.45
☐	HS6	Latrell Sprewell	1.25	.55
☐	HS7	Larry Johnson	1.25	.55
☐	HS8	Eddie Jones	5.00	2.20
☐	HS9	Karl Malone	3.00	1.35
☐	HS10	John Starks	1.25	.55
☐	HS11	Scottie Pippen	6.00	2.70
☐	HS12	Shawn Kemp	6.00	2.70
☐	HS13	Chris Webber	5.00	2.20
☐	HS14	Isaiah Rider	1.25	.55
☐	HS15	Robert Horry	1.00	.45

1995-96 Finest Mystery

Inserted at a rate of one in every first and second series pack, cards from this 44-piece standard-size set were 1.25 times easier to pull than regular issue cards. The set contains a selection of some of the NBA's top stars and rookies. The first twenty-two cards, issued exclusively in first series packs, were designed in three different parallel styles (Bordered, Borderless and Borderless Refractors). The last twenty-two cards, issued exclusively in second series packs, were also designed in three different parallel styles (Bronze, Silver and Gold). Collectors had to peel off a dark protective coating to find

out what version of the card they had obtained. The first series Mystery cards feature a radically different design to the second series. Each first series Bordered card front features a bronze outline, framing a cut-out action shot of the player against a metallic basketball background. The second series Bronze cards feature a mosaic-style, tiled border with bronze-colored features, framing a cut-out action shot of the player. The prices listed below are for the more common Bordered and Bronze cards. Values provided below are for peeled cards.

	MINT	NRMT
COMPLETE SET (44)	50.00	22.00
COMP.BORDER.SER.1 (22)	30.00	13.50
COMP.BRONZE SER.2 (22)	20.00	9.00
COMMON BORDER (M1-M22)	.50	.23
COMMON BRONZE (M23-M44)	.40	.18
SEMISTARS SER.1	.60	.25
SEMISTARS SER.2	.50	.23
UNLISTED STARS SER.1	1.00	.45
UNLISTED STARS SER.2	.75	.35
ONE BORDER PER SER.1 PACK		
ONE BRONZE PER SER.2 PACK		
COMP.BDLS/SILV.SET (44)	325.00	145.00
COMP.BDLS.SER.1 (22)	200.00	90.00
COMP.SILVER SER.2 (22)	125.00	55.00
*BDLS./SILVER: 2X TO 5X HI COLUMN		
*SILVER RCs: 1.5X TO 4X HI		
BDLS: SER.1 STATED ODDS 1:24		
SILVER: SER.2 STATED ODDS 1:24		

		MINT	NRMT
☐ M1	Michael Jordan	12.00	5.50
☐ M2	Grant Hill	6.00	2.70
☐ M3	A.Hardaway	4.00	1.80
☐ M4	Shawn Kemp	3.00	1.35
☐ M5	Kenny Anderson	.60	.25
☐ M6	Charles Barkley	1.50	.70
☐ M7	Latrell Sprewell	.60	.25
☐ M8	Chris Webber	2.50	1.10
☐ M9	Jason Kidd	2.50	1.10
☐ M10	Glenn Robinson	1.25	.55
☐ M11	David Robinson	1.50	.70
☐ M12	Karl Malone	1.50	.70
☐ M13	Larry Johnson	.75	.35
☐ M14	Reggie Miller	1.00	.45
☐ M15	Scottie Pippen	3.00	1.35
☐ M16	Patrick Ewing	1.00	.45
☐ M17	Mitch Richmond	1.00	.45
☐ M18	Glen Rice	1.00	.45
☐ M19	Jamal Mashburn	.75	.35
☐ M20	Juwan Howard	1.50	.70
☐ M21	Hakeem Olajuwon	2.00	.90
☐ M22	Shaquille O'Neal	4.00	1.80
☐ M23	Alonzo Mourning	.75	.35
☐ M24	Dennis Rodman	5.00	2.20
☐ M25	Joe Dumars	.75	.35
☐ M26	Tim Hardaway	1.00	.45
☐ M27	Clyde Drexler	1.00	.45
☐ M28	Jerry Stackhouse	2.50	1.10
☐ M29	John Stockton	.75	.35
☐ M30	Derrick Coleman	.50	.23
☐ M31	Michael Finley	2.50	1.10
☐ M32	Glen Rice	.75	.35
☐ M33	M.Abdul-Rauf	.40	.18
☐ M34	Anthony Mason	.50	.23
☐ M35	Nick Van Exel	.75	.35
☐ M36	Vin Baker	1.50	.70
☐ M37	Horace Grant	.50	.23
☐ M38	John Starks	.50	.23
☐ M39	C.Weatherspoon	.40	.18
☐ M40	Kevin Johnson	.50	.23
☐ M41	Joe Smith	2.50	1.10

		MINT	NRMT
☐ M42	D.Mutombo	.50	.23
☐ M43	D.Stoudamire	5.00	2.20
☐ M44	Antonio McDyess	3.00	1.35

1995-96 Finest Mystery Borderless Refractors/Gold

Randomly inserted into first and second series hobby packs at a rate of one in 96 and retail at one in 80, cards from this 44-card set parallel the more common Mystery Bordered/Bronze issue. Unlike the first series bordered cards, Borderless Refractor card fronts feature an action cutout against a full-bleed, prismatic, metallic basketball background. The second series Gold cards differ from the common second series Bronze cards with their brighter Gold framed front borders. Also, the words "gold" run in small repetitive type diagonally across the background of each card front. The more common Bronze cards have the word "bronze" running across the card fronts. Values provided below are for peeled cards.

		MINT	NRMT
COMP.SET (44)		1400.00	650.00
COMP.BDLS.RF.SER.1 (22)		1000.00	450.00
COMP.GOLD SER.2 (22)		400.00	180.00
COMMON BDLS.RF (M1-M22)		12.00	5.50
COMMON GOLD (M23-M44)		8.00	3.60
SEMISTARS SER.1		15.00	6.75
SEMISTARS SER.2		10.00	4.50
UNLISTED STARS SER.1		25.00	11.00
UNLISTED STARS SER.2		15.00	6.75
BDLS RF: SER.1 STATED ODDS 1:96			
GOLD: SER.2 STATED ODDS 1:96			
CONDITION SENSITIVE SET			

		MINT	NRMT
☐ M1	Michael Jordan	300.00	135.00
☐ M2	Grant Hill	150.00	70.00
☐ M3	A.Hardaway	100.00	45.00
☐ M4	Shawn Kemp	60.00	27.00
☐ M5	Kenny Anderson	15.00	6.75
☐ M6	Charles Barkley	40.00	18.00
☐ M7	Latrell Sprewell	15.00	6.75
☐ M8	Chris Webber	60.00	27.00
☐ M9	Jason Kidd	60.00	27.00

		MINT	NRMT
☐ M10	Glenn Robinson	30.00	13.50
☐ M11	David Robinson	30.00	13.50
☐ M12	Karl Malone	40.00	18.00
☐ M13	Larry Johnson	15.00	6.75
☐ M14	Reggie Miller	25.00	11.00
☐ M15	Scottie Pippen	80.00	36.00
☐ M16	Patrick Ewing	25.00	11.00
☐ M17	Mitch Richmond	25.00	11.00
☐ M18	Glen Rice	25.00	11.00
☐ M19	Jamal Mashburn	15.00	6.75
☐ M20	Juwan Howard	40.00	18.00
☐ M21	Hakeem Olajuwon	50.00	22.00
☐ M22	Shaquille O'Neal	100.00	45.00
☐ M25	Joe Dumars	15.00	6.75
☐ M26	Tim Hardaway	20.00	9.00
☐ M27	Clyde Drexler	20.00	9.00
☐ M28	Jerry Stackhouse	30.00	13.50
☐ M29	John Stockton	15.00	6.75
☐ M30	Derrick Coleman	10.00	4.50
☐ M31	Michael Finley	30.00	13.50
☐ M32	Glen Rice	15.00	6.75
☐ M33	M.Abdul-Rauf	8.00	3.60
☐ M34	Anthony Mason	10.00	4.50
☐ M35	Nick Van Exel	15.00	6.75
☐ M36	Vin Baker	30.00	13.50
☐ M37	Horace Grant	10.00	4.50
☐ M38	John Starks	10.00	4.50
☐ M39	C.Weatherspoon	8.00	3.60
☐ M40	Kevin Johnson	10.00	4.50
☐ M41	Joe Smith	30.00	13.50
☐ M42	D.Mutombo	10.00	4.50
☐ M43	D.Stoudamire	60.00	27.00
☐ M44	Antonio McDyess	40.00	18.00

1995-96 Finest Rack Pack

Randomly inserted into packs at a rate of one in 72, cards from this 7-card set features a selection of top rookies from the 1995-96 campaign. Card fronts feature a colorful "swirl-like" background with a player photo and the set name "Rack Pack" underneath the photo. Card backs feature biographical information, a headshot and a brief commentary. Values below are for unpeeled cards. Peeled cards generally trade for ten to twenty-five percent less.

		MINT	NRMT
COMPLETE SET (7)		100.00	45.00
COMMON CARD (RP1-RP7)		5.00	2.20
SER.2 STATED ODDS 1:72 HOB, 1:96 RET			
☐ RP1	Jerry Stackhouse	15.00	6.75
☐ RP2	Brent Barry	5.00	2.20
☐ RP3	D.Stoudamire	30.00	13.50

RP4 Joe Smith 15.00 6.75
RP5 Michael Finley 15.00 6.75
RP6 Antonio McDyess ... 20.00 9.00
RP7 Rasheed Wallace .. 10.00 4.50

1995-96 Finest Veteran/Rookie

Randomly inserted in second series packs at a rate of one in 24, this 29-card set features rookie/veteran duos from a selection of NBA teams. The cards are dual-sided with each player getting a full photo on a separate side. Prices provided below are for unpeeled cards. Peeled cards generally trade for about ten to twenty-five percent less.

	MINT	NRMT
COMPLETE SET (29)	450.00	200.00
COMMON CARD (RV1-RV29)	4.00	1.80
SEMISTARS	6.00	2.70
UNLISTED STARS	10.00	4.50

SER.2 STATED ODDS 1:24 HOB, 1:18 RET

□ RV1 Joe Smith 20.00 9.00
   Latrell Sprewell
□ RV2 Antonio McDyess .. 25.00 11.00
   D.Mutombo
□ RV3 Jerry Stackhouse .. 20.00 9.00
   C.Weatherspoon
□ RV4 Rasheed Wallace .. 25.00 11.00
   Chris Webber
□ RV5 Kevin Garnett 60.00 27.00
   Tim Gugliotta
□ RV6 Bryant Reeves 10.00 4.50
   Greg Anthony
□ RV7 D.Stoudamire 30.00 13.50
   Willie Anderson
□ RV8 Shawn Respert 20.00 9.00
   Vin Baker
□ RV9 Ed O'Bannon 4.00 1.80
   Armon Gilliam
□ RV10 Kurt Thomas 10.00 4.50
   Alonzo Mourning
□ RV11 Gary Trent 6.00 2.70
   Rod Strickland
□ RV12 Cherokee Parks ... 6.00 2.70
   Jamal Mashburn
□ RV13 Corliss Williamson 10.00 4.50
   Mitch Richmond
□ RV14 Eric Williams 4.00 1.80
   Dino Radja
□ RV15 Brent Barry 6.00 2.70
   Loy Vaught
□ RV16 Alan Henderson ... 6.00 2.70
   Mookie Blaylock

□ RV17 Bob Sura............. 6.00 2.70
   Terrell Brandon
□ RV18 Theo Ratliff 50.00 22.00
   Grant Hill
□ RV19 Randolph Childress 6.00 2.70
   Rod Strickland
□ RV20 Jason Caffey 100.00 45.00
   Michael Jordan
□ RV21 Michael Finley 20.00 9.00
   Kevin Johnson
□ RV22 George Zidek 6.00 2.70
   Larry Johnson
□ RV23 Travis Best 10.00 4.50
   Reggie Miller
□ RV24 Loren Meyer 20.00 9.00
   Jason Kidd
□ RV25 David Vaughn 30.00 13.50
   Shaquille O'Neal
□ RV26 Sherell Ford 25.00 11.00
   Shawn Kemp
□ RV27 Mario Bennett 15.00 6.75
   Charles Barkley
□ RV28 Greg Ostertag 15.00 6.75
   Karl Malone
□ RV29 Cory Alexander 12.00 5.50
   David Robinson

1996-97 Finest

The 1996-97 Finest set was issued in two series totaling 291 cards. The 6-card packs retail for $5.00 each. The series one set is divided into 3-tiers of collectiblity with B1-B100 defined as "common" cards, S101-S127 defined as "uncommon" and inserted at a rate of 1:4 packs and G128-G146 defined as "rare" and inserted at a rate of 1:24 packs. Each card is also arranged into individually designed theme sets - Gladiators, Maestros, Apprentices and Sterling. The series two set is also divided into 3-tiers of collectiblity with cards B147-B246 defined as "common", S247-S273 defined as "uncommon" and inserted at a rate of 1:4 packs and G274-G291 defined as "rare" and inserted at a rate of 1:24 packs. Each card is also arranged into individually designed theme sets - Mainstays, Sterling, Heirs and Foundations. Prices below are for unpeeled cards. Peeled cards generally trade for ten to twenty-five percent less. Card numbers 7 and 134 do not exist. The Christian Laettner bronze, Patrick Ewing gold and Jeff Hornacek gold were all numbered 136. Card number 269 (Kobe Bryant gold) is considered part of the gold set, while card number 289 (Shaquille O'Neal silver) is considered part of the silver set, though they are both out of "set" order. The set is condition sensitive.

	MINT	NRMT
COMPLETE SET (291)	1400.00	650.00
COMPLETE SER.1 (146)	700.00	325.00
COMPLETE SERIES 2 (145)	700.00	325.00
COMP.BRONZE SET (200)	240.00	110.00
COMP.BRONZE SER.1 (100)	200.00	90.00
COMP.BRONZE SER.2 (100)	40.00	18.00
COMMON BRONZE............	.30	.14
SEMISTARS BRONZE..........	.40	.18
UNLISTED STARS BRONZE ...	.60	.25
COMP.SILVER SET (54)....	190.00	85.00
COMP.SILVER SER.1 (27) ..	70.00	32.00
COMP.SILVER SER.2 (27)	120.00	55.00
COMMON SILVER	1.25	.55
SEMISTARS SILVER	1.50	.70
UNLISTED STARS SILVER	2.50	1.10

SILVER: SER.1/2 STATED ODDS 1:4

	MINT	NRMT
COMP.GOLD SET (37)	1000.00	450.00
COMP.GOLD SER.1 (19) ..	450.00	200.00
COMP.GOLD SER.2 (18) ..	550.00	250.00
COMMON GOLD.................	6.00	2.70
SEMISTARS GOLD	8.00	3.60
UNLISTED STARS GOLD	10.00	4.50

GOLD: SER.1/2 STATED ODDS 1:24
CARD NUMBERS 7 AND 134 DO NOT EXIST
LAETTNER B, EWING G AND HORNACEK G NUMBERED 136
NUMBER 269 PART OF GOLD SET
NUMBER 289 PART OF SILVER SET
CONDITION SENSITIVE SET

□ 1 Scottie Pippen B ... 2.00 .90
□ 2 Tim Legler B .... .30 .14
□ 3 Rex Walters B .... .30 .14
□ 4 Calbert Cheaney B .. .30 .14
□ 5 Dennis Rodman B .. 2.50 1.10
□ 6 Tyrone Hill B .... .30 .14
□ 8 Dell Curry B .... .30 .14
□ 9 Olden Polynice B .... .30 .14
□ 10 John Wallace B 5.00 2.20
□ 11 Martin Muursepp B .30 .14
□ 12 Chuck Person B...... .30 .14
□ 13 Grant Hill B 4.00 1.80
□ 14 Shawn Kemp B ..... 2.00 .90
□ 15 B.J. Armstrong B .. .30 .14
□ 16 Gary Trent B .... .30 .14
□ 17 Scott Williams B .... .30 .14
□ 18 Dino Radja B .... .30 .14
□ 19 Roy Rogers B .... 1.00 .45
□ 20 Tony Delk B........... 3.00 1.35
□ 21 Clifford Robinson B. .30 .14
□ 22 Ray Allen B 12.00 5.50
□ 23 Clyde Drexler B .... .75 .35
□ 24 Elliot Perry B .... .30 .14
□ 25 Gary Payton B ...... 1.00 .45
□ 26 Dale Davis B .... .30 .14
□ 27 Horace Grant B ..... .40 .18
□ 28 Brian Evans B ...... 1.00 .45
□ 29 Joe Smith B........... .75 .35
□ 30 Reggie Miller B ..... .60 .25
□ 31 Jermaine O'Neal B.... 4.00 1.80
□ 32 Avery Johnson B .... .30 .14
□ 33 Ed O'Bannon B ...... .30 .14
□ 34 Cedric Ceballos B ... .30 .14
□ 35 Jamal Mashburn B .. .40 .18
□ 36 Michael Williams B .. .30 .14

☐ 37	Detlef Schrempf B	.40	.18
☐ 38	D.Stoudamire B	1.50	.70
☐ 39	Jason Kidd B	1.25	.55
☐ 40	Tom Gugliotta B	.60	.25
☐ 41	Arvydas Sabonis B	.40	.18
☐ 42	Samaki Walker B	2.00	.90
☐ 43	Derek Fisher B	4.00	1.80
☐ 44	Patrick Ewing B	.60	.25
☐ 45	Bryant Reeves B	.40	.18
☐ 46	Mookie Blaylock B	.40	.18
☐ 47	George Zidek B	.30	.14
☐ 48	Jerry Stackhouse B	.75	.35
☐ 49	Vin Baker B	1.25	.55
☐ 50	Michael Jordan B	10.00	4.50
☐ 51	Terrell Brandon B	.60	.25
☐ 52	Karl Malone B	1.00	.45
☐ 53	Lorenzen Wright B	3.00	1.35
☐ 54	S.Abdur-Rahim B	18.00	8.00
☐ 55	Kurt Thomas B	.30	.14
☐ 56	Glen Rice B	.60	.25
☐ 57	Shawn Bradley B	.30	.14
☐ 58	Todd Fuller B	.30	.14
☐ 59	Dale Ellis B	.30	.14
☐ 60	David Robinson B	1.00	.45
☐ 61	Doug Christie B	.30	.14
☐ 62	Stephon Marbury B	25.00	11.00
☐ 63	Hakeem Olajuwon B	1.25	.55
☐ 64	Lindsey Hunter B	.30	.14
☐ 65	A.Hardaway B	2.50	1.10
☐ 66	Kevin Garnett B	5.00	2.20
☐ 67	Kendall Gill B	.40	.18
☐ 68	Sean Elliott B	.30	.14
☐ 69	Allen Iverson B	25.00	11.00
☐ 70	Erick Dampier B	3.00	1.35
☐ 71	Jerome Williams B	1.00	.45
☐ 72	Charles Jones B	.30	.14
☐ 73	Danny Manning B	.40	.18
☐ 74	Kobe Bryant B	80.00	36.00
☐ 75	Steve Nash B	5.00	2.20
☐ 76	Sam Perkins B	.40	.18
☐ 77	Horace Grant B	.40	.18
☐ 78	Alonzo Mourning B	.60	.25
☐ 79	Kerry Kittles B	8.00	3.60
☐ 80	LaPhonso Ellis B	.30	.14
☐ 81	Michael Finley B	.75	.35
☐ 82	Marcus Camby B	8.00	3.60
☐ 83	Antonio McDyess B.	1.00	.45
☐ 84	Antoine Walker B	30.00	13.50
☐ 85	Juwan Howard B	.75	.35
☐ 86	Bryon Russell B	.30	.14
☐ 87	Walter McCarty B	4.00	1.80
☐ 88	Priest Lauderdale B	.30	.14
☐ 89	C.Weatherspoon B	.30	.14
☐ 90	John Stockton B	.60	.25
☐ 91	Mitch Richmond B	.60	.25
☐ 92	Dontae' Jones B	1.50	.70
☐ 93	Michael Smith B	.30	.14
☐ 94	Brent Barry B	.30	.14
☐ 95	Chris Mills B	.30	.14
☐ 96	Dee Brown B	.30	.14
☐ 97	Terry Dehere B	.30	.14
☐ 98	Danny Ferry B	.30	.14
☐ 99	Gheorghe Muresan B	.30	.14
☐ 100	Checklist B	.30	.14
☐ 101	Jim Jackson S	1.50	.70
☐ 102	Cedric Ceballos S	1.25	.55
☐ 103	Glen Rice S	2.50	1.10
☐ 104	Tom Gugliotta S	2.50	1.10
☐ 105	Mario Elie S	1.25	.55
☐ 106	Nick Anderson S	1.25	.55
☐ 107	Glenn Robinson S	2.50	1.10
☐ 108	Terrell Brandon S	2.50	1.10
☐ 109	Tim Hardaway S	3.00	1.35
☐ 110	John Stockton S	2.50	1.10
☐ 111	Brent Barry S	1.25	.55
☐ 112	Mookie Blaylock S	1.50	.70
☐ 113	Tyus Edney S	1.25	.55
☐ 114	Gary Payton S	4.00	1.80
☐ 115	Joe Smith S	3.00	1.35
☐ 116	Karl Malone S	4.00	1.80
☐ 117	Dino Radja S	1.25	.55
☐ 118	Alonzo Mourning S	2.50	1.10
☐ 119	Bryant Stith S	1.25	.55
☐ 120	Derrick McKey S	1.25	.55
☐ 121	Clyde Drexler S	3.00	1.35
☐ 122	Michael Finley S	3.00	1.35
☐ 123	Sean Elliott S	1.25	.55
☐ 124	Hakeem Olajuwon S	5.00	2.20
☐ 125	Joe Dumars S	2.50	1.10
☐ 126	Shawn Bradley S	1.25	.55
☐ 127	Michael Jordan S	30.00	13.50
☐ 128	Latrell Sprewell G	8.00	3.60
☐ 129	A.Hardaway G	40.00	18.00
☐ 130	Grant Hill G	60.00	27.00
☐ 131	D.Stoudamire G	20.00	9.00
☐ 132	David Robinson G	15.00	6.75
☐ 133	Scottie Pippen G	30.00	13.50
☐ 134	Jason Kidd G	20.00	9.00
☐ 136A	Jeff Hornacek G	6.00	2.70
☐ 136B	P.Ewing G UER	10.00	4.50
	Should be card number 134		
☐ 136C	C.Laettner B UER	8.00	3.60
	Should be card number 7		
☐ 137	Jerry Stackhouse G	12.00	5.50
☐ 138	Kevin Garnett G	60.00	27.00
☐ 139	Mitch Richmond G	10.00	4.50
☐ 140	Juwan Howard G	15.00	6.75
☐ 141	Reggie Miller G	10.00	4.50
☐ 142	Christian Laettner G	8.00	3.60
☐ 143	Vin Baker G	20.00	9.00
☐ 144	Shawn Kemp G	30.00	13.50
☐ 145	Dennis Rodman G	40.00	18.00
☐ 146	Shaquille O'Neal G	40.00	18.00
☐ 147	Mookie Blaylock B	.40	.18
☐ 148	Derek Harper B	.30	.14
☐ 149	Gerald Wilkins B	.30	.14
☐ 150	Adam Keefe B	.30	.14
☐ 151	Billy Owens B	.30	.14
☐ 152	Terrell Brandon B	.60	.25
☐ 153	Antonio Davis B	.30	.14
☐ 154	Muggsy Bogues B	.30	.14
☐ 155	Cherokee Parks B	.30	.14
☐ 156	Rasheed Wallace B	.40	.18
☐ 157	Lee Mayberry B	.30	.14
☐ 158	Craig Ehlo B	.30	.14
☐ 159	Todd Fuller B	.30	.14
☐ 160	Charles Barkley B	1.00	.45
☐ 161	Glenn Robinson B	.60	.25
☐ 162	Charles Oakley B	.30	.14
☐ 163	Chris Webber B	1.50	.70
☐ 164	Frank Brickowski B	.30	.14
☐ 165	Mark Jackson B	.30	.14
☐ 166	Jayson Williams B	.40	.18
☐ 167	C.Weatherspoon B	.30	.14
☐ 168	Toni Kukoc B	.40	.18
☐ 169	Alan Henderson B	.30	.14
☐ 170	Tony Delk B	.60	.25
☐ 171	Jamal Mashburn B	.40	.18
☐ 172	Vinny Del Negro B	.30	.14
☐ 173	Greg Ostertag B	.30	.14
☐ 174	Shawn Bradley B	.30	.14
☐ 175	Gheorghe Muresan B	.30	.14
☐ 176	Brent Price B	.30	.14
☐ 177	Rick Fox B	.30	.14
☐ 178	Stacey Augmon B	.30	.14
☐ 179	P.J. Brown B	.30	.14
☐ 180	Jim Jackson B	.40	.18
☐ 181	Hersey Hawkins B	.40	.18
☐ 182	Danny Manning B	.40	.18
☐ 183	Dennis Scott B	.30	.14
☐ 184	Tom Gugliotta B	.60	.25
☐ 185	Tyrone Hill B	.30	.14
☐ 186	Malik Sealy B	.30	.14
☐ 187	John Starks B	.40	.18
☐ 188	Mark Price B	.40	.18
☐ 189	Elden Campbell B	.40	.18
☐ 190	M.Abdul-Rauf B	.30	.14
☐ 191	Will Perdue B	.30	.14
☐ 192	Nate McMillan B	.30	.14
☐ 193	Robert Horry B	.40	.18
☐ 194	Dino Radja B	.30	.14
☐ 195	Loy Vaught B	.40	.18
☐ 196	D.Mutombo B	.40	.18
☐ 197	Eric Montross B	.30	.14
☐ 198	Sasha Danilovic B	.30	.14
☐ 199	Kenny Anderson B	.40	.18
☐ 200	Sean Elliott B	.30	.14
☐ 201	Mark West B	.30	.14
☐ 202	Vlade Divac B	.40	.18
☐ 203	Joe Dumars B	.60	.25
☐ 204	Allan Houston B	.40	.18
☐ 205	Kevin Garnett B	5.00	2.20
☐ 206	Rod Strickland B	.40	.18
☐ 207	Robert Parish B	.40	.18
☐ 208	Jalen Rose B	.30	.14
☐ 209	Armon Gilliam B	.30	.14
☐ 210	Kerry Kittles B	2.00	.90
☐ 211	Derrick Coleman B	.40	.18
☐ 212	Greg Anthony B	.30	.14
☐ 213	Joe Smith B	.75	.35
☐ 214	Steve Smith B	.40	.18
☐ 215	Tim Hardaway B	.75	.35
☐ 216	Tyus Edney B	.30	.14
☐ 217	Steve Nash B	.60	.25
☐ 218	Anthony Mason B	.40	.18
☐ 219	Otis Thorpe B	.40	.18
☐ 220	Eddie Jones B	1.25	.55
☐ 221	Rik Smits B	.40	.18
☐ 222	Isaiah Rider B	.40	.18
☐ 223	Bobby Phills B	.30	.14
☐ 224	Antoine Walker B	6.00	2.70
☐ 225	Rod Strickland B	.40	.18
☐ 226	Hubert Davis B	.30	.14
☐ 227	Eric Williams B	.30	.14
☐ 228	Danny Manning B	.40	.18
☐ 229	Dominique Wilkins B	.60	.25
☐ 230	Brian Shaw B	.30	.14
☐ 231	Larry Johnson B	.40	.18
☐ 232	Kevin Willis B	.30	.14
☐ 233	Bryant Stith B	.30	.14
☐ 234	Blue Edwards B	.30	.14
☐ 235	Robert Pack B	.30	.14
☐ 236	Brian Grant B	.40	.18
☐ 237	Latrell Sprewell B	.40	.18
☐ 238	Glen Rice B	.60	.25
☐ 239	Jerome Williams B	.40	.18
☐ 240	Allen Iverson B	6.00	2.70
☐ 241	Popeye Jones B	.30	.14
☐ 242	Clifford Robinson B	.30	.14
☐ 243	Shaquille O'Neal B	3.00	1.35
☐ 244	Vitaly Potapenko B	1.25	.55
☐ 245	Ervin Johnson B	.30	.14
☐ 246	Checklist	.30	.14
☐ 247	Scottie Pippen B	8.00	3.60
☐ 248	Jason Kidd S	5.00	2.20
☐ 249	Antonio McDyess S	4.00	1.80
☐ 250	Latrell Sprewell S	1.50	.70
☐ 251	Lorenzen Wright S	2.50	1.10
☐ 252	Ray Allen S	5.00	2.20
☐ 253	S.Marbury S	15.00	6.75
☐ 254	Patrick Ewing S	2.50	1.10
☐ 255	A.Hardaway S	10.00	4.50
☐ 256	Kenny Anderson S	1.50	.70
☐ 257	David Robinson S	4.00	1.80
☐ 258	Marcus Camby S	4.00	1.80
☐ 259	S.Abdur-Rahim S	10.00	4.50
☐ 260	Dennis Rodman S	10.00	4.50
☐ 261	Juwan Howard S	3.00	1.35
☐ 262	D.Stoudamire S	6.00	2.70
☐ 263	Shawn Kemp S	8.00	3.60
☐ 264	Mitch Richmond S	2.50	1.10
☐ 265	Jerry Stackhouse S	3.00	1.35
☐ 266	Horace Grant S	1.50	.70
☐ 267	Kerry Kittles S	4.00	1.80
☐ 268	Vin Baker S	5.00	2.20
☐ 269	Kobe Bryant G	120.00	55.00
☐ 270	Reggie Miller S	2.50	1.10
☐ 271	Grant Hill S	15.00	6.75
☐ 272	Oliver Miller S	1.25	.55
☐ 273	Chris Webber S	6.00	2.70
☐ 274	D.Mutombo G	8.00	3.60
☐ 275	A.McDyess G	15.00	6.75
☐ 276	Clyde Drexler G	15.00	6.75
☐ 277	Brent Barry G	8.00	3.60
☐ 278	Tim Hardaway G	15.00	6.75
☐ 279	Glenn Robinson G	10.00	4.50
☐ 280	Allen Iverson G	60.00	27.00
☐ 281	H.Olajuwon G	20.00	9.00
☐ 282	Marcus Camby G	15.00	6.75
☐ 283	John Stockton G	10.00	4.50
☐ 284	S.Abdur-Rahim G	30.00	13.50
☐ 285	Karl Malone G	20.00	9.00
☐ 286	Gary Payton G	20.00	9.00
☐ 287	Stephon Marbury G	60.00	27.00
☐ 288	Alonzo Mourning G	10.00	4.50
☐ 289	Shaquille O'Neal S	10.00	4.50
☐ 290	Charles Barkley G	20.00	9.00
☐ 291	Michael Jordan G	125.00	55.00

1996-97 Finest Refractors

This 291-card set parallels the basic set using the Finest refractive technology. This set is also divided into a 3-tier model of collectiblity using the same common, uncommon and rare themes. A Refractor comon card replaces a common card 1:12 packs and uses the classic Refractor foil. A Refractor uncommon card replaces a common card 1:48 packs and uses a mosaic Refractor foil pattern. A Refractor rare card replaces a common card 1:288 packs and uses a hyper-plaid Refractor foil pattern. Prices below are for unpeeled cards. Peeled cards generally trade for ten to twenty-five percent less. Card numbers 7 and 134 do not exist. The Christian Laettner bronze, Patrick Ewing gold and Jeff Hornacek gold were all numbered 136. Card number 269 (Kobe Bryant gold) is considered part of the gold set, while card number 289 (Shaquille O'Neal silver) is considered part of the silver set, though they are both out of "set" order. The set is condition sensitive.

	MINT	NRMT
COMPLETE SET (291)	7000.00	3200.00
COMP.SERIES 1 (146)	4000.00	1800.00
COMP.SERIES 2 (145)	3000.00	1350.00
COMP.BRNZ.SET (200)	2700.00	1200.00
COMP.BRNZ.SER.1 (100)	2100.00	950.00
COMP.BRNZ.SER.2 (100)	600.00	275.00
COMMON BRONZE	4.00	1.80
SEMISTARS BRONZE	6.00	2.70
UNLISTED STARS BRONZE	12.00	5.50
BRONZE: SER.1/2 STATED ODDS 1:12		
COMP.SILVER SET (54)	1300.00	575.00
COMP.SILVER SER.1 (27)	500.00	220.00
COMP.SILVER SER.2 (27)	800.00	350.00
COMMON SILVER	8.00	3.60
SEMISTARS SILVER	10.00	4.50
UNLISTED STARS SILVER	15.00	6.75
SILVER: SER.1/2 STATED ODDS 1:48		
COMP.GOLD SET (37)	3500.00	1600.00
COMP.GOLD SER.1 (19)	1500.00	700.00
COMP.GOLD SER.2 (18)	2000.00	900.00
COMMON GOLD	20.00	9.00
SEMISTARS GOLD	30.00	13.50
UNLISTED STARS GOLD SER.1	40.00	18.00
UNLISTED STARS GOLD SER.2	50.00	22.00
GOLD: SER.1/2 STATED ODDS 1:288		
CARD NUMBERS 7 AND 134 DO NOT EXIST		
LAETTNER B, EWING G AND HORNACEK G NUMBERED 136		
NUMBER 269 PART OF GOLD SET		
NUMBER 289 PART OF SILVER SET		
CONDITION SENSITIVE SET		

☐ 1	Scottie Pippen B	40.00	18.00
☐ 2	Tim Legler B	4.00	1.80
☐ 3	Rex Walters B	4.00	1.80
☐ 4	Calbert Cheaney B	4.00	1.80
☐ 5	Dennis Rodman B	50.00	22.00
☐ 6	Tyrone Hill B	4.00	1.80
☐ 8	Dell Curry B	4.00	1.80
☐ 9	Olden Polynice B	4.00	1.80
☐ 10	John Wallace B	30.00	13.50
☐ 11	Martin Muursepp B	4.00	1.80
☐ 12	Chuck Person B	4.00	1.80
☐ 13	Grant Hill B	75.00	34.00
☐ 14	Shawn Kemp B	40.00	18.00
☐ 15	B.J. Armstrong B	4.00	1.80
☐ 16	Gary Trent B	4.00	1.80
☐ 17	Scott Williams B	4.00	1.80
☐ 18	Dino Radja B	4.00	1.80
☐ 19	Roy Rogers B	4.00	1.80
☐ 20	Tony Delk B	20.00	9.00
☐ 21	Clifford Robinson B	4.00	1.80
☐ 22	Ray Allen B	60.00	27.00
☐ 23	Clyde Drexler B	15.00	6.75
☐ 24	Elliot Perry B	4.00	1.80
☐ 25	Gary Payton B	20.00	9.00
☐ 26	Dale Davis B	4.00	1.80
☐ 27	Horace Grant B	6.00	2.70
☐ 28	Brian Evans B	4.00	1.80
☐ 29	Joe Smith B	15.00	6.75
☐ 30	Reggie Miller B	12.00	5.50
☐ 31	Jermaine O'Neal B	30.00	13.50
☐ 32	Avery Johnson B	4.00	1.80
☐ 33	Ed O'Bannon B	4.00	1.80
☐ 34	Cedric Ceballos B	4.00	1.80
☐ 35	Jamal Mashburn B	6.00	2.70
☐ 36	Michael Williams B	4.00	1.80
☐ 37	Detlef Schrempf B	6.00	2.70
☐ 38	D.Stoudamire B	30.00	13.50
☐ 39	Jason Kidd B	25.00	11.00
☐ 40	Tom Gugliotta B	12.00	5.50
☐ 41	Arvydas Sabonis B	6.00	2.70
☐ 42	Samaki Walker B	15.00	6.75
☐ 43	Derek Fisher B	20.00	9.00
☐ 44	Patrick Ewing B	12.00	5.50
☐ 45	Bryant Reeves B	4.00	1.80
☐ 46	Mookie Blaylock B	6.00	2.70
☐ 47	George Zidek B	4.00	1.80
☐ 48	Jerry Stackhouse B	15.00	6.75
☐ 49	Vin Baker B	25.00	11.00
☐ 50	Michael Jordan B	150.00	70.00
☐ 51	Terrell Brandon B	12.00	5.50
☐ 52	Karl Malone B	20.00	9.00
☐ 53	Lorenzen Wright B	20.00	9.00
☐ 54	S.Abdur-Rahim B	100.00	45.00
☐ 55	Kurt Thomas B	4.00	1.80
☐ 56	Glen Rice B	12.00	5.50
☐ 57	Shawn Bradley B	4.00	1.80
☐ 58	Todd Fuller B	4.00	1.80
☐ 59	Dale Ellis B	4.00	1.80
☐ 60	David Robinson B	20.00	9.00
☐ 61	Doug Christie B	4.00	1.80
☐ 62	Stephon Marbury B	150.00	70.00
☐ 63	Hakeem Olajuwon B	25.00	11.00
☐ 64	Lindsey Hunter B	4.00	1.80
☐ 65	A.Hardaway B	50.00	22.00
☐ 66	Kevin Garnett B	75.00	34.00
☐ 67	Kendall Gill B	6.00	2.70
☐ 68	Sean Elliott B	4.00	1.80
☐ 69	Allen Iverson B	150.00	70.00
☐ 70	Erick Dampier B	10.00	4.50
☐ 71	Jerome Williams B	6.00	2.70
☐ 72	Charles Jones B	4.00	1.80
☐ 73	Danny Manning B	6.00	2.70
☐ 74	Kobe Bryant B	350.00	160.00
☐ 75	Steve Nash B	30.00	13.50
☐ 76	Sam Perkins B	6.00	2.70
☐ 77	Horace Grant B	6.00	2.70
☐ 78	Alonzo Mourning B	12.00	5.50
☐ 79	Kerry Kittles B	40.00	18.00
☐ 80	LaPhonso Ellis B	4.00	1.80
☐ 81	Michael Finley B	15.00	6.75
☐ 82	Marcus Camby B	40.00	18.00
☐ 83	Antonio McDyess B	20.00	9.00
☐ 84	Antoine Walker B	175.00	80.00
☐ 85	Juwan Howard B	15.00	6.75
☐ 86	Bryon Russell B	4.00	1.80
☐ 87	Walter McCarty B	20.00	9.00
☐ 88	Terry Leadbetter B	4.00	1.80
☐ 89	C.Weatherspoon B	4.00	1.80
☐ 90	John Stockton B	12.00	5.50
☐ 91	Mitch Richmond B	12.00	5.50
☐ 92	Dontae' Jones B	4.00	1.80
☐ 93	Michael Smith B	4.00	1.80
☐ 94	Brent Barry B	4.00	1.80
☐ 95	Chris Mills B	4.00	1.80
☐ 96	Dee Brown B	4.00	1.80
☐ 97	Terry Dehere B	4.00	1.80
☐ 98	Danny Ferry B	4.00	1.80
☐ 99	Gheorghe Muresan B	4.00	1.80
☐ 100	Checklist B	4.00	1.80
☐ 101	Jim Jackson S	10.00	4.50
☐ 102	Cedric Ceballos S	8.00	3.60
☐ 103	Glen Rice S	15.00	6.75
☐ 104	Tom Gugliotta S	15.00	6.75
☐ 105	Mario Elie S	8.00	3.60
☐ 106	Nick Anderson S	8.00	3.60
☐ 107	Glenn Robinson S	15.00	6.75
☐ 108	Terrell Brandon S	15.00	6.75
☐ 109	Tim Hardaway S	20.00	9.00
☐ 110	John Stockton S	15.00	6.75
☐ 111	Brent Barry S	8.00	3.60
☐ 112	Mookie Blaylock S	10.00	4.50
☐ 113	Tyus Edney S	8.00	3.60
☐ 114	Gary Payton S	25.00	11.00
☐ 115	Joe Smith S	20.00	9.00
☐ 116	Karl Malone S	30.00	13.50
☐ 117	Dino Radja S	8.00	3.60
☐ 118	Alonzo Mourning S	15.00	6.75
☐ 119	Bryant Stith S	8.00	3.60
☐ 120	Derrick McKey S	8.00	3.60
☐ 121	Clyde Drexler S	20.00	9.00
☐ 122	Michael Finley S	20.00	9.00
☐ 123	Sean Elliott S	8.00	3.60
☐ 124	Hakeem Olajuwon S	30.00	13.50
☐ 125	Joe Dumars S	15.00	6.75
☐ 126	Shawn Bradley S	8.00	3.60
☐ 127	Michael Jordan S	200.00	90.00
☐ 128	Latrell Sprewell S	30.00	13.50
☐ 129	A.Hardaway G	150.00	70.00
☐ 130	Grant Hill G	250.00	110.00
☐ 131	D.Stoudamire G	100.00	45.00
☐ 132	D.Robinson G	60.00	27.00
☐ 133	Scottie Pippen G	125.00	55.00
☐ 135	Jason Kidd G	80.00	36.00
☐ 136B	P.Ewing G UER	40.00	18.00
	Should be card number 134		
☐ 136C	Jeff Hornacek G	20.00	9.00
☐ 136C	C.Laettner B UER	30.00	13.50
	Should be card number 7		
☐ 137	Jerry Stackhouse G	50.00	22.00
☐ 138	Kevin Garnett G	250.00	110.00
☐ 139	Mitch Richmond G	40.00	18.00
☐ 140	Juwan Howard G	50.00	22.00
☐ 141	Reggie Miller G	40.00	18.00
☐ 142	Christian Laettner G	30.00	13.50
☐ 143	Vin Baker G	80.00	36.00
☐ 144	Shawn Kemp G	100.00	45.00
☐ 145	Dennis Rodman G	150.00	70.00
☐ 146	Shaquille O'Neal G	150.00	70.00
☐ 147	Mookie Blaylock B	6.00	2.70
☐ 148	Derek Harper B	4.00	1.80
☐ 149	Gerald Wilkins B	4.00	1.80
☐ 150	Adam Keefe B	4.00	1.80
☐ 151	Billy Owens B	4.00	1.80
☐ 152	Terrell Brandon B	12.00	5.50
☐ 153	Antonio Davis B	4.00	1.80
☐ 154	Muggsy Bogues B	4.00	1.80
☐ 155	Cherokee Parks B	4.00	1.80
☐ 156	Rasheed Wallace B	6.00	2.70
☐ 157	Lee Mayberry B	4.00	1.80
☐ 158	Craig Ehlo B	4.00	1.80
☐ 159	Todd Fuller B	4.00	1.80
☐ 160	Charles Barkley B	20.00	9.00
☐ 161	Glenn Robinson B	12.00	5.50
☐ 162	Charles Oakley B	4.00	1.80
☐ 163	Chris Webber B	30.00	13.50
☐ 164	Frank Brickowski B	4.00	1.80
☐ 165	Mark Jackson B	4.00	1.80
☐ 166	Jayson Williams B	6.00	2.70
☐ 167	C.Weatherspoon B	4.00	1.80
☐ 168	Toni Kukoc B	6.00	2.70
☐ 169	Alan Henderson B	4.00	1.80
☐ 170	Tony Delk B	12.00	5.50
☐ 171	Jamal Mashburn B	6.00	2.70
☐ 172	Vinny Del Negro B	4.00	1.80
☐ 173	Greg Ostertag B	4.00	1.80

☐ 174 Shawn Bradley B......	4.00	1.80	☐ 260 Dennis Rodman S ..	60.00	27.00		
☐ 175 Gheorghe Muresan B	4.00	1.80	☐ 261 Juwan Howard S	20.00	9.00		
☐ 176 Brent Price B..........	4.00	1.80	☐ 262 D.Stoudamire S......	40.00	18.00		
☐ 177 Rick Fox B..............	4.00	1.80	☐ 263 Shawn Kemp S	50.00	22.00		
☐ 178 Stacey Augmon B....	4.00	1.80	☐ 264 Mitch Richmond S ..	15.00	6.75		
☐ 179 P.J. Brown B............	4.00	1.80	☐ 265 Jerry Stackhouse S	20.00	9.00		
☐ 180 Jim Jackson B..........	6.00	2.70	☐ 266 Horace Grant S	10.00	4.50		
☐ 181 Hersey Hawkins B....	6.00	2.70	☐ 267 Kerry Kittles S	20.00	9.00		
☐ 182 Danny Manning B.....	6.00	2.70	☐ 268 Vin Baker S	30.00	13.50		
☐ 183 Dennis Scott B........	4.00	1.80	☐ 269 Kobe Bryant G	550.00	250.00		
☐ 184 Tom Gugliotta B......	12.00	5.50	☐ 270 Reggie Miller S	15.00	6.75		
☐ 185 Tyrone Hill B............	4.00	1.80	☐ 271 Grant Hill S	100.00	45.00		
☐ 186 Malik Sealy B..........	4.00	1.80	☐ 272 Oliver Miller S	8.00	3.60		
☐ 187 John Starks B..........	6.00	2.70	☐ 273 Chris Webber S	40.00	18.00		
☐ 188 Mark Price B............	4.00	1.80	☐ 274 D.Mutombo G	30.00	13.50		
☐ 189 Elden Campbell B	6.00	2.70	☐ 275 Antonio McDyess G	80.00	36.00		
☐ 190 M.Abdul-Rauf B	4.00	1.80	☐ 276 Clyde Drexler G	60.00	27.00		
☐ 191 Will Perdue B	4.00	1.80	☐ 277 Brent Barry G	30.00	13.50		
☐ 192 Nate McMillan B	4.00	1.80	☐ 278 Tim Hardaway G	60.00	27.00		
☐ 193 Robert Horry B	6.00	2.70	☐ 279 Glenn Robinson G ..	50.00	22.00		
☐ 194 Dino Radja B	4.00	1.80	☐ 280 Allen Iverson G	250.00	110.00		
☐ 195 Loy Vaught B	6.00	2.70	☐ 281 H.Olajuwon G	100.00	45.00		
☐ 196 D.Mutombo B	6.00	2.70	☐ 282 Marcus Camby G	60.00	27.00		
☐ 197 Eric Montross B	4.00	1.80	☐ 283 John Stockton G	50.00	22.00		
☐ 198 Sasha Danilovic B ...	4.00	1.80	☐ 284 S.Abdur-Rahim G ...	150.00	70.00		
☐ 199 Kenny Anderson B ...	6.00	2.70	☐ 285 Karl Malone G	80.00	36.00		
☐ 200 Sean Elliott B	4.00	1.80	☐ 286 Gary Payton G	80.00	36.00		
☐ 201 Mark West B	4.00	1.80	☐ 287 S.Marbury G	250.00	110.00		
☐ 202 Vlade Divac B	6.00	2.70	☐ 288 Alonzo Mourning G .	50.00	22.00		
☐ 203 Joe Dumars B	12.00	5.50	☐ 289 Shaquille O'Neal S..	50.00	22.00		
☐ 204 Allan Houston B	6.00	2.70	☐ 290 Charles Barkley G ..	80.00	36.00		
☐ 205 Kevin Garnett B	75.00	34.00	☐ 291 Michael Jordan G ...	600.00	275.00		
☐ 206 Rod Strickland B	6.00	2.70					
☐ 207 Robert Parish B	6.00	2.70					
☐ 208 Jalen Rose B	4.00	1.80					
☐ 209 Armon Gilliam B	4.00	1.80					
☐ 210 Kerry Kittles B	20.00	9.00					

	MINT	NRMT
COMPLETE SET (326)	900.00	400.00
COMPLETE SERIES 1 (173)	400.00	180.00
COMPLETE SERIES 2 (153)	500.00	220.00
COMP.BRONZE SET (220)	150.00	70.00
COMP.BRONZE SER.1 (120)	100.00	45.00
COMP.BRONZE SER.2 (100)	50.00	22.00
COMMON BRONZE	.25	.11
SEMISTARS BRONZE	.30	.14
UNLISTED STARS BRONZE	.50	.23
COMP.SILVER SET (66)	200.00	90.00
COMP.SILVER SER.1 (33)	100.00	45.00
COMP.SILVER SER.2 (33)	100.00	45.00
COMMON SILVER	.75	.35
SEMISTARS SILVER	1.25	.55
UNLISTED STARS SILVER	2.00	.90
SILVER: SER.1/2 STATED ODDS 1:4		
COMP.GOLD SET (40)	600.00	275.00
COMP.GOLD SER.1 (20)	200.00	90.00
COMP.GOLD SER.2 (20)	400.00	180.00
COMMON GOLD	3.00	1.35
SEMISTARS GOLD	4.00	1.80
UNLISTED STARS GOLD	6.00	2.70
GOLD: SER.1/2 STATED ODDS 1:24		

☐ 211 Derrick Coleman B ..	6.00	2.70
☐ 212 Greg Anthony B	4.00	1.80
☐ 213 Joe Smith B	15.00	6.75
☐ 214 Steve Smith B	6.00	2.70
☐ 215 Tim Hardaway B	15.00	6.75
☐ 216 Tyus Edney B	4.00	1.80
☐ 217 Steve Nash B	12.00	5.50
☐ 218 Anthony Mason B	6.00	2.70
☐ 219 Otis Thorpe B	6.00	2.70
☐ 220 Eddie Jones B	30.00	13.50
☐ 221 Rik Smits B	6.00	2.70
☐ 222 Isaiah Rider B	6.00	2.70
☐ 223 Bobby Phills B	4.00	1.80
☐ 224 Antoine Walker B	50.00	22.00
☐ 225 Rod Strickland B	6.00	2.70
☐ 226 Hubert Davis B	4.00	1.80
☐ 227 Eric Williams B	4.00	1.80
☐ 228 Danny Manning B	6.00	2.70
☐ 229 D.Wilkins B	12.00	5.50
☐ 230 Brian Shaw B	4.00	1.80
☐ 231 Larry Johnson B	6.00	2.70
☐ 232 Kevin Willis B	4.00	1.80
☐ 233 Bryant Stith B	4.00	1.80
☐ 234 Blue Edwards B	4.00	1.80
☐ 235 Robert Pack B	4.00	1.80
☐ 236 Brian Grant B	4.00	1.80
☐ 237 Latrell Sprewell B ...	6.00	2.70
☐ 238 Glen Rice B	12.00	5.50
☐ 239 Jerome Williams B ..	6.00	2.70
☐ 240 Allen Iverson B	80.00	36.00
☐ 241 Popeye Jones B	4.00	1.80
☐ 242 Clifford Robinson B .	4.00	1.80
☐ 243 Shaquille O'Neal B ..	50.00	22.00
☐ 244 Vitaly Potapenko B .	6.00	2.70
☐ 245 Ervin Johnson B	4.00	1.80
☐ 246 Checklist	4.00	1.80
☐ 247 Scottie Pippen S	50.00	22.00
☐ 248 Jason Kidd S	30.00	13.50
☐ 249 Antonio McDyess S .	25.00	11.00
☐ 250 Latrell Sprewell S ...	10.00	4.50
☐ 251 Lorenzen Wright S ..	10.00	4.50
☐ 252 Ray Allen S	25.00	11.00
☐ 253 Stephon Marbury S .	75.00	34.00
☐ 254 Patrick Ewing S	15.00	6.75
☐ 255 A.Hardaway S	60.00	27.00
☐ 256 Kenny Anderson S ..	10.00	4.50
☐ 257 David Robinson S	25.00	11.00
☐ 258 Marcus Camby S	20.00	9.00
☐ 259 S.Abdur-Rahim S	50.00	22.00

1997-98 Finest

The complete set of Finest contained 326 total cards with the series one set containing 173 cards and the series two set containing 153. Both series were released in six card packs that carried a suggested retail price of $5. Like last year, the set is divided into three tiers: bronze, silver and gold. The bronze, or common, cards are the basic and encompass cards 1-120 and 174-273. The silver, or uncommon, cards were inserted at a rate of one in four packs and encompass cards 121-153 and cards 274-306. The gold, or rare, cards were inserted at a rate of one in 24 and encompass cards 154-173 and cards 307-326. Prices listed below are for unpeeled cards. Peeled cards generally trade for 75% of the listed prices.

☐ 1 Scottie Pippen B	1.50	.70
☐ 2 Tim Hardaway B	.60	.25
☐ 3 Charles Outlaw B	.25	.11
☐ 4 Rik Smits B	.30	.14
☐ 5 Dale Ellis B	.25	.11
☐ 6 Clyde Drexler B	.60	.25
☐ 7 Steve Smith B	.30	.14
☐ 8 Nick Anderson B	.25	.11
☐ 9 Juwan Howard B	.50	.23
☐ 10 Cedric Ceballos B	.25	.11
☐ 11 Shawn Bradley B	.25	.11
☐ 12 Loy Vaught B	.30	.14
☐ 13 Todd Day B	.25	.11
☐ 14 Glen Rice B	.50	.23
☐ 15 Bryant Stith B	.25	.11
☐ 16 Bob Sura B	.25	.11
☐ 17 Derrick McKey B	.25	.11
☐ 18 Ray Allen B	.60	.25
☐ 19 Stephon Marbury B	2.50	1.10
☐ 20 David Robinson B	.75	.35
☐ 21 Anthony Peeler B	.25	.11
☐ 22 Isaiah Rider B	.30	.14
☐ 23 Mookie Blaylock B	.30	.14
☐ 24 D.Stoudamire B	1.00	.45
☐ 25 Rod Strickland B	.50	.23
☐ 26 Glenn Robinson B	.50	.23
☐ 27 Chris Webber B	1.25	.55
☐ 28 Christian Laettner B	.25	.11
☐ 29 Joe Dumars B	.50	.23
☐ 30 Mark Price B	.25	.11
☐ 31 Jamal Mashburn B	.30	.14
☐ 32 Danny Manning B	.30	.14
☐ 33 John Stockton B	.50	.23
☐ 34 Detlef Schrempf B	.30	.14
☐ 35 Tyus Edney B	.25	.11
☐ 36 Chris Childs B	.25	.11
☐ 37 Dana Barros B	.25	.11
☐ 38 Bobby Phills B	.25	.11
☐ 39 Michael Jordan B	6.00	2.70
☐ 40 Grant Hill B	3.00	1.35
☐ 41 Brent Barry B	.25	.11
☐ 42 Rony Seikaly B	.25	.11
☐ 43 S.Abdur-Rahim B	1.50	.70
☐ 44 Dominique Wilkins B	.50	.23
☐ 45 Vin Baker B	1.00	.45
☐ 46 Kendall Gill B	.30	.14
☐ 47 Muggsy Bogues B	.25	.11
☐ 48 Hakeem Olajuwon B	1.00	.45
☐ 49 Reggie Miller B	.50	.23
☐ 50 Shaquille O'Neal B	2.00	.90
☐ 51 Antonio McDyess B	.60	.25
☐ 52 Michael Finley B	.50	.23
☐ 53 Jerry Stackhouse B	.50	.23
☐ 54 Brian Grant B	.25	.11
☐ 55 Greg Anthony B	.25	.11
☐ 56 Patrick Ewing B	.50	.23
☐ 57 Allen Iverson B	2.50	1.10
☐ 58 Rasheed Wallace B	.30	.14
☐ 59 Shawn Kemp B	1.50	.70
☐ 60 Bryant Reeves B	.30	.14
☐ 61 Kevin Garnett B	3.00	1.35

#	Player	Gr	Price	Price2
62	Allan Houston B		.30	.14
63	Stacey Augmon B		.25	.11
64	Rick Fox B		.25	.11
65	Derek Harper B		.25	.11
66	Lindsey Hunter B		.25	.11
67	Eddie Jones B		1.00	.45
68	Joe Smith B		.50	.23
69	Alonzo Mourning B		.50	.23
70	LaPhonso Ellis B		.25	.11
71	Tyrone Hill B		.25	.11
72	Charles Barkley B		.75	.35
73	Malik Sealy B		.25	.11
74	Shandon Anderson B		.25	.11
75	Arvydas Sabonis B		.30	.14
76	Tom Gugliotta B		.50	.23
77	A.Hardaway B		2.00	.90
78	Sean Elliott B		.25	.11
79	Marcus Camby B		.50	.23
80	Gary Payton B		.75	.35
81	Kerry Kittles B		.50	.23
82	D.Mutombo B		.30	.14
83	Antoine Walker B		2.50	1.10
84	Terrell Brandon B		.50	.23
85	Otis Thorpe B		.30	.14
86	Mark Jackson B		.25	.11
87	A.C. Green B		.30	.14
88	John Starks B		.30	.14
89	Kenny Anderson B		.30	.14
90	Karl Malone B		.75	.35
91	Mitch Richmond B		.50	.23
92	Derrick Coleman B		.30	.14
93	Horace Grant B		.30	.14
94	John Williams B		.25	.11
95	Jason Kidd B		1.00	.45
96	M.Abdul-Rauf B		.25	.11
97	Walt Williams B		.25	.11
98	Anthony Mason B		.30	.14
99	Latrell Sprewell B		.30	.14
100	Checklist		.25	.11
101	Tim Duncan B		40.00	18.00
102	Keith Van Horn B		25.00	11.00
103	Chauncey Billups B		8.00	3.60
104	Antonio Daniels B		4.00	1.80
105	Tony Battie B		3.00	1.35
106	Tim Thomas B		10.00	4.50
107	Tracy McGrady B		10.00	4.50
108	Adonal Foyle B		2.00	.90
109	Maurice Taylor B		6.00	2.70
110	Austin Croshere B		2.00	.90
111	Bobby Jackson B		4.00	1.80
112	Olivier Saint-Jean B		2.50	1.10
113	John Thomas B		1.25	.55
114	Derek Anderson B		6.00	2.70
115	Brevin Knight B		6.00	2.70
116	Charles Smith B		1.25	.55
117	Johnny Taylor B		1.25	.55
118	Jacque Vaughn B		2.50	1.10
119	Anthony Parker B		1.25	.55
120	Paul Grant B		1.25	.55
121	Stephon Marbury S		10.00	4.50
122	Terrell Brandon S		2.00	.90
123	D.Mutombo S		1.25	.55
124	Patrick Ewing S		2.00	.90
125	Scottie Pippen S		6.00	2.70
126	Antoine Walker S		10.00	4.50
127	Karl Malone S		3.00	1.35
128	Sean Elliott S		.75	.35
129	Chris Webber S		5.00	2.20
130	Shawn Kemp S		6.00	2.70
131	Hakeem Olajuwon S		4.00	1.80
132	Tim Hardaway S		2.50	1.10
133	Glen Rice S		2.00	.90
134	Vin Baker S		4.00	1.80
135	Jim Jackson S		1.25	.55
136	Kevin Garnett S		12.00	5.50
137	Kobe Bryant S		20.00	9.00
138	D.Stoudamire S		4.00	1.80
139	Larry Johnson S		1.25	.55
140	Latrell Sprewell S		1.25	.55
141	Lorenzen Wright S		.75	.35
142	Toni Kukoc S		1.25	.55
143	Allen Iverson S		10.00	4.50
144	Eldon Campbell S		1.25	.55
145	Tom Gugliotta S		2.00	.90
146	David Robinson S		3.00	1.35
147	Jayson Williams S		1.25	.55
148	Shaquille O'Neal S		8.00	3.60
149	Grant Hill S		12.00	5.50
150	Reggie Miller S		2.00	.90
151	Clyde Drexler S		2.50	1.10
152	Ray Allen S		2.50	1.10
153	Eddie Jones S		4.00	1.80
154	Michael Jordan S		80.00	36.00
155	Dominique Wilkins G		6.00	2.70
156	Charles Barkley G		10.00	4.50
157	Jerry Stackhouse G		6.00	2.70
158	Juwan Howard G		6.00	2.70
159	Marcus Camby G		6.00	2.70
160	Christian Laettner G		4.00	1.80
161	Anthony Mason G		4.00	1.80
162	Joe Smith G		6.00	2.70
163	Kerry Kittles G		6.00	2.70
164	Mitch Richmond G		6.00	2.70
165	S.Abdur-Rahim G		20.00	9.00
166	Alonzo Mourning G		6.00	2.70
167	Dennis Rodman G		25.00	11.00
168	Antonio McDyess B		8.00	3.60
169	Shawn Bradley G		3.00	1.35
170	A.Hardaway G		25.00	11.00
171	Jason Kidd G		12.00	5.50
172	Gary Payton G		10.00	4.50
173	John Stockton G		6.00	2.70
174	Allan Houston G		.30	.14
175	Bob Sura B		.25	.11
176	Clyde Drexler B		.60	.25
177	Glenn Robinson B		.50	.23
178	Joe Smith B		.50	.23
179	Larry Johnson B		.30	.14
180	Mitch Richmond B		.50	.23
181	Rony Seikaly B		.25	.11
182	Tyrone Hill B		.25	.11
183	Allen Iverson B		2.50	1.10
184	Brent Barry B		.25	.11
185	D.Stoudamire B		1.00	.45
186	Grant Hill B		3.00	1.35
187	John Stockton B		.50	.23
188	Latrell Sprewell B		.30	.14
189	Mookie Blaylock B		.30	.14
190	Samaki Walker B		.25	.11
191	Vin Baker B		1.00	.45
192	Alonzo Mourning B		.50	.23
193	Brevin Knight B		3.00	1.35
194	Danny Manning B		.30	.14
195	Hakeem Olajuwon B		1.00	.45
196	Johnny Taylor B		.25	.11
197	Lorenzen Wright B		.25	.11
198	Olden Polynice B		.25	.11
199	Scottie Pippen B		1.50	.70
200	Lindsey Hunter B		.25	.11
201	A.Hardaway B		2.00	.90
202	Greg Anthony B		.25	.11
203	David Robinson B		.75	.35
204	Horace Grant B		.30	.14
205	Calbert Cheaney B		.25	.11
206	Loy Vaught B		.30	.14
207	Mario Abdul-Wahad B		1.00	.45
208	Sean Elliott B		.25	.11
209	Rodney Rogers B		.25	.11
210	Anthony Mason B		.30	.14
211	Bryant Reeves B		.30	.14
212	David Wesley B		.25	.11
213	Isaiah Rider B		.30	.14
214	Karl Malone B		.75	.35
215	M.Abdul-Rauf B		.25	.11
216	Patrick Ewing B		.50	.23
217	Shaquille O'Neal B		2.00	.90
218	Antoine Walker B		2.50	1.10
219	Charles Barkley B		.75	.35
220	Dennis Rodman B		2.00	.90
221	Jamal Mashburn B		.30	.14
222	Kendall Gill B		.30	.14
223	Malik Sealy B		.25	.11
224	Rasheed Wallace B		.30	.14
225	S.Abdur-Rahim B		1.50	.70
226	Antonio Daniels B		1.50	.70
227	Charles Oakley B		.25	.11
228	Derek Anderson B		3.00	1.35
229	Jason Kidd B		1.00	.45
230	Kenny Anderson B		.30	.14
231	Marcus Camby B		.50	.23
232	Ray Allen B		.60	.25
233	Shawn Bradley B		.25	.11
234	Antonio McDyess B		.60	.25
235	Chauncey Billups B		2.50	1.10
236	Detlef Schrempf B		.30	.14
237	Jayson Williams B		.30	.14
238	Kerry Kittles B		.50	.23
239	Jalen Rose B		.25	.11
240	Reggie Miller B		.50	.23
241	Shawn Kemp B		1.50	.70
242	Arvydas Sabonis B		.30	.14
243	Tom Gugliotta B		.50	.23
244	D.Mutombo B		.30	.14
245	Jeff Hornacek B		.30	.14
246	Kevin Garnett B		3.00	1.35
247	Matt Maloney B		.25	.11
248	Rex Chapman B		.25	.11
249	Stephon Marbury B		2.50	1.10
250	Austin Croshere B		.50	.23
251	Chris Childs B		.25	.11
252	Eddie Jones B		1.00	.45
253	Jerry Stackhouse B		.50	.23
254	Kevin Johnson B		.30	.14
255	Maurice Taylor B		3.00	1.35
256	Chris Mullin B		.50	.23
257	Terrell Brandon B		.50	.23
258	Avery Johnson B		.25	.11
259	Chris Webber B		1.25	.55
260	Gary Payton B		.75	.35
261	Jim Jackson B		.30	.14
262	Kobe Bryant B		5.00	2.20
263	Michael Finley B		.50	.23
264	Rod Strickland B		.30	.14
265	Tim Hardaway B		.60	.25
266	B.J. Armstrong B		.25	.11
267	Christian Laettner B		.30	.14
268	Glen Rice B		.50	.23
269	Joe Dumars B		.50	.23
270	LaPhonso Ellis B		.25	.11
271	Michael Jordan B		6.00	2.70
272	Ron Mercer B		15.00	6.75
273	Checklist B		.25	.11
274	A.Hardaway S		8.00	3.60
275	Dennis Rodman S		8.00	3.60
276	Gary Payton S		3.00	1.35
277	Jamal Mashburn S		1.25	.55
278	S.Abdur-Rahim S		6.00	2.70
279	Steve Smith S		1.25	.55
280	Tony Battie S		2.50	1.10
281	Alonzo Mourning S		2.00	.90
282	Bobby Jackson S		2.50	1.10
283	Christian Laettner S		1.25	.55
284	Jerry Stackhouse S		2.00	.90
285	Terrell Brandon S		2.00	.90
286	Chauncey Billups S		5.00	2.20
287	Michael Jordan S		25.00	11.00
288	Glenn Robinson S		2.00	.90
289	Jason Kidd S		4.00	1.80
290	Joe Smith S		2.00	.90
291	Michael Finley S		2.00	.90
292	Rod Strickland S		1.25	.55
293	Ron Mercer S		10.00	4.50
294	Tracy McGrady S		8.00	3.60
295	Adonal Foyle S		2.00	.90
296	Marcus Camby S		2.00	.90
297	John Stockton S		2.00	.90
298	Kerry Kittles S		2.00	.90
299	Mitch Richmond S		2.00	.90
300	Shawn Bradley S		.75	.35
301	Anthony Mason S		1.25	.55
302	Antonio Daniels S		3.00	1.35
303	Antonio McDyess S		2.50	1.10
304	Charles Barkley S		3.00	1.35
305	Keith Van Horn S		12.00	5.50
306	Tim Duncan S		15.00	6.75
307	D.Mutombo S		4.00	1.80
308	Grant Hill G		40.00	18.00
309	Shaquille O'Neal G		25.00	11.00
310	Keith Van Horn G		20.00	9.00
311	Shawn Kemp G		20.00	9.00
312	Antoine Walker G		30.00	13.50
313	Hakeem Olajuwon G		12.00	5.50
314	Vin Baker G		12.00	5.50
315	Patrick Ewing G		6.00	2.70
316	Tracy McGrady G		20.00	9.00
317	Glen Rice G		6.00	2.70
318	Reggie Miller G		6.00	2.70
319	Kevin Garnett G		40.00	18.00

			MINT	NRMT
☐	320	Allen Iverson G	30.00	13.50
☐	321	Karl Malone G	10.00	4.50
☐	322	Scottie Pippen G	20.00	9.00
☐	323	Kobe Bryant G	60.00	27.00
☐	324	Stephon Marbury G	30.00	13.50
☐	325	Tim Duncan G	40.00	18.00
☐	326	Chris Webber G	15.00	6.75

1997-98 Finest Embossed

The 106-card embossed semi-parallel is made up of only the silver and gold cards from both series of the basic set. The first 33 cards from both series, or silver, were just embossed and were randomly inserted into packs at a rate of one in 16. The last 20 cards from both series, or gold, were both embossed and die cut. The were randomly inserted at a rate of one in 96. Prices below refer to unpeeled cards. Peeled cards generally trade at about 75% of the listed value. To ascertain values of individual cards, please refer to the multiplier listed below coupled with the value of the base card.

	MINT	NRMT
COMPLETE SET (106)	1450.00	650.00
COMPLETE SERIES 1 (53)	625.00	275.00
COMPLETE SERIES 2 (53)	825.00	375.00
COMP.SILVER SER.1 (33)	175.00	80.00
COMP.SILVER SER.2 (33)	175.00	80.00
COMMON SILVER	1.25	.55
*SILVER STARS: .6X TO 1.5X BASE HI		
*SILVER RCs: .5X TO 1.25X BASE HI		
SILVER: SER.1/2 STATED ODDS 1:16		
COMP.GOLD SER.1 (20)	450.00	200.00
COMP.GOLD SER.2 (20)	650.00	300.00
COMMON GOLD	6.00	2.70
*GOLD STARS: .6X TO 1.5X BASE HI		
GOLD: SER.1/2 STATED ODDS 1:96		

1997-98 Finest Embossed Refractors

This 106-card set parallels the basic series one and two Embossed sets. The first 33 silver embossed refractors from

both sets were randomly inserted into packs at a rate of one in 192. These cards are serially numbered to 263 on the card back. The remaining 20 gold embossed die cut refractors from both sets were randomly inserted at a rate of one in 1,152 packs. These cards are serially numbered to 74 on the card back. Prices below refer to unpeeled cards. Peeled cards generally trade for 75% of the values listed below.

	MINT	NRMT
COMMON SILVER	10.00	4.50
SEMISTARS SILVER	12.00	5.50
UNLISTED STARS SILVER	20.00	9.00
SILVER: SER.1/2 STATED ODDS 1:192		
STATED PRINT RUN 263 SERIAL #'d SETS		
COMMON GOLD	60.00	27.00
GOLD: SER.1/2 STATED ODDS 1:1152		
STATED PRINT RUN 74 SERIAL #'d SETS		

			MINT	NRMT
☐	121	Stephon Marbury S	120.00	55.00
☐	122	Terrell Brandon S	20.00	9.00
☐	123	D.Mutombo S	12.00	5.50
☐	124	Patrick Ewing S	20.00	9.00
☐	125	Scottie Pippen S	80.00	36.00
☐	126	Antoine Walker S	120.00	55.00
☐	127	Karl Malone S	40.00	18.00
☐	128	Sean Elliott S	10.00	4.50
☐	129	Chris Webber S	60.00	27.00
☐	130	Shawn Kemp S	80.00	36.00
☐	131	Hakeem Olajuwon S	50.00	22.00
☐	132	Tim Hardaway S	30.00	13.50
☐	133	Glen Rice S	20.00	9.00
☐	134	Vin Baker S	50.00	22.00
☐	135	Jim Jackson S	12.00	5.50
☐	136	Kevin Garnett S	150.00	70.00
☐	137	Kobe Bryant S	250.00	110.00
☐	138	D.Stoudamire S	50.00	22.00
☐	139	Larry Johnson S	12.00	5.50
☐	140	Latrell Sprewell S	12.00	5.50
☐	141	Lorenzen Wright S	10.00	4.50
☐	142	Toni Kukoc S	12.00	5.50
☐	143	Allen Iverson S	120.00	55.00
☐	144	Elden Campbell S	12.00	5.50
☐	145	Tom Gugliotta S	20.00	9.00
☐	146	David Robinson S	40.00	18.00
☐	147	Jayson Williams S	12.00	5.50
☐	148	Shaquille O'Neal S	100.00	45.00
☐	149	Grant Hill S	150.00	70.00
☐	150	Reggie Miller S	20.00	9.00
☐	151	Clyde Drexler S	30.00	13.50
☐	152	Ray Allen S	30.00	13.50
☐	153	Eddie Jones S	50.00	22.00
☐	154	M.Jordan S	1800.00	800.00
☐	155	D.Wilkins G	60.00	27.00
☐	156	Charles Barkley S	150.00	70.00
☐	157	J.Stackhouse G	100.00	45.00
☐	158	Juwan Howard S	100.00	45.00

			MINT	NRMT
☐	159	Marcus Camby G	100.00	45.00
☐	160	Christian Laettner G	60.00	27.00
☐	161	Anthony Mason G	60.00	27.00
☐	162	Joe Smith G	100.00	45.00
☐	163	Kerry Kittles G	100.00	45.00
☐	164	Mitch Richmond G	100.00	45.00
☐	165	S.Abdur-Rahim G	300.00	135.00
☐	166	Alonzo Mourning G	100.00	45.00
☐	167	Dennis Rodman G	400.00	180.00
☐	168	Antonio McDyess G	125.00	55.00
☐	169	Shawn Bradley G	60.00	27.00
☐	170	A.Hardaway G	400.00	180.00
☐	171	Jason Kidd G	200.00	90.00
☐	172	Gary Payton G	150.00	70.00
☐	173	John Stockton G	100.00	45.00
☐	274	A.Hardaway S	100.00	45.00
☐	275	Dennis Rodman S	100.00	45.00
☐	276	Gary Payton S	40.00	18.00
☐	277	Jamal Mashburn S	12.00	5.50
☐	278	S.Abdur-Rahim S	80.00	36.00
☐	279	Steve Smith S	12.00	5.50
☐	280	Tony Battie S	20.00	9.00
☐	281	Alonzo Mourning S	20.00	9.00
☐	282	Bobby Jackson S	20.00	9.00
☐	283	Christian Laettner S	12.00	5.50
☐	284	Jerry Stackhouse S	20.00	9.00
☐	285	Terrell Brandon S	20.00	9.00
☐	286	Chauncey Billups S	50.00	22.00
☐	287	Michael Jordan S	300.00	135.00
☐	288	Glenn Robinson S	20.00	9.00
☐	289	Jason Kidd S	50.00	22.00
☐	290	Joe Smith S	20.00	9.00
☐	291	Michael Finley S	20.00	9.00
☐	292	Rod Strickland S	12.00	5.50
☐	293	Ron Mercer S	100.00	45.00
☐	294	Tracy McGrady S	80.00	36.00
☐	295	Adonal Foyle S	20.00	9.00
☐	296	Marcus Camby S	20.00	9.00
☐	297	John Stockton S	20.00	9.00
☐	298	Kerry Kittles S	20.00	9.00
☐	299	Mitch Richmond S	20.00	9.00
☐	300	Shawn Bradley S	10.00	4.50
☐	301	Anthony Mason S	12.00	5.50
☐	302	Antonio Daniels S	30.00	13.50
☐	303	Antonio McDyess S	30.00	13.50
☐	304	Charles Barkley S	40.00	18.00
☐	305	Keith Van Horn S	120.00	55.00
☐	306	Tim Duncan S	150.00	70.00
☐	307	D.Mutombo G	60.00	27.00
☐	308	Grant Hill G	600.00	275.00
☐	309	Shaquille O'Neal G	400.00	180.00
☐	310	Keith Van Horn G	500.00	220.00
☐	311	Shawn Kemp G	300.00	135.00
☐	312	Antoine Walker G	500.00	220.00
☐	313	Hakeem Olajuwon G	200.00	90.00
☐	314	Vin Baker G	200.00	90.00
☐	315	Patrick Ewing G	100.00	45.00
☐	316	Tracy McGrady G	300.00	135.00
☐	317	Glen Rice G	100.00	45.00
☐	318	Reggie Miller G	100.00	45.00
☐	319	Kevin Garnett G	600.00	275.00
☐	320	Allen Iverson G	500.00	220.00
☐	321	Karl Malone G	150.00	70.00
☐	322	Scottie Pippen G	300.00	135.00
☐	323	Kobe Bryant G	800.00	350.00
☐	324	Stephon Marbury G	500.00	220.00
☐	325	Tim Duncan G	600.00	275.00
☐	326	Chris Webber G	250.00	110.00

1997-98 Finest Refractors

Randomly inserted into both series packs, this set parallels all three tiers of the basic set. The bronze refractors were inserted at a rate of one in 12. The silver refractors were inserted at a rate of one in 48 and were serially numbered to 1,090 sets. The gold refractors were

inserted at a rate of one in 288 and were serially numbered to 263 sets. Prices below refer to unpeeled cards. Peeled cards generally trade for 75% of the values listed below.

	MINT	NRMT
COMP.SET (326)	5000.00	2200.00
COMP.SERIES 1 (173)	2400.00	1100.00
COMP.SERIES 2 (153)	2600.00	1150.00
COMP.BRNZ SET (220)	1800.00	800.00
COMP.BRNZ SER.1 (120)	1200.00	550.00
COMP.BRNZ SER.2 (100)	600.00	275.00
COMMON BRONZE	2.50	1.10
SEMISTARS BRONZE	3.00	1.35
UNLISTED STARS BRONZE	5.00	2.20
BRONZE: SER.1/2 STATED ODDS 1:12		
COMP.SILVER SET (66)	800.00	350.00
COMP.SILVER SER.1 (33)	400.00	180.00
COMP.SILVER SER.2 (33)	400.00	180.00
COMMON SILVER	4.00	1.80
SEMISTARS SILVER	5.00	2.20
UNLISTED STARS SILVER	8.00	3.60
SILVER: SER.1/2 STATED ODDS 1:48		
STATED PRINT RUN 1090 SERIAL #'d SETS		
COMP.GOLD SET (40)	2400.00	1100.00
COMP.GOLD SER.1 (20)	800.00	350.00
COMP.GOLD SER.2 (20)	1600.00	700.00
COMMON GOLD (154-173)	12.00	5.50
GOLD SEMISTARS	15.00	6.75
GOLD UNLISTED STARS	25.00	11.00
GOLD: SER.1/2 STATED ODDS 1:288		
STATED PRINT RUN 289 SERIAL #'d SETS		

#	Card	MINT	NRMT
1	Scottie Pippen B	15.00	6.75
2	Tim Hardaway B	6.00	2.70
3	Charles Outlaw B	2.50	1.10
4	Rik Smits B	3.00	1.35
5	Dale Ellis B	2.50	1.10
6	Clyde Drexler B	6.00	2.70
7	Steve Smith B	3.00	1.35
8	Nick Anderson B	2.50	1.10
9	Juwan Howard B	5.00	2.20
10	Cedric Ceballos B	2.50	1.10
11	Shawn Bradley B	2.50	1.10
12	Loy Vaught B	3.00	1.35
13	Todd Day B	2.50	1.10
14	Glen Rice B	5.00	2.20
15	Bryant Stith B	2.50	1.10
16	Bob Sura B	2.50	1.10
17	Derrick McKey B	2.50	1.10
18	Ray Allen B	6.00	2.70
19	Stephon Marbury B	25.00	11.00
20	David Robinson B	8.00	3.60
21	Anthony Peeler B	2.50	1.10
22	Isaiah Rider B	3.00	1.35
23	Mookie Blaylock B	3.00	1.35
24	D.Stoudamire B	10.00	4.50
25	Rod Strickland B	3.00	1.35
26	Glenn Robinson B	5.00	2.20
27	Chris Webber B	12.00	5.50
28	Christian Laettner B	3.00	1.35
29	Joe Dumars B	5.00	2.20
30	Mark Price B	2.50	1.10
31	Jamal Mashburn B	3.00	1.35
32	Danny Manning B	3.00	1.35
33	John Stockton B	5.00	2.20
34	Detlef Schrempf B	3.00	1.35
35	Tyus Edney B	2.50	1.10
36	Chris Childs B	2.50	1.10
37	Dana Barros B	2.50	1.10
38	Bobby Phills B	2.50	1.10
39	Michael Jordan B	60.00	27.00
40	Grant Hill B	30.00	13.50
41	Brent Barry B	2.50	1.10
42	Rony Seikaly B	2.50	1.10
43	S.Abdur-Rahim B	15.00	6.75
44	Dominique Wilkins B	5.00	2.20
45	Vin Baker B	10.00	4.50
46	Kendall Gill B	3.00	1.35
47	Muggsy Bogues B	2.50	1.10
48	Hakeem Olajuwon B	10.00	4.50
49	Reggie Miller B	5.00	2.20
50	Shaquille O'Neal B	20.00	9.00
51	Antonio McDyess B	6.00	2.70
52	Michael Finley B	5.00	2.20
53	Jerry Stackhouse B	5.00	2.20
54	Brian Grant B	2.50	1.10
55	Greg Anthony B	2.50	1.10
56	Patrick Ewing B	5.00	2.20
57	Allen Iverson B	25.00	11.00
58	Rasheed Wallace B	3.00	1.35
59	Shawn Kemp B	15.00	6.75
60	Bryant Reeves B	3.00	1.35
61	Kevin Garnett B	30.00	13.50
62	Allan Houston B	3.00	1.35
63	Stacey Augmon B	2.50	1.10
64	Rick Fox B	2.50	1.10
65	Derek Harper B	2.50	1.10
66	Lindsey Hunter B	2.50	1.10
67	Eddie Jones B	10.00	4.50
68	Joe Smith B	5.00	2.20
69	Alonzo Mourning B	5.00	2.20
70	LaPhonso Ellis B	2.50	1.10
71	Tyrone Hill B	2.50	1.10
72	Charles Barkley B	8.00	3.60
73	Malik Sealy B	2.50	1.10
74	Shandon Anderson B	2.50	1.10
75	Arvydas Sabonis B	3.00	1.35
76	Tom Gugliotta B	5.00	2.20
77	A.Hardaway B	20.00	9.00
78	Sean Elliott B	2.50	1.10
79	Marcus Camby B	5.00	2.20
80	Gary Payton B	8.00	3.60
81	Kerry Kittles B	5.00	2.20
82	D.Mutombo B	3.00	1.35
83	Antoine Walker B	25.00	11.00
84	Terrell Brandon B	5.00	2.20
85	Otis Thorpe B	3.00	1.35
86	Mark Jackson B	2.50	1.10
87	A.C. Green B	3.00	1.35
88	John Starks B	3.00	1.35
89	Kenny Anderson B	3.00	1.35
90	Karl Malone B	8.00	3.60
91	Mitch Richmond B	5.00	2.20
92	Derrick Coleman B	3.00	1.35
93	Horace Grant B	3.00	1.35
94	John Williams B	2.50	1.10
95	Jason Kidd B	10.00	4.50
96	M.Abdul-Rauf B	2.50	1.10
97	Walt Williams B	2.50	1.10
98	Anthony Mason B	3.00	1.35
99	Latrell Sprewell B	3.00	1.35
100	Checklist	2.50	1.10
101	Tim Duncan B	225.00	100.00
102	Keith Van Horn B	150.00	70.00
103	Chauncey Billups B	60.00	27.00
104	Antonio Daniels B	40.00	18.00
105	Tony Battie B	30.00	13.50
106	Tim Thomas B	80.00	36.00
107	Tracy McGrady B	80.00	36.00
108	Adonal Foyle B	20.00	9.00
109	Maurice Taylor B	60.00	27.00
110	Austin Croshere B	20.00	9.00
111	Bobby Jackson B	30.00	13.50
112	Olivier Saint-Jean B	25.00	11.00
113	John Thomas B	2.50	1.10
114	Derek Anderson B	60.00	27.00
115	Brevin Knight B	60.00	27.00
116	Charles Smith B	2.50	1.10
117	Johnny Taylor B	2.50	1.10
118	Jacque Vaughn B	20.00	9.00
119	Anthony Parker B	2.50	1.10
120	Paul Grant B	2.50	1.10
121	Stephon Marbury S	40.00	18.00
122	Terrell Brandon S	8.00	3.60
123	D.Mutombo S	5.00	2.20
124	Patrick Ewing S	8.00	3.60
125	Scottie Pippen S	25.00	11.00
126	Antoine Walker S	40.00	18.00
127	Karl Malone S	12.00	5.50
128	Sean Elliott S	4.00	1.80
129	Chris Webber S	20.00	9.00
130	Shawn Kemp S	25.00	11.00
131	Hakeem Olajuwon S	15.00	6.75
132	Tim Hardaway S	10.00	4.50
133	Glen Rice S	8.00	3.60
134	Vin Baker S	15.00	6.75
135	Jim Jackson S	5.00	2.20
136	Kevin Garnett S	50.00	22.00
137	Kobe Bryant S	60.00	27.00
138	D.Stoudamire S	15.00	6.75
139	Larry Johnson S	5.00	2.20
140	Latrell Sprewell S	5.00	2.20
141	Lorenzen Wright S	4.00	1.80
142	Toni Kukoc S	5.00	2.20
143	Allen Iverson S	40.00	18.00
144	Elden Campbell S	3.00	2.20
145	Tom Gugliotta S	8.00	3.60
146	David Robinson S	12.00	5.50
147	Jayson Williams S	5.00	2.20
148	Shaquille O'Neal S	30.00	13.50
149	Grant Hill S	50.00	22.00
150	Reggie Miller S	8.00	3.60
151	Clyde Drexler S	10.00	4.50
152	Ray Allen S	10.00	4.50
153	Eddie Jones S	15.00	6.75
154	Michael Jordan G	400.00	180.00
155	Dominique Wilkins G	25.00	11.00
156	Charles Barkley G	40.00	18.00
157	Jerry Stackhouse G	25.00	11.00
158	Juwan Howard G	25.00	11.00
159	Marcus Camby G	25.00	11.00
160	Christian Laettner G	15.00	6.75
161	Anthony Mason G	15.00	6.75
162	Joe Smith G	25.00	11.00
163	Kerry Kittles G	25.00	11.00
164	Mitch Richmond G	25.00	11.00
165	S.Abdur-Rahim G	80.00	36.00
166	Alonzo Mourning G	25.00	11.00
167	Dennis Rodman G	100.00	45.00
168	Antonio McDyess G	30.00	13.50
169	Shawn Bradley G	12.00	5.50
170	A.Hardaway G	100.00	45.00
171	Jason Kidd G	50.00	22.00
172	Gary Payton G	40.00	18.00
173	John Stockton G	25.00	11.00
174	Allan Houston B	3.00	1.35
175	Bob Sura B	2.50	1.10
176	Clyde Drexler B	6.00	2.70
177	Glenn Robinson B	5.00	2.20
178	Joe Smith B	5.00	2.20
179	Larry Johnson B	3.00	1.35
180	Mitch Richmond B	5.00	2.20
181	Rony Seikaly B	2.50	1.10
182	Tyrone Hill B	2.50	1.10
183	Allen Iverson B	25.00	11.00
184	Brent Barry B	2.50	1.10
185	D.Stoudamire B	10.00	4.50
186	Grant Hill B	30.00	13.50
187	John Stockton B	5.00	2.20
188	Latrell Sprewell B	3.00	1.35
189	Mookie Blaylock B	3.00	1.35
190	Samaki Walker B	2.50	1.10
191	Vin Baker B	10.00	4.50
192	Alonzo Mourning B	6.00	2.70
193	Brevin Knight B	12.00	5.50
194	Danny Manning B	3.00	1.35
195	Hakeem Olajuwon B	10.00	4.50
196	Johnny Taylor B	2.50	1.10
197	Lorenzen Wright B	2.50	1.10
198	Olden Polynice B	2.50	1.10
199	Scottie Pippen B	15.00	6.75
200	Lindsey Hunter B	2.50	1.10
201	A.Hardaway B	20.00	9.00
202	Greg Anthony B	2.50	1.10

☐ 203 David Robinson B	8.00	3.60
☐ 204 Horace Grant B	3.00	1.35
☐ 205 Calbert Cheaney B	2.50	1.10
☐ 206 Loy Vaught B	3.00	1.35
☐ 207 T.Abdul-Wahad B	5.00	2.20
☐ 208 Sean Elliott B	2.50	1.10
☐ 209 Rodney Rogers B	2.50	1.10
☐ 210 Anthony Mason B	3.00	1.35
☐ 211 Bryant Reeves B	3.00	1.35
☐ 212 David Wesley B	2.50	1.10
☐ 213 Isaiah Rider B	3.00	1.35
☐ 214 Karl Malone B	8.00	3.60
☐ 215 M.Abdul-Rauf B	2.50	1.10
☐ 216 Patrick Ewing B	5.00	2.20
☐ 217 Shaquille O'Neal B	20.00	9.00
☐ 218 Antoine Walker B	25.00	11.00
☐ 219 Charles Barkley B	8.00	3.60
☐ 220 Dennis Rodman B	20.00	9.00
☐ 221 Jamal Mashburn B	3.00	1.35
☐ 222 Kendall Gill B	3.00	1.35
☐ 223 Malik Sealy B	2.50	1.10
☐ 224 Rasheed Wallace B	3.00	1.35
☐ 225 S.Abdur-Rahim B	15.00	6.75
☐ 226 Antonio Daniels B	6.00	2.70
☐ 227 Charles Oakley B	2.50	1.10
☐ 228 Derek Anderson B	5.50	
☐ 229 Jason Kidd B	10.00	4.50
☐ 230 Kenny Anderson B	3.00	1.35
☐ 231 Marcus Camby B	5.00	2.20
☐ 232 Ray Allen B	6.00	2.70
☐ 233 Shawn Bradley B	2.50	1.10
☐ 234 Antonio McDyess B	6.00	2.70
☐ 235 Chauncey Billups B	10.00	4.50
☐ 236 Detlef Schrempf B	3.00	1.35
☐ 237 Jayson Williams B	3.00	1.35
☐ 238 Kerry Kittles B	5.00	2.20
☐ 239 Jalen Rose B	2.50	1.10
☐ 240 Reggie Miller B	5.00	2.20
☐ 241 Shawn Kemp B	15.00	6.75
☐ 242 Arvydas Sabonis B	3.00	1.35
☐ 243 Tom Gugliotta B	5.00	2.20
☐ 244 D.Mutombo B	3.00	1.35
☐ 245 Jeff Hornacek B	3.00	1.35
☐ 246 Kevin Garnett B	30.00	13.50
☐ 247 Matt Maloney B	2.50	1.10
☐ 248 Rex Chapman B	2.50	1.10
☐ 249 Stephon Marbury B	25.00	11.00
☐ 250 Austin Croshere B	5.00	2.20
☐ 251 Chris Childs B	2.50	1.10
☐ 252 Eddie Jones B	10.00	4.50
☐ 253 Jerry Stackhouse B	5.00	2.20
☐ 254 Kevin Johnson B	3.00	1.35
☐ 255 Maurice Taylor B	15.00	6.75
☐ 256 Chris Mullin B	5.00	2.20
☐ 257 Terrell Brandon B	5.00	2.20
☐ 258 Avery Johnson B	2.50	1.10
☐ 259 Chris Webber B	12.00	5.50
☐ 260 Gary Payton B	8.00	3.60
☐ 261 Jim Jackson B	3.00	1.35
☐ 262 Kobe Bryant B	50.00	22.00
☐ 263 Michael Finley B	5.00	2.20
☐ 264 Rod Strickland B	3.00	1.35
☐ 265 Tim Hardaway B	6.00	2.70
☐ 266 B.J. Armstrong B	2.50	1.10
☐ 267 Christian Laettner B	3.00	1.35
☐ 268 Glen Rice B	5.00	2.20
☐ 269 Joe Dumars B	5.00	2.20
☐ 270 LaPhonso Ellis B	2.50	1.10
☐ 271 Michael Jordan B	60.00	27.00
☐ 272 Ron Mercer B	125.00	55.00
☐ 273 Checklist	2.50	1.10
☐ 274 A.Hardaway S	30.00	13.50
☐ 275 Dennis Rodman S	30.00	13.50
☐ 276 Gary Payton S	12.00	5.50
☐ 277 Jamal Mashburn S	5.00	2.20
☐ 278 S.Abdur-Rahim S	25.00	11.00
☐ 279 Steve Smith S	5.00	2.20
☐ 280 Tony Battie S	8.00	3.60
☐ 281 Alonzo Mourning S	8.00	3.60
☐ 282 Bobby Jackson S	8.00	3.60
☐ 283 Christian Laettner S	5.00	2.20
☐ 284 Jerry Stackhouse S	8.00	3.60
☐ 285 Terrell Brandon S	8.00	3.60
☐ 286 Chauncey Billups S	15.00	6.75
☐ 287 Michael Jordan S	100.00	45.00
☐ 288 Glenn Robinson S	8.00	3.60

☐ 289 Jason Kidd S	15.00	6.75
☐ 290 Joe Smith S	8.00	3.60
☐ 291 Michael Finley S	8.00	3.60
☐ 292 Rod Strickland S	5.00	2.20
☐ 293 Ron Mercer S	30.00	13.50
☐ 294 Tracy McGrady S	25.00	11.00
☐ 295 Adonal Foyle S	8.00	3.60
☐ 296 Marcus Camby S	8.00	3.60
☐ 297 John Stockton S	8.00	3.60
☐ 298 Kerry Kittles S	8.00	3.60
☐ 299 Mitch Richmond S	8.00	3.60
☐ 300 Shawn Bradley S	4.00	1.80
☐ 301 Anthony Mason S	5.00	2.20
☐ 302 Antonio Daniels S	10.00	4.50
☐ 303 Antonio McDyess S	10.00	4.50
☐ 304 Charles Barkley S	12.00	5.50
☐ 305 Keith Van Horn S	40.00	18.00
☐ 306 Tim Duncan S	50.00	22.00
☐ 307 D.Mutombo S	15.00	6.75
☐ 308 Grant Hill G	150.00	70.00
☐ 309 Shaquille O'Neal G	100.00	45.00
☐ 310 Keith Van Horn G	120.00	55.00
☐ 311 Shawn Kemp G	80.00	36.00
☐ 312 Antoine Walker G	120.00	55.00
☐ 313 H.Olajuwon G	50.00	22.00
☐ 314 Vin Baker G	50.00	22.00
☐ 315 Patrick Ewing G	25.00	11.00
☐ 316 Tracy McGrady G	80.00	36.00
☐ 317 Glen Rice G	25.00	11.00
☐ 318 Reggie Miller G	25.00	11.00
☐ 319 Kevin Garnett G	150.00	70.00
☐ 320 Allen Iverson G	120.00	55.00
☐ 321 Karl Malone G	40.00	18.00
☐ 322 Scottie Pippen G	80.00	36.00
☐ 323 Kobe Bryant G	200.00	90.00
☐ 324 S.Marbury G	120.00	55.00
☐ 325 Tim Duncan G	150.00	70.00
☐ 326 Chris Webber G	60.00	27.00

1994-95 Flair

This 326-card super-premium standard-size set (made by Fleer) was issued in two series. The first series contains 175 cards while the second has 151 cards (including the late addition of Michael Jordan as card #326). Cards were distributed in 10-card "hardpacks" (featuring a two-piece protective design wrapper), each with a suggested retail price of $4.00. The cards have a polyester laminate protective coating on both sides and are made with extra thick 30 point stock. The front has two color action photos blended. The back has one full color action photo with the player's statistics laid on top. Both sides have the player's name stamped in gold foil along with his team. The cards are numbered on the back and checklisted below alphabetically within teams. The first series includes a "Dream Team II" subset (159-172) commemorating the USA's team victory at the 1994 World Championships in Toronto. Rookie Cards of note in this set include Grant Hill, Juwan Howard, Eddie Jones, Jason Kidd, and Glenn Robinson.

	MINT	NRMT
COMPLETE SET (326)	70.00	32.00
COMPLETE SERIES 1 (175)	50.00	9.00
COMPLETE SERIES 2 (151)	50.00	22.00
COMMON CARD (1-175)	.20	.09
COMMON CARD (176-325)	.25	.11
SEMISTARS SER.1	.40	.18
SEMISTARS SER.2	.50	.23
UNLISTED STARS SER.1	.60	.25
UNLISTED STARS SER.2	.75	.35

☐ 1 Stacey Augmon	.20	.09
☐ 2 Mookie Blaylock	.40	.18
☐ 3 Craig Ehlo	.20	.09
☐ 4 Jon Koncak	.20	.09
☐ 5 Andrew Lang	.20	.09
☐ 6 Dee Brown	.20	.09
☐ 7 Sherman Douglas	.20	.09
☐ 8 Acie Earl	.20	.09
☐ 9 Rick Fox	.20	.09
☐ 10 Kevin Gamble	.20	.09
☐ 11 Xavier McDaniel	.20	.09
☐ 12 Dino Radja	.20	.09
☐ 13 Tony Bennett	.20	.09
☐ 14 Dell Curry	.20	.09
☐ 15 Kenny Gattison	.20	.09
☐ 16 Hersey Hawkins	.40	.18
☐ 17 Larry Johnson	.40	.18
☐ 18 Alonzo Mourning	.75	.35
☐ 19 David Wingate	.20	.09
☐ 20 B.J. Armstrong	.20	.09
☐ 21 Steve Kerr	.40	.18
☐ 22 Toni Kukoc	.60	.25
☐ 23 Pete Myers	.20	.09
☐ 24 Scottie Pippen	2.00	.90
☐ 25 Bill Wennington	.20	.09
☐ 26 Terrell Brandon	.60	.25
☐ 27 Brad Daugherty	.20	.09
☐ 28 Tyrone Hill	.20	.09
☐ 29 Bobby Phills	.20	.09
☐ 30 Mark Price	.40	.18
☐ 31 Gerald Wilkins	.20	.09
☐ 32 John Williams	.20	.09
☐ 33 Lucious Harris	.20	.09
☐ 34 Jim Jackson	.40	.18
☐ 35 Jamal Mashburn	.60	.25
☐ 36 Sean Rooks	.20	.09
☐ 37 Doug Smith	.20	.09
☐ 38 M.Abdul-Rauf	.20	.09
☐ 39 LaPhonso Ellis	.40	.18
☐ 40 D.Mutombo	.60	.25
☐ 41 Robert Pack	.20	.09
☐ 42 Rodney Rogers	.20	.09
☐ 43 Brian Williams	.20	.09
☐ 44 Reggie Williams	.20	.09
☐ 45 Joe Dumars	.60	.25
☐ 46 Allan Houston	.40	.18
☐ 47 Lindsey Hunter	.40	.18
☐ 48 Terry Mills	.20	.09
☐ 49 Victor Alexander	.20	.09
☐ 50 Chris Gatling	.20	.09
☐ 51 Billy Owens	.20	.09
☐ 52 Latrell Sprewell	.40	.18
☐ 53 Chris Webber	1.50	.70
☐ 54 Sam Cassell	.60	.25
☐ 55 Carl Herrera	.20	.09

#	Player			#	Player			#	Player		
56	Robert Horry	.40	.18	142	Nate McMillan	.20	.09	228	Scott Brooks	.25	.11
57	Hakeem Olajuwon	1.25	.55	143	Gary Payton	1.00	.45	229	Mario Elie	.25	.11
58	Kenny Smith	.20	.09	144	Sam Perkins	.40	.18	230	Vernon Maxwell	.25	.11
59	Otis Thorpe	.40	.18	145	David Benoit	.20	.09	231	Zan Tabak	.25	.11
60	Antonio Davis	.20	.09	146	Jeff Hornacek	.40	.18	232	Mark Jackson	.50	.23
61	Dale Davis	.20	.09	147	Jay Humphries	.20	.09	233	Derrick McKey	.25	.11
62	Reggie Miller	.60	.25	148	Karl Malone	1.00	.45	234	Tony Massenburg	.25	.11
63	Byron Scott	.40	.18	149	Bryon Russell	.40	.18	235	Lamond Murray	.50	.23
64	Rik Smits	.40	.18	150	Felton Spencer	.20	.09	236	Charles Outlaw	.25	.11
65	Haywoode Workman	.20	.09	151	John Stockton	.60	.25	237	Eric Piatkowski	.25	.11
66	Terry Dehere	.20	.09	152	Rex Chapman	.20	.09	238	Pooh Richardson	.25	.11
67	Harold Ellis	.20	.09	153	Calbert Cheaney	.40	.18	239	Malik Sealy	.25	.11
68	Gary Grant	.20	.09	154	Tom Gugliotta	.60	.25	240	Cedric Ceballos	.50	.23
69	Elmore Spencer	.20	.09	155	Don MacLean	.20	.09	241	Eddie Jones	6.00	2.70
70	Loy Vaught	.40	.18	156	Gheorghe Muresan	.40	.18	242	Anthony Miller	.25	.11
71	Elden Campbell	.40	.18	157	Doug Overton	.20	.09	243	Tony Smith	.25	.11
72	Doug Christie	.20	.09	158	Brent Price	.20	.09	244	Sedale Threatt	.25	.11
73	Vlade Divac	.40	.18	159	Derrick Coleman USA	.20	.09	245	Ledell Eackles	.25	.11
74	George Lynch	.20	.09	160	Joe Dumars USA	.40	.18	246	Kevin Gamble	.25	.11
75	Anthony Peeler	.20	.09	161	Tim Hardaway USA	.60	.25	247	Matt Geiger	.25	.11
76	Nick Van Exel	.60	.25	162	Kevin Johnson USA	.20	.09	248	Brad Lohaus	.25	.11
77	James Worthy	.60	.25	163	Larry Johnson USA	.20	.09	249	Billy Owens	.25	.11
78	Bimbo Coles	.20	.09	164	Shawn Kemp USA	1.00	.45	250	Khalid Reeves	.25	.11
79	Harold Miner	.20	.09	165	Dan Majerle USA	.20	.09	251	Glen Rice	.75	.35
80	John Salley	.20	.09	166	Reggie Miller USA	.40	.18	252	Kevin Willis	.25	.11
81	Rony Seikaly	.20	.09	167	Alonzo Mourning USA	.60	.25	253	Marty Conlon	.25	.11
82	Steve Smith	.40	.18	168	Shaquille O'Neal USA	1.25	.55	254	Eric Mobley	.25	.11
83	Vin Baker	1.50	.70	169	Mark Price USA	.20	.09	255	Johnny Newman	.25	.11
84	Jon Barry	.20	.09	170	Steve Smith USA	.20	.09	256	Ed Pinckney	.25	.11
85	Todd Day	.20	.09	171	Isiah Thomas USA	.40	.18	257	Glenn Robinson	3.00	1.35
86	Lee Mayberry	.20	.09	172	D.Wilkins USA	.40	.18	258	Pat Durham	.25	.11
87	Eric Murdock	.20	.09	173	Checklist	.20	.09	259	Howard Eisley	.25	.11
88	Mike Brown	.20	.09	174	Checklist	.20	.09	260	Winston Garland	.25	.11
89	Christian Laettner	.40	.18	175	Checklist	.20	.09	261	Stacey King	.25	.11
90	Isaiah Rider	.40	.18	176	Tyrone Corbin	.25	.11	262	Donyell Marshall	1.00	.45
91	Doug West	.20	.09	177	Grant Long	.25	.11	263	Sean Rooks	.25	.11
92	Micheal Williams	.20	.09	178	Ken Norman	.25	.11	264	Chris Smith	.25	.11
93	Kenny Anderson	.40	.18	179	Steve Smith	.50	.23	265	Chris Childs	1.00	.45
94	Benoit Benjamin	.20	.09	180	Blue Edwards	.25	.11	266	Sleepy Floyd	.25	.11
95	P.J. Brown	.20	.09	181	Pervis Ellison	.25	.11	267	Armon Gilliam	.25	.11
96	Derrick Coleman	.40	.18	182	Greg Minor	.25	.11	268	Sean Higgins	.25	.11
97	Kevin Edwards	.20	.09	183	Eric Montross	.25	.11	269	Rex Walters	.25	.11
98	Hubert Davis	.20	.09	184	Derek Strong	.25	.11	270	Greg Anthony	.25	.11
99	Patrick Ewing	.60	.25	185	David Wesley	.50	.23	271	Charlie Ward	.50	.23
100	Derek Harper	.40	.18	186	Dominique Wilkins	.75	.35	272	Herb Williams	.25	.11
101	Anthony Mason	.40	.18	187	Michael Adams	.25	.11	273	Monty Williams	.25	.11
102	Charles Oakley	.40	.18	188	Muggsy Bogues	.50	.23	274	Anthony Avent	.25	.11
103	Charles Smith	.20	.09	189	Scott Burrell	.25	.11	275	Anthony Bowie	.25	.11
104	John Starks	.40	.18	190	Darrin Hancock	.25	.11	276	Horace Grant	.50	.23
105	Nick Anderson	.40	.18	191	Robert Parish	.50	.23	277	Donald Royal	.25	.11
106	A.Hardaway	2.50	1.10	192	Jud Buechler	.25	.11	278	Brian Shaw	.25	.11
107	Shaquille O'Neal	2.50	1.10	193	Ron Harper	.50	.23	279	Brooks Thompson	.25	.11
108	Dennis Scott	.20	.09	194	Larry Krystkowiak	.25	.11	280	Derrick Alston	.25	.11
109	Jeff Turner	.20	.09	195	Will Perdue	.25	.11	281	Willie Burton	.25	.11
110	Dana Barros	.20	.09	196	Dickey Simpkins	.25	.11	282	Greg Graham	.25	.11
111	Shawn Bradley	.40	.18	197	Michael Cage	.25	.11	283	B.J. Tyler	.25	.11
112	Jeff Malone	.20	.09	198	Tony Campbell	.25	.11	284	Scott Williams	.25	.11
113	Tim Perry	.20	.09	199	Danny Ferry	.25	.11	285	Sharone Wright	.25	.11
114	C.Weatherspoon	.20	.09	200	Chris Mills	.50	.23	286	Joe Kleine	.25	.11
115	Danny Ainge	.40	.18	201	Popeye Jones	.25	.11	287	Danny Manning	.25	.11
116	Charles Barkley	1.00	.45	202	Jason Kidd	6.00	2.70	288	Elliot Perry	.25	.11
117	A.C. Green	.40	.18	203	Roy Tarpley	.25	.11	289	Wesley Person	1.00	.45
118	Kevin Johnson	.40	.18	204	Lorenzo Williams	.25	.11	290	Trevor Ruffin	.25	.11
119	Dan Majerle	.40	.18	205	Dale Ellis	.25	.11	291	Wayman Tisdale	.25	.11
120	Clyde Drexler	.75	.35	206	Tom Hammonds	.25	.11	292	Mark Bryant	.25	.11
121	Harvey Grant	.20	.09	207	Jalen Rose	.75	.35	293	Chris Dudley	.25	.11
122	Jerome Kersey	.20	.09	208	Reggie Slater	.25	.11	294	Aaron McKie	.25	.11
123	Clifford Robinson	.40	.18	209	Bryant Stith	.25	.11	295	Tracy Murray	.25	.11
124	Rod Strickland	.40	.18	210	Rafael Addison	.25	.11	296	Terry Porter	.25	.11
125	Buck Williams	.40	.18	211	Bill Curley	.25	.11	297	James Robinson	.25	.11
126	Randy Brown	.20	.09	212	Johnny Dawkins	.25	.11	298	Alaa Abdelnaby	.25	.11
127	Olden Polynice	.20	.09	213	Grant Hill	12.00	5.50	299	Duane Causwell	.25	.11
128	Mitch Richmond	.60	.25	214	Mark Macon	.25	.11	300	Brian Grant	.75	.35
129	Lionel Simmons	.20	.09	215	Oliver Miller	.25	.11	301	Bobby Hurley	.25	.11
130	Spud Webb	.40	.18	216	Ivano Newbill	.25	.11	302	Michael Smith	.50	.23
131	Walt Williams	.20	.09	217	Mark West	.25	.11	303	Terry Cummings	.25	.11
132	Willie Anderson	.20	.09	218	Tom Gugliotta	.25	.11	304	Moses Malone	.75	.35
133	Vinny Del Negro	.20	.09	219	Tim Hardaway	1.00	.45	305	Julius Nwosu	.25	.11
134	Sean Elliott	.40	.18	220	Keith Jennings	.25	.11	306	Chuck Person	.25	.11
135	Avery Johnson	.20	.09	221	Dwayne Morton	.25	.11	307	Doc Rivers	.50	.23
136	J.R. Reid	.20	.09	222	Chris Mullin	.75	.35	308	Vincent Askew	.25	.11
137	David Robinson	1.00	.45	223	Ricky Pierce	.25	.11	309	Sarunas Marciulionis	.25	.11
138	Dennis Rodman	2.50	1.10	224	Carlos Rogers	.25	.11	310	Detlef Schrempf	.50	.23
139	Kendall Gill	.40	.18	225	Clifford Rozier	.25	.11	311	Dontonio Wingfield	.25	.11
140	Ervin Johnson	.20	.09	226	Rony Seikaly	.25	.11	312	Antoine Carr	.25	.11
141	Shawn Kemp	2.00	.90	227	Tim Breaux	.25	.11	313	Tom Chambers	.25	.11

		MINT	NRMT
☐ 314	John Crotty	.25	.11
☐ 315	Adam Keefe	.25	.11
☐ 316	Jamie Watson	.50	.23
☐ 317	Mitchell Butler	.25	.11
☐ 318	Kevin Duckworth	.25	.11
☐ 319	Juwan Howard	4.00	1.80
☐ 320	Jim McIlvaine	.25	.11
☐ 321	Scott Skiles	.25	.11
☐ 322	Anthony Tucker	.25	.11
☐ 323	Chris Webber	2.00	.90
☐ 324	Checklist	.25	.11
☐ 325	Checklist	.25	.11
☐ 326	Michael Jordan	15.00	6.75

1994-95 Flair Center Spotlight

Randomly inserted at a rate of one in every 25 first series packs, cards from this 6-card set features dominant centers. The fronts have a 100% etched-foil design with a full color action photo with three shadows of him in red, green and blue. The back also has a color photo with the red, green and blue shadowing on a white background along with player information. The cards are numbered on the back as "X of 6" and are sequenced in alphabetical order.

	MINT	NRMT
COMPLETE SET (6)	50.00	22.00
COMMON CARD (1-6)	5.00	2.20
SER.1 STATED ODDS 1:25		
☐ 1 Patrick Ewing	5.00	2.20
☐ 2 Alonzo Mourning	6.00	2.70
☐ 3 Hakeem Olajuwon	10.00	4.50
☐ 4 Shaquille O'Neal	20.00	9.00
☐ 5 David Robinson	8.00	3.60
☐ 6 Chris Webber	12.00	5.50

1994-95 Flair Hot Numbers

Randomly inserted into first series packs at a rate of one in six, cards from this 20-card standard-size set feature a selection of players who consistently produce big statistics. The player's top statistical numbers

are shown on the front of the card without identifying which category. While some numbers are obvious, like the player's points per game, other statistics are not, like steals and blocks, particularly for multi-talented players. The fronts also have full-color action photos with the team's colors used as the background along with the words "Hot Numbers". The backs also have a color picture with information on what type of player he is. The cards are numbered on the back as "X of 20" and are sequenced in alphabetical order.

	MINT	NRMT
COMPLETE SET (20)	60.00	27.00
COMMON CARD (1-20)	1.00	.45
SEMISTARS	1.50	.70
UNLISTED STARS	2.50	1.10
SER.1 STATED ODDS 1:6		
☐ 1 Vin Baker	6.00	2.70
☐ 2 Sam Cassell	2.50	1.10
☐ 3 Patrick Ewing	2.50	1.10
☐ 4 A.Hardaway	10.00	4.50
☐ 5 Robert Horry	1.00	.45
☐ 6 Shawn Kemp	8.00	3.60
☐ 7 Toni Kukoc	2.50	1.10
☐ 8 Jamal Mashburn	1.50	.70
☐ 9 Reggie Miller	2.50	1.10
☐ 10 D.Mutombo	1.50	.70
☐ 11 Hakeem Olajuwon	5.00	2.20
☐ 12 Shaquille O'Neal	10.00	4.50
☐ 13 Scottie Pippen	8.00	3.60
☐ 14 Isaiah Rider	1.00	.45
☐ 15 David Robinson	4.00	1.80
☐ 16 Latrell Sprewell	1.00	.45
☐ 17 John Starks	1.50	.70
☐ 18 John Stockton	2.50	1.10
☐ 19 Nick Van Exel	2.50	1.10
☐ 20 Chris Webber	6.00	2.70

1994-95 Flair Playmakers

Randomly inserted into second series packs at a rate of one in four, cards from this 10-card standard-size set feature a selection of the best assist men in the NBA. The fronts have a full color action photo with a

hardwood floor in the background. The back also has a color photo with player information set against a hardwood floor. The cards are numbered on the back as "X of 10" and are sequenced in alphabetical order.

	MINT	NRMT
COMPLETE SET (10)	10.00	4.50
COMMON CARD (1-10)	.50	.23
SEMISTARS	.75	.35
UNLISTED STARS	1.25	.55
SER.2 STATED ODDS 1:4		
☐ 1 Kenny Anderson	.75	.35
☐ 2 Mookie Blaylock	.75	.35
☐ 3 Sam Cassell	1.25	.55
☐ 4 A.Hardaway	5.00	2.20
☐ 5 Robert Pack	.50	.23
☐ 6 Scottie Pippen	4.00	1.80
☐ 7 Mark Price	.50	.23
☐ 8 Mitch Richmond	1.25	.55
☐ 9 John Stockton	1.25	.55
☐ 10 Nick Van Exel	1.25	.55

1994-95 Flair Rejectors

Randomly inserted into second series packs at a rate of one in 25, cards from this six-card standard-size set feature a selection of top shot blockers in basketball. The fronts are 100% etched foil that have a full color action photo of the player. The background is three hands in red, green and blue seemingly up to reject a shot. The back also has a player photo along with information on him, such as his blocks per game. The background is nearly identical to the background on the front. The cards are numbered on the back as "X of 6" and are sequenced in alphabetical order.

	MINT	NRMT
COMPLETE SET (6)	60.00	27.00
COMMON CARD (1-6)	3.00	1.35
SEMISTARS	6.00	2.70
SER.2 STATED ODDS 1:25		
☐ 1 Patrick Ewing	6.00	2.70
☐ 2 Alonzo Mourning	8.00	3.60
☐ 3 D.Mutombo	3.00	1.35
☐ 4 Hakeem Olajuwon	12.00	5.50
☐ 5 Shaquille O'Neal	25.00	11.00
☐ 6 David Robinson	10.00	4.50

1994-95 Flair Scoring Power

Randomly inserted into first series packs at a rate of one in eight, cards from this 20-card standard-size set feature a selection of perennial NBA scoring leaders. The fronts emphasize the words scoring power as they are the size of the card laid out horizontally against a black background. There is a player photo in front of the words and another inside. The back also says "Scoring Power" across the entire card horizontally. There is also a player photo with information on him, namely about his scoring. The cards are numbered on the back as "X of 10" and are sequenced in alphabetical order.

	MINT	NRMT
COMPLETE SET (10)	30.00	13.50
COMMON CARD (1-10)	1.00	.45
SEMISTARS	2.50	1.10
SER.1 STATED ODDS 1:8		
☐ 1 Charles Barkley	4.00	1.80
☐ 2 Patrick Ewing	2.50	1.10
☐ 3 Karl Malone	4.00	1.80
☐ 4 Hakeem Olajuwon	5.00	2.20
☐ 5 Shaquille O'Neal	10.00	4.50

☐ 6 Scottie Pippen	8.00	3.60
☐ 7 Mitch Richmond	2.50	1.10
☐ 8 David Robinson	4.00	1.80
☐ 9 Latrell Sprewell	1.00	.45
☐ 10 Dominique Wilkins	1.00	.45

1994-95 Flair Wave of the Future

Randmly inserted into second series packs at a rate of one in seven, cards from this 10-card standard-size set feature a selection of top rookies from the 1994-95 season. Card fronts are laid out horizontally with three color photos of the player. The one in the middle has yellow glow surrounding it and the picture on the left is the same as the middle. The one on the left is a head shot of the color photo used on the back of the card. The back has player information including some college statistics. Both sides of the card have a wave in the background in the team's colors. The cards are numbered on the back as "X of 10" and are sequenced in alphabetical order.

	MINT	NRMT
COMPLETE SET (10)	40.00	18.00
COMMON CARD (1-10)	.75	.35
SEMISTARS	1.25	.55
SER.2 STATED ODDS 1:7		
☐ 1 Brian Grant	1.25	.55
☐ 2 Grant Hill	20.00	9.00
☐ 3 Juwan Howard	8.00	3.60
☐ 4 Eddie Jones	12.00	5.50
☐ 5 Jason Kidd	12.00	5.50
☐ 6 Donyell Marshall	1.25	.55
☐ 7 Eric Montross	.75	.35
☐ 8 Lamond Murray	.75	.35
☐ 9 Wesley Person	1.25	.55
☐ 10 Glenn Robinson	6.00	2.70

1995-96 Flair

These 250-standard size cards comprise Fleer's premium1995-96 Flair set which was issued in two separate series of 150 and

100 cards respectively. Cards were issued in 9-card "hard packs" (featuring a two-piece protective design wrapper) with a suggested retail price of $4.99. Player selection was restricted to recognized starters, top rookies and top players off the bench. Card fronts were upgraded from the previous year, each featuring 100% etched foil designs. Like the previous year, each card was printed on 30-point stock, giving the card twice the thickness of regular issue cards. First and second series cards are numbered alphabetically by team. Two subsets are included in the set: Rookies (199-228) and Style (229-248). Noteworthy Rookie Cards in this set include Michael Finley, Kevin Garnett, Antonio McDyess, Joe Smith, Jerry Stackhouse and D.Stoudamire.

	MINT	NRMT
COMPLETE SET (250)	80.00	36.00
COMPLETE SERIES 1 (150)	40.00	18.00
COMPLETE SERIES 2 (150)	40.00	18.00
COMMON CARD (1-150)	.30	.14
COMMON CARD (151-250)	.20	.09
SEMISTARS SER.1	.60	.25
SEMISTARS SER.2	.40	.18
UNLISTED STARS SER.1	1.00	.45
UNLISTED STARS SER.2	.60	.25
☐ 1 Stacey Augmon	.30	.14
☐ 2 Mookie Blaylock	.60	.25
☐ 3 Grant Long	.30	.14
☐ 4 Steve Smith	.60	.25
☐ 5 Dee Brown	.30	.14
☐ 6 Sherman Douglas	.30	.14
☐ 7 Eric Montross	.30	.14
☐ 8 Dino Radja	.30	.14
☐ 9 David Wesley	.30	.14
☐ 10 Muggsy Bogues	.60	.25
☐ 11 Scott Burrell	.30	.14
☐ 12 Dell Curry	.30	.14
☐ 13 Larry Johnson	.60	.25
☐ 14 Alonzo Mourning	1.00	.45
☐ 15 Michael Jordan	12.00	5.50
☐ 16 Steve Kerr	.60	.25
☐ 17 Toni Kukoc	.60	.25
☐ 18 Scottie Pippen	3.00	1.35
☐ 19 Terrell Brandon	1.00	.45
☐ 20 Tyrone Hill	.30	.14
☐ 21 Chris Mills	.30	.14
☐ 22 Bobby Phills	.30	.14

☐ 23	Mark Price	.30	.14
☐ 24	John Williams	.30	.14
☐ 25	Jim Jackson	.60	.25
☐ 26	Popeye Jones	.30	.14
☐ 27	Jason Kidd	2.50	1.10
☐ 28	Jamal Mashburn	.60	.25
☐ 29	Lorenzo Williams	.30	.14
☐ 30	M.Abdul-Rauf	.30	.14
☐ 31	D.Mutombo	.60	.25
☐ 32	Robert Pack	.30	.14
☐ 33	Jalen Rose	.60	.25
☐ 34	Bryant Stith	.30	.14
☐ 35	Reggie Williams	.30	.14
☐ 36	Joe Dumars	1.00	.45
☐ 37	Grant Hill	6.00	2.70
☐ 38	Allan Houston	.60	.25
☐ 39	Lindsey Hunter	.30	.14
☐ 40	Terry Mills	.30	.14
☐ 41	Chris Gatling	.30	.14
☐ 42	Tim Hardaway	1.25	.55
☐ 43	Donyell Marshall	.60	.25
☐ 44	Chris Mullin	1.00	.45
☐ 45	Carlos Rogers	.30	.14
☐ 46	Clifford Rozier	.30	.14
☐ 47	Latrell Sprewell	.60	.25
☐ 48	Sam Cassell	.60	.25
☐ 49	Clyde Drexler	1.25	.55
☐ 50	Mario Elie	.30	.14
☐ 51	Robert Horry	.30	.14
☐ 52	Hakeem Olajuwon	2.00	.90
☐ 53	Kenny Smith	.30	.14
☐ 54	Antonio Davis	.30	.14
☐ 55	Dale Davis	.30	.14
☐ 56	Mark Jackson	.60	.25
☐ 57	Derrick McKey	.30	.14
☐ 58	Reggie Miller	1.00	.45
☐ 59	Rik Smits	.60	.25
☐ 60	Lamond Murray	.30	.14
☐ 61	Pooh Richardson	.30	.14
☐ 62	Malik Sealy	.30	.14
☐ 63	Loy Vaught	.30	.14
☐ 64	Elden Campbell	.60	.25
☐ 65	Cedric Ceballos	.30	.14
☐ 66	Vlade Divac	.60	.25
☐ 67	Eddie Jones	2.50	1.10
☐ 68	Nick Van Exel	1.00	.45
☐ 69	Bimbo Coles	.30	.14
☐ 70	Billy Owens	.30	.14
☐ 71	Khalid Reeves	.30	.14
☐ 72	Glen Rice	1.00	.45
☐ 73	Kevin Willis	.30	.14
☐ 74	Vin Baker	2.00	.90
☐ 75	Todd Day	.30	.14
☐ 76	Eric Murdock	.30	.14
☐ 77	Glenn Robinson	1.25	.55
☐ 78	Tom Gugliotta	1.00	.45
☐ 79	Christian Laettner	.60	.25
☐ 80	Isaiah Rider	.60	.25
☐ 81	Doug West	.30	.14
☐ 82	Kenny Anderson	.60	.25
☐ 83	P.J. Brown	.30	.14
☐ 84	Derrick Coleman	.60	.25
☐ 85	Armon Gilliam	.30	.14
☐ 86	Chris Morris	.30	.14
☐ 87	Hubert Davis	.30	.14
☐ 88	Patrick Ewing	1.00	.45
☐ 89	Derek Harper	.60	.25
☐ 90	Anthony Mason	.60	.25
☐ 91	Charles Oakley	.30	.14
☐ 92	Charles Smith	.30	.14
☐ 93	John Starks	.60	.25
☐ 94	Nick Anderson	.30	.14
☐ 95	Horace Grant	.60	.25
☐ 96	A.Hardaway	4.00	1.80
☐ 97	Shaquille O'Neal	4.00	1.80
☐ 98	Dennis Scott	.30	.14
☐ 99	Brian Shaw	.30	.14
☐ 100	Dana Barros	.30	.14
☐ 101	Shawn Bradley	.30	.14
☐ 102	C.Weatherspoon	.30	.14
☐ 103	Sharone Wright	.30	.14
☐ 104	Charles Barkley	1.50	.70
☐ 105	A.C. Green	.60	.25
☐ 106	Kevin Johnson	.60	.25
☐ 107	Dan Majerle	.30	.14
☐ 108	Danny Manning	.60	.25
☐ 109	Elliot Perry	.30	.14
☐ 110	Wesley Person	.60	.25
☐ 111	Terry Porter	.30	.14
☐ 112	Clifford Robinson	.30	.14
☐ 113	Rod Strickland	.60	.25
☐ 114	Otis Thorpe	.60	.25
☐ 115	Buck Williams	.30	.14
☐ 116	Brian Grant	.60	.25
☐ 117	Bobby Hurley	.30	.14
☐ 118	Olden Polynice	.30	.14
☐ 119	Mitch Richmond	1.00	.45
☐ 120	Walt Williams	.30	.14
☐ 121	Vinny Del Negro	.30	.14
☐ 122	Sean Elliott	.30	.14
☐ 123	Avery Johnson	.30	.14
☐ 124	David Robinson	1.50	.70
☐ 125	Dennis Rodman	4.00	1.80
☐ 126	Shawn Kemp	3.00	1.35
☐ 127	Nate McMillan	.30	.14
☐ 128	Gary Payton	1.50	.70
☐ 129	Sam Perkins	.60	.25
☐ 130	Detlef Schrempf	.60	.25
☐ 131	B.J. Armstrong	.30	.14
☐ 132	Jerome Kersey	.30	.14
☐ 133	Oliver Miller	.30	.14
☐ 134	John Salley	.30	.14
☐ 135	David Benoit	.30	.14
☐ 136	Antoine Carr	.30	.14
☐ 137	Jeff Hornacek	.60	.25
☐ 138	Karl Malone	1.50	.70
☐ 139	John Stockton	1.00	.45
☐ 140	Greg Anthony	.30	.14
☐ 141	Benoit Benjamin	.30	.14
☐ 142	Blue Edwards	.30	.14
☐ 143	Byron Scott	.30	.14
☐ 144	Calbert Cheaney	.30	.14
☐ 145	Juwan Howard	1.50	.70
☐ 146	Gheorghe Muresan	.30	.14
☐ 147	Scott Skiles	.30	.14
☐ 148	Chris Webber	2.50	1.10
☐ 149	Checklist	.30	.14
☐ 150	Checklist	.30	.14
☐ 151	Stacey Augmon	.20	.09
☐ 152	Mookie Blaylock	.40	.18
☐ 153	Andrew Lang	.20	.09
☐ 154	Steve Smith	.40	.18
☐ 155	Dana Barros	.20	.09
☐ 156	Rick Fox	.20	.09
☐ 157	Kendall Gill	.40	.18
☐ 158	Khalid Reeves	.20	.09
☐ 159	Glen Rice	.60	.25
☐ 160	Dennis Rodman	4.00	1.80
☐ 161	Dan Majerle	.20	.09
☐ 162	Tony Dumas	.20	.09
☐ 163	Dale Ellis	.20	.09
☐ 164	Otis Thorpe	.40	.18
☐ 165	Rony Seikaly	.20	.09
☐ 166	Sam Cassell	.40	.18
☐ 167	Clyde Drexler	.75	.35
☐ 168	Robert Horry	.20	.09
☐ 169	Hakeem Olajuwon	1.25	.55
☐ 170	Ricky Pierce	.20	.09
☐ 171	Rodney Rogers	.20	.09
☐ 172	Brian Williams	.20	.09
☐ 173	Magic Johnson	2.00	.90
☐ 174	Alonzo Mourning	.60	.25
☐ 175	Lee Mayberry	.20	.09
☐ 176	Terry Porter	.20	.09
☐ 177	Shawn Bradley	.40	.18
☐ 178	Jayson Williams	.40	.18
☐ 179	Gary Grant	.20	.09
☐ 180	Jon Koncak	.20	.09
☐ 181	Derrick Coleman	.40	.18
☐ 182	Vernon Maxwell	.20	.09
☐ 183	John Williams	.20	.09
☐ 184	Aaron McKie	.20	.09
☐ 185	Michael Smith	.20	.09
☐ 186	Chuck Person	.20	.09
☐ 187	Hersey Hawkins	.40	.18
☐ 188	Shawn Kemp	.90	.90
☐ 189	Gary Payton	1.00	.45
☐ 190	Detlef Schrempf	.40	.18
☐ 191	Chris Morris	.20	.09
☐ 192	Robert Pack	.20	.09
☐ 193	Willie Anderson EXP	.20	.09
☐ 194	Oliver Miller EXP	.20	.09
☐ 195	Alvin Robertson EXP	.20	.09
☐ 196	Greg Anthony EXP	.20	.09
☐ 197	Blue Edwards EXP	.20	.09
☐ 198	Byron Scott EXP	.20	.09
☐ 199	Cory Alexander	.20	.09
☐ 200	Brent Barry	.60	.25
☐ 201	Travis Best	.40	.18
☐ 202	Jason Caffey	.60	.25
☐ 203	Sasha Danilovic	.20	.09
☐ 204	Tyus Edney	.20	.09
☐ 205	Michael Finley	2.50	1.10
☐ 206	Kevin Garnett	12.00	5.50
☐ 207	Alan Henderson	.60	.25
☐ 208	Antonio McDyess	3.00	1.35
☐ 209	Loren Meyer	.20	.09
☐ 210	Lawrence Moten	.20	.09
☐ 211	Ed O'Bannon	.20	.09
☐ 212	Greg Ostertag	.20	.09
☐ 213	Cherokee Parks	.20	.09
☐ 214	Theo Ratliff	.20	.09
☐ 215	Bryant Reeves	1.50	.70
☐ 216	Shawn Respert	.20	.09
☐ 217	Arvydas Sabonis	1.25	.55
☐ 218	Joe Smith	2.50	1.10
☐ 219	Jerry Stackhouse	2.50	1.10
☐ 220	D.Stoudamire	5.00	2.20
☐ 221	Bob Sura	.40	.18
☐ 222	Kurt Thomas	.40	.18
☐ 223	Gary Trent	.20	.09
☐ 224	David Vaughn	.20	.09
☐ 225	Rasheed Wallace	1.50	.70
☐ 226	Eric Williams	.40	.18
☐ 227	Corliss Williamson	.75	.35
☐ 228	George Zidek	.20	.09
☐ 229	Vin Baker STY	.60	.25
☐ 230	Charles Barkley STY	.60	.25
☐ 231	Patrick Ewing STY	.40	.18
☐ 232	A.Hardaway STY	1.25	.55
☐ 233	Grant Hill STY	2.00	.90
☐ 234	Larry Johnson STY	.20	.09
☐ 235	Michael Jordan STY	4.00	1.80
☐ 236	Jason Kidd STY	.75	.35
☐ 237	Karl Malone STY	.60	.25
☐ 238	Jamal Mashburn STY	.20	.09
☐ 239	Reggie Miller STY	.40	.18
☐ 240	Shaquille O'Neal STY	1.25	.55
☐ 241	Scottie Pippen STY	1.00	.45
☐ 242	Mitch Richmond STY	.40	.18
☐ 243	Clifford Robinson STY	.20	.09
☐ 244	David Robinson STY	.60	.25
☐ 245	Glenn Robinson STY	.60	.25
☐ 246	John Stockton STY	.40	.18
☐ 247	Nick Van Exel STY	.40	.18
☐ 248	Chris Webber STY	.75	.35
☐ 249	Checklist	.20	.09
☐ 250	Checklist	.20	.09

1995-96 Flair Anticipation

Randomly inserted in second series packs at a rate of one in 36, cards from this ten card standard-size set feature a collection of fan favorites.

Borderless fronts have a full-color action raised cutouts and two ghosted images of the same shot in the player's team colors. Backs have a close-up color shot and a player profile. The set is sequenced in alphabetical order.

	MINT	NRMT
COMPLETE SET (10)	150.00	70.00
COMMON CARD (1-10)	5.00	2.20
SER.2 STATED ODDS 1:36		

		MINT	NRMT
□ 1	Grant Hill	30.00	13.50
□ 2	Michael Jordan	60.00	27.00
□ 3	Shawn Kemp	15.00	6.75
□ 4	Jason Kidd	12.00	5.50
□ 5	Alonzo Mourning	5.00	2.20
□ 6	Hakeem Olajuwon	10.00	4.50
□ 7	Shaquille O'Neal	20.00	9.00
□ 8	Glenn Robinson	6.00	2.70
□ 9	Joe Smith	10.00	4.50
□ 10	Jerry Stackhouse	10.00	4.50

1995-96 Flair
Center Spotlight

Randomly inserted in first series packs at a rate of one in 18, cards from this 6-card standard-size set feature a selection of the game's dominant centers. This was the second year in a row Flair included a Center Spotlight insert within their first series product. Each card is printed on clear plastic, with a full color action photo layered on top of a circular designed background. Backs are numbered on the left in gold foil and the player's blue silhouette serves as a background for biography and career highlights which are printed in white. The set is sequenced in alphabetical order.

	MINT	NRMT
COMPLETE SET (6)	25.00	11.00
COMMON CARD (1-6)	1.25	.55
SEMISTARS	4.00	1.80
SER.1 STATED ODDS 1:18		

		MINT	NRMT
□ 1	Vlade Divac	1.25	.55
□ 2	Patrick Ewing	4.00	1.80
□ 3	Alonzo Mourning	4.00	1.80

		MINT	NRMT
□ 4	Hakeem Olajuwon	6.00	2.70
□ 5	Shaquille O'Neal	12.00	5.50
□ 6	David Robinson	5.00	2.20

1995-96 Flair
Class of '95

Seeded in first series packs at the same rate as regular issue cards, these 15-cards were added to the first series Flair product just prior to release. Each card features one of the top rookies from the 1995 NBA draft in their new pro uniforms. Full color, cutout player action shots are placed against a glowing orange basketball backdrop. The set is sequenced in alphabetical order.

	MINT	NRMT
COMPLETE SET (15)	30.00	13.50
COMMON CARD (R1-R15)	.30	.14
SEMISTARS	.60	.25
UNLISTED STARS	1.00	.45
RANDOM INSERTS IN SER.1 PACKS		

		MINT	NRMT
□ R1	Brent Barry	1.00	.45
□ R2	Kevin Garnett	12.00	5.50
□ R3	Antonio McDyess	5.00	2.20
□ R4	Ed O'Bannon	.30	.14
□ R5	Cherokee Parks	.30	.14
□ R6	Bryant Reeves	2.50	1.10
□ R7	Shawn Respert	.30	.14
□ R8	Joe Smith	4.00	1.80
□ R9	Jerry Stackhouse	4.00	1.80
□ R10	D.Stoudamire	8.00	3.60
□ R11	Kurt Thomas	.60	.25
□ R12	Gary Trent	.30	.14
□ R13	Rasheed Wallace	2.50	1.10
□ R14	Eric Williams	.60	.25
□ R15	Corliss Williamson	1.00	.45

1995-96 Flair
Hot Numbers

Randomly inserted in first series packs at rate of one in 36, cards from this 15-card standard-size set showcase the game's top players. Each card is given a three-dimensional effect by the addition of a special lenticular coating (a ribbed plastic material) on the front. The full color

player photos are placed against a swirling background of numbers. The backs continue with the numbers motif that serve as a background for the full-color player cutout. Player's name and short biography are printed in white. The set is sequenced in alphabetical order.

	MINT	NRMT
COMPLETE SET (15)	200.00	90.00
COMMON CARD (1-15)	2.50	1.10
SEMISTARS	6.00	2.70
SER.1 STATED ODDS 1:36		

		MINT	NRMT
□ 1	Charles Barkley	10.00	4.50
□ 2	Grant Hill	40.00	18.00
□ 3	Eddie Jones	15.00	6.75
□ 4	Michael Jordan	80.00	36.00
□ 5	Shawn Kemp	20.00	9.00
□ 6	Jason Kidd	15.00	6.75
□ 7	Karl Malone	10.00	4.50
□ 8	Alonzo Mourning	6.00	2.70
□ 9	D.Mutombo	2.50	1.10
□ 10	Hakeem Olajuwon	12.00	5.50
□ 11	Shaquille O'Neal	25.00	11.00
□ 12	Glenn Robinson	8.00	3.60
□ 13	Dennis Rodman	25.00	11.00
□ 14	Latrell Sprewell	2.50	1.10
□ 15	Chris Webber	15.00	6.75

1995-96 Flair
New Heights

Randomly inserted in second series hobby packs only at a rate of one in 18, cards from this 10-card standard-size set feature some of the more popular players in the hobby. Borderless

fronts have a full-color action cutout with a ghosted image trailing behind. Backs have player profile and biographies. The set is sequenced in alphabetical order.

	MINT	NRMT
COMPLETE SET (10)	75.00	34.00
COMMON CARD (1-10)	2.00	.90
SER.2 STATED ODDS 1:18 HOBBY		
☐ 1 A.Hardaway	12.00	5.50
☐ 2 Grant Hill	20.00	9.00
☐ 3 Larry Johnson	2.00	.90
☐ 4 Michael Jordan	40.00	18.00
☐ 5 Shawn Kemp	10.00	4.50
☐ 6 Karl Malone	5.00	2.20
☐ 7 Hakeem Olajuwon	6.00	2.70
☐ 8 David Robinson	5.00	2.20
☐ 9 Glenn Robinson	4.00	1.80
☐ 10 Chris Webber	8.00	3.60

1995-96 Flair Perimeter Power

Randomly inserted in first series packs at a rate of one in 12, cards from this 15-card set feature players that dominate play from the perimeter. Full-bleed team-color backgrounds include a player cutout with silver foil printing on the front. Backs are printed on a white background with another full-color action player shot.

	MINT	NRMT
COMPLETE SET (15)	15.00	6.75
COMMON CARD (1-15)	.60	.25
SEMISTARS	.75	.35
UNLISTED STARS	1.25	.55
SER.1 STATED ODDS 1:12		
☐ 1 Dana Barros	.60	.25
☐ 2 Clyde Drexler	1.50	.70
☐ 3 A.Hardaway	5.00	2.20
☐ 4 Tim Hardaway	1.50	.70
☐ 5 Dan Majerle	.60	.25
☐ 6 Jamal Mashburn	.75	.35
☐ 7 Reggie Miller	1.25	.55
☐ 8 Gary Payton	2.00	.90
☐ 9 Scottie Pippen	4.00	1.80
☐ 10 Glen Rice	1.25	.55
☐ 11 Mitch Richmond	1.25	.55
☐ 12 Steve Smith	.75	.35
☐ 13 John Starks	.75	.35
☐ 14 John Stockton	1.25	.55
☐ 15 Nick Van Exel	1.25	.55

1995-96 Flair Play Makers

Randomly inserted in second series packs at a rate of one in 54 packs, this set of ten standard-size cards features a selection of some of the league's top playmakers. Fronts are printed in a 3-D lenticular format and feature the player in a full-color action shot. The background is a three-color chalkboard diagram. The diagram background continues on the back and a player profile appears in a screened box next to a full-color action player cutout. The set is sequenced in alphabetical order.

	MINT	NRMT
COMPLETE SET (10)	175.00	80.00
COMMON CARD (1-10)	6.00	2.70
SEMISTARS	8.00	3.60
UNLISTED STARS	12.00	5.50
SER.2 STATED ODDS 1:54		
☐ 1 Clyde Drexler	15.00	6.75
☐ 2 A.Hardaway	50.00	22.00
☐ 3 Jamal Mashburn	6.00	2.70
☐ 4 Reggie Miller	12.00	5.50
☐ 5 Gary Payton	20.00	9.00
☐ 6 Scottie Pippen	40.00	18.00
☐ 7 Mitch Richmond	12.00	5.50
☐ 8 David Robinson	20.00	9.00
☐ 9 Jerry Stackhouse	25.00	11.00
☐ 10 Nick Van Exel	12.00	5.50

1995-96 Flair Wave of the Future

The 10 cards in this standard-size set were randomly inserted at a rate of one in 12 second series packs and feature rookie NBA players with potential for greatness. A full-color player action cutout appears on the front with a watercolor backgound painted in a wave pattern. Backs continue with the wave pattern background and have another full-color action cutout.

The cards are sequenced in alphabetical order.

	MINT	NRMT
COMPLETE SET (10)	40.00	18.00
COMMON CARD (1-10)	1.00	.45
SER.2 STATED ODDS 1:12		
☐ 1 Tyus Edney	1.00	.45
☐ 2 Michael Finley	4.00	1.80
☐ 3 Kevin Garnett	15.00	6.75
☐ 4 Antonio McDyess	5.00	2.20
☐ 5 Ed O'Bannon	1.00	.45
☐ 6 Arvydas Sabonis	2.00	.90
☐ 7 Joe Smith	4.00	1.80
☐ 8 Jerry Stackhouse	4.00	1.80
☐ 9 D.Stoudamire	8.00	3.60
☐ 10 Rasheed Wallace	2.50	1.10

1996-97 Flair Showcase Row 2

The 1996-97 Flair Showcase set was issued in one series totalling 270 cards and was deemed Hobby only for the first time. Each box contained 24 cards per box, five cards per pack with a suggested retail price of $4.99. The set does contain 270 cards, but is essentially a 90-card set with each player having three different front themes: Row 2 (Style), Row 1 (Grace) and Row 0 (Showcase). Each card also contains the following back themes: Showtime, Show Stoppers and Showpiece. By combining the two different themes, collectors can determine the different scarcity levels. For Row 2, or Style, using Style and Showtime (cards 1-30), the odds are 1.5 to one. Using Style and Showpiece (cards 31-60), the odds are one in 2. Using Style and Show Stoppers (cards 61-90), the odds are one in 1.5. A three-card promo strip of Jerry Stackhouse was released and is priced at the end of the set.

	MINT	NRMT
COMPLETE SET (90)	60.00	27.00
COMMON CARD (1-90)	.30	.14
SEMISTARS	.50	.23
UNLISTED STARS	.75	.35
1-30 ODDS 1.5:1		
31-60 ODDS 1:2		
61-90 ODDS 1:1.5		

		MINT	NRMT
☐ 1	A.Hardaway	3.00	1.35
☐ 2	Mitch Richmond	.75	.35
☐ 3	Allen Iverson	8.00	3.60
☐ 4	Charles Barkley	1.25	.55
☐ 5	Juwan Howard	1.00	.45
☐ 6	David Robinson	1.25	.55
☐ 7	Gary Payton	1.25	.55
☐ 8	Kerry Kittles	2.00	.90
☐ 9	Dennis Rodman	3.00	1.35
☐ 10	Shaquille O'Neal	3.00	1.35
☐ 11	Stephon Marbury	8.00	3.60
☐ 12	John Stockton	.75	.35
☐ 13	Glenn Robinson	.75	.35
☐ 14	Hakeem Olajuwon	1.50	.70
☐ 15	Jason Kidd	1.50	.70
☐ 16	Jerry Stackhouse	1.00	.45
☐ 17	Joe Smith	1.00	.45
☐ 18	Reggie Miller	.75	.35
☐ 19	Grant Hill	5.00	2.20
☐ 20	D.Stoudamire	2.00	.90
☐ 21	Kevin Garnett	5.00	2.20
☐ 22	Clyde Drexler	1.00	.45
☐ 23	Michael Jordan	10.00	4.50
☐ 24	Antonio McDyess	1.25	.55
☐ 25	Chris Webber	2.00	.90
☐ 26	Antoine Walker	8.00	3.60
☐ 27	Scottie Pippen	2.50	1.10
☐ 28	Karl Malone	1.25	.55
☐ 29	S.Abdur-Rahim	5.00	2.20
☐ 30	Shawn Kemp	2.50	1.10
☐ 31	Kobe Bryant	20.00	9.00
☐ 32	Derrick Coleman	.50	.23
☐ 33	Alonzo Mourning	.75	.35
☐ 34	Anthony Mason	.50	.23
☐ 35	Ray Allen	2.50	1.10
☐ 36	Arvydas Sabonis	.50	.23
☐ 37	Brian Grant	.30	.14
☐ 38	Bryant Reeves	.50	.23
☐ 39	Christian Laettner	.50	.23
☐ 40	Tom Gugliotta	.75	.35
☐ 41	Latrell Sprewell	.50	.23
☐ 42	Erick Dampier	1.00	.45
☐ 43	Gheorghe Muresan	.30	.14
☐ 44	Glen Rice	.75	.35
☐ 45	Patrick Ewing	.75	.35
☐ 46	Jim Jackson	.50	.23
☐ 47	Michael Finley	.75	.35
☐ 48	Toni Kukoc	.50	.23
☐ 49	Marcus Camby	2.00	.90
☐ 50	Kenny Anderson	.50	.23
☐ 51	Mark Price	.30	.14
☐ 52	Tim Hardaway	1.00	.45
☐ 53	Mookie Blaylock	.50	.23
☐ 54	Steve Smith	.50	.23
☐ 55	Terrell Brandon	.75	.35
☐ 56	Lorenzen Wright	1.00	.45
☐ 57	Sasha Danilovic	.30	.14
☐ 58	Jeff Hornacek	.50	.23
☐ 59	Eddie Jones	1.50	.70
☐ 60	Vin Baker	1.50	.70
☐ 61	Chris Childs	.30	.14
☐ 62	Clifford Robinson	.30	.14
☐ 63	Anthony Peeler	.30	.14
☐ 64	Dino Radja	.30	.14
☐ 65	Joe Dumars	.75	.35
☐ 66	Loy Vaught	.50	.23
☐ 67	Rony Seikaly	.30	.14
☐ 68	Vitaly Potapenko	.30	.14
☐ 69	Chris Gatling	.30	.14
☐ 70	Dale Ellis	.30	.14
☐ 71	Allan Houston	.50	.23
☐ 72	Doug Christie	.30	.14
☐ 73	LaPhonso Ellis	.30	.14
☐ 74	Kendall Gill	.50	.23
☐ 75	Rik Smits	.50	.23
☐ 76	Bobby Phills	.30	.14
☐ 77	Malik Sealy	.30	.14
☐ 78	Sean Elliott	.30	.14
☐ 79	Vlade Divac	.50	.23
☐ 80	David Wesley	.30	.14
☐ 81	Dominique Wilkins	.75	.35
☐ 82	Danny Manning	.50	.23
☐ 83	Detlef Schrempf	.50	.23
☐ 84	Hersey Hawkins	.50	.23
☐ 85	Lindsey Hunter	.30	.14
☐ 86	M.Abdul-Rauf	.30	.14
☐ 87	Shawn Bradley	.30	.14
☐ 88	Horace Grant	.50	.23
☐ 89	Cedric Ceballos	.30	.14
☐ 90	Jamal Mashburn	.50	.23
☐ NNO	J.Stackhouse Promo 3-card strip	3.00	1.35

1996-97 Flair Showcase Row 1

Row 1, or Grace was the middle tier of the Flair Showcase set. Each card contains one of the following back themes: Showtime, Show Stoppers and Showpiece. By combining the two different themes, collectors can determine the different scarcity levels. Using Grace and Show Stoppers (cards 1-30), the odds are one in 2.5. Using Grace and Showtime (cards 31-60), the odds are one in 2. Using Grace and Showpiece (cards 61-90), the odds are one in 3.5. To ascertain values of individual cards, please refer to the multiplier in the header, coupled with the value of the basic card.

	MINT	NRMT
COMPLETE SET (90)	120.00	55.00
COMMON CARD (1-60)	.50	.23
SEMISTARS 1-60	.75	.35
UNLISTED STARS 1-60	1.25	.55
*STARS/RC's 1-60: .75X TO 1.5X ROW 2		
1-30 ODDS 1:2.5		
31-60 ODDS 1:2		
COMMON CARD (61-90)	.60	.25
SEMISTARS 61-90	1.00	.45
UNLISTED STARS 61-90	1.50	.70
*STARS/RC's 61-90: 1X TO 2X ROW 2		
61-90 ODDS 1:3.5		

1996-97 Flair Showcase Row 0

Row 0, or Showcase was the last tier of the Flair Showcase set. Each card contains one of the following back themes: Showtime, Show Stoppers and Showpiece. By combining the two different themes, collectors can determine the different scarcity levels. Using Showcase and Showpiece (cards 1-30), the odds are one in 24. Using Showcase and Show Stoppers (cards 31-60), the odds are one in .10. Finally, by using Showcase and Showtime (cards 61-90), the odds are one in 5.

	MINT	NRMT
COMPLETE SET (90)	1100.00	500.00
COMMON CARD (1-30)	12.00	5.50
1-30 ODDS 1:24		
COMMON CARD (31-60)	2.00	.90
SEMISTARS 31-60	3.00	1.35
UNLISTED STARS 31-60	8.00	3.60
*STARS 31-60: 3X TO 6X ROW 2		
*RC's 31-60: 2.5X TO 5X ROW 2		
31-60 ODDS 1:10		
COMMON CARD (61-90)	.60	.25
SEMISTARS 61-90	1.00	.45
UNLISTED STARS 61-90	1.50	.70
*STARS/RC's 61-90: 1X TO 2X ROW 2		
61-90 ODDS 1:5		

		MINT	NRMT
☐ 1	A.Hardaway	40.00	18.00
☐ 2	Mitch Richmond	12.00	5.50
☐ 3	Allen Iverson	60.00	27.00
☐ 4	Charles Barkley	25.00	11.00
☐ 5	Juwan Howard	15.00	6.75
☐ 6	David Robinson	20.00	9.00
☐ 7	Gary Payton	25.00	11.00
☐ 8	Kerry Kittles	15.00	6.75
☐ 9	Dennis Rodman	40.00	18.00
☐ 10	Shaquille O'Neal	40.00	18.00
☐ 11	Stephon Marbury	60.00	27.00
☐ 12	John Stockton	12.00	5.50
☐ 13	Glenn Robinson	12.00	5.50
☐ 14	Hakeem Olajuwon	25.00	11.00
☐ 15	Jason Kidd	25.00	11.00

□		MINT	NRMT
16	Jerry Stackhouse	15.00	6.75
17	Joe Smith	15.00	6.75
18	Reggie Miller	12.00	5.50
19	Grant Hill	60.00	27.00
20	D.Stoudamire	30.00	13.50
21	Kevin Garnett	60.00	27.00
22	Clyde Drexler	20.00	9.00
23	Michael Jordan	125.00	55.00
24	Antonio McDyess	20.00	9.00
25	Chris Webber	30.00	13.50
26	Antoine Walker	60.00	27.00
27	Scottie Pippen	35.00	16.00
28	Karl Malone	25.00	11.00
29	S.Abdur-Rahim	40.00	18.00
30	Shawn Kemp	35.00	16.00
31	Kobe Bryant	70.00	32.00
32	Derrick Coleman	3.00	1.35
33	Alonzo Mourning	8.00	3.60
34	Anthony Mason	3.00	1.35
35	Ray Allen	12.00	5.50
36	Arvydas Sabonis	3.00	1.35
37	Brian Grant	2.00	.90
38	Bryant Reeves	3.00	1.35
39	Christian Laettner	3.00	1.35
40	Tom Gugliotta	3.00	3.60
41	Latrell Sprewell	3.00	1.35
42	Erick Dampier	8.00	3.60
43	Gheorghe Muresan	2.00	.90
44	Glen Rice	8.00	3.60
45	Patrick Ewing	8.00	3.60
46	Jim Jackson	3.00	1.35
47	Michael Finley	10.00	4.50
48	Toni Kukoc	3.00	1.35
49	Marcus Camby	10.00	4.50
50	Kenny Anderson	3.00	1.35
51	Mark Price	2.00	.90
52	Tim Hardaway	10.00	4.50
53	Mookie Blaylock	3.00	1.35
54	Steve Smith	3.00	1.35
55	Terrell Brandon	8.00	3.60
56	Lorenzen Wright	8.00	3.60
57	Sasha Danilovic	2.00	.90
58	Jeff Hornacek	3.00	1.35
59	Eddie Jones	20.00	9.00
60	Vin Baker	15.00	6.75
61	Chris Childs	.60	.25
62	Clifford Robinson	.60	.25
63	Anthony Peeler	.60	.25
64	Dino Radja	.60	.25
65	Joe Dumars	1.50	.70
66	Loy Vaught	1.00	.45
68	Rony Seikaly	.60	.25
69	Chris Gatling	.60	.25
70	Dale Ellis	.60	.25
71	Allan Houston	1.00	.45
72	Doug Christie	.60	.25
73	LaPhonso Ellis	.60	.25
74	Kendall Gill	1.00	.45
75	Rik Smits	1.00	.45
76	Bobby Phills	.60	.25
77	Malik Sealy	.60	.25
78	Sean Elliott	.60	.25
79	Vlade Divac	1.00	.45
80	David Wesley	.60	.25
81	Dominique Wilkins	1.50	.70
82	Danny Manning	.60	.25
83	Detlef Schrempf	1.00	.45
84	Hersey Hawkins	1.00	.45
85	Lindsey Hunter	1.00	.45
86	M.Abdul-Rauf	.60	.25
87	Shawn Bradley	.60	.25
88	Horace Grant	1.00	.45
89	Cedric Ceballos	.60	.25
90	Jamal Mashburn	1.00	.45

1996-97 Flair Showcase Legacy Collection

Randomly inserted into packs at a rate of one in 30, this 270-card

set parallels the regular set. A couple of differences: card fronts contain a different color holographic background as well as the "Legacy Collection" stamp. Card backs are numbered out of 150 - the first parallel set to be numbered as such. Unlike the basic set, which has several levels of collectibility, the parallel singles are all inserted at the same rate. Each player has three different cards. Prices below reflect values for each individual card.

	MINT	NRMT
COMMON CARD (1-270)	15.00	6.75
SEMISTARS	25.00	11.00
STATED ODDS 1:30		
STATED PRINT RUN 150 SERIAL #'d SETS		
EACH PLAYER HAS THREE DIFF.CARDS		

□		MINT	NRMT
1	A.Hardaway	200.00	90.00
2	Mitch Richmond	50.00	22.00
3	Allen Iverson	250.00	110.00
4	Charles Barkley	80.00	36.00
5	Juwan Howard	60.00	27.00
6	David Robinson	70.00	32.00
7	Gary Payton	80.00	36.00
8	Kerry Kittles	60.00	27.00
9	Dennis Rodman	200.00	90.00
10	Shaquille O'Neal	200.00	90.00
11	Stephon Marbury	250.00	110.00
12	John Stockton	50.00	22.00
13	Glenn Robinson	50.00	22.00
14	Hakeem Olajuwon	100.00	45.00
15	Jason Kidd	100.00	45.00
16	Jerry Stackhouse	60.00	27.00
17	Joe Smith	60.00	27.00
18	Reggie Miller	50.00	22.00
19	Grant Hill	300.00	135.00
20	D.Stoudamire	100.00	45.00
21	Kevin Garnett	300.00	135.00
22	Clyde Drexler	60.00	27.00
23	Michael Jordan	600.00	275.00
24	Antonio McDyess	70.00	32.00
25	Chris Webber	120.00	55.00
26	Antoine Walker	250.00	110.00
27	Scottie Pippen	150.00	70.00
28	Karl Malone	80.00	36.00
29	S.Abdur-Rahim	150.00	70.00
30	Shawn Kemp	150.00	70.00
31	Kobe Bryant	400.00	180.00
32	Derrick Coleman	25.00	11.00
33	Alonzo Mourning	50.00	22.00
34	Anthony Mason	25.00	11.00
35	Ray Allen	70.00	32.00
36	Arvydas Sabonis	25.00	11.00
37	Brian Grant	15.00	6.75
38	Bryant Reeves	25.00	11.00
39	Christian Laettner	25.00	11.00
40	Tom Gugliotta	30.00	13.50
41	Latrell Sprewell	30.00	13.50
42	Erick Dampier	30.00	13.50
43	Gheorghe Muresan	15.00	6.75
44	Glen Rice	50.00	22.00
45	Patrick Ewing	50.00	22.00
46	Jim Jackson	25.00	11.00
47	Michael Finley	60.00	27.00
48	Toni Kukoc	40.00	18.00
49	Marcus Camby	60.00	27.00
50	Kenny Anderson	25.00	11.00
51	Mark Price	15.00	6.75
52	Tim Hardaway	60.00	27.00
53	Mookie Blaylock	25.00	11.00
54	Steve Smith	25.00	11.00
55	Terrell Brandon	40.00	18.00
56	Lorenzen Wright	30.00	13.50
57	Sasha Danilovic	15.00	6.75
58	Jeff Hornacek	25.00	11.00
59	Eddie Jones	100.00	45.00
60	Vin Baker	100.00	45.00
61	Chris Childs	15.00	6.75
62	Clifford Robinson	15.00	6.75
63	Anthony Peeler	15.00	6.75
64	Dino Radja	15.00	6.75
65	Joe Dumars	30.00	13.50
66	Loy Vaught	25.00	11.00
67	Rony Seikaly	15.00	6.75
68	Vitaly Potapenko	25.00	11.00
69	Chris Gatling	15.00	6.75
70	Dale Ellis	15.00	6.75
71	Allan Houston	25.00	11.00
72	Doug Christie	15.00	6.75
73	LaPhonso Ellis	15.00	6.75
74	Kendall Gill	25.00	11.00
75	Rik Smits	25.00	11.00
76	Bobby Phills	15.00	6.75
77	Malik Sealy	15.00	6.75
78	Sean Elliott	15.00	6.75
79	Vlade Divac	25.00	11.00
80	David Wesley	15.00	6.75
81	Dominique Wilkins	30.00	13.50
82	Danny Manning	25.00	11.00
83	Detlef Schrempf	25.00	11.00
84	Hersey Hawkins	25.00	11.00
85	Lindsey Hunter	15.00	6.75
86	M.Abdul-Rauf	15.00	6.75
87	Shawn Bradley	15.00	6.75
88	Horace Grant	25.00	11.00
89	Cedric Ceballos	15.00	6.75
90	Jamal Mashburn	25.00	11.00

1996-97 Flair Showcase Class of '96

Randomly inserted in packs at a rate of one in five, this 20-card set features the top rookies from the class of 1996. Cards feature an embossed design.

	MINT	NRMT
COMPLETE SET (20)	80.00	36.00
COMMON CARD (1-20)	1.25	.55
SEMISTARS	2.00	.90
UNLISTED STARS	3.00	1.35
STATED ODDS 1:5		

		MINT	NRMT
☐ 1	S.Abdur-Rahim	10.00	4.50
☐ 2	Ray Allen	5.00	2.20
☐ 3	Shandon Anderson	3.00	1.35
☐ 4	Kobe Bryant	30.00	13.50
☐ 5	Marcus Camby	4.00	1.80
☐ 6	Erick Dampier	3.00	1.35
☐ 7	Derek Fisher	3.00	1.35
☐ 8	Todd Fuller	1.25	.55
☐ 9	Othella Harrington	2.00	.90
☐ 10	Allen Iverson	15.00	6.75
☐ 11	Kerry Kittles	4.00	1.80
☐ 12	Travis Knight	2.00	.90
☐ 13	Matt Maloney	3.00	1.35
☐ 14	Stephon Marbury	15.00	6.75
☐ 15	Steve Nash	3.00	1.35
☐ 16	Jermaine O'Neal	3.00	1.35
☐ 17	Vitaly Potapenko	2.00	.90
☐ 18	Roy Rogers	1.25	.55
☐ 19	Antoine Walker	15.00	6.75
☐ 20	Lorenzen Wright	3.00	1.35

1996-97 Flair Showcase Hot Shots

Randomly inserted in packs at a rate of one in 90, this 20-card set features some of the best players in the NBA. Card fronts contain a photo of the player over a basketball surrounded by a die-cut flame. A small percentage of the press run contained errors to the names on the front of the cards.

		MINT	NRMT
COMPLETE SET (20)		700.00	325.00
COMMON CARD (1-20)		15.00	6.75
STATED ODDS 1:90			

		MINT	NRMT
☐ 1	Michael Jordan	175.00	80.00
☐ 2	Kevin Garnett	80.00	36.00
☐ 3	D.Stoudamire	30.00	13.50
☐ 4	A.Hardaway	50.00	22.00
☐ 5	Shaquille O'Neal	50.00	22.00
☐ 6	Grant Hill	80.00	36.00
☐ 7	Dennis Rodman	50.00	22.00
☐ 8	Shawn Kemp	40.00	18.00
☐ 9	Scottie Pippen	40.00	18.00
☐ 10	Juwan Howard	15.00	6.75

		MINT	NRMT
☐ 11	Jason Kidd	25.00	11.00
☐ 12	Hakeem Olajuwon	25.00	11.00
☐ 13	Karl Malone	20.00	9.00
☐ 14	Joe Smith	15.00	6.75
☐ 15	David Robinson	20.00	9.00
☐ 16	Jerry Stackhouse	15.00	6.75
☐ 17	Antonio McDyess	20.00	9.00
☐ 18	Clyde Drexler	15.00	6.75
☐ 19	Gary Payton	20.00	9.00
☐ 20	Eddie Jones	25.00	11.00

1997-98 Flair Showcase Row 3

The 1997-98 Flair Showcase set was issued in one series totalling 80 cards. The 5-card packs retailed for $4.99 each. The Row 3 set was broken up into 4 levels with the following odds: Showtime (cards 1-20) at 1:0.9, Showstopper (cards 21-40) at 1:1.1, Showdown (cards 41-60) at 1:1.5 and Showpiece (cards 61-80) at 1:2. A four-card Grant Hill promo strip was also released and is priced at the bottom of the set.

	MINT	NRMT
COMPLETE SET (80)	60.00	27.00
COMMON CARD (1-80)	.30	.14
SEMISTARS	.50	.23
UNLISTED STARS	.75	.35
1-20 STATED ODDS 1:0.9		
21-40 STATED ODDS 1:1.1		
41-60 STATED ODDS 1:1.5		
61-80 STATED ODDS 1:2		

		MINT	NRMT
☐ 1	Michael Jordan	10.00	4.50
☐ 2	Grant Hill	5.00	2.20
☐ 3	Allen Iverson	4.00	1.80
☐ 4	Kevin Garnett	5.00	2.20
☐ 5	Tim Duncan	12.00	5.50
☐ 6	Shawn Kemp	2.50	1.10
☐ 7	Shaquille O'Neal	3.00	1.35
☐ 8	Antoine Walker	4.00	1.80
☐ 9	S.Abdur-Rahim	2.50	1.10
☐ 10	D.Stoudamire	1.50	.70
☐ 11	A.Hardaway	3.00	1.35
☐ 12	Keith Van Horn	10.00	4.50
☐ 13	Dennis Rodman	3.00	1.35
☐ 14	Ron Mercer	8.00	3.60
☐ 15	Stephon Marbury	4.00	1.80
☐ 16	Scottie Pippen	2.50	1.10
☐ 17	Kerry Kittles	.75	.35
☐ 18	Kobe Bryant	6.00	2.70
☐ 19	Marcus Camby	.75	.35
☐ 20	Chauncey Billups	4.00	1.80
☐ 21	Tracy McGrady	6.00	2.70
☐ 22	Joe Smith	.75	.35
☐ 23	Brevin Knight	3.00	1.35
☐ 24	Danny Fortson	2.00	.90
☐ 25	Tim Thomas	6.00	2.70
☐ 26	Gary Payton	1.25	.55
☐ 27	David Robinson	1.25	.55
☐ 28	Hakeem Olajuwon	1.50	.70
☐ 29	Antonio Daniels	2.50	1.10
☐ 30	Antonio McDyess	1.00	.45
☐ 31	Eddie Jones	1.50	.70
☐ 32	Adonal Foyle	1.25	.55
☐ 33	Glenn Robinson	.75	.35
☐ 34	Charles Barkley	1.25	.55
☐ 35	Vin Baker	1.50	.70
☐ 36	Jerry Stackhouse	.75	.35
☐ 37	Ray Allen	1.00	.45
☐ 38	Derek Anderson	3.00	1.35
☐ 39	Isaac Austin	.30	.14
☐ 40	Tony Battie	2.00	.90
☐ 41	Tariq Abdul-Wahad	1.50	.70
☐ 42	D.Mutombo	.50	.23
☐ 43	Clyde Drexler	1.00	.45
☐ 44	Chris Mullin	.75	.35
☐ 45	Tim Hardaway	1.00	.45
☐ 46	Terrell Brandon	.75	.35
☐ 47	John Stockton	.75	.35
☐ 48	Patrick Ewing	.75	.35
☐ 49	Horace Grant	.50	.23
☐ 50	Tom Gugliotta	.75	.35
☐ 51	Mookie Blaylock	.50	.23
☐ 52	Mitch Richmond	.75	.35
☐ 53	Anthony Mason	.50	.23
☐ 54	Michael Finley	.75	.35
☐ 55	Jason Kidd	1.50	.70
☐ 56	Karl Malone	1.25	.55
☐ 57	Reggie Miller	.75	.35
☐ 58	Steve Smith	.50	.23
☐ 59	Glen Rice	.75	.35
☐ 60	Bryant Stith	.30	.14
☐ 61	Loy Vaught	.50	.23
☐ 62	Brian Grant	.30	.14
☐ 63	Joe Dumars	.75	.35
☐ 64	Juwan Howard	.75	.35
☐ 65	Rik Smits	.50	.23
☐ 66	Alonzo Mourning	.75	.35
☐ 67	Allan Houston	.50	.23
☐ 68	Chris Webber	2.00	.90
☐ 69	Kendall Gill	.50	.23
☐ 70	Rony Seikaly	.30	.14
☐ 71	Kenny Anderson	.50	.23
☐ 72	John Wallace	.50	.23
☐ 73	Bryant Reeves	.50	.23
☐ 74	Brian Williams	.30	.14
☐ 75	Larry Johnson	.50	.23
☐ 76	Shawn Bradley	.30	.14
☐ 77	Kevin Johnson	.50	.23
☐ 78	Rod Strickland	.50	.23
☐ 79	Rodney Rogers	.30	.14
☐ 80	Rasheed Wallace	.50	.23
☐ NNO	Grant Hill Promo	5.00	2.20
	4-card strip		

1997-98 Flair Showcase Row 2

The Row 2, or Style, parallels the basic set. The cards have four different combinations: Showstopper (cards 1-20) at 1:3, Showtime (cards 21-40) at 1:2.5, Showpiece (cards 41-60) at 1:4 and Showdown (cards 61-80) at 1:3.5. To ascertain values of individual cards, please refer to the multiplier listed below coupled with the value of the base card.

	MINT	NRMT
COMPLETE SET (80)	200.00	90.00
COMMON CARD (1-80)	.60	.25
SEMISTARS	1.00	.45
*STARS/RCs: .75X TO 2X ROW 3		
1-20 STATED ODDS 1:3		
21-40 STATED ODDS 1:2.5		
41-60 STATED ODDS 1:4		
61-80 STATED ODDS 1:3.5		

1997-98 Flair Showcase Row 1

The Row 1, or Grace, parallels the basic set. The cards have four different combinations: Showdown (cards 1-20) at 1:16, Showpiece (cards 21-40) at 1:24, Showtime (cards 41-60) at 1:6 and Showstopper (cards 61-80) at 1:10. To ascertain values of individual cards, please refer to the multiplier listed below coupled with the value of the base card.

	MINT	NRMT
COMPLETE SET (80)	600.00	275.00
COMMON CARD (1-20)	4.00	1.80
*STARS 1-20: 2X TO 5X ROW 3		
*RCs 1-20: 1.5X TO 4X ROW 3		
1-20 STATED ODDS 1:16		
COMMON CARD (21-40)	2.00	.90
*STARS 21-40: 2.5X TO 6X ROW 3		
*RCs 21-40: 2X TO 5X ROW 3		
21-40 STATED ODDS 1:24		
COMMON CARD (41-60)	1.00	.45
SEMISTARS 41-60	1.50	.70
*STARS/RCs 41-60: 1.25X TO 3X ROW 3		
41-60 STATED ODDS 1:6		
COMMON CARD (61-80)	1.25	.55
SEMISTARS 61-80	2.00	.90
*STARS 61-80: 1.5X TO 4X ROW 3		
61-80 STATED ODDS 1:10		

1997-98 Flair Showcase Row 0

The Row 0, or Showcase, parallels the basic set. The cards have four different combinations: Showpiece (cards 1-20) with serial numbering to 250, Showstopper (cards 21-40) with serial numbering to 1000, Showdown (cards 41-60) with serial numbering to 500 and Showtime (cards 61-80) with serial numbering to 2000.

	MINT	NRMT
COMMON CARD (1-20)	25.00	11.00
STATED PRINT RUN 250 SERIAL #'d SETS		
COMMON CARD (21-40)	6.00	2.70
SEMISTARS 21-40	10.00	4.50
UNLISTED STARS 21-40	15.00	6.75
STATED PRINT RUN 500 SERIAL #'d SETS		
COMMON CARD (41-60)	4.00	1.80
SEMISTARS 41-60	6.00	2.70
UNLISTED STARS 41-60	10.00	4.50
STATED PRINT RUN 1000 SERIAL #'d SETS		
COMMON CARD (61-80)	2.50	1.10
UNLISTED STARS 61-80	4.00	1.80
STATED PRINT RUN 2000 SERIAL #'d SETS		
RANDOM INSERTS IN PACKS		

☐ 1	Michael Jordan	300.00	135.00
☐ 2	Grant Hill	150.00	70.00
☐ 3	Allen Iverson	120.00	55.00
☐ 4	Kevin Garnett	150.00	70.00
☐ 5	Tim Duncan	150.00	70.00
☐ 6	Shawn Kemp	80.00	36.00
☐ 7	Shaquille O'Neal	100.00	45.00
☐ 8	Antoine Walker	120.00	55.00
☐ 9	S.Abdul-Rahim	80.00	36.00
☐ 10	D.Stoudamire	50.00	22.00
☐ 11	A.Hardaway	100.00	45.00
☐ 12	Keith Van Horn	120.00	55.00
☐ 13	Dennis Rodman	100.00	45.00
☐ 14	Ron Mercer	100.00	45.00
☐ 15	Stephon Marbury	120.00	55.00
☐ 16	Scottie Pippen	80.00	36.00
☐ 17	Kerry Kittles	25.00	11.00
☐ 18	Kobe Bryant	200.00	90.00
☐ 19	Marcus Camby	25.00	11.00
☐ 20	Chauncey Billups	50.00	22.00
☐ 21	Tracy McGrady	50.00	22.00
☐ 22	Joe Smith	15.00	6.75
☐ 23	Brevin Knight	25.00	11.00
☐ 24	Danny Fortson	15.00	6.75
☐ 25	Tim Thomas	50.00	22.00
☐ 26	Gary Payton	25.00	11.00
☐ 27	David Robinson	25.00	11.00
☐ 28	Hakeem Olajuwon	30.00	13.50
☐ 29	Antonio Daniels	20.00	9.00
☐ 30	Antonio McDyess	20.00	9.00
☐ 31	Eddie Jones	30.00	13.50

☐ 32	Adonal Foyle	15.00	6.75
☐ 33	Glenn Robinson	15.00	6.75
☐ 34	Charles Barkley	25.00	11.00
☐ 35	Vin Baker	30.00	13.50
☐ 36	Jerry Stackhouse	15.00	6.75
☐ 37	Ray Allen	20.00	9.00
☐ 38	Derek Anderson	25.00	11.00
☐ 39	Isaac Austin	6.00	2.70
☐ 40	Tony Battie	15.00	6.75
☐ 41	Tariq Abdul-Wahad ..	10.00	4.50
☐ 42	D.Mutombo	6.00	2.70
☐ 43	Clyde Drexler	12.00	5.50
☐ 44	Chris Mullin	10.00	4.50
☐ 45	Tim Hardaway	12.00	5.50
☐ 46	Terrell Brandon	10.00	4.50
☐ 47	John Stockton	10.00	4.50
☐ 48	Patrick Ewing	10.00	4.50
☐ 49	Horace Grant	6.00	2.70
☐ 50	Tom Gugliotta	10.00	4.50
☐ 51	Mookie Blaylock	6.00	2.70
☐ 52	Mitch Richmond	10.00	4.50
☐ 53	Anthony Mason	6.00	2.70
☐ 54	Michael Finley	10.00	4.50
☐ 55	Jason Kidd	20.00	9.00
☐ 56	Karl Malone	15.00	6.75
☐ 57	Reggie Miller	10.00	4.50
☐ 58	Steve Smith	6.00	2.70
☐ 59	Glen Rice	10.00	4.50
☐ 60	Bryant Stith	4.00	1.80
☐ 61	Loy Vaught	4.00	1.80
☐ 62	Brian Grant	2.50	1.10
☐ 63	Joe Dumars	6.00	2.70
☐ 64	Juwan Howard	6.00	2.70
☐ 65	Rik Smits	4.00	1.80
☐ 66	Alonzo Mourning	6.00	2.70
☐ 67	Allan Houston	4.00	1.80
☐ 68	Chris Webber	15.00	6.75
☐ 69	Kendall Gill	4.00	1.80
☐ 70	Rony Seikaly	2.50	1.10
☐ 71	Kenny Anderson	4.00	1.80
☐ 72	John Wallace	4.00	1.80
☐ 73	Bryant Reeves	4.00	1.80
☐ 74	Brian Williams	2.50	1.10
☐ 75	Larry Johnson	4.00	1.80
☐ 76	Shawn Bradley	2.50	1.10
☐ 77	Kevin Johnson	4.00	1.80
☐ 78	Rod Strickland	4.00	1.80
☐ 79	Rodney Rogers	2.50	1.10
☐ 80	Rasheed Wallace	4.00	1.80

1997-98 Flair Showcase Legacy Collection

Randomly inserted into packs, the Legacy Collection parallels all 320 basic cards and is serially numbered to 100.

	MINT	NRMT
COMMON CARD (1-320)	15.00	6.75
SEMISTARS	25.00	11.00

RANDOM INSERTS IN PACKS
STATED PRINT RUN 100 SERIAL #'d SETS
EACH PLAYER HAS FOUR DIFFERENT
CARDS

☐ 1 Michael Jordan	700.00	325.00
☐ 2 Grant Hill	300.00	135.00
☐ 3 Allen Iverson	250.00	110.00
☐ 4 Kevin Garnett	300.00	135.00
☐ 5 Tim Duncan	350.00	160.00
☐ 6 Shawn Kemp	150.00	70.00
☐ 7 Shaquille O'Neal	200.00	90.00
☐ 8 Antoine Walker	250.00	110.00
☐ 9 S.Abdur-Rahim	150.00	70.00
☐ 10 D.Stoudamire	100.00	45.00
☐ 11 A.Hardaway	200.00	90.00
☐ 12 Keith Van Horn	250.00	110.00
☐ 13 Dennis Rodman	200.00	90.00
☐ 14 Ron Mercer	200.00	90.00
☐ 15 Stephon Marbury	250.00	110.00
☐ 16 Scottie Pippen	150.00	70.00
☐ 17 Kerry Kittles	50.00	22.00
☐ 18 Kobe Bryant	350.00	160.00
☐ 19 Marcus Camby	50.00	22.00
☐ 20 Chauncey Billups	100.00	45.00
☐ 21 Tracy McGrady	150.00	70.00
☐ 22 Joe Smith	50.00	22.00
☐ 23 Brevin Knight	80.00	36.00
☐ 24 Danny Fortson	50.00	22.00
☐ 25 Tim Thomas	150.00	70.00
☐ 26 Gary Payton	80.00	36.00
☐ 27 David Robinson	80.00	36.00
☐ 28 Hakeem Olajuwon	100.00	45.00
☐ 29 Antonio Daniels	60.00	27.00
☐ 30 Antonio McDyess	60.00	27.00
☐ 31 Eddie Jones	100.00	45.00
☐ 32 Adonal Foyle	40.00	18.00
☐ 33 Glenn Robinson	40.00	18.00
☐ 34 Charles Barkley	80.00	36.00
☐ 35 Vin Baker	100.00	45.00
☐ 36 Jerry Stackhouse	50.00	22.00
☐ 37 Ray Allen	60.00	27.00
☐ 38 Derek Anderson	80.00	36.00
☐ 39 Isaac Austin	15.00	6.75
☐ 40 Tony Battie	50.00	22.00
☐ 41 Tariq Abdul-Wahad	40.00	18.00
☐ 42 D.Mutombo	25.00	11.00
☐ 43 Clyde Drexler	60.00	27.00
☐ 44 Chris Mullin	40.00	18.00
☐ 45 Tim Hardaway	60.00	27.00
☐ 46 Terrell Brandon	40.00	18.00
☐ 47 John Stockton	50.00	22.00
☐ 48 Patrick Ewing	50.00	22.00
☐ 49 Horace Grant	25.00	11.00
☐ 50 Tom Gugliotta	40.00	18.00
☐ 51 Mookie Blaylock	25.00	11.00
☐ 52 Mitch Richmond	50.00	22.00
☐ 53 Anthony Mason	25.00	11.00
☐ 54 Michael Finley	50.00	22.00
☐ 55 Jason Kidd	100.00	45.00
☐ 56 Karl Malone	80.00	36.00
☐ 57 Reggie Miller	50.00	22.00
☐ 58 Steve Smith	25.00	11.00
☐ 59 Glen Rice	50.00	22.00
☐ 60 Bryant Stith	15.00	6.75
☐ 61 Loy Vaught	25.00	11.00
☐ 62 Brian Grant	15.00	6.75
☐ 63 Joe Dumars	40.00	18.00
☐ 64 Juwan Howard	50.00	22.00
☐ 65 Rik Smits	25.00	11.00
☐ 66 Alonzo Mourning	50.00	22.00
☐ 67 Allan Houston	25.00	11.00
☐ 68 Chris Webber	120.00	55.00
☐ 69 Kendall Gill	25.00	11.00
☐ 70 Rony Seikaly	15.00	6.75
☐ 71 Kenny Anderson	25.00	11.00
☐ 72 John Wallace	25.00	11.00
☐ 73 Bryant Reeves	25.00	11.00
☐ 74 Brian Williams	15.00	6.75
☐ 75 Larry Johnson	25.00	11.00
☐ 76 Shawn Bradley	15.00	6.75
☐ 77 Kevin Johnson	25.00	11.00
☐ 78 Rod Strickland	25.00	11.00
☐ 79 Rodney Rogers	15.00	6.75
☐ 80 Rasheed Wallace	25.00	11.00

1997-98 Flair Showcase Wave of the Future

Randomly inserted into packs at one in 20, this 12-card set features some of the top rookies not to be included in the basic set. The cards are enclosed in plastic, which contains a liquid to simulate a water background within the card.

	MINT	NRMT
COMPLETE SET (12)	25.00	11.00
COMMON CARD (1-12)	2.00	.90
SEMISTARS	3.00	1.35
UNLISTED STARS	5.00	2.20
STATED ODDS 1:20		

☐ 1 Corey Beck	2.00	.90
☐ 2 Maurice Taylor	8.00	3.60
☐ 3 Chris Anstey	5.00	2.20
☐ 4 Keith Booth	2.00	.90
☐ 5 Anthony Parker	2.00	.90
☐ 6 Austin Croshere	5.00	2.20
☐ 7 Jacque Vaughn	5.00	2.20
☐ 8 God Shammgod	2.00	.90
☐ 9 Bobby Jackson	5.00	2.20
☐ 10 Johnny Taylor	2.00	.90
☐ 11 Ed Gray	5.00	2.20
☐ 12 Kelvin Cato	5.00	2.20

1961-62 Fleer

The 1961-62 Fleer set was the company's only major basketball issue until the 1986-87 season. The cards were issued in five-cent wax packs. The cards in the set measure the standard 2 1/2" by 3 1/2". Cards numbered 45 to 66 are action shots (designated IA) of players elsewhere in the set. Both the regular cards and the IA cards are numbered alphabetically within that particular subset. No known scarcities exist, although the set is quite popular since it contains the first mainstream basketball cards of many of the game's all-time greats including Elgin Baylor, Wilt Chamberlain, Oscar Robertson and Jerry West. Most cards are frequently found with centering problems

	NRMT	VG-E
COMPLETE SET (66)	4000.00	1800.00
COMMON CARD (1-66)	15.00	6.75
SEMISTARS	20.00	9.00
UNLISTED STARS	25.00	11.00

CONDITION SENSITIVE SET
CARDS PRICED IN NM CONDITION

☐ 1 Al Attles	100.00	30.00
☐ 2 Paul Arizin	40.00	18.00
☐ 3 Elgin Baylor	300.00	135.00
☐ 4 Walt Bellamy	60.00	27.00
☐ 5 Arlen Bockhorn	15.00	6.75
☐ 6 Bob Boozer	25.00	11.00
☐ 7 Carl Braun	30.00	13.50
☐ 8 Wilt Chamberlain	1250.00	550.00
☐ 9 Larry Costello	20.00	9.00
☐ 10 Bob Cousy	250.00	110.00
☐ 11 Walter Dukes	20.00	9.00
☐ 12 Wayne Embry	25.00	11.00
☐ 13 Dave Gambee	15.00	6.75
☐ 14 Tom Gola	40.00	18.00
☐ 15 Sihugo Green	20.00	9.00
☐ 16 Hal Greer	80.00	36.00
☐ 17 Richie Guerin	40.00	18.00
☐ 18 Cliff Hagan	45.00	20.00
☐ 19 Tom Heinsohn	90.00	40.00
☐ 20 Bailey Howell	45.00	20.00
☐ 21 Rod Hundley	55.00	25.00
☐ 22 K.C. Jones	110.00	50.00
☐ 23 Sam Jones	110.00	50.00
☐ 24 Phil Jordan	15.00	6.75
☐ 25 John Kerr	45.00	20.00
☐ 26 Rudy LaRusso	35.00	16.00
☐ 27 George Lee	15.00	6.75
☐ 28 Bob Leonard	20.00	9.00
☐ 29 Clyde Lovellette	50.00	22.00
☐ 30 John McCarthy	15.00	6.75
☐ 31 Tom Meschery	25.00	11.00
☐ 32 Willie Naulls	25.00	11.00
☐ 33 Don Ohl	25.00	11.00
☐ 34 Bob Pettit	90.00	40.00
☐ 35 Frank Ramsey	40.00	18.00
☐ 36 Oscar Robertson	500.00	220.00
☐ 37 Guy Rodgers	25.00	11.00
☐ 38 Bill Russell	500.00	220.00
☐ 39 Dolph Schayes	55.00	25.00
☐ 40 Frank Selvy	20.00	9.00
☐ 41 Gene Shue	25.00	11.00
☐ 42 Jack Twyman	40.00	18.00
☐ 43 Jerry West	650.00	300.00
☐ 44 Len Wilkens UER	160.00	70.00
(Misspelled Wilkins on card front)		
☐ 45 Paul Arizin IA	25.00	11.00
☐ 46 Elgin Baylor IA	100.00	45.00
☐ 47 Wilt Chamberlain IA	375.00	170.00
☐ 48 Larry Costello IA	20.00	9.00
☐ 49 Bob Cousy IA	125.00	55.00
☐ 50 Walter Dukes IA	15.00	6.75
☐ 51 Tom Gola IA	25.00	11.00
☐ 52 Richie Guerin IA	20.00	9.00
☐ 53 Cliff Hagan IA	20.00	9.00

□ 54 Tom Heinsohn IA	45.00	20.00
□ 55 Bailey Howell IA	25.00	11.00
□ 56 John Kerr IA	25.00	11.00
□ 57 Rudy LaRusso IA	20.00	9.00
□ 58 Clyde Lovellette IA	30.00	13.50
□ 59 Bob Pettit IA	40.00	18.00
□ 60 Frank Ramsey IA	25.00	11.00
□ 61 Oscar Robertson IA	175.00	80.00
□ 62 Bill Russell IA	225.00	100.00
□ 63 Dolph Schayes IA	35.00	16.00
□ 64 Gene Shue IA	20.00	9.00
□ 65 Jack Twyman IA	25.00	11.00
□ 66 Jerry West IA	300.00	90.00

1986-87 Fleer

This 132-card standard-size set marks Fleer's return to the basketball card industry after a 25-year hiatus. It also marks what is considered to be the beginning of the modern era of basketball cards. The cards were issued in 12-card wax packs (11 cards plus a sticker) that retailed for 50 cents. Wax boxes consisted of 36 packs. A stick of gum was also included in each pack. The set is checklisted alphabetically by the player's last name. Since only the Star Company had been issuing basketball cards nationally since 1983, most of the players in this Fleer set already had cards which are considered Extended Rookie Cards. However, since this Fleer set was the first nationally distributed through wax packs since the 1981-82 Topps issue, most of the players in the set are considered Rookie Cards including Michael Jordan. Other Rookie Cards, of those that had Star Company cards include Charles Barkley, Clyde Drexler, Patrick Ewing, Hakeem Olajuwon, Isiah Thomas and Dominique Wilkins. Rookie Cards of those that did not previously appear in a set include Joe Dumars, Karl Malone, Chris Mullin and Charles Oakley. Red, white and blue borders surround a color photo that contains a Fleer "Premier" logo in an upper corner. The card backs are printed in red and blue on white card stock. Several cards have "Traded" notations on them if the player was traded subsequent to the photo selection process. It's important to note that some of the more expensive cards in this set (especially Michael Jordan) have been counterfeited in the past few years. Checking key detailed printing areas such as the "Fleer Premier" logo on the front and the players' association logo on the back under eight or ten power magnification usually detects the legitimate from the counterfeits. The cards are condition sensitive due to dark borders and centering problems.

	NRMT-MT	EXC
COMP.w/Stickers (143)	1500.00	700.00
COMP.SET (132)	1400.00	650.00
COMMON CARD (1-132)	2.00	.90
CL (132)	10.00	4.50
SEMISTARS	2.50	1.10
UNLISTED STARS	3.00	1.35

BEWARE COUNTERFEITS
CONDITION SENSITIVE SET
1986-87 THRU 1988-89 PRICED IN NM-MT

□ 1 Kareem Abdul-Jabbar	12.00	5.50
□ 2 Alvan Adams	2.00	.90
□ 3 Mark Aguirre	2.50	1.10
□ 4 Danny Ainge	6.00	2.70
□ 5 John Bagley	2.00	.90
□ 6 Thurl Bailey	2.00	.90
□ 7 Charles Barkley	80.00	36.00
□ 8 Benoit Benjamin	2.50	1.10
□ 9 Larry Bird	40.00	18.00
□ 10 Otis Birdsong	2.00	.90
□ 11 Rolando Blackman	2.00	.90
□ 12 Manute Bol	2.00	.90
□ 13 Sam Bowie	2.50	1.10
□ 14 Joe Barry Carroll	2.00	.90
□ 15 Tom Chambers	4.00	1.80
□ 16 Maurice Cheeks	2.00	.90
□ 17 Michael Cooper	2.50	1.10
□ 18 Wayne Cooper	2.00	.90
□ 19 Pat Cummings	2.00	.90
□ 20 Terry Cummings	2.50	1.10
□ 21 Adrian Dantley	2.50	1.10
□ 22 Brad Davis	2.00	.90
□ 23 Walter Davis	2.00	.90
□ 24 Darryl Dawkins	2.50	1.10
□ 25 Larry Drew	2.00	.90
□ 26 Clyde Drexler	60.00	27.00
□ 27 Joe Dumars	20.00	9.00
□ 28 Mark Eaton	2.00	.90
□ 29 James Edwards	2.00	.90
□ 30 Alex English	2.50	1.10
□ 31 Julius Erving	15.00	6.75
□ 32 Patrick Ewing	50.00	22.00
□ 33 Vern Fleming	2.00	.90
□ 34 Sleepy Floyd	2.00	.90
□ 35 World B. Free	2.00	.90
□ 36 George Gervin	4.00	1.80
□ 37 Artis Gilmore	2.50	1.10
□ 38 Mike Gminski	2.00	.90
□ 39 Rickey Green	2.00	.90
□ 40 Sidney Green	2.00	.90
□ 41 David Greenwood	2.00	.90
□ 42 Darrell Griffith	2.00	.90
□ 43 Bill Hanzlik	2.00	.90
□ 44 Derek Harper	4.00	1.80
□ 45 Gerald Henderson	2.00	.90

□ 46 Roy Hinson	2.00	.90
□ 47 Craig Hodges	2.00	.90
□ 48 Phil Hubbard	2.00	.90
□ 49 Jay Humphries	2.00	.90
□ 50 Dennis Johnson	2.00	.90
□ 51 Eddie Johnson	3.00	1.35
□ 52 Frank Johnson	2.00	.90
□ 53 Magic Johnson	30.00	13.50
□ 54 Marques Johnson	2.00	.90
(Decimal point missing, rookie year scoring avg.)		
□ 55 Steve Johnson UER	2.00	.90
(photo actually David Greenwood)		
□ 56 Vinnie Johnson	2.00	.90
□ 57 Michael Jordan	1000.00	450.00
□ 58 Clark Kellogg	2.00	.90
□ 59 Albert King	2.00	.90
□ 60 Bernard King	2.50	1.10
□ 61 Bill Laimbeer	2.50	1.10
□ 62 Allen Leavell	2.00	.90
□ 63 Lafayette Lever	2.50	1.10
□ 64 Alton Lister	2.00	.90
□ 65 Lewis Lloyd	2.00	.90
□ 66 Maurice Lucas	2.00	.90
□ 67 Jeff Malone	2.00	.90
□ 68 Karl Malone	80.00	36.00
□ 69 Moses Malone	3.00	1.35
□ 70 Cedric Maxwell	2.00	.90
□ 71 Rodney McCray	2.00	.90
□ 72 Xavier McDaniel	2.50	1.10
□ 73 Kevin McHale	3.00	1.35
□ 74 Mike Mitchell	2.00	.90
□ 75 Sidney Moncrief	2.50	1.10
□ 76 Johnny Moore	2.00	.90
□ 77 Chris Mullin	15.00	6.75
□ 78 Larry Nance	4.00	1.80
□ 79 Calvin Natt	2.00	.90
□ 80 Norm Nixon	2.00	.90
□ 81 Charles Oakley	5.00	2.20
□ 82 Hakeem Olajuwon	80.00	36.00
□ 83 Louis Orr	2.00	.90
□ 84 Robert Parish UER	3.00	1.35
(Misspelled Parrish on both sides)		
□ 85 Jim Paxson	2.00	.90
□ 86 Sam Perkins	5.00	2.20
□ 87 Ricky Pierce	2.50	1.10
□ 88 Paul Pressey	2.00	.90
□ 89 Kurt Rambis	2.00	.90
□ 90 Robert Reid	2.00	.90
□ 91 Doc Rivers	4.00	1.80
□ 92 Alvin Robertson	2.00	.90
□ 93 Cliff Robinson	2.00	.90
□ 94 Tree Rollins	2.00	.90
□ 95 Dan Roundfield	2.00	.90
□ 96 Jeff Ruland	2.00	.90
□ 97 Ralph Sampson	2.50	1.10
□ 98 Danny Schayes	2.00	.90
□ 99 Byron Scott	4.00	1.80
□ 100 Purvis Short	2.00	.90
□ 101 Jerry Sichting	2.00	.90
□ 102 Jack Sikma	2.00	.90
□ 103 Derek Smith	2.00	.90
□ 104 Larry Smith	2.00	.90
□ 105 Rory Sparrow	2.00	.90
□ 106 Steve Stipanovich	2.00	.90
□ 107 Terry Teagle	2.00	.90
□ 108 Reggie Theus	2.50	1.10
□ 109 Isiah Thomas	25.00	11.00
□ 110 LaSalle Thompson	2.00	.90
□ 111 Mychal Thompson	2.00	.90
□ 112 Sedale Threatt	2.50	1.10
□ 113 Wayman Tisdale	2.50	1.10
□ 114 Andrew Toney	2.00	.90
□ 115 Kelly Tripucka	2.00	.90
□ 116 Mel Turpin	2.00	.90
□ 117 Kiki Vandeweghe	2.00	.90
□ 118 Jay Vincent	2.00	.90
□ 119 Bill Walton	4.00	1.80
(Missing decimal points on four lines of FG Percentage)		
□ 120 Spud Webb	4.00	1.80
□ 121 Dominique Wilkins	25.00	11.00
□ 122 Gerald Wilkins	2.50	1.10

☐ 123	Buck Williams	4.00	1.80
☐ 124	Gus Williams	2.00	.90
☐ 125	Herb Williams	2.00	.90
☐ 126	Kevin Willis	5.00	2.20
☐ 127	Randy Wittman	2.00	.90
☐ 128	Al Wood	2.00	.90
☐ 129	Mike Woodson	2.00	.90
☐ 130	Orlando Woolridge	2.00	.90
☐ 131	James Worthy	20.00	9.00
☐ 132	Checklist 1-132	10.00	4.50

1986-87 Fleer Stickers

One of these eleven different standard-size stickers was inserted into each 1986-87 Fleer wax pack. The backs of the sticker cards are printed in blue and red on white card stock. The set numbering of the stickers is alphabetical by player's name. Based on the one-to-twelve proportion of stickers to regular cards in the wax packs, there are theoretically an equal number of sticker sets and regular sets. The cards are frequently found off-centered and most card backs are found with wax stains due to packaging.

	NRMT-MT	EXC
COMPLETE SET (11)	140.00	65.00
COMMON STICKER (1-11)	1.50	.70
ONE PER PACK		
CONDITION SENSITIVE SET		

☐ 1	Kareem Abdul-Jabbar	4.00	1.80
☐ 2	Larry Bird	15.00	6.75
☐ 3	Adrian Dantley	1.50	.70
☐ 4	Alex English	1.50	.70
☐ 5	Julius Erving	5.00	2.20
☐ 6	Patrick Ewing	8.00	3.60
☐ 7	Magic Johnson	12.00	5.50
☐ 8	Michael Jordan	100.00	45.00
☐ 9	Hakeem Olajuwon	15.00	6.75
☐ 10	Isiah Thomas	4.00	1.80
☐ 11	Dominique Wilkins	2.50	1.10

1987-88 Fleer

The 1987-88 Fleer basketball set contains 132 standard-size cards. The cards were issued in 12-card wax packs that retailed for 50 cents. A wax box consisted of 36 packs. A sticker card

and stick of gum were included. The fronts are white with gray horizontal stripes. The backs are red, white and blue and show each player's complete NBA statistics. The cards are numbered in alphabetical order by last name. Rookie Cards include Brad Daugherty, A.C. Green, Chuck Person, Terry Porter, Detlef Schrempf and Hot Rod Williams. Other key Rookie Cards in this set, who had already had cards in previous Star sets, are Dale Ellis, John Paxson, and Otis Thorpe. The cards are frequently found off-centered.

	MINT	NRMT
COMPLETE w/Stickers (143)	300.00	135.00
COMPLETE SET (132)	250.00	110.00
COMMON CARD (1-132)	1.50	.70
CL (132) !	3.00	1.35
SEMISTARS	2.00	.90
UNLISTED STARS	2.50	1.10
CONDITION SENSITIVE SET		

☐ 1	Kareem Abdul-Jabbar	8.00	3.60
☐ 2	Alvan Adams	1.50	.70
☐ 3	Mark Aguirre	2.00	.90
☐ 4	Danny Ainge	2.00	.90
☐ 5	John Bagley	1.50	.70
☐ 6	Thurl Bailey UER	1.50	.70
	(reverse negative)		
☐ 7	Greg Ballard	1.50	.70
☐ 8	Gene Banks	1.50	.70
☐ 9	Charles Barkley	20.00	9.00
☐ 10	Benoit Benjamin	1.50	.70
☐ 11	Larry Bird	30.00	13.50
☐ 12	Rolando Blackman	1.50	.70
☐ 13	Manute Bol	1.50	.70
☐ 14	Tony Brown	1.50	.70
☐ 15	Michael Cage	1.50	.70
☐ 16	Joe Barry Carroll	1.50	.70
☐ 17	Bill Cartwright	2.00	.90
☐ 18	Terry Catledge	1.50	.70
☐ 19	Tom Chambers	2.00	.90
☐ 20	Maurice Cheeks	2.00	.90
☐ 21	Michael Cooper	2.00	.90
☐ 22	Dave Corzine	1.50	.70
☐ 23	Terry Cummings	2.00	.90
☐ 24	Adrian Dantley	1.50	.70
☐ 25	Brad Daugherty	2.50	1.10
☐ 26	Walter Davis	1.50	.70
☐ 27	Johnny Dawkins	1.50	.70
☐ 28	James Donaldson	1.50	.70
☐ 29	Larry Drew	1.50	.70
☐ 30	Clyde Drexler	15.00	6.75
☐ 31	Joe Dumars	4.00	1.80
☐ 32	Mark Eaton	1.50	.70

☐ 33	Dale Ellis	2.50	1.10
☐ 34	Alex English	2.00	.90
☐ 35	Julius Erving	12.00	5.50
☐ 36	Mike Evans	1.50	.70
☐ 37	Patrick Ewing	12.00	5.50
☐ 38	Vern Fleming	1.50	.70
☐ 39	Sleepy Floyd	1.50	.70
☐ 40	Artis Gilmore	2.00	.90
☐ 41	Mike Gminski UER	1.50	.70
	(reversed negative)		
☐ 42	A.C. Green	6.00	2.70
☐ 43	Rickey Green	1.50	.70
☐ 44	Sidney Green	1.50	.70
☐ 45	David Greenwood	1.50	.70
☐ 46	Darrell Griffith	1.50	.70
☐ 47	Bill Hanzlik	1.50	.70
☐ 48	Derek Harper	2.00	.90
☐ 49	Ron Harper	8.00	3.60
☐ 50	Gerald Henderson	1.50	.70
☐ 51	Roy Hinson	1.50	.70
☐ 52	Craig Hodges	1.50	.70
☐ 53	Phil Hubbard	1.50	.70
☐ 54	Dennis Johnson	2.00	.90
☐ 55	Eddie Johnson	2.00	.90
☐ 56	Magic Johnson	25.00	11.00
☐ 57	Steve Johnson	1.50	.70
☐ 58	Vinnie Johnson	1.50	.70
☐ 59	Michael Jordan	180.00	80.00
☐ 60	Jerome Kersey	1.50	.70
☐ 61	Bill Laimbeer	2.00	.90
☐ 62	Lafayette Lever UER	1.50	.70
	(Photo actually Otis Smith)		
☐ 63	Cliff Levingston	1.50	.70
☐ 64	Alton Lister	1.50	.70
☐ 65	John Long	1.50	.70
☐ 66	John Lucas	1.50	.70
☐ 67	Jeff Malone	1.50	.70
☐ 68	Karl Malone	20.00	9.00
☐ 69	Moses Malone	2.50	1.10
☐ 70	Cedric Maxwell	1.50	.70
☐ 71	Tim McCormick	1.50	.70
☐ 72	Rodney McCray	1.50	.70
☐ 73	Xavier McDaniel	1.50	.70
☐ 74	Kevin McHale	2.50	1.10
☐ 75	Nate McMillan	2.50	1.10
☐ 76	Sidney Moncrief	1.50	.70
☐ 77	Chris Mullin	3.00	1.35
☐ 78	Larry Nance	2.00	.90
☐ 79	Charles Oakley	2.00	.90
☐ 80	Hakeem Olajuwon	25.00	11.00
☐ 81	Robert Parish UER	2.00	.90
	Misspelled Parrish on both sides)		
☐ 82	Jim Paxson	1.50	.70
☐ 83	John Paxson	2.50	1.10
☐ 84	Sam Perkins	2.00	.90
☐ 85	Chuck Person	2.50	1.10
☐ 86	Jim Petersen	1.50	.70
☐ 87	Ricky Pierce	1.50	.70
☐ 88	Ed Pinckney	1.50	.70
☐ 89	Terry Porter	2.50	1.10
	(College Wisconsin, should be Wisconsin - Stevens Point)		
☐ 90	Paul Pressey	1.50	.70
☐ 91	Robert Reid	1.50	.70
☐ 92	Doc Rivers	2.00	.90
☐ 93	Alvin Robertson	1.50	.70
☐ 94	Tree Rollins	1.50	.70
☐ 95	Ralph Sampson	1.50	.70
☐ 96	Mike Sanders	1.50	.70
☐ 97	Detlef Schrempf	10.00	4.50
☐ 98	Byron Scott	2.00	.90
☐ 99	Jerry Sichting	1.50	.70
☐ 100	Jack Sikma	1.50	.70
☐ 101	Larry Smith	1.50	.70
☐ 102	Rory Sparrow	1.50	.70
☐ 103	Steve Stipanovich	1.50	.70
☐ 104	Jon Sundvold	1.50	.70
☐ 105	Reggie Theus	2.00	.90
☐ 106	Isiah Thomas	6.00	2.70
☐ 107	LaSalle Thompson	1.50	.70
☐ 108	Mychal Thompson	1.50	.70
☐ 109	Otis Thorpe	5.00	2.20
☐ 110	Sedale Threatt	1.50	.70

		MINT	NRMT
□ 111	Waymon Tisdale	1.50	.70
□ 112	Kelly Tripucka	1.50	.70
□ 113	Trent Tucker	1.50	.70
□ 114	Terry Tyler	1.50	.70
□ 115	Darnell Valentine	1.50	.70
□ 116	Kiki Vandeweghe	1.50	.70
□ 117	Darrell Walker	1.50	.70
□ 118	Dominique Wilkins	4.00	1.80
□ 119	Gerald Wilkins	1.50	.70
□ 120	Buck Williams	2.00	.90
□ 121	Herb Williams	.50	.70
□ 122	John Williams	1.50	.70
□ 123	John Williams	2.50	1.10
□ 124	Kevin Willis	2.00	.90
□ 125	David Wingate	1.50	.70
□ 126	Randy Wittman	1.50	.70
□ 127	Leon Wood	1.50	.70
□ 128	Mike Woodson	1.50	.70
□ 129	Orlando Woolridge	1.50	.70
□ 130	James Worthy	4.00	1.80
□ 131	Danny Young	1.50	.70
□ 132	Checklist 1-132	3.00	1.35

1987-88 Fleer Stickers

The 1987-88 Fleer Stickers is an 11-card standard-size set inserted one per wax pack. The fronts are red, white, blue and yellow. The backs are white and blue and contain career highlights. Based on the one-to-twelve proportion of stickers to regular cards in the wax packs, there are theoretically an equal number of sticker sets and regular sets. Virtually all cards from this set have wax-stained backs as a result of the packaging.

		MINT	NRMT
COMPLETE SET (11)		60.00	27.00
COMMON STICKER (1-11)		.50	.23
ONE PER PACK			
□ 1	Magic Johnson	6.00	2.70
□ 2	Michael Jordan	40.00	18.00
	(In text, votes mis-		
	spelled as voites)		
□ 3	Hakeem Olajuwon UER	6.00	2.70
	(Misspelled Olajuwan		
	on card back)		
□ 4	Larry Bird	8.00	3.60
□ 5	Kevin McHale	.75	.35
□ 6	Charles Barkley	5.00	2.20
□ 7	Dominique Wilkins	1.00	.45
□ 8	Kareem Abdul-Jabbar	2.00	.90
□ 9	Mark Aguirre	.50	.23
□ 10	Chuck Person	.50	.23
□ 11	Alex English	.50	.23

1988-89 Fleer

The 1988-89 Fleer basketball set contains 132 standard-size cards. There are 119 regular cards, plus 12 All-Star cards and a checklist. This set was issued in wax packs of 12 cards, gum and a sticker. Wax boxes contained 36 wax packs. The outer borders are white and gray, while the inner borders correspond to the team colors. The backs are greenish and show full NBA statistics with limited biographical information. The set is ordered alphabetically by team with a few exceptions due to late trades. The only subset is All-Stars (120-131). Rookie Cards of note are Muggsy Bogues, Dell Curry, Horace Grant, Mark Jackson, Reggie Miller, Derrick McKey, Scottie Pippen, Mark Price and Dennis Rodman. There is also a Rookie Card of John Stockton who had previously only appeared in Star Company sets.

		MINT	NRMT
COMPLETE w/Stickers (143)	220.00	100.00
COMPLETE SET (132)	200.00	90.00
COMMON CARD (1-132)	.50	.23
CL (132)	.50	.23
SEMISTARS	.75	.35
UNLISTED STARS	1.50	.70
CONDITION SENSITIVE SET		
□ 1	Antoine Carr	.75	.35
□ 2	Cliff Levingston	.50	.23
□ 3	Doc Rivers	.75	.35
□ 4	Spud Webb	.75	.35
□ 5	Dominique Wilkins	1.50	.70
□ 6	Kevin Willis	.75	.35
□ 7	Randy Wittman	.50	.23
□ 8	Danny Ainge	.75	.35
□ 9	Larry Bird	12.00	5.50
□ 10	Dennis Johnson	.50	.23
□ 11	Kevin McHale	1.50	.70
□ 12	Robert Parish	1.50	.70
□ 13	Tyrone Bogues	2.00	.90
□ 14	Dell Curry	1.50	.70
□ 15	Dave Corzine	.50	.23
□ 16	Horace Grant	6.00	2.70
□ 17	Michael Jordan	50.00	22.00
□ 18	Charles Oakley	.75	.35
□ 19	John Paxson	.75	.35

		MINT	NRMT
□ 20	Scottie Pippen UER	50.00	22.00
	(Misspelled Pippin		
	on card back)		
□ 21	Brad Sellers	.50	.23
□ 22	Brad Daugherty	.50	.23
□ 23	Ron Harper	.75	.35
□ 24	Larry Nance	.50	.23
□ 25	Mark Price	2.00	.90
□ 26	Hot Rod Williams	.50	.23
□ 27	Mark Aguirre	.50	.23
□ 28	Rolando Blackman	.50	.23
□ 29	James Donaldson	.50	.23
□ 30	Derek Harper	.75	.35
□ 31	Sam Perkins	.75	.35
□ 32	Roy Tarpley	.50	.23
□ 33	Michael Adams	.75	.35
□ 34	Alex English	.75	.35
□ 35	Lafayette Lever	.50	.23
□ 36	Blair Rasmussen	.50	.23
□ 37	Danny Schayes	.50	.23
□ 38	Jay Vincent	.50	.23
□ 39	Adrian Dantley	.50	.23
□ 40	Joe Dumars	1.50	.70
□ 41	Vinnie Johnson	.50	.23
□ 42	Bill Laimbeer	.75	.35
□ 43	Dennis Rodman	50.00	22.00
□ 44	John Salley	.50	.23
□ 45	Isiah Thomas	1.50	.70
□ 46	Winston Garland	.50	.23
□ 47	Rod Higgins	.50	.23
□ 48	Chris Mullin	1.50	.70
□ 49	Ralph Sampson	.50	.23
□ 50	Joe Barry Carroll	.50	.23
□ 51	Sleepy Floyd	.50	.23
□ 52	Rodney McCray	.50	.23
□ 53	Hakeem Olajuwon	6.00	2.70
□ 54	Purvis Short	.50	.23
□ 55	Vern Fleming	.50	.23
□ 56	John Long	.50	.23
□ 57	Reggie Miller	20.00	9.00
□ 58	Chuck Person	.75	.35
□ 59	Steve Stipanovich	.50	.23
□ 60	Waymon Tisdale	.50	.23
□ 61	Benoit Benjamin	.50	.23
□ 62	Michael Cage	.50	.23
□ 63	Mike Woodson	.50	.23
□ 64	Kareem Abdul-Jabbar	4.00	1.80
□ 65	Michael Cooper	.50	.23
□ 66	A.C. Green	.75	.35
□ 67	Magic Johnson	10.00	4.50
□ 68	Byron Scott	.75	.35
□ 69	Mychal Thompson	.50	.23
□ 70	James Worthy	1.50	.70
□ 71	Duane Washington	.50	.23
□ 72	Kevin Williams	.50	.23
□ 73	Randy Breuer	.50	.23
□ 74	Terry Cummings	.75	.35
□ 75	Paul Pressey	.50	.23
□ 76	Jack Sikma	.50	.23
□ 77	John Bagley	.50	.23
□ 78	Roy Hinson	.50	.23
□ 79	Buck Williams	.75	.35
□ 80	Patrick Ewing	3.00	1.35
□ 81	Sidney Green	.50	.23
□ 82	Mark Jackson	2.50	1.10
□ 83	Kenny Walker	.50	.23
□ 84	Gerald Wilkins	.50	.23
□ 85	Charles Barkley	5.00	2.20
□ 86	Maurice Cheeks	.50	.23
□ 87	Mike Gminski	.50	.23
□ 88	Cliff Robinson	.50	.23
□ 89	Armon Gilliam	1.50	.70
□ 90	Eddie Johnson	.50	.23
□ 91	Mark West	.50	.23
□ 92	Clyde Drexler	4.00	1.80
□ 93	Kevin Duckworth	.50	.23
□ 94	Steve Johnson	.50	.23
□ 95	Jerome Kersey	.50	.23
□ 96	Terry Porter	.50	.23
	(College Wisconsin,		
	should be Wisconsin		
	Stevens Point)		
□ 97	Don Kleine	.50	.23
□ 98	Reggie Theus	.75	.35
□ 99	Otis Thorpe	.75	.35
□ 100	Kenny Smith	1.50	.70

(College NC State, should be North Carolina)

	MINT	NRMT
☐ 101 Greg Anderson	.50	.23
☐ 102 Walter Berry	.50	.23
☐ 103 Frank Brickowski	.50	.23
☐ 104 Johnny Dawkins	.50	.23
☐ 105 Alvin Robertson	.50	.23
☐ 106 Tom Chambers	.50	.23
(Born 6/2/59, should be 6/21/59)		
☐ 107 Dale Ellis	.75	.35
☐ 108 Xavier McDaniel	.50	.23
☐ 109 Derrick McKey	1.50	.70
☐ 110 Nate McMillan UER	.50	.23
(Photo actually Kevin Williams)		
☐ 111 Thurl Bailey	.50	.23
☐ 112 Mark Eaton	.50	.23
☐ 113 Bobby Hansen	.50	.23
☐ 114 Karl Malone	5.00	2.20
☐ 115 John Stockton	25.00	11.00
☐ 116 Bernard King	.50	.23
☐ 117 Jeff Malone	.50	.23
☐ 118 Moses Malone	1.50	.70
☐ 119 John Williams	.50	.23
☐ 120 Michael Jordan AS	20.00	9.00
☐ 121 Mark Jackson AS	1.50	.70
☐ 122 Byron Scott AS	.50	.23
☐ 123 Magic Johnson AS ..	4.00	1.80
☐ 124 Larry Bird AS	5.00	2.20
☐ 125 Dominique Wilkins AS	.75	.35
☐ 126 Hakeem Olajuwon AS	2.50	1.10
☐ 127 John Stockton AS	5.00	2.20
☐ 128 Alvin Robertson AS	.50	.23
☐ 129 Charles Barkley AS	2.00	.90
(Back says Buck Williams is member of Jazz, should be Nets)		
☐ 130 Patrick Ewing AS	1.50	.70
☐ 131 Mark Eaton AS	.50	.23
☐ 132 Checklist 1-132	.50	.23

1988-89 Fleer Stickers

The 1988-89 Fleer Stickers is an 11-card standard-size set issued as a one per card insert along with 12 cards from the regular 132-card set. The fronts are baby blue, red, and white. The backs are blue and pink and contain career highlights. The set is ordered alphabetically. Based on the one-to-twelve proportion of stickers to regular cards in the wax packs, there are theoretically an equal number of sticker sets and regular sets. Virtually all cards from this set have wax-stained backs as a result of the packaging.

	MINT	NRMT
COMPLETE SET (11)	20.00	9.00
COMMON STICKER (1-11)	.25	.11

ONE PER PACK

☐ 1 Mark Aguirre	.25	.11
☐ 2 Larry Bird	5.00	2.20
☐ 3 Clyde Drexler	1.50	.70
☐ 4 Alex English	.25	.11
☐ 5 Patrick Ewing	1.25	.55
☐ 6 Magic Johnson	4.00	1.80
☐ 7 Michael Jordan	15.00	6.75
☐ 8 Karl Malone	2.00	.90
☐ 9 Kevin McHale	.40	.18
☐ 10 Isiah Thomas	.60	.25
☐ 11 Dominique Wilkins	.50	.23

1989-90 Fleer

The 1989-90 Fleer basketball set consists of 168 standard-size cards. The cards were distributed in 15-card wax packs (and one sticker) and in 36-card rack packs. Wax boxes contained 36 packs. The fronts feature color action player photos, with various color borders between white inner and outer borders. The player's name and position appear in the upper left corner, with the team logo superimposed over the upper right corner of the picture. The horizontally oriented backs have black lettering on red, pink, and white background and present career statistics, biographical information, and a performance index. The set is ordered alphabetically in team subsets (with a few exceptions due to late trades). The only subset is All-Star Game Combos (163-167). Rookie Cards of note in this set include Hersey Hawkins, Jeff Hornacek, Kevin Johnson, Reggie Lewis, Dan Majerle, Danny Manning, Mitch Richmond,, Rik Smits, and Rod Strickland. Cards from this set are frequently found off-center.

	MINT	NRMT
COMPLETE w/Stickers (179)	30.00	13.50
COMPLETE SET (168)	25.00	11.00
COMMON CARD (1-168)	.15	.07
SEMISTARS	.25	.11
UNLISTED STARS	.50	.23

☐ 1 John Battle	.15	.07
☐ 2 Jon Koncak	.15	.07
☐ 3 Cliff Levingston	.15	.07
☐ 4 Moses Malone	.50	.23
☐ 5 Doc Rivers	.25	.11
☐ 6 Spud Webb UER	.25	.11
(Points per 48 minutes incorrect at 2.6)		
☐ 7 Dominique Wilkins	.50	.23
☐ 8 Larry Bird	3.00	1.35
☐ 9 Dennis Johnson	.15	.07
☐ 10 Reggie Lewis	.75	.35
☐ 11 Kevin McHale	.25	.23
☐ 12 Robert Parish	.25	.11
☐ 13 Ed Pinckney	.15	.07
☐ 14 Brian Shaw	.50	.23
☐ 15 Rex Chapman	.75	.35
☐ 16 Kurt Rambis	.15	.07
☐ 17 Robert Reid	.15	.07
☐ 18 Kelly Tripucka	.15	.07
☐ 19 Bill Cartwright UER	.15	.07
(First season 1978-80, should be 1979-80)		
☐ 20 Horace Grant	.25	.11
☐ 21 Michael Jordan	10.00	4.50
☐ 22 John Paxson	.15	.07
☐ 23 Scottie Pippen	5.00	2.20
☐ 24 Brad Sellers	.15	.07
☐ 25 Brad Daugherty	.15	.07
☐ 26 Craig Ehlo	.25	.07
☐ 27 Ron Harper	.25	.11
☐ 28 Larry Nance	.25	.11
☐ 29 Mark Price	.25	.11
☐ 30 Mike Sanders	.15	.07
☐ 31A John Williams ERR	.50	.23
☐ 31B John Williams COR	.15	.07
☐ 32 Rolando Blackman UER	.15	.07
(Career blocks and points listed as 1961 and 2127, should be 196 and 12,127)		
☐ 33 Adrian Dantley	.15	.07
☐ 34 James Donaldson	.15	.07
☐ 35 Derek Harper	.25	.11
☐ 36 Sam Perkins	.25	.11
☐ 37 Herb Williams	.15	.07
☐ 38 Michael Adams	.15	.07
☐ 39 Walter Davis	.15	.07
☐ 40 Alex English	.15	.07
☐ 41 Lafayette Lever	.15	.07
☐ 42 Blair Rasmussen	.15	.07
☐ 43 Danny Schayes	.15	.07
☐ 44 Mark Aguirre	.15	.07
☐ 45 Joe Dumars	.50	.23
☐ 46 James Edwards	.15	.07
☐ 47 Vinnie Johnson	.15	.07
☐ 48 Bill Laimbeer	.25	.11
☐ 49 Dennis Rodman	5.00	2.20
☐ 50 Isiah Thomas	.50	.23
☐ 51 John Salley	.15	.07
☐ 52 Manute Bol	.15	.07
☐ 53 Winston Garland	.15	.07
☐ 54 Rod Higgins	.15	.07
☐ 55 Chris Mullin	.50	.23
☐ 56 Mitch Richmond	6.00	2.70
☐ 57 Terry Teagle	.15	.07
☐ 58 Derrick Chievous UER	.15	.07
(Stats correctly say 81 games in '88-89, text says 82)		
☐ 59 Sleepy Floyd	.15	.07
☐ 60 Tim McCormick	.15	.07
☐ 61 Hakeem Olajuwon	1.50	.70
☐ 62 Otis Thorpe	.25	.11
☐ 63 Mike Woodson	.15	.07
☐ 64 Vern Fleming	.15	.07
☐ 65 Reggie Miller	2.00	.90
☐ 66 Chuck Person	.25	.11
☐ 67 Detlef Schrempf	.25	.11
☐ 68 Rik Smits	1.00	.45

☐ 69 Benoit Benjamin	.15	.07
☐ 70 Gary Grant	.15	.07
☐ 71 Danny Manning	1.00	.45
☐ 72 Ken Norman	.15	.07
☐ 73 Charles Smith	.50	.23
☐ 74 Reggie Williams	.15	.07
☐ 75 Michael Cooper	.15	.07
☐ 76 A.C. Green	.25	.11
☐ 77 Magic Johnson	2.50	1.10
☐ 78 Byron Scott	.25	.11
☐ 79 Mychal Thompson	.15	.07
☐ 80 James Worthy	.50	.23
☐ 81 Kevin Edwards	.15	.07
☐ 82 Grant Long	.25	.11
☐ 83 Rony Seikaly	.75	.35
☐ 84 Rory Sparrow	.15	.07
☐ 85 Greg Anderson UER	.15	.07
(Stats show 1988-89 as 19888-89)		
☐ 86 Jay Humphries	.15	.07
☐ 87 Larry Krystkowiak	.15	.07
☐ 88 Ricky Pierce	.15	.07
☐ 89 Paul Pressey	.15	.07
☐ 90 Alvin Robertson	.15	.07
☐ 91 Jack Sikma	.15	.07
☐ 92 Steve Johnson	.15	.07
☐ 93 Rick Mahorn	.15	.07
☐ 94 David Rivers	.15	.07
☐ 95 Joe Barry Carroll	.15	.07
☐ 96 Lester Conner UER	.15	.07
(Garden State in stats, should be Golden State)		
☐ 97 Roy Hinson		.07
☐ 98 Mike McGee	.15	.07
☐ 99 Chris Morris	.50	.23
☐ 100 Patrick Ewing	.75	.35
☐ 101 Mark Jackson	.25	.11
☐ 102 Johnny Newman	.15	.07
☐ 103 Charles Oakley	.25	.11
☐ 104 Rod Strickland	3.00	1.35
☐ 105 Trent Tucker	.15	.07
☐ 106 Kiki Vandeweghe	.15	.07
☐ 107A Gerald Wilkins	.15	.07
(U. of Tennessee)		
☐ 107B Gerald Wilkins	.15	.07
(U. of Tenn.)		
☐ 108 Terry Catledge	.15	.07
☐ 109 Dave Corzine	.15	.07
☐ 110 Scott Skiles	.25	.11
☐ 111 Reggie Theus	.25	.11
☐ 112 Ron Anderson	.15	.07
☐ 113 Charles Barkley	1.25	.55
☐ 114 Scott Brooks	.15	.07
☐ 115 Maurice Cheeks	.15	.07
☐ 116 Mike Gminski	.15	.07
☐ 117 Hersey Hawkins UER	1.00	.45
(Born 9/29/65, should be 9/6/65)		
☐ 118 Christian Welp	.15	.07
☐ 119 Tom Chambers	.25	.07
☐ 120 Armon Gilliam	.15	.07
☐ 121 Jeff Hornacek	.25	.45
☐ 122 Eddie Johnson	.25	.11
☐ 123 Kevin Johnson	1.50	.70
☐ 124 Dan Majerle	1.00	.45
☐ 125 Mark West	.15	.07
☐ 126 Richard Anderson	.15	.07
☐ 127 Mark Bryant	.15	.07
☐ 128 Clyde Drexler	1.00	.45
☐ 129 Kevin Duckworth	.15	.07
☐ 130 Jerome Kersey	.15	.07
☐ 131 Terry Porter	.15	.07
☐ 132 Buck Williams	.25	.11
☐ 133 Danny Ainge	.25	.07
☐ 134 Ricky Berry	.15	.07
☐ 135 Rodney McCray	.15	.07
☐ 136 Jim Petersen	.15	.07
☐ 137 Harold Pressley	.15	.07
☐ 138 Kenny Smith	.15	.07
☐ 139 Wayman Tisdale	.15	.07
☐ 140 Willie Anderson	.15	.07
☐ 141 Frank Brickowski	.15	.07
☐ 142 Terry Cummings	.25	.11
☐ 143 Johnny Dawkins	.15	.07
☐ 144 Vernon Maxwell	.50	.23
☐ 145 Michael Cage	.15	.07

☐ 146 Dale Ellis	.25	.11
☐ 147 Alton Lister	.15	.07
☐ 148 Xavier McDaniel UER	.15	.07
(All-Rookie team in 1985, not 1988)		
☐ 149 Derrick McKey	.15	.07
☐ 150 Nate McMillan	.25	.11
☐ 151 Thurl Bailey	.15	.07
☐ 152 Mark Eaton	.15	.07
☐ 153 Darrell Griffith	.15	.07
☐ 154 Eric Leckner	.15	.07
☐ 155 Karl Malone	1.25	.55
☐ 156 John Stockton	2.00	.90
☐ 157 Mark Alarie	.15	.07
☐ 158 Ledell Eackles	.15	.07
☐ 159 Bernard King	.15	.07
☐ 160 Jeff Malone	.15	.07
☐ 161 Darrell Walker	.15	.07
☐ 162A John Williams ERR	.15	.23
☐ 162B John Williams COR	.15	.07
☐ 163 Karl Malone AS	.50	.23
John Stockton Mark Eaton		
☐ 164 Hakeem Olajuwon AS	.75	.35
Clyde Drexler AS		
☐ 165 Dominique Wilkins AS	.50	.23
Moses Malone AS		
☐ 166 Brad Daugherty AS	.15	.07
Mark Price AS		
Larry Nance AS UER		
Blo says Nance had 204 blocks, should be 206)		
☐ 167 Patrick Ewing AS	.50	.23
Mark Jackson AS		
☐ 168 Checklist 1-168	.10	.05

1989-90 Fleer Stickers

This set of 11 insert standard-size stickers features NBA All-Stars. One All-Star sticker was inserted in each 12-card wax pack. The front has a color action player photo. An aqua stripe with dark blue stars traverses the card top, and the same pattern reappears about halfway down the card face. The words "Fleer '89 All-Stars" appear at the top of the picture, with the player's name and position immediately below the picture. The back has a star pattern similar to the front. A career summary is printed in blue on a white background. Most card backs have problems with wax stains as a result of packaging.

	MINT	NRMT
COMPLETE SET (11)	6.00	2.70
COMMON STICKER (1-11)	.10	.05
SEMISTARS	.15	.07
UNLISTED STARS	.40	.18
ONE PER WAX PACK		
☐ 1 Karl Malone	.60	.25
☐ 2 Hakeem Olajuwon	.75	.35
☐ 3 Michael Jordan	5.00	2.20
☐ 4 Charles Barkley	.60	.25
☐ 5 Magic Johnson	1.25	.55
☐ 6 Isiah Thomas	.40	.18
☐ 7 Patrick Ewing	.40	.18
☐ 8 Dale Ellis	.10	.05
☐ 9 Chris Mullin	.40	.18
☐ 10 Larry Bird	1.50	.70
☐ 11 Tom Chambers	.10	.05

1990-91 Fleer

The 1990-91 Fleer set contains 198 standard-size cards. The cards were available in 15-card wax packs, 23-card cello packs and 36-card rack packs. Wax boxes contained 36 wax packs. There were also 43 card pre-priced packs ($1.49) which contained Rookie Sensation inserts. The fronts feature a color action player photo, with a white inner border and a two-color (red on top and bottom, blue on sides) outer border on a white card face. The team logo is superimposed on the upper left corner of the picture, with the player's name and position appearing below the picture. The backs are printed in black, gray, and yellow, and present biographical and statistical information. The set is ordered alphabetically in team subsets (with a few exceptions due to late trades). The description, All-American, is properly capitalized on the back of cards 134 and 144, but is not capitalized on cards 20, 29, 51, 53, 59, 70, 119, 130, 178, and 192. Rookie Cards of note in the set include Nick Anderson, Mookie Blaylock, Vlade Divac, Sean Elliott, Tim Hardaway, Shawn

Kemp, Glen Rice, and Clifford Robinson.

	MINT	NRMT
COMPLETE SET (198)	6.00	2.70
COMMON CARD (1-198)	.05	.02
SEMISTARS	.08	.04
UNLISTED STARS	.15	.07

		MINT	NRMT
☐ 1	John Battle UER	.05	.02
	(Drafted in '84,		
	should be '85)		
☐ 2	Cliff Levingston	.05	.02
☐ 3	Moses Malone	.15	.07
☐ 4	Kenny Smith	.05	.02
☐ 5	Spud Webb	.08	.04
☐ 6	Dominique Wilkins	.15	.07
☐ 7	Kevin Willis	.08	.04
☐ 8	Larry Bird	.60	.25
☐ 9	Dennis Johnson	.05	.02
☐ 10	Joe Kleine	.05	.02
☐ 11	Reggie Lewis	.08	.04
☐ 12	Kevin McHale	.08	.04
☐ 13	Robert Parish	.08	.04
☐ 14	Jim Paxson	.08	.04
☐ 15	Ed Pinckney	.05	.02
☐ 16	Muggsy Bogues	.08	.04
☐ 17	Rex Chapman	.15	.07
☐ 18	Dell Curry	.05	.02
☐ 19	Armon Gilliam	.05	.02
☐ 20	J.R. Reid	.05	.02
☐ 21	Kelly Tripucka	.05	.02
☐ 22	B.J. Armstrong	.05	.02
☐ 23A	Bill Cartwright ERR	.50	.23
	(No decimal points		
	in FGP and FTP)		
☐ 23B	Bill Cartwright COR	.05	.02
☐ 24	Horace Grant	.08	.04
☐ 25	Craig Hodges	.05	.02
☐ 26	Michael Jordan UER	2.00	.90
	(Led NBA in scoring		
	4 years, not 3)		
☐ 27	Stacey King UER	.05	.02
	(Comma missing between		
	progressed and Stacy)		
☐ 28	John Paxson	.08	.04
☐ 29	Will Perdue	.05	.02
☐ 30	Scottie Pippen UER	.60	.25
	(Born AK, not AK)		
☐ 31	Brad Daugherty	.05	.02
☐ 32	Craig Ehlo	.05	.02
☐ 33	Danny Ferry	.08	.04
☐ 34	Steve Kerr	.15	.07
☐ 35	Larry Nance	.08	.04
☐ 36	Mark Price UER	.08	.04
	(Drafted by Cleveland,		
	should be Dallas)		
☐ 37	Hot Rod Williams	.05	.02
☐ 38	Rolando Blackman	.05	.02
☐ 39A	Adrian Dantley ERR	.50	.23
	(No decimal points		
	in FGP and FTP)		
☐ 39B	Adrian Dantley COR	.05	.02
☐ 40	Brad Davis	.05	.02
☐ 41	James Donaldson UER	.05	.02
	(Text says in committed,		
	should be is committed)		
☐ 42	Derek Harper	.08	.04
☐ 43	Sam Perkins UER	.08	.04
	(First line of text		
	should be intact)		
☐ 44	Bill Wennington	.05	.02
☐ 45	Herb Williams	.05	.02
☐ 46	Michael Adams	.05	.02
☐ 47	Walter Davis	.05	.02
☐ 48	Alex English UER	.05	.02
	(Stats missing from		
	'76-77 through '79-80)		
☐ 49	Bill Hanzlik	.05	.02
☐ 50	Lafayette Lever UER	.05	.02
	(Born AR, not AK)		
☐ 51	Todd Lichti	.05	.02
☐ 52	Blair Rasmussen	.05	.02
☐ 53	Dan Schayes	.05	.02
☐ 54	Mark Aguirre	.05	.02

		MINT	NRMT
☐ 55	Joe Dumars	.15	.07
☐ 56	James Edwards	.05	.02
☐ 57	Vinnie Johnson	.05	.02
☐ 58	Bill Laimbeer	.08	.04
☐ 59	Dennis Rodman UER	.75	.35
	(College misspelled		
	as college on back)		
☐ 60	John Salley	.05	.02
☐ 61	Isiah Thomas	.15	.07
☐ 62	Manute Bol	.05	.02
☐ 63	Tim Hardaway	1.25	.55
☐ 64	Rod Higgins	.05	.02
☐ 65	Sarunas Marciulionis	.05	.02
☐ 66	Chris Mullin	.15	.07
☐ 67	Mitch Richmond	.25	.11
☐ 68	Terry Teagle	.05	.02
☐ 69	Anthony Bowie UER	.05	.02
	(Seasons, not seasons)		
☐ 70	Sleepy Floyd	.05	.02
☐ 71	Buck Johnson	.05	.02
☐ 72	Vernon Maxwell	.05	.02
☐ 73	Hakeem Olajuwon	.30	.14
☐ 74	Otis Thorpe	.08	.04
☐ 75	Mitchell Wiggins	.05	.02
☐ 76	Vern Fleming	.05	.02
☐ 77	George McCloud	.15	.07
☐ 78	Reggie Miller	.20	.09
☐ 79	Chuck Person	.08	.04
☐ 80	Mike Sanders	.05	.02
☐ 81	Detlef Schrempf	.08	.04
☐ 82	Rik Smits	.15	.07
☐ 83	LaSalle Thompson	.05	.02
☐ 84	Benoit Benjamin	.05	.02
☐ 85	Winston Garland	.05	.02
☐ 86	Ron Harper	.08	.04
☐ 87	Danny Manning	.08	.04
☐ 88	Ken Norman	.05	.02
☐ 89	Charles Smith	.05	.02
☐ 90	Michael Cooper	.05	.02
☐ 91	Vlade Divac	.30	.14
☐ 92	A.C. Green	.08	.04
☐ 93	Magic Johnson	.50	.23
☐ 94	Byron Scott	.08	.04
☐ 95	Mychal Thompson UER	.05	.02
	(Missing '78-79 stats		
	from Portland)		
☐ 96	Orlando Woolridge	.05	.02
☐ 97	James Worthy	.15	.07
☐ 98	Sherman Douglas	.08	.04
☐ 99	Kevin Edwards	.05	.02
☐ 100	Grant Long	.05	.02
☐ 101	Glen Rice	1.00	.45
☐ 102	Rony Seikaly UER	.08	.04
	(Ron on front)		
☐ 103	Billy Thompson	.05	.02
☐ 104	Jeff Grayer	.05	.02
☐ 105	Jay Humphries	.05	.02
☐ 106	Ricky Pierce	.05	.02
☐ 107	Paul Pressey	.05	.02
☐ 108	Fred Roberts	.05	.02
☐ 109	Alvin Robertson	.05	.02
☐ 110	Jack Sikma	.05	.02
☐ 111	Randy Breuer	.05	.02
☐ 112	Tony Campbell	.05	.02
☐ 113	Tyrone Corbin	.05	.02
☐ 114	Sam Mitchell UER	.05	.02
	(Mercer University,		
	not Mercer College)		
☐ 115	Tod Murphy UER	.05	.02
	(Born Long Beach,		
	not Lakewood)		
☐ 116	Pooh Richardson	.08	.04
☐ 117	Mookie Blaylock	.30	.14
☐ 118	Sam Bowie	.05	.02
☐ 119	Lester Conner	.05	.02
☐ 120	Dennis Hopson	.05	.02
☐ 121	Chris Morris	.08	.04
☐ 122	Charles Shackleford	.05	.02
☐ 123	Purvis Short	.05	.02
☐ 124	Maurice Cheeks	.05	.02
☐ 125	Patrick Ewing	.15	.07
☐ 126	Mark Jackson	.08	.04
☐ 127A	Johnny Newman ERR	.50	.23
	(Jr. misprinted as		
	J. on card back)		
☐ 127B	Johnny Newman COR	.05	.02

		MINT	NRMT
☐ 128	Charles Oakley	.08	.04
☐ 129	Trent Tucker	.05	.02
☐ 130	Kenny Walker	.05	.02
☐ 131	Gerald Wilkins	.05	.02
☐ 132	Nick Anderson	.25	.11
☐ 133	Terry Catledge	.05	.02
☐ 134	Sidney Green	.05	.02
☐ 135	Otis Smith	.05	.02
☐ 136	Reggie Theus	.08	.04
☐ 137	Sam Vincent	.05	.02
☐ 138	Ron Anderson	.05	.02
☐ 139	Charles Barkley UER	.25	.11
	(FG Percentage .545.)		
☐ 140	Scott Brooks UER	.05	.02
	('89-89 Philadelphia in		
	wrong typeface)		
☐ 141	Johnny Dawkins	.05	.02
☐ 142	Mike Gminski	.05	.02
☐ 143	Hersey Hawkins	.08	.04
☐ 144	Rick Mahorn	.05	.02
☐ 145	Derek Smith	.05	.02
☐ 146	Tom Chambers	.08	.04
☐ 147	Jeff Hornacek	.08	.04
☐ 148	Eddie Johnson	.08	.04
☐ 149	Kevin Johnson	.15	.07
☐ 150A	Dan Majerle ERR	1.00	.45
	(Award in 1988;		
	three-time selection)		
☐ 150B	Dan Majerle COR	.15	.07
	(Award in 1989;		
	three-time selection)		
☐ 151	Tim Perry	.05	.02
☐ 152	Kurt Rambis	.05	.02
☐ 153	Mark West	.05	.02
☐ 154	Clyde Drexler	.20	.09
☐ 155	Kevin Duckworth	.05	.02
☐ 156	Byron Irvin	.05	.02
☐ 157	Jerome Kersey	.05	.02
☐ 158	Terry Porter	.05	.02
☐ 159	Clifford Robinson	.25	.11
☐ 160	Buck Williams	.08	.04
☐ 161	Danny Young	.05	.02
☐ 162	Danny Ainge	.08	.04
☐ 163	Antoine Carr	.05	.02
☐ 164	Pervis Ellison	.08	.04
☐ 165	Rodney McCray	.05	.02
☐ 166	Harold Pressley	.05	.02
☐ 167	Wayman Tisdale	.05	.02
☐ 168	Willie Anderson	.05	.02
☐ 169	Frank Brickowski	.05	.02
☐ 170	Terry Cummings	.05	.02
☐ 171	Sean Elliott	.25	.11
☐ 172	David Robinson	.50	.23
☐ 173	Rod Strickland	.15	.07
☐ 174	David Wingate	.05	.02
☐ 175	Dana Barros	.15	.07
☐ 176	Michael Cage UER	.05	.02
	(Born AR, not AK)		
☐ 177	Dale Ellis	.08	.04
☐ 178	Shawn Kemp	3.00	1.35
☐ 179	Xavier McDaniel	.05	.02
☐ 180	Derrick McKey	.05	.02
☐ 181	Nate McMillan	.08	.04
☐ 182	Thurl Bailey	.05	.02
☐ 183	Mike Brown	.05	.02
☐ 184	Mark Eaton	.05	.02
☐ 185	Blue Edwards	.05	.02
☐ 186	Bobby Hansen	.05	.02
☐ 187	Eric Leckner	.05	.02
☐ 188	Karl Malone	.25	.11
☐ 189	John Stockton	.20	.09
☐ 190	Mark Alarie	.05	.02
☐ 191	Ledell Eackles	.05	.02
☐ 192A	Harvey Grant	.75	.35
	(First name on card		
	front in black)		
☐ 192B	Harvey Grant	.05	.02
	(First name on card		
	front in white)		
☐ 193	Tom Hammonds	.05	.02
☐ 194	Bernard King	.05	.02
☐ 195	Jeff Malone	.05	.02
☐ 196	Darrell Walker	.05	.02
☐ 197	Checklist 1-99	.05	.02
☐ 198	Checklist 100-198	.05	.02

1990-91 Fleer All-Stars

The 12-card All-Star insert standard-size set was randomly inserted in 1990-91 Fleer 12-card packs at a rate of one in five. The fronts feature a color action photo, framed by a basketball hoop and net on an aqua background. An orange stripe at the top represents the bottom of the backboard and has the words "Fleer '90 All-Stars." The player's name and position are given at the bottom between stars. The backs are printed in blue and pink with white borders and have career summaries.

	MINT	NRMT
COMPLETE SET (12)	8.00	3.60
COMMON CARD (1-12)	.15	.07
SEMISTARS	.50	.23
RANDOM INSERTS IN WAX PACKS		

☐ 1 Charles Barkley		.75	.35
☐ 2 Larry Bird		2.00	.90
☐ 3 Hakeem Olajuwon		1.00	.45
☐ 4 Magic Johnson		1.50	.70
☐ 5 Michael Jordan		6.00	2.70
☐ 6 Isiah Thomas		.50	.23
☐ 7 Karl Malone		.75	.35
☐ 8 Tom Chambers		.15	.07
☐ 9 John Stockton		.60	.25
☐ 10 David Robinson		1.50	.70
☐ 11 Clyde Drexler		.60	.25
☐ 12 Patrick Ewing		.50	.23

1990-91 Fleer Rookie Sensations

Randomly inserted in 23-card cello packs, the 1990-91 Fleer Rookie Sensations set consists of 10 standard-size cards. Cards were inserted at a rate of approximately one in five packs. The fronts feature color action player photos, with white and red borders on an aqua background. A basketball overlays the lower left corner of the picture, with the words "Rookie Sensation" in yellow lettering,

and the player's name appearing in white lettering in the bottom red border. The backs are printed in black and red on gray background (with white borders) and present summaries of their college careers and rookie seasons. The key card is David Robinson's first insert.

	MINT	NRMT
COMPLETE SET (10)	25.00	11.00
COMMON CARD (1-10)	.75	.35
SEMISTARS	1.25	.55
RANDOM INSERTS IN CELLO PACKS		

☐ 1 David Robinson UER..	10.00	4.50
(Text has 1988-90 season, should be 1989-90)		
☐ 2 Sean Elliott UER	2.00	.90
(Misspelled Elliot on card front)		
☐ 3 Glen Rice	8.00	3.60
☐ 4 J.R. Reid	.75	.35
☐ 5 Stacey King	.75	.35
☐ 6 Pooh Richardson	1.25	.55
☐ 7 Nick Anderson	2.00	.90
☐ 8 Tim Hardaway	10.00	4.50
☐ 9 Vlade Divac	2.50	1.10
☐ 10 Sherman Douglas	1.25	.55

1990-91 Fleer Update

These cards are the same size and design as the regular issue yet were issued only in complete set form. Factory sets were distributed exclusively through hobby dealers. The set numbering is arranged alphabetically by team. The card numbers have a

"U" prefix. Rookie Cards of note include Dee Brown, Elden Campbell, Cedric Ceballos, Derrick Coleman, Kendall Gill, Chris Jackson, Gary Payton, Drazen Petrovic, Dennis Scott and Loy Vaught. It's interesting to note that this is one of the first sets to actually get current year rookies pictured on trading cards.

	MINT	NRMT
COMPLETE SET (100)	6.00	2.70
COMMON CARD (U1-U100)	.05	.02
SEMISTARS	.15	.07
UNLISTED STARS	.30	.14

☐ U1 Jon Koncak	.05	.02
☐ U2 Tim McCormick	.05	.02
☐ U3 Doc Rivers	.15	.07
☐ U4 Rumeal Robinson	.05	.02
☐ U5 Trevor Wilson	.05	.02
☐ U6 Dee Brown	.30	.14
☐ U7 Dave Popson	.05	.02
☐ U8 Kevin Gamble	.05	.02
☐ U9 Brian Shaw	.30	.14
☐ U10 Michael Smith	.05	.02
☐ U11 Kendall Gill	.60	.25
☐ U12 Johnny Newman	.05	.02
☐ U13 Steve Scheffler	.05	.02
☐ U14 Dennis Hopson	.05	.02
☐ U15 Cliff Levingston	.05	.02
☐ U16 Chucky Brown	.05	.02
☐ U17 John Morton	.05	.02
☐ U18 Gerald Paddio	.05	.02
☐ U19 Alex English	.05	.02
☐ U20 Fat Lever	.05	.02
☐ U21 Rodney McCray	.05	.02
☐ U22 Roy Tarpley	.05	.02
☐ U23 Randy White	.05	.02
☐ U24 Anthony Cook	.05	.02
☐ U25 Chris Jackson	.30	.14
☐ U26 Marcus Liberty	.05	.02
☐ U27 Orlando Woolridge	.05	.02
☐ U28 William Bedford	.05	.02
☐ U29 Lance Blanks	.05	.02
☐ U30 Scott Hastings	.05	.02
☐ U31 Tyrone Hill	.15	.07
☐ U32 Les Jepsen	.05	.02
☐ U33 Steve Johnson	.05	.02
☐ U34 Kevin Pritchard	.05	.02
☐ U35 Dave Jamerson	.05	.02
☐ U36 Kenny Smith	.05	.02
☐ U37 Greg Dreiling	.05	.02
☐ U38 Kenny Williams	.05	.02
☐ U39 Micheal Williams UER	.15	.07
☐ U40 Gary Grant	.05	.02
☐ U41 Bo Kimble	.05	.02
☐ U42 Loy Vaught	.60	.25
☐ U43 Elden Campbell	.60	.25
☐ U44 Sam Perkins	.15	.07
☐ U45 Tony Smith	.05	.02
☐ U46 Terry Teagle	.05	.02
☐ U47 Willie Burton	.15	.07
☐ U48 Bimbo Coles	.30	.14
☐ U49 Terry Davis	.05	.02
☐ U50 Alec Kessler	.05	.02
☐ U51 Greg Anderson	.05	.02
☐ U52 Frank Brickowski	.05	.02
☐ U53 Steve Henson	.05	.02
☐ U54 Brad Lohaus	.05	.02
☐ U55 Dan Schayes	.05	.02
☐ U56 Gerald Glass	.05	.02
☐ U57 Felton Spencer	.15	.07
☐ U58 Doug West	.15	.07
☐ U59 Jud Buechler	.15	.07
☐ U60 Derrick Coleman	.60	.25
☐ U61 Tate George	.05	.02
☐ U62 Reggie Theus	.15	.07
☐ U63 Greg Grant	.05	.02
☐ U64 Jerrod Mustaf	.05	.02

		MINT	NRMT
☐ U65 Eddie Lee Wilkins	.05	.02
☐ U66 Michael Ansley	.05	.02
☐ U67 Jerry Reynolds	.05	.02
☐ U68 Dennis Scott	.40	.18
☐ U69 Manute Bol	.05	.02
☐ U70 Armon Gilliam	.05	.02
☐ U71 Brian Oliver	.05	.02
☐ U72 Kenny Payne	.05	.02
☐ U73 Jayson Williams	.60	.25
☐ U74 Kenny Battle	.05	.02
☐ U75 Cedric Ceballos	.60	.25
☐ U76 Negele Knight	.05	.02
☐ U77 Xavier McDaniel	.05	.02
☐ U78 Alaa Abdelnaby	.05	.02
☐ U79 Danny Ainge	.15	.07
☐ U80 Mark Bryant	.05	.02
☐ U81 Drazen Petrovic	.15	.07
☐ U82 Anthony Bonner	.05	.02
☐ U83 Duane Causwell	.05	.02
☐ U84 Bobby Hansen	.05	.02
☐ U85 Eric Leckner	.05	.02
☐ U86 Travis Mays	.05	.02
☐ U87 Lionel Simmons	.15	.07
☐ U88 Sidney Green	.05	.02
☐ U89 Tony Massenburg	.05	.02
☐ U90 Paul Pressey	.05	.02
☐ U91 Dwayne Schintzius	.05	.02
☐ U92 Gary Payton	3.00	1.35
☐ U93 Olden Polynice	.15	.07
☐ U94 Jeff Malone	.05	.02
☐ U95 Walter Palmer	.05	.02
☐ U96 Delaney Rudd	.05	.02
☐ U97 Pervis Ellison	.15	.07
☐ U98 A.J. English	.05	.02
☐ U99 Greg Foster	.15	.07
☐ U100 Checklist 1-100	.05	.02

1991-92 Fleer

The complete 1991-92 Fleer basketball card set contains 400 standard-size cards. The set was distributed in two series of 240 and 160 cards, respectively. The cards were distributed in 12-card wax packs, 23-card cello packs and 36-card rack packs. Wax boxes contained 36 packs. The fronts feature color action player photos, bordered by a red stripe on the bottom, and gray and red stripes on the top. A 3/4" blue stripe checkered with black NBA logos runs the length of the card and serves as the left border of the picture. The team logo, player's name, and position are printed in white lettering in this stripe. The picture is bordered on the right side by a thin gray stripe and a thicker blue one. The backs present career summaries and are printed with black lettering on various pastel colors, superimposed over a wooden basketball floor background. The cards are numbered and checklisted below alphabetically according to teams within each series. Subsets include All-Stars (210-219), League Leaders (220-226), Slam Dunk (227-232), All Star Game Highlights (233-238) and Team Leaders (372-398). Rookie Cards of note include Kenny Anderson, Stacey Augmon, Terrell Brandon, Larry Johnson, Anthony Mason, D.Mutombo, Steve Smith, and John Starks.

	MINT	NRMT
COMPLETE SET (400)	10.00	4.50
COMPLETE SERIES 1 (240)	5.00	2.20
COMPLETE SERIES 2 (160)	5.00	2.20
COMMON CARD (1-400)	.05	.02
SEMISTARS	.08	.04
UNLISTED STARS	.15	.07

☐ 1 John Battle	.05	.02
☐ 2 Jon Koncak	.05	.02
☐ 3 Rumeal Robinson	.05	.02
☐ 4 Spud Webb	.08	.04
☐ 5 Bob Weiss CO	.05	.02
☐ 6 Dominique Wilkins	.15	.07
☐ 7 Kevin Willis	.05	.02
☐ 8 Larry Bird	.60	.25
☐ 9 Dee Brown	.05	.02
☐ 10 Chris Ford CO	.05	.02
☐ 11 Kevin Gamble	.05	.02
☐ 12 Reggie Lewis	.08	.04
☐ 13 Kevin McHale	.08	.04
☐ 14 Robert Parish	.08	.04
☐ 15 Ed Pinckney	.05	.02
☐ 16 Brian Shaw	.05	.02
☐ 17 Muggsy Bogues	.08	.04
☐ 18 Rex Chapman	.08	.04
☐ 19 Dell Curry	.05	.02
☐ 20 Kendall Gill	.08	.04
☐ 21 Eric Leckner	.05	.02
☐ 22 Gene Littles CO	.05	.02
☐ 23 Johnny Newman	.05	.02
☐ 24 J.R. Reid	.05	.02
☐ 25 B.J. Armstrong	.05	.02
☐ 26 Bill Cartwright	.05	.02
☐ 27 Horace Grant	.08	.04
☐ 28 Phil Jackson CO	.08	.04
☐ 29 Michael Jordan	2.00	.90
☐ 30 Cliff Levingston	.05	.02
☐ 31 John Paxson	.05	.02
☐ 32 Will Perdue	.05	.02
☐ 33 Scottie Pippen	.50	.23
☐ 34 Brad Daugherty	.05	.02
☐ 35 Craig Ehlo	.05	.02
☐ 36 Danny Ferry	.05	.02
☐ 37 Larry Nance	.08	.04
☐ 38 Mark Price	.08	.04
☐ 39 Darnell Valentine	.05	.02
☐ 40 Hot Rod Williams	.05	.02
☐ 41 Lenny Wilkens CO	.08	.04
☐ 42 Richie Adubato CO	.05	.02
☐ 43 Rolando Blackman	.05	.02
☐ 44 James Donaldson	.05	.02
☐ 45 Derek Harper	.08	.04
☐ 46 Rodney McCray	.05	.02
☐ 47 Randy White	.05	.02
☐ 48 Herb Williams	.05	.02
☐ 49 Chris Jackson	.05	.02
☐ 50 Marcus Liberty	.05	.02
☐ 51 Todd Lichti	.05	.02
☐ 52 Blair Rasmussen	.05	.02
☐ 53 Paul Westhead CO	.05	.02
☐ 54 Reggie Williams	.05	.02
☐ 55 Joe Wolf	.05	.02
☐ 56 Orlando Woolridge	.05	.02
☐ 57 Mark Aguirre	.05	.02
☐ 58 Chuck Daly CO	.15	.07
☐ 59 Joe Dumars	.15	.07
☐ 60 James Edwards	.05	.02
☐ 61 Vinnie Johnson	.05	.02
☐ 62 Bill Laimbeer	.08	.04
☐ 63 Dennis Rodman	.60	.25
☐ 64 Isiah Thomas	.15	.07
☐ 65 Tim Hardaway	.30	.14
☐ 66 Rod Higgins	.05	.02
☐ 67 Tyrone Hill	.08	.04
☐ 68 Sarunas Marciulionis	.05	.02
☐ 69 Chris Mullin	.15	.07
☐ 70 Don Nelson CO	.08	.04
☐ 71 Mitch Richmond	.20	.09
☐ 72 Tom Tolbert	.05	.02
☐ 73 Don Chaney CO	.05	.02
☐ 74 Eric(Sleepy) Floyd	.05	.02
☐ 75 Buck Johnson	.05	.02
☐ 76 Vernon Maxwell	.05	.02
☐ 77 Hakeem Olajuwon	.30	.14
☐ 78 Kenny Smith	.05	.02
☐ 79 Larry Smith	.05	.02
☐ 80 Otis Thorpe	.08	.04
☐ 81 Vern Fleming	.05	.02
☐ 82 Bob Hill CO	.05	.02
☐ 83 Reggie Miller	.15	.07
☐ 84 Chuck Person	.05	.02
☐ 85 Detlef Schrempf	.08	.04
☐ 86 Rik Smits	.08	.04
☐ 87 LaSalle Thompson	.05	.02
☐ 88 Micheal Williams	.05	.02
☐ 89 Gary Grant	.05	.02
☐ 90 Ron Harper	.08	.04
☐ 91 Bo Kimble	.05	.02
☐ 92 Danny Manning	.08	.04
☐ 93 Ken Norman	.05	.02
☐ 94 Olden Polynice	.05	.02
☐ 95 Mike Schuler CO	.05	.02
☐ 96 Charles Smith	.05	.02
☐ 97 Vlade Divac	.08	.04
☐ 98 Mike Dunleavy CO	.05	.02
☐ 99 A.C. Green	.08	.04
☐ 100 Magic Johnson	.50	.23
☐ 101 Sam Perkins	.08	.04
☐ 102 Byron Scott	.08	.04
☐ 103 Terry Teagle	.05	.02
☐ 104 James Worthy	.15	.07
☐ 105 Willie Burton	.05	.02
☐ 106 Bimbo Coles	.05	.02
☐ 107 Sherman Douglas	.05	.02
☐ 108 Kevin Edwards	.05	.02
☐ 109 Grant Long	.05	.02
☐ 110 Kevin Loughery CO	.05	.02
☐ 111 Glen Rice	.25	.11
☐ 112 Rony Seikaly	.05	.02
☐ 113 Frank Brickowski	.05	.02
☐ 114 Dale Ellis	.08	.04
☐ 115 Del Harris CO	.05	.02
☐ 116 Jay Humphries	.05	.02
☐ 117 Fred Roberts	.05	.02
☐ 118 Alvin Robertson	.05	.02
☐ 119 Dan Schayes	.05	.02
☐ 120 Jack Sikma	.08	.04
☐ 121 Tony Campbell	.05	.02
☐ 122 Tyrone Corbin	.05	.02
☐ 123 Sam Mitchell	.05	.02
☐ 124 Tod Murphy	.05	.02
☐ 125 Pooh Richardson	.05	.02
☐ 126 Jimmy Rodgers CO	.05	.02
☐ 127 Felton Spencer	.05	.02
☐ 128 Mookie Blaylock	.08	.04
☐ 129 Sam Bowie	.05	.02
☐ 130 Derrick Coleman	.25	.11
☐ 131 Chris Dudley	.05	.02
☐ 132 Bill Fitch CO	.05	.02
☐ 133 Chris Morris	.05	.02
☐ 134 Drazen Petrovic	.08	.04
☐ 135 Maurice Cheeks	.05	.02
☐ 136 Patrick Ewing	.15	.07

☐ 137	Mark Jackson	.08	.04
☐ 138	Charles Oakley	.08	.04
☐ 139	Pat Riley CO	.08	.04
☐ 140	Trent Tucker	.05	.02
☐ 141	Kiki Vandeweghe	.05	.02
☐ 142	Gerald Wilkins	.05	.02
☐ 143	Nick Anderson	.08	.04
☐ 144	Terry Catledge	.05	.02
☐ 145	Matt Guokas CO	.05	.02
☐ 146	Jerry Reynolds	.05	.02
☐ 147	Dennis Scott	.08	.04
☐ 148	Scott Skiles	.05	.02
☐ 149	Otis Smith	.05	.02
☐ 150	Ron Anderson	.05	.02
☐ 151	Charles Barkley	.25	.11
☐ 152	Johnny Dawkins	.05	.02
☐ 153	Armon Gilliam	.05	.02
☐ 154	Hersey Hawkins	.08	.04
☐ 155	Jim Lynam CO	.05	.02
☐ 156	Rick Mahorn	.05	.02
☐ 157	Brian Oliver	.05	.02
☐ 158	Tom Chambers	.05	.02
☐ 159	C.Fitzsimmons CO	.05	.02
☐ 160	Jeff Hornacek	.08	.04
☐ 161	Kevin Johnson	.15	.07
☐ 162	Negele Knight	.05	.02
☐ 163	Dan Majerle	.08	.04
☐ 164	Xavier McDaniel	.05	.02
☐ 165	Mark West	.05	.02
☐ 166	Rick Adelman CO	.05	.02
☐ 167	Danny Ainge	.08	.04
☐ 168	Clyde Drexler	.20	.09
☐ 169	Kevin Duckworth	.05	.02
☐ 170	Jerome Kersey	.05	.02
☐ 171	Terry Porter	.05	.02
☐ 172	Clifford Robinson	.08	.04
☐ 173	Buck Williams	.08	.04
☐ 174	Antoine Carr	.05	.02
☐ 175	Duane Causwell	.05	.02
☐ 176	Jim Les	.05	.02
☐ 177	Travis Mays	.05	.02
☐ 178	Dick Motta CO	.05	.02
☐ 179	Lionel Simmons	.05	.02
☐ 180	Rory Sparrow	.05	.02
☐ 181	Wayman Tisdale	.05	.02
☐ 182	Willie Anderson	.05	.02
☐ 183	Larry Brown CO	.05	.02
☐ 184	Terry Cummings	.05	.02
☐ 185	Sean Elliott	.08	.04
☐ 186	Paul Pressey	.05	.02
☐ 187	David Robinson	.30	.14
☐ 188	Rod Strickland	.15	.07
☐ 189	Benoit Benjamin	.05	.02
☐ 190	Eddie Johnson	.08	.04
☐ 191	K.C. Jones CO	.08	.04
☐ 192	Shawn Kemp	.75	.35
☐ 193	Derrick McKey	.05	.02
☐ 194	Gary Payton	.40	.18
☐ 195	Ricky Pierce	.05	.02
☐ 196	Sedale Threatt	.05	.02
☐ 197	Thurl Bailey	.05	.02
☐ 198	Mark Eaton	.05	.02
☐ 199	Blue Edwards	.05	.02
☐ 200	Jeff Malone	.05	.02
☐ 201	Karl Malone	.25	.11
☐ 202	Jerry Sloan CO	.08	.04
☐ 203	John Stockton	.15	.07
☐ 204	Ledell Eackles	.05	.02
☐ 205	Pervis Ellison	.05	.02
☐ 206	A.J. English	.05	.02
☐ 207	Harvey Grant	.05	.02
☐ 208	Bernard King	.05	.02
☐ 209	Wes Unseld CO	.08	.04
☐ 210	Kevin Johnson AS	.08	.04
☐ 211	Michael Jordan AS	1.00	.45
☐ 212	Dominique Wilkins AS	.08	.04
☐ 213	Charles Barkley AS	.15	.07
☐ 214	Hakeem Olajuwon AS	.15	.07
☐ 215	Patrick Ewing AS	.15	.07
☐ 216	Tim Hardaway AS	.15	.07
☐ 217	John Stockton AS	.15	.07
☐ 218	Chris Mullin AS	.08	.04
☐ 219	Karl Malone AS	.15	.07
☐ 220	Michael Jordan LL	1.00	.45
☐ 221	John Stockton LL	.15	.07
☐ 222	Alvin Robertson LL	.05	.02
☐ 223	Hakeem Olajuwon LL	.15	.07
☐ 224	Buck Williams LL	.05	.02
☐ 225	David Robinson LL	.15	.07
☐ 226	Reggie Miller LL	.15	.07
☐ 227	Blue Edwards SD	.05	.02
☐ 228	Dee Brown SD	.05	.02
☐ 229	Rex Chapman SD	.05	.02
☐ 230	Kenny Smith SD	.05	.02
☐ 231	Shawn Kemp SD	.40	.18
☐ 232	Kendall Gill SD	.05	.02
☐ 233	'91 All Star Game	.50	.23
	Enemies - A Love Story (East Bench Scene)		
☐ 234	Clyde Drexler ASG	.15	.07
	Kevin McHale ASG		
☐ 235	Alvin Robertson ASG	.05	.02
☐ 236	Patrick Ewing ASG	.08	.04
	Karl Malone ASG		
☐ 237	'91 All Star Game	.25	.11
	Just Me and the Boys Michael Jordan Magic Johnson David Robinson Patrick Ewing		
☐ 238	Michael Jordan ASG	.50	.23
☐ 239	Checklist 1-120	.05	.02
☐ 240	Checklist 121-240	.05	.02
☐ 241	Stacey Augmon	.15	.07
☐ 242	Maurice Cheeks	.05	.02
☐ 243	Paul Graham	.05	.02
☐ 244	Rodney Monroe	.05	.02
☐ 245	Blair Rasmussen	.05	.02
☐ 246	Alexander Volkov	.05	.02
☐ 247	John Bagley	.05	.02
☐ 248	Rick Fox	.15	.07
☐ 249	Rickey Green	.05	.02
☐ 250	Joe Kleine	.05	.02
☐ 251	Stojko Vrankovic	.05	.02
☐ 252	Allan Bristow CO	.05	.02
☐ 253	Kenny Gattison	.05	.02
☐ 254	Mike Gminski	.05	.02
☐ 255	Larry Johnson	.60	.25
☐ 256	Bobby Hansen	.05	.02
☐ 257	Craig Hodges	.05	.02
☐ 258	Stacey King	.05	.02
☐ 259	Scott Williams	.05	.02
☐ 260	John Battle	.05	.02
☐ 261	Winston Bennett	.05	.02
☐ 262	Terrell Brandon	.75	.35
☐ 263	Henry James	.05	.02
☐ 264	Steve Kerr	.08	.04
☐ 265	Jimmy Oliver	.05	.02
☐ 266	Brad Davis	.05	.02
☐ 267	Terry Davis	.05	.02
☐ 268	Donald Hodge	.05	.02
☐ 269	Mike Iuzzolino	.05	.02
☐ 270	Fat Lever	.05	.02
☐ 271	Doug Smith	.05	.02
☐ 272	Greg Anderson	.05	.02
☐ 273	Kevin Brooks	.05	.02
☐ 274	Walter Davis	.05	.02
☐ 275	Winston Garland	.05	.02
☐ 276	Mark Macon	.05	.02
☐ 277	D.Mutombo	.50	.23
	(Fleer '91 on front)		
☐ 277B	D.Mutombo	.50	.23
	(Fleer '91-92 on front)		
☐ 278	William Bedford	.05	.02
☐ 279	Lance Blanks	.05	.02
☐ 280	John Salley	.05	.02
☐ 281	Charles Thomas	.05	.02
☐ 282	Darrell Walker	.05	.02
☐ 283	Orlando Woolridge	.05	.02
☐ 284	Victor Alexander	.05	.02
☐ 285	Vincent Askew	.05	.02
☐ 286	Mario Elie	.15	.07
☐ 287	Alton Lister	.05	.02
☐ 288	Billy Owens	.15	.07
☐ 289	Matt Bullard	.05	.02
☐ 290	Carl Herrera	.05	.02
☐ 291	Tree Rollins	.05	.02
☐ 292	John Turner	.05	.02
☐ 293	Dale Davis UER	.15	.07
	(Photo on back actually Sean Green)		
☐ 294	Sean Green	.05	.02
☐ 295	Kenny Williams	.05	.02
☐ 296	James Edwards	.05	.02
☐ 297	LeRon Ellis	.05	.02
☐ 298	Doc Rivers	.08	.04
☐ 299	Loy Vaught	.08	.04
☐ 300	Elden Campbell	.05	.02
☐ 301	Jack Haley	.05	.02
☐ 302	Keith Owens	.05	.02
☐ 303	Tony Smith	.05	.02
☐ 304	Sedale Threatt	.05	.02
☐ 305	Keith Askins	.05	.02
☐ 306	Alec Kessler	.05	.02
☐ 307	John Morton	.05	.02
☐ 308	Alan Ogg	.05	.02
☐ 309	Steve Smith	.40	.18
☐ 310	Lester Conner	.05	.02
☐ 311	Jeff Grayer	.05	.02
☐ 312	Frank Hamblen CO	.05	.02
☐ 313	Steve Henson	.05	.02
☐ 314	Larry Krystkowiak	.05	.02
☐ 315	Moses Malone	.15	.07
☐ 316	Thurl Bailey	.05	.02
☐ 317	Randy Breuer	.05	.02
☐ 318	Scott Brooks	.05	.02
☐ 319	Gerald Glass	.05	.02
☐ 320	Luc Longley	.20	.09
☐ 321	Doug West	.05	.02
☐ 322	Kenny Anderson	.30	.14
☐ 323	Tate George	.05	.02
☐ 324	Terry Mills	.15	.07
☐ 325	Greg Anthony	.15	.07
☐ 326	Anthony Mason	.30	.14
☐ 327	Tim McCormick	.05	.02
☐ 328	Xavier McDaniel	.05	.02
☐ 329	Brian Quinnett	.05	.02
☐ 330	John Starks	.20	.09
☐ 331	Stanley Roberts	.05	.02
☐ 332	Jeff Turner	.05	.02
☐ 333	Sam Vincent	.05	.02
☐ 334	Brian Williams	.15	.07
☐ 335	Manute Bol	.05	.02
☐ 336	Kenny Payne	.05	.02
☐ 337	Charles Shackleford	.05	.02
☐ 338	Jayson Williams	.15	.07
☐ 339	Cedric Ceballos	.08	.04
☐ 340	Andrew Lang	.05	.02
☐ 341	Jerrod Mustaf	.05	.02
☐ 342	Tim Perry	.05	.02
☐ 343	Kurt Rambis	.05	.02
☐ 344	Alaa Abdelnaby	.05	.02
☐ 345	Robert Pack	.08	.04
☐ 346	Danny Young	.05	.02
☐ 347	Anthony Bonner	.05	.02
☐ 348	Pete Chilcutt	.05	.02
☐ 349	Rex Hughes CO	.05	.02
☐ 350	Mitch Richmond	.20	.09
☐ 351	Dwayne Schintzius	.05	.02
☐ 352	Spud Webb	.08	.04
☐ 353	Antoine Carr	.05	.02
☐ 354	Sidney Green	.05	.02
☐ 355	Vinnie Johnson	.05	.02
☐ 356	Greg Sutton	.05	.02
☐ 357	Dana Barros	.05	.02
☐ 358	Michael Cage	.05	.02
☐ 359	Marty Conlon	.05	.02
☐ 360	Rich King	.05	.02
☐ 361	Nate McMillan	.05	.02
☐ 362	David Benoit	.08	.04
☐ 363	Mike Brown	.05	.02
☐ 364	Tyrone Corbin	.05	.02
☐ 365	Eric Murdock	.05	.02
☐ 366	Delaney Rudd	.05	.02
☐ 367	Michael Adams	.05	.02
☐ 368	Tom Hammonds	.05	.02
☐ 369	Larry Stewart	.05	.02
☐ 370	Andre Turner	.05	.02
☐ 371	David Wingate	.05	.02
☐ 372	Dominique Wilkins TL	.08	.04
☐ 373	Larry Bird TL	.30	.14
☐ 374	Rex Chapman TL	.05	.02
☐ 375	Michael Jordan TL	1.00	.45
☐ 376	Brad Daugherty TL	.05	.02
☐ 377	Derek Harper TL	.05	.02
☐ 378	D.Mutombo TL	.15	.07
☐ 379	Joe Dumars TL	.08	.04
☐ 380	Chris Mullin TL	.08	.04

☐ 381 Hakeem Olajuwon TL	.15	.07
☐ 382 Chuck Person TL	.05	.02
☐ 383 Charles Smith TL	.05	.02
☐ 384 James Worthy TL	.08	.04
☐ 385 Glen Rice TL	.15	.07
☐ 386 Alvin Robertson TL	.05	.02
☐ 387 Tony Campbell TL	.05	.02
☐ 388 Derrick Coleman TL	.05	.02
☐ 389 Patrick Ewing TL	.15	.07
☐ 390 Scott Skiles TL	.05	.02
☐ 391 Charles Barkley TL	.15	.07
☐ 392 Kevin Johnson TL	.08	.04
☐ 393 Clyde Drexler TL	.15	.07
☐ 394 Lionel Simmons TL	.05	.02
☐ 395 David Robinson TL	.15	.07
☐ 396 Ricky Pierce TL	.05	.02
☐ 397 John Stockton TL	.15	.07
☐ 398 Michael Adams TL	.05	.02
☐ 399 Checklist	.05	.02
☐ 400 Checklist	.05	.02

1991-92 Fleer Dikembe Mutombo

This 12-card standard-size set was randomly inserted in 1991-92 Fleer second series 12-card wax packs at a rate of approximately one in six. The set highlights the accomplishments of then Denver Nuggets' rookie D.Mutombo. The front borders are dark red and checkered with miniature black NBA logos. The background of the color action photo is ghosted so that the featured player stands out, and the color of the lettering on the front is mustard. On a pink background, the back has a color close-up photo and a summary of the player's performance. Mutombo autographed over 2,000 of these cards which were also randomly inserted into packs. Those cards inserted in packs feature embossed Fleer logos for authenticity.

	MINT	NRMT
COMPLETE SET (12)	5.00	2.20
COMMON MUTOMBO (1-12)	.50	.23
RANDOM INSERTS IN ALL SER.2 PACKS		
☐ 1 Dikembe Mutombo	.50	.23
Childhood in Zaire		
☐ 2 Dikembe Mutombo	.50	.23

	Georgetown Start	
☐ 3 Dikembe Mutombo	.50	.23
Arrival on		
college scene		
☐ 4 Dikembe Mutombo	.50	.23
Capping college career		
☐ 5 Dikembe Mutombo	.50	.23
NBA Draft		
☐ 6 Dikembe Mutombo	.50	.23
First NBA games		
☐ 7 Dikembe Mutombo	.50	.23
Offensive skills		
☐ 8 Dikembe Mutombo	.50	.23
What he has meant		
to the Nuggets		
☐ 9 Dikembe Mutombo	.50	.23
Work Habits		
☐ 10 Dikembe Mutombo	.50	.23
Charmed Denver		
☐ 11 Dikembe Mutombo	.50	.23
The Future		
☐ 12 Dikembe Mutombo	.50	.23
The Mutombo Legend		
☐ AU Dikembe Mutombo	80.00	36.00
(Certified autograph)		

1991-92 Fleer Pro-Visions

This six-card standard-size set showcases outstanding NBA players. The set was distributed as a random insert in 1991-92 Fleer first series 12-card plastic-wrap packs at a rate of approximately one per six packs. The fronts feature a color player portrait by sports artist Terry Smith. The portrait is bordered on all sides by white, with the player's name in red lettering below the picture. The backs present biographical information and career summary in black lettering on a color background (with white borders).

	MINT	NRMT
COMPLETE SET (6)	4.00	1.80
COMMON CARD (1-6)	.25	.11
RANDOM INSERTS IN ALL SER.1 PACKS		
☐ 1 David Robinson	.50	.23
☐ 2 Michael Jordan	3.00	1.35
☐ 3 Charles Barkley	.40	.18
☐ 4 Patrick Ewing	.25	.11
☐ 5 Karl Malone	.40	.18
☐ 6 Magic Johnson	.75	.35

1991-92 Fleer Rookie Sensations

This 10-card standard-size set showcases outstanding rookies from the 1990-91 season. The set was distributed as a random insert in 1991-92 Fleer 23-card cello packs at a rate of approximately two in every three packs. The card fronts feature a color player photo inside a basketball rim and net. The picture is bordered in magenta on all sides. The words "Rookie Sensations" appear above the picture, and player information is given below the picture. An orange basketball with the words "Fleer '91" appears in the upper left corner on both sides of the card. The back has a magenta border and includes highlights of the player's rookie season.

	MINT	NRMT
COMPLETE SET (10)	8.00	3.60
COMMON CARD (1-10)	.50	.23
SEMISTARS	.75	.35
UNLISTED STARS	1.50	.70
RANDOM INSERTS IN SER.1 CELLO PACKS		
☐ 1 Lionel Simmons	.50	.23
☐ 2 Dennis Scott	.75	.35
☐ 3 Derrick Coleman	1.50	.70
☐ 4 Kendall Gill	1.50	.70
☐ 5 Travis Mays	.50	.23
☐ 6 Felton Spencer	.50	.23
☐ 7 Willie Burton	.50	.23
☐ 8 Chris Jackson	.50	.23
☐ 9 Gary Payton	6.00	2.70
☐ 10 Dee Brown	.50	.23

1991-92 Fleer Schoolyard

This six-card standard-size set of "Schoolyard Stars" was inserted one per 1991-92 Fleer 36-card rack packs. The card front features color action player photos. The photos are bordered on the left and bottom by a black stripe and a broken pink

stripe. Yellow stripes traverse the card top and bottom, and the background is a gray cement-colored design. The back has a similar layout and presents a basketball tip in black lettering on white.

	MINT	NRMT
COMPLETE SET (6)	8.00	3.60
COMMON CARD (1-6)	.75	.35
SEMISTARS	1.50	.70
ONE PER SER.1 RACK PACK		

		MINT	NRMT
☐ 1	Chris Mullin	3.00	1.35
☐ 2	Isiah Thomas	3.00	1.35
☐ 3	Kevin McHale	1.50	.70
☐ 4	Kevin Johnson	3.00	1.35
☐ 5	Karl Malone	6.00	2.70
☐ 6	Alvin Robertson	.75	.35

1991-92 Fleer Dominique Wilkins

Cards from this 12-card insert standard-size set were randomly inserted in 1991-92 Fleer second series 12-card wax packs at a rate of approximately one per six. The set highlights the career of superstar Dominique Wilkins. The front borders are dark red and checkered with miniature black NBA logos. The background of the color action photo is ghosted so that the featured player stands out, and the color of the lettering on the front is mustard. On a pink background, the back has a color close-up

photo and a summary of the player's performance. Wilkins personally autographed over 2,000 of these cards which were also randomly inserted in packs. Those cards inserted in packs feature embossed Fleer logos for authenticity.

		MINT	NRMT
COMPLETE SET (12)		4.00	1.80
COMMON WILKINS (1-12)		.40	.18
RANDOM INSERTS IN ALL SER.2 PACKS			
☐ 1	Dominique Wilkins Overview	.40	.18
☐ 2	Dominique Wilkins College	.40	.18
☐ 3	Dominique Wilkins Early years	.40	.18
☐ 4	Dominique Wilkins Early Career	.40	.18
☐ 5	Dominique Wilkins Dominique Emerges	.40	.18
☐ 6	Dominique Wilkins Another milestone	.40	.18
☐ 7	Dominique Wilkins Wilkins continues to shine	.40	.18
☐ 8	Dominique Wilkins Best all-round season	.40	.18
☐ 9	Dominique Wilkins Charitable Causes	.40	.18
☐ 10	Dominique Wilkins Durability	.40	.18
☐ 11	Dominique Wilkins Career Numbers	.40	.18
☐ 12	Dominique Wilkins Future	.40	.18
☐ AU	Dominique Wilkins (Certified autograph)	80.00	36.00

1992-93 Fleer

The complete 1992-93 Fleer basketball set contains 444 standard-size cards. The set was distributed in two series of 264 and 180 cards, respectively. First series cards were distributed in 17-card plastic-wrap packs, 32-card cello packs, and 42-card rack packs. Second series cards were distributed in 15-card plastic-wrap packs and 32-card cello packs. The fronts display color action player photos, enclosed by metallic bronze borders and accented on the right by two pebble-grain col-

ored stripes. On a tan pebble-grain background, the horizontally oriented backs have a color close-up photo in the shape of the lane under the basket. Biography, career statistics, and player profile are included on the backs. The cards are numbered on the back and checklisted below alphabetically according to teams. Subsets include League Leaders (238-245), Award Winners (246-249), Pro-Visions (250-255), Schoolyard Stars (256-264) and Slam Dunk (265-300). The Slam Dunk subset is divided into five categories: Power, Grace, Champions, Little Big Men, and Great Defenders. Randomly inserted throughout the packs were more than 3,000 (Slam Dunk subset) cards signed by former NBA players Darryl Dawkins and Kenny Walker as well as by current NBA star Shawn Kemp. According to Fleer's advertising material, odds of finding a signed Slam Dunk card are one in 5,000 packs. Rookie Cards of note include Tom Gugliotta, Robert Horry, Christian Laettner, Alonzo Mourning, Shaquille O'Neal, Latrell Sprewell and Clarence Weatherspoon. A second series mail-in offer featuring an "All-Star Slam Dunk Team" card and an issue of Inside Stuff was available (expiring 6/30/93) in return for ten second series wrappers plus a dollar.

	MINT	NRMT
COMPLETE SET (444)	30.00	13.50
COMPLETE SERIES 1 (264)	15.00	6.75
COMPLETE SERIES 2 (180)	15.00	6.75
COMMON CARD (1-444)	.05	.02
SEMISTARS	.10	.05
UNLISTED STARS	.25	.11
SLM DNK AUs: SER.2 STATED ODDS 1:5,000		

		MINT	NRMT
☐ 1	Stacey Augmon	.10	.05
☐ 2	Duane Ferrell	.05	.02
☐ 3	Paul Graham	.05	.02
☐ 4A	Jon Koncak (Shooting pose on back)	.05	.02
☐ 4B	Jon Koncak (No ball visible in photo on back)	.05	.02
☐ 5	Blair Rasmussen	.05	.02
☐ 6	Rumeal Robinson	.05	.02
☐ 7	Bob Weiss CO	.05	.02
☐ 8	Dominique Wilkins	.25	.11
☐ 9	Kevin Willis	.05	.02
☐ 10	John Bagley	.05	.02
☐ 11	Larry Bird	1.00	.45
☐ 12	Dee Brown	.05	.02
☐ 13	Chris Ford CO	.05	.02
☐ 14	Rick Fox	.10	.05
☐ 15	Kevin Gamble	.05	.02
☐ 16	Reggie Lewis	.10	.05
☐ 17	Kevin McHale	.25	.11

18	Robert Parish	.10	.05
19	Ed Pinckney	.05	.02
20	Muggsy Bogues	.10	.05
21	Allan Bristow CO	.05	.02
22	Dell Curry	.05	.02
23	Kenny Gattison	.05	.02
24	Kendall Gill	.05	.02
25	Larry Johnson	.30	.14
26	Johnny Newman	.05	.02
27	J.R. Reid	.05	.02
28	B.J. Armstrong	.05	.02
29	Bill Cartwright	.05	.02
30	Horace Grant	.10	.05
31	Phil Jackson CO	.10	.05
32	Michael Jordan	3.00	1.35
33	Stacey King	.05	.02
34	Cliff Levingston	.05	.02
35	John Paxson	.10	.05
36	Scottie Pippen	.75	.35
37	Scott Williams	.05	.02
38	John Battle	.05	.02
39	Terrell Brandon	.40	.18
40	Brad Daugherty	.05	.02
41	Craig Ehlo	.05	.02
42	Larry Nance	.10	.05
43	Mark Price	.05	.02
44	Mike Sanders	.05	.02
45	Lenny Wilkens CO	.10	.05
46	John Hot Rod Williams	.05	.02
47	Richie Adubato CO	.05	.02
48	Terry Davis	.05	.02
49	Derek Harper	.10	.05
50	Donald Hodge	.05	.02
51	Mike Iuzzolino	.05	.02
52	Rodney McCray	.05	.02
53	Doug Smith	.05	.02
54	Greg Anderson	.05	.02
55	Winston Garland	.05	.02
56	Dan Issel CO	.05	.02
57	Chris Jackson	.05	.02
58	Marcus Liberty	.05	.02
59	Mark Macon	.05	.02
60	D.Mutombo	.25	.11
61	Reggie Williams	.05	.02
62	Mark Aguirre	.05	.02
63	Joe Dumars	.25	.11
64	Bill Laimbeer	.10	.05
65	Olden Polynice	.05	.02
66	Dennis Rodman	1.00	.45
67	Ron Rothstein CO	.05	.02
68	John Salley	.05	.02
69	Isiah Thomas	.25	.11
70	Darrell Walker	.05	.02
71	Orlando Woolridge	.05	.02
72	Victor Alexander	.05	.02
73	Mario Elie	.10	.05
74	Tim Hardaway	.40	.18
75	Tyrone Hill	.05	.02
76	Sarunas Marciulionis	.05	.02
77	Chris Mullin	.25	.11
78	Don Nelson CO	.10	.05
79	Billy Owens	.10	.05
80	Sleepy Floyd UER	.05	.02

(Went past 4000 assist mark, not 2000)

81	Avery Johnson	.05	.02
82	Buck Johnson	.05	.02
83	Vernon Maxwell	.05	.02
84	Hakeem Olajuwon	.50	.23
85	Kenny Smith	.05	.02
86	Otis Thorpe	.10	.05
87	Rudy Tomjanovich CO	.10	.05
88	Dale Davis	.05	.02
89	Vern Fleming	.05	.02
90	Bob Hill CO	.05	.02
91	Reggie Miller	.25	.11
92	Chuck Person	.05	.02
93	Detlef Schrempf	.10	.05
94	Rik Smits	.10	.05
95	LaSalle Thompson	.05	.02
96	Micheal Williams	.05	.02
97	Larry Brown CO	.10	.05
98	James Edwards	.05	.02
99	Gary Grant	.05	.02
100	Ron Harper	.05	.02
101	Danny Manning	.10	.05

102	Ken Norman	.05	.02
103	Doc Rivers	.10	.05
104	Charles Smith	.05	.02
105	Loy Vaught	.10	.05
106	Elden Campbell	.10	.05
107	Vlade Divac	.10	.05
108	A.C. Green	.10	.05
109	Sam Perkins	.10	.05
110	Randy Pfund CO	.05	.02
111	Byron Scott	.10	.05
112	Terry Teagle	.05	.02
113	Sedale Threatt	.05	.02
114	James Worthy	.25	.11
115	Willie Burton	.05	.02
116	Bimbo Coles	.05	.02
117	Kevin Edwards	.05	.02
118	Grant Long	.05	.02
119	Kevin Loughery CO	.05	.02
120	Glen Rice	.30	.14
121	Rony Seikaly	.05	.02
122	Brian Shaw	.05	.02
123	Steve Smith	.25	.11
124	Frank Brickowski	.05	.02
125	Mike Dunleavy CO	.05	.02
126	Blue Edwards	.05	.02
127	Moses Malone	.25	.11
128	Eric Murdock	.05	.02
129	Fred Roberts	.05	.02
130	Alvin Robertson	.05	.02
131	Thurl Bailey	.05	.02
132	Tony Campbell	.05	.02
133	Gerald Glass	.05	.02
134	Luc Longley	.10	.05
135	Sam Mitchell	.05	.02
136	Pooh Richardson	.05	.02
137	Jimmy Rodgers CO	.05	.02
138	Felton Spencer	.05	.02
139	Doug West	.05	.02
140	Kenny Anderson	.25	.11
141	Mookie Blaylock	.10	.05
142	Sam Bowie	.05	.02
143	Derrick Coleman	.10	.05
144	Chucky DaLy CO	.10	.05
145	Terry Mills	.10	.05
146	Chris Morris	.05	.02
147	Drazen Petrovic	.05	.02
148	Greg Anthony	.05	.02
149	Rolando Blackman	.05	.02
150	Patrick Ewing	.25	.11
151	Mark Jackson	.05	.02
152	Anthony Mason	.25	.11
153	Xavier McDaniel	.05	.02
154	Charles Oakley	.10	.05
155	Pat Riley CO	.10	.05
156	John Starks	.10	.05
157	Gerald Wilkins	.05	.02
158	Nick Anderson	.10	.05
159	Anthony Bowie	.05	.02
160	Terry Catledge	.05	.02
161	Matt Guokas CO	.05	.02
162	Stanley Roberts	.05	.02
163	Dennis Scott	.10	.05
164	Scott Skiles	.05	.02
165	Brian Williams	.05	.02
166	Ron Anderson	.05	.02
167	Manute Bol	.05	.02
168	Johnny Dawkins	.05	.02
169	Armon Gilliam	.05	.02
170	Hersey Hawkins	.10	.05
171	Jeff Hornacek	.10	.05
172	Andrew Lang	.05	.02
173	Doug Moe CO	.05	.02
174	Tim Perry	.05	.02
175	Jeff Ruland	.05	.02
176	Charles Shackleford	.05	.02
177	Danny Ainge	.10	.05
178	Charles Barkley	.40	.18
179	Cedric Ceballos	.10	.05
180	Tom Chambers	.05	.02
181	Kevin Johnson	.25	.11
182	Dan Majerle	.10	.05
183	Mark West UER	.05	.02

(Needs 33 blocks to reach 1000, not 31)

184	Paul Westphal CO	.05	.02
185	Rick Adelman CO	.05	.02

186	Clyde Drexler	.30	.14
187	Kevin Duckworth	.05	.02
188	Jerome Kersey	.05	.02
189	Robert Pack	.05	.02
190	Terry Porter	.05	.02
191	Clifford Robinson	.10	.05
192	Rod Strickland	.25	.11
193	Buck Williams	.10	.05
194	Anthony Bonner	.05	.02
195	Duane Causwell	.05	.02
196	Mitch Richmond	.25	.11
197	Garry St. Jean CO	.05	.02
198	Lionel Simmons	.05	.02
199	Wayman Tisdale	.05	.02
200	Spud Webb	.10	.05
201	Willie Anderson	.05	.02
202	Antoine Carr	.05	.02
203	Terry Cummings	.10	.05
204	Sean Elliott	.10	.05
205	Dale Ellis	.05	.02
206	Vinnie Johnson	.05	.02
207	David Robinson	.40	.18
208	Jerry Tarkanian CO	.05	.02
209	Benoit Benjamin	.05	.02
210	Michael Cage	.05	.02
211	Eddie Johnson	.05	.02
212	George Karl CO	.10	.05
213	Shawn Kemp	1.00	.45
214	Derrick McKey	.05	.02
215	Nate McMillan	.05	.02
216	Gary Payton	.50	.23
217	Ricky Pierce	.05	.02
218	David Benoit	.05	.02
219	Mike Brown	.05	.02
220	Tyrone Corbin	.05	.02
221	Mark Eaton	.05	.02
222	Jay Humphries	.05	.02
223	Larry Krystkowiak	.05	.02
224	Jeff Malone	.05	.02
225	Karl Malone	.40	.18
226	Jerry Sloan CO	.10	.05
227	John Stockton	.25	.11
228	Michael Adams	.05	.02
229	Rex Chapman	.05	.02
230	Ledell Eackles	.05	.02
231	Pervis Ellison	.05	.02
232	A.J. English	.05	.02
233	Harvey Grant	.05	.02
234	LaBradford Smith	.05	.02
235	Larry Stewart	.05	.02
236	Wes Unseld CO	.10	.05
237	David Wingate	.05	.02
238	Michael Jordan LL	1.50	.70

Scoring

239	Dennis Rodman LL	.50	.23

Rebounding

| 240 | John Stockton LL | .25 | .11 |

Assists/Steals

| 241 | Buck Williams LL | .05 | .02 |

Field Goal Percentage

| 242 | Mark Price LL | .05 | .02 |

Free Throw Percentage

| 243 | Dana Barros LL | .05 | .02 |

Three Point Percentage

| 244 | David Robinson LL | .25 | .11 |

Shots Blocked

| 245 | Chris Mullin LL | .10 | .05 |

Minutes Played

| 246 | Michael Jordan MVP | 1.50 | .70 |
| 247 | L.Johnson ROY UER | .25 | .11 |

(Scoring average was 19.2, not 19.7)

| 248 | David Robinson | .25 | .11 |

Defensive Player of the Year

| 249 | Detlef Schrempf | .05 | .02 |

Sixth Man of the Year

250	Clyde Drexler PV	.25	.11
251	Tim Hardaway PV	.25	.11
252	Kevin Johnson PV	.10	.05
253	Larry Johnson PV UER	.25	.11

(Scoring average was 19.2, not 19.7)

254	Scottie Pippen PV	.40	.18
255	Isiah Thomas PV	.10	.05
256	Larry Bird SY	.50	.23

☐ 257 Brad Daugherty SY	.05	.02	☐ 343 Latrell Sprewell	.75	.35	☐ 429 Avery Johnson	.05	.02
☐ 258 Kevin Johnson SY	.10	.05	☐ 344 Scott Brooks	.05	.02	☐ 430 Dana Barros	.05	.02
☐ 259 Larry Johnson SY	.25	.11	☐ 345 Matt Bullard	.05	.02	☐ 431 Rich King	.05	.02
☐ 260 Scottie Pippen SY	.40	.18	☐ 346 Carl Herrera	.05	.02	☐ 432 Isaac Austin	.10	.05
☐ 261 Dennis Rodman SY	.50	.23	☐ 347 Robert Horry	.40	.18	☐ 433 John Crotty	.05	.02
☐ 262 Checklist 1	.05	.02	☐ 348 Tree Rollins	.05	.02	☐ 434 Stephen Howard	.05	.02
☐ 263 Checklist 2	.05	.02	☐ 349 Greg Dreiling	.05	.02	☐ 435 Jay Humphries	.05	.02
☐ 264 Checklist 3	.05	.02	☐ 350 George McCloud	.05	.02	☐ 436 Larry Krystkowiak	.05	.02
☐ 265 Charles Barkley SD	.25	.11	☐ 351 Sam Mitchell	.05	.02	☐ 437 Tom Gugliotta	.75	.35
☐ 266 Shawn Kemp SD	.50	.23	☐ 352 Pooh Richardson	.05	.02	☐ 438 Buck Johnson	.05	.02
☐ 267 Dan Majerle SD	.05	.02	☐ 353 Malik Sealy	.10	.05	☐ 439 Charles Jones	.05	.02
☐ 268 Karl Malone SD	.25	.11	☐ 354 Kenny Williams	.05	.02	☐ 440 Don MacLean	.05	.02
☐ 269 Buck Williams SD	.05	.02	☐ 355 Jaren Jackson	.05	.02	☐ 441 Doug Overton	.05	.02
☐ 270 Clyde Drexler SD	.25	.11	☐ 356 Mark Jackson	.10	.05	☐ 442 Brent Price	.10	.05
☐ 271 Sean Elliott SD	.05	.02	☐ 357 Stanley Roberts	.05	.02	☐ 443 Checklist 1	.05	.02
☐ 272 Ron Harper SD	.05	.02	☐ 358 Elmore Spencer	.05	.02	☐ 444 Checklist 2	.05	.02
☐ 273 Michael Jordan SD	1.50	.70	☐ 359 Kiki Vandeweghe	.05	.02	☐ SD266 Shawn Kemp AU 250.00	110.00	
☐ 274 James Worthy SD	.10	.05	☐ 360 John S. Williams	.05	.02	(Certified Autograph)		
☐ 275 Cedric Ceballos SD	.05	.02	☐ 361 Randy Woods	.05	.02	☐ SD277 Darrell Walker AU 25.00	11.00	
☐ 276 Larry Nance SD	.05	.02	☐ 362 Duane Cooper	.05	.02	(Certified Autograph)		
☐ 277 Kenny Walker SD	.05	.02	☐ 363 James Edwards	.05	.02	☐ SD300 Darryl Dawkins AU 40.00	18.00	
☐ 278 Spud Webb SD	.10	.05	☐ 364 Anthony Peeler	.10	.05	(Certified Autograph)		
☐ 279 Dominique Wilkins SD	.10	.05	☐ 365 Tony Smith	.05	.02	☐ NNO Slam Dunk Wrapper 3.00	1.35	
☐ 280 Terrell Brandon SD	.25	.11	☐ 366 Keith Askins	.05	.02	Exchange		
☐ 281 Dee Brown SD	.05	.02	☐ 367 Matt Geiger	.10	.05			
☐ 282 Kevin Johnson SD	.10	.05	☐ 368 Alec Kessler	.05	.02			
☐ 283 Doc Rivers SD	.05	.02	☐ 369 Harold Miner	.10	.05			
☐ 284 Byron Scott SD	.05	.02	☐ 370 John Salley	.05	.02			
☐ 285 Manute Bol SD	.05	.02	☐ 371 Anthony Avent	.05	.02			
☐ 286 D.Mutombo SD	.25	.11	☐ 372 Todd Day	.05	.02			
☐ 287 Robert Parish SD	.05	.02	☐ 373 Blue Edwards	.05	.02			
☐ 288 David Robinson SD	.25	.11	☐ 374 Brad Lohaus	.05	.02			
☐ 289 Dennis Rodman SD	.50	.23	☐ 375 Lee Mayberry	.05	.02			
☐ 290 Blue Edwards SD	.05	.02	☐ 376 Eric Murdock	.05	.02			
☐ 291 Patrick Ewing SD	.25	.11	☐ 377 Dan Schayes	.05	.02			
☐ 292 Larry Johnson SD	.25	.11	☐ 378 Lance Blanks	.05	.02			
☐ 293 Jerome Kersey SD	.05	.02	☐ 379 Christian Laettner	.60	.25			
☐ 294 Hakeem Olajuwon SD	.25	.11	☐ 380 Bob McCann	.05	.02			
☐ 295 Stacey Augmon SD	.05	.02	☐ 381 Chuck Person	.05	.02			
☐ 296 Derrick Coleman SD	.05	.02	☐ 382 Brad Sellers	.05	.02			
☐ 297 Kendall Gill SD	.05	.02	☐ 383 Chris Smith	.05	.02			
☐ 298 Shaquille O'Neal SD	1.25	.55	☐ 384 Micheal Williams	.05	.02			
☐ 299 Scottie Pippen SD	.40	.18	☐ 385 Rafael Addison	.05	.02			
☐ 300 Darryl Dawkins SD	.05	.02	☐ 386 Chucky Brown	.05	.02			
☐ 301 Mookie Blaylock	.10	.05	☐ 387 Chris Dudley	.05	.02			
☐ 302 Adam Keefe	.05	.02	☐ 388 Tate George	.05	.02			
☐ 303 Travis Mays	.05	.02	☐ 389 Rick Mahorn	.05	.02			
☐ 304 Morlon Wiley	.05	.02	☐ 390 Rumeal Robinson	.05	.02			
☐ 305 Sherman Douglas	.05	.02	☐ 391 Jayson Williams	.10	.05			
☐ 306 Joe Kleine	.05	.02	☐ 392 Eric Anderson	.05	.02			
☐ 307 Xavier McDaniel	.05	.02	☐ 393 Rolando Blackman	.05	.02			
☐ 308 Tony Bennett	.05	.02	☐ 394 Tony Campbell	.05	.02			
☐ 309 Tom Hammonds	.05	.02	☐ 395 Hubert Davis	.05	.05			
☐ 310 Kevin Lynch	.05	.02	☐ 396 Doc Rivers	.10	.05			
☐ 311 Alonzo Mourning	1.25	.55	☐ 397 Charles Smith	.05	.02			
☐ 312 David Wingate	.05	.02	☐ 398 Herb Williams	.05	.02			
☐ 313 Rodney McCray	.05	.02	☐ 399 Litterial Green	.05	.02			
☐ 314 Will Perdue	.05	.02	☐ 400 Greg Kite	.05	.02			
☐ 315 Trent Tucker	.05	.02	☐ 401 Shaquille O'Neal	4.00	1.80			
☐ 316 Corey Williams	.05	.02	☐ 402 Jerry Reynolds	.05	.02			
☐ 317 Danny Ferry	.05	.02	☐ 403 Jeff Turner	.05	.02			
☐ 318 Jay Guidinger	.05	.02	☐ 404 Greg Grant	.05	.02			
☐ 319 Jerome Lane	.05	.02	☐ 405 Jeff Hornacek	.10	.05			
☐ 320 Gerald Wilkins	.05	.02	☐ 406 Andrew Lang	.05	.02			
☐ 321 Stephen Bardo	.05	.02	☐ 407 Kenny Payne	.05	.02			
☐ 322 Walter Bond	.05	.02	☐ 408 Tim Perry	.05	.02			
☐ 323 Brian Howard	.05	.02	☐ 409 C.Weatherspoon	.25	.11			
☐ 324 Tracy Moore	.05	.02	☐ 410 Danny Ainge	.10	.05			
☐ 325 Sean Rooks	.05	.02	☐ 411 Charles Barkley	.40	.18			
☐ 326 Randy White	.05	.02	☐ 412 Negele Knight	.05	.02			
☐ 327 Kevin Brooks	.05	.02	☐ 413 Oliver Miller	.10	.05			
☐ 328 LaPhonso Ellis	.40	.18	☐ 414 Jerrod Mustaf	.05	.02			
☐ 329 Scott Hastings	.05	.02	☐ 415 Mark Bryant	.05	.02			
☐ 330 Todd Lichti	.05	.02	☐ 416 Mario Elie	.10	.05			
☐ 331 Robert Pack	.05	.02	☐ 417 Dave Johnson	.05	.02			
☐ 332 Bryant Stith	.10	.05	☐ 418 Tracy Murray	.05	.02			
☐ 333 Gerald Glass	.05	.02	☐ 419 Reggie Smith	.05	.02			
☐ 334 Terry Mills	.10	.05	☐ 420 Rod Strickland	.25	.11			
☐ 335 Isaiah Morris	.05	.02	☐ 421 Randy Brown	.05	.02			
☐ 336 Mark Randall	.05	.02	☐ 422 Pete Chilcutt	.05	.02			
☐ 337 Danny Young	.05	.02	☐ 423 Jim Les	.05	.02			
☐ 338 Chris Gatling	.05	.02	☐ 424 Walt Williams	.25	.11			
☐ 339 Jeff Grayer	.05	.02	☐ 425 Lloyd Daniels	.05	.02			
☐ 340 Byron Houston	.05	.02	☐ 426 Vinny Del Negro	.05	.02			
☐ 341 Keith Jennings	.05	.02	☐ 427 Dale Ellis	.05	.02			
☐ 342 Alton Lister	.05	.02	☐ 428 Sidney Green	.05	.02			

1992-93 Fleer All-Stars

This 24-card standard-size set was randomly inserted in both series 17-card packs and features outstanding players from the Eastern (1-12) and Western (13-24) Conference. According to Fleer's advertising materials, the odds of pulling an All-Star insert are approximately one per nine packs. The horizontal fronts display two color images of the featured player against a gradated silver-blue background. The cards are bordered by a darker silver-blue, and the player's name is gold-foil stamped at the lower right corner. The Orlando All-Star Weekend logo is in the upper right and the team logo in the lower left corner. The backs are white with silver-blue borders and present career highlights, the player's name, and the Orlando All-Star Weekend logo. The cards are numbered on the back in alphabetical order.

	MINT	NRMT
COMPLETE SET (24)	100.00	45.00
COMMON CARD (1-24)	1.00	.45
SEMISTARS	2.50	1.10
UNLISTED STARS	4.00	1.80
SER.1 STATED ODDS 1:9		
CONDITION SENSITIVE SET		

		MINT	NRMT
☐ 1	Michael Adams	1.00	.45
☐ 2	Charles Barkley	6.00	2.70
☐ 3	Brad Daugherty	1.00	.45
☐ 4	Joe Dumars	4.00	1.80
☐ 5	Patrick Ewing	4.00	1.80
☐ 6	Michael Jordan	50.00	22.00
☐ 7	Reggie Lewis	2.50	1.10
☐ 8	Scottie Pippen	12.00	5.50
☐ 9	Mark Price	1.00	.45
☐ 10	Dennis Rodman	15.00	6.75
☐ 11	Isiah Thomas	4.00	1.80
☐ 12	Kevin Willis	1.00	.45
☐ 13	Clyde Drexler	5.00	2.20
☐ 14	Tim Hardaway	6.00	2.70
☐ 15	Jeff Hornacek	2.50	1.10
☐ 16	Dan Majerle	2.50	1.10
☐ 17	Karl Malone	6.00	2.70
☐ 18	Chris Mullin	4.00	1.80
☐ 19	D.Mutombo	4.00	1.80
☐ 20	Hakeem Olajuwon	8.00	3.60
☐ 21	David Robinson	6.00	2.70
☐ 22	John Stockton	4.00	1.80
☐ 23	Otis Thorpe	2.50	1.10
☐ 24	James Worthy	4.00	1.80

1992-93 Fleer Larry Johnson

Larry Johnson, the 1991-92 NBA Rookie of the Year, is featured in this 15-card signature series. The first 12 cards were available as random inserts in all forms of Fleer's first series packaging. The odds of pulling a Larry Johnson insert from a 17-card pack were one in 18, from a 32-card cello pack were one in 13 and from a 42-card rack pack were one in six. In addition, Larry personally autographed more than 2,000 of these cards, which were randomly inserted in the wax packs. These cards feature embossed Fleer logos on front for authenticity. According to Fleer's advertising materials, the odds of finding a signed Larry Johnson were approximately one in 15,000 packs. Collectors were also able to

receive three additional Johnson cards and the premiere edition of NBA Inside Stuff magazine by sending in ten wrappers and $1.00 in a mail-in offer expiring 6/30/93. These standard-size cards feature color player photos framed by thin orange and blue borders on a silver-blue card face. The player's name and the words "NBA Rookie of the Year" are gold foil-stamped at the top. The backs feature an orange panel that summarizes Johnson's game and demeanor. His name and "NBA Rookie of the Year" appear at the top in a lighter orange.

		MINT	NRMT
COMPLETE SET (12)		10.00	4.50
COMMON L.JOHNSON (1-12)	1.25	.55
SER.1 STATED ODDS 1:18		
COMMON SEND-OFF (13-15)	4.00	1.80
THREE CARDS PER 10 SER.1 WRAPPERS		

		MINT	NRMT
☐ 1	Larry Johnson (Holdin' up Hornets' home jersey)	1.25	.55
☐ 2	Larry Johnson (Driving through traffic against Knicks)	1.25	.55
☐ 3	Larry Johnson (Turned to the side, holding ball over head)	1.25	.55
☐ 4	Larry Johnson (Shooting jumpshot)	1.25	.55
☐ 5	Larry Johnson (Smiling, holding ball at chest level)	1.25	.55
☐ 6	Larry Johnson (Dribbling into a no-look pass)	1.25	.55
☐ 7	Larry Johnson (Posting up down low)	1.25	.55
☐ 8	Larry Johnson (Shooting ball in lane)	1.25	.55
☐ 9	Larry Johnson (Going for tip-in in home jersey)	1.25	.55
☐ 10	Larry Johnson (In warm-up suit)	1.25	.55
☐ 11	Larry Johnson (High-fiving during pre-game introductions)	1.25	.55
☐ 12	Larry Johnson (Dribbling with his left hand)	1.25	.55
☐ 13	Larry Johnson (Going up for a rebound)	4.00	1.80
☐ 14	Larry Johnson (Away from ball photo)	4.00	1.80
☐ 15	Larry Johnson (Charlotte skyline in background)	4.00	1.80
☐ AU	Larry Johnson AU. (Certified autograph)	100.00	45.00

1992-93 Fleer Rookie Sensations

Randomly inserted in first series 32-card cello packs, this set features 12 of the top rookies from the 1991-92 season. According to information released by Fleer,

the odds of pulling a Rookie Sensation is approximately one per five packs. Measuring the standard size, the cards feature the player in action against a computer generated team emblem on a gradated purple background. The words "Rookie Sensations" and the player's name are gold foil-stamped at the bottom. The backs display career highlights on a mint-green face with a purple border. The cards are numbered on the back in alphabetical order.

	MINT	NRMT
COMPLETE SET (12)	25.00	11.00
COMMON CARD (1-12)	1.00	.45
SEMISTARS	2.00	.90
UNLISTED STARS	5.00	2.20
SER.1 STATED ODDS 1:5 CELLO		

		MINT	NRMT
☐ 1	Greg Anthony	1.00	.45
☐ 2	Stacey Augmon	2.00	.90
☐ 3	Terrell Brandon	8.00	3.60
☐ 4	Rick Fox	2.00	.90
☐ 5	Larry Johnson	6.00	2.70
☐ 6	Mark Macon	1.00	.45
☐ 7	D.Mutombo	5.00	2.20
☐ 8	Billy Owens	2.00	.90
☐ 9	Stanley Roberts	1.00	.45
☐ 10	Doug Smith	1.00	.45
☐ 11	Steve Smith	5.00	2.20
☐ 12	Larry Stewart	1.00	.45

1992-93 Fleer Sharpshooters

Randomly inserted in second series 15-card plastic-wrap packs, these 18 standard-size cards feature some of the NBA's best shooters. According to Fleer's advertising materials, the odds of finding a Sharpshooter card are approximately one in three packs. The color action photos on the fronts are odd-shaped, overlaying a purple geometric shape and resting on a silver card face. The "Sharp Shooter" logo is gold-foil stamped at the upper left corner, while the player's name is gold-foil stamped below the picture. On a wheat-colored panel inside blue borders, the backs present a player profile.

	MINT	NRMT
COMPLETE SET (18)	20.00	9.00
COMMON CARD (1-18)	.50	.23
SEMISTARS	1.00	.45
UNLISTED STARS	4.00	1.80
SER.2 STATED ODDS 1:3		

		MINT	NRMT
☐ 1	Reggie Miller	4.00	1.80
☐ 2	Dana Barros	.50	.23
☐ 3	Jeff Hornacek	1.00	.45
☐ 4	Drazen Petrovic	.50	.23
☐ 5	Glen Rice	5.00	2.20
☐ 6	Terry Porter	.50	.23
☐ 7	Mark Price	.50	.23
☐ 8	Michael Adams	.50	.23
☐ 9	Hersey Hawkins	1.00	.45
☐ 10	Chuck Person	.50	.23
☐ 11	John Stockton	4.00	1.80
☐ 12	Dale Ellis	.50	.23
☐ 13	Clyde Drexler	5.00	2.20
☐ 14	Mitch Richmond	4.00	1.80
☐ 15	Craig Ehlo	.50	.23
☐ 16	Dell Curry	.50	.23
☐ 17	Chris Mullin	4.00	1.80
☐ 18	Rolando Blackman	.50	.23

1992-93 Fleer Team Leaders

The 1992-93 Fleer Team Leaders were inserted into five of every six first series 42-card rack packs. A Larry Johnson Signature Series insert card replaced a Team Leader in every sixth rack pack. These 27 standard size cards feature a key member of each NBA team. The color action photos on the

front are surrounded by thick dark blue borders, covered by a slick UV coating and stamped with gold foil printing. Because of the dark borders, these cards are condition sensitive. The full-color card backs include a player head shot accompanied by written text summarizing the player's career. The cards are numbered on the back in alphabetical order by team. A low production run of rack packs has contributed largely to the popularity of this set.

	MINT	NRMT
COMPLETE SET (27)	300.00	135.00
COMMON CARD (1-27)	2.50	1.10
SEMISTARS	5.00	2.20
UNLISTED STARS	12.00	5.50
ONE TL OR JOHNSON PER SER.1 RACK PACK		
CONDITION SENSITIVE SET		

		MINT	NRMT
☐ 1	Dominique Wilkins	12.00	5.50
☐ 2	Reggie Lewis	5.00	2.20
☐ 3	Larry Johnson	5.00	2.20
☐ 4	Michael Jordan	150.00	70.00
☐ 5	Mark Price	2.50	1.10
☐ 6	Terry Davis	2.50	1.10
☐ 7	D.Mutombo	12.00	5.50
☐ 8	Isiah Thomas	12.00	5.50
☐ 9	Chris Mullin	12.00	5.50
☐ 10	Hakeem Olajuwon	25.00	11.00
☐ 11	Reggie Miller	12.00	5.50
☐ 12	Danny Manning	5.00	2.20
☐ 13	James Worthy	12.00	5.50
☐ 14	Glen Rice	15.00	6.75
☐ 15	Alvin Robertson	2.50	1.10
☐ 16	Tony Campbell	2.50	1.10
☐ 17	Derrick Coleman	5.00	2.20
☐ 18	Patrick Ewing	12.00	5.50
☐ 19	Scott Skiles	2.50	1.10
☐ 20	Hersey Hawkins	5.00	2.20
☐ 21	Kevin Johnson	12.00	5.50
☐ 22	Clyde Drexler	15.00	6.75
☐ 23	Mitch Richmond	12.00	5.50
☐ 24	David Robinson	20.00	9.00
☐ 25	Ricky Pierce	2.50	1.10
☐ 26	Karl Malone	20.00	9.00
☐ 27	Pervis Ellison	2.50	1.10

1992-93 Fleer Total D

The 1992-93 Fleer Total D cards were randomly inserted into second series 32-card cello packs. According to Fleer's advertising

materials, the odds of pulling a Total D card were approximately one per five packs. These 15 standard size cards feature some of the NBA's top defensive players. Card fronts feature colorized players against a black border, covered with a slick UV coating and gold stamped lettering. Because of these black borders, the cards are condition sensitive. The full-color card backs feature small player head shots accompanied by text describing the player's defensive abilities.

	MINT	NRMT
COMPLETE SET (15)	100.00	45.00
COMMON CARD (1-15)	1.50	.70
SEMISTARS	2.50	1.10
UNLISTED STARS	4.00	1.80
SER.2 STATED ODDS 1:5 CELLO		
CONDITION SENSITIVE SET		

		MINT	NRMT
☐ 1	David Robinson	6.00	2.70
☐ 2	Dennis Rodman	15.00	6.75
☐ 3	Scottie Pippen	12.00	5.50
☐ 4	Joe Dumars	4.00	1.80
☐ 5	Michael Jordan	50.00	22.00
☐ 6	John Stockton	4.00	1.80
☐ 7	Patrick Ewing	4.00	1.80
☐ 8	Micheal Williams	1.50	.70
☐ 9	Larry Nance	2.50	1.10
☐ 10	Buck Williams	2.50	1.10
☐ 11	Alvin Robertson	1.50	.70
☐ 12	D.Mutombo	4.00	1.80
☐ 13	Mookie Blaylock	2.50	1.10
☐ 14	Hakeem Olajuwon	8.00	3.60
☐ 15	Rony Seikaly	1.50	.70

1993-94 Fleer

The 1993-94 Fleer basketball card set contains 400 standard-size cards. The set was issued in two series consisting of 240 and 160 cards. Cards were primarily distributed in 15-card wax packs (1.29 suggested retail) and 21-card cello packs (1.99). Unlike the first series packs, all second series packs contained an insert card. There are 36 packs per wax box. The fronts are UV-coated and feature color action player photos and are enclosed by white borders. The player's name appears in the lower left and is superimposed over a colorful florescent background. The backs feature full-color printing and bold graphics combining the player's picture, name, and complete statistics. With the exception of card numbers 131, 174, and 216, the cards are numbered and checklisted below alphabetically in team order. Subsets are NBA League Leaders (221-228), NBA Award Winners (229-232), Pro-Visions (223-237), and checklists (238-240). Players traded since the first series are pictured with their new team in a 160-card second series (241-400) offering. Rookie Cards of note include Vin Baker, A.Hardaway, Jamal Mashburn, Nick Van Exel and Chris Webber.

	MINT	NRMT
COMPLETE SET (400)	20.00	9.00
COMPLETE SERIES 1 (240)	10.00	4.50
COMPLETE SERIES 2 (160)	10.00	4.50
COMMON CARD (1-400)	.05	.02
SEMISTARS	.10	.05
UNLISTED STARS	.25	.11

#	Player	MINT	NRMT
☐ 1	Stacey Augmon	.05	.02
☐ 2	Mookie Blaylock	.10	.05
☐ 3	Duane Ferrell	.05	.02
☐ 4	Paul Graham	.05	.02
☐ 5	Adam Keefe	.05	.02
☐ 6	Jon Koncak	.05	.02
☐ 7	Dominique Wilkins	.25	.11
☐ 8	Kevin Willis	.05	.02
☐ 9	Alaa Abdelnaby	.05	.02
☐ 10	Dee Brown	.05	.02
☐ 11	Sherman Douglas	.05	.02
☐ 12	Rick Fox	.05	.02
☐ 13	Kevin Gamble	.05	.02
☐ 14	Reggie Lewis	.10	.05
☐ 15	Xavier McDaniel	.05	.02
☐ 16	Robert Parish	.10	.05
☐ 17	Muggsy Bogues	.10	.05
☐ 18	Dell Curry	.05	.02
☐ 19	Kenny Gattison	.05	.02
☐ 20	Kendall Gill	.10	.05
☐ 21	Larry Johnson	.25	.11
☐ 22	Alonzo Mourning	.40	.18
☐ 23	Johnny Newman	.05	.02
☐ 24	David Wingate	.05	.02
☐ 25	B.J. Armstrong	.05	.02
☐ 26	Bill Cartwright	.05	.02
☐ 27	Horace Grant	.10	.05
☐ 28	Michael Jordan	3.00	1.35
☐ 29	Stacey King	.05	.02
☐ 30	John Paxson	.05	.02
☐ 31	Will Perdue	.05	.02
☐ 32	Scottie Pippen	.75	.35
☐ 33	Scott Williams	.05	.02
☐ 34	Terrell Brandon	.25	.11
☐ 35	Brad Daugherty	.05	.02
☐ 36	Craig Ehlo	.05	.02
☐ 37	Danny Ferry	.05	.02
☐ 38	Larry Nance	.10	.05
☐ 39	Mark Price	.05	.02
☐ 40	Mike Sanders	.05	.02
☐ 41	Gerald Wilkins	.05	.02
☐ 42	John(Hot Rod) Williams	.05	.02
☐ 43	Terry Davis	.05	.02
☐ 44	Derek Harper	.10	.05
☐ 45	Mike Iuzzolino	.05	.02
☐ 46	Jim Jackson	.25	.11
☐ 47	Sean Rooks	.05	.02
☐ 48	Doug Smith	.05	.02
☐ 49	Randy White	.05	.02
☐ 50	M.Abdul-Rauf	.05	.02
☐ 51	LaPhonso Ellis	.10	.05
☐ 52	Marcus Liberty	.05	.02
☐ 53	Mark Macon	.05	.02
☐ 54	D.Mutombo	.25	.11
☐ 55	Robert Pack	.05	.02
☐ 56	Bryant Stith	.05	.02
☐ 57	Reggie Williams	.05	.02
☐ 58	Mark Aguirre	.05	.02
☐ 59	Joe Dumars	.25	.11
☐ 60	Bill Laimbeer	.05	.02
☐ 61	Terry Mills	.05	.02
☐ 62	Olden Polynice	.05	.02
☐ 63	Alvin Robertson	.05	.02
☐ 64	Dennis Rodman	1.00	.45
☐ 65	Isiah Thomas	.25	.11
☐ 66	Victor Alexander	.05	.02
☐ 67	Tim Hardaway	.30	.14
☐ 68	Tyrone Hill	.05	.02
☐ 69	Byron Houston	.05	.02
☐ 70	Sarunas Marciulionis	.05	.02
☐ 71	Chris Mullin	.25	.11
☐ 72	Billy Owens	.05	.02
☐ 73	Latrell Sprewell	.25	.11
☐ 74	Scott Brooks	.05	.02
☐ 75	Matt Bullard	.05	.02
☐ 76	Carl Herrera	.05	.02
☐ 77	Robert Horry	.05	.02
☐ 78	Vernon Maxwell	.05	.02
☐ 79	Hakeem Olajuwon	.50	.23
☐ 80	Kenny Smith	.05	.02
☐ 81	Otis Thorpe	.10	.05
☐ 82	Dale Davis	.05	.02
☐ 83	Vern Fleming	.05	.02
☐ 84	George McCloud	.05	.02
☐ 85	Reggie Miller	.25	.11
☐ 86	Sam Mitchell	.05	.02
☐ 87	Pooh Richardson	.05	.02
☐ 88	Detlef Schrempf	.10	.05
☐ 89	Rik Smits	.05	.02
☐ 90	Gary Grant	.05	.02
☐ 91	Ron Harper	.10	.05
☐ 92	Mark Jackson	.10	.05
☐ 93	Danny Manning	.05	.02
☐ 94	Ken Norman	.05	.02
☐ 95	Stanley Roberts	.05	.02
☐ 96	Loy Vaught	.05	.02
☐ 97	John Williams	.05	.02
☐ 98	Elden Campbell	.10	.05
☐ 99	Doug Christie	.05	.02
☐ 100	Duane Cooper	.05	.02
☐ 101	Vlade Divac	.10	.05
☐ 102	A.C. Green	.05	.02
☐ 103	Anthony Peeler	.05	.02
☐ 104	Sedale Threatt	.05	.02
☐ 105	James Worthy	.25	.11
☐ 106	Bimbo Coles	.05	.02
☐ 107	Grant Long	.05	.02
☐ 108	Harold Miner	.05	.02
☐ 109	Glen Rice	.25	.11
☐ 110	John Salley	.05	.02
☐ 111	Rony Seikaly	.05	.02
☐ 112	Brian Shaw	.05	.02
☐ 113	Steve Smith	.10	.05
☐ 114	Anthony Avent	.05	.02
☐ 115	Jon Barry	.05	.02
☐ 116	Frank Brickowski	.05	.02
☐ 117	Todd Day	.05	.02
☐ 118	Blue Edwards	.05	.02
☐ 119	Brad Lohaus	.05	.02
☐ 120	Lee Mayberry	.05	.02
☐ 121	Eric Murdock	.05	.02
☐ 122	Thurl Bailey	.05	.02
☐ 123	Christian Laettner	.25	.11
☐ 124	Luc Longley	.10	.05
☐ 125	Chuck Person	.05	.02
☐ 126	Felton Spencer	.05	.02
☐ 127	Doug West	.05	.02
☐ 128	Micheal Williams	.05	.02
☐ 129	Rafael Addison	.05	.02
☐ 130	Kenny Anderson	.10	.05
☐ 131	Sam Bowie	.05	.02
☐ 132	Chucky Brown	.05	.02
☐ 133	Derrick Coleman	.10	.05
☐ 134	Chris Dudley	.05	.02
☐ 135	Chris Morris	.05	.02
☐ 136	Rumeal Robinson	.05	.02
☐ 137	Greg Anthony	.05	.02
☐ 138	Rolando Blackman	.05	.02
☐ 139	Tony Campbell	.05	.02
☐ 140	Hubert Davis	.05	.02
☐ 141	Patrick Ewing	.25	.11
☐ 142	Anthony Mason	.10	.05
☐ 143	Charles Oakley	.10	.05
☐ 144	Doc Rivers	.10	.05
☐ 145	Charles Smith	.05	.02
☐ 146	John Starks	.10	.05
☐ 147	Nick Anderson	.10	.05
☐ 148	Anthony Bowie	.05	.02
☐ 149	Shaquille O'Neal	1.00	.45
☐ 150	Donald Royal	.05	.02
☐ 151	Dennis Scott	.10	.05
☐ 152	Scott Skiles	.05	.02
☐ 153	Tom Tolbert	.05	.02
☐ 154	Jeff Turner	.05	.02
☐ 155	Ron Anderson	.05	.02
☐ 156	Johnny Dawkins	.05	.02
☐ 157	Hersey Hawkins	.10	.05
☐ 158	Jeff Hornacek	.10	.05
☐ 159	Andrew Lang	.05	.02
☐ 160	Tim Perry	.05	.02
☐ 161	C.Weatherspoon	.05	.02
☐ 162	Danny Ainge	.10	.05
☐ 163	Charles Barkley	.40	.18
☐ 164	Cedric Ceballos	.10	.05
☐ 165	Tom Chambers	.05	.02
☐ 166	Richard Dumas	.05	.02
☐ 167	Kevin Johnson	.10	.05
☐ 168	Negele Knight	.05	.02
☐ 169	Dan Majerle	.10	.05
☐ 170	Oliver Miller	.05	.02
☐ 171	Mark West	.05	.02
☐ 172	Mark Bryant	.05	.02
☐ 173	Clyde Drexler	.30	.14
☐ 174	Kevin Duckworth	.05	.02
☐ 175	Mario Elie	.05	.02
☐ 176	Jerome Kersey	.05	.02
☐ 177	Terry Porter	.05	.02
☐ 178	Clifford Robinson	.10	.05
☐ 179	Rod Strickland	.10	.05
☐ 180	Buck Williams	.05	.02
☐ 181	Anthony Bonner	.05	.02
☐ 182	Duane Causwell	.05	.02
☐ 183	Mitch Richmond	.25	.11
☐ 184	Lionel Simmons	.05	.02
☐ 185	Wayman Tisdale	.05	.02
☐ 186	Spud Webb	.10	.05
☐ 187	Walt Williams	.10	.05
☐ 188	Antoine Carr	.05	.02
☐ 189	Terry Cummings	.05	.02
☐ 190	Lloyd Daniels	.05	.02
☐ 191	Vinny Del Negro	.05	.02
☐ 192	Sean Elliott	.10	.05
☐ 193	Dale Ellis	.05	.02
☐ 194	Avery Johnson	.05	.02
☐ 195	J.R. Reid	.05	.02
☐ 196	David Robinson	.40	.18
☐ 197	Michael Cage	.05	.02
☐ 198	Eddie Johnson	.05	.02
☐ 199	Shawn Kemp	.75	.35
☐ 200	Derrick McKey	.05	.02
☐ 201	Nate McMillan	.05	.02
☐ 202	Gary Payton	.40	.18
☐ 203	Sam Perkins	.10	.05
☐ 204	Ricky Pierce	.05	.02
☐ 205	David Benoit	.05	.02
☐ 206	Tyrone Corbin	.05	.02
☐ 207	Mark Eaton	.05	.02
☐ 208	Jay Humphries	.05	.02
☐ 209	Larry Krystkowiak	.05	.02
☐ 210	Jeff Malone	.05	.02
☐ 211	Karl Malone	.40	.18
☐ 212	John Stockton	.25	.11
☐ 213	Michael Adams	.05	.02
☐ 214	Rex Chapman	.05	.02
☐ 215	Pervis Ellison	.05	.02
☐ 216	Harvey Grant	.05	.02
☐ 217	Tom Gugliotta	.25	.11
☐ 218	Buck Johnson	.05	.02

☐ 219 LaBradford Smith	.05	.02
☐ 220 Larry Stewart	.05	.02
☐ 221 B.J. Armstrong LL	.05	.02
3-Pt Field Goal		
Percentage Leader		
☐ 222 Cedric Ceballos LL	.05	.02
FG Percentage Leader		
☐ 223 Larry Johnson LL	.10	.05
Minutes Played Leader		
☐ 224 Michael Jordan LL	1.50	.70
Scoring/Steals Leader		
☐ 225 Hakeem Olajuwon LL	.25	.11
Shot Block Leader		
☐ 226 Mark Price LL	.05	.02
FT Percentage Leader		
☐ 227 Dennis Rodman LL	.50	.23
Rebounding Leader		
☐ 228 John Stockton LL	.10	.05
Assists Leader		
☐ 229 Charles Barkley AW	.25	.11
Most Valuable Player		
☐ 230 Hakeem Olajuwon AW	.25	.11
Defensive POY		
☐ 231 Shaquille O'Neal AW	.50	.23
Rookie of the Year		
☐ 232 Clifford Robinson AW	.05	.02
Sixth Man Award		
☐ 233 Shawn Kemp PV	.40	.18
☐ 234 Alonzo Mourning PV	.25	.11
☐ 235 Hakeem Olajuwon PV	.25	.11
☐ 236 John Stockton PV	.10	.05
☐ 237 Dominique Wilkins PV	.10	.05
☐ 238 Checklist 1-85	.05	.02
☐ 239 Checklist 86-165	.05	.02
☐ 240 Checklist 166-240 UER	.05	.02
(237 listed as Cliff Robinson;		
should be Dominique Wilkins)		
☐ 241 Doug Edwards	.05	.02
☐ 242 Craig Ehlo	.05	.02
☐ 243 Andrew Lang	.05	.02
☐ 244 Kenny Whatley	.05	.02
☐ 245 Chris Corchiani	.05	.02
☐ 246 Acie Earl	.05	.02
☐ 247 Jimmy Oliver	.05	.02
☐ 248 Ed Pinckney	.05	.02
☐ 249 Dino Radja	.10	.05
☐ 250 Matt Wenstrom	.05	.02
☐ 251 Tony Bennett	.05	.02
☐ 252 Scott Burrell	.25	.11
☐ 253 LeRon Ellis	.05	.02
☐ 254 Hersey Hawkins	.10	.05
☐ 255 Eddie Johnson	.05	.02
☐ 256 Corie Blount	.05	.02
☐ 257 Jo Jo English	.05	.02
☐ 258 Dave Johnson	.05	.02
☐ 259 Steve Kerr	.10	.05
☐ 260 Toni Kukoc	.60	.25
☐ 261 Pete Myers	.05	.02
☐ 262 Bill Wennington	.05	.02
☐ 263 John Battle	.05	.02
☐ 264 Tyrone Hill	.05	.02
☐ 265 Gerald Madkins	.05	.02
☐ 266 Chris Mills	.40	.18
☐ 267 Bobby Phills	.05	.02
☐ 268 Greg Dreiling	.05	.02
☐ 269 Lucious Harris	.05	.02
☐ 270 Donald Hodge	.05	.02
☐ 271 Popeye Jones	.05	.02
☐ 272 Tim Legler	.05	.02
☐ 273 Fat Lever	.05	.02
☐ 274 Jamal Mashburn	.60	.25
☐ 275 Darren Morningstar	.05	.02
☐ 276 Tom Hammonds	.05	.02
☐ 277 Darnell Mee	.05	.02
☐ 278 Rodney Rogers	.05	.02
☐ 279 Brian Williams	.05	.02
☐ 280 Greg Anderson	.05	.02
☐ 281 Sean Elliott	.10	.05
☐ 282 Allan Houston	.50	.23
☐ 283 Lindsey Hunter	.25	.11
☐ 284 Marcus Liberty	.05	.02
☐ 285 Mark Macon	.05	.02
☐ 286 David Wood	.05	.02
☐ 287 Jud Buechler	.05	.02
☐ 288 Chris Gatling	.05	.02
☐ 289 Josh Grant	.05	.02

☐ 290 Jeff Grayer	.05	.02
☐ 291 Avery Johnson	.05	.02
☐ 292 Chris Webber	1.50	.70
☐ 293 Sam Cassell	.60	.25
☐ 294 Mario Elie	.05	.02
☐ 295 Richard Petruska	.05	.02
☐ 296 Eric Riley	.05	.02
☐ 297 Antonio Davis	.10	.05
☐ 298 Scott Haskin	.05	.02
☐ 299 Derrick McKey	.05	.02
☐ 300 Byron Scott	.10	.05
☐ 301 Malik Sealy	.05	.02
☐ 302 LaSalle Thompson	.05	.02
☐ 303 Kenny Williams	.05	.02
☐ 304 Haywoode Workman	.05	.02
☐ 305 Mark Aguirre	.05	.02
☐ 306 Terry Dehere	.05	.02
☐ 307 Bob Martin	.05	.02
☐ 308 Elmore Spencer	.05	.02
☐ 309 Tom Tolbert	.05	.02
☐ 310 Randy Woods	.05	.02
☐ 311 Sam Bowie	.05	.02
☐ 312 James Edwards	.05	.02
☐ 313 Antonio Harvey	.05	.02
☐ 314 George Lynch	.05	.02
☐ 315 Tony Smith	.05	.02
☐ 316 Nick Van Exel	.75	.35
☐ 317 Manute Bol	.05	.02
☐ 318 Willie Burton	.05	.02
☐ 319 Matt Geiger	.05	.02
☐ 320 Alec Kessler	.05	.02
☐ 321 Vin Baker	1.50	.70
☐ 322 Ken Norman	.05	.02
☐ 323 Dan Schayes	.05	.02
☐ 324 Derek Strong	.05	.02
☐ 325 Mike Brown	.05	.02
☐ 326 Brian Davis	.05	.02
☐ 327 Tellis Frank	.05	.02
☐ 328 Marlon Maxey	.05	.02
☐ 329 Isaiah Rider	.30	.14
☐ 330 Chris Smith	.05	.02
☐ 331 Benoit Benjamin	.05	.02
☐ 332 P.J. Brown	.05	.02
☐ 333 Kevin Edwards	.05	.02
☐ 334 Armon Gilliam	.05	.02
☐ 335 Rick Mahorn	.05	.02
☐ 336 Dwayne Schintzius	.05	.02
☐ 337 Rex Walters	.05	.02
☐ 338 David Wesley	.25	.11
☐ 339 Jayson Williams	.10	.05
☐ 340 Anthony Bonner	.05	.02
☐ 341 Herb Williams	.05	.02
☐ 342 Litterial Green	.05	.02
☐ 343 A.Hardaway	3.00	1.35
☐ 344 Greg Kite	.05	.02
☐ 345 Larry Krystkowiak	.05	.02
☐ 346 Todd Lichti	.05	.02
☐ 347 Keith Tower	.05	.02
☐ 348 Dana Barros	.05	.02
☐ 349 Shawn Bradley	.30	.14
☐ 350 Michael Curry	.05	.02
☐ 351 Greg Graham	.05	.02
☐ 352 Warren Kidd	.05	.02
☐ 353 Moses Malone	.25	.11
☐ 354 Orlando Woolridge	.05	.02
☐ 355 Duane Cooper	.05	.02
☐ 356 Joe Courtney	.05	.02
☐ 357 A.C. Green	.10	.05
☐ 358 Frank Johnson	.05	.02
☐ 359 Joe Kleine	.05	.02
☐ 360 Malcolm Mackey	.05	.02
☐ 361 Jerrod Mustaf	.05	.02
☐ 362 Chris Dudley	.05	.02
☐ 363 Harvey Grant	.05	.02
☐ 364 Tracy Murray	.05	.02
☐ 365 James Robinson	.05	.02
☐ 366 Reggie Smith	.05	.02
☐ 367 Kevin Thompson	.05	.02
☐ 368 Randy Breuer	.05	.02
☐ 369 Randy Brown	.05	.02
☐ 370 Evers Burns	.05	.02
☐ 371 Pete Chilcutt	.05	.02
☐ 372 Bobby Hurley	.10	.05
☐ 373 Jim Les	.05	.02
☐ 374 Mike Peplowski	.05	.02
☐ 375 Willie Anderson	.05	.02

☐ 376 Sleepy Floyd	.05	.02
☐ 377 Negele Knight	.05	.02
☐ 378 Dennis Rodman	1.00	.45
☐ 379 Chris Whitney	.05	.02
☐ 380 Vincent Askew	.05	.02
☐ 381 Kendall Gill	.10	.05
☐ 382 Ervin Johnson	.10	.05
☐ 383 Chris King	.05	.02
☐ 384 Rich King	.05	.02
☐ 385 Steve Scheffler	.05	.02
☐ 386 Detlef Schrempf	.10	.05
☐ 387 Tom Chambers	.05	.02
☐ 388 John Crotty	.05	.02
☐ 389 Bryon Russell	.25	.11
☐ 390 Felton Spencer	.05	.02
☐ 391 Luther Wright	.05	.02
☐ 392 Mitchell Butler	.05	.02
☐ 393 Calbert Cheaney	.25	.11
☐ 394 Kevin Duckworth	.05	.02
☐ 395 Don MacLean	.05	.02
☐ 396 Gheorghe Muresan	.30	.14
☐ 397 Doug Overton	.05	.02
☐ 398 Brent Price	.05	.02
☐ 399 Checklist	.05	.02
☐ 400 Checklist	.05	.02

1993-94 Fleer All-Stars

Randomly inserted in 1993-94 Fleer first series 15-card packs, this 24-card standard-size set features 12 players from the Eastern Conference (1-12) and the Western Conference (13-24) that participated in the 1992-93 All-Star Game in Salt Lake City. According to wrapper information, All-Stars are randomly inserted into one of every 10 packs. The fronts are UV-coated and feature color action player photos enclosed by purple borders. The NBA All-Star logo appears in the lower left or right corner. The player's name is stamped in gold foil and appears at the bottom. The backs are also UV-coated and feature a full-color shot of the player along with a statistical performance sketch from the previous year. Each division's All-Stars are in alphabetical order.

	MINT	NRMT
COMPLETE SET (24)	80.00	36.00
COMMON CARD (1-24)	1.00	.45
SEMISTARS	1.50	.70
UNLISTED STARS	2.50	1.10
SER.1 STATED ODDS 1:10 HOBBY		

		MINT	NRMT
☐ 1	Brad Daugherty	1.00	.45
☐ 2	Joe Dumars	2.50	1.10
☐ 3	Patrick Ewing	2.50	1.10
☐ 4	Larry Johnson	2.50	1.10
☐ 5	Michael Jordan	30.00	13.50
☐ 6	Larry Nance	1.50	.70
☐ 7	Shaquille O'Neal	10.00	4.50
☐ 8	Scottie Pippen UER	8.00	3.60
	(Name spelled Pipen on front)		
☐ 9	Mark Price	1.00	.45
☐ 10	Detlef Schrempf	1.50	.70
☐ 11	Isiah Thomas	2.50	1.10
☐ 12	Dominique Wilkins	2.50	1.10
☐ 13	Charles Barkley	4.00	1.80
☐ 14	Clyde Drexler	3.00	1.35
☐ 15	Sean Elliott	1.50	.70
☐ 16	Tim Hardaway	3.00	1.35
☐ 17	Shawn Kemp	8.00	3.60
☐ 18	Dan Majerle	1.00	.45
☐ 19	Karl Malone	4.00	1.80
☐ 20	Danny Manning	1.00	.45
☐ 21	Hakeem Olajuwon	5.00	2.20
☐ 22	Terry Porter	1.00	.45
☐ 23	David Robinson	4.00	1.80
☐ 24	John Stockton	2.50	1.10

1993-94 Fleer Clyde Drexler

Randomly inserted in all 1993-94 Fleer first series packs at an approximate rate of one in six, this 12-card standard-size set captures the greatest moments in Drexler's career. Drexler autographed more than 2,000 of his cards. These cards are embossed with Fleer logos for authenticity. Odds of getting a signed card were approximately 1 in 7,000 packs. The collector could acquire three additional cards and an issue of NBA Inside Stuff magazine through a mail-in for ten wrappers plus 1.50. The offer expired June 10, 1994. An additional card (No. 16) was offered free to collectors who subscribed to NBA Inside Stuff magazine. Since 12 cards were issued through packs, a 12-card set is considered com-

plete. All 16 cards have the same basic design with the front featuring a unique two photo design, one color, and the other red-screened, serving as the background. The player's name as well as the Fleer logo appear at the top of the card in gold foil. The bottom of the cards carries the words "Career Highlights," also stamped in gold foil. The back of the cards carry information about Drexler, with another red-screened photo again as the background. The cards are numbered on the back. The first twelve cards are numbered "X of 12" and the last four cards are simply numbered 13, 14, 15 and 16.

		MINT	NRMT
COMPLETE SET (12)		5.00	2.20
COMMON DREXLER (1-12)		.50	.23
SER.1 STATED ODDS 1:6			
DREXLER AU: SER.1 STATED ODDS 1:7,000			
COMMON SEND-OFF (13-15)		2.00	.90
THREE CARDS PER 10 SER.1 WRAPPERS			

		MINT	NRMT
☐ 1	Clyde Drexler	.50	.23
	(Ball in right hand, pointing with left)		
☐ 2	Clyde Drexler	.50	.23
	(Holding ball aloft with right hand)		
☐ 3	Clyde Drexler	.50	.23
	(Wearing red shoes, left-hand dribble)		
☐ 4	Clyde Drexler	.50	.23
	(Wearing red shoes, right-hand dribble)		
☐ 5	Clyde Drexler	.50	.23
	(Making ready to slam dunk with both hands)		
☐ 6	Clyde Drexler	.50	.23
	(Wearing white shoes, right-hand dribble)		
☐ 7	Clyde Drexler	.50	.23
	(Right-hand dribble, half of ball visible)		
☐ 8	Clyde Drexler	.50	.23
	(Right hand under ball, left hand alongside)		
☐ 9	Clyde Drexler	.50	.23
	(Receiving or passing ball)		
☐ 10	Clyde Drexler	.50	.23
	(Both hands above head; right hand near ball)		
☐ 11	Clyde Drexler	.50	.23
	(Left foot off floor; right-hand dribble)		
☐ 12	Clyde Drexler	.50	.23
	(In NBA All-Star uniform)		
☐ 13	Clyde Drexler	2.00	.90
	(Right-hand dribble, looking over defense)		
☐ 14	Clyde Drexler	2.00	.90
	(Dribbling down court with right hand)		
☐ 15	Clyde Drexler	2.00	.90
	(Shooting, with Pippen defending)		
☐ 16	Clyde Drexler	2.00	.90
	(Bringing ball up court black uniform)		
☐ AU	Clyde Drexler AU	125.00	55.00
	(Certified autograph)		

1993-94 Fleer First Year Phenoms

These 10 standard-size cards feature top rookies from the 1993-94 season. Cards were randomly inserted in 1993-94 Fleer second-series 15-card wax and 21-card jumbo packs. The insertion rate was approximately one in four wax packs and one in three cello packs. The yellow-bordered fronts feature color player action cutouts superposed upon purple, yellow, and black fluorescent basketball court designs. The player's name appears vertically in gold foil near one corner, and the gold-foil set logo appears at the bottom left. The horizontal back sports a similar florescent design. A color player close-up cutout appears on one side; his name, team, and career highlights appear on the other. The cards are numbered on the back as "X of 10" and sequenced in alphabetical order.

	MINT	NRMT
COMPLETE SET (10)	8.00	3.60
COMMON CARD (1-10)	.25	.11
SEMISTARS	.30	.14
UNLISTED STARS	.50	.23
SER.2 STATED ODDS 1:4 HOBBY, 1:3 CELLO		

		MINT	NRMT
☐ 1	Shawn Bradley	.50	.23
☐ 2	A.Hardaway	5.00	2.20
☐ 3	Lindsey Hunter	.50	.23
☐ 4	Bobby Hurley	.25	.11
☐ 5	Toni Kukoc	.75	.35
☐ 6	Jamal Mashburn	.75	.35
☐ 7	Dino Radja	.30	.14
☐ 8	Isaiah Rider	.50	.23
☐ 9	Nick Van Exel	1.00	.45
☐ 10	Chris Webber	2.00	.90

1993-94 Fleer Internationals

This 12-card insert standard-size set features NBA players born outside the United States.

Fleer All-Defensive The cards were randomly inserted in first series 15-card packs at a rate of one in 10. The fronts are UV-coated and feature a color player photo superimposed over a map of his country of origin. The player's name appears at the top of the card and is gold foil stamped. The backs are also UV-coated and feature a color shot of the player along with a brief biographical sketch. The set is sequenced in alphabetical order.

	MINT	NRMT
COMPLETE SET (12)	4.00	1.80
COMMON CARD (1-12)	.25	.11
SEMISTARS	.60	.25
UNLISTED STARS	1.25	.55
SER.1 STATED ODDS 1:10		

		MINT	NRMT
□ 1	Alaa Abdelnaby	.25	.11
□ 2	Vlade Divac	.60	.25
□ 3	Patrick Ewing	1.25	.55
□ 4	Carl Herrera	.25	.11
□ 5	Luc Longley	.60	.25
□ 6	Sarunas Marciulionis	.25	.11
□ 7	D.Mutombo	1.25	.55
□ 8	Rumeal Robinson	.25	.11
□ 9	Detlef Schrempf	.60	.25
□ 10	Rony Seikaly	.25	.11
□ 11	Rik Smits	.60	.25
□ 12	Dominique Wilkins	1.25	.55

1993-94 Fleer Living Legends

These six standard-size cards honoring veteran superstars were randomly inserted in 1993-

94 Fleer second series 15-card (ratio of one in 37) and 21-card (one in 24) packs. The horizontal fronts feature color player action cutouts superimposed upon a borderless metallic motion-streaked background. The player's name and the set's logo appear at the bottom in gold foil. The horizontal back carries a color player close-up cutout on one side; his name, team, and career highlights appear on the other. The cards are numbered on the back as "X of 6" and are sequenced in alphabetical order

	MINT	NRMT
COMPLETE SET (6)	25.00	11.00
COMMON CARD (1-6)	.75	.35
SEMISTARS	1.50	.70
SER.2 STATED ODDS 1:37 HOB, 1:24 JUM		

		MINT	NRMT
□ 1	Charles Barkley	2.50	1.10
□ 2	Larry Bird	6.00	2.70
□ 3	Patrick Ewing	1.50	.70
□ 4	Michael Jordan	20.00	9.00
□ 5	Hakeem Olajuwon	3.00	1.35
□ 6	Dominique Wilkins	.75	.35

1993-94 Fleer Lottery Exchange

This 11-card standard-size set features the top players from the 1993 NBA Draft. Card fronts resemble that of the basic Fleer issue with the exception of a notation of what number pick the player was. Backs have a photo and statistics. The set could be obtained in exchange for the Draft Exchange card that was randomly inserted (one in 180) in first series packs. The expiration date was April 1, 1994. The cards are numbered on the back in draft order.

	MINT	NRMT
COMPLETE SET (11)	20.00	9.00
COMMON CARD (1-11)	.50	.23
SEMISTARS	1.00	.45
UNLISTED STARS	1.25	.55

ONE SET PER EXCHANGE CARD BY MAIL		
EXCH.CARD: SER.1 STATED ODDS 1:180		

		MINT	NRMT
□ 1	Chris Webber	5.00	2.20
□ 2	Shawn Bradley	1.25	.55
□ 3	A.Hardaway	12.00	5.50
□ 4	Jamal Mashburn	2.00	.90
□ 5	Isaiah Rider	1.25	.55
□ 6	Calbert Cheaney	1.25	.55
□ 7	Bobby Hurley	1.00	.45
□ 8	Vin Baker	5.00	2.20
□ 9	Rodney Rogers	.50	.23
□ 10	Lindsey Hunter	1.25	.55
□ 11	Allan Houston	1.50	.70
□ NNO	Exp. Exchange Card	.50	.23

1993-94 Fleer NBA Superstars

These 20 standard-size cards featuring NBA stars were randomly inserted in 1993-94 Fleer second-series 15-card packs. The fronts feature color player action cutouts superimposed upon multiple color action shots on the right side and the player's name in team color-coded vertical block lettering on the left. The set's title appears vertically along the left edge in gold foil. The horizontal back carries a color player close-up cutout on one side; his name, team, and career highlights appear on the other. The cards are numbered on the back as "X of 20" and are sequenced in alphabetical order.

	MINT	NRMT
COMPLETE SET (20)	20.00	9.00
COMMON CARD (1-20)	.25	.11
SEMISTARS	.40	.18
UNLISTED STARS	.75	.35
RANDOM INSERTS IN SER.2 HOBBY PACKS		

		MINT	NRMT
□ 1	M.Abdul-Rauf	.25	.11
□ 2	Charles Barkley	1.25	.55
□ 3	Derrick Coleman	.40	.18
□ 4	Clyde Drexler	1.00	.45
□ 5	Joe Dumars	.75	.35
□ 6	Patrick Ewing	.75	.35
□ 7	Michael Jordan	10.00	4.50
□ 8	Shawn Kemp	2.50	1.10
□ 9	Christian Laettner	.75	.35
□ 10	Karl Malone	1.25	.55
□ 11	Danny Manning	.25	.11
□ 12	Reggie Miller	.75	.35
□ 13	Alonzo Mourning	1.25	.55

	MINT	NRMT
☐ 14 Chris Mullin	.75	.35
☐ 15 Hakeem Olajuwon	1.50	.70
☐ 16 Shaquille O'Neal	3.00	1.35
☐ 17 Mark Price	.25	.11
☐ 18 Mitch Richmond	.75	.35
☐ 19 David Robinson	1.25	.55
☐ 20 Dominique Wilkins	.75	.35

1993-94 Fleer Rookie Sensations

Randomly inserted in 29-card series one jumbo packs, these 24 standard-size UV-coated cards feature top rookies from the 1992-93 season. Odds of finding a Rookie Sensations card are approximately one in every five packs. The cards feature color player action photos on the fronts with silver-colored borders. Each player photo is superimposed upon a card design that has a basketball "earth" at the card bottom radiating "spotlight" beams that shade from yellow to magenta on a sky blue background. The player's name and the Rookie Sensations logo, both stamped in gold foil, appear in the lower left. Bordered in silver, the backs feature color close-ups of the players in the lower right or left. Blue "sky" and two intersecting yellow-to-magenta "spotlight" beams form the background. The player's name appears in silver-colored lettering at the top of the card above the player's NBA rookie-year highlights. The set is sequenced in alphabetical order.

	MINT	NRMT
COMPLETE SET (24)	50.00	22.00
COMMON CARD (1-24)	1.00	.45
SEMISTARS	2.00	.90
UNLISTED STARS	4.00	1.80
SER.1 STATED ODDS 1:5 CELLO		
☐ 1 Anthony Avent	1.00	.45
☐ 2 Doug Christie	1.00	.45
☐ 3 Lloyd Daniels	1.00	.45
☐ 4 Hubert Davis	1.00	.45
☐ 5 Todd Day	1.00	.45

	MINT	NRMT
☐ 6 Richard Dumas	1.00	.45
☐ 7 LaPhonso Ellis	2.00	.90
☐ 8 Tom Gugliotta	4.00	1.80
☐ 9 Robert Horry	2.00	.90
☐ 10 Byron Houston	1.00	.45
☐ 11 Jim Jackson UER	4.00	1.80

(Text on back states he played in Big East; he played in Big Ten)

	MINT	NRMT
☐ 12 Adam Keefe	1.00	.45
☐ 13 Christian Laettner	4.00	1.80
☐ 14 Lee Mayberry	1.00	.45
☐ 15 Oliver Miller	1.00	.45
☐ 16 Harold Miner	1.00	.45
☐ 17 Alonzo Mourning	6.00	2.70
☐ 18 Shaquille O'Neal	15.00	6.75
☐ 19 Anthony Peeler	1.00	.45
☐ 20 Sean Rooks	1.00	.45
☐ 21 Latrell Sprewell	4.00	1.80
☐ 22 Bryant Stith	1.00	.45
☐ 23 C.Weatherspoon	1.00	.45
☐ 24 Walt Williams	2.00	.90

1993-94 Fleer Sharpshooters

These 10 standard-size cards were randomly inserted in 1993-94 Fleer second-series 15-card packs. The fronts feature color player action cutouts superimposed upon color-screened action shots. The player's name appears at the upper right in gold foil. The set's logo appears at the bottom left. The black horizontal back carries a color player-close-up cutout on one side; his name, card title, and career highlights appear on the other. The cards are numbered on the back as "X of 10" and are sequenced in alphabetical order.

	MINT	NRMT
COMPLETE SET (10)	30.00	13.50
COMMON CARD (1-10)	1.00	.45
SEMISTARS	1.50	.70
UNLISTED STARS	2.00	.90
RANDOM INSERTS IN SER.2 HOBBY PACKS		
☐ 1 Tom Gugliotta	2.00	.90
☐ 2 Jim Jackson	2.00	.90
☐ 3 Michael Jordan	25.00	11.00
☐ 4 Dan Majerle	1.50	.70
☐ 5 Mark Price	1.00	.45
☐ 6 Glen Rice	2.00	.90
☐ 7 Mitch Richmond	2.00	.90
☐ 8 Latrell Sprewell	2.00	.90
☐ 9 John Starks	1.50	.70
☐ 10 Dominique Wilkins	2.00	.90

1993-94 Fleer Towers of Power

These 30 standard-size cards were randomly inserted in 1993-94 Fleer second series 21-card jumbo packs at an approximate rate of two in every three packs. The fronts feature color player action cutouts superposed upon borderless backgrounds of city skylines. The player's name appears in gold foil in a lower corner. The gold-foil set logo appears in an upper corner. The back has the same borderless skyline background photo as the front and carries a color player cutout on one side, and his career highlights on the other. The cards are numbered on the back as "X of 30" and sequenced in alphabetical order.

	MINT	NRMT
COMPLETE SET (30)	60.00	27.00
COMMON CARD (1-30)	.75	.35
SEMISTARS	1.50	.70
UNLISTED STARS	2.50	1.10
SER.2 STATED ODDS 2:3 CELLO		
☐ 1 Charles Barkley	4.00	1.80
☐ 2 Shawn Bradley	2.50	1.10
☐ 3 Derrick Coleman	1.50	.70
☐ 4 Brad Daugherty	.75	.35
☐ 5 Dale Davis	.75	.35
☐ 6 Vlade Divac	1.50	.70
☐ 7 Patrick Ewing	2.50	1.10
☐ 8 Horace Grant	1.50	.70
☐ 9 Tom Gugliotta	2.50	1.10
☐ 10 Larry Johnson	2.50	1.10
☐ 11 Shawn Kemp	8.00	3.60
☐ 12 Christian Laettner	2.50	1.10
☐ 13 Karl Malone	4.00	1.80
☐ 14 Danny Manning	.75	.35
☐ 15 Jamal Mashburn	4.00	1.80
☐ 16 Oliver Miller	.75	.35
☐ 17 Alonzo Mourning	4.00	1.80
☐ 18 D.Mutombo	1.50	.70
☐ 19 Ken Norman	.75	.35
☐ 20 Hakeem Olajuwon	5.00	2.20
☐ 21 Shaquille O'Neal	10.00	4.50
☐ 22 Robert Parish	1.50	.70
☐ 23 Olden Polynice	.75	.35
☐ 24 Clifford Robinson	.75	.70
☐ 25 David Robinson	4.00	1.80
☐ 26 Dennis Rodman	10.00	4.50
☐ 27 Rony Seikaly	.75	.35
☐ 28 Wayman Tisdale	.75	.35

□ 29 Chris Webber	10.00	4.50
□ 30 Dominique Wilkins	2.50	1.10

1994-95 Fleer

The 390 cards comprising Fleer's '94-95 base-brand standard-size set were distributed in two separate series of 240 and 150 cards each. Cards were distributed in 15-card packs (SRP $1.29), 21-card magazine cello packs (SRP $1.99) and 23-card retail jumbo packs (SRP $2.27). The cards feature color player action shots on their white-bordered fronts. The player's name, team, and position appear in team-colored lettering set on an irregular team-colored foil patch at the lower left. The black-bordered back carries a color player action shot on the left side, with the player's name, biography, team logo, and statistics displayed on a team-colored background on the right. The cards are numbered on the back and grouped alphabetically within teams. Unlike previous years, there were no subset cards featured in this set. Each pack contained at least one card insert card. One in every 72 packs (Hot Packs) contained only inserts. Rookie Cards of note in this set include Grant Hill, Juwan Howard, Eddie Jones, Jason Kidd and Glenn Robinson.

	MINT	NRMT
COMPLETE SET (390)	24.00	11.00
COMPLETE SERIES 1 (240)	12.00	5.50
COMPLETE SERIES 2 (150)	12.00	5.50
COMMON CARD (1-390)	.05	.02
SEMISTARS	.10	.05
UNLISTED STARS	.25	.11

□ 1 Stacey Augmon	.05	.02
□ 2 Mookie Blaylock	.10	.05
□ 3 Craig Ehlo	.05	.02
□ 4 Duane Ferrell	.05	.02
□ 5 Adam Keefe	.05	.02
□ 6 Jon Koncak	.05	.02
□ 7 Andrew Lang	.05	.02
□ 8 Danny Manning	.05	.02
□ 9 Kevin Willis	.05	.02
□ 10 Dee Brown	.05	.02
□ 11 Sherman Douglas	.05	.02
□ 12 Acie Earl	.05	.02
□ 13 Rick Fox	.05	.02
□ 14 Kevin Gamble	.05	.02
□ 15 Xavier McDaniel	.05	.02
□ 16 Robert Parish	.10	.05
□ 17 Ed Pinckney	.05	.02
□ 18 Dino Radja	.05	.02
□ 19 Muggsy Bogues	.10	.05
□ 20 Frank Brickowski	.05	.02
□ 21 Scott Burrell	.05	.02
□ 22 Dell Curry	.05	.02
□ 23 Kenny Gattison	.05	.02
□ 24 Hersey Hawkins	.10	.05
□ 25 Eddie Johnson	.05	.02
□ 26 Larry Johnson	.10	.05
□ 27 Alonzo Mourning	.30	.14
□ 28 David Wingate	.05	.02
□ 29 B.J. Armstrong	.05	.02
□ 30 Horace Grant	.10	.05
□ 31 Steve Kerr	.10	.05
□ 32 Toni Kukoc	.25	.11
□ 33 Luc Longley	.10	.05
□ 34 Pete Myers	.05	.02
□ 35 Scottie Pippen	.75	.35
□ 36 Bill Wennington	.05	.02
□ 37 Scott Williams	.05	.02
□ 38 Terrell Brandon	.25	.11
□ 39 Brad Daugherty	.05	.02
□ 40 Tyrone Hill	.05	.02
□ 41 Chris Mills	.10	.05
□ 42 Larry Nance	.05	.02
□ 43 Bobby Phills	.05	.02
□ 44 Mark Price	.05	.02
□ 45 Gerald Wilkins	.05	.02
□ 46 John Williams	.05	.02
□ 47 Lucious Harris	.05	.02
□ 48 Donald Hodge	.05	.02
□ 49 Jim Jackson	.10	.05
□ 50 Popeye Jones	.05	.02
□ 51 Tim Legler	.05	.02
□ 52 Fat Lever	.05	.02
□ 53 Jamal Mashburn	.25	.11
□ 54 Sean Rooks	.05	.02
□ 55 Doug Smith	.05	.02
□ 56 M.Abdul-Rauf	.05	.02
□ 57 LaPhonso Ellis	.05	.02
□ 58 D.Mutombo	.25	.11
□ 59 Robert Pack	.05	.02
□ 60 Rodney Rogers	.05	.02
□ 61 Bryant Stith	.05	.02
□ 62 Brian Williams	.05	.02
□ 63 Reggie Williams	.05	.02
□ 64 Greg Anderson	.05	.02
□ 65 Joe Dumars	.25	.11
□ 66 Sean Elliott	.10	.05
□ 67 Allan Houston	.25	.11
□ 68 Lindsey Hunter	.05	.02
□ 69 Terry Mills	.05	.02
□ 70 Victor Alexander	.05	.02
□ 71 Chris Gatling	.05	.02
□ 72 Tim Hardaway	.30	.14
□ 73 Keith Jennings	.05	.02
□ 74 Avery Johnson	.05	.02
□ 75 Chris Mullin	.25	.11
□ 76 Billy Owens	.05	.02
□ 77 Latrell Sprewell	.10	.05
□ 78 Chris Webber	.60	.25
□ 79 Scott Brooks	.05	.02
□ 80 Sam Cassell	.25	.11
□ 81 Mario Elie	.05	.02
□ 82 Carl Herrera	.05	.02
□ 83 Robert Horry	.10	.05
□ 84 Vernon Maxwell	.05	.02
□ 85 Hakeem Olajuwon	.50	.23
□ 86 Kenny Smith	.05	.02
□ 87 Otis Thorpe	.10	.05
□ 88 Antonio Davis	.05	.02
□ 89 Dale Davis	.05	.02
□ 90 Vern Fleming	.05	.02
□ 91 Derrick McKey	.05	.02
□ 92 Reggie Miller	.25	.11
□ 93 Pooh Richardson	.05	.02
□ 94 Byron Scott	.10	.05
□ 95 Rik Smits	.10	.05
□ 96 Haywoode Workman	.05	.02
□ 97 Terry Dehere	.05	.02
□ 98 Harold Ellis	.05	.02
□ 99 Gary Grant	.05	.02
□ 100 Ron Harper	.10	.05
□ 101 Mark Jackson	.10	.05
□ 102 Stanley Roberts	.05	.02
□ 103 Elmore Spencer	.05	.02
□ 104 Loy Vaught	.10	.05
□ 105 Dominique Wilkins	.25	.11
□ 106 Elden Campbell	.10	.05
□ 107 Doug Christie	.05	.02
□ 108 Vlade Divac	.10	.05
□ 109 George Lynch	.05	.02
□ 110 Anthony Peeler	.05	.02
□ 111 Tony Smith	.05	.02
□ 112 Sedale Threatt	.05	.02
□ 113 Nick Van Exel	.25	.11
□ 114 James Worthy	.25	.11
□ 115 Bimbo Coles	.05	.02
□ 116 Grant Long	.05	.02
□ 117 Harold Miner	.05	.02
□ 118 Glen Rice	.25	.11
□ 119 John Salley	.05	.02
□ 120 Rony Seikaly	.05	.02
□ 121 Brian Shaw	.05	.02
□ 122 Steve Smith	.10	.05
□ 123 Vin Baker	.60	.25
□ 124 Jon Barry	.05	.02
□ 125 Todd Day	.05	.02
□ 126 Blue Edwards	.05	.02
□ 127 Lee Mayberry	.05	.02
□ 128 Eric Murdock	.05	.02
□ 129 Ken Norman	.05	.02
□ 130 Derek Strong	.05	.02
□ 131 Thurl Bailey	.05	.02
□ 132 Stacey King	.05	.02
□ 133 Christian Laettner	.10	.05
□ 134 Chuck Person	.10	.05
□ 135 Isaiah Rider	.10	.05
□ 136 Chris Smith	.05	.02
□ 137 Doug West	.05	.02
□ 138 Micheal Williams	.05	.02
□ 139 Kenny Anderson	.10	.05
□ 140 Benoit Benjamin	.05	.02
□ 141 P.J. Brown	.05	.02
□ 142 Derrick Coleman	.10	.05
□ 143 Kevin Edwards	.05	.02
□ 144 Armon Gilliam	.05	.02
□ 145 Chris Morris	.05	.02
□ 146 Johnny Newman	.05	.02
□ 147 Greg Anthony	.05	.02
□ 148 Anthony Bonner	.05	.02
□ 149 Hubert Davis	.05	.02
□ 150 Patrick Ewing	.25	.11
□ 151 Derek Harper	.10	.05
□ 152 Anthony Mason	.10	.05
□ 153 Charles Oakley	.10	.05
□ 154 Doc Rivers	.05	.02
□ 155 Charles Smith	.10	.05
□ 156 John Starks	.10	.05
□ 157 Nick Anderson	.10	.05
□ 158 Anthony Avent	.05	.02
□ 159 A.Hardaway	1.00	.45
□ 160 Shaquille O'Neal	1.00	.45
□ 161 Donald Royal	.05	.02
□ 162 Dennis Scott	.10	.05
□ 163 Scott Skiles	.05	.02
□ 164 Jeff Turner	.05	.02
□ 165 Dana Barros	.05	.02
□ 166 Shawn Bradley	.10	.05
□ 167 Greg Graham	.05	.02
□ 168 Eric Leckner	.05	.02
□ 169 Jeff Malone	.05	.02
□ 170 Moses Malone	.25	.11
□ 171 Tim Perry	.05	.02
□ 172 C.Weatherspoon	.05	.02
□ 173 Orlando Woolridge	.05	.02
□ 174 Danny Ainge	.10	.05
□ 175 Charles Barkley	.40	.18
□ 176 Cedric Ceballos	.10	.05
□ 177 A.C. Green	.10	.05
□ 178 Kevin Johnson	.10	.05
□ 179 Joe Kleine	.05	.02
□ 180 Dan Majerle	.05	.02
□ 181 Oliver Miller	.05	.02

182	Mark West	.05	.02
183	Clyde Drexler	.30	.14
184	Harvey Grant	.05	.02
185	Jerome Kersey	.05	.02
186	Tracy Murray	.05	.02
187	Terry Porter	.05	.02
188	Clifford Robinson	.10	.05
189	James Robinson	.05	.02
190	Rod Strickland	.05	.02
191	Buck Williams	.10	.05
192	Duane Causwell	.05	.02
193	Bobby Hurley	.05	.02
194	Olden Polynice	.05	.02
195	Mitch Richmond	.25	.11
196	Lionel Simmons	.05	.02
197	Wayman Tisdale	.05	.02
198	Spud Webb	.10	.05
199	Walt Williams	.05	.02
200	Trevor Wilson	.05	.02
201	Willie Anderson	.05	.02
202	Antoine Carr	.05	.02
203	Terry Cummings	.05	.02
204	Vinny Del Negro	.05	.02
205	Dale Ellis	.05	.02
206	Negele Knight	.05	.02
207	J.R. Reid	.05	.02
208	David Robinson	.40	.18
209	Dennis Rodman	1.00	.45
210	Vincent Askew	.05	.02
211	Michael Cage	.05	.02
212	Kendall Gill	.10	.05
213	Shawn Kemp	.75	.35
214	Nate McMillan	.05	.02
215	Gary Payton	.40	.18
216	Sam Perkins	.10	.05
217	Ricky Pierce	.05	.02
218	Detlef Schrempf	.10	.05
219	David Benoit	.05	.02
220	Tom Chambers	.05	.02
221	Tyrone Corbin	.05	.02
222	Jeff Hornacek	.10	.05
223	Jay Humphries	.05	.02
224	Karl Malone	.40	.18
225	Bryon Russell	.10	.05
226	Felton Spencer	.05	.02
227	John Stockton	.25	.11
228	Michael Adams	.05	.02
229	Rex Chapman	.05	.02
230	Calbert Cheaney	.10	.05
231	Kevin Duckworth	.05	.02
232	Pervis Ellison	.05	.02
233	Tom Gugliotta	.25	.11
234	Don MacLean	.05	.02
235	Gheorghe Muresan	.10	.05
236	Brent Price	.05	.02
237	Toronto Raptors Logo Card	.05	
238	Checklist	.05	.02
239	Checklist	.05	.02
240	Checklist	.05	.02
241	Sergei Bazarevich	.05	.02
242	Tyrone Corbin	.05	.02
243	Grant Long	.05	.02
244	Ken Norman	.05	.02
245	Steve Smith	.10	.05
246	Fred Vinson	.05	.02
247	Blue Edwards	.05	.02
248	Greg Minor	.05	.02
249	Eric Montross	.05	.02
250	Derek Strong	.05	.02
251	David Wesley	.10	.05
252	Dominique Wilkins	.25	.11
253	Michael Adams	.05	.02
254	Tony Bennett	.05	.02
255	Darrin Hancock	.05	.02
256	Robert Parish	.10	.05
257	Corie Blount	.05	.02
258	Jud Buechler	.05	.02
259	Greg Foster	.05	.02
260	Ron Harper	.10	.05
261	Larry Krystkowiak	.05	.02
262	Will Perdue	.05	.02
263	Dickey Simpkins	.05	.02
264	Michael Cage	.05	.02
265	Tony Campbell	.05	.02
266	Terry Davis	.05	.02
267	Tony Dumas	.05	.02
268	Jason Kidd	2.00	.90
269	Roy Tarpley	.05	.02
270	Morlon Wiley	.05	.02
271	Lorenzo Williams	.05	.02
272	Dale Ellis	.05	.02
273	Tom Hammonds	.05	.02
274	Cliff Levingston	.05	.02
275	Darnell Mee	.05	.02
276	Jalen Rose	.25	.11
277	Reggie Slater	.05	.02
278	Bill Curley	.05	.02
279	Johnny Dawkins	.05	.02
280	Grant Hill	3.00	1.35
281	Eric Leckner	.05	.02
282	Mark Macon	.05	.02
283	Oliver Miller	.05	.02
284	Mark West	.05	.02
285	Manute Bol	.05	.02
286	Tom Gugliotta	.25	.11
287	Ricky Pierce	.05	.02
288	Carlos Rogers	.05	.02
289	Clifford Rozier	.05	.02
290	Rony Seikaly	.05	.02
291	Tim Breaux	.05	.02
292	Chris Jent	.05	.02
293	Eric Riley	.05	.02
294	Zan Tabak	.05	.02
295	Duane Ferrell	.05	.02
296	Mark Jackson	.10	.05
297	John Williams	.05	.02
298	Matt Fish	.05	.02
299	Tony Massenburg	.05	.02
300	Lamond Murray	.10	.05
301	Charles Outlaw	.05	.02
302	Eric Piatkowski	.05	.02
303	Pooh Richardson	.05	.02
304	Randy Woods	.05	.02
305	Sam Bowie	.05	.02
306	Cedric Ceballos	.10	.05
307	Antonio Harvey	.05	
308	Eddie Jones	2.00	.90
309	Anthony Miller	.05	.02
310	Ledell Eackles	.05	.02
311	Kevin Gamble	.05	.02
312	Brad Lohaus	.05	.02
313	Billy Owens	.05	.02
314	Khalid Reeves	.05	.02
315	Kevin Willis	.05	.02
316	Marty Conlon	.05	.02
317	Eric Mobley	.05	.02
318	Johnny Newman	.05	.02
319	Ed Pinckney	.05	.02
320	Glenn Robinson	1.00	.45
321	Mike Brown	.05	.02
322	Pat Durham	.05	.02
323	Howard Eisley	.05	.02
324	Andres Guibert	.05	.02
325	Donyell Marshall	.30	.14
326	Sean Rooks	.05	.02
327	Yinka Dare	.05	.02
328	Sleepy Floyd	.05	.02
329	Sean Higgins	.05	.02
330	Rick Mahorn	.05	.02
331	Rex Walters	.05	.02
332	Jayson Williams	.10	.05
333	Charlie Ward	.10	.05
334	Herb Williams	.05	.02
335	Monty Williams	.05	.02
336	Anthony Bowie	.05	.02
337	Horace Grant	.10	.05
338	Geert Hammink	.05	.02
339	Tree Rollins	.05	.02
340	Brian Shaw	.05	.02
341	Brooks Thompson	.05	.02
342	Derrick Alston	.05	.02
343	Willie Burton	.05	.02
344	Jaren Jackson	.05	.02
345	B.J. Tyler	.05	.02
346	Scott Williams	.05	.02
347	Sharone Wright	.05	.02
348	Antonio Lang	.05	.02
349	Danny Manning	.05	.02
350	Elliot Perry	.05	.02
351	Wesley Person	.30	.14
352	Trevor Ruffin	.05	.02
353	Dan Schayes	.05	.02
354	Aaron Swinson	.05	.02
355	Wayman Tisdale	.05	.02
356	Mark Bryant	.05	.02
357	Chris Dudley	.05	.02
358	James Edwards	.05	.02
359	Aaron McKie	.05	.02
360	Alaa Abdelnaby	.05	.02
361	Frank Brickowski	.05	.02
362	Randy Brown	.05	.02
363	Brian Grant	.25	.11
364	Michael Smith	.10	.05
365	Henry Turner	.05	.02
366	Sean Elliott	.10	.05
367	Avery Johnson	.05	.02
368	Moses Malone	.25	.11
369	Julius Nwosu	.05	.02
370	Chuck Person	.05	.02
371	Chris Whitney	.05	.02
372	Bill Cartwright	.05	.02
373	Byron Houston	.05	.02
374	Ervin Johnson	.05	.02
375	Sarunas Marciulionis	.05	.02
376	Antoine Carr	.05	.02
377	John Crotty	.05	.02
378	Adam Keefe	.05	.02
379	Jamie Watson	.10	.05
380	Mitchell Butler	.05	.02
381	Juwan Howard	1.25	.55
382	Jim McIlvaine	.05	.02
383	Doug Overton	.05	.02
384	Scott Skiles	.05	.02
385	Larry Stewart	.05	.02
386	Kenny Walker	.05	.02
387	Chris Webber	.60	.25
388	Vancouver Grizzlies Logo Card	.05	.02
389	Checklist		.02
390	Checklist		.02

1994-95 Fleer All-Defensive

Randomly inserted in all first-series packs at a rate of one in nine, these 10 standard-size cards feature first and second All-NBA Defensive teams. Card fronts are borderless with color player action shots that have been faded to black-and-white. The player's name and first or second team designation appear in silver-foil lettering near the bottom. On a color-screened background, the back carries a color player cutout on one side and career highlights on the other. The cards are numbered on the back as "X of

10" and are sequenced in alphabetical order.

	MINT	NRMT
COMPLETE SET (10)	6.00	2.70
COMMON CARD (1-10)	.25	.11
SEMISTARS	.40	.18
SER.1 STATED ODDS 1:9 HOBBY/RETAIL		

		MINT	NRMT
☐ 1	Mookie Blaylock	.40	.18
☐ 2	Charles Oakley	.40	.18
☐ 3	Hakeem Olajuwon	1.50	.70
☐ 4	Gary Payton	1.25	.55
☐ 5	Scottie Pippen	2.50	1.10
☐ 6	Horace Grant	.40	.18
☐ 7	Nate McMillan	.25	.11
☐ 8	David Robinson	1.25	.55
☐ 9	Dennis Rodman	3.00	1.35
☐ 10	Latrell Sprewell	.40	.18

1994-95 Fleer All-Stars

Randomly inserted in 15-card first-series packs at a rate of one in two, these 26 standard-size cards feature borderless fronts with color player action shots and backgrounds that fade to black-and-white. The player's name and first or second team designation appear in silver-foil lettering near the bottom. On a color-screened background, the back carries a color player cutout on one side and career highlights on the other.

	MINT	NRMT
COMPLETE SET (26)	30.00	13.50
COMMON CARD (1-26)	.50	.23
SEMISTARS	.75	.35
UNLISTED STARS	1.50	.70
SER.1 STATED ODDS 1:2 HOBBY		

		MINT	NRMT
☐ 1	Kenny Anderson	.75	.35
☐ 2	B.J. Armstrong	.50	.23
☐ 3	Mookie Blaylock	.75	.35
☐ 4	Derrick Coleman	.75	.35
☐ 5	Patrick Ewing	1.50	.70
☐ 6	Horace Grant	.75	.35
☐ 7	Alonzo Mourning	2.00	.90
☐ 8	Charles Oakley	.75	.35
☐ 9	Shaquille O'Neal	6.00	2.70
☐ 10	Scottie Pippen	5.00	2.20
☐ 11	Mark Price	.50	.23
☐ 12	John Starks	.75	.35
☐ 13	Dominique Wilkins	1.50	.70
☐ 14	Charles Barkley	2.50	1.10
☐ 15	Clyde Drexler	2.00	.90
☐ 16	Kevin Johnson	.75	.35
☐ 17	Shawn Kemp	5.00	2.20
☐ 18	Karl Malone	2.50	1.10
☐ 19	Danny Manning	.50	.23
☐ 20	Hakeem Olajuwon	3.00	1.35
☐ 21	Gary Payton	2.50	1.10
☐ 22	Mitch Richmond	1.50	.70
☐ 23	Clifford Robinson	.75	.35
☐ 24	David Robinson	2.50	1.10
☐ 25	Latrell Sprewell	.75	.35
☐ 26	John Stockton	1.50	.70

1994-95 Fleer Award Winners

These four standard-size cards were random inserts in all first series packs at an approximate rate of one in 22. The set highlights four NBA award winners from the 1993-94 season. The horizontal fronts feature multiple player images. The player's name and his award appear at the bottom in gold-foil lettering. The horizontal back carries a color player close-up on one side and career highlights on the other. The cards are numbered "X of 4" and are sequenced in alphabetical order.

	MINT	NRMT
COMPLETE SET (4)	4.00	1.80
COMMON CARD (1-4)	.25	.11
SER.1 STATED ODDS 1:22 HOBBY/RETAIL		

		MINT	NRMT
☐ 1	Dell Curry	.25	.11
☐ 2	Don MacLean	.25	.11
☐ 3	Hakeem Olajuwon	2.00	.90
☐ 4	Chris Webber	2.50	1.10

1994-95 Fleer Career Achievement

Randomly inserted in all first series packs at rate of one in 37, these six standard-size cards feature veteran NBA superstars. The fronts feature color player cutouts on their borderless

metallic fronts. The player's name appears in gold-foil lettering in a lower corner. The back carries a color player close-up in a lower corner, with career highlights appearing above and alongside. The cards are numbered on the back as "X of 6" and are sequenced in alphabetical order.

	MINT	NRMT
COMPLETE SET (6)	20.00	9.00
COMMON CARD (1-6)	1.00	.45
SEMISTARS	3.00	1.35
SER.1 STATED ODDS 1:37 HOBBY/RETAIL		

		MINT	NRMT
☐ 1	Patrick Ewing	3.00	1.35
☐ 2	Karl Malone	5.00	2.20
☐ 3	Hakeem Olajuwon	6.00	2.70
☐ 4	Robert Parish	1.00	.45
☐ 5	Scottie Pippen	10.00	4.50
☐ 6	Dominique Wilkins	1.00	.45

1994-95 Fleer First Year Phenoms

Randomly inserted into all second series packs at a rate of one in five, cards from this 10-card standard-size set feature a selection of the top rookies from 1994. These borderless cards feature a full color, cut-out player photo bursting forth from the center of the card, against a multi-imaged, shaded photo background. Card backs feature brief text on each player. The set is sequenced in alphabetical order.

	MINT	NRMT
COMPLETE SET (10)	15.00	6.75
COMMON CARD (1-10)	.40	.18
SEMISTARS	.75	.35
SER.2 STATED ODDS 1:5 HOBBY/RETAIL		

		MINT	NRMT
☐ 1	Grant Hill	8.00	3.60
☐ 2	Jason Kidd	5.00	2.20
☐ 3	Donyell Marshall	.75	.35
☐ 4	Eric Montross	.40	.18
☐ 5	Lamond Murray	.40	.18
☐ 6	Wesley Person	.75	.35
☐ 7	Khalid Reeves	.40	.18
☐ 8	Glenn Robinson	2.50	1.10
☐ 9	Jalen Rose	.75	.35
☐ 10	Sharone Wright	.40	.18

1994-95 Fleer League Leaders

Randomly inserted in all first series Fleer packs at an approximate rate of one in 11, these eight standard-size cards showcase league statistical leaders from the 1993-94 season. Card fronts feature a horizontal design with color player cutouts set on hardwood backgrounds. The player's name and the category in which he led the NBA appear in gold-foil lettering at the bottom. On a hardwood background, the horizontal back carries a color player close-up on one side and career highlights on the other. The cards are numbered on the back as "X of 8" and are sequenced in alphabetical order.

	MINT	NRMT
COMPLETE SET (8)	6.00	2.70
COMMON CARD (1-8)	.25	.11
SEMISTARS	.50	.23
UNLISTED STARS	.75	.35
SER.1 STATED ODDS 1:11 HOBBY/RETAIL		

		MINT	NRMT
☐ 1	M.Abdul-Rauf	.25	.11
☐ 2	Nate McMillan	.25	.11
☐ 3	Tracy Murray	.25	.11
☐ 4	D.Mutombo	.50	.23
☐ 5	Shaquille O'Neal	3.00	1.35
☐ 6	David Robinson	1.25	.55
☐ 7	Dennis Rodman	3.00	1.35
☐ 8	John Stockton	.75	.35

1994-95 Fleer Lottery Exchange

This 11-card standard-size set was available exclusively by redeeming the Fleer Lottery Exchange card, which was randomly inserted into all first series packs at a rate of one in 175. The expiration date for the redemption was April 1st, 1995. Card design is very similar to the basic issue Fleer cards except for the Lottery Pick logo on front.

	MINT	NRMT
COMPLETE SET (11)	25.00	11.00
COMMON CARD (1-11)	.40	.18
SEMISTARS	.75	.35
ONE SET PER EXCHANGE CARD BY MAIL		
EXCH.CARD: SER.1 STATED ODDS 1:175		

		MINT	NRMT
☐ 1	Glenn Robinson	3.00	1.35
☐ 2	Jason Kidd	6.00	2.70
☐ 3	Grant Hill	10.00	4.50
☐ 4	Donyell Marshall	.75	.35
☐ 5	Juwan Howard	4.00	1.80
☐ 6	Sharone Wright	.40	.18
☐ 7	Lamond Murray	.40	.18
☐ 8	Brian Grant	.75	.35
☐ 9	Eric Montross	.40	.18
☐ 10	Eddie Jones	6.00	2.70
☐ 11	Carlos Rogers	.40	.18
☐ NNO	Lottery Exchange Card	1.00	.45

1994-95 Fleer Pro-Visions

Randomly inserted in all first-series packs at a rate of one in five, these nine standard-size

cards highlight some top NBA stars. Borderless fronts feature color paintings of the players on fanciful backgrounds. The player's name appears in gold-foil lettering in a lower corner. The back carries career highlights on a colorful ghosted abstract background.

	MINT	NRMT
COMPLETE SET (9)	4.00	1.80
COMMON CARD (1-9)	.15	.07
SEMISTARS	.20	.09
UNLISTED STARS	.30	.14
SER.1 STATED ODDS 1:5 HOBBY/RETAIL		

		MINT	NRMT
☐ 1	Jamal Mashburn	.30	.14
☐ 2	John Starks	.20	.09
☐ 3	Toni Kukoc	.30	.14
☐ 4	Derrick Coleman	.20	.09
☐ 5	Chris Webber	1.00	.45
☐ 6	Dennis Rodman	1.50	.70
☐ 7	Gary Payton	.60	.25
☐ 8	A.Hardaway	1.50	.70
☐ 9	Dan Majerle	.15	.07

1994-95 Fleer Rookie Sensations

Randomly inserted at a rate of one in three first-series 21-card cello packs, these 25 standard-size cards feature a selection of the top rookies from the 1993-94 season. Card fronts feature color player action cutouts "breaking out" of borderless multicolored backgrounds. The player's name appears in gold-foil lettering in a lower corner. The back carries another color player action cutout on one side, and career highlights within a colored panel on the other. The cards are numbered on the back as "X of 25" and are sequenced in alphabetical order.

	MINT	NRMT
COMPLETE SET (25)	25.00	11.00
COMMON CARD (1-25)	.50	.23
SEMISTARS	1.00	.45
UNLISTED STARS	2.00	.90
SER.1 STATED ODDS 1:3 CELLO		

		MINT	NRMT
☐ 1	Vin Baker	5.00	2.20
☐ 2	Shawn Bradley	1.00	.45
☐ 3	P.J. Brown	.50	.23
☐ 4	Sam Cassell	2.00	.90
☐ 5	Calbert Cheaney	1.00	.45
☐ 6	Antonio Davis	.50	.23
☐ 7	Acie Earl	.50	.23
☐ 8	Harold Ellis	.50	.23
☐ 9	A.Hardaway	8.00	3.60
☐ 10	Allan Houston	2.00	.90
☐ 11	Lindsey Hunter	1.00	.45
☐ 12	Bobby Hurley	.50	.23
☐ 13	Popeye Jones	.50	.23
☐ 14	Toni Kukoc	2.00	.90
☐ 15	George Lynch	.50	.23
☐ 16	Jamal Mashburn	2.00	.90
☐ 17	Chris Mills	1.00	.45
☐ 18	Gheorghe Muresan	1.00	.45
☐ 19	Dino Radja	.50	.23
☐ 20	Isaiah Rider	1.00	.45
☐ 21	James Robinson	.50	.23
☐ 22	Rodney Rogers	.50	.23
☐ 23	Bryon Russell	1.00	.45
☐ 24	Nick Van Exel	2.00	.90
☐ 25	Chris Webber	5.00	2.20

1994-95 Fleer Sharpshooters

Randomly inserted exclusively into second series retail packs at a rate of one in seven, cards from this 10-card standard-size set feature a selection of the NBA's best long-distance shoot ers. Card fronts feature color player photos cut out against a neon basketball background overlapped by a basketball net. The set is sequenced in alphabetical order.

		MINT	NRMT
	COMPLETE SET (10)	15.00	6.75
	COMMON CARD (1-10)	1.00	.45
	SEMISTARS	2.00	.90
	UNLISTED STARS	4.00	1.80
	SER.2 STATED ODDS 1:7 RETAIL		
☐ 1	Dell Curry	1.00	.45
☐ 2	Joe Dumars	4.00	1.80
☐ 3	Dale Ellis	1.00	.45
☐ 4	Dan Majerle	2.00	.90
☐ 5	Reggie Miller	4.00	1.80
☐ 6	Mark Price	1.00	.45
☐ 7	Glen Rice	4.00	1.80
☐ 8	Mitch Richmond	4.00	1.80
☐ 9	Dennis Scott	2.00	.90
☐ 10	Latrell Sprewell	2.00	.90

1994-95 Fleer Superstars

Randomly inserted into all second series packs at a rate of one in 37, cards from this six-card set feature a selection of veteran NBA stars with true Hall of Fame potential. Card fronts feature psychedelic, etched-foil backgrounds against a full color, cut out player photo. The set is sequenced in alphabetical order.

		MINT	NRMT
	COMPLETE SET (6)	20.00	9.00
	COMMON CARD (1-6)	1.00	.45
	SEMISTARS	1.50	.70
	UNLISTED STARS	3.00	1.35
	SER.2 STATED ODDS 1:37 HOBBY/RETAIL		
☐ 1	Charles Barkley	5.00	2.20
☐ 2	Patrick Ewing	3.00	1.35
☐ 3	Hakeem Olajuwon	6.00	2.70
☐ 4	Robert Parish	1.00	.45
☐ 5	Scottie Pippen	10.00	4.50
☐ 6	Dominique Wilkins	1.50	.70

1994-95 Fleer Team Leaders

Randomly inserted into all second series packs at a rate of one in three, cards from this nine-card standard-size set each feature three key players from an NBA team. Horizontal card fronts feature three full color, cut out player photos against a

computer-enhanced graphic background. The backs have a head shot of all three players and infomation on them. The cards are numbered "X of 9." There are two variations of card #3. The error version lists Joe Dumars as a Houston Rocket. The corrected version lists him as a Detroit Piston. It appears that equal quantities of both versions exist.

		MINT	NRMT
	COMPLETE SET (9)	4.00	1.80
	COMMON CARD (1-9)	.25	.11
	SEMISTARS	.50	.23
	SER.2 STATED ODDS 1:3 HOBBY/RETAIL		
☐ 1	Mookie Blaylock Dominique Wilkins Alonzo Mourning	.50	.23
☐ 2	Scottie Pippen Mark Price Jamal Mashburn	1.00	.45
☐ 3	D.Mutombo ERR Joe Dumars Detroit Pistons Latrell Sprewell Card has Dumars with Rockets	.60	.25
☐ 3A	D.Mutombo COR Joe Dumars Latrell Sprewell	.60	.25
☐ 4	Hakeem Olajuwon Reggie Miller Loy Vaught	.75	.35
☐ 5	Vlade Divac Glen Rice Vin Baker	.60	.25
☐ 6	Isaiah Rider Kenny Anderson Patrick Ewing	.25	.11
☐ 7	Shaquille O'Neal C.Weatherspoon Charles Barkley	1.50	.70
☐ 8	Rod Strickland Mitch Richmond David Robinson	.75	.35
☐ 9	Shawn Kemp John Stockton Rex Chapman	1.00	.45

1994-95 Fleer Total D

Randomly inserted exclusively into second series hobby packs at a rate of one in seven, cards from this 10-card standard-size set feature a selection of the NBA's top defensive players. The fronts are laid out horizontally with a color photo and the player's name and team is in gold-foil at the bottom. "Total D" is in the background many times with a variety of colors set behind that. The backs have a head shot and information and why the player is so good defensively with a similar background to the front. The cards are numbered "X of 10" and are sequenced in alphabetical order.

	MINT	NRMT
COMPLETE SET (10)	10.00	4.50
COMMON CARD (1-10)	.50	.23
SEMISTARS	.60	.25
UNLISTED STARS	1.25	.55
SER.2 STATED ODDS 1:7 HOBBY		

☐ 1 Mookie Blaylock	.60	.25
☐ 2 Nate McMillan	.50	.23
☐ 3 D.Mutombo	1.25	.55
☐ 4 Charles Oakley	.60	.25
☐ 5 Hakeem Olajuwon	2.50	1.10
☐ 6 Gary Payton	2.00	.90
☐ 7 Scottie Pippen	4.00	1.80
☐ 8 David Robinson	2.00	.90
☐ 9 Latrell Sprewell	.60	.25
☐ 10 John Stockton	1.25	.55

1994-95 Fleer Towers of Power

Randomly inserted exclusively into second series 21-card retail packs at a rate of one in five, cards from this 10-card standard-size set feature a selection of the top centers and power forwards in the NBA. The fronts have a color-action photo surrounded by a yellow glow with a tower in the background. The words "Tower of Power" are at the bottom in gold-foil. The backs are the same except for a different photo and player information at the bottom. The cards are numbered "X of 10" and are sequenced in alphabetical order.

	MINT	NRMT
COMPLETE SET (10)	30.00	13.50
COMMON CARD (1-10)	1.00	.45
SEMISTARS	2.00	.90
SER.2 STATED ODDS 1:5 CELLO		

☐ 1 Charles Barkley	3.00	1.35
☐ 2 Patrick Ewing	2.00	.90
☐ 3 Shawn Kemp	6.00	2.70
☐ 4 Karl Malone	3.00	1.35
☐ 5 Alonzo Mourning	2.50	1.10
☐ 6 D.Mutombo	1.00	.45
☐ 7 Hakeem Olajuwon	4.00	1.80
☐ 8 Shaquille O'Neal	8.00	3.60
☐ 9 David Robinson	3.00	1.35
☐ 10 Chris Webber	5.00	2.20

1994-95 Fleer Triple Threats

Randomly inserted in all first-series packs at an approximate rate of one in nine, these 10 standard-size cards spotlight some top NBA stars. Card fronts feature borderless fronts with multiple color player action cutouts on black backgrounds highlighted by colorful basketball court designs. The player's name appears in gold-foil lettering in a lower corner. This background design continues on the back, which carries a color player cutout on one side and career highlights in a ghosted strip on the other. The cards are numbered on the back as "X of 10" and are sequenced in alphabetical order.

	MINT	NRMT
COMPLETE SET (10)	6.00	2.70
COMMON CARD (1-10)	.25	.11
SEMISTARS	.50	.23
SER.1 STATED ODDS 1:9 HOBBY/RETAIL		

☐ 1 Mookie Blaylock	.25	.11
☐ 2 Patrick Ewing	.50	.23
☐ 3 Shawn Kemp	1.50	.70
☐ 4 Karl Malone	.75	.35
☐ 5 Reggie Miller	.50	.23
☐ 6 Hakeem Olajuwon	1.00	.45
☐ 7 Shaquille O'Neal	2.00	.90
☐ 8 Scottie Pippen	1.50	.70
☐ 9 David Robinson	.75	.35
☐ 10 Latrell Sprewell	.25	.11

1994-95 Fleer Young Lions

Randomly inserted into all second series packs at a rate of one in five, cards from this 6-card standard-size set feature a selection of popular players with three years or less of NBA experience. Fronts feature a player photo on the left and a lion photo on the right. In the bottom

right corner there is gold-foil stamping of a lion, the term "Young Lion" and the player's name. The back has a brief biography and another player photo. The card is numbered in the lower right as "X" of 6. The set is sequenced in alphabetical order.

	MINT	NRMT
COMPLETE SET (6)	8.00	3.60
COMMON CARD (1-6)	.60	.25
SER.2 STATED ODDS 1:5 HOBBY/RETAIL		

☐ 1 Vin Baker	2.00	.90
☐ 2 A.Hardaway	3.00	1.35
☐ 3 Larry Johnson	.60	.25
☐ 4 Alonzo Mourning	1.00	.45
☐ 5 Shaquille O'Neal	3.00	1.35
☐ 6 Chris Webber	2.00	.90

1995-96 Fleer

The 1995-96 Fleer set was issued in two separate series of 200 and 150 cards, respectively, for a total of 350. Cards were distributed in 11-card hobby and retail packs (SRP $1.49) and 17-card retail pre-priced packs (SRP $2.29). Each pack contains at least two insert cards. Special Hot Packs, containing a selection of only insert cards, were randomly seeded into one in every 72 packs. The borderless fronts feature four different background designs (one for each division) against a cut-out color player action shot. The *backs have a color-action photo and the same picture set against a pixeled background, along with statistics. The cards are grouped alphabetically within teams. The set concludes with the following topical subsets: Rookies (280-319) and Firm Foundations (320-348). Rookie Cards of note in this set include Michael Finley, Kevin Garnett, Antonio McDyess, Joe Smith, Jerry Stackhouse and D.Stoudamire.*

	MINT	NRMT
COMPLETE SET (350)	40.00	18.00
COMPLETE SERIES 1 (200)	20.00	9.00
COMPLETE SERIES 2 (150)	20.00	9.00
COMMON CARD (1-350)	.10	.05
SEMISTARS	.15	.07
UNLISTED STARS	.25	.11

#	Player	MINT	NRMT
1	Stacey Augmon	.10	.05
2	Mookie Blaylock	.15	.07
3	Craig Ehlo	.10	.05
4	Andrew Lang	.10	.05
5	Grant Long	.10	.05
6	Ken Norman	.10	.05
7	Steve Smith	.15	.07
8	Dee Brown	.10	.05
9	Sherman Douglas	.10	.05
10	Eric Montross	.10	.05
11	Dino Radja	.10	.05
12	David Wesley	.10	.05
13	Dominique Wilkins	.25	.11
14	Muggsy Bogues	.15	.07
15	Scott Burrell	.10	.05
16	Dell Curry	.10	.05
17	Hersey Hawkins	.15	.07
18	Larry Johnson	.15	.07
19	Alonzo Mourning	.25	.11
20	Robert Parish	.15	.07
21	B.J. Armstrong	.10	.05
22	Michael Jordan	3.00	1.35
23	Steve Kerr	.15	.07
24	Toni Kukoc	.15	.07
25	Will Perdue	.10	.05
26	Scottie Pippen	.75	.35
27	Terrell Brandon	.25	.11
28	Tyrone Hill	.10	.05
29	Chris Mills	.10	.05
30	Bobby Phills	.10	.05
31	Mark Price	.10	.05
32	John Williams	.10	.05
33	Lucious Harris	.10	.05
34	Jim Jackson	.15	.07
35	Popeye Jones	.10	.05
36	Jason Kidd	.60	.25
37	Jamal Mashburn	.15	.07
38	George McCloud	.10	.05
39	Roy Tarpley	.10	.05
40	Lorenzo Williams	.10	.05
41	M.Abdul-Rauf	.10	.05
42	Dale Ellis	.10	.05
43	LaPhonso Ellis	.15	.07
44	D.Mutombo	.15	.07
45	Robert Pack	.10	.05
46	Rodney Rogers	.10	.05
47	Jalen Rose	.15	.07
48	Bryant Stith	.10	.05
49	Reggie Williams	.10	.05
50	Joe Dumars	.25	.11
51	Grant Hill	1.50	.70
52	Allan Houston	.15	.07
53	Lindsey Hunter	.10	.05
54	Oliver Miller	.10	.05
55	Terry Mills	.10	.05
56	Mark West	.10	.05
57	Chris Gatling	.10	.05
58	Tim Hardaway	.30	.14
59	Donyell Marshall	.15	.07
60	Chris Mullin	.25	.11
61	Carlos Rogers	.10	.05
62	Clifford Rozier	.10	.05
63	Rony Seikaly	.10	.05
64	Latrell Sprewell	.15	.07
65	Sam Cassell	.15	.07
66	Clyde Drexler	.30	.14
67	Mario Elie	.10	.05
68	Carl Herrera	.10	.05
69	Robert Horry	.10	.05
70	Vernon Maxwell	.10	.05
71	Hakeem Olajuwon	.50	.23
72	Kenny Smith	.10	.05
73	Dale Davis	.10	.05
74	Mark Jackson	.15	.07
75	Derrick McKey	.10	.05
76	Reggie Miller	.25	.11
77	Sam Mitchell	.10	.05
78	Byron Scott	.10	.05
79	Rik Smits	.10	.05
80	Terry Dehere	.10	.05
81	Tony Massenburg	.10	.05
82	Lamond Murray	.10	.05
83	Pooh Richardson	.10	.05
84	Malik Sealy	.10	.05
85	Loy Vaught	.10	.05
86	Elden Campbell	.15	.07
87	Cedric Ceballos	.15	.07
88	Vlade Divac	.15	.07
89	Eddie Jones	.60	.25
90	Anthony Peeler	.10	.05
91	Sedale Threatt	.10	.05
92	Nick Van Exel	.25	.11
93	Bimbo Coles	.10	.05
94	Matt Geiger	.10	.05
95	Billy Owens	.10	.05
96	Khalid Reeves	.10	.05
97	Glen Rice	.25	.11
98	John Salley	.10	.05
99	Kevin Willis	.10	.05
100	Vin Baker	.50	.23
101	Marty Conlon	.10	.05
102	Todd Day	.10	.05
103	Lee Mayberry	.10	.05
104	Eric Murdock	.10	.05
105	Glenn Robinson	.30	.14
106	Winston Garland	.10	.05
107	Tom Gugliotta	.25	.11
108	Christian Laettner	.15	.07
109	Isaiah Rider	.15	.07
110	Sean Rooks	.10	.05
111	Doug West	.10	.05
112	Kenny Anderson	.15	.07
113	Benoit Benjamin	.10	.05
114	P.J. Brown	.10	.05
115	Derrick Coleman	.15	.07
116	Armon Gilliam	.10	.05
117	Chris Morris	.10	.05
118	Rex Walters	.10	.05
119	Hubert Davis	.10	.05
120	Patrick Ewing	.25	.11
121	Derek Harper	.15	.07
122	Anthony Mason	.15	.07
123	Charles Oakley	.15	.07
124	Charles Smith	.10	.05
125	John Starks	.15	.07
126	Nick Anderson	.10	.05
127	Anthony Bowie	.10	.05
128	Horace Grant	.15	.07
129	A.Hardaway	1.00	.45
130	Shaquille O'Neal	1.00	.45
131	Donald Royal	.10	.05
132	Dennis Scott	.10	.05
133	Brian Shaw	.10	.05
134	Derrick Alston	.10	.05
135	Dana Barros	.10	.05
136	Shawn Bradley	.15	.07
137	Willie Burton	.10	.05
138	C.Weatherspoon	.10	.05
139	Scott Williams	.10	.05
140	Sharone Wright	.10	.05
141	Danny Ainge	.15	.07
142	Charles Barkley	.40	.18
143	A.C. Green	.15	.07
144	Kevin Johnson	.15	.07
145	Dan Majerle	.10	.05
146	Danny Manning	.15	.07
147	Elliot Perry	.10	.05
148	Wesley Person	.15	.07
149	Wayman Tisdale	.10	.05
150	Chris Dudley	.10	.05
151	Jerome Kersey	.10	.05
152	Aaron McKie	.10	.05
153	Terry Porter	.10	.05
154	Clifford Robinson	.10	.05
155	James Robinson	.10	.05
156	Rod Strickland	.15	.07
157	Otis Thorpe	.15	.07
158	Buck Williams	.10	.05
159	Brian Grant	.15	.07
160	Bobby Hurley	.10	.05
161	Olden Polynice	.10	.05
162	Mitch Richmond	.25	.11
163	Michael Smith	.10	.05
164	Spud Webb	.15	.07
165	Walt Williams	.10	.05
166	Terry Cummings	.10	.05
167	Vinny Del Negro	.10	.05
168	Sean Elliott	.10	.05
169	Avery Johnson	.10	.05
170	Chuck Person	.10	.05
171	J.R. Reid	.10	.05
172	Doc Rivers	.15	.07
173	David Robinson	.40	.18
174	Dennis Rodman	1.00	.45
175	Vincent Askew	.10	.05
176	Kendall Gill	.15	.07
177	Shawn Kemp	.75	.35
178	Sarunas Marciulionis	.10	.05
179	Nate McMillan	.10	.05
180	Gary Payton	.40	.18
181	Sam Perkins	.15	.07
182	Detlef Schrempf	.15	.07
183	David Benoit	.10	.05
184	Antoine Carr	.10	.05
185	Blue Edwards	.10	.05
186	Jeff Hornacek	.15	.07
187	Adam Keefe	.10	.05
188	Karl Malone	.40	.18
189	Felton Spencer	.10	.05
190	John Stockton	.25	.11
191	Rex Chapman	.10	.05
192	Calbert Cheaney	.10	.05
193	Juwan Howard	.40	.18
194	Don MacLean	.10	.05
195	Gheorghe Muresan	.10	.05
196	Scott Skiles	.10	.05
197	Chris Webber	.60	.25
198	Checklist	.10	.05
199	Checklist	.10	.05
200	Checklist	.10	.05
201	Stacey Augmon	.10	.05
202	Mookie Blaylock	.15	.07
203	Grant Long	.10	.05
204	Ken Norman	.10	.05
205	Steve Smith	.15	.07
206	Spud Webb	.15	.07
207	Dana Barros	.10	.05
208	Rick Fox	.10	.05
209	Kendall Gill	.10	.05
210	Khalid Reeves	.10	.05
211	Glen Rice	.25	.11
212	Luc Longley	.10	.05
213	Dennis Rodman	1.50	.70
214	Dan Majerle	.10	.05
215	Tony Dumas	.10	.05
216	Tom Hammonds	.10	.05
217	Elmore Spencer	.10	.05
218	Otis Thorpe	.15	.07
219	B.J. Armstrong	.10	.05
220	Sam Cassell	.15	.07
221	Clyde Drexler	.30	.14
222	Mario Elie	.10	.05
223	Robert Horry	.10	.05
224	Hakeem Olajuwon	.50	.23
225	Kenny Smith	.10	.05
226	Antonio Davis	.10	.05
227	Eddie Johnson	.10	.05
228	Ricky Pierce	.10	.05
229	Eric Piatkowski	.10	.05
230	Rodney Rogers	.10	.05

		MINT	NRMT
☐ 231 Brian Williams	.10	.05
☐ 232 Corie Blount	.10	.05
☐ 233 George Lynch	.10	.05
☐ 234 Kevin Gamble	.10	.05
☐ 235 Alonzo Mourning	.25	.11
☐ 236 Eric Mobley	.10	.05
☐ 237 Terry Porter	.10	.05
☐ 238 Micheal Williams	.10	.05
☐ 239 Kevin Edwards	.10	.05
☐ 240 Vern Fleming	.10	.05
☐ 241 Charlie Ward	.10	.05
☐ 242 Jon Koncak	.10	.05
☐ 243 Richard Dumas	.10	.05
☐ 244 Jeff Malone	.10	.05
☐ 245 Vernon Maxwell	.10	.05
☐ 246 John Williams	.10	.05
☐ 247 Harvey Grant	.10	.05
☐ 248 Dontonio Wingfield	.10	.05
☐ 249 Tyrone Corbin	.10	.05
☐ 250 Sarunas Marciulionis	.10	.05
☐ 251 Will Perdue	.10	.05
☐ 252 Hersey Hawkins	.15	.07
☐ 253 Ervin Johnson	.10	.05
☐ 254 Shawn Kemp	.75	.35
☐ 255 Gary Payton	.40	.18
☐ 256 Sam Perkins	.15	.07
☐ 257 Detlef Schrempf	.15	.07
☐ 258 Chris Morris	.10	.05
☐ 259 Robert Pack	.10	.05
☐ 260 Willie Anderson ET	.10	.05
☐ 261 Jimmy King ET	.10	.05
☐ 262 Oliver Miller ET	.10	.05
☐ 263 Tracy Murray ET	.10	.05
☐ 264 Ed Pinckney ET	.10	.05
☐ 265 Alvin Robertson ET	.10	.05
☐ 266 Carlos Rogers ET	.10	.05
☐ 267 John Salley ET	.10	.05
☐ 268 D.Stoudamire ET	.75	.35
☐ 269 Zan Tabak ET	.10	.05
☐ 270 Ashraf Amaya ET	.10	.05
☐ 271 Greg Anthony ET	.10	.05
☐ 272 Benoit Benjamin ET	.10	.05
☐ 273 Blue Edwards ET	.10	.05
☐ 274 Kenny Gattison ET	.10	.05
☐ 275 Antonio Harvey ET	.10	.05
☐ 276 Chris King ET	.10	.05
☐ 277 Lawrence Moten ET	.10	.05
☐ 278 Bryant Reeves ET	.25	.11
☐ 279 Byron Scott ET	.10	.05
☐ 280 Cory Alexander	.10	.05
☐ 281 Jerome Allen	.10	.05
☐ 282 Brent Barry	.25	.11
☐ 283 Mario Bennett	.10	.05
☐ 284 Travis Best	.15	.07
☐ 285 Junior Burrough	.10	.05
☐ 286 Jason Caffey	.25	.11
☐ 287 Randolph Childress	.10	.05
☐ 288 Sasha Danilovic	.10	.05
☐ 289 Mark Davis	.10	.05
☐ 290 Tyus Edney	.10	.05
☐ 291 Michael Finley	1.00	.45
☐ 292 Sherrell Ford	.10	.05
☐ 293 Kevin Garnett	3.00	1.35
☐ 294 Alan Henderson	.25	.11
☐ 295 Frankie King	.10	.05
☐ 296 Jimmy King	.10	.05
☐ 297 Donny Marshall	.10	.05
☐ 298 Antonio McDyess	1.25	.55
☐ 299 Loren Meyer	.10	.05
☐ 300 Lawrence Moten	.10	.05
☐ 301 Ed O'Bannon	.10	.05
☐ 302 Greg Ostertag	.10	.05
☐ 303 Cherokee Parks	.10	.05
☐ 304 Theo Ratliff	.25	.11
☐ 305 Bryant Reeves	.60	.25
☐ 306 Shawn Respert	.10	.05
☐ 307 Lou Roe	.10	.05
☐ 308 Arvydas Sabonis	.50	.23
☐ 309 Joe Smith	1.00	.45
☐ 310 Jerry Stackhouse	1.00	.45
☐ 311 D.Stoudamire	2.00	.90
☐ 312 Bob Sura	.15	.07
☐ 313 Kurt Thomas	.15	.07
☐ 314 Gary Trent	.10	.05
☐ 315 David Vaughn	.10	.05
☐ 316 Rasheed Wallace	.60	.25
☐ 317 Eric Williams	.15	.07
☐ 318 Corliss Williamson	.30	.14
☐ 319 George Zidek	.10	.05
☐ 320 Mookie Blaylock FF	.10	.05
☐ 321 Dino Radja FF	.10	.05
☐ 322 Larry Johnson FF	.10	.05
☐ 323 Michael Jordan FF	1.50	.70
☐ 324 Tyrone Hill FF	.10	.05
☐ 325 Jason Kidd FF	.30	.14
☐ 326 D.Mutombo FF	.10	.05
☐ 327 Grant Hill FF	.75	.35
☐ 328 Joe Smith FF	.40	.18
☐ 329 Hakeem Olajuwon FF	.25	.11
☐ 330 Reggie Miller FF	.15	.07
☐ 331 Loy Vaught FF	.10	.05
☐ 332 Nick Van Exel FF	.15	.07
☐ 333 Alonzo Mourning FF	.15	.07
☐ 334 Glenn Robinson FF	.25	.11
☐ 335 Kevin Garnett FF	1.25	.55
☐ 336 Kenny Anderson FF	.10	.05
☐ 337 Patrick Ewing FF	.15	.07
☐ 338 Shaquille O'Neal FF	.50	.23
☐ 339 Jerry Stackhouse FF	.40	.18
☐ 340 Charles Barkley FF	.25	.11
☐ 341 Clifford Robinson FF	.10	.05
☐ 342 Mitch Richmond FF	.15	.07
☐ 343 David Robinson FF	.25	.11
☐ 344 Shawn Kemp FF	.40	.18
☐ 345 D.Stoudamire FF	.75	.35
☐ 346 Karl Malone FF	.25	.11
☐ 347 Bryant Reeves FF	.25	.11
☐ 348 Chris Webber FF	.30	.14
☐ 349 Checklist (201-319)	.10	.05
☐ 350 Checklist (320-350/ins.)	.10	.05

1995-96 Fleer All-Stars

Randomly inserted in all first series packs at an approximate rate of one in three, these thirteen dual-player, double-sided standard-size cards feature members of the 1994-95 Eastern and Western Conference All-Star squads. Only All-Star MVP Mitch Richmond is given his own card. Both sides have a full-color action photo taken at the All-Star game with the West having a purple background and the East a green background. The bottoms have the Phoenix All-Star Weekend insignia with the player's name and conference in gold-foil. The cards are numbered "X of 13."

	MINT	NRMT
COMPLETE SET (13)	6.00	2.70
COMMON CARD (1-13)	.25	.11
SEMISTARS	.30	.14
UNLISTED STARS	.60	.25
SER.1 STATED ODDS 1:3 HOBBY/RETAIL		

		MINT	NRMT
☐ 1 Grant Hill	2.00	.90
Charles Barkley		
☐ 2 Scottie Pippen	1.50	.70
Shawn Kemp		
☐ 3 Shaquille O'Neal	1.50	.70
Hakeem Olajuwon		
☐ 4 A.Hardaway	1.25	.55
Dan Majerle		
☐ 5 Reggie Miller	.30	.14
Latrell Sprewell		
☐ 6 Vin Baker	.75	.35
Cedric Ceballos		
☐ 7 Tyrone Hill	.30	.14
Karl Malone		
☐ 8 Larry Johnson	.25	.11
Detlef Schrempf		
☐ 9 Patrick Ewing	.60	.25
David Robinson		
☐ 10 Alonzo Mourning	.60	.25
D.Mutombo		
☐ 11 Dana Barros	.30	.14
Gary Payton		
☐ 12 Joe Dumars	.60	.25
John Stockton		
☐ 13 M.Richmond AS MVP	.60	.25

1995-96 Fleer Class Encounters

Randomly inserted in all second series packs at a rate of one in two, this 40-card standard-size set highlights the first 20 players of the 1995 draft and 20 of the most sucessful players from the 1994 draft. Full-bleed fronts have gold foil printing and one full-color action shot as the main background. Three head shots of the original appear in increasing size on the right side. Horizontal backs have a white-bordered, off-center head shot with a player profile printed in black type on a red background. Each group of cards is sequenced in alphabetical order.

	MINT	NRMT
COMPLETE SET (40)	25.00	11.00
COMMON CARD (1-40)	.25	.11
SEMISTARS	.40	.18

UNLISTED STARS .75 .35
SER.2 STATED ODDS 1:2 HOBBY/RETAIL

		MINT	NRMT
☐ 1	Derrick Alston	.25	.11
☐ 2	Brian Grant	.40	.18
☐ 3	Grant Hill	5.00	2.20
☐ 4	Juwan Howard	1.25	.55
☐ 5	Eddie Jones	2.00	.90
☐ 6	Jason Kidd	2.00	.90
☐ 7	Donyell Marshall	.40	.18
☐ 8	Anthony Miller	.25	.11
☐ 9	Eric Mobley	.25	.11
☐ 10	Eric Montross	.25	.11
☐ 11	Lamond Murray	.25	.11
☐ 12	Wesley Person	.40	.18
☐ 13	Eric Piatkowski	.25	.11
☐ 14	Khalid Reeves	.25	.11
☐ 15	Glenn Robinson	1.00	.45
☐ 16	Carlos Rogers	.25	.11
☐ 17	Jalen Rose	.40	.18
☐ 18	Clifford Rozier	.25	.11
☐ 19	Michael Smith	.25	.11
☐ 20	Sharone Wright	.25	.11
☐ 21	Brent Barry	.75	.35
☐ 22	Jason Caffey	.75	.35
☐ 23	Randolph Childress	.25	.11
☐ 24	Kevin Garnett	6.00	2.70
☐ 25	Alan Henderson	.75	.35
☐ 26	Antonio McDyess	2.50	1.10
☐ 27	Ed O'Bannon	.25	.11
☐ 28	Cherokee Parks	.25	.11
☐ 29	Theo Ratliff	.75	.35
☐ 30	Bryant Reeves	1.25	.55
☐ 31	Shawn Respert	.25	.11
☐ 32	Joe Smith	2.00	.90
☐ 33	Jerry Stackhouse	2.00	.90
☐ 34	D.Stoudamire	4.00	1.80
☐ 35	Bob Sura	.40	.18
☐ 36	Kurt Thomas	.40	.18
☐ 37	Gary Trent	.25	.11
☐ 38	Rasheed Wallace	1.25	.55
☐ 39	Eric Williams	.40	.18
☐ 40	Corliss Williamson	.75	.35

1995-96 Fleer Double Doubles

Randomly inserted in all first series packs at an approximate rate of one in three, these 12 cards feature players who averaged double figures per game in two statistical categories during the 1994-95 season. Full-bleed fronts features the player in two, split-shot color action photos separated by the words "Double Double" which are printed in the player's team colors. The player is again featured in full-color on the back with a career synopsis and '94-95 stats printed in black type. The set is sequenced in alphabetical order.

		MINT	NRMT
COMPLETE SET (12)		6.00	2.70
COMMON CARD (1-12)		.25	.11
SEMISTARS		.40	.18
UNLISTED STARS		.50	.23
SER.1 STATED ODDS 1:3 HOBBY/RETAIL			
☐ 1	Vin Baker	1.00	.45
☐ 2	Vlade Divac	.40	.18
☐ 3	Patrick Ewing	.50	.23
☐ 4	Tyrone Hill	.25	.11
☐ 5	Popeye Jones	.25	.11
☐ 6	Shawn Kemp	1.50	.70
☐ 7	Karl Malone	.75	.35
☐ 8	D.Mutombo	.40	.18
☐ 9	Hakeem Olajuwon	1.00	.45
☐ 10	Shaquille O'Neal	2.00	.90
☐ 11	David Robinson	.75	.35
☐ 12	John Stockton	.50	.23

1995-96 Fleer End to End

Randomly inserted in all second series packs at a rate of one in four, cards from this 20-card set focus on the NBA's leaders at both ends of the court. Borderless, horizontal fronts are split between two panels, one having a blue background with "End to End" in repeating print, and the other with a full-color action player shot. A player cutout is placed in the middle of the two panels. Horizontal backs have a full-color action cutout and a player profile.

		MINT	NRMT
COMPLETE SET (20)		25.00	11.00
COMMON CARD (1-20)		.25	.11
SEMISTARS		.40	.18
UNLISTED STARS		.75	.35
SER.2 STATED ODDS 1:4 HOBBY/RETAIL			
☐ 1	Mookie Blaylock	.40	.18
☐ 2	Vlade Divac	.40	.18
☐ 3	Clyde Drexler	1.00	.45
☐ 4	Patrick Ewing	.75	.35
☐ 5	Horace Grant	.25	.11
☐ 6	A.Hardaway	3.00	1.35
☐ 7	Grant Hill	5.00	2.20
☐ 8	Eddie Jones	2.00	.90
☐ 9	Michael Jordan	10.00	4.50
☐ 10	Jason Kidd	2.00	.90
☐ 11	Alonzo Mourning	.75	.35
☐ 12	D.Mutombo	.40	.18
☐ 13	Hakeem Olajuwon	1.50	.70
☐ 14	Shaquille O'Neal	3.00	1.35
☐ 15	Gary Payton	1.25	.55
☐ 16	Scottie Pippen	2.50	1.10
☐ 17	David Robinson	1.25	.55
☐ 18	Latrell Sprewell	.40	.18
☐ 19	John Stockton	.75	.35
☐ 20	Rod Strickland	.40	.18

1995-96 Fleer Flair Hardwood Leaders

Issued one per pack in all first series packs, these 27 super-premium, double-thick Flair style standard-size cards feature each team's statistical leader or award winner from the 1994-95 season. The fronts have a color action photo with the key as the background. The backs have a color photo with a hardwood background and player information. The entire 27-card set was also issued as a commemorative sheet most notably distributed as a wrapper redemption at the San Antonio All-Star Jam Session show. The set is sequenced in alphabetical order by team.

		MINT	NRMT
COMPLETE SET (27)		20.00	9.00
COMMON CARD (1-27)		.25	.11
SEMISTARS		.40	.18
UNLISTED STARS		.60	.25
ONE PER SER.1 PACK			
☐ 1	Mookie Blaylock	.40	.18
☐ 2	Dominique Wilkins	.60	.25
☐ 3	Alonzo Mourning	.60	.25
☐ 4	Michael Jordan	8.00	3.60
☐ 5	Mark Price	.25	.11
☐ 6	Jim Jackson	.40	.18
☐ 7	D.Mutombo	.40	.18
☐ 8	Grant Hill	4.00	1.80
☐ 9	Tim Hardaway	.75	.35
☐ 10	Hakeem Olajuwon	1.25	.55
☐ 11	Reggie Miller	.60	.25
☐ 12	Loy Vaught	.25	.11
☐ 13	Cedric Ceballos	.25	.11
☐ 14	Glen Rice	.60	.25
☐ 15	Glenn Robinson	.75	.35
☐ 16	Christian Laettner	.40	.18

		MINT	NRMT
☐ 17	Derrick Coleman	.40	.18
☐ 18	Patrick Ewing	.60	.25
☐ 19	Shaquille O'Neal	2.50	1.10
☐ 20	Dana Barros	.25	.11
☐ 21	Charles Barkley	1.00	.45
☐ 22	Clifford Robinson	.25	.11
☐ 23	Mitch Richmond	.60	.25
☐ 24	David Robinson	1.00	.45
☐ 25	Gary Payton	1.00	.45
☐ 26	Karl Malone	1.00	.45
☐ 27	Chris Webber	1.50	.70

1995-96 Fleer Franchise Futures

Randomly inserted into all first series packs at an approximate rate of one in 37, these nine etched-foil standard-size cards feature a selection of the game's hottest young stars. The fronts have a full-color action photo with a huge basketball and fire underneath it in the background. The backs have a color photo with a similar yet less snazzy version of the front background. The set is sequenced in alphabetical order.

	MINT	NRMT
COMPLETE SET (9)	40.00	18.00
COMMON CARD (1-9)	1.50	.70
SEMISTARS	2.00	.90
UNLISTED STARS	3.00	1.35
SER.1 STATED ODDS 1:37 HOBBY/RETAIL		

		MINT	NRMT
☐ 1	Vin Baker	6.00	2.70
☐ 2	A.Hardaway	12.00	5.50
☐ 3	Jim Jackson	1.50	.70
☐ 4	Jamal Mashburn	2.00	.90
☐ 5	Alonzo Mourning	3.00	1.35
☐ 6	D.Mutombo	2.00	.90
☐ 7	Shaquille O'Neal	12.00	5.50
☐ 8	Nick Van Exel	3.00	1.35
☐ 9	Chris Webber	8.00	3.60

1995-96 Fleer Rookie Phenoms

The 10 cards in this set were randomly inserted in second series hobby packs at a rate of one in 24 and highlight the play of the NBA's best rook-

ies. Borderless fronts are gold and silver foil finished with a full-color action cutout. Backs carry an extreme vertical color shot on the left and a player profile on the right.

	MINT	NRMT
COMPLETE SET (10)	60.00	27.00
COMMON CARD (1-10)	1.00	.45
SER.2 STATED ODDS 1:24 HOBBY		
COMP.HOT PACK SET (10)	20.00	9.00
HP CARDS: 33% VALUE		
HP: SER.2 STATED ODDS 1:72 HOBBY		

		MINT	NRMT
☐ 1	Kevin Garnett	25.00	11.00
☐ 2	Antonio McDyess	8.00	3.60
☐ 3	Ed O'Bannon	1.00	.45
☐ 4	Bryant Reeves	4.00	1.80
☐ 5	Shawn Respert	1.00	.45
☐ 6	Joe Smith	6.00	2.70
☐ 7	Jerry Stackhouse	6.00	2.70
☐ 8	D.Stoudamire	12.00	5.50
☐ 9	Gary Trent	1.00	.45
☐ 10	Rasheed Wallace	4.00	1.80

1995-96 Fleer Rookie Sensations

Randomly inserted exclusively into first series 17-card retail pre-priced packs at an approximate rate of one in five, these 15 cards spotlight the top rookies from the 1994-95 season. The fronts have a full-color action photo with the words "Rookie Sensation" in gold-foil around a basketball. The backs have a full-color photo with play-

er information at the bottom in a yellow haze.

	MINT	NRMT
COMPLETE SET (15)	25.00	11.00
COMMON CARD (1-15)	.75	.35
SEMISTARS	1.50	.70
UNLISTED STARS	2.50	1.10
SER.1 STATED ODDS 1:5 CELLO		

		MINT	NRMT
☐ 1	Brian Grant	1.50	.70
☐ 2	Grant Hill	15.00	6.75
☐ 3	Juwan Howard	4.00	1.80
☐ 4	Eddie Jones	6.00	2.70
☐ 5	Jason Kidd	6.00	2.70
☐ 6	Donyell Marshall	1.50	.70
☐ 7	Eric Montross	.75	.35
☐ 8	Lamond Murray	.75	.35
☐ 9	Wesley Person	1.50	.70
☐ 10	Khalid Reeves	.75	.35
☐ 11	Glenn Robinson	3.00	1.35
☐ 12	Jalen Rose	1.50	.70
☐ 13	Clifford Rozier	.75	.35
☐ 14	Michael Smith	.75	.35
☐ 15	Sharone Wright	.75	.35

1995-96 Fleer Stackhouse's Scrapbook

Randomly inserted into all second series packs at a rate one in every 24, these two cards represent the first part of a multi-series, eight-card, cross-brand set devoted to Fleer spokesperson Jerry Stackhouse.

	MINT	NRMT
COMPLETE SET (8)	30.00	13.50
COMP.FLEER SER.1 (2)	4.00	1.80
COMP.ULTRA SER.2 (2)	4.00	1.80
COMP.FLAIR SER.3 (2)	15.00	6.75
COMP.METAL SER.4 (2)	10.00	4.50
COMMON FLEER (S1-S2)	2.50	1.10
COMMON ULTRA (S3-S4)	3.00	1.35
COMMON FLAIR (S5-S6)	8.00	3.60
COMMON METAL (S7-S8)	4.00	1.80
SER.2 STATED ODDS 1:24 FLEER PRODUCTS		

		MINT	NRMT
☐ S1	Jerry Stackhouse	2.50	1.10
☐ S2	Jerry Stackhouse	2.50	1.10

1995-96 Fleer Total D

Randomly inserted into first series 11-card hobby and retail

packs at an approximate rate of one in five, these 12 standard-size cards feature a selection of the NBA's top defenders. The fronts have a color-action photo with the player's name and "Total D" on the side in gold-foil. The horizontal backs are split between a color action player photo on the left and a player profile printed in white and set against a gradated color background on the right. The set is sequenced in alphabetical order.

	MINT	NRMT
COMPLETE SET (12)	15.00	6.75
COMMON CARD (1-12)	.25	.11
SEMISTARS	.40	.18
UNLISTED STARS	.60	.25
SER.1 STATED ODDS 1:5 HOBBY/RETAIL		

		MINT	NRMT
☐ 1	Mookie Blaylock	.25	.11
☐ 2	Patrick Ewing	.60	.25
☐ 3	Michael Jordan	8.00	3.60
☐ 4	Alonzo Mourning	.60	.25
☐ 5	D.Mutombo	.40	.18
☐ 6	Hakeem Olajuwon	1.25	.55
☐ 7	Shaquille O'Neal	2.50	1.10
☐ 8	Gary Payton	1.00	.45
☐ 9	Scottie Pippen	2.00	.90
☐ 10	David Robinson	1.00	.45
☐ 11	Dennis Rodman	2.50	1.10
☐ 12	John Stockton	.60	.25

1995-96 Fleer Total O

Randomly inserted in second series retail packs only at a rate of one in 12, cards from this 10-card standard-size set spotlight the NBA's offensive talent. Borderless fronts capture the player in a full-color action cutout with two red foil rings surrounding the image. All are on a backdrop of a basketball in the hands of a shooter and "Total O" is printed in silver foil on the ball. Backs are split between a full-color action player shot and a colored rock background containing a player profile printed in white type.

	MINT	NRMT
COMPLETE SET (10)	40.00	18.00
COMMON CARD (1-10)	.75	.35
SEMISTARS	1.00	.45
UNLISTED STARS	1.50	.70
COMP.HOT PACK SET (10)	25.00	11.00
HP CARDS: 66% VALUE		
HP: SER.2 STATED ODDS 1:72 RETAIL		

		MINT	NRMT
☐ 1	Grant Hill	10.00	4.50
☐ 2	Michael Jordan	25.00	11.00
☐ 3	Jamal Mashburn	.75	.35
☐ 4	Reggie Miller	1.50	.70
☐ 5	Hakeem Olajuwon	3.00	1.35
☐ 6	Shaquille O'Neal	6.00	2.70
☐ 7	Mitch Richmond	1.50	.70
☐ 8	David Robinson	2.50	1.10
☐ 9	Glenn Robinson	2.00	.90
☐ 10	Jerry Stackhouse	3.00	1.35

1995-96 Fleer Towers of Power

The big "Earth Shakers" of the NBA are represented in this 10-card set. Cards were randomly inserted into one in every 54 second series packs. Borderless fronts have etched copper foil designs and a full-color action player cutout. Backs are a three-tone color screen with a one-color action shot near the top right. A player profile appears in black type on the bottom half.

	MINT	NRMT
COMPLETE SET (10)	80.00	36.00
COMMON CARD (1-10)	5.00	2.20
SER.2 STATED ODDS 1:54 HOBBY/RETAIL		

		MINT	NRMT
☐ 1	Shawn Kemp	15.00	6.75
☐ 2	Karl Malone	8.00	3.60
☐ 3	Antonio McDyess	12.00	5.50
☐ 4	Alonzo Mourning	5.00	2.20
☐ 5	Hakeem Olajuwon	10.00	4.50
☐ 6	Shaquille O'Neal	20.00	9.00
☐ 7	David Robinson	8.00	3.60
☐ 8	Glenn Robinson	6.00	2.70
☐ 9	Joe Smith	10.00	4.50
☐ 10	Chris Webber	12.00	5.50

1996-97 Fleer

The 1996-97 Fleer set was issued in two series totalling 300 cards. Both series had 150 cards issued in 11-card packs carrying a suggested retail price of $1.49 each. Card fronts contain a full-bleed photo with the player's last name in ghosted white letters and their first name in gold foil laid over it. The player's team name is also in gold foil under the player's first name. Card backs are horizontal with the team colors setting the background along with a basketball and the team logo. A photo of the player is provided along with statistical and biographical information. Cards are sequenced alphabetically within team order. The only subset is Hardwood Leaders (120-148). No Rookie Cards are featured in the first series. Card #83 (Jerry Stackhouse) was also used for promotional purposes.

	MINT	NRMT
COMPLETE SET (300)	35.00	16.00
COMPLETE SERIES 1 (150)	15.00	6.75
COMPLETE SERIES 2 (150)	20.00	9.00
COMMON CARD (1-300)	.10	.05
SEMISTARS	.15	.07
UNLISTED STARS	.25	.11

		MINT	NRMT
☐ 1	Stacey Augmon	.10	.05
☐ 2	Mookie Blaylock	.15	.07
☐ 3	Christian Laettner	.15	.07
☐ 4	Grant Long	.10	.05
☐ 5	Steve Smith	.15	.07
☐ 6	Rick Fox	.10	.05
☐ 7	Dino Radja	.10	.05
☐ 8	Eric Williams	.10	.05
☐ 9	Kenny Anderson	.15	.07
☐ 10	Dell Curry	.10	.05
☐ 11	Larry Johnson	.15	.07
☐ 12	Glen Rice	.25	.11

#	Player			#	Player			#	Player		
13	Michael Jordan	3.00	1.35	99	Avery Johnson	.10	.05	185	B.J. Armstrong	.10	.05
14	Toni Kukoc	.15	.07	100	David Robinson	.40	.18	186	Todd Fuller	.10	.05
15	Scottie Pippen	.75	.35	101	Hersey Hawkins	.15	.07	187	Ray Owes	.10	.05
16	Dennis Rodman	1.00	.45	102	Shawn Kemp	.75	.35	188	Mark Price	.10	.05
17	Terrell Brandon	.25	.11	103	Gary Payton	.30	.14	189	Felton Spencer	.10	.05
18	Chris Mills	.10	.05	104	Detlef Schrempf	.15	.07	190	Charles Barkley	.40	.18
19	Bobby Phills	.05	.05	105	Oliver Miller	.10	.05	191	Mario Elie	.10	.05
20	Bob Sura	.10	.05	106	Tracy Murray	.10	.05	192	Othella Harrington	.15	.07
21	Jim Jackson	.15	.07	107	D.Stoudamire	.60	.25	193	Matt Maloney	.40	.18
22	Jason Kidd	.50	.23	108	Sharone Wright	.10	.05	194	Brent Price	.10	.05
23	Jamal Mashburn	.15	.07	109	Jeff Hornacek	.15	.07	195	Kevin Willis	.10	.05
24	George McCloud	.10	.05	110	Karl Malone	.40	.18	196	Travis Best	.10	.05
25	M.Abdul-Rauf	.10	.05	111	John Stockton	.25	.11	197	Erick Dampier	.30	.14
26	Antonio McDyess	.40	.18	112	Greg Anthony	.10	.05	198	Antonio Davis	.10	.05
27	D.Mutombo	.15	.07	113	Bryant Reeves	.15	.07	199	Jalen Rose	.10	.05
28	Jalen Rose	.10	.05	114	Byron Scott	.15	.07	200	Pooh Richardson	.10	.05
29	Bryant Stith	.10	.05	115	Calbert Cheaney	.10	.05	201	Rodney Rogers	.10	.05
30	Joe Dumars	.25	.11	116	Juwan Howard	.25	.11	202	Lorenzen Wright	.30	.14
31	Grant Hill	1.50	.70	117	Gheorghe Muresan	.10	.05	203	Kobe Bryant	5.00	2.20
32	Allan Houston	.15	.07	118	Rasheed Wallace	.15	.07	204	Derek Fisher	.30	.14
33	Theo Ratliff	.10	.05	119	Chris Webber	.60	.25	205	Travis Knight	.10	.05
34	Otis Thorpe	.15	.07	120	Mookie Blaylock HL	.10	.05	206	Shaquille O'Neal	1.00	.45
35	Chris Mullin	.25	.11	121	Dino Radja HL	.10	.05	207	Byron Scott	.15	.07
36	Joe Smith	.30	.14	122	Larry Johnson HL	.10	.05	208	P.J. Brown	.10	.05
37	Latrell Sprewell	.15	.07	123	Michael Jordan HL	1.50	.70	209	Sasha Danilovic	.10	.05
38	Kevin Willis	.10	.05	124	Terrell Brandon HL	.15	.07	210	Dan Majerle	.15	.07
39	Sam Cassell	.15	.07	125	Jason Kidd HL	.25	.11	211	Martin Muursepp	.10	.05
40	Clyde Drexler	.30	.14	126	Antonio McDyess HL	.25	.11	212	Ray Allen	.75	.35
41	Robert Horry	.15	.07	127	Grant Hill HL	.75	.35	213	Armon Gilliam	.10	.05
42	Hakeem Olajuwon	.50	.23	128	Latrell Sprewell HL	.10	.05	214	Andrew Lang	.10	.05
43	Dale Davis	.10	.05	129	Hakeem Olajuwon HL	.25	.11	215	Moochie Norris	.10	.05
44	Mark Jackson	.10	.05	130	Reggie Miller HL	.15	.07	216	Kevin Garnett	1.50	.70
45	Derrick McKey	.10	.05	131	Loy Vaught HL	.10	.05	217	Tom Gugliotta	.25	.11
46	Reggie Miller	.25	.11	132	Cedric Ceballos HL	.10	.05	218	Shane Heal	.10	.05
47	Rik Smits	.15	.07	133	Alonzo Mourning HL	.15	.07	219	Stephon Marbury	2.50	1.10
48	Brent Barry	.10	.05	134	Vin Baker HL	.25	.11	220	Stojko Vrankovic	.10	.05
49	Malik Sealy	.10	.05	135	Isaiah Rider HL	.10	.05	221	Kerry Kittles	.60	.25
50	Loy Vaught	.15	.07	136	Armon Gilliam HL	.10	.05	222	Robert Pack	.10	.05
51	Brian Williams	.10	.05	137	Patrick Ewing HL	.15	.07	223	Jayson Williams	.15	.07
52	Elden Campbell	.15	.07	138	Shaquille O'Neal HL	.50	.23	224	Allan Houston	.15	.07
53	Cedric Ceballos	.10	.05	139	Jerry Stackhouse HL	.25	.11	225	Larry Johnson	.10	.05
54	Vlade Divac	.15	.07	140	Charles Barkley HL	.25	.11	226	Dontae' Jones	.10	.05
55	Eddie Jones	.50	.23	141	Clifford Robinson HL	.10	.05	227	Walter McCarty	.15	.07
56	Nick Van Exel	.25	.11	142	Mitch Richmond HL	.15	.07	228	John Wallace	.40	.18
57	Tim Hardaway	.30	.14	143	David Robinson HL	.25	.11	229	Charlie Ward	.10	.05
58	Alonzo Mourning	.25	.11	144	Shawn Kemp HL	.40	.18	230	Brian Evans	.10	.05
59	Kurt Thomas	.10	.05	145	D.Stoudamire HL	.30	.14	231	Amal McCaskill	.10	.05
60	Walt Williams	.10	.05	146	Karl Malone HL	.25	.11	232	Brian Shaw	.10	.05
61	Vin Baker	.50	.23	147	Bryant Reeves HL	.10	.05	233	Mark Davis	.10	.05
62	Sherman Douglas	.10	.05	148	Juwan Howard HL	.25	.11	234	Lucious Harris	.10	.05
63	Glenn Robinson	.25	.11	149	Checklist	.10	.05	235	Allen Iverson	2.50	1.10
64	Kevin Garnett	1.50	.70	150	Checklist	.10	.05	236	Sam Cassell	.15	.07
65	Tom Gugliotta	.25	.11	151	Alan Henderson	.10	.05	237	Robert Horry	.15	.07
66	Isaiah Rider	.15	.07	152	Priest Lauderdale	.10	.05	238	Danny Manning	.15	.07
67	Shawn Bradley	.10	.05	153	D.Mutombo	.15	.07	239	Steve Nash	.40	.18
68	Chris Childs	.10	.05	154	Dana Barros	.10	.05	240	Kenny Anderson	.15	.07
69	Armon Gilliam	.10	.05	155	Todd Day	.10	.05	241	Aleksandar Djordjevic	.10	.05
70	Ed O'Bannon	.10	.05	156	Brett Szabo	.10	.05	242	Jermaine O'Neal	.40	.18
71	Patrick Ewing	.25	.11	157	Antoine Walker	2.50	1.10	243	Isaiah Rider	.15	.07
72	Derek Harper	.10	.05	158	Scott Burrell	.10	.05	244	Rasheed Wallace	.15	.07
73	Anthony Mason	.15	.07	159	Tony Delk	.30	.14	245	M.Abdul-Rauf	.10	.05
74	Charles Oakley	.10	.05	160	Vlade Divac	.15	.07	246	Michael Smith	.10	.05
75	John Starks	.15	.07	161	Matt Geiger	.10	.05	247	Corliss Williamson	.15	.07
76	Nick Anderson	.10	.05	162	Anthony Mason	.15	.07	248	Vernon Maxwell	.10	.05
77	Horace Grant	.15	.07	163	Malik Rose	.10	.05	249	Charles Smith	.10	.05
78	A.Hardaway	1.00	.45	164	Ron Harper	.15	.07	250	Dominique Wilkins	.25	.11
79	Shaquille O'Neal	1.00	.45	165	Scott Kerr	.10	.05	251	Craig Ehlo	.10	.05
80	Dennis Scott	.10	.05	166	Luc Longley	.10	.05	252	Jim McIlvaine	.10	.05
81	Derrick Coleman	.10	.05	167	Danny Ferry	.10	.05	253	Sam Perkins	.15	.07
82	Vernon Maxwell	.10	.05	168	Tyrone Hill	.10	.05	254	Marcus Camby	.60	.25
83	Jerry Stackhouse	.30	.14	169	Vitaly Potapenko	.15	.07	255	Popeye Jones	.10	.05
84	C.Weatherspoon	.10	.05	170	Tony Dumas	.10	.05	256	Donald Whiteside	.10	.05
85	Charles Barkley	.40	.18	171	Chris Gatling	.10	.05	257	Walt Williams	.10	.05
86	Michael Finley	.30	.14	172	Oliver Miller	.10	.05	258	Jeff Hornacek	.15	.07
87	Kevin Johnson	.15	.07	173	Eric Montross	.10	.05	259	Karl Malone	.40	.18
88	Wesley Person	.10	.05	174	Samaki Walker	.30	.14	260	Bryon Russell	.10	.05
89	Clifford Robinson	.10	.05	175	Darvin Ham	.10	.05	261	John Stockton	.25	.11
90	Arvydas Sabonis	.15	.07	176	Mark Jackson	.10	.05	262	S.Abdur-Rahim	1.50	.70
91	Rod Strickland	.10	.05	177	Ervin Johnson	.10	.05	263	Anthony Peeler	.10	.05
92	Gary Trent	.10	.05	178	Stacey Augmon	.10	.05	264	Roy Rogers	.10	.05
93	Tyus Edney	.10	.05	179	Joe Dumars	.25	.11	265	Tim Legler	.10	.05
94	Brian Grant	.10	.05	180	Grant Hill	1.50	.70	266	Tracy Murray	.10	.05
95	Billy Owens	.10	.05	181	Grant Long	.10	.05	267	Rod Strickland	.10	.05
96	Mitch Richmond	.25	.11	182	Terry Mills	.10	.05	268	Ben Wallace	.10	.05
97	Vinny Del Negro	.10	.05	183	Otis Thorpe	.15	.07	269	Kevin Garnett CB	.75	.35
98	Sean Elliott	.10	.05	184	Jerome Williams	.15	.07	270	Allan Houston CB	.10	.05

		MINT	NRMT
☐ 271	Eddie Jones CB	.25	.11
☐ 272	Jamal Mashburn CB	.10	.05
☐ 273	Antonio McDyess CB	.25	.11
☐ 274	Glenn Robinson CB	.15	.07
☐ 275	Joe Smith CB	.25	.11
☐ 276	Steve Smith CB	.10	.05
☐ 277	Jerry Stackhouse CB	.25	.11
☐ 278	D.Stoudamire CB	.30	.14
☐ 279	Hakeem Olajuwon AS	.25	.11
☐ 280	Charles Barkley AS	.25	.11
☐ 281	Patrick Ewing AS	.15	.07
☐ 282	Michael Jordan AS	1.50	.70
☐ 283	Clyde Drexler AS	.25	.11
☐ 284	Karl Malone AS	.25	.11
☐ 285	John Stockton AS	.15	.07
☐ 286	David Robinson AS	.25	.11
☐ 287	Scottie Pippen AS	.40	.18
☐ 288	Shawn Kemp AS	.40	.18
☐ 289	Shaquille O'Neal AS	.50	.23
☐ 290	Mitch Richmond AS	.15	.07
☐ 291	Reggie Miller AS	.15	.07
☐ 292	Alonzo Mourning AS	.15	.07
☐ 293	Gary Payton AS	.25	.11
☐ 294	A.Hardaway AS	.50	.23
☐ 295	Grant Hill AS	.75	.35
☐ 296	Dennis Rodman AS	.50	.23
☐ 297	Juwan Howard AS	.25	.11
☐ 298	Jason Kidd AS	.25	.11
☐ 299	Checklist	.10	.05
☐ 300	Checklist	.10	.05

1996-97 Fleer Decade of Excellence

Randomly inserted exclusively into both series hobby packs at a rate of one in 72, this 20-card set features reprints from the popular 1986-87 debut Fleer set. Card fronts are designated with the card name "Fleer Decade of Excellence 1986-1996" in gold foil to distinguish the card from the original issue. Card backs are identical to the 1986-87 release, but with a "1996" copyright.

		MINT	NRMT
COMPLETE SET (20)		180.00	80.00
COMPLETE SERIES 1 (10)		120.00	55.00
COMPLETE SERIES 2 (10)		60.00	27.00
COMMON CARD (1-20)		5.00	2.20
SEMISTARS		8.00	3.60
SER.1/2 STATED ODDS 1:72 HOBBY			
☐ 1	Clyde Drexler	10.00	4.50
☐ 2	Joe Dumars	5.00	2.20
☐ 3	Derek Harper	5.00	2.20
☐ 4	Michael Jordan	80.00	36.00

		MINT	NRMT
☐ 5	Karl Malone	12.00	5.50
☐ 6	Chris Mullin	5.00	2.20
☐ 7	Charles Oakley	5.00	2.20
☐ 8	Sam Perkins	5.00	2.20
☐ 9	Ricky Pierce	5.00	2.20
☐ 10	Buck Williams	5.00	2.20
☐ 11	Charles Barkley	12.00	5.50
☐ 12	Patrick Ewing	8.00	3.60
☐ 13	Eddie Johnson	5.00	2.20
☐ 14	Hakeem Olajuwon	15.00	6.75
☐ 15	Robert Parish	5.00	2.20
☐ 16	Byron Scott	5.00	2.20
☐ 17	Wayman Tisdale	5.00	2.20
☐ 18	Gerald Wilkins	5.00	2.20
☐ 19	Herb Williams	5.00	2.20
☐ 20	Kevin Willis	5.00	2.20

1996-97 Fleer Franchise Futures

Randomly inserted exclusively into first series hobby packs at a rate of one in 54, this 10-card set features young stars that may be the future of their respecive teams. Card fronts feature an embossed photo with the card name "Franchise Future" running along the left side of the card in silver foil. The player's name is also treated with silver foil at the bottom of the card. Card backs feature a brief commentary on the player and are numbered "X of 10".

		MINT	NRMT
COMPLETE SET (10)		25.00	11.00
COMMON CARD (1-10)		1.25	.55
SER.1 STATED ODDS 1:54 HOBBY			
☐ 1	Kevin Garnett	8.00	3.60
☐ 2	A.Hardaway	5.00	2.20
☐ 3	Grant Hill	8.00	3.60
☐ 4	Juwan Howard	1.50	.70
☐ 5	Jason Kidd	2.50	1.10
☐ 6	Antonio McDyess	2.00	.90
☐ 7	Glenn Robinson	1.25	.55
☐ 8	Joe Smith	1.50	.70
☐ 9	Jerry Stackhouse	1.50	.70
☐ 10	D.Stoudamire	3.00	1.35

1996-97 Fleer Game Breakers

Randomly inserted exclusively into first series retail packs at a rate of one in 48, this 15-card set features some of the top duos from the NBA. The card fronts are made of plastic and feature color action shots of both player's represented. Both player's last names are in gold foil at the bottom under the Game Breakers card name. Card backs feature a background of the team's colors with a brief commentary on each individual player and are numbered "X of 15".

		MINT	NRMT
COMPLETE SET (15)		250.00	110.00
COMMON PAIR (1-15)		5.00	2.20
SER.1 STATED ODDS 1:48 RETAIL			
☐ 1	Michael Jordan Scottie Pippen	100.00	45.00
☐ 2	Jim Jackson Jason Kidd	10.00	4.50
☐ 3	Grant Hill Allan Houston	30.00	13.50
☐ 4	Joe Smith Latrell Sprewell	5.00	2.20
☐ 5	Clyde Drexler Hakeem Olajuwon	15.00	6.75
☐ 6	Cedric Ceballos Nick Van Exel	5.00	2.20
☐ 7	Tim Hardaway Alonzo Mourning	10.00	4.50
☐ 8	Vin Baker Glenn Robinson	12.00	5.50
☐ 9	Kevin Garnett Isaiah Rider	25.00	11.00
☐ 10	A.Hardaway Shaquille O'Neal	30.00	13.50
☐ 11	Jerry Stackhouse C.Weatherspoon	5.00	2.20
☐ 12	Charles Barkley Michael Finley	12.00	5.50
☐ 13	Sean Elliott David Robinson	8.00	3.60
☐ 14	Shawn Kemp Gary Payton	20.00	9.00
☐ 15	Karl Malone John Stockton	12.00	5.50

1996-97 Fleer Lucky 13

Randomly inserted into all first series packs at a rate of one in 30, this 13-card set features cards that are redeemable for the top 13 player's selected in the 1996 NBA Draft. Card fronts

contain a colorful background with a number from 1-13. Whatever card number is on the front corresponds to the rookie selected at that spot in the 1996 NBA draft and can be redeemed for a special card featuring that player. The expiration date for this redemption is April 1, 1997. Cards are numbered on the back as "X of 13".

	MINT	NRMT
COMPLETE SET (13)	70.00	32.00
COMMON CARD (1-13)	1.25	.55
SEMISTARS	1.50	.70
UNLISTED STARS	2.50	1.10
EXCH.CARDS: SER.1 STATED ODDS 1:30		

		MINT	NRMT
☐ 1	Allen Iverson	12.00	5.50
☐ 2	Marcus Camby	3.00	1.35
☐ 3	S.Abdur-Rahim	8.00	3.60
☐ 4	Stephon Marbury	12.00	5.50
☐ 5	Ray Allen	4.00	1.80
☐ 6	Antoine Walker	12.00	5.50
☐ 7	Lorenzen Wright	2.50	1.10
☐ 8	Kerry Kittles	3.00	1.35
☐ 9	Samaki Walker	2.50	1.10
☐ 10	Erick Dampier	2.50	1.10
☐ 11	Todd Fuller	1.25	.55
☐ 12	Vitaly Potapenko	1.50	.70
☐ 13	Kobe Bryant	25.00	11.00
☐ NNO	Expired Trade Cards	.50	.23

1996-97 Fleer Rookie Rewind

Randomly inserted in all first series packs at a rate of one in 24, this 15-card set takes a look back at the top rookies from the 1995-96 class. Card fronts con-

tain team colors in the background with both the card name "Rookie Rewind" and the player's last name treated in gold foil. Card backs contain another player shot and a brief commentary. Card backs are numbered as "X of 15".

	MINT	NRMT
COMPLETE SET (15)	30.00	13.50
COMMON CARD (1-15)	1.00	.45
SEMISTARS	1.50	.70
UNLISTED STARS	2.50	1.10
SER.1 STATED ODDS 1:24 HOBBY/RETAIL		

		MINT	NRMT
☐ 1	Brent Barry	1.00	.45
☐ 2	Tyus Edney	1.00	.45
☐ 3	Michael Finley	3.00	1.35
☐ 4	Kevin Garnett	15.00	6.75
☐ 5	Antonio McDyess	4.00	1.80
☐ 6	Bryant Reeves	1.50	.70
☐ 7	Arvydas Sabonis	1.50	.70
☐ 8	Joe Smith	3.00	1.35
☐ 9	Jerry Stackhouse	3.00	1.35
☐ 10	D.Stoudamire	6.00	2.70
☐ 11	Bob Sura	1.00	.45
☐ 12	Kurt Thomas	1.00	.45
☐ 13	Gary Trent	1.00	.45
☐ 14	Rasheed Wallace	1.50	.70
☐ 15	Eric Williams	1.00	.45

1996-97 Fleer Rookie Sensations

Randomly inserted into all second series packs at a rate of one in 90, this 15-card set features etched-foil and embossing and focuses on the top rookies from the 1996-97 season.

	MINT	NRMT
COMPLETE SET (15)	225.00	100.00
COMMON CARD (1-15)	4.00	1.80
SEMISTARS	5.00	2.20
UNLISTED STARS	8.00	3.60
SER.2 STATED ODDS 1:90 HOBBY/RETAIL		

		MINT	NRMT
☐ 1	S.Abdur-Rahim	25.00	11.00
☐ 2	Ray Allen	12.00	5.50
☐ 3	Kobe Bryant	70.00	32.00
☐ 4	Marcus Camby	10.00	4.50
☐ 5	Erick Dampier	8.00	3.60
☐ 6	Tony Delk	8.00	3.60
☐ 7	Allen Iverson	40.00	18.00
☐ 8	Kerry Kittles	10.00	4.50
☐ 9	Stephon Marbury	40.00	18.00
☐ 10	Steve Nash	4.00	1.80
☐ 11	Roy Rogers	4.00	1.80

		MINT	NRMT
☐ 12	Antoine Walker	40.00	18.00
☐ 13	Samaki Walker	8.00	3.60
☐ 14	John Wallace	8.00	3.60
☐ 15	Lorenzen Wright	8.00	3.60

1996-97 Fleer Stackhouse's All-Fleer

Randomly inserted in first series nine-card packs at a rate of one in 12 and one per special first series retail pack, this 12-card set features some of the top player's in the NBA as seen through Fleer Spokesman Jerry Stackhouse's eyes. Card fronts contain team colors in the background and have both the card name and the player's name running vertical in gold foil. Card backs contain a brief statistical summary and are numbered as "X of 12".

	MINT	NRMT
COMPLETE SET (12)	20.00	9.00
COMMON CARD (1-12)	1.00	.45
SER.1 STATED ODDS 1:12 HOBBY/RETAIL		
ONE PER SPECIAL SER.1 RETAIL PACK		

		MINT	NRMT
☐ 1	Charles Barkley	1.25	.55
☐ 2	A.Hardaway	3.00	1.35
☐ 3	Grant Hill	5.00	2.20
☐ 4	Michael Jordan	10.00	4.50
☐ 5	Shawn Kemp	2.50	1.10
☐ 6	Jason Kidd	1.50	.70
☐ 7	Karl Malone	1.25	.55
☐ 8	Hakeem Olajuwon	1.50	.70
☐ 9	Shaquille O'Neal	3.00	1.35
☐ 10	Gary Payton	1.00	.45
☐ 11	Scottie Pippen	2.50	1.10
☐ 12	David Robinson	1.25	.55

1996-97 Fleer Stackhouse's Scrapbook

Randomly inserted into all first series packs at a rate of one in 24, cards from this two-card set highlight moments from Stackhouse's rookie year. In addition, they are the last instal-

Iment to the cross-brand insert from all of the 1995-96 Fleer products.

	MINT	NRMT
COMPLETE SET (2)	5.00	2.20
COMMON STACK. (S9-S10)..	2.50	1.10

SER.1 STATED ODDS 1:24 HOB/RET

| □ S9 Jerry Stackhouse | 2.50 | 1.10 |
| □ S10 Jerry Stackhouse | 2.50 | 1.10 |

1996-97 Fleer Swing Shift

Randomly inserted into all second series packs at a rate of one in 6, this 15-card set focuses on players who can not only play well from the outside, but who can also post up down low. Card fronts feature a "shattered" glass colored background.

	MINT	NRMT
COMPLETE SET (15)	15.00	6.75
COMMON CARD (1-15)	.40	.18
SEMISTARS	.50	.23
UNLISTED STARS	.75	.35

SER.2 STATED ODDS 1:6 HOBBY/RETAIL

□ 1 Ray Allen	1.25	.55
□ 2 Charles Barkley	1.25	.55
□ 3 Michael Finley	1.00	.45
□ 4 A.Hardaway	3.00	1.35
□ 5 Grant Hill	5.00	2.20
□ 6 Jim Jackson	.40	.18
□ 7 Eddie Jones	1.50	.70
□ 8 Kerry Kittles	1.00	.45
□ 9 Reggie Miller	.75	.35
□ 10 Gary Payton	1.25	.55
□ 11 Scottie Pippen	2.50	1.10
□ 12 Mitch Richmond	.75	.35
□ 13 Steve Smith	.50	.23
□ 14 Latrell Sprewell	.50	.23
□ 15 Jerry Stackhouse	1.00	.45

1996-97 Fleer Thrill Seekers

Randomly inserted into second series hobby packs only at a rate of one in 240, this 15-card set uses Lenticular technology and showcases NBA players who know how to "thrill" NBA fans.

	MINT	NRMT
COMPLETE SET (15)	750.00	350.00
COMMON CARD (1-15)	15.00	6.75

SER.2 STATED ODDS 1:240 HOBBY

□ 1 S.Abdur-Rahim	50.00	22.00
□ 2 Charles Barkley	25.00	11.00
□ 3 A.Hardaway	60.00	27.00
□ 4 Grant Hill	100.00	45.00
□ 5 Allen Iverson	80.00	36.00
□ 6 Michael Jordan	200.00	90.00
□ 7 Shawn Kemp	50.00	22.00
□ 8 Jason Kidd	30.00	13.50
□ 9 Stephon Marbury	80.00	36.00
□ 10 Antonio McDyess	25.00	11.00
□ 11 Reggie Miller	15.00	6.75
□ 12 Alonzo Mourning	15.00	6.75
□ 13 Shaquille O'Neal	60.00	27.00
□ 14 David Robinson	25.00	11.00
□ 15 D.Stoudamire	40.00	18.00

1996-97 Fleer Total O

Randomly inserted into second series retail packs only at a rate of one in 44, this 10-card set features NBA players known for

their offensive ability. Cards are printed on clear plastic stock and card fronts feature half of a colorful basketball in the background.

	MINT	NRMT
COMPLETE SET (10)	125.00	55.00
COMMON CARD (1-10)	4.00	1.80

SER.2 STATED ODDS 1:44 RETAIL

□ 1 A.Hardaway	15.00	6.75
□ 2 Grant Hill	25.00	11.00
□ 3 Juwan Howard	5.00	2.20
□ 4 Michael Jordan	50.00	22.00
□ 5 Shawn Kemp	12.00	5.50
□ 6 Karl Malone	6.00	2.70
□ 7 Alonzo Mourning	4.00	1.80
□ 8 Hakeem Olajuwon	8.00	3.60
□ 9 Shaquille O'Neal	15.00	6.75
□ 10 Jerry Stackhouse	5.00	2.20

1996-97 Fleer Towers of Power

Randomly inserted into all second series packs at a rate of one in 30, this 10-card set focuses on the dominent men of the NBA. Card fronts feature etched foil.

	MINT	NRMT
COMPLETE SET (10)	40.00	18.00
COMMON CARD (1-10)	2.00	.90

SER.2 STATED ODDS 1:30 HOBBY/RETAIL

□ 1 S.Abdur-Rahim	6.00	2.70
□ 2 Marcus Camby	2.50	1.10
□ 3 Patrick Ewing	2.00	.90
□ 4 Kevin Garnett	12.00	5.50
□ 5 Shawn Kemp	6.00	2.70
□ 6 Hakeem Olajuwon	4.00	1.80
□ 7 Shaquille O'Neal	8.00	3.60
□ 8 David Robinson	3.00	1.35
□ 9 Dennis Rodman	8.00	3.60
□ 10 Joe Smith	2.50	1.10

1997-98 Fleer

This 350-card set was released in two series with 10-card packs that carried a suggested retail price of $1.49 and $1.59. The cards carry a Textured Legend matte finish that makes the cards idea for autographs. The

cards feature full-bleed action photos with the player's name appearing in gold foil block type at the bottom. The player's team and position are in gold foil script below the name. The backs carry career statistics.

	MINT	NRMT
COMPLETE SET (350)	40.00	18.00
COMPLETE SERIES 1 (200)	20.00	9.00
COMPLETE SERIES 2 (150)	20.00	9.00
COMMON CARD (1-350)	.10	.05
SEMISTARS	.15	.07
UNLISTED STARS	.25	.11
COMP.CRYSTAL SET (345)	240.00	110.00
COMP.CRYSTAL SER.1 (197)	120.00	55.00
COMP.CRYSTAL SER.2 (148)	120.00	55.00
COMMON CRYSTAL	.50	.23
*CRYSTAL STARS: 2X TO 5X HI COLUMN		
*CRYSTAL RCs: 2X TO 4X HI		
CRYSTAL: SER.1/2 STATED ODDS 1:2 HOB		
COMP.TIFFANY SET (345)	1800.00	800.00
COMP.TIFFANY SER.1 (197)	800.00	350.00
COMP.TIFFANY SER.2 (148)	1000.00	450.00
COMMON TIFFANY (1-197)	3.00	1.35
COMMON TIFFANY (200-348)	4.00	1.80
*TIFFANY SER.1 STARS: 15X TO 30X HI		
*TIFFANY SER.2 STARS: 20X TO 40X HI		
*TIFFANY SER.2 RCs: 10X TO 20X HI		
TIFFANY: SER.1/2 STARED ODDS 1:20 HOB		

□ 1 A.Hardaway	1.00	.45
□ 2 Mitch Richmond	.25	.11
□ 3 Allen Iverson	1.25	.55
□ 4 Chris Webber	.60	.25
□ 5 Sasha Danilovic	.10	.05
□ 6 Avery Johnson	.10	.05
□ 7 Kenny Anderson	.15	.07
□ 8 Antoine Walker	1.25	.55
□ 9 Nick Van Exel	.25	.11
□ 10 Mookie Blaylock	.15	.07
□ 11 Wesley Person	.10	.05
□ 12 Vlade Divac	.15	.07
□ 13 Glenn Robinson	.25	.11
□ 14 Chris Mills	.10	.05
□ 15 Latrell Sprewell	.15	.07
□ 16 Jayson Williams	.15	.07
□ 17 Travis Best	.10	.05
□ 18 Charlie Ward	.10	.05
□ 19 Theo Ratliff	.10	.05
□ 20 Gary Payton	.40	.18
□ 21 Marcus Camby	.25	.11
□ 22 Clyde Drexler	.30	.14
□ 23 Michael Jordan	3.00	1.35
□ 24 Antonio McDyess	.30	.14
□ 25 Stephon Marbury	1.25	.55
□ 26 Isaac Austin	.10	.05
□ 27 S.Abdur-Rahim	.75	.35
□ 28 Malik Sealy	.10	.05
□ 29 Arvydas Sabonis	.15	.07
□ 30 Kerry Kittles	.25	.11
□ 31 Reggie Miller	.25	.11
□ 32 Karl Malone	.40	.18
□ 33 Grant Hill	1.50	.70
□ 34 Hakeem Olajuwon	.50	.23
□ 35 Danny Ferry	.10	.05
□ 36 Dominique Wilkins	.25	.11
□ 37 Armon Gilliam	.10	.05
□ 38 Danny Manning	.15	.07
□ 39 Larry Johnson	.15	.07
□ 40 Dino Radja	.10	.05
□ 41 Jason Caffey	.10	.05
□ 42 Jerry Stackhouse	.25	.11
□ 43 Alonzo Mourning	.25	.11
□ 44 Shawn Bradley	.10	.05
□ 45 Bo Outlaw	.10	.05
□ 46 Bryon Russell	.10	.05
□ 47 Doug West	.10	.05
□ 48 Lawrence Moten	.10	.05
□ 49 Dale Ellis	.10	.05
□ 50 Kobe Bryant	2.00	.90
□ 51 Carlos Rogers	.10	.05
□ 52 Todd Fuller	.10	.05
□ 53 Tyus Edney	.10	.05
□ 54 Horace Grant	.15	.07
□ 55 D.Mutombo	.15	.07
□ 56 Jim McIlvaine	.10	.05
□ 57 Harvey Grant	.10	.05
□ 58 Dean Garrett	.10	.05
□ 59 Samaki Walker	.10	.05
□ 60 Johnny Newman	.10	.05
□ 61 Antonio Davis	.10	.05
□ 62 Jamal Mashburn	.15	.07
□ 63 Muggsy Bogues	.10	.05
□ 64 Rod Strickland	.25	.11
□ 65 Craig Ehlo	.10	.05
□ 66 Rex Walters	.10	.05
□ 67 Bob Sura	.10	.05
□ 68 Travis Knight	.10	.05
□ 69 Toni Kukoc	.15	.07
□ 70 Antonio Davis	.10	.05
□ 71 Mario Elie	.10	.05
□ 72 Popeye Jones	.10	.05
□ 73 David Wesley	.10	.05
□ 74 John Wallace	.15	.07
□ 75 Calbert Cheaney	.10	.05
□ 76 Grant Long	.10	.05
□ 77 Will Perdue	.10	.05
□ 78 Rasheed Wallace	.15	.07
□ 79 Chris Gatling	.10	.05
□ 80 Corliss Williamson	.15	.07
□ 81 B.J. Armstrong	.10	.05
□ 82 Brian Shaw	.10	.05
□ 83 Darrick Martin	.10	.05
□ 84 Vinny Del Negro	.10	.05
□ 85 Tony Delk	.10	.05
□ 86 Greg Anthony	.10	.05
□ 87 Mark Davis	.10	.05
□ 88 Anthony Goldwire	.10	.05
□ 89 Rex Chapman	.10	.05
□ 90 Stojko Vrankovic	.10	.05
□ 91 Dennis Rodman	1.00	.45
□ 92 Detlef Schrempf	.15	.07
□ 93 Henry James	.10	.05
□ 94 Tracy Murray	.10	.05
□ 95 Voshon Lenard	.10	.05
□ 96 Sharone Wright	.10	.05
□ 97 Ed O'Bannon	.10	.05
□ 98 Gerald Wilkins	.10	.05
□ 99 Kevin Willis	.10	.05
□ 100 Shaquille O'Neal	1.00	.45
□ 101 Jim Jackson	.15	.07
□ 102 Mark Price	.10	.05
□ 103 Patrick Ewing	.25	.11
□ 104 Lorenzen Wright	.10	.05
□ 105 Tyrone Hill	.10	.05
□ 106 Ray Allen	.30	.14
□ 107 Jermaine O'Neal	.15	.07
□ 108 Anthony Mason	.15	.07
□ 109 M.Abdul-Rauf	.10	.05
□ 110 Terry Mills	.10	.05
□ 111 Gheorghe Muresan	.10	.05
□ 112 Mark Jackson	.10	.05
□ 113 Greg Ostertag	.10	.05
□ 114 Kevin Johnson	.15	.07
□ 115 Anthony Peeler	.10	.05
□ 116 Rony Seikaly	.10	.05
□ 117 Keith Askins	.10	.05
□ 118 Todd Day	.10	.05
□ 119 Chris Childs	.10	.05
□ 120 Chris Carr	.10	.05
□ 121 Erick Strickland	.25	.11
□ 122 Elden Campbell	.15	.07
□ 123 Elliot Perry	.10	.05
□ 124 Pooh Richardson	.10	.05
□ 125 Juwan Howard	.25	.11
□ 126 Ervin Johnson	.10	.05
□ 127 Eric Montross	.10	.05
□ 128 Otis Thorpe	.15	.07
□ 129 Hersey Hawkins	.15	.07
□ 130 Bimbo Coles	.10	.05
□ 131 Olden Polynice	.10	.05
□ 132 Christian Laettner	.15	.07
□ 133 Sean Elliott	.15	.07
□ 134 Othella Harrington	.10	.05
□ 135 Erick Dampier	.15	.07
□ 136 Vitaly Potapenko	.10	.05
□ 137 Doug Christie	.10	.05
□ 138 Luc Longley	.15	.07
□ 139 C.Weatherspoon	.10	.05
□ 140 Gary Trent	.10	.05
□ 141 Shandon Anderson	.10	.05
□ 142 Sam Perkins	.15	.07
□ 143 Derek Harper	.10	.05
□ 144 Robert Horry	.10	.05
□ 145 Roy Rogers	.10	.05
□ 146 John Starks	.15	.07
□ 147 Tyrone Corbin	.10	.05
□ 148 Andrew Lang	.10	.05
□ 149 Derek Strong	.10	.05
□ 150 Joe Smith	.25	.11
□ 151 Ron Harper	.15	.07
□ 152 Sam Cassell	.15	.07
□ 153 Brent Barry	.10	.05
□ 154 LaPhonso Ellis	.10	.05
□ 155 Matt Geiger	.10	.05
□ 156 Steve Nash	.10	.05
□ 157 Michael Smith	.10	.05
□ 158 Eric Williams	.10	.05
□ 159 Tom Gugliotta	.25	.11
□ 160 Monty Williams	.10	.05
□ 161 Lindsey Hunter	.10	.05
□ 162 Oliver Miller	.10	.05
□ 163 Brent Price	.10	.05
□ 164 Derrick McKey	.10	.05
□ 165 Robert Pack	.10	.05
□ 166 Derrick Coleman	.10	.05
□ 167 Isaiah Rider	.15	.07
□ 168 Dan Majerle	.15	.07
□ 169 Jeff Hornacek	.15	.07
□ 170 Terrell Brandon	.25	.11
□ 171 Nate McMillan	.10	.05
□ 172 Cedric Ceballos	.10	.05
□ 173 Derek Fisher	.10	.05
□ 174 Rodney Rogers	.10	.05
□ 175 Blue Edwards	.10	.05
□ 176 Brooks Thompson	.10	.05
□ 177 Sherman Douglas	.10	.05
□ 178 Sam Mitchell	.10	.05
□ 179 Charles Oakley	.10	.05
□ 180 Greg Minor	.10	.05
□ 181 Chris Mullin	.25	.11
□ 182 P.J. Brown	.10	.05
□ 183 Stacey Augmon	.10	.05
□ 184 Don MacLean	.10	.05
□ 185 Aaron McKie	.10	.05
□ 186 Dale Davis	.10	.05
□ 187 Vernon Maxwell	.10	.05
□ 188 Dell Curry	.10	.05
□ 189 Kendall Gill	.15	.07
□ 190 Billy Owens	.10	.05
□ 191 Steve Kerr	.10	.05
□ 192 Matt Maloney	.10	.05
□ 193 Dennis Scott	.10	.05
□ 194 A.C. Green	.15	.07
□ 195 George McCloud	.10	.05
□ 196 Walt Williams	.10	.05
□ 197 Eldridge Recasner	.10	.05
□ 198 Checklist	.10	.05
(Hawks/Bucks)		
□ 199 Checklist	.10	.05
(T'wolves/Wizards)		
□ 200 Checklist	.10	.05
(inserts)		
□ 201 Tim Duncan	3.00	1.35
□ 202 Tim Thomas	1.50	.70

□			
203	Clifford Rozier	.10	.05
204	Bryant Reeves	.15	.07
205	Glen Rice	.25	.11
206	Darrell Armstrong	.10	.05
207	Juwan Howard	.25	.11
208	John Stockton	.25	.11
209	Antonio McDyess	.30	.14
210	James Cotton	.10	.05
211	Brian Grant	.10	.05
212	Chris Whitney	.10	.05
213	Antonio Davis	.10	.05
214	Kendall Gill	.15	.07
215	Adonal Foyle	.30	.14
216	Dean Garrett	.10	.05
217	Dennis Scott	.10	.05
218	Zydrunas Ilgauskas	.15	.07
219	Antonio Daniels	.60	.25
220	Derek Harper	.10	.05
221	Travis Knight	.10	.05
222	Bobby Hurley	.10	.05
223	Greg Anderson	.10	.05
224	Rod Strickland	.15	.07
225	David Benoit	.10	.05
226	Tracy McGrady	1.50	.70
227	Brian Williams	.10	.05
228	James Robinson	.10	.05
229	Randy Brown	.10	.05
230	Greg Foster	.10	.05
231	Reggie Miller	.25	.11
232	Eric Montross	.10	.05
233	Malik Rose	.10	.05
234	Charles Barkley	.40	.18
235	Tony Battie	.50	.23
236	Terry Mills	.10	.05
237	Jerald Honeycutt	.10	.05
238	Bubba Wells	.10	.05
239	John Wallace	.15	.07
240	Jason Kidd	.50	.23
241	Mark Price	.10	.05
242	Ron Mercer	2.00	.90
243	Derrick Coleman	.15	.07
244	Fred Hoiberg	.10	.05
245	Wesley Person	.10	.05
246	Eddie Jones	.50	.23
247	Allan Houston	.15	.07
248	Keith Van Horn	2.50	1.10
249	Johnny Newman	.10	.05
250	Kevin Garnett	1.50	.70
251	Latrell Sprewell	.15	.07
252	Tracy Murray	.10	.05
253	Charles O'Bannon	.10	.05
254	Lamond Murray	.10	.05
255	Jerry Stackhouse	.25	.11
256	Rik Smits	.15	.07
257	Alan Henderson	.10	.05
258	Tariq Abdul-Wahad	.40	.18
259	Nick Anderson	.10	.05
260	Calbert Cheaney	.10	.05
261	Scottie Pippen	.75	.35
262	Rodrick Rhodes	.30	.14
263	Derek Anderson	.75	.35
264	Dana Barros	.10	.05
265	Todd Day	.10	.05
266	Michael Finley	.25	.11
267	Kevin Edwards	.10	.05
268	Terrell Brandon	.25	.11
269	Bobby Phills	.10	.05
270	Kelvin Cato	.30	.14
271	Vin Baker	.50	.23
272	Eric Washington	.25	.11
273	Jim Jackson	.15	.07
274	Joe Dumars	.25	.11
275	David Robinson	.40	.18
276	Jayson Williams	.15	.07
277	Travis Best	.10	.05
278	Kurt Thomas	.10	.05
279	Otis Thorpe	.15	.07
280	D.Stoudamire	.50	.23
281	John Williams	.10	.05
282	Loy Vaught	.15	.07
283	Charles Outlaw	.10	.05
284	Todd Fuller	.10	.05
285	Terry Dehere	.10	.05
286	C.Weatherspoon	.10	.05
287	Danny Fortson	.50	.23
288	Howard Eisley	.10	.05
289	Steve Smith	.15	.07
290	Chris Webber	.60	.25
291	Shawn Kemp	.75	.35
292	Sam Cassell	.15	.07
293	Rick Fox	.10	.05
294	Walter McCarty	.10	.05
295	Mark Jackson	.10	.05
296	Chris Mills	.10	.05
297	Jacque Vaughn	.40	.18
298	Shawn Respert	.10	.05
299	Scot Burrell	.10	.05
300	Allen Iverson	1.25	.55
301	Charles Smith	.10	.05
302	Ervin Johnson	.10	.05
303	Hubert Davis	.10	.05
304	Eddie Johnson	.10	.05
305	Erick Dampier	.10	.05
306	Eric Williams	.10	.05
307	Anthony Johnson	.10	.05
308	David Wesley	.10	.05
309	Eric Piatkowski	.10	.05
310	Austin Croshere	.30	.14
311	Malik Sealy	.10	.05
312	George McCloud	.10	.05
313	Anthony Parker	.10	.05
314	Cedric Henderson	.30	.14
315	John Thomas	.10	.05
316	Corey Alexander	.10	.05
317	Johnny Taylor	.10	.05
318	Chris Mullin	.25	.11
319	J.R. Reid	.10	.05
320	George Lynch	.10	.05
321	Lawrence Funderburke	.25	.11
322	God Shammgod	.10	.05
323	Bobby Jackson	.50	.23
324	Khalid Reeves	.10	.05
325	Zan Tabak	.10	.05
326	Chris Gatling	.10	.05
327	Alvin Williams	.30	.14
328	Scot Pollard	.10	.05
329	Kerry Kittles	.25	.11
330	Tim Hardaway	.30	.14
331	Maurice Taylor	.75	.35
332	Keith Booth	.10	.05
333	Chris Morris	.10	.05
334	Bryant Stith	.10	.05
335	Terry Cummings	.10	.05
336	Ed Gray	.30	.14
337	Eric Snow	.10	.05
338	Clifford Robinson	.10	.05
339	Chris Dudley	.10	.05
340	Chauncey Billups	1.00	.45
341	Paul Grant	.10	.05
342	Tyrone Hill	.10	.05
343	Joe Smith	.25	.11
344	Sean Rooks	.10	.05
345	Harvey Grant	.10	.05
346	Dale Davis	.10	.05
347	Brevin Knight	.75	.35
348	Serge Zwikker	.10	.05
349	Checklist (Hawks/Kings)	.10	.05
350	Checklist (Spurs/Wizards/Inserts)	.10	.05

1997-98 Fleer Decade of Excellence

Randomly inserted in series one hobby packs only at a rate of one in 36, this 12-card set showcases players that have been in the NBA for 10 or more years using photos from the 1987-88 season and graphic design showcasing the 1987-88 Fleer basketball design.

	MINT	NRMT
COMPLETE SET (12)	125.00	55.00
COMMON CARD (1-12)	3.00	1.35
UNLISTED STARS	5.00	2.20
SER.1 STATED ODDS 1:36 HOBBY		
COMP.RARE TRAD. SET (12)	450.00	200.00
COMMON RARE TRAD. (1-12)	12.00	5.50
*RARE TRAD: 2X TO 4X HI COLUMN		
RARE TRAD: SER.1 STATED ODDS 1:360 HOB		

□			
1	Charles Barkley	8.00	3.60
2	Clyde Drexler	6.00	2.70
3	Patrick Ewing	5.00	2.20
4	Kevin Johnson	3.00	1.35
5	Michael Jordan	60.00	27.00
6	Karl Malone	8.00	3.60
7	Reggie Miller	5.00	2.20
8	Hakeem Olajuwon	10.00	4.50
9	Scottie Pippen	15.00	6.75
10	Dennis Rodman	20.00	9.00
11	John Stockton	5.00	2.20
12	Dominique Wilkins	5.00	2.20

1997-98 Fleer Diamond Ink

Inserted one per pack in different Fleer products, these cards could be exchanged for autographed mini-basketballs from Fleer/SkyBox. Points came in 1, 5 and 10 denominations. Balls were exchangable when 500 total points of any particular player were collected. In addition, the first 100 balls were serially numbered. The program expired December 31, 1998. The cards are not numbered and are listed below in alphabetical order.

	MINT	NRMT
T.BATTIE POINT	.12	.05
C.BILLUPS POINT	.20	.09
K.BRYANT POINT	.75	.35
D.FORTSON POINT	.12	.05
K.GARNETT POINT	.50	.23
G.HILL POINT	1.50	.70
S.MARBURY POINT	.30	.14
A.MCDYESS POINT	.12	.05
T.MCGRADY POINT	.20	.09
J.SMITH POINT	.12	.05
T.THOMAS POINT	.20	.09
A.WALKER POINT	.30	.14

ONE PER SER.1 ULTRA PACK
ONE PER SER.2 FLEER PACK
ONE PER FLAIR PACK
PRICES LISTED PER POINT
EXCH.500 POINTS FOR SIGNED MINI-BALL
EXCH.500 HILL POINTS FOR SIGNED JERSEY

1997-98 Fleer Flair Hardwood Leaders

Randomly inserted in all series one packs at a rate of one in six, this 29-card set features the heavier stock associated with the Flair brand. One player or "leader" from each team is depicted in the set.

	MINT	NRMT
COMPLETE SET (29)	50.00	22.00
COMMON CARD (1-29)	.50	.23
SEMISTARS	.60	.25
UNLISTED STARS	1.00	.45
SER.1 STATED ODDS 1:6 HOBBY/RETAIL		

		MINT	NRMT
□ 1	Christian Laettner	.50	.23
□ 2	Antoine Walker	5.00	2.20
□ 3	Glen Rice	1.00	.45
□ 4	Michael Jordan	15.00	6.75
□ 5	Terrell Brandon	.50	.23
□ 6	Michael Finley	1.00	.45
□ 7	Antonio McDyess	1.25	.55
□ 8	Grant Hill	6.00	2.70
□ 9	Latrell Sprewell	.60	.25
□ 10	Hakeem Olajuwon	2.00	.90
□ 11	Reggie Miller	1.00	.45
□ 12	Loy Vaught	.50	.23
□ 13	Shaquille O'Neal	4.00	1.80
□ 14	Alonzo Mourning	1.00	.45
□ 15	Vin Baker	2.00	.90
□ 16	Kevin Garnett	6.00	2.70
□ 17	Kerry Kittles	1.00	.45
□ 18	Patrick Ewing	1.00	.45
□ 19	A.Hardaway	4.00	1.80
□ 20	Jerry Stackhouse	1.00	.45
□ 21	Jason Kidd	2.00	.90
□ 22	Kenny Anderson	.50	.23
□ 23	Mitch Richmond	1.00	.45
□ 24	David Robinson	1.50	.70
□ 25	Shawn Kemp	3.00	1.35

		MINT	NRMT
□ 26	D.Stoudamire	2.00	.90
□ 27	Karl Malone	1.50	.70
□ 28	S.Abdur-Rahim	3.00	1.35
□ 29	Chris Webber	2.50	1.10

1997-98 Fleer Franchise Futures

Randomly inserted in series one retail packs only at a rate of one in 36, this 10-card set focuses on players with up to three years experience who are up their team's future. The cards feature a die cut design with a full etched foil front.

	MINT	NRMT
COMPLETE SET (10)	90.00	40.00
COMMON CARD (1-10)	3.00	1.35
SER.1 STATED ODDS 1:36 RETAIL		

		MINT	NRMT
□ 1	S.Abdur-Rahim	10.00	4.50
□ 2	Ray Allen	4.00	1.80
□ 3	Kobe Bryant	25.00	11.00
□ 4	Kevin Garnett	20.00	9.00
□ 5	Grant Hill	20.00	9.00
□ 6	Juwan Howard	3.00	1.35
□ 7	Allen Iverson	15.00	6.75
□ 8	Kerry Kittles	3.00	1.35
□ 9	Joe Smith	3.00	1.35
□ 10	D.Stoudamire	6.00	2.70

1997-98 Fleer Game Breakers

Randomly inserted in all series one packs at a rate of one in 288, this 12-card dual player set features some of the NBA's best duos. Card fronts carry etched-foil.

	MINT	NRMT
COMPLETE SET (12)	550.00	250.00
COMMON CARD (1-12)	12.00	5.50
SER.1 STATED ODDS 1:288 HOBBY/RETAIL		

		MINT	NRMT
□ 1	Michael Jordan Dennis Rodman	150.00	70.00
□ 2	Joe Dumars Grant Hill	60.00	27.00
□ 3	Joe Smith Latrell Sprewell	12.00	5.50
□ 4	Charles Barkley Hakeem Olajuwon	40.00	18.00
□ 5	Eddie Jones Shaquille O'Neal	60.00	27.00
□ 6	Kevin Garnett Stephon Marbury	80.00	36.00
□ 7	Nick Anderson A.Hardaway	40.00	18.00
□ 8	Allen Iverson Jerry Stackhouse	40.00	18.00
□ 9	Shawn Kemp Gary Payton	50.00	22.00
□ 10	Marcus Camby D.Stoudamire	20.00	9.00
□ 11	Karl Malone John Stockton	25.00	11.00
□ 12	Juwan Howard Chris Webber	40.00	18.00

1997-98 Fleer Goudey Greats

Randomly inserted into series two packs at a rate of one in four, this 15-card set features some of today's players in the Goudey card style from yesteryear complete with commentary from NBA Hall of Famer Nate "Tiny" Archibald.

	MINT	NRMT
COMPLETE SET (15)	15.00	6.75
COMMON CARD (1-15)	.60	.25
SER.2 STATED ODDS 1:4 HOBBY/RETAIL		

		MINT	NRMT
□ 1	Ray Allen	.75	.35
□ 2	Clyde Drexler	.75	.35
□ 3	Patrick Ewing	.60	.25
□ 4	A.Hardaway	2.50	1.10
□ 5	Grant Hill	4.00	1.80
□ 6	Stephon Marbury	3.00	1.35
□ 7	Alonzo Mourning	.60	.25
□ 8	Shaquille O'Neal	2.50	1.10
□ 9	Gary Payton	1.00	.45
□ 10	Scottie Pippen	2.00	.90
□ 11	David Robinson	1.00	.45
□ 12	Joe Smith	.60	.25
□ 13	John Stockton	.60	.25
□ 14	D.Stoudamire	1.25	.55
□ 15	Antoine Walker	3.00	1.35

1997-98 Fleer Key Ingredients

Randomly inserted in series one retail packs only at a rate of one in two, this 15-card set features players who are the "key" to their teams' success.

	MINT	NRMT
COMPLETE SET (15)	8.00	3.60
COMMON CARD (1-15)	.30	.14
SER.1 STATED ODDS 1:2 RETAIL		
COMP.GOLD SET (15)	50.00	22.00
COMMON GOLD (1-15)	2.00	.90
*GOLD: 3X TO 6X HI COLUMN		
GOLD: SER.1 STATED ODDS 1:18 HOB/RET		

			MINT	NRMT
☐ 1	Charles Barkley		.50	.23
☐ 2	Marcus Camby		.30	.14
☐ 3	A.Hardaway		1.25	.55
☐ 4	Juwan Howard		.30	.14
☐ 5	Shawn Kemp		1.00	.45
☐ 6	Karl Malone		.50	.23
☐ 7	Stephon Marbury		1.50	.70
☐ 8	Alonzo Mourning		.30	.14
☐ 9	Shaquille O'Neal		1.25	.55
☐ 10	Scottie Pippen		1.00	.45
☐ 11	Mitch Richmond		.30	.14
☐ 12	David Robinson		.50	.23
☐ 13	Joe Smith		.30	.14
☐ 14	Jerry Stackhouse		.30	.14
☐ 15	Antoine Walker		1.50	.70

1997-98 Fleer Million Dollar Moments

These cards were inserted one per pack in all 1997-98 Fleer basketball products. The set contains 50 cards. If a collector

put together the complete set, they could win the Grand Prize of $1,000,000. The game ended on August 31, 1998. Cards numbered 46-50 are the tougher cards to pull. They are not priced below.

	MINT	NRMT
COMPLETE SET (45)	6.00	2.70
COMMON CARD (1-45)	.05	.02
SEMISTARS	.10	.05
UNLISTED STARS	.15	.07
ONE PER FLEER/ULTRA PACK		

		MINT	NRMT
☐ 1	Checklist (1-50)	.05	.02
☐ 2	Mark Jackson	.05	.02
☐ 3	Charles Barkley	.25	.11
☐ 4	Terrell Brandon	.15	.07
☐ 5	Wayman Tisdale	.05	.02
☐ 6	Clyde Drexler	.20	.09
☐ 7	Patrick Ewing	.15	.07
☐ 8	Kevin Garnett	1.00	.45
☐ 9	Tom Gugliotta	.15	.07
☐ 10	A.Hardaway	.60	.25
☐ 11	Tim Hardaway	.15	.07
☐ 12	Grant Hill	1.00	.45
☐ 13	Allen Iverson	.75	.35
☐ 14	Shawn Kemp	.50	.23
☐ 15	Jason Kidd	.15	.07
☐ 16	Charles Oakley	.05	.02
☐ 17	Karl Malone	.25	.11
☐ 18	Alonzo Mourning	.15	.07
☐ 19	Shaquille O'Neal	.60	.25
☐ 20	Hakeem Olajuwon	.30	.14
☐ 21	Chris Webber	.40	.18
☐ 22	Scottie Pippen	.50	.23
☐ 23	Glen Rice	.15	.07
☐ 24	Mitch Richmond	.15	.07
☐ 25	David Robinson	.25	.11
☐ 26	Dennis Rodman	.60	.25
☐ 27	Jerry Stackhouse	.15	.07
☐ 28	John Stockton	.15	.07
☐ 29	Mookie Blaylock	.10	.05
☐ 30	Muggsy Bogues	.05	.02
☐ 31	Kobe Bryant	1.25	.55
☐ 32	Rex Chapman	.05	.02
☐ 33	Joe Dumars	.15	.07
☐ 34	Dale Ellis	.05	.02
☐ 35	Horace Grant	.10	.05
☐ 36	Jeff Hornacek	.10	.05
☐ 37	D.Stoudamire	.30	.14
☐ 38	Kevin Johnson	.10	.05
☐ 39	Larry Johnson	.10	.05
☐ 40	Toni Kukoc	.10	.05
☐ 41	Danny Manning	.10	.05
☐ 42	Stephon Marbury	.60	.25
☐ 43	Reggie Miller	.15	.07
☐ 44	Chris Mullin	.15	.07
☐ 45	D.Mutombo	.10	.05

1997-98 Fleer Rookie Rewind

Randomly inserted in all series one packs at a rate of one in four, this 10-card set takes a look back at some of the best rookies from the 1996-97 season.

	MINT	NRMT
COMPLETE SET (10)	20.00	9.00
COMMON CARD (1-10)	.40	.18
SEMISTARS	.60	.25
UNLISTED STARS	1.00	.45
SER.1 STATED ODDS 1:4 HOBBY/RETAIL		

		MINT	NRMT
☐ 1	S.Abdur-Rahim	3.00	1.35
☐ 2	Ray Allen	1.25	.55
☐ 3	Kobe Bryant	8.00	3.60
☐ 4	Marcus Camby	1.00	.45
☐ 5	Allen Iverson	5.00	2.20
☐ 6	Kerry Kittles	1.00	.45
☐ 7	Matt Maloney	.40	.18
☐ 8	Stephon Marbury	5.00	2.20
☐ 9	Roy Rogers	.40	.18
☐ 10	Antoine Walker	5.00	2.20

1997-98 Fleer Rookie Sensations

Randomly inserted into series two packs at a rate of one in eight, this 10-card set features color photos of some of the top rookies from the 1997 class.

	MINT	NRMT
COMPLETE SET (10)	40.00	18.00
COMMON CARD (1-10)	1.25	.55
UNLISTED STARS	2.00	.90
SER.2 STATED ODDS 1:8 HOBBY/RETAIL		

		MINT	NRMT
☐ 1	Derek Anderson	3.00	1.35
☐ 2	Tony Battie	2.00	.90
☐ 3	Chauncey Billups	4.00	1.80
☐ 4	Austin Croshere	1.25	.55
☐ 5	Antonio Daniels	2.50	1.10
☐ 6	Tim Duncan	12.00	5.50
☐ 7	Tracy McGrady	6.00	2.70
☐ 8	Ron Mercer	8.00	3.60
☐ 9	Tim Thomas	6.00	2.70
☐ 10	Keith Van Horn	10.00	4.50

1997-98 Fleer Soaring Stars

Randomly inserted into series two retail packs at a rate of 1:2, this 20-card set showcases

players who make headlines for their teams.

	MINT	NRMT
COMPLETE SET (20)	15.00	6.75
COMMON CARD (1-20)	.20	.09
SEMISTARS	.25	.11
UNLISTED STARS	.40	.18
SER.2 STATED ODDS 1:2 RETAIL		
COMP.HIGH FLY (20)	60.00	27.00
COMMON HIGH FLY (1-20) ..	1.00	.45
*HIGH FLY STARS: 2X TO 4X HI COLUMN		
HIGH FLY: SER.2 STATED ODDS 1:24 H/R		

		MINT	NRMT
☐ 1	S.Abdur-Rahim	1.25	.55
☐ 2	Ray Allen	.50	.23
☐ 3	Charles Barkley	.60	.25
☐ 4	Kobe Bryant	3.00	1.35
☐ 5	Marcus Camby	.40	.18
☐ 6	Kevin Garnett	2.50	1.10
☐ 7	Tim Hardaway	.50	.23
☐ 8	Eddie Jones	.75	.35
☐ 9	Michael Jordan	5.00	2.20
☐ 10	Shawn Kemp	1.25	.55
☐ 11	Jason Kidd	.75	.35
☐ 12	Kerry Kittles	.40	.18
☐ 13	Karl Malone	.60	.25
☐ 14	Antonio McDyess	.50	.23
☐ 15	Glen Rice	.40	.18
☐ 16	Mitch Richmond	.40	.18
☐ 17	Latrell Sprewell	.20	.09
☐ 18	Jerry Stackhouse	.40	.18
☐ 19	Antoine Walker	2.00	.90
☐ 20	Chris Webber	1.00	.45

1997-98 Fleer Thrill Seekers

Randomly inserted into series two packs at a rate of one in 288, this 10-card set highlights some of the NBA's ultimate crowd pleasers. The cards feature matte finish frames and 100% etched silver holofoil

background and spot UV coating.

	MINT	NRMT
COMPLETE SET (10)	400.00	180.00
COMMON CARD (1-10)	8.00	3.60
SER.2 STATED ODDS 1:288 HOBBY/RETAIL		

		MINT	NRMT
☐ 1	S.Abdur-Rahim	25.00	11.00
☐ 2	Kobe Bryant	60.00	27.00
☐ 3	Tim Duncan	50.00	22.00
☐ 4	A.Hardaway	30.00	13.50
☐ 5	Grant Hill	50.00	22.00
☐ 6	Allen Iverson	40.00	18.00
☐ 7	Michael Jordan	100.00	45.00
☐ 8	Stephon Marbury	40.00	18.00
☐ 9	Dennis Rodman	30.00	13.50
☐ 10	Joe Smith	8.00	3.60

1997-98 Fleer Total 0

Randomly inserted into series two retail packs only at a rate of one in 18, this 10-card set focuses on key offensive players.

	MINT	NRMT
COMPLETE SET (10)	50.00	22.00
COMMON CARD (1-10)	1.50	.70
SER.2 STATED ODDS 1:18 RETAIL		

		MINT	NRMT
☐ 1	A.Hardaway	6.00	2.70
☐ 2	Grant Hill	10.00	4.50
☐ 3	Juwan Howard	1.50	.70
☐ 4	Allen Iverson	8.00	3.60
☐ 5	Michael Jordan	20.00	9.00
☐ 6	Karl Malone	2.50	1.10
☐ 7	Stephon Marbury	8.00	3.60
☐ 8	Hakeem Olajuwon	3.00	1.35
☐ 9	Shaquille O'Neal	6.00	2.70
☐ 10	D.Stoudamire	3.00	1.35

1997-98 Fleer Towers of Power

Randomly inserted into series two packs at a rate of one in 18, this 12-card set features some of the NBA's most dominate big men. Cards feature a die cut design.

	MINT	NRMT
COMPLETE SET (12)	40.00	18.00
COMMON CARD (1-12)	1.50	.70
SER.2 STATED ODDS 1:18 HOBBY/RETAIL		

		MINT	NRMT
☐ 1	S.Abdur-Rahim	5.00	2.20
☐ 2	Marcus Camby	1.50	.70
☐ 3	Patrick Ewing	1.50	.70
☐ 4	Kevin Garnett	10.00	4.50
☐ 5	Shawn Kemp	5.00	2.20
☐ 6	Karl Malone	2.50	1.10
☐ 7	Hakeem Olajuwon	3.00	1.35
☐ 8	Shaquille O'Neal	6.00	2.70
☐ 9	Dennis Rodman	6.00	2.70
☐ 10	Joe Smith	1.50	.70
☐ 11	Antoine Walker	8.00	3.60
☐ 12	Chris Webber	4.00	1.80

1997-98 Fleer Zone

Randomly inserted into series two hobby packs only at a rate of one in 36, this 15-card set focuses on players known for getting into a "zone" during a game. Card design includes silver rainbow holofoil and a 100% etched foil background.

	MINT	NRMT
COMPLETE SET (15)	150.00	70.00
COMMON CARD (1-15)	3.00	1.35
SER.2 STATED ODDS 1:36 HOBBY		

		MINT	NRMT
☐ 1	S.Abdur-Rahim	10.00	4.50
☐ 2	Kobe Bryant	25.00	11.00
☐ 3	Marcus Camby	3.00	1.35
☐ 4	Tim Duncan	20.00	9.00
☐ 5	Kevin Garnett	20.00	9.00
☐ 6	A.Hardaway	12.00	5.50
☐ 7	Grant Hill	20.00	9.00
☐ 8	Juwan Howard	3.00	1.35
☐ 9	Allen Iverson	15.00	6.75
☐ 10	Michael Jordan	40.00	18.00
☐ 11	Hakeem Olajuwon	6.00	2.70
☐ 12	Gary Payton	5.00	2.20
☐ 13	Scottie Pippen	10.00	4.50
☐ 14	Glen Rice	3.00	1.35
☐ 15	Keith Van Horn	15.00	6.75

1998-99 Fleer

The 1998-99 Fleer Series I set was issued with a total of 150 cards. The packs were issued with 10 cards per pack carrying a suggested retail price of $1.59. The set contains the topical subset: Plus Factor (133-147).

	MINT	NRMT
COMPLETE SERIES 1 (150)	20.00	9.00
COMMON CARD (1-150)	.10	.05
SEMISTARS	.15	.07
COMP.VINT.61 SER.1 (147)	70.00	32.00
COMMON VINT.61 (1-147)	.30	.14
*VINT.61 STARS: 1.25X TO 3X HI COLUMN		
VINT.61: SER.1 STATED ODDS 1:1 HOB		

		MINT	NRMT
☐ 1	Kobe Bryant	2.00	.90
☐ 2	Corliss Williamson	.15	.07
☐ 3	Allen Iverson	1.00	.45
☐ 4	Michael Finley	.20	.09
☐ 5	Juwan Howard	.25	.11
☐ 6	Marcus Camby	.20	.09
☐ 7	Toni Kukoc	.15	.07
☐ 8	Antoine Walker	1.00	.45
☐ 9	Stephon Marbury	1.00	.45
☐ 10	Tim Hardaway	.30	.14
☐ 11	Zydrunas Ilgauskas	.15	.07
☐ 12	John Stockton	.25	.11
☐ 13	Glenn Robinson	.20	.09
☐ 14	Isaiah Rider	.15	.07
☐ 15	Danny Fortson	.20	.09
☐ 16	Donyell Marshall	.15	.07
☐ 17	Chris Mullin	.20	.09
☐ 18	S.Abdur-Rahim	.60	.25
☐ 19	Bobby Phills	.10	.05
☐ 20	Gary Payton	.40	.18
☐ 21	Derrick Coleman	.15	.07
☐ 22	Larry Johnson	.15	.07
☐ 23	Michael Jordan	3.00	1.35
☐ 24	Danny Manning	.15	.07
☐ 25	Nick Anderson	.10	.05
☐ 26	Chris Gatling	.10	.05
☐ 27	Steve Smith	.15	.07
☐ 28	Chris Webber	.60	.25
☐ 29	Terrell Brandon	.20	.09
☐ 30	Rasheed Wallace	.15	.07
☐ 31	Reggie Miller	.25	.11
☐ 32	Karl Malone	.40	.18
☐ 33	Grant Hill	1.50	.70
☐ 34	Hakeem Olajuwon	.50	.23
☐ 35	Erick Dampier	.10	.05
☐ 36	Vin Baker	.50	.23
☐ 37	Tim Thomas	.75	.35
☐ 38	Mark Price	.10	.05
☐ 39	Shawn Bradley	.10	.05
☐ 40	Calbert Cheaney	.10	.05
☐ 41	Glen Rice	.25	.11
☐ 42	Kevin Willis	.10	.05
☐ 43	Chris Carr	.10	.05
☐ 44	Keith Van Horn	1.25	.55
☐ 45	Jamal Mashburn	.15	.07
☐ 46	Eddie Jones	.50	.23

☐ 47	Brevin Knight	.30	.14
☐ 48	Olden Polynice	.10	.05
☐ 49	Bobby Jackson	.20	.09
☐ 50	David Robinson	.40	.18
☐ 51	Patrick Ewing	.25	.11
☐ 52	Samaki Walker	.10	.05
☐ 53	Antonio Daniels	.25	.11
☐ 54	Rodney Rogers	.10	.05
☐ 55	D.Mutombo	.15	.07
☐ 56	Tracy McGrady	.75	.35
☐ 57	Walt Williams	.10	.05
☐ 58	Walter McCarty	.10	.05
☐ 59	Detlef Schrempf	.15	.07
☐ 60	Ervin Johnson	.10	.05
☐ 61	Michael Smith	.10	.05
☐ 62	Clifford Robinson	.10	.05
☐ 63	Brian Williams	.10	.05
☐ 64	Shandon Anderson	.10	.05
☐ 65	P.J. Brown	.10	.05
☐ 66	Scottie Pippen	.75	.35
☐ 67	Anthony Peeler	.10	.05
☐ 68	Tony Delk	.10	.05
☐ 69	David Wesley	.10	.05
☐ 70	John Starks	.15	.07
☐ 71	Nick Van Exel	.20	.09
☐ 72	Kerry Kittles	.20	.09
☐ 73	Tony Battie	.20	.09
☐ 74	Lamond Murray	.10	.05
☐ 75	A.Hardaway	1.00	.45
☐ 76	Jalen Rose	.10	.05
☐ 77	Derek Anderson	.30	.14
☐ 78	Avery Johnson	.10	.05
☐ 79	Michael Stewart	.15	.07
☐ 80	Brian Shaw	.10	.05
☐ 81	Chauncey Billups	.40	.18
☐ 82	Kenny Anderson	.15	.07
☐ 83	Bryon Russell	.10	.05
☐ 84	Jason Kidd	.50	.23
☐ 85	Tyrone Hill	.10	.05
☐ 86	Jim McIlvaine	.10	.05
☐ 87	Brian Grant	.10	.05
☐ 88	Bryant Stith	.10	.05
☐ 89	Brent Price	.10	.05
☐ 90	John Wallace	.15	.07
☐ 91	Dennis Rodman	1.00	.45
☐ 92	Alonzo Mourning	.25	.11
☐ 93	Bimbo Coles	.10	.05
☐ 94	Chris Anstey	.15	.07
☐ 95	Lindsey Hunter	.10	.05
☐ 96	Ed Gray	.15	.07
☐ 97	Chris Mills	.10	.05
☐ 98	Rick Fox	.10	.05
☐ 99	Lorenzen Wright	.10	.05
☐ 100	Kevin Garnett	1.50	.70
☐ 101	Shawn Kemp	.75	.35
☐ 102	Mark Jackson	.10	.05
☐ 103	Sam Cassell	.15	.07
☐ 104	Monty Williams	.10	.05
☐ 105	Ron Mercer	1.00	.45
☐ 106	Bryant Reeves	.15	.07
☐ 107	Tracy Murray	.10	.05
☐ 108	Ray Allen	.25	.11
☐ 109	Maurice Taylor	.30	.14
☐ 110	Jerome Williams	.10	.05
☐ 111	Horace Grant	.15	.07
☐ 112	Tariq Abdul-Wahad	.10	.05
☐ 113	Travis Knight	.10	.05
☐ 114	Kendall Gill	.15	.07
☐ 115	Aaron McKie	.10	.05
☐ 116	Dean Garrett	.10	.05
☐ 117	Jeff Hornacek	.15	.07
☐ 118	Todd Fuller	.10	.05
☐ 119	Arvydas Sabonis	.15	.07
☐ 120	Voshon Lenard	.10	.05
☐ 121	Steve Nash	.15	.07
☐ 122	Cedric Henderson	.15	.07
☐ 123	Rodrick Rhodes	.10	.05
☐ 124	Mookie Blaylock	.15	.07
☐ 125	Hersey Hawkins	.15	.07
☐ 126	Doug Christie	.10	.05
☐ 127	Eric Piatkowski	.10	.05
☐ 128	Sean Elliott	.15	.07
☐ 129	Anthony Mason	.15	.07
☐ 130	Allan Houston	.15	.07
☐ 131	Antonio Davis	.10	.05
☐ 132	Hubert Davis	.10	.05

☐ 133	Rod Strickland PF	.10	.05
☐ 134	Jason Kidd PF	.25	.11
☐ 135	Mark Jackson PF	.10	.05
☐ 136	Marcus Camby PF	.15	.07
☐ 137	D.Mutombo PF	.10	.05
☐ 138	Shawn Bradley PF	.10	.05
☐ 139	Dennis Rodman PF	.50	.23
☐ 140	Jayson Williams PF	.10	.05
☐ 141	Tim Duncan PF	.75	.35
☐ 142	Michael Jordan PF	1.50	.70
☐ 143	Shaquille O'Neal PF	.50	.23
☐ 144	Karl Malone PF	.20	.09
☐ 145	Mookie Blaylock PF	.10	.05
☐ 146	Brevin Knight PF	.20	.09
☐ 147	Doug Christie PF	.10	.05
☐ 148	Checklist	.10	.05
☐ 149	Checklist	.10	.05
☐ 150	Checklist	.10	.05
☐ S44	K.Van Horn SAMPLE	2.00	.90

1998-99 Fleer Electrifying

Randomly inserted in series one packs at a rate of one in 72, this 10-card set features player's who consistently have electrifying performances. The card fronts feature a gold patterned full-foil background with embossed "electricity".

	MINT	NRMT
COMPLETE SET (10)	200.00	90.00
COMMON CARD (1-10)	8.00	3.60
SER.1 STATED ODDS 1:72 HOB/RET		

		MINT	NRMT
☐ 1	Kobe Bryant	40.00	18.00
☐ 2	Kevin Garnett	30.00	13.50
☐ 3	A.Hardaway	20.00	9.00
☐ 4	Grant Hill	30.00	13.50
☐ 5	Allen Iverson	20.00	9.00
☐ 6	Michael Jordan	60.00	27.00
☐ 7	Shawn Kemp	15.00	6.75
☐ 8	Stephon Marbury	20.00	9.00
☐ 9	Gary Payton	8.00	3.60
☐ 10	Dennis Rodman	20.00	9.00

1998-99 Fleer Great Expectations

Randomly inserted in series one packs at a rate of one in 20, this 10-card set features players that represent the future of the NBA. The card fronts are bordered in gold holofoil with a matte finish background.

	MINT	NRMT
COMPLETE SET (10)	50.00	22.00
COMMON CARD (1-10)	1.50	.70
SER.1 STATED ODDS 1:20 HOB/RET		

		MINT	NRMT
☐ 1	S.Abdur-Rahim	4.00	1.80
☐ 2	Ray Allen	1.50	.70
☐ 3	Kobe Bryant	12.00	5.50
☐ 4	Tim Duncan	10.00	4.50
☐ 5	Kevin Garnett	10.00	4.50
☐ 6	Grant Hill	10.00	4.50
☐ 7	Allen Iverson	6.00	2.70
☐ 8	Stephon Marbury	6.00	2.70
☐ 9	Keith Van Horn	8.00	3.60
☐ 10	Antoine Walker	6.00	2.70

1998-99 Fleer Lucky 13

Randomly inserted in series one packs at a rate of 1:96, this 13-card set features cards that were redeemable for corresponding draft picks.

	MINT	NRMT
COMPLETE SET (13)	150.00	70.00
COMMON CARD (1-13)	5.00	2.20
SER.1 STATED ODDS 1:96 HOB/RET		

		MINT	NRMT
☐ 1	M.Olowokandi Trade	30.00	13.50
☐ 2	Mike Bibby Trade	25.00	11.00
☐ 3	Raef Lafrentz Trade	15.00	6.75
☐ 4	Antawn Jamison Trade	25.00	11.00
☐ 5	Vince Carter Trade	15.00	6.75
☐ 6	Robert Traylor Trade	15.00	6.75
☐ 7	Jason Williams Trade	10.00	4.50
☐ 8	Larry Hughes Trade	12.00	5.50
☐ 9	Dirk Nowitzki Trade	8.00	3.60
☐ 10	Paul Pierce Trade	12.00	5.50
☐ 11	Bonzi Wells Trade	8.00	3.60
☐ 12	Michael Doleac Trade	5.00	2.20
☐ 13	Keon Clark Trade	5.00	2.20

1998-99 Fleer Rookie Rewind

Randomly inserted in series one packs at one in 36, this 10-card set featues the players named by the NBA to the 1997-98 NBA All-Rookie Team. The card fronts feature silver hologoil accents and embossing.

	MINT	NRMT
COMPLETE SET (10)	40.00	18.00
COMMON CARD (1-10)	1.50	.70
SER.1 STATED ODDS 1:36 HOB/RET		

		MINT	NRMT
☐ 1	Derek Anderson	3.00	1.35
☐ 2	Tim Duncan	15.00	6.75
☐ 3	Cedric Henderson	1.50	.70
☐ 4	Zydrunas Ilgauskas	1.50	.70
☐ 5	Bobby Jackson	2.00	.90
☐ 6	Brevin Knight	3.00	1.35
☐ 7	Ron Mercer	10.00	4.50
☐ 8	Maurice Taylor	3.00	1.35
☐ 9	Tim Thomas	8.00	3.60
☐ 10	Keith Van Horn	12.00	5.50

1998-99 Fleer Timeless Memories

Randomly inserted into series one packs at a rate of one in 12, this 10-card set features players that make the moments great. Card fronts feature the player's face in a watch face with clouds swirling below.

	MINT	NRMT
COMPLETE SET (10)	15.00	6.75
COMMON CARD (1-10)	.75	.35
SER.1 STATED ODDS 1:12 HOB/RET		

		MINT	NRMT
☐ 1	S.Abdur-Rahim	2.00	.90
☐ 2	Ray Allen	.75	.35
☐ 3	Vin Baker	1.50	.70
☐ 4	A.Hardaway	3.00	1.35
☐ 5	Tim Hardaway	1.00	.45
☐ 6	Shaquille O'Neal	3.00	1.35
☐ 7	Scottie Pippen	2.50	1.10
☐ 8	David Robinson	1.25	.55
☐ 9	Dennis Rodman	3.00	1.35
☐ 10	Antoine Walker	3.00	1.35

1989-90 Hoops

The 1989-90 Hoops set contains 352 standard-size cards. The cards were issued in two series of 300 and 52 cards. Hoops' initial venture in the basketball market helped spark the basketball card boom of 1989-90. The cards were issued in 15-card packs. The fronts feature color action player photos, bordered by a basketball lane in one of the team's colors. On a white card face the player's name appears in black lettering above the picture. The backs have head shots of the players, biographical information and statistics printed on a pale yellow background with white borders. The cards are numbered on the back. The key Rookie Card in this set is David Robinson (138). This is his lone Rookie Card. Beware of Robinson counterfeits which are distinguishable primarily by comparison to a real card or under magnification. Other Rookie Cards of note include Hersey Hawkins, Jeff Hornacek, Kevin Johnson, Steve Kerr, Reggie Lewis, Dan Majerle, Danny Manning, Mitch Richmond, Rik Smits and Rod Strickland. The second series features the premier cards of the expansion teams (Minnesota and Orlando), traded players, a special NBA Championship card of the Detroit Pistons and a Robinson In Action (310) card. Since the original Detroit Pistons

World Champs card (No. 353A) was so difficult for collectors to find in packs, Hoops produced another edition (353B) of the card that was available direct from the company free of charge. If a collector wished to acquire two or more from the company, additional copies were available for 35 cents per card. The set is considered complete with the less difficult version. The short prints (SP below) in the first series are those cards which were dropped to make room for the new second series cards on the printing sheet.

	MINT	NRMT
COMPLETE SET (352)	25.00	11.00
COMPLETE SERIES 1 (300)	20.00	9.00
COMPLETE SERIES 2 (52)	5.00	2.20
COMMON CARD (1-352)	.05	.02
COMMON SP	.15	.07
SEMISTARS	.10	.05
SEMISTARS SP	.25	.11
UNLISTED STARS	.25	.11
BEWARE ROBINSON 138 COUNTERFEIT		

□ 1 Joe Dumars	.25	.11
□ 2 Tree Rollins	.05	.02
□ 3 Kenny Walker	.05	.02
□ 4 Mychal Thompson	.05	.02
□ 5 Alvin Robertson SP	.15	.07
□ 6 Vinny Del Negro	.25	.11
□ 7 Greg Anderson SP	.15	.07
□ 8 Rod Strickland	1.00	.45
□ 9 Ed Pinckney	.05	.02
□ 10 Dale Ellis	.05	.02
□ 11 Chuck Daly CO	.25	.11
□ 12 Eric Leckner	.05	.02
□ 13 Charles Davis	.05	.02
□ 14 Cotton Fitzsimmons CO	.05	.02
(No NBA logo on back in bottom right)		
□ 15 Byron Scott	.10	.05
□ 16 Derrick Chievous	.05	.02
□ 17 Reggie Lewis	.25	.11
□ 18 Jim Paxson	.05	.02
□ 19 Tony Campbell	.05	.02
□ 20 Rolando Blackman	.05	.02
□ 21 Michael Jordan AS	1.50	.70
□ 22 Cliff Levingston	.05	.02
□ 23 Roy Tarpley	.05	.02
□ 24 Harold Pressley UER	.05	.02
(Cinderella misspelled as cindarella)		
□ 25 Larry Nance	.10	.05
□ 26 Chris Morris	.25	.11
□ 27 Bob Hansen UER	.05	.02
(Drafted in '84, should say '83)		
□ 28 Mark Price AS	.05	.02
□ 29 Reggie Miller	.60	.25
□ 30 Karl Malone	.40	.18
□ 31 Sidney Lowe SP	.15	.07
□ 32 Ron Anderson	.05	.02
□ 33 Mike Gminski	.05	.02
□ 34 Scott Brooks	.05	.02
□ 35 Kevin Johnson	.50	.23
□ 36 Mark Bryant	.05	.02
□ 37 Rik Smits	.30	.14
□ 38 Tim Perry	.05	.02
□ 39 Ralph Sampson	.05	.02
□ 40 Danny Manning UER	.30	.14
(Missing 1988 in draft info)		
□ 41 Kevin Edwards	.05	.02
□ 42 Paul Mokeski	.05	.02
□ 43 Dale Ellis AS	.05	.02

□ 44 Walter Berry	.05	.02
□ 45 Chuck Person	.10	.05
□ 46 Rick Mahorn SP	.15	.07
□ 47 Joe Kleine	.05	.02
□ 48 Brad Daugherty AS	.05	.02
□ 49 Mike Woodson	.05	.02
□ 50 Brad Daugherty	.05	.02
□ 51 Shelton Jones SP	.15	.07
□ 52 Michael Adams	.05	.02
□ 53 Wes Unseld CO	.05	.02
□ 54 Rex Chapman	.25	.11
□ 55 Kelly Tripucka	.05	.02
□ 56 Rickey Green	.05	.02
□ 57 Frank Johnson SP	.15	.07
□ 58 Johnny Newman	.05	.02
□ 59 Billy Thompson	.05	.02
□ 60 Stu Jackson CO	.05	.02
□ 61 Walter Davis	.05	.02
□ 62 Brian Shaw SP UER	.25	.11
(Gary Grant led rookies in assists, not Shaw)		
□ 63 Gerald Wilkins	.05	.02
□ 64 Armon Gilliam	.05	.02
□ 65 Maurice Cheeks SP	.15	.07
□ 66 Jack Sikma	.05	.02
□ 67 Harvey Grant	.05	.02
□ 68 Jim Lynam CO	.05	.02
□ 69 Clyde Drexler AS	.15	.07
□ 70 Xavier McDaniel	.05	.02
□ 71 Danny Young	.05	.02
□ 72 Fennis Dembo	.05	.02
□ 73 Mark Acres SP	.15	.07
□ 74 Brad Lohaus SP	.15	.07
□ 75 Manute Bol	.05	.02
□ 76 Purvis Short	.05	.02
□ 77 Allen Leavell	.05	.02
□ 78 Johnny Dawkins SP	.15	.07
□ 79 Paul Pressey	.05	.02
□ 80 Patrick Ewing	.25	.11
□ 81 Bill Wennington	.25	.11
□ 82 Danny Schayes	.05	.02
□ 83 Derek Smith	.05	.02
□ 84 Moses Malone AS	.10	.05
□ 85 Jeff Malone	.05	.02
□ 86 Otis Smith SP	.15	.07
□ 87 Trent Tucker	.05	.02
□ 88 Robert Reid	.05	.02
□ 89 John Paxson	.05	.02
□ 90 Chris Mullin	.25	.11
□ 91 Tom Garrick	.05	.02
□ 92 Willis Reed SP UER	.25	.11
(Gambling, should be Grambling)		
□ 93 Dave Corzine SP	.15	.07
□ 94 Mark Alarie	.05	.02
□ 95 Mark Aguirre	.05	.02
□ 96 Charles Barkley AS	.20	.09
□ 97 Sidney Green SP	.15	.07
□ 98 Kevin Willis	.10	.05
□ 99 Dave Hoppen	.05	.02
□ 100 Terry Cummings SP	.25	.11
□ 101 Dwayne Washington SP	.15	.07
□ 102 Larry Brown CO	.10	.05
□ 103 Kevin Duckworth	.05	.02
□ 104 Uwe Blab SP	.15	.07
□ 105 Terry Porter	.05	.02
□ 106 Craig Ehlo	.05	.02
□ 107 Don Casey CO	.05	.02
□ 108 Pat Riley CO	.25	.11
□ 109 John Salley	.05	.02
□ 110 Charles Barkley	.40	.18
□ 111 Sam Bowie SP	.15	.07
□ 112 Earl Cureton	.05	.02
□ 113 Craig Hodges UER	.05	.02
(3-pointing shooting)		
□ 114 Benoit Benjamin	.05	.02
□ 115A Spud Webb ERR SP	.25	.11
(Signed 9/27/89)		
□ 115B Spud Webb COR	.10	.05
(Second series; signed 9/26/85)		
□ 116 Karl Malone AS	.15	.11
□ 117 Sleepy Floyd	.05	.02
□ 118 John Williams	.05	.02
□ 119 Michael Holton	.05	.02

□ 120 Alex English	.05	.02
□ 121 Dennis Johnson	.05	.02
□ 122 Wayne Cooper SP	.15	.07
□ 123A Don Chaney CO	.05	.02
(Line next to NBA coaching record)		
□ 123B Don Chaney CO	.05	.02
(No line)		
□ 124 A.C. Green	.10	.05
□ 125 Adrian Dantley	.05	.02
□ 126 Del Harris CO	.05	.02
□ 127 Dick Harter CO	.05	.02
□ 128 Reggie Williams	.05	.02
□ 129 Bill Hanzlik	.05	.02
□ 130 Dominique Wilkins	.25	.11
□ 131 Herb Williams	.05	.02
□ 132 Steve Johnson SP	.15	.07
□ 133 Alex English AS	.05	.02
□ 134 Darrell Walker	.05	.02
□ 135 Bill Laimbeer	.10	.05
□ 136 Fred Roberts	.05	.02
□ 137 Hersey Hawkins	.30	.14
□ 138 David Robinson	12.00	5.50
□ 139 Brad Sellers SP	.15	.07
□ 140 John Stockton	.60	.25
□ 141 Grant Long	.10	.05
□ 142 Marc Iavaroni AS	.15	.07
□ 143 Steve Alford SP	.15	.07
□ 144 Jeff Lamp SP	.15	.07
□ 145 Buck Williams SP UER	.25	.11
(Won ROY in '81, should say '82)		
□ 146 Mark Jackson AS	.05	.02
□ 147 Jim Petersen	.05	.02
□ 148 Steve Stipanovich SP	.15	.07
□ 149 Sam Vincent SP	.15	.07
□ 150 Larry Bird	1.00	.45
□ 151 Jon Koncak	.05	.02
□ 152 Olden Polynice	.10	.05
□ 153 Randy Breuer	.05	.02
□ 154 John Battle	.05	.02
□ 155 Mark Eaton	.05	.02
□ 156 Kevin McHale AS UER	.10	.05
(No TM on Celtics logo on back)		
□ 157 Jerry Sichting SP	.15	.07
□ 158 Pat Cummings SP	.15	.07
□ 159 Patrick Ewing AS	.10	.05
□ 160 Mark Price	.05	.02
□ 161 Jerry Reynolds CO	.05	.02
□ 162 Ken Norman	.05	.02
□ 163 John Bagley SP UER	.15	.07
(Picked in '83, should say '82)		
□ 164 Christian Welp SP	.15	.07
□ 165 Reggie Theus SP	.25	.11
□ 166 Magic Johnson AS	.40	.18
□ 167 John Long SP	.05	.02
(Picked in '79, should say '78)		
□ 168 Larry Smith SP	.15	.07
□ 169 Charles Shackleford	.05	.02
□ 170 Tom Chambers	.05	.02
□ 171A John MacLeod CO SP	.25	.11
ERR (NBA logo in wrong place)		
□ 171B John MacLeod CO	.05	.02
COR (Second series)		
□ 172 Ron Rothstein CO	.05	.02
□ 173 Joe Wolf	.05	.02
□ 174 Mark Eaton AS	.05	.02
□ 175 Jon Sundvold	.05	.02
□ 176 Scott Hastings SP	.15	.07
□ 177 Isiah Thomas AS	.10	.05
□ 178 Hakeem Olajuwon AS	.25	.11
□ 179 Mike Fratello CO	.10	.05
□ 180 Hakeem Olajuwon	.50	.23
□ 181 Randolph Keys	.05	.02
□ 182 Richard Anderson SP	.05	.02
(Trail Blazers on front should be all caps)		
□ 183 Dan Majerle	.30	.14
□ 184 Derek Harper	.10	.05
□ 185 Robert Parish	.10	.05
□ 186 Ricky Berry SP	.15	.07
□ 187 Michael Cooper	.05	.02

☐ 188	Vinnie Johnson	.10	.05
☐ 189	James Donaldson	.05	.02
☐ 190	Clyde Drexler UER	.30	.14
	(4th pick, should		
	be 14th)		
☐ 191	Jay Vincent SP	.15	.07
☐ 192	Nate McMillan	.10	.05
☐ 193	Kevin Duckworth AS	.05	.02
☐ 194	Ledell Eackles	.05	.02
☐ 195	Eddie Johnson	.10	.05
☐ 196	Terry Teagle	.05	.02
☐ 197	Tom Chambers AS	.05	.02
☐ 198	Joe Barry Carroll	.05	.02
☐ 199	Dennis Hopson	.05	.02
☐ 200	Michael Jordan	3.00	1.35
☐ 201	Jerome Lane	.05	.02
☐ 202	Greg Kite	.05	.02
☐ 203	David Rivers SP	.15	.07
☐ 204	Sylvester Gray	.05	.02
☐ 205	Ron Harper	.10	.05
☐ 206	Frank Brickowski	.05	.02
☐ 207	Rory Sparrow	.05	.02
☐ 208	Gerald Henderson	.05	.02
☐ 209	Rod Higgins UER	.05	.02
	('85-86 stats should		
	also include San		
	Antonio and Seattle)		
☐ 210	James Worthy	.25	.11
☐ 211	Dennis Rodman	1.50	.70
☐ 212	Ricky Pierce	.05	.02
☐ 213	Charles Oakley	.10	.05
☐ 214	Steve Colter	.05	.02
☐ 215	Danny Ainge	.10	.05
☐ 216	Lenny Wilkens CO UER	.10	.05
	(No NBA logo on back		
	in bottom right)		
☐ 217	Larry Nance AS	.05	.02
☐ 218	Muggsy Bogues	.10	.05
☐ 219	James Worthy AS	.10	.05
☐ 220	Lafayette Lever	.05	.02
☐ 221	Quintin Dailey SP	.15	.07
☐ 222	Lester Conner	.05	.02
☐ 223	Jose Ortiz	.05	.02
☐ 224	Micheal Williams SP	.25	.11
	UER (Misspelled		
	Michael on card)		
☐ 225	Wayman Tisdale	.05	.02
☐ 226	Mike Sanders SP	.15	.07
☐ 227	Jim Farmer SP	.15	.07
☐ 228	Mark West	.05	.02
☐ 229	Jeff Hornacek	.30	.14
☐ 230	Chris Mullin AS	.05	.02
☐ 231	Vern Fleming	.05	.02
☐ 232	Kenny Smith	.05	.02
☐ 233	Derrick McKey	.05	.02
☐ 234	Dominique Wilkins AS	.10	.05
☐ 235	Willie Anderson	.05	.02
☐ 236	Keith Lee SP	.15	.07
☐ 237	Buck Johnson	.05	.02
☐ 238	Randy Wittman	.05	.02
☐ 239	Terry Catledge SP	.15	.07
☐ 240	Bernard King	.05	.02
☐ 241	Darrell Griffith	.05	.02
☐ 242	Horace Grant	.10	.05
☐ 243	Rony Seikaly	.25	.11
☐ 244	Scottie Pippen	1.50	.70
☐ 245	Michael Cage UER	.05	.02
	(Picked in '85,		
	should say '84)		
☐ 246	Kurt Rambis	.05	.02
☐ 247	Morlon Wiley SP	.15	.07
☐ 248	Ronnie Grandison	.05	.02
☐ 249	Scott Skiles SP	.25	.11
☐ 250	Isiah Thomas	.25	.11
☐ 251	Thurl Bailey	.05	.02
☐ 252	Doc Rivers	.10	.05
☐ 253	Stuart Gray SP	.15	.07
☐ 254	John Williams	.05	.02
☐ 255	Bill Cartwright	.05	.02
☐ 256	Terry Cummings AS	.05	.02
☐ 257	Rodney McCray	.05	.02
☐ 258	Larry Krystkowiak	.05	.02
☐ 259	Will Perdue	.05	.02
☐ 260	Mitch Richmond	1.50	.70
☐ 261	Blair Rasmussen	.05	.02
☐ 262	Charles Smith	.25	.11

☐ 263	Tyrone Corbin SP	.15	.07
☐ 264	Kelvin Upshaw	.05	.02
☐ 265	Otis Thorpe	.10	.05
☐ 266	Phil Jackson CO	.25	.11
☐ 267	Jerry Sloan CO	.10	.05
☐ 268	John Shasky	.05	.02
☐ 269A	B. Bickerstaff CO SP	.25	.11
	ERR (Born 2/11/44)		
☐ 269B	B. Bickerstaff CO	.05	.02
	COR (Second series;		
	Born 11/2/43)		
☐ 270	Magic Johnson	.75	.35
☐ 271	Vernon Maxwell	.10	.05
☐ 272	Tim McCormick	.05	.02
☐ 273	Don Nelson CO	.10	.05
☐ 274	Gary Grant	.05	.02
☐ 275	Sidney Moncrief SP	.15	.07
☐ 276	Roy Hinson	.05	.02
☐ 277	Jimmy Rodgers CO	.05	.02
☐ 278	Antoine Carr	.05	.02
☐ 279A	O.Woolridge SP	.25	.11
	ERR (No Trademark)		
☐ 279B	O.Woolridge	.05	.02
	COR (Second series)		
☐ 280	Kevin McHale	.25	.11
☐ 281	LaSalle Thompson	.05	.02
☐ 282	Detlef Schrempf	.10	.05
☐ 283	Doug Moe CO	.05	.02
☐ 284A	James Edwards	.25	.11
	(Small black line		
	next to card number)		
☐ 284B	James Edwards	.05	.02
	(No small black line)		
☐ 285	Jerome Kersey	.05	.02
☐ 286	Sam Perkins	.10	.05
☐ 287	Sedale Threatt	.05	.02
☐ 288	Tim Kempton SP	.15	.07
☐ 289	Mark McNamara	.05	.02
☐ 290	Moses Malone	.25	.11
☐ 291	Rick Adelman CO UER	.05	.02
	(Chemekata misspelled		
	as Chemketa)		
☐ 292	Dick Versace CO	.05	.02
☐ 293	Alton Lister SP	.15	.07
☐ 294	Winston Garland	.05	.02
☐ 295	Kiki Vandeweghe	.05	.02
☐ 296	Brad Davis	.05	.02
☐ 297	John Stockton AS	.30	.14
☐ 298	Jay Humphries	.05	.02
☐ 299	Dell Curry	.05	.02
☐ 300	Mark Jackson	.10	.05
☐ 301	Morlon Wiley	.05	.02
☐ 302	Reggie Theus	.10	.05
☐ 303	Otis Smith	.05	.02
☐ 304	Tod Murphy	.05	.02
☐ 305	Sidney Green	.05	.02
☐ 306	Shelton Jones	.05	.02
☐ 307	Mark Acres	.05	.02
☐ 308	Terry Catledge	.05	.02
☐ 309	Larry Smith	.05	.02
☐ 310	David Robinson IA	1.50	.70
☐ 311	Johnny Dawkins	.05	.02
☐ 312	Terry Cummings	.10	.05
☐ 313	Sidney Lowe	.05	.02
☐ 314	Bill Musselman CO	.05	.02
☐ 315	Buck Williams UER	.10	.05
	(Won ROY in '81,		
	should say '82)		
☐ 316	Mel Turpin	.05	.02
☐ 317	Scott Hastings	.05	.02
☐ 318	Scott Skiles	.10	.05
☐ 319	Tyrone Corbin	.05	.02
☐ 320	Maurice Cheeks	.05	.02
☐ 321	Matt Guokas CO	.05	.02
☐ 322	Jeff Turner	.05	.02
☐ 323	David Wingate	.05	.02
☐ 324	Steve Johnson	.05	.02
☐ 325	Alton Lister	.05	.02
☐ 326	Ken Bannister	.05	.02
☐ 327	Bill Fitch CO UER	.05	.02
	(Copyright missing		
	on bottom of back)		
☐ 328	Sam Vincent	.05	.02
☐ 329	Larry Drew	.05	.02
☐ 330	Rick Mahorn	.05	.02
☐ 331	Christian Welp	.05	.02

☐ 332	Brad Lohaus	.05	.02
☐ 333	Frank Johnson	.05	.02
☐ 334	Jim Farmer	.05	.02
☐ 335	Wayne Cooper	.05	.02
☐ 336	Mike Brown	.05	.02
☐ 337	Sam Bowie	.05	.02
☐ 338	Kevin Gamble	.05	.02
☐ 339	Jerry Ice Reynolds	.05	.02
☐ 340	Mike Sanders	.05	.02
☐ 341	Bill Jones UER	.05	.02
	(Center on front,		
	should be F)		
☐ 342	Greg Anderson	.05	.02
☐ 343	Dave Corzine	.05	.02
☐ 344	Micheal Williams UER	.05	.02
	(Misspelled Michael		
	on card)		
☐ 345	Jay Vincent	.05	.02
☐ 346	David Rivers	.05	.02
☐ 347	Caldwell Jones UER	.05	.02
	(He was not starting		
	center on '83 Sixers)		
☐ 348	Brad Sellers	.05	.02
☐ 349	Scott Roth	.05	.02
☐ 350	Alvin Robertson	.05	.02
☐ 351	Steve Kerr	.60	.25
☐ 352	Stuart Gray	.05	.02
☐ 353A	World Champions SP	4.00	1.80
☐ 353B	World Champ. UER	.50	.23
	(George Blaha mis-		
	spelled Blanha)		

1990-91 Hoops

The complete 1990-91 Hoops basketball set contains 440 standard-size cards. The set was distributed in two series of 336 and 104 cards, respectively. The cards were issued in 15-card plastic-wrap packs which came 36 to a box. On the front the color action player photo appears in the shape of a basketball lane, bordered by gold on the All-Star cards (1-26) and by silver on the regular issues (27-331, 336). The player's name and the stripe below the picture are printed in one of the team's colors. The team logo at the lower right corner rounds out the card face. The back of the regular issue has a color head shot and biographical informa-tion as well as college and pro statistics, framed by a basket-ball lane. The set is arranged alphabetically according to teams. Subsets are Coaches

(305-331/343-354), *NBA Finals (337-342), Team checklists (355-381), Inside Stuff (382-385), Stay in School (386-387), Don't Foul Out (388-389), Lottery Selections (390-400), and Updates (401-438). Some of the All-Star cards (card numbers 2, 6, and 8) can be found with or without a printing mistake, i.e., no T in the trademark logo on the card back. A few of the cards (card numbers 14, 66, 144, and 279) refer to the player as "all America" rather than "All America." The following cards can be found with or without a black line under the card number, height, and birthplace: 20, 23, 24, 29, and 87. Rookie Cards of note included in the set are Nick Anderson, Mookie Blaylock, Derrick Coleman, Vlade Divac, Sean Elliott, Kendall Gill, Tim Hardaway, Chris Jackson, Shawn Kemp, Gary Payton, Drazen Petrovic, Glen Rice, Clifford Robinson and Dennis Scott. The short prints (SP below) in the first series are those cards which were dropped to make room for the new second series cards on the printing sheet.*

	MINT	NRMT
COMPLETE SET (440)	15.00	6.75
COMPLETE SERIES 1 (336)	10.00	4.50
COMPLETE SERIES 2 (104)..	5.00	2.20
COMMON CARD (1-440)	.05	.02
COMMON	.10	.05
SEMISTARS	.08	.04
UNLISTED STARS	.15	.07

☐ 1 Charles Barkley AS SP....	.25	.11
☐ 2 Larry Bird AS SP	.60	.25
☐ 3 Joe Dumars AS SP	.15	.07
☐ 4 Patrick Ewing AS SP	.15	.07
(A-S blocks listed as 1, should be 5) UER		
☐ 5 Michael Jordan AS SP....	2.00	.90
(Won Slam Dunk in '87 and '88, not '86 and '88) UER		
☐ 6 Kevin McHale AS SP	.10	.05
☐ 7 Reggie Miller AS SP	.15	.07
☐ 8 Robert Parish AS SP	.10	.05
☐ 9 Scottie Pippen AS SP	.60	.25
☐ 10 Dennis Rodman AS SP ..	.75	.35
☐ 11 Isiah Thomas AS SP	.15	.07
☐ 12 Dominique Wilkins AS SP	.15	.07
☐ 13A All-Star Checklist SP ..	.25	.11
ERR (No card number)		
☐ 13B All-Star Checklist SP ..	.10	.05
COR (Card number on back)		
☐ 14 B.Blackman AS SP	.10	.05
☐ 15 Tom Chambers AS SP...	.10	.05
☐ 16 Clyde Drexler AS SP	.20	.09
☐ 17 A.C. Green AS SP	.10	.05
☐ 18 Magic Johnson AS SP ..	.50	.23
☐ 19 Kevin Johnson AS SP ..	.15	.07
☐ 20 Lafayette Lever AS SP .	.10	.05
☐ 21 Karl Malone AS SP	.25	.11
☐ 22 Chris Mullin AS SP	.15	.07

☐ 23 Hakeem Olajuwon AS SP	.30	.14
☐ 24 David Robinson AS SP .	.50	.23
☐ 25 John Stockton AS SP...	.20	.09
☐ 26 James Worthy AS SP ...	.15	.07
☐ 27 John Battle	.05	.02
☐ 28 Jon Koncak	.05	.02
☐ 29 Cliff Levingston SP	.10	.05
☐ 30 John Long SP	.10	.05
☐ 31 Moses Malone	.15	.07
☐ 32 Doc Rivers	.08	.04
☐ 33 Kenny Smith SP	.10	.05
☐ 34 Alexander Volkov	.05	.02
☐ 35 Spud Webb	.08	.04
☐ 36 Dominique Wilkins	.15	.07
☐ 37 Kevin Willis	.08	.04
☐ 38 John Bagley	.05	.02
☐ 39 Larry Bird	.60	.25
☐ 40 Kevin Gamble	.05	.02
☐ 41 Dennis Johnson SP	.05	.02
☐ 42 Joe Kleine	.05	.02
☐ 43 Reggie Lewis	.08	.04
☐ 44 Kevin McHale	.08	.04
☐ 45 Robert Parish	.08	.04
☐ 46 Jim Paxson SP	.08	.04
☐ 47 Ed Pinckney	.05	.02
☐ 48 Brian Shaw	.15	.07
☐ 49 Richard Anderson SP ..	.10	.05
☐ 50 Muggsy Bogues	.08	.04
☐ 51 Rex Chapman	.15	.07
☐ 52 Dell Curry	.05	.02
☐ 53 Kenny Gattison	.05	.02
☐ 54 Armon Gilliam	.05	.02
☐ 55 Dave Hoppen	.05	.02
☐ 56 Randolph Keys	.05	.02
☐ 57 J.R. Reid	.05	.02
☐ 58 Robert Reid SP	.10	.05
☐ 59 Kelly Tripucka	.05	.02
☐ 60 B.J. Armstrong	.08	.04
☐ 61 Bill Cartwright	.05	.02
☐ 62 Charles Davis SP	.10	.05
☐ 63 Horace Grant	.08	.04
☐ 64 Craig Hodges	.05	.02
☐ 65 Michael Jordan	2.00	.90
☐ 66 Stacey King	.05	.02
☐ 67 John Paxson	.08	.04
☐ 68 Will Perdue	.05	.02
☐ 69 Scottie Pippen	.60	.25
☐ 70 Winston Bennett	.05	.02
☐ 71 Chucky Brown	.05	.02
☐ 72 Derrick Chievous	.05	.02
☐ 73 Brad Daugherty	.05	.02
☐ 74 Craig Ehlo	.05	.02
☐ 75 Steve Kerr	.15	.07
☐ 76 Paul Mokeski SP	.10	.05
☐ 77 John Morton	.05	.02
☐ 78 Larry Nance	.08	.04
☐ 79 Mark Price	.08	.04
☐ 80 Hot Rod Williams	.05	.02
☐ 81 Steve Alford	.05	.02
☐ 82 Rolando Blackman	.05	.02
☐ 83 Adrian Dantley SP	.05	.02
☐ 84 Brad Davis	.05	.02
☐ 85 James Donaldson	.05	.02
☐ 86 Derek Harper	.08	.04
☐ 87 Sam Perkins	.08	.04
☐ 88 Roy Tarpley	.05	.02
☐ 89 Bill Wennington SP	.10	.05
☐ 90 Herb Williams	.05	.02
☐ 91 Michael Adams	.05	.02
☐ 92 Walter Davis UER	.05	.02
(Born NC, not PA)		
☐ 93 Walter Davis UER	.05	.02
(Born NC, not PA)		
☐ 94 Alex English SP	.05	.02
☐ 95 Bill Hanzlik	.05	.02
☐ 96 Jerome Lane	.05	.02
☐ 97 Lafayette Lever SP	.10	.05
☐ 98 Todd Lichti	.05	.02
☐ 99 Blair Rasmussen	.05	.02
☐ 100 Danny Schayes SP	.10	.05
☐ 101 Mark Aguirre	.05	.02
☐ 102 William Bedford	.05	.02
☐ 103 Joe Dumars	.15	.07
☐ 104 James Edwards	.05	.02
☐ 105 Scott Hastings	.05	.02
☐ 106 Gerald Henderson SP .	.10	.05
☐ 107 Vinnie Johnson	.05	.02

☐ 108 Bill Laimbeer	.08	.04
☐ 109 Dennis Rodman	.75	.35
☐ 110 John Salley	.05	.02
☐ 111 Isiah Thomas UER	.15	.07
(No position listed on the card)		
☐ 112 Manute Bol SP	.10	.05
☐ 113 Tim Hardaway	1.25	.55
☐ 114 Rod Higgins	.05	.02
☐ 115 Sarunas Marciulionis..	.05	.02
☐ 116 Chris Mullin UER	.15	.07
(Born Brooklyn, NY, not New York, NY)		
☐ 117 Jim Petersen	.05	.02
☐ 118 Mitch Richmond	.25	.11
☐ 119 Mike Smrek	.05	.02
☐ 120 Terry Teagle SP	.10	.05
☐ 121 Tom Tolbert	.05	.02
☐ 122 Christian Welp SP	.10	.05
☐ 123 Byron Dinkins SP	.10	.05
☐ 124 Eric(Sleepy) Floyd	.05	.02
☐ 125 Buck Johnson	.05	.02
☐ 126 Vernon Maxwell	.05	.02
☐ 127 Hakeem Olajuwon	.30	.14
☐ 128 Larry Smith	.05	.02
☐ 129 Otis Thorpe	.08	.04
☐ 130 Mitchell Wiggins SP ..	.10	.05
☐ 131 Mike Woodson	.05	.02
☐ 132 Greg Dreiling	.05	.02
☐ 133 Vern Fleming	.05	.02
☐ 134 Rickey Green SP	.10	.05
☐ 135 Reggie Miller	.20	.09
☐ 136 Chuck Person	.08	.04
☐ 137 Mike Sanders	.05	.02
☐ 138 Detlef Schrempf	.10	.05
☐ 139 Rik Smits	.15	.07
☐ 140 LaSalle Thompson	.05	.02
☐ 141 Randy Wittman	.05	.02
☐ 142 Benoit Benjamin	.05	.02
☐ 143 Winston Garland	.05	.02
☐ 144 Tom Garrick	.05	.02
☐ 145 Gary Grant	.05	.02
☐ 146 Ron Harper	.08	.04
☐ 147 Danny Manning	.08	.04
☐ 148 Jeff Martin	.05	.02
☐ 149 Ken Norman	.05	.02
☐ 150 David Rivers SP	.10	.05
☐ 151 Charles Smith	.05	.02
☐ 152 Joe Wolf SP	.10	.05
☐ 153 Michael Cooper SP	.10	.05
☐ 154 Vlade Divac UER	.30	.14
(Height 6'11", should be 7'1")		
☐ 155 Larry Drew	.05	.02
☐ 156 A.C. Green	.08	.04
☐ 157 Magic Johnson	.50	.23
☐ 158 Mark McNamara SP ..	.05	.02
☐ 159 Byron Scott	.08	.04
☐ 160 Mychal Thompson	.05	.02
☐ 161 Jay Vincent SP	.10	.05
☐ 162 Orlando Woolridge SP	.10	.05
☐ 163 James Worthy	.15	.07
☐ 164 Sherman Douglas	.08	.04
☐ 165 Kevin Edwards	.05	.02
☐ 166 Tellis Frank SP	.10	.05
☐ 167 Grant Long	.05	.02
☐ 168 Glen Rice	1.00	.45
☐ 169A Rony Seikaly	.08	.04
(Athens)		
☐ 169B Rony Seikaly	.08	.04
(Beirut)		
☐ 170 Rory Sparrow SP	.10	.05
☐ 171A Jon Sundvold	.05	.02
(First series)		
☐ 171B Billy Thompson	.05	.02
(Second series)		
☐ 172A Billy Thompson	.05	.02
(First series)		
☐ 172B Jon Sundvold	.05	.02
(Second series)		
☐ 173 Greg Anderson	.05	.02
☐ 174 Jeff Grayer	.05	.02
☐ 175 Jay Humphries	.05	.02
☐ 176 Frank Kornet	.05	.02
☐ 177 Larry Krystkowiak	.05	.02
☐ 178 Brad Lohaus	.05	.02

☐ 179 Ricky Pierce	.05	.02
☐ 180 Paul Pressey SP	.10	.05
☐ 181 Fred Roberts	.05	.02
☐ 182 Alvin Robertson	.05	.02
☐ 183 Jack Sikma	.05	.02
☐ 184 Randy Breuer	.05	.02
☐ 185 Tony Campbell	.05	.02
☐ 186 Tyrone Corbin	.05	.02
☐ 187 Sidney Lowe SP	.10	.05
☐ 188 Sam Mitchell	.05	.02
☐ 189 Tod Murphy	.05	.02
☐ 190 Pooh Richardson	.08	.04
☐ 191 Scott Roth SP	.05	.02
☐ 192 Brad Sellers SP	.10	.05
☐ 193 Mookie Blaylock	.30	.14
☐ 194 Sam Bowie	.05	.02
☐ 195 Lester Conner	.05	.02
☐ 196 Derrick Gervin	.05	.02
☐ 197 Jack Haley	.05	.02
☐ 198 Roy Hinson	.05	.02
☐ 199 Dennis Hopson SP	.10	.05
☐ 200 Chris Morris	.08	.04
☐ 201 Purvis Short SP	.10	.05
☐ 202 Maurice Cheeks	.05	.02
☐ 203 Patrick Ewing	.15	.07
☐ 204 Stuart Gray	.05	.02
☐ 205 Mark Jackson	.08	.04
☐ 206 Johnny Newman SP	.10	.05
☐ 207 Charles Oakley	.08	.04
☐ 208 Trent Tucker	.05	.02
☐ 209 Kiki Vandeweghe	.05	.02
☐ 210 Kenny Walker	.05	.02
☐ 211 Eddie Lee Wilkins	.05	.02
☐ 212 Gerald Wilkins	.05	.02
☐ 213 Mark Acres	.05	.02
☐ 214 Nick Anderson	.25	.11
☐ 215 Michael Ansley UER (Ranked first, not third)	.05	.02
☐ 216 Terry Catledge	.05	.02
☐ 217 Dave Corzine SP	.10	.05
☐ 218 Sidney Green SP	.10	.05
☐ 219 Jerry Reynolds	.05	.02
☐ 220 Scott Skiles	.05	.02
☐ 221 Otis Smith	.05	.02
☐ 222 Reggie Theus SP	.08	.04
☐ 223A Sam Vincent (Shows Michael Jordan)	1.50	.70
☐ 223B Sam Vincent (Second series and shows Sam dribbling)	.05	.02
☐ 224 Ron Anderson	.05	.02
☐ 225 Charles Barkley	.25	.11
☐ 226 Scott Brooks SP UER (Born French Camp, not Lathron, Cal.)	.10	.05
☐ 227 Johnny Dawkins	.05	.02
☐ 228 Mike Gminski	.05	.02
☐ 229 Hersey Hawkins	.08	.04
☐ 230 Rick Mahorn	.05	.02
☐ 231 Derek Smith SP	.10	.05
☐ 232 Bob Thornton	.05	.02
☐ 233 Kenny Battle	.05	.02
☐ 234A Tom Chambers (First series; Forward on front)	.05	.02
☐ 234B Tom Chambers (Second series; Guard on front)	.05	.02
☐ 235 Greg Grant SP	.10	.05
☐ 236 Jeff Hornacek	.08	.04
☐ 237 Eddie Johnson	.08	.04
☐ 238A Kevin Johnson (First series; Guard on front)	.15	.07
☐ 238B Kevin Johnson (Second series; Forward on front)	.15	.07
☐ 239 Dan Majerle	.15	.07
☐ 240 Tim Perry	.05	.02
☐ 241 Kurt Rambis	.05	.02
☐ 242 Mark West	.05	.02
☐ 243 Mark Bryant	.05	.02
☐ 244 Wayne Cooper	.05	.02
☐ 245 Clyde Drexler	.20	.09
☐ 246 Kevin Duckworth	.05	.02
☐ 247 Jerome Kersey	.05	.02
☐ 248 Drazen Petrovic	.08	.04
☐ 249A Terry Porter ERR (No NBA symbol on back)	.50	.23
☐ 249B Terry Porter COR	.05	.02
☐ 250 Clifford Robinson	.25	.11
☐ 251 Buck Williams	.08	.04
☐ 252 Danny Young	.05	.02
☐ 253 Danny Ainge SP UER (Middle name Ray misspelled as Rae on back)	.08	.04
☐ 254 Randy Allen SP	.10	.05
☐ 255 Antoine Carr	.05	.02
☐ 256 Vinny Del Negro SP	.10	.05
☐ 257 Pervis Ellison SP	.10	.05
☐ 258 Greg Kite SP	.10	.05
☐ 259 Rodney McCray SP	.10	.05
☐ 260 Harold Pressley SP	.10	.05
☐ 261 Ralph Sampson	.05	.02
☐ 262 Wayman Tisdale	.05	.02
☐ 263 Willie Anderson	.05	.02
☐ 264 Uwe Blab SP	.10	.05
☐ 265 Frank Brickowski SP	.10	.05
☐ 266 Terry Cummings	.05	.02
☐ 267 Sean Elliott	.25	.11
☐ 268 Caldwell Jones SP	.10	.05
☐ 269 Johnny Moore SP	.10	.05
☐ 270 David Robinson	.50	.23
☐ 271 Rod Strickland	.15	.07
☐ 272 Reggie Williams	.05	.02
☐ 273 David Wingate SP	.10	.05
☐ 274 Dana Barros UER (Born April, not March)	.15	.07
☐ 275 Michael Cage UER (Drafted '84, not '85)	.05	.02
☐ 276 Quintin Dailey	.05	.02
☐ 277 Dale Ellis	.08	.04
☐ 278 Steve Johnson SP	.10	.05
☐ 279 Shawn Kemp	3.00	1.35
☐ 280 Xavier McDaniel	.05	.02
☐ 281 Derrick McKey	.05	.02
☐ 282 Nate McMillan	.08	.04
☐ 283 Olden Polynice	.05	.02
☐ 284 Sedale Threatt	.05	.02
☐ 285 Thurl Bailey	.05	.02
☐ 286 Mike Brown	.05	.02
☐ 287 Mark Eaton UER (72nd pick, not 82nd)	.05	.02
☐ 288 Blue Edwards	.05	.02
☐ 289 Darrell Griffith	.05	.02
☐ 290 Robert Hansen SP	.10	.05
☐ 291 Eric Leckner SP	.10	.05
☐ 292 Karl Malone	.25	.11
☐ 293 Delaney Rudd	.05	.02
☐ 294 John Stockton	.20	.09
☐ 295 Mark Alarie	.05	.02
☐ 296 Ledell Eackles SP	.10	.05
☐ 297 Harvey Grant	.05	.02
☐ 298A Tom Hammonds (No rookie logo on front)	.05	.02
☐ 298B Tom Hammonds (Rookie logo on front)	.05	.02
☐ 299 Charles Jones	.05	.02
☐ 300 Bernard King	.05	.02
☐ 301 Jeff Malone SP	.10	.05
☐ 302 Mel Turpin SP	.10	.05
☐ 303 Darrell Walker	.05	.02
☐ 304 John Williams	.05	.02
☐ 305 Bob Weiss CO	.05	.02
☐ 306 Chris Ford CO	.05	.02
☐ 307 Gene Littles CO	.05	.02
☐ 308 Phil Jackson CO	.15	.07
☐ 309 Lenny Wilkens CO	.08	.04
☐ 310 Richie Adubato CO	.05	.02
☐ 311 Doug Moe CO SP	.10	.05
☐ 312 Chuck Daly CO	.08	.04
☐ 313 Don Nelson CO	.08	.04
☐ 314 Don Chaney CO	.05	.02
☐ 315 Dick Versace CO	.05	.02
☐ 316 Mike Schuler CO	.05	.02
☐ 317 Pat Riley CO SP	.15	.07
☐ 318 Ron Rothstein CO	.05	.02
☐ 319 Del Harris CO	.05	.02
☐ 320 Bill Musselman CO	.05	.02
☐ 321 Bill Fitch CO	.05	.02
☐ 322 Stu Jackson CO	.05	.02
☐ 323 Matt Guokas CO	.05	.02
☐ 324 Jim Lynam CO	.05	.02
☐ 325 Cotton Fitzsimmons CO	.05	.02
☐ 326 Rick Adelman CO	.05	.02
☐ 327 Dick Motta CO	.05	.02
☐ 328 Larry Brown CO	.08	.04
☐ 329 K.C. Jones CO	.05	.02
☐ 330 Jerry Sloan CO	.08	.04
☐ 331 Wes Unseld CO	.05	.02
☐ 332 Checklist 1 SP	.10	.05
☐ 333 Checklist 2 SP	.10	.05
☐ 334 Checklist 3 SP	.10	.05
☐ 335 Checklist 4 SP	.10	.05
☐ 336 Danny Ferry SP	.25	.11
☐ 337 Pistons Celebrate Dennis Rodman	.15	.07
☐ 338 Buck Williams FIN Dennis Rodman	.15	.07
☐ 339 Joe Dumars FIN Isiah Thomas	.15	.07
☐ 340 Jerome Kersey FIN Isiah Thomas	.08	.04
☐ 341A V.Johnson FIN ERR. No headline on back	.05	.02
☐ 341B Vinnie Johnson COR	.05	.02
☐ 342 Pistons Celebrate UER James Edwards Player named as Sidney Green is really David Greenwood	.05	.02
☐ 343 K.C. Jones CO	.05	.02
☐ 344 Wes Unseld CO	.05	.02
☐ 345 Don Nelson CO	.08	.04
☐ 346 Bob Weiss CO	.05	.02
☐ 347 Chris Ford CO	.05	.02
☐ 348 Phil Jackson CO	.15	.07
☐ 349 Lenny Wilkens CO	.08	.04
☐ 350 Don Chaney CO	.05	.02
☐ 351 Mike Dunleavy CO	.05	.02
☐ 352 Matt Guokas CO	.05	.02
☐ 353 Rick Adelman CO	.05	.02
☐ 354 Jerry Sloan CO	.08	.04
☐ 355 Dominique Wilkins TC	.08	.04
☐ 356 Larry Bird TC	.30	.14
☐ 357 Rex Chapman TC	.05	.02
☐ 358 Michael Jordan TC ..	1.00	.45
☐ 359 Mark Price TC	.05	.02
☐ 360 Rolando Blackman TC	.05	.02
☐ 361 Michael Adams TC UER (Westhead should be card 422, not 440)	.05	.02
☐ 362 Joe Dumars TC UER (Gerald Henderson's name and number not listed)	.08	.04
☐ 363 Chris Mullin TC	.08	.04
☐ 364 Hakeem Olajuwon TC	.15	.07
☐ 365 Reggie Miller TC	.15	.07
☐ 366 Danny Manning TC	.05	.02
☐ 367 Magic Johnson TC UER (Dunleavy listed as 439, should be 351)	.25	.11
☐ 368 Rony Seikaly TC	.05	.02
☐ 369 Alvin Robertson TC	.05	.02
☐ 370 Pooh Richardson TC	.05	.02
☐ 371 Chris Morris TC	.05	.02
☐ 372 Patrick Ewing TC	.15	.07
☐ 373 Nick Anderson TC	.15	.07
☐ 374 Charles Barkley TC	.15	.07
☐ 375 Kevin Johnson TC	.08	.04
☐ 376 Clyde Drexler TC	.15	.07
☐ 377 Wayman Tisdale TC	.05	.02
☐ 378 David Robinson TC (Basketball fully visible)	.25	.11
☐ 378B David Robinson TC (Basketball partially visible)	.25	.11
☐ 379 Xavier McDaniel TC	.05	.02
☐ 380 Karl Malone TC	.15	.07
☐ 381 Bernard King TC	.05	.02
☐ 382 Michael Jordan TC Playground	1.00	.45
☐ 383 Karl Malone horseback	.15	.07
☐ 384 European Imports (Vlade Divac Sarunas Marciulionis)	.05	.02
☐ 385 Super Streaks Stay In School	1.00	.45

(Magic Johnson and Michael Jordan)

#	Card	MINT	NRMT
☐ 386	Johnny Newman	.05	.02
	(Stay in School)		
☐ 387	Dell Curry	.05	.02
	(Stay in School)		
☐ 388	Patrick Ewing	.15	.07
	(Don't Foul Out)		
☐ 389	Isiah Thomas	.15	.07
	(Don't Foul Out)		
☐ 390	Derrick Coleman LS	.30	.14
☐ 391	Gary Payton LS	1.25	.55
☐ 392	Chris Jackson LS	.05	.02
☐ 393	Dennis Scott LS	.20	.09
☐ 394	Kendall Gill LS	.30	.14
☐ 395	Felton Spencer LS	.08	.04
☐ 396	Lionel Simmons LS	.08	.04
☐ 397	Bo Kimble LS	.05	.02
☐ 398	Willie Burton LS	.08	.04
☐ 399	Rumeal Robinson LS	.05	.02
☐ 400	Tyrone Hill LS	.05	.02
☐ 401	Tim McCormick	.05	.02
☐ 402	Sidney Moncrief	.05	.02
☐ 403	Johnny Newman	.05	.02
☐ 404	Dennis Hopson	.05	.02
☐ 405	Cliff Levingston	.05	.02
☐ 406A	Danny Ferry ERR	.30	.14
	(No position on front of card)		
☐ 406B	Danny Ferry COR	.15	.07
☐ 407	Alex English	.05	.02
☐ 408	Lafayette Lever	.05	.02
☐ 409	Rodney McCray	.05	.02
☐ 410	Mike Dunleavy CO	.05	.02
☐ 411	Orlando Woolridge	.05	.02
☐ 412	Joe Wolf	.05	.02
☐ 413	Tree Rollins	.05	.02
☐ 414	Kenny Smith	.05	.02
☐ 415	Sam Perkins	.08	.04
☐ 416	Terry Teagle	.05	.02
☐ 417	Frank Brickowski	.05	.02
☐ 418	Danny Schayes	.05	.02
☐ 419	Scott Brooks	.05	.02
☐ 420	Reggie Theus	.08	.04
☐ 421	Greg Grant	.05	.02
☐ 422	Paul Westhead CO	.05	.02
☐ 423	Greg Kite	.05	.02
☐ 424	Manute Bol	.05	.02
☐ 425	Rickey Green	.05	.02
☐ 426	Ed Nealy	.05	.02
☐ 427	Danny Ainge	.08	.04
☐ 428	Bobby Hansen	.05	.02
☐ 429	Eric Leckner	.05	.02
☐ 430	Rory Sparrow	.05	.02
☐ 431	Bill Wennington	.05	.02
☐ 432	Paul Pressey	.05	.02
☐ 433	David Greenwood	.05	.02
☐ 434	Mark McNamara	.05	.02
☐ 435	Sidney Green	.05	.02
☐ 436	Dave Corzine	.05	.02
☐ 437	Jeff Malone	.05	.02
☐ 438	Pervis Ellison	.08	.04
☐ 439	Checklist 5	.05	.02
☐ 440	Checklist 6	.05	.02
☐ NNO	David Robinson and All-Rookie Team (No stats on back)	1.25	.55
☐ NNO	David Robinson and All-Rookie Team (Stats on back)	5.00	2.20

1991-92 Hoops

The complete 1991-92 Hoops basketball set contains 590 standard-size cards. The set was released in two series of 330 and 260 cards, respectively. For the first time, second series packs contained only second series cards. The fronts feature color action player photos, with

SEDALE THREATT

different color borders on a white card face. The player's name is printed in black lettering in the upper left corner, and the team logo is superimposed over the lower left corner of the picture. In a horizontal format the backs have color head shots and biographical information on the left side, while the right side presents college and pro statistics. The cards are numbered on the back and checklisted below alphabetically within team order. Subsets are Coaches (221-247), All-Stars East (248-260), All-Stars West (261-273), Teams (274-300), Centennial Card honoring James Naismith (301), Inside Stuff (302-305), League Leaders (306-313), Milestones (314-318), NBA yearbook (319-324), Public Service messages (325-327/544/545), Supreme Court (449-502), Art Cards (503-529), Active Leaders (530-537), NBA Hoops Tribune (538-543), Draft Picks (546-556), USA Basketball 1976 (557), USA Basketball 1984 (558-564), USA Basketball 1988 (565-574) and USA Basketball 1992 (575-588). Rookie Cards of note include Kenny Anderson, Stacey Augmon, Terrell Brandon, Larry Johnson, Anthony Mason, D.Mutombo, Steve Smith, and John Starks. A short-printed Naismith card, numbered CC1, was inserted into wax packs. It features a colorized photo of Dr. Naismith standing between two peach baskets like those used in the first basketball game. The back narrates the invention of the game of basketball. An unnumbered Centennial card featuring the Centennial logo was also available via a mail-in offer. Second series packs featured a randomly inserted Gold Foil USA Basketball logo card.

A special individually numbered (out of 10,000) "Head of the Class" (showing the top six draft picks from 1991) card was made available to the first 10,000 fans requesting one along with three wrappers from each series of 1991-92 Hoops cards. The card is numbered 'of 10,000' and features tiny pictures of the top six players selected in the 1991 NBA draft.

	MINT	NRMT
COMPLETE SET (590)	25.00	11.00
COMPLETE SERIES 1 (330)	10.00	4.50
COMPLETE SERIES 2 (260)	15.00	6.75
COMMON CARD (1-590)	.05	.02
SEMISTARS	.10	.05
UNLISTED STARS	.25	.11

#	Card	MINT	NRMT
☐ 1	John Battle	.05	.02
☐ 2	Moses Malone UER	.25	.11
	(119 rebounds 1982-83, should be 1194)		
☐ 3	Sidney Moncrief	.05	.02
☐ 4	Doc Rivers	.10	.05
☐ 5	Rumeal Robinson UER	.05	.02
	(Back says 11th pick in 1990, should be 10th)		
☐ 6	Spud Webb	.10	.05
☐ 7	Dominique Wilkins	.25	.11
☐ 8	Kevin Willis	.05	.02
☐ 9	Larry Bird	1.00	.45
☐ 10	Dee Brown	.05	.02
☐ 11	Kevin Gamble	.05	.02
☐ 12	Joe Kleine	.05	.02
☐ 13	Reggie Lewis	.10	.05
☐ 14	Kevin McHale	.10	.05
☐ 15	Robert Parish	.10	.05
☐ 16	Ed Pinckney	.05	.02
☐ 17	Brian Shaw	.05	.02
☐ 18	Muggsy Bogues	.10	.05
☐ 19	Rex Chapman	.10	.05
☐ 20	Dell Curry	.05	.02
☐ 21	Kendall Gill	.10	.05
☐ 22	Mike Gminski	.05	.02
☐ 23	Johnny Newman	.05	.02
☐ 24	J.R. Reid	.05	.02
☐ 25	Kelly Tripucka	.05	.02
☐ 26	B.J. Armstrong	.05	.02
	(B.J. on front, Benjamin Roy on back)		
☐ 27	Bill Cartwright	.05	.02
☐ 28	Horace Grant	.10	.05
☐ 29	Craig Hodges	.05	.02
☐ 30	Michael Jordan	3.00	1.35
☐ 31	Stacey King	.05	.02
☐ 32	Cliff Levingston	.05	.02
☐ 33	John Paxson	.10	.05
☐ 34	Scottie Pippen	.75	.35
☐ 35	Chucky Brown	.05	.02
☐ 36	Brad Daugherty	.05	.02
☐ 37	Craig Ehlo	.05	.02
☐ 38	Danny Ferry	.05	.02
☐ 39	Larry Nance	.10	.05
☐ 40	Mark Price	.10	.05
☐ 41	Darnell Valentine	.05	.02
☐ 42	Hot Rod Williams	.05	.02
☐ 43	Rolando Blackman	.10	.05
☐ 44	Brad Davis	.05	.02
☐ 45	James Donaldson	.05	.02
☐ 46	Derek Harper	.10	.05
☐ 47	Fat Lever	.05	.02
☐ 48	Rodney McCray	.05	.02
☐ 49	Roy Tarpley	.05	.02
☐ 50	Herb Williams	.05	.02
☐ 51	Michael Adams	.05	.02
☐ 52	Chris Jackson UER	.05	.02
	(Born in Mississippi, not Michigan)		
☐ 53	Jerome Lane	.05	.02

☐ 54	Todd Lichti		.02
☐ 55	Blair Rasmussen	.05	.02
☐ 56	Reggie Williams	.05	.02
☐ 57	Joe Wolf	.05	.02
☐ 58	Orlando Woolridge	.05	.02
☐ 59	Mark Aguirre	.05	.02
☐ 60	Joe Dumars	.25	.11
☐ 61	James Edwards	.05	.02
☐ 62	Vinnie Johnson	.05	.02
☐ 63	Bill Laimbeer	.05	.02
☐ 64	Dennis Rodman	1.00	.45
☐ 65	John Salley	.05	.02
☐ 66	Isiah Thomas	.25	.11
☐ 67	Tim Hardaway	.50	.23
☐ 68	Rod Higgins	.05	.02
☐ 69	Tyrone Hill	.10	.05
☐ 70	Alton Lister	.05	.02
☐ 71	Sarunas Marciulionis	.05	.02
☐ 72	Chris Mullin	.25	.11
☐ 73	Mitch Richmond	.30	.14
☐ 74	Tom Tolbert	.05	.02
☐ 75	Eric(Sleepy) Floyd	.05	.02
☐ 76	Buck Johnson	.05	.02
☐ 77	Vernon Maxwell	.05	.02
☐ 78	Hakeem Olajuwon	.50	.23
☐ 79	Kenny Smith	.05	.02
☐ 80	Larry Smith	.05	.02
☐ 81	Otis Thorpe	.10	.05
☐ 82	David Wood	.05	.02
☐ 83	Vern Fleming	.05	.02
☐ 84	Reggie Miller	.25	.11
☐ 85	Chuck Person	.05	.02
☐ 86	Mike Sanders	.05	.02
☐ 87	Detlef Schrempf	.10	.05
☐ 88	Rik Smits	.10	.05
☐ 89	LaSalle Thompson	.05	.02
☐ 90	Micheal Williams	.05	.02
☐ 91	Winston Garland	.05	.02
☐ 92	Gary Grant	.05	.02
☐ 93	Ron Harper	.10	.05
☐ 94	Danny Manning	.05	.02
☐ 95	Jeff Martin	.05	.02
☐ 96	Ken Norman	.05	.02
☐ 97	Olden Polynice	.05	.02
☐ 98	Charles Smith	.05	.02
☐ 99	Vlade Divac	.05	.02
☐ 100	A.C. Green	.10	.05
☐ 101	Magic Johnson	.75	.35
☐ 102	Sam Perkins	.05	.02
☐ 103	Byron Scott	.05	.02
☐ 104	Terry Teagle	.05	.02
☐ 105	Mychal Thompson	.05	.02
☐ 106	James Worthy	.25	.11
☐ 107	Willie Burton	.05	.02
☐ 108	Bimbo Coles	.05	.02
☐ 109	Terry Davis	.05	.02
☐ 110	Sherman Douglas	.05	.02
☐ 111	Kevin Edwards	.05	.02
☐ 112	Alec Kessler	.05	.02
☐ 113	Glen Rice	.40	.18
☐ 114	Rony Seikaly	.05	.02
☐ 115	Frank Brickowski	.05	.02
☐ 116	Dale Ellis	.10	.05
☐ 117	Jay Humphries	.05	.02
☐ 118	Brad Lohaus	.05	.02
☐ 119	Fred Roberts	.05	.02
☐ 120	Alvin Robertson	.05	.02
☐ 121	Danny Schayes	.05	.02
☐ 122	Jack Sikma	.05	.02
☐ 123	Randy Breuer	.05	.02
☐ 124	Tony Campbell	.05	.02
☐ 125	Tyrone Corbin	.05	.02
☐ 126	Gerald Glass	.05	.02
☐ 127	Sam Mitchell	.05	.02
☐ 128	Tod Murphy	.05	.02
☐ 129	Pooh Richardson	.05	.02
☐ 130	Felton Spencer	.05	.02
☐ 131	Mookie Blaylock	.10	.05
☐ 132	Sam Bowie	.05	.02
☐ 133	Jud Buechler	.05	.02
☐ 134	Derrick Coleman	.10	.05
☐ 135	Chris Dudley	.05	.02
☐ 136	Chris Morris	.05	.02
☐ 137	Drazen Petrovic	.05	.02
☐ 138	Reggie Theus	.10	.05
☐ 139	Maurice Cheeks	.05	.02
☐ 140	Patrick Ewing	.25	.11
☐ 141	Mark Jackson	.10	.05
☐ 142	Charles Oakley	.10	.05
☐ 143	Trent Tucker	.05	.02
☐ 144	Kiki Vandeweghe	.05	.02
☐ 145	Kenny Walker	.05	.02
☐ 146	Gerald Wilkins	.05	.02
☐ 147	Nick Anderson	.10	.05
☐ 148	Michael Ansley	.05	.02
☐ 149	Terry Catledge	.05	.02
☐ 150	Jerry Reynolds	.05	.02
☐ 151	Dennis Scott	.10	.05
☐ 152	Scott Skiles	.05	.02
☐ 153	Otis Smith	.05	.02
☐ 154	Sam Vincent	.05	.02
☐ 155	Ron Anderson	.05	.02
☐ 156	Charles Barkley	.40	.18
☐ 157	Manute Bol	.05	.02
☐ 158	Johnny Dawkins	.05	.02
☐ 159	Armon Gilliam	.05	.02
☐ 160	Rickey Green	.05	.02
☐ 161	Hersey Hawkins	.10	.05
☐ 162	Rick Mahorn	.05	.02
☐ 163	Tom Chambers	.05	.02
☐ 164	Jeff Hornacek	.10	.05
☐ 165	Kevin Johnson	.25	.11
☐ 166	Andrew Lang	.05	.02
☐ 167	Dan Majerle	.10	.05
☐ 168	Xavier McDaniel	.05	.02
☐ 169	Kurt Rambis	.05	.02
☐ 170	Mark West	.05	.02
☐ 171	Danny Ainge	.10	.05
☐ 172	Mark Bryant	.05	.02
☐ 173	Walter Davis	.05	.02
☐ 174	Clyde Drexler	.30	.14
☐ 175	Kevin Duckworth	.05	.02
☐ 176	Jerome Kersey	.05	.02
☐ 177	Terry Porter	.05	.02
☐ 178	Clifford Robinson	.10	.05
☐ 179	Buck Williams	.05	.02
☐ 180	Anthony Bonner	.05	.02
☐ 181	Antoine Carr	.05	.02
☐ 182	Duane Causwell	.05	.02
☐ 183	Bobby Hansen	.05	.02
☐ 184	Travis Mays	.05	.02
☐ 185	Lionel Simmons	.05	.02
☐ 186	Rory Sparrow	.05	.02
☐ 187	Wayman Tisdale	.05	.02
☐ 188	Willie Anderson	.05	.02
☐ 189	Terry Cummings	.05	.02
☐ 190	Sean Elliott	.10	.05
☐ 191	Sidney Green	.05	.02
☐ 192	David Greenwood	.05	.02
☐ 193	Paul Pressey	.05	.02
☐ 194	David Robinson	.50	.23
☐ 195	Dwayne Schintzius	.05	.02
☐ 196	Rod Strickland	.25	.11
☐ 197	Benoit Benjamin	.05	.02
☐ 198	Michael Cage	.05	.02
☐ 199	Eddie Johnson	.10	.05
☐ 200	Shawn Kemp	1.25	.55
☐ 201	Derrick McKey	.05	.02
☐ 202	Gary Payton	.60	.25
☐ 203	Ricky Pierce	.05	.02
☐ 204	Sedale Threatt	.05	.02
☐ 205	Thurl Bailey	.05	.02
☐ 206	Mike Brown	.05	.02
☐ 207	Mark Eaton	.05	.02
☐ 208	Blue Edwards UER	.05	.02
	(Forward/guard on front, guard on back)		
☐ 209	Darrell Griffith	.05	.02
☐ 210	Jeff Malone	.05	.02
☐ 211	Karl Malone	.40	.18
☐ 212	John Stockton	.25	.11
☐ 213	Ledell Eackles	.05	.02
☐ 214	Pervis Ellison	.05	.02
☐ 215	A.J. English	.05	.02
☐ 216	Harvey Grant	.05	.02
	(Shown boxing out twin brother Horace)		
☐ 217	Charles Jones	.05	.02
☐ 218	Bernard King	.05	.02
☐ 219	Darrell Walker	.05	.02
☐ 220	John Williams	.05	.02
☐ 221	Bob Weiss CO	.05	.02
☐ 222	Chris Ford CO	.05	.02
☐ 223	Gene Littles CO	.05	.02
☐ 224	Phil Jackson CO	.10	.05
☐ 225	Lenny Wilkens CO	.10	.05
☐ 226	Richie Adubato CO	.05	.02
☐ 227	Paul Westhead CO	.05	.02
☐ 228	Chuck Daly CO	.10	.05
☐ 229	Don Nelson CO	.10	.05
☐ 230	Don Chaney CO	.05	.02
☐ 231	Bob Hill CO UER	.05	.02
	(Coached under Ted Owens, not Ted Owen)		
☐ 232	Mike Schuler CO	.05	.02
☐ 233	Mike Dunleavy CO	.05	.02
☐ 234	Kevin Loughery CO	.05	.02
☐ 235	Del Harris CO	.05	.02
☐ 236	Jimmy Rodgers CO	.05	.02
☐ 237	Bill Fitch CO	.05	.02
☐ 238	Pat Riley CO	.10	.05
☐ 239	Matt Guokas CO	.05	.02
☐ 240	Jim Lynam CO	.05	.02
☐ 241	Cotton Fitzsimmons CO	.05	.02
☐ 242	Rick Adelman CO	.05	.02
☐ 243	Dick Motta CO	.05	.02
☐ 244	Larry Brown CO	.05	.02
☐ 245	K.C. Jones CO	.10	.05
☐ 246	Jerry Sloan CO	.10	.05
☐ 247	Wes Unseld CO	.10	.05
☐ 248	Charles Barkley AS	.25	.11
☐ 249	Brad Daugherty AS	.05	.02
☐ 250	Joe Dumars AS	.10	.05
☐ 251	Patrick Ewing AS	.25	.11
☐ 252	Hersey Hawkins AS	.05	.02
☐ 253	Michael Jordan AS	1.50	.70
☐ 254	Bernard King AS	.05	.02
☐ 255	Kevin McHale AS	.05	.02
☐ 256	Robert Parish AS	.05	.02
☐ 257	Ricky Pierce AS	.05	.02
☐ 258	Alvin Robertson AS	.05	.02
☐ 259	Dominique Wilkins AS	.10	.05
☐ 260	Chris Ford CO AS	.05	.02
☐ 261	Tom Chambers AS	.05	.02
☐ 262	Clyde Drexler AS	.25	.11
☐ 263	Kevin Duckworth AS	.05	.02
☐ 264	Tim Hardaway AS	.25	.11
☐ 265	Kevin Johnson AS	.10	.05
☐ 266	Magic Johnson AS	.40	.18
☐ 267	Karl Malone AS	.25	.11
☐ 268	Chris Mullin AS	.10	.05
☐ 269	Terry Porter AS	.05	.02
☐ 270	David Robinson AS	.25	.11
☐ 271	John Stockton AS	.25	.11
☐ 272	James Worthy AS	.10	.05
☐ 273	Rick Adelman CO AS	.05	.02
☐ 274	Atlanta Hawks	.05	.02
	Team Card UER (Actually began as Tri-Cities Blackhawks)		
☐ 275	Boston Celtics	.05	.02
	Team Card UER (No NBA Hoops logo on card front)		
☐ 276	Charlotte Hornets	.05	.02
	Team Card		
☐ 277	Chicago Bulls	.05	.02
	Team Card		
☐ 278	Cleveland Cavaliers	.05	.02
	Team Card		
☐ 279	Dallas Mavericks	.05	.02
	Team Card		
☐ 280	Denver Nuggets	.05	.02
	Team Card		
☐ 281	Detroit Pistons	.05	.02
	Team Card UER (Pistons not NBA Finalists until 1988; Ft. Wayne Pistons in Finals in 1955 and 1956)		
☐ 282	Golden State Warriors	.05	.02
	Team Card		
☐ 283	Houston Rockets	.05	.02
	Team Card		
☐ 284	Indiana Pacers	.05	.02
	Team Card		
☐ 285	Los Angeles Clippers	.05	.02
	Team Card		

□ 286 Los Angeles Lakers .05	.02
Team Card	
□ 287 Miami Heat .05	.02
Team Card	
□ 288 Milwaukee Bucks .05	.02
Team Card	
□ 289 Minnesota T'wolves .05	.02
Team Card	
□ 290 New Jersey Nets .05	.02
Team Card	
□ 291 New York Knicks .05	.02
Team Card UER	
(Golden State not mentioned as an active charter member of NBA)	
□ 292 Orlando Magic .05	.02
Team Card	
□ 293 Philadelphia 76ers .05	.02
Team Card	
□ 294 Phoenix Suns .05	.02
Team Card	
□ 295 Portland Trail Blazers .05	.02
Team Card	
□ 296 Sacramento Kings .05	.02
Team Card	
□ 297 San Antonio Spurs .05	.02
Team Card	
□ 298 Seattle Supersonics .05	.02
Team Card	
□ 299 Utah Jazz .05	.02
Team Card	
□ 300 Washington Bullets .05	.02
Team Card	
□ 301 James Naismith .10	.05
Centennial Card	
□ 302 Kevin Johnson IS .10	.05
□ 303 Reggie Miller IS .25	.11
□ 304 Hakeem Olajuwon IS .25	.11
□ 305 Robert Parish IS .05	.02
□ 306 Scoring Leaders 1.00	.45
Michael Jordan	
Karl Malone	
□ 307 3-Point FG Percent .05	.02
League Leaders	
Jim Les	
Trent Tucker	
□ 308 Free Throw Percent .05	.02
League Leaders	
Reggie Miller	
Jeff Malone	
□ 309 Blocks League Leaders .25	.11
Hakeem Olajuwon	
David Robinson	
□ 310 Steals League Leaders .05	.02
Alvin Robertson	
John Stockton	
□ 311 Rebounds LL UER .50	.23
David Robinson	
Dennis Rodman	
(Robinson credited as playing for Houston)	
□ 312 Assists League Leaders .30	.14
John Stockton	
Magic Johnson	
□ 313 Field Goal Percent .10	.05
League Leaders	
Buck Williams	
Robert Parish	
□ 314 Larry Bird UER .50	.23
Milestone	
(Should be card 315 to fit Milestone sequence)	
□ 315 Alex English .10	.05
Moses Malone	
Milestone UER	
(Should be card 314 and be a League Leader card)	
□ 316 Magic Johnson .40	.18
Milestone	
□ 317 Michael Jordan 1.50	.70
Milestone	
□ 318 Moses Malone .10	.05
Milestone	
□ 319 Larry Bird .50	.23
NBA Yearbook	
Look Back	

□ 320 Maurice Cheeks .05	.02
NBA Yearbook	
Look Back	
□ 321 Magic Johnson .40	.18
NBA Yearbook	
Look Back	
□ 322 Bernard King .05	.02
NBA Yearbook	
Look Back	
□ 323 Moses Malone .10	.05
NBA Yearbook	
Look Back	
□ 324 Robert Parish .05	.02
NBA Yearbook	
Look Back	
□ 325 All-Star Jam .10	.05
Jammin' With Will Smith	
(Stay in School)	
□ 326 All-Star Jam .10	.05
Jammin' With The Boys and Will Smith	
(Stay in School)	
□ 327 David Robinson .25	.11
Leave Alcohol Out	
□ 328 Checklist 1 .05	.02
□ 329 Checklist 2 UER .05	.02
(Card front is from 330)	
□ 330 Checklist 3 UER .05	.02
(Card front is from 329; card 327 listed operation, should be celebration)	
□ 331 Maurice Cheeks .05	.02
□ 332 Duane Ferrell .05	.02
□ 333 Jon Koncak .05	.02
□ 334 Gary Leonard .05	.02
□ 335 Travis Mays .05	.02
□ 336 Blair Rasmussen .05	.02
□ 337 Alexander Volkov .05	.02
□ 338 John Bagley .05	.02
□ 339 Rickey Green UER .05	.02
(Ricky on front)	
□ 340 Derek Smith .05	.02
□ 341 Stojko Vrankovic .05	.02
□ 342 Anthony Frederick .05	.02
□ 343 Kenny Gattison .05	.02
□ 344 Eric Leckner .05	.02
□ 345 Will Perdue .05	.02
□ 346 Scott Williams .05	.02
□ 347 John Battle .05	.02
□ 348 Winston Bennett .05	.02
□ 349 Henry James .05	.02
□ 350 Steve Kerr .10	.05
□ 351 John Morton .05	.02
□ 352 Terry Davis .05	.02
□ 353 Randy White .05	.02
□ 354 Greg Anderson .05	.02
□ 355 Anthony Cook .05	.02
□ 356 Walter Davis .05	.02
□ 357 Winston Garland .05	.02
□ 358 Scott Hastings .05	.02
□ 359 Marcus Liberty .05	.02
□ 360 William Bedford .05	.02
□ 361 Lance Blanks .05	.02
□ 362 Brad Sellers .05	.02
□ 363 Darrell Walker .05	.02
□ 364 Orlando Woolridge .05	.02
□ 365 Vincent Askew .05	.02
□ 366 Mario Elie .25	.11
□ 367 Jim Petersen .05	.02
□ 368 Matt Bullard .05	.02
□ 369 Gerald Henderson .05	.02
□ 370 Dave Jamerson .05	.02
□ 371 Tree Rollins .05	.02
□ 372 Greg Dreiling .05	.02
□ 373 George McCloud .05	.02
□ 374 Kenny Williams .05	.02
□ 375 Randy Wittman .05	.02
□ 376 Tony Brown .05	.02
□ 377 Lanard Copeland .05	.02
□ 378 James Edwards .05	.02
□ 379 Bo Kimble .05	.02
□ 380 Doc Rivers .10	.05
□ 381 Loy Vaught .10	.05
□ 382 Elden Campbell .25	.11
□ 383 Jack Haley .05	.02

□ 384 Tony Smith .05	.02
□ 385 Sedale Threatt .05	.02
□ 386 Keith Askins .05	.02
□ 387 Grant Long .05	.02
□ 388 Alan Ogg .05	.02
□ 389 Jon Sundvold .05	.02
□ 390 Lester Conner .05	.02
□ 391 Jeff Grayer .05	.02
□ 392 Steve Henson .05	.02
□ 393 Larry Krystkowiak .05	.02
□ 394 Moses Malone .25	.11
□ 395 Scott Brooks .05	.02
□ 396 Tellis Frank .05	.02
□ 397 Doug West .05	.02
□ 398 Rafael Addison .05	.02
□ 399 Dave Feitl .05	.02
□ 400 Tate George .05	.02
□ 401 Terry Mills .25	.11
□ 402 Tim McCormick .05	.02
□ 403 Xavier McDaniel .05	.02
□ 404 Anthony Mason .50	.23
□ 405 Brian Quinnett .05	.02
□ 406 John Starks .30	.14
□ 407 Mark Acres .05	.02
□ 408 Greg Kite .05	.02
□ 409 Jeff Turner .05	.02
□ 410 Morlon Wiley .05	.02
□ 411 Dave Hoppen .05	.02
□ 412 Brian Oliver .05	.02
□ 413 Kenny Payne .05	.02
□ 414 Charles Shackleford .05	.02
□ 415 Mitchell Wiggins .05	.02
□ 416 Jayson Williams .25	.11
□ 417 Cedric Ceballos .10	.05
□ 418 Negele Knight .05	.02
□ 419 Andrew Lang .05	.02
□ 420 Jerrod Mustaf .05	.02
□ 421 Ed Nealy .05	.02
□ 422 Tim Perry .05	.02
□ 423 Alaa Abdelnaby .05	.02
□ 424 Wayne Cooper .05	.02
□ 425 Danny Young .05	.02
□ 426 Dennis Hopson .05	.02
□ 427 Les Jepsen .05	.02
□ 428 Jim Les .05	.02
□ 429 Mitch Richmond .30	.14
□ 430 Dwayne Schintzius .05	.02
□ 431 Spud Webb .10	.05
□ 432 Jud Buechler .05	.02
□ 433 Antoine Carr .05	.02
□ 434 Tom Garrick .05	.02
□ 435 Sean Higgins .05	.02
□ 436 Avery Johnson .10	.05
□ 437 Tony Massenburg .05	.02
□ 438 Dana Barros .05	.02
□ 439 Quintin Dailey .05	.02
□ 440 Bart Kofoed .05	.02
□ 441 Nate McMillan .05	.02
□ 442 Delaney Rudd .05	.02
□ 443 Michael Adams .05	.02
□ 444 Mark Alarie .05	.02
□ 445 Greg Foster .05	.02
□ 446 Tom Hammonds .05	.02
□ 447 Andre Turner .05	.02
□ 448 David Wingate .05	.02
□ 449 Dominique Wilkins SC .10	.05
□ 450 Kevin Willis SC .05	.02
□ 451 Larry Bird SC .50	.23
□ 452 Robert Parish SC .05	.02
□ 453 Rex Chapman SC .05	.02
□ 454 Kendall Gill SC .05	.02
□ 455 Michael Jordan SC 1.50	.70
□ 456 Scottie Pippen SC .40	.18
□ 457 Brad Daugherty SC .05	.02
□ 458 Larry Nance SC .05	.02
□ 459 Rolando Blackman SC .05	.02
□ 460 Derek Harper SC .05	.02
□ 461 Chris Jackson SC .05	.02
□ 462 Todd Lichti SC .05	.02
□ 463 Joe Dumars SC .10	.05
□ 464 Isiah Thomas SC .10	.05
□ 465 Tim Hardaway SC .25	.11
□ 466 Chris Mullin SC .25	.11
□ 467 Hakeem Olajuwon SC .25	.11
□ 468 Otis Thorpe SC .05	.02
□ 469 Reggie Miller SC .25	.11

☐ 470 Detlef Schrempf SC....	.05	.02
☐ 471 Ron Harper SC	.05	.02
☐ 472 Charles Smith SC	.05	.02
☐ 473 Magic Johnson SC	.40	.18
☐ 474 James Worthy SC	.10	.05
☐ 475 Sherman Douglas SC	.05	.02
☐ 476 Rony Seikaly SC	.05	.02
☐ 477 Jay Humphries SC	.05	.02
☐ 478 Alvin Robertson SC	.05	.02
☐ 479 Tyrone Corbin SC	.05	.02
☐ 480 Pooh Richardson SC ..	.05	.02
☐ 481 Sam Bowie SC	.05	.02
☐ 482 Derrick Coleman SC	.05	.02
☐ 483 Patrick Ewing SC	.25	.11
☐ 484 Charles Oakley SC	.05	.02
☐ 485 Dennis Scott SC	.05	.02
☐ 486 Scott Skiles SC	.05	.02
☐ 487 Charles Barkley SC	.25	.11
☐ 488 Hersey Hawkins SC	.05	.02
☐ 489 Tom Chambers SC	.05	.02
☐ 490 Kevin Johnson SC	.10	.05
☐ 491 Clyde Drexler SC	.25	.11
☐ 492 Terry Porter SC	.05	.02
☐ 493 Lionel Simmons SC	.05	.02
☐ 494 Wayman Tisdale SC	.05	.02
☐ 495 Terry Cummings SC	.05	.02
☐ 496 David Robinson SC	.25	.11
☐ 497 Shawn Kemp SC	.60	.25
☐ 498 Ricky Pierce SC	.05	.02
☐ 499 Karl Malone SC	.25	.11
☐ 500 John Stockton SC	.25	.11
☐ 501 Harvey Grant SC	.05	.02
☐ 502 Bernard King SC	.05	.02
☐ 503 Travis Mays Art	.05	.02
☐ 504 Kevin McHale Art	.05	.02
☐ 505 Muggsy Bogues Art	.05	.02
☐ 506 Scottie Pippen Art	.40	.18
☐ 507 Brad Daugherty Art	.05	.02
☐ 508 Derek Harper Art	.05	.02
☐ 509 Chris Jackson Art	.05	.02
☐ 510 Isiah Thomas Art	.10	.05
☐ 511 Tim Hardaway Art	.25	.11
☐ 512 Otis Thorpe Art	.05	.02
☐ 513 Chuck Person Art	.05	.02
☐ 514 Ron Harper Art	.05	.02
☐ 515 James Worthy Art	.10	.05
☐ 516 Sherman Douglas Art	.05	.02
☐ 517 Dale Ellis Art	.05	.02
☐ 518 Tony Campbell Art	.05	.02
☐ 519 Derrick Coleman Art ..	.05	.02
☐ 520 Gerald Wilkins Art	.05	.02
☐ 521 Scott Skiles Art	.05	.02
☐ 522 Manute Bol Art	.05	.02
☐ 523 Tom Chambers Art	.05	.02
☐ 524 Terry Porter Art	.05	.02
☐ 525 Lionel Simmons Art ..	.05	.02
☐ 526 Sean Elliott Art	.05	.02
☐ 527 Shawn Kemp Art	.60	.25
☐ 528 John Stockton Art	.25	.11
☐ 529 Harvey Grant Art	.05	.02
☐ 530 Michael Adams	.05	.02
All-Time Active Leader		
Three-Point Field Goals		
☐ 531 Charles Barkley	.25	.11
All-Time Active Leader		
Field Goal Percentage		
☐ 532 Larry Bird	.50	.23
All-Time Active Leader		
Free Throw Percentage		
☐ 533 Maurice Cheeks	.05	.02
All-Time Active Leader		
Steals		
☐ 534 Mark Eaton	.05	.02
All-Time Active Leader		
Blocks		
☐ 535 Magic Johnson	.40	.18
All-Time Active Leader		
Assists		
☐ 536 Michael Jordan	1.50	.70
All-Time Active Leader		
Scoring Average		
☐ 537 Moses Malone	.10	.05
All-Time Active Leader		
Rebounds		
☐ 538 Sam Perkins FIN	.05	.02
☐ 539 Scottie Pippen FIN	.25	.11

James Worthy		
☐ 540 Vlade Divac FIN	.10	.05
☐ 541 John Paxson FIN	.10	.05
☐ 542 Michael Jordan FIN .	1.50	.70
Magic Johnson)		
☐ 543 Michael Jordan FIN ..		.70
NBA Champs, kissing trophy)		
☐ 544 Otis Smith	.05	.02
Stay in School		
☐ 545 Jeff Turner	.05	.02
Stay in School		
☐ 546 Larry Johnson	1.00	.45
☐ 547 Kenny Anderson	.50	.23
☐ 548 Billy Owens	.25	.11
☐ 549 D.Mutombo	.75	.35
☐ 550 Steve Smith	.60	.25
☐ 551 Doug Smith	.05	.02
☐ 552 Luc Longley	.30	.14
☐ 553 Mark Macon	.05	.02
☐ 554 Stacey Augmon	.25	.11
☐ 555 Brian Williams	.25	.11
☐ 556 Terrell Brandon	1.25	.55
☐ 557 Walter Davis	.05	.02
Team USA 1976		
☐ 558 Vern Fleming	.05	.02
Team USA 1984		
☐ 559 Joe Kleine	.05	.02
Team USA 1984		
☐ 560 Jon Koncak	.05	.02
Team USA 1984		
☐ 561 Sam Perkins	.05	.02
Team USA 1984		
☐ 562 Alvin Robertson	.05	.02
Team USA 1984		
☐ 563 Wayman Tisdale	.05	.02
Team USA 1984		
☐ 564 Jeff Turner	.05	.02
Team USA 1984		
☐ 565 Willie Anderson	.05	.02
Team USA 1988		
☐ 566 Stacey Augmon	.25	.11
Team USA 1988		
☐ 567 Bimbo Coles	.05	.02
Team USA 1988		
☐ 568 Jeff Grayer	.05	.02
Team USA 1988		
☐ 569 Hersey Hawkins	.05	.02
Team USA 1988		
☐ 570 Dan Majerle	.05	.02
Team USA 1988		
☐ 571 Danny Manning	.05	.02
Team USA 1988		
☐ 572 J.R. Reid	.05	.02
Team USA 1988		
☐ 573 Mitch Richmond	.60	.25
Team USA 1988		
☐ 574 Charles Smith	.05	.02
Team USA 1988		
☐ 575 Charles Barkley	.75	.35
Team USA 1992		
☐ 576 Larry Bird	2.00	.90
Team USA 1992		
☐ 577 Patrick Ewing	.50	.23
Team USA 1992		
☐ 578 Magic Johnson	1.50	.70
Team USA 1992		
☐ 579 Michael Jordan	6.00	2.70
Team USA 1992		
☐ 580 Karl Malone	.75	.35
Team USA 1992		
☐ 581 Chris Mullin	.25	.11
Team USA 1992		
☐ 582 Scottie Pippen	1.50	.70
Team USA 1992		
☐ 583 David Robinson	1.00	.45
Team USA 1992		
☐ 584 John Stockton	.50	.23
Team USA 1992		
☐ 585 Chuck Daly CO	.10	.05
Team USA 1992		
☐ 586 Lenny Wilkens CO	.10	.05
Team USA 1992		
☐ 587 P.J. Carlesimo CO	.05	.02
Team USA 1992		
☐ 588 Mike Krzyzewski CO ..	.40	.18
Team USA 1992		

☐ 589 Checklist Card 1	.05	.02
☐ 590 Checklist Card 2	.05	.02
☐ CC1 Dr.James Naismith .	1.00	.45
☐ XX Head of the Class ..	20.00	9.00
Kenny Anderson		
Larry Johnson		
D.Mutombo		
Billy Owens		
Doug Smith		
Steve Smith		
☐ NNO Team USA SP	.50	.23
Title Card		
☐ NNO Centennial Card	1.00	.45
(Sendaway)		

1991-92 Hoops All-Star MVP's

This six-card standard-size insert set commemorates the most valuable player of the NBA All-Star games from 1986 to 1991. Two cards were inserted in each second series rack pack. On a white card face, the front features non-action color photos framed by either a blue (7, 9, 12) or red (8, 10, 11) border. The top thicker border is jagged and displays the player's name, while the year the award was received appears in a colored box in the lower left corner. The backs have the same design and feature a color action photo from the All-Star game. The cards are numbered on the back by Roman numerals.

	MINT	NRMT
COMPLETE SET (6)	20.00	9.00
COMMON CARD (7-12)	.50	.23
SEMISTARS	.75	.35
ROMAN NUMERAL NUMBERED		
TWO PER SER.2 RACK PACK		

☐ 7 Isiah Thomas	1.50	.70
(Numbered VII)		
☐ 8 Tom Chambers	.50	.23
(Numbered VIII)		
☐ 9 Michael Jordan	15.00	6.75
(Numbered IX)		
☐ 10 Karl Malone	2.00	.90
(Numbered X)		
☐ 11 Magic Johnson	4.00	1.80
(Numbered XI)		
☐ 12 Charles Barkley	2.00	.90
(Numbered XII)		

1991-92 Hoops Slam Dunk

This six-card standard size insert set of "Slam Dunk Champions" features the winners of the All-Star weekend slam dunk competition from 1984 to 1991. The cards were issued two per first series 47-card rack pack. The front has a color photo of the player dunking the ball, with royal blue borders on a white card face. The player's name appears in orange lettering in a purple stripe above the picture, and the year the player won is given in a "Slam Dunk Champion" emblem overlaying the lower left corner of the picture. The design of the back is similar to the front, only with an extended caption on a yellow-green background. A drawing of a basketball entering a rim appears at the upper left corner. The cards are numbered on the back by Roman numerals.

	MINT	NRMT
COMPLETE SET (6)	15.00	6.75
COMMON CARD (1-6)	.50	.23
TWO PER SER.1 RACK PACK		
☐ 1 Larry Nance (Numbered I)	.75	.35
☐ 2 Dominique Wilkins (Numbered II)	1.00	.45
☐ 3 Spud Webb (Numbered III)	.75	.35
☐ 4 Michael Jordan (Numbered IV)	15.00	6.75
☐ 5 Kenny Walker (Numbered V)	.50	.23
☐ 6 Dee Brown (Numbered VI)	.50	.23

1992-93 Hoops

The complete 1992-93 Hoops basketball set contains 490 standard-size cards. The set was released in two series of 350 and 140 cards, respectively. Both series packs contained 12 cards each with a suggested retail price of 79 cents each. Reported production quantities were 20,000 20-box wax cases of the first series and approximately 14,000 20-box wax cases of the second series. The basic card fronts display color action player photos surrounded by white borders. A color stripe reflecting one of the team's colors cuts across the picture and the player's name is printed vertically in a transparent stripe bordering the left side of the picture. The horizontally oriented backs carry a color head shot, biography, career highlights, and complete statistics (college and pro). The cards are checklisted below alphabetically according to teams. Subsets include Coaches (239-265), Team cards (266-292), Magic All-Stars East (293-305), NBA All-Stars West (306-319), League Leaders (320-327), Magic Moments (328-331), NBA Inside Stuff (332-333), NBA Stay in School (334-335), Basketball Tournament of the Americas (336-347) and Trivia (481-485). Rookie cards, scattered throughout the set, have a gold rather than a ghosted white stripe. The team logo appears in the lower left corner and intersects a team color-coded stripe that contains the player's position. The horizontal backs show a white background and include statistics (collegiate and pro), biographies, and career summaries. A close-up photo is at the upper left. Rookie Cards of note include Tom Gugliotta, Robert Horry, Christian Laettner, Alonzo Mourning, Shaquille O'Neal, Bobby Phills, Latrell Sprewell and C.Weatherspoon. A Magic Johnson "Commemorative Card" and a Patrick Ewing "Ultimate Game" card were randomly inserted in first series foil packs. One-thousand of each were autographed. The odds of pulling an autographed card were one in 14,400 packs. Also randomly inserted into second series foil packs were a Patrick Ewing Art card (reported odds were one per 21 packs), a Chicago Bulls Championship card (reported odds were one per 32 packs) and a John Stockton "Ultimate Game" card (reported odds were one per 92 packs). Stockton autographed 1,633 of these cards (reported odds were one per 5,732 packs). Also randomly inserted into first series packs was a USA Basketball Team card. A Barcelona Plastic card was also randomly inserted in first series packs at a rate of approximately one per 720 packs.

	MINT	NRMT
COMPLETE SET (490)	35.00	16.00
COMPLETE SERIES 1 (350)	15.00	6.75
COMPLETE SERIES 2 (140)	20.00	9.00
COMMON CARD (1-350)	.05	.02
COMMON CARD (351-490)	.10	.05
SEMISTARS SER.1	.10	.05
SEMISTARS SER.2	.20	.09
UNLISTED STARS SER.1	.25	.11
UNLISTED STARS SER.2	.40	.18
AC1: SER.2 STATED ODDS 1:21		
SU1: SER.2 STATED ODDS 1:92, 1:5,732 AU		
TR1: SER.2 STATED ODDS 1:32		
BAR.PLASTIC: SER.1 STATED ODDS 1:720		
MAGIC AU: SER.1 STATED ODDS 1:14,400		
EWING AU: SER.1 STATED ODDS 1:14,400		
☐ 1 Stacey Augmon	.10	.05
☐ 2 Maurice Cheeks	.05	.02
☐ 3 Duane Ferrell	.05	.02
☐ 4 Paul Graham	.05	.02
☐ 5 Jon Koncak	.05	.02
☐ 6 Blair Rasmussen	.05	.02
☐ 7 Rumeal Robinson	.05	.02
☐ 8 Dominique Wilkins	.25	.11
☐ 9 Kevin Willis	.05	.02
☐ 10 Larry Bird	1.00	.45
☐ 11 Dee Brown	.05	.02
☐ 12 Sherman Douglas	.05	.02
☐ 13 Rick Fox	.10	.05
☐ 14 Kevin Gamble	.05	.02
☐ 15 Reggie Lewis	.10	.05
☐ 16 Kevin McHale	.25	.11
☐ 17 Robert Parish	.10	.05
☐ 18 Ed Pinckney UER (Wrong trade info, Kleine to Sacramento and Lohaus to Boston)	.05	.02
☐ 19 Muggsy Bogues	.10	.05
☐ 20 Dell Curry	.05	.02
☐ 21 Kenny Gattison	.05	.02
☐ 22 Kendall Gill	.10	.05
☐ 23 Mike Gminski	.05	.02
☐ 24 Larry Johnson	.30	.14
☐ 25 Johnny Newman	.05	.02
☐ 26 J.R. Reid	.05	.02
☐ 27 B.J. Armstrong	.05	.02
☐ 28 Bill Cartwright	.05	.02
☐ 29 Horace Grant	.10	.05
☐ 30 Michael Jordan	3.00	1.35

31	Stacey King	.05	.02
32	John Paxson	.10	.05
33	Will Perdue	.05	.02
34	Scottie Pippen	.75	.35
35	Scott Williams	.05	.02
36	John Battle	.05	.02
37	Terrell Brandon	.40	.18
38	Brad Daugherty	.05	.02
39	Craig Ehlo	.05	.02
40	Danny Ferry	.05	.02
41	Henry James	.05	.02
42	Larry Nance	.10	.05
43	Mark Price	.05	.02
44	Hot Rod Williams	.05	.02
45	Rolando Blackman	.05	.02
46	Terry Davis	.05	.02
47	Derek Harper	.10	.05
48	Mike Iuzzolino	.05	.02
49	Fat Lever	.05	.02
50	Rodney McCray	.05	.02
51	Doug Smith	.05	.02
52	Randy White	.05	.02
53	Herb Williams	.05	.02
54	Greg Anderson	.05	.02
55	Winston Garland	.05	.02
56	Chris Jackson	.05	.02
57	Marcus Liberty	.05	.02
58	Todd Lichti	.05	.02
59	Mark Macon	.05	.02
60	D.Mutombo	.25	.11
61	Reggie Williams	.05	.02
62	Mark Aguirre	.05	.02
63	William Bedford	.05	.02
64	Joe Dumars	.25	.11
65	Bill Laimbeer	.10	.05
66	Dennis Rodman	1.00	.45
67	John Salley	.05	.02
68	Isiah Thomas	.25	.11
69	Darrell Walker	.05	.02
70	Orlando Woolridge	.05	.02
71	Victor Alexander	.05	.02
72	Mario Elie	.10	.05
73	Chris Gatling	.05	.02
74	Tim Hardaway	.40	.18
75	Tyrone Hill	.05	.02
76	Alton Lister	.05	.02
77	Sarunas Marciulionis	.05	.02
78	Chris Mullin	.25	.11
79	Billy Owens	.10	.05
80	Matt Bullard	.05	.02
81	Sleepy Floyd	.05	.02
82	Avery Johnson	.05	.02
83	Buck Johnson	.05	.02
84	Vernon Maxwell	.05	.02
85	Hakeem Olajuwon	.50	.23
86	Kenny Smith	.05	.02
87	Larry Smith	.05	.02
88	Otis Thorpe	.10	.05
89	Dale Davis	.10	.05
90	Vern Fleming	.05	.02
91	George McCloud	.05	.02
92	Reggie Miller	.25	.11
93	Chuck Person	.05	.02
94	Detlef Schrempf	.10	.05
95	Rik Smits	.10	.05
96	LaSalle Thompson	.05	.02
97	Micheal Williams	.05	.02
98	James Edwards	.05	.02
99	Gary Grant	.05	.02
100	Ron Harper	.10	.05
101	Danny Manning	.10	.05
102	Ken Norman	.05	.02
103	Olden Polynice	.05	.02
104	Doc Rivers	.10	.05
105	Charles Smith	.05	.02
106	Loy Vaught	.10	.05
107	Elden Campbell	.10	.05
108	Vlade Divac	.10	.05
109	A.C. Green	.10	.05
110	Sam Perkins	.10	.05
111	Byron Scott	.10	.05
112	Tony Smith	.05	.02
113	Terry Teagle	.05	.02
114	Sedale Threatt	.05	.02
115	James Worthy	.25	.11
116	Willie Burton	.05	.02
117	Bimbo Coles	.05	.02
118	Kevin Edwards	.05	.02
119	Alec Kessler	.05	.02
120	Grant Long	.05	.02
121	Glen Rice	.30	.14
122	Rony Seikaly	.05	.02
123	Brian Shaw	.05	.02
124	Steve Smith	.25	.11
125	Frank Brickowski	.05	.02
126	Dale Ellis	.05	.02
127	Jeff Grayer	.05	.02
128	Jay Humphries	.05	.02
129	Larry Krystkowiak	.05	.02
130	Moses Malone	.25	.11
131	Fred Roberts	.05	.02
132	Alvin Robertson	.05	.02
133	Dan Schayes	.05	.02
134	Thurl Bailey	.05	.02
135	Scott Brooks	.05	.02
136	Tony Campbell	.05	.02
137	Gerald Glass	.05	.02
138	Luc Longley	.10	.05
139	Sam Mitchell	.05	.02
140	Pooh Richardson	.05	.02
141	Felton Spencer	.05	.02
142	Doug West	.05	.02
143	Rafael Addison	.05	.02
144	Kenny Anderson	.25	.11
145	Mookie Blaylock	.10	.05
146	Sam Bowie	.05	.02
147	Derrick Coleman	.10	.05
148	Chris Dudley	.05	.02
149	Terry Mills	.10	.05
150	Chris Morris	.05	.02
151	Drazen Petrovic	.05	.02
152	Greg Anthony	.05	.02
153	Patrick Ewing	.25	.11
154	Mark Jackson	.10	.05
155	Anthony Mason	.25	.11
156	Xavier McDaniel	.05	.02
157	Charles Oakley	.10	.05
158	John Starks	.10	.05
159	Gerald Wilkins	.05	.02
160	Nick Anderson	.10	.05
161	Terry Catledge	.05	.02
162	Jerry Reynolds	.05	.02
163	Stanley Roberts	.05	.02
164	Dennis Scott	.10	.05
165	Scott Skiles	.05	.02
166	Jeff Turner	.05	.02
167	Sam Vincent	.05	.02
168	Brian Williams	.10	.05
169	Ron Anderson	.05	.02
170	Charles Barkley	.40	.18
171	Manute Bol	.05	.02
172	Johnny Dawkins	.05	.02
173	Armon Gilliam	.05	.02
174	Hersey Hawkins	.10	.05
175	Brian Oliver	.05	.02
176	Charles Shackleford	.05	.02
177	Jayson Williams	.10	.05
178	Cedric Ceballos	.10	.05
179	Tom Chambers	.05	.02
180	Jeff Hornacek	.05	.02
181	Kevin Johnson	.25	.11
182	Negele Knight	.05	.02
183	Andrew Lang	.05	.02
184	Dan Majerle	.10	.05
185	Tim Perry	.05	.02
186	Mark West	.05	.02
187	Alaa Abdelnaby	.05	.02
188	Danny Ainge	.10	.05
189	Clyde Drexler	.30	.14
190	Kevin Duckworth	.05	.02
191	Jerome Kersey	.05	.02
192	Robert Pack	.05	.02
193	Terry Porter	.05	.02
194	Clifford Robinson	.10	.05
195	Buck Williams	.05	.02
196	Anthony Bonner	.05	.02
197	Duane Causwell	.05	.02
198	Pete Chilcutt	.05	.02
199	Dennis Hopson	.05	.02
200	Mitch Richmond	.25	.11
201	Lionel Simmons	.05	.02
202	Wayman Tisdale	.05	.02
203	Spud Webb	.10	.05
204	Willie Anderson	.05	.02
205	Antoine Carr	.05	.02
206	Terry Cummings	.10	.05
207	Sean Elliott	.10	.05
208	Sidney Green	.05	.02
209	David Robinson	.40	.18
210	Rod Strickland	.25	.11
211	Greg Sutton	.05	.02
212	Dana Barros	.05	.02
213	Benoit Benjamin	.05	.02
214	Michael Cage	.05	.02
215	Eddie Johnson	.05	.02
216	Shawn Kemp	1.00	.45
217	Derrick McKey	.05	.02
218	Nate McMillan	.05	.02
219	Gary Payton	.50	.23
220	Ricky Pierce	.05	.02
221	David Benoit	.05	.02
222	Mike Brown	.05	.02
223	Tyrone Corbin	.05	.02
224	Mark Eaton	.05	.02
225	Blue Edwards	.05	.02
226	Jeff Malone	.05	.02
227	Karl Malone	.40	.18
228	Eric Murdock	.05	.02
229	John Stockton	.25	.11
230	Michael Adams	.05	.02
231	Rex Chapman	.05	.02
232	Ledell Eackles	.05	.02
233	Pervis Ellison	.05	.02
234	A.J. English	.05	.02
235	Harvey Grant	.05	.02
236	Charles Jones	.05	.02
237	LaBradford Smith	.05	.02
238	Larry Stewart	.05	.02
239	Bob Weiss CO	.05	.02
240	Chris Ford CO	.05	.02
241	Allan Bristow CO	.05	.02
242	Phil Jackson CO	.10	.05
243	Lenny Wilkens CO	.10	.05
244	Richie Adubato CO	.05	.02
245	Dan Issel CO	.05	.02
246	Ron Rothstein CO	.05	.02
247	Don Nelson CO	.10	.05
248	Rudy Tomjanovich CO	.10	.05
249	Bob Hill CO	.05	.02
250	Larry Brown CO	.10	.05
251	Randy Pfund CO	.05	.02
252	Kevin Loughery CO	.05	.02
253	Mike Dunleavy CO	.05	.02
254	Jimmy Rodgers CO	.05	.02
255	Chuck Daly CO	.10	.05
256	Pat Riley CO	.10	.05
257	Matt Guokas CO	.05	.02
258	Doug Moe CO	.05	.02
259	Paul Westphal CO	.05	.02
260	Rick Adelman CO	.05	.02
261	Garry St. Jean CO	.05	.02
262	Jerry Tarkanian CO	.05	.02
263	George Karl CO	.10	.05
264	Jerry Sloan CO	.10	.05
265	Wes Unseld CO	.10	.05
266	Atlanta Hawks Team Card	.05	.02
267	Boston Celtics Team Card	.05	.02
268	Charlotte Hornets Team Card	.05	.02
269	Chicago Bulls Team Card	.05	.02
270	Cleveland Cavaliers Team Card	.05	.02
271	Dallas Mavericks Team Card	.05	.02
272	Denver Nuggets Team Card	.05	.02
273	Detroit Pistons Team Card	.05	.02
274	Golden State Warriors Team Card	.05	.02
275	Houston Rockets Team Card	.05	.02
276	Indiana Pacers Team Card	.05	.02
277	Los Angeles Clippers	.05	.02

		MINT	NRMT
☐ 466	Vinny Del Negro	.10	.05
☐ 467	Dale Ellis	.10	.05
☐ 468	Larry Smith	.10	.05
☐ 469	David Wood	.10	.05
☐ 470	Rich King	.10	.05
☐ 471	Isaac Austin	.20	.09
☐ 472	John Crotty	.10	.05
☐ 473	Stephen Howard	.10	.05
☐ 474	Jay Humphries	.10	.05
☐ 475	Larry Krystkowiak	.10	.05
☐ 476	Tom Gugliotta	1.25	.55
☐ 477	Buck Johnson	.10	.05
☐ 478	Don MacLean	.10	.05
☐ 479	Doug Overton	.10	.05
☐ 480	Brent Price	.20	.09
☐ 481	David Robinson TRIV	.40	.18
	Blocks		
☐ 482	Magic Johnson TRIV..	.60	.25
	Assists		
☐ 483	John Stockton TRIV ...	.20	.09
	Steals		
☐ 484	Patrick Ewing TRIV	.20	.09
	Points		
☐ 485	Answer Card TRIV......	.40	.18
	Magic Johnson		
	David Robinson		
	Patrick Ewing		
	John Stockton		
☐ 486	John Stockton	.20	.09
	Stay in School		
☐ 487	Ahmad Rashad	.20	.09
	Willow Bay		
	Inside Stuff		
☐ 488	Rookie Checklist	.10	.05
☐ 489	Checklist 1..............	.05	.02
☐ 490	Checklist 2..............	.05	.02
☐ AC1	Patrick Ewing Art	.50	.23
☐ SU1	John Stockton AU	100.00	45.00
	(Certified autograph)		
☐ SU1	John Stockton Game	1.50	.70
	His Ultimate Game		
☐ TR1	NBA Championship..	3.00	1.35
	Michael Jordan		
	Clyde Drexler		
☐ NNO	Team USA	1.50	.70
☐ NNO	Barcelona Plastic ..	30.00	13.50
☐ NNO	M.Johnson Comm ..	1.00	.45
☐ NNO	M.Johnson AU.......	200.00	90.00
☐ NNO	Patrick Ewing Game..	.50	.23
	His Ultimate Game		
☐ NNO	Patrick Ewing AU	100.00	45.00
	(Certified autograph)		

1992-93 Hoops Draft Redemption

A "Lottery Exchange Card" randomly inserted (reportedly at a rate of one per 360 packs) in 1992-93 Hoops first series 12-card foil packs entitled the collector to receive this NBA Draft Redemption Lottery Exchange set. It consists of ten standard size cards of the top 1992 NBA Draft Picks. The first eleven players drafted are represented, with the exception of Jim Jackson, the late-signing fourth pick. Insert sets began to be mailed out during the week of January 4, 1993, and the redemption period expired on March 31, 1993. According to SkyBox International media releases a total of 25,876 sets were released to the public; 24,461 Lottery Exchange cards were redeemed. An additional 415 sets were claimed through a second chance drawing (select-ed from 149,166 mail-in entries). Finally, 1,000 more sets were released for public relations and promotional use. A reserve of 1,000 sets were held for replacement of damaged sets and 500 sets were kept for SkyBox International archives. In the color photos on the fronts, the players appear in dress attire in front of a gray studio background, except for cards C and J. The player's name is printed in white in a hardwood floor border design at the bottom of the card. An NBA Draft icon overlaps the border and the photo. A one inch tall hardwood design number at the upper left corner indicates the order the players were drafted. The horizontal backs display white backgrounds with a similar hardwood stripe containing the player's name across the top. A shad-owed close-up photo is dis-played next to college statistics and a player profile. The cards are lettered on the back. Sets still in the factory-sealed bags are valued at a premium of up to 20 percent above the complete set price below.

	MINT	NRMT
COMPLETE SET (10)	50.00	22.00
COMMON CARD (A-J)	1.50	.70
SEMISTARS	2.00	.90
UNLISTED STARS	3.00	1.35
ONE PER EXCHANGE CARD BY MAIL		
EXCH.CARD: SER.1 STATED ODDS 1:360		
☐ A Shaquille O'Neal	30.00	13.50
☐ B Alonzo Mourning.......	10.00	4.50
☐ C Christian Laettner	5.00	2.20
☐ D LaPhonso Ellis	3.00	1.35
☐ E Tom Gugliotta	6.00	2.70
☐ F Walt Williams	2.00	.90
☐ G Todd Day	1.50	.70
☐ H C.Weatherspoon	2.00	.90
☐ I Adam Keefe	1.50	.70
☐ J Robert Horry	3.00	1.35
☐ NNO Draft Red. Card	.50	.23

	MINT	NRMT
	(Stamped)	
☐ NNO Draft Red. Card	2.00	.90
	(Unstamped)	

1992-93 Hoops Magic's All-Rookies

This 10-card standard size set was randomly inserted into Hoops second series 12-card foil packs. They were inserted at a rate of one in 30 packs. The set features Magic Johnson's selections of the top rookies from the 1992-93 season. The cards show color action player photos and have a gold foil stripe containing the player's name down the left edge and a thinner stripe across the bottom printed with the city's name. The Magic's All-Rookie Team logo appears in the lower left corner. The backs display a small close-up picture of Magic Johnson in a yellow Los Angeles Lakers' warm-up jacket. A yellow stripe down the left edge contains the set name (Magic's All-Rookie Team) and the card number. The white background is printed in black with Magic's evaluation of the player.

	MINT	NRMT
COMPLETE SET (10)	110.00	50.00
COMMON CARD (1-10)	2.00	.90
SEMISTARS	4.00	1.80
UNLISTED STARS	6.00	2.70
SER.2 STATED ODDS 1:30		
☐ 1 Shaquille O'Neal	60.00	27.00
☐ 2 Alonzo Mourning......	20.00	9.00
☐ 3 Christian Laettner	10.00	4.50
☐ 4 LaPhonso Ellis..........	6.00	2.70
☐ 5 Tom Gugliotta	12.00	5.50
☐ 6 Walt Williams	4.00	1.80
☐ 7 Todd Day	2.00	.90
☐ 8 C.Weatherspoon	4.00	1.80
☐ 9 Robert Horry	6.00	2.70
☐ 10 Harold Miner	2.00	.90

1992-93 Hoops More Magic Moments

Randomly inserted (at a reported rate of one card per 195 packs) into 1992-93 Hoops second series 12-card packs, this three-card standard-size set commemorates Magic Johnson's return to training camp and pre-season game action. Each card features a color player photo bordered in white. Team color-coded bars and lettering accent the picture on the left edge and below, and a team color-coded star overwritten with the words "More Magic" appears at the lower left corner. Over ghosted photos similar or identical to the front photos, the backs summarize Magic's return, his performance in his first game, his performance in his last game, and his decision to retire again. The cards are numbered on the back with an "M" prefix.

	MINT	NRMT
COMPLETE SET (3)	70.00	32.00
COMMON MAGIC (M1-M3)	25.00	11.00
SER.2 STATED ODDS 1:195		
☐ M1 Magic in Trng Camp Fall 1992	25.00	11.00
☐ M2 L.A. Lakers vs. Philadelphia October 20, 1992	25.00	11.00
☐ M3 L.A. Lakers vs. Cleveland October 30, 1992	25.00	11.00

1992-93 Hoops Supreme Court

This 10-card, standard-size set was randomly inserted (at a reported rate of one card per 11 packs) in Hoops second series 12-card foil packs and features color action player photos on the front. A gold foil stripe frames the pictures which are surrounded by a hardwood floor design. The player's name is printed in gold foil down the left side. A gray and burnt-orange logo printed with the words "Supreme Court 1992-93" appears in the lower left corner. A purple stripe containing the phrase "The Fan's Choice" runs across the bottom of the picture. Hoops promoted The Supreme Court Sweepstakes, which offered fans the opportunity to select the ten players who appeared in this subset. The backs are white with black print. A small color player photo with rounded corners is displayed next to a personal profile. The cards are numbered on the back with an "SC" prefix.

	MINT	NRMT
COMPLETE SET (10)	30.00	13.50
COMMON CARD (SC1-SC10)	1.50	.70
SER.2 STATED ODDS 1:11		
☐ SC1 Michael Jordan	20.00	9.00
☐ SC2 Scottie Pippen	5.00	2.20
☐ SC3 David Robinson	2.50	1.10
☐ SC4 Patrick Ewing	1.00	.45
☐ SC5 Clyde Drexler	2.00	.90
☐ SC6 Karl Malone	2.50	1.10
☐ SC7 Charles Barkley	2.50	1.10
☐ SC8 John Stockton	1.00	.45
☐ SC9 Chris Mullin	1.00	.45
☐ SC10 Magic Johnson	5.00	2.20

1993-94 Hoops

This 421-card standard-size set was issued in separate series of 300 and 121 cards. Cards were distributed in 13-card foil (12 basic cards plus one gold card) and 26-card jumbo (24 basic and two gold cards) packs. Cards feature full-bleed glossy color player photos on the fronts. Each player's name and team logo appear in team colors along a ghosted band at the bottom. The back presents a color head shot of the player in a small rectangle bordered with a team color in the top right corner. Alongside is his jersey number and position within a team-colored bar. The player's name and a short biography are printed on a hardwood floor design at the top. Below, the player's college and NBA stats, displayed in separate tables on a white background, round out the card. The cards are numbered on the back and listed alphabetically within team order. Subsets are Coaches (230-256), All-Stars (257-282), League Leaders (283-290), Boys and Girls Club (291), Hoops Tribune (292-297), and Checklists (298-300/419-420). Rookie Cards of note include Vin Baker, A.Hardaway, Jamal Mashburn, Nick Van Exel and Chris Webber.

	MINT	NRMT
COMPLETE SET (421)	20.00	9.00
COMPLETE SERIES 1 (300)	12.00	5.50
COMPLETE SERIES 2 (121)	8.00	3.60
COMMON CARD (1-421)	.05	.02
SEMISTARS	.10	.05
UNLISTED STARS	.25	.11
COMP.GOLD SET (421)	60.00	27.00
COMP.GOLD SERIES 1 (300)	35.00	16.00
COMP.GOLD SERIES 2 (121)	25.00	11.00
COMM.GOLD CARD (1-421)	.10	.05
*GOLD STARS: 1.25X TO 2.5X HI COLUMN		
*GOLD RCs: 1X TO 2X HI		
ONE GOLD PER PACK		
TWO GOLD PER JUMBO PACK		
DR1: SER.2 STATED ODDS 1:18		
BOTH AUs: SER.2 STATED ODDS 1:13,886		
☐ 1 Stacey Augmon	.05	.02
☐ 2 Mookie Blaylock	.10	.05
☐ 3 Duane Ferrell	.05	.02
☐ 4 Paul Graham	.05	.02
☐ 5 Adam Keefe	.05	.02
☐ 6 Blair Rasmussen	.05	.02
☐ 7 Dominique Wilkins	.25	.11
☐ 8 Kevin Willis	.05	.02
☐ 9 Alaa Abdelnaby	.05	.02
☐ 10 Dee Brown	.05	.02
☐ 11 Sherman Douglas	.05	.02
☐ 12 Rick Fox	.05	.02
☐ 13 Kevin Gamble	.05	.02
☐ 14 Joe Kleine	.05	.02
☐ 15 Xavier McDaniel	.05	.02
☐ 16 Robert Parish	.10	.05
☐ 17 Tony Bennett	.05	.02

18	Muggsy Bogues	.10	.05
19	Dell Curry	.05	.02
20	Kenny Gattison	.05	.02
21	Kendall Gill	.10	.05
22	Larry Johnson	.25	.11
23	Alonzo Mourning	.40	.18
24	Johnny Newman	.05	.02
25	B.J. Armstrong	.05	.02
26	Bill Cartwright	.05	.02
27	Horace Grant	.10	.05
28	Michael Jordan	3.00	1.35
29	Stacey King	.05	.02
30	John Paxson	.05	.02
31	Will Perdue	.05	.02
32	Scottie Pippen	.75	.35
33	Scott Williams	.05	.02
34	Moses Malone	.25	.11
35	John Battle	.05	.02
36	Terrell Brandon	.25	.11
37	Brad Daugherty	.05	.02
38	Craig Ehlo	.05	.02
39	Danny Ferry	.05	.02
40	Larry Nance	.10	.05
41	Mark Price	.05	.02
42	Gerald Wilkins	.05	.02
43	John Williams	.05	.02
44	Terry Davis	.05	.02
45	Derek Harper	.10	.05
46	Donald Hodge	.05	.02
47	Mike Iuzzolino	.05	.02
48	Jim Jackson	.25	.11
49	Sean Rooks	.05	.02
50	Doug Smith	.05	.02
51	Randy White	.05	.02
52	M.Abdul-Rauf	.05	.02
53	LaPhonso Ellis	.10	.05
54	Marcus Liberty	.05	.02
55	Mark Macon	.05	.02
56	D.Mutombo	.25	.11
57	Robert Pack	.05	.02
58	Bryant Stith	.05	.02
59	Reggie Williams	.05	.02
60	Mark Aguirre	.05	.02
61	Joe Dumars	.25	.11
62	Bill Laimbeer	.05	.02
63	Terry Mills	.05	.02
64	Olden Polynice	.05	.02
65	Alvin Robertson	.05	.02
66	Dennis Rodman	1.00	.45
67	Isiah Thomas	.25	.11
68	Victor Alexander	.05	.02
69	Tim Hardaway	.30	.14
70	Tyrone Hill	.05	.02
71	Byron Houston	.05	.02
72	Sarunas Marciulionis	.05	.02
73	Chris Mullin	.25	.11
74	Billy Owens	.05	.02
75	Latrell Sprewell	.25	.11
76	Scott Brooks	.05	.02
77	Matt Bullard	.05	.02
78	Carl Herrera	.05	.02
79	Robert Horry	.10	.05
80	Vernon Maxwell	.05	.02
81	Hakeem Olajuwon	.50	.23
82	Kenny Smith	.05	.02
83	Otis Thorpe	.10	.05
84	Dale Davis	.05	.02
85	Vern Fleming	.05	.02
86	George McCloud	.05	.02
87	Reggie Miller	.25	.11
88	Sam Mitchell	.05	.02
89	Pooh Richardson	.05	.02
90	Detlef Schrempf	.10	.05
91	Malik Sealy	.05	.02
92	Rik Smits	.05	.02
93	Gary Grant	.05	.02
94	Ron Harper	.05	.02
95	Mark Jackson	.10	.05
96	Danny Manning	.05	.02
97	Ken Norman	.05	.02
98	Stanley Roberts	.05	.02
99	Elmore Spencer	.05	.02
100	Loy Vaught	.10	.05
101	John Williams	.05	.02
102	Randy Woods	.05	.02
103	Benoit Benjamin	.05	.02
104	Elden Campbell	.10	.05
105	Doug Christie UER	.05	.02
	(Has uniform number on front and 35 on back)		
106	Vlade Divac	.10	.05
107	Anthony Peeler	.05	.02
108	Tony Smith	.05	.02
109	Sedale Threatt	.05	.02
110	James Worthy	.25	.11
111	Bimbo Coles	.05	.02
112	Grant Long	.05	.02
113	Harold Miner	.05	.02
114	Glen Rice	.25	.11
115	John Salley	.05	.02
116	Rony Seikaly	.05	.02
117	Brian Shaw	.05	.02
118	Steve Smith	.10	.05
119	Anthony Avent	.05	.02
120	Jon Barry	.05	.02
121	Frank Brickowski	.05	.02
122	Todd Day	.05	.02
123	Blue Edwards	.05	.02
124	Brad Lohaus	.05	.02
125	Lee Mayberry	.05	.02
126	Eric Murdock	.05	.02
127	Derek Strong	.05	.02
128	Thurl Bailey	.05	.02
129	Christian Laettner	.25	.11
130	Luc Longley	.10	.05
131	Marlon Maxey	.05	.02
132	Chuck Person	.05	.02
133	Chris Smith	.05	.02
134	Doug West	.05	.02
135	Micheal Williams	.05	.02
136	Rafael Addison	.05	.02
137	Kenny Anderson	.10	.05
138	Sam Bowie	.05	.02
139	Chucky Brown	.05	.02
140	Derrick Coleman	.10	.05
141	Chris Morris	.05	.02
142	Rumeal Robinson	.05	.02
143	Greg Anthony	.05	.02
144	Rolando Blackman	.05	.02
145	Hubert Davis	.05	.02
146	Patrick Ewing	.25	.11
147	Anthony Mason	.10	.05
148	Charles Oakley	.05	.02
149	Doc Rivers	.10	.05
150	Charles Smith	.05	.02
151	John Starks	.10	.05
152	Nick Anderson	.10	.05
153	Anthony Bowie	.05	.02
154	Litterial Green	.05	.02
155	Shaquille O'Neal	1.00	.45
156	Donald Royal	.05	.02
157	Dennis Scott	.05	.02
158	Scott Skiles	.05	.02
159	Tom Tolbert	.05	.02
160	Jeff Turner	.05	.02
161	Ron Anderson	.05	.02
162	Johnny Dawkins	.05	.02
163	Hersey Hawkins	.05	.02
164	Jeff Hornacek	.05	.02
165	Andrew Lang	.05	.02
166	Tim Perry	.05	.02
167	C.Weatherspoon	.05	.02
168	Danny Ainge	.10	.05
169	Charles Barkley	.40	.18
170	Cedric Ceballos	.10	.05
171	Richard Dumas	.05	.02
172	Kevin Johnson	.10	.05
173	Dan Majerle	.10	.05
174	Oliver Miller	.05	.02
175	Mark West	.05	.02
176	Clyde Drexler	.30	.14
177	Kevin Duckworth	.05	.02
178	Mario Elie	.05	.02
179	Dave Johnson	.05	.02
180	Jerome Kersey	.05	.02
181	Tracy Murray	.05	.02
182	Terry Porter	.05	.02
183	Clifford Robinson	.10	.05
184	Rod Strickland	.05	.02
185	Buck Williams	.10	.05
186	Anthony Bonner	.05	.02
187	Randy Brown	.05	.02
188	Duane Causwell	.05	.02
189	Pete Chilcutt	.05	.02
190	Mitch Richmond	.25	.11
191	Lionel Simmons	.05	.02
192	Wayman Tisdale	.05	.02
193	Spud Webb	.10	.05
194	Walt Williams	.10	.05
195	Willie Anderson	.05	.02
196	Antoine Carr	.05	.02
197	Terry Cummings	.05	.02
198	Lloyd Daniels	.05	.02
199	Sean Elliott	.10	.05
200	Dale Ellis	.05	.02
201	Avery Johnson	.05	.02
202	J.R. Reid	.05	.02
203	David Robinson	.40	.18
204	Dana Barros	.05	.02
205	Michael Cage	.05	.02
206	Eddie Johnson	.05	.02
207	Shawn Kemp	.75	.35
208	Derrick McKey	.05	.02
209	Nate McMillan	.05	.02
210	Gary Payton	.40	.18
211	Sam Perkins	.10	.05
212	Ricky Pierce	.05	.02
213	David Benoit	.05	.02
214	Tyrone Corbin	.05	.02
215	Mark Eaton	.05	.02
216	Jay Humphries	.05	.02
217	Jeff Malone	.05	.02
218	Karl Malone	.40	.18
219	John Stockton	.25	.11
220	Michael Adams	.05	.02
221	Rex Chapman	.05	.02
222	Pervis Ellison	.05	.02
223	Harvey Grant	.05	.02
224	Tom Gugliotta	.25	.11
225	Don MacLean	.05	.02
226	Doug Overton	.05	.02
227	Brent Price	.05	.02
228	LaBradford Smith	.05	.02
229	Larry Stewart	.05	.02
230	Lenny Wilkens CO	.10	.05
231	Chris Ford CO	.05	.02
232	Allan Bristow CO	.05	.02
233	Phil Jackson CO	.10	.05
234	Mike Fratello CO	.10	.05
235	Quinn Buckner CO	.05	.02
236	Dan Issel CO	.05	.02
237	Don Chaney CO	.05	.02
238	Don Nelson CO	.10	.05
239	Rudy Tomjanovich CO	.10	.05
240	Larry Brown CO	.10	.05
241	Bob Weiss CO	.05	.02
242	Randy Pfund CO	.05	.02
243	Kevin Loughery CO	.05	.02
244	Mike Dunleavy CO	.05	.02
245	Sidney Lowe CO	.05	.02
246	Chuck Daly CO	.10	.05
247	Pat Riley CO	.10	.05
248	Brian Hill CO	.05	.02
249	Fred Carter CO	.05	.02
250	Paul Westphal CO	.05	.02
251	Rick Adelman CO	.05	.02
252	Garry St. Jean CO	.05	.02
253	John Lucas CO	.05	.02
254	George Karl CO	.10	.05
255	Jerry Sloan CO	.10	.05
256	Wes Unseld CO	.05	.02
257	Michael Jordan AS	1.50	.70
258	Isiah Thomas AS	.10	.05
259	Scottie Pippen AS	.40	.18
260	Larry Johnson AS	.10	.05
261	Dominique Wilkins AS	.10	.05
262	Joe Dumars AS	.10	.05
263	Mark Price AS	.05	.02
264	Shaquille O'Neal AS	.50	.23
265	Patrick Ewing AS	.10	.05
266	Larry Nance AS	.05	.02
267	Detlef Schrempf AS	.05	.02
268	Brad Daugherty AS	.05	.02
269	Charles Barkley AS	.25	.11
270	Clyde Drexler AS	.25	.11
271	Sean Elliott AS	.10	.05
272	Tim Hardaway AS	.25	.11
273	Shawn Kemp AS	.40	.18

□ 274 Dan Majerle AS	.05	.02
□ 275 Karl Malone AS	.25	.11
□ 276 Danny Manning AS	.05	.02
□ 277 Hakeem Olajuwon AS	.25	.11
□ 278 Terry Porter AS	.05	.02
□ 279 David Robinson AS	.25	.11
□ 280 John Stockton AS	.10	.05
□ 281 East Team Photo	.05	.02
□ 282 West Team Photo	.05	.02
□ 283 Scoring	.75	.35
Michael Jordan		
Dominique Wilkins		
Karl Malone		
□ 284 Rebounding	.50	.23
Dennis Rodman		
Shaquille O'Neal		
D.Mutombo		
□ 285 Field Goal Percentage	.05	.02
Cedric Ceballos		
Brad Daugherty		
Dale Davis		
□ 286 Assists	.10	.05
John Stockton		
Tim Hardaway		
Scott Skiles		
□ 287 Free Throw Percentage	.05	.02
Mark Price		
M.Abdul-Rauf		
Eddie Johnson		
□ 288 3-point FG Percentage	.05	.02
B.J. Armstrong		
Chris Mullin		
Kenny Smith		
□ 289 Steals	.75	.35
Michael Jordan		
Mookie Blaylock		
John Stockton		
□ 290 Blocks	.40	.18
Hakeem Olajuwon		
Shaquille O'Neal		
D.Mutombo		
□ 291 Boys and Girls Club	.10	.05
David Robinson		
□ 292 B.J. Armstrong TRIB	.05	.02
□ 293 Scottie Pippen TRIB	.40	.18
□ 294 Kevin Johnson TRIB	.05	.02
□ 295 Charles Barkley TRIB	.25	.11
□ 296 Richard Dumas TRIB	.05	.02
□ 297 Horace Grant CL	.05	.02
□ 298 David Robinson CL	.05	.02
□ 299 David Robinson CL	.05	.02
□ 300 David Robinson CL	.05	.02
□ 301 Craig Ehlo	.05	.02
□ 302 Jon Koncak	.05	.02
□ 303 Andrew Lang	.05	.02
□ 304 Chris Corchiani	.05	.02
□ 305 Acie Earl	.05	.02
□ 306 Dino Radja	.10	.05
□ 307 Scott Burrell	.25	.11
□ 308 Hersey Hawkins	.10	.05
□ 309 Eddie Johnson	.05	.02
□ 310 David Wingate	.05	.02
□ 311 Corie Blount	.05	.02
□ 312 Steve Kerr	.10	.05
□ 313 Toni Kukoc	.60	.25
□ 314 Pete Myers	.05	.02
□ 315 Jay Guidinger	.05	.02
□ 316 Tyrone Hill	.05	.02
□ 317 Gerald Madkins	.05	.02
□ 318 Chris Mills	.40	.18
□ 319 Bobby Phills	.05	.02
□ 320 Lucious Harris	.05	.02
□ 321 Popeye Jones	.05	.02
□ 322 Fat Lever	.05	.02
□ 323 Jamal Mashburn	.60	.25
□ 324 Darren Morningstar	.05	.02
(See also 334)		
□ 325 Kevin Brooks	.05	.02
□ 326 Tom Hammonds	.05	.02
□ 327 Darnell Mee	.05	.02
□ 328 Rodney Rogers	.05	.02
□ 329 Brian Williams	.05	.02
□ 330 Greg Anderson	.05	.02
□ 331 Sean Elliott	.10	.05
□ 332 Allan Houston	.50	.23
□ 333 Lindsey Hunter	.25	.11
□ 334 David Wood UER	.05	.02
(Card misnumbered 324)		
□ 335 Jud Buechler	.05	.02
□ 336 Chris Gatling	.05	.02
□ 337 Josh Grant	.05	.02
□ 338 Jeff Grayer	.05	.02
□ 339 Keith Jennings	.05	.02
□ 340 Avery Johnson	.05	.02
□ 341 Chris Webber	1.50	.70
□ 342 Sam Cassell	.60	.25
□ 343 Mario Elie	.05	.02
□ 344 Eric Riley	.05	.02
□ 345 Antonio Davis	.10	.05
□ 346 Scott Haskin	.05	.02
□ 347 Gerald Paddio	.05	.02
□ 348 LaSalle Thompson	.05	.02
□ 349 Ken Williams	.05	.02
□ 350 Mark Aguirre	.05	.02
□ 351 Terry Dehere	.05	.02
□ 352 Henry James	.05	.02
□ 353 Sam Bowie	.05	.02
□ 354 George Lynch	.05	.02
□ 355 Kurt Rambis	.05	.02
□ 356 Nick Van Exel	.75	.35
□ 357 Trevor Wilson	.05	.02
□ 358 Keith Askins	.05	.02
□ 359 Manute Bol	.05	.02
□ 360 Willie Burton	.05	.02
□ 361 Matt Geiger	.05	.02
□ 362 Alec Kessler	.05	.02
□ 363 Vin Baker	1.50	.70
□ 364 Ken Norman	.05	.02
□ 365 Dan Schayes	.05	.02
□ 366 Mike Brown	.05	.02
□ 367 Isaiah Rider	.30	.14
□ 368 Benoit Benjamin	.05	.02
□ 369 P.J. Brown	.05	.02
□ 370 Kevin Edwards	.05	.02
□ 371 Armon Gilliam	.05	.02
□ 372 Rick Mahorn	.05	.02
□ 373 Dwayne Schintzius	.05	.02
□ 374 Rex Walters	.05	.02
□ 375 Jayson Williams	.10	.05
□ 376 Eric Anderson	.05	.02
□ 377 Anthony Bonner	.05	.02
□ 378 Tony Campbell	.05	.02
□ 379 Herb Williams	.05	.02
□ 380 A.Hardaway	3.00	1.35
□ 381 Greg Kite	.05	.02
□ 382 Larry Krystkowiak	.05	.02
□ 383 Todd Lichti	.05	.02
□ 384 Dana Barros	.05	.02
□ 385 Shawn Bradley	.30	.14
□ 386 Greg Graham	.05	.02
□ 387 Warren Kidd	.05	.02
□ 388 Eric Leckner	.05	.02
□ 389 Moses Malone	.25	.11
□ 390 A.C. Green	.10	.05
□ 391 Frank Johnson	.05	.02
□ 392 Joe Kleine	.05	.02
□ 393 Malcolm Mackey	.05	.02
□ 394 Jerrod Mustaf	.05	.02
□ 395 Mark Bryant	.05	.02
□ 396 Chris Dudley	.05	.02
□ 397 Harvey Grant	.05	.02
□ 398 James Robinson	.05	.02
□ 399 Reggie Smith	.05	.02
□ 400 Randy Brown	.05	.02
□ 401 Bobby Hurley	.10	.05
□ 402 Jim Les	.05	.02
□ 403 Vinny Del Negro	.05	.02
□ 404 Sleepy Floyd	.05	.02
□ 405 Dennis Rodman	1.00	.45
□ 406 Chris Whitney	.05	.02
□ 407 Vincent Askew	.05	.02
□ 408 Kendall Gill	.10	.05
□ 409 Ervin Johnson	.10	.05
□ 410 Rich King	.05	.02
□ 411 Detlef Schrempf	.10	.05
□ 412 Tom Chambers	.05	.02
□ 413 John Crotty	.05	.02
□ 414 Felton Spencer	.05	.02
□ 415 Luther Wright	.05	.02
□ 416 Calbert Cheaney	.25	.11
□ 417 Kevin Duckworth	.05	.02
□ 418 Gheorghe Muresan	.30	.14
□ 419 David Robinson CL	.05	.02
□ 420 David Robinson CL	.05	.02
□ 421 David Robinson CL	.05	.02
□ DR1 David Robinson	.40	.18
Commemorative 1989		
Rookie Card		
□ MB1 Magic Johnson	.50	.23
Larry Bird		
Commemorative		
□ NNO David Robinson	80.00	36.00
Autograph Card		
□ NNO David Robinson	10.00	4.50
Expired Voucher		
□ NNO Magic Johnson	400.00	180.00
Larry Bird		
Autograph Card		
□ NNO Magic Johnson	30.00	13.50
Larry Bird		
Expired Voucher		

1993-94 Hoops Admiral's Choice

Randomly inserted in second series 13-card foil and 26-card jumbo packs at a rate of one in 12, this five-card standard-size set features David Robinson's selection of the best starting five players in the game today. The cards have borderless fronts with color player photos. The player's name appears in gold-foil lettering at the top. The white back features a color player photo on the left with the player profile on the right. The cards are numbered on the back with an "AC" prefix.

	MINT	NRMT
COMPLETE SET (5)	3.00	1.35
COMMON CARD (AC1-AC5)	.25	.11
SER.2 STATED ODDS 1:12		
□ AC1 Shawn Kemp	1.00	.45
□ AC2 Derrick Coleman	.25	.11
□ AC3 Kenny Anderson	.25	.11
□ AC4 Shaquille O'Neal	1.25	.55
□ AC5 Chris Webber	2.00	.90

1993-94 Hoops David's Best

Inserted into one in every ten first series 1993-94 Hoops 13-card foil packs, these UV-coated

cards feature color action photos of David Robinson against featured opponents. The "David's Best" logo runs across the bottom of the card in "golden crystal-foil" lettering. The back of the cards present Robinson's stat line from the selected game and a brief synopsis of the highlights. The cards are numbered on the back with a "DB" prefix.

	MINT	NRMT
COMPLETE SET (5)	2.00	.90
COMMON D.ROB. (DB1-DB5)	.50	.23
SER.1 STATED ODDS 1:10		
☐ DB1 David Robinson (Vs. Lakers)	.50	.23
☐ DB2 David Robinson (Vs. Magic)	.50	.23
☐ DB3 David Robinson (Vs. Trail Blazers)	.50	.23
☐ DB4 David Robinson (Vs. Warriors)	.50	.23
☐ DB5 David Robinson (Vs. Hornets)	.50	.23

1993-94 Hoops Draft Redemption

For the second consecutive year, a redemption card was randomly inserted into series one packs at a rate of one in 360. The card could be sent in for this 11-card standard-size set by March 31, 1994. The cards feature a full-color head photo on the front. The player's name appears centered at the top in gold foil. The player's draft number also appears in gold foil at the upper right. The horizontal back features a color player head shot on the left, with player statistics and biography alongside on the right. The cards are numbered on the back with an "LP" prefix and sequenced in draft lottery order.

	MINT	NRMT
COMPLETE SET (11)	40.00	18.00
COMMON CARD (LP1-LP11)	1.00	.45
SEMISTARS	1.50	.70
UNLISTED STARS	2.50	1.10
ONE SET PER EXCHANGE CARD BY MAIL		
EXCH.CARD: SER.1 STATED ODDS 1:360		
☐ LP1 Chris Webber	10.00	4.50
☐ LP2 Shawn Bradley	2.50	1.10
☐ LP3 A.Hardaway	25.00	11.00
☐ LP4 Jamal Mashburn	4.00	1.80
☐ LP5 Isaiah Rider	2.50	1.10
☐ LP6 Calbert Cheaney	2.50	1.10
☐ LP7 Bobby Hurley	1.50	.70
☐ LP8 Vin Baker	10.00	4.50
☐ LP9 Rodney Rogers	1.00	.45
☐ LP10 Lindsey Hunter	2.50	1.10
☐ LP11 Allan Houston	3.00	1.35
☐ NNO Red. Lottery Card	.25	.11
☐ NNO Unred. Lottery Card	1.50	.70

1993-94 Hoops Face to Face

Randomly inserted in first series 13-card foil packs at a rate of one in 20, these 12 standard-size cards feature a standout rookie from 1992-93 on one side and a veteran All-Star with similar skills on the other. The full-bleed glossy color player action photos on both sides are reproduced over metallic-type backgrounds. On both sides, the Face to Face logo and the player's name appears at the bottom. The cards are numbered on the second side with an "FTF" prefix.

	MINT	NRMT
COMPLETE SET (12)	30.00	13.50
COMMON CARD (1-12)	.75	.35
SEMISTARS	1.25	.55
SER.1 STATED ODDS 1:20		
FTF PREFIX ON CARD NUMBERS		
☐ 1 Shaquille O'Neal David Robinson	6.00	2.70
☐ 2 Alonzo Mourning Patrick Ewing	3.00	1.35
☐ 3 Christian Laettner Shawn Kemp	4.00	1.80
☐ 4 Jim Jackson Clyde Drexler	2.50	1.10
☐ 5 LaPhonso Ellis Larry Johnson	1.25	.55
☐ 6 C.Weatherspoon Charles Barkley	2.50	1.10
☐ 7 Tom Gugliotta Karl Malone	3.00	1.35
☐ 8 Walt Williams Magic Johnson	4.00	1.80
☐ 9 Robert Horry Scottie Pippen	4.00	1.80
☐ 10 Harold Miner Michael Jordan	15.00	6.75
☐ 11 Todd Day Chris Mullin	.75	.35
☐ 12 Richard Dumas Dominique Wilkins	1.25	.55

1993-94 Hoops Magic's All-Rookies

Randomly inserted in second-series 13-card foil and 26-card jumbo packs at a rate of one in 30, this 10-card standard size set features Magic Johnson's projected All-Rookie team for 1993-94. The borderless front features a full-color action shot with the player's name in a gold foil strip at the bottom. The borderless back features an italicized player profile written by Magic Johnson set against a ghosted background photo of Magic.

	MINT	NRMT
COMPLETE SET (10)	40.00	18.00
COMMON CARD (1-10)	1.00	.45
SEMISTARS	1.50	.70
UNLISTED STARS	2.50	1.10
SER.2 STATED ODDS 1:30		
☐ 1 Chris Webber	10.00	4.50
☐ 2 Shawn Bradley	2.50	1.10
☐ 3 A.Hardaway	25.00	11.00
☐ 4 Jamal Mashburn	5.00	2.20

		MINT	NRMT
□ 5	Isaiah Rider	2.50	1.10
□ 6	Calbert Cheaney	1.50	.70
□ 7	Bobby Hurley	1.00	.45
□ 8	Vin Baker	10.00	4.50
□ 9	Lindsey Hunter	1.50	.70
□ 10	Toni Kukoc	4.00	1.80

□ HS21	Charles Barkley	.25	.11
□ HS22	Clifford Robinson	.10	.05
□ HS23	Lionel Simmons	.05	.02
□ HS24	David Robinson	.25	.11
□ HS25	Shawn Kemp	.25	.11
□ HS26	Karl Malone	.25	.11
□ HS27	Rex Chapman	.05	.02
□ HS28	Answer Card	.05	.02

1993-94 Hoops Scoops

Randomly inserted in second series 13-card foil packs, this 28-card set measures the standard size. Photos feature unique above the rim photography of a star player from each of the 27 NBA teams. Cards are either horizontal or vertical. The player's name, his team's name, and logo appear in a black bar under the photo, while the NBA Hoops Scoops logo appears in the upper right or left corner. On a white background, the backs carry trivia questions about the teams. The cards are numbered on the back with an "HS" prefix. These cards are as plentiful as the regular issue cards.

	MINT	NRMT
COMPLETE SET (28)	1.00	.45
COMMON CARD (HS1-HS28)	.05	.02
SEMISTARS	.10	.05
UNLISTED STARS	.25	.11

*GOLD CARDS:1.25X TO 2.5X HI COLUMN
RANDOM INSERTS IN SER.2 PACKS

□ HS1	Dominique Wilkins	.25	.11
□ HS2	Robert Parish	.10	.05
□ HS3	Alonzo Mourning	.25	.11
□ HS4	Scottie Pippen	.25	.11
□ HS5	Larry Nance	.05	.02
□ HS6	Derek Harper	.05	.02
□ HS7	Reggie Williams	.05	.02
□ HS8	Bill Laimbeer	.05	.02
□ HS9	Tim Hardaway	.25	.11
□ HS10	H.Olajuwon UER	.25	.11

(Robert Horry is featured player)

□ HS11	LaSalle Thompson	.05	.02
□ HS12	Danny Manning	.05	.02
□ HS13	James Worthy	.25	.11
□ HS14	Grant Long	.05	.02
□ HS15	Blue Edwards	.05	.02
□ HS16	Christian Laettner	.25	.11
□ HS17	Derrick Coleman	.10	.05
□ HS18	Patrick Ewing	.25	.11
□ HS19	Nick Anderson	.05	.02
□ HS20	C.Weatherspoon	.05	.02

1993-94 Hoops Supreme Court

Randomly inserted into second series 13-card foil and 26-card jumbo packs, this 11-card standard-size set reflects the All-NBA team as chosen by media members that report on the hobby. Card fronts feature full-color action player photos set against a wood grain vertical bar with the player's name centered at the top in silver-foil lettering. The backs carry color player action shots along the left side and player statistics along the right side. The cards are numbered on the back with an "SC" prefix.

	MINT	NRMT
COMPLETE SET (11)	12.00	5.50
COMMON CARD (SC1-SC11)	.40	.18
SEMISTARS	.50	.23

SER.2 STATED ODDS 1:11

□ SC1	Charles Barkley	.75	.35
□ SC2	David Robinson	.75	.35
□ SC3	Patrick Ewing	.50	.23
□ SC4	Shaquille O'Neal	2.00	.90
□ SC5	Larry Johnson	.40	.18
□ SC6	Karl Malone	.75	.35
□ SC7	Alonzo Mourning	.75	.35
□ SC8	John Stockton	.50	.23
□ SC9	H.Olajuwon UER	1.00	.45

(Name spelled Olajuon on front)

□ SC10	Scottie Pippen	1.50	.70
□ SC11	Michael Jordan	6.00	2.70

1994-95 Hoops

The 450 standard-size cards comprising the '94-95 Hoops set were distributed in two separate series of 300 and 150 cards each. Cards were issued in 12-card hobby and retail packs (suggested retail price first series $0.99, second series $1.19) and 24-card retail jumbo packs. All second series packs contained at least one insert card (12-card packs had one insert and 24-card jumbo packs had two). Cards feature borderless color player action shots on the front. The player's name, position, and team name appear in white lettering within a team colored stripe near the bottom. The white back carries a color player head shot at the upper left, with the player's name and brief biography appearing alongside to the right. Statistics and career highlights follow below. The cards are numbered on the back and grouped alphabetically within teams. Subsets include All-Stars (224-251), League Leaders (252-258), Award Winners (259-265), Tribune (266-273), Coaches (274-295/383-388), Team Cards (391-420), Top This (421-430) and Gold Mine (431-450). A special Shaquille O'Neal Press Sheet (featuring 100 of his previously issued Hoops and SkyBox cards in an uncut poster-size format) was available by sending in thirty-two first series wrappers along with a check or money order for $1.50. As a special bonus 100 Press Sheets were autographed by O'Neal and randomly mailed out to collectors who responded to the promotion, which expired on March 1st, 1995. A special Grant Hill Commemorative card was available by sending in two second series wrappers along with a check or money order for $3.00 before the June 15th expiration date. Rookie Cards of note include Grant Hill, Juwan Howard, Eddie Jones, Jason Kidd and Glenn Robinson.

	MINT	NRMT
COMPLETE SET (450)	24.00	11.00
COMPLETE SERIES 1 (300)	12.00	5.50
COMPLETE SERIES 2 (150)	12.00	5.50
COMMON CARD (1-450)	.05	.02
SEMISTARS	.10	.05
UNLISTED STARS	.25	.11

#	Player	MINT	NRMT
1	Stacey Augmon	.05	.02
2	Mookie Blaylock	.05	.02
3	Doug Edwards	.05	.02
4	Craig Ehlo	.05	.02
5	Jon Koncak	.05	.02
6	Danny Manning	.05	.02
7	Kevin Willis	.05	.02
8	Dee Brown	.05	.02
9	Sherman Douglas	.05	.02
10	Acie Earl	.05	.02
11	Kevin Gamble	.05	.02
12	Xavier McDaniel	.05	.02
13	Robert Parish	.10	.05
14	Dino Radja	.05	.02
15	Tony Bennett	.05	.02
16	Muggsy Bogues	.10	.05
17	Scott Burrell	.05	.02
18	Dell Curry	.05	.02
19	Hersey Hawkins	.10	.05
20	Eddie Johnson	.05	.02
21	Larry Johnson	.10	.05
22	Alonzo Mourning	.30	.14
23	B.J. Armstrong	.05	.02
24	Corie Blount	.05	.02
25	Bill Cartwright	.05	.02
26	Horace Grant	.10	.05
27	Toni Kukoc	.25	.11
28	Luc Longley	.10	.05
29	Pete Myers	.05	.02
30	Scottie Pippen	.75	.35
31	Scott Williams	.05	.02
32	Terrell Brandon	.25	.11
33	Brad Daugherty	.05	.02
34	Tyrone Hill	.05	.02
35	Chris Mills	.10	.05
36	Larry Nance	.05	.02
37	Bobby Phills	.05	.02
38	Mark Price	.05	.02
39	Gerald Wilkins	.05	.02
40	John(Hot Rod) Williams	.05	.02
41	Terry Davis	.05	.02
42	Lucious Harris	.05	.02
43	Jim Jackson	.10	.05
44	Popeye Jones	.05	.02
45	Tim Legler	.05	.02
46	Jamal Mashburn	.25	.11
47	Sean Rooks	.05	.02
48	M.Abdul-Rauf	.05	.02
49	LaPhonso Ellis	.10	.05
50	D.Mutombo	.25	.11
51	Robert Pack	.05	.02
52	Rodney Rogers	.05	.02
53	Bryant Stith	.05	.02
54	Brian Williams	.05	.02
55	Reggie Williams	.05	.02
56	Greg Anderson	.05	.02
57	Joe Dumars	.25	.11
58	Sean Elliott	.10	.05
59	Allan Houston	.25	.11
60	Lindsey Hunter	.10	.05
61	Mark Macon	.05	.02
62	Terry Mills	.05	.02
63	Victor Alexander	.05	.02
64	Chris Gatling	.05	.02
65	Tim Hardaway	.30	.14
66	Avery Johnson	.05	.02
67	Sarunas Marciulionis	.05	.02
68	Chris Mullin	.25	.11
69	Billy Owens	.05	.02
70	Latrell Sprewell	.10	.05
71	Chris Webber	.60	.25
72	Matt Bullard	.05	.02
73	Sam Cassell	.25	.11
74	Mario Elie	.05	.02
75	Carl Herrera	.05	.02
76	Robert Horry	.10	.05
77	Vernon Maxwell	.05	.02
78	Hakeem Olajuwon	.50	.23
79	Kenny Smith	.05	.02
80	Otis Thorpe	.10	.05
81	Antonio Davis	.05	.02
82	Dale Davis	.05	.02
83	Vern Fleming	.05	.02
84	Scott Haskin	.05	.02
85	Derrick McKey	.05	.02
86	Reggie Miller	.25	.11
87	Byron Scott	.10	.05
88	Rik Smits	.10	.05
89	Haywoode Workman	.05	.02
90	Terry Dehere	.05	.02
91	Harold Ellis	.05	.02
92	Gary Grant	.05	.02
93	Ron Harper	.05	.02
94	Mark Jackson	.10	.05
95	Stanley Roberts	.05	.02
96	Loy Vaught	.10	.05
97	Dominique Wilkins	.25	.11
98	Elden Campbell	.10	.05
99	Doug Christie	.05	.02
100	Vlade Divac	.10	.05
101	Reggie Jordan	.05	.02
102	George Lynch	.05	.02
103	Anthony Peeler	.05	.02
104	Sedale Threatt	.05	.02
105	Nick Van Exel	.25	.11
106	James Worthy	.25	.11
107	Bimbo Coles	.05	.02
108	Matt Geiger	.05	.02
109	Grant Long	.05	.02
110	Harold Miner	.05	.02
111	Glen Rice	.25	.11
112	John Salley	.05	.02
113	Rony Seikaly	.05	.02
114	Brian Shaw	.05	.02
115	Steve Smith	.10	.05
116	Vin Baker	.60	.25
117	Jon Barry	.05	.02
118	Todd Day	.05	.02
119	Lee Mayberry	.05	.02
120	Eric Murdock	.05	.02
121	Ken Norman	.05	.02
122	Mike Brown	.05	.02
123	Stacey King	.05	.02
124	Christian Laettner	.10	.05
125	Chuck Person	.05	.02
126	Isaiah Rider	.10	.05
127	Chris Smith	.05	.02
128	Doug West	.05	.02
129	Micheal Williams	.05	.02
130	Kenny Anderson	.10	.05
131	Benoit Benjamin	.05	.02
132	P.J. Brown	.05	.02
133	Derrick Coleman	.10	.05
134	Kevin Edwards	.05	.02
135	Armon Gilliam	.05	.02
136	Chris Morris	.05	.02
137	Rex Walters	.05	.02
138	David Wesley	.05	.02
139	Greg Anthony	.05	.02
140	Anthony Bonner	.05	.02
141	Hubert Davis	.05	.02
142	Patrick Ewing	.25	.11
143	Derek Harper	.10	.05
144	Anthony Mason	.10	.05
145	Charles Oakley	.10	.05
146	Charles Smith	.05	.02
147	John Starks	.10	.05
148	Nick Anderson	.10	.05
149	Anthony Avent	.05	.02
150	Anthony Bowie	.05	.02
151	A.Hardaway	1.00	.45
152	Shaquille O'Neal	1.00	.45
153	Donald Royal	.05	.02
154	Dennis Scott	.10	.05
155	Scott Skiles	.05	.02
156	Jeff Turner	.05	.02
157	Dana Barros	.05	.02
158	Shawn Bradley	.10	.05
159	Greg Graham	.05	.02
160	Warren Kidd	.05	.02
161	Eric Leckner	.05	.02
162	Jeff Malone	.05	.02
163	Tim Perry	.05	.02
164	C.Weatherspoon	.05	.02
165	Danny Ainge	.10	.05
166	Charles Barkley	.40	.18
167	Cedric Ceballos	.10	.05
168	A.C. Green	.10	.05
169	Kevin Johnson	.10	.05
170	Malcolm Mackey	.05	.02
171	Dan Majerle	.10	.05
172	Oliver Miller	.05	.02
173	Mark West	.05	.02
174	Clyde Drexler	.30	.14
175	Chris Dudley	.05	.02
176	Harvey Grant	.05	.02
177	Tracy Murray	.05	.02
178	Terry Porter	.05	.02
179	Clifford Robinson	.10	.05
180	James Robinson	.05	.02
181	Rod Strickland	.10	.05
182	Buck Williams	.05	.02
183	Duane Causwell	.05	.02
184	Bobby Hurley	.05	.02
185	Olden Polynice	.05	.02
186	Mitch Richmond	.25	.11
187	Lionel Simmons	.05	.02
188	Wayman Tisdale	.05	.02
189	Spud Webb	.10	.05
190	Walt Williams	.05	.02
191	Willie Anderson	.05	.02
192	Lloyd Daniels	.05	.02
193	Vinny Del Negro	.05	.02
194	Dale Ellis	.05	.02
195	J.R. Reid	.05	.02
196	David Robinson	.40	.18
197	Dennis Rodman	1.00	.45
198	Kendall Gill	.10	.05
199	Ervin Johnson	.05	.02
200	Shawn Kemp	.75	.35
201	Chris King	.05	.02
202	Nate McMillan	.05	.02
203	Gary Payton	.40	.18
204	Sam Perkins	.05	.02
205	Ricky Pierce	.05	.02
206	Detlef Schrempf	.10	.05
207	David Benoit	.05	.02
208	Tom Chambers	.05	.02
209	Tyrone Corbin	.05	.02
210	Jeff Hornacek	.10	.05
211	Karl Malone	.40	.18
212	Bryon Russell	.10	.05
213	Felton Spencer	.05	.02
214	John Stockton	.25	.11
215	Luther Wright	.05	.02
216	Michael Adams	.05	.02
217	Mitchell Butler	.05	.02
218	Rex Chapman	.05	.02
219	Calbert Cheaney	.10	.05
220	Pervis Ellison	.05	.02
221	Tom Gugliotta	.25	.11
222	Don MacLean	.05	.02
223	Gheorghe Muresan	.10	.05
224	Kenny Anderson AS	.05	.02
225	B.J. Armstrong AS	.05	.02
226	Mookie Blaylock AS	.05	.02
227	Derrick Coleman AS	.05	.02
228	Patrick Ewing AS	.10	.05
229	Horace Grant AS	.05	.02
230	Alonzo Mourning AS	.25	.11
231	Shaquille O'Neal AS	.50	.23
232	Charles Oakley AS	.05	.02
233	Scottie Pippen AS	.40	.18
234	Mark Price AS	.05	.02
235	John Starks AS	.05	.02
236	Dominique Wilkins AS	.10	.05
237	East Team	.05	.02
238	Charles Barkley AS	.25	.11
239	Clyde Drexler AS	.25	.11
240	Kevin Johnson AS	.05	.02
241	Shawn Kemp AS	.40	.18
242	Karl Malone AS	.25	.11
243	Danny Manning AS	.05	.02
244	Hakeem Olajuwon AS	.25	.11
245	Gary Payton AS	.25	.11
246	Mitch Richmond AS	.10	.05
247	Clifford Robinson AS	.05	.02
248	David Robinson AS	.25	.11
249	Latrell Sprewell AS	.05	.02
250	John Stockton AS	.10	.05

☐ 251	West Team	.05	.02
☐ 252	Tracy Murray LL	.05	.02
	B.J. Armstrong		
	Reggie Miller		
☐ 253	John Stockton LL	.10	.05
	Muggsy Bogues		
	Mookie Blaylock		
☐ 254	D.Mutombo LL	.25	.11
	Hakeem Olajuwon		
	Houston Rockets		
	David Robinson		
☐ 255	M.Abdul-Rauf LL	.05	.02
	Reggie Miller		
	Indiana Pacers		
	Ricky Pierce		
☐ 256	Dennis Rodman LL	.40	.18
	Shaquille O'Neal		
	Kevin Willis		
☐ 257	David Robinson LL	.40	.18
	Shaquille O'Neal		
	Hakeem Olajuwon		
☐ 258	Nate McMillan LL	.25	.11
	Scottie Pippen		
	Mookie Blaylock		
☐ 259	Chris Webber AW	.30	.14
☐ 260	Hakeem Olajuwon AW	.25	.11
☐ 261	Hakeem Olajuwon AW	.25	.11
☐ 262	Dell Curry AW	.05	.02
☐ 263	Scottie Pippen AW	.40	.18
☐ 264	A.Hardaway AW	.50	.23
☐ 265	Don MacLean AW	.05	.02
☐ 266	Hakeem Olajuwon FIN	.25	.11
☐ 267	Derek Harper FIN	.05	.02
☐ 268	Sam Cassell FIN	.05	.02
☐ 269	Hakeem Olajuwon	.25	.11
	Tribute		
☐ 270	Patrick Ewing FIN	.10	.05
	Hakeem Olajuwon		
☐ 271	Carl Herrera FIN	.05	.02
☐ 272	Vernon Maxwell FIN	.05	.02
☐ 273	Hakeem Olajuwon FIN	.25	.11
☐ 274	Lenny Wilkens CO	.10	.05
☐ 275	Chris Ford CO	.05	.02
☐ 276	Allan Bristow CO	.05	.02
☐ 277	Phil Jackson CO	.10	.05
☐ 278	Mike Fratello CO	.10	.05
☐ 279	Dick Motta CO	.05	.02
☐ 280	Dan Issel CO	.10	.05
☐ 281	Don Chaney CO	.05	.02
☐ 282	Don Nelson CO	.10	.05
☐ 283	Rudy Tomjanovich CO	.10	.05
☐ 284	Larry Brown CO	.10	.05
☐ 285	Del Harris CO UER	.05	.02
	(Back refers to Ralph Sampson		
	and Akeem Olajuwon as part o		
	'80-'81 Rockets)		
☐ 286	Kevin Loughery CO	.05	.02
☐ 287	Mike Dunleavy CO	.05	.02
☐ 288	Sidney Lowe CO	.05	.02
☐ 289	Pat Riley CO	.10	.05
☐ 290	Brian Hill CO	.05	.02
☐ 291	John Lucas CO	.10	.05
☐ 292	Paul Westphal CO	.05	.02
☐ 293	Garry St. Jean CO	.05	.02
☐ 294	George Karl CO	.10	.05
☐ 295	Jerry Sloan CO	.10	.05
☐ 296	Magic Johnson	.75	.35
	Commemorative		
☐ 297	Denzel Washington	.10	.05
☐ 298	Checklist	.05	.02
☐ 299	Checklist	.05	.02
☐ 300	Checklist	.05	.02
☐ 301	Sergei Bazarevich	.05	.02
☐ 302	Tyrone Corbin	.05	.02
☐ 303	Grant Long	.05	.02
☐ 304	Ken Norman	.05	.02
☐ 305	Steve Smith	.10	.05
☐ 306	Blue Edwards	.05	.02
☐ 307	Greg Minor	.05	.02
☐ 308	Eric Montross	.05	.02
☐ 309	Dominique Wilkins	.25	.11
☐ 310	Michael Adams	.05	.02
☐ 311	Darrin Hancock	.05	.02
☐ 312	Robert Parish	.10	.05
☐ 313	Ron Harper	.10	.05
☐ 314	Dickey Simpkins	.05	.02
☐ 315	Michael Cage	.05	.02
☐ 316	Tony Dumas	.05	.02
☐ 317	Jason Kidd	2.00	.90
☐ 318	Roy Tarpley	.05	.02
☐ 319	Dale Ellis	.05	.02
☐ 320	Jalen Rose	.25	.11
☐ 321	Bill Curley	.05	.02
☐ 322	Grant Hill	3.00	1.35
☐ 323	Oliver Miller	.05	.02
☐ 324	Mark West	.05	.02
☐ 325	Tom Gugliotta	.25	.11
☐ 326	Ricky Pierce	.05	.02
☐ 327	Carlos Rogers	.05	.02
☐ 328	Clifford Rozier	.05	.02
☐ 329	Rony Seikaly	.05	.02
☐ 330	Tim Breaux	.05	.02
☐ 331	Duane Ferrell	.05	.02
☐ 332	Mark Jackson	.10	.05
☐ 333	Lamond Murray	.10	.05
☐ 334	Charles Outlaw	.05	.02
☐ 335	Eric Piatkowski	.05	.02
☐ 336	Pooh Richardson	.05	.02
☐ 337	Malik Sealy	.05	.02
☐ 338	Cedric Ceballos	.10	.05
☐ 339	Eddie Jones	2.00	.90
☐ 340	Anthony Miller	.05	.02
☐ 341	Kevin Gamble	.05	.02
☐ 342	Brad Lohaus	.05	.02
☐ 343	Billy Owens	.05	.02
☐ 344	Khalid Reeves	.05	.02
☐ 345	Kevin Willis	.05	.02
☐ 346	Eric Mobley	.05	.02
☐ 347	Johnny Newman	.05	.02
☐ 348	Ed Pinckney	.05	.02
☐ 349	Glenn Robinson	1.00	.45
☐ 350	Howard Eisley	.05	.02
☐ 351	Donyell Marshall	.30	.14
☐ 352	Vinny Dare	.05	.02
☐ 353	Charlie Ward	.10	.05
☐ 354	Monty Williams	.05	.02
☐ 355	Horace Grant	.10	.05
☐ 356	Brian Shaw	.05	.02
☐ 357	Brooks Thompson	.05	.02
☐ 358	Derrick Alston	.05	.02
☐ 359	B.J. Tyler	.05	.02
☐ 360	Scott Williams	.05	.02
☐ 361	Sharone Wright	.05	.02
☐ 362	Antonio Lang	.05	.02
☐ 363	Danny Manning	.05	.02
☐ 364	Wesley Person	.30	.14
☐ 365	Wayman Tisdale	.05	.02
☐ 366	Trevor Ruffin	.05	.02
☐ 367	Aaron McKie	.05	.02
☐ 368	Brian Grant	.25	.11
☐ 369	Michael Smith	.10	.05
☐ 370	Sean Elliott	.10	.05
☐ 371	Avery Johnson	.05	.02
☐ 372	Chuck Person	.05	.02
☐ 373	Bill Cartwright	.05	.02
☐ 374	Sarunas Marciulionis	.05	.02
☐ 375	Dontonio Wingfield	.05	.02
☐ 376	Antoine Carr	.05	.02
☐ 377	Jamie Watson	.10	.05
☐ 378	Juwan Howard	1.25	.55
☐ 379	Jim McIlvaine	.05	.02
☐ 380	Scott Skiles	.05	.02
☐ 381	Anthony Tucker	.05	.02
☐ 382	Chris Webber	.60	.25
☐ 383	Bill Fitch CO	.05	.02
☐ 384	Bill Blair CO	.05	.02
☐ 385	Butch Beard CO	.05	.02
☐ 386	P.J. Carlesimo CO	.05	.02
☐ 387	Bob Hill CO	.05	.02
☐ 388	Jim Lynam CO	.05	.02
☐ 389	Checklist 4	.05	.02
☐ 390	Checklist 5	.05	.02
☐ 391	Atlanta Hawks TC	.05	.02
☐ 392	Boston Celtics TC	.05	.02
☐ 393	Charlotte Hornets TC	.05	.02
☐ 394	Chicago Bulls TC	.05	.02
☐ 395	Cleveland Cavaliers TC	.05	.02
☐ 396	Dallas Mavericks TC	.05	.02
☐ 397	Denver Nuggets TC	.05	.02
☐ 398	Detroit Pistons TC	.05	.02
☐ 399	Golden State	.05	.02
	Warriors TC		
☐ 400	Houston Rockets TC	.05	.02
☐ 401	Indiana Pacers TC	.05	.02
☐ 402	L.A. Clippers TC	.05	.02
☐ 403	Los Angeles Lakers TC	.05	.02
☐ 404	Miami Heat TC	.05	.02
☐ 405	Milwaukee Bucks TC	.05	.02
☐ 406	Minnesota	.05	.02
	Timberwolves TC		
☐ 407	New Jersey Nets TC	.05	.02
☐ 408	New York Knicks TC	.05	.02
☐ 409	Orlando Magic TC	.05	.02
☐ 410	Philadelphia 76ers TC	.05	.02
☐ 411	Phoenix Suns TC	.05	.02
☐ 412	Portland Trail	.05	.02
	Blazers TC		
☐ 413	Sacramento Kings TC	.05	.02
☐ 414	San Antonio Spurs TC	.05	.02
☐ 415	Seattle Supersonics TC	.05	.02
☐ 416	Utah Jazz TC	.05	.02
☐ 417	Washington Bullets TC	.05	.02
☐ 418	Toronto Raptors TC	.05	.02
☐ 419	Vancouver Grizzlies TC	.05	.02
☐ 420	NBA Logo Card	.05	.02
☐ 421	Glenn Robinson TOP	.40	.18
	Chris Webber		
☐ 422	Jason Kidd TOP	.40	.18
	Shawn Bradley		
☐ 423	Grant Hill TOP	1.00	.45
	A.Hardaway		
☐ 424	Donyell Marshall TOP	.25	.11
	Jamal Mashburn		
☐ 425	Juwan Howard TOP	.30	.14
	Isaiah Rider		
☐ 426	Sharone Wright TOP	.05	.02
	Calbert Cheaney		
☐ 427	Lamond Murray TOP	.05	.02
	Bobby Hurley		
☐ 428	Brian Grant TOP	.40	.18
	Vin Baker		
☐ 429	Eric Montross TOP	.05	.02
	Rodney Rogers		
☐ 430	Eddie Jones TOP	.40	.18
	Lindsey Hunter		
☐ 431	Craig Ehlo GM	.05	.02
☐ 432	Dino Radja GM	.05	.02
☐ 433	Toni Kukoc GM	.10	.05
☐ 434	Mark Price GM	.05	.02
☐ 435	Latrell Sprewell GM	.05	.02
☐ 436	Sam Cassell GM	.05	.02
☐ 437	Vernon Maxwell GM	.05	.02
☐ 438	H.Workman GM	.05	.02
☐ 439	Harold Ellis GM	.05	.02
☐ 440	Cedric Ceballos GM	.05	.02
☐ 441	Vlade Divac GM	.05	.02
☐ 442	Nick Van Exel GM	.10	.05
☐ 443	John Starks GM	.05	.02
☐ 444	Scott Williams GM	.05	.02
☐ 445	Clifford Robinson GM	.05	.02
☐ 446	Spud Webb GM	.10	.05
☐ 447	Avery Johnson GM	.05	.02
☐ 448	Dennis Rodman GM	.50	.23
☐ 449	S.Marciulionis GM	.05	.02
☐ 450	Nate McMillan GM	.05	.02
☐ NNO	G.Hill Wrapper Exch.	6.00	2.70
☐ NNO	Shaq Sheet Wrap.	400.00	180.00
	Exchange Autograph		
☐ NNO	Shaq Sht Wrap.Exch.	30.00	13.50

1994-95 Hoops Big Numbers

Randomly inserted in first series hobby and retail foil packs at a rate of one in 30, this 12 standard-size set features color player action cutouts on their black horizontal and borderless fronts. The player's name and a number representing his Big Number accomplishment appear

in silver-foil lettering offset to one side. The white horizontal back carries a color player head shot at the right, with a description of his Big Number accomplishment appearing alongside. The cards are numbered on the back with a "BN" prefix.

	MINT	NRMT
COMPLETE SET (12)	50.00	22.00
COMMON CARD (BN1-BN12)	1.25	.55
SEMISTARS	1.50	.70
UNLISTED STARS	2.50	1.10
SER.1 STATED ODDS 1:30		
*RAINBOW CARDS: EQUAL VALUE TO SILVER		
ONE RAINBOW PER SER.1 RETAIL PACK		

		MINT	NRMT
☐ BN1	David Robinson	4.00	1.80
☐ BN2	Jamal Mashburn	1.50	.70
☐ BN3	Hakeem Olajuwon	5.00	2.20
☐ BN4	Patrick Ewing	2.50	1.10
☐ BN5	Shaquille O'Neal	10.00	4.50
☐ BN6	Latrell Sprewell	1.25	.55
☐ BN7	Chris Webber	6.00	2.70
☐ BN8	A.Hardaway	10.00	4.50
☐ BN9	Scottie Pippen	8.00	3.60
☐ BN10	Isaiah Rider	1.25	.55
☐ BN11	Alonzo Mourning	3.00	1.35
☐ BN12	Charles Barkley	4.00	1.80

1994-95 Hoops Draft Redemption

For the third straight year, a redemption card was randomly inserted into first series packs at a rate of one in 360. The card could be sent in for this 11-card standard size set on or before the June 15th, 1995 deadline. The cards feature a full-color

player photo cut out against a computer-generated background with a big number (corresponding to the player's draft selection) zooming out of the side. This set is sequenced in draft order.

	MINT	NRMT
COMPLETE SET (11)	25.00	11.00
COMMON CARD (1-11)	.50	.23
SEMISTARS	1.00	.45
ONE SET PER EXCHANGE CARD BY MAIL		
EXCH.CARD: SER.1 STATED ODDS 1:360		

		MINT	NRMT
☐ 1	Glenn Robinson	4.00	1.80
☐ 2	Jason Kidd	8.00	3.60
☐ 3	Grant Hill	12.00	5.50
☐ 4	Donyell Marshall	1.00	.45
☐ 5	Juwan Howard	5.00	2.20
☐ 6	Sharone Wright	.50	.23
☐ 7	Lamond Murray	.50	.23
☐ 8	Brian Grant	1.00	.45
☐ 9	Eric Montross	.50	.23
☐ 10	Eddie Jones	8.00	3.60
☐ 11	Carlos Rogers	.50	.23
☐ NNO	Exp. Exchange Card	1.00	.45

1994-95 Hoops Magic's All-Rookies

Randomly inserted into all second series packs (12-card hobby and retail packs at a rate of one in twelve, 24-card retail jumbo packs at an approximate rate of slightly greater than one per pack), cards from this 12-card standard-size set feature a selection of top rookies from the 1994-95 season. The fronts have a color action photo with different color backgrounds for each card with designs in them. The word "Magic's" is in the upper right corner and "All-Rookie" is three-dimensionally encompassing the player. The backs have a picture of Magic Johnson holding the card showing the front. On the left side it says "Magic's All-Rookie Team" and there is player commentary at the bottom.

	MINT	NRMT
COMPLETE SET (10)	20.00	9.00
COMMON CARD (AR1-AR10)	.50	.23
SEMISTARS	.60	.25
SER.2 STATED ODDS 1:12		
COMPLETE FOIL SET (10)	50.00	22.00
*FOIL CARDS:1.25X to 2.5X HI COLUMN		
SER.2 STATED ODDS 1:36		
FAR PREFIX ON CARD NUMBER		

		MINT	NRMT
☐ AR1	Glenn Robinson	2.50	1.10
☐ AR2	Jason Kidd	5.00	2.20
☐ AR3	Grant Hill	8.00	3.60
☐ AR4	Donyell Marshall	.60	.25
☐ AR5	Juwan Howard	3.00	1.35
☐ AR6	Sharone Wright	.50	.23
☐ AR7	Brian Grant	.60	.25
☐ AR8	Eddie Jones	5.00	2.20
☐ AR9	Jalen Rose	.60	.25
☐ AR10	Wesley Person	.60	.25

1994-95 Hoops Power Ratings

Inserted one per pack into all second series packs, cards from this 54-card standard-size set feature a selection of the top players in the NBA. Cards feature a photo of the player silhouetted over flame-thrower graphics. Backs present a second photo and colorful bar chart of the players stats in seven key categories. Two players per team were included in this set.

	MINT	NRMT
COMPLETE SET (54)	10.00	4.50
COMMON CARD (PR1-PR54)	.10	.05
SEMISTARS	.25	.11
UNLISTED STARS	.50	.23
ONE PER SERIES 2 PACK		

		MINT	NRMT
☐ PR1	Mookie Blaylock	.25	.11
☐ PR2	Stacey Augmon	.10	.05
☐ PR3	Dino Radja	.10	.05
☐ PR4	Dominique Wilkins	.50	.23
☐ PR5	Larry Johnson	.25	.11
☐ PR6	Alonzo Mourning	.60	.25
☐ PR7	Toni Kukoc	.50	.23
☐ PR8	Scottie Pippen	1.50	.70
☐ PR9	John Williams	.10	.05
☐ PR10	Mark Price	.10	.05
☐ PR11	Jim Jackson	.25	.11
☐ PR12	Jamal Mashburn	.50	.23
☐ PR13	Dale Ellis	.10	.05
☐ PR14	LaPhonso Ellis	.25	.11
☐ PR15	Joe Dumars	.50	.23
☐ PR16	Lindsey Hunter	.25	.11
☐ PR17	Latrell Sprewell	.25	.11

		MINT	NRMT
☐ PR18	Chris Mullin	.50	.23
☐ PR19	Vernon Maxwell	.10	.05
☐ PR20	Hakeem Olajuwon	1.00	.45
☐ PR21	Mark Jackson	.25	.11
☐ PR22	Reggie Miller	.50	.23
☐ PR23	Pooh Richardson	.10	.05
☐ PR24	Loy Vaught	.25	.11
☐ PR25	Vlade Divac	.25	.11
☐ PR26	Nick Van Exel	.50	.23
☐ PR27	Glen Rice	.50	.23
☐ PR28	Billy Owens	.10	.05
☐ PR29	Vin Baker	1.25	.55
☐ PR30	Eric Murdock	.10	.05
☐ PR31	Christian Laettner	.25	.11
☐ PR32	Isaiah Rider	.25	.11
☐ PR33	Kenny Anderson	.25	.11
☐ PR34	Derrick Coleman	.25	.11
☐ PR35	Patrick Ewing	.50	.23
☐ PR36	John Starks	.25	.11
☐ PR37	Nick Anderson	.25	.11
☐ PR38	A.Hardaway	2.00	.90
☐ PR39	Shawn Bradley	.25	.11
☐ PR40	C.Weatherspoon	.10	.05
☐ PR41	Charles Barkley	.75	.35
☐ PR42	Kevin Johnson	.25	.11
☐ PR43	Clyde Drexler	.60	.25
☐ PR44	Clifford Robinson	.25	.11
☐ PR45	Mitch Richmond	.50	.23
☐ PR46	Olden Polynice	.10	.05
☐ PR47	Sean Elliott	.25	.11
☐ PR48	Chuck Person	.10	.05
☐ PR49	Shawn Kemp	1.50	.70
☐ PR50	Gary Payton	.75	.35
☐ PR51	Jeff Hornacek	.25	.11
☐ PR52	Karl Malone	.75	.35
☐ PR53	Rex Chapman	.10	.05
☐ PR54	Don MacLean	.10	.05

1994-95 Hoops Predators

Randomly inserted into all second series packs (one in every twelve 12-card packs and two per 24-card jumbo pack), cards from this 8-card standard-size set feature eight league leaders from the 1993-94 season. Design is very similar to the Power Ratings inserts. The set is sequenced in alphabetical order. There was also a Jumbo card of the David Robinson Predator inserted into Series 2 Sam's boxes. That card is listed below at the end of the set.

	MINT	NRMT
COMPLETE SET (8)	4.00	1.80
COMMON CARD (P1-P8)	.15	.07
SEMISTARS	.25	.11

☐ UNLISTED STARS	.50	.23
SER.2 STATED ODDS 1:12		
☐ P1 M.Abdul-Rauf	.15	.07
☐ P2 D.Mutombo	.25	.11
☐ P3 Shaquille O'Neal	2.00	.90
☐ P4 Tracy Murray	.15	.07
☐ P5 David Robinson	.75	.35
☐ P6 Dennis Rodman	2.00	.90
☐ P7 Nate McMillan	.15	.07
☐ P8 John Stockton	.50	.23
☐ NNO D.Robinson Jumbo	3.00	1.35

1994-95 Hoops Supreme Court

Randomly inserted in first series hobby and retail packs at a rate of one in four, the 50 standard-size parallel cards comprising the '94-95 Hoops Supreme Court set feature a selection of the top stars within the basic issue first series Hoops set. Unlike the regular issue cards, each Supreme Court insert features a special embossed gold-foil logo on the card front. The cards are also numbered on the back with an "SC" prefix, player head shot at the upper left, with the player's name and brief biography appearing alongside to the right. Statistics and career highlights follow below.

	MINT	NRMT
COMPLETE SET (50)	20.00	9.00
COMMON CARD (SC1-SC50)	.25	.11
SEMISTARS	.40	.18
UNLISTED STARS	.75	.35
SER.1 STATED ODDS 1:4		

		MINT	NRMT
☐ SC1	Mookie Blaylock	.40	.18
☐ SC2	Danny Manning	.25	.11
☐ SC3	Dino Radja	.25	.11
☐ SC4	Larry Johnson	.40	.18
☐ SC5	Alonzo Mourning	1.00	.45
☐ SC6	B.J. Armstrong	.25	.11
☐ SC7	Horace Grant	.40	.18
☐ SC8	Toni Kukoc	.75	.35
☐ SC9	Brad Daugherty	.25	.11
☐ SC10	Mark Price	.25	.11
☐ SC11	Jim Jackson	.40	.18
☐ SC12	Jamal Mashburn	.75	.35
☐ SC13	D.Mutombo	.75	.35
☐ SC14	Joe Dumars	.75	.35
☐ SC15	Lindsey Hunter	.40	.18
☐ SC16	Tim Hardaway	1.00	.45
☐ SC17	Chris Mullin	.75	.35
☐ SC18	Sam Cassell	.75	.35
☐ SC19	Hakeem Olajuwon	1.50	.70
☐ SC20	Reggie Miller	.75	.35
☐ SC21	Dominique Wilkins	.75	.35
☐ SC22	Nick Van Exel	.75	.35
☐ SC23	Harold Miner	.25	.11
☐ SC24	Steve Smith	.40	.18
☐ SC25	Vin Baker	2.00	.90
☐ SC26	Christian Laettner	.40	.18
☐ SC27	Isaiah Rider	.40	.18
☐ SC28	Kenny Anderson	.40	.18
☐ SC29	Derrick Coleman	.40	.18
☐ SC30	Patrick Ewing	.75	.35
☐ SC31	John Starks	.40	.18
☐ SC32	A.Hardaway	3.00	1.35
☐ SC33	Shaquille O'Neal	3.00	1.35
☐ SC34	Shawn Bradley	.40	.18
☐ SC35	C.Weatherspoon	.25	.11
☐ SC36	Charles Barkley	1.25	.55
☐ SC37	Kevin Johnson	.40	.18
☐ SC38	Oliver Miller	.25	.11
☐ SC39	Clyde Drexler	1.00	.45
☐ SC40	Clifford Robinson	.40	.18
☐ SC41	Mitch Richmond	.75	.35
☐ SC42	Bobby Hurley	.25	.11
☐ SC43	David Robinson	1.25	.55
☐ SC44	Dennis Rodman	3.00	1.35
☐ SC45	Gary Payton	1.25	.55
☐ SC46	Shawn Kemp	2.50	1.10
☐ SC47	John Stockton	.75	.35
☐ SC48	Karl Malone	1.25	.55
☐ SC49	Calbert Cheaney	.40	.18
☐ SC50	Tom Gugliotta	.60	.25

1995-96 Hoops

The 1995-96 Hoops basketball set was issued in two series of 250 and 150 standard-size cards respectively for a total of 400. Series one cards were issued in 12-card hobby and retail packs (SRP $1.29) and 20-card retail jumbo packs (SRP $1.99). Series two cards were issued in 8-card packs for $.99 each. Fronts have a full-color action photo with the player's name in gold foil surrounded by his team's color. The backs have a color photo with pro and college career statistics. Cards are grouped alphabetically within teams. The following subsets are featured: Coaches (171-197), Sizzlin' Sophs (198-207), Milestones (208-217), Buzzer

Beaters (218-227), Pipeline (228-232), Class Acts (233-242), Triple Threats (243-247), Player/Coach Updates (291-333), Coaches (334-337), Expansion Teams (338-357), Earthshakers (358-372), Rock/House (373-387) and Wicked Dishes (388-397). A special Grant Hill Tribute card, featuring a clear acetate center, was randomly inserted into one in every 360 series one packs. All insert cards feature 3-D technology. A pair of Grant Hill 3-D glasses was available by sending in two first series wrappers and a check or money order for $3.50. In addition, a limited edition Grant Hill Commemorative Co-Rookie of the Year card was available by sending in a check or money order for $9.95 plus two series one wrappers. Both promotions were detailed on first series wrappers and expired December 31, 1995. Rookie Cards of note in this set include Michael Finley, Kevin Garnett, Antonio McDyess, Joe Smith, Jerry Stackhouse and D.Stoudamire.

	MINT	NRMT
COMPLETE SET (400)	35.00	16.00
COMPLETE SERIES 1 (250)	20.00	9.00
COMPLETE SERIES 2 (150)	15.00	6.75
COMMON CARD (1-400)		.05
SEMISTARS	.15	.07
UNLISTED STARS	.25	.11
HILL TRIB: SER.1 STATED ODDS 1:360		

□ 1 Stacey Augmon		.05
□ 2 Mookie Blaylock	.15	.07
□ 3 Craig Ehlo	.10	.05
□ 4 Andrew Lang	.10	.05
□ 5 Grant Long	.10	.05
□ 6 Ken Norman	.10	.05
□ 7 Steve Smith	.15	.07
□ 8 Dee Brown	.10	.05
□ 9 Sherman Douglas	.10	.05
□ 10 Pervis Ellison	.10	.05
□ 11 Eric Montross	.10	.05
□ 12 Dino Radja	.10	.05
□ 13 Dominique Wilkins	.25	.11
□ 14 Muggsy Bogues	.15	.07
□ 15 Scott Burrell	.10	.05
□ 16 Dell Curry	.10	.05
□ 17 Hersey Hawkins	.15	.07
□ 18 Larry Johnson	.15	.07
□ 19 Alonzo Mourning	.25	.11
□ 20 B.J. Armstrong	.10	.05
□ 21 Michael Jordan	3.00	1.35
□ 22 Toni Kukoc	.15	.07
□ 23 Will Perdue	.10	.05
□ 24 Scottie Pippen	.75	.35
□ 25 Dickey Simpkins	.10	.05
□ 26 Terrell Brandon	.25	.11
□ 27 Tyrone Hill	.10	.05
□ 28 Chris Mills	.10	.05
□ 29 Bobby Phills	.10	.05
□ 30 Mark Price	.10	.05
□ 31 John Williams	.10	.05
□ 32 Tony Dumas	.10	.05
□ 33 Jim Jackson	.15	.07
□ 34 Popeye Jones	.10	.05

□ 35 Jason Kidd	.60	.25
□ 36 Jamal Mashburn	.15	.07
□ 37 Roy Tarpley	.10	.05
□ 38 M.Abdul-Rauf	.10	.05
□ 39 LaPhonso Ellis	.15	.07
□ 40 D.Mutombo	.15	.07
□ 41 Robert Pack	.10	.05
□ 42 Rodney Rogers	.10	.05
□ 43 Jalen Rose	.15	.07
□ 44 Bryant Stith	.10	.05
□ 45 Joe Dumars	.25	.11
□ 46 Grant Hill	1.50	.70
□ 47 Allan Houston	.15	.07
□ 48 Lindsey Hunter	.10	.05
□ 49 Oliver Miller	.10	.05
□ 50 Terry Mills	.10	.05
□ 51 Chris Gatling	.10	.05
□ 52 Tim Hardaway	.30	.14
□ 53 Donyell Marshall	.15	.07
□ 54 Chris Mullin	.25	.11
□ 55 Carlos Rogers	.10	.05
□ 56 Clifford Rozier	.10	.05
□ 57 Rony Seikaly	.10	.05
□ 58 Latrell Sprewell	.15	.07
□ 59 Sam Cassell	.10	.05
□ 60 Clyde Drexler	.30	.14
□ 61 Robert Horry	.10	.05
□ 62 Vernon Maxwell	.10	.05
□ 63 Hakeem Olajuwon	.50	.23
□ 64 Kenny Smith	.10	.05
□ 65 Dale Davis	.10	.05
□ 66 Mark Jackson	.15	.07
□ 67 Derrick McKey	.10	.05
□ 68 Reggie Miller	.25	.11
□ 69 Byron Scott	.10	.05
□ 70 Rik Smits	.15	.07
□ 71 Terry Dehere	.10	.05
□ 72 Lamond Murray	.10	.05
□ 73 Eric Piatkowski	.10	.05
□ 74 Pooh Richardson	.10	.05
□ 75 Malik Sealy	.10	.05
□ 76 Loy Vaught	.10	.05
□ 77 Elden Campbell	.15	.07
□ 78 Cedric Ceballos	.10	.05
□ 79 Vlade Divac	.15	.07
□ 80 Eddie Jones	.60	.25
□ 81 Sedale Threatt	.10	.05
□ 82 Nick Van Exel	.25	.11
□ 83 Bimbo Coles	.10	.05
□ 84 Harold Miner	.10	.05
□ 85 Billy Owens	.10	.05
□ 86 Khalid Reeves	.10	.05
□ 87 Glen Rice	.25	.11
□ 88 Kevin Willis	.10	.05
□ 89 Vin Baker	.50	.23
□ 90 Marty Conlon	.10	.05
□ 91 Todd Day	.10	.05
□ 92 Eric Mobley	.10	.05
□ 93 Eric Murdock	.10	.05
□ 94 Glenn Robinson	.30	.14
□ 95 Winston Garland	.10	.05
□ 96 Tom Gugliotta	.25	.11
□ 97 Christian Laettner	.15	.07
□ 98 Isaiah Rider	.15	.07
□ 99 Sean Rooks	.10	.05
□ 100 Doug West	.10	.05
□ 101 Kenny Anderson	.15	.07
□ 102 Benoit Benjamin	.10	.05
□ 103 Derrick Coleman	.15	.07
□ 104 Kevin Edwards	.10	.05
□ 105 Armon Gilliam	.10	.05
□ 106 Chris Morris	.10	.05
□ 107 Patrick Ewing	.25	.11
□ 108 Derek Harper	.15	.07
□ 109 Anthony Mason	.15	.07
□ 110 Charles Oakley	.10	.05
□ 111 Charles Smith	.10	.05
□ 112 John Starks	.15	.07
□ 113 Monty Williams	.10	.05
□ 114 Nick Anderson	.10	.05
□ 115 Horace Grant	.15	.07
□ 116 A.Hardaway	1.00	.45
□ 117 Shaquille O'Neal	1.00	.45
□ 118 Dennis Scott	.10	.05
□ 119 Brian Shaw	.10	.05
□ 120 Dana Barros	.10	.05

□ 121 Shawn Bradley	.15	.07
□ 122 Willie Burton	.10	.05
□ 123 Jeff Malone	.10	.05
□ 124 C.Weatherspoon	.10	.05
□ 125 Sharone Wright	.10	.05
□ 126 Charles Barkley	.40	.18
□ 127 A.C. Green	.15	.07
□ 128 Kevin Johnson	.15	.07
□ 129 Dan Majerle	.15	.07
□ 130 Danny Manning	.15	.07
□ 131 Elliot Perry	.10	.05
□ 132 Wesley Person	.15	.07
□ 133 Chris Dudley	.10	.05
□ 134 Clifford Robinson	.10	.05
□ 135 James Robinson	.10	.05
□ 136 Rod Strickland	.15	.07
□ 137 Otis Thorpe	.15	.07
□ 138 Buck Williams	.10	.05
□ 139 Brian Grant	.15	.07
□ 140 Olden Polynice	.10	.05
□ 141 Mitch Richmond	.25	.11
□ 142 Michael Smith	.10	.05
□ 143 Spud Webb	.15	.07
□ 144 Walt Williams	.10	.05
□ 145 Vinny Del Negro	.10	.05
□ 146 Sean Elliott	.10	.05
□ 147 Avery Johnson	.10	.05
□ 148 Chuck Person	.10	.05
□ 149 David Robinson	.40	.18
□ 150 Dennis Rodman	1.00	.45
□ 151 Kendall Gill	.15	.07
□ 152 Ervin Johnson	.10	.05
□ 153 Shawn Kemp	.75	.35
□ 154 Nate McMillan	.10	.05
□ 155 Gary Payton	.40	.18
□ 156 Detlef Schrempf	.15	.07
□ 157 Dontonio Wingfield	.10	.05
□ 158 David Benoit	.10	.05
□ 159 Jeff Hornacek	.15	.07
□ 160 Karl Malone	.40	.18
□ 161 Felton Spencer	.10	.05
□ 162 John Stockton	.25	.11
□ 163 Jamie Watson	.10	.05
□ 164 Rex Chapman	.10	.05
□ 165 Calbert Cheaney	.10	.05
□ 166 Juwan Howard	.40	.18
□ 167 Don MacLean	.10	.05
□ 168 Gheorghe Muresan	.10	.05
□ 169 Scott Skiles	.10	.05
□ 170 Chris Webber	.60	.25
□ 171 Lenny Wilkens CO	.15	.07
□ 172 Allan Bristow CO	.10	.05
□ 173 Phil Jackson CO	.15	.07
□ 174 Mike Fratello CO	.15	.07
□ 175 Dick Motta CO	.10	.05
□ 176 Bernie Bickerstaff CO	.10	.05
□ 177 Doug Collins CO	.15	.07
□ 178 Rick Adelman CO	.10	.05
□ 179 Rudy Tomjanovich CO	.15	.07
□ 180 Larry Brown CO	.15	.07
□ 181 Bill Fitch CO	.10	.05
□ 182 Del Harris CO	.10	.05
□ 183 Mike Dunleavy CO	.10	.05
□ 184 Bill Blair CO	.10	.05
□ 185 Butch Beard CO	.10	.05
□ 186 Pat Riley CO	.15	.07
□ 187 Brian Hill CO	.10	.05
□ 188 John Lucas CO	.15	.07
□ 189 Paul Westphal CO	.10	.05
□ 190 P.J. Carlesimo CO	.10	.05
□ 191 Garry St. Jean CO	.10	.05
□ 192 Bob Hill CO	.10	.05
□ 193 George Karl CO	.10	.05
□ 194 Brendan Malone CO	.10	.05
□ 195 Jerry Sloan CO	.15	.07
□ 196 Kevin Pritchard	.10	.05
□ 197 Jim Lynam CO	.10	.05
□ 198 Brian Grant SS	.10	.05
□ 199 Grant Hill SS	.75	.35
□ 200 Juwan Howard SS	.25	.11
□ 201 Eddie Jones SS	.30	.14
□ 202 Jason Kidd SS	.30	.14
□ 203 Donyell Marshall SS	.10	.05
□ 204 Eric Montross SS	.10	.05
□ 205 Glenn Robinson SS	.25	.11
□ 206 Jalen Rose SS	.10	.05

□ 207 Sharone Wright SS	.10	.05
□ 208 Dana Barros MS	.10	.05
□ 209 Joe Dumars MS	.15	.07
□ 210 A.C. Green MS	.10	.05
□ 211 Grant Hill MS	.75	.35
□ 212 Karl Malone MS	.25	.11
□ 213 Reggie Miller MS	.15	.07
□ 214 Glen Rice MS	.15	.07
□ 215 John Stockton MS	.15	.07
□ 216 Lenny Wilkens MS	.15	.07
□ 217 Dominique Wilkins MS	.15	.07
□ 218 Kenny Anderson BB	.10	.05
□ 219 Mookie Blaylock BB	.10	.05
□ 220 Larry Johnson BB	.10	.05
□ 221 Shawn Kemp BB	.40	.18
□ 222 Toni Kukoc BB	.10	.05
□ 223 Jamal Mashburn BB	.10	.05
□ 224 Glen Rice BB	.15	.07
□ 225 Mitch Richmond BB	.15	.07
□ 226 Latrell Sprewell BB	.10	.05
□ 227 Rod Strickland BB	.10	.05
□ 228 Michael Adams PL Darrick Martin	.10	.05
□ 229 Craig Ehlo PL Jerome Harmon	.10	.05
□ 230 Mario Elie PL George McCloud	.10	.05
□ 231 Anthony Mason PL Chucky Brown	.10	.05
□ 232 John Starks PL Tim Legler	.10	.05
□ 233 Muggsy Bogues CA	.10	.05
□ 234 Joe Dumars CA	.15	.07
□ 235 LaPhonso Ellis CA	.10	.05
□ 236 Patrick Ewing CA	.15	.07
□ 237 Grant Hill CA	.75	.35
□ 238 Kevin Johnson CA	.10	.05
□ 239 Dan Majerle CA	.10	.05
□ 240 Karl Malone CA	.25	.11
□ 241 Hakeem Olajuwon CA	.25	.11
□ 242 David Robinson CA	.25	.11
□ 243 Dana Barros TT	.10	.05
□ 244 Scott Burrell TT	.10	.05
□ 245 Reggie Miller TT	.15	.07
□ 246 Glen Rice TT	.15	.07
□ 247 John Stockton TT	.15	.07
□ 248 Checklist #1	.10	.05
□ 249 Checklist #2	.10	.05
□ 250 Checklist #3	.10	.05
□ 251 Alan Henderson	.25	.11
□ 252 Junior Burrough	.10	.05
□ 253 Eric Williams	.15	.07
□ 254 George Zidek	.10	.05
□ 255 Jason Caffey	.25	.11
□ 256 Donny Marshall	.10	.05
□ 257 Bob Sura	.15	.07
□ 258 Loren Meyer	.10	.05
□ 259 Cherokee Parks	.10	.05
□ 260 Antonio McDyess	1.25	.55
□ 261 Theo Ratliff	.25	.11
□ 262 Lou Roe	.10	.05
□ 263 Andrew DeClercq	.10	.05
□ 264 Joe Smith	1.00	.45
□ 265 Travis Best	.15	.07
□ 266 Brent Barry	.25	.11
□ 267 Frankie King	.10	.05
□ 268 Sasha Danilovic	.15	.05
□ 269 Kurt Thomas	.15	.07
□ 270 Shawn Respert	.10	.05
□ 271 Jerome Allen	.10	.05
□ 272 Kevin Garnett	3.00	1.35
□ 273 Ed O'Bannon	.10	.05
□ 274 David Vaughn	.10	.05
□ 275 Jerry Stackhouse	1.00	.45
□ 276 Mario Bennett	.10	.05
□ 277 Michael Finley	1.00	.45
□ 278 Randolph Childress	.10	.05
□ 279 Arvydas Sabonis	.50	.23
□ 280 Gary Trent	.10	.05
□ 281 Tyus Edney	.10	.05
□ 282 Corliss Williamson	.30	.14
□ 283 Cory Alexander	.10	.05
□ 284 Sherrell Ford	.10	.05
□ 285 Jimmy King	.10	.05
□ 286 D.Stoudamire	2.00	.90
□ 287 Greg Ostertag	.10	.05
□ 288 Lawrence Moten	.10	.05
□ 289 Bryant Reeves	.60	.25
□ 290 Rasheed Wallace	.60	.25
□ 291 Spud Webb	.15	.07
□ 292 Dana Barros	.10	.05
□ 293 Rick Fox	.10	.05
□ 294 Kendall Gill	.15	.07
□ 295 Khalid Reeves	.10	.05
□ 296 Glen Rice	.25	.11
□ 297 Luc Longley	.15	.05
□ 298 Dennis Rodman	1.50	.70
□ 299 Dan Majerle	.10	.05
□ 300 Lorenzo Williams	.10	.05
□ 301 Dale Ellis	.10	.05
□ 302 Reggie Williams	.10	.05
□ 303 Otis Thorpe	.15	.07
□ 304 B.J. Armstrong	.10	.05
□ 305 Pete Chilcutt	.10	.05
□ 306 Mario Elie	.10	.05
□ 307 Antonio Davis	.10	.05
□ 308 Ricky Pierce	.10	.05
□ 309 Rodney Rogers	.10	.05
□ 310 Brian Williams	.10	.05
□ 311 Corie Blount	.10	.05
□ 312 George Lynch	.10	.05
□ 313 Alonzo Mourning	.25	.11
□ 314 Lee Mayberry	.10	.05
□ 315 Terry Porter	.10	.05
□ 316 P.J. Brown	.10	.05
□ 317 Hubert Davis	.10	.05
□ 318 Charlie Ward	.10	.05
□ 319 Jon Koncak	.10	.05
□ 320 Derrick Coleman	.15	.07
□ 321 Richard Dumas	.10	.05
□ 322 Vernon Maxwell	.10	.05
□ 323 Wayman Tisdale	.10	.05
□ 324 Dontonio Wingfield	.10	.05
□ 325 Tyrone Corbin	.10	.05
□ 326 Bobby Hurley	.10	.05
□ 327 Will Perdue	.10	.05
□ 328 J.R. Reid	.10	.05
□ 329 Hersey Hawkins	.15	.07
□ 330 Sam Perkins	.15	.07
□ 331 Adam Keefe	.10	.05
□ 332 Chris Morris	.10	.05
□ 333 Robert Pack	.10	.05
□ 334 M.L. Carr CO	.10	.05
□ 335 Pat Riley CO	.15	.07
□ 336 Don Nelson CO	.10	.05
□ 337 Brian Winters CO	.10	.05
□ 338 Willie Anderson ET	.10	.05
□ 339 Acie Earl ET	.10	.05
□ 340 Jimmy King ET	.10	.05
□ 341 Oliver Miller ET	.10	.05
□ 342 Tracy Murray ET	.10	.05
□ 343 Ed Pinckney ET	.10	.05
□ 344 Alvin Robertson ET	.10	.05
□ 345 Carlos Rogers ET	.10	.05
□ 346 John Saliey ET	.10	.05
□ 347 D.Stoudamire ET	.75	.35
□ 348 Zan Tabak ET	.10	.05
□ 349 Greg Anthony ET	.10	.05
□ 350 Blue Edwards ET	.10	.05
□ 351 Kenny Gattison ET	.10	.05
□ 352 Antonio Harvey ET	.10	.05
□ 353 Chris King ET	.10	.05
□ 354 Darrick Martin ET	.10	.05
□ 355 Lawrence Moten ET	.10	.05
□ 356 Bryant Reeves ET	.25	.11
□ 357 Byron Scott ET	.10	.05
□ 358 Michael Jordan ES	1.50	.70
□ 359 D.Mutombo ES	.10	.05
□ 360 Grant Hill ES	.75	.35
□ 361 Robert Horry ES	.10	.05
□ 362 Alonzo Mourning ES	.15	.07
□ 363 Vin Baker ES	.25	.11
□ 364 Isaiah Rider ES	.10	.05
□ 365 Charles Oakley ES	.10	.05
□ 366 Shaquille O'Neal ES	.50	.23
□ 367 Jerry Stackhouse ES	.40	.18
□ 368 C.Weatherspoon ES	.10	.05
□ 369 Charles Barkley ES	.25	.11
□ 370 Sean Elliott ES	.10	.05
□ 371 Shawn Kemp ES	.40	.18
□ 372 Chris Webber ES	.30	.14
□ 373 Spud Webb RH	.10	.05
□ 374 Muggsy Bogues RH	.10	.05
□ 375 Toni Kukoc RH	.10	.05
□ 376 Dennis Rodman RH	.75	.35
□ 377 Jamal Mashburn RH	.10	.05
□ 378 Jalen Rose RH	.10	.05
□ 379 Clyde Drexler RH	.25	.11
□ 380 Mark Jackson RH	.10	.05
□ 381 Clyde Ceballos RH	.10	.05
□ 382 Nick Van Exel RH	.15	.07
□ 383 John Starks RH	.10	.05
□ 384 Vernon Maxwell RH	.10	.05
□ 385 Shawn Kemp RH	.40	.18
□ 386 Gary Payton RH	.25	.11
□ 387 Karl Malone RH	.25	.11
□ 388 Mookie Blaylock WD	.10	.05
□ 389 Muggsy Bogues WD	.10	.05
□ 390 Jason Kidd WD	.30	.14
□ 391 Tim Hardaway WD	.25	.11
□ 392 Nick Van Exel WD	.15	.07
□ 393 Kenny Anderson WD	.10	.05
□ 394 A.Hardaway WD	.50	.23
□ 395 Rod Strickland WD	.10	.05
□ 396 Avery Johnson WD	.10	.05
□ 397 John Stockton WD	.15	.07
□ 398 Grant Hill SPEC	.75	.35
□ 399 Checklist (251-367)	.10	.05
□ 400 CL (368-400/Ins.)	.10	.05
□ NNO Grant Hill Co-ROY Exchange	20.00	9.00
□ NNO Grant Hill Sweepstakes	1.00	.45
□ NNO Grant Hill Tribute	40.00	18.00

1995-96 Hoops Block Party

Randomly inserted into all first series packs at an approximate rate of one in two packs, these 25 standard-size cards highlight the top shot-blockers in the NBA. The fronts have a full-color action photo with a multi-colored, computer-generated background and the words "Block Party" at the top in gold-foil. The backs have a color photo on the left side with a similar background to the front with player information and statistics on the right.

	MINT	NRMT
COMPLETE SET (25)	5.00	2.20
COMMON CARD (1-25)	.15	.07
SEMISTARS	.25	.11
UNLISTED STARS	.40	.18
SER.1 STATED ODDS 1:2 HOBBY/RETAIL		

□ 1 Oliver Miller	.15	.07
□ 2 Dennis Rodman	1.50	.70

☐ 3 Scottie Pippen	1.25	.55
☐ 4 D.Mutombo	.25	.11
☐ 5 Vlade Divac	.25	.11
☐ 6 Brian Grant	.25	.11
☐ 7 Alonzo Mourning	.40	.18
☐ 8 Hakeem Olajuwon	.75	.35
☐ 9 Patrick Ewing	.40	.18
☐ 10 Shawn Kemp	1.25	.55
☐ 11 Vin Baker	.75	.35
☐ 12 Horace Grant	.25	.11
☐ 13 Dale Davis	.15	.07
☐ 14 Juwan Howard	.60	.25
☐ 15 Eddie Jones	1.00	.45
☐ 16 Eric Montross	.15	.07
☐ 17 Tyrone Hill	.15	.07
☐ 18 Tom Gugliotta	.40	.18
☐ 19 Shawn Bradley	.25	.11
☐ 20 Dan Majerle	.15	.07
☐ 21 Loy Vaught	.15	.07
☐ 22 Donyell Marshall	.25	.11
☐ 23 Chris Webber	1.00	.45
☐ 24 Derrick Coleman	.25	.11
☐ 25 Walt Williams	.15	.07

1995-96 Hoops Grant Hill Dunks/Slams

Cards D1-D5 were randomly inserted exclusively into one in every 36 first series 12-card hobby packs, while cards S1-S5 were randomly inserted exclusively into one in every 36 first series retail 12-card packs. All cards are foil-coated, featuring an assortment of Grant Hill dunking and slamming photos. The fronts each carry an oversized letter, so that cards D1-D5 spell out "DUNK!!!," and cards S1-S5 spell out "SLAM!". All cards are designed to be viewed through special Grant Hill 3-D glasses which were available through an on-wrapper offer.

	MINT	NRMT
COMPLETE SET (10)	40.00	18.00
COMPLETE DUNKS SET (5)	20.00	9.00
COMPLETE SLAMS SET (5)	20.00	9.00
COMMON DUNK/SLAM (D1-D5)	5.00	2.20
DUNK: SER.1 STATED ODDS 1:36 RETAIL		
SLAM: SER.1 STATED ODDS 1:36 HOBBY		

☐ S1 Grant Hill	5.00	2.20
	S-Card	
☐ S2 Grant Hill	5.00	2.20

	L-Card	
☐ S3 Grant Hill	5.00	2.20
	A-Card	
☐ S4 Grant Hill	5.00	2.20
	M-Card	
☐ S5 Grant Hill	5.00	2.20
	I-Card	
☐ D1 Grant Hill	5.00	2.20
	D-Card	
☐ D2 Grant Hill	5.00	2.20
	U-Card	
☐ D3 Grant Hill	5.00	2.20
	N-Card	
☐ D4 Grant Hill	5.00	2.20
	K-Card	
☐ D5 Grant Hill	5.00	2.20
	!!!-Card	

1995-96 Hoops Grant's All-Rookies

Randomly inserted in all second series packs at a rate of one in 64, this 10-card standard-size set continues the tradition of the Magic's All-Rookies sets featured in earlier Hoops products. New spokesperson Grant Hill replaces Magic Johnson, picking 10 players who may follow in his own footsteps. Hill is pictured alongside the featured rookie on the horizontal fronts. The left side of the card contains a silver hologram strip with "Top 10" cut out to give the card a 3-D look when viewed with the Grant Hill 3-D glasses. Backs carry another full color cutout shot of the player set against the borderless color background. The "Top 10" logo is once again placed on the back. The player's name is printed across the top in gold and a player profile is printed in white. The set is sequenced in alphabetical order by team.

	MINT	NRMT
COMPLETE SET (10)	60.00	27.00
COMMON CARD (AR1-AR10)	1.50	.70
SEMISTARS	2.50	1.10
SER.2 STATED ODDS 1:64 HOBBY/RETAIL		

☐ AR1 Cherokee Parks	1.50	.70
☐ AR2 Antonio McDyess	10.00	4.50
☐ AR3 Theo Ratliff	2.50	1.10
☐ AR4 Joe Smith	8.00	3.60

☐ AR5 Shawn Respert	1.50	.70
☐ AR6 Kevin Garnett	25.00	11.00
☐ AR7 Ed O'Bannon	1.50	.70
☐ AR8 Jerry Stackhouse	8.00	3.60
☐ AR9 D.Stoudamire	15.00	6.75
☐ AR10 Rasheed Wallace	5.00	2.20

1995-96 Hoops HoopStars

Randomly inserted in all second series packs at a rate of one in 16, this 12-card standard-size set presents top players on multi-colored cards featuring color foils for the HoopStars logo and player name. The set is sequenced in alphabetical order by team.

	MINT	NRMT
COMPLETE SET (12)		6.75
COMMON CARD (HS1-HS12)	.60	.25
SEMISTARS	.75	.35
UNLISTED STARS	1.25	.55
SER.2 STATED ODDS 1:16 HOBBY/RETAIL		

☐ HS1 Scottie Pippen	4.00	1.80
☐ HS2 Jim Jackson	.60	.25
☐ HS3 Antonio McDyess	3.00	1.35
☐ HS4 Clyde Drexler	1.50	.70
☐ HS5 Alonzo Mourning	1.25	.55
☐ HS6 Glenn Robinson	1.50	.70
☐ HS7 Patrick Ewing	1.25	.55
☐ HS8 A.Hardaway	5.00	2.20
☐ HS9 Shawn Kemp	4.00	1.80
☐ HS10 Karl Malone	2.00	.90
☐ HS11 Juwan Howard	2.00	.90
☐ HS12 Rasheed Wallace	1.50	.70

1995-96 Hoops Hot List

Randomly inserted in second series hobby packs only at a rate of one in 32, this 10-card standard-size set features full-bleed fronts with a full-color player cutout set against a blue foil background. Player's name is printed vertically in copper foil on a purple foil strip. HOT is printed diagonally across the front. Backs feature a full-color action shot with the player's stats printed below the photo.

The set is sequenced in alphabetically order by team.

	MINT	NRMT
COMPLETE SET (10)	50.00	22.00
COMMON CARD (1-10)	1.25	.55
SER.2 STATED ODDS 1:32 HOBBY		

		MINT	NRMT
☐ 1	Michael Jordan	25.00	11.00
☐ 2	Jason Kidd	5.00	2.20
☐ 3	Jamal Mashburn	1.25	.55
☐ 4	Grant Hill	12.00	5.50
☐ 5	Joe Smith	4.00	1.80
☐ 6	Hakeem Olajuwon	4.00	1.80
☐ 7	Glenn Robinson	2.50	1.10
☐ 8	Shaquille O'Neal	8.00	3.60
☐ 9	Jerry Stackhouse	4.00	1.80
☐ 10	David Robinson	3.00	1.35

1995-96 Hoops Number Crunchers

Randomly inserted into all first series packs at an approximate rate of one in two packs, these 25 standard-size cards highlight players that attained notable statistical achievements during the 1994-95 season. The fronts have a color-action photo with the player's number in a multi-color background and the word "Crunchers" spelled out on a tic-tac-toe board in the lower left corner in gold-foil. The backs have a color-action photo with a huge multi-colored ball in the background along with player information and statistics.

	MINT	NRMT
COMPLETE SET (25)	10.00	4.50
COMMON CARD (1-25)	.15	.07
SEMISTARS	.25	.11
UNLISTED STARS	.40	.18
SER.1 STATED ODDS 1:2 HOBBY/RETAIL		

		MINT	NRMT
☐ 1	Michael Jordan	5.00	2.20
☐ 2	Shaquille O'Neal	1.50	.70
☐ 3	Grant Hill	2.50	1.10
☐ 4	Detlef Schrempf	.25	.11
☐ 5	Kenny Anderson	.25	.11
☐ 6	A.Hardaway	1.50	.70
☐ 7	Latrell Sprewell	.25	.11
☐ 8	Jamal Mashburn	.25	.11
☐ 9	Nick Van Exel	.40	.18
☐ 10	Charles Barkley	.60	.25
☐ 11	Mitch Richmond	.40	.18
☐ 12	David Robinson	.60	.25
☐ 13	Gary Payton	.60	.25
☐ 14	Rod Strickland	.25	.11
☐ 15	Glenn Robinson	.50	.23
☐ 16	Reggie Miller	.40	.18
☐ 17	Karl Malone	.60	.25
☐ 18	Jim Jackson	.25	.11
☐ 19	Clyde Drexler	.50	.23
☐ 20	Glen Rice	.40	.18
☐ 21	Isaiah Rider	.25	.11
☐ 22	Cedric Ceballos	.15	.07
☐ 23	John Stockton	.40	.18
☐ 24	Jason Kidd	1.00	.45
☐ 25	Mookie Blaylock	.25	.11

1995-96 Hoops Power Palette

Randomly inserted in second series retail packs only at a rate of one in 32, this 10-card set is a parallel version of the Hoops SkyView insert. Unlike the acetate-centered SkyView cards, the more common Power Palette feature metallic foil backgrounds.

	MINT	NRMT
COMPLETE SET (10)	60.00	27.00
COMMON CARD (1-10)	2.50	1.10
SER.2 STATED ODDS 1:32 RETAIL		

		MINT	NRMT
☐ 1	Michael Jordan	25.00	11.00
☐ 2	Jason Kidd	5.00	2.20
☐ 3	Grant Hill	12.00	5.50
☐ 4	Joe Smith	4.00	1.80
☐ 5	Hakeem Olajuwon	4.00	1.80
☐ 6	Glenn Robinson	2.50	1.10
☐ 7	A.Hardaway	8.00	3.60
☐ 8	Shaquille O'Neal	8.00	3.60
☐ 9	Jerry Stackhouse	4.00	1.80
☐ 10	Charles Barkley	3.00	1.35

1995-96 Hoops SkyView

Randomly inserted in all second series packs at a rate of one in 480, cards from this 10-card standard-size set are extra-thick and replace two basic issue cards in the pack. The front of the card presents a die-cut action photo over a multi-color plastic acetate window. The set is sequenced in alphabetical order by team.

	MINT	NRMT
COMPLETE SET (10)	100.00	45.00
COMMON CARD (SV1-SV10)	5.00	2.20
SER.2 STATED ODDS 1:480 HOBBY/RETAIL		

		MINT	NRMT
☐ SV1	Michael Jordan	60.00	27.00
☐ SV2	Jason Kidd	10.00	4.50
☐ SV3	Grant Hill	25.00	11.00
☐ SV4	Joe Smith	8.00	3.60
☐ SV5	Hakeem Olajuwon	8.00	3.60
☐ SV6	Glenn Robinson	5.00	2.20
☐ SV7	A.Hardaway	15.00	6.75
☐ SV8	Shaquille O'Neal	15.00	6.75
☐ SV9	Jerry Stackhouse	8.00	3.60
☐ SV10	Charles Barkley	6.00	2.70

1995-96 Hoops Slamland

Inserted into all second series packs at a rate of one per pack, cards from this 50-card standard-size set showcase top stars printed over one of five different animated "Slamland" backgrounds. The card fronts feature the player's name, area of expertise and a distinctive foil-stamped Slamland designation. The set is sequenced in alphabetical order by team.

	MINT	NRMT
COMPLETE SET (50)	8.00	3.60
COMMON CARD (SL1-SL50)	.05	.02
SEMISTARS	.15	.07
UNLISTED STARS	.25	.11
ONE PER SER.2 PACK		

		MINT	NRMT
☐ SL1	Stacey Augmon	.05	.02
☐ SL2	Steve Smith	.15	.07
☐ SL3	Eric Montross	.05	.02
☐ SL4	Dino Radja	.05	.02
☐ SL5	Dell Curry	.05	.02
☐ SL6	Larry Johnson	.15	.07
☐ SL7	Scottie Pippen	.75	.35
☐ SL8	Dennis Rodman	1.50	.70
☐ SL9	Tyrone Hill	.05	.02
☐ SL10	Jim Jackson	.15	.07
☐ SL11	Jamal Mashburn	.15	.07
☐ SL12	D.Mutombo	.15	.07
☐ SL13	Joe Dumars	.25	.11
☐ SL14	Grant Hill	1.50	.70
☐ SL15	Allan Houston	.15	.07
☐ SL16	Donyell Marshall	.15	.07
☐ SL17	Latrell Sprewell	.15	.07
☐ SL18	Sam Cassell	.15	.07
☐ SL19	Hakeem Olajuwon	.50	.23
☐ SL20	Reggie Miller	.25	.11
☐ SL21	Loy Vaught	.05	.02
☐ SL22	Vlade Divac	.15	.07
☐ SL23	Eddie Jones	.60	.25
☐ SL24	Alonzo Mourning	.25	.11
☐ SL25	Kevin Willis	.05	.02
☐ SL26	Vin Baker	.50	.23
☐ SL27	Glenn Robinson	.30	.14
☐ SL28	Tom Gugliotta	.25	.11
☐ SL29	Kenny Anderson	.15	.07
☐ SL30	Derrick Coleman	.15	.07
☐ SL31	Patrick Ewing	.25	.11
☐ SL32	John Starks	.15	.07
☐ SL33	Dennis Scott	.05	.02
☐ SL34	Jerry Stackhouse	.75	.35
☐ SL35	Charles Barkley	.40	.18
☐ SL36	Kevin Johnson	.15	.07
☐ SL37	Danny Manning	.15	.07
☐ SL38	Clifford Robinson	.05	.02
☐ SL39	Brian Grant	.15	.07
☐ SL40	Mitch Richmond	.25	.11
☐ SL41	Walt Williams	.05	.02
☐ SL42	David Robinson	.40	.18
☐ SL43	Gary Payton	.40	.18
☐ SL44	Detlef Schrempf	.15	.07
☐ SL45	D.Stoudamire	1.50	.70
☐ SL46	Karl Malone	.40	.18
☐ SL47	John Stockton	.25	.11
☐ SL48	Bryant Reeves	.50	.23
☐ SL49	Juwan Howard	.40	.18
☐ SL50	Chris Webber	.60	.25

1995-96 Hoops Top Ten

Randomly inserted into all first series packs at an approximate rate of one in 12, these 10 standard-size cards feature a selection of former lottery picks that are on their way to or have already attained great success in the NBA. The fronts are laid out horizontally with a color-action photo and a wide strip down the left side that reads

"Top" with 10 in the middle of the O. The background on each card is different and has a multi-colored cloudy look. The backs have the same background as the front with a color-action photo and player information at the top.

		MINT	NRMT
COMPLETE SET (10)		30.00	13.50
COMMON CARD (AR1-AR10)		1.00	.45
SEMISTARS		1.25	.55
SER.1 STATED ODDS 1:12 HOBBY/RETAIL			

		MINT	NRMT
☐ AR1	Shaquille O'Neal	5.00	2.20
☐ AR2	Grant Hill	8.00	3.60
☐ AR3	Chris Webber	3.00	1.35
☐ AR4	Jamal Mashburn	1.00	.45
☐ AR5	A.Hardaway	5.00	2.20
☐ AR6	Alonzo Mourning	1.25	.55
☐ AR7	Michael Jordan	15.00	6.75
☐ AR8	Charles Barkley	2.00	.90
☐ AR9	Glenn Robinson	1.50	.70
☐ AR10	Jason Kidd	3.00	1.35

1996-97 Hoops

The 1996-97 Hoops set was issued in two series. The first series had a total of 200 cards, while the second series contained 150. Both series had 9-card packs that carried a suggested retail price of $1.29 each. Card fronts contain a full bleed action shot with the player's name written in gold foil diagonally across the bottom right. Card backs have a small photo of the player in the top left corner with complete college

and pro statistics as well as biographical information. The cards are grouped alphabetically within team order. Some Rookie Cards that were included in the second series were S.Abdur-Rahim, Kobe Bryant, Marcus Camby, Allen Iverson, Stephon Marbury and Antoine Walker. Also, a Grant Hill Z-Force Preview card was randomly inserted into series one packs at a rate of one in 360 packs. It previewed the inaugural edition of SkyBox Z-Force. A non-numbered two-card promo sheet was also issued which featured a regular issue Grant Hill card and a HIPnotized Jerry Stackhouse.

	MINT	NRMT
COMPLETE SET (350)	30.00	13.50
COMPLETE SERIES 1 (200)	15.00	6.75
COMPLETE SERIES 2 (150)	15.00	6.75
COMMON CARD (1-350)	.10	.05
SEMISTARS	.15	.07
UNLISTED STARS	.25	.11
COMP.SILVER SET (98)	50.00	22.00
COMMON SILVER (1-98)	.30	.14
*SILVER: 1.5X TO 3X HI COLUMN		
SILVER: ONE PER SPECIAL SER.1		
RET.PACK		
HILL Z-F: SER.1 STATED ODDS 1:360 H/R		
AUTOGRAPHICS LISTED UNDER SKYBOX		

		MINT	NRMT
☐ 1	Stacey Augmon	.10	.05
☐ 2	Mookie Blaylock	.15	.07
☐ 3	Alan Henderson	.10	.05
☐ 4	Christian Laettner	.15	.07
☐ 5	Grant Long	.10	.05
☐ 6	Steve Smith	.15	.07
☐ 7	Dana Barros	.10	.05
☐ 8	Todd Day	.10	.05
☐ 9	Rick Fox	.10	.05
☐ 10	Eric Montross	.10	.05
☐ 11	Dino Radja	.10	.05
☐ 12	Eric Williams	.10	.05
☐ 13	Kenny Anderson	.15	.07
☐ 14	Scott Burrell	.10	.05
☐ 15	Dell Curry	.10	.05
☐ 16	Matt Geiger	.10	.05
☐ 17	Larry Johnson	.15	.07
☐ 18	Glen Rice	.25	.11
☐ 19	Ron Harper	.15	.07
☐ 20	Michael Jordan	3.00	1.35
☐ 21	Steve Kerr	.10	.05
☐ 22	Toni Kukoc	.15	.07
☐ 23	Luc Longley	.15	.07
☐ 24	Scottie Pippen	.75	.35
☐ 25	Dennis Rodman	1.00	.45
☐ 26	Terrell Brandon	.25	.11
☐ 27	Danny Ferry	.10	.05
☐ 28	Tyrone Hill	.10	.05
☐ 29	Chris Mills	.10	.05
☐ 30	Bobby Phills	.10	.05
☐ 31	Bob Sura	.10	.05
☐ 32	Tony Dumas	.10	.05
☐ 33	Jim Jackson	.15	.07
☐ 34	Popeye Jones	.10	.05
☐ 35	Jason Kidd	.50	.23
☐ 36	Jamal Mashburn	.15	.07
☐ 37	George McCloud	.10	.05
☐ 38	Cherokee Parks	.10	.05
☐ 39	M.Abdul-Rauf	.10	.05
☐ 40	LaPhonso Ellis	.10	.05
☐ 41	Antonio McDyess	.40	.18
☐ 42	D.Mutombo	.15	.07
☐ 43	Jalen Rose	.10	.05

44	Bryant Stith	.10	.05
45	Joe Dumars	.25	.11
46	Grant Hill	1.50	.70
47	Allan Houston	.15	.07
48	Lindsey Hunter	.10	.05
49	Terry Mills	.10	.05
50	Theo Ratliff	.10	.05
51	Otis Thorpe	.10	.05
52	B.J. Armstrong	.10	.05
53	Donyell Marshall	.10	.05
54	Chris Mullin	.25	.11
55	Joe Smith	.30	.14
56	Rony Seikaly	.10	.05
57	Latrell Sprewell	.15	.07
58	Mark Bryant	.10	.05
59	Sam Cassell	.15	.07
60	Clyde Drexler	.30	.14
61	Mario Elie	.10	.05
62	Robert Horry	.15	.07
63	Hakeem Olajuwon	.23	.23
64	Travis Best	.10	.05
65	Antonio Davis	.10	.05
66	Mark Jackson	.10	.05
67	Derrick McKey	.10	.05
68	Reggie Miller	.25	.11
69	Rik Smits	.15	.07
70	Brent Barry	.10	.05
71	Terry Dehere	.10	.05
72	Pooh Richardson	.10	.05
73	Rodney Rogers	.10	.05
74	Loy Vaught	.15	.07
75	Brian Williams	.10	.05
76	Elden Campbell	.10	.05
77	Cedric Ceballos	.10	.05
78	Vlade Divac	.10	.05
79	Eddie Jones	.50	.23
80	Anthony Peeler	.10	.05
81	Nick Van Exel	.25	.11
82	Sasha Danilovic	.10	.05
83	Tim Hardaway	.30	.14
84	Alonzo Mourning	.25	.11
85	Kurt Thomas	.10	.05
86	Walt Williams	.10	.05
87	Vin Baker	.50	.23
88	Sherman Douglas	.10	.05
89	Johnny Newman	.10	.05
90	Shawn Respert	.10	.05
91	Glenn Robinson	.25	.11
92	Kevin Garnett	1.50	.70
93	Tom Gugliotta	.25	.11
94	Andrew Lang	.10	.05
95	Sam Mitchell	.10	.05
96	Isaiah Rider	.15	.07
97	Shawn Bradley	.10	.05
98	P.J. Brown	.10	.05
99	Chris Childs	.10	.05
100	Armon Gilliam	.10	.05
101	Ed O'Bannon	.10	.05
102	Jayson Williams	.15	.07
103	Hubert Davis	.10	.05
104	Patrick Ewing	.25	.11
105	Anthony Mason	.15	.07
106	Charles Oakley	.10	.05
107	John Starks	.15	.07
108	Charlie Ward	.10	.05
109	Nick Anderson	.10	.05
110	Horace Grant	.15	.07
111	A.Hardaway	1.00	.45
112	Shaquille O'Neal	1.00	.45
113	Dennis Scott	.10	.05
114	Brian Shaw	.10	.05
115	Derrick Coleman	.15	.07
116	Vernon Maxwell	.10	.05
117	Trevor Ruffin	.10	.05
118	Jerry Stackhouse	.30	.14
119	C.Weatherspoon	.10	.05
120	Charles Barkley	.40	.18
121	Michael Finley	.30	.14
122	A.C. Green	.15	.07
123	Kevin Johnson	.15	.07
124	Danny Manning	.15	.07
125	Wesley Person	.10	.05
126	John Williams	.10	.05
127	Harvey Grant	.10	.05
128	Aaron McKie	.10	.05
129	Clifford Robinson	.10	.05
130	Arvydas Sabonis	.15	.07
131	Rod Strickland	.15	.07
132	Gary Trent	.10	.05
133	Tyus Edney	.10	.05
134	Brian Grant	.15	.07
135	Billy Owens	.10	.05
136	Olden Polynice	.10	.05
137	Mitch Richmond	.25	.11
138	Corliss Williamson	.15	.07
139	Vinny Del Negro	.10	.05
140	Sean Elliott	.10	.05
141	Avery Johnson	.10	.05
142	Chuck Person	.10	.05
143	David Robinson	.40	.18
144	Charles Smith	.10	.05
145	Sherrell Ford	.10	.05
146	Hersey Hawkins	.15	.07
147	Shawn Kemp	.75	.35
148	Nate McMillan	.10	.05
149	Gary Payton	.30	.14
150	Detlef Schrempf	.15	.07
151	Oliver Miller	.10	.05
152	Tracy Murray	.10	.05
153	Carlos Rogers	.10	.05
154	D.Stoudamire	.60	.25
155	Zan Tabak	.10	.05
156	Sharone Wright	.10	.05
157	Antoine Carr	.10	.05
158	Jeff Hornacek	.15	.07
159	Adam Keefe	.10	.05
160	Karl Malone	.40	.18
161	Chris Morris	.10	.05
162	John Stockton	.25	.11
163	Greg Anthony	.10	.05
164	Blue Edwards	.10	.05
165	Chris King	.10	.05
166	Lawrence Moten	.10	.05
167	Bryant Reeves	.15	.07
168	Byron Scott	.15	.07
169	Calbert Cheaney	.10	.05
170	Juwan Howard	.30	.14
171	Tim Legler	.10	.05
172	Gheorghe Muresan	.10	.05
173	Rasheed Wallace	.15	.07
174	Chris Webber	.60	.25
175	Steve Smith BF	.10	.05
176	Michael Jordan BF	1.50	.70
177	Scottie Pippen BF	.40	.18
178	Dennis Rodman BF	.50	.23
179	Allan Houston BF	.10	.05
180	Hakeem Olajuwon BF	.25	.11
181	Patrick Ewing BF	.15	.07
182	A.Hardaway BF	.50	.23
183	Shaquille O'Neal BF	.50	.23
184	Charles Barkley BF	.25	.11
185	Arvydas Sabonis BF	.10	.05
186	David Robinson BF	.25	.11
187	Shawn Kemp BF	.40	.18
188	Gary Payton BF	.25	.11
189	Karl Malone BF	.25	.11
190	Kenny Anderson PLA	.15	.07
191	Toni Kukoc PLA	.10	.05
192	Brent Barry PLA	.10	.05
193	Cedric Ceballos PLA	.10	.05
194	Shawn Bradley PLA	.10	.05
195	Charles Oakley PLA	.10	.05
196	Dennis Scott PLA	.10	.05
197	Clifford Robinson PLA	.10	.05
198	Mitch Richmond PLA	.15	.07
199	Checklist	.10	.05
200	Checklist	.10	.05
201	D.Mutombo	.15	.07
202	Dee Brown	.10	.05
203	David Wesley	.10	.05
204	Vlade Divac	.10	.05
205	Anthony Mason	.15	.07
206	Chris Gatling	.10	.05
207	Eric Montross	.10	.05
208	Ervin Johnson	.10	.05
209	Stacey Augmon	.10	.05
210	Joe Dumars	.25	.11
211	Grant Hill	1.50	.70
212	Charles Barkley	.40	.18
213	Jalen Rose	.10	.05
214	Lamond Murray	.10	.05
215	Shaquille O'Neal	1.00	.45
216	P.J. Brown	.10	.05
217	Dan Majerle	.15	.07
218	Armon Gilliam	.10	.05
219	Andrew Lang	.10	.05
220	Kevin Garnett	1.50	.70
221	Tom Gugliotta	.25	.11
222	Cherokee Parks	.10	.05
223	Doug West	.10	.05
224	Kendall Gill	.15	.07
225	Robert Pack	.10	.05
226	Allan Houston	.10	.07
227	Larry Johnson	.15	.07
228	Rony Seikaly	.10	.05
229	Gerald Wilkins	.10	.05
230	Michael Cage	.10	.05
231	Lucious Harris	.10	.05
232	Sam Cassell	.15	.07
233	Robert Horry	.15	.07
234	Kenny Anderson	.15	.07
235	Isaiah Rider	.15	.07
236	Rasheed Wallace	.15	.07
237	M.Abdul-Rauf	.10	.05
238	Vernon Maxwell	.10	.05
239	Dominique Wilkins	.25	.11
240	Jim McIlvaine	.10	.05
241	Hubert Davis	.10	.05
242	Popeye Jones	.10	.05
243	Walt Williams	.10	.05
244	Karl Malone	.40	.18
245	John Stockton	.25	.11
246	Anthony Peeler	.10	.05
247	Tracy Murray	.10	.05
248	Rod Strickland	.15	.07
249	Lenny Wilkens CO	.10	.05
250	M.L. Carr CO	.10	.05
251	Dave Cowens CO	.10	.05
252	Phil Jackson CO	.15	.07
253	Mike Fratello CO	.10	.05
254	Jim Cleamons CO	.10	.05
255	Dick Motta CO	.10	.05
256	Doug Collins CO	.10	.05
257	Rick Adelman CO	.10	.05
258	Rudy Tomjanovich CO	.15	.07
259	Larry Brown CO	.15	.07
260	Bill Fitch CO	.10	.05
261	Del Harris CO	.10	.05
262	Pat Riley CO	.15	.07
263	Chris Ford CO	.10	.05
264	Flip Saunders CO	.10	.05
265	John Calipari CO	.15	.07
266	Jeff Van Gundy CO	.10	.05
267	Brian Hill CO	.10	.05
268	Johnny Davis CO	.10	.05
269	Danny Ainge CO	.15	.07
270	P.J. Carlesimo CO	.10	.05
271	Garry St. Jean CO	.10	.05
272	Bob Hill CO	.10	.05
273	George Karl CO	.15	.07
274	Darrell Walker CO	.10	.05
275	Jerry Sloan CO	.15	.07
276	Brian Winters CO	.10	.05
277	Jim Lynam CO	.10	.05
278	S.Abdur-Rahim	1.50	.70
279	Ray Allen	.75	.35
280	Shandon Anderson	.30	.14
281	Kobe Bryant	5.00	2.20
282	Marcus Camby	.60	.25
283	Erick Dampier	.30	.14
284	Emanual Davis	.10	.05
285	Tony Delk	.30	.14
286	Brian Evans	.10	.05
287	Derek Fisher	.30	.14
288	Todd Fuller	.10	.05
289	Dean Garrett	.10	.05
290	Reggie Geary	.10	.05
291	Darvin Ham	.10	.05
292	Othella Harrington	.15	.07
293	Shane Heal	.10	.05
294	Mark Hendrickson	.10	.05
295	Allen Iverson	2.50	1.10
296	Dontae' Jones	.10	.05
297	Kerry Kittles	.60	.25
298	Priest Lauderdale	.10	.05
299	Matt Maloney	.40	.18
300	Stephon Marbury	2.50	1.10
301	Walter McCarty	.15	.07

☐ 302 Jeff McInnis	.10	.05
☐ 303 Martin Muursepp	.10	.05
☐ 304 Steve Nash	.40	.18
☐ 305 Moochie Norris	.10	.05
☐ 306 Jermaine O'Neal	.40	.18
☐ 307 Vitaly Potapenko	.15	.07
☐ 308 Virginius Praskevicius	.10	.05
☐ 309 Roy Rogers	.10	.05
☐ 310 Malik Rose	.10	.05
☐ 311 James Scott	.10	.05
☐ 312 Antoine Walker	2.50	1.10
☐ 313 Samaki Walker	.30	.14
☐ 314 Ben Wallace	.10	.05
☐ 315 John Wallace	.40	.18
☐ 316 Jerome Williams	.15	.07
☐ 317 Lorenzen Wright	.30	.14
☐ 318 Charles Barkley ST	.25	.11
☐ 319 Derrick Coleman ST	.10	.05
☐ 320 Michael Finley ST	.15	.07
☐ 321 Stephon Marbury ST	1.25	.55
☐ 322 Reggie Miller ST	.15	.07
☐ 323 Alonzo Mourning ST	.15	.07
☐ 324 Shaquille O'Neal ST	.50	.23
☐ 325 Gary Payton ST	.25	.11
☐ 326 Dennis Rodman ST	.50	.23
☐ 327 D.Stoudamire ST	.30	.14
☐ 328 Vin Baker CBG	.25	.11
☐ 329 Clyde Drexler CBG	.25	.11
☐ 330 Patrick Ewing CBG	.15	.07
☐ 331 A.Hardaway CBG	.50	.23
☐ 332 Grant Hill CBG	.75	.35
☐ 333 Juwan Howard CBG	.25	.11
☐ 334 Larry Johnson CBG	.10	.05
☐ 335 Michael Jordan CBG	1.50	.70
☐ 336 Shawn Kemp CBG	.40	.18
☐ 337 Jason Kidd CBG	.25	.11
☐ 338 Karl Malone CBG	.25	.11
☐ 339 Reggie Miller CBG	.15	.07
☐ 340 Hakeem Olajuwon CBG	.25	.11
☐ 341 Scottie Pippen CBG	.40	.18
☐ 342 Mitch Richmond CBG	.15	.07
☐ 343 David Robinson CBG UER back David Robinsinon	.25	.11
☐ 344 Dennis Rodman CBG	.50	.23
☐ 345 Joe Smith CBG	.25	.11
☐ 346 Jerry Stackhouse CBG	.25	.11
☐ 347 John Stockton CBG	.15	.07
☐ 348 Jerry Stackhouse BG	.25	.11
☐ 349 CL (201-350/inserts)	.10	.05
☐ 350 Checklist (inserts)	.10	.05
☐ NNO G.Hill Z-Force Prev.	20.00	9.00
☐ NNO Grant Hill Jerry Stackhouse Promo	5.00	2.20

1996-97 Hoops Fly With

FLY WITH
Gary Payton
Seattle Sonics

Randomly inserted in series two retail packs only at a rate of one in 24, this 10-card set focuses on the high-flying acrobats of ten NBA players. Cards feature clear plastic stock and a cloud background on the fronts.

	MINT	NRMT
COMPLETE SET (10)	30.00	13.50
COMMON CARD (1-10)	2.50	1.10
SER.2 STATED ODDS 1:24 RETAIL		
☐ 1 Charles Barkley	4.00	1.80
☐ 2 Juwan Howard	3.00	1.35
☐ 3 Jason Kidd	5.00	2.20
☐ 4 Alonzo Mourning	2.50	1.10
☐ 5 Gary Payton	4.00	1.80
☐ 6 David Robinson	4.00	1.80
☐ 7 Dennis Rodman	10.00	4.50
☐ 8 Joe Smith	3.00	1.35
☐ 9 Jerry Stackhouse	3.00	1.35
☐ 10 D.Stoudamire	6.00	2.70

1996-97 Hoops Grant's All-Rookies

Randomly inserted in all series two packs at a rate of one in 360, this 11-card set features the SkyView technology as Grant Hill selects his picks for the best rookies from the 1996-97 class. Despite no serial numbering, the stated print run for the set was 996 of each card.

	MINT	NRMT
COMPLETE SET (11)	350.00	160.00
COMMON CARD (1-11)	8.00	3.60
SER.2 STATED ODDS 1:360 HOBBY/RETAIL STATED PRINT RUN 996 SETS		
☐ 1 S.Abdur-Rahim	40.00	18.00
☐ 2 Ray Allen	20.00	9.00
☐ 3 Kobe Bryant	100.00	45.00
☐ 4 Marcus Camby	15.00	6.75
☐ 5 Grant Hill	60.00	27.00
☐ 6 Allen Iverson	60.00	27.00
☐ 7 Kerry Kittles	15.00	6.75
☐ 8 Stephon Marbury	60.00	27.00
☐ 9 Antoine Walker	60.00	27.00
☐ 10 Samaki Walker	8.00	3.60
☐ 11 Lorenzen Wright	8.00	3.60

1996-97 Hoops Head to Head

Randomly inserted at a rate of one in 24 packs, this 10-card set features dual-player cards of either teammates or young players. Card fronts contain action photos of both players and the logo "Head to Head" in gold foil at the bottom of the card. In addition, the logo and both of

the player's first names are treated with a diamond-like element. Card backs are divided into four quadrants with two of them featuring action shots and the other two featuring a brief commentary on each player. Card backs are numbered with a "HH" prefix.

	MINT	NRMT
COMPLETE SET (10)	40.00	18.00
COMMON PAIR (HH1-HH10)	2.50	1.10
SER.1 STATED ODDS 1:24 HOBBY/RETAIL		
☐ HH1 Larry Johnson Glenn Rice	2.50	1.10
☐ HH2 Michael Jordan Scottie Pippen	20.00	9.00
☐ HH3 Jason Kidd Grant Hill	10.00	4.50
☐ HH4 Clyde Drexler Hakeem Olajuwon	5.00	2.20
☐ HH5 Vin Baker Glenn Robinson	4.00	1.80
☐ HH6 A.Hardaway Shaquille O'Neal	8.00	3.60
☐ HH7 Antonio McDyess Jerry Stackhouse	4.00	1.80
☐ HH8 Sean Elliott David Robinson	2.50	1.10
☐ HH9 Joe Smith D.Stoudamire	5.00	2.20
☐ HH10 Karl Malone John Stockton	2.50	1.10

1996-97 Hoops HIPnotized

Randomly inserted at a rate of one in four packs, this 20-card set features some of the top players in the game. Card fronts

are full bleed action shots with a swirling background. The logo "HIPnotized" and the player's last name are in gold foil. Card backs are horizontal with statistical and biographical information as well as a having a brief commentary next to the photo. Cards are numbered with a "H" prefix.

	MINT	NRMT
COMPLETE SET (20)	15.00	6.75
COMMON CARD (H1-H20)	.30	.14
SEMISTARS	.50	.23
UNLISTED STARS	.75	.35
SER.1 STATED ODDS 1:4 HOBBY/RETAIL		

		MINT	NRMT
☐ H1	Steve Smith	.50	.23
☐ H2	Dana Barros	.30	.14
☐ H3	Larry Johnson	.50	.23
☐ H4	Dennis Rodman	3.00	1.35
☐ H5	Terrell Brandon	.75	.35
☐ H6	Jason Kidd	1.50	.70
☐ H7	Grant Hill	5.00	2.20
☐ H8	Clyde Drexler	1.00	.45
☐ H9	Reggie Miller	.75	.35
☐ H10	Alonzo Mourning	.75	.35
☐ H11	Glenn Robinson	.75	.35
☐ H12	Patrick Ewing	.75	.35
☐ H13	Shaquille O'Neal	3.00	1.35
☐ H14	Jerry Stackhouse	1.00	.45
☐ H15	Charles Barkley	1.25	.55
☐ H16	Clifford Robinson	.30	.14
☐ H17	Mitch Richmond	.75	.35
☐ H18	David Robinson	1.25	.55
☐ H19	Gary Payton	1.00	.45
☐ H20	Juwan Howard	1.00	.45

1996-97 Hoops Hot List

Randomly inserted in series two hobby packs only at a rate of one in 48, this 20-card set features a flamed front on clear plastic stock.

	MINT	NRMT
COMPLETE SET (20)	150.00	70.00
COMMON CARD (1-20)	2.00	.90
SEMISTARS	2.50	1.10
UNLISTED STARS	4.00	1.80
SER.2 STATED ODDS 1:48 HOBBY		

		MINT	NRMT
☐ 1	Vin Baker	8.00	3.60
☐ 2	Patrick Ewing	4.00	1.80
☐ 3	Michael Finley	5.00	2.20
☐ 4	Kevin Garnett	25.00	11.00

		MINT	NRMT
☐ 5	A.Hardaway	15.00	6.75
☐ 6	Grant Hill	25.00	11.00
☐ 7	Allan Houston	2.50	1.10
☐ 8	Michael Jordan	50.00	22.00
☐ 9	Shawn Kemp	12.00	5.50
☐ 10	Christian Laettner	2.50	1.10
☐ 11	Karl Malone	6.00	2.70
☐ 12	Antonio McDyess	6.00	2.70
☐ 13	Reggie Miller	4.00	1.80
☐ 14	Hakeem Olajuwon	8.00	3.60
☐ 15	Shaquille O'Neal	15.00	6.75
☐ 16	Scottie Pippen	12.00	5.50
☐ 17	Mitch Richmond	4.00	1.80
☐ 18	Isaiah Rider	2.00	.90
☐ 19	Rod Strickland	2.50	1.10
☐ 20	Chris Webber	10.00	4.50

1996-97 Hoops Rookie Headliners

Randomly inserted at a rate of one in 72 hobby packs, this 10-card set focuses on some of the best rookies from the 1995-96 class. Card fronts are designed similar to a game ticket with both the left and right borders in gold foil. The action shot of the player is located between the two borders and the player's last name is in gold foil on top of the photo. Card backs have a shot of the player in the middle of the card against a light gold background along with a brief commentary on the player. The player's rookie statistics are located along the left border. Card backs are numbered as "X of 10".

	MINT	NRMT
COMPLETE SET (10)	60.00	27.00
COMMON CARD (1-10)	1.50	.70
SEMISTARS	2.00	.90
UNLISTED STARS	5.00	2.20
SER.1 STATED ODDS 1:72 HOBBY		

		MINT	NRMT
☐ 1	Antonio McDyess	8.00	3.60
☐ 2	Joe Smith	6.00	2.70
☐ 3	Brent Barry	1.50	.70
☐ 4	Kevin Garnett	30.00	13.50
☐ 5	Jerry Stackhouse	6.00	2.70
☐ 6	Michael Finley	6.00	2.70
☐ 7	Arvydas Sabonis	2.00	.90
☐ 8	Tyus Edney	1.50	.70
☐ 9	D.Stoudamire	12.00	5.50
☐ 10	Bryant Reeves	2.00	.90

1996-97 Hoops Rookies

Randomly inserted in all series two packs at one in six, this 30-card set focuses on the season's best first year players. Card fronts carry a gold foiled background.

	MINT	NRMT
COMPLETE SET (30)	50.00	22.00
COMMON CARD (1-30)	.50	.23
SEMISTARS	1.00	.45
UNLISTED STARS	1.50	.70
SER.2 STATED ODDS 1:6 HOBBY/RETAIL		

		MINT	NRMT
☐ 1	S.Abdur-Rahim	5.00	2.20
☐ 2	Ray Allen	2.50	1.10
☐ 3	Kobe Bryant	15.00	6.75
☐ 4	Marcus Camby	2.00	.90
☐ 5	Erick Dampier	1.50	.70
☐ 6	Emanual Davis	.50	.23
☐ 7	Tony Delk	.50	.23
☐ 8	Brian Evans	.50	.23
☐ 9	Derek Fisher	1.50	.70
☐ 10	Todd Fuller	.50	.23
☐ 11	Othella Harrington	1.00	.45
☐ 12	Allen Iverson	8.00	3.60
☐ 13	Dontae' Jones	.50	.23
☐ 14	Kerry Kittles	2.00	.90
☐ 15	Priest Lauderdale	.50	.23
☐ 16	Matt Maloney	1.50	.70
☐ 17	Stephon Marbury	8.00	3.60
☐ 18	Walter McCarty	1.00	.45
☐ 19	Jeff McInnis	.50	.23
☐ 20	Martin Muursepp	.50	.23
☐ 21	Steve Nash	1.50	.70
☐ 22	Moochie Norris	.50	.23
☐ 23	Jermaine O'Neal	1.50	.70
☐ 24	Vitaly Potapenko	1.00	.45
☐ 25	Roy Rogers	.50	.23
☐ 26	Antoine Walker	8.00	3.60
☐ 27	Samaki Walker	1.50	.70
☐ 28	John Wallace	1.50	.70
☐ 29	Jerome Williams	1.00	.45
☐ 30	Lorenzen Wright	1.50	.70

1996-97 Hoops Starting Five

Randomly inserted in all series two packs at one in 12, this 29-card set features each team's starting five. Card fronts feature a full shot of the team's primary player with the other four starters in gold boxes at the bottom of the card.

	MINT	NRMT
COMPLETE SET (29)	50.00	22.00
COMMON CARD (1-29)	.50	.23
SEMISTARS	.75	.35
UNLISTED STARS	1.25	.55
SER.2 STATED ODDS 1:12 HOBBY/RETAIL		

- □ 1 Mookie Blaylock ..... .75 .35
  - Christian Laettner
  - D.Mutombo
  - Ken Norman
  - Steve Smith
  - Atlanta Hawks
- □ 2 Dana Barros ..... .50 .23
  - Dee Brown
  - Todd Day
  - Rick Fox
  - Dino Radja
  - Boston Celtics
- □ 3 Tyrone Bogues ..... .75 .35
  - Dell Curry
  - Vlade Divac
  - Anthony Mason
  - Glen Rice
  - Charlotte Hornets
- □ 4 Michael Jordan 12.00 5.50
  - Toni Kukoc
  - Luc Longley
  - Scottie Pippen
  - Dennis Rodman
  - Chicago Bulls
- □ 5 Terrell Brandon ..... .75 .35
  - Tyrone Hill
  - Chris Mills
  - Bobby Phills
  - Vitaly Potapenko
  - Cleveland Cavaliers
- □ 6 Chris Gatling ..... 2.00 .90
  - Jim Jackson
  - Jason Kidd
  - Jamal Mashburn
  - Oliver Miller
  - Dallas Mavericks
- □ 7 LaPhonso Ellis ..... 1.50 .70
  - Mark Jackson
  - Ervin Johnson
  - Antonio McDyess
  - Bryant Stith
  - Denver Nuggets
- □ 8 Stacey Augmon 8.00 3.60
  - Joe Dumars
  - Grant Hill
  - Lindsey Hunter
  - Otis Thorpe
  - Detroit Pistons
- □ 9 Chris Mullin ..... 1.50 .70
  - Mark Price
  - Felton Spencer
  - Joe Smith
  - Latrell Sprewell
  - Golden State Warriors
- □ 10 Charles Barkley 2.50 1.10
  - Clyde Drexler
  - Hakeem Olajuwon
  - Brent Price
  - Kevin Willis
  - Houston Rockets
- □ 11 Dale Davis ..... 1.25 .55
  - Duane Ferrell
  - Reggie Miller
  - Jalen Rose
  - Rik Smits
  - Indiana Pacers
- □ 12 Terry Dehere ..... .50 .23
  - Charles Outlaw
  - Pooh Richardson
  - Rodney Rogers
  - Loy Vaught
  - Los Angeles Clippers
- □ 13 Elden Campbell 6.00 2.70
  - Cedric Ceballos
  - Eddie Jones
  - Shaquille O'Neal
  - Nick Van Exel
  - Los Angeles Lakers
- □ 14 P.J. Brown ..... 1.25 .55
  - Tim Hardaway
  - Dan Majerle
  - Alonzo Mourning
  - Kurt Thomas
  - Miami Heat
- □ 15 Ray Allen ..... 1.50 .70
  - Vin Baker
  - Sherman Douglas
  - Andrew Lang
  - Glenn Robinson
  - Milwaukee Bucks
- □ 16 Kevin Garnett 6.00 2.70
  - Tom Gugliotta
  - Stephon Marbury
  - Cherokee Parks
  - James Robinson
  - Minnesota Timberwolves
- □ 17 Shawn Bradley ..... .50 .23
  - Kendall Gill
  - Ed O'Bannon
  - Khalid Reeves
  - Jayson Williams
  - New Jersey Nets
- □ 18 Patrick Ewing ..... 1.25 .55
  - Allan Houston
  - Larry Johnson
  - Charles Oakley
  - John Starks
  - New York Knicks
- □ 19 Nick Anderson 5.00 2.20
  - Horace Grant
  - A.Hardaway
  - Dennis Scott
  - Rony Seikaly
  - Orlando Magic
- □ 20 Michael Cage 2.50 1.10
  - Derrick Coleman
  - Allen Iverson
  - Jerry Stackhouse
  - C.Weatherspoon
  - Philadelphia 76'ers
- □ 21 Sam Cassell ..... .75 .35
  - Michael Finley
  - Robert Horry
  - Kevin Johnson
  - Danny Manning
  - Phoenix Suns
- □ 22 Kenny Anderson ..... .50 .23
  - Isaiah Rider
  - Clifford Robinson
  - Arvydas Sabonis
  - Rasheed Wallace
  - Portland Trail Blazers
- □ 23 M.Abdul-Rauf ..... .50 .23
  - Brian Grant
  - Billy Owens
  - Olden Polynice
  - Mitch Richmond
  - Sacramento Kings
- □ 24 Avery Johnson ..... 1.50 .70
  - Vernon Maxwell
  - David Robinson
  - Charles Smith
  - Dominique Wilkins
  - San Antonio Spurs
- □ 25 Hersey Hawkins 4.00 1.80
  - Shawn Kemp
  - Gary Payton
  - Sam Perkins
  - Detlef Schrempf
  - Seattle Supersonics
- □ 26 Marcus Camby ..... 1.50 .70
  - Hubert Davis
  - Popeye Jones
  - D.Stoudamire
  - Walt Williams
  - Toronto Raptors
- □ 27 Jeff Hornacek ..... 1.50 .70
  - Adam Keefe
  - Karl Malone
  - Greg Ostertag
  - John Stockton
  - Utah Jazz
- □ 28 S.Abdur-Rahim 4.00 1.80
  - George Lynch
  - Lee Mayberry
  - Anthony Peeler
  - Bryant Reeves
  - Vancouver Grizzlies
- □ 29 Calbert Cheaney ..... 1.50 .70
  - Juwan Howard
  - Gheorghe Muresan
  - Rod Strickland
  - Chris Webber
  - Washington Bullets

1996-97 Hoops Superfeats

Randomly inserted at a rate of one in 36 retail packs, this 10-card set features players who had super "feats" during the 1995-96 NBA season. Card fronts feature a colorful background with a full color action shot of the player on top. The player's name and the logo "Superfeats" are treated with gold foil. Card backs feature another action shot of the player and a brief commentary on the extraordinary achievements the player had the previous season. Card backs are also numbered as "X of 10".

	MINT	NRMT
COMPLETE SET (10)	100.00	45.00
COMMON CARD (1-10)	2.00	.90
SEMISTARS	3.00	1.35
SER.1 STATED ODDS 1:36 RETAIL		

- □ 1 Michael Jordan 60.00 27.00
- □ 2 Jason Kidd 6.00 2.70
- □ 3 Grant Hill 20.00 9.00
- □ 4 Hakeem Olajuwon 6.00 2.70
- □ 5 Alonzo Mourning 3.00 1.35
- □ 6 Anthony Mason ..... 2.00 .90

	MINT	NRMT
☐ 7 A.Hardaway	12.00	5.50
☐ 8 Jerry Stackhouse	4.00	1.80
☐ 9 Shawn Kemp	10.00	4.50
☐ 10 D.Stoudamire	8.00	3.60

1997-98 Hoops

The 1997-98 Hoops set was released in two series, with each 165-card series distributed in 10-card packs with a suggested retail price of $.99. Card fronts feature color player images on computer graphic treatment backgrounds. The set includes the League Leaders subset (1-8) and two checklist cards (164-165). The backs carry player information and statistics. A Grant Hill promo card was issued to preview the product. It is priced below.

	MINT	NRMT
COMPLETE SET (330)	30.00	13.50
COMPLETE SERIES 1 (165)	12.00	5.50
COMPLETE SERIES 2 (165)	18.00	8.00
COMMON CARD (1-330)	.10	.05
SEMISTARS	.15	.07
UNLISTED STARS	.25	.11
AUTOGRAPHICS LISTED UNDER SKYBOX		

☐ 1 Michael Jordan LL	1.50	.70	☐ 30 Dennis Rodman	1.00	.45
☐ 2 Dennis Rodman LL	.60	.25	☐ 31 Terrell Brandon	.25	.11
☐ 3 Mark Jackson LL	.10	.05	☐ 32 Danny Ferry	.10	.05
☐ 4 Shawn Bradley LL	.10	.05	☐ 33 Tyrone Hill	.10	.05
☐ 5 Glen Rice LL	.15	.07	☐ 34 Bobby Phills	.10	.05
☐ 6 Mookie Blaylock LL	.10	.05	☐ 35 Vitaly Potapenko	.10	.05
☐ 7 Gheorghe Muresan LL	.10	.05	☐ 36 Shawn Bradley	.10	.05
☐ 8 Mark Price LL	.10	.05	☐ 37 Sasha Danilovic	.10	.05
☐ 9 Tyrone Corbin	.10	.05	☐ 38 Derek Harper	.10	.05
☐ 10 Christian Laettner	.15	.07	☐ 39 Martin Muursepp	.10	.05
☐ 11 Priest Lauderdale	.10	.05	☐ 40 Robert Pack	.10	.05
☐ 12 D.Mutombo	.15	.07	☐ 41 Khalid Reeves	.10	.05
☐ 13 Steve Smith	.25	.11	☐ 42 Vincent Askew	.10	.05
☐ 14 Todd Day	.10	.05	☐ 43 Dale Ellis	.10	.05
☐ 15 Rick Fox	.10	.05	☐ 44 LaPhonso Ellis	.10	.05
☐ 16 Brett Szabo	.10	.05	☐ 45 Antonio McDyess	.30	.14
☐ 17 Antoine Walker	1.25	.55	☐ 46 Bryant Stith	.10	.05
☐ 18 David Wesley	.10	.05	☐ 47 Joe Dumars	.25	.11
☐ 19 Muggsy Bogues	.10	.05	☐ 48 Grant Hill	1.50	.70
☐ 20 Dell Curry	.10	.05	☐ 49 Lindsey Hunter	.10	.05
☐ 21 Tony Delk	.10	.05	☐ 50 Aaron McKie	.10	.05
☐ 22 Anthony Mason	.15	.07	☐ 51 Theo Ratliff	.10	.05
☐ 23 Glen Rice	.25	.11	☐ 52 Scott Burrell	.10	.05
☐ 24 Malik Rose	.10	.05	☐ 53 Todd Fuller	.10	.05
☐ 25 Steve Kerr	.10	.05	☐ 54 Chris Mullin	.25	.11
☐ 26 Toni Kukoc	.15	.07	☐ 55 Mark Price	.10	.05
☐ 27 Luc Longley	.10	.05	☐ 56 Joe Smith	.25	.11
☐ 28 Robert Parish	.15	.07	☐ 57 Latrell Sprewell	.15	.07
☐ 29 Scottie Pippen	.75	.35	☐ 58 Clyde Drexler	.30	.14
			☐ 59 Mario Elie	.10	.05
			☐ 60 Othella Harrington	.10	.05
			☐ 61 Matt Maloney	.10	.05
			☐ 62 Hakeem Olajuwon	.50	.23
			☐ 63 Kevin Willis	.10	.05
			☐ 64 Travis Best	.10	.05
			☐ 65 Erick Dampier	.15	.07
			☐ 66 Antonio Davis	.10	.05
			☐ 67 Dale Davis	.10	.05
			☐ 68 Mark Jackson	.10	.05
			☐ 69 Reggie Miller	.25	.11
			☐ 70 Brent Barry	.10	.05
			☐ 71 Darrick Martin	.10	.05
			☐ 72 Charles Outlaw	.10	.05
			☐ 73 Loy Vaught	.10	.05
			☐ 74 Lorenzen Wright	.10	.05
			☐ 75 Kobe Bryant	2.00	.90
			☐ 76 Derek Fisher	.10	.05
			☐ 77 Robert Horry	.10	.05
			☐ 78 Eddie Jones	.50	.23
			☐ 79 Travis Knight	.10	.05
			☐ 80 George McCloud	.10	.05
			☐ 81 Shaquille O'Neal	1.00	.45
			☐ 82 P.J. Brown	.10	.05
			☐ 83 Tim Hardaway	.30	.14
			☐ 84 Voshon Lenard	.10	.05
			☐ 85 Jamal Mashburn	.15	.07
			☐ 86 Alonzo Mourning	.25	.11
			☐ 87 Ray Allen	.30	.14
			☐ 88 Vin Baker	.50	.23
			☐ 89 Sherman Douglas	.10	.05
			☐ 90 Armon Gilliam	.10	.05
			☐ 91 Glenn Robinson	.25	.11
			☐ 92 Kevin Garnett	1.50	.70
			☐ 93 Dean Garrett	.10	.05
			☐ 94 Tom Gugliotta	.10	.05
			☐ 95 Stephon Marbury	1.25	.55
			☐ 96 Doug West	.10	.05
			☐ 97 Chris Gatling	.10	.05
			☐ 98 Kendall Gill	.15	.07
			☐ 99 Kerry Kittles	.25	.11
			☐ 100 Jayson Williams	.15	.07
			☐ 101 Chris Childs	.10	.05
			☐ 102 Patrick Ewing	.25	.11
			☐ 103 Allan Houston	.15	.07
			☐ 104 Larry Johnson	.15	.07
			☐ 105 Charles Oakley	.15	.07
			☐ 106 John Starks	.15	.07
			☐ 107 John Wallace	.15	.07
			☐ 108 Nick Anderson	.10	.05
			☐ 109 Horace Grant	.15	.07
			☐ 110 A.Hardaway	1.00	.45
			☐ 111 Rony Seikaly	.10	.05
			☐ 112 Derek Strong	.10	.05
			☐ 113 Derrick Coleman	.10	.05
			☐ 114 Allen Iverson	1.25	.55
			☐ 115 Doug Overton	.10	.05

☐ 116 Jerry Stackhouse	.25	.11
☐ 117 Rex Walters	.10	.05
☐ 118 Cedric Ceballos	.10	.05
☐ 119 Kevin Johnson	.15	.07
☐ 120 Jason Kidd	.50	.23
☐ 121 Steve Nash	.10	.05
☐ 122 Wesley Person	.10	.05
☐ 123 Kenny Anderson	.15	.07
☐ 124 Jermaine O'Neal	.15	.07
☐ 125 Isaiah Rider	.15	.07
☐ 126 Arvydas Sabonis	.15	.07
☐ 127 Gary Trent	.10	.05
☐ 128 Tyus Edney	.10	.05
☐ 129 Brian Grant	.10	.05
☐ 130 Olden Polynice	.10	.05
☐ 131 Mitch Richmond	.25	.11
☐ 132 Corliss Williamson	.15	.07
☐ 133 Vinny Del Negro	.10	.05
☐ 134 Sean Elliott	.10	.05
☐ 135 Avery Johnson	.10	.05
☐ 136 Will Perdue	.10	.05
☐ 137 Dominique Wilkins	.25	.11
☐ 138 Craig Ehlo	.10	.05
☐ 139 Hersey Hawkins	.15	.07
☐ 140 Shawn Kemp	.75	.35
☐ 141 Jim McIlvaine	.10	.05
☐ 142 Sam Perkins	.10	.07
☐ 143 Detlef Schrempf	.15	.07
☐ 144 Marcus Camby	.25	.11
☐ 145 Doug Christie	.10	.05
☐ 146 Popeye Jones	.10	.05
☐ 147 D.Stoudamire	.50	.23
☐ 148 Walt Williams	.10	.05
☐ 149 Jeff Hornacek	.15	.07
☐ 150 Karl Malone	.40	.18
☐ 151 Greg Ostertag	.10	.05
☐ 152 Bryon Russell	.10	.05
☐ 153 John Stockton	.25	.11
☐ 154 S.Abdur-Rahim	.75	.35
☐ 155 Greg Anthony	.10	.05
☐ 156 Anthony Peeler	.10	.05
☐ 157 Bryant Reeves	.15	.07
☐ 158 Roy Rogers	.10	.05
☐ 159 Calbert Cheaney	.10	.05
☐ 160 Juwan Howard	.25	.11
☐ 161 Gheorghe Muresan	.10	.05
☐ 162 Rod Strickland	.25	.11
☐ 163 Chris Webber	.60	.25
☐ 164 Checklist	.10	.05
☐ 165 Checklist	.10	.05
☐ 166 Tim Duncan	3.00	1.35
☐ 167 Chauncey Billups	1.00	.45
☐ 168 Keith Van Horn	2.50	1.10
☐ 169 Tracy McGrady	1.50	.70
☐ 170 John Thomas	.10	.05
☐ 171 Tim Thomas	1.50	.70
☐ 172 Ron Mercer	2.00	.90
☐ 173 Scot Pollard	.10	.05
☐ 174 Jason Lawson	.10	.05
☐ 175 Keith Booth	.10	.05
☐ 176 Adonal Foyle	.30	.14
☐ 177 Bubba Wells	.10	.05
☐ 178 Derek Anderson	.75	.35
☐ 179 Rodrick Rhodes	.30	.14
☐ 180 Kelvin Cato	.30	.14
☐ 181 Serge Zwikker	.10	.05
☐ 182 Ed Gray	.30	.14
☐ 183 Brevin Knight	.75	.35
☐ 184 Alvin Williams	.30	.14
☐ 185 Paul Grant	.10	.05
☐ 186 Austin Croshere	.30	.14
☐ 187 Chris Crawford	.10	.05
☐ 188 Anthony Johnson	.10	.05
☐ 189 James Cotton	.10	.05
☐ 190 James Collins	.10	.05
☐ 191 Tony Battie	.50	.23
☐ 192 Tariq Abdul-Wahad	.40	.18
☐ 193 Danny Fortson	.30	.14
☐ 194 Maurice Taylor	.75	.35
☐ 195 Bobby Jackson	.50	.23
☐ 196 Charles Smith	.10	.05
☐ 197 Johnny Taylor	.10	.05
☐ 198 Jerald Honeycutt	.10	.05
☐ 199 Mario Milic	.10	.05
☐ 200 Anthony Parker	.10	.05
☐ 201 Jacque Vaughn	.40	.18

□			
202	Antonio Daniels	.60	.25
203	Charles O'Bannon	.10	.05
204	God Shammgod	.10	.05
205	Kebu Stewart	.10	.05
206	Mookie Blaylock	.15	.07
207	Chucky Brown	.10	.05
208	Alan Henderson	.10	.05
209	Dana Barros	.10	<05
210	Tyus Edney	.10	.05
211	Travis Knight	.10	.05
212	Walter McCarty	.10	.05
213	Vlade Divac	.15	.07
214	Matt Geiger	.10	.05
215	Bobby Phills	.10	.05
216	J.R. Reid	.10	.05
217	David Wesley	.10	.05
218	Scott Burrell	.10	.05
219	Ron Harper	.15	.07
220	Michael Jordan	3.00	1.35
221	Bill Wennington	.10	.05
222	Mitchell Butler	.10	.05
223	Zydrunas Ilgauskas	.15	.07
224	Shawn Kemp	.75	.35
225	Wesley Person	.10	.05
226	Shawnelle Scott	.10	.05
227	Bob Sura	.10	.05
228	Hubert Davis	.10	.05
229	Michael Finley	.25	.11
230	Dennis Scott	.10	.05
231	Erick Strickland	.15	.07
232	Samaki Walker	.10	.05
233	Dean Garrett	.10	.05
234	Priest Lauderdale	.10	.05
235	Eric Williams	.10	.05
236	Grant Long	.10	.05
237	Malik Sealy	.10	.05
238	Brian Williams	.10	.05
239	Muggsy Bogues	.10	.05
240	Bimbo Coles	.10	.05
241	Brian Shaw	.10	.05
242	Joe Smith	.25	.11
243	Latrell Sprewell	.15	.07
244	Charles Barkley	.40	.18
245	Emanual Davis	.10	.05
246	Brent Price	.10	.05
247	Reggie Miller	.25	.11
248	Chris Mullin	.25	.11
249	Jalen Rose	.10	.05
250	Rik Smits	.15	.07
251	Mark West	.10	.05
252	Lamond Murray	.10	.05
253	Pooh Richardson	.10	.05
254	Rodney Rogers	.10	.05
255	Stojko Vrankovic	.10	.05
256	Jon Barry	.10	.05
257	Corie Blount	.10	.05
258	Elden Campbell	.15	.07
259	Rick Fox	.10	.05
260	Nick Van Exel	.25	.11
261	Isaac Austin	.10	.05
262	Dan Majerle	.15	.07
263	Terry Mills	.10	.05
264	Mark Strickland	.10	.05
265	Terrell Brandon	.25	.11
266	Tyrone Hill	.10	.05
267	Ervin Johnson	.10	.05
268	Andrew Lang	.10	.05
269	Elliot Perry	.10	.05
270	Chris Carr	.10	.05
271	Reggie Jordan	.10	.05
272	Sam Mitchell	.10	.05
273	Stanley Roberts	.10	.05
274	Michael Cage	.10	.05
275	Sam Cassell	.15	.07
276	Lucious Harris	.10	.05
277	Kerry Kittles	.25	.11
278	Don MacLean	.10	.05
279	Chris Dudley	.10	.05
280	Chris Mills	.10	.05
281	Charlie Ward	.10	.05
282	Buck Williams	.10	.05
283	Herb Williams	.10	.05
284	Derek Harper	.10	.05
285	Mark Price	.10	.05
286	Gerald Wilkins	.10	.05
287	Allen Iverson	1.25	.55

□			
288	Jim Jackson	.15	.07
289	Eric Montross	.10	.05
290	Jerry Stackhouse	.25	.11
291	C.Weatherspoon	.10	.05
292	Tom Chambers	.10	.05
293	Rex Chapman	.10	.05
294	Danny Manning	.15	.07
295	Antonio McDyess	.30	.14
296	Clifford Robinson	.10	.05
297	Stacey Augmon	.10	.05
298	Brian Grant	.10	.05
299	Rasheed Wallace	.15	.07
300	M.Abdul-Rauf	.10	.05
301	Terry Dehere	.10	.05
302	Billy Owens	.10	.05
303	Michael Smith	.10	.05
304	Cory Alexander	.10	.05
305	Chuck Person	.10	.05
306	David Robinson	.40	.18
307	Charles Smith	.10	.05
308	Monty Williams	.10	.05
309	Vin Baker	.50	.23
310	Jerome Kersey	.10	.05
311	Nate McMillan	.10	.05
312	Gary Payton	.40	.18
313	Eric Snow	.10	.05
314	Carlos Rogers	.10	.05
315	Zan Tabak	.10	.05
316	John Wallace	.15	.07
317	Sharone Wright	.10	.05
318	Shandon Anderson	.10	.05
319	Antoine Carr	.10	.05
320	Howard Eisley	.10	.05
321	Chris Morris	.10	.05
322	Pete Chilcutt	.10	.05
323	George Lynch	.10	.05
324	Chris Robinson	.10	.05
325	Otis Thorpe	.15	.07
326	Harvey Grant	.10	.05
327	Darvin Ham	.10	.05
328	Juwan Howard	.25	.11
329	Ben Wallace	.10	.05
330	Chris Webber	.60	.25
NNO	Grant Hill Promo	3.00	1.35

1997-98 Hoops Chairman of the Boards

Randomly inserted into series two packs at a rate of one in 9, this 10-card set focuses on some of the players considered the best rebounders in the NBA. The card fronts carry 100% etched silver foil. Card backs carry a "CB" prefix.

		MINT	NRMT
COMPLETE SET (10)		20.00	9.00
COMMON CARD (CB1-CB10)		.50	.23
SEMISTARS		.60	.25

		MINT	NRMT
UNLISTED STARS		1.00	.45
SER.2 STATED ODDS 1:9 HOBBY/RETAIL			

□			
CB1	Shaquille O'Neal	4.00	1.80
CB2	D.Mutombo	.60	.25
CB3	Dennis Rodman	4.00	1.80
CB4	Patrick Ewing	1.00	.45
CB5	Charles Barkley	1.50	.70
CB6	Karl Malone	1.50	.70
CB7	Rasheed Wallace	.50	.23
CB8	Chris Webber	2.50	1.10
CB9	Tim Duncan	6.00	2.70
CB10	Kevin Garnett	6.00	2.70

1997-98 Hoops Chill with Hill

Randomly inserted in series one packs at a rate of one in 10, this 10-card set features candid photos of Grant Hill on foil backgrounds which present a photographic essay on a day in his life.

	MINT	NRMT
COMPLETE SET (10)	15.00	6.75
COMMON HILL (1-10)	2.00	.90
SER.1 STATED ODDS 1:10 HOB/RET		

□			
1	Grant Hill	2.00	.90
	Tonight's the night		
2	Grant Hill	2.00	.90
	Stars from different worlds		
3	Grant Hill	2.00	.90
	Lots of questions		
4	Grant Hill	2.00	.90
	Another Challenge		
5	Grant Hill	2.00	.90
	Obey your thirst		
6	Grant Hill	2.00	.90
	All-Star Game		
7	Grant Hill	2.00	.90
	In the rafters at Cameron		
8	Grant Hill	2.00	.90
	The importance of education		
9	Grant Hill	2.00	.90
	I start preparing mentally..		
10	Grant Hill	2.00	.90
	I wouldn't trade this..		

1997-98 Hoops Dish N Swish

Randomly inserted in series one retail packs only at a rate of one in 18, this 10-card set features the top point guards in the league who are adept at both passing and shooting.

	MINT	NRMT
COMPLETE SET (10)	60.00	27.00
COMMON CARD (DS1-DS10)	1.25	.55
UNLISTED STARS	2.00	.90
SER.1 STATED ODDS 1:18 RETAIL		

		MINT	NRMT
□ DS1	Mookie Blaylock	1.25	.55
□ DS2	Terrell Brandon	1.50	.70
□ DS3	A.Hardaway	8.00	3.60
□ DS4	Allen Iverson	10.00	4.50
□ DS5	Michael Jordan	30.00	13.50
□ DS6	Jason Kidd	4.00	1.80
□ DS7	Stephon Marbury	10.00	4.50
□ DS8	Gary Payton	3.00	1.35
□ DS9	John Stockton	2.00	.90
□ DS10	D.Stoudamire	4.00	1.80

1997-98 Hoops Frequent Flyer Club

Randomly inserted in series one hobby packs only at a rate of one in 36, this 20-card set features color photos of players with great dunking ability on a cloud background. The horizontal cards are printed on a special foil-stamped card with rounded corners. Card backs are numbered with a "FF" prefix.

	MINT	NRMT
COMPLETE SET (20)	125.00	55.00
COMMON CARD (FF1-FF20)	1.25	.55
SEMISTARS	1.50	.70
UNLISTED STARS	2.50	1.10
SER.1 STATED ODDS 1:36 HOBBY		
COMP.UPGRADE SET (20)	500.00	220.00
COMN. UPGRADE (FF1-FF20)	6.00	2.70
*UPGRADE: 2X TO 4X HI COLUMN		
UPGRADE: SER.1 STATED ODDS 1:360 HOB		

		MINT	NRMT
□ FF1	Christian Laettner	1.50	.70
□ FF2	Antoine Walker	12.00	5.50
□ FF3	Glen Rice	2.50	1.10
□ FF4	Michael Jordan	30.00	13.50
□ FF5	Dennis Rodman	10.00	4.50
□ FF6	Grant Hill	15.00	6.75
□ FF7	Latrell Sprewell	1.50	.70
□ FF8	Charles Barkley	4.00	1.80
□ FF9	Kobe Bryant	20.00	9.00
□ FF10	Shaquille O'Neal	10.00	4.50
□ FF11	Ray Allen	3.00	1.35
□ FF12	Kevin Garnett	15.00	6.75
□ FF13	Kerry Kittles	2.50	1.10
□ FF14	A.Hardaway	10.00	4.50
□ FF15	Jerry Stackhouse	2.50	1.10
□ FF16	Cedric Ceballos	1.25	.55
□ FF17	Shawn Kemp	8.00	3.60
□ FF18	Marcus Camby	2.50	1.10
□ FF19	Juwan Howard	2.50	1.10
□ FF20	Chris Webber	6.00	2.70

1997-98 Hoops Great Shots

Inserted one per series two pack, this 30-card set features some of the best NBA players on mini-posters that measure 5"x7".

	MINT	NRMT
COMPLETE SET (30)	8.00	3.60
COMMON CARD (1-30)	.10	.05
SEMISTARS	.12	.05
UNLISTED STARS	.15	.07
ONE PER SERIES 2 PACK		

		MINT	NRMT
□ 1	D.Mutombo	.12	.05
□ 2	Antoine Walker	.75	.35
□ 3	Glen Rice	.15	.07
□ 4	Dennis Rodman	.60	.25
□ 5	Derek Anderson	.30	.14
	Brevin Knight		
□ 6	Michael Finley	.15	.07
□ 7	Danny Fortson	.20	.09
	Tony Battle		
	Bobby Jackson		
□ 8	Grant Hill	1.00	.45
□ 9	Joe Smith	.15	.07
□ 10	Charles Barkley	.25	.11
□ 11	Reggie Miller	.15	.07
□ 12	Lamond Murray	.10	.05
□ 13	Kobe Bryant	1.25	.55
□ 14	Alonzo Mourning	.15	.07
□ 15	Ray Allen	.20	.09
□ 16	Kevin Garnett	1.00	.45
□ 17	Stephon Marbury	.75	.35
□ 18	Kerry Kittles	.15	.07
□ 19	Patrick Ewing	.15	.07
□ 20	A.Hardaway	.60	.25
□ 21	Allen Iverson	.75	.35
□ 22	Jason Kidd	.30	.14
□ 23	Rasheed Wallace	.12	.05
□ 24	Mitch Richmond	.15	.07
□ 25	David Robinson	.25	.11
□ 26	Gary Payton	.25	.11
□ 27	D.Stoudamire	.30	.14
□ 28	John Stockton	.15	.07
□ 29	S.Abdur-Rahim	.50	.23
□ 30	Chris Webber	.40	.18

1997-98 Hoops High Voltage

Randomly inserted in series two hobby packs at a rate of one in 36, this 20-card set features fan favorites who can electrify a crowd. Card fronts carry a holo-foil background. Card backs are numbered with a "HV" prefix.

	MINT	NRMT
COMPLETE SET (20)	175.00	80.00
COMMON CARD (HV1-HV20)	2.50	1.10
SER.2 STATED ODDS 1:36 HOBBY		

		MINT	NRMT
□ HV1	Kobe Bryant	20.00	9.00
□ HV2	Eddie Jones	5.00	2.20
□ HV3	Ray Allen	3.00	1.35
□ HV4	A.Hardaway	10.00	4.50
□ HV5	Grant Hill	15.00	6.75
□ HV6	S.Abdur-Rahim	8.00	3.60
□ HV7	Marcus Camby	2.50	1.10
□ HV8	Allen Iverson	12.00	5.50
□ HV9	Kerry Kittles	2.50	1.10
□ HV10	Kevin Garnett	15.00	6.75
□ HV11	Stephon Marbury	12.00	5.50
□ HV12	Chris Webber	6.00	2.70
□ HV13	Antoine Walker	12.00	5.50
□ HV14	Michael Jordan	30.00	13.50
□ HV15	Tim Duncan	15.00	6.75
□ HV16	Dennis Rodman	10.00	4.50
□ HV17	Scottie Pippen	8.00	3.60
□ HV18	Shawn Kemp	8.00	3.60
□ HV19	Hakeem Olajuwon	5.00	2.20
□ HV20	Karl Malone	4.00	1.80

1997-98 Hoops High Voltage 500

This 20-card parallel set was randomly inserted into hobby packs of series two Hoops. These cards, as opposed to the base High Voltage insert, are serially numbered to 500 and feature a "Light Fantastic" background. Card backs are numbered with a "HV" prefix.

	MINT	NRMT
COMPLETE SET (20)	800.00	350.00
COMMON CARD (HV1-HV20)	12.00	5.50
RANDOM INSERTS IN SER.2 HOBBY		
STATED PRINT RUN 500 SERIAL #'d SETS		
☐ HV1 Kobe Bryant	100.00	45.00
☐ HV2 Eddie Jones	25.00	11.00
☐ HV3 Ray Allen	15.00	6.75
☐ HV4 A.Hardaway	50.00	22.00
☐ HV5 Grant Hill	80.00	36.00
☐ HV6 S.Abdur-Rahim	40.00	18.00
☐ HV7 Marcus Camby	12.00	5.50
☐ HV8 Allen Iverson	60.00	27.00
☐ HV9 Kerry Kittles	12.00	5.50
☐ HV10 Kevin Garnett	80.00	36.00
☐ HV11 Stephon Marbury	60.00	27.00
☐ HV12 Chris Webber	30.00	13.50
☐ HV13 Antoine Walker	60.00	27.00
☐ HV14 Michael Jordan	160.00	70.00
☐ HV15 Tim Duncan	80.00	36.00
☐ HV16 Dennis Rodman	50.00	22.00
☐ HV17 Scottie Pippen	40.00	18.00
☐ HV18 Shawn Kemp	40.00	18.00
☐ HV19 Hakeem Olajuwon	25.00	11.00
☐ HV20 Karl Malone	20.00	9.00

1997-98 Hoops HOOPerstars

Randomly inserted in series one packs at a rate of one in 288, this 10-card die cut set features the best and brightest NBA stars on etched foil backgrounds. Card backs are numbered with a "H" prefix.

	MINT	NRMT
COMPLETE SET (10)	300.00	135.00
COMMON CARD (H1-H10)	8.00	3.60
SER.1 STATED ODDS 1:288 HOBBY/RETAIL		
☐ H1 Michael Jordan	100.00	45.00
☐ H2 Grant Hill	50.00	22.00
☐ H3 Shaquille O'Neal	30.00	13.50
☐ H4 Ray Allen	10.00	4.50
☐ H5 Stephon Marbury	40.00	18.00
☐ H6 A.Hardaway	30.00	13.50
☐ H7 Allen Iverson	40.00	18.00
☐ H8 Shawn Kemp	25.00	11.00
☐ H9 Marcus Camby	8.00	3.60
☐ H10 S.Abdur-Rahim	25.00	11.00

1997-98 Hoops 911

Randomly inserted in series two packs at a rate of one in 288, this 10-card set features a two-piece card with some of the NBA's best "emergency" play-

ers. The card is contained in a lazer-cut sleeve. Card backs are numbered with a "N" prefix.

	MINT	NRMT
COMPLETE SET (10)	300.00	135.00
COMMON CARD (N1-N10)	15.00	6.75
SER.2 STATED ODDS 1:288 HOB/RET		
☐ N1 Michael Jordan	100.00	45.00
☐ N2 Grant Hill	50.00	22.00
☐ N3 Shawn Kemp	25.00	11.00
☐ N4 Stephon Marbury	40.00	18.00
☐ N5 D.Stoudamire	15.00	6.75
☐ N6 Shaquille O'Neal	30.00	13.50
☐ N7 S.Abdur-Rahim	25.00	11.00
☐ N8 Allen Iverson	40.00	18.00
☐ N9 Antoine Walker	40.00	18.00
☐ N10 A.Hardaway	30.00	13.50

1997-98 Hoops Rock the House

Randomly inserted in series two retail packs at a rate of one in 18, this 10-card set features some of the NBA's most crowd pleasing players. Card backs are numbered with a "RH" prefix.

	MINT	NRMT
COMPLETE SET (10)	70.00	32.00
COMMON CARD (RH1-RH10)	2.00	.90
SER.2 STATED ODDS 1:18 RETAIL		
☐ RH1 A.Hardaway	8.00	3.60
☐ RH2 Stephon Marbury	10.00	4.50
☐ RH3 Grant Hill	12.00	5.50
☐ RH4 Shaquille O'Neal	8.00	3.60
☐ RH5 Kerry Kittles	2.00	.90
☐ RH6 Michael Jordan	30.00	13.50
☐ RH7 Ray Allen	2.50	1.10
☐ RH8 D.Stoudamire	4.00	1.80

| ☐ RH9 Kevin Garnett | 12.00 | 5.50 |
| ☐ RH10 Shawn Kemp | 6.00 | 2.70 |

1997-98 Hoops Rookie Headliners

Randomly inserted in series one packs at a rate of one in 48, this 10-card set showcases the top rookies from the 1996-97 season with silhouetted action shots and a portrait shot on foil with a newspaper print background. Card backs are numbered with a "RH" prefix.

	MINT	NRMT
COMPLETE SET (10)	60.00	27.00
COMMON CARD (RH1-RH10)	1.25	.55
SEMISTARS	1.50	.70
UNLISTED STARS	2.50	1.10
SER.1 STATED ODDS 1:48 HOBBY/RETAIL		
☐ RH1 Antoine Walker	12.00	5.50
☐ RH2 Matt Maloney	1.25	.55
☐ RH3 Kobe Bryant	20.00	9.00
☐ RH4 Ray Allen	3.00	1.35
☐ RH5 Stephon Marbury	12.00	5.50
☐ RH6 Kerry Kittles	2.50	1.10
☐ RH7 John Wallace	1.50	.70
☐ RH8 Allen Iverson	12.00	5.50
☐ RH9 Marcus Camby	2.50	1.10
☐ RH10 S.Abdur-Rahim	8.00	3.60

1997-98 Hoops Talkin' Hoops

Inserted one in every series one pack, this 30-card set features color player photos of top NBA players with a commentary on the player by NBC personality

Bill Walton. Card backs are numbered with a "TH" prefix.

	MINT	NRMT
COMPLETE SET (30)	15.00	6.75
COMMON CARD (TH1-TH30)	.15	.07
SEMISTARS	.20	.09
UNLISTED STARS	.30	.14
ONE PER SER.1 PACK		

		MINT	NRMT
☐ TH1	Christian Laettner	.20	.09
☐ TH2	Antoine Walker	1.50	.70
☐ TH3	Glen Rice	.30	.14
☐ TH4	Dennis Rodman	1.25	.55
☐ TH5	Scottie Pippen	1.00	.45
☐ TH6	Terrell Brandon	.30	.14
☐ TH7	Michael Finley	.30	.14
☐ TH8	Grant Hill	2.00	.90
☐ TH9	Joe Smith	.30	.14
☐ TH10	Charles Barkley	.50	.23
☐ TH11	Hakeem Olajuwon	.60	.25
☐ TH12	Reggie Miller	.30	.14
☐ TH13	Loy Vaught	.15	.07
☐ TH14	Shaquille O'Neal	1.25	.55
☐ TH15	Kobe Bryant	2.50	1.10
☐ TH16	Kevin Garnett	2.00	.90
☐ TH17	Tom Gugliotta	.30	.14
☐ TH18	Kerry Kittles	.30	.14
☐ TH19	John Wallace	.20	.09
☐ TH20	Patrick Ewing	.30	.14
☐ TH21	Jerry Stackhouse	.30	.14
☐ TH22	David Robinson	.50	.23
☐ TH23	Gary Payton	.50	.23
☐ TH24	Shawn Kemp	1.00	.45
☐ TH25	D.Stoudamire	.60	.25
☐ TH26	John Stockton	.30	.14
☐ TH27	Karl Malone	.50	.23
☐ TH28	S.Abdur-Rahim	1.00	.45
☐ TH29	Juwan Howard	.30	.14
☐ TH30	Chris Webber	.75	.35

1997-98 Hoops Top of the World

Randomly inserted in series two packs at a rate of one in 48, this 15-card set features 15 of the top rookies from the 1997 draft class. Card backs are numbered with a "TW" prefix.

	MINT	NRMT
COMPLETE SET (15)	100.00	45.00
COMMON CARD (TW1-TW15)	1.50	.70
SEMISTARS	2.50	1.10
UNLISTED STARS	4.00	1.80
SER.2 STATED ODDS 1:48 HOB/RET		

		MINT	NRMT
☐ TW1	Tim Duncan	25.00	11.00
☐ TW2	Tim Thomas	12.00	5.50
☐ TW3	Tony Battie	4.00	1.80
☐ TW4	Keith Van Horn	20.00	9.00
☐ TW5	Antonio Daniels	5.00	2.20
☐ TW6	Derek Anderson	6.00	2.70
☐ TW7	Chauncey Billups	8.00	3.60
☐ TW8	Tracy McGrady	12.00	5.50
☐ TW9	Danny Fortson	4.00	1.80
☐ TW10	Austin Croshere	2.50	1.10
☐ TW11	Tariq Abdul-Wahad	2.50	1.10
☐ TW12	Adonal Foyle	2.50	1.10
☐ TW13	Rodrick Rhodes	2.50	1.10
☐ TW14	Ron Mercer	15.00	6.75
☐ TW15	Charles Smith	1.50	.70

1993-94 Jam Session

This 240-card set was issued in 1993 by Fleer and features oversized cards measuring approximately 2 1/2" by 4 3/4". Cards were issued in 12-card packs (36 per box) with a suggested retail pack price of 1.59. One insert card is included in every pack. The full-bleed fronts feature glossy color action player photos. Across the bottom edge of the picture appears a team color-coded bar with the player's name, position and team. The NBA Jam Session logo is superposed on the lower right corner. The backs are divided in half vertically with the left side carrying a second action shot and on the right side a panel with a background that fades from green to white. On the panel appears biography, career highlights, statistics and team logo. The cards are numbered on the back and checklisted below alphabetically within and according to teams. Rookie Cards of note include A.Hardaway, Jamal Mashburn and Chris Webber.

	MINT	NRMT
COMPLETE SET (240)	30.00	13.50
COMMON CARD (1-240)	.10	.05
SEMISTARS	.25	.11
UNLISTED STARS	.50	.23

		MINT	NRMT
☐ 1	Stacey Augmon	.10	.05
☐ 2	Mookie Blaylock	.25	.11
☐ 3	Doug Edwards	.10	.05
☐ 4	Duane Ferrell	.10	.05
☐ 5	Paul Graham	.10	.05
☐ 6	Adam Keefe	.10	.05
☐ 7	Jon Koncak	.10	.05
☐ 8	Dominique Wilkins	.50	.23
☐ 9	Kevin Willis	.10	.05
☐ 10	Alaa Abdelnaby	.10	.05
☐ 11	Dee Brown	.10	.05
☐ 12	Sherman Douglas	.10	.05
☐ 13	Rick Fox	.10	.05
☐ 14	Kevin Gamble	.10	.05
☐ 15	Xavier McDaniel	.10	.05
☐ 16	Robert Parish	.25	.11
☐ 17	Muggsy Bogues	.25	.11
☐ 18	Scott Burrell	.50	.23
☐ 19	Dell Curry	.10	.05
☐ 20	Kenny Gattison	.10	.05
☐ 21	Hersey Hawkins	.25	.11
☐ 22	Eddie Johnson	.10	.05
☐ 23	Larry Johnson	.50	.23
☐ 24	Alonzo Mourning	.75	.35
☐ 25	Johnny Newman	.10	.05
☐ 26	David Wingate	.10	.05
☐ 27	B.J. Armstrong	.10	.05
☐ 28	Corie Blount	.10	.05
☐ 29	Bill Cartwright	.10	.05
☐ 30	Horace Grant	.25	.11
☐ 31	Stacey King	.10	.05
☐ 32	John Paxson	.10	.05
☐ 33	Michael Jordan	6.00	2.70
☐ 34	Scottie Pippen	1.50	.70
☐ 35	Scott Williams	.10	.05
☐ 36	Terrell Brandon	.50	.23
☐ 37	Brad Daugherty	.10	.05
☐ 38	Danny Ferry	.10	.05
☐ 39	Tyrone Hill	.10	.05
☐ 40	Chris Mills	.75	.35
☐ 41	Larry Nance	.25	.11
☐ 42	Mark Price	.25	.11
☐ 43	Gerald Wilkins	.10	.05
☐ 44	John Williams	.10	.05
☐ 45	Terry Davis	.10	.05
☐ 46	Derek Harper	.25	.11
☐ 47	Donald Hodge	.10	.05
☐ 48	Jim Jackson	.50	.23
☐ 49	Jamal Mashburn	1.25	.55
☐ 50	Sean Rooks	.10	.05
☐ 51	Doug Smith	.10	.05
☐ 52	M.Abdul-Rauf	.10	.05
☐ 53	Kevin Brooks	.10	.05
☐ 54	LaPhonso Ellis	.25	.11
☐ 55	Mark Macon	.10	.05
☐ 56	D.Mutombo	.50	.23
☐ 57	Rodney Rogers	.10	.05
☐ 58	Bryant Stith	.10	.05
☐ 59	Reggie Williams	.10	.05
☐ 60	Joe Dumars	.50	.23
☐ 61	Sean Elliott	.25	.11
☐ 62	Bill Laimbeer	.10	.05
☐ 63	Terry Mills	.10	.05
☐ 64	Olden Polynice	.10	.05
☐ 65	Alvin Robertson	.10	.05
☐ 66	Isiah Thomas	.50	.23
☐ 67	Victor Alexander	.10	.05
☐ 68	Chris Gatling	.10	.05
☐ 69	Tim Hardaway	.60	.25
☐ 70	Byron Houston	.10	.05
☐ 71	Sarunas Marciulionis	.10	.05
☐ 72	Chris Mullin	.50	.23
☐ 73	Billy Owens	.10	.05
☐ 74	Latrell Sprewell	.50	.23
☐ 75	Chris Webber	3.00	1.35
☐ 76	Scott Brooks	.10	.05
☐ 77	Matt Bullard	.10	.05
☐ 78	Sam Cassell	1.25	.55
☐ 79	Mario Elie	.10	.05
☐ 80	Carl Herrera	.10	.05
☐ 81	Robert Horry	.25	.11
☐ 82	Vernon Maxwell	.10	.05
☐ 83	Hakeem Olajuwon	1.00	.45
☐ 84	Kenny Smith	.10	.05
☐ 85	Otis Thorpe	.25	.11
☐ 86	Dale Davis	.10	.05
☐ 87	Vern Fleming	.10	.05
☐ 88	Scott Haskin	.10	.05
☐ 89	Reggie Miller	.50	.23
☐ 90	Sam Mitchell	.10	.05

□			
□ 91	Pooh Richardson	.10	.05
□ 92	Detlef Schrempf	.25	.11
□ 93	Malik Sealy	.10	.05
□ 94	Rik Smits	.25	.11
□ 95	Terry Dehere	.10	.05
□ 96	Ron Harper	.25	.11
□ 97	Mark Jackson	.25	.11
□ 98	Danny Manning	.10	.05
□ 99	Stanley Roberts	.10	.05
□ 100	Loy Vaught	.25	.11
□ 101	John Williams	.10	.05
□ 102	Sam Bowie	.10	.05
□ 103	Elden Campbell	.25	.11
□ 104	Doug Christie	.10	.05
□ 105	Vlade Divac	.25	.11
□ 106	James Edwards	.10	.05
□ 107	George Lynch	.10	.05
□ 108	Anthony Peeler	.10	.05
□ 109	Sedale Threatt	.10	.05
□ 110	James Worthy	.50	.23
□ 111	Bimbo Coles	.10	.05
□ 112	Grant Long	.10	.05
□ 113	Harold Miner	.10	.05
□ 114	Glen Rice	.50	.23
□ 115	John Salley	.10	.05
□ 116	Rony Seikaly	.10	.05
□ 117	Brian Shaw	.10	.05
□ 118	Steve Smith	.25	.11
□ 119	Anthony Avent	.10	.05
□ 120	Vin Baker	3.00	1.35
□ 121	Jon Barry	.10	.05
□ 122	Frank Brickowski	.10	.05
□ 123	Todd Day	.10	.05
□ 124	Blue Edwards	.10	.05
□ 125	Brad Lohaus	.10	.05
□ 126	Lee Mayberry	.10	.05
□ 127	Eric Murdock	.10	.05
□ 128	Ken Norman	.10	.05
□ 129	Thurl Bailey	.10	.05
□ 130	Mike Brown	.10	.05
□ 131	Christian Laettner	.50	.23
□ 132	Luc Longley	.25	.11
□ 133	Chuck Person	.10	.05
□ 134	Chris Smith	.10	.05
□ 135	Doug West	.10	.05
□ 136	Micheal Williams	.10	.05
□ 137	Kenny Anderson	.25	.11
□ 138	Benoit Benjamin	.10	.05
□ 139	Derrick Coleman	.25	.11
□ 140	Armon Gilliam	.10	.05
□ 141	Rick Mahorn	.10	.05
□ 142	Chris Morris	.10	.05
□ 143	Rumeal Robinson	.10	.05
□ 144	Rex Walters	.10	.05
□ 145	Greg Anthony	.10	.05
□ 146	Rolando Blackman	.10	.05
□ 147	Tony Campbell	.10	.05
□ 148	Hubert Davis	.10	.05
□ 149	Patrick Ewing	.50	.23
□ 150	Anthony Mason	.25	.11
□ 151	Charles Oakley	.25	.11
□ 152	Doc Rivers	.25	.11
□ 153	Charles Smith	.10	.05
□ 154	John Starks	.25	.11
□ 155	Herb Williams	.10	.05
□ 156	Nick Anderson	.25	.11
□ 157	Anthony Bowie	.10	.05
□ 158	Litterial Green	.10	.05
□ 159	A.Hardaway	8.00	3.60
□ 160	Shaquille O'Neal	2.00	.90
□ 161	Donald Royal	.10	.05
□ 162	Dennis Scott	.25	.11
□ 163	Scott Skiles	.10	.05
□ 164	Jeff Turner	.10	.05
□ 165	Dana Barros	.10	.05
□ 166	Shawn Bradley	.60	.25
□ 167	Johnny Dawkins	.10	.05
□ 168	Greg Graham	.10	.05
□ 169	Jeff Hornacek	.25	.11
□ 170	Moses Malone	.50	.23
□ 171	Tim Perry	.10	.05
□ 172	C.Weatherspoon	.10	.05
□ 173	Danny Ainge	.25	.11
□ 174	Charles Barkley	.75	.35
□ 175	Cedric Ceballos	.25	.11
□ 176	A.C. Green	.25	.11

□			
□ 177	Frank Johnson	.10	.05
□ 178	Kevin Johnson	.25	.11
□ 179	Negele Knight	.10	.05
□ 180	Malcolm Mackey	.10	.05
□ 181	Dan Majerle	.25	.11
□ 182	Oliver Miller	.10	.05
□ 183	Mark West	.10	.05
□ 184	Clyde Drexler	.60	.25
□ 185	Chris Dudley	.10	.05
□ 186	Harvey Grant	.10	.05
□ 187	Jerome Kersey	.10	.05
□ 188	Terry Porter	.10	.05
□ 189	Clifford Robinson	.25	.11
□ 190	James Robinson	.10	.05
□ 191	Rod Strickland	.25	.11
□ 192	Buck Williams	.25	.11
□ 193	Randy Brown	.10	.05
□ 194	Duane Causwell	.10	.05
□ 195	Bobby Hurley	.25	.11
□ 196	Mitch Richmond	.50	.23
□ 197	Lionel Simmons	.10	.05
□ 198	Wayman Tisdale	.10	.05
□ 199	Spud Webb	.25	.11
□ 200	Walt Williams	.25	.11
□ 201	Willie Anderson	.10	.05
□ 202	Antoine Carr	.10	.05
□ 203	Terry Cummings	.10	.05
□ 204	Lloyd Daniels	.10	.05
□ 205	Vinny Del Negro	.10	.05
□ 206	Sleepy Floyd	.10	.05
□ 207	Avery Johnson	.10	.05
□ 208	J.R. Reid	.10	.05
□ 209	David Robinson	.75	.35
□ 210	Dennis Rodman	2.00	.90
□ 211	Michael Cage	.10	.05
□ 212	Kendall Gill	.25	.11
□ 213	Ervin Johnson	.25	.11
□ 214	Shawn Kemp	1.50	.70
□ 215	Derrick McKey	.10	.05
□ 216	Nate McMillan	.10	.05
□ 217	Gary Payton	.75	.35
□ 218	Sam Perkins	.25	.11
□ 219	Ricky Pierce	.10	.05
□ 220	Isaac Austin	.10	.05
□ 221	David Benoit	.10	.05
□ 222	Tom Chambers	.10	.05
□ 223	Tyrone Corbin	.10	.05
□ 224	Mark Eaton	.10	.05
□ 225	Jay Humphries	.10	.05
□ 226	Jeff Malone	.10	.05
□ 227	Karl Malone	.75	.35
□ 228	John Stockton	.50	.23
□ 229	Luther Wright	.10	.05
□ 230	Michael Adams	.10	.05
□ 231	Calbert Cheaney	.50	.23
□ 232	Kevin Duckworth	.10	.05
□ 233	Pervis Ellison	.10	.05
□ 234	Tom Gugliotta	.50	.23
□ 235	Buck Johnson	.10	.05
□ 236	Doug Overton	.10	.05
□ 237	LaBradford Smith	.10	.05
□ 238	Larry Stewart	.10	.05
□ 239	Checklist	.10	.05
□ 240	Checklist	.10	.05

1993-94 Jam Session Gamebreakers

Randomly inserted into 12-card packs at a rate of one in four, this eight-card 2 1/2" by 4 3/4" set features some of the NBA's top players. The borderless fronts feature color action cutouts on multicolored backgrounds highlighted by grid lines. The player's name appears in gold foil at the lower

left. The back features a color player head shot with a screened background similar to the front. The player's name appears above the photo, career highlights appear below. The cards are numbered on the back as "X of 8."

	MINT	NRMT
COMPLETE SET (8)	4.00	1.80
COMMON CARD (1-8)	.25	.11
SEMISTARS	.50	.23
UNLISTED STARS	.75	.35
STATED ODDS 1:4		

□ 1	Charles Barkley	1.25	.55
□ 2	Tim Hardaway	1.00	.45
□ 3	Kevin Johnson	.50	.23
□ 4	Dan Majerle	.50	.23
□ 5	Scottie Pippen	2.50	1.10
□ 6	Mark Price	.25	.11
□ 7	John Starks	.50	.23
□ 8	Dominique Wilkins	.75	.35

1993-94 Jam Session Rookie Standouts

Randomly inserted in 12-card packs at a rate of one in four, this oversized (2 1/2" by 4 3/4") eight-card set features borderless fronts with full-color player action photos. The player's name appears in gold-foil lettering in the lower left corner. The back features a color player action head shot with the player's statistics below. The cards

are numbered on the back as "X of 8."

	MINT	NRMT
COMPLETE SET (8)	20.00	9.00
COMMON (1-8)	.50	.23
SEMISTARS	.75	.35
UNLISTED ALLS	1.25	.55
STATED ODDS 1:4		
☐ 1 Vin Baker	5.00	2.20
☐ 2 Shawn Bradley	1.25	.55
☐ 3 Calbert Cheaney	.75	.35
☐ 4 A.Hardaway UER	12.00	5.50
Text states drafted after		
senior year instead of junior		
☐ 5 Bobby Hurley	.50	.23
☐ 6 Jamal Mashburn	2.00	.90
☐ 7 Rodney Rogers	.50	.23
☐ 8 Chris Webber	5.00	2.20

1993-94 Jam Session Second Year Stars

Randomly inserted into Jam Session 12-card packs at a rate of one in four, this eight-card 2 1/2" by 4 3/4" set features some of the NBA's top second-year players. The borderless fronts feature a color action cutout on a rainbow-colored background. The player's name appears in gold foil in the lower right. The back features a color player head-shot with screened rainbow background. The player's name appears above the photo with a player profile displayed below. The cards are numbered on the back as "X of 8."

	MINT	NRMT
COMPLETE SET (8)	5.00	2.20
COMMON (1-8)	.25	.11
SEMISTARS	.40	.18
UNLISTED STARS	.75	.35
STATED ODDS 1:4		
☐ 1 Tom Gugliotta	.75	.35
☐ 2 Jim Jackson	.75	.35
☐ 3 Christian Laettner	.75	.35
☐ 4 Oliver Miller	.25	.11
☐ 5 Harold Miner	.25	.11
☐ 6 Alonzo Mourning	1.25	.55
☐ 7 Shaquille O'Neal	3.00	1.35
☐ 8 Walt Williams	.40	.18

1993-94 Jam Session Slam Dunk Heroes

Randomly inserted in 12-card Jam Session packs at a rate of one in four, this eight-card 2 1/2" by 4 3/4" set features some of the NBA's top slam dunkers. The borderless fronts feature color action cutouts on multicolored posterized background. The player's name appears vertically in gold foil near the bottom. The back features a color player head shot. The player's name appears above the photo, a player profile is displayed below. The cards are numbered on the back as "X of 8."

	MINT	NRMT
COMPLETE SET (8)	10.00	4.50
COMMON CARD (1-8)	.60	.25
SEMISTARS	.75	.35
STATED ODDS 1:4		
☐ 1 Patrick Ewing	.75	.35
☐ 2 Larry Johnson	.60	.25
☐ 3 Shawn Kemp	2.50	1.10
☐ 4 Karl Malone	1.25	.55
☐ 5 Alonzo Mourning	1.25	.55
☐ 6 Hakeem Olajuwon	1.50	.70
☐ 7 Shaquille O'Neal	3.00	1.35
☐ 8 David Robinson	1.25	.55

1994-95 Jam Session

The complete 1994-95 Jam Session set consists of 200 oversized (2 1/2" by 4 3/4") cards. The cards were issued in 12-card packs with 36 packs per box. Each pack has one card from one of the four insert sets. Suggested retail price was $1.59 per pack. Cello packs consisting of three player cards and a cover card were given away at McDonald's restaurants

in the Phoenix area to promote the Jam Session featured at the NBA All-Star weekend. The fronts have full-bleed color action photos that are tightly cropped so the player takes up a larger percentage of the card than in most sets. The NBA Jam Session logo is superimposed on the lower right corner and the player's name and team is just above it in the teams color. The backs have color-action photos on the right side with statistics and information on the left that is set against the color of the player's team. The entire card is UV coated as are all the insert sets. The cards are numbered on the back and grouped alphabetically within teams. Rookie Cards of note in this set include Grant Hill, Eddie Jones and Jason Kidd.

	MINT	NRMT
COMPLETE SET (200)	30.00	13.50
COMMON CARD (1-200)	.10	.05
SEMISTARS	.25	.11
UNLISTED STARS	.50	.23
☐ 1 Stacey Augmon	.10	.05
☐ 2 Mookie Blaylock	.25	.11
☐ 3 Tyrone Corbin	.10	.05
☐ 4 Craig Ehlo	.10	.05
☐ 5 Ken Norman	.10	.05
☐ 6 Kevin Willis	.10	.05
☐ 7 Dee Brown	.10	.05
☐ 8 Sherman Douglas	.10	.05
☐ 9 Acie Earl	.10	.05
☐ 10 Blue Edwards	.10	.05
☐ 11 Pervis Ellison	.10	.05
☐ 12 Rick Fox	.10	.05
☐ 13 Xavier McDaniel	.10	.05
☐ 14 Eric Montross	.10	.05
☐ 15 Dino Radja	.10	.05
☐ 16 Dominique Wilkins	.50	.23
☐ 17 Michael Adams	.10	.05
☐ 18 Muggsy Bogues	.25	.11
☐ 19 Dell Curry	.10	.05
☐ 20 Kenny Gattison	.10	.05
☐ 21 Hersey Hawkins	.25	.11
☐ 22 Larry Johnson	.25	.11
☐ 23 Alonzo Mourning	.60	.25
☐ 24 Robert Parish	.25	.11
☐ 25 B.J. Armstrong	.10	.05
☐ 26 Ron Harper	.25	.11
☐ 27 Steve Kerr	.25	.11
☐ 28 Toni Kukoc	.50	.23
☐ 29 Pete Myers	.10	.05

□ 30	Will Perdue	.10	.05
□ 31	Scottie Pippen	1.50	.70
□ 32	Terrell Brandon	.50	.23
□ 33	Michael Cage	.10	.05
□ 34	Brad Daugherty	.10	.05
□ 35	Chris Mills	.25	.11
□ 36	Bobby Phills	.10	.05
□ 37	Mark Price	.10	.05
□ 38	Gerald Wilkins	.10	.05
□ 39	John Williams	.10	.05
□ 40	Jim Jackson	.25	.11
□ 41	Jason Kidd	4.00	1.80
□ 42	Jamal Mashburn	.50	.23
□ 43	Sean Rooks	.10	.05
□ 44	Doug Smith	.10	.05
□ 45	M.Abdul-Rauf	.10	.05
□ 46	LaPhonso Ellis	.25	.11
□ 47	D.Mutombo	.50	.23
□ 48	Robert Pack	.10	.05
□ 49	Rodney Rogers	.10	.05
□ 50	Jalen Rose	.50	.23
□ 51	Bryant Stith	.10	.05
□ 52	Reggie Williams	.10	.05
□ 53	Bill Curley	.10	.05
□ 54	Joe Dumars	.50	.23
□ 55	Grant Hill	6.00	2.70
□ 56	Allan Houston	.50	.23
□ 57	Lindsey Hunter	.25	.11
□ 58	Oliver Miller	.10	.05
□ 59	Terry Mills	.10	.05
□ 60	Mark West	.10	.05
□ 61	Chris Gatling	.10	.05
□ 62	Tim Hardaway	.60	.25
□ 63	Chris Mullin	.50	.23
□ 64	Billy Owens	.10	.05
□ 65	Ricky Pierce	.10	.05
□ 66	Latrell Sprewell	.25	.11
□ 67	Chris Webber	1.25	.55
□ 68	Sam Cassell	.50	.23
□ 69	Mario Elie	.10	.05
□ 70	Carl Herrera	.10	.05
□ 71	Robert Horry	.25	.11
□ 72	Vernon Maxwell	.10	.05
□ 73	Hakeem Olajuwon	1.00	.45
□ 74	Kenny Smith	.10	.05
□ 75	Otis Thorpe	.25	.11
□ 76	Antonio Davis	.10	.05
□ 77	Dale Davis	.10	.05
□ 78	Mark Jackson	.25	.11
□ 79	Derrick McKey	.10	.05
□ 80	Reggie Miller	.50	.23
□ 81	Byron Scott	.25	.11
□ 82	Rik Smits	.25	.11
□ 83	Haywoode Workman	.10	.05
□ 84	Gary Grant	.10	.05
□ 85	Pooh Richardson	.10	.05
□ 86	Stanley Roberts	.10	.05
□ 87	Elmore Spencer	.10	.05
□ 88	Loy Vaught	.25	.11
□ 89	Elden Campbell	.10	.05
□ 90	Cedric Ceballos	.25	.11
□ 91	Doug Christie	.10	.05
□ 92	Vlade Divac	.25	.11
□ 93	Eddie Jones	4.00	1.80
□ 94	George Lynch	.10	.05
□ 95	Anthony Peeler	.10	.05
□ 96	Nick Van Exel	.50	.23
□ 97	James Worthy	.50	.23
□ 98	Grant Long	.10	.05
□ 99	Harold Miner	.10	.05
□ 100	Glen Rice	.50	.23
□ 101	John Salley	.10	.05
□ 102	Rony Seikaly	.10	.05
□ 103	Steve Smith	.25	.11
□ 104	Vin Baker	1.25	.55
□ 105	Jon Barry	.10	.05
□ 106	Todd Day	.10	.05
□ 107	Lee Mayberry	.10	.05
□ 108	Eric Murdock	.10	.05
□ 109	Stacey King	.10	.05
□ 110	Christian Laettner	.25	.11
□ 111	Donyell Marshall	.60	.25
□ 112	Isaiah Rider	.25	.11
□ 113	Doug West	.10	.05
□ 114	Micheal Williams	.10	.05
□ 115	Kenny Anderson	.25	.11
□ 116	P.J. Brown	.10	.05
□ 117	Derrick Coleman	.25	.11
□ 118	Yinka Dare	.10	.05
□ 119	Kevin Edwards	.10	.05
□ 120	Armon Gilliam	.10	.05
□ 121	Chris Morris	.10	.05
□ 122	Anthony Bonner	.10	.05
□ 123	Hubert Davis	.10	.05
□ 124	Patrick Ewing	.50	.23
□ 125	Derek Harper	.25	.11
□ 126	Anthony Mason	.25	.11
□ 127	Charles Oakley	.25	.11
□ 128	Doc Rivers	.25	.11
□ 129	Charles Smith	.10	.05
□ 130	John Starks	.25	.11
□ 131	Charlie Ward	.25	.11
□ 132	Nick Anderson	.25	.11
□ 133	Anthony Bowie	.10	.05
□ 134	Horace Grant	.25	.11
□ 135	A.Hardaway	2.00	.90
□ 136	Shaquille O'Neal	2.00	.90
□ 137	Dennis Scott	.25	.11
□ 138	Jeff Turner	.10	.05
□ 139	Dana Barros	.10	.05
□ 140	Shawn Bradley	.25	.11
□ 141	Johnny Dawkins	.10	.05
□ 142	Jeff Malone	.10	.05
□ 143	Tim Perry	.10	.05
□ 144	C.Weatherspoon	.10	.05
□ 145	Scott Williams	.10	.05
□ 146	Danny Ainge	.25	.11
□ 147	Charles Barkley	.75	.35
□ 148	A.C. Green	.25	.11
□ 149	Kevin Johnson	.25	.11
□ 150	Joe Kleine	.10	.05
□ 151	Antonio Lang	.10	.05
□ 152	Dan Majerle	.25	.11
□ 153	Danny Manning	.10	.05
□ 154	Wayman Tisdale	.10	.05
□ 155	Clyde Drexler	.60	.25
□ 156	Harvey Grant	.10	.05
□ 157	Tracy Murray	.10	.05
□ 158	Terry Porter	.10	.05
□ 159	Clifford Robinson	.25	.11
□ 160	Rod Strickland	.25	.11
□ 161	Buck Williams	.25	.11
□ 162	Bobby Hurley	.10	.05
□ 163	Olden Polynice	.10	.05
□ 164	Mitch Richmond	.50	.23
□ 165	Lionel Simmons	.10	.05
□ 166	Spud Webb	.25	.11
□ 167	Walt Williams	.10	.05
□ 168	Willie Anderson	.10	.05
□ 169	Terry Cummings	.10	.05
□ 170	Vinny Del Negro	.10	.05
□ 171	Sean Elliott	.25	.11
□ 172	Avery Johnson	.10	.05
□ 173	Chuck Person	.10	.05
□ 174	J.R. Reid	.10	.05
□ 175	David Robinson	.75	.35
□ 176	Dennis Rodman	2.00	.90
□ 177	Bill Cartwright	.10	.05
□ 178	Kendall Gill	.25	.11
□ 179	Shawn Kemp	1.50	.70
□ 180	Nate McMillan	.10	.05
□ 181	Gary Payton	.75	.35
□ 182	Sam Perkins	.25	.11
□ 183	Detlef Schrempf	.25	.11
□ 184	David Benoit	.10	.05
□ 185	Jeff Hornacek	.25	.11
□ 186	Jay Humphries	.10	.05
□ 187	Karl Malone	.75	.35
□ 188	Bryon Russell	.25	.11
□ 189	Felton Spencer	.10	.05
□ 190	John Stockton	.50	.23
□ 191	Mitchell Butler	.10	.05
□ 192	Rex Chapman	.10	.05
□ 193	Calbert Cheaney	.25	.11
□ 194	Tom Gugliotta	.50	.23
□ 195	Don MacLean	.10	.05
□ 196	Gheorghe Muresan	.25	.11
□ 197	Scott Skiles	.10	.05
□ 198	Checklist	.10	.05
□ 199	Checklist	.10	.05
□ 200	Checklist	.10	.05

1994-95
Jam Session
Flashing Stars

This eight card oversized (2 1/2" by 4 3/4") set was randomly inserted in 12-packs at a rate of approximately one in two. The set is composed of the flashiest players in the game like A.Hardaway and Reggie Miller. The fronts have full-bleed color action photos similar to the regular set but the background has swirling colors. The player's name and words "Flashing Star" are in gold foil at the bottom. The NBA Jam Session logo is superimposed on the upper right corner. The backs have color action photos and information explaining he is a "Flashing star." The cards are numbered on the back as "X of 8" and are sequenced in alphabetical order.

	MINT	NRMT
COMPLETE SET (8)	5.00	2.20
COMMON CARD (1-8)	.25	.11
SEMISTARS	.50	.23
UNLISTED STARS	.75	.35
STATED ODDS 1:2		

□ 1	A.Hardaway	3.00	1.35
□ 2	Robert Horry	.25	.11
□ 3	Dan Majerle	.50	.23
□ 4	Reggie Miller	.75	.35
□ 5	Mitch Richmond	.75	.35
□ 6	Isaiah Rider	.50	.23
□ 7	Latrell Sprewell	.50	.23
□ 8	Dominique Wilkins	.75	.35

1994-95
Jam Session
Gamebreakers

This eight card oversized (2 1/2" by 4 3/4") set was randomly inserted in 12-card packs at a rate of one in four. The set is composed of players who can take control of the game. The fronts have full-bleed color

action photos similar to the regular set but the background is a basketball going through a net. The player image is also pushed out slightly which can also be seen from the back to give it a 3-D look. The NBA Jam Session logo is superimposed on the upper right corner. The backs have three layers to it. The background has two colors that are different on each card. A full-color action photo of the player is the middle layer. Up front is the player name in the middle and player information is a hazy white box underneath. The cards are numbered on the back as "X of 8" and are sequenced in alphabetical order.

	MINT	NRMT
COMPLETE SET (8)	10.00	4.50
COMMON CARD (1-8)	.75	.35
STATED ODDS 1:4		

		MINT	NRMT
☐ 1	Charles Barkley	1.25	.55
☐ 2	Patrick Ewing	.75	.35
☐ 3	Karl Malone	1.25	.55
☐ 4	Alonzo Mourning	1.00	.45
☐ 5	Hakeem Olajuwon	1.50	.70
☐ 6	Shaquille O'Neal	3.00	1.35
☐ 7	Scottie Pippen	2.50	1.10
☐ 8	David Robinson	1.25	.55

1994-95 Jam Session Rookie Standouts

This 20-card oversized (2 1/2" by 4 3/4") set was available exclusively via mail. Information on obtaining the set was on the packs and you had to pay $3.95 to receive the set. The wrapper offer expired on June 30th, 1995. The set contains a selection of the top rookies from the 1994-95 season. The fronts have full-bleed color action photos on a painted background with a black and white action photo in the looming behind.

The NBA Jam Session logo is superimposed on the upper left corner. The player's name and the "Rookie Standout" with a basketball under it are in gold foil at the bottom of the card. The backs have a full color action photo also on a painted background and information on the rookie particularly about his college career. The cards are numbered on the back as "X of 20" and are sequenced in alphabetical order.

	MINT	NRMT
COMPLETE SET (20)	15.00	6.75
COMMON CARD (1-20)	.25	.11
SEMISTARS	.50	.23
SET WAS AVAILABLE BY WRAPPER OFFER		

		MINT	NRMT
☐ 1	Brian Grant	.50	.23
☐ 2	Grant Hill	6.00	2.70
☐ 3	Juwan Howard	2.50	1.10
☐ 4	Eddie Jones	4.00	1.80
☐ 5	Jason Kidd	4.00	1.80
☐ 6	Donyell Marshall	.50	.23
☐ 7	Eric Montross	.25	.11
☐ 8	Lamond Murray	.25	.11
☐ 9	Wesley Person	.50	.23
☐ 10	Khalid Reeves	.25	.11
☐ 11	Glenn Robinson	2.00	.90
☐ 12	Carlos Rogers	.25	.11
☐ 13	Jalen Rose	.50	.23
☐ 14	Clifford Rozier	.25	.11
☐ 15	Dickey Simpkins	.25	.11
☐ 16	Michael Smith	.25	.11
☐ 17	Anthony Tucker	.25	.11
☐ 18	Charlie Ward	.25	.11
☐ 19	Monty Williams	.25	.11
☐ 20	Sharone Wright	.25	.11

1994-95 Jam Session Second Year Stars

This eight card oversized (2 1/2" by 4 3/4") set was randomly inserted in 12-card packs at a rate of one in four. The set consists of the best rookies from the 93-94 crop. The fronts are laid out horizontally and have full-bleed color action photos. The player is surrounded by a glowing yellow. The background has

a close-up of his face from the action shot and copies of the shot in television screens behind that. The bottom says the player's name and "Second Year Star" in gold foil. The backs are laid out vertically with a full color action photo also surrounded by a glowing yellow on the left with player information on the right. The background is the same player photo set in numerous television screens similar to the front. The cards are numbered on the back as "X of 8" and are sequenced in alphabetical order.

	MINT	NRMT
COMPLETE SET (8)	8.00	3.60
COMMON CARD (1-8)	.25	.11
SEMISTARS	.40	.18
UNLISTED STARS	.75	.35
STATED ODDS 1:4		

		MINT	NRMT
☐ 1	Vin Baker	2.00	.90
☐ 2	A.Hardaway	3.00	1.35
☐ 3	Lindsey Hunter	.40	.18
☐ 4	Toni Kukoc	.75	.35
☐ 5	Jamal Mashburn	.75	.35
☐ 6	Dino Radja	.25	.11
☐ 7	Isaiah Rider	.40	.18
☐ 8	Chris Webber	2.00	.90

1994-95 Jam Session Slam Dunk Heroes

Cards from this eight-card over-sized (2 1/2 by 4 3/4") set were

randomly inserted in packs at a rate of one in 36. The set is made up of players who jam with authority, namely centers and forwards. The cards have a 100% etched foil design. The fronts have a full color action photo with the player's name and the words "Slam Dunk Hero" boxing in a net are at the bottom in gold foil. The backs have a fuller color action photo on the left with player information on the right. The background on both the fronts and backs have a psychedelic look to it with basketballs floating about. The cards are numbered on the back as "X of 8" and are sequenced in alphabetical order.

	MINT	NRMT
COMPLETE SET (8)	75.00	34.00
COMMON CARD (1-8)	3.00	1.35
SEMISTARS	4.00	1.80
UNLISTED STARS	6.00	2.70
STATED ODDS 1:36		

		MINT	NRMT
☐ 1	Charles Barkley	10.00	4.50
☐ 2	Larry Johnson	3.00	1.35
☐ 3	Shawn Kemp	20.00	9.00
☐ 4	Jamal Mashburn	4.00	1.80
☐ 5	D.Mutombo	6.00	2.70
☐ 6	Hakeem Olajuwon	12.00	5.50
☐ 7	Shaquille O'Neal	25.00	11.00
☐ 8	Chris Webber	15.00	6.75

1995-96 Jam Session

The 1995-96 NBA Jam Session regular card set was issued in one series of 118 cards with 2 checklist cards. Cards were distributed in eight card hobby and retail packs carrying a suggested retail price of $1.59. Forty of the cards are called "Connection Collection" and feature two players that form a unique tandem. The 78 regular cards are full-bleed color player action photos with a strip at the top with the word "JAM" repeating. Backs include a full color action player

shot with a screened strip containing the players biography, a short personality profile, a player rating and NBA career summary. The "Connection Collection" cards are borderless with one-color backgrounds and a full-color action player cutout. Backs of the Connection Collection cards feature an extreme vertical and skewed full-color action photo of the player with a player biography, career stats and a short player profile. Cards are grouped alphabetically by team name. There are no Rookie Cards in this set.

	MINT	NRMT
COMPLETE SET (120)	25.00	11.00
COMMON CARD (1-120)	.15	.07
SEMISTARS	.20	.09
UNLISTED STARS	.40	.18
COMP.DIE CUT SET (120)	60.00	27.00
COMMON DIE CUT (1-120)	.30	.14
*DIE CUT STARS: 1.25X TO 2.5X HI COLUMN		
ONE DIE CUT PER PACK		
HILL TRIB: STATED ODDS 1:360		

		MINT	NRMT
☐ 1	Stacey Augmon CC	.15	.07
☐ 2	Mookie Blaylock	.20	.07
☐ 3	Grant Long	.15	.07
☐ 4	Steve Smith	.20	.07
☐ 5	Dee Brown CC	.15	.07
☐ 6	Sherman Douglas	.15	.07
☐ 7	Eric Montross	.15	.07
☐ 8	Dino Radja	.15	.07
☐ 9	Muggsy Bogues CC	.20	.09
☐ 10	Scott Burrell	.15	.07
☐ 11	Larry Johnson CC	.20	.07
☐ 12	Alonzo Mourning	.40	.18
☐ 13	Michael Jordan CC	5.00	2.20
☐ 14	Steve Kerr	.20	.09
☐ 15	Toni Kukoc CC	.20	.07
☐ 16	Scottie Pippen	1.25	.55
☐ 17	Terrell Brandon	.40	.18
☐ 18	Tyrone Hill	.15	.07
☐ 19	Mark Price CC	.15	.07
☐ 20	John Williams	.15	.07
☐ 21	Jim Jackson	.20	.07
☐ 22	Popeye Jones CC	.15	.07
☐ 23	Jason Kidd CC	1.00	.45
☐ 24	Jamal Mashburn	.20	.09
☐ 25	M.Abdul-Rauf	.15	.07
☐ 26	D.Mutombo CC	.20	.09
☐ 27	Robert Pack CC	.15	.07
☐ 28	Jalen Rose	.20	.09
☐ 29	Joe Dumars CC	.40	.18
☐ 30	Grant Hill CC	2.50	1.10
☐ 31	Allan Houston	.20	.09
☐ 32	Terry Mills	.15	.07
☐ 33	Chris Gatling	.15	.07
☐ 34	Tim Hardaway CC	.50	.23
☐ 35	Donyell Marshall	.20	.09
☐ 36	Chris Mullin CC	.40	.18
☐ 37	Latrell Sprewell	.20	.09
☐ 38	Sam Cassell	.20	.09
☐ 39	Clyde Drexler CC	.50	.23
☐ 40	Robert Horry	.15	.07
☐ 41	Hakeem Olajuwon CC	.75	.35
☐ 42	Kenny Smith	.15	.07
☐ 43	Dale Davis	.15	.07
☐ 44	Mark Jackson	.20	.09
☐ 45	Reggie Miller CC	.40	.18
☐ 46	Rik Smits	.20	.09
☐ 47	Lamond Murray	.15	.07
☐ 48	Pooh Richardson CC	.15	.07
☐ 49	Malik Sealy	.15	.07
☐ 50	Loy Vaught	.15	.07
☐ 51	Cedric Ceballos	.15	.07
☐ 52	Vlade Divac	.20	.09
☐ 53	Eddie Jones	1.00	.45
☐ 54	Nick Van Exel	.40	.18
☐ 55	Billy Owens	.15	.07
☐ 56	Khalid Reeves	.15	.07
☐ 57	Glen Rice CC	.40	.18
☐ 58	Kevin Willis	.15	.07
☐ 59	Vin Baker	.75	.35
☐ 60	Todd Day	.15	.07
☐ 61	Eric Murdock	.15	.07
☐ 62	Glenn Robinson CC	.50	.23
☐ 63	Tom Gugliotta	.40	.18
☐ 64	Christian Laettner CC	.20	.09
☐ 65	Isaiah Rider CC	.20	.09
☐ 66	Doug West	.15	.07
☐ 67	Kenny Anderson	.20	.09
☐ 68	P.J. Brown	.15	.07
☐ 69	Derrick Coleman	.20	.09
☐ 70	Armon Gilliam	.15	.07
☐ 71	Patrick Ewing CC	.40	.18
☐ 72	Derek Harper	.20	.09
☐ 73	Charles Oakley	.15	.07
☐ 74	John Starks CC	.20	.09
☐ 75	Horace Grant CC	.20	.09
☐ 76	A.Hardaway CC	1.50	.70
☐ 77	Shaquille O'Neal CC	1.50	.70
☐ 78	Dennis Scott	.15	.07
☐ 79	Dana Barros CC	.15	.07
☐ 80	Shawn Bradley	.20	.09
☐ 81	C.Weatherspoon	.15	.07
☐ 82	Sharone Wright	.15	.07
☐ 83	Charles Barkley CC	.60	.25
☐ 84	Kevin Johnson CC	.20	.09
☐ 85	Dan Majerle CC	.15	.07
☐ 86	Wesley Person CC	.20	.09
☐ 87	Harvey Grant	.15	.07
☐ 88	Clifford Robinson	.15	.07
☐ 89	Rod Strickland	.20	.09
☐ 90	Buck Williams	.15	.07
☐ 91	Brian Grant	.20	.09
☐ 92	Olden Polynice	.15	.07
☐ 93	Mitch Richmond	.40	.18
☐ 94	Walt Williams	.15	.07
☐ 95	Sean Elliott	.15	.07
☐ 96	Avery Johnson	.15	.07
☐ 97	David Robinson CC	.60	.25
☐ 98	Dennis Rodman	1.50	.70
☐ 99	Shawn Kemp CC	1.25	.55
☐ 100	Nate McMillan	.15	.07
☐ 101	Gary Payton	.60	.25
☐ 102	Detlef Schrempf	.20	.09
☐ 103	Willie Anderson	.15	.07
☐ 104	Jerome Kersey	.15	.07
☐ 105	Oliver Miller	.15	.07
☐ 106	Ed Pinckney CC	.15	.07
☐ 107	David Benoit	.15	.07
☐ 108	Jeff Hornacek CC	.20	.09
☐ 109	Karl Malone CC	.60	.25
☐ 110	John Stockton	.40	.18
☐ 111	Greg Anthony	.15	.07
☐ 112	Benoit Benjamin	.15	.07
☐ 113	Blue Edwards	.15	.07
☐ 114	Kenny Gattison	.15	.07
☐ 115	Calbert Cheaney	.15	.07
☐ 116	Juwan Howard	.60	.25
☐ 117	Gheorghe Muresan CC	.15	.07
☐ 118	Chris Webber CC	1.00	.45
☐ 119	Checklist	.15	.07
☐ 120	Checklist	.15	.07
☐ NNO	Grant Hill	50.00	22.00
	Foil Tribute		

1995-96 Jam Session Fuel Injectors

Randomly inserted into all packs at a rate of one in 36, these nine cards feature hot stars of the '90s. Borderless fronts have

two-toned backgrounds with the player in a full-color action cutout. The player's image has a fuzzy outline, giving it an electric look. A screened box contains the player's biography and a player profile. The player's career summary appears in black type near the bottom of the card. The set is sequenced in alphabetical order.

	MINT	NRMT
COMPLETE SET (9)	90.00	40.00
COMMON CARD (1-9)	3.00	1.35
SEMISTARS	5.00	2.20
STATED ODDS 1:36 HOBBY/RETAIL		

		MINT	NRMT
☐ 1	Grant Hill	30.00	13.50
☐ 2	Larry Johnson	5.00	2.20
☐ 3	Eddie Jones	12.00	5.50
☐ 4	Jason Kidd	12.00	5.50
☐ 5	Hakeem Olajuwon	10.00	4.50
☐ 6	Shaquille O'Neal	20.00	9.00
☐ 7	Scottie Pippen	15.00	6.75
☐ 8	Glenn Robinson	6.00	2.70
☐ 9	Latrell Sprewell	3.00	1.35

1995-96 Jam Session Pop-Ups

Seeded at a rate of one per pack these pop-up cards highlight the play of 25 NBA standouts. Fronts feature the player in full-color action with a crowd background printed with horizontal lines. The cards are perforated around the player's image so that it can be separated from the rest of the card, popped out and displayed standing. Card backs give instructions on how to assemble the card for display. The set is sequenced in alphabetical order. Prices below are for mint unperforated cards.

	MINT	NRMT
COMPLETE SET (25)	8.00	3.60
COMMON CARD (1-25)	.15	.07
SEMISTARS	.40	.18
UNLISTED STARS	.60	.25
ONE PER PACK		

		MINT	NRMT
☐ 1	Kenny Anderson	.40	.18
☐ 2	Charles Barkley	1.00	.45
☐ 3	Mookie Blaylock	.40	.18
☐ 4	Muggsy Bogues	.40	.18
☐ 5	Shawn Bradley	.40	.18
☐ 6	Sam Cassell	.40	.18
☐ 7	Clyde Drexler	.75	.35
☐ 8	Brian Grant	.40	.18
☐ 9	Horace Grant	.40	.18
☐ 10	Tim Hardaway	.75	.35
☐ 11	Michael Jordan	4.00	1.80
☐ 12	Jim Jackson	.40	.18
☐ 13	Shawn Kemp	2.00	.90
☐ 14	Christian Laettner	.40	.18
☐ 15	Dan Majerle	.15	.07
☐ 16	Eric Montross	.15	.07
☐ 17	Alonzo Mourning	.60	.25
☐ 18	Gheorghe Muresan	.15	.07
☐ 19	Lamond Murray	.15	.07
☐ 20	D.Mutombo	.40	.18
☐ 21	Charles Oakley	.15	.07
☐ 22	Scottie Pippen	2.00	.90
☐ 23	Mark Price	.15	.07
☐ 24	Glen Rice	.60	.25
☐ 25	Clifford Robinson	.15	.07

1995-96 Jam Session Pop-Ups Bonus

Randomly inserted exclusively in retail packs at a rate of one in 24, this five-card set features a selection of NBA stars. The card fronts are borderless with a full-color action shot set against a crowd background with horizontal fading lines. The player's image is perforated for pop-out assembly. The unnumbered backs include instruction for assembly of the cards. The set is sequenced in alphabetical order. Prices below refer to mint unperforated cards.

	MINT	NRMT
COMPLETE SET (5)	30.00	13.50
COMMON CARD (1-5)	3.00	1.35
STATED ODDS 1:24 RETAIL		

		MINT	NRMT
☐ 1	Patrick Ewing	3.00	1.35
☐ 2	Grant Hill	20.00	9.00
☐ 3	Glenn Robinson	4.00	1.80
☐ 4	Jason Kidd	8.00	3.60
☐ 5	Jerry Stackhouse	6.00	2.70

1995-96 Jam Session Rookies

Randomly inserted in packs at a rate of one in six, cards from this 10-card set highlight the '95-96 freshman crop. Borderless fronts include a full-color player action cutout with stars winding around the player's image. "Rookie" is printed in a spiraling pattern and serves as the background. Numbered backs feature the player in a full-color cutout pose standing on a hovering star and the background continues with the spiraling pattern with the word "rookie". The player's last name appears over his head.

	MINT	NRMT
COMPLETE SET (10)	15.00	6.75
COMMON CARD (1-10)	.75	.35
SEMISTARS	1.25	.55
STATED ODDS 1:6 HOBBY/RETAIL		

		MINT	NRMT
☐ 1	Joe Smith	4.00	1.80
☐ 2	Antonio McDyess	5.00	2.20
☐ 3	Jerry Stackhouse	4.00	1.80
☐ 4	Rasheed Wallace	2.50	1.10
☐ 5	Bryant Reeves	2.50	1.10
☐ 6	Shawn Respert	.75	.35
☐ 7	Cherokee Parks	.75	.35
☐ 8	Alan Henderson	1.25	.55
☐ 9	George Zidek	.75	.35
☐ 10	Sherrell Ford	.75	.35

1995-96
Jam Session
Show Stoppers

Randomly inserted exclusively in hobby packs at a rate of one in 48, this set of nine cards is the rarest of the '95-96 Jam Session collection and features some of the game's best players. The full-bleed fronts show the player in a full-color cutout against a sparkling, etched blue-foil background The players name is stamped in gold foil at the bottom of the card in all caps. A digital image of the player serves as a background and a smaller full-color action player shot appears on the bottom half of the card. The player's biography and profile wrap around the color shot and his NBA totals appear at the bottom of the card. The set is sequenced in alphabetical order and is condition sensitive due to the etched foil edges.

	MINT	NRMT
COMPLETE SET (9)	250.00	110.00
COMMON CARD (1-9)	5.00	2.20
SEMISTARS	8.00	3.60
CONDITION SENSITIVE SET		
STATED ODDS 1:48 HOBBY		

□ 1 A.Hardaway	40.00	18.00
□ 2 Grant Hill	60.00	27.00
□ 3 Michael Jordan	125.00	55.00
□ 4 Karl Malone	12.00	5.50
□ 5 Jamal Mashburn	5.00	2.20
□ 6 Reggie Miller	8.00	3.60
□ 7 David Robinson	12.00	5.50
□ 8 John Stockton	8.00	3.60
□ 9 Chris Webber	20.00	9.00

1995-96 Metal

The 1995-96 premiere issue of Metal basketball by Fleer/ SkyBox consists of 220 standard-size cards issued in two separate series of 120 and 100 cards respectively. The eight-

card packs carried a suggested retail price of $2.49 each. Borderless fronts feature the player in a full-color action cutout against a multicolored, hand engraved, metallic foil background. Backs picture the player in a full-color action shot with his team's logo printed at the bottom. The only subset is Nuts and Bolts (209-218). Rookie Cards of note include Michael Finley, Kevin Garnett, Antonio McDyess, Joe Smith, Jerry Stackhouse and Damon Stoudamire.

	MINT	NRMT
COMPLETE SET (220)	45.00	20.00
COMPLETE SERIES 1 (120)	25.00	11.00
COMPLETE SERIES 2 (100)	20.00	9.00
COMMON CARD (1-120)	.15	.07
COMMON CARD (121-220)	.10	.05
SEMISTARS SER.1	.30	.14
SEMISTARS SER.2	.25	.11
UNLISTED STARS SER.1	.50	.23
UNLISTED STARS SER.2	.40	.18
COMP.SILV.SPOT.SET (120)	80.00	36.00
COMMON SILV.SPOT (1-120)	.50	.23
*SILV.SPOT.STARS: 1.5X TO 3X HI COLUMN		
ONE SILVER SPOTLIGHT PER SER.1 PACK		

□ 1 Stacey Augmon	.15	.07
□ 2 Mookie Blaylock	.30	.14
□ 3 Grant Long	.15	.07
□ 4 Steve Smith	.30	.14
□ 5 Dee Brown	.15	.07
□ 6 Sherman Douglas	.15	.07
□ 7 Eric Montross	.15	.07
□ 8 Dino Radja	.15	.07
□ 9 Muggsy Bogues	.30	.14
□ 10 Scott Burrell	.15	.07
□ 11 Larry Johnson	.30	.14
□ 12 Alonzo Mourning	.50	.23
□ 13 Michael Jordan	6.00	2.70
□ 14 Toni Kukoc	.30	.14
□ 15 Scottie Pippen	1.50	.70
□ 16 Terrell Brandon	.50	.23
□ 17 Tyrone Hill	.15	.07
□ 18 Mark Price	.15	.07
□ 19 John Williams	.15	.07
□ 20 Jim Jackson	.30	.14
□ 21 Popeye Jones	.15	.07
□ 22 Jason Kidd	1.25	.55
□ 23 Jamal Mashburn	.30	.14
□ 24 Mahmoud Abdul-Rauf	.15	.07
□ 25 Dikembe Mutombo	.30	.14
□ 26 Robert Pack	.15	.07
□ 27 Jalen Rose	.30	.14
□ 28 Joe Dumars	.50	.23
□ 29 Grant Hill	3.00	1.35
□ 30 Lindsey Hunter	.15	.07
□ 31 Terry Mills	.15	.07
□ 32 Tim Hardaway	.60	.25
□ 33 Donyell Marshall	.30	.14
□ 34 Chris Mullin	.50	.23
□ 35 Clifford Rozier	.15	.07
□ 36 Latrell Sprewell	.30	.14
□ 37 Sam Cassell	.30	.14
□ 38 Clyde Drexler	.60	.25
□ 39 Robert Horry	.15	.07
□ 40 Hakeem Olajuwon	1.00	.45
□ 41 Kenny Smith	.15	.07
□ 42 Dale Davis	.15	.07
□ 43 Mark Jackson	.30	.14
□ 44 Derrick McKey	.15	.07
□ 45 Reggie Miller	.50	.23
□ 46 Rik Smits	.30	.14
□ 47 Lamond Murray	.15	.07
□ 48 Pooh Richardson	.15	.07
□ 49 Malik Sealy	.15	.07
□ 50 Loy Vaught	.15	.07
□ 51 Elden Campbell	.30	.14
□ 52 Cedric Ceballos	.15	.07
□ 53 Vlade Divac	.30	.14
□ 54 Eddie Jones	1.25	.55
□ 55 Nick Van Exel	.50	.23
□ 56 Bimbo Coles	.15	.07
□ 57 Billy Owens	.15	.07
□ 58 Khalid Reeves	.15	.07
□ 59 Glen Rice	.50	.23
□ 60 Kevin Willis	.15	.07
□ 61 Vin Baker	1.00	.45
□ 62 Todd Day	.15	.07
□ 63 Eric Murdock	.15	.07
□ 64 Glenn Robinson	.60	.25
□ 65 Tom Gugliotta	.50	.23
□ 66 Christian Laettner	.30	.14
□ 67 Isaiah Rider	.30	.14
□ 68 Kenny Anderson	.30	.14
□ 69 P.J. Brown	.15	.07
□ 70 Derrick Coleman	.30	.14
□ 71 Patrick Ewing	.50	.23
□ 72 Anthony Mason	.30	.14
□ 73 Charles Oakley	.15	.07
□ 74 John Starks	.30	.14
□ 75 Nick Anderson	.15	.07
□ 76 Horace Grant	.30	.14
□ 77 Anfernee Hardaway	2.00	.90
□ 78 Shaquille O'Neal	2.00	.90
□ 79 Dennis Scott	.15	.07
□ 80 Dana Barros	.15	.07
□ 81 Shawn Bradley	.30	.14
□ 82 Clarence Weatherspoon	.15	.07
□ 83 Sharone Wright	.15	.07
□ 84 Charles Barkley	.75	.35
□ 85 Kevin Johnson	.30	.14
□ 86 Dan Majerle	.15	.07
□ 87 Danny Manning	.30	.14
□ 88 Wesley Person	.30	.14
□ 89 Clifford Robinson	.15	.07
□ 90 Rod Strickland	.30	.14
□ 91 Otis Thorpe	.30	.14
□ 92 Buck Williams	.15	.07
□ 93 Brian Grant	.30	.14
□ 94 Olden Polynice	.15	.07
□ 95 Mitch Richmond	.50	.23
□ 96 Walt Williams	.15	.07
□ 97 Sean Elliott	.15	.07
□ 98 Avery Johnson	.15	.07
□ 99 David Robinson	.75	.35
□ 100 Dennis Rodman	2.00	.90
□ 101 Shawn Kemp	1.50	.70
□ 102 Nate McMillan	.15	.07
□ 103 Gary Payton	.75	.35
□ 104 Detlef Schrempf	.30	.14
□ 105 B.J. Armstrong	.15	.07
□ 106 Oliver Miller	.15	.07
□ 107 John Salley	.15	.07
□ 108 David Benoit	.15	.07
□ 109 Jeff Hornacek	.30	.14
□ 110 Karl Malone	.75	.35
□ 111 John Stockton	.50	.23
□ 112 Greg Anthony	.15	.07
□ 113 Benoit Benjamin	.15	.07
□ 114 Byron Scott	.15	.07
□ 115 Calbert Cheaney	.15	.07

☐ 116 Juwan Howard	.75	.35
☐ 117 Gheorghe Muresan	.15	.07
☐ 118 Chris Webber	1.25	.55
☐ 119 Checklist	.15	.07
☐ 120 Checklist	.15	.07
☐ 121 Stacey Augmon	.15	.07
☐ 122 Mookie Blaylock	.25	.11
☐ 123 Alan Henderson	.40	.18
☐ 124 Andrew Lang	.15	.07
☐ 125 Ken Norman	.15	.07
☐ 126 Steve Smith	.25	.11
☐ 127 Dana Barros	.15	.07
☐ 128 Rick Fox	.15	.07
☐ 129 Eric Williams	.25	.11
☐ 130 Kendall Gill	.25	.11
☐ 131 Khalid Reeves	.15	.07
☐ 132 Glen Rice	.40	.18
☐ 133 George Zidek	.15	.07
☐ 134 Dennis Rodman	2.50	1.10
☐ 135 Danny Ferry	.15	.07
☐ 136 Dan Majerle	.15	.07
☐ 137 Chris Mills	.15	.07
☐ 138 Bobby Phills	.15	.07
☐ 139 Bob Sura	.25	.11
☐ 140 Tony Dumas	.15	.07
☐ 141 Dale Ellis	.15	.07
☐ 142 Don MacLean	.15	.07
☐ 143 Antonio McDyess	2.00	.90
☐ 144 Bryant Stith	.15	.07
☐ 145 Allan Houston	.25	.11
☐ 146 Theo Ratliff	.40	.18
☐ 147 Otis Thorpe	.15	.07
☐ 148 B.J. Armstrong	.15	.07
☐ 149 Rony Seikaly	.15	.07
☐ 150 Joe Smith	1.50	.70
☐ 151 Sam Cassell	.25	.11
☐ 152 Clyde Drexler	.50	.23
☐ 153 Robert Horry	.15	.07
☐ 154 Hakeem Olajuwon	.75	.35
☐ 155 Antonio Davis	.15	.07
☐ 156 Ricky Pierce	.15	.07
☐ 157 Brent Barry	.40	.18
☐ 158 Terry Dehere	.15	.07
☐ 159 Rodney Rogers	.15	.07
☐ 160 Brian Williams	.15	.07
☐ 161 Magic Johnson	1.25	.55
☐ 162 Sasha Danilovic	.15	.07
☐ 163 Alonzo Mourning	.40	.18
☐ 164 Kurt Thomas	.25	.11
☐ 165 Sherman Douglas	.15	.07
☐ 166 Shawn Respert	.15	.07
☐ 167 Kevin Garnett	5.00	2.20
☐ 168 Terry Porter	.15	.07
☐ 169 Shawn Bradley	.15	.07
☐ 170 Kevin Edwards	.15	.07
☐ 171 Ed O'Bannon	.15	.07
☐ 172 Jayson Williams	.25	.11
☐ 173 Derek Harper	.15	.07
☐ 174 Charles Smith	.15	.07
☐ 175 Brian Shaw	.15	.07
☐ 176 Derrick Coleman	.25	.11
☐ 177 Vernon Maxwell	.15	.07
☐ 178 Trevor Ruffin	.15	.07
☐ 179 Jerry Stackhouse	1.50	.70
☐ 180 Michael Finley	1.50	.70
☐ 181 A.C. Green	.25	.11
☐ 182 John Williams	.15	.07
☐ 183 Aaron McKie	.15	.07
☐ 184 Arvydas Sabonis	.75	.35
☐ 185 Gary Trent	.15	.07
☐ 186 Tyus Edney	.15	.07
☐ 187 Sarunas Marciulionis	.15	.07
☐ 188 Michael Smith	.15	.07
☐ 189 Corliss Williamson	.50	.23
☐ 190 Vinny Del Negro	.15	.07
☐ 191 Hersey Hawkins	.25	.11
☐ 192 Shawn Kemp	1.25	.55
☐ 193 Gary Payton	.60	.25
☐ 194 Sam Perkins	.25	.11
☐ 195 Detlef Schrempf	.25	.11
☐ 196 Willie Anderson	.15	.07
☐ 197 Oliver Miller	.15	.07
☐ 198 Tracy Murray	.15	.07
☐ 199 Alvin Robertson	.15	.07
☐ 200 Damon Stoudamire	3.00	1.35
☐ 201 Chris Morris	.15	.07

☐ 202 Greg Anthony	.15	.07
☐ 203 Blue Edwards	.15	.07
☐ 204 Eric Murdock	.15	.07
☐ 205 Bryant Reeves	1.00	.45
☐ 206 Byron Scott	.15	.07
☐ 207 Robert Pack	.15	.07
☐ 208 Rasheed Wallace	1.00	.45
☐ 209 Anfernee Hardaway NB	.75	.35
☐ 210 Grant Hill NB	1.25	.55
☐ 211 Larry Johnson NB	.15	.07
☐ 212 Michael Jordan NB	2.50	1.10
☐ 213 Jason Kidd NB	.50	.23
☐ 214 Karl Malone NB	.40	.18
☐ 215 Shaquille O'Neal NB	.75	.35
☐ 216 Scottie Pippen NB	.60	.25
☐ 217 David Robinson NB	.40	.18
☐ 218 Glenn Robinson NB	.40	.18
☐ 219 Checklist	.15	.07
☐ 220 Checklist	.15	.07

1995-96 Metal Maximum Metal

Randomly inserted in all series one packs at a rate of one in 36, cards from this 10-card standard-size set highlight some NBA impact players. These cards have a basketball-shaped die cut design and feature a full-color player action cutout on the front. The background is a silver foil diamond-plate basketball going through a hoop. Backs continue with the diamond plate basketball and hoop background and also feature a full-color player cutout. The player's name and a player profile are printed on the back. The set is sequenced in alphabetical order.

	MINT	NRMT
COMPLETE SET (10)	80.00	36.00
COMMON CARD (1-10)	3.00	1.35
SER.1 STATED ODDS 1:36 HOBBY/RETAIL		

☐ 1 Charles Barkley	5.00	2.20
☐ 2 Patrick Ewing	3.00	1.35
☐ 3 Grant Hill	20.00	9.00
☐ 4 Michael Jordan	40.00	18.00
☐ 5 Shawn Kemp	10.00	4.50
☐ 6 Karl Malone	5.00	2.20
☐ 7 Hakeem Olajuwon	6.00	2.70
☐ 8 Shaquille O'Neal	12.00	5.50
☐ 9 Mitch Richmond	3.00	1.35
☐ 10 David Robinson	5.00	2.20

1995-96 Metal Metal Force

Randomly inserted exclusively in second series retail packs at a rate of one in 54, cards from this 15-card set feature a selection of the NBA's top stars and rookies. Each card is made of a clear plastic material and comes with a protective coating on front. Prices provided below refer to unpeeled cards. Peeled cards generally trade for ten to twenty-five percent less.

	MINT	NRMT
COMPLETE SET (15)	175.00	80.00
COMMON CARD (1-15)	4.00	1.80
SEMISTARS	5.00	2.20
UNLISTED STARS	8.00	3.60
SER.2 STATED ODDS 1:54 RETAIL		

☐ 1 Vin Baker	15.00	6.75
☐ 2 Charles Barkley	12.00	5.50
☐ 3 Cedric Ceballos	4.00	1.80
☐ 4 Grant Hill	50.00	22.00
☐ 5 Larry Johnson	5.00	2.20
☐ 6 Magic Johnson	25.00	11.00
☐ 7 Shawn Kemp	25.00	11.00
☐ 8 Karl Malone	12.00	5.50
☐ 9 Jamal Mashburn	5.00	2.20
☐ 10 Scottie Pippen	25.00	11.00
☐ 11 Glenn Robinson	10.00	4.50
☐ 12 Dennis Rodman	50.00	22.00
☐ 13 Joe Smith	12.00	5.50
☐ 14 Jerry Stackhouse	12.00	5.50
☐ 15 Chris Webber	20.00	9.00

1995-96 Metal Molten Metal

Randomly inserted in all series one packs at a rate of one in 72, cards from this 10-card set feature a selection of up and coming NBA stars. The fronts feature full-color action cutouts set against stamped multicolored laminated foil backgrounds. Borderless backs feature the player in a full-color action cutout and a white box surrounds a player profile which is printed in white

```
COMP.SILV.SPOT.SET (10) 20.00    9.00
*SILV.SPOTLIGHT: 1.25X TO 2.5X HI COL-
UMN
RANDOM INSERTS IN ALL SER.1 PACKS

□ R1 Brent Barry ............... .30    .14
□ R2 Antonio McDyess..... 2.50   1.10
□ R3 Ed O'Bannon............. .30    .14
□ R4 Cherokee Parks......... .30    .14
□ R5 Bryant Reeves.......... 1.25    .55
□ R6 Shawn Respert.......... .30    .14
□ R7 Joe Smith............... 2.00    .90
□ R8 Jerry Stackhouse...... 2.00    .90
□ R9 Gary Trent.............. .30    .14
□ R10 Rasheed Wallace...... 1.25    .55
```

type. The set is sequenced in alphabetical order.

```
                    MINT   NRMT
COMPLETE SET (10) ...... 175.00  80.00
COMMON CARD (1-10) ...... 4.00   1.80
SEMISTARS ............... 6.00   2.70
UNLISTED STARS ......... 10.00   4.50
SER.1 STATED ODDS 1:72 HOBBY/RETAIL

□ 1 Anfernee Hardaway .... 40.00  18.00
□ 2 Grant Hill............. 60.00  27.00
□ 3 Robert Horry........... 4.00   1.80
□ 4 Eddie Jones............ 25.00  11.00
□ 5 Toni Kukoc............. 6.00   2.70
□ 6 Jamal Mashburn......... 6.00   2.70
□ 7 Alonzo Mourning........ 10.00   4.50
□ 8 Glenn Robinson......... 12.00   5.50
□ 9 Latrell Sprewell....... 6.00   2.70
□ 10 Chris Webber.......... 25.00  11.00
```

1995-96 Metal Rookie Roll Call

Spotlighting the '95-96 rookie class, cards from this 10-card standard-size set were randomly inserted in both series one hobby and retail packs. Though these cards are considered inserts, they were distributed at the same rate as regular issue cards. The cards display hand-engraved, metalized foil designs and are numbered on the back. The set is sequenced in alphabetical order.

```
                  MINT   NRMT
COMPLETE SET (10) ......... 8.00   3.60
COMMON CARD (R1-R10)...... .30    .14
```

1995-96 Metal Scoring Magnets

Randomly inserted exclusively into second series hobby packs at a rate of one in 54, cards from this 8-card set feature a selection of the NBA's top scoring threats. Card fronts have embossed player shots with the card name "Scoring Magnet" in silver foil running vertical along both sides of the player. Card backs contain a brief commentary and are numbered as "X of 8".

```
                   MINT    NRMT
COMPLETE SET (8) ...... 150.00  70.00
COMMON CARD (1-8) ........ 8.00   3.60
SER.2 STATED ODDS 1:54 HOBBY

□ 1 Anfernee Hardaway .... 20.00   9.00
□ 2 Grant Hill............ 30.00  13.50
□ 3 Magic Johnson......... 15.00   6.75
□ 4 Michael Jordan........ 60.00  27.00
□ 5 Jason Kidd............ 12.00   5.50
□ 6 Hakeem Olajuwon....... 10.00   4.50
□ 7 Shaquille O'Neal...... 20.00   9.00
□ 8 David Robinson......... 8.00   3.60
```

1995-96 Metal Slick Silver

Randomly inserted exclusively into first series hobby packs at a rate of one in seven, cards from this 10-card standard-size set highlight the league's premier point and shooting guards. The clear acetate cards feature the player in a full-color action shot

with a trail of ghost images on the front. Backs feature a player profile printed on the player's reverse silhouette. The set is sequenced in alphabetical order.

```
                  MINT   NRMT
COMPLETE SET (10) ...... 40.00  18.00
COMMON CARD (1-10) ...... 1.00    .45
SEMISTARS ............... 1.25    .55
UNLISTED STARS .......... 2.00    .90
SER.1 STATED ODDS 1:7 HOBBY/RETAIL

□ 1 Kenny Anderson......... 1.25    .55
□ 2 Anfernee Hardaway ..... 8.00   3.60
□ 3 Michael Jordan........ 25.00  11.00
□ 4 Jason Kidd............. 5.00   2.20
□ 5 Reggie Miller.......... 2.00    .90
□ 6 Gary Payton............ 3.00   1.35
□ 7 Mitch Richmond......... 2.00    .90
□ 8 Latrell Sprewell....... 1.00    .45
□ 9 John Stockton.......... 2.00    .90
□ 10 Nick Van Exel......... 2.00    .90
```

1995-96 Metal Steel Towers

Randomly inserted exclusively into series one retail and magazine packs at a rate of one in four, cards from this 10-card insert set focus on the leagues top big men. Full-bleed fronts have silver foil backgrounds and are stamped with skyscraper designs. Backs are two-toned according to player's team colors and feature a full-color action shot and a player profile printed next to it. Skyscraper designs also appear in the back-

ground on the backs. The set is sequenced in alphabetical order.

	MINT	NRMT
COMPLETE SET (10)	15.00	6.75
COMMON CARD (1-10)	.50	.23
SEMISTARS	1.00	.45
UNLISTED STARS	1.50	.70
SER.1 STATED ODDS 1:4 RETAIL		

			MINT	NRMT
☐ 1	Shawn Bradley		.50	.23
☐ 2	Vlade Divac		1.00	.45
☐ 3	Patrick Ewing		1.50	.70
☐ 4	Alonzo Mourning		1.50	.70
☐ 5	Dikembe Mutombo		1.00	.45
☐ 6	Hakeem Olajuwon		3.00	1.35
☐ 7	Shaquille O'Neal		6.00	2.70
☐ 8	David Robinson		2.50	1.10
☐ 9	Rik Smits		1.00	.45
☐ 10	Kevin Willis		.50	.23

1995-96 Metal Tempered Steel

Randomly inserted into all second series packs at a rate of one in 12, cards from this 12-card set feature a selection of top rookies from the 1995-96 season. Card fronts have a colorful foil-etched background with the the "Tempered Steel" logo written in cursive running along the left side. Card backs feature an action shot and a brief commentary next to it. Card backs are numbered as "X of 12".

	MINT	NRMT
COMPLETE SET (12)	30.00	13.50
COMMON CARD (1-12)	1.25	.55
SEMISTARS	1.50	.70
UNLISTED STARS	2.50	1.10
SER.2 STATED ODDS 1:12 HOBBY/RETAIL		

		MINT	NRMT
☐ 1 Sasha Danilovic		1.25	.55
☐ 2 Tyus Edney		1.25	.55
☐ 3 Michael Finley		5.00	2.20
☐ 4 Kevin Garnett		15.00	6.75
☐ 5 Antonio McDyess		6.00	2.70
☐ 6 Bryant Reeves		3.00	1.35
☐ 7 Arvydas Sabonis		2.50	1.10
☐ 8 Joe Smith		5.00	2.20
☐ 9 Jerry Stackhouse		5.00	2.20
☐ 10 Damon Stoudamire		10.00	4.50
☐ 11 Rasheed Wallace		3.00	1.35
☐ 12 Eric Williams		1.50	.70

1996-97 Metal

Produced by Fleer/SkyBox, the 1996 Metal set is comprised of 250 cards with eight-card packs carrying a suggested retail price of $2.49. Borderless fronts feature the player in a full-color action cutout against an etched color and silver foil background. The player's name is printed in silver foil and embossed along the right side of the card. Backs picture the player in a full-color action shot with his team's logo printed at the bottom against a "steel" background. The player's name and statistics run vertically along the right side of the card. The cards are grouped alphabetically within teams and checklisted below alphabetically according to team. The Series one Fresh Foundation subset contains the Rookie Cards of Stephon Marbury, Shareef Abdur-Rahim, Ray Allen, Kobe Bryant and Steve Nash. Card #73 (Jerry Stackhouse) was also used for promotional purposes.

	MINT	NRMT
COMPLETE SET (250)	45.00	20.00
COMPLETE SERIES 1 (150)	25.00	11.00
COMPLETE SERIES 2 (100)	20.00	9.00
COMMON CARD (1-250)	.15	.07
SEMISTARS	.20	.09
UNLISTED STARS	.40	.18

		MINT	NRMT
☐ 1 Mookie Blaylock		.20	.09
☐ 2 Christian Laettner		.20	.09
☐ 3 Steve Smith		.20	.09
☐ 4 Dana Barros		.15	.07
☐ 5 Rick Fox		.15	.07
☐ 6 Dino Radja		.15	.07
☐ 7 Eric Williams		.15	.07
☐ 8 Dell Curry		.15	.07
☐ 9 Matt Geiger		.15	.07
☐ 10 Glen Rice		.40	.18
☐ 11 Michael Jordan		5.00	2.20
☐ 12 Toni Kukoc		.20	.09
☐ 13 Luc Longley		.20	.09
☐ 14 Scottie Pippen		1.25	.55
☐ 15 Dennis Rodman		1.50	.70
☐ 16 Terrell Brandon		.40	.18
☐ 17 Danny Ferry		.15	.07
☐ 18 Chris Mills		.15	.07
☐ 19 Bobby Phills		.15	.07

		MINT	NRMT
☐ 20 Bob Sura		.15	.07
☐ 21 Jim Jackson		.20	.09
☐ 22 Jason Kidd		.75	.35
☐ 23 Jamal Mashburn		.20	.09
☐ 24 George McCloud		.15	.07
☐ 25 LaPhonso Ellis		.15	.07
☐ 26 Antonio McDyess		.60	.25
☐ 27 Bryant Stith		.15	.07
☐ 28 Joe Dumars		.40	.18
☐ 29 Grant Hill		2.50	1.10
☐ 30 Theo Ratliff		.15	.07
☐ 31 Otis Thorpe		.20	.09
☐ 32 Chris Mullin		.40	.18
☐ 33 Joe Smith		.50	.23
☐ 34 Latrell Sprewell		.20	.09
☐ 35 Sam Cassell		.20	.09
☐ 36 Clyde Drexler		.50	.23
☐ 37 Robert Horry		.20	.09
☐ 38 Hakeem Olajuwon		.75	.35
☐ 39 Antonio Davis		.15	.07
☐ 40 Dale Davis		.15	.07
☐ 41 Derrick McKey		.15	.07
☐ 42 Reggie Miller		.40	.18
☐ 43 Rik Smits		.20	.09
☐ 44 Brent Barry		.15	.07
☐ 45 Malik Sealy		.15	.07
☐ 46 Loy Vaught		.20	.09
☐ 47 Elden Campbell		.20	.09
☐ 48 Cedric Ceballos		.15	.07
☐ 49 Eddie Jones		.75	.35
☐ 50 Nick Van Exel		.40	.18
☐ 51 Sasha Danilovic		.15	.07
☐ 52 Tim Hardaway		.50	.23
☐ 53 Alonzo Mourning		.40	.18
☐ 54 Kurt Thomas		.15	.07
☐ 55 Vin Baker		.75	.35
☐ 56 Sherman Douglas		.15	.07
☐ 57 Glenn Robinson		.40	.18
☐ 58 Kevin Garnett		2.50	1.10
☐ 59 Tom Gugliotta		.40	.18
☐ 60 Doug West		.15	.07
☐ 61 Shawn Bradley		.15	.07
☐ 62 Ed O'Bannon		.15	.07
☐ 63 Jayson Williams		.20	.09
☐ 64 Patrick Ewing		.40	.18
☐ 65 Charles Oakley		.20	.09
☐ 66 John Starks		.20	.09
☐ 67 Nick Anderson		.15	.07
☐ 68 Horace Grant		.20	.09
☐ 69 Anfernee Hardaway		1.50	.70
☐ 70 Dennis Scott		.15	.07
☐ 71 Brian Shaw		.15	.07
☐ 72 Derrick Coleman		.20	.09
☐ 73 Jerry Stackhouse		.50	.23
☐ 74 Clarence Weatherspoon		.15	.07
☐ 75 Charles Barkley		.60	.25
☐ 76 Michael Finley		.50	.23
☐ 77 Kevin Johnson		.20	.09
☐ 78 Wesley Person		.15	.07
☐ 79 Aaron McKie		.15	.07
☐ 80 Clifford Robinson		.15	.07
☐ 81 Arvydas Sabonis		.20	.09
☐ 82 Gary Trent		.15	.07
☐ 83 Tyus Edney		.15	.07
☐ 84 Brian Grant		.15	.07
☐ 85 Billy Owens		.15	.07
☐ 86 Olden Polynice		.15	.07
☐ 87 Mitch Richmond		.40	.18
☐ 88 Vinny Del Negro		.15	.07
☐ 89 Sean Elliott		.15	.07
☐ 90 Avery Johnson		.15	.07
☐ 91 David Robinson		.60	.25
☐ 92 Hersey Hawkins		.20	.09
☐ 93 Shawn Kemp		1.25	.55
☐ 94 Gary Payton		.60	.25
☐ 95 Sam Perkins		.20	.09
☐ 96 Detlef Schrempf		.20	.09
☐ 97 Doug Christie		.15	.07
☐ 98 Damon Stoudamire		1.00	.45
☐ 99 Sharone Wright		.15	.07
☐ 100 Jeff Hornacek		.20	.09
☐ 101 Karl Malone		.60	.25
☐ 102 John Stockton		.40	.18
☐ 103 Greg Anthony		.15	.07
☐ 104 Blue Edwards		.15	.07
☐ 105 Bryant Reeves		.20	.09

106	Juwan Howard	.50	.23
107	Gheorghe Muresan	.15	.07
108	Chris Webber	1.00	.45
109	Kenny Anderson OTM	.20	.09
110	Stacey Augmon OTM	.15	.07
111	Chris Childs OTM	.15	.07
112	Vlade Divac OTM	.15	.07
113	Allan Houston OTM	.15	.07
114	Mark Jackson OTM	.15	.07
115	Larry Johnson OTM	.15	.07
116	Grant Long OTM	.15	.07
117	Anthony Mason OTM	.15	.07
118	D.Mutombo OTM	.15	.07
119	Shaquille O'Neal OTM	.75	.35
120	Isaiah Rider OTM	.15	.07
121	Rod Strickland OTM	.15	.07
122	Rasheed Wallace OTM	.15	.07
123	Jalen Rose OTM	.15	.07
124	A.Hardaway MET	.75	.35
125	Tim Hardaway MET	.40	.18
126	Allan Houston MET	.15	.07
127	Eddie Jones MET	.40	.18
128	Michael Jordan MET	2.50	1.10
129	Reggie Miller MET	.20	.09
130	Glen Rice MET	.20	.09
131	Mitch Richmond MET	.20	.09
132	Steve Smith MET	.15	.07
133	John Stockton MET	.20	.09
134	Stephon Marbury FF	4.00	1.80
135	S.Abdur-Rahim FF	2.50	1.10
136	Ray Allen FF	1.25	.55
137	Kobe Bryant FF	8.00	3.60
138	Steve Nash FF	.60	.25
139	Grant Hill MS	1.25	.55
140	Jason Kidd MS	.40	.18
141	Karl Malone MS	.40	.18
142	Hakeem Olajuwon MS	.40	.18
143	Shaquille O'Neal MS	.75	.35
144	Gary Payton MS	.40	.18
145	Scottie Pippen MS	.60	.25
146	Jerry Stackhouse MS	.40	.18
147	Damon Stoudamire MS	.50	.23
148	Rod Strickland MS	.15	.07
149	Checklist (1-102)	.15	.07
150	CL (103-150/inserts)	.15	.07
151	Tyrone Corbin	.15	.07
152	Dikembe Mutombo	.20	.09
153	Antoine Walker	4.00	1.80
154	David Wesley	.15	.07
155	Vlade Divac	.20	.09
156	Anthony Mason	.20	.09
157	Ron Harper	.15	.07
158	Steve Kerr	.15	.07
159	Robert Parish	.20	.09
160	Tyrone Hill	.15	.07
161	Vitaly Potapenko	.20	.09
162	Sam Cassell	.20	.09
163	Chris Gatling	.15	.07
164	Samaki Walker	.50	.23
165	Dale Ellis	.15	.07
166	Mark Jackson	.15	.07
167	Ervin Johnson	.15	.07
168	Grant Hill	2.50	1.10
169	Lindsey Hunter	.15	.07
170	Todd Fuller	.15	.07
171	Mark Price	.15	.07
172	Charles Barkley	.60	.25
173	Othella Harrington	.20	.09
174	Matt Maloney	.60	.25
175	Kevin Willis	.15	.07
176	Travis Best	.15	.07
177	Erick Dampier	.50	.23
178	Jalen Rose	.15	.07
179	Rodney Rogers	.15	.07
180	Lorenzen Wright	.50	.23
181	Kobe Bryant	4.00	1.80
182	Robert Horry	.20	.09
183	Shaquille O'Neal	1.50	.70
184	P.J. Brown	.15	.07
185	Dan Majerle	.20	.09
186	Ray Allen	.60	.25
187	Armon Gilliam	.15	.07
188	Andrew Lang	.15	.07
189	Stephon Marbury	2.00	.90
190	Stojko Vrankovic	.15	.07
191	Kendall Gill	.20	.09
192	Kerry Kittles	1.00	.45
193	Robert Pack	.15	.07
194	Chris Childs	.15	.07
195	Allan Houston	.20	.09
196	Larry Johnson	.20	.09
197	John Wallace	.60	.25
198	Rony Seikaly	.15	.07
199	Gerald Wilkins	.15	.07
200	Lucious Harris	.15	.07
201	Allen Iverson	4.00	1.80
202	Cedric Ceballos	.15	.07
203	Jason Kidd	.75	.35
204	Danny Manning	.20	.09
205	Steve Nash	.40	.18
206	Kenny Anderson	.20	.09
207	Isaiah Rider	.20	.09
208	Rasheed Wallace	.20	.09
209	Mahmoud Abdul-Rauf	.15	.07
210	Corliss Williamson	.20	.09
211	Vernon Maxwell	.15	.07
212	Dominique Wilkins	.40	.18
213	Craig Ehlo	.15	.07
214	Jim McIlvaine	.15	.07
215	Marcus Camby	1.00	.45
216	Hubert Davis	.15	.07
217	Walt Williams	.15	.07
218	Shandon Anderson	.50	.23
219	Bryon Russell	.15	.07
220	Shareef Abdur-Rahim	1.25	.55
221	Roy Rogers	.15	.07
222	Tracy Murray	.15	.07
223	Rod Strickland	.20	.09
224	Kevin Garnett MET	1.25	.55
225	Karl Malone MET	.40	.18
226	Alonzo Mourning MET	.20	.09
227	Hakeem Olajuwon MET	.40	.18
228	Gary Payton MET	.40	.18
229	Scottie Pippen MET	.60	.25
230	David Robinson MET	.40	.18
231	Dennis Rodman MET	.75	.35
232	Latrell Sprewell MET	.15	.07
233	Jerry Stackhouse MET	.40	.18
234	Marcus Camby FF	.50	.23
235	Todd Fuller FF	.15	.07
236	Allen Iverson FF	2.00	.90
237	Kerry Kittles FF	.50	.23
238	Roy Rogers FF	.15	.07
239	Anfernee Hardaway MS	.75	.35
240	Juwan Howard MS	.40	.18
241	Michael Jordan MS	2.50	1.10
242	Shawn Kemp MS	.60	.25
243	Gary Payton MS	.40	.18
244	Mitch Richmond MS	.20	.09
245	Glenn Robinson MS	.20	.09
246	John Stockton MS	.20	.09
247	Damon Stoudamire MS	.50	.23
248	Chris Webber MS	.50	.23
249	Checklist	.15	.07
250	Checklist	.15	.07

1996-97 Metal Precious Metal

Randomly inserted into hobby packs at a rate of one in 36, this 98-card set is a parallel of the Series two set only (minus the checklists). These cards differ from the basic set with a fade in the etched foil background.

	MINT	NRMT
COMPLETE SET (98)	1100.00	500.00
COMMON CARD (151-248)	4.00	1.80
SEMISTARS	6.00	2.70
UNLISTED STARS	10.00	4.50
SER.2 STATED ODDS 1:36 HOBBY		

151	Tyrone Corbin	4.00	1.80
152	Dikembe Mutombo	6.00	2.70
153	Antoine Walker	50.00	22.00
154	David Wesley	4.00	1.80
155	Vlade Divac	6.00	2.70
156	Anthony Mason	6.00	2.70
157	Ron Harper	4.00	1.80
158	Steve Kerr	4.00	1.80
159	Robert Parish	6.00	2.70
160	Tyrone Hill	4.00	1.80
161	Vitaly Potapenko	6.00	2.70
162	Sam Cassell	6.00	2.70
163	Chris Gatling	4.00	1.80
164	Samaki Walker	10.00	4.50
165	Dale Ellis	4.00	1.80
166	Mark Jackson	4.00	1.80
167	Ervin Johnson	4.00	1.80
168	Grant Hill	60.00	27.00
169	Lindsey Hunter	4.00	1.80
170	Todd Fuller	4.00	1.80
171	Mark Price	4.00	1.80
172	Charles Barkley	15.00	6.75
173	Othella Harrington	10.00	4.50
174	Matt Maloney	10.00	4.50
175	Kevin Willis	4.00	1.80
176	Travis Best	4.00	1.80
177	Erick Dampier	4.00	1.80
178	Jalen Rose	4.00	1.80
179	Rodney Rogers	4.00	1.80
180	Lorenzen Wright	10.00	4.50
181	Kobe Bryant	120.00	55.00
182	Robert Horry	6.00	2.70
183	Shaquille O'Neal	40.00	18.00
184	P.J. Brown	4.00	1.80
185	Dan Majerle	6.00	2.70
186	Ray Allen	15.00	6.75
187	Armon Gilliam	4.00	1.80
188	Andrew Lang	4.00	1.80
189	Stephon Marbury	50.00	22.00
190	Stojko Vrankovic	4.00	1.80
191	Kendall Gill	6.00	2.70
192	Kerry Kittles	12.00	5.50
193	Robert Pack	4.00	1.80
194	Chris Childs	4.00	1.80
195	Allan Houston	6.00	2.70
196	Larry Johnson	6.00	2.70
197	John Wallace	10.00	4.50
198	Rony Seikaly	4.00	1.80
199	Gerald Wilkins	4.00	1.80
200	Lucious Harris	4.00	1.80
201	Allen Iverson	50.00	22.00
202	Cedric Ceballos	4.00	1.80
203	Jason Kidd	20.00	9.00
204	Danny Manning	6.00	2.70
205	Steve Nash	10.00	4.50
206	Kenny Anderson	6.00	2.70
207	Isaiah Rider	6.00	2.70
208	Rasheed Wallace	4.00	1.80
209	Mahmoud Abdul-Rauf	4.00	1.80
210	Corliss Williamson	6.00	2.70
211	Vernon Maxwell	4.00	1.80
212	Dominique Wilkins	10.00	4.50
213	Craig Ehlo	4.00	1.80
214	Jim McIlvaine	4.00	1.80
215	Marcus Camby	12.00	5.50
216	Hubert Davis	4.00	1.80
217	Walt Williams	4.00	1.80
218	Shandon Anderson	10.00	4.50
219	Bryon Russell	4.00	1.80
220	Shareef Abdur-Rahim	30.00	13.50
221	Roy Rogers	4.00	1.80
222	Tracy Murray	4.00	1.80

☐ 223 Rod Strickland	6.00	2.70
☐ 224 Kevin Garnett MET	60.00	27.00
☐ 225 Karl Malone MET....	15.00	6.75
☐ 226 Alonzo Mourning MET	6.00	2.70
☐ 227 Hakeem Olajuwon MET	20.00	9.00
☐ 228 Gary Payton MET ..	15.00	6.75
☐ 229 Scottie Pippen MET	30.00	13.50
☐ 230 David Robinson MET	15.00	6.75
☐ 231 Dennis Rodman MET	40.00	18.00
☐ 232 Latrell Sprewell MET	4.00	1.80
☐ 233 Jerry Stackhouse MET	12.00	5.50
☐ 234 Marcus Camby FF ..	10.00	4.50
☐ 235 Todd Fuller FF	4.00	1.80
☐ 236 Allen Iverson FF......	25.00	11.00
☐ 237 Kerry Kittles FF	10.00	4.50
☐ 238 Roy Rogers FF.......	4.00	1.80
☐ 239 Anfernee Hardaway MS	40.00	18.00
☐ 240 Juwan Howard MS	12.00	5.50
☐ 241 Michael Jordan MS	250.00	110.00
☐ 242 Shawn Kemp MS...	30.00	13.50
☐ 243 Gary Payton MS ...	15.00	6.75
☐ 244 Mitch Richmond MS	6.00	2.70
☐ 245 Glenn Robinson MS	6.00	2.70
☐ 246 John Stockton MS...	6.00	2.70
☐ 247 Damon Stoudamire MS	25.00	11.00
☐ 248 Chris Webber MS ..	25.00	11.00

1996-97 Metal
Cyber-Metal

Randomly inserted in all series two packs at a rate of one in 6, this 20-card set features NBA players as "Terminator-type" characters.

	MINT	NRMT
COMPLETE SET (20)	40.00	18.00
COMMON CARD (1-20)	1.25	.55
SEMISTARS	1.50	.70
SER.2 STATED ODDS 1:6 HOBBY/RETAIL		

☐ 1 Shareef Abdur-Rahim	5.00	2.20
☐ 2 Ray Allen	2.50	1.10
☐ 3 Vin Baker	3.00	1.35
☐ 4 Charles Barkley	2.50	1.10
☐ 5 Kobe Bryant	15.00	6.75
☐ 6 Patrick Ewing	1.50	.70
☐ 7 Jason Kidd	3.00	1.35
☐ 8 Karl Malone	2.50	1.10
☐ 9 Stephon Marbury	8.00	3.60
☐ 10 Reggie Miller	1.50	.70
☐ 11 Alonzo Mourning	1.50	.70
☐ 12 Hakeem Olajuwon	3.00	1.35
☐ 13 Gary Payton	2.50	1.10
☐ 14 Scottie Pippen	5.00	2.20
☐ 15 Mitch Richmond	1.50	.70
☐ 16 David Robinson	2.50	1.10
☐ 17 Joe Smith	2.00	.90
☐ 18 Latrell Sprewell	1.25	.55
☐ 19 John Stockton	1.50	.70
☐ 20 Chris Webber	4.00	1.80

1996-97 Metal
Decade of
Excellence

Randomly inserted in all first series packs at a rate of one in 100, this 10 card set features metalized foil replicas of the 1986-87 Fleer NBA cards. Card backs carry a "M" prefix.

	MINT	NRMT
COMPLETE SET (10)	50.00	22.00
COMMON CARD (M1-M10) ..	2.50	1.10
SER.1 STATED ODDS 1:100 HOBBY/RETAIL		

☐ M1 Clyde Drexler	4.00	1.80
☐ M2 Joe Dumars	2.50	1.10
☐ M3 Derek Harper	2.50	1.10
☐ M4 Michael Jordan	40.00	18.00
☐ M5 Karl Malone	5.00	2.20
☐ M6 Chris Mullin	2.50	1.10
☐ M7 Charles Oakley	2.50	1.10
☐ M8 Sam Perkins	2.50	1.10
☐ M9 Ricky Pierce	2.50	1.10
☐ M10 Buck Williams	2.50	1.10

1996-97 Metal
Freshly Forged

Randomly inserted in all series two packs at a rate of one in 24, this 15-card set focuses on younger players and features an original art illustrated background on each card.

	MINT	NRMT
COMPLETE SET (15)	100.00	45.00
COMMON CARD (1-15)	2.50	1.10
SER.2 STATED ODDS 1:24 HOBBY/RETAIL		

☐ 1 Shareef Abdur-Rahim	8.00	3.60
☐ 2 Ray Allen	4.00	1.80
☐ 3 Kobe Bryant	20.00	9.00
☐ 4 Marcus Camby	3.00	1.35
☐ 5 Kevin Garnett	15.00	6.75
☐ 6 Anfernee Hardaway	10.00	4.50
☐ 7 Grant Hill	15.00	6.75
☐ 8 Allen Iverson	12.00	5.50
☐ 9 Jason Kidd	5.00	2.20
☐ 10 Stephon Marbury	12.00	5.50
☐ 11 Glenn Robinson	2.50	1.10
☐ 12 Joe Smith	3.00	1.35
☐ 13 Jerry Stackhouse	3.00	1.35
☐ 14 Damon Stoudamire	6.00	2.70
☐ 15 Antoine Walker	12.00	5.50

1996-97 Metal
Maximum Metal

The first ten cards were randomly inserted in first series hobby packs only at a rate of one in 180. This 10-card set features embossed metalized cards of ten of the fan's favorite impact players. The fronts display color action player images with a metallic foil basketball in the background. The backs carry player information. The final ten cards were randomly inserted in second series retail packs only at a rate of one in 120. These cards feature the same design used in series one.

	MINT	NRMT
COMPLETE SET (20)	400.00	180.00
COMPLETE SERIES 1 (10)	300.00	135.00
COMPLETE SERIES 2 (10)	100.00	45.00
COMMON CARD (1-20)	5.00	2.20
1-10: SER.1 STATED ODDS 1:180 HOBBY		
11-20: SER.2 STATED ODDS 1:120 RETAIL		

☐ 1 Charles Barkley	15.00	6.75
☐ 2 Anfernee Hardaway	40.00	18.00
☐ 3 Grant Hill	60.00	27.00
☐ 4 Michael Jordan	125.00	55.00
☐ 5 Jason Kidd	20.00	9.00
☐ 6 Karl Malone	15.00	6.75
☐ 7 Hakeem Olajuwon	20.00	9.00
☐ 8 Gary Payton	15.00	6.75
☐ 9 David Robinson	15.00	6.75
☐ 10 Damon Stoudamire	25.00	11.00
☐ 11 Juwan Howard	6.00	2.70
☐ 12 Shawn Kemp	15.00	6.75
☐ 13 Kerry Kittles	6.00	2.70
☐ 14 Stephon Marbury	25.00	11.00
☐ 15 Dennis Rodman	20.00	9.00
☐ 16 Joe Smith	6.00	2.70
☐ 17 Jerry Stackhouse	6.00	2.70

	MINT	NRMT
☐ 18 John Stockton	5.00	2.20
☐ 19 Antoine Walker	25.00	11.00
☐ 20 Chris Webber	12.00	5.50

1996-97 Metal Metal Edge

Randomly inserted in all first series packs at a rate of one in 36, this 15-card set features players known for their aggressiveness in driving to the basket. The fronts display a color player photo a geometric metallic foil background. The backs carry player information.

	MINT	NRMT
COMPLETE SET (15)	80.00	36.00
COMMON CARD (1-15)	2.00	.90
SEMISTARS	2.50	1.10
UNLISTED STARS	4.00	1.80
SER.1 STATED ODDS 1:36 HOBBY/RETAIL		

		MINT	NRMT
☐ 1	Charles Barkley	6.00	2.70
☐ 2	Jamal Mashburn	2.00	.90
☐ 3	Alonzo Mourning	4.00	1.80
☐ 4	Gary Payton	6.00	2.70
☐ 5	Scottie Pippen	12.00	5.50
☐ 6	Steve Smith	2.50	1.10
☐ 7	Latrell Sprewell	2.50	1.10
☐ 8	John Stockton	4.00	1.80
☐ 9	Nick Van Exel	4.00	1.80
☐ 10	Chris Webber	10.00	4.50
☐ 11	Stephon Marbury	15.00	6.75
☐ 12	Shareef Abdur-Rahim	10.00	4.50
☐ 13	Ray Allen	5.00	2.20
☐ 14	Antoine Walker	15.00	6.75
☐ 15	Kobe Bryant	30.00	13.50

1996-97 Metal Minted Metal Redemption

These redemption cards were randomly inserted into hobby packs of series two at one in 720 packs and were exchangeable for Highland Mint cards. The selected two players are the Fleer Spokesmen, Grant Hill and Jerry Stackhouse. The expiration date for the cards was March 1, 1998. Both players have the following redemptions available: All-Metal 14kt.

gold, Gold-plated, Silver and Bronze cards. Both the Gold and the Solid Gold cards for each player are not priced below due to lack of market information.

	MINT	NRMT
COMP.BRONZE SET (2)	110.00	50.00
COMMON CARD (1-2)	40.00	18.00
*SILVER: 1.5X HI COLUMN		
SER.2 STATED ODDS 1:720 HOBBY FOR ANY		
PLAYERS LISTED ALPHABETICALLY		

		MINT	NRMT
☐ 1	Grant Hill Bronze	80.00	36.00
☐ 2	Jerry Stackhouse Bronze	40.00	18.00
☐ 3	Grant Hill Silver	120.00	55.00
☐ 4	Jerry Stackhouse Silver	60.00	27.00

1996-97 Metal Molten Metal

The first ten cards were randomly inserted in series one retail packs only at a rate of one in 180. This 10-card set features some of the hottest up and coming stars who have one to three years NBA experience. The fronts display color action player photos on a 3-D background. The backs carry player information. The final twenty cards were randomly inserted in series two hobby packs at a rate of one in 72. The second series cards feature embossed technology.

	MINT	NRMT
COMPLETE SET (30)	600.00	275.00
COMPLETE SERIES 1 (10)	250.00	110.00
COMPLETE SERIES 2 (20)	350.00	160.00
COMMON CARD (1-10)	12.00	5.50
COMMON CARD (11-30)	5.00	2.70
SEMISTARS SER.2	6.00	2.70
UNLISTED STARS SER.2	8.00	3.60
1-10: SER.1 STATED ODDS 1:180 RETAIL		
11-30: SER.2 STATED ODDS 1:72 HOBBY		

		MINT	NRMT
☐ 1	Michael Finley	12.00	5.50
☐ 2	Kevin Garnett	60.00	27.00
☐ 3	Anfernee Hardaway	40.00	18.00
☐ 4	Grant Hill	60.00	27.00
☐ 5	Juwan Howard	12.00	5.50
☐ 6	Jason Kidd	20.00	9.00
☐ 7	Antonio McDyess	15.00	6.75
☐ 8	Joe Smith	12.00	5.50
☐ 9	Jerry Stackhouse	12.00	5.50
☐ 10	Damon Stoudamire	20.00	9.00
☐ 11	Shareef Abdur-Rahim	25.00	11.00
☐ 12	Ray Allen	12.00	5.50
☐ 13	Charles Barkley	12.00	5.50
☐ 14	Terrell Brandon	8.00	3.60
☐ 15	Marcus Camby	10.00	4.50
☐ 16	Tom Gugliotta	8.00	3.60
☐ 17	Allen Iverson	40.00	18.00
☐ 18	Michael Jordan	100.00	45.00
☐ 19	Kerry Kittles	10.00	4.50
☐ 20	Karl Malone	12.00	5.50
☐ 21	Hakeem Olajuwon	15.00	6.75
☐ 22	Shaquille O'Neal	30.00	13.50
☐ 23	Gary Payton	12.00	5.50
☐ 24	Scottie Pippen	25.00	11.00
☐ 25	David Robinson	12.00	5.50
☐ 26	Glenn Robinson	8.00	3.60
☐ 27	Joe Smith	10.00	4.50
☐ 28	Latrell Sprewell	5.00	2.20
☐ 29	Antoine Walker	40.00	18.00
☐ 30	Chris Webber	20.00	9.00

1996-97 Metal Net-Rageous

Randomly inserted in all series two packs at a rate of one in 288, this 10-card set features some of the best players in the NBA against a die-cut background.

	MINT	NRMT
COMPLETE SET (10)	500.00	220.00
COMMON CARD (1-10)	15.00	6.75
SER.2 STATED ODDS 1:288 HOBBY/RETAIL		

		MINT	NRMT
☐ 1	Kevin Garnett	80.00	36.00
☐ 2	Anfernee Hardaway	50.00	22.00
☐ 3	Grant Hill	80.00	36.00
☐ 4	Juwan Howard	15.00	6.75
☐ 5	Michael Jordan	150.00	70.00
☐ 6	Shawn Kemp	40.00	18.00
☐ 7	Shaquille O'Neal	50.00	22.00

	MINT	NRMT
☐ 8 Dennis Rodman	50.00	22.00
☐ 9 Jerry Stackhouse	15.00	6.75
☐ 10 Damon Stoudamire	30.00	13.50

1996-97 Metal Platinum Portraits

Randomly inserted in all series two packs at a rate of one in 96, this 10-card set focuses on NBA stars using up-close profile photography. Card fronts feature a head shot of the player against a silver metalized background.

	MINT	NRMT
COMPLETE SET (10)	150.00	70.00
COMMON CARD (1-10)	8.00	3.60
SER.2 STATED ODDS 1:96 HOBBY/RETAIL		

		MINT	NRMT
☐ 1	Charles Barkley	8.00	3.60
☐ 2	Kevin Garnett	30.00	13.50
☐ 3	Anfernee Hardaway	20.00	9.00
☐ 4	Grant Hill	30.00	13.50
☐ 5	Michael Jordan	60.00	27.00
☐ 6	Shawn Kemp	15.00	6.75
☐ 7	Karl Malone	8.00	3.60
☐ 8	Shaquille O'Neal	20.00	9.00
☐ 9	Hakeem Olajuwon	10.00	4.50
☐ 10	Damon Stoudamire	12.00	5.50

1996-97 Metal Power Tools

Randomly inserted in all first series packs at a rate of one in 18, this 10-card set features color action player cutouts of power players on etched foil backgrounds of machine gears. The backs carry player information.

	MINT	NRMT
COMPLETE SET (10)	30.00	13.50
COMMON CARD (1-10)	1.00	.45
SEMISTARS	1.50	.70
SER.1 STATED ODDS 1:18 HOBBY/RETAIL		

		MINT	NRMT
☐ 1	Vin Baker	5.00	2.20
☐ 2	Charles Barkley	4.00	1.80
☐ 3	Horace Grant	1.00	.45
☐ 4	Juwan Howard	3.00	1.35
☐ 5	Larry Johnson	1.50	.70
☐ 6	Shawn Kemp	8.00	3.60
☐ 7	Karl Malone	4.00	1.80
☐ 8	Antonio McDyess	4.00	1.80
☐ 9	Dennis Rodman	10.00	4.50
☐ 10	Joe Smith	3.00	1.35

1996-97 Metal Steel Slammin'

Randomly inserted in all first series packs at a rate of one in 72, this 10-card set features the NBA's top slam-dunkers performing their craft on a metal die-cut card. The fronts display a color action player image on a metallic background. The backs carry player information.

	MINT	NRMT
COMPLETE SET (10)	160.00	70.00
COMMON CARD (1-10)	2.50	1.10
SER.1 STATED ODDS 1:72 HOBBY/RETAIL		

		MINT	NRMT
☐ 1	Brent Barry	2.50	1.10
☐ 2	Clyde Drexler	8.00	3.60
☐ 3	Michael Finley	8.00	3.60
☐ 4	Kevin Garnett	40.00	18.00
☐ 5	Eddie Jones	12.00	5.50
☐ 6	Michael Jordan	80.00	36.00
☐ 7	Shawn Kemp	20.00	9.00
☐ 8	Shaquille O'Neal	25.00	11.00
☐ 9	Joe Smith	8.00	3.60
☐ 10	Jerry Stackhouse	8.00	3.60

1997-98 Metal Universe

The Metal Universe set was issued in only one series, containing 125 cards that came in nine card packs with a suggest-

ed retail price of $2.49. Card fronts contain an action shot of the player with some form of a "cartoon" scene surrounding the player. The player's name is against a silver bar running along the card bottom. Card back contains a photo and statistics.

	MINT	NRMT
COMPLETE SET (125)	25.00	11.00
COMMON CARD (1-125)	.15	.07
SEMISTARS	.20	.09
UNLISTED STARS	.40	.18
COMMON REEBOK BRONZE	.20	.09
*REEBOK BRONZE: .25X TO .5X HI COLUMN		
COMMON REEBOK GOLD	.60	.25
*REEBOK GOLD: 1.5X TO 3X HI		
COMMON REEBOK SILVER	.30	.14
*REEBOK SILVERS: .5X TO 1X HI		
REEBOK: ONE PER SER.1 PACK		
AUTOGRAPHICS LISTED UNDER SKYBOX		

		MINT	NRMT
☐ 1	Charles Barkley	.60	.25
☐ 2	Dell Curry	.15	.07
☐ 3	Derek Fisher	.15	.07
☐ 4	Derek Harper	.15	.07
☐ 5	Avery Johnson	.15	.07
☐ 6	Steve Smith	.20	.09
☐ 7	Alonzo Mourning	.40	.18
☐ 8	Rod Strickland	.20	.09
☐ 9	Chris Mullin	.40	.18
☐ 10	Rony Seikaly	.15	.07
☐ 11	Vin Baker	.75	.35
☐ 12	Austin Croshere	.50	.23
☐ 13	Vinny Del Negro	.15	.07
☐ 14	Sherman Douglas	.15	.07
☐ 15	Priest Lauderdale	.15	.07
☐ 16	Cedric Ceballos	.15	.07
☐ 17	LaPhonso Ellis	.15	.07
☐ 18	Luc Longley	.20	.09
☐ 19	Brian Grant	.15	.07
☐ 20	Allen Iverson	2.00	.90
☐ 21	Anthony Mason	.20	.09
☐ 22	Bryant Reeves	.20	.09
☐ 23	Michael Jordan	5.00	2.20
☐ 24	Dale Ellis	.15	.07
☐ 25	Terrell Brandon	.40	.18
☐ 26	Patrick Ewing	.40	.18
☐ 27	Allan Houston	.20	.09
☐ 28	Damon Stoudamire	.75	.35
☐ 29	Lucy Vaught	.20	.09
☐ 30	Walt Williams	.15	.07
☐ 31	Shareef Abdur-Rahim	1.25	.55
☐ 32	Mario Elie	.15	.07
☐ 33	Juwan Howard	.40	.18
☐ 34	Tom Gugliotta	.40	.18
☐ 35	Glen Rice	.40	.18
☐ 36	Isaiah Rider	.20	.09
☐ 37	Arvydas Sabonis	.20	.09
☐ 38	Derrick Coleman	.20	.09
☐ 39	Kevin Willis	.15	.07
☐ 40	Kendall Gill	.20	.09

1997-98 Metal Universe Precious Metal Gems

Serially numbered to 150, this 123-card set is a parallel to the basic set. The card fronts feature a full color red background for 90% of the production run, while a full green color background accounts for the remaining 10%. To ascertain values of the green cards, please refer to the multiplier listed below coupled with the value of the red card.

		MINT	NRMT
	COMMON RED (1-123)	15.00	6.75
	SEMISTARS RED	25.00	11.00
	RANDOM INSERTS IN HOBBY PACKS		
	STATED PRINT RUN 100 SERIAL #'d SETS		
	COMMON GREEN (1-123) .. 80.00	36.00
	*GREEN STARS: 5X TO 8X RED GEMS HI	
	*GREEN RCs: 3X TO 6X RED	
	FIRST 10 CARDS OF PRINT RUN ARE GREEN	

☐ 41	John Wallace	.20	.09
☐ 42	Tracy McGrady	2.50	1.10
☐ 43	Travis Best	.15	.07
☐ 44	Malik Rose	.15	.07
☐ 45	Anfernee Hardaway	1.50	.70
☐ 46	Roy Rogers	.15	.07
☐ 47	Kerry Kittles	.40	.18
☐ 48	Matt Maloney	.15	.07
☐ 49	Antonio McDyess	.50	.23
☐ 50	Shaquille O'Neal	1.50	.70
☐ 51	George McCloud	.15	.07
☐ 52	Wesley Person	.15	.07
☐ 53	Shawn Bradley	.15	.07
☐ 54	Antonio Davis	.15	.07
☐ 55	P.J. Brown	.15	.07
☐ 56	Joe Dumars	.40	.18
☐ 57	Horace Grant	.20	.09
☐ 58	Steve Kerr	.15	.07
☐ 59	Hakeem Olajuwon	.75	.35
☐ 60	Tim Hardaway	.50	.23
☐ 61	Toni Kukoc	.20	.09
☐ 62	Ron Mercer	3.00	1.35
☐ 63	Gary Payton	.60	.25
☐ 64	Grant Hill	2.50	1.10
☐ 65	Detlef Schrempf		.09
☐ 66	Tim Duncan	5.00	2.20
☐ 67	Shawn Kemp	1.25	.55
☐ 68	Voshon Lenard	.15	.07
☐ 69	Othella Harrington	.15	.07
☐ 70	Hersey Hawkins	.20	.09
☐ 71	Lindsey Hunter	.15	.07
☐ 72	Antoine Walker	2.00	.90
☐ 73	Jamal Mashburn	.20	.09
☐ 74	Kenny Anderson	.20	.09
☐ 75	Todd Day	.15	.07
☐ 76	Todd Fuller	.15	.07
☐ 77	Jermaine O'Neal	.20	.09
☐ 78	David Robinson	.60	.25
☐ 79	Erick Dampier	.15	.07
☐ 80	Keith Van Horn	4.00	1.80
☐ 81	Kobe Bryant	3.00	1.35
☐ 82	Chris Childs		.07
☐ 83	Scottie Pippen	1.25	.55
☐ 84	Marcus Camby	.40	.18
☐ 85	Danny Ferry	.15	.07
☐ 86	Jeff Hornacek	.20	.09
☐ 87	Charles Outlaw	.15	.07
☐ 88	Larry Johnson	.20	.09
☐ 89	Tony Delk	.15	.07
☐ 90	Stephon Marbury	2.00	.90
☐ 91	Robert Pack	.15	.07
☐ 92	Chris Webber	1.00	.45
☐ 93	Clyde Drexler	.50	.23
☐ 94	Eddie Jones	.75	.35
☐ 95	Jerry Stackhouse	.40	.18
☐ 96	Tyrone Hill	.15	.07
☐ 97	Karl Malone	.60	.25
☐ 98	Reggie Miller	.40	.18
☐ 99	Bryon Russell	.15	.07
☐ 100	Dale Davis	.15	.07
☐ 101	Steve Nash	.20	.09
☐ 102	Vitaly Potapenko	.15	.07
☐ 103	Nick Anderson	.15	.07
☐ 104	Ray Allen	.50	.23
☐ 105	Sean Elliott	.15	.07
☐ 106	Dikembe Mutombo	.20	.09
☐ 107	Dennis Rodman	1.50	.70
☐ 108	Lorenzen Wright	.15	.07
☐ 109	Kevin Garnett	2.50	1.10
☐ 110	Christian Laettner	.20	.09
☐ 111	Mitch Richmond	.40	.18
☐ 112	Joe Smith	.40	.18
☐ 113	Jason Kidd	.75	.35
☐ 114	Glenn Robinson	.40	.18
☐ 115	Mark Price	.15	.07
☐ 116	Mark Jackson	.15	.07
☐ 117	Bobby Phills	.15	.07
☐ 118	John Starks	.20	.09
☐ 119	John Stockton	.40	.18
☐ 120	Mookie Blaylock	.20	.09
☐ 121	Dean Garrett	.15	.07
☐ 122	Olden Polynice	.15	.07
☐ 123	Latrell Sprewell	.20	.09
☐ 124	Checklist	.15	.07
☐ 125	Checklist	.15	.07

☐ 1	Charles Barkley	60.00	27.00
☐ 2	Dell Curry	15.00	6.75
☐ 3	Derek Fisher	15.00	6.75
☐ 4	Derek Harper	15.00	6.75
☐ 5	Steve Smith	25.00	11.00
☐ 6	Avery Johnson	15.00	6.75
☐ 7	Alonzo Mourning	40.00	18.00
☐ 8	Rod Strickland	25.00	11.00
☐ 9	Chris Mullin	40.00	18.00
☐ 10	Rony Seikaly	15.00	6.75
☐ 11	Vin Baker	80.00	36.00
☐ 12	Austin Croshere	40.00	18.00
☐ 13	Vinny Del Negro	15.00	6.75
☐ 14	Sherman Douglas	15.00	6.75
☐ 15	Priest Lauderdale	15.00	6.75
☐ 16	Cedric Ceballos	15.00	6.75
☐ 17	LaPhonso Ellis	15.00	6.75
☐ 18	Luc Longley	25.00	11.00
☐ 19	Brian Grant	15.00	6.75
☐ 20	Allen Iverson	200.00	90.00
☐ 21	Anthony Mason	25.00	11.00
☐ 22	Bryant Reeves	25.00	11.00
☐ 23	Michael Jordan	750.00	350.00
☐ 23G	M.Jordan Green	8500.00	3800.00
☐ 24	Dale Ellis	15.00	6.75
☐ 25	Terrell Brandon	30.00	13.50
☐ 26	Patrick Ewing	40.00	18.00
☐ 27	Allan Houston	25.00	11.00
☐ 28	Damon Stoudamire	75.00	34.00
☐ 29	Loy Vaught	25.00	11.00
☐ 30	Walt Williams	15.00	6.75
☐ 31	Shareef Abdur-Rahim	150.00	70.00
☐ 32	Mario Elie	15.00	6.75

☐ 33	Juwan Howard	40.00	18.00
☐ 34	Tom Gugliotta	40.00	18.00
☐ 35	Glen Rice	40.00	18.00
☐ 36	Isaiah Rider	25.00	11.00
☐ 37	Arvydas Sabonis	25.00	11.00
☐ 38	Derrick Coleman	25.00	11.00
☐ 39	Kevin Willis	15.00	6.75
☐ 40	Kendall Gill	25.00	11.00
☐ 41	John Wallace	25.00	11.00
☐ 42	Tracy McGrady	125.00	55.00
☐ 43	Travis Best	15.00	6.75
☐ 44	Malik Rose	15.00	6.75
☐ 45	Anfernee Hardaway	225.00	100.00
☐ 46	Roy Rogers	15.00	6.75
☐ 47	Kerry Kittles	40.00	18.00
☐ 48	Matt Maloney	15.00	6.75
☐ 49	Antonio McDyess	50.00	22.00
☐ 50	Shaquille O'Neal	150.00	70.00
☐ 51	George McCloud	15.00	6.75
☐ 52	Wesley Person	15.00	6.75
☐ 53	Shawn Bradley	15.00	6.75
☐ 54	Antonio Davis	15.00	6.75
☐ 55	P.J. Brown	15.00	6.75
☐ 56	Joe Dumars	40.00	18.00
☐ 57	Horace Grant	25.00	11.00
☐ 58	Steve Kerr	15.00	6.75
☐ 59	Hakeem Olajuwon	80.00	36.00
☐ 60	Tim Hardaway	60.00	27.00
☐ 61	Toni Kukoc	40.00	18.00
☐ 62	Ron Mercer	150.00	70.00
☐ 63	Gary Payton	60.00	27.00
☐ 64	Grant Hill	250.00	110.00
☐ 65	Detlef Schrempf	25.00	11.00
☐ 66	Tim Duncan	250.00	110.00
☐ 67	Shawn Kemp	125.00	55.00
☐ 68	Voshon Lenard	15.00	6.75
☐ 69	Othella Harrington	15.00	6.75
☐ 70	Hersey Hawkins	25.00	11.00
☐ 71	Lindsey Hunter	15.00	6.75
☐ 72	Antoine Walker	200.00	90.00
☐ 73	Jamal Mashburn	25.00	11.00
☐ 74	Kenny Anderson	25.00	11.00
☐ 75	Todd Day	15.00	6.75
☐ 76	Todd Fuller	15.00	6.75
☐ 77	Jermaine O'Neal	25.00	11.00
☐ 78	David Robinson	60.00	27.00
☐ 79	Erick Dampier	15.00	6.75
☐ 80	Keith Van Horn	200.00	90.00
☐ 81	Kobe Bryant	500.00	220.00
☐ 82	Chris Childs	15.00	6.75
☐ 83	Scottie Pippen	150.00	70.00
☐ 84	Marcus Camby	40.00	18.00
☐ 85	Danny Ferry	15.00	6.75
☐ 86	Jeff Hornacek	25.00	11.00
☐ 87	Charles Outlaw	15.00	6.75
☐ 88	Larry Johnson	25.00	11.00
☐ 89	Tony Delk	15.00	6.75
☐ 90	Stephon Marbury	200.00	90.00
☐ 91	Robert Pack	15.00	6.75
☐ 92	Chris Webber	150.00	70.00
☐ 93	Clyde Drexler	50.00	22.00
☐ 94	Eddie Jones	80.00	36.00
☐ 95	Jerry Stackhouse	40.00	18.00
☐ 96	Tyrone Hill	15.00	6.75
☐ 97	Karl Malone	60.00	27.00
☐ 98	Reggie Miller	40.00	18.00
☐ 99	Bryon Russell	15.00	6.75
☐ 100	Dale Davis	15.00	6.75
☐ 101	Steve Nash	25.00	11.00
☐ 102	Vitaly Potapenko	15.00	6.75
☐ 103	Nick Anderson	15.00	6.75
☐ 104	Ray Allen	50.00	22.00
☐ 105	Sean Elliott	15.00	6.75
☐ 106	Dikembe Mutombo	25.00	11.00
☐ 107	Dennis Rodman	150.00	70.00
☐ 108	Lorenzen Wright	15.00	6.75
☐ 109	Kevin Garnett	250.00	110.00
☐ 110	Christian Laettner	25.00	11.00
☐ 111	Mitch Richmond	40.00	18.00
☐ 112	Joe Smith	40.00	18.00
☐ 113	Jason Kidd	80.00	36.00
☐ 114	Glenn Robinson	30.00	13.50
☐ 115	Mark Price	15.00	6.75
☐ 116	Mark Jackson	15.00	6.75
☐ 117	Bobby Phills	15.00	6.75
☐ 118	John Starks	25.00	11.00

□ 119	John Stockton	40.00	18.00
□ 120	Mookie Blaylock	25.00	11.00
□ 121	Dean Garrett	15.00	6.75
□ 122	Olden Polynice	15.00	6.75
□ 123	Latrell Sprewell	25.00	11.00

1997-98 Metal Universe Gold Universe

Randomly inserted in retail packs only at a rate of one in 120, this 10-card set features some of the shining stars of the NBA.

	MINT	NRMT
COMPLETE SET (10)	100.00	45.00
COMMON CARD (1-10)	4.00	1.80
SEMISTARS	5.00	2.20
UNLISTED STARS	8.00	3.60
STATED ODDS 1:120 RETAIL		

□ 1	Damon Stoudamire	15.00	6.75
□ 2	Shawn Kemp	25.00	11.00
□ 3	John Stockton	8.00	3.60
□ 4	Jerry Stackhouse	8.00	3.60
□ 5	John Wallace	4.00	1.80
□ 6	Juwan Howard	8.00	3.60
□ 7	David Robinson	12.00	5.50
□ 8	Gary Payton	12.00	5.50
□ 9	Joe Smith	8.00	3.60
□ 10	Charles Barkley	12.00	5.50

1997-98 Metal Universe Planet Metal

Randomly inserted in packs at a rate of one in 24, this 15-card set focuses on the NBA's best

depicted as a universe. Card fronts feature a silver metallic background with a "swirling" planet in the background.

	MINT	NRMT
COMPLETE SET (15)	125.00	55.00
COMMON CARD (1-15)	2.50	1.10
STATED ODDS 1:24 HOBBY/RETAIL		

□ 1	Michael Jordan	30.00	13.50
□ 2	Allen Iverson	12.00	5.50
□ 3	Kobe Bryant	20.00	9.00
□ 4	Shaquille O'Neal	10.00	4.50
□ 5	Stephon Marbury	12.00	5.50
□ 6	Marcus Camby	2.50	1.10
□ 7	Anfernee Hardaway	10.00	4.50
□ 8	Kevin Garnett	15.00	6.75
□ 9	Shareef Abdur-Rahim	8.00	3.60
□ 10	Dennis Rodman	10.00	4.50
□ 11	Grant Hill	15.00	6.75
□ 12	Hakeem Olajuwon	5.00	2.20
□ 13	David Robinson	4.00	1.80
□ 14	Charles Barkley	4.00	1.80
□ 15	Gary Payton	4.00	1.80

1997-98 Metal Universe Platinum Portraits

Randomly inserted in packs at a rate of one in 288, this 15-card set features NBA stars in a Hall of Fame plaque treatment. The cards feature a matrix-etching the form a picture of the player's face.

	MINT	NRMT
COMPLETE SET (15)	750.00	350.00
COMMON CARD (1-15)	12.00	5.50
STATED ODDS 1:288 HOBBY/RETAIL		

□ 1	Michael Jordan	150.00	70.00
□ 2	Allen Iverson	60.00	27.00
□ 3	Kobe Bryant	100.00	45.00
□ 4	Shaquille O'Neal	50.00	22.00
□ 5	Stephon Marbury	60.00	27.00
□ 6	Marcus Camby	12.00	5.50
□ 7	Anfernee Hardaway	50.00	22.00
□ 8	Kevin Garnett	80.00	36.00
□ 9	Shareef Abdur-Rahim	40.00	18.00
□ 10	Dennis Rodman	50.00	22.00
□ 11	Ray Allen	15.00	6.75
□ 12	Grant Hill	80.00	36.00
□ 13	Kerry Kittles	12.00	5.50
□ 14	Antoine Walker	60.00	27.00
□ 15	Scottie Pippen	40.00	18.00

1997-98 Metal Universe Silver Slams

Randomly inserted in packs at one in 6, this 20-card set focuses on the young rising stars of the NBA. The cards feature black and white photos of the players against colorful foilboard.

	MINT	NRMT
COMPLETE SET (20)	25.00	11.00
COMMON CARD (1-20)	.50	.23
SEMISTARS	.75	.35
UNLISTED STARS	1.25	.55
STATED ODDS 1:6 HOBBY/RETAIL		

□ 1	Ray Allen	1.50	.70
□ 2	Kerry Kittles	1.25	.55
□ 3	Antoine Walker	6.00	2.70
□ 4	Scottie Pippen	4.00	1.80
□ 5	Damon Stoudamire	2.50	1.10
□ 6	Shawn Kemp	4.00	1.80
□ 7	Jerry Stackhouse	1.25	.55
□ 8	John Wallace	.50	.23
□ 9	Juwan Howard	1.25	.55
□ 10	Gary Payton	2.00	.90
□ 11	Joe Smith	1.25	.55
□ 12	Terrell Brandon	1.25	.55
□ 13	Hakeem Olajuwon	2.50	1.10
□ 14	Tom Gugliotta	1.25	.55
□ 15	Glen Rice	1.25	.55
□ 16	Charles Barkley	2.00	.90
□ 17	David Robinson	2.00	.90
□ 18	Patrick Ewing	1.25	.55
□ 19	Christian Laettner	.75	.35
□ 20	Chris Webber	3.00	1.35

1997-98 Metal Universe Titanium

Randomly inserted in hobby packs only at a rate of one in 72, this 20-card set features some of the NBA's most explosive players on die cut cards. The cards are on clear plastic stock with the script in a light-blue foil.

	MINT	NRMT
COMPLETE SET (20)	400.00	180.00
COMMON CARD (1-20)	6.00	2.70
STATED ODDS 1:72 HOBBY		

		MINT	NRMT
☐ 1	Michael Jordan	80.00	36.00
☐ 2	Allen Iverson	30.00	13.50
☐ 3	Kobe Bryant	50.00	22.00
☐ 4	Shaquille O'Neal	25.00	11.00
☐ 5	Stephon Marbury	30.00	13.50
☐ 6	Marcus Camby	6.00	2.70
☐ 7	Anfernee Hardaway	25.00	11.00
☐ 8	Kevin Garnett	40.00	18.00
☐ 9	Shareef Abdur-Rahim	20.00	9.00
☐ 10	Dennis Rodman	25.00	11.00
☐ 11	Ray Allen	8.00	3.60
☐ 12	Grant Hill	40.00	18.00
☐ 13	Kerry Kittles	6.00	2.70
☐ 14	Antoine Walker	30.00	13.50
☐ 15	Scottie Pippen	20.00	9.00
☐ 16	Damon Stoudamire	12.00	5.50
☐ 17	Shawn Kemp	20.00	9.00
☐ 18	Hakeem Olajuwon	12.00	5.50
☐ 19	Jerry Stackhouse	6.00	2.70
☐ 20	Juwan Howard	6.00	2.70

1997-98 Metal Universe Championship

The 1997-98 Metal Universe Championship set was issued in one series totalling 100 cards. The debut set was issued in eight-card packs which carried a suggested retail price of $2.69.

	MINT	NRMT
COMPLETE SET (100)	25.00	11.00
COMMON CARD (1-100)	.15	.07
SEMISTARS	.20	.09
UNLISTED STARS	.40	.18
AUTOGRAPHICS LISTED UNDER SKYBOX		

☐ 1	Shaquille O'Neal	1.50	.70
☐ 2	Chris Mills	.15	.07
☐ 3	Tariq Abdul-Wahad	.60	.25
☐ 4	Adonal Foyle	.50	.23
☐ 5	Kendall Gill	.20	.09
☐ 6	Vin Baker	.75	.35

☐ 7	Chauncey Billups	1.50	.70
☐ 8	Bobby Jackson	.75	.35
☐ 9	Keith Van Horn	4.00	1.80
☐ 10	Avery Johnson	.15	.07
☐ 11	Juwan Howard	.40	.18
☐ 12	Steve Smith	.20	.09
☐ 13	Alonzo Mourning	.40	.18
☐ 14	Anfernee Hardaway	1.50	.70
☐ 15	Sean Elliott	.15	.07
☐ 16	Danny Fortson	.75	.35
☐ 17	John Stockton	.40	.18
☐ 18	John Thomas	.15	.07
☐ 19	Lorenzen Wright	.15	.07
☐ 20	Mark Price	.15	.07
☐ 21	Rasheed Wallace	.20	.09
☐ 22	Ray Allen	.50	.23
☐ 23	Michael Jordan	5.00	2.20
☐ 24	John Wallace	.20	.09
☐ 25	Bryant Reeves	.20	.09
☐ 26	Allen Iverson	2.00	.90
☐ 27	Antoine Walker	2.00	.90
☐ 28	Terrell Brandon	.40	.18
☐ 29	Damon Stoudamire	.75	.35
☐ 30	Antonio Daniels	1.00	.45
☐ 31	Corey Beck	.15	.07
☐ 32	Tyrone Hill	.15	.07
☐ 33	Grant Hill	2.50	1.10
☐ 34	Tim Thomas	2.50	1.10
☐ 35	Clifford Robinson	.15	.07
☐ 36	Tracy McGrady	2.50	1.10
☐ 37	Chris Webber	1.00	.45
☐ 38	Austin Croshere	.50	.23
☐ 39	Reggie Miller	.40	.18
☐ 40	Derek Anderson	1.25	.55
☐ 41	Kevin Garnett	2.50	1.10
☐ 42	Kevin Johnson	.20	.09
☐ 43	Antonio McDyess	.50	.23
☐ 44	Brevin Knight	1.25	.55
☐ 45	Charles Barkley	.60	.25
☐ 46	Tom Gugliotta	.40	.18
☐ 47	Jason Kidd	.75	.35
☐ 48	Marcus Camby	.40	.18
☐ 49	God Shammgod	.15	.07
☐ 50	Wesley Person	.15	.07
☐ 51	Clyde Drexler	.50	.23
☐ 52	Paul Grant	.15	.07
☐ 53	Rod Strickland	.20	.09
☐ 54	Tony Delk	.15	.07
☐ 55	Stephon Marbury	2.00	.90
☐ 56	Detlef Schrempf	.20	.09
☐ 57	Joe Smith	.40	.18
☐ 58	Sam Cassell	.20	.09
☐ 59	Gary Payton	.60	.25
☐ 60	Chris Crawford	.15	.07
☐ 61	Hakeem Olajuwon	.75	.35
☐ 62	Dennis Rodman	1.50	.70
☐ 63	Eddie Jones	.75	.35
☐ 64	Mitch Richmond	.40	.18
☐ 65	David Wesley	.15	.07
☐ 66	Tony Battie	.75	.35
☐ 67	Isaac Austin	.15	.07
☐ 68	Isaiah Rider	.20	.09
☐ 69	Jacque Vaughn	.60	.25
☐ 70	Tim Hardaway	.50	.23
☐ 71	Darrell Armstrong	.15	.07
☐ 72	Tim Duncan	5.00	2.20
☐ 73	Glen Rice	.40	.18
☐ 74	Bubba Wells	.15	.07
☐ 75	Maurice Taylor	1.25	.55
☐ 76	Kelvin Cato	.50	.23
☐ 77	Shareef Abdur-Rahim	1.25	.55
☐ 78	Shawn Kemp	1.25	.55
☐ 79	Michael Finley	.40	.18
☐ 80	Chris Mullin	.40	.18
☐ 81	Ron Mercer	3.00	1.35
☐ 82	Brian Williams	.15	.07
☐ 83	Kerry Kittles	.40	.18
☐ 84	David Robinson	.60	.25
☐ 85	Scottie Pippen	1.25	.55
☐ 86	Kobe Bryant	3.00	1.35
☐ 87	Anthony Johnson	.15	.07
☐ 88	Karl Malone	.60	.25
☐ 89	Mookie Blaylock	.20	.09
☐ 90	Joe Dumars	.40	.18
☐ 91	Patrick Ewing	.40	.18
☐ 92	Bobby Phills	.15	.07

☐ 93	Dennis Scott	.15	.07
☐ 94	Rodney Rogers	.15	.07
☐ 95	Jim Jackson	.20	.09
☐ 96	Kenny Anderson	.20	.09
☐ 97	Jerry Stackhouse	.40	.18
☐ 98	Larry Johnson	.20	.09
☐ 99	Checklist	.15	.07
☐ 100	Checklist	.15	.07

1997-98 Metal Universe Championship Precious Metal Gems

Randomly inserted into packs, this 98-card set parallels the regular base set, minus the checklists. The cards are serially numbered to 50 on the back.

	MINT	NRMT
COMMON CARD (1-98)	30.00	13.50
SEMISTARS	40.00	18.00
RANDOM INSERTS IN PACKS		
STATED PRINT RUN 50 SERIAL #'d SETS		

☐ 1	Shaquille O'Neal	250.00	110.00
☐ 2	Chris Mills	30.00	13.50
☐ 3	Tariq Abdul-Wahad	50.00	22.00
☐ 4	Adonal Foyle	60.00	27.00
☐ 5	Kendall Gill	40.00	18.00
☐ 6	Vin Baker	125.00	55.00
☐ 7	Chauncey Billups	125.00	55.00
☐ 8	Bobby Jackson	60.00	27.00
☐ 9	Keith Van Horn	350.00	160.00
☐ 10	Avery Johnson	30.00	13.50
☐ 11	Juwan Howard	60.00	27.00
☐ 12	Steve Smith	40.00	18.00
☐ 13	Alonzo Mourning	60.00	27.00
☐ 14	Anfernee Hardaway	250.00	110.00
☐ 15	Sean Elliott	30.00	13.50
☐ 16	Danny Fortson	60.00	27.00
☐ 17	John Stockton	60.00	27.00
☐ 18	John Thomas	30.00	13.50
☐ 19	Lorenzen Wright	30.00	13.50
☐ 20	Mark Price	30.00	13.50
☐ 21	Rasheed Wallace	40.00	18.00
☐ 22	Ray Allen	80.00	36.00
☐ 23	Michael Jordan	1400.00	650.00
☐ 24	John Wallace	40.00	18.00
☐ 25	Bryant Reeves	40.00	18.00
☐ 26	Allen Iverson	300.00	135.00
☐ 27	Antoine Walker	300.00	135.00
☐ 28	Terrell Brandon	50.00	22.00
☐ 29	Damon Stoudamire	125.00	55.00
☐ 30	Antonio Daniels	80.00	36.00
☐ 31	Corey Beck	30.00	13.50
☐ 32	Tyrone Hill	30.00	13.50
☐ 33	Grant Hill	400.00	180.00
☐ 34	Tim Thomas	200.00	90.00

☐ 35	Clifford Robinson	30.00	13.50
☐ 36	Tracy McGrady	200.00	90.00
☐ 37	Chris Webber	150.00	70.00
☐ 38	Austin Croshere	60.00	27.00
☐ 39	Reggie Miller	60.00	27.00
☐ 40	Derek Anderson	100.00	45.00
☐ 41	Kevin Garnett	400.00	180.00
☐ 42	Kevin Johnson	40.00	18.00
☐ 43	Antonio McDyess	80.00	36.00
☐ 44	Brevin Knight	100.00	45.00
☐ 45	Charles Barkley	100.00	45.00
☐ 46	Tom Gugliotta	60.00	27.00
☐ 47	Jason Kidd	150.00	70.00
☐ 48	Marcus Camby	60.00	27.00
☐ 49	God Shammgod	30.00	13.50
☐ 50	Wesley Person	30.00	13.50
☐ 51	Clyde Drexler	80.00	36.00
☐ 52	Paul Grant	30.00	13.50
☐ 53	Rod Strickland	40.00	18.00
☐ 54	Tony Delk	30.00	13.50
☐ 55	Stephon Marbury	300.00	135.00
☐ 56	Detlef Schrempf	40.00	18.00
☐ 57	Joe Smith	60.00	27.00
☐ 58	Sam Cassell	40.00	18.00
☐ 59	Gary Payton	100.00	45.00
☐ 60	Chris Crawford	30.00	13.50
☐ 61	Hakeem Olajuwon	125.00	55.00
☐ 62	Dennis Rodman	250.00	110.00
☐ 63	Eddie Jones	150.00	70.00
☐ 64	Mitch Richmond	60.00	27.00
☐ 65	David Wesley	30.00	13.50
☐ 66	Tony Battie	60.00	27.00
☐ 67	Isaac Austin	30.00	13.50
☐ 68	Isaiah Rider	40.00	18.00
☐ 69	Jacque Vaughn	50.00	22.00
☐ 70	Tim Hardaway	90.00	40.00
☐ 71	Darrell Armstrong	30.00	13.50
☐ 72	Tim Duncan	400.00	180.00
☐ 73	Glen Rice	60.00	27.00
☐ 74	Bubba Wells	30.00	13.50
☐ 75	Maurice Taylor	100.00	45.00
☐ 76	Kelvin Cato	60.00	27.00
☐ 77	Shareef Abdur-Rahim	200.00	90.00
☐ 78	Shawn Kemp	200.00	90.00
☐ 79	Michael Finley	60.00	27.00
☐ 80	Chris Mullin	60.00	27.00
☐ 81	Ron Mercer	250.00	110.00
☐ 82	Brian Williams	30.00	13.50
☐ 83	Kerry Kittles	60.00	27.00
☐ 84	David Robinson	100.00	45.00
☐ 85	Scottie Pippen	200.00	90.00
☐ 86	Kobe Bryant	500.00	220.00
☐ 87	Anthony Johnson	30.00	13.50
☐ 88	Karl Malone	100.00	45.00
☐ 89	Mookie Blaylock	40.00	18.00
☐ 90	Joe Dumars	60.00	27.00
☐ 91	Patrick Ewing	60.00	27.00
☐ 92	Bobby Phills	30.00	13.50
☐ 93	Dennis Scott	30.00	13.50
☐ 94	Rodney Rogers	30.00	13.50
☐ 95	Jim Jackson	40.00	18.00
☐ 96	Kenny Anderson	40.00	18.00
☐ 97	Jerry Stackhouse	60.00	27.00
☐ 98	Larry Johnson	40.00	18.00

1997-98 Metal Universe Championship All-Millenium Team

Randomly inserted into packs at a rate of one in six, this 20-card set features top veterans and rising stars pictured against etched-foil fronts.

	MINT	NRMT
COMPLETE SET (20)	40.00	18.00
COMMON CARD (1-20)	.75	.35
STATED ODDS 1:6		

☐ 1	Stephon Marbury	4.00	1.80
☐ 2	Shareef Abdur-Rahim	2.50	1.10
☐ 3	Karl Malone	1.25	.55
☐ 4	Scottie Pippen	2.50	1.10
☐ 5	Michael Jordan	10.00	4.50
☐ 6	Marcus Camby	.75	.35
☐ 7	Kobe Bryant	6.00	2.70
☐ 8	Allen Iverson	4.00	1.80
☐ 9	Kerry Kittles	.75	.35
☐ 10	Ray Allen	1.00	.45
☐ 11	Dennis Rodman	2.50	1.10
☐ 12	Damon Stoudamire	1.50	.70
☐ 13	Antoine Walker	4.00	1.80
☐ 14	Anfernee Hardaway	3.00	1.35
☐ 15	Hakeem Olajuwon	1.50	.70
☐ 16	Shawn Kemp	2.50	1.10
☐ 17	Antonio Daniels	1.00	.45
☐ 18	Juwan Howard	.75	.35
☐ 19	Gary Payton	1.25	.55
☐ 20	Tim Duncan	5.00	2.20

1997-98 Metal Universe Championship Championship Galaxy

Randomly inserted into packs at a rate of one in 192, this 15-card set pays tribute to players who currently wear NBA Championship rings and many young players who hope to obtain one in the future. The cards feature a foiled background with a double-etched player image surrounded by a "riveted" border.

	MINT	NRMT
COMPLETE SET (15)	500.00	220.00
COMMON CARD (1-15)	8.00	3.60
STATED ODDS 1:192		

☐ 1	Michael Jordan	100.00	45.00
☐ 2	Allen Iverson	40.00	18.00
☐ 3	Kobe Bryant	60.00	27.00
	UER front Kobe, Bryant		
☐ 4	Shaquille O'Neal	30.00	13.50
☐ 5	Stephon Marbury	40.00	18.00
☐ 6	Marcus Camby	8.00	3.60
☐ 7	Anfernee Hardaway	30.00	13.50
☐ 8	Kevin Garnett	50.00	22.00
☐ 9	Shareef Abdur-Rahim	25.00	11.00
☐ 10	Dennis Rodman	30.00	13.50
☐ 11	Grant Hill	50.00	22.00
☐ 12	Kerry Kittles	8.00	3.60
☐ 13	Antoine Walker	40.00	18.00
☐ 14	Scottie Pippen	25.00	11.00
☐ 15	Damon Stoudamire	15.00	6.75

1997-98 Metal Universe Championship Future Champions

Randomly inserted into packs at a rate of one in 18, this 15-card set focuses on rookie players. The cards appear three-dimensional with an action photo encased in a copper frame that is die cut at the bottom.

	MINT	NRMT
COMPLETE SET (15)	60.00	27.00
COMMON CARD (1-15)	1.25	.55
SEMISTARS	1.50	.70
UNLISTED STARS	2.50	1.10
STATED ODDS 1:18		

☐ 1	Tim Duncan	15.00	6.75
☐ 2	Tony Battie	2.50	1.10
☐ 3	Keith Van Horn	12.00	5.50
☐ 4	Antonio Daniels	3.00	1.35
☐ 5	Chauncey Billups	5.00	2.20
☐ 6	Ron Mercer	10.00	4.50
☐ 7	Tracy McGrady	8.00	3.60
☐ 8	Danny Fortson	2.50	1.10
☐ 9	Brevin Knight	4.00	1.80
☐ 10	Derek Anderson	4.00	1.80
☐ 11	Bobby Jackson	2.50	1.10
☐ 12	Jacque Vaughn	1.50	.70
☐ 13	Tim Thomas	8.00	3.60
☐ 14	Austin Croshere	1.25	.55
☐ 15	Kelvin Cato	1.25	.55

1997-98 Metal Universe Championship Hardware

Randomly inserted into packs at a rate of one in 360, this 15-card set focuses on players who have a shot to one day take home an NBA honor, such as Scoring Champion, Rookie of the Year and MVP. The cards feature dual foils with an embossed background.

	MINT	NRMT
COMPLETE SET (15)	1000.00	450.00
COMMON CARD (1-15)	15.00	6.75
STATED ODDS 1:360		

		MINT	NRMT
☐ 1	Stephon Marbury	80.00	36.00
☐ 2	Shareef Abdur-Rahim	50.00	22.00
☐ 3	Shaquille O'Neal	60.00	27.00
☐ 4	Scottie Pippen	50.00	22.00
☐ 5	Michael Jordan	200.00	90.00
☐ 6	Marcus Camby	15.00	6.75
☐ 7	Kobe Bryant	125.00	55.00
☐ 8	Kevin Garnett	100.00	45.00
☐ 9	Kerry Kittles	15.00	6.75
☐ 10	Grant Hill	100.00	45.00
☐ 11	Dennis Rodman	60.00	27.00
☐ 12	Tim Duncan	100.00	45.00
☐ 13	Antonio Daniels	20.00	9.00
☐ 14	Anfernee Hardaway	60.00	27.00
☐ 15	Allen Iverson	80.00	36.00

1997-98 Metal Universe Championship Trophy Case

Randomly inserted into packs at a rate of one in 96, this 10-card set features ten of the best players in the NBA presented on a 3-D sculptured embossed background.

	MINT	NRMT
COMPLETE SET (10)	100.00	45.00
COMMON CARD (1-10)	4.00	1.80
STATED ODDS 1:96		

		MINT	NRMT
☐ 1	Kevin Garnett	25.00	11.00
☐ 2	Grant Hill	25.00	11.00
☐ 3	Damon Stoudamire	8.00	3.60
☐ 4	Shaquille O'Neal	15.00	6.75
☐ 5	Ray Allen	5.00	2.20
☐ 6	Gary Payton	6.00	2.70
☐ 7	Shawn Kemp	12.00	5.50
☐ 8	Hakeem Olajuwon	8.00	3.60
☐ 9	John Stockton	4.00	1.80
☐ 10	Antoine Walker	20.00	9.00

1997 Pinnacle Inside WNBA

The 1997 Pinnacle Inside set was issued in one series totalling 82 cards and honors the first women playing in the WNBA. The set was distributed in cans containing ten cards each with a suggested retail price of $2.99. The fronts feature color action player photos with player information on the backs. The set contains the topical subsets: Hoops Scoops (57-72), and Style , Grace (73-80). Scheduled release date is October, 1997.

	MINT	NRMT
COMPLETE SET (81)	40.00	18.00
COMMON CARD (1-81)	.15	.07
SEMISTARS	.20	.09
UNLISTED STARS	.30	.14
ALL NON-SUBSET CARDS ARE RCs		

COMP.COURT SET (81)	250.00	110.00
COMMON COURT (1-81)	1.00	.45
*COURT: 3X TO 6X HI COLUMN		
COURT: STATED ODDS 1:7		

☐ 1	Lisa Leslie	4.00	1.80
☐ 2	Cynthia Cooper	4.00	1.80
☐ 3	Rebecca Lobo	3.00	1.35
☐ 4	Michele Timms	1.25	.55
☐ 5	Ruthie Bolton-Holifield	2.50	1.10
☐ 6	Michelle Edwards	.75	.35
☐ 7	Vicky Bullett	.40	.18
☐ 8	Tammi Reiss	.75	.35
☐ 9	Penny Toler	.30	.14
☐ 10	Tia Jackson	.15	.07
☐ 11	Rhonda Mapp	.20	.09
☐ 12	Elena Baranova	1.00	.45
☐ 13	Tina Thompson	1.00	.45
☐ 14	Merlakia Jones	.40	.18
☐ 15	Tora Suber	.30	.14
☐ 16	Sophia Witherspoon	.40	.18
☐ 17	Tajama Abraham	.15	.07
☐ 18	Jessie Hicks	.15	.07
☐ 19	Tina Nicholson	.15	.07
☐ 20	Tiffany Woosley	.15	.07
☐ 21	Chantel Tremitiere	.15	.07
☐ 22	Deanna Charles	.15	.07
☐ 23	Nancy Lieberman-Cline	2.00	.90
☐ 24	Denique Graves	.15	.07
☐ 25	Toni Foster	.30	.14
☐ 26	Sheryl Swoopes	4.00	1.80
☐ 27	Kym Hampton	.40	.18
☐ 28	Sharon Manning	.15	.07
☐ 29	J.Lawrence Braxton	.15	.07
☐ 30	Sue Wicks	.30	.14
☐ 31	Lady Hardmon	.15	.07
☐ 32	Jamila Wideman	.30	.14
☐ 33	Bridgette Gordon	.15	.07
☐ 34	Lynette Woodard	1.25	.55
☐ 35	Kim Perrot	.40	.18
☐ 36	Teresa Weatherspoon	.40	.18
☐ 37	Andrea Stinson	1.25	.55
☐ 38	Janeth Arcain	.15	.07
☐ 39	Pamela McGee	.30	.14
☐ 40	Tamecka Dixon	.40	.18
☐ 41	Wendy Palmer	1.25	.55
☐ 42	Umeki Webb	.15	.07
☐ 43	Isabelle Fijalkowski	.15	.07
☐ 44	Jennifer Gillom	1.25	.55
☐ 45	Latasha Byears	.40	.18
☐ 46	Haixia Zheng	.15	.07
☐ 47	Kisha Ford	.15	.07
☐ 48	Eva Nemcova	.30	.14
☐ 49	Penny Moore	.40	.18
☐ 50	Mwadi Mabika	.15	.07
☐ 51	Kim Williams	.15	.07
☐ 52	Wanda Guyton	.15	.07
☐ 53	Vickie Johnson	.40	.18
☐ 54	Deborah Carter	.15	.07
☐ 55	Bridget Pettis	.15	.07
☐ 56	Andrea Congreaves	.15	.07
☐ 57	Haixia Zheng HS	.15	.07
☐ 58	Tammi Reiss HS	.40	.18
☐ 59	Jennifer Gillom HS	.60	.25
☐ 60	Bridgette Gordon HS	.15	.07
☐ 61	J.Lawrence Braxton HS	.15	.07
☐ 62	Cynthia Cooper HS	2.00	.90
☐ 63	T.Weatherspoon HS	.30	.14
☐ 64	Andrea Stinson HS	.50	.23
☐ 65	N.Lieberman-Cline HS	1.00	.45
☐ 66	Andrea Congreaves HS	.15	.07
☐ 67	Sophia Witherspoon HS	.30	.14
☐ 68	Vicky Bullett HS	.30	.14
☐ 69	R. Bolton-Holifield HS	1.25	.55
☐ 70	Tina Thompson HS	.50	.23
☐ 71	Lynette Woodard HS	.60	.25
☐ 72	Jamila Wideman HS	.20	.09
☐ 73	Lisa Leslie SG	2.00	.90
☐ 74	Wendy Palmer SG	.60	.25
☐ 75	Michele Timms SG	.60	.25
☐ 76	R. Bolton-Holifield SG	1.25	.55
☐ 77	Andrea Stinson SG	.60	.25
☐ 78	Lynette Woodard SG	.60	.25
☐ 79	Cynthia Cooper SG	2.00	.90
☐ 80	Rebecca Lobo SG	1.50	.70
☐ 81	Checklist	.15	.07

1997 Pinnacle Inside WNBA Executive Collection

Randomly inserted in cans at the rate of one in 47, this 82-card limited production set is parallel to the base set and is printed on prismatic foil with gold foil stamped accents.

	MINT	NRMT
COMMON CARD (1-81)	8.00	3.60
SEMISTARS	12.00	5.50
UNLISTED STARS	15.00	6.75
STATED ODDS 1:47		

		MINT	NRMT
☐ 1	Lisa Leslie	200.00	90.00
☐ 2	Cynthia Cooper	200.00	90.00
☐ 3	Rebecca Lobo	150.00	70.00
☐ 4	Michele Timms	60.00	27.00
☐ 5	Ruthie Bolton-Holifield	125.00	55.00
☐ 6	Michelle Edwards	40.00	18.00
☐ 7	Vicky Bullett	20.00	9.00
☐ 8	Tammi Reiss	40.00	18.00
☐ 9	Penny Toler	15.00	6.75
☐ 10	Tia Jackson	8.00	3.60
☐ 11	Rhonda Mapp	12.00	5.50
☐ 12	Elena Baranova	50.00	22.00
☐ 13	Tina Thompson	50.00	22.00
☐ 14	Merlakia Jones	20.00	9.00
☐ 15	Tora Suber	15.00	6.75
☐ 16	Sophia Witherspoon	20.00	9.00
☐ 17	Tajama Abraham	8.00	3.60
☐ 18	Jessie Hicks	8.00	3.60
☐ 19	Tina Nicholson	8.00	3.60
☐ 20	Tiffany Woosley	8.00	3.60
☐ 21	Chantel Tremitiere	8.00	3.60
☐ 22	Daedra Charles	8.00	3.60
☐ 23	Nancy Lieberman-Cline	100.00	45.00
☐ 24	Denique Graves	8.00	3.60
☐ 25	Toni Foster	15.00	6.75
☐ 26	Sheryl Swoopes	200.00	90.00
☐ 27	Kym Hampton	20.00	9.00
☐ 28	Sharon Manning	8.00	3.60
☐ 29	J.Lawrence Braxton	8.00	3.60
☐ 30	Sue Wicks	15.00	6.75
☐ 31	Lady Hardmon	8.00	3.60
☐ 32	Jamila Wideman	15.00	6.75
☐ 33	Bridgette Gordon	8.00	3.60
☐ 34	Lynette Woodard	60.00	27.00
☐ 35	Kim Perrot	20.00	9.00
☐ 36	Teresa Weatherspoon	20.00	9.00
☐ 37	Andrea Stinson	60.00	27.00
☐ 38	Janeth Arcain	8.00	3.60
☐ 39	Pamela McGee	15.00	6.75
☐ 40	Tamecka Dixon	20.00	9.00
☐ 41	Wendy Palmer	60.00	27.00
☐ 42	Umeki Webb	8.00	3.60
☐ 43	Isabelle Fijalkowski	8.00	3.60
☐ 44	Jennifer Gillom	60.00	27.00
☐ 45	Latasha Byears	20.00	9.00
☐ 46	Haixia Zheng	8.00	3.60
☐ 47	Kisha Ford	8.00	3.60
☐ 48	Eva Nemcova	15.00	6.75
☐ 49	Penny Moore	20.00	9.00
☐ 50	Mwadi Mabika	8.00	3.60
☐ 51	Kim Williams	8.00	3.60
☐ 52	Wanda Guyton	8.00	3.60
☐ 53	Vickie Johnson	20.00	9.00
☐ 54	Deborah Carter	8.00	3.60
☐ 55	Bridget Pettis	8.00	3.60
☐ 56	Andrea Congreaves	8.00	3.60
☐ 57	Haixia Zheng HS	8.00	3.60
☐ 58	Tammi Reiss HS	20.00	9.00
☐ 59	Jennifer Gillom HS	30.00	13.50
☐ 60	Bridgette Gordon HS	8.00	3.60
☐ 61	J.Lawrence Braxton HS	8.00	3.60
☐ 62	Cynthia Cooper	75.00	34.00
☐ 63	T.Weatherspoon HS	15.00	6.75
☐ 64	Elena Baranova HS	25.00	11.00
☐ 65	N.Lieberman-Cline HS	50.00	22.00
☐ 66	Andrea Congreaves HS	8.00	3.60
☐ 67	Sophia Witherspoon HS	15.00	6.75
☐ 68	Vicky Bullett HS	15.00	6.75
☐ 69	R.Bolton-Holifield HS	60.00	27.00
☐ 70	Tina Thompson HS	25.00	11.00
☐ 71	Lynette Woodard HS	30.00	13.50
☐ 72	Jamila Wideman HS	12.00	5.50
☐ 73	Lisa Leslie SG	100.00	45.00
☐ 74	Wendy Palmer SG	50.00	22.00
☐ 75	Michele Timms SG	30.00	13.50
☐ 76	R.Bolton-Holifield SG	60.00	27.00
☐ 77	Andrea Stinson SG	30.00	13.50
☐ 78	Lynette Woodard SG	30.00	13.50
☐ 79	Cynthia Cooper SG	100.00	45.00
☐ 80	Rebecca Lobo SG	80.00	36.00
☐ 81	Checklist	8.00	3.60

1997 Pinnacle Inside WNBA Cans

This set of 17 cans feature color action photos of the stars of the league's inaugural season along with their team's logo. Two player cans per team were issued. Each can contained ten cards. A special WNBA can was also distributed.

	MINT	NRMT
COMPLETE SET (17)	15.00	6.75
COMMON CAN (1-17)	.40	.18
SEMISTARS	.50	.23
UNLISTED STARS	.60	.25
COMMON SEALED CAN	4.00	1.80

		MINT	NRMT
☐ 1	Andrea Stinson	1.00	.45
☐ 2	Vicky Bullett	.75	.35
☐ 3	Lynette Woodard	1.00	.45
☐ 4	Michelle Edwards	.75	.35
☐ 5	Cynthia Cooper	3.00	1.35
☐ 6	Tina Thompson	.75	.35
☐ 7	Lisa Leslie	3.00	1.35
☐ 8	Jamila Wideman	.60	.25
☐ 9	Teresa Weatherspoon	.75	.35
☐ 10	Rebecca Lobo	2.50	1.10
☐ 11	Michele Timms	1.00	.45
☐ 12	Bridget Pettis	.40	.18
☐ 13	Bridgette Gordon	.40	.18
☐ 14	Ruthie Bolton-Holifield	2.00	.90
☐ 15	Wendy Palmer	1.00	.45
☐ 16	Elena Baranova	.75	.35
☐ 17	WNBA League	2.00	.90

1997 Pinnacle Inside WNBA My Town

Randomly inserted in cans at the rate of one in 19, this eight-card insert set features color photos of franchise players printed on a holographic foil card stock with a micro-etched backdrop of the player's team city.

	MINT	NRMT
COMPLETE SET (8)	125.00	55.00
COMMON CARD (1-8)	5.00	2.20
STATED ODDS 1:19		

		MINT	NRMT
☐ 1	Lisa Leslie	40.00	18.00
☐ 2	Lady Hardmon	5.00	2.20
☐ 3	Michele Timms	12.00	5.50
☐ 4	Ruthie Bolton-Holifield	25.00	11.00
☐ 5	Andrea Stinson	12.00	5.50
☐ 6	Michelle Edwards	8.00	3.60
☐ 7	Cynthia Cooper	40.00	18.00
☐ 8	Rebecca Lobo	30.00	13.50

1997 Pinnacle Inside WNBA Team Development

Randomly inserted in cans at the rate of one in 19, this eight-card set features color photos of the WNBA first round draft picks printed on an all-foil card stock with foil stamped treatments.

	MINT	NRMT
COMPLETE SET (8)	55.00	25.00
COMMON CARD (1-8)	6.00	2.70
STATED ODDS 1:19		

		MINT	NRMT
☐ 1	Tina Thompson	20.00	9.00
☐ 2	Pamela McGee	6.00	2.70

		MINT	NRMT
□ 3	Jamila Wideman	6.00	2.70
□ 4	Eva Nemcova	8.00	3.60
□ 5	Tammi Reiss	15.00	6.75
□ 6	Sue Wicks	6.00	2.70
□ 7	Tora Suber	6.00	2.70
□ 8	Toni Foster	6.00	2.70

1998 Pinnacle WNBA

The 1998 Pinnacle WNBA set was issued in one series totalling 85 cards. Each pack came with 10 cards with a suggested retail price of $2.49. This was the second year that Pinnacle distributed the only cards for the WNBA. The card fronts carried either an action or posed player shot, and their statistics from the first year of the WNBA.

	MINT	NRMT
COMPLETE SET (85)	25.00	11.00
COMMON CARD (1-85)	.10	.05
SEMISTARS	.15	.07
COMP.COURT SET (85)	80.00	36.00
COMMON COURT (1-85)	.30	.14
*COURT: 1.25X TO 3X HI COLUMN		
COURT: STATED ODDS 1:3		

		MINT	NRMT
□ 1	Rhonda Blades	.50	.23
□ 2	Lisa Leslie	3.00	1.35
□ 3	Jennifer Gillom	1.00	.45
□ 4	Ruthie Bolton-Holifield	2.00	.90
□ 5	Wendy Palmer	1.00	.45
□ 6	Sophia Witherspoon	.30	.14
□ 7	Eva Nemcova	.30	.14
□ 8	Andrea Stinson	1.00	.45
□ 9	Heidi Burge	.10	.05
□ 10	Cynthia Cooper	3.00	1.35
□ 11	Christy Smith	.10	.05
□ 12	Penny Moore	.30	.14
□ 13	Penny Toler	.25	.11
□ 14	Bridget Pettis	.10	.05
□ 15	Tora Suber	.25	.11
□ 16	Elena Baranova	.75	.35
□ 17	Rebecca Lobo	2.50	1.10
□ 18	Isabelle Fijalkowski	.10	.05
□ 19	Vicky Bullett	.30	.14
□ 20	Tina Thompson	.75	.35
□ 21	Andrea Kuklova	.10	.05
□ 22	Rita Williams	.50	.23
□ 23	Tamecka Dixon	.30	.14
□ 24	Michele Timms	1.00	.45
□ 25	Bridgette Gordon	.10	.05
□ 26	Tammi Reiss	.60	.25
□ 27	Kym Hampton	.30	.14
□ 28	Janice Braxton	.10	.05
□ 29	Rhonda Mapp	.15	.07
□ 30	Janeth Arcain	.15	.07
□ 31	Lynette Woodard	1.00	.45
□ 32	Tammy Jackson	.10	.05
□ 33	Haixia Zheng	.10	.05
□ 34	Toni Foster	.25	.11
□ 35	Chantel Tremitiere	.10	.05
□ 36	Vickie Johnson	.30	.14
□ 37	Michelle Edwards	.60	.25
□ 38	Wanda Guyton	.15	.07
□ 39	Kim Perrot	.30	.14
□ 40	Sheryl Swoopes	3.00	1.35
□ 41	Merlakia Jones	.30	.14
□ 42	Teresa Weatherspoon	.30	.14
□ 43	Kim Williams	.10	.05
□ 44	Lady Hardmon	.10	.05
□ 45	Latasha Byears	.30	.14
□ 46	Umeki Webb	.10	.05
□ 47	Pamela McGee	.25	.11
□ 48	Nikki McCray	3.00	1.35
□ 49	Cindy Brown	2.00	.90
□ 50	Tiffany Woosley	.10	.05
□ 51	Andrea Congreaves	.10	.05
□ 52	Jamila Wideman	.25	.11
□ 53	Mwadi Mabika	.10	.05
□ 54	Murriel Page	.75	.35
□ 55	Mikiko Hagiwara	.10	.05
□ 56	Linda Burgess	.30	.14
□ 57	Olympia Scott	.10	.05
□ 58	Dena Head	.10	.05
□ 59	Quacy Barnes	.10	.05
□ 60	Suzie McDonnell-Serio	.60	.25
□ 61	Trena Trice	.10	.05
□ 62	Rushia Brown	.10	.05
□ 63	Kisha Ford	.10	.05
□ 64	Sharon Manning	.10	.05
□ 65	Tangela Smith	.10	.05
□ 66	Jim Lewis CO	.10	.05
□ 67	N.Lieberman-Cline CO	1.50	.70
□ 68	Van Chancellor CO	.15	.07
□ 69	Denise Taylor CO	.10	.05
□ 70	Heidi VanDerveer CO	.10	.05
□ 71	Marynell Meadors CO	.10	.05
□ 72	L.Hill-MacDonald CO	.10	.05
□ 73	Nancy Darsch CO	.10	.05
□ 74	Cheryl Miller CO	3.00	1.35
□ 75	Julie Rousseau CO	.10	.05
□ 76	Rebecca Lobo P	1.25	.55
□ 77	Jennifer Gillom P	.50	.23
□ 78	Janeth Arcain P	.10	.05
□ 79	Rhonda Mapp P	.10	.05
□ 80	Cynthia Cooper P	1.50	.70
□ 81	Tina Thompson P	.40	.18
□ 82	Kym Hampton P	.15	.07
□ 83	Cynthia Cooper P	1.50	.70
□ 84	Checklist	.10	.05
□ 85	Checklist	.10	.05
□ S66	Sheryl Swoopes	2.00	.90
	Sample		

1998 Pinnacle WNBA Arena Collection

Randomly inserted in packs at a rate of one in 19, this 85-card set parallels the basic set. The

cards feature gold foil, rather than the common silver and features the title "Arena Collection" above the player's name. The cards are also produced on a silver sparkle foil.

	MINT	NRMT
COMPLETE SET (85)	500.00	220.00
COMMON CARD (1-85)	1.50	.70
SEMISTARS	2.50	1.10
STATED ODDS 1:19		

		MINT	NRMT
□ 1	Rhonda Blades	3.00	1.35
□ 2	Lisa Leslie	40.00	18.00
□ 3	Jennifer Gillom	12.00	5.50
□ 4	Ruthie Bolton-Holifield	25.00	11.00
□ 5	Wendy Palmer	12.00	5.50
□ 6	Sophia Witherspoon	4.00	1.80
□ 7	Eva Nemcova	4.00	1.80
□ 8	Andrea Stinson	12.00	5.50
□ 9	Heidi Burge	1.50	.70
□ 10	Cynthia Cooper	40.00	18.00
□ 11	Christy Smith	1.50	.70
□ 12	Penny Moore	4.00	1.80
□ 13	Penny Toler	3.00	1.35
□ 14	Bridget Pettis	1.50	.70
□ 15	Tora Suber	3.00	1.35
□ 16	Elena Baranova	10.00	4.50
□ 17	Rebecca Lobo	30.00	13.50
□ 18	Isabelle Fijalkowski	1.50	.70
□ 19	Vicky Bullett	4.00	1.80
□ 20	Tina Thompson	10.00	4.50
□ 21	Andrea Kuklova	1.50	.70
□ 22	Rita Williams	3.00	1.35
□ 23	Tamecka Dixon	4.00	1.80
□ 24	Michele Timms	12.00	5.50
□ 25	Bridgette Gordon	1.50	.70
□ 26	Tammi Reiss	8.00	3.60
□ 27	Kym Hampton	4.00	1.80
□ 28	Janice Braxton	1.50	.70
□ 29	Rhonda Mapp	2.50	1.10
□ 30	Janeth Arcain	2.50	1.10
□ 31	Lynette Woodard	12.00	5.50
□ 32	Tammy Jackson	1.50	.70
□ 33	Haixia Zheng	1.50	.70
□ 34	Toni Foster	3.00	1.35
□ 35	Chantel Tremitiere	1.50	.70
□ 36	Vickie Johnson	4.00	1.80
□ 37	Michelle Edwards	8.00	3.60
□ 38	Wanda Guyton	2.50	1.10
□ 39	Kim Perrot	4.00	1.80
□ 40	Sheryl Swoopes	40.00	18.00
□ 41	Merlakia Jones	4.00	1.80
□ 42	Teresa Weatherspoon	4.00	1.80
□ 43	Kim Williams	1.50	.70
□ 44	Lady Hardmon	1.50	.70
□ 45	Latasha Byears	4.00	1.80
□ 46	Umeki Webb	1.50	.70
□ 47	Pamela McGee	3.00	1.35
□ 48	Nikki McCray	20.00	9.00
□ 49	Cindy Brown	12.00	5.50
□ 50	Tiffany Woosley	1.50	.70
□ 51	Andrea Congreaves	1.50	.70
□ 52	Jamila Wideman	3.00	1.35

☐ 53 Mwadi Mabika	1.50	.70
☐ 54 Murriel Page	5.00	2.20
☐ 55 Mikiko Hagiwara	1.50	.70
☐ 56 Linda Burgess	3.00	1.35
☐ 57 Olympia Scott	1.50	.70
☐ 58 Dena Head	1.50	.70
☐ 59 Quacy Barnes	1.50	.70
☐ 60 Suzie McDonnell-Serio	4.00	1.80
☐ 61 Trena Trice	1.50	.70
☐ 62 Rushia Brown	1.50	.70
☐ 63 Kisha Ford	1.50	.70
☐ 64 Sharon Manning	1.50	.70
☐ 65 Tangela Smith	1.50	.70
☐ 66 Jim Lewis CO	1.50	.70
☐ 67 N.Lieberman-Cline CO	20.00	9.00
☐ 68 Van Chancellor CO	2.50	1.10
☐ 69 Denise Taylor CO	1.50	.70
☐ 70 Heidi VanDerveer CO	1.50	.70
☐ 71 Marynell Meadors CO	1.50	.70
☐ 72 L. Hill-MacDonald CO	1.50	.70
☐ 73 Nancy Darsch CO	1.50	.70
☐ 74 Cheryl Miller CO	40.00	18.00
☐ 75 Julie Rousseau CO	1.50	.70
☐ 76 Rebecca Lobo P	15.00	6.75
☐ 77 Jennifer Gillom P	6.00	2.70
☐ 78 Janeth Arcain P	1.50	.70
☐ 79 Rhonda Mapp P	1.50	.70
☐ 80 Cynthia Cooper P	20.00	9.00
☐ 81 Tina Thompson P	5.00	2.20
☐ 82 Kym Hampton P	2.50	1.10
☐ 83 Cynthia Cooper P	20.00	9.00
☐ 84 Checklist	1.50	.70
☐ 85 Checklist	1.50	.70

1998 Pinnacle WNBA Coast to Coast

Randomly inserted in packs at a rate of one in 9, this 10-card set features players who can take it from one end of the court to another. The card fronts feature a player photo against silver foil with "Coast 2 Coast" running along the bottom of the card. The card backs feature commentary.

	MINT	NRMT
COMPLETE SET (10)	30.00	13.50
COMMON CARD (1-10)	1.00	.45
STATED ODDS 1:9		

☐ 1 Lynette Woodard	3.00	1.35
☐ 2 Nikki McCray	5.00	2.20
☐ 3 Lisa Leslie	10.00	4.50
☐ 4 Andrea Stinson	3.00	1.35
☐ 5 Eva Nemcova	1.00	.45
☐ 6 Cynthia Cooper	10.00	4.50
☐ 7 Teresa Weatherspoon	1.00	.45
☐ 8 Wendy Palmer	3.00	1.35

1998 Pinnacle WNBA Number Ones

Randomly inserted into packs at a rate of one in 19, this 9-card set features number one draft picks. The card fronts are on silver foil with "Number 1 Ones" across the bottom. Card backs feature a black and white background of the card front with a brief commentary on the player.

	MINT	NRMT
COMPLETE SET (9)	120.00	55.00
COMMON CARD (1-9)	5.00	2.20
STATED ODDS 1:19		

☐ 1 Malgorzata Dydek	40.00	18.00
☐ 2 Ticha Penicheiro	12.00	5.50
☐ 3 Murriel Page	10.00	4.50
☐ 4 Korie Hlede	25.00	11.00
☐ 5 Allison Feaster	5.00	2.20
☐ 6 Cindy Blodgett	25.00	11.00
☐ 7 Tracy Reid	25.00	11.00
☐ 8 Alicia Thompson	5.00	2.20
☐ 9 Nyree Roberts	5.00	2.20

1998 Pinnacle WNBA Planet Pinnacle

Randomly inserted into packs at a rate of one in 9, this 10-card set features international players. The card fronts feature a posed player shot in a black and red "swirl" against silver foil. Card backs contain a facial shot with commentary.

	MINT	NRMT
COMPLETE SET (10)	20.00	9.00
COMMON CARD (1-10)	.50	.23
STATED ODDS 1:9		

☐ 1 Korie Hlede	3.00	1.35
☐ 2 Eva Nemcova	1.00	.45
☐ 3 Haixia Zheng	.50	.23
☐ 4 Michele Timms	3.00	1.35
☐ 5 Ticha Penicheiro	1.50	.70
☐ 6 Elena Baranova	2.50	1.10
☐ 7 Rebecca Lobo	8.00	3.60
☐ 8 Isabelle Fijalkowski	.50	.23
☐ 9 Andrea Congreaves	.50	.23
☐ 10 Sheryl Swoopes	10.00	4.50

1990-91 SkyBox

This 1990-91 set marks SkyBox's entry into the basketball card market. The complete set contains 423 standard-size cards featuring NBA players. The set was released in two series of 300 and 123 cards, respectively. Foil packs for each series contained 15 cards. However, the second series packs contained a mix of players from both series. The second series cards replaced 123 cards from the first series, which then became short-prints compared to other cards in the first series. The front features an action shot of the player on a computer-generated background of various color schemes. The player's name appears in a black stripe at the bottom with the team logo superimposed at the left lower corner. The photo is bordered in gold. The back presents head shots of the player with gold borders on white background. Player statistics are given in a box below the photo. The cards are checklisted below alphabetically according to team. Subsets are Coaches (301-327), Team Checklists (328-354), Lottery

☐ 9 Ruthie Bolton-Holifield	6.00	2.70
☐ 10 Michele Timms	3.00	1.35

Picks (355-365), Updates (366-420), and Checklists (421-423). Rookie Cards of note included in the set are Nick Anderson, Mookie Blaylock, Derrick Coleman, Vlade Divac, Sean Elliott, Danny Ferry, Kendall Gill, Tim Hardaway, Chris Jackson, Avery Johnson, Shawn Kemp, Gary Payton, Drazen Petrovic, Glen Rice, Clifford Robinson and Dennis Scott. First series single prints (SP) are noted below.

	MINT	NRMT
COMPLETE SET (423)	20.00	9.00
COMPLETE SERIES 1 (300)	12.00	5.50
COMPLETE SERIES 2 (123)..	8.00	3.60
COMMON CARD (1-300)	.05	.02
COMMON CARD (301-423) ..	.10	.05
COMMON SP	.10	.05
SEMISTARS SER.1	.10	.05
SEMISTARS SER.2	.30	.14
UNLISTED STARS SER.1	.25	.11
UNLISTED STARS SER.2	.60	.25

#	Player	MINT	NRMT
1	John Battle	.05	.02
2	Duane Ferrell SP	.10	.05
3	Jon Koncak	.05	.02
4	Cliff Levingston SP	.10	.05
5	John Long SP	.10	.05
6	Moses Malone	.25	.11
7	Doc Rivers	.05	.02
8	Kenny Smith SP	.10	.05
9	Alexander Volkov	.05	.02
10	Spud Webb	.10	.05
11	Dominique Wilkins	.25	.11
12	Kevin Willis	.10	.05
13	John Bagley	.05	.02
14	Larry Bird	1.00	.45
15	Kevin Gamble	.05	.02
16	Dennis Johnson SP	.05	.02
17	Joe Kleine	.05	.02
18	Reggie Lewis	.10	.05
19	Kevin McHale	.10	.05
20	Robert Parish	.10	.05
21	Jim Paxson SP	.10	.05
22	Ed Pinckney	.05	.02
23	Brian Shaw	.25	.11
24	Michael Smith	.05	.02
25	Richard Anderson SP ..	.10	.05
26	Muggsy Bogues	.10	.05
27	Rex Chapman	.25	.11
28	Dell Curry	.05	.02
29	Armon Gilliam	.05	.02
30	Michael Holton SP	.10	.05
31	Dave Hoppen	.05	.02
32	J.R. Reid	.05	.02
33	Robert Reid SP	.10	.05
34	Brian Rowsom SP	.10	.05
35	Kelly Tripucka	.05	.02
36	Michael Williams SP .. UER (Misspelled Michael on card)	.10	.05
37	B.J. Armstrong	.05	.02
38	Bill Cartwright	.05	.02
39	Horace Grant	.10	.05
40	Craig Hodges	.05	.02
41	Michael Jordan	3.00	1.35
42	Stacey King	.05	.02
43	Ed Nealy SP	.10	.05
44	John Paxson	.05	.02
45	Will Perdue	.05	.02
46	Scottie Pippen	1.00	.45
47	Jeff Sanders SP	.10	.05
48	Winston Bennett	.05	.02
49	Chucky Brown	.05	.02
50	Brad Daugherty	.05	.02
51	Craig Ehlo	.05	.02
52	Steve Kerr	.25	.11
53	Paul Mokeski SP	.10	.05
54	John Morton	.05	.02
55	Larry Nance	.10	.05
56	Mark Price	.10	.05
57	Tree Rollins SP	.10	.05
58	Hot Rod Williams	.05	.02
59	Steve Alford	.05	.02
60	Rolando Blackman	.05	.02
61	Adrian Dantley SP	.05	.02
62	Brad Davis	.05	.02
63	James Donaldson	.05	.02
64	Derek Harper	.10	.05
65	Anthony Jones SP	.10	.05
66	Sam Perkins SP	.10	.05
67	Roy Tarpley	.05	.02
68	Bill Wennington SP	.10	.05
69	Randy White	.05	.02
70	Herb Williams	.05	.02
71	Michael Adams	.05	.02
72	Joe Barry Carroll SP	.10	.05
73	Walter Davis	.05	.02
74	Alex English SP	.05	.02
75	Bill Hanzlik	.05	.02
76	Tim Kempton SP	.05	.02
77	Jerome Lane	.05	.02
78	Lafayette Lever SP	.10	.05
79	Todd Lichti	.05	.02
80	Blair Rasmussen	.05	.02
81	Dan Schayes SP	.10	.05
82	Mark Aguirre	.05	.02
83	William Bedford	.05	.02
84	Joe Dumars	.25	.11
85	James Edwards	.05	.02
86	David Greenwood SP ..	.10	.05
87	Scott Hastings	.05	.02
88	Gerald Henderson SP	.10	.05
89	Vinnie Johnson	.05	.02
90	Bill Laimbeer	.10	.05
91	Dennis Rodman (SkyBox logo in upper right or left)	1.25	.55
91B	Dennis Rodman (SkyBox logo in upper left corner)	1.00	.45
92	John Salley	.05	.02
93	Isiah Thomas	.25	.11
94	Manute Bol SP	.10	.05
95	Tim Hardaway	2.00	.90
96	Rod Higgins	.05	.02
97	Sarunas Marciulionis	.05	.02
98	Chris Mullin	.25	.11
99	Jim Petersen	.05	.02
100	Mitch Richmond	.40	.18
101	Mike Smrek	.05	.02
102	Terry Teagle SP	.10	.05
103	Tom Tolbert	.05	.02
104	Kelvin Upshaw SP	.10	.05
105	Anthony Bowie SP	.10	.05
106	Adrian Caldwell	.05	.02
107	Eric(Sleepy) Floyd	.05	.02
108	Buck Johnson	.05	.02
109	Vernon Maxwell	.05	.02
110	Hakeem Olajuwon	.50	.23
111	Larry Smith	.05	.02
112A	Otis Thorpe ERR (Front photo actually Mitchell Wiggins)	.50	.23
112B	Otis Thorpe COR	.10	.05
113A	M. Wiggins SP ERR (Front photo actually Otis Thorpe)	.50	.23
113B	M. Wiggins SP COR	.10	.05
114	Vern Fleming	.05	.02
115	Rickey Green SP	.10	.05
116	George McCloud	.25	.11
117	Reggie Miller	.30	.14
118A	Dyron Nix SP ERR.. (Back photo actually Wayman Tisdale)	1.50	.70
118B	Dyron Nix SP COR ..	.10	.05
119	Chuck Person	.10	.05
120	Mike Sanders	.05	.02
121	Detlef Schrempf	.10	.05
122	Rik Smits	.25	.11
123	LaSalle Thompson	.05	.02
124	Benoit Benjamin	.05	.02
125	Winston Garland	.05	.02
126	Tom Garrick	.05	.02
127	Gary Grant	.05	.02
128	Ron Harper	.10	.05
129	Danny Manning	.10	.05
130	Jeff Martin	.05	.02
131	Ken Norman	.05	.02
132	Charles Smith	.05	.02
133	Joe Wolf SP	.10	.05
134	Michael Cooper SP ..	.10	.05
135	Vlade Divac	.50	.23
136	Larry Drew	.05	.02
137	A.C. Green	.10	.05
138	Magic Johnson	.75	.35
139	Mark McNamara SP ..	.05	.02
140	Byron Scott	.10	.05
141	Mychal Thompson	.05	.02
142	Orlando Woolridge SP	.10	.05
143	James Worthy	.25	.11
144	Terry Davis	.05	.02
145	Sherman Douglas	.10	.05
146	Kevin Edwards	.05	.02
147	Tellis Frank SP	.10	.05
148	Scott Haffner SP	.10	.05
149	Grant Long	.05	.02
150	Glen Rice	1.50	.70
151	Rony Seikaly	.10	.05
152	Rory Sparrow SP	.10	.05
153	Jon Sundvold	.05	.02
154	Billy Thompson	.05	.02
155	Greg Anderson	.05	.02
156	Ben Coleman SP	.10	.05
157	Jeff Grayer	.05	.02
158	Jay Humphries	.05	.02
159	Frank Kornet	.05	.02
160	Larry Krystkowiak	.05	.02
161	Brad Lohaus	.05	.02
162	Ricky Pierce	.05	.02
163	Paul Pressey SP	.10	.05
164	Fred Roberts	.05	.02
165	Alvin Robertson	.05	.02
166	Jack Sikma	.05	.02
167	Randy Breuer	.05	.02
168	Tony Campbell	.05	.02
169	Tyrone Corbin	.05	.02
170	Sidney Lowe SP	.10	.05
171	Sam Mitchell	.05	.02
172	Tod Murphy	.05	.02
173	Pooh Richardson	.10	.05
174	Donald Royal SP	.10	.05
175	Brad Sellers SP	.10	.05
176	Mookie Blaylock	.50	.23
177	Sam Bowie	.05	.02
178	Lester Conner	.05	.02
179	Derrick Gervin	.05	.02
180	Jack Haley	.05	.02
181	Roy Hinson	.05	.02
182	Dennis Hopson SP	.10	.05
183	Chris Morris	.10	.05
184	Pete Myers SP	.10	.05
185	Purvis Short SP	.10	.05
186	Maurice Cheeks	.05	.02
187	Patrick Ewing	.25	.11
188	Stuart Gray	.05	.02
189	Mark Jackson	.10	.05
190	Johnny Newman SP ..	.10	.05
191	Charles Oakley	.10	.05
192	Brian Quinnett	.05	.02
193	Trent Tucker	.05	.02
194	Kiki Vandeweghe	.05	.02
195	Kenny Walker	.05	.02
196	Eddie Lee Wilkins	.05	.02
197	Gerald Wilkins	.05	.02
198	Mark Acres	.05	.02
199	Nick Anderson	.40	.18
200	Michael Ansley	.05	.02
201	Terry Catledge	.05	.02
202	Dave Corzine SP	.10	.05
203	Sidney Green SP	.10	.05
204	Jerry Reynolds	.05	.02
205	Scott Skiles	.05	.02
206	Otis Smith	.05	.02
207	Reggie Theus SP	.10	.05
208	Jeff Turner	.05	.02
209	Sam Vincent	.05	.02
210	Ron Anderson	.05	.02

□ 211 Charles Barkley	.40	.18
□ 212 Scott Brooks SP	.10	.05
□ 213 Lanard Copeland SP	.10	.05
□ 214 Johnny Dawkins	.05	.02
□ 215 Mike Gminski	.05	.02
□ 216 Hersey Hawkins	.10	.05
□ 217 Rick Mahorn	.05	.02
□ 218 Derek Smith SP	.10	.05
□ 219 Bob Thornton	.05	.02
□ 220 Tom Chambers	.05	.02
□ 221 Greg Grant SP	.10	.05
□ 222 Jeff Hornacek	.10	.05
□ 223 Eddie Johnson	.10	.05
□ 224A Kevin Johnson	.25	.11
(SkyBox logo in lower right corner)		
□ 224B Kevin Johnson	.25	.11
(SkyBox logo in upper right corner)		
□ 225 Andrew Lang	.25	.11
□ 226 Dan Majerle	.25	.11
□ 227 Mike McGee SP	.10	.05
□ 228 Tim Perry	.05	.02
□ 229 Kurt Rambis	.05	.02
□ 230 Mark West	.05	.02
□ 231 Mark Bryant	.05	.02
□ 232 Wayne Cooper	.05	.02
□ 233 Clyde Drexler	.30	.14
□ 234 Kevin Duckworth	.05	.02
□ 235 Byron Irvin SP	.10	.05
□ 236 Jerome Kersey	.05	.02
□ 237 Drazen Petrovic	.30	.14
□ 238 Terry Porter	.05	.02
□ 239 Clifford Robinson	.40	.18
□ 240 Buck Williams	.10	.05
□ 241 Danny Young	.05	.02
□ 242 Danny Ainge SP	.10	.05
□ 243 Randy Allen SP	.10	.05
□ 244A Antoine Carr SP	.15	.07
(Wearing Atlanta jersey on back)		
□ 244B Antoine Carr SP	.05	.02
(Wearing Sacramento jersey on back)		
□ 245 Vinny Del Negro SP	.10	.05
□ 246 Pervis Ellison SP	.10	.05
□ 247 Greg Kite SP	.10	.05
□ 248 Rodney McCray SP	.10	.05
□ 249 Harold Pressley SP	.10	.05
□ 250 Ralph Sampson	.05	.02
□ 251 Wayman Tisdale	.05	.02
□ 252 Willie Anderson	.05	.02
□ 253 Uwe Blab SP	.10	.05
□ 254 Frank Brickowski SP	.10	.05
□ 255 Terry Cummings	.05	.02
□ 256 Sean Elliott	.40	.18
□ 257 Caldwell Jones SP	.10	.05
□ 258 Johnny Moore SP	.10	.05
□ 259 Zarko Paspalj SP	.10	.05
□ 260 David Robinson	.75	.35
□ 261 Rod Strickland	.25	.11
□ 262 David Wingate SP	.10	.05
□ 263 Dana Barros	.25	.11
□ 264 Michael Cage	.05	.02
□ 265 Quintin Dailey	.05	.02
□ 266 Dale Ellis	.10	.05
□ 267 Steve Johnson SP	.10	.05
□ 268 Shawn Kemp	5.00	2.20
□ 269 Xavier McDaniel	.05	.02
□ 270 Derrick McKey	.05	.02
□ 271A N.McMillan SP ERR	.20	.09
(Back photo actually Olden Polynice; first series)		
□ 271B Nate McMillan COR	.10	.05
(second series)		
□ 272 Olden Polynice	.10	.05
□ 273 Sedale Threatt	.05	.02
□ 274 Thurl Bailey	.05	.02
□ 275 Mike Brown	.05	.02
□ 276 Mark Eaton	.05	.02
□ 277 Blue Edwards	.05	.02
□ 278 Darrell Griffith	.05	.02
□ 279 Bobby Hansen SP	.10	.05
□ 280 Eric Johnson	.05	.02
□ 281 Eric Leckner SP	.10	.05
□ 282 Karl Malone	.40	.18
□ 283 Delaney Rudd	.05	.02
□ 284 John Stockton	.30	.14
□ 285 Mark Alarie	.05	.02
□ 286 Steve Colter SP	.10	.05
□ 287 Ledell Eackles SP	.10	.05
□ 288 Harvey Grant	.05	.02
□ 289 Tom Hammonds	.05	.02
□ 290 Charles Jones	.05	.02
□ 291 Bernard King	.05	.02
□ 292 Jeff Malone SP	.10	.05
□ 293 Darrell Walker	.05	.02
□ 294 John Williams	.05	.02
□ 295 Checklist 1 SP	.10	.05
□ 296 Checklist 2 SP	.10	.05
□ 297 Checklist 3 SP	.10	.05
□ 298 Checklist 4 SP	.10	.05
□ 299 Checklist 5 SP	.10	.05
□ 300 Danny Ferry SP	.50	.23
□ 301 Bob Weiss CO	.10	.05
□ 302 Chris Ford CO	.10	.05
□ 303 Gene Littles CO	.10	.05
□ 304 Phil Jackson CO	.30	.14
□ 305 Lenny Wilkens CO	.30	.14
□ 306 Richie Adubato CO	.10	.05
□ 307 Paul Westhead CO	.10	.05
□ 308 Chuck Daly CO	.30	.14
□ 309 Don Nelson CO	.30	.14
□ 310 Don Chaney CO	.10	.05
□ 311 Dick Versace CO	.10	.05
□ 312 Mike Schuler CO	.10	.05
□ 313 Mike Dunleavy CO	.10	.05
□ 314 Ron Rothstein CO	.10	.05
□ 315 Del Harris CO	.10	.05
□ 316 Bill Musselman CO	.10	.05
□ 317 Bill Fitch CO	.10	.05
□ 318 Stu Jackson CO	.10	.05
□ 319 Matt Guokas CO	.10	.05
□ 320 Jim Lynam CO	.10	.05
□ 321 Cotton Fitzsimmons CO	.10	.05
□ 322 Rick Adelman CO	.10	.05
□ 323 Dick Motta CO	.10	.05
□ 324 Larry Brown CO	.10	.05
□ 325 K.C. Jones CO	.30	.14
□ 326 Jerry Sloan CO	.30	.14
□ 327 Wes Unseld CO	.10	.05
□ 328 Atlanta Hawks TC	.10	.05
□ 329 Boston Celtics TC	.10	.05
□ 330 Charlotte Hornets TC	.10	.05
□ 331 Chicago Bulls TC	.30	.14
□ 332 Cleveland Cavaliers TC	.10	.05
□ 333 Dallas Mavericks TC	.10	.05
□ 334 Denver Nuggets TC	.10	.05
□ 335 Detroit Pistons TC	.10	.05
□ 336 Golden State Warriors TC	.10	.05
□ 337 Houston Rockets TC	.10	.05
□ 338 Indiana Pacers TC	.10	.05
□ 339 Los Angeles Clippers TC	.10	.05
□ 340 Los Angeles Lakers TC	.10	.05
□ 341 Miami Heat TC	.10	.05
□ 342 Milwaukee Bucks TC	.10	.05
□ 343 Minn. Timberwolves TC	.10	.05
□ 344 New Jersey Nets TC	.10	.05
□ 345 New York Knicks TC	.10	.05
□ 346 Orlando Magic TC	.10	.05
□ 347 Philadelphia 76ers TC	.10	.05
□ 348 Phoenix Suns TC	.10	.05
□ 349 Portland Trail Blazers TC	.10	.05
□ 350 Sacramento Kings TC	.10	.05
□ 351 San Antonio Spurs TC	.10	.05
□ 352 Seattle SuperSonics TC	.10	.05
□ 353 Utah Jazz TC	.10	.05
□ 354 Washington Bullets TC	.10	.05
□ 355 Rumeal Robinson	.10	.05
□ 356 Kendall Gill	1.25	.55
□ 357 Chris Jackson	.60	.25
□ 358 Tyrone Hill	.50	.23
□ 359 Bo Kimble	.10	.05
□ 360 Willie Burton	.30	.14
□ 361 Felton Spencer	.30	.14
□ 362 Derrick Coleman	1.25	.55
□ 363 Dennis Scott	.75	.35
□ 364 Lionel Simmons	.30	.14
□ 365 Gary Payton	5.00	2.20
□ 366 Tim McCormick	.10	.05
□ 367 Sidney Moncrief	.10	.05
□ 368 Kenny Gattison	.10	.05
□ 369 Randolph Keys	.10	.05
□ 370 Johnny Newman	.10	.05
□ 371 Dennis Hopson	.10	.05
□ 372 Cliff Levingston	.10	.05
□ 373 Derrick Chievous	.10	.05
□ 374 Danny Ferry	.30	.14
□ 375 Alex English	.10	.05
□ 376 Lafayette Lever	.10	.05
□ 377 Rodney McCray	.10	.05
□ 378 T.R. Dunn	.10	.05
□ 379 Corey Gaines	.10	.05
□ 380 Avery Johnson	.60	.25
□ 381 Joe Wolf	.10	.05
□ 382 Orlando Woolridge	.10	.05
□ 383 Tree Rollins	.10	.05
□ 384 Steve Johnson	.10	.05
□ 385 Kenny Smith	.10	.05
□ 386 Mike Woodson	.10	.05
□ 387 Greg Dreiling	.10	.05
□ 388 Micheal Williams	.30	.14
□ 389 Randy Wittman	.10	.05
□ 390 Ken Bannister	.10	.05
□ 391 Sam Perkins	.30	.14
□ 392 Terry Teagle	.10	.05
□ 393 Milt Wagner	.10	.05
□ 394 Frank Brickowski	.10	.05
□ 395 Dan Schayes	.10	.05
□ 396 Scott Brooks	.10	.05
□ 397 Doug West	.30	.14
□ 398 Chris Dudley	.10	.05
□ 399 Reggie Theus	.30	.14
□ 400 Greg Grant	.10	.05
□ 401 Greg Kite	.10	.05
□ 402 Mark McNamara	.10	.05
□ 403 Manute Bol	.10	.05
□ 404 Rickey Green	.10	.05
□ 405 Kenny Battle	.10	.05
□ 406 Ed Nealy	.10	.05
□ 407 Danny Ainge	.30	.14
□ 408 Steve Colter	.10	.05
□ 409 Bobby Hansen	.10	.05
□ 410 Eric Leckner	.10	.05
□ 411 Rory Sparrow	.10	.05
□ 412 Bill Wennington	.10	.05
□ 413 Sidney Green	.10	.05
□ 414 David Greenwood	.10	.05
□ 415 Paul Pressey	.10	.05
□ 416 Reggie Williams	.10	.05
□ 417 Dave Corzine	.10	.05
□ 418 Jeff Malone	.10	.05
□ 419 Pervis Ellison	.10	.05
□ 420 Byron Irvin	.10	.05
□ 421 Checklist 1	.05	.05
□ 422 Checklist 2	.05	.05
□ 423 Checklist 3	.05	.05
□ NNO SkyBox Salutes the NBA	5.00	2.20

1991-92 SkyBox

The complete 1991-92 SkyBox basketball set contains 659 standard-size cards. The set was released in two series of 350 and 309 cards, respectively.

This year SkyBox did not package both first and second series cards in second series packs. The cards were available in 15-card fin-sealed foil packs that feature four different mail-in offers on the back, or 62-card blister packs that contain two (of four) SkyBox logo cards not available in the 15-card foil packs. The fronts feature color action player photos overlaying multi-colored computer-generated geometric shapes and stripes. The pictures are borderless and the card face is white. The player's name appears in different color lettering at the bottom of each card, with the team logo in the lower right corner. In a trapezoid shape, the backs have non-action color player photos. At the bottom biographical and statistical information appear inside a color-striped diagonal. The cards are numbered and checklisted below alphabetically within team order. Subsets are Stats (298-307), Best Single Game Performance (308-312), NBA All-Star Weekend Highlights (313-317), NBA All-Rookie Team (318-322), GQ's "NBA All-Star Style Team" (323-327), Centennial Highlights (328-332), Great Moments from the NBA Finals (333-337), Stay in School (338-344), Checklists (345-350), Team Logos (351-377), Coaches (378-404), Game Frames (405-431), Sixth Man (432-458), Teamwork (459-485), Rising Stars (486-512), Lottery Picks (513-523), Centennial (524-529), 1992 USA Basketball Team (530-546), 1988 USA Basketball Team (547-556), 1984 USA Basketball Team (557-563), The Magic of SkyBox (564-571), SkyBox Salutes (572-576), Skymasters (577-588), Shooting Stars (589-602), Small School Sensations (603-609), NBA Stay in School (610-614), Player Updates (615-653), and Checklists (654-659). As part of a promotion with Cheerios, real SkyBox cards from the basic set were inserted into specially marked 10-ounce and 15-ounce cereal boxes. These cereal boxes appeared on store shelves in December 1991 and January 1992, and they depicted images of SkyBox

cards on the front, back, and side panels. An unnumbered gold foil-stamped 1992 USA Basketball Team photo card was randomly inserted into second series foil packs, while the blister packs featured two-card sets of NBA MVPs from the same team for consecutive years. As a mail-in offer a limited Clyde Drexler Olympic card was sent to the first 10,000 respondents in return for ten SkyBox wrappers and 1.00 for postage and handling. Rookie Cards of note include Kenny Anderson, Stacey Augmon, Terrell Brandon, Larry Johnson, Dikembe Mutombo, Steve Smith and John Starks.

		MINT	NRMT
	COMPLETE SET (659)	60.00	27.00
	COMPLETE SERIES 1 (350)	20.00	9.00
	COMPLETE SERIES 2 (309)	40.00	18.00
	COMMON CARD (1-659)	.05	.02
	SEMISTARS	.20	.09
	UNLISTED STARS	.40	.18
□ 1	John Battle	.05	.02
□ 2	Duane Ferrell	.05	.02
□ 3	Jon Koncak	.05	.02
□ 4	Moses Malone	.40	.18
□ 5	Tim McCormick	.05	.02
□ 6	Sidney Moncrief	.05	.02
□ 7	Doc Rivers	.20	.09
□ 8	Rumeal Robinson UER (Drafted 11th, should say 10th)	.05	.02
□ 9	Spud Webb	.20	.09
□ 10	Dominique Wilkins	.40	.18
□ 11	Kevin Willis	.05	.02
□ 12	Larry Bird	1.50	.70
□ 13	Dee Brown	.05	.02
□ 14	Kevin Gamble	.05	.02
□ 15	Joe Kleine	.05	.02
□ 16	Reggie Lewis	.20	.09
□ 17	Kevin McHale	.20	.09
□ 18	Robert Parish	.20	.09
□ 19	Ed Pinckney	.05	.02
□ 20	Brian Shaw	.05	.02
□ 21	Michael Smith	.05	.02
□ 22	Stojko Vrankovic	.05	.02
□ 23	Muggsy Bogues	.20	.09
□ 24	Rex Chapman	.20	.09
□ 25	Dell Curry	.05	.02
□ 26	Kenny Gattison	.05	.02
□ 27	Kendall Gill	.20	.09
□ 28	Mike Gminski	.05	.02
□ 29	Randolph Keys	.05	.02
□ 30	Eric Leckner	.05	.02
□ 31	Johnny Newman	.05	.02
□ 32	J.R. Reid	.05	.02
□ 33	Kelly Tripucka	.20	.09
□ 34	B.J. Armstrong	.05	.02
□ 35	Bill Cartwright	.05	.02
□ 36	Horace Grant	.20	.09
□ 37	Craig Hodges	.05	.02
□ 38	Dennis Hopson	.05	.02
□ 39	Michael Jordan	5.00	2.20
□ 40	Stacey King	.05	.02
□ 41	Cliff Levingston	.05	.02
□ 42	John Paxson	.20	.09
□ 43	Will Perdue	.05	.02
□ 44	Scottie Pippen	1.25	.55
□ 45	Winston Bennett	.05	.02
□ 46	Chucky Brown	.05	.02
□ 47	Brad Daugherty	.05	.02
□ 48	Craig Ehlo	.05	.02
□ 49	Danny Ferry	.05	.02
□ 50	Steve Kerr	.20	.09
□ 51	John Morton	.05	.02
□ 52	Larry Nance	.20	.09
□ 53	Mark Price	.05	.02
□ 54	Darnell Valentine	.05	.02
□ 55	John Williams	.05	.02
□ 56	Steve Alford	.05	.02
□ 57	Rolando Blackman	.05	.02
□ 58	Brad Davis	.05	.02
□ 59	James Donaldson	.05	.02
□ 60	Derek Harper	.20	.09
□ 61	Fat Lever	.05	.02
□ 62	Rodney McCray	.05	.02
□ 63	Roy Tarpley	.05	.02
□ 64	Kelvin Upshaw	.05	.02
□ 65	Randy White	.05	.02
□ 66	Herb Williams	.05	.02
□ 67	Michael Adams	.05	.02
□ 68	Greg Anderson	.05	.02
□ 69	Anthony Cook	.05	.02
□ 70	Chris Jackson	.05	.02
□ 71	Jerome Lane	.05	.02
□ 72	Marcus Liberty	.05	.02
□ 73	Todd Lichti	.05	.02
□ 74	Blair Rasmussen	.05	.02
□ 75	Reggie Williams	.05	.02
□ 76	Joe Wolf	.05	.02
□ 77	Orlando Woolridge	.05	.02
□ 78	Mark Aguirre	.05	.02
□ 79	William Bedford	.05	.02
□ 80	Lance Blanks	.05	.02
□ 81	Joe Dumars	.40	.18
□ 82	James Edwards	.05	.02
□ 83	Scott Hastings	.05	.02
□ 84	Vinnie Johnson	.05	.02
□ 85	Bill Laimbeer	.20	.09
□ 86	Dennis Rodman	1.50	.70
□ 87	John Salley	.05	.02
□ 88	Isiah Thomas	.40	.18
□ 89	Mario Elie	.40	.18
□ 90	Tim Hardaway	.75	.35
□ 91	Rod Higgins	.05	.02
□ 92	Tyrone Hill	.20	.09
□ 93	Les Jepsen	.05	.02
□ 94	Alton Lister	.05	.02
□ 95	Sarunas Marciulionis	.05	.02
□ 96	Chris Mullin	.40	.18
□ 97	Jim Petersen	.05	.02
□ 98	Mitch Richmond	.50	.23
□ 99	Tom Tolbert	.05	.02
□ 100	Adrian Caldwell	.05	.02
□ 101	Eric(Sleepy) Floyd	.05	.02
□ 102	Dave Jamerson	.05	.02
□ 103	Buck Johnson	.05	.02
□ 104	Vernon Maxwell	.05	.02
□ 105	Hakeem Olajuwon	.75	.35
□ 106	Kenny Smith	.05	.02
□ 107	Larry Smith	.05	.02
□ 108	Otis Thorpe	.20	.09
□ 109	Kennard Winchester	.05	.02
□ 110	David Wood	.05	.02
□ 111	Greg Dreiling	.05	.02
□ 112	Vern Fleming	.05	.02
□ 113	George McCloud	.05	.02
□ 114	Reggie Miller	.40	.18
□ 115	Chuck Person	.05	.02
□ 116	Mike Sanders	.05	.02
□ 117	Detlef Schrempf	.20	.09
□ 118	Rik Smits	.20	.09
□ 119	LaSalle Thompson	.05	.02
□ 120	Kenny Williams	.05	.02
□ 121	Michal Williams	.05	.02
□ 122	Ken Bannister	.05	.02
□ 123	Winston Garland	.05	.02
□ 124	Gary Grant	.05	.02
□ 125	Ron Harper	.20	.09
□ 126	Bo Kimble	.05	.02
□ 127	Danny Manning	.20	.09
□ 128	Jeff Martin	.05	.02
□ 129	Ken Norman	.05	.02
□ 130	Olden Polynice	.05	.02
□ 131	Charles Smith	.05	.02
□ 132	Loy Vaught	.20	.09
□ 133	Elden Campbell	.20	.09
□ 134	Vlade Divac	.20	.09

□ 135	Larry Drew	.05	.02
□ 136	A.C. Green	.20	.09
□ 137	Magic Johnson	1.25	.55
□ 138	Sam Perkins	.20	.09
□ 139	Byron Scott	.05	.02
□ 140	Tony Smith	.05	.02
□ 141	Terry Teagle	.05	.02
□ 142	Mychal Thompson	.05	.02
□ 143	James Worthy	.40	.18
□ 144	Willie Burton	.05	.02
□ 145	Bimbo Coles	.05	.02
□ 146	Terry Davis	.05	.02
□ 147	Sherman Douglas	.05	.02
□ 148	Kevin Edwards	.05	.02
□ 149	Alec Kessler	.05	.02
□ 150	Grant Long	.05	.02
□ 151	Glen Rice	.60	.25
□ 152	Rony Seikaly	.05	.02
□ 153	Jon Sundvold	.05	.02
□ 154	Billy Thompson	.05	.02
□ 155	Frank Brickowski	.05	.02
□ 156	Lester Conner	.05	.02
□ 157	Jeff Grayer	.05	.02
□ 158	Jay Humphries	.05	.02
□ 159	Larry Krystkowiak	.05	.02
□ 160	Brad Lohaus	.05	.02
□ 161	Dale Ellis	.20	.09
□ 162	Fred Roberts	.05	.02
□ 163	Alvin Robertson	.05	.02
□ 164	Danny Schayes	.05	.02
□ 165	Jack Sikma	.05	.02
□ 166	Randy Breuer	.05	.02
□ 167	Scott Brooks	.05	.02
□ 168	Tony Campbell	.05	.02
□ 169	Tyrone Corbin	.05	.02
□ 170	Gerald Glass	.05	.02
□ 171	Sam Mitchell	.05	.02
□ 172	Tod Murphy	.05	.02
□ 173	Pooh Richardson	.05	.02
□ 174	Felton Spencer	.05	.02
□ 175	Bob Thornton	.05	.02
□ 176	Doug West	.05	.02
□ 177	Mookie Blaylock	.20	.09
□ 178	Sam Bowie	.05	.02
□ 179	Jud Buechler	.05	.02
□ 180	Derrick Coleman	.20	.09
□ 181	Chris Dudley	.05	.02
□ 182	Tate George	.05	.02
□ 183	Jack Haley	.05	.02
□ 184	Terry Mills	.40	.18
□ 185	Chris Morris	.05	.02
□ 186	Drazen Petrovic	.20	.09
□ 187	Reggie Theus	.20	.09
□ 188	Maurice Cheeks	.05	.02
□ 189	Patrick Ewing	.40	.18
□ 190	Mark Jackson	.20	.09
□ 191	Jerrod Mustaf	.05	.02
□ 192	Charles Oakley	.20	.09
□ 193	Brian Quinnett	.05	.02
□ 194	John Starks	.50	.23
□ 195	Trent Tucker	.05	.02
□ 196	Kiki Vandeweghe	.05	.02
□ 197	Kenny Walker	.05	.02
□ 198	Gerald Wilkins	.05	.02
□ 199	Mark Acres	.05	.02
□ 200	Nick Anderson	.20	.09
□ 201	Michael Ansley	.05	.02
□ 202	Terry Catledge	.05	.02
□ 203	Greg Kite	.05	.02
□ 204	Jerry Reynolds	.05	.02
□ 205	Dennis Scott	.20	.09
□ 206	Scott Skiles	.05	.02
□ 207	Otis Smith	.05	.02
□ 208	Jeff Turner	.05	.02
□ 209	Sam Vincent	.05	.02
□ 210	Ron Anderson	.05	.02
□ 211	Charles Barkley	.60	.25
□ 212	Manute Bol	.05	.02
□ 213	Johnny Dawkins	.05	.02
□ 214	Armon Gilliam	.05	.02
□ 215	Rickey Green	.05	.02
□ 216	Hersey Hawkins	.20	.09
□ 217	Rick Mahorn	.05	.02
□ 218	Brian Oliver	.05	.02
□ 219	Andre Turner	.05	.02
□ 220	Jayson Williams	.40	.18

□ 221	Joe Barry Carroll	.05	.02
□ 222	Cedric Ceballos	.20	.09
□ 223	Tom Chambers	.05	.02
□ 224	Jeff Hornacek	.20	.09
□ 225	Kevin Johnson	.40	.18
□ 226	Negele Knight	.05	.02
□ 227	Andrew Lang	.05	.02
□ 228	Dan Majerle	.20	.09
□ 229	Xavier McDaniel	.05	.02
□ 230	Kurt Rambis	.05	.02
□ 231	Mark West	.05	.02
□ 232	Alaa Abdelnaby	.05	.02
□ 233	Danny Ainge	.20	.09
□ 234	Mark Bryant	.05	.02
□ 235	Wayne Cooper	.05	.02
□ 236	Walter Davis	.05	.02
□ 237	Clyde Drexler	.50	.23
□ 238	Kevin Duckworth	.05	.02
□ 239	Jerome Kersey	.05	.02
□ 240	Terry Porter	.05	.02
□ 241	Clifford Robinson	.20	.09
□ 242	Buck Williams	.20	.09
□ 243	Anthony Bonner	.05	.02
□ 244	Antoine Carr	.05	.02
□ 245	Duane Causwell	.05	.02
□ 246	Bobby Hansen	.05	.02
□ 247	Jim Les	.05	.02
□ 248	Travis Mays	.05	.02
□ 249	Ralph Sampson	.05	.02
□ 250	Lionel Simmons	.05	.02
□ 251	Rory Sparrow	.05	.02
□ 252	Wayman Tisdale	.05	.02
□ 253	Bill Wennington	.05	.02
□ 254	Willie Anderson	.05	.02
□ 255	Terry Cummings	.05	.02
□ 256	Sean Elliott	.20	.09
□ 257	Sidney Green	.05	.02
□ 258	David Greenwood	.05	.02
□ 259	Avery Johnson	.20	.09
□ 260	Paul Pressey	.05	.02
□ 261	David Robinson	.75	.35
□ 262	Dwayne Schintzius	.05	.02
□ 263	Rod Strickland	.40	.18
□ 264	David Wingate	.05	.02
□ 265	Dana Barros	.05	.02
□ 266	Benoit Benjamin	.05	.02
□ 267	Michael Cage	.05	.02
□ 268	Quintin Dailey	.05	.02
□ 269	Ricky Pierce	.05	.02
□ 270	Eddie Johnson	.20	.09
□ 271	Shawn Kemp	2.00	.90
□ 272	Derrick McKey	.05	.02
□ 273	Nate McMillan	.05	.02
□ 274	Gary Payton	1.00	.45
□ 275	Sedale Threatt	.05	.02
□ 276	Thurl Bailey	.05	.02
□ 277	Mike Brown	.05	.02
□ 278	Tony Brown	.05	.02
□ 279	Mark Eaton	.05	.02
□ 280	Blue Edwards	.05	.02
□ 281	Darrell Griffith	.05	.02
□ 282	Jeff Malone	.05	.02
□ 283	Karl Malone	.60	.25
□ 284	Delaney Rudd	.05	.02
□ 285	John Stockton	.40	.18
□ 286	Andy Toolson	.05	.02
□ 287	Mark Alarie	.05	.02
□ 288	Ledell Eackles	.05	.02
□ 289	Pervis Ellison	.05	.02
□ 290	A.J. English	.05	.02
□ 291	Harvey Grant	.05	.02
□ 292	Tom Hammonds	.05	.02
□ 293	Charles James	.05	.02
□ 294	Bernard King	.05	.02
□ 295	Darrell Walker	.05	.02
□ 296	John Williams	.05	.02
□ 297	Haywoode Workman	.05	.02
□ 298	Muggsy Bogues Assist-to-Turnover Ratio Leader	.05	.02
□ 299	Lester Conner Steal-to Turnover Ratio Leader	.05	.02
□ 300	Michael Adams Largest One-Year Scoring Improvement	.05	.02

□ 301	Chris Mullin Most Minutes Per Game	.20	.09
□ 302	Otis Thorpe Most Consecutive Games Played	.05	.02
□ 303	Mitch Richmond Chris Mullin Tim Hardaway Highest Scoring Trio	.40	.18
□ 304	Darrell Walker Top Rebounding Guard	.05	.02
□ 305	Jerome Lane Rebounds Per 48 Minutes	.05	.02
□ 306	John Stockton Assists Per 48 Minutes	.40	.18
□ 307	Michael Jordan Points Per 48 Minutes	2.50	1.10
□ 308	Michael Adams Best Single Game Performance: Points	.05	.02
□ 309	Larry Smith Jerome Lane Best Single Game Performance: Rebounds	.05	.02
□ 310	Scott Skiles Best Single Game Performance: Assists	.05	.02
□ 311	Hakeem Olajuwon David Robinson Best Single Game Performance: Blocks	.60	.25
□ 312	Alvin Robertson Best Single Game Performance: Steals	.05	.02
□ 313	Stay in School Jam	.05	.02
□ 314	Craig Hodges Three-Point Shootout	.05	.02
□ 315	Dee Brown Slam-Dunk Championship	.05	.02
□ 316	Charles Barkley All-Star Game MVP	.40	.18
□ 317	Behind the Scenes Charles Barkley Joe Dumars Kevin McHale	.40	.18
□ 318	Derrick Coleman ART	.05	.02
□ 319	Lionel Simmons ART	.05	.02
□ 320	Dennis Scott ART	.05	.02
□ 321	Kendall Gill ART	.05	.02
□ 322	Dee Brown ART	.05	.02
□ 323	Magic Johnson GQ All-Star Team	.60	.25
□ 324	Hakeem Olajuwon GQ All-Star Team	.40	.18
□ 325	Kevin Willis Dominique Wilkins GQ All-Star Team	.20	.09
□ 326	Kevin Willis Dominique Wilkins GQ All-Star Team	.20	.09
□ 327	Gerald Wilkins GQ All-Star Team	.05	.02
□ 328	1891-1991 Basketball Centennial Logo	.05	.02
□ 329	Old-Fashioned Ball	.05	.02
□ 330	Women Take the Court	.05	.02
□ 331	The Peach Basket	.05	.02
□ 332	James A. Naismith Founder of Basketball	.20	.09
□ 333	Magic Johnson FIN Michael Jordan FIN	2.00	.90
□ 334	Michael Jordan FIN	2.50	1.10
□ 335	Vlade Divac FIN	.05	.02
□ 336	John Paxson FIN	.05	.02
□ 337	Bulls Starting Five Great Moments from the NBA Finals	1.25	.55
□ 338	Language Arts Stay in School	.05	.02
□ 339	Mathematics Stay in School	.05	.02
□ 340	Vocational Education Stay in School	.05	.02
□ 341	Social Studies Stay in School	.05	.02
□ 342	Physical Education	.05	.02

Stay in School
☐ 343 Art .... .05 .02
Stay in School
☐ 344 Science .... .05 .02
Stay in School
☐ 345 Checklist 1 (1-60) ...... .05 .02
☐ 346 Checklist 2 (61-120) .. .05 .02
☐ 347 Checklist 3 (121-180) .. .05 .02
☐ 348 Checklist 4 (181-244) .. .05 .02
☐ 349 Checklist 5 (245-305) .. .05 .02
☐ 350 Checklist 6 (306-350) .. .05 .02
☐ 351 Atlanta Hawks .... .05 .02
　Team Logo
☐ 352 Boston Celtics .... .05 .02
　Team Logo
☐ 353 Charlotte Hornets .... .05 .02
　Team Logo
☐ 354 Chicago Bulls .... .05 .02
　Team Logo
☐ 355 Cleveland Cavaliers .... .05 .02
　Team Logo
☐ 356 Dallas Mavericks .... .05 .02
　Team Logo
☐ 357 Denver Nuggets .... .05 .02
　Team Logo
☐ 358 Detroit Pistons .... .05 .02
　Team Logo
☐ 359 Golden State Warriors .05 .02
　Team Logo
☐ 360 Houston Rockets .... .05 .02
　Team Logo
☐ 361 Indiana Pacers .... .05 .02
　Team Logo
☐ 362 Los Angeles Clippers .. .05 .02
　Team Logo
☐ 363 Los Angeles Lakers .... .05 .02
　Team Logo
☐ 364 Miami Heat .... .05 .02
　Team Logo
☐ 365 Milwaukee Bucks .... .05 .02
　Team Logo
☐ 366 Minnesota T'wolves ..... .05 .02
　Team Logo
☐ 367 New Jersey Nets .... .05 .02
　Team Logo
☐ 368 New York Knicks .... .05 .02
　Team Logo
☐ 369 Orlando Magic............ .05 .02
　Team Logo
☐ 370 Philadelphia 76ers ...... .05 .02
　Team Logo
☐ 371 Phoenix Suns .... .05 .02
　Team Logo
☐ 372 Portland Trail Blazers .. .05 .02
　Team Logo
☐ 373 Sacramento Kings ...... .05 .02
　Team Logo
☐ 374 San Antonio Spurs ..... .05 .02
　Team Logo
☐ 375 Seattle Supersonics .... .05 .02
　Team Logo
☐ 376 Utah Jazz .... .05 .02
　Team Logo
☐ 377 Washington Bullets .... .05 .02
　Team Logo
☐ 378 Bob Weiss CO .... .05 .02
☐ 379 Chris Ford CO .... .05 .02
☐ 380 Allan Bristow CO .... .05 .02
☐ 381 Phil Jackson CO .... .20 .09
☐ 382 Lenny Wilkens CO .... .20 .09
☐ 383 Richie Adubato CO ...... .05 .02
☐ 384 Paul Westhead CO ...... .05 .02
☐ 385 Chuck Daly CO .... .20 .09
☐ 386 Don Nelson CO .... .20 .09
☐ 387 Don Chaney CO .... .05 .02
☐ 388 Bob Hill CO .... .05 .02
☐ 389 Mike Schuler CO .... .05 .02
☐ 390 Mike Dunleavy CO .... .05 .02
☐ 391 Kevin Loughery CO ...... .05 .02
☐ 392 Del Harris CO .... .05 .02
☐ 393 Jimmy Rodgers CO ...... .05 .02
☐ 394 Bill Fitch CO .... .05 .02
☐ 395 Pat Riley CO .... .20 .09
☐ 396 Matt Guokas CO .... .05 .02
☐ 397 Jim Lynam CO............. .05 .02
☐ 398 Cotton Fitzsimmons CO .05 .02

☐ 399 Rick Adelman CO .... .05 .02
☐ 400 Dick Motta CO............ .05 .02
☐ 401 Larry Brown CO........... .05 .02
☐ 402 K.C. Jones CO............ .20 .09
☐ 403 Jerry Sloan CO .... .20 .09
☐ 404 Wes Unseld CO .... .05 .02
☐ 405 Mo Cheeks GF............ .05 .02
☐ 406 Dee Brown GF .... .05 .02
☐ 407 Rex Chapman GF .... .05 .02
☐ 408 Michael Jordan GF .. 2.50 1.10
☐ 409 John Williams GF .... .05 .02
☐ 410 James Donaldson GF .. .05 .02
☐ 411 Dikembe Mutombo GF .40 .18
☐ 412 Isiah Thomas GF .... .20 .09
☐ 413 Tim Hardaway GF .... .40 .18
☐ 414 Hakeem Olajuwon GF .. .40 .18
☐ 415 Detlef Schrempf GF ..... .05 .02
☐ 416 Danny Manning GF ...... .05 .02
☐ 417 Magic Johnson GF ...... .60 .25
☐ 418 Bimbo Coles GF .... .05 .02
☐ 419 Alvin Robertson GF ..... .05 .02
☐ 420 Sam Mitchell GF .... .05 .02
☐ 421 Sam Bowie GF .... .05 .02
☐ 422 Mark Jackson GF .... .05 .02
☐ 423 Orlando Magic............ .05 .02
　Game Frame
☐ 424 Charles Barkley GF .... .40 .18
☐ 425 Dan Majerle GF .... .05 .02
☐ 426 Robert Pack GF .... .05 .02
☐ 427 Wayman Tisdale GF..... .05 .02
☐ 428 David Robinson GF ...... .40 .18
☐ 429 Nate McMillan GF .... .05 .02
　Seattle Supersonics
☐ 430 Karl Malone GF .... .40 .18
☐ 431 Michael Adams GF ...... .05 .02
☐ 432 Duane Ferrell SM .... .05 .02
☐ 433 Kevin McHale SM .... .05 .02
☐ 434 Dell Curry SM .... .05 .02
☐ 435 B.J. Armstrong SM ...... .05 .02
☐ 436 John Williams SM .... .05 .02
☐ 437 Brad Davis SM .... .05 .02
☐ 438 Marcus Liberty SM ...... .05 .02
☐ 439 Mark Aguirre SM .... .05 .02
☐ 440 Rod Higgins SM .... .05 .02
☐ 441 Eric(Sleepy) Floyd SM .. .05 .02
☐ 442 Detlef Schrempf SM .... .05 .02
☐ 443 Loy Vaught SM .... .05 .02
☐ 444 Terry Teagle SM .... .05 .02
☐ 445 Kevin Edwards SM ...... .05 .02
☐ 446 Dale Ellis SM .... .05 .02
☐ 447 Tod Murphy SM .... .05 .02
☐ 448 Chris Dudley SM .... .05 .02
☐ 449 Mark Jackson SM .... .05 .02
☐ 450 Jerry Reynolds SM ...... .05 .02
☐ 451 Ron Anderson SM ...... .05 .02
☐ 452 Dan Majerle SM .... .05 .02
☐ 453 Danny Ainge SM .... .05 .02
☐ 454 Jim Les SM .... .05 .02
☐ 455 Paul Pressey SM .... .05 .02
☐ 456 Ricky Pierce SM .... .05 .02
☐ 457 Mike Brown SM........... .05 .02
☐ 458 Ledell Eackles SM ...... .05 .02
☐ 459 Atlanta Hawks .... .20 .09
　Teamwork
　(Dominique Wilkins
　and Kevin Willis)
☐ 460 Boston Celtics .... .40 .18
　Teamwork
　(Larry Bird and
　Robert Parish)
☐ 461 Charlotte Hornets .... .05 .02
　Teamwork
　(Rex Chapman and
　Kendall Gill)
☐ 462 Chicago Bulls .... 1.50 .70
　Teamwork
　(Michael Jordan and
　Scottie Pippen)
☐ 463 Cleveland Cavaliers .... .05 .02
　Teamwork
　(Craig Ehlo and
　Mark Price)
☐ 464 Dallas Mavericks .... .05 .02
　Teamwork
　(Derek Harper and
　Rolando Blackman)

☐ 465 Denver Nuggets.......... .05 .02
　Teamwork
　(Reggie Williams and
　Chris Jackson)
☐ 466 Detroit Pistons .... .20 .09
　Teamwork
　(Isiah Thomas and
　Bill Laimbeer)
☐ 467 Golden State Warriors .20 .09
　Teamwork
　(Tim Hardaway and
　Chris Mullin)
☐ 468 Houston Rockets .... .05 .02
　Teamwork
　(Vernon Maxwell and
　Kenny Smith)
☐ 469 Indiana Pacers .... .20 .09
　Teamwork
　(Detlef Schrempf and
　Reggie Miller)
☐ 470 Los Angeles Clippers.. .05 .02
　Teamwork
　(Charles Smith and
　Danny Manning)
☐ 471 Los Angeles Lakers .. .40 .18
　Teamwork
　(Magic Johnson and
　James Worthy)
☐ 472 Miami Heat .... .40 .18
　Teamwork
　(Glen Rice and
　Rony Seikaly)
☐ 473 Milwaukee Bucks .... .05 .02
　Teamwork
　(Jay Humphries and
　Alvin Robertson)
☐ 474 Minnesota T'wolves .... .05 .02
　Teamwork
　(Tony Campbell and
　Pooh Richardson)
☐ 475 New Jersey Nets .... .05 .02
　Teamwork
　(Derrick Coleman and
　Sam Bowie)
☐ 476 New York Knicks .... .20 .09
　Teamwork
　(Patrick Ewing and
　Charles Oakley)
☐ 477 Orlando Magic............ .05 .02
　Teamwork
　(Dennis Scott and
　Scott Skiles)
☐ 478 Philadelphia 76ers ..... .40 .18
　Teamwork
　(Charles Barkley and
　Hersey Hawkins)
☐ 479 Phoenix Suns .... .20 .09
　Teamwork
　(Kevin Johnson and
　Tom Chambers)
☐ 480 Portland Trail Blazers .40 .18
　Teamwork
　(Clyde Drexler and
　Terry Porter)
☐ 481 Sacramento Kings ...... .05 .02
　Teamwork
　(Lionel Simmons and
　Wayman Tisdale)
☐ 482 San Antonio Spurs ..... .05 .02
　Teamwork
　(Terry Cummings and
　Sean Elliott)
☐ 483 Seattle Supersonics ... .05 .02
　Teamwork
　(Eddie Johnson and
　Ricky Pierce)
☐ 484 Utah Jazz................. .40 .18
　Teamwork
　(Karl Malone and
　John Stockton)
☐ 485 Washington Bullets .... .05 .02
　Teamwork
　(Harvey Grant and
　Bernard King)
☐ 486 Rumeal Robinson RS .05 .02
☐ 487 Dee Brown RS........... .05 .02

☐ 488	Kendall Gill RS	.05	.02
☐ 489	B.J. Armstrong RS	.05	.02
☐ 490	Danny Ferry RS	.05	.02
☐ 491	Randy White RS	.05	.02
☐ 492	Chris Jackson RS	.05	.02
☐ 493	Lance Blanks RS	.05	.02
☐ 494	Tim Hardaway RS	.40	.18
☐ 495	Vernon Maxwell RS	.05	.02
☐ 496	Micheal Williams RS	.05	.02
☐ 497	Charles Smith RS	.05	.02
☐ 498	Vlade Divac RS	.05	.02
☐ 499	Willie Burton RS	.05	.02
☐ 500	Jeff Grayer RS	.05	.02
☐ 501	Pooh Richardson RS	.05	.02
☐ 502	Derrick Coleman RS	.05	.02
☐ 503	John Starks RS	.40	.18
☐ 504	Dennis Scott RS	.05	.02
☐ 505	Hersey Hawkins RS	.05	.02
☐ 506	Negele Knight RS	.05	.02
☐ 507	Clifford Robinson RS	.05	.02
☐ 508	Lionel Simmons RS	.05	.02
☐ 509	David Robinson RS	.40	.18
☐ 510	Gary Payton RS	.50	.23
☐ 511	Blue Edwards RS	.05	.02
☐ 512	Harvey Grant RS	.05	.02
☐ 513	Larry Johnson	1.50	.70
☐ 514	Kenny Anderson	.75	.35
☐ 515	Billy Owens	.40	.18
☐ 516	Dikembe Mutombo	1.25	.55
☐ 517	Steve Smith	1.00	.45
☐ 518	Doug Smith	.05	.02
☐ 519	Luc Longley	.50	.23
☐ 520	Mark Macon	.05	.02
☐ 521	Stacey Augmon	.40	.18
☐ 522	Brian Williams	.40	.18
☐ 523	Terrell Brandon	2.00	.90
☐ 524	The Ball	.05	.02
☐ 525	The Basket	.05	.02
☐ 526	The 24-second Shot Clock	.05	.02
☐ 527	The Game Program	.05	.02
☐ 528	The Championship Gift	.05	.02
☐ 529	Championship Trophy	.05	.02
☐ 530	Charles Barkley USA	1.25	.55
☐ 531	Larry Bird USA	3.00	1.35
☐ 532	Patrick Ewing USA	.75	.35
☐ 533	Magic Johnson USA	2.50	1.10
☐ 534	Michael Jordan USA	10.00	4.50
☐ 535	Karl Malone USA	1.25	.55
☐ 536	Chris Mullin USA	.40	.18
☐ 537	Scottie Pippen USA	2.50	1.10
☐ 538	David Robinson USA	1.50	.70
☐ 539	John Stockton USA	.75	.35
☐ 540	Chuck Daly CO USA	.20	.09
☐ 541	P.J. Carlesimo CO USA	.05	.02
☐ 542	M.Krzyzewski CO USA	.60	.25
☐ 543	Lenny Wilkens CO USA	.20	.09
☐ 544	Team USA Card 1	2.50	1.10
☐ 545	Team USA Card 2	2.50	1.10
☐ 546	Team USA Card 3	2.50	1.10
☐ 547	Willie Anderson USA	.05	.02
☐ 548	Stacey Augmon USA	.40	.18
☐ 549	Bimbo Coles USA	.05	.02
☐ 550	Jeff Grayer USA	.05	.02
☐ 551	Hersey Hawkins USA	.05	.02
☐ 552	Dan Majerle USA	.05	.02
☐ 553	Danny Manning USA	.05	.02
☐ 554	J.R. Reid USA	.05	.02
☐ 555	Mitch Richmond USA	1.00	.45
☐ 556	Charles Smith USA	.05	.02
☐ 557	Vern Fleming USA	.05	.02
☐ 558	Joe Kleine USA	.05	.02
☐ 559	Jon Koncak USA	.05	.02
☐ 560	Sam Perkins USA	.05	.02
☐ 561	Alvin Robertson USA	.05	.02
☐ 562	Wayman Tisdale USA	.05	.02
☐ 563	Jeff Turner USA	.05	.02
☐ 564	Tony Campbell (Magic of SkyBox)	.05	.02
☐ 565	Joe Dumars (Magic of SkyBox)	.20	.09
☐ 566	Horace Grant (Magic of SkyBox)	.05	.02
☐ 567	Reggie Lewis (Magic of SkyBox)	.05	.02
☐ 568	Hakeem Olajuwon (Magic of SkyBox)	.40	.18
☐ 569	Sam Perkins (Magic of SkyBox)	.05	.02
☐ 570	Chuck Person (Magic of SkyBox)	.05	.02
☐ 571	Buck Williams (Magic of SkyBox)	.05	.02
☐ 572	Michael Jordan (SkyBox Salutes)	2.50	1.10
☐ 573	Bernard King (NBA All-Star)	.05	.02
☐ 574	Moses Malone (SkyBox Salutes)	.20	.09
☐ 575	Robert Parish (SkyBox Salutes)	.05	.02
☐ 576	Pat Riley CO (SkyBox Salutes)	.20	.09
☐ 577	Dee Brown (SkyMaster)	.05	.02
☐ 578	Rex Chapman (SkyMaster)	.05	.02
☐ 579	Clyde Drexler (SkyMaster)	.40	.18
☐ 580	Blue Edwards (SkyMaster)	.05	.02
☐ 581	Ron Harper (SkyMaster)	.05	.02
☐ 582	Kevin Johnson (SkyMaster)	.20	.09
☐ 583	Michael Jordan (SkyMaster)	2.50	1.10
☐ 584	Shawn Kemp (SkyMaster)	1.00	.45
☐ 585	Xavier McDaniel (SkyMaster)	.05	.02
☐ 586	Scottie Pippen (SkyMaster)	.60	.25
☐ 587	Kenny Smith (SkyMaster)	.05	.02
☐ 588	Dominique Wilkins (SkyMaster)	.20	.09
☐ 589	Michael Adams (Shooting Star)	.05	.02
☐ 590	Danny Ainge (Shooting Star)	.05	.02
☐ 591	Larry Bird (Shooting Star)	.75	.35
☐ 592	Dale Ellis (Shooting Star)	.05	.02
☐ 593	Hersey Hawkins (Shooting Star)	.05	.02
☐ 594	Jeff Hornacek (Shooting Star)	.05	.02
☐ 595	Jeff Malone (Shooting Star)	.05	.02
☐ 596	Reggie Miller (Shooting Star)	.40	.18
☐ 597	Chris Mullin (Shooting Star)	.20	.09
☐ 598	John Paxson (Shooting Star)	.05	.02
☐ 599	Drazen Petrovic (Shooting Star)	.05	.02
☐ 600	Ricky Pierce (Shooting Star)	.05	.02
☐ 601	Mark Price (Shooting Star)	.05	.02
☐ 602	Dennis Scott (Shooting Star)	.05	.02
☐ 603	Manute Bol (Small School Sensation)	.05	.02
☐ 604	Jerome Kersey (Small School Sensation)	.05	.02
☐ 605	Charles Oakley (Small School Sensation)	.05	.02
☐ 606	Scottie Pippen (Small School Sensation)	.60	.25
☐ 607	Terry Porter (Small School Sensation)	.05	.02
☐ 608	Dennis Rodman (Small School Sensation)	.75	.35
☐ 609	Sedale Threatt (Small School Sensation)	.05	.02
☐ 610	Business (Stay in School)	.05	.02
☐ 611	Engineering (Stay in School)	.05	.02
☐ 612	Law (Stay in School)	.05	.02
☐ 613	Liberal Arts (Stay in School)	.05	.02
☐ 614	Medicine (Stay in School)	.05	.02
☐ 615	Maurice Cheeks	.05	.02
☐ 616	Travis Mays	.05	.02
☐ 617	Blair Rasmussen	.05	.02
☐ 618	Alexander Volkov	.05	.02
☐ 619	Rickey Green	.05	.02
☐ 620	Bobby Hansen	.05	.02
☐ 621	John Battle	.05	.02
☐ 622	Terry Davis	.05	.02
☐ 623	Walter Davis	.05	.02
☐ 624	Winston Garland	.05	.02
☐ 625	Scott Hastings	.05	.02
☐ 626	Brad Sellers	.05	.02
☐ 627	Darrell Walker	.05	.02
☐ 628	Orlando Woolridge	.05	.02
☐ 629	Tony Brown	.05	.02
☐ 630	James Edwards	.05	.02
☐ 631	Doc Rivers	.20	.09
☐ 632	Jack Haley	.05	.02
☐ 633	Sedale Threatt	.05	.02
☐ 634	Moses Malone	.40	.18
☐ 635	Thurl Bailey	.05	.02
☐ 636	Rafael Addison	.05	.02
☐ 637	Tim McCormick	.05	.02
☐ 638	Xavier McDaniel	.05	.02
☐ 639	Charles Shackleford	.05	.02
☐ 640	Mitchell Wiggins	.05	.02
☐ 641	Jerrod Mustaf	.05	.02
☐ 642	Dennis Hopson	.05	.02
☐ 643	Les Jepsen	.05	.02
☐ 644	Mitch Richmond	.50	.23
☐ 645	Dwayne Schintzius	.05	.02
☐ 646	Spud Webb	.20	.09
☐ 647	Jud Buechler	.05	.02
☐ 648	Antoine Carr	.05	.02
☐ 649	Tyrone Corbin	.05	.02
☐ 650	Michael Adams	.05	.02
☐ 651	Ralph Sampson	.05	.02
☐ 652	Andre Turner	.05	.02
☐ 653	David Wingate	.05	.02
☐ 654	Checklist 'S' (351-404)	.05	.02
☐ 655	Checklist 'K' (405-458)		.02
☐ 656	Checklist 'Y' (459-512)		.02
☐ 657	Checklist 'B' (513-563)		.02
☐ 658	Checklist 'O' (564-614)		.02
☐ 659	Checklist 'X' (615-659)	.05	.02
☐ NNO	Clyde Drexler USA (Send-away)	75.00	34.00
☐ NNO	Team USA Card	12.00	5.50

1991-92 SkyBox Blister Inserts

The first four inserts were featured in series one blister packs, while the last two were inserted in series two blister packs. The cards measure the standard size. The first four have logos on their front and comments on the back. The last two are double-sided cards and display most valuable players from the same team for two consecutive years. The cards are numbered on the back with Roman numerals.

Isiah Thomas
NBA Finals MVP 1990

	MINT	NRMT
COMPLETE SET (6)	2.50	1.10
COMMON CARD (1-4)	.25	.11
COMMON CARD (5-6)	.50	.23

ONE CARD PER BLISTER PACK

		MINT	NRMT
☐ 1	USA Basketball	.25	.11
	(Numbered I)		
☐ 2	Stay in School	.25	.11
	It's Your Best Move		
	(Numbered II)		
☐ 3	Orlando All-Star	.25	.11
	Weekend		
	(Numbered III)		
☐ 4	Inside Stuff	.25	.11
	(Numbered IV)		
☐ 5	Magic Johnson	1.00	.45
	and James Worthy		
	Back to Back		
	NBA Finals MVP 1987/1988		
	(Numbered V)		
☐ 6	Joe Dumars	.50	.23
	and Isiah Thomas		
	Back to Back		
	NBA Finals MVP 1989/1990		
	(Numbered VI)		

1992-93 SkyBox

The complete 1992-93 SkyBox basketball set contains 413 standard-size cards. The set was released in two series of 327 and 86 cards, respectively. Both series foil packs contained 12 cards each with 36 packs to a box. Suggested retail price was $1.15 per pack. Reported production quantities were approximately 15,000 20-box cases for the first series and 15,000 20-box cases for the second series. The new front design features computer-gen-erated screens of color blended with full-bleed color action photos. The backs carry full-bleed non-action close-up photos overlaid by a column displaying complete statistics and a color stripe with a personal "bio-bit." Cards of second series rookies have a gold seal in the other lower corner. In addition, the second series Draft Pick rookie cards were printed in shorter supply than the other cards in the second series set. First series cards are checklisted below alphabetically according team order. Subsets are Coaches (255-281), Team Tix (282-308), 1992 NBA All-Star Weekend Highlights (309-313), 1992 NBA Finals (314-318), 1992 NBA All-Rookie Team (319), and Public Service (230-321). The set concludes with checklist cards (322-327). The cards are numbered on the back. Special gold-foil stamped cards of Magic Johnson and David Robinson, some personally autographed, were randomly inserted in first series foil packs. Versions of these Johnson and Robinson cards with sparkling silver foil were also produced and one of each accompanied the first 7,500 cases ordered exclusively by hobby accounts. According to SkyBox approximately one of every 36 packs contained either a Magic Johnson or David Robinson SP card. The "Head of the Class" mail-away card features the first six 1992 NBA draft picks. The card was made available to the first 20,000 fans through a mail-in offer for three wrappers from each series of 1992-93 SkyBox cards plus 3.25 for postage and handling. The horizontal front features three color, cut-out player photos against a black background. Three wide vertical stripes in shades of red and violet run behind the players. A gold bar near the bottom carries the phrase "Head of the Class 1992 Top NBA Draft Picks." The back features three player photos similar to the ones on the front. The background design is the same except the wide stripes are green, orange, and blue. A white bar at the lower right corner carries the serial number and production run (20,000). Rookie Cards of note include Tom Gugliotta, Robert Horry, Christian Laettner, Alonzo Mourning, Shaquille O'Neal, Latrell Sprewell and Clarence Weatherspoon.

	MINT	NRMT
COMPLETE SET (413)	50.00	22.00
COMPLETE SERIES 1 (327)	30.00	13.50
COMPLETE SERIES 2 (86)	20.00	9.00
COMMON CARD (1-413)	.10	.05
SEMISTARS	.25	.11
UNLISTED STARS	.50	.23

		MINT	NRMT
☐ 1	Stacey Augmon	.25	.11
☐ 2	Maurice Cheeks	.10	.05
☐ 3	Duane Ferrell	.10	.05
☐ 4	Paul Graham	.10	.05
☐ 5	Jon Koncak	.10	.05
☐ 6	Blair Rasmussen	.10	.05
☐ 7	Rumeal Robinson	.10	.05
☐ 8	Dominique Wilkins	.50	.23
☐ 9	Kevin Willis	.10	.05
☐ 10	Larry Bird	2.00	.90
☐ 11	Dee Brown	.10	.05
☐ 12	Sherman Douglas	.10	.05
☐ 13	Rick Fox	.25	.11
☐ 14	Kevin Gamble	.10	.05
☐ 15	Reggie Lewis	.25	.11
☐ 16	Kevin McHale	.50	.23
☐ 17	Robert Parish	.25	.11
☐ 18	Ed Pinckney	.10	.05
☐ 19	Muggsy Bogues	.10	.05
☐ 20	Dell Curry	.10	.05
☐ 21	Kenny Gattison	.10	.05
☐ 22	Kendall Gill	.25	.11
☐ 23	Mike Gminski	.10	.05
☐ 24	Tom Hammonds	.10	.05
☐ 25	Larry Johnson	.60	.25
☐ 26	Johnny Newman	.10	.05
☐ 27	J.R. Reid	.10	.05
☐ 28	B.J. Armstrong	.10	.05
☐ 29	Bill Cartwright	.10	.05
☐ 30	Horace Grant	.25	.11
☐ 31	Michael Jordan	6.00	2.70
☐ 32	Stacey King	.10	.05
☐ 33	John Paxson	.25	.11
☐ 34	Will Perdue	.10	.05
☐ 35	Scottie Pippen	1.50	.70
☐ 36	Scott Williams	.10	.05
☐ 37	John Battle	.10	.05
☐ 38	Terrell Brandon	.75	.35
☐ 39	Brad Daugherty	.10	.05
☐ 40	Craig Ehlo	.10	.05
☐ 41	Danny Ferry	.10	.05
☐ 42	Henry James	.10	.05
☐ 43	Larry Nance	.25	.11
☐ 44	Mark Price	.10	.05
☐ 45	Mike Sanders	.10	.05
☐ 46	Hot Rod Williams	.10	.05
☐ 47	Rolando Blackman	.10	.05
☐ 48	Terry Davis	.10	.05
☐ 49	Derek Harper	.25	.11
☐ 50	Donald Hodge	.10	.05
☐ 51	Mike Iuzzolino	.10	.05
☐ 52	Fat Lever	.10	.05
☐ 53	Rodney McCray	.10	.05
☐ 54	Doug Smith	.10	.05
☐ 55	Randy White	.10	.05
☐ 56	Herb Williams	.10	.05
☐ 57	Greg Anderson	.10	.05
☐ 58	Walter Davis	.10	.05
☐ 59	Winston Garland	.10	.05
☐ 60	Chris Jackson	.10	.05
☐ 61	Marcus Liberty	.10	.05
☐ 62	Todd Lichti	.10	.05
☐ 63	Mark Macon	.10	.05
☐ 64	Dikembe Mutombo	.50	.23
☐ 65	Reggie Williams	.10	.05
☐ 66	Mark Aguirre	.10	.05
☐ 67	William Bedford	.10	.05

☐ 68	Lance Blanks	.10	.05
☐ 69	Joe Dumars	.50	.23
☐ 70	Bill Laimbeer	.25	.11
☐ 71	Dennis Rodman	2.00	.90
☐ 72	John Salley	.10	.05
☐ 73	Isiah Thomas	.50	.23
☐ 74	Darrell Walker	.10	.05
☐ 75	Orlando Woolridge	.10	.05
☐ 76	Victor Alexander	.10	.05
☐ 77	Mario Elie	.25	.11
☐ 78	Chris Gatling	.10	.05
☐ 79	Tim Hardaway	.75	.35
☐ 80	Tyrone Hill	.10	.05
☐ 81	Alton Lister	.10	.05
☐ 82	Sarunas Marciulionis	.10	.05
☐ 83	Chris Mullin	.50	.23
☐ 84	Billy Owens	.25	.11
☐ 85	Matt Bullard	.10	.05
☐ 86	Sleepy Floyd	.10	.05
☐ 87	Avery Johnson	.10	.05
☐ 88	Buck Johnson	.10	.05
☐ 89	Vernon Maxwell	.10	.05
☐ 90	Hakeem Olajuwon	1.00	.45
☐ 91	Kenny Smith	.10	.05
☐ 92	Larry Smith	.10	.05
☐ 93	Otis Thorpe	.25	.11
☐ 94	Dale Davis	.10	.05
☐ 95	Vern Fleming	.10	.05
☐ 96	George McCloud	.10	.05
☐ 97	Reggie Miller	.50	.23
☐ 98	Chuck Person	.10	.05
☐ 99	Detlef Schrempf	.25	.11
☐ 100	Rik Smits	.25	.11
☐ 101	LaSalle Thompson	.10	.05
☐ 102	Micheal Williams	.10	.05
☐ 103	James Edwards	.10	.05
☐ 104	Gary Grant	.10	.05
☐ 105	Ron Harper	.25	.11
☐ 106	Bo Kimble	.10	.05
☐ 107	Danny Manning	.25	.11
☐ 108	Ken Norman	.10	.05
☐ 109	Olden Polynice	.10	.05
☐ 110	Doc Rivers	.25	.11
☐ 111	Charles Smith	.10	.05
☐ 112	Loy Vaught	.25	.11
☐ 113	Elden Campbell	.10	.05
☐ 114	Vlade Divac	.25	.11
☐ 115	A.C. Green	.25	.11
☐ 116	Jack Haley	.10	.05
☐ 117	Sam Perkins	.25	.11
☐ 118	Byron Scott	.25	.11
☐ 119	Tony Smith	.10	.05
☐ 120	Sedale Threatt	.10	.05
☐ 121	James Worthy	.50	.23
☐ 122	Keith Askins	.10	.05
☐ 123	Willie Burton	.10	.05
☐ 124	Bimbo Coles	.10	.05
☐ 125	Kevin Edwards	.10	.05
☐ 126	Alec Kessler	.10	.05
☐ 127	Grant Long	.10	.05
☐ 128	Glen Rice	.60	.25
☐ 129	Rony Seikaly	.10	.05
☐ 130	Brian Shaw	.10	.05
☐ 131	Steve Smith	.50	.23
☐ 132	Frank Brickowski	.10	.05
☐ 133	Dale Ellis	.10	.05
☐ 134	Jeff Grayer	.10	.05
☐ 135	Jay Humphries	.10	.05
☐ 136	Larry Krystkowiak	.10	.05
☐ 137	Moses Malone	.50	.23
☐ 138	Fred Roberts	.10	.05
☐ 139	Alvin Robertson	.10	.05
☐ 140	Dan Schayes	.10	.05
☐ 141	Thurl Bailey	.10	.05
☐ 142	Scott Brooks	.10	.05
☐ 143	Tony Campbell	.10	.05
☐ 144	Gerald Glass	.10	.05
☐ 145	Luc Longley	.25	.11
☐ 146	Sam Mitchell	.10	.05
☐ 147	Pooh Richardson	.10	.05
☐ 148	Felton Spencer	.10	.05
☐ 149	Doug West	.10	.05
☐ 150	Rafael Addison	.10	.05
☐ 151	Kenny Anderson	.50	.23
☐ 152	Mookie Blaylock	.25	.11
☐ 153	Sam Bowie	.10	.05
☐ 154	Derrick Coleman	.25	.11
☐ 155	Chris Dudley	.10	.05
☐ 156	Tate George	.10	.05
☐ 157	Terry Mills	.25	.11
☐ 158	Chris Morris	.10	.05
☐ 159	Drazen Petrovic	.10	.05
☐ 160	Greg Anthony	.10	.05
☐ 161	Patrick Ewing	.50	.23
☐ 162	Mark Jackson	.25	.11
☐ 163	Anthony Mason	.50	.23
☐ 164	Tim McCormick	.10	.05
☐ 165	Xavier McDaniel	.10	.05
☐ 166	Charles Oakley	.25	.11
☐ 167	John Starks	.25	.11
☐ 168	Gerald Wilkins	.10	.05
☐ 169	Nick Anderson	.25	.11
☐ 170	Terry Catledge	.10	.05
☐ 171	Jerry Reynolds	.10	.05
☐ 172	Stanley Roberts	.10	.05
☐ 173	Dennis Scott	.10	.05
☐ 174	Scott Skiles	.10	.05
☐ 175	Jeff Turner	.10	.05
☐ 176	Sam Vincent	.10	.05
☐ 177	Brian Williams	.25	.11
☐ 178	Ron Anderson	.10	.05
☐ 179	Charles Barkley	.75	.35
☐ 180	Manute Bol	.10	.05
☐ 181	Johnny Dawkins	.10	.05
☐ 182	Armon Gilliam	.10	.05
☐ 183	Greg Grant	.10	.05
☐ 184	Hersey Hawkins	.25	.11
☐ 185	Brian Oliver	.10	.05
☐ 186	Charles Shackleford	.10	.05
☐ 187	Jayson Williams	.25	.11
☐ 188	Cedric Ceballos	.25	.11
☐ 189	Tom Chambers	.25	.11
☐ 190	Jeff Hornacek	.25	.11
☐ 191	Kevin Johnson	.50	.23
☐ 192	Negele Knight	.10	.05
☐ 193	Andrew Lang	.10	.05
☐ 194	Dan Majerle	.25	.11
☐ 195	Jerrod Mustaf	.10	.05
☐ 196	Tim Perry	.10	.05
☐ 197	Mark West	.10	.05
☐ 198	Alaa Abdelnaby	.10	.05
☐ 199	Danny Ainge	.25	.11
☐ 200	Mark Bryant	.10	.05
☐ 201	Clyde Drexler	.60	.25
☐ 202	Kevin Duckworth	.10	.05
☐ 203	Jerome Kersey	.10	.05
☐ 204	Robert Pack	.10	.05
☐ 205	Terry Porter	.10	.05
☐ 206	Clifford Robinson	.25	.11
☐ 207	Buck Williams	.25	.11
☐ 208	Anthony Bonner	.10	.05
☐ 209	Randy Brown	.10	.05
☐ 210	Duane Causwell	.10	.05
☐ 211	Pete Chilcutt	.10	.05
☐ 212	Dennis Hopson	.10	.05
☐ 213	Jim Les	.10	.05
☐ 214	Mitch Richmond	.50	.23
☐ 215	Lionel Simmons	.10	.05
☐ 216	Wayman Tisdale	.10	.05
☐ 217	Spud Webb	.25	.11
☐ 218	Willie Anderson	.10	.05
☐ 219	Antoine Carr	.10	.05
☐ 220	Terry Cummings	.25	.11
☐ 221	Sean Elliott	.25	.11
☐ 222	Sidney Green	.10	.05
☐ 223	Vinnie Johnson	.10	.05
☐ 224	David Robinson	.75	.35
☐ 225	Rod Strickland	.50	.23
☐ 226	Greg Sutton	.10	.05
☐ 227	Dana Barros	.10	.05
☐ 228	Benoit Benjamin	.10	.05
☐ 229	Michael Cage	.10	.05
☐ 230	Eddie Johnson	.10	.05
☐ 231	Shawn Kemp	2.00	.90
☐ 232	Derrick McKey	.10	.05
☐ 233	Nate McMillan	.10	.05
☐ 234	Gary Payton	1.00	.45
☐ 235	Ricky Pierce	.10	.05
☐ 236	David Benoit	.10	.05
☐ 237	Mike Brown	.10	.05
☐ 238	Tyrone Corbin	.10	.05
☐ 239	Mark Eaton	.10	.05
☐ 240	Blue Edwards	.10	.05
☐ 241	Jeff Malone	.10	.05
☐ 242	Karl Malone	.75	.35
☐ 243	Eric Murdock	.10	.05
☐ 244	John Stockton	.50	.23
☐ 245	Michael Adams	.10	.05
☐ 246	Rex Chapman	.10	.05
☐ 247	Ledell Eackles	.10	.05
☐ 248	Pervis Ellison	.10	.05
☐ 249	A.J. English	.10	.05
☐ 250	Harvey Grant	.10	.05
☐ 251	Charles Jones	.10	.05
☐ 252	Bernard King	.10	.05
☐ 253	LaBradford Smith	.10	.05
☐ 254	Larry Stewart	.10	.05
☐ 255	Bob Weiss CO	.10	.05
☐ 256	Chris Ford CO	.10	.05
☐ 257	Allan Bristow CO	.10	.05
☐ 258	Phil Jackson CO	.25	.11
☐ 259	Lenny Wilkens CO	.25	.11
☐ 260	Richie Adubato CO	.10	.05
☐ 261	Dan Issel CO	.10	.05
☐ 262	Ron Rothstein CO	.10	.05
☐ 263	Don Nelson CO	.10	.05
☐ 264	Rudy Tomjanovich CO	.25	.11
☐ 265	Bob Hill CO	.10	.05
☐ 266	Larry Brown CO	.25	.11
☐ 267	Randy Pfund CO	.10	.05
☐ 268	Kevin Loughery CO	.10	.05
☐ 269	Mike Dunleavy CO	.10	.05
☐ 270	Jimmy Rodgers CO	.10	.05
☐ 271	Chuck Daly CO	.25	.11
☐ 272	Pat Riley CO	.25	.11
☐ 273	Matt Guokas CO	.10	.05
☐ 274	Doug Moe CO	.10	.05
☐ 275	Paul Westphal CO	.10	.05
☐ 276	Rick Adelman CO	.10	.05
☐ 277	Garry St. Jean CO	.10	.05
☐ 278	Jerry Tarkanian CO	.10	.05
☐ 279	George Karl CO	.25	.11
☐ 280	Jerry Sloan CO	.25	.11
☐ 281	Wes Unseld CO	.25	.11
☐ 282	Dominique Wilkins TT	.25	.11
☐ 283	Reggie Lewis TT	.10	.05
☐ 284	Kendall Gill TT	.10	.05
☐ 285	Horace Grant TT	.10	.05
☐ 286	Brad Daugherty TT	.10	.05
☐ 287	Derek Harper TT	.10	.05
☐ 288	Chris Jackson TT	.10	.05
☐ 289	Isiah Thomas TT	.25	.11
☐ 290	Chris Mullin TT	.25	.11
☐ 291	Kenny Smith TT	.10	.05
☐ 292	Reggie Miller TT	.50	.23
☐ 293	Ron Harper TT	.10	.05
☐ 294	Vlade Divac TT	.25	.11
☐ 295	Glen Rice TT	.50	.23
☐ 296	Moses Malone TT	.25	.11
☐ 297	Doug West TT	.10	.05
☐ 298	Derrick Coleman TT	.10	.05
☐ 299	Patrick Ewing TT	.50	.23
	(See also card 305)		
☐ 300	Scott Skiles TT	.10	.05
☐ 301	Hersey Hawkins TT	.10	.05
☐ 302	Kevin Johnson TT	.25	.11
☐ 303	Clifford Robinson TT	.10	.05
☐ 304	Spud Webb TT	.25	.11
☐ 305	D.Robinson TT COR	.50	.23
☐ 305A	D.Robinson TT ERR	.10	.05
	(Card misnumbered as 299)		
☐ 306	Shawn Kemp TT	1.00	.45
☐ 307	John Stockton TT	.50	.23
☐ 308	Pervis Ellison TT	.10	.05
☐ 309	Craig Hodges AS	.10	.05
☐ 310	M.Johnson A-S MVP	.75	.35
☐ 311	Cedric Ceballos	.10	.05
	Slam Dunk Champ		
☐ 312	Karl Malone ASG	.50	.23
☐ 313	Dennis Rodman ASG	.50	.23
☐ 314	Michael Jordan MVP	3.00	1.35
☐ 315	Clyde Drexler FIN	.50	.23
☐ 316	Danny Ainge PO	.10	.05
☐ 317	Scottie Pippen PO	.75	.35
☐ 318	NBA Champs	.10	.05
☐ 319	Larry Johnson ART	.25	.11
	Dikembe Mutombo		
☐ 320	NBA Stay in School	.10	.05

☐ 321	Boys and Girls 10	.05
	Clubs of America	
☐ 322	Checklist 1...............10	.05
☐ 323	Checklist 2...............10	.05
☐ 324	Checklist 3...............10	.05
☐ 325	Checklist 4...............10	.05
☐ 326	Checklist 5...............10	.05
☐ 327	Checklist 6...............10	.05
☐ 328	Adam Keefe...............10	.05
☐ 329	Sean Rooks 10	.05
☐ 330	Xavier McDaniel 10	.05
☐ 331	Kiki Vandeweghe.......10	.05
☐ 332	Alonzo Mourning.... 2.50	1.10
☐ 333	Rodney McCray.........10	.05
☐ 334	Gerald Wilkins 10	.05
☐ 335	Tony Bennett.............10	.05
☐ 336	LaPhonso Ellis..........75	.35
☐ 337	Bryant Stith 25	.11
☐ 338	Isaiah Morris 10	.05
☐ 339	Olden Polynice 10	.05
☐ 340	Jeff Grayer................10	.05
☐ 341	Byron Houston 10	.05
☐ 342	Latrell Sprewell...... 1.50	.70
☐ 343	Scott Brooks 10	.05
☐ 344	Frank Johnson...........10	.05
☐ 345	Robert Horry..............75	.35
☐ 346	David Wood 10	.05
☐ 347	Sam Mitchell 10	.05
☐ 348	Pooh Richardson........10	.05
☐ 349	Malik Sealy 25	.11
☐ 350	Morlon Wiley 10	.05
☐ 351	Mark Jackson 25	.11
☐ 352	Stanley Roberts 10	.05
☐ 353	Elmore Spencer..........10	.05
☐ 354	John Williams 10	.05
☐ 355	Randy Woods 10	.05
☐ 356	James Edwards...........10	.05
☐ 357	Jeff Sanders 10	.05
☐ 358	Magic Johnson........ 1.50	.70
☐ 359	Anthony Peeler 25	.11
☐ 360	Harold Miner..............25	.11
☐ 361	John Salley 10	.05
☐ 362	Alaa Abdelnaby..........10	.05
☐ 363	Todd Day...................10	.05
☐ 364	Blue Edwards.............10	.05
☐ 365	Lee Mayberry 10	.05
☐ 366	Eric Murdock..............10	.05
☐ 367	Mookie Blaylock 25	.11
☐ 368	Anthony Avent............10	.05
☐ 369	Christian Laettner ... 1.25	.55
☐ 370	Chuck Person 10	.05
☐ 371	Chris Smith 10	.05
☐ 372	Micheal Williams 10	.05
☐ 373	Rolando Blackman 10	.05
☐ 374	Tony Campbell UER 10	.05
	(Back photo actually	
	Alvin Robertson)	
☐ 375	Hubert Davis..............25	.11
☐ 376	Travis Mays...............10	.05
☐ 377	Doc Rivers.................25	.11
☐ 378	Charles Smith 10	.05
☐ 379	Rumeal Robinson 10	.05
☐ 380	Vinny Del Negro 10	.05
☐ 381	Steve Kerr 25	.11
☐ 382	Shaquille O'Neal 8.00	3.60
☐ 383	Donald Royal 10	.05
☐ 384	Jeff Hornacek 25	.11
☐ 385	Andrew Lang..............10	.05
☐ 386	Tim Perry UER 10	.05
	(Alvin Robertson pictured on back)	
☐ 387	C.Weatherspoon 50	.23
☐ 388	Danny Ainge 75	.35
☐ 389	Charles Barkley 75	.35
☐ 390	Tim Kempton..............10	.05
☐ 391	Oliver Miller...............25	.11
☐ 392	Dave Johnson 10	.05
☐ 393	Tracy Murray..............25	.11
☐ 394	Rod Strickland............50	.23
☐ 395	Marty Conlon 10	.05
☐ 396	Walt Williams 50	.23
☐ 397	Lloyd Daniels.............10	.05
☐ 398	Dale Ellis 10	.05
☐ 399	Dave Hoppen..............10	.05
☐ 400	Larry Smith................10	.05
☐ 401	Doug Overton 10	.05
☐ 402	Isaac Austin...............25	.11

☐ 403	Jay Humphries 05	
☐ 404	Larry Krystkowiak 10	.05
☐ 405	Tom Gugliotta 1.50	.70
☐ 406	Buck Johnson 10	.05
☐ 407	Don MacLean 10	.05
☐ 408	Marlon Maxey.............10	.05
☐ 409	Corey Williams 10	.05
☐ 410	Special Olympics........25	.11
	Dan Majerle	
☐ 411	Checklist 1................10	.05
☐ 412	Checklist 2................10	.05
☐ 413	Checklist 3................10	.05
☐ NNO	David Robinson AU 125.00	55.00
☐ NNO	Magic Johnson AU 200.00	90.00
☐ NNO	David Robinson 4.00	1.80
	The Admiral Comes	
	Prepared	
☐ NNO	Head of the Class... 30.00	13.50
	LaPhonso Ellis	
	Tom Gugliotta	
	Christian Laettner	
	Alonzo Mourning	
	Shaquille O'Neal	
	Walt Williams	
☐ NNO	Magic Johnson 6.00	2.70
	The Magic Never Ends	

1992-93 SkyBox Draft Picks

This 25-card standard-size insert set showcases the first round picks from the 1992 NBA Draft. The cards were randomly inserted into 12-card (both series) foil packs. According to SkyBox, approximately one out of every eight packs contained a Draft Pick card. The card numbering (1-27) reflects the actual order in which each player was selected. Six players (2, 10-11, 15-16, 18) available by the first series cut-off date were issued in first series foil packs, while the rest of the first round picks who signed NBA contracts were issued in second series packs. DP4 and DP17, intended for Jim Jackson and Doug Christie respectively, were not issued with this set because neither player signed a professional contract in time to be included in the second series. They were issued in 1993-94 first series packs. The fronts display an opaque metallic gold rectangle

set off from the player. On a gradated gold background, the backs present player profiles. A white rectangle that runs vertically the length of the card contains statistics. The team logo is superimposed on this rectangle. The cards are numbered on the back with a "DP" prefix.

	MINT	NRMT
COMPLETE SET (25)	45.00	20.00
COMPLETE SERIES 1 (6) ...	10.00	4.50
COMPLETE SERIES 2 (19)..	35.00	16.00
COMMON CARD..................	.50	.23
SEMISTARS	1.25	.55
UNLISTED STARS	2.00	.90
SER.1/2 STATED ODDS 1:8		
4/17 ISSUED THE NEXT YEAR		

☐ DP1	Shaquille O'Neal 20.00	9.00
☐ DP2	Alonzo Mourning 6.00	2.70
☐ DP3	Christian Laettner 3.00	1.35
☐ DP4	Not issued	
	.... (Player unsigned)	
☐ DP5	LaPhonso Ellis 2.00	.90
☐ DP6	Tom Gugliotta....... 4.00	1.80
☐ DP7	Walt Williams 1.25	.55
☐ DP8	Todd Day .... .50	.23
☐ DP9	C.Weatherspoon 1.25	.55
☐ DP10	Adam Keefe .... .50	.23
☐ DP11	Robert Horry......... 2.00	.90
☐ DP12	Harold Miner.......... 1.25	.55
☐ DP13	Bryant Stith 1.25	.55
☐ DP14	Malik Sealy 1.25	.55
☐ DP15	Anthony Peeler 1.25	.55
☐ DP16	Randy Woods .... .50	.23
☐ DP17	Not issued	
	.... (Player unsigned)	
☐ DP18	Tracy Murray 1.25	.55
☐ DP19	Don MacLean .... .50	.23
☐ DP20	Hubert Davis......... 1.25	.55
☐ DP21	Jon Barry .... .50	.23
☐ DP22	Oliver Miller 1.25	.55
☐ DP23	Lee Mayberry .... .50	.23
☐ DP24	Latrell Sprewell..... 4.00	1.80
☐ DP25	Elmore Spencer ...... .50	.23
☐ DP26	Dave Johnson .... .50	.23
☐ DP27	Byron Houston .... .50	.23

1992-93 SkyBox Olympic Team

Each card in this 12-card standard-size set features an action photo of a team member and his complete statistics from the Olympic Games. According to SkyBox, the cards were randomly inserted into 12-card first series foil packs at a rate of approximately one per six. The backs tell the story of U.S. Men's Olympic Team, from scrimmage in Monte Carlo to the medal ceremony in Barcelona. The cards are numbered on the back with a "USA" prefix.

	MINT	NRMT
COMPLETE SET (12)	50.00	22.00
COMMON CARD (1-12)	2.00	.90

SER.1 STATED ODDS 1:6
USA PREFIX ON CARD NUMBER

		MINT	NRMT
☐ 1	Clyde Drexler	2.50	1.10
☐ 2	Chris Mullin	2.00	.90
☐ 3	John Stockton	2.00	.90
☐ 4	Karl Malone	3.00	1.35
☐ 5	Scottie Pippen	6.00	2.70
☐ 6	Larry Bird	8.00	3.60
☐ 7	Charles Barkley	3.00	1.35
☐ 8	Patrick Ewing	2.00	.90
☐ 9	Christian Laettner	3.00	1.35
☐ 10	David Robinson	3.00	1.35
☐ 11	Michael Jordan	25.00	11.00
☐ 12	Magic Johnson	6.00	2.70

1992-93 SkyBox David Robinson

This ten-card standard-size insert set provides a look at Robinson at various stages of his life. Included are photos from his childhood, indulging in hobbies, with his family at the Naval Academy and his present day super stardom. The first five cards were randomly inserted in first series 12-card foil packs, while the second five were found in second series packs. According to SkyBox, approximately one of every eight packs contains a David Robinson insert card. The cards feature a different design than the regular issue cards. The fronts display color photos tilted slightly to the left with a special seal overlaying the upper left corner. The surrounding card face shows two colors.

	MINT	NRMT
COMPLETE SET (10)	4.00	1.80
COMPLETE SERIES 1 (5)	2.00	.90

COMPLETE SERIES 2 (5)	2.00	.90
COMMON D.ROB. (R1-R10)	.50	.23

SER.1/2 STATED ODDS 1:8

☐ R1	David Robinson Childhood	.50	.23
☐ R2	David Robinson At Ease	.50	.23
☐ R3	David Robinson College	.50	.23
☐ R4	David Robinson College	.50	.23
☐ R5	David Robinson At Ease	.50	.23
☐ R6	David Robinson College	.50	.23
☐ R7	David Robinson College	.50	.23
☐ R8	David Robinson Doug Drotman Awards	.50	.23
☐ R9	David Robinson Awards	.50	.23
☐ R10	David Robinson At Ease	.50	.23

1992-93 SkyBox School Ties

Randomly inserted in 1992-93 SkyBox second series 12-card foil packs at a reported rate of one per four, this 18-card standard-size set consists of six different three-card "School Ties" interlocking cards. When the three cards in each puzzle are placed together, they create a montage of active NBA players from one particular college. The fronts feature several color player photos that have team color-coded picture frames. The team logo appears in a team color-coded banner that is superimposed across the bottom of the picture. The backs have brightly colored backgrounds and display information about the college, the players, and a checklist of the players on the three-card puzzle. The cards are numbered on the back with an "ST" prefix.

	MINT	NRMT
COMPLETE SET (18)	15.00	6.75
COMMON CARD (ST1-ST18)	.25	.11

SEMISTARS	.50	.23

SER.2 STATED ODDS 1:4

☐ ST1	Patrick Ewing Alonzo Mourning Georgetown	2.50	1.10
☐ ST2	Dikembe Mutombo Eric Floyd Georgetown	.50	.23
☐ ST3	Reggie Williams David Wingate Georgetown	.25	.11
☐ ST4	Kenny Anderson Duane Ferrell Georgia Tech	.40	.18
☐ ST5	Tom Hammonds Jon Barry Mark Price Georgia Tech	.25	.11
☐ ST6	John Salley Dennis Scott Georgia Tech	.50	.23
☐ ST7	Rafael Addison Dave Johnson Syracuse	.25	.11
☐ ST8	Billy Owens Derrick Coleman Rony Seikaly Syracuse	.50	.23
☐ ST9	Sherman Douglas Danny Schayes Syracuse	.25	.11
☐ ST10	Nick Anderson Kendall Gill Illinois	.40	.18
☐ ST11	Derek Harper Eddie Johnson Illinois	.25	.11
☐ ST12	Marcus Liberty Ken Norman Illinois	.25	.11
☐ ST13	Greg Anthony Stacey Augmon Nevada-Las Vegas	.50	.23
☐ ST14	Armon Gilliam Larry Johnson Sidney Green Nevada-Las Vegas	.40	.18
☐ ST15	Elmore Spencer Gerald Paddio Nevada-Las Vegas	.25	.11
☐ ST16	James Worthy Michael Jordan Sam Perkins North Carolina	12.00	5.50
☐ ST17	J.R. Reid Pete Chilcutt Brad Daugherty Rick Fox North Carolina	.25	.11
☐ ST18	Hubert Davis Kenny Smith Scott Williams North Carolina	.50	.23

1992-93 SkyBox Thunder and Lightning

Randomly inserted into second series 12-card foil packs at a reported rate of one per 40 packs, each card in this nine-card standard-size set features a pair of teammates. There is a photo on each side. The catchword on the front is "Thunder", referring to a dominant power player, while "Lightning" on the back captures the speed of a

guard. The cards are highlighted by a litho-foil printing which gives a foil-look to the graphics around the basketball. The cards have color action player photos against a dark background, with computer enhancement around the ball and player. On the front, the power player's name appears at the bottom and is underlined by a thin yellow stripe. The word "Thunder" appears below the stripe. On the horizontal backs, the speed player's name is displayed in the upper right with the same yellow underline, but the word "Lightning" appears below it. The cards are numbered on the back with a "TL" prefix.

	MINT	NRMT
COMPLETE SET (9)	40.00	18.00
COMMON PAIR (TL1-TL9)	1.50	.70
SEMISTARS	3.00	1.35
UNLISTED STARS	4.00	1.80
SER.2 STATED ODDS 1:40		
☐ TL1 Dikembe Mutombo	4.00	1.80
Mark Macon		
☐ TL2 Buck Williams	6.00	2.70
Clyde Drexler		
☐ TL3 Charles Barkley	8.00	3.60
Kevin Johnson		
☐ TL4 Pervis Ellison	1.50	.70
Michael Adams		
☐ TL5 Larry Johnson	3.00	1.35
Tyrone Bogues		
☐ TL6 Brad Daugherty	1.50	.70
Mark Price		
☐ TL7 Shawn Kemp	20.00	9.00
Gary Payton		
☐ TL8 Karl Malone	12.00	5.50
John Stockton		
☐ TL9 Billy Owens	6.00	2.70
Tim Hardaway		

1993-94 SkyBox

The 1993-94 SkyBox basketball set contains 341 standard-size cards that were issued in series of 191 and 150 respectively. Cards were issued in 12-card packs with 36 packs per box. The cards feature full-bleed color action photos with a wide white stripe down one side of the front containing the player's name, position, and team. The SkyBox Premium foil stamp logo appears superimposed on the front. The backs display a second player close-up shot on the top half, and the player's statistics and scouting report on the bottom half. The cards are numbered on the back and grouped alphabetically within team order. Subsets are Playoff Performances (4-21), Changing Faces (292-318), and Costacos Brothers Poster Cards (319-338). Rookie Cards of note include Vin Baker, Anfernee Hardaway, Allan Houston, Jamal Mashburn, Nick Van Exel and Chris Webber. The odds of finding a Head of the Class card are one in 360 first series packs. It was redeemable for a Head of the Class card featuring the top six 1993 draft picks. The redemption date was April 15, 1994.

	MINT	NRMT
COMPLETE SET (341)	30.00	13.50
COMPLETE SERIES 1 (191)	15.00	6.75
COMPLETE SERIES 2 (150)	15.00	6.75
COMMON CARD (1-341)	.05	.02
SEMISTARS	.15	.07
UNLISTED STARS	.30	.14
DP4/DP17: SER.1 STATED ODDS 1:36		
HOC EXCH: SER.1 STATED ODDS 1:360		

		MINT	NRMT
☐ 1	Checklist	.05	.02
☐ 2	Checklist	.05	.02
☐ 3	Checklist	.05	.02
☐ 4	Larry Johnson PO	.15	.07
☐ 5	Alonzo Mourning PO	.30	.14
☐ 6	Hakeem Olajuwon PO	.30	.14
☐ 7	Brad Daugherty PO	.05	.02
☐ 8	Oliver Miller PO	.05	.02
☐ 9	David Robinson PO	.30	.14
☐ 10	Patrick Ewing PO	.15	.07
☐ 11	Ricky Pierce PO	.05	.02
☐ 12	Sam Perkins PO	.05	.02
☐ 13	John Starks PO	.05	.02
☐ 14	Michael Jordan PO	2.00	.90
☐ 15	Dan Majerle PO	.05	.02
☐ 16	Scottie Pippen PO	.50	.23
☐ 17	Shawn Kemp PO	.50	.23
☐ 18	Charles Barkley PO	.30	.14
☐ 19	Horace Grant PO	.05	.02
☐ 20	Kevin Johnson PO	.05	.02
☐ 21	John Paxson PO	.05	.02
☐ 22	David Robinson IS	.30	.14
☐ 23	NBA On NBC	.05	.02
☐ 24	Stacey Augmon	.05	.02
☐ 25	Mookie Blaylock	.15	.07
☐ 26	Craig Ehlo	.05	.02
☐ 27	Adam Keefe	.05	.02
☐ 28	Dominique Wilkins	.30	.14
☐ 29	Kevin Willis	.05	.02
☐ 30	Dee Brown	.05	.02
☐ 31	Sherman Douglas	.05	.02
☐ 32	Rick Fox	.05	.02
☐ 33	Kevin Gamble	.05	.02
☐ 34	Xavier McDaniel	.05	.02
☐ 35	Robert Parish	.15	.07
☐ 36	Muggsy Bogues	.15	.07
☐ 37	Dell Curry	.05	.02
☐ 38	Kendall Gill	.15	.07
☐ 39	Larry Johnson	.30	.14
☐ 40	Alonzo Mourning	.50	.23
☐ 41	Johnny Newman	.05	.02
☐ 42	B.J. Armstrong	.05	.02
☐ 43	Bill Cartwright	.05	.02
☐ 44	Horace Grant	.15	.07
☐ 45	Michael Jordan	4.00	1.80
☐ 46	John Paxson	.05	.02
☐ 47	Scottie Pippen	1.00	.45
☐ 48	Scott Williams	.05	.02
☐ 49	Terrell Brandon	.30	.14
☐ 50	Brad Daugherty	.05	.02
☐ 51	Larry Nance	.15	.07
☐ 52	Mark Price	.05	.02
☐ 53	Gerald Wilkins	.05	.02
☐ 54	John Williams	.05	.02
☐ 55	Terry Davis	.05	.02
☐ 56	Derek Harper	.15	.07
☐ 57	Jim Jackson	.30	.14
☐ 58	Sean Rooks	.05	.02
☐ 59	Doug Smith	.05	.02
☐ 60	Mahmoud Abdul-Rauf	.15	.07
☐ 61	LaPhonso Ellis	.15	.07
☐ 62	Mark Macon	.05	.02
☐ 63	Dikembe Mutombo	.30	.14
☐ 64	Bryant Stith	.05	.02
☐ 65	Reggie Williams	.05	.02
☐ 66	Joe Dumars	.30	.14
☐ 67	Bill Laimbeer	.05	.02
☐ 68	Terry Mills	.05	.02
☐ 69	Alvin Robertson	.05	.02
☐ 70	Dennis Rodman	1.25	.55
☐ 71	Isiah Thomas	.30	.14
☐ 72	Victor Alexander	.05	.02
☐ 73	Tim Hardaway	.40	.18
☐ 74	Tyrone Hill	.05	.02
☐ 75	Sarunas Marciulionis	.05	.02
☐ 76	Chris Mullin	.30	.14
☐ 77	Billy Owens	.05	.02
☐ 78	Latrell Sprewell	.30	.14
☐ 79	Robert Horry	.15	.07
☐ 80	Vernon Maxwell	.05	.02
☐ 81	Hakeem Olajuwon	.60	.25
☐ 82	Kenny Smith	.05	.02
☐ 83	Otis Thorpe	.15	.07
☐ 84	Dale Davis	.05	.02
☐ 85	Reggie Miller	.30	.14
☐ 86	Pooh Richardson	.05	.02
☐ 87	Detlef Schrempf	.15	.07
☐ 88	Malik Sealy	.05	.02
☐ 89	Rik Smits	.05	.02
☐ 90	Ron Harper	.15	.07
☐ 91	Mark Jackson	.15	.07
☐ 92	Danny Manning	.05	.02
☐ 93	Stanley Roberts	.05	.02
☐ 94	Loy Vaught	.15	.07
☐ 95	Randy Woods	.05	.02
☐ 96	Sam Bowie	.05	.02
☐ 97	Doug Christie	.05	.02
☐ 98	Vlade Divac	.15	.07
☐ 99	Anthony Peeler	.05	.02
☐ 100	Sedale Threatt	.05	.02
☐ 101	James Worthy	.30	.14
☐ 102	Grant Long	.05	.02
☐ 103	Harold Miner	.05	.02
☐ 104	Glen Rice	.30	.14
☐ 105	John Salley	.05	.02
☐ 106	Rony Seikaly	.05	.02

☐ 107	Steve Smith	.15	.07
☐ 108	Anthony Avent	.05	.02
☐ 109	Jon Barry	.05	.02
☐ 110	Frank Brickowski	.05	.02
☐ 111	Blue Edwards	.05	.02
☐ 112	Todd Day	.05	.02
☐ 113	Lee Mayberry	.05	.02
☐ 114	Eric Murdock	.05	.02
☐ 115	Thurl Bailey	.05	.02
☐ 116	Christian Laettner	.30	.14
☐ 117	Chuck Person	.05	.02
☐ 118	Doug West	.05	.02
☐ 119	Micheal Williams	.05	.02
☐ 120	Kenny Anderson	.15	.07
☐ 121	Benoit Benjamin	.05	.02
☐ 122	Derrick Coleman	.15	.07
☐ 123	Chris Morris	.05	.02
☐ 124	Rumeal Robinson	.05	.02
☐ 125	Rolando Blackman	.05	.02
☐ 126	Patrick Ewing	.30	.14
☐ 127	Anthony Mason	.15	.07
☐ 128	Charles Oakley	.15	.07
☐ 129	Doc Rivers	.15	.07
☐ 130	Charles Smith	.05	.02
☐ 131	John Starks	.15	.07
☐ 132	Nick Anderson	.15	.07
☐ 133	Shaquille O'Neal	1.25	.55
☐ 134	Donald Royal	.05	.02
☐ 135	Dennis Scott	.15	.07
☐ 136	Scott Skiles	.05	.02
☐ 137	Brian Williams	.05	.02
☐ 138	Johnny Dawkins	.05	.02
☐ 139	Hersey Hawkins	.15	.07
☐ 140	Jeff Hornacek	.15	.07
☐ 141	Andrew Lang	.05	.02
☐ 142	Tim Perry	.05	.02
☐ 143	C.Weatherspoon	.05	.02
☐ 144	Danny Ainge	.15	.07
☐ 145	Charles Barkley	.50	.23
☐ 146	Cedric Ceballos	.15	.07
☐ 147	Kevin Johnson	.15	.07
☐ 148	Oliver Miller	.05	.02
☐ 149	Dan Majerle	.15	.07
☐ 150	Clyde Drexler	.40	.18
☐ 151	Harvey Grant	.05	.02
☐ 152	Jerome Kersey	.05	.02
☐ 153	Terry Porter	.05	.02
☐ 154	Clifford Robinson	.15	.07
☐ 155	Rod Strickland	.15	.07
☐ 156	Buck Williams	.15	.07
☐ 157	Mitch Richmond	.30	.14
☐ 158	Lionel Simmons	.05	.02
☐ 159	Wayman Tisdale	.05	.02
☐ 160	Spud Webb	.15	.07
☐ 161	Walt Williams	.15	.07
☐ 162	Antoine Carr	.05	.02
☐ 163	Lloyd Daniels	.05	.02
☐ 164	Sean Elliott	.15	.07
☐ 165	Dale Ellis	.05	.02
☐ 166	Avery Johnson	.05	.02
☐ 167	J.R. Reid	.05	.02
☐ 168	David Robinson	.50	.23
☐ 169	Shawn Kemp	1.00	.45
☐ 170	Derrick McKey	.05	.02
☐ 171	Nate McMillan	.05	.02
☐ 172	Gary Payton	.50	.23
☐ 173	Sam Perkins	.15	.07
☐ 174	Ricky Pierce	.05	.02
☐ 175	Tyrone Corbin	.05	.02
☐ 176	Jay Humphries	.05	.02
☐ 177	Jeff Malone	.05	.02
☐ 178	Karl Malone	.50	.23
☐ 179	John Stockton	.30	.14
☐ 180	Michael Adams	.05	.02
☐ 181	Kevin Duckworth	.05	.02
☐ 182	Pervis Ellison	.05	.02
☐ 183	Tom Gugliotta	.30	.14
☐ 184	Don MacLean	.05	.02
☐ 185	Brent Price	.05	.02
☐ 186	George Lynch	.05	.02
☐ 187	Rex Walters	.05	.02
☐ 188	Shawn Bradley	.40	.18
☐ 189	Ervin Johnson	.15	.07
☐ 190	Luther Wright	.05	.02
☐ 191	Calbert Cheaney	.30	.14
☐ 192	Craig Ehlo	.05	.02
☐ 193	Duane Ferrell	.05	.02
☐ 194	Paul Graham	.05	.02
☐ 195	Andrew Lang	.05	.02
☐ 196	Chris Corchiani	.05	.02
☐ 197	Acie Earl	.05	.02
☐ 198	Dino Radja	.15	.07
☐ 199	Ed Pinckney	.05	.02
☐ 200	Tony Bennett	.05	.02
☐ 201	Scott Burrell	.30	.14
☐ 202	Kenny Gattison	.05	.02
☐ 203	Hersey Hawkins	.15	.07
☐ 204	Eddie Johnson	.05	.02
☐ 205	Corie Blount	.05	.02
☐ 206	Steve Kerr	.15	.07
☐ 207	Toni Kukoc	.75	.35
☐ 208	Pete Myers	.05	.02
☐ 209	Danny Ferry	.05	.02
☐ 210	Tyrone Hill	.05	.02
☐ 211	Gerald Madkins	.05	.02
☐ 212	Chris Mills	.50	.23
☐ 213	Lucious Harris	.05	.02
☐ 214	Popeye Jones	.05	.02
☐ 215	Jamal Mashburn	.75	.35
☐ 216	Darnell Mee	.05	.02
☐ 217	Rodney Rogers	.05	.02
☐ 218	Brian Williams	.05	.02
☐ 219	Greg Anderson	.05	.02
☐ 220	Sean Elliott	.15	.07
☐ 221	Allan Houston	.60	.25
☐ 222	Lindsey Hunter	.30	.14
☐ 223	Chris Gatling	.05	.02
☐ 224	Josh Grant	.05	.02
☐ 225	Keith Jennings	.05	.02
☐ 226	Avery Johnson	.05	.02
☐ 227	Chris Webber	2.00	.90
☐ 228	Sam Cassell	.75	.35
☐ 229	Mario Elie	.05	.02
☐ 230	Richard Petruska	.05	.02
☐ 231	Eric Riley	.05	.02
☐ 232	Antonio Davis	.15	.07
☐ 233	Scott Haskin	.05	.02
☐ 234	Derrick McKey	.05	.02
☐ 235	Mark Aguirre	.05	.02
☐ 236	Terry Dehere	.05	.02
☐ 237	Gary Grant	.05	.02
☐ 238	Randy Woods	.05	.02
☐ 239	Sam Bowie	.05	.02
☐ 240	Elden Campbell	.15	.07
☐ 241	Nick Van Exel	1.00	.45
☐ 242	Manute Bol	.05	.02
☐ 243	Brian Shaw	.05	.02
☐ 244	Vin Baker	2.00	.90
☐ 245	Brad Lohaus	.05	.02
☐ 246	Ken Norman	.05	.02
☐ 247	Derek Strong	.05	.02
☐ 248	Dan Schayes	.05	.02
☐ 249	Mike Brown	.05	.02
☐ 250	Luc Longley	.15	.07
☐ 251	Isaiah Rider	.40	.18
☐ 252	Kevin Edwards	.05	.02
☐ 253	Armon Gilliam	.05	.02
☐ 254	Greg Anthony	.05	.02
☐ 255	Anthony Bonner	.05	.02
☐ 256	Tony Campbell	.05	.02
☐ 257	Hubert Davis	.05	.02
☐ 258	Litterial Green	.05	.02
☐ 259	Anfernee Hardaway	4.00	1.80
☐ 260	Larry Krystkowiak	.05	.02
☐ 261	Todd Lichti	.05	.02
☐ 262	Dana Barros	.05	.02
☐ 263	Greg Graham	.05	.02
☐ 264	Warren Kidd	.05	.02
☐ 265	Moses Malone	.30	.14
☐ 266	A.C. Green	.15	.07
☐ 267	Joe Kleine	.05	.02
☐ 268	Malcolm Mackey	.05	.02
☐ 269	Mark Bryant	.05	.02
☐ 270	Chris Dudley	.05	.02
☐ 271	Harvey Grant	.05	.02
☐ 272	James Robinson	.05	.02
☐ 273	Dragan Tarlac	.05	.02
☐ 274	Bobby Hurley	.15	.07
☐ 275	Jim Les	.05	.02
☐ 276	Willie Anderson	.05	.02
☐ 277	Terry Cummings	.05	.02
☐ 278	Vinny Del Negro	.05	.02
☐ 279	Sleepy Floyd	.05	.02
☐ 280	Dennis Rodman	1.25	.55
☐ 281	Vincent Askew	.05	.02
☐ 282	Kendall Gill	.15	.07
☐ 283	Steve Scheffler	.05	.02
☐ 284	Detlef Schrempf	.15	.07
☐ 285	David Benoit	.05	.02
☐ 286	Tom Chambers	.05	.02
☐ 287	Felton Spencer	.05	.02
☐ 288	Rex Chapman	.05	.02
☐ 289	Kevin Duckworth	.05	.02
☐ 290	Gheorghe Muresan	.40	.18
☐ 291	Kenny Walker	.05	.02
☐ 292	Andrew Lang CF / Craig Ehlo	.05	.02
☐ 293	Dino Radja CF / Acie Earl	.05	.02
☐ 294	Eddie Johnson CF / Hersey Hawkins	.05	.02
☐ 295	Toni Kukoc CF / Corie Blount	.15	.07
☐ 296	Tyrone Hill CF / Chris Mills	.05	.02
☐ 297	Jamal Mashburn CF / Popeye Jones	.30	.14
☐ 298	Darnell Mee CF / Rodney Rogers	.05	.02
☐ 299	Lindsey Hunter CF / Allan Houston	.15	.07
☐ 300	Chris Webber CF / Avery Johnson	.50	.23
☐ 301	Sam Cassell CF / Mario Elie	.30	.14
☐ 302	Derrick McKey CF / Antonio Davis	.05	.02
☐ 303	Terry Dehere CF / Mark Aguirre	.05	.02
☐ 304	Nick Van Exel CF / George Lynch	.30	.14
☐ 305	Harold Miner CF / Steve Smith	.05	.02
☐ 306	Ken Norman CF / Vin Baker	.30	.14
☐ 307	Mike Brown CF / Isaiah Rider	.15	.07
☐ 308	Kevin Edwards CF / Rex Walters	.05	.02
☐ 309	Hubert Davis CF / Anthony Bonner	.05	.02
☐ 310	Anfernee Hardaway CF / Larry Krystkowiak	1.25	.55
☐ 311	Moses Malone CF / Shawn Bradley	.30	.14
☐ 312	Joe Kleine CF / A.C. Green	.05	.02
☐ 313	Harvey Grant CF / Chris Dudley	.05	.02
☐ 314	Bobby Hurley CF / Mitch Richmond	.30	.14
☐ 315	Sleepy Floyd CF / Dennis Rodman	.30	.14
☐ 316	Kendall Gill CF / Detlef Schrempf	.05	.02
☐ 317	Felton Spencer CF / Luther Wright	.05	.02
☐ 318	Calbert Cheaney CF / Kevin Duckworth	.05	.02
☐ 319	Karl Malone PC	.30	.14
☐ 320	Alonzo Mourning PC	.30	.14
☐ 321	Scottie Pippen PC	.50	.23
☐ 322	Mark Price PC	.05	.02
☐ 323	LaPhonso Ellis PC	.05	.02
☐ 324	Joe Dumars PC	.15	.07
☐ 325	Chris Mullin PC	.05	.02
☐ 326	Ron Harper PC	.05	.02
☐ 327	Glen Rice PC	.15	.07
☐ 328	Christian Laettner PC	.15	.07
☐ 329	Kenny Anderson PC	.05	.02
☐ 330	John Starks PC	.05	.02
☐ 331	Shaquille O'Neal PC	.60	.25
☐ 332	Charles Barkley PC	.30	.14
☐ 333	Clifford Robinson PC	.05	.02
☐ 334	Clyde Drexler PC	.30	.14
☐ 335	Mitch Richmond PC	.15	.07
☐ 336	David Robinson PC	.30	.14
☐ 337	Shawn Kemp PC	.50	.23

		MINT	NRMT
☐ 338	John Stockton PC	.15	.07
☐ 339	Checklist 4...............	.05	.02
☐ 340	Checklist 5...............	.05	.02
☐ 341	Checklist 6...............	.05	.02
☐ DP4	Jim Jackson	1.50	.70
☐ DP17	Doug Christie	.40	.18
☐ NNO	Head of the Class ..	2.00	.90
	Expired Exchange		
☐ NNO	HOC Card..............	30.00	13.50
	Shawn Bradley		
	Calbert Cheaney		
	Anfernee Hardaway		
	Jamal Mashburn		
	Isaiah Rider		
	Chris Webber		

1993-94 SkyBox All-Rookies

Randomly inserted in first series 12-card packs at a rate of one in 36, this standard-size five-card set features top rookies from the 1992-93 season. The design features borderless fronts with color action player cutouts set against metallic game-crowd backgrounds. The player's name appears in gold-foil lettering at the upper left. The white back carries a color player head shot along with career highlights.

	MINT	NRMT
COMPLETE SET (5)	15.00	6.75
COMMON CARD (AR1-AR5) ..	.75	.35
SEMISTARS	1.50	.70
UNLISTED STARS	2.00	.90
SER.1 STATED ODDS 1:36		

		MINT	NRMT
☐ AR1	Shaquille O'Neal	10.00	4.50
☐ AR2	Alonzo Mourning	3.00	1.35
☐ AR3	Christian Laettner	1.50	.70
☐ AR4	Tom Gugliotta.........	2.00	.90
☐ AR5	LaPhonso Ellis	.75	.35

1993-94 SkyBox Center Stage

Randomly inserted in first series packs at a rate of one in 12, this 9-card standard-size set showcases some of the best players in the NBA. Card fronts feature borderless fronts with color action player cutouts placed against black backgrounds. The

player's name is centered at the top in prismatic silver-foil lettering. The white back features a color action player cutout and player biography.

	MINT	NRMT
COMPLETE SET (9)	35.00	16.00
COMMON CARD (CS1-CS9)..	1.00	.45
SEMISTARS	1.50	.70
SER.1 STATED ODDS 1:12		

		MINT	NRMT
☐ CS1	Michael Jordan	25.00	11.00
☐ CS2	Shaquille O'Neal	8.00	3.60
☐ CS3	Charles Barkley......	3.00	1.35
☐ CS4	John Starks	1.50	.70
☐ CS5	Larry Johnson	1.50	.70
☐ CS6	Hakeem Olajuwon ..	4.00	1.80
☐ CS7	Kenny Anderson	1.50	.70
☐ CS8	Mahmoud Abdul-Rauf	1.00	.45
☐ CS9	Clifford Robinson	1.50	.70

1993-94 SkyBox Draft Picks

These 26 standard-size cards were random inserts in both first series (Nos. 2, 6-8, 12, 15) and second series (the other 20) 12-card packs. The odds of finding one of these cards are one in every 12 packs. Card No. 26 was scheduled to be LSU center Geert Hammink. Hammink decided to play in Europe and his card was pulled. The fronts feature a color player action cutout set off to one side and superposed upon a ghosted posed color player photo. The player's name, the team that

drafted him, and his draft pick number appear at the top. The white back carries the player's name, career highlights, and pre-NBA statistics. The cards are numbered on the back with a "DP" prefix. The set is sequenced in draft order.

	MINT	NRMT
COMPLETE SET (26)	50.00	22.00
COMPLETE SERIES 1 (9)....	10.00	4.50
COMPLETE SERIES 2 (17)..	40.00	18.00
COMMON CARD (1-26)	.50	.23
SEMISTARS	1.00	.45
UNLISTED STARS	2.50	1.10
NUMBER 26 NEVER ISSUED		
SER.1/2 STATED ODDS 1:12		

		MINT	NRMT
☐ DP1	Chris Webber	10.00	4.50
☐ DP2	Shawn Bradley	2.50	1.10
☐ DP3	Anfernee Hardaway ..	25.00	11.00
☐ DP4	Jamal Mashburn.....	4.00	1.80
☐ DP5	Isaiah Rider	2.50	1.10
☐ DP6	Calbert Cheaney	2.50	1.10
☐ DP7	Bobby Hurley	1.00	.45
☐ DP8	Vin Baker	10.00	4.50
☐ DP9	Rodney Rogers.......	.50	.23
☐ DP10	Lindsey Hunter	2.50	1.10
☐ DP11	Allan Houston	3.00	1.35
☐ DP12	George Lynch	.50	.23
☐ DP13	Terry Dehere.........	.50	.23
☐ DP14	Scott Haskin	.50	.23
☐ DP15	Doug Edwards	.50	.23
☐ DP16	Rex Walters	.50	.23
☐ DP17	Greg Graham	.50	.23
☐ DP18	Luther Wright	.50	.23
☐ DP19	Acie Earl	.50	.23
☐ DP20	Scott Burrell	2.50	1.10
☐ DP21	James Robinson.....	.50	.23
☐ DP22	Chris Mills	2.50	1.10
☐ DP23	Ervin Johnson.......	.50	.45
☐ DP24	Sam Cassell	4.00	1.80
☐ DP25	Corie Blount	.50	.23
☐ DP26	Not Issued		
☐ DP27	Malcolm Mackey......	.50	.23

1993-94 SkyBox Dynamic Dunks

These nine standard-size cards were random inserts in second series 12-card packs. The odds of finding one of these cards are one in every 36 packs. The horizontal fronts feature color dunking-action player cutouts superposed upon borderless black and gold metallic backgrounds. The player's name appears in

gold lettering at the bottom right. The horizontal black back carries another color dunking-action player photo. The player's name and a comment on his dunking style appear in white lettering beneath the photo. The set is sequenced in alphabetical order.

	MINT	NRMT
COMPLETE SET (9)	25.00	11.00
COMMON CARD (D1-D9)	.50	.23
SEMISTARS	.75	.35
SER.2 STATED ODDS 1:36		

		MINT	NRMT
☐ D1	Nick Anderson	.50	.23
☐ D2	Charles Barkley	2.50	1.10
☐ D3	Robert Horry	.75	.35
☐ D4	Michael Jordan	20.00	9.00
☐ D5	Shawn Kemp	5.00	2.20
☐ D6	Anthony Mason	.75	.35
☐ D7	Alonzo Mourning	2.00	.90
☐ D8	Hakeem Olajuwon	3.00	1.35
☐ D9	Dominique Wilkins	.75	.35

1993-94 SkyBox Shaq Talk

The 1993-94 SkyBox Shaq Talk set consists of 10 cards that were randomly inserted in first (cards 1-5) and second series (6-10) 12-card packs. The odds of finding one of these cards are reportedly one in every 36 packs. The standard size cards spotlight Shaquille O'Neal. The fronts feature cut-out action shots of Shaq over a ghosted background. The set title is superimposed across the top of the card in red lettering. The white backs have a ghosted SkyBox Premium logo. At the top is a quote from Shaquille regarding game strategy and below is player critique by a basketball analyst. The cards are numbered on the back with a "Shaq Talk" prefix.

	MINT	NRMT
COMPLETE SET (10)	40.00	18.00
COMPLETE SERIES 1 (5)	20.00	9.00
COMPLETE SERIES 2 (5)	20.00	9.00

		MINT	NRMT
	COMMON SHAQ (1-10)	5.00	2.20
SER.1/2 STATED ODDS 1:36			
SHAQ TALK PREFIX ON CARD NUMBER			
☐ 1	Shaquille O'Neal The Rebound	5.00	2.20
☐ 2	Shaquille O'Neal The Block (Blocking David Robinson's shot)	5.00	2.20
☐ 3	Shaquille O'Neal The Postup	5.00	2.20
☐ 4	Shaquille O'Neal The Dunk	5.00	2.20
☐ 5	Shaquille O'Neal Defense	5.00	2.20
☐ 6	Shaquille O'Neal Scoring	5.00	2.20
☐ 7	Shaquille O'Neal Passing	5.00	2.20
☐ 8	Shaquille O'Neal Rejections	5.00	2.20
☐ 9	Shaquille O'Neal Confidence	5.00	2.20
☐ 10	Shaquille O'Neal Legends	5.00	2.20

1993-94 SkyBox Showdown Series

These 12 standard-size cards were random inserts in first (cards 1-6) and second series (7-12) 12-card packs. The odds of finding one of these cards are one in every six packs. Each front features a borderless color action photo of the two players involved in the "Showdown." Both players' names appear, one vs. the other, in gold lettering within a metallic black stripe near the bottom. The horizontal white back carries a color player close-up for each player on each side. The players' names appear beneath each photo. Comparative statistics fill in the area between the two player photos.

	MINT	NRMT
COMPLETE SET (12)	6.00	2.70
COMPLETE SERIES 1 (6)	3.00	1.35
COMPLETE SERIES 2 (6)	3.00	1.35
COMMON PAIR (SS1-SS12)	.25	.11
SEMISTARS	.40	.18
UNLISTED STARS	.50	.23
SER.1/2 STATED ODDS 1:6		

		MINT	NRMT
☐ SS1	Alonzo Mourning Patrick Ewing	.40	.18
☐ SS2	Shaquille O'Neal Patrick Ewing	1.00	.45
☐ SS3	Alonzo Mourning Shaquille O'Neal	1.25	.55
☐ SS4	Hakeem Olajuwon Dikembe Mutombo	.50	.23
☐ SS5	David Robinson Hakeem Olajuwon	.60	.25
☐ SS6	David Robinson Dikembe Mutombo	.40	.18
☐ SS7	Shawn Kemp Karl Malone	.75	.35
☐ SS8	Larry Johnson Charles Barkley	.40	.18
☐ SS9	Dominique Wilkins Scottie Pippen	.50	.23
☐ SS10	Joe Dumars Reggie Miller	.25	.11
☐ SS11	Clyde Drexler Micheal Jordan	2.00	.90
☐ SS12	Magic Johnson Larry Bird	1.50	.70

1993-94 SkyBox Thunder and Lightning

Randomly inserted in second series packs at a rate of one in 12 packs, this standard-size nine-card set features players pictured on both sides. On one side a guard would be featured and a forward or center on the other side. Borderless on either side, the color action player cutouts set against metallic backgrounds.

	MINT	NRMT
COMPLETE SET (9)	20.00	9.00
COMMON PAIR (1-9)	.50	.23
SEMISTARS	.60	.25
UNLISTED STARS	1.00	.45
SER.2 STATED ODDS 1:12		

		MINT	NRMT
☐ TL1	Jamal Mashburn Jim Jackson	2.00	.90
☐ TL2	Harold Miner Steve Smith	.50	.23
☐ TL3	Isaiah Rider Micheal Williams	.50	.23
☐ TL4	Derrick Coleman Kenny Anderson	.60	.25
☐ TL5	Patrick Ewing John Starks	1.00	.45

		MINT	NRMT
☐ TL6	Shaquille O'Neal	12.00	5.50
	Anfernee Hardaway		
☐ TL7	Shawn Bradley	.50	.23
	Jeff Hornacek		
☐ TL8	Walt Williams	.60	.25
	Bobby Hurley		
☐ TL9	Dennis Rodman	6.00	2.70
	David Robinson		

1993-94 SkyBox USA Tip-Off

The 13-card 1993-94 SkyBox USA Tip-Off set could be only acquired by sending in the USA Exchange card. The USA Exchange cards were randomly inserted in SkyBox series two packs. The Tip-Off redemption expiration was 6/15/94. It should be noted that Michael Jordan is not part of the set. Card fronts and backs feature studio photos of players in their USA Basketball uniforms.

		MINT	NRMT
COMPLETE SET (14)		25.00	11.00
COMMON CARD (1-13)		.75	.35
SEMISTARS		1.00	.45
UNLISTED STARS		1.25	.55
ONE SET PER EXCHANGE CARD BY MAIL			
EXCH.CARD: SER.2 STATED ODDS 1:240			
☐ 1	Steve Smith	4.00	1.80
	Magic Johnson		
☐ 2	Larry Johnson	2.50	1.10
	Charles Barkley		
☐ 3	Patrick Ewing	2.50	1.10
	Alonzo Mourning		
☐ 4	Shawn Kemp	5.00	2.20
	Karl Malone		
☐ 5	Chris Mullin	.75	.35
	Dan Majerle		
☐ 6	John Stockton	1.25	.55
	Mark Price		
☐ 7	Christian Laettner	1.00	.45
	Derrick Coleman		
☐ 8	Dominique Wilkins	1.50	.70
	Clyde Drexler		
☐ 9	Joe Dumars	3.00	1.35
	Scottie Pippen		
☐ 10	David Robinson	6.00	2.70
	Shaquille O'Neal		
☐ 11	Reggie Miller	5.00	2.20
☐ 12	Tim Hardaway	1.25	.55
☐ 13	Isiah Thomas	.75	.35
☐ NNO	Checklist	.25	.11
☐ NNO	Expired USA Exchange	1.50	.70

1994-95 SkyBox

The 350 standard-size cards that comprise the 1994-95 SkyBox set were issued in two separate series of 200 and 150 cards respectively. Cards were distributed in 12-card hobby and retail packs with a suggested retail price of $1.99 each. Unlike first series packs, each second series pack contained an insert card. Card fronts feature full-bleed action photos with the player's name running down the upper-left corner. The cards are grouped alphabetically within teams and checklisted below alphabetically according to teams. Subsets are NBA on NBC (176-185), Dynamic Duals (186-197), USA Basketball (198), Checklists (298-300), SkySlams (301-313), SkyShots (314-325), SkySwats (326-338), and SkyPilots (339-350). Every first series pack contained an Action and Drama Instant Win game card, offering the chance to play one-on-one with Magic Johnson, or receive a number of other prizes including autographed Hakeem Olajuwon or David Robinson jerseys, a dual autographed Olajuwon/Robinson card or an exclusive Magic Johnson exchange card available only through this promotion. A special three-card panel featuring Johnson, Olajuwon and Robinson was available by mailing in forty first series wrappers before the June 30th, 1995 deadline. Also, three Master Series Preview Press Sheet Exchange cards were randomly seeded into one in every 360 first series packs. The cards were redeemable for 50-card uncut press sheets of SkyBox's new super-premium Emotion cards. The expiration

date for the Emotion Press Sheets was March 1, 1995. As a final note, approximately one in every 360 first series retail packs contained an unannounced Hakeem Olajuwon Gold "stealth" card. Approximately one in every 360 second series retail packs contained an unannounced Grant Hill Gold "stealth" card. A standard-size promo card featuring Hakeem Olajuwon was issued to preview the set; a 3 1/2" by 5" jumbo version, distinguished by a gold foil autograph, was issued as a chiptopper in retail boxes. Three 5" by 7" jumbo featuring Grant Hill were also issued as chiptoppers. Series 1 Sam's retail boxes contained a jumbo Grant Hill Hoops rookie card, Series 2 retail boxes contained a jumbo Grant Hill SkyBox rookie card and Series 2 vintage retail boxes contained a jumbo replica of his Slammin' Universe card. Rookie Cards in this set include Grant Hill, Jason Kidd and Glenn Robinson.

	MINT	NRMT
COMPLETE SET (350)	30.00	13.50
COMPLETE SERIES 1 (200)	15.00	6.75
COMPLETE SERIES 2 (150)	15.00	6.75
COMMON CARD (1-200)	.10	.05
COMMON CARD (201-350)	.05	.02
SEMISTARS SER.1	.20	.09
SEMISTARS SER.2	.10	.05
UNLISTED STARS SER.1	.40	.18
UNLISTED STARS SER.2	.25	.11
GHO: SER.2 STATED ODDS 1:360 RETAIL		
OLAJ.GLD: SER.1 STATED ODDS 1:360 RET		
DUAL AU: SER.2 STATED ODDS 1:15,000		
☐ 1 Stacey Augmon	.10	.05
☐ 2 Mookie Blaylock	.20	.09
☐ 3 Doug Edwards	.10	.05
☐ 4 Craig Ehlo	.10	.05
☐ 5 Adam Keefe	.10	.05
☐ 6 Danny Manning	.10	.05
☐ 7 Kevin Willis	.10	.05
☐ 8 Dee Brown	.10	.05
☐ 9 Sherman Douglas	.10	.05
☐ 10 Acie Earl	.10	.05
☐ 11 Kevin Gamble	.10	.05
☐ 12 Xavier McDaniel	.10	.05
☐ 13 Dino Radja	.10	.05
☐ 14 Muggsy Bogues	.20	.09
☐ 15 Scott Burrell	.10	.05
☐ 16 Dell Curry	.10	.05
☐ 17 LeRon Ellis	.10	.05
☐ 18 Hersey Hawkins	.20	.09
☐ 19 Larry Johnson	.20	.09
☐ 20 Alonzo Mourning	.50	.23
☐ 21 B.J. Armstrong	.10	.05
☐ 22 Corie Blount	.10	.05
☐ 23 Horace Grant	.20	.09
☐ 24 Toni Kukoc	.40	.18
☐ 25 Luc Longley	.20	.09
☐ 26 Scottie Pippen	1.25	.55
☐ 27 Scott Williams	.10	.05
☐ 28 Terrell Brandon	.40	.18
☐ 29 Brad Daugherty	.10	.05
☐ 30 Tyrone Hill	.10	.05
☐ 31 Chris Mills	.20	.09

32	Bobby Phills	.10	.05
33	Mark Price	.10	.05
34	Gerald Wilkins	.10	.05
35	Lucious Harris	.10	.05
36	Jim Jackson	.20	.09
37	Popeye Jones	.10	.05
38	Jamal Mashburn	.40	.18
39	Sean Rooks	.10	.05
40	Mahmoud Abdul-Rauf	.10	.05
41	LaPhonso Ellis	.20	.09
42	Dikembe Mutombo	.40	.18
43	Robert Pack	.10	.05
44	Rodney Rogers	.10	.05
45	Bryant Stith	.10	.05
46	Reggie Williams	.10	.05
47	Joe Dumars	.40	.18
48	Sean Elliott	.20	.09
49	Allan Houston	.40	.18
50	Lindsey Hunter	.20	.09
51	Terry Mills	.10	.05
52	Victor Alexander	.10	.05
53	Tim Hardaway	.50	.23
54	Chris Mullin	.40	.18
55	Billy Owens	.10	.05
56	Latrell Sprewell	.20	.09
57	Chris Webber	1.00	.45
58	Sam Cassell	.40	.18
59	Carl Herrera	.10	.05
60	Robert Horry	.20	.09
61	Vernon Maxwell	.10	.05
62	Hakeem Olajuwon	.75	.35
63	Kenny Smith	.10	.05
64	Otis Thorpe	.20	.09
65	Antonio Davis	.10	.05
66	Dale Davis	.10	.05
67	Derrick McKey	.10	.05
68	Reggie Miller	.40	.18
69	Pooh Richardson	.10	.05
70	Rik Smits	.20	.09
71	Haywoode Workman	.10	.05
72	Terry Dehere	.10	.05
73	Harold Ellis	.10	.05
74	Ron Harper	.20	.09
75	Mark Jackson	.20	.09
76	Loy Vaught	.10	.05
77	Dominique Wilkins	.40	.18
78	Elden Campbell	.10	.05
79	Doug Christie	.10	.05
80	Vlade Divac	.20	.09
81	George Lynch	.10	.05
82	Anthony Peeler	.10	.05
83	Sedale Threatt	.10	.05
84	Nick Van Exel	.40	.18
85	Harold Miner	.10	.05
86	Glen Rice	.40	.18
87	John Salley	.10	.05
88	Rony Seikaly	.10	.05
89	Brian Shaw	.10	.05
90	Steve Smith	.20	.09
91	Vin Baker	1.00	.45
92	Jon Barry	.10	.05
93	Todd Day	.10	.05
94	Blue Edwards	.10	.05
95	Lee Mayberry	.10	.05
96	Eric Murdock	.10	.05
97	Mike Brown	.10	.05
98	Stacey King	.10	.05
99	Christian Laettner	.20	.09
100	Isaiah Rider	.20	.09
101	Doug West	.10	.05
102	Micheal Williams	.10	.05
103	Kenny Anderson	.20	.09
104	P.J. Brown	.10	.05
105	Derrick Coleman	.20	.09
106	Kevin Edwards	.10	.05
107	Chris Morris	.10	.05
108	Rex Walters	.10	.05
109	Hubert Davis	.10	.05
110	Patrick Ewing	.40	.18
111	Derek Harper	.20	.09
112	Anthony Mason	.20	.09
113	Charles Oakley	.20	.09
114	Charles Smith	.10	.05
115	John Starks	.20	.09
116	Nick Anderson	.20	.09
117	Anfernee Hardaway	1.50	.70
118	Shaquille O'Neal	1.50	.70
119	Donald Royal	.10	.05
120	Dennis Scott	.20	.09
121	Scott Skiles	.10	.05
122	Dana Barros	.10	.05
123	Shawn Bradley	.20	.09
124	Johnny Dawkins	.10	.05
125	Greg Graham	.10	.05
126	C.Weatherspoon	.10	.05
127	Danny Ainge	.20	.09
128	Charles Barkley	.60	.25
129	Cedric Ceballos	.20	.09
130	A.C. Green	.20	.09
131	Kevin Johnson	.20	.09
132	Dan Majerle	.20	.09
133	Oliver Miller	.10	.05
134	Clyde Drexler	.50	.23
135	Harvey Grant	.10	.05
136	Tracy Murray	.10	.05
137	Terry Porter	.10	.05
138	Clifford Robinson	.20	.09
139	James Robinson	.10	.05
140	Rod Strickland	.20	.09
141	Bobby Hurley	.10	.05
142	Olden Polynice	.10	.05
143	Mitch Richmond	.40	.18
144	Lionel Simmons	.10	.05
145	Wayman Tisdale	.10	.05
146	Spud Webb	.20	.09
147	Walt Williams	.10	.05
148	Willie Anderson	.10	.05
149	Vinny Del Negro	.10	.05
150	Dale Ellis	.10	.05
151	J.R. Reid	.10	.05
152	David Robinson	.60	.25
153	Dennis Rodman	1.50	.70
154	Kendall Gill	.20	.09
155	Shawn Kemp	1.25	.55
156	Nate McMillan	.10	.05
157	Gary Payton	.60	.25
158	Sam Perkins	.20	.09
159	Ricky Pierce	.10	.05
160	Detlef Schrempf	.20	.09
161	David Benoit	.10	.05
162	Tyrone Corbin	.10	.05
163	Jeff Hornacek	.20	.09
164	Jay Humphries	.10	.05
165	Karl Malone	.60	.25
166	Bryon Russell	.20	.09
167	Felton Spencer	.10	.05
168	John Stockton	.40	.18
169	Michael Adams	.10	.05
170	Rex Chapman	.10	.05
171	Calbert Cheaney	.20	.09
172	Pervis Ellison	.10	.05
173	Tom Gugliotta	.40	.18
174	Don MacLean	.10	.05
175	Gheorghe Muresan	.20	.09
176	Charles Barkley NBC	.40	.18
177	Charles Oakley NBC	.10	.05
178	Hakeem Olajuwon NBC	.40	.18
179	D.Mutombo NBC	.20	.09
180	Scottie Pippen NBC	.60	.25
181	Sam Cassell NBC	.40	.18
182	Karl Malone NBC	.40	.18
183	Reggie Miller PO	.20	.09
184	Patrick Ewing NBC	.20	.09
185	Vernon Maxwell NBC	.10	.05
186	Anfernee Hardaway DD / Steve Smith	.40	.18
187	Chris Webber DD / Shaquille O'Neal	.50	.23
188	Jamal Mashburn DD / Rodney Rogers	.20	.09
189	Toni Kukoc DD / Dino Radja	.20	.09
190	Lindsey Hunter DD / Kenny Anderson	.10	.05
191	Latrell Sprewell DD / Jimmy Jackson	.10	.05
192	C.Weatherspoon / Vin Baker DD	.40	.18
193	Calbert Cheaney DD / Chris Mills	.20	.09
194	Isaiah Rider DD / Robert Horry	.10	.05
195	Sam Cassell DD / Nick Van Exel	.10	.05
196	Gheorghe Muresan DD / Shawn Bradley	.10	.05
197	LaPhonso Ellis DD / Tom Gugliotta	.20	.09
198	USA Basketball Card	.10	.05
199	Checklist	.10	.05
200	Checklist	.10	.05
201	Sergei Bazarevich	.05	.02
202	Tyrone Corbin	.05	.02
203	Grant Long	.05	.02
204	Ken Norman	.05	.02
205	Steve Smith	.15	.07
206	Blue Edwards	.05	.02
207	Greg Minor	.05	.02
208	Eric Montross	.05	.02
209	Dominique Wilkins	.15	.07
210	Michael Adams	.05	.02
211	Kenny Gattison	.05	.02
212	Darrin Hancock	.05	.02
213	Robert Parish	.10	.05
214	Ron Harper	.10	.05
215	Steve Kerr	.05	.02
216	Will Perdue	.05	.02
217	Dickey Simpkins	.05	.02
218	John Battle	.05	.02
219	Michael Cage	.05	.02
220	Tony Dumas	.05	.02
221	Jason Kidd	2.00	.90
222	Roy Tarpley	.05	.02
223	Dale Ellis	.05	.02
224	Jalen Rose	.15	.07
225	Bill Curley	.05	.02
226	Grant Hill	3.00	1.35
227	Oliver Miller	.05	.02
228	Mark West	.05	.02
229	Tom Gugliotta	.25	.11
230	Ricky Pierce	.05	.02
231	Carlos Rogers	.05	.02
232	Clifford Rozier	.05	.02
233	Rony Seikaly	.05	.02
234	Tim Breaux	.05	.02
235	Duane Ferrell	.05	.02
236	Mark Jackson	.10	.05
237	Byron Scott	.10	.05
238	John Williams	.05	.02
239	Lamond Murray	.10	.05
240	Eric Piatkowski	.05	.02
241	Pooh Richardson	.05	.02
242	Malik Sealy	.05	.02
243	Cedric Ceballos	.10	.05
244	Eddie Jones	2.00	.90
245	Anthony Miller	.05	.02
246	Tony Smith	.05	.02
247	Kevin Gamble	.05	.02
248	Brad Lohaus	.05	.02
249	Billy Owens	.05	.02
250	Khalid Reeves	.10	.05
251	Kevin Willis	.05	.02
252	Eric Mobley	.05	.02
253	Johnny Newman	.05	.02
254	Ed Pinckney	.05	.02
255	Glenn Robinson	1.00	.45
256	Howard Eisley	.05	.02
257	Donyell Marshall	.30	.14
258	Yinka Dare	.05	.02
259	Sean Higgins	.05	.02
260	Jayson Williams	.10	.05
261	Charlie Ward	.05	.05
262	Monty Williams	.05	.02
263	Horace Grant	.10	.05
264	Brian Shaw	.05	.02
265	Brooks Thompson	.05	.02
266	Derrick Alston	.05	.02
267	B.J. Tyler	.05	.02
268	Scott Williams	.05	.02
269	Sharone Wright	.05	.02
270	Antonio Lang	.05	.02
271	Danny Manning	.05	.02
272	Wesley Person	.30	.14
273	Trevor Ruffin	.05	.02
274	Wayman Tisdale	.05	.02
275	Jerome Kersey	.05	.02
276	Aaron McKie	.05	.02
277	Frank Brickowski	.05	.02

☐ 278 Brian Grant	.25	.11	☐ NNO Emotion Exchange A 1.00		.45
☐ 279 Michael Smith	.10	.05	Expired		
☐ 280 Terry Cummings	.05	.02	☐ NNO Emotion Exchange B 1.00		.45
☐ 281 Sean Elliott	.10	.05	Expired		
☐ 282 Avery Johnson	.05	.02	☐ NNO Emotion Exchange C 1.00		.45
☐ 283 Moses Malone	.25	.11	Expired		
☐ 284 Chuck Person	.05	.02	☐ NNO 3rd Prize Game Card .25		.11
☐ 285 Vincent Askew	.05	.02	Expired		
☐ 286 Bill Cartwright	.05	.02	☐ NNO Hakeem Olajuwon 250.00		110.00
☐ 287 Sarunas Marciulionis	.05	.02	David Robinson AU		
☐ 288 Dontonio Wingfield	.05	.02	☐ NNO Magic Johnson 5.00		2.20
☐ 289 Jay Humphries	.05	.02	Exchange Card		
☐ 290 Adam Keefe	.05	.02	☐ NNO Three-Card Panel 4.00		1.80
☐ 291 Jamie Watson	.05	.02	Magic Johnson		
☐ 292 Kevin Duckworth	.05	.02	Hakeem Olajuwon		
☐ 293 Juwan Howard	1.25	.55	David Robinson		
☐ 294 Jim McIlvaine	.05	.02			
☐ 295 Scott Skiles	.05	.02			
☐ 296 Anthony Tucker	.05	.02			
☐ 297 Chris Webber	.60	.25			
☐ 298 Checklist 201-265	.05	.02			
☐ 299 Checklist 266-345	.05	.02			
☐ 300 CL 346-350/Inserts	.05	.02			
☐ 301 Vin Baker SSL	.30	.14			
☐ 302 Charles Barkley SSL	.25	.11			
☐ 303 Derrick Coleman SSL	.15	.07			
☐ 304 Clyde Drexler SSL	.15	.07			
☐ 305 LaPhonso Ellis SSL	.05	.02			
☐ 306 Larry Johnson SSL	.05	.02			
☐ 307 Shawn Kemp SSL	.40	.18			
☐ 308 Karl Malone SSL	.15	.07			
☐ 309 Jamal Mashburn SSL	.15	.07			
☐ 310 Scottie Pippen SSL	.40	.18			
☐ 311 Dominique Wilkins SSL	.10	.05			
☐ 312 Walt Williams SSL	.05	.02			
☐ 313 Sharone Wright SSL	.05	.02			
☐ 314 B.J. Armstrong SSH	.05	.02			
☐ 315 Joe Dumars SSH	.10	.05			
☐ 316 Tony Dumas SSH	.05	.02			
☐ 317 Tim Hardaway SSH	.15	.07			
☐ 318 Toni Kukoc SSH	.15	.07			
☐ 319 Danny Manning SSH	.05	.02			
☐ 320 Reggie Miller SSH	.15	.07			
☐ 321 Chris Mullin SSH	.10	.05			
☐ 322 Wesley Person SSH	.10	.05			
☐ 323 John Starks SSH	.05	.02			
☐ 324 John Stockton SSH	.15	.07			
☐ 325 C. Weatherspoon SSH	.05	.02			
☐ 326 Shawn Bradley SSW	.05	.02			
☐ 327 Vlade Divac SSW	.05	.02			
☐ 328 Patrick Ewing SSW	.15	.07			
☐ 329 Christian Laettner SSW	.05	.02			
☐ 330 Eric Montross SSW	.05	.02			
☐ 331 G.Muresan SSW	.05	.02			
☐ 332 D.Mutombo SSW	.15	.07			
☐ 333 Hakeem Olajuwon SSW	.25	.11			
☐ 334 Robert Parish SSW	.05	.02			
☐ 335 David Robinson SSW	.25	.11			
☐ 336 Dennis Rodman SSW	.50	.23			
☐ 337 Rony Seikaly SSW	.05	.02			
☐ 338 Rik Smits SSW	.05	.02			
☐ 339 Kenny Anderson SPI	.05	.02			
☐ 340 Dee Brown SPI	.05	.02			
☐ 341 Bobby Hurley SPI	.05	.02			
☐ 342 Kevin Johnson SPI	.05	.02			
☐ 343 Jason Kidd SPI	.75	.35			
☐ 344 Gary Payton SPI	.25	.11			
☐ 345 Mark Price SPI	.05	.02			
☐ 346 Khalid Reeves SPI	.05	.02			
☐ 347 Jalen Rose SPI	.10	.05			
☐ 348 Latrell Sprewell SPI	.05	.02			
☐ 349 B.J. Tyler SPI	.05	.02			
☐ 350 Charlie Ward SPI	.05	.02			
☐ GHO Grant Hill	30.00	13.50			
Gold					
☐ NNO Hakeem Olajuwon 12.00		5.50			
Gold					
☐ NNO Grant Hill 10.00		4.50			
SkyBox Jumbo					
☐ NNO Grant Hill 10.00		4.50			
Hoops Jumbo					
☐ NNO Grant Hill 10.00		4.50			
Slammin' Universe					
Jumbo Card					
☐ NNO Emotion Sheet A .. 30.00		13.50			
☐ NNO Emotion Sheet B .. 30.00		13.50			

1994-95 SkyBox Center Stage

Randomly inserted in all first series packs at a rate of one in 72, cards from this nine-card standard-size set feature a selection of the game's top stars. Card fronts feature full-color player photos over etched-foil backgrounds.

	MINT	NRMT
COMPLETE SET (9)	70.00	32.00
COMMON CARD (CS1-CS9)	4.00	1.80
SER.1 STATED ODDS 1:72		
☐ CS1 Hakeem Olajuwon	8.00	3.60
☐ CS2 Shaquille O'Neal	15.00	6.75
☐ CS3 Anfernee Hardaway	15.00	6.75
☐ CS4 Chris Webber	10.00	4.50
☐ CS5 Scottie Pippen	12.00	5.50
☐ CS6 David Robinson	6.00	2.70
☐ CS7 Latrell Sprewell	4.00	1.80
☐ CS8 Charles Barkley	6.00	2.70
☐ CS9 Alonzo Mourning	5.00	2.20

1994-95 SkyBox Draft Picks

These 27 standard-size cards were random inserts in both first series (Nos. 2, 9, 10, 14 and 18) and second series (the other 22) packs. The first series cards were randomly seeded into one in every 45 packs. The second series cards were randomly seeded into one in every 18 packs. The set features all twenty-seven first round draft selections from the 1994 NBA draft. The foil card fronts feature a head shot of each player. The cards are numbered with a "DP" prefix. The set is sequenced in draft order.

	MINT	NRMT
COMPLETE SET (27)	90.00	40.00
COMPLETE SERIES 1 (5)	25.00	11.00
COMPLETE SERIES 2 (22)	65.00	29.00
COMMON CARD (1-27)	1.00	.45
SEMISTARS	2.50	1.10
SER.1 STATED ODDS 1:45		
SER.2 STATED ODDS 1:18		
☐ DP1 Glenn Robinson	10.00	4.50
☐ DP2 Jason Kidd	20.00	9.00
☐ DP3 Grant Hill	30.00	13.50
☐ DP4 Donyell Marshall	2.50	1.10
☐ DP5 Juwan Howard	12.00	5.50
☐ DP6 Sharone Wright	1.00	.45
☐ DP7 Lamond Murray	1.00	.45
☐ DP8 Brian Grant	2.50	1.10
☐ DP9 Eric Montross	1.00	.45
☐ DP10 Eddie Jones	20.00	9.00
☐ DP11 Carlos Rogers	1.00	.45
☐ DP12 Khalid Reeves	1.00	.45
☐ DP13 Jalen Rose	2.50	1.10
☐ DP14 Yinka Dare	1.00	.45
☐ DP15 Eric Piatkowski	1.00	.45
☐ DP16 Clifford Rozier	1.00	.45
☐ DP17 Aaron McKie	1.00	.45
☐ DP18 Eric Mobley	1.00	.45
☐ DP19 Tony Dumas	1.00	.45
☐ DP20 B.J. Tyler	1.00	.45
☐ DP21 Dickey Simpkins	1.00	.45
☐ DP22 Bill Curley	1.00	.45
☐ DP23 Wesley Person	2.50	1.10
☐ DP24 Monty Williams	1.00	.45
☐ DP25 Greg Minor	1.00	.45
☐ DP26 Charlie Ward	1.00	.45
☐ DP27 Brooks Thompson	1.00	.45

1994-95 SkyBox Grant Hill

Randomly inserted exclusively into one in every 36 second series hobby packs, cards from this 5-card standard-size set highlight the Detroit rookie, and SkyBox spokesperson, in various action shots. Full-color photos are set against a psychedelic background.

	MINT	NRMT
COMPLETE SET (5)	40.00	18.00
COMMON HILL (GH1-GH5)	10.00	4.50
SER.2 STATED ODDS 1:36 HOBBY		
□ GH1 Grant Hill	10.00	4.50
(Two-handed jam; back turned)		
□ GH2 Grant Hill	10.00	4.50
(One arm jam)		
□ GH3 Grant Hill	10.00	4.50
(Dribbling)		
□ GH4 Grant Hill	10.00	4.50
(Driving to hoop at left)		
□ GH5 Grant Hill	10.00	4.50
(Two-handed jam)		

1994-95 SkyBox Head of the Class

This 6-card standard-size set was available exclusively by mailing in the SkyBox Head of the Class exchange card before the June 15th, 1995 deadline. The Head of the Class exchange card was randomly inserted into one in every 480 first series packs. SkyBox selected six top rookies from the 1994-95 NBA season to be featured in the set. Card fronts feature a full-color player photo against a computer generated textured background. The set is sequenced in alphabetical order.

	MINT	NRMT
COMPLETE SET (6)	50.00	22.00
COMMON CARD (1-6)	1.50	.70
ONE SET PER HOC EXCHANGE CARD		
EXCH.CARD: SER.1 STATED ODDS 1:480		

		MINT	NRMT
□ 1	Grant Hill	25.00	11.00
□ 2	Juwan Howard	10.00	4.50
□ 3	Jason Kidd	15.00	6.75
□ 4	Donyell Marshall	2.00	.90
□ 5	Glenn Robinson	8.00	3.60
□ 6	Sharone Wright	1.50	.70
□ NNO	HOC Exchange Card	2.00	.90
	Expired		
□ NNO	Checklist Card	.25	.11

1994-95 SkyBox Ragin' Rookies

Randomly inserted into all first series packs at a rate of one in five, cards from this 24-card set feature a selection of the top rookies from the 1993 NBA draft. Full-color action photos feature a scratched border design.

		MINT	NRMT
COMPLETE SET (24)		25.00	11.00
COMMON CARD (RR1-RR24)		.75	.35
SEMISTARS		1.25	.55
UNLISTED STARS		2.50	1.10
SER.1 STATED ODDS 1:5			
□ RR1	Dino Radja	.75	.35
□ RR2	Corie Blount	.75	.35
□ RR3	Toni Kukoc	2.50	1.10
□ RR4	Chris Mills	1.25	.55
□ RR5	Jamal Mashburn	2.50	1.10
□ RR6	Rodney Rogers	.75	.35
□ RR7	Allan Houston	2.50	1.10
□ RR8	Lindsey Hunter	1.25	.55
□ RR9	Chris Webber	6.00	2.70
□ RR10	Sam Cassell	2.50	1.10
□ RR11	Antonio Davis	.75	.35
□ RR12	Terry Dehere	.75	.35
□ RR13	Nick Van Exel	2.50	1.10
□ RR14	George Lynch	.75	.35
□ RR15	Vin Baker	6.00	2.70
□ RR16	Isaiah Rider	1.25	.55
□ RR17	P.J. Brown	.75	.35
□ RR18	Anfernee Hardaway	10.00	4.50
□ RR19	Shawn Bradley	1.25	.55
□ RR20	James Robinson	.75	.35
□ RR21	Bobby Hurley	.75	.35
□ RR22	Ervin Johnson	.75	.35
□ RR23	Bryon Russell	1.25	.55
□ RR24	Calbert Cheaney	1.25	.55

1994-95 SkyBox Revolution

Randomly inserted into second series packs at a rate of one in 72, cards from this 10-card standard-size set feature a selection of NBA stars. The horizontal fronts feature full-color player photos against etched-foil backgrounds featuring team colors. The set is sequenced in alphabetical order.

		MINT	NRMT
COMPLETE SET (10)		70.00	32.00
COMMON CARD (R1-R10)		2.00	.90
SEMISTARS		3.00	1.35
UNLISTED STARS		4.00	1.80
SER.2 STATED ODDS 1:72			
□ R1	Patrick Ewing	4.00	1.80
□ R2	Grant Hill	25.00	11.00
□ R3	Jamal Mashburn	3.00	1.35
□ R4	Alonzo Mourning	5.00	2.20
□ R5	Dikembe Mutombo	3.00	1.35
□ R6	Shaquille O'Neal	15.00	6.75
□ R7	Scottie Pippen	12.00	5.50
□ R8	Glenn Robinson	8.00	3.60
□ R9	Latrell Sprewell	2.00	.90
□ R10	Chris Webber	10.00	4.50

1994-95 SkyBox SkyTech Force

Randomly inserted into second series packs at a rate of one in two, cards from this 30-card standard-size set feature a selection of the NBA's top stars. Card fronts feature foil backgrounds. The player's name is in gold foil on the bottom while the words "SkyTech Force" is printed vertically on the right. The backs contain some career information as well as a color action photo. The cards are *numbered in the upper right with an "SF" prefix and are sequenced in alphabetical order.*

	MINT	NRMT
COMPLETE SET (30)	10.00	4.50
COMMON CARD (SF1-SF30)	.15	.07
SEMISTARS	.30	.14
UNLISTED STARS	.60	.25
SER.2 STATED ODDS 1:2		

		MINT	NRMT
☐	SF1 Kenny Anderson	.30	.14
☐	SF2 B.J. Armstrong	.15	.07
☐	SF3 Charles Barkley	1.00	.45
☐	SF4 Shawn Bradley	.30	.14
☐	SF5 LaPhonso Ellis	.30	.14
☐	SF6 Anfernee Hardaway	2.50	1.10
☐	SF7 Bobby Hurley	.15	.07
☐	SF8 Kevin Johnson	.30	.14
☐	SF9 Larry Johnson	.30	.14
☐	SF10 Shawn Kemp	2.00	.90
☐	SF11 Jason Kidd	4.00	1.80
☐	SF12 Christian Laettner	.30	.14
☐	SF13 Karl Malone	1.00	.45
☐	SF14 Danny Manning	.15	.07
☐	SF15 Chris Mills	.30	.14
☐	SF16 Chris Mullin	.60	.25
☐	SF17 Lamond Murray	.30	.14
☐	SF18 Charles Oakley	.30	.14
☐	SF19 Hakeem Olajuwon	1.25	.55
☐	SF20 Gary Payton	1.00	.45
☐	SF21 Mark Price	.15	.07
☐	SF22 Dino Radja	.15	.07
☐	SF23 Mitch Richmond	.60	.25
☐	SF24 Clifford Robinson	.30	.14
☐	SF25 David Robinson	1.00	.45
☐	SF26 Dennis Rodman	2.50	1.10
☐	SF27 Dickey Simpkins	.15	.07
☐	SF28 John Starks	.30	.14
☐	SF29 John Stockton	.60	.25
☐	SF30 Charlie Ward	.30	.14

1994-95 SkyBox Slammin' Universe

Randomly inserted into second series packs at a rate of one in two, cards from this 30-card standard-size set feature a selection of the NBA's top dunkers. The horizontal card fronts feature full-color player action shots against a wild "galaxy" background. The cards are numbered with a "SU" prefix and are sequenced in alphabetical order.

	MINT	NRMT
COMPLETE SET (30)	10.00	4.50
COMMON CARD (SU1-SU30)	.15	.07

		MINT	NRMT
SEMISTARS		.30	.14
UNLISTED STARS		.60	.25
SER.2 STATED ODDS 1:2			

☐	SU1 Vin Baker	1.50	.70
☐	SU2 Dee Brown	.15	.07
☐	SU3 Derrick Coleman	.30	.14
☐	SU4 Clyde Drexler	.75	.35
☐	SU5 Joe Dumars	.60	.25
☐	SU6 Tony Dumas	.15	.07
☐	SU7 Patrick Ewing	.60	.25
☐	SU8 Horace Grant	.30	.14
☐	SU9 Tom Gugliotta	.60	.25
☐	SU10 Grant Hill	6.00	2.70
☐	SU11 Jim Jackson	.30	.14
☐	SU12 Toni Kukoc	.60	.25
☐	SU13 Donyell Marshall	.60	.25
☐	SU14 Jamal Mashburn	.60	.25
☐	SU15 Reggie Miller	.60	.25
☐	SU16 Eric Montross	.15	.07
☐	SU17 Alonzo Mourning	.75	.35
☐	SU18 Dikembe Mutombo	.60	.25
☐	SU19 Shaquille O'Neal	2.50	1.10
☐	SU20 Glen Rice	.60	.25
☐	SU21 Isaiah Rider	.30	.14
☐	SU22 Glenn Robinson	2.00	.90
☐	SU23 Jalen Rose	.60	.25
☐	SU24 Detlef Schrempf	.30	.14
☐	SU25 Steve Smith	.30	.14
☐	SU26 Latrell Sprewell	.30	.14
☐	SU27 Rod Strickland	.30	.14
☐	SU28 B.J. Tyler	.15	.07
☐	SU29 Nick Van Exel	.60	.25
☐	SU30 Dominique Wilkins	.60	.25

1995-96 SkyBox

The 1995-96 SkyBox set was issued in two series of 150 and 151 standard-size cards, for a total of 301. The cards were issued in 12-card regular packs at a suggested retail price of $1.99, and jumbo packs of 20 were sold at $3.99. Full-bleed fronts feature a full-color action player cutout against a one-color background of either blue, cyan, yellow or magenta. A computer-generated flame streaks out from the basketball the player is holding. Backs feature a one-color player action shot in a vertical strip on the right side of the cards and a full color close-up shot at the bottom. The top right features a player biography and career stats. The set is arranged and checklisted below alphabetically

according to teams by city. Subsets are Front and Center (125-133), Turning Point (134-142), Expansion Teams (143-148), Rookies (219-248), Honor Roll (249-298) and Checklists (299-300). Key Rookie Cards include Michael Finley, Kevin Garnett, Antonio McDyess, Joe Smith, Jerry Stackhouse and Damon Stoudamire. A 5" by 7" jumbo featuring Grant Hill (card #226) was issued as a chiptopper in retail boxes. In addition, parallel lenticular versions of the Grant Hill and Jerry Stackhouse Meltdown inserts were available through a second series wrapper offer. Both cards are unnumbered and feature nifty moving backgrounds in which a steel wall turns to goo as fireworks explode. Collectors had to send in two wrappers along with a check or money order for $9.99 per card before the December 31st, 1996 deadline.

	MINT	NRMT
COMPLETE SET (301)	35.00	16.00
COMPLETE SERIES 1 (150)	15.00	6.75
COMPLETE SERIES 2 (151)	20.00	9.00
COMMON CARD (1-301)		.05
SEMISTARS	.15	.07
UNLISTED STARS	.30	.14

☐	1 Stacey Augmon	.10	.05
☐	2 Mookie Blaylock	.15	.07
☐	3 Grant Long	.10	.05
☐	4 Steve Smith	.15	.07
☐	5 Dee Brown	.10	.05
☐	6 Sherman Douglas	.10	.05
☐	7 Eric Montross	.10	.05
☐	8 Dino Radja	.10	.05
☐	9 Dominique Wilkins	.30	.14
☐	10 Muggsy Bogues	.15	.07
☐	11 Scott Burrell	.10	.05
☐	12 Dell Curry	.10	.05
☐	13 Larry Johnson	.15	.07
☐	14 Alonzo Mourning	.30	.14
☐	15 Michael Jordan UER	4.00	1.80
	Career block total is wrong		
☐	16 Steve Kerr	.15	.07
☐	17 Toni Kukoc	.15	.07
☐	18 Scottie Pippen	1.00	.45
☐	19 Terrell Brandon	.30	.14
☐	20 Tyrone Hill	.10	.05
☐	21 Chris Mills	.10	.05
☐	22 Mark Price	.10	.05
☐	23 John Williams	.10	.05
☐	24 Tony Dumas	.10	.05
☐	25 Jim Jackson	.15	.07
☐	26 Popeye Jones	.10	.05
☐	27 Jason Kidd	.75	.35
☐	28 Jamal Mashburn	.15	.07
☐	29 LaPhonso Ellis	.15	.07
☐	30 Dikembe Mutombo	.15	.07
☐	31 Robert Pack	.10	.05
☐	32 Jalen Rose	.10	.05
☐	33 Bryant Stith	.10	.05
☐	34 Joe Dumars	.30	.14
☐	35 Grant Hill	2.00	.90
☐	36 Allan Houston	.15	.07
☐	37 Lindsey Hunter	.10	.05
☐	38 Chris Gatling	.10	.05
☐	39 Tim Hardaway	.40	.18
☐	40 Donyell Marshall	.15	.07

41	Chris Mullin	.30	.14
42	Carlos Rogers	.10	.05
43	Latrell Sprewell	.15	.07
44	Sam Cassell	.15	.07
45	Clyde Drexler	.40	.18
46	Robert Horry	.10	.05
47	Hakeem Olajuwon	.60	.25
48	Kenny Smith	.10	.05
49	Dale Davis	.10	.05
50	Mark Jackson	.10	.05
51	Reggie Miller	.30	.14
52	Rik Smits	.15	.07
53	Lamond Murray	.10	.05
54	Eric Piatkowski	.10	.05
55	Pooh Richardson	.10	.05
56	Rodney Rogers	.10	.05
57	Loy Vaught	.10	.05
58	Elden Campbell	.15	.07
59	Cedric Ceballos	.10	.05
60	Vlade Divac	.15	.07
61	Eddie Jones	.75	.35
62	Anthony Peeler	.10	.05
63	Nick Van Exel	.30	.14
64	Bimbo Coles	.10	.05
65	Billy Owens	.10	.05
66	Khalid Reeves	.10	.05
67	Glen Rice	.30	.14
68	Kevin Willis	.10	.05
69	Vin Baker	.60	.25
70	Todd Day	.10	.05
71	Eric Murdock	.10	.05
72	Glenn Robinson	.40	.18
73	Tom Gugliotta	.30	.14
74	Christian Laettner	.15	.07
75	Isaiah Rider	.15	.07
76	Doug West	.10	.05
77	Kenny Anderson	.15	.07
78	P.J. Brown	.10	.05
79	Derrick Coleman	.10	.05
80	Armon Gilliam	.10	.05
81	Patrick Ewing	.30	.14
82	Derek Harper	.15	.07
83	Anthony Mason	.15	.07
84	Charles Oakley	.10	.05
85	John Starks	.15	.07
86	Nick Anderson	.15	.07
87	Horace Grant	.15	.07
88	Anfernee Hardaway	1.25	.55
89	Shaquille O'Neal	1.25	.55
90	Dana Barros	.10	.05
91	Shawn Bradley	.15	.07
92	Clarence Weatherspoon	.10	.05
93	Sharone Wright	.10	.05
94	Charles Barkley	.50	.23
95	Kevin Johnson	.15	.07
96	Dan Majerle	.10	.05
97	Danny Manning	.15	.07
98	Wesley Person	.15	.07
99	Clifford Robinson	.10	.05
100	Rod Strickland	.15	.07
101	Otis Thorpe	.15	.07
102	Buck Williams	.10	.05
103	Brian Grant	.15	.07
104	Olden Polynice	.10	.05
105	Mitch Richmond	.30	.14
106	Walt Williams	.10	.05
107	Vinny Del Negro	.10	.05
108	Sean Elliott	.10	.05
109	Avery Johnson	.10	.05
110	David Robinson	.50	.23
111	Dennis Rodman	1.25	.55
112	Shawn Kemp	1.00	.45
113	Gary Payton	.50	.23
114	Sam Perkins	.15	.07
115	Detlef Schrempf	.15	.07
116	David Benoit	.10	.05
117	Jeff Hornacek	.10	.05
118	Karl Malone	.50	.23
119	John Stockton	.30	.14
120	Calbert Cheaney	.10	.05
121	Juwan Howard	.50	.23
122	Don MacLean	.10	.05
123	Gheorghe Muresan	.10	.05
124	Chris Webber	.75	.35
125	Robert Horry FC	.10	.05
126	Mark Jackson FC	.10	.05
127	Steve Smith FC	.10	.05
128	Lamond Murray FC	.10	.05
129	Christian Laettner FC	.10	.05
130	Kenny Anderson FC	.10	.05
131	Anthony Mason FC	.10	.05
132	Kevin Johnson FC	.10	.05
133	Jeff Hornacek FC	.10	.05
134	Larry Johnson TP	.10	.05
135	Popeye Jones TP	.10	.05
136	Allan Houston TP	.10	.05
137	Chris Gatling TP	.10	.05
138	Sam Cassell TP	.10	.05
139	Anthony Peeler TP	.10	.05
140	Vin Baker TP	.30	.14
141	Dana Barros TP	.10	.05
142	Gheorghe Muresan TP	.10	.05
143	Toronto Raptors	.10	.05
144	Vancouver Grizzlies	.10	.05
145	Glen Rice EXP / Muggsy Bogues EXP	.15	.07
146	Nick Anderson EXP / Christian Laettner EXP	.15	.07
147	John Salley TF	.10	.05
148	Greg Anthony TF	.10	.05
149	Checklist #1	.10	.05
150	Checklist #2	.10	.05
151	Craig Ehlo	.10	.05
152	Spud Webb	.15	.07
153	Dana Barros	.10	.05
154	Lucious Harris	.10	.05
155	Kendall Gill	.15	.07
156	Khalid Reeves	.10	.05
157	Glen Rice	.30	.14
158	Luc Longley	.15	.07
159	Dennis Rodman	2.00	.90
160	Dickey Simpkins	.10	.05
161	Danny Ferry	.10	.05
162	Dan Majerle	.10	.05
163	Bobby Phills	.10	.05
164	Lucious Harris	.10	.05
165	George McCloud	.10	.05
166	Mahmoud Abdul-Rauf	.10	.05
167	Don MacLean	.10	.05
168	Reggie Williams	.10	.05
169	Terry Mills	.10	.05
170	Otis Thorpe	.15	.07
171	B.J. Armstrong	.10	.05
172	Rony Seikaly	.10	.05
173	Chucky Brown	.10	.05
174	Mario Elie	.10	.05
175	Antonio Davis	.10	.05
176	Ricky Pierce	.10	.05
177	Terry Dehere	.10	.05
178	Rodney Rogers	.10	.05
179	Malik Sealy	.10	.05
180	Brian Williams	.10	.05
181	Sedale Threatt	.10	.05
182	Alonzo Mourning	.30	.14
183	Lee Mayberry	.10	.05
184	Sean Rooks	.10	.05
185	Shawn Bradley	.15	.07
186	Kevin Edwards	.10	.05
187	Hubert Davis	.10	.05
188	Charles Smith	.10	.05
189	Charlie Ward	.10	.05
190	Dennis Scott	.10	.05
191	Brian Shaw	.10	.05
192	Derrick Coleman	.15	.07
193	Richard Dumas	.10	.05
194	Vernon Maxwell	.10	.05
195	A.C. Green	.15	.07
196	Elliot Perry	.10	.05
197	John Williams	.10	.05
198	Aaron McKie	.10	.05
199	Bobby Hurley	.10	.05
200	Michael Smith	.10	.05
201	J.R. Reid	.10	.05
202	Hersey Hawkins	.10	.07
203	Willie Anderson	.10	.05
204	Tracy Murray	.10	.05
205	Alvin Robertson	.10	.05
206	Alvin Robertson	.10	.05
207	Carlos Rogers UEP (Card says Rodney Rogers on front with picture)	.15	.07
208	John Salley	.10	.05
209	Zan Tabak	.10	.05
210	Adam Keefe	.10	.05
211	Chris Morris	.10	.05
212	Greg Anthony	.10	.05
213	Blue Edwards	.10	.05
214	Kenny Gattison	.10	.05
215	Antonio Harvey	.10	.05
216	Chris King	.10	.05
217	Byron Scott	.10	.05
218	Robert Pack	.10	.05
219	Alan Henderson	.30	.14
220	Eric Williams	.15	.07
221	George Zidek	.10	.05
222	Jason Caffey	.30	.14
223	Bob Sura	.15	.07
224	Cherokee Parks	.10	.05
225	Antonio McDyess	1.50	.70
226	Theo Ratliff	.30	.14
227	Joe Smith	1.25	.55
228	Travis Best	.15	.07
229	Brent Barry	.30	.14
230	Sasha Danilovic	.10	.05
231	Kurt Thomas	.15	.07
232	Shawn Respert	.10	.05
233	Kevin Garnett	4.00	1.80
234	Ed O'Bannon	.10	.05
235	Jerry Stackhouse	1.25	.55
236	Michael Finley	1.25	.55
237	Mario Bennett	.10	.05
238	Randolph Childress	.10	.05
239	Arvydas Sabonis	.60	.25
240	Gary Trent	.10	.05
241	Tyus Edney	.10	.05
242	Corliss Williamson	.40	.18
243	Cory Alexander	.10	.05
244	Damon Stoudamire	2.50	1.10
245	Greg Ostertag	.10	.05
246	Lawrence Moten	.10	.05
247	Bryant Reeves	.75	.35
248	Rasheed Wallace	.75	.35
249	Muggsy Bogues HR	.10	.05
250	Dell Curry HR	.10	.05
251	Scottie Pippen HR	.50	.23
252	Danny Ferry HR	.10	.05
253	M.Abdul-Rauf HR	.10	.05
254	Joe Dumars HR	.15	.07
255	Tim Hardaway HR	.30	.14
256	Chris Mullin HR	.15	.07
257	Hakeem Olajuwon HR	.30	.14
258	Kenny Smith HR	.10	.05
259	Reggie Miller HR	.15	.07
260	Rik Smits HR	.10	.05
261	Vlade Divac HR	.10	.05
262	Doug West HR	.10	.05
263	Patrick Ewing HR	.15	.07
264	Charles Oakley HR	.10	.05
265	Nick Anderson HR	.10	.05
266	Dennis Scott HR	.10	.05
267	Jeff Turner HR	.10	.05
268	Charles Barkley HR	.30	.14
269	Kevin Johnson HR	.10	.05
270	Clifford Robinson HR	.10	.05
271	Buck Williams HR	.10	.05
272	Lionel Simmons HR	.10	.05
273	David Robinson HR	.30	.14
274	Gary Payton HR	.30	.14
275	Karl Malone HR	.30	.14
276	John Stockton HR	.15	.07
277	Steve Smith HR	.10	.05
278	Michael Jordan ELE	2.00	.90
279	Jim Jackson ELE	.10	.05
280	Jason Kidd ELE	.40	.18
281	Jamal Mashburn ELE	.10	.05
282	Dikembe Mutombo ELE	.10	.05
283	Grant Hill ELE	1.00	.45
284	Tim Hardaway ELE	.30	.14
285	Clyde Drexler ELE	.30	.14
286	Cedric Ceballos ELE	.10	.05
287	Gary Payton ELE	.25	.11
288	Billy Owens ELE	.10	.05
289	Vin Baker ELE	.30	.14
290	Glenn Robinson ELE	.30	.14
291	Kenny Anderson ELE	.10	.05
292	A.Hardaway ELE	.60	.25
293	Shaquille O'Neal ELE	.60	.25
294	Charles Barkley ELE	.30	.14
295	Rod Strickland ELE	.10	.05

☐	296 Mitch Richmond ELE..	.15	.07
☐	297 Juwan Howard ELE...	.30	.14
☐	298 Chris Webber ELE	.40	.18
☐	299 Checklist #1	.10	.05
☐	300 Checklist #2	.10	.05
☐	301 Magic Johnson	1.00	.45
☐	PR Grant Hill JUMBO ...	10.00	4.50
☐	NNO Grant Hill	35.00	16.00
	Meltdown Exchange		
☐	NNO Jerry Stackhouse ..	20.00	9.00
	Meltdown Exchange		

1995-96 SkyBox Atomic

Randomly inserted in all series one packs at a rate of one in four regular packs and one in three jumbo packs, this 15-card standard-size set highlights the play of the NBA's power men. Borderless fronts have etched foil backgrounds with a full-color action player cutout. An atomic symbol surrounds the ball the player is holding and the player's name, team and position are stamped in gold foil at the middle left of the card. Skybox's "Atomic" logo is printed at the bottom left. Backs are numbered with the prefix "A" and have a faded, one color action shot of the player and continues with the basketball as the center of an atomic symbol. Player biography and an inset color photo are set against red bars on the bottom half of the card.

	MINT	NRMT
COMPLETE SET (15)	8.00	3.60
COMMON CARD (A1-A15)	.30	.14
SEMISTARS	.50	.23
SER.1 STATED ODDS 1:4 HOBBY/RETAIL		

☐	A1 Eric Montross	.30	.14
☐	A2 Charles Oakley	.30	.14
☐	A3 Rik Smits	.50	.23
☐	A4 Vlade Divac	.50	.23
☐	A5 Buck Williams	.30	.14
☐	A6 Vin Baker	1.50	.70
☐	A7 Glenn Robinson	1.00	.45
☐	A8 Isaiah Rider	.50	.23
☐	A9 Derrick Coleman	.50	.23
☐	A10 C.Weatherspoon	.30	.14

☐	A11 Sharone Wright..........	.30	.14
☐	A12 Brian Grant	.50	.23
☐	A13 Jim Jackson	.50	.23
☐	A14 Clyde Drexler	1.00	.45
☐	A15 Anfernee Hardaway ..	3.00	1.35

1995-96 SkyBox Close-Ups

A short player history is the focus of this nine-card standard-size set that features both established players and up-and-coming rookies. The cards were randomly inserted in all series one packs at a rate of one in nine regular packs and one in six jumbo packs. They were also inserted one per special series one Wal-Mart retail pack. Borderless fronts feature an extreme color close-up of the player's face set against an etched foil background. The player's first name is stamped in gold foil script against his last name which is printed larger and in full block letters. The SkyBox logo and "Close-Up" are stamped in gold foil at the bottom left of the card. The backs feature a stretched one-color player photo on the right side of the card. The left side has the player's name, team logo and a short player history printed in black type. The set is sequenced in alphabetical order by team.

	MINT	NRMT
COMPLETE SET (9)	20.00	9.00
COMMON CARD (C1-C9)	2.00	.90
SER.1 STATED ODDS 1:9 RETAIL		
ONE PER SPECIAL SER.1 RETAIL PACK		

☐	C1 Scottie Pippen	6.00	2.70
☐	C2 Grant Hill	12.00	5.50
☐	C3 Clyde Drexler	2.50	1.10
☐	C4 Nick Van Exel	2.00	.90
☐	C5 Tom Gugliotta	2.00	.90
☐	C6 Patrick Ewing	2.00	.90
☐	C7 Charles Barkley	3.00	1.35
☐	C8 Karl Malone	3.00	1.35
☐	C9 Juwan Howard	3.00	1.35

1995-96 SkyBox Dynamic

Randomly inserted at a rate of one in four series one regular packs and one in three series one jumbo packs, this 12-card standard-size set features the most intense NBA players. Fronts feature a full-color action player photo handling a ball that is exploding. The player is set against a bright red etched foil background with the "Dynamic" logo scrawled at an angle across the bottom. The player's name is printed on the bottom right of the card. Full-bleed, one-color backs are numbered with the prefix "D" and picture the player in an action shot and a full color close-up inset. The player's name is printed in white caps and a player profile is printed in black type on tilted red bars. The set is sequenced in alphabetical team order.

	MINT	NRMT
COMPLETE SET (12)	6.00	2.70
COMMON CARD (D1-D12).....	.25	.11
SEMISTARS	.40	.18
UNLISTED STARS	.60	.25
SER.1 STATED ODDS 1:4 HOBBY/RETAIL		

☐	D1 Larry Johnson............	.40	.18
☐	D2 Alonzo Mourning	.60	.25
☐	D3 Dikembe Mutombo	.40	.18
☐	D4 Jalen Rose	.40	.18
☐	D5 Grant Hill	4.00	1.80
☐	D6 Latrell Sprewell	.40	.18
☐	D7 Reggie Miller	.60	.25
☐	D8 John Starks...............	.40	.18
☐	D9 Calbert Cheaney	.25	.11
☐	D10 Dennis Rodman	2.50	1.10
☐	D11 Detlef Schrempf	.40	.18
☐	D12 Chris Webber	1.50	.70

1995-96 SkyBox High Hopes

Randomly inserted in all second series packs at a rate of one in 18, this 20-card set focuses on the hot young stars of the NBA. Borderless fronts feature the

player in a full-color action cutout, with "High Hopes" spelled out in red and yellow spark and flame block letters on a black background. The player's name is printed in gold foil at the bottom. Backs have another full-color action cutout set against a black background with a player profile printed in white type. "High Hopes" is printed vertically on the right side.

	MINT	NRMT
COMPLETE SET (20)	60.00	27.00
COMMON CARD (HH1-HH20)	.75	.35
SEMISTARS	1.50	.70
UNLISTED STARS	2.50	1.10
SER.2 STATED ODDS 1:18 H/R, 1:12 JUM		

		MINT	NRMT
☐	HH1 Alan Henderson	2.50	1.10
☐	HH2 Eric Williams	1.50	.70
☐	HH3 George Zidek	.75	.35
☐	HH4 Bob Sura	.75	.35
☐	HH5 Cherokee Parks	.75	.35
☐	HH6 Antonio McDyess	6.00	2.70
☐	HH7 Joe Smith	5.00	2.20
☐	HH8 Brent Barry	2.50	1.10
☐	HH9 Shawn Respert	.75	.35
☐	HH10 Kevin Garnett	20.00	9.00
☐	HH11 Ed O'Bannon	.75	.35
☐	HH12 Jerry Stackhouse	5.00	2.20
☐	HH13 Michael Finley	5.00	2.20
☐	HH14 Arvydas Sabonis	2.50	1.10
☐	HH15 Gary Trent	.75	.35
☐	HH16 Tyus Edney	.75	.35
☐	HH17 Damon Stoudamire	10.00	4.50
☐	HH18 Greg Ostertag	.75	.35
☐	HH19 Bryant Reeves	3.00	1.35
☐	HH20 Rasheed Wallace	3.00	1.35

1995-96 SkyBox Hot Sparks

Randomly inserted in second series hobby packs only at a rate of one in 12, this 10-card set notes the players who make things happen in the NBA. Fronts have a full-color action cutout with the player's name printed vertically in gold foil on the right side. A mauve computerized image serves as a background. A similar but darker background appears on the

back with another full-color action cutout and a player profile printed in white type.

	MINT	NRMT
COMPLETE SET (11)	30.00	13.50
COMMON CARD (HS1-HS11)	1.00	.45
SEMISTARS	1.25	.55
UNLISTED STARS	2.00	.90
SER.2 STATED ODDS 1:12 HOBBY		

		MINT	NRMT
☐	HS1 Mookie Blaylock	1.00	.45
☐	HS2 Jason Kidd	5.00	2.20
☐	HS3 Tim Hardaway	2.50	1.10
☐	HS4 Nick Van Exel	2.00	.90
☐	HS5 Kenny Anderson	1.25	.55
☐	HS6 Anfernee Hardaway	8.00	3.60
☐	HS7 Rod Strickland	1.25	.55
☐	HS8 Gary Payton	3.00	1.35
☐	HS9 Damon Stoudamire	8.00	3.60
☐	HS10 John Stockton	2.00	.90
☐	HS11 Magic Johnson	6.00	2.70

1995-96 SkyBox Kinetic

Randomly inserted in all first series at a rate of one in four (and one in three jumbo), cards from this 9-card standard-size set highlight the NBA's speed demons. Full-bleed fronts have swirling color swoops and surround a full-color player cutout set against an etched foil background. Player's name and team name are printed in silver foil at the bottom. Borderless backs feature a one-color player cutout and continues with the swoosh patterns. A full-color head shot

is inset with a white border and a player profile is printed in black type on gold bars.

	MINT	NRMT
COMPLETE SET (9)	2.00	.90
COMMON CARD (K1-K9)	.25	.11
SEMISTARS	.40	.18
UNLISTED STARS	.60	.25
SER.1 STATED ODDS 1:4 HOBBY/RETAIL		

		MINT	NRMT
☐	K1 Mookie Blaylock	.40	.18
☐	K2 Tim Hardaway	.75	.35
☐	K3 Lamond Murray UER	.25	.11
	Mach is spelled Mock		
☐	K4 Stacey Augmon	.25	.11
☐	K5 Nick Van Exel	.60	.25
☐	K6 Khalid Reeves	.25	.11
☐	K7 Kenny Anderson	.40	.18
☐	K8 Rod Strickland	.40	.18
☐	K9 Gary Payton	1.00	.45

1995-96 SkyBox Larger Than Life

Randomly inserted in first series regular and jumbo packs at a rate of one in 48 and one in 36 respectively, this 10-card standard-size set showcases those players who have established themselves in the NBA. A sunburst design is etched into gold foil and serves as a background for the fronts which include a full-color action player cutout. The "Larger Than Life" logo is printed diagonally and upwards from the bottom right and tapers up to the SkyBox logo. The player's first name is printed in lower case black type just above his last name which appears in all caps red type. Backs continue with the sunburst pattern on the gold type. A player profile is printed in black type on the right side and a full-color action cutout appears on the left side. The set is sequenced in alphabetical team order.

	MINT	NRMT
COMPLETE SET (10)	100.00	45.00

	MINT	NRMT
COMMON CARD (L1-L10)	4.00	1.80

SER.1 STATED ODDS 1:48 HOBBY/RETAIL

☐ L1	Michael Jordan	50.00	22.00
☐ L2	Jason Kidd	10.00	4.50
☐ L3	Grant Hill	25.00	11.00
☐ L4	Hakeem Olajuwon	8.00	3.60
☐ L5	Glenn Robinson	5.00	2.20
☐ L6	Patrick Ewing	4.00	1.80
☐ L7	Shaquille O'Neal	15.00	6.75
☐ L8	Charles Barkley	6.00	2.70
☐ L9	David Robinson	6.00	2.70
☐ L10	John Stockton	4.00	1.80

1995-96 SkyBox Lottery Exchange

Hobbyists received this 13-card set after collecting the three separate Lottery Exchange cards randomly inserted into first series packs (each card was seeded at a rate of 1:40 packs). The expiration date for exchanging the cards was June 15th, 1996. The set consists of the first thirteen players selected in the 1995 NBA draft. Card fronts feature a full-color player action cutout set against a murky colored background.

	MINT	NRMT
COMPLETE SET (13)	40.00	18.00
COMMON CARD (1-13)	1.00	.45

ONE SET PER THREE EXCH.CARDS BY MAIL
EXCH.CARDS: SER.1 STATED ODDS 1:40

☐ 1	Joe Smith	4.00	1.80
☐ 2	Antonio McDyess	5.00	2.20
☐ 3	Jerry Stackhouse	4.00	1.80
☐ 4	Rasheed Wallace	2.50	1.10
☐ 5	Kevin Garnett	12.00	5.50
☐ 6	Bryant Reeves	2.50	1.10
☐ 7	Damon Stoudamire	8.00	3.60
☐ 8	Shawn Respert	1.00	.45
☐ 9	Ed O'Bannon	1.00	.45
☐ 10	Kurt Thomas	1.00	.45
☐ 11	Gary Trent	1.00	.45
☐ 12	Cherokee Parks	1.00	.45
☐ 13	Corliss Williamson	2.00	.90
☐ NNO	Exchange Card 1	1.00	.45
	Expired		
☐ NNO	Exchange Card 2	1.00	.45
	Expired		
☐ NNO	Exchange Card 3	1.00	.45
	Expired		

1995-96 SkyBox Meltdown

Randomly inserted in second series regular packs at a rate of one in 54 and jumbo packs at a rate of one in 42, this 10-card set is a tribute to the league's hottest scorers. Borderless fronts have a foil finish with an image of blue melting metal. A full-color player cutout appears on the front with his name and team printed on the bottom. Blue metal showers down in a cascade on the back with a full-color action cutout and a player profile printed in white type.

	MINT	NRMT
COMPLETE SET (10)	125.00	55.00
COMMON CARD (M1-M10)	2.00	.90

SER.2 STATED ODDS 1:54 H/R, 1.42 JUM

☐ M1	Michael Jordan	50.00	22.00
☐ M2	Dan Majerle	2.00	.90
☐ M3	Jason Kidd	10.00	4.50
☐ M4	Antonio McDyess	10.00	4.50
☐ M5	Grant Hill	25.00	11.00
☐ M6	Joe Smith	8.00	3.60
☐ M7	Hakeem Olajuwon	8.00	3.60
☐ M8	Shaquille O'Neal	15.00	6.75
☐ M9	Jerry Stackhouse	8.00	3.60
☐ M10	David Robinson	6.00	2.70

1995-96 SkyBox Rookie Prevue

Randomly inserted in first series packs at a rate of one in nine,

this 20-card standard-size set focuses on the hot rookies of 1994-95. The borderless fronts include a full-color action player cutout on the right. The player's last name is printed in gold foil across the top with his first name in smaller type underneath the last name. The background is a red and gold sunburst pattern with "Rookie Prevue" in bold block letters on the bottom left. Backs also carry the "Rookie Prevue" logo at the bottom left and a player action cutout on the right. The background continues the red and gold sunburst design and the player's name and a short profile is printed in black type on the upper left side of the back. The set is sequenced in draft order.

	MINT	NRMT
COMPLETE SET (20)	75.00	34.00
COMMON CARD (RP1-RP20)	1.00	.45
SEMISTARS	2.50	1.10
UNLISTED STARS	4.00	1.80

SER.1 STATED ODDS 1:9 HOBBY/RETAIL

☐ RP1	Joe Smith	8.00	3.60
☐ RP2	Antonio McDyess	10.00	4.50
☐ RP3	Jerry Stackhouse	8.00	3.60
☐ RP4	Rasheed Wallace	5.00	2.20
☐ RP5	Bryant Reeves	5.00	2.20
☐ RP6	Damon Stoudamire	15.00	6.75
☐ RP7	Shawn Respert	1.00	.45
☐ RP8	Ed O'Bannon	1.00	.45
☐ RP9	Kurt Thomas	2.50	1.10
☐ RP10	Gary Trent	1.00	.45
☐ RP11	Cherokee Parks	1.00	.45
☐ RP12	Corliss Williamson	4.00	1.80
☐ RP13	Eric Williams	2.50	1.10
☐ RP14	Brent Barry	4.00	1.80
☐ RP15	Alan Henderson	4.00	1.80
☐ RP16	Bob Sura	2.50	1.10
☐ RP17	Theo Ratliff	4.00	1.80
☐ RP18	Randolph Childress	1.00	.45
☐ RP19	Michael Finley	8.00	3.60
☐ RP20	George Zidek	1.00	.45

1995-96 SkyBox Standouts

Randomly inserted in first series packs at a rate of one in 18 regular packs and one in 36 jumbo packs, this 12-card standard-size set spotlights the play of the NBA's hot rookies. The fronts feature the player in a full-color action cutout set against a metallic copper foil. The player stands on top of a circular "Skybox Standouts" logo and his name is stamped in gold foil at the upper right corner. A full-color action player cutout appears on the back and is set against the "Standouts" logo. A player profile appears on the top left of the card and the player's name and team are printed in a reverse type process on a strip of light blue across the bottom.

	MINT	NRMT
COMPLETE SET (12)	40.00	18.00
COMMON CARD (S1-S12)	1.50	.70
SEMISTARS	2.00	.90
UNLISTED STARS	3.00	1.35
SER.1 STATED ODDS 1:18 H/R, 1:36 JUM		

		MINT	NRMT
☐ S1	Alonzo Mourning	3.00	1.35
☐ S2	Scottie Pippen	10.00	4.50
☐ S3	Danny Manning	1.50	.70
☐ S4	Jamal Mashburn	2.00	.90
☐ S5	Latrell Sprewell	2.00	.90
☐ S6	Reggie Miller	3.00	1.35
☐ S7	Anfernee Hardaway	12.00	5.50
☐ S8	Brian Grant	2.00	.90
☐ S9	Shawn Kemp	10.00	4.50
☐ S10	Clifford Robinson	1.50	.70
☐ S11	Joe Dumars	3.00	1.35
☐ S12	Chris Webber	8.00	3.60

1995-96 SkyBox Standouts Hobby

Randomly inserted exclusively into first series hobby packs at a rate of one in 18, this six-card set is a tribute to the league's best. Borderless fronts have gold foil paper and the player's name is stamped in the upper right in a lighter gold foil. A full-color action player cutout appears and stand directly on a circular pattern that reads "Skybox Standouts." Backs have another full-color action

cutout with a player profile, the Skybox medallion and a granite-like strip with the player's name and team etched inside.

	MINT	NRMT
COMPLETE SET (6)	90.00	40.00
COMMON CARD (SH1-SH6)	8.00	3.60
SER.1 STATED ODDS 1:18 HOBBY		

		MINT	NRMT
☐ SH1	Michael Jordan	50.00	22.00
☐ SH2	Jason Kidd	10.00	4.50
☐ SH3	Hakeem Olajuwon	8.00	3.60
☐ SH4	Eddie Jones	10.00	4.50
☐ SH5	Shaquille O'Neal	15.00	6.75
☐ SH6	Grant Hill	25.00	11.00

1995-96 SkyBox USA Basketball

Randomly inserted in second series retail packs at a rate of one in 12 and in every second series jumbo pack and one per series two special retail pack, this set features the first ten players selected to the 1996 USA men's basketball team. Card fronts feature full-color action cutouts of Team USA members pictured in their Olympic togs set against a gray background of a globe.

	MINT	NRMT
COMPLETE SET (10)	25.00	11.00
COMMON CARD (U1-U10)	1.25	.55
SER.2 STATED ODDS 1:12 RETAIL		
ONE PER SPECIAL SER.2 RETAIL PACK		

		MINT	NRMT
☐ U1	Anfernee Hardaway	5.00	2.20
☐ U2	Grant Hill	8.00	3.60
☐ U3	Karl Malone	2.00	.90
☐ U4	Reggie Miller	1.25	.55
☐ U5	Scottie Pippen	4.00	1.80
☐ U6	Hakeem Olajuwon	2.50	1.10
☐ U7	Shaquille O'Neal	5.00	2.20
☐ U8	David Robinson	2.00	.90
☐ U9	Glenn Robinson	1.50	.70
☐ U10	John Stockton	1.25	.55

1996-97 SkyBox

The 1996-97 Skybox set was issued with a total of 281 cards.

The set was issued in two series with series one totaling 131 cards and series two totaling 150. The 12-card packs retail for $2.99 each. The cards are grouped alphabetically within teams. Rookie cards that were available in the first series included Shareef Abdur-Rahim, Kobe Bryant, Marcus Camby, Allen Iverson, Stephon Marbury and Antoine Walker. A Jerry Stackhouse promo was released before the set that is identical to the regular issue card except it does not have a card number on the back. It is listed below at the end of the set.

	MINT	NRMT
COMPLETE SET (281)	40.00	18.00
COMPLETE SERIES 1 (131)	25.00	11.00
COMPLETE SERIES 2 (150)	15.00	6.75
COMMON CARD (1-281)	.10	.05
SEMISTARS	.15	.07
UNLISTED STARS	.30	.14
COMP.RUBY SET (279)	2300.00	1050.00
COMP.RUBY SER.1 (131)	1500.00	700.00
COMP.RUBY SER.2 (148)	800.00	350.00
COMMON RUBY	4.00	1.80
*STARS: 20X TO 40X HI COLUMN		
*RCs: 10X TO 20X HI		
RUBY: ONE PER SER.1/2 HOBBY BOX		

		MINT	NRMT
☐ 1	Mookie Blaylock	.15	.07
☐ 2	Alan Henderson	.10	.05
☐ 3	Christian Laettner	.15	.07
☐ 4	Dikembe Mutombo	.15	.07
☐ 5	Steve Smith	.15	.07
☐ 6	Dana Barros	.10	.05
☐ 7	Rick Fox	.10	.05
☐ 8	Dino Radja	.10	.05
☐ 9	Antoine Walker	3.00	1.35
☐ 10	Eric Williams	.10	.05
☐ 11	Dell Curry	.10	.05
☐ 12	Tony Delk	.40	.18
☐ 13	Matt Geiger	.10	.05
☐ 14	Glen Rice	.30	.14
☐ 15	Ron Harper	.15	.07
☐ 16	Michael Jordan	4.00	1.80
☐ 17	Toni Kukoc	.15	.07
☐ 18	Scottie Pippen	1.00	.45
☐ 19	Dennis Rodman	1.25	.55
☐ 20	Terrell Brandon	.30	.14
☐ 21	Danny Ferry	.10	.05
☐ 22	Chris Mills	.10	.05
☐ 23	Bobby Phills	.10	.05
☐ 24	Vitaly Potapenko	.15	.07
☐ 25	Jim Jackson	.15	.07
☐ 26	Jason Kidd	.60	.25

27	Jamal Mashburn	.15	.07
28	George McCloud	.10	.05
29	Samaki Walker	.40	.18
30	LaPhonso Ellis	.10	.05
31	Antonio McDyess	.50	.23
32	Bryant Stith	.10	.05
33	Joe Dumars	.30	.14
34	Grant Hill	2.00	.90
35	Lindsey Hunter	.10	.05
36	Theo Ratliff	.10	.05
37	Otis Thorpe	.10	.07
38	Todd Fuller	.10	.05
39	Chris Mullin	.30	.14
40	Joe Smith	.40	.18
41	Latrell Sprewell	.15	.07
42	Charles Barkley	.50	.23
43	Clyde Drexler	.40	.18
44	Mario Elie	.10	.05
45	Hakeem Olajuwon	.60	.25
46	Erick Dampier	.40	.18
47	Dale Davis	.10	.05
48	Derrick McKey	.10	.05
49	Reggie Miller	.30	.14
50	Rik Smits	.15	.07
51	Brent Barry	.10	.05
52	Rodney Rogers	.10	.05
53	Loy Vaught	.15	.07
54	Lorenzen Wright	.40	.18
55	Kobe Bryant	6.00	2.70
56	Cedric Ceballos	.10	.05
57	Eddie Jones	.60	.25
58	Shaquille O'Neal	1.25	.55
59	Nick Van Exel	.30	.14
60	Tim Hardaway	.40	.18
61	Alonzo Mourning	.30	.14
62	Kurt Thomas	.10	.05
63	Ray Allen	1.00	.45
64	Vin Baker	.25	.11
65	Shawn Respert	.10	.05
66	Glenn Robinson	.30	.14
67	Kevin Garnett	2.00	.90
68	Tom Gugliotta	.30	.14
69	Stephon Marbury	3.00	1.35
70	Sam Mitchell	.10	.05
71	Shawn Bradley	.10	.05
72	Kendall Gill	.15	.07
73	Kerry Kittles	.75	.35
74	Ed O'Bannon	.10	.05
75	Patrick Ewing	.30	.14
76	Larry Johnson	.15	.07
77	Charles Oakley	.10	.05
78	John Starks	.15	.07
79	John Wallace	.50	.23
80	Nick Anderson	.10	.05
81	Horace Grant	.15	.07
82	Anfernee Hardaway	1.25	.55
83	Dennis Scott	.10	.05
84	Derrick Coleman	.15	.07
85	Allen Iverson	3.00	1.35
86	Jerry Stackhouse	.40	.18
87	Clarence Weatherspoon	.10	.05
88	Michael Finley	.40	.18
89	Robert Horry	.15	.07
90	Kevin Johnson	.15	.07
91	Steve Nash	.50	.23
92	Wesley Person	.10	.05
93	Aaron McKie	.10	.05
94	Jermaine O'Neal	.50	.23
95	Clifford Robinson	.10	.05
96	Arvydas Sabonis	.15	.07
97	Gary Trent	.10	.05
98	Tyus Edney	.10	.05
99	Brian Grant	.10	.05
100	Mitch Richmond	.30	.14
101	Billy Owens	.10	.05
102	Corliss Williamson	.15	.07
103	Vinny Del Negro	.10	.05
104	Sean Elliott	.10	.05
105	Avery Johnson	.10	.05
106	Chuck Person	.10	.05
107	David Robinson	.50	.23
108	Hersey Hawkins	.15	.07
109	Shawn Kemp	1.00	.45
110	Gary Payton	.50	.23
111	Sam Perkins	.15	.07
112	Detlef Schrempf	.15	.07
113	Marcus Camby	.75	.35
114	Carlos Rogers	.10	.05
115	Damon Stoudamire	.75	.35
116	Zan Tabak	.10	.05
117	Antoine Carr	.10	.05
118	Jeff Hornacek	.15	.07
119	Karl Malone	.50	.23
120	Chris Morris	.10	.05
121	John Stockton	.30	.14
122	Shareef Abdur-Rahim	2.00	.90
123	Greg Anthony	.10	.05
124	Bryant Reeves	.15	.07
125	Roy Rogers	.10	.05
126	Calbert Cheaney	.10	.05
127	Juwan Howard	.40	.18
128	Gheorghe Muresan	.10	.05
129	Chris Webber	.75	.35
130	Checklist	.10	.05
131	Checklist	.10	.05
132	Jon Barry	.10	.05
133	Christian Laettner	.15	.07
134	Dikembe Mutombo	.15	.07
135	Dee Brown	.10	.05
136	Todd Day	.10	.05
137	David Wesley	.10	.05
138	Vlade Divac	.15	.07
139	Anthony Goldwire	.10	.05
140	Anthony Mason	.15	.07
141	Jason Caffey	.10	.05
142	Luc Longley	.15	.07
143	Tyrone Hill	.10	.05
144	Antonio Lang	.10	.05
145	Sam Cassell	.15	.07
146	Chris Gatling	.10	.05
147	Eric Montross	.10	.05
148	Ervin Johnson	.10	.05
149	Sarunas Marciulionis	.10	.05
150	Stacey Augmon	.10	.05
151	Grant Long	.10	.05
152	Terry Mills	.10	.05
153	Kenny Smith	.10	.05
154	B.J. Armstrong	.10	.05
155	Bimbo Coles	.10	.05
156	Charles Barkley	.50	.23
157	Brent Price	.10	.05
158	Duane Ferrell	.10	.05
159	Jalen Rose	.10	.05
160	Terry Dehere	.10	.05
161	Charles Outlaw	.10	.05
162	Corie Blount	.10	.05
163	Shaquille O'Neal	1.25	.55
164	Rumeal Robinson	.10	.05
165	P.J. Brown	.10	.05
166	Ronnie Grandison	.10	.05
167	Sherman Douglas	.10	.05
168	Johnny Newman	.10	.05
169	James Robinson	.10	.05
170	Doug West	.10	.05
171	Robert Pack	.10	.05
172	Khalid Reeves	.10	.05
173	Chris Childs	.10	.05
174	Allan Houston	.15	.07
175	Charlie Ward	.10	.05
176	Darrell Armstrong	.10	.05
177	Gerald Wilkins	.10	.05
178	Lucious Harris	.10	.05
179	Robert Horry	.15	.07
180	Danny Manning	.15	.07
181	Kenny Anderson	.15	.07
182	Isaiah Rider	.10	.05
183	Rasheed Wallace	.15	.07
184	Mahmoud Abdul-Rauf	.10	.05
185	Cory Alexander	.10	.05
186	Vernon Maxwell	.10	.05
187	Dominique Wilkins	.30	.14
188	Nate McMillan	.10	.05
189	Larry Stewart	.10	.05
190	Doug Christie	.10	.05
191	Hubert Davis	.10	.05
192	Walt Williams	.10	.05
193	Adam Keefe	.10	.05
194	Greg Ostertag	.10	.05
195	John Stockton	.30	.14
196	George Lynch	.10	.05
197	Lee Mayberry	.10	.05
198	Tracy Murray	.10	.05
199	Rod Strickland	.15	.07
200	S.Abdur-Rahim ROO	1.00	.45
201	Ray Allen ROO	.50	.23
202	S.Anderson ROO	.40	.18
203	Kobe Bryant ROO	3.00	1.35
204	Marcus Camby ROO	.40	.18
205	Erick Dampier ROO	.30	.14
206	Emanual Davis ROO	.10	.05
207	Tony Delk ROO	.30	.14
208	Brian Evans ROO	.10	.05
209	Derek Fisher ROO	.40	.18
210	Todd Fuller ROO	.10	.05
211	Dean Garrett ROO	.10	.05
212	Reggie Geary ROO	.10	.05
213	Darvin Ham ROO	.10	.05
214	Othella Harrington ROO	.15	.07
215	Shane Heal ROO	.10	.05
216	Allen Iverson ROO	1.50	.70
217	Dontae' Jones ROO	.10	.05
218	Kerry Kittles ROO	.40	.18
219	Priest Lauderdale ROO	.10	.05
220	Randy Livingston ROO	.10	.05
221	Matt Maloney ROO	.50	.23
222	Stephon Marbury ROO	1.50	.70
223	Walter McCarty ROO	.15	.07
224	Amal McCaskill ROO	.10	.05
225	Jeff McInnis ROO	.10	.05
226	Martin Muursepp ROO	.10	.05
227	Steve Nash ROO	.30	.14
228	Ruben Nembhard ROO	.10	.05
229	Jermaine O'Neal ROO	.30	.14
230	Vitaly Potapenko ROO	.30	.14
231	V.Praskevicius ROO	.10	.05
232	Roy Rogers ROO	.10	.05
233	Malik Rose ROO	.10	.05
234	Antoine Walker ROO	1.50	.70
235	Samaki Walker ROO	.30	.14
236	Ben Wallace ROO	.10	.05
237	John Wallace ROO	.30	.14
238	Jerome Williams ROO	.15	.07
239	Lorenzen Wright ROO	.30	.14
240	Sam Cassell PM	.10	.05
241	Anfernee Hardaway PM	.60	.25
242	Tim Hardaway PM	.30	.14
243	Grant Hill PM	1.00	.45
244	Allan Houston PM	.10	.05
245	Juwan Howard PM	.30	.14
246	Kevin Johnson PM	.15	.07
247	Michael Jordan PM	2.00	.90
248	Jason Kidd PM	.30	.14
249	Karl Malone PM	.30	.14
250	Reggie Miller PM	.15	.07
251	Gary Payton PM	.30	.14
252	Wesley Person PM	.10	.05
253	Glen Rice PM	.15	.07
254	David Robinson PM	.30	.14
255	Steve Smith PM	.10	.05
256	Latrell Sprewell PM	.10	.05
257	Jerry Stackhouse PM	.30	.14
258	Rod Strickland PM	.10	.05
259	Nick Van Exel PM	.15	.07
260	Charles Barkley DT	.30	.14
261	Dale Davis DT	.10	.05
262	Patrick Ewing DT	.15	.07
263	Michael Finley DT	.15	.07
264	Chris Gatling DT	.10	.05
265	Armon Gilliam DT	.10	.05
266	Tyrone Hill DT	.10	.05
267	Robert Horry DT	.10	.05
268	Mark Jackson DT	.10	.05
269	Shawn Kemp DT	.50	.23
270	Jamal Mashburn DT	.10	.05
271	Anthony Mason DT	.10	.05
272	Alonzo Mourning DT	.15	.07
273	Dikembe Mutombo DT	.10	.05
274	Shaquille O'Neal DT	.60	.25
275	Isaiah Rider DT	.10	.05
276	Dennis Rodman DT	.60	.25
277	Damon Stoudamire DT	.40	.18
278	Chris Webber DT	.40	.18
279	Jayson Williams DT	.10	.05
280	Checklist (132-239)	.10	.05
281	Checklist (240-281/inserts)	.10	.05
NNO	J.Stackhouse Promo	3.00	1.35

1996-97 SkyBox Autographics Black

Randomly inserted in the following 1996-97 products: Hoops series one and two, SkyBox series one and two, SkyBox Z-Force series one and two and SkyBox EX2000 all at a rate of one in 72, this set features autographs of some of the top stars in the NBA. Card design is identical for each issue and several players had their cards seeded into more than one of the aforementioned products. Card fronts feature a background in the particular player's team colors and an action shot of the player. Most of the cards were autographed vertically along the left side. Card backs are black with a spotlight photo, the player's name and career statistics. The first 100 cards of each player were autographed in blue ink and the remaining number were in black. A couple exceptions include Hakeem Olajuwon and Scottie Pippen, who autographed all of their cards in blue ink only. Also, Kevin Garnett autographed two-thirds of his cards in blue and the rest in black. The cards below are not numbered and are listed alphabetically. As far as set value, the set is considered complete with the Kevin Garnett Black, Hakeem Olajuwon Blue and the Scottie Pippen Blue. Both Olajuwon and Pippen are also listed under the Blue set. Recently, some news of counterfeits have surfaced. The focal cards being reproduced include the Grant Hill, Kevin Garnett and Scottie Pippen. These cards feature no chipping on the edges, a lighter color of black on

the back, a fuzzy copyright line and, in general, a poor autograph. These do, however, have the SkyBox logo stamped on the card.

	MINT	NRMT
COMP. BLACK AU SET (95)	3500.00	1600.00
COMMON BLACK AU CARD	10.00	4.50
COMMON BLUE AU CARD	20.00	9.00
SEMISTARS BLACK	15.00	6.75
SEMISTARS BLUE	30.00	13.50

STATED ODDS:1:72 FLEER/SKYBOX PROD.
*BLUE INK AU: 1.25X to 2X IN COLUMN
BLUES: RANDOM INS.IN SKYBOX PRODUCTS
ALL OLAJUWON CARDS SIGNED IN BLUE
ALL PIPPEN CARDS SIGNED IN BLUE
GARNETT BLUE CARDS: 2:1 VERSUS BLACK
NO JOHN WALLACE BLUE AU's EXIST
SET INCLUDES #'s 22A, 61 AND 68
CARDS LISTED BELOW ALPHABETICALLY
BEWARE COUNTERFEITS

		MINT	NRMT
☐ 1	Ray Allen	80.00	36.00
☐ 2	Kenny Anderson	35.00	16.00
☐ 3	Nick Anderson	30.00	13.50
☐ 4	B.J. Armstrong	10.00	4.50
☐ 5	Vincent Askew	10.00	4.50
☐ 6	Dana Barros	10.00	4.50
☐ 7	Brent Barry	20.00	9.00
☐ 8	Travis Best	10.00	4.50
☐ 9	Muggsy Bogues	10.00	4.50
☐ 10	P.J. Brown	10.00	4.50
☐ 11	Randy Brown	20.00	9.00
☐ 12	Marcus Camby	60.00	27.00
☐ 13	Chris Childs	15.00	6.75
☐ 14	Dell Curry	10.00	4.50
☐ 15	Andrew DeClercq	10.00	4.50
☐ 16	Tony Delk	35.00	16.00
☐ 17	Sherman Douglas	10.00	4.50
☐ 18	Clyde Drexler	150.00	70.00
☐ 19	Tyus Edney	10.00	4.50
☐ 20	Michael Finley	40.00	18.00
☐ 21	Rick Fox	10.00	4.50
☐ 22A	Kevin Garnett	300.00	135.00
☐ 23	Matt Geiger	10.00	4.50
☐ 24	Kendall Gill	30.00	13.50
☐ 25	Brian Grant	10.00	4.50
☐ 26	Tim Hardaway	60.00	27.00
☐ 27	Grant Hill	300.00	135.00
☐ 28	Tyrone Hill	10.00	4.50
☐ 29	Allan Houston	30.00	13.50
☐ 30	Juwan Howard	250.00	110.00
☐ 31	Zydrunas Ilgauskas	35.00	16.00
☐ 32	Jim Jackson	15.00	6.75
☐ 33	Mark Jackson	15.00	6.75
☐ 34	Eddie Jones	125.00	55.00
☐ 35	Adam Keefe	10.00	4.50
☐ 36	Steve Kerr	20.00	9.00
☐ 37	Kerry Kittles	80.00	36.00
☐ 38	Toni Kukoc	40.00	18.00
☐ 39	Andrew Lang	10.00	4.50
☐ 40	Voshon Lenard	15.00	6.75
☐ 41	Grant Long	10.00	4.50
☐ 42	Luc Longley	30.00	13.50
☐ 43	George Lynch	10.00	4.50
☐ 44	Don MacLean	10.00	4.50
☐ 45	Stephon Marbury	150.00	70.00
☐ 46	Lee Mayberry	10.00	4.50
☐ 47	Walter McCarty	30.00	13.50
☐ 48	George McCloud	10.00	4.50
☐ 49	Antonio McDyess	90.00	40.00
☐ 50	Nate McMillan	10.00	4.50
☐ 51	Chris Mills	10.00	4.50
☐ 52	Sam Mitchell	10.00	4.50
☐ 53	Eric Montross	10.00	4.50
☐ 54	Chris Morris	10.00	4.50
☐ 55	Lawrence Moten	10.00	4.50
☐ 56	Alonzo Mourning	175.00	80.00
☐ 57	Gheorghe Muresan	10.00	4.50
☐ 58	Steve Nash	60.00	27.00
☐ 59	Ed O'Bannon	10.00	4.50
☐ 60	Charles Oakley	25.00	11.00
☐ 61	Hakeem Olajuwon Blue	200.00	90.00
☐ 62	Greg Ostertag	10.00	4.50
☐ 63	Billy Owens	10.00	4.50
☐ 64	Sam Perkins	15.00	6.75
☐ 65	Chuck Person	10.00	4.50
☐ 66	Wesley Person	10.00	4.50
☐ 67	Bobby Phills	10.00	4.50
☐ 68	Scottie Pippen	300.00	135.00
	Blue Ink		
☐ 69	Theo Ratliff	10.00	4.50
☐ 70	Glen Rice	60.00	27.00
☐ 71	Rodney Rogers	10.00	4.50
☐ 72	Byron Scott	15.00	6.75
☐ 73	Dennis Scott	10.00	4.50
☐ 74	Joe Smith	60.00	27.00
☐ 75	Kenny Smith	10.00	4.50
☐ 76	Rik Smits	15.00	6.75
☐ 77	Eric Snow	10.00	4.50
☐ 78	Latrell Sprewell	25.00	11.00
☐ 79	Jerry Stackhouse	60.00	27.00
☐ 80	John Starks	30.00	13.50
☐ 81	Bryant Stith	10.00	4.50
☐ 82	Damon Stoudamire	150.00	70.00
☐ 83	Rod Strickland	120.00	55.00
☐ 84	Bob Sura	15.00	6.75
☐ 85	Zan Tabak	10.00	4.50
☐ 86	Loy Vaught	15.00	6.75
☐ 87	Antoine Walker	150.00	70.00
☐ 88	Samaki Walker	25.00	11.00
☐ 89	John Wallace	60.00	27.00
☐ 90	Bill Wennington	15.00	6.75
☐ 91	David Wesley	10.00	4.50
☐ 92	Doug West	10.00	4.50
☐ 93	Monty Williams	10.00	4.50
☐ 94	Joe Wolf	10.00	4.50
☐ 95	Sharone Wright	10.00	4.50

1996-97 SkyBox Close-Ups

Randomly inserted in all series one packs at a rate of one in 24, this 9-card set features a die cut design and gives collectors a close-up view of players in action with a crystal ball in the background.

	MINT	NRMT
COMPLETE SET (9)	40.00	18.00
COMMON CARD (CU1-CU9)	2.50	1.10

SER.1 STATED ODDS 1:24 HOBBY/RETAIL

		MINT	NRMT
☐ CU1	Anfernee Hardaway	10.00	4.50
☐ CU2	Grant Hill	15.00	6.75
☐ CU3	Juwan Howard	3.00	1.35
☐ CU4	Jason Kidd	5.00	2.20
☐ CU5	Shawn Kemp	8.00	3.60
☐ CU6	Alonzo Mourning	2.50	1.10
☐ CU7	Hakeem Olajuwon	5.00	2.20
☐ CU8	Jerry Stackhouse	3.00	1.35
☐ CU9	Damon Stoudamire	6.00	2.70

1996-97 SkyBox Emerald Autograph Exchange

Loosely inserted one in 20 hobby boxes as exchange cards, this 5-card set features autographed base cards. Each card contains green "emerald" foil rather than the standard gold foil. Most of the redemption autographs were returned signed in black ink, however, Marcus Camby redemptions were available in both blue and black ink. The expiration date was February 1, 1998.

	MINT	NRMT
COMPLETE SET (5)	450.00	200.00
COMMON CARD (E1-E5)	50.00	22.00
SER.2 STATED ODDS 1:20 HOBBY BOXES		

		MINT	NRMT
☐ E1	Ray Allen	60.00	27.00
☐ E2	Marcus Camby	50.00	22.00
☐ E3	Grant Hill	300.00	135.00
☐ E4	Kerry Kittles	60.00	27.00
☐ E5	Jerry Stackhouse	50.00	22.00

1996-97 SkyBox Golden Touch

Randomly inserted in all series two packs at a rate of one in 240, this set focuses on veterans and rookies who can make just about any shot on the court.

Cards carry a heavily die cut design.

	MINT	NRMT
COMPLETE SET (10)	350.00	160.00
COMMON CARD (1-10)	6.00	2.70
SEMISTARS	8.00	3.60
SER.2 STATED ODDS 1:240 HOBBY/RETAIL		

		MINT	NRMT
☐ 1	Vin Baker	25.00	11.00
☐ 2	Terrell Brandon	8.00	3.60
☐ 3	Allan Houston	6.00	2.70
☐ 4	Allen Iverson	60.00	27.00
☐ 5	Michael Jordan	150.00	70.00
☐ 6	Shawn Kemp	40.00	18.00
☐ 7	Karl Malone	20.00	9.00
☐ 8	Stephon Marbury	60.00	27.00
☐ 9	Latrell Sprewell	6.00	2.70
☐ 10	Damon Stoudamire	30.00	13.50

1996-97 SkyBox Intimidators

Randomly inserted in all series two packs at a rate of one in 8, this 20-card set focuses on players who can intimidate on the court. Card fronts feature the player's name and team written vertically around the shot of the player.

	MINT	NRMT
COMPLETE SET (20)	40.00	18.00
COMMON CARD (1-20)	.60	.25
SEMISTARS	1.00	.45
UNLISTED STARS	1.50	.70
SER.2 STATED ODDS 1:8 HOBBY/RETAIL		

		MINT	NRMT
☐ 1	Shareef Abdur-Rahim	5.00	2.20
☐ 2	Charles Barkley	2.50	1.10
☐ 3	Marcus Camby	2.00	.90
☐ 4	Elden Campbell	1.00	.45
☐ 5	Derrick Coleman	1.00	.25
☐ 6	Patrick Ewing	1.50	.70
☐ 7	Michael Finley	2.00	.90
☐ 8	Kevin Garnett	10.00	4.50
☐ 9	Jim Jackson	1.00	.45
☐ 10	Anthony Mason	1.00	.45
☐ 11	Antonio McDyess	2.50	1.10
☐ 12	Alonzo Mourning	1.50	.70
☐ 13	Gheorghe Muresan	.60	.25
☐ 14	Dikembe Mutombo	1.00	.45
☐ 15	Shaquille O'Neal	6.00	2.70
☐ 16	Isaiah Rider	.60	.25
☐ 17	Clifford Robinson	.60	.25
☐ 18	David Robinson	2.50	1.10
☐ 19	Dennis Rodman	6.00	2.70
☐ 20	Clarence Weatherspoon	.60	.25

1996-97 SkyBox Larger Than Life

Randomly inserted in series one hobby packs only at a rate of one in 180, this 18-card set features cards that are presented in 4-color image action photos horizontally. The images are set against a background featuring the player's portrait in the shadow. The player's names are gold foil stamped. Card backs feature a "B" prefix.

	MINT	NRMT
COMPLETE SET (18)	650.00	300.00
COMMON CARD (B1-B18)	6.00	2.70
SEMISTARS	10.00	4.50
SER.1 STATED ODDS 1:180 HOBBY		

		MINT	NRMT
☐ B1	Shareef Abdur-Rahim	40.00	18.00
☐ B2	Marcus Camby	15.00	6.75
☐ B3	Kevin Garnett	60.00	27.00
☐ B4	Anfernee Hardaway	40.00	18.00
☐ B5	Grant Hill	60.00	27.00
☐ B6	Allen Iverson	60.00	27.00
☐ B7	Michael Jordan	175.00	80.00
☐ B8	Shawn Kemp	30.00	13.50
☐ B9	Stephon Marbury	60.00	27.00
☐ B10	Jamal Mashburn	6.00	2.70
☐ B11	Antonio McDyess	15.00	6.75
☐ B12	Alonzo Mourning	10.00	4.50
☐ B13	Dikembe Mutombo	6.00	2.70
☐ B14	Hakeem Olajuwon	20.00	9.00
☐ B15	Shaquille O'Neal	40.00	18.00
☐ B16	Dennis Rodman	40.00	18.00
☐ B17	Jerry Stackhouse	12.00	5.50
☐ B18	Damon Stoudamire	25.00	11.00

1996-97 SkyBox Net Set

Randomly inserted in series two hobby packs only at a rate of one in 48, this 20-card set focuses on the league's superstars.

	MINT	NRMT
COMPLETE SET (20)	250.00	110.00
COMMON CARD (1-20)	5.00	2.20
SER.2 STATED ODDS 1:48 HOBBY		

		MINT	NRMT
☐ 1	Vin Baker	10.00	4.50
☐ 2	Clyde Drexler	6.00	2.70
☐ 3	Patrick Ewing	5.00	2.20
☐ 4	Anfernee Hardaway	20.00	9.00
☐ 5	Grant Hill	30.00	13.50
☐ 6	Juwan Howard	6.00	2.70

		MINT	NRMT
☐ 7	Allen Iverson	25.00	11.00
☐ 8	Michael Jordan	60.00	27.00
☐ 9	Shawn Kemp	15.00	6.75
☐ 10	Jason Kidd	10.00	4.50
☐ 11	Karl Malone	8.00	3.60
☐ 12	Stephon Marbury	25.00	11.00
☐ 13	Alonzo Mourning	5.00	2.20
☐ 14	Hakeem Olajuwon	10.00	4.50
☐ 15	Shaquille O'Neal	20.00	9.00
☐ 16	Scottie Pippen	15.00	6.75
☐ 17	David Robinson	8.00	3.60
☐ 18	Joe Smith	6.00	2.70
☐ 19	Damon Stoudamire	12.00	5.50
☐ 20	Chris Webber	12.00	5.50

1996-97 SkyBox New Edition

Randomly inserted in series two retail packs only at a rate of one in 36, this 10-card set focuses on rookies featuring a die cut design that looks similar to the front of a video game machine.

	MINT	NRMT
COMPLETE SET (10)	70.00	32.00
COMMON CARD (1-10)	1.50	.70
SEMISTARS	2.00	.90
UNLISTED STARS	3.00	1.35
SER.2 STATED ODDS 1:36 RETAIL		
☐ 1 Shareef Abdur-Rahim	10.00	4.50
☐ 2 Ray Allen	5.00	2.20
☐ 3 Kobe Bryant	30.00	13.50
☐ 4 Marcus Camby	4.00	1.80
☐ 5 Allen Iverson	15.00	6.75
☐ 6 Kerry Kittles	4.00	1.80
☐ 7 Matt Maloney	3.00	1.35
☐ 8 Stephon Marbury	15.00	6.75
☐ 9 Steve Nash	3.00	1.35
☐ 10 Samaki Walker	1.50	.70

1996-97 SkyBox Rookie Prevue

Randomly inserted in series one packs at a rate of one in 54, this 18-card set focuses on the top 18 players from the 1996 NBA Draft. Card fronts feature a foil background. Card backs are numbered with a "R" prefix.

		MINT	NRMT
COMPLETE SET (18)		200.00	90.00
COMMON CARD (R1-R18)		2.50	1.10
SEMISTARS		5.00	2.20
UNLISTED STARS		8.00	3.60
SER.1 STATED ODDS 1:54 HOBBY/RETAIL			
☐ R1	Shareef Abdur-Rahim	25.00	11.00
☐ R2	Ray Allen	12.00	5.50
☐ R3	Kobe Bryant	75.00	34.00
☐ R4	Marcus Camby	10.00	4.50
☐ R5	Erick Dampier	8.00	3.60
☐ R6	Tony Delk	8.00	3.60
☐ R7	Brian Evans	2.50	1.10
☐ R8	Todd Fuller	2.50	1.10
☐ R9	Allen Iverson	40.00	18.00
☐ R10	Kerry Kittles	10.00	4.50
☐ R11	Stephon Marbury	40.00	18.00
☐ R12	Steve Nash	8.00	3.60
☐ R13	Vitaly Potapenko	5.00	2.20
☐ R14	Roy Rogers	2.50	1.10
☐ R15	Antoine Walker	40.00	18.00
☐ R16	Samaki Walker	8.00	3.60
☐ R17	John Wallace	8.00	3.60
☐ R18	Lorenzen Wright	8.00	3.60

1996-97 SkyBox Standouts

Randomly inserted in series one retail packs only at a rate of one in 180, this 9-card set features laser cut photos of standout NBA players which are silhouetted over a foil background which contains a giant basketball net graphic. Card backs are numbered with a "SO" prefix.

		MINT	NRMT
COMPLETE SET (9)		150.00	70.00
COMMON CARD (SO1-SO9)		10.00	4.50
SER.1 STATED ODDS 1:180 RETAIL			
☐ SO1	Grant Hill	60.00	27.00
☐ SO2	Juwan Howard	12.00	5.50
☐ SO3	Jason Kidd	20.00	9.00
☐ SO4	Reggie Miller	10.00	4.50
☐ SO5	Shaquille O'Neal	40.00	18.00
☐ SO6	Gary Payton	15.00	6.75
☐ SO7	Scottie Pippen	30.00	13.50
☐ SO8	Mitch Richmond	10.00	4.50
☐ SO9	Joe Smith	12.00	5.50

1996-97 SkyBox Thunder and Lightning

Randomly inserted in all series two packs at a rate of one in 144, this 10-card multi-player set focuses on some of the NBA's most deadly combinations. The "outside" card contains the first player while the second player is contained inside the first one.

		MINT	NRMT
COMPLETE SET (10)		225.00	100.00
COMMON CARD (1-10)		5.00	2.20
SER.2 STATED ODDS 1:144 HOBBY/RETAIL			
☐ 1	Michael Jordan Scottie Pippen	80.00	36.00
☐ 2	Kevin Johnson Danny Manning	5.00	2.20
☐ 3	Grant Hill Joe Dumars	40.00	18.00
☐ 4	Latrell Sprewell Joe Smith	8.00	3.60
☐ 5	Charles Barkley Hakeem Olajuwon	25.00	11.00
☐ 6	Vin Baker Glenn Robinson	20.00	9.00
☐ 7	Patrick Ewing Larry Johnson	12.00	5.50
☐ 8	Shawn Kemp Gary Payton	30.00	13.50
☐ 9	Karl Malone John Stockton	20.00	9.00
☐ 10	Juwan Howard Chris Webber	25.00	11.00

1996-97 SkyBox Triple Threats

The first nine cards were randomly inserted into first series packs at roughly one per pack. The bonus Triple Threat cards were randomly inserted in first series packs at a rate of one in 240, and feature three members from the NBA Champion Chicago Bulls. These cards differed from the first nine by the use of a metallic background. All card backs were numbered with a "TT" prefix.

	MINT	NRMT
COMPLETE SET (9)	1.50	.70
COMMON CARD (TT1-TT12)	.10	.05
SEMISTARS	.15	.07
UNLISTED STARS	.30	.14

SPs: SER.1 STATED ODDS 1:720 HOB/RET
SPs NOT CONSIDERED PART OF SET
*RUBIES: 20X TO 40X HI COLUMN
RUBIES: ONE PER HOBBY BOX
SPs DO NOT HAVE RUBY PARALLEL

		MINT	NRMT
☐ TT1	Chris Mullin	.30	.14
☐ TT2	Joe Smith	.40	.18
☐ TT3	Latrell Sprewell	.15	.07
☐ TT4	Avery Johnson	.10	.05
☐ TT5	Sean Elliott	.10	.05
☐ TT6	David Robinson	.50	.23
☐ TT7	John Stockton	.30	.14
☐ TT8	Karl Malone	.50	.23
☐ TT9	Jeff Hornacek	.15	.07
☐ TT10	Dennis Rodman SP	20.00	9.00
☐ TT11	Michael Jordan SP	60.00	27.00
☐ TT12	Scottie Pippen SP	15.00	6.75

1997-98 SkyBox

This 250-card set features borderless color action player images printed on 20 pt. stock with holographic foil stamping and was distributed in eight-card packs with a suggested retail price of $2.59. The backs carry information about the player and career statistics. The second series contained the subset "Team SkyBox" that was inserted into packs at a rate of one in four.

	MINT	NRMT
COMPLETE SET (250)	90.00	40.00
COMPLETE SERIES 1 (125)	25.00	11.00
COMPLETE SERIES 2 (125)	70.00	32.00
COMMON CARD (1-250)	.15	.07
SEMISTARS	.20	.09
UNLISTED STARS	.40	.18

TEAM SKYBOX SUBSET 1:4 HOB/RET
COMMON REEBOK BRONZE .. .20 .09
*REEBOK BRONZE: .25X TO .5X HI COLUMN
COMMON REEBOK GOLD ...... .60 .25
*REEBOK GOLD: 1.5X TO 3X HI
COMMON REEBOK SILVER ... .30 .14
*REEBOK SILVER: .5X TO 1X HI
REEBOK: ONE PER SER.1 PACK

		MINT	NRMT
☐ 1	Grant Hill	2.50	1.10
☐ 2	Matt Maloney	.15	.07
☐ 3	Vinny Del Negro	.15	.07
☐ 4	Kevin Willis	.15	.07
☐ 5	Mark Jackson	.15	.07
☐ 6	Ray Allen	.50	.23
☐ 7	Derrick Coleman	.20	.09
☐ 8	Isaiah Rider	.20	.09
☐ 9	Rod Strickland	.20	.09
☐ 10	Danny Ferry	.15	.07
☐ 11	Antonio Davis	.15	.07
☐ 12	Glenn Robinson	.40	.18
☐ 13	Cedric Ceballos	.15	.07
☐ 14	Sean Elliott	.15	.07
☐ 15	Walt Williams	.15	.07
☐ 16	Glen Rice	.40	.18
☐ 17	Clyde Drexler	.50	.23
☐ 18	Sherman Douglas	.15	.07
☐ 19	Othella Harrington	.15	.07
☐ 20	John Stockton	.40	.18
☐ 21	Priest Lauderdale	.15	.07
☐ 22	Khalid Reeves	.15	.07
☐ 23	Kobe Bryant	3.00	1.35
☐ 24	Vin Baker	.75	.35
☐ 25	Steve Nash	.20	.09
☐ 26	Jeff Hornacek	.20	.09
☐ 27	Tyrone Corbin	.15	.07
☐ 28	Charles Barkley	.60	.25
☐ 29	Michael Jordan	5.00	2.20
☐ 30	Latrell Sprewell	.20	.09
☐ 31	Anfernee Hardaway	1.50	.70
☐ 32	Steve Kerr	.15	.07
☐ 33	Joe Smith	.40	.18
☐ 34	Jermaine O'Neal	.20	.09
☐ 35	Ron Mercer	3.00	1.35
☐ 36	Antonio McDyess	.50	.23
☐ 37	Patrick Ewing	.40	.18
☐ 38	Avery Johnson	.15	.07
☐ 39	Toni Kukoc	.20	.09
☐ 40	Sam Perkins	.20	.09
☐ 41	Voshon Lenard	.15	.07
☐ 42	Detlef Schrempf	.20	.09
☐ 43	Horace Grant	.20	.09
☐ 44	Luc Longley	.20	.09
☐ 45	Todd Fuller	.15	.07
☐ 46	Tim Hardaway	.50	.23
☐ 47	Nick Anderson	.15	.07
☐ 48	Scottie Pippen	1.25	.55
☐ 49	Lindsey Hunter	.15	.07
☐ 50	Shawn Kemp	1.25	.55
☐ 51	Larry Johnson	.20	.09
☐ 52	Shawn Bradley	.15	.07
☐ 53	Martin Muursepp	.15	.07
☐ 54	Jamal Mashburn	.20	.09
☐ 55	John Starks	.20	.09
☐ 56	Rony Seikaly	.15	.07
☐ 57	Gary Payton	.60	.25
☐ 58	Juwan Howard	.40	.18
☐ 59	Vitaly Potapenko	.15	.07
☐ 60	Reggie Miller	.40	.18
☐ 61	Alonzo Mourning	.40	.18
☐ 62	Roy Rogers	.15	.07
☐ 63	Antoine Walker	2.00	.90
☐ 64	Joe Dumars	.40	.18
☐ 65	Allan Houston	.40	.18
☐ 66	Hersey Hawkins	.20	.09
☐ 67	Dell Curry	.15	.07
☐ 68	Tony Delk	.20	.09
☐ 69	Mookie Blaylock	.20	.09
☐ 70	Derek Harper	.15	.07
☐ 71	Loy Vaught	.20	.09
☐ 72	Tom Gugliotta	.40	.18
☐ 73	Mitch Richmond	.40	.18
☐ 74	Dikembe Mutombo	.20	.09
☐ 75	Tony Battie	.75	.35
☐ 76	Derek Fisher	.15	.07
☐ 77	Jason Kidd	.75	.35
☐ 78	Shareef Abdur-Rahim	1.25	.55
☐ 79	Tracy McGrady	2.50	1.10
☐ 80	Anthony Mason	.20	.09
☐ 81	Mario Elie	.15	.07
☐ 82	Karl Malone	.60	.25
☐ 83	Mark Price	.15	.07
☐ 84	Steve Smith	.20	.09
☐ 85	LaPhonso Ellis	.15	.07
☐ 86	Robert Horry	.20	.09
☐ 87	Wesley Person	.15	.07
☐ 88	Marcus Camby	.40	.18
☐ 89	Antonio Daniels	1.00	.45
☐ 90	Eddie Jones	.75	.35
☐ 91	Gary Trent	.15	.07
☐ 92	Danny Fortson	.75	.35
☐ 93	Chris Childs	.15	.07
☐ 94	David Robinson	.60	.25
☐ 95	Bryant Reeves	.20	.09
☐ 96	Chris Webber	1.00	.45
☐ 97	P.J. Brown	.15	.07
☐ 98	Tyrone Hill	.15	.07
☐ 99	Dale Davis	.15	.07
☐ 100	Allen Iverson	2.00	.90
☐ 101	Jerry Stackhouse	.75	.35
☐ 102	Arvydas Sabonis	.20	.09
☐ 103	Damon Stoudamire	.75	.35
☐ 104	Tim Thomas	2.50	1.10
☐ 105	Christian Laettner	.20	.09
☐ 106	Robert Pack	.15	.07
☐ 107	Lorenzen Wright	.15	.07
☐ 108	Olden Polynice	.15	.07
☐ 109	Terrell Brandon	.40	.18
☐ 110	Theo Ratliff	.15	.07
☐ 111	Kevin Garnett	2.50	1.10
☐ 112	Tim Duncan	5.00	2.20
☐ 113	Bryon Russell	.15	.07
☐ 114	Chauncey Billups	1.50	.70
☐ 115	Dale Ellis	.15	.07
☐ 116	Shaquille O'Neal	1.50	.70
☐ 117	Keith Van Horn	4.00	1.80
☐ 118	Kenny Anderson	.20	.09
☐ 119	Dennis Rodman	1.50	.70
☐ 120	Hakeem Olajuwon	.75	.35
☐ 121	Stephon Marbury	2.00	.90
☐ 122	Kendall Gill	.20	.09
☐ 123	Kerry Kittles	.40	.18
☐ 124	Checklist	.15	.07
☐ 125	Checklist	.15	.07
☐ 126	Anthony Johnson	.40	.18
☐ 127	Chris Anstey	.40	.18
☐ 128	Dean Garrett	.15	.07
☐ 129	Rik Smits	.20	.09
☐ 130	Tracy Murray	.15	.07
☐ 131	Charles O'Bannon	.15	.07
☐ 132	Eldridge Recasner	.15	.07
☐ 133	Johnny Taylor	.15	.07
☐ 134	Priest Lauderdale	.15	.07
☐ 135	Rod Strickland	.20	.09
☐ 136	Alan Henderson	.15	.07
☐ 137	Austin Croshere	.50	.23
☐ 138	Buck Williams	.15	.07

□ 139 Clifford Robinson	.15	.07
□ 140 Darrell Armstrong	.15	.07
□ 141 Dennis Scott	.15	.07
□ 142 Carl Herrera	.15	.07
□ 143 Maurice Taylor	1.25	.55
□ 144 Chris Gatling	.15	.07
□ 145 Alvin Williams	.50	.23
□ 146 Antonio McDyess	.50	.23
□ 147 Chauncey Billups	.75	.35
□ 148 George McCloud	.15	.07
□ 149 George Lynch	.15	.07
□ 150 John Thomas	.15	.07
□ 151 Jayson Williams	.20	.09
□ 152 Otis Thorpe	.20	.09
□ 153 Serge Zwikker	.15	.07
□ 154 Chris Crawford	.15	.07
□ 155 Muggsy Bogues	.15	.07
□ 156 Mark Jackson	.15	.07
□ 157 Dontonio Wingfield	.15	.07
□ 158 Rodrick Rhodes	.50	.23
□ 159 Sam Cassell	.20	.09
□ 160 Hubert Davis	.15	.07
□ 161 C.Weatherspoon	.15	.07
□ 162 Eddie Johnson	.15	.07
□ 163 Jacque Vaughn	.60	.25
□ 164 Mark Price	.15	.07
□ 165 Terry Dehere	.15	.07
□ 166 Travis Knight	.15	.07
□ 167 Charles Smith	.15	.07
□ 168 David Wesley	.15	.07
□ 169 David Wingate	.15	.07
□ 170 Todd Day	.15	.07
□ 171 Adonal Foyle	.50	.23
□ 172 Chris Mills	.15	.07
□ 173 Paul Grant	.15	.07
□ 174 Adam Keefe	.15	.07
□ 175 Erick Dampier	.15	.07
UER back Eric		
□ 176 Ervin Johnson	.15	.07
□ 177 Lamond Murray	.15	.07
□ 178 Vlade Divac	.20	.09
□ 179 Bobby Phills	.15	.07
□ 180 Brian Williams	.15	.07
□ 181 Chris Dudley	.15	.07
□ 182 Tyrone Hill	.15	.07
□ 183 Donyell Marshall	.15	.07
□ 184 Kevin Gamble	.15	.07
□ 185 Scot Pollard	.15	.07
□ 186 Cherokee Parks	.15	.07
□ 187 Terry Mills	.15	.07
□ 188 Glen Rice	.40	.18
□ 189 Shawn Respert	.15	.07
□ 190 Terrell Brandon	.40	.18
□ 191 Keith Closs	.15	.07
□ 192 Tariq Abdul-Wahad	.60	.25
□ 193 Wesley Person	.15	.07
□ 194 Chuck Person	.15	.07
□ 195 Derek Anderson	1.25	.55
□ 196 Jon Barry	.15	.07
□ 197 Chris Mullin	.40	.18
□ 198 Ed Gray	.50	.23
□ 199 Charlie Ward	.15	.07
□ 200 Kelvin Cato	.50	.23
□ 201 Michael Finley	.40	.18
□ 202 Rick Fox	.15	.07
□ 203 Scott Burrell	.15	.07
□ 204 Vin Baker	.75	.35
□ 205 Eric Snow	.15	.07
□ 206 Isaac Austin	.15	.07
□ 207 Keith Booth	.15	.07
□ 208 Brian Grant	.15	.07
□ 209 Chris Webber	1.00	.45
□ 210 Eric Williams	.15	.07
□ 211 Jim Jackson	.20	.09
□ 212 Anthony Parker	.15	.07
□ 213 Brevin Knight	1.25	.55
□ 214 Cory Alexander	.15	.07
□ 215 James Robinson	.15	.07
□ 216 Bobby Jackson	.75	.35
□ 217 Charles Outlaw	.15	.07
□ 218 God Shammgod	.15	.07
□ 219 James Cotton	.15	.07
□ 220 Jud Buechler	.15	.07
□ 221 Shandon Anderson	.15	.07
□ 222 Kevin Johnson	.20	.09
□ 223 Chris Morris	.15	.07

□ 224 S.Abdur-Rahim TS	2.50	1.10
□ 225 Ray Allen TS	1.00	.45
□ 226 Kobe Bryant TS	8.00	3.60
□ 227 Marcus Camby TS	.75	.35
□ 228 Antonio Daniels TS	1.00	.45
□ 229 Tim Duncan TS	5.00	2.20
□ 230 Kevin Garnett TS	5.00	2.20
□ 231 Anfernee Hardaway TS	3.00	1.35
□ 232 Grant Hill TS	5.00	2.20
□ 233 Allen Iverson TS	4.00	1.80
□ 234 Bobby Jackson TS	.75	.35
□ 235 Michael Jordan TS	10.00	4.50
□ 236 Shawn Kemp TS	2.50	1.10
□ 237 Karl Malone TS	1.25	.55
□ 238 Stephon Marbury TS	4.00	1.80
□ 239 Hakeem Olajuwon TS	1.50	.70
□ 240 Shaquille O'Neal TS	3.00	1.35
□ 241 Gary Payton TS	1.25	.55
□ 242 Scottie Pippen TS	2.50	1.10
□ 243 David Robinson TS	1.25	.55
□ 244 Dennis Rodman TS	3.00	1.35
□ 245 Jerry Stackhouse TS	.75	.35
□ 246 Damon Stoudamire TS	1.50	.70
□ 247 Keith Van Horn TS	4.00	1.80
□ 248 Antoine Walker TS	4.00	1.80
□ 249 Grant Hill CL	.60	.25
□ 250 Hakeem Olajuwon CL	.40	.18
□ NNO Allen Iverson	40.00	18.00
Ruby Shoe		
□ NNO Allen Iverson	12.00	5.50
Gold Shoe		
□ NNO Allen Iverson	100.00	45.00
Emerald Shoe		
□ NNO Allen Iverson	5.00	2.20
Silver Shoe		
□ NNO Allen Iverson	2.50	1.10
Bronze Shoe		

1997-98 SkyBox Star Rubies

This 248-card set is a hobby only parallel version of the regular set. The fronts contained a "splattered" red background and red-foil on the "SkyBox" logo. Fewer than 50 sets were produced and serially numbered.

	MINT	NRMT
COMMON CARD	40.00	18.00
SEMISTARS	50.00	22.00
RANDOM INS.IN BOTH SERIES HOB.PACKS		
STATED PRINT RUN 50 SERIAL #'d SETS		
SUBSETS ARE NOT SP'S IN PARALLEL SET		

□ 1 Grant Hill	500.00	220.00
□ 2 Matt Maloney	40.00	18.00
□ 3 Vinny Del Negro	40.00	18.00
□ 4 Kevin Willis	40.00	18.00
□ 5 Mark Jackson	40.00	18.00
□ 6 Ray Allen	100.00	45.00
□ 7 Derrick Coleman	50.00	22.00
□ 8 Isaiah Rider	50.00	22.00

□ 9 Rod Strickland	50.00	22.00
□ 10 Danny Ferry	40.00	18.00
□ 11 Antonio Davis	40.00	18.00
□ 12 Glenn Robinson	60.00	27.00
□ 13 Cedric Ceballos	40.00	18.00
□ 14 Sean Elliott	40.00	18.00
□ 15 Walt Williams	40.00	18.00
□ 16 Glen Rice	80.00	36.00
□ 17 Clyde Drexler	100.00	45.00
□ 18 Sherman Douglas	40.00	18.00
□ 19 Othella Harrington	40.00	18.00
□ 20 John Stockton	80.00	36.00
□ 21 Priest Lauderdale	40.00	18.00
□ 22 Khalid Reeves	40.00	18.00
□ 23 Kobe Bryant	750.00	350.00
□ 24 Vin Baker	150.00	70.00
□ 25 Steve Nash	50.00	22.00
□ 26 Jeff Hornacek	50.00	22.00
□ 27 Tyrone Corbin	40.00	18.00
□ 28 Charles Barkley	125.00	55.00
□ 29 Michael Jordan	2000.00	900.00
□ 30 Latrell Sprewell	50.00	22.00
□ 31 Anfernee Hardaway	450.00	200.00
□ 32 Steve Kerr	40.00	18.00
□ 33 Joe Smith	80.00	36.00
□ 34 Jermaine O'Neal	50.00	22.00
□ 35 Ron Mercer	300.00	135.00
□ 36 Antonio McDyess	100.00	45.00
□ 37 Patrick Ewing	80.00	36.00
□ 38 Avery Johnson	40.00	18.00
□ 39 Toni Kukoc	80.00	36.00
□ 40 Sam Perkins	50.00	22.00
□ 41 Voshon Lenard	40.00	18.00
□ 42 Detlef Schrempf	50.00	22.00
□ 43 Horace Grant	50.00	22.00
□ 44 Luc Longley	50.00	22.00
□ 45 Todd Fuller	40.00	18.00
□ 46 Tim Hardaway	150.00	70.00
□ 47 Nick Anderson	40.00	18.00
□ 48 Scottie Pippen	250.00	110.00
□ 49 Lindsey Hunter	40.00	18.00
□ 50 Shawn Kemp	250.00	110.00
□ 51 Larry Johnson	50.00	22.00
□ 52 Shawn Bradley	40.00	18.00
□ 53 Martin Muursepp	40.00	18.00
□ 54 Jamal Mashburn	50.00	22.00
□ 55 John Starks	50.00	22.00
□ 56 Rony Seikaly	40.00	18.00
□ 57 Gary Payton	125.00	55.00
□ 58 Juwan Howard	80.00	36.00
□ 59 Vitaly Potapenko	40.00	18.00
□ 60 Reggie Miller	80.00	36.00
□ 61 Alonzo Mourning	80.00	36.00
□ 62 Roy Rogers	40.00	18.00
□ 63 Antoine Walker	400.00	180.00
□ 64 Joe Dumars	60.00	27.00
□ 65 Allan Houston	50.00	22.00
□ 66 Hersey Hawkins	50.00	22.00
□ 67 Dell Curry	40.00	18.00
□ 68 Tony Delk	40.00	18.00
□ 69 Mookie Blaylock	50.00	22.00
□ 70 Derek Harper	40.00	18.00
□ 71 Loy Vaught	50.00	22.00
□ 72 Tom Gugliotta	60.00	27.00
□ 73 Mitch Richmond	80.00	36.00
□ 74 Dikembe Mutombo	50.00	22.00
□ 75 Tony Battie	40.00	18.00
□ 76 Derek Fisher	40.00	18.00
□ 77 Jason Kidd	160.00	70.00
□ 78 Shareef Abdur-Rahim	250.00	110.00
□ 79 Tracy McGrady	250.00	110.00
□ 80 Anthony Mason	50.00	22.00
□ 81 Mario Elie	40.00	18.00
□ 82 Karl Malone	125.00	55.00
□ 83 Mark Price	40.00	18.00
□ 84 Steve Smith	50.00	22.00
□ 85 LaPhonso Ellis	40.00	18.00
□ 86 Robert Horry	50.00	22.00
□ 87 Wesley Person	40.00	18.00
□ 88 Marcus Camby	80.00	36.00
□ 89 Antonio Daniels	100.00	45.00
□ 90 Eddie Jones	160.00	70.00
□ 91 Gary Trent	40.00	18.00
□ 92 Danny Fortson	80.00	36.00
□ 93 Chris Childs	40.00	18.00
□ 94 David Robinson	125.00	55.00

			MINT	NRMT
☐ 95	Bryant Reeves		50.00	22.00
☐ 96	Chris Webber		200.00	90.00
☐ 97	P.J. Brown		40.00	18.00
☐ 98	Tyrone Hill		40.00	18.00
☐ 99	Dale Davis		40.00	18.00
☐ 100	Allen Iverson		400.00	180.00
☐ 101	Jerry Stackhouse		80.00	36.00
☐ 102	Arvydas Sabonis		50.00	22.00
☐ 103	Damon Stoudamire		150.00	70.00
☐ 104	Tim Thomas		250.00	110.00
☐ 105	Christian Laettner		50.00	22.00
☐ 106	Robert Pack		40.00	18.00
☐ 107	Lorenzen Wright		40.00	18.00
☐ 108	Olden Polynice		40.00	18.00
☐ 109	Terrell Brandon		60.00	27.00
☐ 110	Theo Ratliff		40.00	18.00
☐ 111	Kevin Garnett		500.00	220.00
☐ 112	Tim Duncan		500.00	220.00
☐ 113	Bryon Russell		40.00	18.00
☐ 114	Chauncey Billups		150.00	70.00
☐ 115	Dale Ellis		40.00	18.00
☐ 116	Shaquille O'Neal		300.00	135.00
☐ 117	Keith Van Horn		400.00	180.00
☐ 118	Kenny Anderson		50.00	22.00
☐ 119	Dennis Rodman		300.00	135.00
☐ 120	Hakeem Olajuwon		150.00	70.00
☐ 121	Stephon Marbury		400.00	180.00
☐ 122	Kendall Gill		50.00	22.00
☐ 123	Kerry Kittles		80.00	36.00
☐ 126	Anthony Johnson		40.00	18.00
☐ 127	Chris Anstey		60.00	27.00
☐ 128	Dean Garrett		40.00	18.00
☐ 129	Rik Smits		50.00	22.00
☐ 130	Tracy Murray		40.00	18.00
☐ 131	Charles O'Bannon		40.00	18.00
☐ 132	Eldridge Recasner		40.00	18.00
☐ 133	Johnny Taylor		40.00	18.00
☐ 134	Priest Lauderdale		40.00	18.00
☐ 135	Rod Strickland		50.00	22.00
☐ 136	Alan Henderson		40.00	18.00
☐ 137	Austin Croshere		60.00	27.00
☐ 138	Buck Williams		40.00	18.00
☐ 139	Clifford Robinson		40.00	18.00
☐ 140	Darrell Armstrong		40.00	18.00
☐ 141	Dennis Scott		40.00	18.00
☐ 142	Carl Herrera		40.00	18.00
☐ 143	Maurice Taylor		125.00	55.00
☐ 144	Chris Gatling		40.00	18.00
☐ 145	Alvin Williams		60.00	27.00
☐ 146	Antonio McDyess		100.00	45.00
☐ 147	Chauncey Billups		125.00	55.00
☐ 148	George McCloud		40.00	18.00
☐ 149	George Lynch		40.00	18.00
☐ 150	John Thomas		40.00	18.00
☐ 151	Jayson Williams		50.00	22.00
☐ 152	Otis Thorpe		50.00	22.00
☐ 153	Serge Zwikker		40.00	18.00
☐ 154	Chris Crawford		40.00	18.00
☐ 155	Muggsy Bogues		40.00	18.00
☐ 156	Mark Jackson		40.00	18.00
☐ 157	Dontonio Wingfield		40.00	18.00
☐ 158	Rodrick Rhodes		60.00	27.00
☐ 159	Sam Cassell		50.00	22.00
☐ 160	Hubert Davis		40.00	18.00
☐ 161	C.Weatherspoon		40.00	18.00
☐ 162	Eddie Johnson		40.00	18.00
☐ 163	Jacque Vaughn		60.00	27.00
☐ 164	Mark Price		40.00	18.00
☐ 165	Terry Dehere		40.00	18.00
☐ 166	Travis Knight		40.00	18.00
☐ 167	Charles Smith		40.00	18.00
☐ 168	David Wesley		40.00	18.00
☐ 169	David Wingate		40.00	18.00
☐ 170	Todd Day		40.00	18.00
☐ 171	Adonal Foyle		60.00	27.00
☐ 172	Chris Mills		40.00	18.00
☐ 173	Paul Grant		40.00	18.00
☐ 174	Adam Keefe		40.00	18.00
☐ 175	Erick Dampier		40.00	18.00
	UER Back spelled Eric			
☐ 176	Ervin Johnson		40.00	18.00
☐ 177	Lamond Murray		40.00	18.00
☐ 178	Vlade Divac		50.00	22.00
☐ 179	Bobby Phills		40.00	18.00
☐ 180	Brian Williams		40.00	18.00
☐ 181	Chris Dudley		40.00	18.00

			MINT	NRMT
☐ 182	Tyrone Hill		40.00	18.00
☐ 183	Donyell Marshall		40.00	18.00
☐ 184	Kevin Gamble		40.00	18.00
☐ 185	Scot Pollard		40.00	18.00
☐ 186	Cherokee Parks		40.00	18.00
☐ 187	Terry Mills		40.00	18.00
☐ 188	Glen Rice		80.00	36.00
☐ 189	Shawn Respert		40.00	18.00
☐ 190	Terrell Brandon		60.00	27.00
☐ 191	Keith Closs		40.00	18.00
☐ 192	Tariq Abdul-Wahad		60.00	27.00
☐ 193	Wesley Person		40.00	18.00
☐ 194	Chuck Person		40.00	18.00
☐ 195	Derek Anderson		125.00	55.00
☐ 196	Jon Barry		40.00	18.00
☐ 197	Chris Mullin		60.00	27.00
☐ 198	Ed Gray		60.00	27.00
☐ 199	Charlie Ward		40.00	18.00
☐ 200	Kelvin Cato		60.00	27.00
☐ 201	Michael Finley		80.00	36.00
☐ 202	Rick Fox		40.00	18.00
☐ 203	Scott Burrell		40.00	18.00
☐ 204	Vin Baker		150.00	70.00
☐ 205	Eric Snow		40.00	18.00
☐ 206	Isaac Austin		40.00	18.00
☐ 207	Keith Booth		40.00	18.00
☐ 208	Brian Grant		40.00	18.00
☐ 209	Chris Webber		200.00	90.00
☐ 210	Eric Williams		40.00	18.00
☐ 211	Jim Jackson		50.00	22.00
☐ 212	Anthony Parker		40.00	18.00
☐ 213	Brevin Knight		125.00	55.00
☐ 214	Cory Alexander		40.00	18.00
☐ 215	James Robinson		40.00	18.00
☐ 216	Bobby Jackson		80.00	36.00
☐ 217	Charles Outlaw		40.00	18.00
☐ 218	God Shammgod		40.00	18.00
☐ 219	James Cotton		40.00	18.00
☐ 220	Jud Buechler		40.00	18.00
☐ 221	Shandon Anderson		40.00	18.00
☐ 222	Kevin Johnson		50.00	22.00
☐ 223	Chris Morris		40.00	18.00
☐ 224	S.Abdur-Rahim TS		200.00	90.00
☐ 225	Ray Allen TS		80.00	36.00
☐ 226	Kobe Bryant TS		600.00	275.00
☐ 227	Marcus Camby TS		60.00	27.00
☐ 228	Antonio Daniels TS		80.00	36.00
☐ 229	Tim Duncan TS		400.00	180.00
☐ 230	Kevin Garnett TS		400.00	180.00
☐ 231	A.Hardaway TS		300.00	135.00
☐ 232	Grant Hill TS		400.00	180.00
☐ 233	Allen Iverson TS		300.00	135.00
☐ 234	Bobby Jackson TS		60.00	27.00
☐ 235	Michael Jordan TS		1600.00	700.00
☐ 236	Shawn Kemp TS		200.00	90.00
☐ 237	Karl Malone TS		100.00	45.00
☐ 238	Stephon Marbury TS		300.00	135.00
☐ 239	Hakeem Olajuwon TS		125.00	55.00
☐ 240	Shaquille O'Neal TS		250.00	110.00
☐ 241	Gary Payton TS		100.00	45.00
☐ 242	Scottie Pippen TS		200.00	90.00
☐ 243	David Robinson TS		100.00	45.00
☐ 244	Dennis Rodman TS		250.00	110.00
☐ 245	Jerry Stackhouse TS		60.00	27.00
☐ 246	D.Stoudamire TS		125.00	55.00
☐ 247	Keith Van Horn TS		350.00	160.00
☐ 248	Antoine Walker TS		300.00	135.00
☐ 249	Grant Hill CL		300.00	135.00
☐ 250	Hakeem Olajuwon CL		100.00	45.00

1997-98 SkyBox And One

This 10-card set was randomly inserted in series one packs at a rate of one in 96. When the seal was removed from these die cut cards, it could be opened in four directions to reveal a larger player photo in a diamond-shaped "poster" with silver and

gold foils. An extra bonus card of the same player is hiding inside.

		MINT	NRMT
COMPLETE SET (10)		200.00	90.00
COMMON CARD (1-10)		5.00	2.20
SER. 1 STATED ODDS 1:96 HOB/RET			
☐ 1	Shawn Kemp	15.00	6.75
☐ 2	Hakeem Olajuwon	10.00	4.50
☐ 3	Charles Barkley	8.00	3.60
☐ 4	Antoine Walker	25.00	11.00
☐ 5	Dennis Rodman	20.00	9.00
☐ 6	Tim Duncan	30.00	13.50
☐ 7	Marcus Camby	5.00	2.20
☐ 8	Keith Van Horn	25.00	11.00
☐ 9	Shareef Abdur-Rahim	15.00	6.75
☐ 10	Michael Jordan	60.00	27.00

1997-98 SkyBox Autographics

Randomly inserted in-packs of all Fleer/SkyBox products, this set features autographs of some of the NBA's best players. For Hoops 1, these were inserted at a rate of one in 240 hobby and retail packs. For Hoops 2, these were inserted at a rate of one in 144 hobby and retail. For Metal and Metal Championship, these cards were inserted one in 120 hobby and retail. For SkyBox Premium 1 and 2, these cards were inserted one in 72 packs. For SkyBox E-X2001, these cards were inserted one in 60 packs. For SkyBox Z-Force 1 and 2, these cards were inserted one in 120 packs. Both Tracy McGrady and Rasheed Wallace only have Century Marks cards - no regular ones. Those cards are included in the set price, but are priced in the Century Mark set. The cards are not numbered and listed below alphabetically.

	MINT	NRMT
COMPLETE SET (119)	4800.00	2200.00
COMMON AUTOGRAPH	10.00	4.50
COMMON CENTURY MARK	30.00	13.50
SEMISTARS	15.00	6.75
CENTURY MARKS: 1.25X TO 3X HI COLUMN		
C.M: STATED PRT.RUN 100 SERIAL #'d		
SETS		
ALL MCGRADY CARDS ARE CEN.MARKS		
ALL R.WALLACE CARDS ARE CEN.MARKS		
SET INCLUDES #'s 71 AND 108		
STATED ODDS 1:240 HOOPS 1		
STATED ODDS 1:144 HOOPS 2		
STATED ODDS 1:96 METAL		
STATED ODDS 1:72 METAL		
STATED ODDS 1:72 METAL CHAMP.		
STATED ODDS 1:72 SKYBOX 1,2		
STATED ODDS 1:60 SKY.E-X2001		
STATED ODDS 1:120 Z-FORCE 1,2		
CARDS LISTED BELOW ALPHABETICALLY		

		MINT	NRMT
☐ 1	Shareef Abdur-Rahim	150.00	70.00
☐ 2	Cory Alexander	10.00	4.50
☐ 3	Kenny Anderson	25.00	11.00
☐ 4	Nick Anderson	20.00	9.00
☐ 5	Stacey Augmon	10.00	4.50
☐ 6	Isaac Austin	10.00	4.50
☐ 7	Vin Baker	100.00	45.00
☐ 8	Charles Barkley	300.00	135.00
☐ 9	Dana Barros	10.00	4.50
☐ 10	Brent Barry	10.00	4.50
☐ 11	Tony Battie	40.00	18.00
☐ 12	Travis Best	10.00	4.50
☐ 13	Corie Blount	10.00	4.50
☐ 14	P.J. Brown	10.00	4.50
☐ 15	Randy Brown	20.00	9.00
☐ 16	Jud Buechler	20.00	9.00
☐ 17	Marcus Camby	50.00	22.00
☐ 18	Elden Campbell	15.00	6.75
☐ 19	Chris Carr	10.00	4.50
☐ 20	Kelvin Cato	40.00	18.00
☐ 21	Duane Causwell	10.00	4.50
☐ 22	Rex Chapman	35.00	16.00
☐ 23	Calbert Cheaney	10.00	4.50
☐ 24	Randolph Childress	10.00	4.50
☐ 25	Derrick Coleman	30.00	13.50
☐ 26	Austin Croshere	25.00	11.00
☐ 27	Dell Curry	10.00	4.50
☐ 28	Ben Davis	10.00	4.50
☐ 29	Mark Davis	10.00	4.50
☐ 30	Andrew DeClercq	10.00	4.50
☐ 31	Tony Delk	25.00	11.00
☐ 32	Vlade Divac	15.00	6.75
☐ 33	Clyde Drexler	125.00	55.00
☐ 34	Joe Dumars	50.00	22.00
☐ 35	Howard Eisley	10.00	4.50
☐ 36	Danny Ferry	10.00	4.50
☐ 37	Michael Finley	25.00	11.00
☐ 38	Derek Fisher	25.00	11.00
☐ 39	Danny Fortson	40.00	18.00
☐ 40	Todd Fuller	10.00	4.50
☐ 41	Chris Gatling	10.00	4.50
☐ 42	Matt Geiger	10.00	4.50
☐ 43	Brian Grant	10.00	4.50
☐ 44	Tom Gugliotta	70.00	32.00
☐ 45	Tim Hardaway	80.00	36.00
☐ 46	Ron Harper	25.00	11.00
☐ 47	Othella Harrington	10.00	4.50
☐ 48	Grant Hill	300.00	135.00
☐ 49	Tyrone Hill	10.00	4.50
☐ 50	Allan Houston	35.00	16.00
☐ 51	Juwan Howard	80.00	36.00
☐ 52	Lindsey Hunter	30.00	13.50
☐ 53	Bobby Hurley	10.00	4.50
☐ 54	Jim Jackson	20.00	9.00
☐ 55	Avery Johnson	10.00	4.50
☐ 56	Eddie Johnson	10.00	4.50
☐ 57	Ervin Johnson	10.00	4.50
☐ 58	Larry Johnson	40.00	18.00
☐ 59	Popeye Jones	10.00	4.50
☐ 60	Adam Keefe	10.00	4.50
☐ 61	Steve Kerr	20.00	9.00
☐ 62	Kerry Kittles	75.00	34.00
☐ 63	Brevin Knight	60.00	27.00
☐ 64	Travis Knight	20.00	9.00
☐ 65	George Lynch	10.00	4.50
☐ 66	Don MacLean	10.00	4.50
☐ 67	Stephon Marbury	175.00	80.00
☐ 68	Donny Marshall	10.00	4.50
☐ 69	Walter McCarty	10.00	4.50
☐ 70	Antonio McDyess	60.00	27.00
☐ 71	Ron Mercer	150.00	70.00
☐ 72	Reggie Miller	200.00	90.00
☐ 73	Chris Mills	10.00	4.50
☐ 74	Sam Mitchell	10.00	4.50
☐ 75	Chris Morris	10.00	4.50
☐ 76	Alonzo Mourning	100.00	45.00
☐ 77	Chris Mullin	35.00	16.00
☐ 78	Dikembe Mutombo	50.00	22.00
☐ 79	Anthony Parker	25.00	11.00
☐ 80	Sam Perkins	15.00	6.75
☐ 81	Elliott Perry	10.00	4.50
☐ 82	Bobby Phills	10.00	4.50
☐ 83	Eric Piatkowski	10.00	4.50
☐ 84	Scottie Pippen	250.00	110.00
☐ 85	Vitaly Potapenko	10.00	4.50
☐ 86	Brent Price	10.00	4.50
☐ 87	Theo Ratliff	10.00	4.50
☐ 88	Glen Rice	60.00	27.00
☐ 89	Glenn Robinson	50.00	22.00
☐ 90	Dennis Rodman	450.00	200.00
☐ 91	Roy Rogers	10.00	4.50
☐ 92	Malik Rose	10.00	4.50
☐ 93	Joe Smith	60.00	27.00
☐ 94	Tony Smith	10.00	4.50
☐ 95	Eric Snow	10.00	4.50
☐ 96	Jerry Stackhouse	80.00	36.00
☐ 97	Pistons Uniform		
☐ 98	Jerry Stackhouse	60.00	27.00
	Sixers Uniform		
☐ 99	John Starks	30.00	13.50
☐ 100	Bryant Stith	10.00	4.50
☐ 101	Erick Strickland	15.00	6.75
☐ 102	Rod Strickland	50.00	22.00
☐ 103	Nick Van Exel	70.00	32.00
☐ 104	Keith Van Horn	250.00	110.00
☐ 105	David Vaughn	10.00	4.50
☐ 106	Jacque Vaughn	25.00	11.00
☐ 107	Antoine Walker	150.00	70.00
☐ 109	C.Weatherspoon	10.00	4.50
☐ 110	David Wesley	10.00	4.50
☐ 111	Dominique Wilkins	60.00	27.00
☐ 112	Gerald Wilkins	10.00	4.50
☐ 113	Eric Williams	10.00	4.50
☐ 114	John Williams	10.00	4.50
☐ 115	Lorenzo Williams	10.00	4.50
☐ 116	Monty Williams	10.00	4.50
☐ 117	Scott Williams	10.00	4.50
☐ 118	Walt Williams	10.00	4.50
☐ 119	Lorenzen Wright	10.00	4.50

KEVIN GARNETT

	MINT	NRMT
COMPLETE SET (15)	250.00	110.00
COMMON CARD (CA1-CA15)	5.00	2.20
SER.2 STATED ODDS 1:96 HOB/RET		

		MINT	NRMT
☐ CA1	Allen Iverson	25.00	11.00
☐ CA2	Kobe Bryant	40.00	18.00
☐ CA3	Michael Jordan	60.00	27.00
☐ CA4	Shaquille O'Neal	20.00	9.00
☐ CA5	Stephon Marbury	25.00	11.00
☐ CA6	Shareef Abdur-Rahim	15.00	6.75
☐ CA7	Marcus Camby	5.00	2.20
☐ CA8	Kevin Garnett	30.00	13.50
☐ CA9	Dennis Rodman	20.00	9.00
☐ CA10	Anfernee Hardaway	20.00	9.00
☐ CA11	Ray Allen	6.00	2.70
☐ CA12	Scottie Pippen	15.00	6.75
☐ CA13	Shawn Kemp	15.00	6.75
☐ CA14	Hakeem Olajuwon	10.00	4.50
☐ CA15	John Stockton	5.00	2.20

1997-98 SkyBox Golden Touch

Randomly inserted into series two packs at a rate of one in 360, this 15-card die cut set features some of the NBA's biggest superstars on embossed satin gold-foil. Card backs are numbered with a "GT" prefix.

	MINT	NRMT
COMPLETE SET (15)	1000.00	450.00
COMMON CARD (GT1-GT15)	15.00	6.75
SER.2 STATED ODDS 1:360 HOB/RET		

		MINT	NRMT
☐ GT1	Michael Jordan	200.00	90.00
☐ GT2	Allen Iverson	80.00	36.00
☐ GT3	Kobe Bryant	125.00	55.00
☐ GT4	Shaquille O'Neal	60.00	27.00
☐ GT5	Stephon Marbury	80.00	36.00
☐ GT6	Marcus Camby	15.00	6.75
☐ GT7	Anfernee Hardaway	60.00	27.00
☐ GT8	Kevin Garnett	100.00	45.00
☐ GT9	Shareef Abdur-Rahim	50.00	22.00

1997-98 SkyBox Competitive Advantage

Randomly inserted into series two packs at a rate of one in 96, this 15-card set features some of the best players on die cut, matte finished cards. The cards feature a background of Mount Olympus. Card backs are numbered with a "CA" prefix.

		MINT	NRMT
☐ GT10	Dennis Rodman	60.00	27.00
☐ GT11	Grant Hill	100.00	45.00
☐ GT12	Kerry Kittles	15.00	6.75
☐ GT13	Antoine Walker	80.00	36.00
☐ GT14	Scottie Pippen	50.00	22.00
☐ GT15	Damon Stoudamire	30.00	13.50

1997-98 SkyBox Jam Pack

Randomly inserted into series two packs at a rate of one in 18, this 15-card set features stars on the rise on 100% holofoil cardboard. The fronts feature a scenic background that has the players "walking on water". Card backs carry a "JP" prefix.

	MINT	NRMT
COMPLETE SET (15)	60.00	27.00
COMMON CARD (JP1-JP15)	1.50	.70
SEMISTARS	2.00	.90
UNLISTED STARS	3.00	1.35
SER.2 STATED ODDS 1:18 HOB/RET		
☐ JP1 Ray Allen	4.00	1.80
☐ JP2 Damon Stoudamire	6.00	2.70
☐ JP3 Shawn Kemp	10.00	4.50
☐ JP4 Hakeem Olajuwon	6.00	2.70
☐ JP5 Jerry Stackhouse	3.00	1.35
☐ JP6 John Wallace	1.50	.70
☐ JP7 Juwan Howard	3.00	1.35
☐ JP8 David Robinson	5.00	2.20
☐ JP9 Gary Payton	5.00	2.20
☐ JP10 Joe Smith	3.00	1.35
☐ JP11 Charles Barkley	5.00	2.20
☐ JP12 Terrell Brandon	3.00	1.35
☐ JP13 Vin Baker	6.00	2.70
☐ JP14 Antonio McDyess	4.00	1.80
☐ JP15 Tim Duncan	20.00	9.00

1997-98 SkyBox Next Game

Randomly inserted in series one packs at the rate of one in six, this 15-card set features color photos of the 1997-98 season's top NBA rookies. The backs carry player information.

	MINT	NRMT
COMPLETE SET (15)	30.00	13.50
COMMON CARD (1-15)	.60	.25
SEMISTARS	.75	.35
UNLISTED STARS	1.25	.55
SER.1 STATED ODDS 1:6 HOB/RET		

		MINT	NRMT
☐ 1	Derek Anderson	2.00	.90
☐ 2	Tony Battie	1.25	.55
☐ 3	Chauncey Billups	2.50	1.10
☐ 4	Kelvin Cato	.60	.25
☐ 5	Austin Croshere	.60	.25
☐ 6	Antonio Daniels	1.50	.70
☐ 7	Tim Duncan	8.00	3.60
☐ 8	Danny Fortson	1.25	.55
☐ 9	Adonal Foyle	.60	.25
☐ 10	Tracy McGrady	4.00	1.80
☐ 11	Ron Mercer	5.00	2.20
☐ 12	Olivier Saint-Jean	.75	.35
☐ 13	Maurice Taylor	2.00	.90
☐ 14	Tim Thomas	4.00	1.80
☐ 15	Keith Van Horn	6.00	2.70

1997-98 SkyBox Premium Players

Randomly inserted in series one packs at the rate of one in 192, this 15-card set features letter box photography in the background and a player highlighted in the foreground with silver rainbow foil and team colors.

	MINT	NRMT
COMPLETE SET (15)	500.00	220.00
COMMON CARD (1-15)	8.00	3.60
SER 1 STATED ODDS 1:192 HOB/RET		
☐ 1 Michael Jordan	110.00	50.00
☐ 2 Allen Iverson	40.00	18.00
☐ 3 Kobe Bryant	60.00	27.00
☐ 4 Shaquille O'Neal	30.00	13.50
☐ 5 Stephon Marbury	40.00	18.00
☐ 6 Marcus Camby	8.00	3.60
☐ 7 Anfernee Hardaway	30.00	13.50
☐ 8 Kevin Garnett	50.00	22.00
☐ 9 Shareef Abdur-Rahim	25.00	11.00
☐ 10 Dennis Rodman	30.00	13.50
☐ 11 Ray Allen	10.00	4.50
☐ 12 Grant Hill	50.00	22.00

		MINT	NRMT
☐ 13	Kerry Kittles	8.00	3.60
☐ 14	Karl Malone	12.00	5.50
☐ 15	Scottie Pippen	25.00	11.00

1997-98 SkyBox Rock 'n Fire

Randomly inserted in series one packs at the rate of one in 18, this 10-card set is reversible and featues a color action photo of a rising basketball star on one side and his portrait on the other with silver foil highlights. The card slides into a frame which carries more player information.

	MINT	NRMT
COMPLETE SET (10)	80.00	36.00
COMMON CARD (1-10)	2.50	1.10
SER 1 STATED ODDS 1:18 HOB/RET		
☐ 1 Allen Iverson	12.00	5.50
☐ 2 Kobe Bryant	20.00	9.00
☐ 3 Shaquille O'Neal	10.00	4.50
☐ 4 Stephon Marbury	12.00	5.50
☐ 5 Marcus Camby	2.50	1.10
☐ 6 Anfernee Hardaway	10.00	4.50
☐ 7 Kevin Garnett	15.00	6.75
☐ 8 Shareef Abdur-Rahim	8.00	3.60
☐ 9 Damon Stoudamire	5.00	2.20
☐ 10 Grant Hill	15.00	6.75

1997-98 SkyBox Silky Smooth

Randomly inserted in series one packs at the rate of one in 360, this 10-card set features a glossy color action player photo with silver and gold holofoil and viewed through a matte coated, laser-cut net which can be opened to expose the card.

	MINT	NRMT
COMPLETE SET (10)	800.00	350.00
COMMON CARD (1-10)	25.00	11.00
SER.1 STATED ODDS 1:360 HOB/RET		
☐ 1 Michael Jordan	200.00	90.00
☐ 2 Allen Iverson	80.00	36.00
☐ 3 Kobe Bryant	125.00	55.00
☐ 4 Shaquille O'Neal	60.00	27.00
☐ 5 Stephon Marbury	80.00	36.00
☐ 6 Gary Payton	25.00	11.00
☐ 7 Anfernee Hardaway	60.00	27.00
☐ 8 Kevin Garnett	100.00	45.00
☐ 9 Scottie Pippen	50.00	22.00
☐ 10 Grant Hill	100.00	45.00

1997-98 SkyBox Star Search

Randomly inserted into series two packs at a rate of one in six, this 15-card set features the top prospects from the 1997 Draft Class. The card fronts, when closed, feature a small photo of the player in front of a curtain. The fronts can be opened to "raise the curtain" on these players to reveal an action shot. Card backs are numbered with a "SS" prefix.

	MINT	NRMT
COMPLETE SET (15)	30.00	13.50
COMMON CARD (SS1-SS15)	.60	.25
SEMISTARS	.75	.35
UNLISTED STARS	1.25	.55
SER.2 STATED ODDS 1:6 HOB/RET		
☐ SS1 Tim Duncan	8.00	3.60
☐ SS2 Tony Battie	1.25	.55
☐ SS3 Keith Van Horn	6.00	2.70
☐ SS4 Antonio Daniels	1.50	.70
☐ SS5 Chauncey Billups	2.50	1.10
☐ SS6 Ron Mercer	5.00	2.20
☐ SS7 Tracy McGrady	4.00	1.80
☐ SS8 Danny Fortson	1.25	.55
☐ SS9 Brevin Knight	2.00	.90
☐ SS10 Derek Anderson	2.00	.90
☐ SS11 Bobby Jackson	1.25	.55
☐ SS12 Jacque Vaughn	.75	.35
☐ SS13 Tim Thomas	4.00	1.80
☐ SS14 Austin Croshere	.60	.25
☐ SS15 Kelvin Cato	.60	.25

1997-98 SkyBox Thunder and Lightning

Randomly inserted into series two packs at a rate of one in 192, this 15-card set features a combination of rainbow holofoil and phosphorescent pigmentation to highlight a collection of stars who use their physical prowess to the team's advantage. Unlike past years, which featured two players, this only features one. One side features the player as "thunder" in his home uniform while the flip side shows him as "lightning" in his away uniform. Card backs are numbered with a "TL" prefix.

	MINT	NRMT
COMPLETE SET (15)	500.00	220.00
COMMON CARD (TL1-TL15)	8.00	3.60
SER.2 STATED ODDS 1:192 HOB/RET		
☐ TL1 Stephon Marbury	40.00	18.00
☐ TL2 Shareef Abdur-Rahim	25.00	11.00
☐ TL3 Shaquille O'Neal	30.00	13.50
☐ TL4 Scottie Pippen	25.00	11.00
☐ TL5 Michael Jordan	100.00	45.00
☐ TL6 Marcus Camby	8.00	3.60
☐ TL7 Kobe Bryant	60.00	27.00
☐ TL8 Kevin Garnett	50.00	22.00
☐ TL9 Kerry Kittles	8.00	3.60
☐ TL10 Grant Hill	50.00	22.00
☐ TL11 Dennis Rodman	30.00	13.50
☐ TL12 Damon Stoudamire	15.00	6.75
☐ TL13 Antoine Walker	40.00	18.00
☐ TL14 Anfernee Hardaway	30.00	13.50
☐ TL15 Allen Iverson	40.00	18.00

1996-97 SkyBox E-X2000

The SkyBox E-X2000 set was issued in one series totalling 80 cards. Cards were available in 2-card packs with a suggested retail price of $3.99. Card designs are similar to the 1995-96 Hoops SkyView insert with a clear plastic design inside of a frame with a photo of the player overlapped. The cards are

designated as Condition Sensitive due to the easy nature of damaging the cards. A Grant Hill Emerald exchange card was also inserted at one in 500 packs. This card was exchangeable for a Grant Hill autographed ball. Reportedly, only 75 balls were signed for the promotion. Also available to dealers who purchased a case was a blow-up Grant Hill E-X2000 card which was serial numbered to 3000. A regular issue-size Grant Hill promo card was also released and is listed below at the end of the set.

	MINT	NRMT
COMPLETE SET (82)	130.00	57.50
COMMON CARD (1-82)	.50	.23
SEMISTARS	.60	.25
UNLISTED STARS	1.00	.45
AUTOGRAPHICS LISTED UNDER SKYBOX		
EMERALD EXCH: STATED ODDS 1:500		
CONDITION SENSITIVE SET		
☐ 1 Christian Laettner	.60	.25
☐ 2 Dikembe Mutombo	.60	.25
☐ 3 Steve Smith	.60	.25
☐ 4 Antoine Walker	20.00	9.00
☐ 5 David Wesley	.50	.23
☐ 6 Tony Delk	2.00	.90
☐ 7 Anthony Mason	.50	.23
☐ 8 Glen Rice	1.00	.45
☐ 9 Michael Jordan	15.00	6.75
☐ 10 Scottie Pippen	3.00	1.35
☐ 11 Dennis Rodman	4.00	1.80
☐ 12 Terrell Brandon	1.00	.45
☐ 13 Chris Mills	.50	.23
☐ 14 Shawn Bradley	.50	.23
☐ 15 Michael Finley	1.25	.55
☐ 16 Dale Ellis	.50	.23
☐ 17 Antonio McDyess	1.50	.70
☐ 18 Joe Dumars	1.00	.45
☐ 19 Grant Hill	6.00	2.70
☐ 20 Chris Mullin	1.00	.45
☐ 21 Joe Smith	1.25	.55
☐ 22 Latrell Sprewell	.60	.25
☐ 23 Charles Barkley	1.50	.70
☐ 24 Clyde Drexler	1.25	.55
☐ 25 Hakeem Olajuwon	2.00	.90
☐ 26 Erick Dampier	2.00	.90
☐ 27 Reggie Miller	1.00	.45
☐ 28 Loy Vaught	.60	.25
☐ 29 Lorenzen Wright	2.00	.90
☐ 30 Kobe Bryant	50.00	22.00
☐ 31 Eddie Jones	2.00	.90
☐ 32 Shaquille O'Neal	4.00	1.80
☐ 33 Nick Van Exel	1.00	.45
☐ 34 Tim Hardaway	1.25	.55
☐ 35 Jamal Mashburn	.60	.25

☐ 36 Alonzo Mourning	1.00	.45
☐ 37 Ray Allen	8.00	3.60
☐ 38 Vin Baker	2.00	.90
☐ 39 Glenn Robinson	1.00	.45
☐ 40 Kevin Garnett	6.00	2.70
☐ 41 Tom Gugliotta	1.00	.45
☐ 42 Stephon Marbury	15.00	6.75
☐ 43 Kendall Gill	.60	.25
☐ 44 Jim Jackson	.60	.25
☐ 45 Kerry Kittles	5.00	2.20
☐ 46 Patrick Ewing	1.00	.45
☐ 47 Larry Johnson	.60	.25
☐ 48 John Wallace	3.00	1.35
☐ 49 Nick Anderson	.50	.23
☐ 50 Horace Grant	.60	.25
☐ 51 Anfernee Hardaway	4.00	1.80
☐ 52 Derrick Coleman	.60	.25
☐ 53 Allen Iverson	15.00	6.75
☐ 54 Jerry Stackhouse	1.25	.55
☐ 55 Cedric Ceballos	.50	.23
☐ 56 Kevin Johnson	.60	.25
☐ 57 Jason Kidd	2.00	.90
☐ 58 Clifford Robinson	.50	.23
☐ 59 Arvydas Sabonis	.60	.25
☐ 60 Rasheed Wallace	.60	.25
☐ 61 Mahmoud Abdul-Rauf	.50	.23
☐ 62 Brian Grant	.50	.23
☐ 63 Mitch Richmond	1.00	.45
☐ 64 Sean Elliott	.50	.23
☐ 65 David Robinson	1.50	.70
☐ 66 Dominique Wilkins	1.00	.45
☐ 67 Shawn Kemp	3.00	1.35
☐ 68 Gary Payton	1.50	.70
☐ 69 Detlef Schrempf	.60	.25
☐ 70 Marcus Camby	4.00	1.80
☐ 71 Damon Stoudamire	2.50	1.10
☐ 72 Walt Williams	.50	.23
☐ 73 Shandon Anderson	2.50	1.10
☐ 74 Karl Malone	1.00	.70
☐ 75 John Stockton	1.00	.45
☐ 76 Shareef Abdur-Rahim	12.00	5.50
☐ 77 Bryant Reeves	.60	.25
☐ 78 Roy Rogers	1.25	.55
☐ 79 Juwan Howard	1.25	.55
☐ 80 Chris Webber	2.50	1.10
☐ 81 Checklist	.25	.11
☐ 82 Checklist	.25	.11
☐ NNO Grant Hill Blow-Up/3000	40.00	18.00
☐ NNO Grant Hill Promo	5.00	2.20
☐ NNO Grant Hill Emerald Exchange	400.00	180.00

1996-97 SkyBox E-X2000 Credentials

Randomly inserted in packs, this 80-card set is a parallel to the basic set. Numbered out of 499, these cards feature an alternate foil and background image. The

---

cards are considered Condition Sensitive due to the easy nature of damaging the cards.

	MINT	NRMT
COMPLETE SET (80)	2500.00	1100.00
COMMON CARD (1-80)	10.00	4.50
SEMISTARS	15.00	6.75
UNLISTED STARS	25.00	11.00
RANDOM INSERTS IN PACKS		
STATED PRINT RUN 499 SERIAL #'d SETS		
CONDITION SENSITIVE SET		

☐ 1 Christian Laettner	15.00	6.75
☐ 2 Dikembe Mutombo	15.00	6.75
☐ 3 Steve Smith	15.00	6.75
☐ 4 Antoine Walker	150.00	70.00
☐ 5 David Wesley	10.00	4.50
☐ 6 Tony Delk	25.00	11.00
☐ 7 Anthony Mason	15.00	6.75
☐ 8 Glen Rice	25.00	11.00
☐ 9 Michael Jordan	350.00	160.00
☐ 10 Scottie Pippen	75.00	34.00
☐ 11 Dennis Rodman	100.00	45.00
☐ 12 Terrell Brandon	25.00	11.00
☐ 13 Chris Mills	10.00	4.50
☐ 14 Shawn Bradley	10.00	4.50
☐ 15 Michael Finley	30.00	13.50
☐ 16 Dale Ellis	10.00	4.50
☐ 17 Antonio McDyess	40.00	18.00
☐ 18 Joe Dumars	25.00	11.00
☐ 19 Grant Hill	150.00	70.00
☐ 20 Chris Mullin	25.00	11.00
☐ 21 Joe Smith	30.00	13.50
☐ 22 Latrell Sprewell	15.00	6.75
☐ 23 Charles Barkley	40.00	18.00
☐ 24 Clyde Drexler	30.00	13.50
☐ 25 Hakeem Olajuwon	50.00	22.00
☐ 26 Erick Dampier	25.00	11.00
☐ 27 Reggie Miller	25.00	11.00
☐ 28 Loy Vaught	15.00	6.75
☐ 29 Lorenzen Wright	25.00	11.00
☐ 30 Kobe Bryant	200.00	90.00
☐ 31 Eddie Jones	50.00	22.00
☐ 32 Shaquille O'Neal	100.00	45.00
☐ 33 Nick Van Exel	25.00	11.00
☐ 34 Tim Hardaway	30.00	13.50
☐ 35 Jamal Mashburn	15.00	6.75
☐ 36 Alonzo Mourning	25.00	11.00
☐ 37 Ray Allen	40.00	18.00
☐ 38 Vin Baker	50.00	22.00
☐ 39 Glenn Robinson	25.00	11.00
☐ 40 Kevin Garnett	150.00	70.00
☐ 41 Tom Gugliotta	25.00	11.00
☐ 42 Stephon Marbury	125.00	55.00
☐ 43 Kendall Gill	15.00	6.75
☐ 44 Jim Jackson	15.00	6.75
☐ 45 Kerry Kittles	30.00	13.50
☐ 46 Patrick Ewing	25.00	11.00
☐ 47 Larry Johnson	15.00	6.75
☐ 48 John Wallace	25.00	11.00
☐ 49 Nick Anderson	10.00	4.50
☐ 50 Horace Grant	15.00	6.75
☐ 51 Anfernee Hardaway	100.00	45.00
☐ 52 Derrick Coleman	15.00	6.75
☐ 53 Allen Iverson	125.00	55.00
☐ 54 Jerry Stackhouse	30.00	13.50
☐ 55 Cedric Ceballos	10.00	4.50
☐ 56 Kevin Johnson	15.00	6.75
☐ 57 Jason Kidd	50.00	22.00
☐ 58 Clifford Robinson	10.00	4.50
☐ 59 Arvydas Sabonis	15.00	6.75
☐ 60 Rasheed Wallace	15.00	6.75
☐ 61 Mahmoud Abdul-Rauf	10.00	4.50
☐ 62 Brian Grant	10.00	4.50
☐ 63 Mitch Richmond	25.00	11.00
☐ 64 Sean Elliott	10.00	4.50
☐ 65 David Robinson	40.00	18.00
☐ 66 Dominique Wilkins	25.00	11.00
☐ 67 Shawn Kemp	75.00	34.00
☐ 68 Gary Payton	40.00	18.00
☐ 69 Detlef Schrempf	15.00	6.75
☐ 70 Marcus Camby	30.00	13.50
☐ 71 Damon Stoudamire	60.00	27.00
☐ 72 Walt Williams	10.00	4.50
☐ 73 Shandon Anderson	25.00	11.00
☐ 74 Karl Malone	40.00	18.00
☐ 75 John Stockton	25.00	11.00
☐ 76 Shareef Abdur-Rahim	75.00	34.00
☐ 77 Bryant Reeves	15.00	6.75
☐ 78 Roy Rogers	10.00	4.50
☐ 79 Juwan Howard	30.00	13.50
☐ 80 Chris Webber	60.00	27.00

1996-97 SkyBox E-X2000 A Cut Above

Randomly inserted in packs at a rate of one in 288, this 10-card set features a sawblade die cut at the top of the card.

	MINT	NRMT
COMPLETE SET (10)	600.00	275.00
COMMON CARD (1-10)	15.00	6.75
STATED ODDS 1:288		

☐ 1 Kevin Garnett	80.00	36.00
☐ 2 Anfernee Hardaway	50.00	22.00
☐ 3 Grant Hill	80.00	36.00
☐ 4 Allen Iverson	60.00	27.00
☐ 5 Michael Jordan	200.00	90.00
☐ 6 Shawn Kemp	40.00	18.00
☐ 7 Hakeem Olajuwon	25.00	11.00
☐ 8 Shaquille O'Neal	50.00	22.00
☐ 9 Glenn Robinson	15.00	6.75
☐ 10 Dennis Rodman	50.00	22.00

1996-97 SkyBox E-X2000 Net Assets

Randomly inserted in packs at a rate of one in 20, this 20-card

set features a precision cut net in the background of the card.

	MINT	NRMT
COMPLETE SET (20)	250.00	110.00
COMMON CARD (1-20)	3.00	1.35
SEMISTARS	5.00	2.20
STATED ODDS 1:20		

		MINT	NRMT
☐ 1	Ray Allen	8.00	3.60
☐ 2	Charles Barkley	8.00	3.60
☐ 3	Patrick Ewing	5.00	2.20
☐ 4	Kevin Garnett	30.00	13.50
☐ 5	Anfernee Hardaway	20.00	9.00
☐ 6	Grant Hill	30.00	13.50
☐ 7	Allen Iverson	25.00	11.00
☐ 8	Michael Jordan	60.00	27.00
☐ 9	Jason Kidd	10.00	4.50
☐ 10	Kerry Kittles	6.00	2.70
☐ 11	Karl Malone	8.00	3.60
☐ 12	Alonzo Mourning	5.00	2.20
☐ 13	Shaquille O'Neal	20.00	9.00
☐ 14	Gary Payton	8.00	3.60
☐ 15	Bryant Reeves	3.00	1.35
☐ 16	David Robinson	8.00	3.60
☐ 17	Dennis Rodman	20.00	9.00
☐ 18	Joe Smith	6.00	2.70
☐ 19	Damon Stoudamire	12.00	5.50
☐ 20	Chris Webber	12.00	5.50

1996-97 SkyBox E-X2000 Star Date 2000

Randomly inserted in packs at a rate of one in 9, this 15-card set features many of the players from the 1996-97 rookie class on a futuristic outer space background.

	MINT	NRMT
COMPLETE SET (15)	80.00	36.00
COMMON CARD (1-15)	1.50	.70
STATED ODDS 1:9		

		MINT	NRMT
☐ 1	Shareef Abdur-Rahim	8.00	3.60
☐ 2	Ray Allen	4.00	1.80
☐ 3	Kobe Bryant	20.00	9.00
☐ 4	Marcus Camby	3.00	1.35
☐ 5	Erick Dampier	1.50	.70
☐ 6	Juwan Howard	3.00	1.35
☐ 7	Allen Iverson	12.00	5.50
☐ 8	Jason Kidd	5.00	2.20
☐ 9	Kerry Kittles	3.00	1.35
☐ 10	Stephon Marbury	12.00	5.50
☐ 11	Jamal Mashburn	1.50	.70
☐ 12	Antonio McDyess	4.00	1.80
☐ 13	Joe Smith	3.00	1.35
☐ 14	Damon Stoudamire	6.00	2.70
☐ 15	Antoine Walker	12.00	5.50

1997-98 SkyBox E-X2001

The 1997-98 SkyBox E-X2001 hobby set only was issued in one series totalling 82 cards - 80 basic and two checklists. Each pack contained two cards that carried a suggested retail price of $3.99. The cards feature a semi-clear plastic background with the player die cut over the top of the card. A Grant Hill sample card was also released and is listed at the end of the base set.

	MINT	NRMT
COMPLETE SET (82)	125.00	55.00
COMMON CARD (1-82)	.50	.23
SEMISTARS	.60	.25
UNLISTED STARS	1.00	.45

		MINT	NRMT
☐ 1	Grant Hill	6.00	2.70
☐ 2	Kevin Garnett	6.00	2.70
☐ 3	Allen Iverson	5.00	2.20
☐ 4	Anfernee Hardaway	4.00	1.80
☐ 5	Dennis Rodman	4.00	1.80
☐ 6	Shawn Kemp	3.00	1.35
☐ 7	Shaquille O'Neal	4.00	1.80
☐ 8	Kobe Bryant	10.00	4.50
☐ 9	Michael Jordan	15.00	6.75
☐ 10	Marcus Camby	1.00	.45
☐ 11	Scottie Pippen	3.00	1.35
☐ 12	Antoine Walker	5.00	2.20
☐ 13	Stephon Marbury	5.00	2.20
☐ 14	Shareef Abdur-Rahim	3.00	1.35
☐ 15	Jerry Stackhouse	1.00	.45
☐ 16	Eddie Jones	2.00	.90
☐ 17	Charles Barkley	1.50	.70
☐ 18	David Robinson	1.50	.70
☐ 19	Karl Malone	1.50	.70
☐ 20	Damon Stoudamire	2.00	.90
☐ 21	Patrick Ewing	1.00	.45
☐ 22	Kerry Kittles	1.00	.45
☐ 23	Gary Payton	1.50	.70
☐ 24	Glenn Robinson	1.00	.45
☐ 25	Hakeem Olajuwon	2.00	.90
☐ 26	John Starks	.60	.25
☐ 27	John Stockton	1.00	.45
☐ 28	Vin Baker	2.00	.90
☐ 29	Reggie Miller	1.00	.45
☐ 30	Clyde Drexler	1.25	.55
☐ 31	Alonzo Mourning	1.00	.45
☐ 32	Juwan Howard	1.00	.45
☐ 33	Ray Allen	1.25	.55
☐ 34	Christian Laettner	.60	.25
☐ 35	Terrell Brandon	1.00	.45
☐ 36	Sean Elliott	.50	.23
☐ 37	Rod Strickland	.60	.25
☐ 38	Rodney Rogers	.50	.23
☐ 39	Donyell Marshall	.50	.23
☐ 40	David Wesley	.50	.23
☐ 41	Sam Cassell	.60	.25
☐ 42	Cedric Ceballos	.50	.23
☐ 43	Mahmoud Abdul-Rauf	.50	.23
☐ 44	Rik Smits	.60	.25
☐ 45	Lindsey Hunter	.50	.23
☐ 46	Michael Finley	1.00	.45
☐ 47	Steve Smith	.60	.25
☐ 48	Larry Johnson	.60	.25
☐ 49	Dikembe Mutombo	.60	.25
☐ 50	Tom Gugliotta	1.00	.45
☐ 51	Joe Dumars	1.00	.45
☐ 52	Glen Rice	1.00	.45
☐ 53	Bryant Reeves	.60	.25
☐ 54	Tim Hardaway	1.25	.55
☐ 55	Isaiah Rider	.60	.25
☐ 56	Rasheed Wallace	.60	.25
☐ 57	Jason Kidd	2.00	.90
☐ 58	Joe Smith	1.00	.45
☐ 59	Chris Webber	2.50	1.10
☐ 60	Mitch Richmond	1.00	.45
☐ 61	Antonio McDyess	1.25	.55
☐ 62	Bobby Jackson	4.00	1.80
☐ 63	Derek Anderson	6.00	2.70
☐ 64	Kelvin Cato	2.50	1.10
☐ 65	Jacque Vaughn	3.00	1.35
☐ 66	Tariq Abdul-Wahad	3.00	1.35
☐ 67	Johnny Taylor	1.25	.55
☐ 68	Chris Anstey	2.00	.90
☐ 69	Maurice Taylor	6.00	2.70
☐ 70	Antonio Daniels	5.00	2.20
☐ 71	Chauncey Billups	8.00	3.60
☐ 72	Austin Croshere	2.50	1.10
☐ 73	Brevin Knight	6.00	2.70
☐ 74	Keith Van Horn	20.00	9.00
☐ 75	Tim Duncan	40.00	18.00
☐ 76	Danny Fortson	4.00	1.80
☐ 77	Tim Thomas	12.00	5.50
☐ 78	Tony Battie	4.00	1.80
☐ 79	Tracy McGrady	12.00	5.50
☐ 80	Ron Mercer	15.00	6.75
☐ 81	Checklist (1-82)	.50	.23
☐ 82	Checklist (inserts)	.50	.23
☐ S1	Grant Hill SAMPLE	8.00	3.60

1997-98 SkyBox E-X2001 Essential Credentials Future

Randomly inserted into packs, the Essential Credential Future features multi-tiered serial numbering cards. These cards are distinguished by their orange/pink glow edge stock. Each card is sequentially numbered with the amount of cards being equal to the opposite of their Essential Credentials Now card. For example, card number

1 has 80 serial numbered cards, while card number 80 has only one card. The tougher cards are not priced, but have been listed below for checklisting.

	MINT	NRMT
COMMON CARD (1-80)	400.00	18.00
SEMISTARS	50.00	22.00

RANDOM INSERTS IN PACKS
PRINT RUNS IN PARENTHESIS BELOW

		MINT	NRMT
☐ 1	Grant Hill (80	400.00	180.00
☐ 2	Kevin Garnett (79)	400.00	180.00
☐ 3	Allen Iverson (78)	300.00	135.00
☐ 4	A.Hardaway (77)	250.00	110.00
☐ 5	Dennis Rodman (76)	250.00	110.00
☐ 6	Shawn Kemp (75)	200.00	90.00
☐ 7	Shaquille O'Neal (74)	250.00	110.00
☐ 8	Kobe Bryant (73)	600.00	275.00
☐ 9	Michael Jordan (72)	1200.00	550.00
☐ 10	Marcus Camby (71)	60.00	27.00
☐ 11	Scottie Pippen (70)	200.00	90.00
☐ 12	Antoine Walker (69)	300.00	135.00
☐ 13	Stephon Marbury (68)	300.00	135.00
☐ 14	S.Abdur-Rahim (67)	200.00	90.00
☐ 15	Jerry Stackhouse (66)	60.00	27.00
☐ 16	Eddie Jones (65)	125.00	55.00
☐ 17	Charles Barkley (64)	100.00	45.00
☐ 18	David Robinson (63)	100.00	45.00
☐ 19	Karl Malone (62)	100.00	45.00
☐ 20	D.Stoudamire (61)	125.00	55.00
☐ 21	Patrick Ewing (60)	80.00	36.00
☐ 22	Kerry Kittles (59)	80.00	36.00
☐ 23	Gary Payton (58)	125.00	55.00
☐ 24	Glenn Robinson (57)	60.00	27.00
☐ 25	Hakeem Olajuwon (56)	150.00	70.00
☐ 26	John Starks (55)	50.00	22.00
☐ 27	John Stockton (54)	80.00	36.00
☐ 28	Vin Baker (53)	150.00	70.00
☐ 29	Reggie Miller (52)	80.00	36.00
☐ 30	Clyde Drexler (51)	100.00	45.00
☐ 31	Alonzo Mourning (50)	80.00	36.00
☐ 32	Juwan Howard (49)	80.00	36.00
☐ 33	Ray Allen (48)	100.00	45.00
☐ 34	Christian Laettner (47)	50.00	22.00
☐ 35	Terrell Brandon (46)	60.00	27.00
☐ 36	Sean Elliott (45)	40.00	18.00
☐ 37	Rod Strickland (44)	50.00	22.00
☐ 38	Rodney Rogers (43)	40.00	18.00
☐ 39	Donyell Marshall (42)	40.00	18.00
☐ 40	David Wesley (41)	40.00	18.00
☐ 41	Sam Cassell (40)	60.00	27.00
☐ 42	Cedric Ceballos (39)	40.00	18.00
☐ 43	M.Abdul-Rauf (38)	40.00	18.00
☐ 44	Rik Smits (37)	60.00	27.00
☐ 45	Lindsey Hunter (36)	60.00	27.00
☐ 46	Michael Finley (35)	100.00	45.00
☐ 47	Steve Smith (34)	60.00	27.00
☐ 48	Larry Johnson (33)	60.00	27.00
☐ 49	Dikembe Mutombo (32)	60.00	27.00
☐ 50	Tom Gugliotta (31)	60.00	27.00
☐ 51	Joe Dumars (30)	80.00	36.00
☐ 52	Glen Rice (29)	125.00	55.00
☐ 53	Bryant Reeves (28)	80.00	36.00
☐ 54	Tim Hardaway (27)	160.00	70.00
☐ 55	Isaiah Rider (26)	80.00	36.00
☐ 56	Rasheed Wallace (25)	80.00	36.00
☐ 57	Jason Kidd (24)	300.00	135.00
☐ 58	Joe Smith (23)	125.00	55.00
☐ 59	Chris Webber (22)	350.00	160.00
☐ 60	Mitch Richmond (21)	150.00	70.00
☐ 61	Antonio McDyess (20)	200.00	90.00
☐ 62	Bobby Jackson (19)	150.00	70.00
☐ 63	Derek Anderson (18)	250.00	110.00
☐ 64	Kelvin Cato (17)	100.00	45.00
☐ 65	Jacque Vaughn (16)	125.00	55.00
☐ 66	Tariq Abdul-Wahad (15)		
☐ 67	Johnny Taylor (14)		
☐ 68	Chris Anstey (13)		
☐ 69	Maurice Taylor (12)		
☐ 70	Antonio Daniels (11)		
☐ 71	Chauncey Billups (10)		
☐ 72	Austin Croshere (9)		
☐ 73	Brevin Knight (8)		
☐ 74	Keith Van Horn (7)		
☐ 75	Tim Duncan (6)		
☐ 76	Danny Fortson (5)		
☐ 77	Tim Thomas (4)		
☐ 78	Tony Battle (3)		
☐ 79	Tracy McGrady (2)		
☐ 80	Ron Mercer (1)		

1997-98 SkyBox E-X2001 Essential Credentials Now

Randomly inserted into packs, the Essential Credential Now features multi-tiered serial numbering cards. These cards are distinguished by their yellow/green glow edge stock. Each card is sequentially numbered with the amount of cards being equal to the player's card number. For example, card number 1 has only one card and card number 80 has eighty serial number cards. The tougher cards have not been priced, but are listed below for checklisting.

	MINT	NRMT
COMMON CARD (1-80)	40.00	18.00
SEMISTARS	50.00	22.00

RANDOM INSERTS IN PACKS
PRINT RUNS IN PARENTHESIS BELOW

		MINT	NRMT
☐ 1	Grant Hill (1)		
☐ 2	Kevin Garnett (2)		
☐ 3	Allen Iverson (3)		
☐ 4	Anfernee Hardaway (4)		
☐ 5	Dennis Rodman (5)		
☐ 6	Shawn Kemp (6)		
☐ 7	Shaquille O'Neal (7)		
☐ 8	Kobe Bryant (8)		
☐ 9	Michael Jordan (9)		
☐ 10	Marcus Camby (10)		
☐ 11	Scottie Pippen (11)		
☐ 12	Antoine Walker (12)		
☐ 13	Stephon Marbury (13)		
☐ 14	Shareef Abdur-Rahim (14)		
☐ 15	Jerry Stackhouse (15)		
☐ 16	Eddie Jones (16)	400.00	180.00
☐ 17	Charles Barkley (17)	300.00	135.00
☐ 18	David Robinson (18)	300.00	135.00
☐ 19	Karl Malone (19)	300.00	135.00
☐ 20	D.Stoudamire (20)	300.00	135.00
☐ 21	Patrick Ewing (21)	150.00	70.00
☐ 22	Kerry Kittles (22)	150.00	70.00
☐ 23	Gary Payton (23)	200.00	90.00
☐ 24	Glenn Robinson (24)	100.00	45.00
☐ 25	H.Olajuwon (25)	250.00	110.00
☐ 26	John Starks (26)	60.00	27.00
☐ 27	John Stockton (27)	150.00	70.00
☐ 28	Vin Baker (28)	250.00	110.00
☐ 29	Reggie Miller (29)	160.00	70.00
☐ 30	Clyde Drexler (30)	160.00	70.00
☐ 31	Alonzo Mourning (31)	100.00	45.00
☐ 32	Juwan Howard (32)	100.00	45.00
☐ 33	Ray Allen (33)	125.00	55.00
☐ 34	Christian Laettner (34)	60.00	27.00
☐ 35	Terrell Brandon (35)	80.00	36.00
☐ 36	Sean Elliott (36)	40.00	18.00
☐ 37	Rod Strickland (37)	60.00	27.00
☐ 38	Rodney Rogers (38)	40.00	18.00
☐ 39	Donyell Marshall (39)	60.00	27.00
☐ 40	David Wesley (40)	40.00	18.00
☐ 41	Sam Cassell (41)	50.00	22.00
☐ 42	Cedric Ceballos (42)	40.00	18.00
☐ 43	M.Abdul-Rauf (43)	40.00	18.00
☐ 44	Rik Smits (44)	50.00	22.00
☐ 45	Lindsey Hunter (45)	40.00	18.00
☐ 46	Michael Finley (46)	80.00	36.00
☐ 47	Steve Smith (47)	50.00	22.00
☐ 48	Larry Johnson (48)	50.00	22.00
☐ 49	Dikembe Mutombo (49)	50.00	22.00
☐ 50	Tom Gugliotta (50)	50.00	22.00
☐ 51	Joe Dumars (51)	50.00	22.00
☐ 52	Glen Rice (52)	80.00	36.00
☐ 53	Bryant Reeves (53)	50.00	22.00
☐ 54	Tim Hardaway (54)	110.00	50.00
☐ 55	Isaiah Rider (55)	50.00	22.00
☐ 56	Rasheed Wallace (56)	50.00	22.00
☐ 57	Jason Kidd (57)	150.00	70.00
☐ 58	Joe Smith (58)	80.00	36.00
☐ 59	Chris Webber (59)	200.00	90.00
☐ 60	Mitch Richmond (60)	80.00	36.00
☐ 61	Antonio McDyess (61)	100.00	45.00
☐ 62	Bobby Jackson (62)	60.00	27.00
☐ 63	Derek Anderson (63)	100.00	45.00
☐ 64	Kelvin Cato (64)	50.00	22.00
☐ 65	Jacque Vaughn (65)	50.00	22.00
☐ 66	Tariq Abdul-Wahad (66)	50.00	22.00
☐ 67	Johnny Taylor (67)	40.00	18.00
☐ 68	Chris Anstey (68)	50.00	22.00
☐ 69	Maurice Taylor (69)	100.00	45.00
☐ 70	Antonio Daniels (70)	80.00	36.00
☐ 71	Chauncey Billups (71)	125.00	55.00
☐ 72	Austin Croshere (72)	50.00	22.00
☐ 73	Brevin Knight (73)	100.00	45.00
☐ 74	Keith Van Horn (74)	350.00	160.00
☐ 75	Tim Duncan (75)	400.00	180.00
☐ 76	Danny Fortson (76)	60.00	27.00
☐ 77	Tim Thomas (77)	200.00	90.00
☐ 78	Tony Battle (78)	60.00	27.00
☐ 79	Tracy McGrady (79)	200.00	90.00
☐ 80	Ron Mercer (80)	250.00	110.00

1997-98 SkyBox E-X2001 Gravity Denied

Randomly inserted into packs at a rate of one in 24, this 20-card set features two die cut pieces, that form an "aerodynamic"

photo of these NBA players in three separate windows.

	MINT	NRMT
COMPLETE SET (20)	200.00	90.00
COMMON CARD (1-20)	3.00	1.35
STATED ODDS 1:24		
☐ 1 Vin Baker	6.00	2.70
☐ 2 Charles Barkley	5.00	2.20
☐ 3 Tony Battie	3.00	1.35
☐ 4 Kobe Bryant	25.00	11.00
☐ 5 Patrick Ewing	3.00	1.35
☐ 6 Kevin Garnett	20.00	9.00
☐ 7 Anfernee Hardaway	12.00	5.50
☐ 8 Grant Hill	20.00	9.00
☐ 9 Michael Jordan	50.00	22.00
☐ 10 Shawn Kemp	10.00	4.50
☐ 11 Kerry Kittles	3.00	1.35
☐ 12 Karl Malone	5.00	2.20
☐ 13 Tracy McGrady	10.00	4.50
☐ 14 Hakeem Olajuwon	6.00	2.70
☐ 15 Shaquille O'Neal	12.00	5.50
☐ 16 Scottie Pippen	10.00	4.50
☐ 17 Jerry Stackhouse	3.00	1.35
☐ 18 Tim Thomas	10.00	4.50
☐ 19 Antoine Walker	15.00	6.75
☐ 20 Chris Webber	8.00	3.60

1997-98 SkyBox E-X2001 Jam-Balaya

Randomly inserted into packs at a rate of one in 720, this 15-card set features the NBA's best jammers on a die cut background in the shape of an oval.

	MINT	NRMT
COMPLETE SET (15)	1500.00	700.00
COMMON CARD (1-15)	50.00	22.00
STATED ODDS 1:720		
☐ 1 Allen Iverson	125.00	55.00
☐ 2 Anfernee Hardaway	100.00	45.00
☐ 3 Dennis Rodman	100.00	45.00
☐ 4 Grant Hill	150.00	70.00
☐ 5 Kevin Garnett	150.00	70.00
☐ 6 Michael Jordan	350.00	160.00
☐ 7 Shaquille O'Neal	100.00	45.00
☐ 8 Tim Duncan	150.00	70.00
☐ 9 Keith Van Horn	125.00	55.00
☐ 10 Stephon Marbury	125.00	55.00
☐ 11 Shareef Abdur-Rahim	80.00	36.00
☐ 12 Kobe Bryant	200.00	90.00
☐ 13 Damon Stoudamire	50.00	22.00
☐ 14 Scottie Pippen	80.00	36.00
☐ 15 Eddie Jones	50.00	22.00

1997-98 SkyBox E-X2001 Star Date 2001

Randomly inserted into packs at a rate of one in 12, this 15-card set features some of the best young stars in the NBA. The cards have a die cut "galaxy" background with silver rainbow holofoil.

	MINT	NRMT
COMPLETE SET (15)	80.00	36.00
COMMON CARD (1-15)	1.50	.70
SEMISTARS	2.00	.90
UNLISTED STARS	3.00	1.35
STATED ODDS 1:12		
☐ 1 Shareef Abdur-Rahim	5.00	2.20
☐ 2 Tony Battie	3.00	1.35
☐ 3 Kobe Bryant	12.00	5.50
☐ 4 Antonio Daniels	4.00	1.80
☐ 5 Tim Duncan	20.00	9.00
☐ 6 Adonal Foyle	2.00	.90
☐ 7 Allen Iverson	8.00	3.60
☐ 8 Matt Maloney	1.50	.70
☐ 9 Stephon Marbury	8.00	3.60
☐ 10 Tracy McGrady	10.00	4.50
☐ 11 Ron Mercer	12.00	5.50
☐ 12 Tim Thomas	10.00	4.50
☐ 13 Keith Van Horn	15.00	6.75
☐ 14 Jacque Vaughn	2.00	.90
☐ 15 Antoine Walker	8.00	3.60

1995-96 SkyBox E-XL

The 1995-96 Skybox E-XL set was issued in one series totalling 100 cards. Only the top veterans and rookies in the

league were selected for inclusion within this premium brand set. The 6-card packs retailed for $4.99 each. Cards are numbered alphabetically within teams. The only subset is Untouchable (91-99). The product picks up where the 1994-95 SkyBox Emotion issue left off. Each player card features silhouetted action photo over a multi-colored background, framed by one of five different shaped die cut window designs. Only the player image and multi-colored backgrounds are UV coated. The rest of the card is non-UV coated, giving the card a unique look and feel. A non-numbered Grant Hill promo card was issued to preview the set.

	MINT	NRMT
COMPLETE SET (100)	50.00	22.00
COMMON CARD (1-100)	.25	.11
SEMISTARS	.40	.18
UNLISTED STARS	.60	.25
COMPLETE BLUE SET (100)	100.00	45.00
COMMON BLUE (1-100)	.30	.14
*BLUE STARS:1.25X TO 2.5X HI COLUMN		
*BLUE RCs: 1X TO 2X HI		
ONE OR MORE BLUES PER PACK		
☐ 1 Stacey Augmon	.25	.11
☐ 2 Mookie Blaylock	.40	.18
☐ 3 Christian Laettner	.40	.18
☐ 4 Dana Barros	.25	.11
☐ 5 Dino Radja	.25	.11
☐ 6 Eric Williams	.40	.18
☐ 7 Kenny Anderson	.40	.18
☐ 8 Larry Johnson	.40	.18
☐ 9 Glen Rice	.60	.25
☐ 10 Michael Jordan	8.00	3.60
☐ 11 Toni Kukoc	.40	.18
☐ 12 Scottie Pippen	2.00	.90
☐ 13 Dennis Rodman	4.00	1.80
☐ 14 Terrell Brandon	.60	.25
☐ 15 Bobby Phills	.25	.11
☐ 16 Bob Sura	.40	.18
☐ 17 Jim Jackson	.40	.18
☐ 18 Jason Kidd	1.50	.70
☐ 19 Jamal Mashburn	.40	.18
☐ 20 Mahmoud Abdul-Rauf	.25	.11
☐ 21 Antonio McDyess	3.00	1.35
☐ 22 Dikembe Mutombo	.40	.18
☐ 23 Joe Dumars	.60	.25
☐ 24 Grant Hill	4.00	1.80
☐ 25 Allan Houston	.40	.18
☐ 26 Joe Smith	2.50	1.10
☐ 27 Latrell Sprewell	.40	.18
☐ 28 Kevin Willis	.25	.11
☐ 29 Sam Cassell	.40	.18
☐ 30 Clyde Drexler	.75	.35
☐ 31 Robert Horry	.25	.11
☐ 32 Hakeem Olajuwon	1.25	.55
☐ 33 Derrick McKey	.25	.11
☐ 34 Reggie Miller	.60	.25
☐ 35 Rik Smits	.40	.18
☐ 36 Brent Barry	.60	.25
☐ 37 Loy Vaught	.25	.11
☐ 38 Brian Williams	.25	.11
☐ 39 Cedric Ceballos	.25	.11
☐ 40 Magic Johnson	2.00	.90
☐ 41 Nick Van Exel	.60	.25
☐ 42 Tim Hardaway	.75	.35
☐ 43 Alonzo Mourning	.60	.25
☐ 44 Kurt Thomas	.40	.18
☐ 45 Walt Williams	.25	.11
☐ 46 Vin Baker	1.25	.55

☐ 47 Shawn Respert	.25	.11
☐ 48 Glenn Robinson	.75	.35
☐ 49 Kevin Garnett	8.00	3.60
☐ 50 Tom Gugliotta	.60	.25
☐ 51 Isaiah Rider	.40	.18
☐ 52 Shawn Bradley	.40	.18
☐ 53 Chris Childs	.25	.11
☐ 54 Ed O'Bannon	.25	.11
☐ 55 Patrick Ewing	.60	.25
☐ 56 Anthony Mason	.40	.18
☐ 57 Charles Oakley	.25	.11
☐ 58 Horace Grant	.40	.18
☐ 59 Anfernee Hardaway	2.50	1.10
☐ 60 Shaquille O'Neal	2.50	1.10
☐ 61 Derrick Coleman	.40	.18
☐ 62 Jerry Stackhouse	2.50	1.10
☐ 63 Clarence Weatherspoon	.25	.11
☐ 64 Charles Barkley	1.00	.45
☐ 65 Michael Finley	2.50	1.10
☐ 66 Kevin Johnson	.40	.18
☐ 67 Clifford Robinson	.25	.11
☐ 68 Arvydas Sabonis	1.25	.55
☐ 69 Rod Strickland	.40	.18
☐ 70 Tyus Edney	.25	.11
☐ 71 Billy Owens	.25	.11
☐ 72 Mitch Richmond	.60	.25
☐ 73 Sean Elliott	.25	.11
☐ 74 Avery Johnson	.25	.11
☐ 75 David Robinson	1.00	.45
☐ 76 Shawn Kemp	2.00	.90
☐ 77 Gary Payton	1.00	.45
☐ 78 Detlef Schrempf	.40	.18
☐ 79 Tracy Murray	.25	.11
☐ 80 Damon Stoudamire	5.00	2.20
☐ 81 Sharone Wright	.25	.11
☐ 82 Jeff Hornacek	.40	.18
☐ 83 Karl Malone	1.00	.45
☐ 84 John Stockton	.60	.25
☐ 85 Greg Anthony	.25	.11
☐ 86 Bryant Reeves	1.50	.70
☐ 87 Byron Scott	.25	.11
☐ 88 Juwan Howard	1.00	.45
☐ 89 Gheorghe Muresan	.25	.11
☐ 90 Rasheed Wallace	1.50	.70
☐ 91 Steve Smith UNT	.25	.11
☐ 92 Dikembe Mutombo UNT	.25	.11
☐ 93 Brent Barry UNT	.40	.18
☐ 94 Glenn Robinson UNT	.60	.25
☐ 95 Armon Gilliam UNT	.25	.11
☐ 96 Nick Anderson UNT	.25	.11
☐ 97 Gary Trent UNT	.25	.11
☐ 98 Brian Grant UNT	.25	.11
☐ 99 Bryant Reeves UNT	.60	.25
☐ 100 Checklist	.25	.11
☐ NNO Grant Hill Promo	5.00	2.20

1995-96 SkyBox E-XL A Cut Above

Randomly inserted in hobby and retail packs at a rate of one in 130, this 10-card die-cut insert set features a selection of the NBA's elite stars. Each card front features a unique framing

of two different, die-cut photos surrounded by a blue border. Card backs contain an action photo and brief commentary and are numbered as "X of 10".

	MINT	NRMT
COMPLETE SET (10)	150.00	70.00
COMMON CARD (1-10)	12.00	5.50
STATED ODDS 1:130		
☐ 1 Scottie Pippen	30.00	13.50
☐ 2 Jason Kidd	20.00	9.00
☐ 3 Grant Hill	50.00	22.00
☐ 4 Joe Smith	12.00	5.50
☐ 5 Hakeem Olajuwon	12.00	5.50
☐ 6 Magic Johnson	15.00	6.75
☐ 7 Shaquille O'Neal	30.00	13.50
☐ 8 Jerry Stackhouse	12.00	5.50
☐ 9 Charles Barkley	12.00	5.50
☐ 10 David Robinson	12.00	5.50

1995-96 SkyBox E-XL Natural Born Thrillers

Randomly inserted in hobby and retail packs at a rate of one in 48, this 10-card set highlights a selection of crowd-pleasing players who do incredible things on the court. Each card features a multi-layered die-cut design. Card backs are black and textured with the player's name and a brief commentary in gold foil. The cards are numbered as "X of 10". A non-numbered Jerry Stackhouse card was sent out to preview the set.

	MINT	NRMT
COMPLETE SET (10)	250.00	110.00
COMMON CARD (1-10)	8.00	3.60
STATED ODDS 1:48		
☐ 1 Michael Jordan	100.00	45.00
☐ 2 Antonio McDyess	15.00	6.75
☐ 3 Grant Hill	40.00	18.00
☐ 4 Clyde Drexler	8.00	3.60
☐ 5 Kevin Garnett	40.00	18.00
☐ 6 Anfernee Hardaway	25.00	11.00
☐ 7 Jerry Stackhouse	12.00	5.50
☐ 8 Michael Finley	12.00	5.50
☐ 9 Shawn Kemp	20.00	9.00
☐ 10 Damon Stoudamire	25.00	11.00
☐ NNO J.Stackhouse Promo	3.00	1.35

1995-96 SkyBox E-XL No Boundaries

Randomly inserted exclusively in hobby packs at a rate of one in 18, this 10-card set features players that can bust open a game on a special die cut designed card. Card fronts have metallic backgrounds with an action shot of the player and the player's name which is written in gold foil. Card backs feature a head shot of the player in a die-cut circle. The cards are numbered as "X of 10".

	MINT	NRMT
COMPLETE SET (10)	80.00	36.00
COMMON CARD (1-10)	4.00	1.80
STATED ODDS 1:18 HOBBY		
☐ 1 Michael Jordan	50.00	22.00
☐ 2 Antonio McDyess	10.00	4.50
☐ 3 Hakeem Olajuwon	8.00	3.60
☐ 4 Magic Johnson	12.00	5.50
☐ 5 Vin Baker	8.00	3.60
☐ 6 Patrick Ewing	4.00	1.80
☐ 7 Anfernee Hardaway	15.00	6.75
☐ 8 Jerry Stackhouse	8.00	3.60
☐ 9 Gary Payton	6.00	2.70
☐ 10 Damon Stoudamire	15.00	6.75

1995-96 SkyBox E-XL Unstoppable

Randomly inserted in hobby and retail packs at a rate of one in 6, this 20-card set features 10 players who are "unstoppable" inside the paint and 10 who are "unstoppable" from outside. Card fronts have a large action shot of the player with the player's name written vertically along the border. Card backs have a textured background photo with a brief commentary on the player. The cards are numbered as "X of 20".

	MINT	NRMT
COMPLETE SET (20)	50.00	22.00
COMMON CARD (1-20)	1.25	.55
SEMISTARS	1.50	.70
UNLISTED STARS	2.50	1.10
STATED ODDS 1:6		

□ 1 Alan Henderson	2.50	1.10
□ 2 Glen Rice	2.50	1.10
□ 3 Scottie Pippen	8.00	3.60
□ 4 Dennis Rodman	12.00	5.50
□ 5 Terrell Brandon	2.50	1.10
□ 6 Jason Kidd	6.00	2.70
□ 7 Grant Hill	15.00	6.75
□ 8 Joe Smith	5.00	2.20
□ 9 Sam Cassell	1.50	.70
□ 10 Reggie Miller	2.50	1.10
□ 11 Alonzo Mourning	2.50	1.10
□ 12 Shaquille O'Neal	10.00	4.50
□ 13 Charles Barkley	4.00	1.80
□ 14 Clifford Robinson	1.25	.55
□ 15 Sean Elliott	1.25	.55
□ 16 David Robinson	4.00	1.80
□ 17 Shawn Kemp	8.00	3.60
□ 18 Karl Malone	4.00	1.80
□ 19 John Stockton	2.50	1.10
□ 20 Juwan Howard	4.00	1.80

1996-97 SkyBox
Z-Force

The inaugural edtion of SkyBox Z-Force has a total of 200 cards. The eight-card hobby and retail packs carry a suggested retail price of $2.49 each. Card fronts contain an action shot of the player against an "explosive-type" background. The player's name is in block letters at the top of the card and the SkyBox Z-Force logo is outlined in gold foil along the bottom right of the card. Card backs contain a hardwood floor design in the

background with a player shot over it. Statistical and biographical information is also located on the back. The cards are grouped alphabetically within teams. The series two cards feature the same graphics as series one, but a thicker card stock. A Grant Hill Total Z card was inserted in series two packs at a rate of one in 900 packs. The card is a one-shot leather card. Series two packs also featured a 10-card redemption for a full set of the 1996-97 SkyBox Autographics program. The tough card number was card #5. Also, a non-numbered two-card promo sheet was also issued for the first series which features a basic card of Grant Hill and Jerry Stackhouse. For the second series, a Grant Hill promo was released that mirrored his regular issue card bearing the words "Promotion Sample" on the front and back. The two promos are listed below at the end of the set.

	MINT	NRMT
COMPLETE SET (200)	40.00	18.00
COMPLETE SERIES 1 (100)	20.00	9.00
COMPLETE SERIES 2 (100)	20.00	9.00
COMMON CARD (1-100)	.15	.07
COMMON CARD (101-200)	.10	.05
SEMISTARS SER.1	.20	.09
SEMISTARS SER.2	.15	.07
UNLISTED STARS SER.1	.40	.18
UNLISTED STARS SER.2	.30	.14
HILL Z: SER.2 STATED ODDS 1:900		
HOB/RET		
AUTOGRAPHICS LISTED UNDER SKYBOX		

□ 1 Mookie Blaylock	.20	.09
□ 2 Alan Henderson	.15	.07
□ 3 Christian Laettner	.20	.09
□ 4 Steve Smith	.20	.09
□ 5 Rick Fox	.15	.07
□ 6 Dino Radja	.15	.07
□ 7 Eric Williams	.15	.07
□ 8 Muggsy Bogues	.15	.07
□ 9 Larry Johnson	.20	.09
□ 10 Glen Rice	.40	.18
□ 11 Michael Jordan	5.00	2.20
□ 12 Toni Kukoc	.20	.09
□ 13 Scottie Pippen	1.25	.55
□ 14 Dennis Rodman	1.50	.70
□ 15 Terrell Brandon	.40	.18
□ 16 Bobby Phills	.15	.07
□ 17 Bob Sura	.15	.07
□ 18 Jim Jackson	.20	.09
□ 19 Jason Kidd	.75	.35
□ 20 Jamal Mashburn	.20	.09
□ 21 George McCloud	.15	.07
□ 22 Mahmoud Abdul-Rauf	.15	.07
□ 23 Antonio McDyess	.60	.25
□ 24 Dikembe Mutombo	.20	.09
□ 25 Joe Dumars	.40	.18
□ 26 Grant Hill	2.50	1.10
□ 27 Allan Houston	.20	.09
□ 28 Otis Thorpe	.20	.09
□ 29 Chris Mullin	.40	.18
□ 30 Joe Smith	.50	.23
□ 31 Latrell Sprewell	.20	.09
□ 32 Sam Cassell	.20	.09
□ 33 Clyde Drexler	.50	.23

□ 34 Robert Horry	.20	.09
□ 35 Hakeem Olajuwon	.75	.35
□ 36 Travis Best	.15	.07
□ 37 Dale Davis	.15	.07
□ 38 Reggie Miller	.40	.18
□ 39 Rik Smits	.20	.09
□ 40 Brent Barry	.15	.07
□ 41 Loy Vaught	.20	.09
□ 42 Brian Williams	.15	.07
□ 43 Cedric Ceballos	.15	.07
□ 44 Eddie Jones	.75	.35
□ 45 Nick Van Exel	.40	.18
□ 46 Tim Hardaway	.50	.23
□ 47 Alonzo Mourning	.40	.18
□ 48 Kurt Thomas	.15	.07
□ 49 Walt Williams	.15	.07
□ 50 Vin Baker	.75	.35
□ 51 Glenn Robinson	.40	.18
□ 52 Kevin Garnett	2.50	1.10
□ 53 Tom Gugliotta	.40	.18
□ 54 Isaiah Rider	.20	.09
□ 55 Shawn Bradley	.15	.07
□ 56 Chris Childs	.15	.07
□ 57 Jayson Williams	.20	.09
□ 58 Patrick Ewing	.40	.18
□ 59 Anthony Mason	.20	.09
□ 60 Charles Oakley	.15	.07
□ 61 Nick Anderson	.15	.07
□ 62 Horace Grant	.20	.09
□ 63 Anfernee Hardaway	1.50	.70
□ 64 Shaquille O'Neal	1.50	.70
□ 65 Dennis Scott	.15	.07
□ 66 Jerry Stackhouse	.50	.23
□ 67 Clarence Weatherspoon	.15	.07
□ 68 Charles Barkley	.60	.25
□ 69 Michael Finley	.60	.25
□ 70 Kevin Johnson	.20	.09
□ 71 Clifford Robinson	.15	.07
□ 72 Arvydas Sabonis	.20	.09
□ 73 Rod Strickland	.20	.09
□ 74 Tyus Edney	.15	.07
□ 75 Brian Grant	.15	.07
□ 76 Billy Owens	.15	.07
□ 77 Mitch Richmond	.40	.18
□ 78 Vinny Del Negro	.15	.07
□ 79 Sean Elliott	.15	.07
□ 80 Avery Johnson	.15	.07
□ 81 David Robinson	.60	.25
□ 82 Hersey Hawkins	.20	.09
□ 83 Shawn Kemp	1.25	.55
□ 84 Gary Payton	.60	.25
□ 85 Detlef Schrempf	.20	.09
□ 86 Doug Christie	.15	.07
□ 87 Damon Stoudamire	1.00	.45
□ 88 Sharone Wright	.15	.07
□ 89 Jeff Hornacek	.20	.09
□ 90 Karl Malone	.60	.25
□ 91 John Stockton	.40	.18
□ 92 Greg Anthony	.15	.07
□ 93 Bryant Reeves	.20	.09
□ 94 Byron Scott	.20	.09
□ 95 Juwan Howard	.50	.23
□ 96 Gheorghe Muresan	.15	.07
□ 97 Rasheed Wallace	.20	.09
□ 98 Chris Webber	1.00	.45
□ 99 Checklist	.15	.07
□ 100 Checklist	.15	.07
□ 101 Dikembe Mutombo	.10	.05
□ 102 Dee Brown	.10	.05
□ 103 Dell Curry	.10	.05
□ 104 Vlade Divac	.15	.07
□ 105 Anthony Mason	.15	.07
□ 106 Robert Parish	.15	.07
□ 107 Oliver Miller	.10	.05
□ 108 Eric Montross	.10	.05
□ 109 Ervin Johnson	.10	.05
□ 110 Stacey Augmon	.10	.05
□ 111 Charles Barkley	.50	.23
□ 112 Jalen Rose	.10	.05
□ 113 Rodney Rogers	.10	.05
□ 114 Shaquille O'Neal	1.25	.55
□ 115 Dan Majerle	.15	.07
□ 116 Kendall Gill	.15	.07
□ 117 Khalid Reeves	.10	.05
□ 118 Allan Houston	.15	.07
□ 119 Larry Johnson	.15	.07

☐ 120	John Starks	.15	.07
☐ 121	Rony Seikaly	.10	.05
☐ 122	Gerald Wilkins	.10	.05
☐ 123	Michael Cage	.10	.05
☐ 124	Derrick Coleman	.15	.07
☐ 125	Sam Cassell	.15	.07
☐ 126	Danny Manning	.15	.07
☐ 127	Robert Horry	.15	.07
☐ 128	Kenny Anderson	.15	.07
☐ 129	Isaiah Rider	.15	.07
☐ 130	Rasheed Wallace	.15	.07
☐ 131	Mahmoud Abdul-Rauf	.10	.05
☐ 132	Vernon Maxwell	.10	.05
☐ 133	Dominique Wilkins	.30	.14
☐ 134	Hubert Davis	.10	.05
☐ 135	Popeye Jones	.10	.05
☐ 136	Anthony Peeler	.10	.05
☐ 137	Tracy Murray	.10	.05
☐ 138	Rod Strickland	.15	.07
☐ 139	Shareef Abdur-Rahim	2.00	.90
☐ 140	Ray Allen	1.00	.45
☐ 141	Shandon Anderson	.40	.18
☐ 142	Kobe Bryant	6.00	2.70
☐ 143	Marcus Camby	.40	.35
☐ 144	Erick Dampier	.40	.18
☐ 145	Emanual Davis	.10	.05
☐ 146	Tony Delk	.40	.18
☐ 147	Todd Fuller	.10	.05
☐ 148	Darvin Ham	.10	.05
☐ 149	Othella Harrington	.15	.07
☐ 150	Shane Heal	.10	.05
☐ 151	Allen Iverson	3.00	1.35
☐ 152	Dontae' Jones	.10	.05
☐ 153	Kerry Kittles	.75	.35
☐ 154	Priest Lauderdale	.10	.05
☐ 155	Matt Maloney	.50	.23
☐ 156	Stephon Marbury	3.00	1.35
☐ 157	Walter McCarty	.15	.07
☐ 158	Steve Nash	.50	.23
☐ 159	Jermaine O'Neal	.50	.23
☐ 160	Ray Owens	.10	.05
☐ 161	Vitaly Potapenko	.15	.07
☐ 162	Roy Rogers	.10	.05
☐ 163	Antoine Walker	3.00	1.35
☐ 164	Samaki Walker	.40	.18
☐ 165	Ben Wallace	.10	.05
☐ 166	John Wallace	.50	.23
☐ 167	Jerome Williams	.15	.07
☐ 168	Lorenzen Wright	.40	.18
☐ 169	Vin Baker ZUP	.30	.14
☐ 170	Charles Barkley ZUP	.30	.14
☐ 171	Patrick Ewing ZUP	.15	.07
☐ 172	Michael Finley ZUP	.15	.07
☐ 173	Kevin Garnett ZUP	1.00	.45
☐ 174	A.Hardaway ZUP	.60	.25
☐ 175	Grant Hill ZUP	1.00	.45
☐ 176	Juwan Howard ZUP	.30	.14
☐ 177	Jim Jackson ZUP	.10	.05
☐ 178	Eddie Jones ZUP	.30	.14
☐ 179	Michael Jordan ZUP	2.00	.90
☐ 180	Shawn Kemp ZUP	.50	.23
☐ 181	Jason Kidd ZUP	.30	.14
☐ 182	Karl Malone ZUP	.30	.14
☐ 183	Antonio McDyess ZUP	.30	.14
☐ 184	Reggie Miller ZUP	.15	.07
☐ 185	Alonzo Mourning ZUP	.15	.07
☐ 186	Hakeem Olajuwon ZUP	.30	.14
☐ 187	Shaquille O'Neal ZUP	.60	.25
☐ 188	Gary Payton ZUP	.30	.14
☐ 189	Mitch Richmond ZUP	.15	.07
☐ 190	Clifford Robinson ZUP	.10	.05
☐ 191	David Robinson ZUP	.30	.14
☐ 192	Glenn Robinson ZUP	.15	.07
☐ 193	Dennis Rodman ZUP	.50	.25
☐ 194	Joe Smith ZUP	.30	.14
☐ 195	Jerry Stackhouse ZUP	.30	.14
☐ 196	John Stockton ZUP	.15	.07
☐ 197	D.Stoudamire ZUP	.40	.18
☐ 198	Chris Webber ZUP	.40	.18
☐ 199	Checklist (101-157)	.10	.05
☐ 200	CL (158-200/ins.)	.10	.05
☐ NNO	Grant Hill	2.20	
	Jerry Stackhouse Promo		
☐ NNO	Grant Hill Promo	5.00	
☐ NNO	Grant Hill Total Z	40.00	18.00

1996-97 SkyBox Z-Force Z-Cling

Inserted one per series one pack, this 100-card set is a semi-parallel to the regular set. The card fronts are identical to the basic issue, but the card backs are blank outside of the player's name and the card number. 96 of the original 100 cards are parallels. The exceptions are Shaquille O'Neal, which has him in a Laker uniform on the parallel, the Byron Scott card (#94), which was never issued and the two checklist cards. The Byron Scott card and the two checklists were replaced with the following rookies: Ray Allen (#R1), Stephon Marbury (#R2) and Shareef Abdur-Rahim (#R3), thus making the set complete at 100 cards. To ascertain values of individual cards, please refer to the multiplier in the header, coupled with the value of the basic card.

	MINT	NRMT
COMPLETE SET (100)	50.00	22.00
COMMON CARD (1-100)	.20	.09
UNLISTED STARS	.40	.18
*Z-CLING: 1.25X TO 2.5X BASIC		
ONE IN EVERY SER.1 PACK		
TWO PER SPECIAL SER.1 RETAIL PACK		
NUMBER 94 NEVER ISSUED		

		MINT	NRMT
☐ 64	Shaquille O'Neal	5.00	2.20
	Lakers uniform		
☐ R1	Ray Allen	3.00	1.35
☐ R2	Stephon Marbury	10.00	4.50
☐ R3	Shareef Abdur-Rahim	6.00	2.70

1996-97 SkyBox Z-Force Big Men on the Court

Randomly inserted in series two packs at a rate of one in 240, this 10-card die-cut set feature some of the league's top play-

ers. The cards are printed with silver foil with the insert set name "Big Men on the Court" in the background.

	MINT	NRMT
COMPLETE SET (10)	450.00	200.00
COMMON CARD (1-10)	12.00	5.50
SER.2 STATED ODDS 1:240 HOBBY/RETAIL		
COMP.BMOC Z-P.SET (10)	900.00	400.00
COMMON BMOC Z-P.(1-10)	25.00	11.00
*BMOC Z-PEAT STARS: 1.25X TO 2X		
BMOC Z-P: SER.2 STATED ODDS 1:1,120 H/R		

		MINT	NRMT
☐ 1	Charles Barkley	20.00	9.00
☐ 2	Anfernee Hardaway	50.00	22.00
☐ 3	Grant Hill	80.00	36.00
☐ 4	Michael Jordan	150.00	70.00
☐ 5	Shawn Kemp	40.00	18.00
☐ 6	Alonzo Mourning	12.00	5.50
☐ 7	Hakeem Olajuwon	25.00	11.00
☐ 8	Shaquille O'Neal	50.00	22.00
☐ 9	Scottie Pippen	40.00	18.00
☐ 10	David Robinson	20.00	9.00

1996-97 SkyBox Z-Force Little Big Men

Randomly inserted in series two retail packs only at a rate of one in 36, this 10-card set focuses on some of the NBA's smaller superstars. Card fronts contain buildings in the background on silver foil.

	MINT	NRMT
COMPLETE SET (10)	50.00	22.00
COMMON CARD (1-10)	2.00	.90
SEMISTARS	2.50	1.10

	UNLISTED STARS	4.00	1.80
	SER.2 STATED ODDS 1:36 RETAIL		

		MINT	NRMT
□ 1	Kenny Anderson	2.50	1.10
□ 2	Mookie Blaylock	2.50	1.10
□ 3	Muggsy Bogues	2.00	.90
□ 4	Terrell Brandon	4.00	1.80
□ 5	Allen Iverson	20.00	9.00
□ 6	Avery Johnson	2.00	.90
□ 7	Kevin Johnson	2.50	1.10
□ 8	Stephon Marbury	20.00	9.00
□ 9	Gary Payton	6.00	2.70
□ 10	Nick Van Exel	4.00	1.80

1996-97 SkyBox Z-Force Slam Cam

Randomly inserted in series one hobby and retail packs at a rate of one in 240, this 9-card set features some of the top slam dunkers in the game. Card fronts contain a kaleidoscopic color background with an action photo laid on top. The player's name and the set name "Slam Cam" are loctated above the photo. Card backs are horizontal with the set name in the background with another action shot of the player. The cards are numbered with a "SC" prefix.

		MINT	NRMT
	COMPLETE SET (9)	350.00	160.00
	COMMON CARD (SC1-SC9)	15.00	6.75
	SER.1 STATED ODDS 1:240 HOBBY/RETAIL		

		MINT	NRMT
□ SC1	Clyde Drexler	15.00	6.75
□ SC2	Michael Finley	15.00	6.75
□ SC3	Anfernee Hardaway	50.00	22.00
□ SC4	Grant Hill	70.00	32.00
□ SC5	Michael Jordan	150.00	70.00
□ SC6	Shawn Kemp	40.00	18.00
□ SC7	Karl Malone	20.00	9.00
□ SC8	Antonio McDyess	20.00	9.00
□ SC9	Shaquille O'Neal	50.00	22.00

1996-97 SkyBox Z-Force Swat Team

Randomly inserted in series one hobby packs only at a rate of one in 72, this 9-card set features some of the leagues best blockers. Card front backgrounds are prismatic with the logo "Swat Team" designed into

it. An action shot of the player is laid on top with their names directly underneath. Card backs contain the same type background as the front, without the prismatic foil. The cards are numbered with a "ST" prefix.

		MINT	NRMT
	COMPLETE SET (9)	100.00	45.00
	COMMON CARD (ST1-ST9)	3.00	1.35
	SEMISTARS	6.00	2.70
	SER.1 STATED ODDS 1:72 HOBBY		

		MINT	NRMT
□ ST1	Patrick Ewing	6.00	2.70
□ ST2	Kevin Garnett	40.00	18.00
□ ST3	Alonzo Mourning	6.00	2.70
□ ST4	Dikembe Mutombo	3.00	1.35
□ ST5	Hakeem Olajuwon	12.00	5.50
□ ST6	Shaquille O'Neal	25.00	11.00
□ ST7	David Robinson	10.00	4.50
□ ST8	Dennis Rodman	25.00	11.00
□ ST9	Joe Smith	8.00	3.60

1996-97 SkyBox Z-Force Vortex

Randomly inserted in series one retail packs only at a rate of one in 36, this 15-card set features embossed card fronts with a swirl background. The action shot of the player is located in the middle of the card with the player's name in gold foil block letters directly below. Card backs are horizontal with a similar background and have a brief commentary along with another action shot. The cards are numbered as "Vortex/X".

		MINT	NRMT
	COMPLETE SET (15)	100.00	45.00
	COMMON CARD (V1-V15)	2.00	.90
	SEMISTARS	2.50	1.10
	UNLISTED STARS	4.00	1.80
	SER.1 STATED ODDS 1:36 RETAIL		

		MINT	NRMT
□ V1	Charles Barkley	6.00	2.70
□ V2	Anfernee Hardaway	15.00	6.75
□ V3	Grant Hill	25.00	11.00
□ V4	Juwan Howard	5.00	2.20
□ V5	Michael Jordan	50.00	22.00
□ V6	Jason Kidd	8.00	3.60
□ V7	Reggie Miller	4.00	1.80
□ V8	Gary Payton	6.00	2.70
□ V9	Scottie Pippen	12.00	5.50
□ V10	Mitch Richmond	4.00	1.80
□ V11	Glenn Robinson	4.00	1.80
□ V12	Arvydas Sabonis	2.00	.90
□ V13	Jerry Stackhouse	5.00	2.20
□ V14	John Stockton	4.00	1.80
☒ V15	Damon Stoudamire	10.00	4.50

1996-97 SkyBox Z-Force Zebut

Randomly inserted in series two hobby packs only at a rate of one in 24, this 20-card set is embossed and printed on silver foil. The set focuses on first year players from the 96-97 class.

		MINT	NRMT
	COMPLETE SET (20)	150.00	70.00
	COMMON CARD (1-20)	1.50	.70
	SEMISTARS	3.00	1.35
	UNLISTED STARS	5.00	2.20
	SER.2 STATED ODDS 1:24 HOBBY		
	COMP.ZEBUT Z-P SET (20)	600.00	275.00
	COMMON ZEBUT Z-P (1-20)	6.00	2.70
	*ZEBUT Z-PEAT RC's: 2X TO 4X		
	ZEBUT Z-P: SER.2 STATED ODDS 1:240 HOB		

		MINT	NRMT
□ 1	Shareef Abdur-Rahim	15.00	6.75
□ 2	Ray Allen	8.00	3.60
□ 3	Kobe Bryant	50.00	22.00
□ 4	Marcus Camby	6.00	2.70
□ 5	Erick Dampier	5.00	2.20
□ 6	Todd Fuller	1.50	.70
□ 7	Othella Harrington	3.00	1.35
□ 8	Allen Iverson	25.00	11.00
□ 9	Kerry Kittles	6.00	2.70
□ 10	Priest Lauderdale	1.50	.70
□ 11	Stephon Marbury	25.00	11.00
□ 12	Steve Nash	5.00	2.20
□ 13	Jermaine O'Neal	5.00	2.20
□ 14	Kaya Owens	1.50	.70
□ 15	Vitaly Potapenko	3.00	1.35
□ 16	Roy Rogers	1.50	.70
□ 17	Antoine Walker	25.00	11.00

☐ 18 Samaki Walker	5.00	2.20
☐ 19 John Wallace	5.00	2.20
☐ 20 Lorenzen Wright	5.00	2.20

1996-97 SkyBox Z-Force Zensations

Randomly inserted in all series two packs at a rate of one in 6, this 20-card set features a foil-stamped background and focuses on veterans and rookies. Card fronts feature the player spotlighted.

	MINT	NRMT
COMPLETE SET (20)	30.00	13.50
COMMON CARD (1-20)	.60	.25
SEMISTARS	.75	.35
UNLISTED STARS	1.25	.55
SER.2 STATED ODDS 1:6 HOBBY/RETAIL		

☐ 1 Shareef Abdur-Rahim	5.00	2.20
☐ 2 Ray Allen	2.50	1.10
☐ 3 Nick Anderson	.60	.25
☐ 4 Vin Baker	2.50	1.10
☐ 5 Mookie Blaylock	.75	.35
☐ 6 Calbert Cheaney	.60	.25
☐ 7 Kevin Garnett	8.00	3.60
☐ 8 Horace Grant	.75	.35
☐ 9 Tim Hardaway	1.50	.70
☐ 10 Allen Iverson	8.00	3.60
☐ 11 Avery Johnson	.60	.25
☐ 12 Kevin Johnson	.75	.35
☐ 13 Danny Manning	.75	.35
☐ 14 Stephon Marbury	8.00	3.60
☐ 15 Jamal Mashburn	.75	.35
☐ 16 Glen Rice	1.25	.55
☐ 17 Isaiah Rider	.75	.35
☐ 18 Latrell Sprewell	.75	.35
☐ 19 Rod Strickland	.75	.35
☐ 20 Nick Van Exel	1.25	.55

1997-98 SkyBox Z-Force

This 210-card set was issued in two series, distributed in eight-card packs with a suggested retail price of $1.59. The fronts feature borderless color action player photos printed on 14 pt. card stock with gold foil stamping and UV coating. The player's

name is written vertically down the side in different foil colors. The backs carry another player photo and player information.

	MINT	NRMT
COMPLETE SET (210)	25.00	11.00
COMPLETE SERIES 1 (110)	10.00	4.50
COMPLETE SERIES 2 (100)	15.00	6.75
COMMON CARD (1-210)	.10	.05
SEMISTARS	.15	.07
UNLISTED STARS	.25	.11
COMP.RAVE SET (208)	3400.00	1500.00
COMP.RAVE SER.1 (1-108)	2000.00	900.00
COMP.RAVE SER.2 (111-210)	1400.00	650.00
COMMON RAVE	6.00	2.70
*RAVE STARS: 30X TO 60X HI COLUMN		
*RAVE RCs: 15X TO 30X HI		
RAVE: RANDOM INS.IN SER.1/2 HOB PACKS		
RAVE: STATED PRINT RUN 399 SERIAL #'d SETS		
CARD NUMBER 143 DOES NOT EXIST		
BAKER AND McGRADY BOTH #'d 172		
AUTOGRAPHICS LISTED UNDER SKYBOX		

☐ 1 Anfernee Hardaway	1.00	.45
☐ 2 Mitch Richmond	.25	.11
☐ 3 Stephon Marbury	1.25	.55
☐ 4 Charles Barkley	.40	.18
☐ 5 Juwan Howard	.25	.11
☐ 6 Avery Johnson	.10	.05
☐ 7 Rex Chapman	.10	.05
☐ 8 Antoine Walker	1.25	.55
☐ 9 Nick Van Exel	.25	.11
☐ 10 Tim Hardaway	.30	.14
☐ 11 Clarence Weatherspoon	.10	.05
☐ 12 John Stockton	.25	.11
☐ 13 Glenn Robinson	.25	.11
☐ 14 Anthony Mason	.15	.07
☐ 15 Latrell Sprewell	.15	.07
☐ 16 Kendall Gill	.10	.05
☐ 17 Terry Mills	.10	.05
☐ 18 Mookie Blaylock	.15	.07
☐ 19 Michael Finley	.25	.11
☐ 20 Gary Payton	.40	.18
☐ 21 Kevin Garnett	1.50	.70
☐ 22 Clyde Drexler	.30	.14
☐ 23 Michael Jordan	3.00	1.35
☐ 24 Antonio McDyess	.30	.14
☐ 25 Nick Anderson	.10	.05
☐ 26 Patrick Ewing	.25	.11
☐ 27 Anthony Peeler	.10	.05
☐ 28 Doug Christie	.10	.05
☐ 29 Bobby Phills	.10	.05
☐ 30 Kerry Kittles	.25	.11
☐ 31 Reggie Miller	.25	.11
☐ 32 Karl Malone	.40	.18
☐ 33 Grant Hill	1.50	.70
☐ 34 Shaquille O'Neal	1.00	.45
☐ 35 Loy Vaught	.15	.07
☐ 36 Kenny Anderson	.15	.07
☐ 37 Wesley Person	.10	.05
☐ 38 Jamal Mashburn	.15	.07
☐ 39 Christian Laettner	.15	.07
☐ 40 Shawn Kemp	.75	.35
☐ 41 Glen Rice	.25	.11
☐ 42 Vin Baker	.50	.23

☐ 43 Popeye Jones	.10	.05
☐ 44 Derrick Coleman	.15	.07
☐ 45 Rik Smits	.15	.07
☐ 46 Dale Ellis	.10	.05
☐ 47 Rod Strickland	.15	.07
☐ 48 Mark Price	.15	.07
☐ 49 Toni Kukoc	.25	.11
☐ 50 David Robinson	.40	.18
☐ 51 John Wallace	.15	.07
☐ 52 Samaki Walker	.10	.05
☐ 53 Shareef Abdur-Rahim	.75	.35
☐ 54 Rodney Rogers	.10	.05
☐ 55 Dikembe Mutombo	.15	.07
☐ 56 Rony Seikaly	.10	.05
☐ 57 Matt Maloney	.10	.05
☐ 58 Chris Webber	.60	.25
☐ 59 Robert Horry	.15	.07
☐ 60 Rasheed Wallace	.15	.07
☐ 61 Jeff Hornacek	.15	.07
☐ 62 Walt Williams	.10	.05
☐ 63 Detlef Schrempf	.15	.07
☐ 64 Dan Majerle	.15	.07
☐ 65 Dell Curry	.10	.05
☐ 66 Scottie Pippen	.75	.35
☐ 67 Greg Anthony	.10	.05
☐ 68 Mahmoud Abdul-Rauf	.10	.05
☐ 69 Cedric Ceballos	.10	.05
☐ 70 Terrell Brandon	.25	.11
☐ 71 Arvydas Sabonis	.15	.07
☐ 72 Malik Sealy	.10	.05
☐ 73 Dean Garrett	.10	.05
☐ 74 Joe Dumars	.25	.11
☐ 75 Joe Smith	.25	.11
☐ 76 Shawn Bradley	.10	.05
☐ 77 Gheorghe Muresan	.10	.05
☐ 78 Dale Davis	.10	.05
☐ 79 Bryant Stith	.10	.05
☐ 80 Lorenzen Wright	.10	.05
☐ 81 Chris Childs	.10	.05
☐ 82 Bryon Russell	.10	.05
☐ 83 Steve Smith	.15	.07
☐ 84 Jerry Stackhouse	.25	.11
☐ 85 Hersey Hawkins	.15	.07
☐ 86 Ray Allen	.30	.14
☐ 87 Dominique Wilkins	.25	.11
☐ 88 Kobe Bryant	2.00	.90
☐ 89 Tom Gugliotta	.25	.11
☐ 90 Dennis Scott	.10	.05
☐ 91 Dennis Rodman	1.00	.45
☐ 92 Bryant Reeves	.15	.07
☐ 93 Vlade Divac	.15	.07
☐ 94 Jason Kidd	.50	.23
☐ 95 Mario Elie	.10	.05
☐ 96 Lindsey Hunter	.10	.05
☐ 97 Olden Polynice	.10	.05
☐ 98 Allan Houston	.15	.07
☐ 99 Alonzo Mourning	.25	.11
☐ 100 Allen Iverson	1.25	.55
☐ 101 LaPhonso Ellis	.10	.05
☐ 102 Bob Sura	.10	.05
☐ 103 Chris Mullin	.25	.11
☐ 104 Sam Cassell	.15	.07
☐ 105 Eric Williams	.10	.05
☐ 106 Antonio Davis	.10	.05
☐ 107 Marcus Camby	.25	.11
☐ 108 Isaiah Rider	.15	.07
☐ 109 Checklist	.10	.05
(Atlanta Hawks-Phoenix Suns)		
☐ 110 Checklist	.10	.05
(Portland-inserts)		
☐ 111 Tim Duncan	3.00	1.35
☐ 112 Joe Smith	.25	.11
☐ 113 Shawn Kemp	.75	.35
☐ 114 Terry Mills	.10	.05
☐ 115 Jacque Vaughn	.40	.18
☐ 116 Ron Mercer	2.00	.90
☐ 117 Brian Williams	.10	.05
☐ 118 Rik Smits	.15	.07
☐ 119 Eric Williams	.10	.05
☐ 120 Tim Thomas	1.50	.70
☐ 121 Damon Stoudamire	.50	.23
☐ 122 God Shammgod	.10	.05
☐ 123 Tyrone Hill	.10	.05
☐ 124 Elden Campbell	.15	.07
☐ 125 Keith Van Horn	2.50	1.10
☐ 126 Brian Grant	.10	.05

127	Antonio McDyess	.30 .14
128	Darrell Armstrong	.10 .05
129	Sam Perkins	.15 .07
130	Chris Mills	.10 .05
131	Reggie Miller	.25 .11
132	Chris Gatling	.10 .05
133	Ed Gray	.30 .14
134	Hakeem Olajuwon	.50 .23
135	Chris Webber	.60 .25
136	Kendall Gill	.15 .07
137	Wesley Person	.10 .05
138	Derrick Coleman	.15 .07
139	Dana Barros	.10 .05
140	Dennis Scott	.10 .05
141	Paul Grant	.10 .05
142	Scott Burrell	.10 .05
143	Does not Exist	
144	Austin Croshere	.30 .14
145	Maurice Taylor	.75 .35
146	Kevin Johnson	.15 .07
147	Tony Battie	.50 .23
148	Tariq Abdul-Wahad	.40 .18
149	Johnny Taylor	.10 .05
150	Allen Iverson	1.25 .55
151	Terrell Brandon	.25 .11
152	Derek Anderson	.75 .35
153	Calbert Cheaney	.10 .05
154	Jayson Williams	.10 .05
155	Rick Fox	.10 .05
156	John Thomas	.10 .05
157	David Wesley	.10 .05
158	Bobby Jackson	.50 .23
159	Kelvin Cato	.30 .14
160	Vinny Del Negro	.10 .05
161	Adonal Foyle	.30 .14
162	Larry Johnson	.15 .07
163	Brevin Knight	.75 .35
164	Rod Strickland	.15 .07
165	Rodrick Rhodes	.30 .14
166	Scot Pollard	.10 .05
167	Sam Cassell	.15 .07
168	Jerry Stackhouse	.25 .11
169	Mark Jackson	.10 .05
170	John Wallace	.15 .07
171	Horace Grant	.15 .07
172A	Vin Baker	.50 .23
172B	Tracy McGrady	1.50 .70
173	Eddie Jones	.50 .23
174	Kerry Kittles	.25 .11
175	Antonio Daniels	.60 .25
176	Alan Henderson	.10 .05
177	Sean Elliott	.10 .05
178	John Starks	.15 .07
179	Chauncey Billups	1.00 .45
180	Juwan Howard	.10 .05
181	Bobby Phills	.10 .05
182	Latrell Sprewell	.15 .07
183	Jim Jackson	.15 .07
184	Danny Fortson	.50 .23
185	Zydrunas Ilgauskas	.15 .07
186	Clifford Robinson	.10 .05
187	Chris Mullin	.25 .11
188	Greg Ostertag	.10 .05
189	Antoine Walker ZUP	.60 .25
190	Michael Jordan ZUP	1.50 .70
191	Scottie Pippen ZUP	.40 .18
192	Dennis Rodman ZUP	.50 .23
193	Grant Hill ZUP	.75 .35
194	Clyde Drexler ZUP	.25 .11
195	Kobe Bryant ZUP	1.00 .45
196	Shaquille O'Neal ZUP	.50 .23
197	Alonzo Mourning ZUP	.15 .07
198	Ray Allen ZUP	.25 .11
199	Kevin Garnett ZUP	.75 .35
200	Stephon Marbury ZUP	.60 .25
201	A.Hardaway ZUP	.50 .23
202	Jason Kidd ZUP	.25 .11
203	David Robinson ZUP	.25 .11
204	Gary Payton ZUP	.25 .11
205	Marcus Camby ZUP	.25 .07
206	Karl Malone ZUP	.25 .11
207	John Stockton ZUP	.25 .07
208	S.Abdur-Rahim ZUP	.40 .18
209	Charles Barkley CL	.25 .11
210	Gary Payton CL	.25 .11

1997-98 SkyBox Z-Force Super Rave

Randomly inserted in series two hobby packs only, this 100-card set parallels the series two set. The cards are serially numbered to 50.

		MINT	NRMT
COMMON CARD (111-210)		30.00	13.50
SEMISTARS		40.00	18.00

RANDOM INSERTS IN SER.2 HOBBY PACKS
STATED PRINT RUN 50 SERIAL #'d SETS
CARD NUMBER 143 DOES NOT EXIST
BAKER AND MCGRADY BOTH #'d 172

111	Tim Duncan	400.00	180.00
112	Joe Smith	60.00	27.00
113	Shawn Kemp	200.00	90.00
114	Terry Mills	30.00	13.50
115	Jacque Vaughn	50.00	22.00
116	Ron Mercer	250.00	110.00
117	Brian Williams	30.00	13.50
118	Rik Smits	40.00	18.00
119	Eric Williams	30.00	13.50
120	Tim Thomas	200.00	90.00
121	Damon Stoudamire	125.00	55.00
122	God Shammgod	30.00	13.50
123	Tyrone Hill	30.00	13.50
124	Elden Campbell	40.00	18.00
125	Keith Van Horn	350.00	160.00
126	Brian Grant	30.00	13.50
127	Antonio McDyess	80.00	36.00
128	Darrell Armstrong	30.00	13.50
129	Sam Perkins	40.00	18.00
130	Chris Mills	30.00	13.50
131	Reggie Miller	60.00	27.00
132	Chris Gatling	30.00	13.50
133	Ed Gray	50.00	22.00
134	Hakeem Olajuwon	125.00	55.00
135	Chris Webber	160.00	70.00
136	Kendall Gill	40.00	18.00
137	Wesley Person	30.00	13.50
138	Derrick Coleman	40.00	18.00
139	Dana Barros	30.00	13.50
140	Dennis Scott	30.00	13.50
141	Paul Grant	30.00	13.50
142	Scott Burrell	30.00	13.50
143	Does not Exist		
144	Austin Croshere	50.00	22.00
145	Maurice Taylor	100.00	45.00
146	Kevin Johnson	40.00	18.00
147	Tony Battie	60.00	27.00
148	Olivier Saint-Jean	50.00	22.00
149	Johnny Taylor	30.00	13.50
150	Allen Iverson	300.00	135.00
151	Terrell Brandon	50.00	22.00
152	Derek Anderson	100.00	45.00
153	Calbert Cheaney	30.00	13.50
154	Jayson Williams	40.00	18.00
155	Rick Fox	30.00	13.50
156	John Thomas	30.00	13.50
157	David Wesley	30.00	13.50
158	Bobby Jackson	60.00	27.00
159	Kelvin Cato	50.00	22.00
160	Vinny Del Negro	30.00	13.50
161	Adonal Foyle	50.00	22.00
162	Larry Johnson	40.00	18.00
163	Brevin Knight	100.00	45.00
164	Rod Strickland	40.00	18.00
165	Rodrick Rhodes	50.00	22.00
166	Scot Pollard	30.00	13.50
167	Sam Cassell	40.00	18.00
168	Jerry Stackhouse	60.00	27.00
169	Mark Jackson	30.00	13.50
170	John Wallace	40.00	18.00
171	Horace Grant	40.00	18.00
172A	Vin Baker	125.00	55.00
172B	Tracy McGrady	200.00	90.00
173	Eddie Jones	125.00	55.00
174	Kerry Kittles	60.00	27.00
175	Antonio Daniels	80.00	36.00
176	Alan Henderson	30.00	13.50
177	Sean Elliott	30.00	13.50
178	John Starks	40.00	18.00
179	Chauncey Billups	125.00	55.00
180	Juwan Howard	60.00	27.00
181	Bobby Phills	30.00	13.50
182	Latrell Sprewell	40.00	18.00
183	Jim Jackson	40.00	18.00
184	Danny Fortson	60.00	27.00
185	Zydrunas Ilgauskas	40.00	18.00
186	Clifford Robinson	30.00	13.50
187	Chris Mullin	50.00	22.00
188	Greg Ostertag	30.00	13.50
189	Antoine Walker ZUP	300.00	135.00
190	M.Jordan ZUP	1600.00	700.00
191	Scottie Pippen ZUP	200.00	90.00
192	Dennis Rodman ZUP	250.00	110.00
193	Grant Hill ZUP	400.00	180.00
194	Clyde Drexler ZUP	80.00	36.00
195	Kobe Bryant ZUP	600.00	275.00
196	Shaquille O'Neal ZUP	250.00	110.00
197	Alonzo Mourning ZUP	60.00	27.00
198	Ray Allen ZUP	80.00	36.00
199	Kevin Garnett ZUP	400.00	180.00
200	S.Marbury ZUP	300.00	135.00
201	A.Hardaway ZUP	250.00	110.00
202	Jason Kidd ZUP	150.00	70.00
203	David Robinson ZUP	100.00	45.00
204	Gary Payton ZUP	100.00	45.00
205	Marcus Camby ZUP	60.00	27.00
206	Karl Malone ZUP	100.00	45.00
207	John Stockton ZUP	60.00	27.00
208	S.Abdur-Rahim ZUP	200.00	90.00
209	Charles Barkley CL	70.00	32.00
210	Gary Payton CL	70.00	32.00

1997-98 SkyBox Z-Force Big Men on Court

Randomly inserted in series two packs at a rate of one in 288, this 15-card set features some of the best players on the court.

The cards are produced on special mulit-dimensional thermoplastic card stock.

	MINT	NRMT
COMPLETE SET (15)	800.00	350.00
COMMON CARD (1-15)	12.00	5.50
SER.2 STATED ODDS 1:288 HOB/RET		

		MINT	NRMT
☐ 1	Shareef Abdur-Rahim	40.00	18.00
☐ 2	Kobe Bryant	100.00	45.00
☐ 3	Marcus Camby	12.00	5.50
☐ 4	Tim Duncan	80.00	36.00
☐ 5	Kevin Garnett	80.00	36.00
☐ 6	Anfernee Hardaway	50.00	22.00
☐ 7	Grant Hill	80.00	36.00
☐ 8	Allen Iverson	60.00	27.00
☐ 9	Michael Jordan	150.00	70.00
☐ 10	Shawn Kemp	40.00	18.00
☐ 11	Stephon Marbury	60.00	27.00
☐ 12	Shaquille O'Neal	50.00	22.00
☐ 13	Scottie Pippen	40.00	18.00
☐ 14	Dennis Rodman	50.00	22.00
☐ 15	Antoine Walker	60.00	27.00

1997-98 SkyBox Z-Force Boss

Randomly inserted in series one packs at a rate of one in six, this 20-card set features color action player photos of top players on the courts. The card fronts feature a photo of the player embossed against a hardwood floor background. The backs carry player information.

	MINT	NRMT
COMPLETE SET (20)	40.00	18.00
COMMON CARD (1-20)	.75	.35
SER.1 STATED ODDS 1:6 HOBBY/RETAIL		
COMP.SUP.BOSS SET (20)	150.00	70.00
COMMON SUP.BOSS (1-20)	2.00	.90
*SUP.BOSS: 1.25X TO 3X HI COLUMN		
SUP.BOSS: SER.1 STATED ODDS 1:36 H/R		

		MINT	NRMT
☐ 1	Shareef Abdur-Rahim	2.50	1.10
☐ 2	Ray Allen	1.00	.45
☐ 3	Kobe Bryant	6.00	2.70
☐ 4	Marcus Camby	.75	.35
☐ 5	Kevin Garnett	5.00	2.20
☐ 6	Anfernee Hardaway	3.00	1.35
☐ 7	Grant Hill	5.00	2.20
☐ 8	Allen Iverson	4.00	1.80
☐ 9	Eddie Jones	1.50	.70
☐ 10	Michael Jordan	10.00	4.50
☐ 11	Shawn Kemp	2.50	1.10
☐ 12	Kerry Kittles	.75	.35
☐ 13	Stephon Marbury	4.00	1.80
☐ 14	Shaquille O'Neal	3.00	1.35
☐ 15	Hakeem Olajuwon	1.50	.70

		MINT	NRMT
☐ 16	Scottie Pippen	2.50	1.10
☐ 17	Dennis Rodman	3.00	1.35
☐ 18	Joe Smith	.75	.35
☐ 19	Damon Stoudamire	1.50	.70
☐ 20	Antoine Walker	4.00	1.80

1997-98 SkyBox Z-Force Fast Track

Randomly inserted in series one packs at a rate of one in 24, this 12-card set features color action photos of players who are on the road to NBA stardom. Card fronts contain a yellow background with the title "Fast Track" having a felt-feel. The backs carry player information.

	MINT	NRMT
COMPLETE SET (12)	40.00	18.00
COMMON CARD (1-12)	2.00	.90
SER.1 STATED ODDS 1:24 HOBBY/RETAIL		

		MINT	NRMT
☐ 1	Ray Allen	2.50	1.10
☐ 2	Kobe Bryant	15.00	6.75
☐ 3	Marcus Camby	2.00	.90
☐ 4	Juwan Howard	2.00	.90
☐ 5	Eddie Jones	4.00	1.80
☐ 6	Kerry Kittles	2.00	.90
☐ 7	Antonio McDyess	2.50	1.10
☐ 8	Joe Smith	2.00	.90
☐ 9	Jerry Stackhouse	2.00	.90
☐ 10	Damon Stoudamire	4.00	1.80
☐ 11	Antoine Walker	10.00	4.50
☐ 12	Chris Webber	5.00	2.20

1997-98 SkyBox Z-Force Limited Access

Randomly inserted in series one retail packs only at a rate of one in 18, this 10-card set features color player photos on a bi-fold card with in-depth statistical analysis.

	MINT	NRMT
COMPLETE SET (10)	60.00	27.00
COMMON CARD (1-10)	2.00	.90
SER.1 STATED ODDS 1:18 RETAIL		

		MINT	NRMT
☐ 1	Shareef Abdur-Rahim	6.00	2.70
☐ 2	Ray Allen	2.50	1.10
☐ 3	Charles Barkley	3.00	1.35
☐ 4	Anfernee Hardaway	8.00	3.60
☐ 5	Juwan Howard	2.00	.90

		MINT	NRMT
☐ 6	Michael Jordan	25.00	11.00
☐ 7	Stephon Marbury	10.00	4.50
☐ 8	Shaquille O'Neal	8.00	3.60
☐ 9	Dennis Rodman	8.00	3.60
☐ 10	Antoine Walker	10.00	4.50

1997-98 SkyBox Z-Force Quick Strike

Randomly inserted in series two packs at a rate of one in 96, this 12-card set focuses on players who can light up the scoreboard in the blink of an eye. Card fronts feature holofoil backing on clear plastic stock.

	MINT	NRMT
COMPLETE SET (12)	200.00	90.00
COMMON CARD (1-12)	8.00	3.60
SER.2 STATED ODDS 1:96 HOB/RET		

		MINT	NRMT
☐ 1	Shareef Abdur-Rahim	12.00	5.50
☐ 2	Anfernee Hardaway	15.00	6.75
☐ 3	Grant Hill	25.00	11.00
☐ 4	Allen Iverson	20.00	9.00
☐ 5	Michael Jordan	50.00	22.00
☐ 6	Stephon Marbury	20.00	9.00
☐ 7	Hakeem Olajuwon	8.00	3.60
☐ 8	Scottie Pippen	12.00	5.50
☐ 9	Damon Stoudamire	8.00	3.60
☐ 10	Keith Van Horn	20.00	9.00
☐ 11	Antoine Walker	20.00	9.00
☐ 12	Chris Webber	10.00	4.50

1997-98 SkyBox Z-Force Rave Reviews

Randomly inserted in series one packs at a rate of one in 288,

this 12-card set features color action photos of players who generate incredible numbers on the court and continually make the headlines. The backs carry player information.

	MINT	NRMT
COMPLETE SET (12)	500.00	220.00
COMMON CARD (1-12)	20.00	9.00
SER.1 STATED ODDS 1:288 HOBBY/RETAIL		

		MINT	NRMT
☐ 1	Shareef Abdur-Rahim	30.00	13.50
☐ 2	Kevin Garnett	60.00	27.00
☐ 3	Anfernee Hardaway	40.00	18.00
☐ 4	Grant Hill	60.00	27.00
☐ 5	Allen Iverson	50.00	22.00
☐ 6	Michael Jordan	120.00	55.00
☐ 7	Shawn Kemp	30.00	13.50
☐ 8	Stephon Marbury	50.00	22.00
☐ 9	Shaquille O'Neal	40.00	18.00
☐ 10	Hakeem Olajuwon	20.00	9.00
☐ 11	Scottie Pippen	30.00	13.50
☐ 12	Dennis Rodman	40.00	18.00

1997-98 SkyBox
Z-Force Slam Cam

Randomly inserted in series two packs at a rate of one in 36, this 12-card set features NBA players who play their game above the rim. The card fronts feature a black and white film footage background on plastic stock.

	MINT	NRMT
COMPLETE SET (12)	100.00	45.00
COMMON CARD (1-12)	2.50	1.10
SER.2 STATED ODDS 1:36 HOB/RET		

		MINT	NRMT
☐ 1	Kobe Bryant	20.00	9.00
☐ 2	Marcus Camby	2.50	1.10

		MINT	NRMT
☐ 3	Tim Duncan	15.00	6.75
☐ 4	Kevin Garnett	15.00	6.75
☐ 5	Michael Jordan	30.00	13.50
☐ 6	Shawn Kemp	8.00	3.60
☐ 7	Karl Malone	4.00	1.80
☐ 8	Antonio McDyess	3.00	1.35
☐ 9	Shaquille O'Neal	10.00	4.50
☐ 10	Joe Smith	2.50	1.10
☐ 11	Jerry Stackhouse	2.50	1.10
☐ 12	Chris Webber	6.00	2.70

1997-98 SkyBox
Z-Force
Star Gazing

Randomly inserted in series two retail packs at a rate of one in 18, this 15-card set features some of the NBA's best against a dark foil-board background.

	MINT	NRMT
COMPLETE SET (15)	100.00	45.00
COMMON CARD (1-15)	2.00	.90
SER.2 STATED ODDS 1:18 RETAIL		

		MINT	NRMT
☐ 1	Shareef Abdur-Rahim	6.00	2.70
☐ 2	Kobe Bryant	15.00	6.75
☐ 3	Marcus Camby	2.00	.90
☐ 4	Kevin Garnett	12.00	5.50
☐ 5	Anfernee Hardaway	8.00	3.60
☐ 6	Grant Hill	12.00	5.50
☐ 7	Allen Iverson	10.00	4.50
☐ 8	Stephon Marbury	10.00	4.50
☐ 9	Hakeem Olajuwon	4.00	1.80
☐ 10	Shaquille O'Neal	8.00	3.60
☐ 11	Scottie Pippen	6.00	2.70
☐ 12	Dennis Rodman	8.00	3.60
☐ 13	Damon Stoudamire	4.00	1.80
☐ 14	Keith Van Horn	10.00	4.50
☐ 15	Antoine Walker	10.00	4.50

1997-98 SkyBox
Z-Force
Total Impact

Randomly inserted in series one packs at a rate of one in 48, this 12-card set features color action photos of players who can hurt their opponents with their many skills. Card fronts carry a player shot against a diffracting foil background. The backs carry player information.

	MINT	NRMT
COMPLETE SET (12)	75.00	34.00
COMMON CARD (1-12)	2.50	1.10
SER.1 STATED ODDS 1:48 HOBBY/RETAIL		

		MINT	NRMT
☐ 1	Kobe Bryant	20.00	9.00
☐ 2	Marcus Camby	2.50	1.10
☐ 3	Kevin Garnett	15.00	6.75
☐ 4	Grant Hill	15.00	6.75
☐ 5	Allen Iverson	12.00	5.50
☐ 6	Eddie Jones	5.00	2.20
☐ 7	Shawn Kemp	8.00	3.60
☐ 8	Kerry Kittles	2.50	1.10
☐ 9	Hakeem Olajuwon	5.00	2.20
☐ 10	Scottie Pippen	8.00	3.60
☐ 11	Joe Smith	2.50	1.10
☐ 12	Chris Webber	6.00	2.70

1997-98 SkyBox
Z-Force Zebut

Randomly inserted in series two packs at a rate of one in 24, this 12-card set features rookie phenoms who are destined for the NBA spotlight. Each player is set against a spotlight with a 100% die cut foil background.

	MINT	NRMT
COMPLETE SET (12)	40.00	18.00
COMMON CARD (1-12)	1.00	.45
SEMISTARS	1.25	.55
UNLISTED STARS	2.00	.90
SER.2 STATED ODDS 1:24 HOB/RET		

		MINT	NRMT
☐ 1	Derek Anderson	3.00	1.35
☐ 2	Tony Battie	2.00	.90
☐ 3	Chauncey Billups	4.00	1.80
☐ 4	Austin Croshere	1.00	.45
☐ 5	Antonio Daniels	2.50	1.10
☐ 6	Tim Duncan	12.00	5.50
☐ 7	Danny Fortson	2.00	.90
☐ 8	Tracy McGrady	6.00	2.70
☐ 9	Ron Mercer	8.00	3.60
☐ 10	Tariq Abdul-Wahad	1.25	.55
☐ 11	Tim Thomas	6.00	2.70
☐ 12	Keith Van Horn	10.00	4.50

1997-98 SkyBox Z-Force Zensations

Randomly inserted in series two packs at a rate of one in 6, this 25-card set features die cut, mulit-colored cards showcasing the league's marquee players.

	MINT	NRMT
COMPLETE SET (25)	20.00	9.00
COMMON CARD (1-25)	.40	.18
SEMISTARS	.50	.23
UNLISTED STARS	.75	.35
SER.2 STATED ODDS 1:6 HOB/RET		

□ 1 Ray Allen	1.00	.45
□ 2 Vin Baker	1.50	.70
□ 3 Charles Barkley	1.25	.55
□ 4 Clyde Drexler	1.00	.45
□ 5 Patrick Ewing	.75	.35
□ 6 Juwan Howard	.75	.35
□ 7 Eddie Jones	1.50	.70
□ 8 Shawn Kemp	2.50	1.10
□ 9 Jason Kidd	1.50	.70
□ 10 Kerry Kittles	.75	.35
□ 11 Karl Malone	1.25	.55
□ 12 Antonio McDyess	1.00	.45
□ 13 Hakeem Olajuwon	1.50	.70
□ 14 Gary Payton	1.25	.55
□ 15 Glen Rice	.75	.35
□ 16 Mitch Richmond	.75	.35
□ 17 David Robinson	1.25	.55
□ 18 Dennis Rodman	3.00	1.35
□ 19 Joe Smith	.75	.35
□ 20 Latrell Sprewell	.40	.18
□ 21 Jerry Stackhouse	.75	.35
□ 22 John Stockton	.75	.35
□ 23 Damon Stoudamire	1.50	.70
□ 24 Rasheed Wallace	.50	.23
□ 25 Chris Webber	2.00	.90

1994-95 SP

The complete 1994-95 SP set (issued by Upper Deck) consists

of 165-card standard size cards issued in eight-card packs (suggested retail price $3.99). Boxes were distributed exclusively to hobby dealers. The set features full-bleed fronts with color action photos. There is a gold strip down the left side with the player name while the team name is at the bottom. The backs feature another color action photo with the statistics at the bottom and a gold hologram at the bottom left. The only subset is Premier Prospects (1-30) which highlights rookies. Unlike the regular player cards, these rookie-focused cards have a full-bleed gold foil background with a silver foil pyramid at the bottom with the player's name in it. The backs feature a vertical color player photo on the right and statistics on the left. After the Premier Prospects subset, the cards are grouped alphabetically within teams. Two parallel Michael Jordan cards (red and silver), both numbered MJ1, were randomly inserted in packs. The cards feature feature photos from Jordan's return with the words "He's Back March 19, 1995" in red foil. The red version was inserted at a ratio of one in every 30 packs. The silver version was inserted at a ratio of one in every 192 packs. Rookie Cards of note in this set include Grant Hill, Juwan Howard, Eddie Jones, Jason Kidd and Glenn Robinson.

	MINT	NRMT
COMPLETE SET (165)	30.00	13.50
COMMON CARD (1-165)	.15	.07
SEMISTARS	.30	.14
UNLISTED STARS	.60	.25
COMP.DIE CUT SET (165)	60.00	27.00
COMMON DIE CUT (D1-D165)	.30	.14
*DIE CUT STARS: 1.25X TO 2.5X HI CLMN		
*DIE CUT RCs: 1X TO 2X HI		
ONE DIE CUT PER PACK		
MJ1R: STATED ODDS 1:30		
MJ1S: STATED ODDS 1:192		

□ 1 Glenn Robinson FOIL	2.50	1.10
□ 2 Jason Kidd FOIL	5.00	2.20
□ 3 Grant Hill FOIL	8.00	3.60
□ 4 Donyell Marshall FOIL	.75	.35
□ 5 Juwan Howard FOIL	3.00	1.35
□ 6 Sharone Wright FOIL	.15	.07
□ 7 Lamond Murray FOIL	.30	.14
□ 8 Brian Grant FOIL	.60	.25
□ 9 Eric Montross FOIL	.15	.07
□ 10 Eddie Jones FOIL	5.00	2.20
□ 11 Carlos Rogers FOIL	.15	.07
□ 12 Khalid Reeves FOIL	.15	.07
□ 13 Jalen Rose FOIL	.60	.25
□ 14 Eric Piatkowski FOIL	.15	.07
□ 15 Clifford Rozier FOIL	.15	.07
□ 16 Aaron McKie FOIL	.15	.07
□ 17 Eric Mobley FOIL	.15	.07
□ 18 Tony Dumas FOIL	.15	.07
□ 19 B.J. Tyler FOIL	.15	.07
□ 20 Dickey Simpkins FOIL	.15	.07
□ 21 Bill Curley FOIL	.15	.07
□ 22 Wesley Person FOIL	.75	.35
□ 23 Monty Williams FOIL	.15	.07
□ 24 Greg Minor FOIL	.15	.07
□ 25 Charlie Ward FOIL	.30	.14
□ 26 Brooks Thompson FOIL	.15	.07
□ 27 Trevor Ruffin FOIL	.15	.07
□ 28 Derrick Alston FOIL	.15	.07
□ 29 Michael Smith FOIL	.30	.14
□ 30 Dontonio Wingfield FOIL	.15	.07
□ 31 Stacey Augmon	.15	.07
□ 32 Steve Smith	.30	.14
□ 33 Mookie Blaylock	.30	.14
□ 34 Grant Long	.15	.07
□ 35 Ken Norman	.15	.07
□ 36 Dominique Wilkins	.60	.25
□ 37 Dino Radja	.15	.07
□ 38 Dee Brown	.15	.07
□ 39 David Wesley	.30	.14
□ 40 Rick Fox	.15	.07
□ 41 Alonzo Mourning	.75	.35
□ 42 Larry Johnson	.30	.14
□ 43 Hersey Hawkins	.30	.14
□ 44 Scott Burrell	.15	.07
□ 45 Muggsy Bogues	.30	.14
□ 46 Scottie Pippen	2.00	.90
□ 47 Toni Kukoc	.60	.25
□ 48 B.J. Armstrong	.15	.07
□ 49 Will Perdue	.15	.07
□ 50 Ron Harper	.30	.14
□ 51 Mark Price	.15	.07
□ 52 Tyrone Hill	.15	.07
□ 53 Chris Mills	.30	.14
□ 54 John Williams	.15	.07
□ 55 Bobby Phills	.15	.07
□ 56 Jim Jackson	.30	.14
□ 57 Jamal Mashburn	.60	.25
□ 58 Popeye Jones	.15	.07
□ 59 Roy Tarpley	.15	.07
□ 60 Lorenzo Williams	.15	.07
□ 61 Mahmoud Abdul-Rauf	.15	.07
□ 62 Rodney Rogers	.15	.07
□ 63 Bryant Stith	.15	.07
□ 64 Dikembe Mutombo	.60	.25
□ 65 Robert Pack	.15	.07
□ 66 Joe Dumars	.60	.25
□ 67 Terry Mills	.15	.07
□ 68 Oliver Miller	.15	.07
□ 69 Lindsey Hunter	.30	.14
□ 70 Mark West	.15	.07
□ 71 Latrell Sprewell	.30	.14
□ 72 Tim Hardaway	.75	.35
□ 73 Ricky Pierce	.15	.07
□ 74 Rony Seikaly	.15	.07
□ 75 Tom Gugliotta	.60	.25
□ 76 Hakeem Olajuwon	1.25	.55
□ 77 Clyde Drexler	.75	.35
□ 78 Vernon Maxwell	.15	.07
□ 79 Robert Horry	.30	.14
□ 80 Sam Cassell	.60	.25
□ 81 Reggie Miller	.60	.25
□ 82 Rik Smits	.30	.14
□ 83 Derrick McKey	.15	.07
□ 84 Mark Jackson	.15	.07
□ 85 Dale Davis	.15	.07
□ 86 Loy Vaught	.30	.14
□ 87 Terry Dehere	.15	.07
□ 88 Malik Sealy	.15	.07
□ 89 Pooh Richardson	.15	.07
□ 90 Tony Massenburg	.15	.07
□ 91 Cedric Ceballos	.30	.14
□ 92 Nick Van Exel	.60	.25
□ 93 George Lynch	.15	.07
□ 94 Vlade Divac	.30	.14
□ 95 Elden Campbell	.30	.14
□ 96 Glen Rice	.60	.25
□ 97 Kevin Willis	.15	.07
□ 98 Billy Owens	.15	.07
□ 99 Bimbo Coles	.15	.07
□ 100 Harold Miner	.15	.07
□ 101 Vin Baker	1.50	.70
□ 102 Todd Day	.15	.07

		MINT	NRMT
☐ 103 Marty Conlon	.15		.07
☐ 104 Lee Mayberry	.15		.07
☐ 105 Eric Murdock	.15		.07
☐ 106 Isaiah Rider	.30		.14
☐ 107 Doug West	.15		.07
☐ 108 Christian Laettner	.30		.14
☐ 109 Sean Rooks	.15		.07
☐ 110 Stacey King	.15		.07
☐ 111 Derrick Coleman	.30		.14
☐ 112 Kenny Anderson	.30		.14
☐ 113 Chris Morris	.15		.07
☐ 114 Armon Gilliam	.15		.07
☐ 115 Benoit Benjamin	.15		.07
☐ 116 Patrick Ewing	.60		.25
☐ 117 Charles Oakley	.30		.14
☐ 118 John Starks	.30		.14
☐ 119 Derek Harper	.30		.14
☐ 120 Charles Smith	.15		.07
☐ 121 Shaquille O'Neal	2.50		1.10
☐ 122 Anfernee Hardaway	2.50		1.10
☐ 123 Nick Anderson	.30		.14
☐ 124 Horace Grant	.30		.14
☐ 125 Donald Royal	.15		.07
☐ 126 C.Weatherspoon	.15		.07
☐ 127 Dana Barros	.15		.07
☐ 128 Jeff Malone	.15		.07
☐ 129 Willie Burton	.15		.07
☐ 130 Shawn Bradley	.30		.14
☐ 131 Charles Barkley	1.00		.45
☐ 132 Kevin Johnson	.30		.14
☐ 133 Danny Manning	.15		.07
☐ 134 Dan Majerle	.30		.14
☐ 135 A.C. Green	.30		.14
☐ 136 Otis Thorpe	.30		.14
☐ 137 Clifford Robinson	.30		.14
☐ 138 Rod Strickland	.30		.14
☐ 139 Buck Williams	.30		.14
☐ 140 James Robinson	.15		.07
☐ 141 Mitch Richmond	.60		.25
☐ 142 Walt Williams	.15		.07
☐ 143 Olden Polynice	.15		.07
☐ 144 Spud Webb	.30		.14
☐ 145 Duane Causwell	.15		.07
☐ 146 David Robinson	1.00		.45
☐ 147 Dennis Rodman	2.50		1.10
☐ 148 Sean Elliott	.30		.14
☐ 149 Avery Johnson	.15		.07
☐ 150 J.R. Reid	.15		.07
☐ 151 Shawn Kemp	2.00		.90
☐ 152 Gary Payton	1.00		.45
☐ 153 Detlef Schrempf	.30		.14
☐ 154 Nate McMillan	.15		.07
☐ 155 Kendall Gill	.30		.14
☐ 156 Karl Malone	1.00		.45
☐ 157 John Stockton	.60		.25
☐ 158 Jeff Hornacek	.30		.14
☐ 159 Felton Spencer	.15		.07
☐ 160 David Benoit	.15		.07
☐ 161 Chris Webber	1.50		.70
☐ 162 Rex Chapman	.15		.07
☐ 163 Don MacLean	.15		.07
☐ 164 Calbert Cheaney	.30		.14
☐ 165 Scott Skiles	.15		.07
☐ P23 Michael Jordan Red	15.00		6.75
☐ MJ1R Michael Jordan Red	6.00		2.70
☐ MJ1S Michael Jordan Silver	25.00		11.00

1994-95 SP Holoviews

Cards from this 36-card standard size set were randomly inserted in packs at a rate of one in five. The set features a mixture of NBA stars coupled with a wide selection of 1994-95 rookies. The fronts feature color action photos with a hologram of the

company spokesperson Shawn Kemp on the left with the player's name in silver just to the right. In addition, a holographic head shot of each player is placed in the lower left corner. The backs have a black and white photo on the right and player information on the left.

	MINT	NRMT
COMPLETE SET (36)	75.00	34.00
COMMON CARD (PC1-PC36)	1.00	.45
SEMISTARS	1.50	.70
UNLISTED STARS	3.00	1.35
STATED ODDS 1:5		
COMP.DIE CUT SET (36)	300.00	135.00
COMMON DC (DPC1-DPC36)	3.00	1.35
*DIE CUTS: 1.5X TO 3X HI COLUMN		
DIE CUTS: STATED ODDS 1:75		

		MINT	NRMT
☐ PC1 Eric Montross	1.00		.45
☐ PC2 Dominique Wilkins	3.00		1.35
☐ PC3 Larry Johnson	1.50		.70
☐ PC4 Dickey Simpkins	1.00		.45
☐ PC5 Jalen Rose	3.00		1.35
☐ PC6 Latrell Sprewell	1.50		.70
☐ PC7 Carlos Rogers	1.00		.45
☐ PC8 Lamond Murray	1.50		.70
☐ PC9 Eddie Jones	12.00		5.50
☐ PC10 Cedric Ceballos	1.50		.70
☐ PC11 Khalid Reeves	1.00		.45
☐ PC12 Glenn Robinson	6.00		2.70
☐ PC13 Christian Laettner	1.50		.70
☐ PC14 Derrick Coleman	1.50		.70
☐ PC15 Vin Baker	8.00		3.60
☐ PC16 Donyell Marshall	3.00		1.35
☐ PC17 Kenny Anderson	1.50		.70
☐ PC18 Sharone Wright	1.00		.45
☐ PC19 Wesley Person	3.00		1.35
☐ PC20 Brian Grant	3.00		1.35
☐ PC21 Mitch Richmond	3.00		1.35
☐ PC22 Shawn Kemp	10.00		4.50
☐ PC23 Gary Payton	5.00		2.20
☐ PC24 Juwan Howard	8.00		3.60
☐ PC25 Stacey Augmon	1.00		.45
☐ PC26 Aaron McKie	1.00		.45
☐ PC27 Clifford Rozier	1.00		.45
☐ PC28 Eric Piatkowski	1.00		.45
☐ PC29 Shaquille O'Neal	12.00		5.50
☐ PC30 Charlie Ward	1.50		.70
☐ PC31 Monty Williams	1.00		.45
☐ PC32 Jason Kidd	12.00		5.50
☐ PC33 Bill Curley	1.00		.45
☐ PC34 Grant Hill	20.00		9.00
☐ PC35 Jamal Mashburn	3.00		1.35
☐ PC36 Nick Van Exel	3.00		1.35

1995-96 SP

The 1995-96 Upper Deck SP set was issued in one series totalling 167 cards. The 8-card packs, distributed exclusively to hobby outlets, retailed for $4.19 each. The first 147 cards are grouped by team alphabetically by city. The set ends with the rookie-based subset Premier Prospects (148-167) which feature a totally different design to the basic cards. Card stock thickness was upgraded from the previous year. A special Hakeem Olajuwon Commemorative card (celebrating his achievement of becoming only the ninth player in NBA history to score 20,000 points and grab 10,000 rebounds) was randomly seeded into 1 in every 359 packs. Rookie Cards of note in this set include Michael Finley, Kevin Garnett, Antonio McDyess, Jerry Stackhouse and Damon Stoudamire.

	MINT	NRMT
COMPLETE SET (167)	30.00	13.50
COMMON CARD (1-167)	.15	.07
SEMISTARS	.20	.09
UNLISTED STARS	.40	.18
C1: STATED ODDS 1:359		

		MINT	NRMT
☐ 1 Stacey Augmon	.15		.07
☐ 2 Mookie Blaylock	.20		.09
☐ 3 Andrew Lang	.15		.07
☐ 4 Steve Smith	.20		.09
☐ 5 Spud Webb	.20		.09
☐ 6 Dana Barros	.15		.07
☐ 7 Dee Brown	.15		.07
☐ 8 Todd Day	.15		.07
☐ 9 Rick Fox	.15		.07
☐ 10 Eric Montross	.15		.07
☐ 11 Dino Radja	.15		.07
☐ 12 Kenny Anderson	.20		.09
☐ 13 Scott Burrell	.15		.07
☐ 14 Dell Curry	.15		.07
☐ 15 Matt Geiger	.15		.07
☐ 16 Larry Johnson	.20		.09
☐ 17 Glen Rice	.40		.18
☐ 18 Steve Ward	.20		.09
☐ 19 Toni Kukoc	.20		.09
☐ 20 Luc Longley	.20		.09
☐ 21 Scottie Pippen	1.25		.55
☐ 22 Dennis Rodman	3.00		1.35
☐ 23 Michael Jordan	5.00		2.20
☐ 24 Terrell Brandon	.40		.18
☐ 25 Michael Cage	.15		.07
☐ 26 Danny Ferry	.15		.07
☐ 27 Chris Mills	.15		.07
☐ 28 Bobby Phills	.15		.07
☐ 29 Tony Dumas	.15		.07

	Player	MINT	NRMT
□ 30	Jim Jackson	.20	.09
□ 31	Popeye Jones	.15	.07
□ 32	Jason Kidd	1.00	.45
□ 33	Jamal Mashburn	.20	.09
□ 34	Mahmoud Abdul-Rauf	.15	.07
□ 35	LaPhonso Ellis	.20	.09
□ 36	Dikembe Mutombo	.20	.09
□ 37	Jalen Rose	.20	.09
□ 38	Bryant Stith	.15	.07
□ 39	Joe Dumars	.40	.18
□ 40	Grant Hill	2.50	1.10
□ 41	Lindsey Hunter	.15	.07
□ 42	Allan Houston	.20	.09
□ 43	Otis Thorpe	.20	.09
□ 44	B.J. Armstrong	.15	.07
□ 45	Tim Hardaway	.50	.23
□ 46	Chris Mullin	.40	.18
□ 47	Latrell Sprewell	.20	.09
□ 48	Rony Seikaly	.15	.07
□ 49	Sam Cassell	.20	.09
□ 50	Clyde Drexler	.50	.23
□ 51	Robert Horry	.15	.07
□ 52	Hakeem Olajuwon	.75	.35
□ 53	Kenny Smith	.15	.07
□ 54	Dale Davis	.15	.07
□ 55	Derrick McKey	.15	.07
□ 56	Reggie Miller	.40	.18
□ 57	Ricky Pierce	.15	.07
□ 58	Rik Smits	.20	.09
□ 59	Lamond Murray	.15	.07
□ 60	Rodney Rogers	.15	.07
□ 61	Malik Sealy	.15	.07
□ 62	Loy Vaught	.15	.07
□ 63	Brian Williams	.15	.07
□ 64	Elden Campbell	.20	.09
□ 65	Cedric Ceballos	.15	.07
□ 66	Magic Johnson	1.25	.55
□ 67	Eddie Jones	1.00	.45
□ 68	Nick Van Exel	.40	.18
□ 69	Bimbo Coles	.15	.07
□ 70	Alonzo Mourning	.40	.18
□ 71	Billy Owens	.15	.07
□ 72	Kevin Willis	.15	.07
□ 73	Vin Baker	.75	.35
□ 74	Benoit Benjamin	.15	.07
□ 75	Sherman Douglas	.15	.07
□ 76	Lee Mayberry	.15	.07
□ 77	Glenn Robinson	.50	.23
□ 78	Tom Gugliotta	.40	.18
□ 79	Christian Laettner	.20	.09
□ 80	Sam Mitchell	.15	.07
□ 81	Terry Porter	.15	.07
□ 82	Isaiah Rider	.20	.09
□ 83	Shawn Bradley	.20	.09
□ 84	P.J. Brown	.15	.07
□ 85	Kendall Gill	.20	.09
□ 86	Armon Gilliam	.15	.07
□ 87	Jayson Williams	.20	.09
□ 88	Patrick Ewing	.40	.18
□ 89	Derek Harper	.20	.09
□ 90	Anthony Mason	.20	.09
□ 91	Charles Oakley	.20	.09
□ 92	John Starks	.20	.09
□ 93	Nick Anderson	.15	.07
□ 94	Horace Grant	.20	.09
□ 95	Anfernee Hardaway	1.50	.70
□ 96	Shaquille O'Neal	1.50	.70
□ 97	Dennis Scott	.15	.07
□ 98	Derrick Coleman	.20	.09
□ 99	Vernon Maxwell	.15	.07
□ 100	Trevor Ruffin	.15	.07
□ 101	C.Weatherspoon	.15	.07
□ 102	Sharone Wright	.15	.07
□ 103	Charles Barkley	.60	.25
□ 104	A.C. Green	.20	.09
□ 105	Kevin Johnson	.20	.09
□ 106	Wesley Person	.20	.09
□ 107	John Williams	.15	.07
□ 108	Chris Dudley	.15	.07
□ 109	Harvey Grant	.15	.07
□ 110	Aaron McKie	.15	.07
□ 111	Clifford Robinson	.15	.07
□ 112	Rod Strickland	.20	.09
□ 113	Brian Grant	.20	.09
□ 114	Sarunas Marciulionis	.15	.07
□ 115	Olden Polynice	.15	.07
□ 116	Mitch Richmond	.40	.18
□ 117	Walt Williams	.15	.07
□ 118	Vinny Del Negro	.15	.07
□ 119	Sean Elliott	.15	.07
□ 120	Avery Johnson	.15	.07
□ 121	Chuck Person	.15	.07
□ 122	David Robinson	.60	.25
□ 123	Hersey Hawkins	.20	.09
□ 124	Shawn Kemp	1.25	.55
□ 125	Gary Payton	.60	.25
□ 126	Sam Perkins	.20	.09
□ 127	Detlef Schrempf	.20	.09
□ 128	Oliver Miller	.15	.07
□ 129	Tracy Murray	.15	.07
□ 130	Ed Pinckney	.15	.07
□ 131	Alvin Robertson	.15	.07
□ 132	Zan Tabak	.15	.07
□ 133	Jeff Hornacek	.20	.09
□ 134	Adam Keefe	.15	.07
□ 135	Karl Malone	.60	.25
□ 136	Chris Morris	.15	.07
□ 137	John Stockton	.40	.18
□ 138	Greg Anthony	.15	.07
□ 139	Blue Edwards	.15	.07
□ 140	Kenny Gattison	.15	.07
□ 141	Chris King	.15	.07
□ 142	Byron Scott	.15	.07
□ 143	Calbert Cheaney	.15	.07
□ 144	Juwan Howard	.60	.25
□ 145	Gheorghe Muresan	.15	.07
□ 146	Robert Pack	.15	.07
□ 147	Chris Webber	1.00	.45
□ 148	Alan Henderson	.40	.18
□ 149	Eric Williams	.20	.09
□ 150	George Zidek	.15	.07
□ 151	Bob Sura	.20	.09
□ 152	Antonio McDyess	2.00	.90
□ 153	Theo Ratliff	.40	.18
□ 154	Joe Smith	1.50	.70
□ 155	Brent Barry	.40	.18
□ 156	Sasha Danilovic	.15	.07
□ 157	Kurt Thomas	.20	.09
□ 158	Shawn Respert	.15	.07
□ 159	Kevin Garnett	6.00	2.70
□ 160	Ed O'Bannon	.15	.07
□ 161	Jerry Stackhouse	1.50	.70
□ 162	Michael Finley	1.50	.70
□ 163	Arvydas Sabonis	.75	.35
□ 164	Cory Alexander	.15	.07
□ 165	Damon Stoudamire	3.00	1.35
□ 166	Bryant Reeves	1.00	.45
□ 167	Rasheed Wallace	1.00	.45
□ C1	Hakeem Olajuwon	15.00	6.75
	Commemorative		

1995-96 SP All-Stars

Randomly inserted in packs at a rate of one in 5, this 30-card set features 24 players from the 1996 NBA All-Star game in addition to several future All-Star athletes. Each card features a double die-cut design and silver foil stamping.

		MINT	NRMT
COMPLETE SET (30)		70.00	32.00
COMMON CARD (AS1-AS30)		.60	.25
SEMISTARS		.75	.35
UNLISTED STARS		1.25	.55
STATED ODDS 1:5			
COMP.GOLD SET (30)		600.00	275.00
COMMON GOLD (AS1-AS30)		5.00	2.20
*GOLD STARS: 4X TO 8X HI COLUMN			
*GOLD RCs: 3X TO 6X HI			
GOLD: STATED ODDS 1:61			

	Player	MINT	NRMT
□ AS1	Anfernee Hardaway	5.00	2.20
□ AS2	Michael Jordan	20.00	9.00
□ AS3	Grant Hill	8.00	3.60
□ AS4	Scottie Pippen	4.00	1.80
□ AS5	Shaquille O'Neal	5.00	2.20
□ AS6	Vin Baker	2.50	1.10
□ AS7	Terrell Brandon	1.25	.55
□ AS8	Patrick Ewing	1.25	.55
□ AS9	Juwan Howard	2.00	.90
□ AS10	Reggie Miller	1.25	.55
□ AS11	Alonzo Mourning	1.25	.55
□ AS12	Glen Rice	1.25	.55
□ AS13	Clyde Drexler	1.50	.70
□ AS14	Jason Kidd	3.00	1.35
□ AS15	Charles Barkley	2.00	.90
□ AS16	Shawn Kemp	4.00	1.80
□ AS17	Hakeem Olajuwon	2.50	1.10
□ AS18	Sean Elliott	.60	.25
□ AS19	Karl Malone	2.00	.90
□ AS20	Dikembe Mutombo	.75	.35
□ AS21	Gary Payton	2.00	.90
□ AS22	Mitch Richmond	1.25	.55
□ AS23	David Robinson	2.00	.90
□ AS24	John Stockton	1.25	.55
□ AS25	Jerry Stackhouse	2.50	1.10
□ AS26	Damon Stoudamire	5.00	2.20
□ AS27	Rasheed Wallace	1.50	.70
□ AS28	Kevin Garnett	10.00	4.50
□ AS29	Antonio McDyess	3.00	1.35
□ AS30	Joe Smith	2.50	1.10

1995-96 SP Holoviews

Randomly inserted in packs at a rate of one in 7, this 40-card set features a selection of young-sters and veteran stars from all 29 teams. Each card utilizes the special Holoview technology and features four holographic head shot images in the back-ground.

	MINT	NRMT
COMPLETE SET (40)	125.00	55.00
COMMON CARD (PC1-PC40)	1.00	.45

	MINT	NRMT
SEMISTARS	1.50	.70
UNLISTED STARS	2.50	1.10
STATED ODDS 1:7		
COMP.DIE CUT SET (40)	500.00	220.00
COMMON CARD (PC1-PC40)	4.00	1.80
*DIE CUTS: 2X TO 4X HI COLUMN		
DIE CUT: STATED ODDS 1:76		
PC1 Mookie Blaylock	1.50	.70
PC2 Eric Williams	1.50	.70
PC3 Larry Johnson	1.50	.70
PC4 George Zidek	1.00	.45
PC5 Michael Jordan	30.00	13.50
PC6 Bob Sura	1.50	.70
PC7 Jason Kidd	6.00	2.70
PC8 Cherokee Parks	1.00	.45
PC9 Antonio McDyess	6.00	2.70
PC10 Grant Hill	15.00	6.75
PC11 Theo Ratliff	2.50	1.10
PC12 Joe Smith	5.00	2.20
PC13 Latrell Sprewell	1.50	.70
PC14 Hakeem Olajuwon	5.00	2.20
PC15 Travis Best	1.50	.70
PC16 Brent Barry	2.50	1.10
PC17 Nick Van Exel	1.50	.70
PC18 Kurt Thomas	1.50	.70
PC19 Shawn Respert	1.00	.45
PC20 Glenn Robinson	3.00	1.35
PC21 Christian Laettner	1.50	.70
PC22 Ed O'Bannon	1.00	.45
PC23 Patrick Ewing	2.50	1.10
PC24 Anfernee Hardaway	10.00	4.50
PC25 Shaquille O'Neal	10.00	4.50
PC26 Jerry Stackhouse	5.00	2.20
PC27 Mario Bennett	1.00	.45
PC28 Michael Finley	5.00	2.20
PC29 Randolph Childress	1.00	.45
PC30 Brian Grant	1.50	.70
PC31 Mitch Richmond	2.50	1.10
PC32 Cory Alexander	1.00	.45
PC33 David Robinson	4.00	1.80
PC34 Sherrell Ford	1.00	.45
PC35 Shawn Kemp	8.00	3.60
PC36 Damon Stoudamire	10.00	4.50
PC37 Greg Ostertag	1.00	.45
PC38 Bryant Reeves	3.00	1.35
PC39 Juwan Howard	4.00	1.80
PC40 Rasheed Wallace	3.00	1.35

1996-97 SP

The 1996-97 SP set was issued in one series totalling 146 cards. The set contains the topical subset Premier Prospects (127-146). Cards were issued in 8-card packs with a suggested retail price of $3.99. Card fronts feature a player shot with his name running horizontally across the bottom and the player's team running vertically across the side.

	MINT	NRMT
COMPLETE SET (146)	35.00	16.00
COMMON CARD (1-146)	.15	.07
SEMISTARS	.20	.09
UNLISTED STARS	.40	.18
1 Mookie Blaylock	.20	.09
2 Christian Laettner	.20	.09
3 Dikembe Mutombo	.20	.09
4 Steve Smith	.20	.09
5 Dana Barros	.15	.07
6 Rick Fox	.15	.07
7 Dino Radja	.15	.07
8 Eric Williams	.15	.07
9 Dell Curry	.15	.07
10 Vlade Divac	.20	.09
11 Anthony Mason	.20	.09
12 Glen Rice	.40	.18
13 Scottie Pippen	1.25	.55
14 Toni Kukoc	.20	.09
15 Luc Longley	.20	.09
16 Michael Jordan	5.00	2.20
17 Dennis Rodman	1.50	.70
18 Terrell Brandon	.40	.18
19 Tyrone Hill	.15	.07
20 Bobby Phills	.15	.07
21 Bob Sura	.15	.07
22 Chris Gatling	.15	.07
23 Jim Jackson	.20	.09
24 Sam Cassell	.20	.09
25 Jamal Mashburn	.20	.09
26 Dale Ellis	.15	.07
27 LaPhonso Ellis	.15	.07
28 Mark Jackson	.15	.07
29 Antonio McDyess	.60	.25
30 Bryant Stith	.15	.07
31 Joe Dumars	.40	.18
32 Grant Hill	2.50	1.10
33 Lindsey Hunter	.15	.07
34 Otis Thorpe	.20	.09
35 Chris Mullin	.40	.18
36 Mark Price	.15	.07
37 Joe Smith	.50	.23
38 Latrell Sprewell	.20	.09
39 Charles Barkley	.60	.25
40 Clyde Drexler	.50	.23
41 Mario Elie	.15	.07
42 Hakeem Olajuwon	.75	.35
43 Travis Best	.15	.07
44 Dale Davis	.15	.07
45 Reggie Miller	.40	.18
46 Rik Smits	.20	.09
47 Pooh Richardson	.15	.07
48 Rodney Rogers	.15	.07
49 Malik Sealy	.15	.07
50 Loy Vaught	.20	.09
51 Elden Campbell	.20	.09
52 Robert Horry	.20	.09
53 Eddie Jones	.75	.35
54 Shaquille O'Neal	1.50	.70
55 Nick Van Exel	.40	.18
56 Sasha Danilovic	.15	.07
57 Tim Hardaway	.50	.23
58 Dan Majerle	.20	.09
59 Alonzo Mourning	.40	.18
60 Vin Baker	.75	.35
61 Sherman Douglas	.15	.07
62 Armon Gilliam	.15	.07
63 Glenn Robinson	.40	.18
64 Kevin Garnett	2.50	1.10
65 Tom Gugliotta	.40	.18
66 Terry Porter	.15	.07
67 Doug West	.15	.07
68 Shawn Bradley	.15	.07
69 Kendall Gill	.20	.09
70 Robert Pack	.15	.07
71 Jayson Williams	.20	.09
72 Chris Childs	.15	.07
73 Patrick Ewing	.40	.18
74 Allan Houston	.20	.09
75 Larry Johnson	.20	.09
76 John Starks	.15	.07
77 Nick Anderson	.15	.07
78 Horace Grant	.20	.09
79 Anfernee Hardaway	1.50	.70
80 Dennis Scott	.15	.07
81 Derrick Coleman	.20	.09
82 Mark Davis	.15	.07
83 Jerry Stackhouse	.50	.23
84 Clarence Weatherspoon	.15	.07
85 Cedric Ceballos	.15	.07
86 Kevin Johnson	.20	.09
87 Jason Kidd	.75	.35
88 Danny Manning	.20	.09
89 Wesley Person	.15	.07
90 Kenny Anderson	.20	.09
91 Isaiah Rider	.20	.09
92 Clifford Robinson	.15	.07
93 Arvydas Sabonis	.20	.09
94 Rasheed Wallace	.20	.09
95 Mahmoud Abdul-Rauf	.15	.07
96 Brian Grant	.15	.07
97 Olden Polynice	.15	.07
98 Mitch Richmond	.40	.18
99 Corliss Williamson	.20	.09
100 Sean Elliott	.15	.07
101 Avery Johnson	.15	.07
102 David Robinson	.60	.25
103 Dominique Wilkins	.40	.18
104 Hersey Hawkins	.20	.09
105 Jim McIlvaine	.15	.07
106 Shawn Kemp	1.25	.55
107 Gary Payton	.60	.25
108 Detlef Schrempf	.20	.09
109 Doug Christie	.15	.07
110 Popeye Jones	.15	.07
111 Damon Stoudamire	1.00	.45
112 Walt Williams	.15	.07
113 Jeff Hornacek	.20	.09
114 Karl Malone	.60	.25
115 Greg Ostertag	.15	.07
116 Bryon Russell	.15	.07
117 John Stockton	.40	.18
118 Greg Anthony	.15	.07
119 Blue Edwards	.15	.07
120 Anthony Peeler	.15	.07
121 Bryant Reeves	.20	.09
122 Calbert Cheaney	.15	.07
123 Juwan Howard	.50	.23
124 Gheorghe Muresan	.15	.07
125 Rod Strickland	.20	.09
126 Chris Webber	1.00	.45
127 Antoine Walker	4.00	1.80
128 Tony Delk	.50	.23
129 Vitaly Potapenko	.20	.09
130 Samaki Walker	.50	.23
131 Todd Fuller	.15	.07
132 Erick Dampier	.50	.23
133 Lorenzen Wright	.50	.23
134 Kobe Bryant	8.00	3.60
135 Derek Fisher	.50	.23
136 Ray Allen	1.25	.55
137 Stephon Marbury	4.00	1.80
138 Kerry Kittles	1.00	.45
139 Walter McCarty	.20	.09
140 John Wallace	.60	.25
141 Allen Iverson	4.00	1.80
142 Steve Nash	.60	.25
143 Jermaine O'Neal	.60	.25
144 Marcus Camby	1.00	.45
145 Shareef Abdur-Rahim	2.50	1.10
146 Roy Rogers	.15	.07

1996-97 SP Game Film

Randomly inserted in packs at a rate of one in 120, this 10-card set uses slide photography and video film to capture the moves of each particular player. Card backs contain a "GF" prefix.

	MINT	NRMT
COMPLETE SET (10)	400.00	180.00
COMMON CARD (GF1-GF10)	6.00	2.70
SEMISTARS	10.00	4.50
STATED ODDS 1:120		

		MINT	NRMT
☐ GF1	Michael Jordan	125.00	55.00
☐ GF2	Kevin Garnett	60.00	27.00
☐ GF3	Charles Barkley	15.00	6.75
☐ GF4	Anfernee Hardaway	40.00	18.00
☐ GF5	Shaquille O'Neal ...	40.00	18.00
☐ GF6	Jim Jackson	6.00	2.70
☐ GF7	Dennis Rodman	40.00	18.00
☐ GF8	Alonzo Mourning ...	10.00	4.50
☐ GF9	Grant Hill	60.00	27.00
☐ GF10	Shawn Kemp	30.00	13.50

1996-97 SP Holoviews

Randomly inserted in packs at a rate of one in 10, this 40-card set features the top NBA players with Holoview technology. Unlike past years, there is no die-cut parallel. Card backs are numbered with a "PC" prefix.

		MINT	NRMT
COMPLETE SET (40)		300.00	135.00
COMMON CARD (PC1-PC40)		1.50	.70
SEMISTARS		2.00	.90
UNLISTED STARS		3.00	1.35
STATED ODDS 1:10			

☐ PC1	Mookie Blaylock	2.00	.90
☐ PC2	Antoine Walker	20.00	9.00
☐ PC3	Eric Williams.........	1.50	.70
☐ PC4	Tony Delk	3.00	1.35
☐ PC5	Michael Jordan	40.00	18.00
☐ PC6	Dennis Rodman	12.00	5.50
☐ PC7	Vitaly Potapenko....	2.00	.90
☐ PC8	Bob Sura	1.50	.70
☐ PC9	Jamal Mashburn	2.00	.90
☐ PC10	Antonio McDyess ...	5.00	2.20
☐ PC11	Grant Hill..............	20.00	9.00
☐ PC12	Joe Smith	4.00	1.80
☐ PC13	Latrell Sprewell......	2.00	.90
☐ PC14	Charles Barkley	5.00	2.20
☐ PC15	Hakeem Olajuwon ..	6.00	2.70
☐ PC16	Erick Dampier	3.00	1.35
☐ PC17	Lorenzen Wright	3.00	1.35

☐ PC18	Kobe Bryant	40.00	18.00
☐ PC19	Shaquille O'Neal ..	12.00	5.50
☐ PC20	Alonzo Mourning ..	3.00	1.35
☐ PC21	Ray Allen	6.00	2.70
☐ PC22	Kevin Garnett	20.00	9.00
☐ PC23	Stephon Marbury ..	20.00	9.00
☐ PC24	Kerry Kittles	5.00	2.20
☐ PC25	Walter McCarty	2.00	.90
☐ PC26	John Wallace	3.00	1.35
☐ PC27	Anfernee Hardaway	12.00	5.50
☐ PC28	Allen Iverson	20.00	9.00
☐ PC29	Jerry Stackhouse ..	4.00	1.80
☐ PC30	Steve Nash	3.00	1.35
☐ PC31	Jermaine O'Neal ...	3.00	1.35
☐ PC32	Brian Grant	1.50	.70
☐ PC33	Mitch Richmond	3.00	1.35
☐ PC34	David Robinson	5.00	2.20
☐ PC35	Shawn Kemp.........	10.00	4.50
☐ PC36	Marcus Camby	5.00	2.20
☐ PC37	Damon Stoudamire	8.00	3.60
☐ PC38	John Stockton	3.00	1.35
☐ PC39	Shareef Abdur-Rahim	12.00	5.50
☐ PC40	Juwan Howard	4.00	1.80

1996-97 SP Inside Info

Inserted as a chiptopper at one per box, this 17-card set features several action and portrait photos of the players. In addition, each card has a special slide-out portion containing more information. The basic set contains 16 cards and the 17th is for Michael Jordan commemorating his 25,000 point.

		MINT	NRMT
COMPLETE SET (17)		225.00	100.00
COMMON CARD		2.50	1.10
SEMISTARS		4.00	1.80
ONE PER BOX			
*GOLD: 1.5X TO 3X HI COLUMN			
GOLD: RANDOM INSERTS IN BOXES			

☐ IN1	Charles Barkley	6.00	2.70
☐ IN2	Kevin Garnett........	25.00	11.00
☐ IN3	Anfernee Hardaway	15.00	6.75
☐ IN4	Grant Hill	25.00	11.00
☐ IN5	Allen Iverson	20.00	9.00
☐ IN6	Jason Kidd	8.00	3.60
☐ IN7	Shawn Kemp	12.00	5.50
☐ IN8	Antonio McDyess ...	6.00	2.70
☐ IN9	Dikembe Mutombo .	2.50	1.10
☐ IN10	Shaquille O'Neal ...	15.00	6.75
☐ IN11	Hakeem Olajuwon ..	8.00	3.60
☐ IN12	Dennis Rodman	15.00	6.75
☐ IN13	Jerry Stackhouse ...	5.00	2.20
☐ IN14	John Stockton	4.00	1.80
☐ IN15	Damon Stoudamire	10.00	4.50
☐ IN16	Chris Webber	10.00	4.50
☐ IN17	Michael Jordan 25K	60.00	27.00

1996-97 SP SPx Force

Randomly inserted in packs at a rate of one in 360, this 5-card set features the holoview technology of four players per card divided into particular themes: Scoring, Rebounding, Playmakers, Defenders and All-Around Talents. In addition, the All-Around Talents card also came in four different auto-graphed versions, with each player individually signing 100 cards. Each of the autographed cards are sequentially numbered.

	MINT	NRMT
COMPLETE SET (5)	300.00	135.00
COMMON CARD (F1-F5)	50.00	22.00
STATED ODDS 1:360		
AUTOGRAPHS NUMBERED TO 100		

		MINT	NRMT
☐ F1	Michael Jordan ...... Jerry Stackhouse Mitch Richmond Latrell Sprewell	100.00	45.00
☐ F2	Shawn Kemp .... Dennis Rodman Charles Barkley Juwan Howard	50.00	22.00
☐ F3	Mookie Blaylock ..... Nick Van Exel Stephon Marbury Damon Stoudamire	50.00	22.00
☐ F4	Marcus Camby .... Erick Dampier Anfernee Hardaway Antonio McDyess	50.00	22.00
☐ F5	Michael Jordan ...... Anfernee Hardaway Shawn Kemp Damon Stoudamire	110.00	50.00
☐ F5A	M.Jordan AU ...... Numbered to 100	2500.00	1100.00
☐ F5B	A.Hardaway AU .... Numbered to 100	600.00	275.00
☐ F5C	Shawn Kemp AU .. Numbered to 100	300.00	135.00
☐ F5D	D.Stoudamire AU .. Numbered to 100	250.00	110.00

1997-98 SP Authentic

This is the first year that the brand name SP has changed

over to SP Authentic, due to the heavy inclusion of autographs and memorabilia. The set size is 176 cards which were issued in five-card packs which carried a suggested retail price of $4.99.

	MINT	NRMT
COMPLETE SET (176)	80.00	36.00
COMMON CARD (1-176)	.25	.11
SEMISTARS	.40	.18
UNLISTED STARS	.60	.25

☐ 1 Steve Smith	.40		.18
☐ 2 Dikembe Mutombo	.40		.18
☐ 3 Christian Laettner	.40		.18
☐ 4 Mookie Blaylock	.40		.18
☐ 5 Alan Henderson	.25		.11
☐ 6 Antoine Walker	3.00		1.35
☐ 7 Ron Mercer	10.00		4.50
☐ 8 Walter McCarty	.25		.11
☐ 9 Kenny Anderson	.40		.18
☐ 10 Travis Knight	.25		.11
☐ 11 Dana Barros	.25		.11
☐ 12 Glen Rice	.60		.25
☐ 13 Vlade Divac	.40		.18
☐ 14 Dell Curry	.25		.11
☐ 15 David Wesley	.25		.11
☐ 16 Bobby Phills	.25		.11
☐ 17 Anthony Mason	.40		.18
☐ 18 Toni Kukoc	.40		.18
☐ 19 Dennis Rodman	2.50		1.10
☐ 20 Ron Harper	.40		.18
☐ 21 Steve Kerr	.25		.11
☐ 22 Scottie Pippen	2.00		.90
☐ 23 Michael Jordan	8.00		3.60
☐ 24 Shawn Kemp	2.00		.90
☐ 25 Wesley Person	.25		.11
☐ 26 Derek Anderson	4.00		1.80
☐ 27 Zydrunas Ilgauskas	.40		.18
☐ 28 Brevin Knight	4.00		1.80
☐ 29 Michael Finley	.60		.25
☐ 30 Shawn Bradley	.25		.11
☐ 31 A.C. Green	.40		.18
☐ 32 Hubert Davis	.25		.11
☐ 33 Dennis Scott	.25		.11
☐ 34 Tony Battie	2.50		1.10
☐ 35 Bobby Jackson	2.50		1.10
☐ 36 LaPhonso Ellis	.25		.11
☐ 37 Bryant Stith	.25		.11
☐ 38 Dean Garrett	.25		.11
☐ 39 Danny Fortson	2.50		1.10
☐ 40 Grant Hill	4.00		1.80
☐ 41 Brian Williams	.25		.11
☐ 42 Lindsey Hunter	.25		.11
☐ 43 Malik Sealy	.25		.11
☐ 44 Jerry Stackhouse	.60		.25
☐ 45 Muggsy Bogues	.25		.11
☐ 46 Joe Smith	.25		.11
☐ 47 Donyell Marshall	.25		.11
☐ 48 Erick Dampier	.25		.11
☐ 49 Bimbo Coles	.25		.11
☐ 50 Charles Barkley	1.00		.45
☐ 51 Hakeem Olajuwon	1.25		.55
☐ 52 Clyde Drexler	.75		.35
☐ 53 Kevin Willis	.25		.11
☐ 54 Mario Elie	.25		.11
☐ 55 Reggie Miller	.60		.25
☐ 56 Rik Smits	.40		.18
☐ 57 Chris Mullin	.40		.18
☐ 58 Antonio Davis	.25		.11
☐ 59 Dale Davis	.25		.11
☐ 60 Mark Jackson	.25		.11
☐ 61 Brent Barry	.25		.11
☐ 62 Loy Vaught	.40		.18
☐ 63 Rodney Rogers	.25		.11
☐ 64 Lamond Murray	.25		.11
☐ 65 Maurice Taylor	4.00		1.80
☐ 66 Shaquille O'Neal	2.50		1.10
☐ 67 Eddie Jones	1.25		.55
☐ 68 Kobe Bryant	5.00		2.20
☐ 69 Nick Van Exel	.60		.25
☐ 70 Robert Horry	.40		.18
☐ 71 Tim Hardaway	.75		.35
☐ 72 Jamal Mashburn	.40		.18
☐ 73 Alonzo Mourning	.60		.25
☐ 74 Isaac Austin	.25		.11
☐ 75 P.J. Brown	.25		.11
☐ 76 Ray Allen	.75		.35
☐ 77 Glenn Robinson	.60		.25
☐ 78 Ervin Johnson	.25		.11
☐ 79 Terrell Brandon	.60		.25
☐ 80 Tyrone Hill	.25		.11
☐ 81 Stephon Marbury	3.00		1.35
☐ 82 Kevin Garnett	4.00		1.80
☐ 83 Tom Gugliotta	.60		.25
☐ 84 Chris Carr	.25		.11
☐ 85 Cherokee Parks	.25		.11
☐ 86 Sam Cassell	.40		.18
☐ 87 Chris Gatling	.25		.11
☐ 88 Kendall Gill	.40		.18
☐ 89 Keith Van Horn	12.00		5.50
☐ 90 Jayson Williams	.40		.18
☐ 91 Kerry Kittles	.60		.25
☐ 92 Patrick Ewing	.60		.25
☐ 93 Larry Johnson	.40		.18
☐ 94 Chris Childs	.25		.11
☐ 95 John Starks	.40		.18
☐ 96 Charles Oakley	.25		.11
☐ 97 Allan Houston	.40		.18
☐ 98 Mark Price	.25		.11
☐ 99 Anfernee Hardaway	2.50		1.10
☐ 100 Rony Seikaly	.25		.11
☐ 101 Horace Grant	.40		.18
☐ 102 Charles Outlaw	.25		.11
☐ 103 C.Weatherspoon	.25		.11
☐ 104 Allen Iverson	3.00		1.35
☐ 105 Jim Jackson	.40		.18
☐ 106 Theo Ratliff	.25		.11
☐ 107 Tim Thomas	8.00		3.60
☐ 108 Danny Manning	.40		.18
☐ 109 Jason Kidd	1.25		.55
☐ 110 Kevin Johnson	.40		.18
☐ 111 Rex Chapman	.25		.11
☐ 112 Clifford Robinson	.25		.11
☐ 113 Antonio McDyess	.75		.35
☐ 114 Damon Stoudamire	1.25		.55
☐ 115 Isaiah Rider	.40		.18
☐ 116 Arvydas Sabonis	.40		.18
☐ 117 Rasheed Wallace	.40		.18
☐ 118 Brian Grant	.25		.11
☐ 119 Gary Trent	.25		.11
☐ 120 Mitch Richmond	.60		.25
☐ 121 Corliss Williamson	.40		.18
☐ 122 Lawrence Funderburke	1.25		.55
☐ 123 Olden Polynice	.25		.11
☐ 124 Billy Owens	.25		.11
☐ 125 Avery Johnson	.25		.11
☐ 126 Sean Elliott	.25		.11
☐ 127 David Robinson	1.00		.45
☐ 128 Tim Duncan	15.00		6.75
☐ 129 Jaren Jackson	.25		.11
☐ 130 Detlef Schrempf	.40		.18
☐ 131 Gary Payton	1.00		.45
☐ 132 Vin Baker	1.25		.55
☐ 133 Hersey Hawkins	.40		.18
☐ 134 Dale Ellis	.25		.11
☐ 135 Sam Perkins	.40		.18
☐ 136 Marcus Camby	.60		.25
☐ 137 John Wallace	.40		.18
☐ 138 Doug Christie	.25		.11
☐ 139 Chauncey Billups	5.00		2.20
☐ 140 Walt Williams	.25		.11
☐ 141 Karl Malone	1.00		.45
☐ 142 Bryon Russell	.25		.11
☐ 143 Jeff Hornacek	.40		.18
☐ 144 Greg Ostertag	.25		.11
☐ 145 John Stockton	.60		.25
☐ 146 Shandon Anderson	.25		.11
☐ 147 Shareef Abdur-Rahim	2.00		.90
☐ 148 Bryant Reeves	.40		.18
☐ 149 Antonio Daniels	3.00		1.35
☐ 150 Otis Thorpe	.40		.18
☐ 151 Blue Edwards	.25		.11
☐ 152 Chris Webber	1.50		.70
☐ 153 Juwan Howard	.60		.25
☐ 154 Rod Strickland	.40		.18
☐ 155 Calbert Cheaney	.25		.11
☐ 156 Tracy Murray	.25		.11
☐ 157 Chauncey Billups	2.50		1.10
☐ 158 Ed Gray	1.50		.70
☐ 159 Tony Battie FW	1.25		.55
☐ 160 Keith Van Horn FW	6.00		2.70
☐ 161 Cedric Henderson	1.50		.70
☐ 162 Kelvin Cato	1.50		.70
☐ 163 Tariq Abdul-Wahad	2.00		.90
☐ 164 Derek Anderson FW	2.00		.90
☐ 165 Tim Duncan FW	8.00		3.60
☐ 166 Tracy McGrady	8.00		3.60
☐ 167 Ron Mercer FW	5.00		2.20
☐ 168 Bobby Jackson FW	1.25		.55
☐ 169 Antonio Daniels FW	1.50		.70
☐ 170 Zydrunas Ilgauskas FW	.40		.18
☐ 171 Maurice Taylor FW	2.00		.90
☐ 172 Tim Thomas FW	4.00		1.80
☐ 173 Brevin Knight FW	2.00		.90
☐ 174 L.Funderburke FW	.60		.25
☐ 175 Jacque Vaughn	2.00		.90
☐ 176 Danny Fortson FW	1.25		.55

1997-98 SP Authentic Authentics

Randomly inserted into packs at an overall rate of one in 288, this 20-card set features redemption cards for various pieces of memorabilia (both signed and unsigned) from Michael Jordan, Anfernee Hardaway and Shawn Kemp. The cards are not numbered and are listed below in alphabetical order by player. Some cards are not priced below due to insufficient market information.

	MINT	NRMT
COMMON CARD	40.00	18.00
OVERALL STATED ODDS 1:288		
JORDAN GAME NIGHT SERIAL #'d TO 100		

FIVE DIFFERENT JORDAN GAME NIGHT CARDS
AUTOGRAPHED ITEMS LABELED WITH AU
PRINT RUNS LISTED IN PARENTHESIS

		MINT	NRMT
☐ AH1	Anfernee Hardaway Signed Black Jersey	600.00	275.00
☐ AH2	Anfernee Hardaway Signed Blue Jersey	500.00	220.00
☐ AH3	Anfernee Hardaway Signed Sports Illustrated	100.00	45.00
☐ AH4	Anfernee Hardaway Signed 8x10 photo	40.00	18.00
☐ MJ1	Michael Jordan.. Signed Jersey	2500.00	1100.00
☐ MJ2	Michael Jordan.. Signed 16x20 Photo	700.00	325.00
☐ MJ3	Michael Jordan.. Unsigned 2-card set	60.00	27.00
☐ MJ4	Michael Jordan.. Unsigned 8x10 Photo	60.00	27.00
☐ MJ5	Michael Jordan.. Unsigned Gold Card	80.00	36.00
☐ MJ6	Michael Jordan.. Unsigned Game Night Card	400.00	180.00
☐ MJ6B	Michael Jordan.. Unsigned Game Night Card	400.00	180.00
☐ MJ6C	Michael Jordan.. Unsigned Game Night Card	400.00	180.00
☐ MJ6D	Michael Jordan.. Unsigned Game Night Card	400.00	180.00
☐ MJ6E	Michael Jordan.. Unsigned Game Night Card	400.00	180.00
☐ MJ7	Michael Jordan.. Unsigned Blow-up Poster	80.00	36.00
☐ MJ8	Michael Jordan.. Signed Game Night Card	7000.00	3200.00
☐ SK1	Shawn Kemp..... Signed Sonics Jersey	500.00	220.00
☐ SK2	Shawn Kemp..... Signed All-Star Photo	100.00	45.00
☐ SK3	Shawn Kemp..... Signed Mini-ball	100.00	45.00
☐ NNO	SP Uncut Sheet (200)	150.00	70.00

1997-98 SP Authentic BuyBack

Randomly inserted into packs at a rate of one in 309 packs, this 36-card set features 15 different player autographs on past SP issued cards and/or inserts. Each card is different in regards to how many each player signed, but those numbers were not disclosed. Some cards are not priced below due to insufficient market information.

		MINT	NRMT
	COMMON CARD (1-15)	60.00	27.00

STATED ODDS 1:309 PACKS
CARDS NUMBERED BELOW ALPHABETICALLY

☐ 1	S.Abdur-Rahim '96/7	100.00	45.00
☐ 2	Vin Baker '94/5		
☐ 3	Vin Baker '95/6	100.00	45.00
☐ 4	Vin Baker '96/6AS		
☐ 5	Clyde Drexler '94/5	100.00	45.00
☐ 6	Clyde Drexler '95/6	100.00	45.00
☐ 7	Clyde Drexler '96/7	125.00	55.00
☐ 8	A.Hardaway '94/5	250.00	110.00
☐ 9	A.Hardaway '95/6	200.00	90.00
☐ 10	Anfernee Hardaway '96/7		
☐ 11	Tim Hardaway '94/5	80.00	36.00
☐ 12	Tim Hardaway '95/6		
☐ 13	Tim Hardaway '96/7		
☐ 14	Juwan Howard '94/5	100.00	45.00
☐ 15	Juwan Howard '95/6	70.00	32.00
☐ 16	Juwan Howard '95/6AS	100.00	45.00
☐ 17	Juwan Howard '96/7		
☐ 18	Eddie Jones '94/5 ..	125.00	55.00
☐ 19	Eddie Jones '95/6 ..	80.00	36.00
☐ 20	Eddie Jones '96/7		
☐ 21	M.Jordan '94MJ1R	3500.00	1600.00
☐ 22	Jason Kidd '94/5	125.00	55.00
☐ 23	Jason Kidd '95/6		
☐ 24	Jason Kidd '95/6AS		
☐ 25	Jason Kidd '96/7		
☐ 26	Kerry Kittles '96/7 ..	75.00	34.00
☐ 27	Karl Malone '94/5 ..	125.00	55.00
☐ 28	Karl Malone '95/6		
☐ 29	Glen Rice '95/6AS....	60.00	27.00
☐ 30	Glen Rice '96/7	80.00	36.00
☐ 31	Mitch Richmond '94/5	60.00	27.00
☐ 32	Mitch Richmond '95/6	60.00	27.00
☐ 33	Mitch Richmond '96/7		
☐ 34	Damon Stoudamire '95/6		
☐ 35	Damon Stoudamire '96/7		
☐ 36	Antoine Walker '96/7	150.00	70.00

1997-98 SP Authentic Premium Portraits

Randomly inserted into packs at a rate of one in 1,528, this seven-card set features an autograph from some of the top stars in the NBA. Card backs are numbered with the player's initials.

		MINT	NRMT
	COMPLETE SET (7)	1200.00	550.00
	COMMON CARD	100.00	45.00

STATED ODDS 1:1,528

☐ DP	Damon Stoudamire	200.00	90.00
☐ EP	Eddie Jones	250.00	110.00
☐ JP	Jason Kidd	250.00	110.00

☐ KP	Kerry Kittles	150.00	70.00
☐ MP	Dikembe Mutombo	100.00	45.00
☐ RP	Glen Rice	175.00	80.00
☐ TP	Tim Hardaway	200.00	90.00

1997-98 SP Authentic Profiles 1

Randomly inserted into packs at a rate of one in three, this 40-card set profiles some of the leagues best players. Card backs are numbered with a "P" prefix.

		MINT	NRMT
	COMPLETE SET (40)	80.00	36.00
	COMMON CARD (P1-P40)	.50	.23
	SEMISTARS	.60	.25
	UNLISTED STARS	1.00	.45

STATED ODDS 1:3

	COMP.PRO.2 SET (40)......	250.00	110.00
	COMMON PRO.2	1.25	.55

*PRO.2: 1X TO 2.5X HI COLUMN
PRO.2: STATED ODDS 1:12

☐ P1	Michael Jordan	12.00	5.50
☐ P2	Glen Rice	1.00	.45
☐ P3	Brent Barry	.50	.23
☐ P4	LaPhonso Ellis	.50	.23
☐ P5	Allen Iverson	5.00	2.20
☐ P6	Dikembe Mutombo	.60	.25
☐ P7	Charles Barkley	1.50	.70
☐ P8	Antoine Walker	5.00	2.20
☐ P9	Karl Malone	1.50	.70
☐ P10	Jason Kidd	2.00	.90
☐ P11	Gary Payton	1.50	.70
☐ P12	Kevin Garnett	6.00	2.70
☐ P13	Keith Van Horn	8.00	3.60
☐ P14	Glenn Robinson	1.00	.45
☐ P15	Michael Finley	1.00	.45
☐ P16	Hakeem Olajuwon	2.00	.90
☐ P17	Chris Webber	2.50	1.10
☐ P18	Mitch Richmond	1.00	.45
☐ P19	Marcus Camby	1.00	.45
☐ P20	Tim Hardaway	1.25	.55
☐ P21	Shawn Kemp	3.00	1.35
☐ P22	Reggie Miller	1.00	.45
☐ P23	Shaquille O'Neal	4.00	1.80
☐ P24	Chauncey Billups	3.00	1.35
☐ P25	Grant Hill	6.00	2.70
☐ P26	Shareef Abdur-Rahim	3.00	1.35
☐ P27	David Robinson	1.50	.70
☐ P28	Scottie Pippen	3.00	1.35
☐ P29	Juwan Howard	1.00	.45
☐ P30	Anfernee Hardaway	4.00	1.80
☐ P31	Jerry Stackhouse	1.00	.45
☐ P32	Kobe Bryant	8.00	3.60
☐ P33	Patrick Ewing	1.00	.45
☐ P34	Alonzo Mourning	1.00	.45
☐ P35	John Stockton	1.00	.45
☐ P36	Kenny Anderson	.60	.25

		MINT	NRMT
☐ P37	Tim Duncan	10.00	4.50
☐ P38	Stephon Marbury	5.00	2.20
☐ P39	Dennis Rodman	4.00	1.80
☐ P40	Joe Smith	1.00	.45

1997-98 SP Authentic Profiles 3

Randomly inserted into packs, this 40-card set parallels both the regular Profiles 1 and 2, but is die cut and is serially numbered on the back to 100. Card backs carry a "P" prefix.

		MINT	NRMT
COMMON CARD (P1-P40)		15.00	6.75
SEMISTARS		25.00	11.00
RANDOM INSERTS IN PACKS			
STATED PRINT RUN 100 SERIAL #'d SETS			
☐ P1	Michael Jordan	600.00	275.00
☐ P2	Glen Rice	40.00	18.00
☐ P3	Brent Barry	15.00	6.75
☐ P4	LaPhonso Ellis	15.00	6.75
☐ P5	Allen Iverson	200.00	90.00
☐ P6	Dikembe Mutombo	25.00	11.00
☐ P7	Charles Barkley	60.00	27.00
☐ P8	Antoine Walker	200.00	90.00
☐ P9	Karl Malone	60.00	27.00
☐ P10	Jason Kidd	80.00	36.00
☐ P11	Gary Payton	60.00	27.00
☐ P12	Kevin Garnett	250.00	110.00
☐ P13	Keith Van Horn	200.00	90.00
☐ P14	Glenn Robinson	30.00	13.50
☐ P15	Michael Finley	40.00	18.00
☐ P16	Hakeem Olajuwon	80.00	36.00
☐ P17	Chris Webber	100.00	45.00
☐ P18	Mitch Richmond	40.00	18.00
☐ P19	Marcus Camby	40.00	18.00
☐ P20	Tim Hardaway	50.00	22.00
☐ P21	Shawn Kemp	125.00	55.00
☐ P22	Reggie Miller	40.00	18.00
☐ P23	Shaquille O'Neal	150.00	70.00
☐ P24	Chauncey Billups	80.00	36.00
☐ P25	Grant Hill	250.00	110.00
☐ P26	Shareef Abdur-Rahim	125.00	55.00
☐ P27	David Robinson	60.00	27.00
☐ P28	Scottie Pippen	125.00	55.00
☐ P29	Juwan Howard	40.00	18.00
☐ P30	Anfernee Hardaway	150.00	70.00
☐ P31	Jerry Stackhouse	40.00	18.00
☐ P32	Kobe Bryant	300.00	135.00
☐ P33	Patrick Ewing	40.00	18.00
☐ P34	Alonzo Mourning	40.00	18.00
☐ P35	John Stockton	40.00	18.00
☐ P36	Kenny Anderson	25.00	11.00
☐ P37	Tim Duncan	250.00	110.00
☐ P38	Stephon Marbury	200.00	90.00
☐ P39	Dennis Rodman	150.00	70.00
☐ P40	Joe Smith	40.00	18.00

1997-98 SP Authentic Sign of the Times

Randomly inserted into packs at a rate of one in 42, this 22-card set features autographs of several different NBA players. Card backs are numbered with the player's initials.

		MINT	NRMT
COMPLETE SET (23)		750.00	350.00
COMMON CARD		15.00	6.75
STATED ODDS 1:42			
☐ AH	Allan Houston	20.00	9.00
☐ AJ	Avery Johnson	15.00	6.75
☐ BB	Brent Barry	20.00	9.00
☐ BW	Brian Williams	15.00	6.75
☐ CM	Chris Mullin	20.00	9.00
☐ DM	Dikembe Mutombo	25.00	11.00
☐ DS	Damon Stoudamire	50.00	22.00
☐ EJ	Eddie Jones	80.00	36.00
☐ GM	Gheorghe Muresan	20.00	9.00
☐ GP	Gary Payton	100.00	45.00
☐ GR	Glen Rice	40.00	18.00
☐ HW	Juwan Howard	60.00	27.00
☐ KJ	Kevin Johnson	30.00	13.50
☐ KK	Kerry Kittles	40.00	18.00
☐ LH	Lindsey Hunter	15.00	6.75
☐ MB	Mookie Blaylock	15.00	6.75
☐ MR	Mitch Richmond	40.00	18.00
☐ SC	Sam Cassell	20.00	9.00
☐ SE	Sean Elliott	15.00	6.75
☐ TE	Terrell Brandon	40.00	18.00
☐ TG	Tom Gugliotta	40.00	18.00
☐ TH	Tim Hardaway	70.00	32.00
☐ VB	Vin Baker	60.00	27.00

1997-98 SP Authentic Sign of the Times Stars and Rookies

Randomly inserted into packs at a rate of one in 113, this 11-card set features autographs of some of the top stars and rookies from 1997-98. Card backs are numbered with the player's initials. Some cards are not priced below due to insufficient market information.

		MINT	NRMT
COMMON CARD		50.00	22.00
STATED ODDS 1:113			
☐ AW	Antoine Walker	100.00	45.00
☐ CD	Clyde Drexler		
☐ CH	Chauncey Billups	60.00	27.00
☐ JK	Jason Kidd	100.00	45.00
☐ JS	John Stockton	70.00	32.00
☐ KM	Karl Malone	80.00	36.00
☐ KV	Keith Van Horn	120.00	55.00
☐ MJ	Michael Jordan		
☐ RO	Ron Mercer	100.00	45.00
☐ SA	Shareef Abdur-Rahim	100.00	45.00
☐ TB	Tony Battie	50.00	22.00

1994-95 SP Championship

The premier edition of the 1994-95 SP Championship series (made by Upper Deck) consists of 135 standard size cards issued in six-card foil packs, each with a suggested retail price of $2.99. SP Championship cards were shipped exclusively to retail outlets. Card fronts feature full-bleed, color action photos with a foil SP Championship logo. The player's name runs up the side of the card in small gold foil print. Team name is contained in a foil oval. After a Road to the Finals (1-27) subset, the cards are grouped alphabetically within team order. Rookie Cards of note in this set include Grant Hill, Juwan Howard, Eddie Jones, Jason Kidd and Glenn Robinson.

	MINT	NRMT
COMPLETE SET (135)	30.00	13.50
COMMON CARD (1-135)	.10	.05
SEMISTARS	.20	.09
UNLISTED STARS	.40	.18
COMP.DIE CUT SET (135)	60.00	27.00
COMMON DIE CUT (1-135)	.25	.11

*DIE CUT STARS: 1.25X TO 2.5X HI COL-
UMN
*DIE CUT RCs: 1X TO 2X HI
ONE DIE CUT PER PACK

☐ 1 Mookie Blaylock RF	.10	.05
☐ 2 Dominique Wilkins RF	.20	.09
☐ 3 Alonzo Mourning RF	.40	.18
☐ 4 Michael Jordan RF	4.00	1.80
☐ 5 Mark Price RF	.10	.05
☐ 6 Jamal Mashburn RF	.20	.09
☐ 7 Dikembe Mutombo RF	.20	.09
☐ 8 Grant Hill RF	2.00	.90
☐ 9 Latrell Sprewell RF	.10	.05
☐ 10 Hakeem Olajuwon RF	.40	.18
☐ 11 Reggie Miller RF	.20	.09
☐ 12 Loy Vaught RF	.10	.05
☐ 13 Nick Van Exel RF	.20	.09
☐ 14 Glen Rice RF	.20	.09
☐ 15 Glenn Robinson RF	.60	.25
☐ 16 Isaiah Rider RF	.10	.05
☐ 17 Kenny Anderson RF	.10	.05
☐ 18 Patrick Ewing RF	.20	.09
☐ 19 Shaquille O'Neal RF	.75	.35
☐ 20 Dana Barros RF	.20	.09
☐ 21 Charles Barkley RF	.40	.18
☐ 22 Clifford Robinson RF	.10	.05
☐ 23 Mitch Richmond RF	.20	.09
☐ 24 David Robinson RF	.40	.18
☐ 25 Shawn Kemp RF	.60	.25
☐ 26 Karl Malone RF	.40	.18
☐ 27 Chris Webber RF	.50	.23
☐ 28 Stacey Augmon	.10	.05
☐ 29 Mookie Blaylock	.20	.09
☐ 30 Grant Long	.10	.05
☐ 31 Steve Smith	.20	.09
☐ 32 Dee Brown	.10	.05
☐ 33 Eric Montross	.10	.05
☐ 34 Dino Radja	.10	.05
☐ 35 Dominique Wilkins	.40	.18
☐ 36 Muggsy Bogues	.20	.09
☐ 37 Scott Burrell	.10	.05
☐ 38 Larry Johnson	.20	.09
☐ 39 Alonzo Mourning	.50	.23
☐ 40 B.J. Armstrong	.10	.05
☐ 41 Michael Jordan	8.00	3.60
☐ 42 Toni Kukoc	.40	.18
☐ 43 Scottie Pippen	1.25	.55
☐ 44 Tyrone Hill	.10	.05
☐ 45 Chris Mills	.20	.09
☐ 46 Mark Price	.10	.05
☐ 47 John Williams	.10	.05
☐ 48 Jim Jackson	.20	.09
☐ 49 Jason Kidd	3.00	1.35
☐ 50 Jamal Mashburn	.40	.18
☐ 51 Roy Tarpley	.10	.05
☐ 52 Mahmoud Abdul-Rauf	.10	.05
☐ 53 Dikembe Mutombo	.40	.18
☐ 54 Rodney Rogers	.10	.05
☐ 55 Bryant Stith	.10	.05
☐ 56 Joe Dumars	.40	.18
☐ 57 Grant Hill	5.00	2.20
☐ 58 Lindsey Hunter	.20	.09
☐ 59 Terry Mills	.10	.05
☐ 60 Tim Hardaway	.50	.23
☐ 61 Donyell Marshall	.50	.23
☐ 62 Chris Mullin	.40	.18
☐ 63 Latrell Sprewell	.20	.09
☐ 64 Sam Cassell	.40	.18
☐ 65 Clyde Drexler	.50	.23
☐ 66 Vernon Maxwell	.10	.05
☐ 67 Hakeem Olajuwon	.75	.35
☐ 68 Dale Davis	.10	.05
☐ 69 Mark Jackson	.20	.09
☐ 70 Reggie Miller	.40	.18
☐ 71 Rik Smits	.20	.09
☐ 72 Terry Dehere	.10	.05
☐ 73 Lamond Murray	.20	.09
☐ 74 Pooh Richardson	.10	.05
☐ 75 Loy Vaught	.20	.09
☐ 76 Cedric Ceballos	.20	.09
☐ 77 Vlade Divac	.20	.09
☐ 78 Eddie Jones	3.00	1.35
☐ 79 Nick Van Exel	.40	.18
☐ 80 Bimbo Coles	.10	.05
☐ 81 Billy Owens	.10	.05
☐ 82 Glen Rice	.60	.25
☐ 83 Kevin Willis	.10	.05
☐ 84 Vin Baker	1.00	.45
☐ 85 Marty Conlon	.10	.05
☐ 86 Eric Murdock	.10	.05
☐ 87 Glenn Robinson	1.50	.70
☐ 88 Tom Gugliotta	.40	.18
☐ 89 Christian Laettner	.20	.09
☐ 90 Isaiah Rider	.20	.09
☐ 91 Doug West	.10	.05
☐ 92 Kenny Anderson	.20	.09
☐ 93 Benoit Benjamin	.10	.05
☐ 94 Derrick Coleman	.20	.09
☐ 95 Armon Gilliam	.10	.05
☐ 96 Patrick Ewing	.40	.18
☐ 97 Derek Harper	.20	.09
☐ 98 Charles Oakley	.20	.09
☐ 99 John Starks	.20	.09
☐ 100 Nick Anderson	.20	.09
☐ 101 Horace Grant	.20	.09
☐ 102 Anfernee Hardaway	1.50	.70
☐ 103 Shaquille O'Neal	1.50	.70
☐ 104 Dana Barros	.10	.05
☐ 105 Shawn Bradley	.20	.09
☐ 106 C.Weatherspoon	.10	.05
☐ 107 Sharone Wright	.10	.05
☐ 108 Charles Barkley	.60	.25
☐ 109 Kevin Johnson	.20	.09
☐ 110 Dan Majerle	.20	.09
☐ 111 Wesley Person	.50	.23
☐ 112 Terry Porter	.10	.05
☐ 113 Clifford Robinson	.20	.09
☐ 114 Rod Strickland	.20	.09
☐ 115 Buck Williams	.20	.09
☐ 116 Brian Grant	.40	.18
☐ 117 Mitch Richmond	.40	.18
☐ 118 Spud Webb	.20	.09
☐ 119 Walt Williams	.10	.05
☐ 120 Vinny Del Negro	.10	.05
☐ 121 Sean Elliott	.20	.09
☐ 122 David Robinson	.60	.25
☐ 123 Dennis Rodman	1.50	.70
☐ 124 Kendall Gill	.20	.09
☐ 125 Shawn Kemp	1.25	.55
☐ 126 Gary Payton	.60	.25
☐ 127 Detlef Schrempf	.20	.09
☐ 128 David Benoit	.10	.05
☐ 129 Jeff Hornacek	.20	.09
☐ 130 Karl Malone	.60	.25
☐ 131 John Stockton	.40	.18
☐ 132 Rex Chapman	.10	.05
☐ 133 Calbert Cheaney	.20	.09
☐ 134 Juwan Howard	2.00	.90
☐ 135 Chris Webber	1.00	.45

player action photos. The set is sequenced in alphabetical order.

	MINT	NRMT
COMPLETE SET (10)	50.00	22.00
COMMON CARD (F1-F10)	1.25	.55
SEMISTARS	2.50	1.10
STATED ODDS 1:40		
COMP.DIE CUT SET (10)	300.00	135.00
*DIE CUTS: 3X TO 6X HI COLUMN		
DIE CUTS: STATED ODDS 1:300		

☐ F1 Brian Grant	1.25	.55
☐ F2 Anfernee Hardaway	10.00	4.50
☐ F3 Grant Hill	15.00	6.75
☐ F4 Eddie Jones	10.00	4.50
☐ F5 Jamal Mashburn	2.50	1.10
☐ F6 Shaquille O'Neal	10.00	4.50
☐ F7 Isaiah Rider	1.25	.55
☐ F8 Glenn Robinson	5.00	2.20
☐ F9 Latrell Sprewell	1.25	.55
☐ F10 Chris Webber	6.00	2.70

1994-95 SP Championship Playoff Heroes

1994-95 SP Championship Future Playoff Heroes

Randomly inserted at a rate of 1 in every 40 packs, this 10-card standard-size set spotlights up-and-coming NBA stars who figure to be Playoff Heroes in the coming years. Unlike the glossy regular issue cards, these inserts feature a throwback design element incorporating basic cardboard-style backgrounds against glossy color

Randomly inserted at a rate of one in every 15 packs, this 10-card standard size set features active NBA Playoff performers. Unlike the glossy regular issue cards, these inserts feature a throwback design element incorporating basic cardboard-style backgrounds against glossy color player action photos. A number of cards slipped through production with scuffed logos on front. In addition, some others also had "Future Playoff Heroes" logos rather than the *regular "Playoff Heroes" logos. None of these variations trade for a premium. The set is sequenced in alphabetical order.*

	MINT	NRMT
COMPLETE SET (10)	50.00	22.00
COMMON CARD (P1-P10)	1.00	.45
SEMISTARS	1.50	.70
UNLISTED STARS	2.50	1.10
STATED ODDS 1:15		
COMP.DIE CUT SET (10)	250.00	110.00
*DIE CUTS: 2.5X TO 5X HI COLUMN		
DIE CUTS: STATED ODDS 1:225		

		MINT	NRMT
☐ P1	Charles Barkley	4.00	1.80
☐ P2	Michael Jordan	30.00	13.50
☐ P3	Shawn Kemp	8.00	3.60
☐ P4	Moses Malone	1.00	.45
☐ P5	Reggie Miller	2.50	1.10
☐ P6	Alonzo Mourning	3.00	1.35
☐ P7	Dikembe Mutombo	1.50	.70
☐ P8	Hakeem Olajuwon	5.00	2.20
☐ P9	Robert Parish	1.00	.45
☐ P10	John Stockton	2.50	1.10

1995-96 SP Championship

The 1995-96 SP Championship set was issued in one series totaling 146 cards. The 6-card packs retailed for $2.99 each. The set, issued in early-May, 1996 to retail outlets only, features full color action shots against an all-foil background with player name, team and a head shot along the front borders. The set is sequenced in alphabetical order by team and includes many of the top stars in the 1996 playoffs along with a special subset: Race for the Playoffs (118-146). Rookie Cards of note include Michael Finley, Kevin Garnett, Antonio McDyess, Jerry Stackhouse and Damon Stoudamire.

	MINT	NRMT
COMPLETE SET (146)	40.00	18.00
COMMON CARD (1-146)	.15	.07
SEMISTARS	.20	.09
UNLISTED STARS	.40	.18

		MINT	NRMT
☐ 1	Stacey Augmon	.15	.07
☐ 2	Mookie Blaylock	.20	.09
☐ 3	Alan Henderson	.40	.18
☐ 4	Steve Smith	.20	.09
☐ 5	Dana Barros	.15	.07
☐ 6	Dee Brown	.15	.07
☐ 7	Eric Montross	.15	.07
☐ 8	Dino Radja	.15	.07
☐ 9	Eric Williams	.20	.09
☐ 10	Kenny Anderson	.20	.09
☐ 11	Larry Johnson	.20	.09
☐ 12	Glen Rice	.40	.18
☐ 13	George Zidek	.15	.07
☐ 14	Toni Kukoc	.20	.09
☐ 15	Scottie Pippen	1.25	.55
☐ 16	Dennis Rodman	2.50	1.10
☐ 17	Michael Jordan	5.00	2.20
☐ 18	Terrell Brandon	.40	.18
☐ 19	Danny Ferry	.15	.07
☐ 20	Chris Mills	.15	.07
☐ 21	Bobby Phills	.15	.07
☐ 22	Jim Jackson	.20	.09
☐ 23	Popeye Jones	.15	.07
☐ 24	Jason Kidd	1.00	.45
☐ 25	Jamal Mashburn	.20	.09
☐ 26	Mahmoud Abdul-Rauf	.15	.07
☐ 27	Dale Ellis	.15	.07
☐ 28	Antonio McDyess	2.00	.90
☐ 29	Dikembe Mutombo	.20	.09
☐ 30	Joe Dumars	.40	.18
☐ 31	Grant Hill	2.50	1.10
☐ 32	Allan Houston	.20	.09
☐ 33	Otis Thorpe	.20	.09
☐ 34	Tim Hardaway	.50	.23
☐ 35	Chris Mullin	.40	.18
☐ 36	Latrell Sprewell	.20	.09
☐ 37	Joe Smith	1.50	.70
☐ 38	Sam Cassell	.20	.09
☐ 39	Clyde Drexler	.50	.23
☐ 40	Robert Horry	.15	.07
☐ 41	Hakeem Olajuwon	.75	.35
☐ 42	Dale Davis	.15	.07
☐ 43	Derrick McKey	.15	.07
☐ 44	Reggie Miller	.40	.18
☐ 45	Rik Smits	.20	.09
☐ 46	Brent Barry	.40	.18
☐ 47	Lamond Murray	.15	.07
☐ 48	Loy Vaught	.15	.07
☐ 49	Brian Williams	.15	.07
☐ 50	Cedric Ceballos	.15	.07
☐ 51	Magic Johnson	1.25	.55
☐ 52	Eddie Jones	1.00	.45
☐ 53	Nick Van Exel	.40	.18
☐ 54	Stanis Dolivic	.15	.07
☐ 55	Alonzo Mourning	.40	.18
☐ 56	Billy Owens	.15	.07
☐ 57	Kevin Willis	.15	.07
☐ 58	Vin Baker	.75	.35
☐ 59	Sherman Douglas	.15	.07
☐ 60	Lee Mayberry	.15	.07
☐ 61	Glenn Robinson	.50	.23
☐ 62	Kevin Garnett	5.00	2.20
☐ 63	Tom Gugliotta	.40	.18
☐ 64	Christian Laettner	.20	.09
☐ 65	Isaiah Rider	.20	.09
☐ 66	Chris Childs	.15	.07
☐ 67	Kendall Gill	.15	.07
☐ 68	Armon Gilliam	.15	.07
☐ 69	Ed O'Bannon	.15	.07
☐ 70	Patrick Ewing	.40	.18
☐ 71	Derek Harper	.20	.09
☐ 72	Charles Oakley	.15	.07
☐ 73	John Starks	.20	.09
☐ 74	Horace Grant	.20	.09
☐ 75	Anfernee Hardaway	1.50	.70
☐ 76	Shaquille O'Neal	1.50	.70
☐ 77	Dennis Scott	.15	.07
☐ 78	Derrick Coleman	.20	.09
☐ 79	Trevor Ruffin	.15	.07
☐ 80	Jerry Stackhouse	1.50	.70
☐ 81	Clarence Weatherspoon	.15	.07
☐ 82	Charles Barkley	.60	.25
☐ 83	Michael Finley	1.50	.70
☐ 84	Kevin Johnson	.20	.09
☐ 85	Danny Manning	.20	.09
☐ 86	Randolph Childress	.15	.07
☐ 87	Clifford Robinson	.15	.07
☐ 88	Arvydas Sabonis	.75	.35
☐ 89	Rod Strickland	.20	.09
☐ 90	Tyus Edney	.15	.07
☐ 91	Brian Grant	.20	.09
☐ 92	Mitch Richmond	.40	.18
☐ 93	Walt Williams	.15	.07
☐ 94	Sean Elliott	.15	.07
☐ 95	Avery Johnson	.15	.07
☐ 96	Chuck Person	.15	.07
☐ 97	David Robinson	.60	.25
☐ 98	Shawn Kemp	1.25	.55
☐ 99	Gary Payton	.60	.25
☐ 100	Sam Perkins	.20	.09
☐ 101	Detlef Schrempf	.20	.09
☐ 102	Ed Pinckney	.15	.07
☐ 103	Tracy Murray	.15	.07
☐ 104	Alvin Robertson	.15	.07
☐ 105	Damon Stoudamire	3.00	1.35
☐ 106	Jeff Hornacek	.20	.09
☐ 107	Karl Malone	.60	.25
☐ 108	Chris Morris	.15	.07
☐ 109	John Stockton	.40	.18
☐ 110	Greg Anthony	.15	.07
☐ 111	Blue Edwards	.15	.07
☐ 112	Bryant Reeves	1.00	.45
☐ 113	Byron Scott	.15	.07
☐ 114	Juwan Howard	.60	.25
☐ 115	Gheorghe Muresan	.15	.07
☐ 116	Rasheed Wallace	1.00	.45
☐ 117	Chris Webber	1.00	.45
☐ 118	Mookie Blaylock RP	.15	.07
☐ 119	Dana Barros RP	.15	.07
☐ 120	Larry Johnson RP	.15	.07
☐ 121	Michael Jordan RP	2.50	1.10
☐ 122	Terrell Brandon RP	.20	.09
☐ 123	Jason Kidd RP	.50	.23
☐ 124	M.Abdul-Rauf RP	.15	.07
☐ 125	Grant Hill RP	1.25	.55
☐ 126	Latrell Sprewell RP	.15	.07
☐ 127	Hakeem Olajuwon RP	.40	.18
☐ 128	Reggie Miller RP	.20	.09
☐ 129	Loy Vaught RP	.15	.07
☐ 130	Magic Johnson RP	.60	.25
☐ 131	Alonzo Mourning RP	.20	.09
☐ 132	Vin Baker RP	.40	.18
☐ 133	Tom Gugliotta RP	.20	.09
☐ 134	Ed O'Bannon RP	.15	.07
☐ 135	Patrick Ewing RP	.20	.09
☐ 136	Anfernee Hardaway RP	.75	.35
☐ 137	Jerry Stackhouse RP	.60	.25
☐ 138	Charles Barkley RP	.40	.18
☐ 139	Clifford Robinson RP	.15	.07
☐ 140	Mitch Richmond RP	.20	.09
☐ 141	David Robinson RP	.40	.18
☐ 142	Shawn Kemp RP	.60	.25
☐ 143	Damon Stoudamire RP	1.25	.55
☐ 144	John Stockton RP	.20	.09
☐ 145	Bryant Reeves RP	.40	.18
☐ 146	Juwan Howard RP	.40	.18

1995-96 SP Championship Champions of the Court

Randomly inserted in packs at a rate of one in 6, cards from this 30-card set feature one top star from each NBA team and an additional card of Michael Jordan. In this special horizontal design, there is one action color photo on the left side and the same action photo in black and white on the right side. The main feature of the card is a cel photo featuring a headshot with a protective film covering the cell photo on the front of the card.

When you turn the card over you see the same photo of the player. Each card is printed on special transparent chromium material. Unpeeled cards are priced below. Peeled cards are valued at about ten to twenty-five percent less.

	MINT	NRMT
COMPLETE SET (30)	125.00	55.00
COMMON CARD (C1-C30)	1.00	.45
SEMISTARS	1.50	.70
UNLISTED STARS	2.50	1.10
STATED ODDS 1:6		
COMP.DIE CUT SET (30)	800.00	350.00
COMMON DIE CUT (C1-C30)	4.00	1.80
*DIE CUT STARS: 2.5X TO 5X HI COLUMN		
*DIE CUT RCs: 2X TO 4X HI		
DIE CUT: STATED ODDS 1:75		

		MINT	NRMT
☐ C1	Steve Smith	1.50	.70
☐ C2	Dino Radja	1.00	.45
☐ C3	Glen Rice	2.50	1.10
☐ C4	Scottie Pippen	8.00	3.60
☐ C5	Terrell Brandon	2.50	1.10
☐ C6	Jason Kidd	6.00	2.70
☐ C7	Dikembe Mutombo	1.50	.70
☐ C8	Grant Hill	15.00	6.75
☐ C9	Joe Smith	5.00	2.20
☐ C10	Hakeem Olajuwon	5.00	2.20
☐ C11	Reggie Miller	2.50	1.10
☐ C12	Loy Vaught	1.00	.45
☐ C13	Magic Johnson	8.00	3.60
☐ C14	Alonzo Mourning	2.50	1.10
☐ C15	Vin Baker	5.00	2.20
☐ C16	Kevin Garnett	15.00	6.75
☐ C17	Ed O'Bannon	1.00	.45
☐ C18	Patrick Ewing	2.50	1.10
☐ C19	Shaquille O'Neal	10.00	4.50
☐ C20	Jerry Stackhouse	5.00	2.20
☐ C21	Charles Barkley	4.00	1.80
☐ C22	Clifford Robinson	1.00	.45
☐ C23	Mitch Richmond	2.50	1.10
☐ C24	David Robinson	4.00	1.80
☐ C25	Shawn Kemp	8.00	3.60
☐ C26	Damon Stoudamire	10.00	4.50
☐ C27	John Stockton	2.50	1.10
☐ C28	Bryant Reeves	3.00	1.35
☐ C29	Juwan Howard	4.00	1.80
☐ C30	Michael Jordan	30.00	13.50

1995-96 SP Championship Championship Shots

Inserted at a rate of one per magazine and Wal-Mart pack, as well as randomly in one in every three regular retail packs, this 20-card set features intense, closeup shots of many of the top NBA stars. Despite their status as inserts, these cards are actually easier to pull from packs than regular-issue cards. The design is highlighted by a horizontal, silver-foil, saw-tooth die cut element on the side border.

	MINT	NRMT
COMPLETE SET (20)	30.00	13.50
COMMON CARD (S1-S20)	.25	.11
SEMISTARS	.50	.23
UNLISTED STARS	.75	.35
STATED ODDS 1:3		
ONE PER SPECIAL RETAIL PACK		
COMP.GOLD SET (20)	300.00	135.00
COMMON GOLD (S1-S20)	2.00	.90
*GOLD STARS: 5X TO 10X HI COLUMN		
*GOLD RCs: 4X TO 8X HI		
GOLD: STATED ODDS 1:62		

		MINT	NRMT
☐ S1	Antonio McDyess	2.50	1.10
☐ S2	Nick Van Exel	.75	.35
☐ S3	Michael Finley	2.00	.90
☐ S4	Anfernee Hardaway	3.00	1.35
☐ S5	Latrell Sprewell	.50	.23
☐ S6	Brian Grant	.50	.23
☐ S7	Juwan Howard	1.25	.55
☐ S8	Ed O'Bannon	.25	.11
☐ S9	Kevin Garnett	6.00	2.70
☐ S10	Charles Barkley	1.25	.55
☐ S11	Joe Smith	2.00	.90
☐ S12	Patrick Ewing	.75	.35
☐ S13	Brent Barry	.75	.35
☐ S14	Dennis Rodman	5.00	2.20
☐ S15	Jerry Stackhouse	2.00	.90
☐ S16	Michael Jordan	10.00	4.50
☐ S17	Jalen Rose	.50	.23
☐ S18	Jamal Mashburn	.50	.23
☐ S19	Theo Ratliff	.75	.35
☐ S20	Shaquille O'Neal	3.00	1.35

1996 SPx

The premier edition of Upper Deck's super-premium SPx basketball set contains 50 cards featuring only the top stars and youngsters in the NBA. The set marked a number of technological "firsts" in the basketball card market including first stand-alone all-Holoview set and first complete, perimeter die cut set. To create the holoview imagery, each athlete was videotaped while rotating on a turntable. The individual frames of videotape were then synthesized to produce a 50-degree, three-dimensional picture. Each card features super premium 32 point thick stock. Each pack contained only one card and carried a suggested retail price of $2.99. Each box contained 36 packs. In addition, to the 50 regular cards, a special Record Breaker card commemorating Michael Jordan's eighth scoring title (1:75 packs) and Tribute card commemorating Anfernee Hardaway's accomplishments in the NBA (1:24 packs) were issued. Also, two separate trade cards were available for signed Jordan and Hardaway cards. The odds of receiving a Jordan trade card were 1:34,560 packs. The Hardaway trade card was more than 25 times easier to pull at a rate of 1,345 packs.

	MINT	NRMT
COMPLETE SET (50)	80.00	36.00
COMMON CARD (1-50)	.75	.35
SEMISTARS	1.00	.45
UNLISTED STARS	1.50	.70
COMP.GOLD SET (50)	250.00	110.00
COMMON GOLD (1-50)	1.50	.70
GOLD: 1X TO 2X HI COLUMN		
GOLD: STATED ODDS 1:7		
R1: STATED ODDS 1:75		
T1: STATED ODDS 1:95		

		MINT	NRMT
☐ 1	Stacey Augmon	.75	.35
☐ 2	Mookie Blaylock	1.00	.45
☐ 3	Eric Montross	.75	.35
☐ 4	Eric Williams	.75	.35
☐ 5	Larry Johnson	1.00	.45
☐ 6	George Zidek	.75	.35
☐ 7	Jason Caffey	.75	.35
☐ 8	Michael Jordan	20.00	9.00
☐ 9	Chris Mills	.75	.35
☐ 10	Bob Sura	.75	.35
☐ 11	Jason Kidd	4.00	1.80
☐ 12	Jamal Mashburn	1.00	.45
☐ 13	Antonio McDyess	3.00	1.35
☐ 14	Jalen Rose	.75	.35
☐ 15	Grant Hill	10.00	4.50
☐ 16	Theo Ratliff	.75	.35
☐ 17	Joe Smith	2.50	1.10
☐ 18	Latrell Sprewell	1.00	.45
☐ 19	Hakeem Olajuwon	3.00	1.35
☐ 20	Reggie Miller	1.50	.70

□ 21 Rik Smits	1.00	.45
□ 22 Brent Barry	.75	.35
□ 23 Lamond Murray	.75	.35
□ 24 Magic Johnson	5.00	2.20
□ 25 Eddie Jones	4.00	1.80
□ 26 Nick Van Exel	1.50	.70
□ 27 Alonzo Mourning	1.50	.70
□ 28 Kurt Thomas	.75	.35
□ 29 Vin Baker	3.00	1.35
□ 30 Glenn Robinson	2.00	.90
□ 31 Kevin Garnett	10.00	4.50
□ 32 Ed O'Bannon	.75	.35
□ 33 Patrick Ewing	1.50	.70
□ 34 Anfernee Hardaway	6.00	2.70
□ 35 Shaquille O'Neal	6.00	2.70
□ 36 Jerry Stackhouse	2.50	1.10
□ 37 Charles Barkley	2.50	1.10
□ 38 Michael Finley	2.50	1.10
□ 39 Randolph Childress	.75	.35
□ 40 Gary Trent	.75	.35
□ 41 Brian Grant	.75	.35
□ 42 Mitch Richmond	1.50	.70
□ 43 David Robinson	2.50	1.10
□ 44 Shawn Kemp	5.00	2.20
□ 45 Gary Payton	2.50	1.10
□ 46 Damon Stoudamire	6.00	2.70
□ 47 Karl Malone	2.50	1.10
□ 48 John Stockton	1.50	.70
□ 49 Bryant Reeves	1.00	.45
□ 50 Rasheed Wallace	1.00	.45
□ R1 Michael Jordan	20.00	9.00
Record Breaker		
□ T1 Anfernee Hardaway	6.00	2.70
Tribute		
□ NNO Michael Jordan	700.00	325.00
Expired Exchange		
□ NNO Michael Jordan	3000.00	1350.00
Certified Autograph		
□ NNO Anfernee Hardaway	40.00	18.00
Expired Exchange		
□ NNO Anfernee Hardaway	200.00	90.00
Certified Autograph		

1996 SPx Holoview Heroes

Cards in this set of ten were randomly issued at a rate of one in every 24 packs and feature ten NBA players with the potential to be named to the NBA Hall of Fame. These die-cut cards feature a combination of lithograph and holoview technology.

	MINT	NRMT
COMPLETE SET (10)	80.00	36.00
COMMON CARD (H1-H10)	4.00	1.80
STATED ODDS 1:24		

□ H1 Michael Jordan	30.00	13.50
□ H2 Jason Kidd	6.00	2.70
□ H3 Grant Hill	15.00	6.75
□ H4 Joe Smith	4.00	1.80
□ H5 Magic Johnson	8.00	3.60
□ H6 Antonio McDyess	5.00	2.20
□ H7 Anfernee Hardaway	10.00	4.50
□ H8 Jerry Stackhouse	4.00	1.80
□ H9 Damon Stoudamire	10.00	4.50
□ H10 Shaquille O'Neal	10.00	4.50

1997 SPx

The 1997 SPx set was issued in one series totaling 50 cards and was distributed in one-card packs at a suggested retail of $3.49. This perimeter die-cut set features combinations of holographic, lithographic and Holoview images printed on super premium 32 point card stock. The cards were released after the 1997 NBA Playoffs and carry information from the first half of the 1996-97 NBA season. The cards are numbered with an "SPx" prefix. A Michael Jordan "sample" card was released prior to the regular set. It is listed below at the end of the set.

	MINT	NRMT
COMPLETE SET (50)	100.00	45.00
COMMON CARD (1-50)	.75	.35
SEMISTARS	1.00	.45
UNLISTED STARS	1.50	.70
COMP.GOLD SET (50)	250.00	110.00
COMMON GOLD (1-50)	1.50	.70
*GOLD: 1X TO 2X HI COLUMN		
GOLD: STATED ODDS 1:9		
SPX PREFIX ON CARDS		

□ 1 Mookie Blaylock	1.00	.45
□ 2 Antoine Walker	8.00	3.60
□ 3 Eric Williams	.75	.35
□ 4 Tony Delk	.75	.35
□ 5 Michael Jordan	20.00	9.00
□ 6 Dennis Rodman	6.00	2.70
□ 7 Vitaly Potapenko	.75	.35
□ 8 Bob Sura	.75	.35
□ 9 Jamal Mashburn	1.00	.45
□ 10 Samaki Walker	.75	.35
□ 11 Antonio McDyess	2.00	.90
□ 12 Joe Dumars	1.50	.70
□ 13 Grant Hill	10.00	4.50
□ 14 Joe Smith	1.50	.70
□ 15 Latrell Sprewell	1.00	.45
□ 16 Charles Barkley	2.50	1.10
□ 17 Hakeem Olajuwon	3.00	1.35
□ 18 Erick Dampier	.75	.35
□ 19 Reggie Miller	1.50	.70
□ 20 Brent Barry	.75	.35
□ 21 Lorenzen Wright	.75	.35
□ 22 Kobe Bryant	12.00	5.50
□ 23 Eddie Jones	3.00	1.35
□ 24 Shaquille O'Neal	6.00	2.70
□ 25 Alonzo Mourning	1.50	.70
□ 26 Kurt Thomas	.75	.35
□ 27 Vin Baker	3.00	1.35
□ 28 Glenn Robinson	1.50	.70
□ 29 Kevin Garnett	10.00	4.50
□ 30 Stephon Marbury	8.00	3.60
□ 31 Kerry Kittles	1.50	.70
□ 32 Patrick Ewing	1.50	.70
□ 33 Larry Johnson	1.00	.45
□ 34 Anfernee Hardaway	6.00	2.70
□ 35 Allen Iverson	8.00	3.60
□ 36 Jerry Stackhouse	1.50	.70
□ 37 Kevin Johnson	1.00	.45
□ 38 Steve Nash	1.00	.45
□ 39 Jermaine O'Neal	1.00	.45
□ 40 Mitch Richmond	1.50	.70
□ 41 David Robinson	2.50	1.10
□ 42 Shawn Kemp	5.00	2.20
□ 43 Gary Payton	2.50	1.10
□ 44 Marcus Camby	1.50	.70
□ 45 Damon Stoudamire	3.00	1.35
□ 46 Karl Malone	2.50	1.10
□ 47 John Stockton	1.50	.70
□ 48 Shareef Abdur-Rahim	5.00	2.20
□ 49 Bryant Reeves	1.00	.45
□ 50 Juwan Howard	1.50	.70
□ NNO Michael Jordan	15.00	6.75
Promo		

1997 SPx Holoview Heroes

Randomly inserted in packs at a rate of one in 75, this 20-card set features color photos of some of the best performers in the NBA on a vertical die-cut card format. Card backs are numbered with a "H" prefix.

	MINT	NRMT
COMPLETE SET (20)	300.00	135.00
COMMON CARD (H1-H20)	6.00	2.70
STATED ODDS 1:75		

□ H1 Michael Jordan	80.00	36.00
□ H2 Grant Hill	40.00	18.00
□ H3 Reggie Miller	6.00	2.70
□ H4 Joe Smith	6.00	2.70
□ H5 Kevin Garnett	40.00	18.00
□ H6 Mitch Richmond	6.00	2.70
□ H7 Allen Iverson	30.00	13.50
□ H8 Patrick Ewing	6.00	2.70
□ H9 Hakeem Olajuwon	12.00	5.50
□ H10 David Robinson	10.00	4.50
□ H11 Anfernee Hardaway	25.00	11.00
□ H12 Juwan Howard	6.00	2.70
□ H13 Gary Payton	10.00	4.50
□ H14 Dennis Rodman	25.00	11.00
□ H15 Shaquille O'Neal	25.00	11.00
□ H16 Charles Barkley	10.00	4.50

☐ H17 Damon Stoudamire 12.00 5.50
☐ H18 Shawn Kemp 20.00 9.00
☐ H19 Glenn Robinson 6.00 2.70
☐ H20 John Stockton 6.00 2.70

1997 SPx ProMotion

Randomly inserted in packs at a rate of one in 430, this five-card set features back-to-back Holoview images. Card fronts actually picture three shots of the player.

	MINT	NRMT
COMPLETE SET (5)	175.00	80.00
COMMON CARD (1-5)	12.00	5.50
STATED ODDS 1:430		

☐ 1 Michael Jordan 120.00 55.00
☐ 2 Damon Stoudamire 15.00 6.75
☐ 3 Anfernee Hardaway 40.00 18.00
☐ 4 Shawn Kemp 30.00 13.50
☐ 5 Antonio McDyess 12.00 5.50

1997 SPx ProMotion Autographs

This five-card set is a parallel set to the regular SPx Pro Motion set and is similar in design. The difference is the autograph of the pictured player on the card. Only 100 of these autographed cards are available for each player and are hand numbered.

	MINT	NRMT
COMPLETE SET (5)	3000.00	1350.00
COMMON CARD (1-5)	125.00	55.00
RANDOM INSERTS IN PACKS		
CARDS NUMBERED TO 100		

☐ 1 Michael Jordan 2500.00 1100.00
☐ 2 Damon Stoudamire 250.00 110.00
☐ 3 Anfernee Hardaway 400.00 180.00
☐ 4 Shawn Kemp 300.00 135.00
☐ 5 Antonio McDyess 125.00 55.00

1997-98 SPx

The 1998 SPx set was the final that used the "holoview" tech-

nology. The 50-card set was packaged in three-card packs with a suggested retail price of $5.99. The set also featured redemption cards for a "Piece of History" which was a framed, uncut, Hardcourt HoloView sheet. That card is priced at the bottom of the set.

	MINT	NRMT
COMPLETE SET (50)	75.00	34.00
COMMON CARD (1-50)	.50	.23
SEMISTARS	.60	.25
UNLISTED STARS	1.00	.45
COMP.SKY SET (50)	100.00	45.00
COMMON SKY	.60	.25
*SKY STARS: .5X TO 1.2X HI COLUMN		
*SKY RCs: .4X TO 1X HI		
SKY: ONE PER PACK		
COMP.BRONZE SET (50) ..	150.00	70.00
COMMON BRONZE	1.00	.45
*BRONZE STARS: .75X TO 2X HI		
*BRONZE RCs: .6X TO 1.5X HI		
BRONZE: STATED ODDS 1:3		
COMP.SILVER SET (50)	350.00	160.00
COMMON SILVER	2.00	.90
*SILVER STARS: 1.5X TO 4X HI		
*SILVER RCs: 1.25X TO 3X HI		
SILVER: STATED ODDS 1:6		
COMP.GOLD SET (50)	700.00	325.00
COMMON GOLD	4.00	1.80
*GOLD STARS: 3X TO 8X HI		
*GOLD RCs: 2.5X TO 6X HI		
GOLD: STATED ODDS 1:17		

☐ 1 Mookie Blaylock .60 .25
☐ 2 Dikembe Mutombo .60 .25
☐ 3 Chauncey Billups 4.00 1.80
☐ 4 Antoine Walker 5.00 2.20
☐ 5 Glen Rice 1.00 .45
☐ 6 Michael Jordan 12.00 5.50
☐ 7 Scottie Pippen 3.00 1.35
☐ 8 Dennis Rodman 4.00 1.80
☐ 9 Shawn Kemp 3.00 1.35
☐ 10 Michael Finley 1.00 .45
☐ 11 Tony Battie 2.00 .90
☐ 12 LaPhonso Ellis .50 .23
☐ 13 Grant Hill 6.00 2.70
☐ 14 Joe Dumars 1.00 .45
☐ 15 Joe Smith 1.00 .45
☐ 16 Clyde Drexler 1.25 .55
☐ 17 Charles Barkley 1.50 .70
☐ 18 Hakeem Olajuwon 2.00 .90
☐ 19 Reggie Miller 1.00 .45
☐ 20 Brent Barry .50 .23
☐ 21 Kobe Bryant 8.00 3.60
☐ 22 Shaquille O'Neal 4.00 1.80
☐ 23 Alonzo Mourning 1.00 .45
☐ 24 Glenn Robinson 1.00 .45
☐ 25 Kevin Garnett 6.00 2.70
☐ 26 Stephon Marbury 5.00 2.20
☐ 27 Keith Van Horn 10.00 4.50
☐ 28 Patrick Ewing 1.00 .45

☐ 29 Anfernee Hardaway 4.00 1.80
☐ 30 Allen Iverson 5.00 2.20
☐ 31 Kevin Johnson .60 .25
☐ 32 Antonio McDyess 1.25 .55
☐ 33 Jason Kidd 2.00 .90
☐ 34 Kenny Anderson .60 .25
☐ 35 Rasheed Wallace .60 .25
☐ 36 Mitch Richmond 1.00 .45
☐ 37 Tim Duncan 12.00 5.50
☐ 38 David Robinson 1.50 .70
☐ 39 Vin Baker 2.00 .90
☐ 40 Gary Payton 1.50 .70
☐ 41 Marcus Camby 1.00 .45
☐ 42 Tracy McGrady 6.00 2.70
☐ 43 Damon Stoudamire 2.00 .90
☐ 44 Karl Malone 1.50 .70
☐ 45 John Stockton 1.00 .45
☐ 46 Shareef Abdur-Rahim 3.00 1.35
☐ 47 Antonio Daniels 2.50 1.10
☐ 48 Bryant Reeves .60 .25
☐ 49 Juwan Howard 1.00 .45
☐ 50 Chris Webber 2.50 1.10
☐ T1 Piece of History Trade 200.00 90.00

1997-98 SPx Grand Finale

Randomly inserted into packs, this 50-card parallel set features serial numbering to 50 on the card backs.

	MINT	NRMT
COMMON CARD (1-50)	40.00	18.00
SEMISTARS	50.00	22.00
RANDOM INSERTS IN PACKS		
STATED PRINT RUN 50 SERIAL #'d SETS		

☐ 1 Mookie Blaylock 50.00 22.00
☐ 2 Dikembe Mutombo 50.00 22.00
☐ 3 Chauncey Billups 150.00 70.00
☐ 4 Antoine Walker 400.00 180.00
☐ 5 Glen Rice 80.00 36.00
☐ 6 Michael Jordan 1200.00 550.00
☐ 7 Scottie Pippen 250.00 110.00
☐ 8 Dennis Rodman 300.00 135.00
☐ 9 Shawn Kemp 250.00 110.00
☐ 10 Michael Finley 80.00 36.00
☐ 11 Tony Battie 80.00 36.00
☐ 12 LaPhonso Ellis 40.00 18.00
☐ 13 Grant Hill 500.00 220.00
☐ 14 Joe Dumars 80.00 36.00
☐ 15 Joe Smith 80.00 36.00
☐ 16 Clyde Drexler 100.00 45.00
☐ 17 Charles Barkley 125.00 55.00
☐ 18 Hakeem Olajuwon 150.00 70.00
☐ 19 Reggie Miller 80.00 36.00
☐ 20 Brent Barry 40.00 18.00
☐ 21 Kobe Bryant 600.00 275.00
☐ 22 Shaquille O'Neal 300.00 135.00
☐ 23 Alonzo Mourning 80.00 36.00
☐ 24 Glenn Robinson 60.00 27.00
☐ 25 Kevin Garnett 500.00 220.00
☐ 26 Stephon Marbury 400.00 180.00
☐ 27 Keith Van Horn 400.00 180.00
☐ 28 Patrick Ewing 80.00 36.00
☐ 29 Anfernee Hardaway 300.00 135.00
☐ 30 Allen Iverson 400.00 180.00
☐ 31 Kevin Johnson 50.00 22.00
☐ 32 Antonio McDyess 100.00 45.00
☐ 33 Jason Kidd 150.00 70.00
☐ 34 Kenny Anderson 50.00 22.00
☐ 35 Rasheed Wallace 50.00 22.00
☐ 36 Mitch Richmond 80.00 36.00
☐ 37 Tim Duncan 500.00 220.00
☐ 38 David Robinson 125.00 55.00
☐ 39 Vin Baker 80.00 36.00
☐ 40 Gary Payton 125.00 55.00
☐ 41 Marcus Camby 80.00 36.00
☐ 42 Tracy McGrady 250.00 110.00
☐ 43 Damon Stoudamire 150.00 70.00
☐ 44 Karl Malone 125.00 55.00

☐ 45	John Stockton	80.00	36.00
☐ 46	Shareef Abdur-Rahim	250.00	110.00
☐ 47	Antonio Daniels	100.00	45.00
☐ 48	Bryant Reeves	50.00	22.00
☐ 49	Juwan Howard	80.00	36.00
☐ 50	Chris Webber	200.00	90.00

1997-98 SPx Hardcourt Holoview

Randomly inserted into packs at a rate of one in 54, this 20-card set features key NBA players using several "holoview" poses.

	MINT	NRMT
COMPLETE SET (20)	400.00	180.00
COMMON CARD (HH1-HH20)	3.00	1.35
SEMISTARS	4.00	1.80
UNLISTED STARS	6.00	2.70
STATED ODDS 1:54		

☐ HH1	Michael Jordan	80.00	36.00
☐ HH2	Allen Iverson	30.00	13.50
☐ HH3	Antoine Walker	30.00	13.50
☐ HH4	Chris Webber	15.00	6.75
☐ HH5	Glenn Robinson	4.00	1.80
☐ HH6	Kevin Garnett	40.00	18.00
☐ HH7	Shareef Abdur-Rahim	20.00	9.00
☐ HH8	Keith Van Horn	30.00	13.50
☐ HH9	Kobe Bryant	50.00	22.00
☐ HH10	Glen Rice	6.00	2.70
☐ HH11	Damon Stoudamire	12.00	5.50
☐ HH12	Hakeem Olajuwon	12.00	5.50
☐ HH13	Mookie Blaylock	3.00	1.35
☐ HH14	Shaquille O'Neal	25.00	11.00
☐ HH15	Stephon Marbury	30.00	13.50
☐ HH16	Chauncey Billups	12.00	5.50
☐ HH17	Anfernee Hardaway	25.00	11.00
☐ HH18	Tim Duncan	40.00	18.00
☐ HH19	Mitch Richmond	6.00	2.70
☐ HH20	Grant Hill	40.00	18.00

1997-98 SPx ProMotion

Randomly inserted into packs at a rate of one in 252, this 10-card set features the player against several "holoview" poses.

	MINT	NRMT
COMPLETE SET (10)	550.00	250.00
COMMON CARD (PM1-PM10)	20.00	9.00
STATED ODDS 1:252		

☐ PM1	Michael Jordan	150.00	70.00
☐ PM2	Shaquille O'Neal	50.00	22.00
☐ PM3	Tim Duncan	80.00	36.00
☐ PM4	Shareef Abdur-Rahim	40.00	18.00
☐ PM5	Grant Hill	80.00	36.00
☐ PM6	Karl Malone	20.00	9.00
☐ PM7	Anfernee Hardaway	50.00	22.00
☐ PM8	Keith Van Horn	60.00	27.00
☐ PM9	Kevin Garnett	80.00	36.00
☐ PM10	Damon Stoudamire	25.00	11.00

1992-93 Stadium Club

The complete 1992-93 Stadium Club basketball set (created by

Topps) consists of 400 standard-size cards, having been issued in two 200-card series. Both first and second series packs contained 15 cards with a suggested retail price of $1.79 per pack. Topps also issued, late in the season, second series 23-card jumbo packs. A Stadium Club membership form was inserted in every 15-card pack. The basic card fronts feature full-bleed color action player photos. The team name and player's name appear in gold foil stripes that cut across the bottom of the card and intersect the Stadium Club logo. On a colorful background of a basketball in a net, the horizontal backs present biography, The Sporting News Skills Rating System, player evaluation, 1991-92 season and career statistics, and a miniature representation of the player's first Topps card, which is contusingly referenced as "Topps Rookie Card" by Topps. The first series closes and the second series begins with a Members Choice (191-211) subset. Rookie Cards of note include Tom Gugliotta, Robert Horry, Christian Laettner, Alonzo Mourning, Shaquille O'Neal, Latrell Sprewell and Clarence Weatherspoon.

	MINT	NRMT
COMPLETE SET (400)	60.00	27.00
COMPLETE SERIES 1 (200)	20.00	9.00
COMPLETE SERIES 2 (200)	40.00	18.00
COMMON CARD (1-400)	.10	.05
SEMISTARS	.30	.14
UNLISTED STARS	.60	.25

☐ 1	Michael Jordan	8.00	3.60
☐ 2	Greg Anthony	.10	.05
☐ 3	Otis Thorpe	.30	.14
☐ 4	Jim Les	.10	.05
☐ 5	Kevin Willis	.10	.05
☐ 6	Derek Harper	.30	.14
☐ 7	Elden Campbell	.30	.14
☐ 8	A.J. English	.10	.05
☐ 9	Kenny Gattison	.10	.05
☐ 10	Drazen Petrovic	.10	.05

☐ 11	Chris Mullin	.60	.25
☐ 12	Mark Price	.10	.05
☐ 13	Karl Malone	1.00	.45
☐ 14	Gerald Glass	.10	.05
☐ 15	Negele Knight	.10	.05
☐ 16	Mark Macon	.10	.05
☐ 17	Michael Cage	.10	.05
☐ 18	Kevin Edwards	.10	.05
☐ 19	Sherman Douglas	.10	.05
☐ 20	Ron Harper	.30	.14
☐ 21	Clifford Robinson	.30	.14
☐ 22	Byron Scott	.30	.14
☐ 23	Antoine Carr	.10	.05
☐ 24	Greg Dreiling	.10	.05
☐ 25	Bill Laimbeer	.30	.14
☐ 26	Hersey Hawkins	.30	.14
☐ 27	Will Perdue	.10	.05
☐ 28	Todd Lichti	.10	.05
☐ 29	Gary Grant	.10	.05
☐ 30	Sam Perkins	.30	.14
☐ 31	Jayson Williams	.30	.14
☐ 32	Magic Johnson	2.00	.90
☐ 33	Larry Bird	2.50	1.10
☐ 34	Chris Morris	.10	.05
☐ 35	Nick Anderson	.30	.14
☐ 36	Scott Hastings	.10	.05
☐ 37	Ledell Eackles	.10	.05
☐ 38	Robert Pack	.10	.05
☐ 39	Dana Barros	.30	.14
☐ 40	Anthony Bonner	.10	.05
☐ 41	J.R. Reid	.10	.05
☐ 42	Tyrone Hill	.10	.05
☐ 43	Rik Smits	.30	.14
☐ 44	Kevin Duckworth	.10	.05
☐ 45	LaSalle Thompson	.10	.05
☐ 46	Brian Williams	.30	.14
☐ 47	Willie Anderson	.10	.05
☐ 48	Ken Norman	.10	.05
☐ 49	Mike Iuzzolino	.10	.05
☐ 50	Isiah Thomas	.60	.25
☐ 51	Alec Kessler	.10	.05
☐ 52	Johnny Dawkins	.10	.05
☐ 53	Avery Johnson	.10	.05
☐ 54	Stacey Augmon	.30	.14
☐ 55	Charles Oakley	.30	.14
☐ 56	Rex Chapman	.10	.05
☐ 57	Charles Shackleford	.10	.05
☐ 58	Jeff Ruland	.10	.05
☐ 59	Craig Ehlo	.10	.05
☐ 60	Jon Koncak	.10	.05
☐ 61	Danny Schayes	.10	.05
☐ 62	David Benoit	.10	.05
☐ 63	Robert Parish	.30	.14
☐ 64	Mookie Blaylock	.30	.14
☐ 65	Sean Elliott	.30	.14
☐ 66	Mark Aguirre	.10	.05
☐ 67	Scott Williams	.10	.05
☐ 68	Doug West	.10	.05
☐ 69	Kenny Anderson	.60	.25
☐ 70	Randy Brown	.10	.05
☐ 71	Muggsy Bogues	.30	.14
☐ 72	Spud Webb	.30	.14
☐ 73	Sedale Threatt	.10	.05
☐ 74	Chris Gatling	.10	.05
☐ 75	Derrick McKey	.10	.05
☐ 76	Sleepy Floyd	.10	.05
☐ 77	Chris Jackson	.10	.05
☐ 78	Thurl Bailey	.10	.05
☐ 79	Steve Smith	.60	.25
☐ 80	Jerrod Mustaf	.10	.05
☐ 81	Anthony Bowie	.10	.05
☐ 82	John Williams	.10	.05
☐ 83	Paul Graham	.10	.05
☐ 84	Willie Burton	.10	.05
☐ 85	Vernon Maxwell	.10	.05
☐ 86	Stacey King	.10	.05
☐ 87	B.J. Armstrong	.10	.05
☐ 88	Kevin Gamble	.10	.05
☐ 89	Terry Catledge	.10	.05
☐ 90	Jeff Malone	.10	.05
☐ 91	Sam Bowie	.10	.05
☐ 92	Orlando Woolridge	.10	.05
☐ 93	Steve Kerr	.30	.14
☐ 94	Eric Leckner	.10	.05
☐ 95	Loy Vaught	.30	.14
☐ 96	Jud Buechler	.10	.05

97	Doug Smith	.10	.05
98	Sidney Green	.10	.05
99	Jerome Kersey	.10	.05
100	Patrick Ewing	.60	.25
101	Ed Nealy	.10	.05
102	Shawn Kemp	2.50	1.10
103	Luc Longley	.30	.14
104	George McCloud	.10	.05
105	Ron Anderson	.10	.05
106	Moses Malone UER	.60	.25
	(Rookie Card is 1975-76, not 1976-77)		
107	Tony Smith	.10	.05
108	Terry Porter	.10	.05
109	Blair Rasmussen	.10	.05
110	Bimbo Coles	.10	.05
111	Grant Long	.10	.05
112	John Battle	.10	.05
113	Brian Oliver	.10	.05
114	Tyrone Corbin	.10	.05
115	Benoit Benjamin	.10	.05
116	Rick Fox	.30	.14
117	Rafael Addison	.10	.05
118	Danny Young	.10	.05
119	Fat Lever	.10	.05
120	Terry Cummings	.30	.14
121	Felton Spencer	.10	.05
122	Joe Kleine	.10	.05
123	Johnny Newman	.10	.05
124	Gary Payton	1.25	.55
125	Kurt Rambis	.10	.05
126	Vlade Divac	.30	.14
127	John Paxson	.30	.14
128	Lionel Simmons	.10	.05
129	Randy Wittman	.10	.05
130	Winston Garland	.10	.05
131	Jerry Reynolds	.10	.05
132	Dell Curry	.10	.05
133	Fred Roberts	.10	.05
134	Michael Adams	.10	.05
135	Charles Jones	.10	.05
136	Frank Brickowski	.10	.05
137	Alton Lister	.10	.05
138	Horace Grant	.30	.14
139	Greg Sutton	.10	.05
140	John Starks	.30	.14
141	Detlef Schrempf	.30	.14
142	Rodney Monroe	.10	.05
143	Pete Chilcutt	.10	.05
144	Mike Brown	.10	.05
145	Rony Seikaly	.10	.05
146	Donald Hodge	.10	.05
147	Kevin McHale	.60	.25
148	Ricky Pierce	.10	.05
149	Brian Shaw	.10	.05
150	Reggie Williams	.10	.05
151	Kendall Gill	.30	.14
152	Tom Chambers	.10	.05
153	Jack Haley	.10	.05
154	Terrell Brandon	1.00	.45
155	Dennis Scott	.30	.14
156	Mark Randall	.10	.05
157	Kenny Payne	.10	.05
158	Bernard King	.10	.05
159	Tate George	.10	.05
160	Scott Skiles	.10	.05
161	Pervis Ellison	.10	.05
162	Marcus Liberty	.10	.05
163	Rumeal Robinson	.10	.05
164	Anthony Mason	.60	.25
165	Les Jepsen	.10	.05
166	Kenny Smith	.10	.05
167	Randy White	.10	.05
168	Dee Brown	.10	.05
169	Chris Dudley	.10	.05
170	Armon Gilliam	.10	.05
171	Eddie Johnson	.10	.05
172	A.C. Green	.30	.14
173	Darrell Walker	.10	.05
174	Bill Cartwright	.10	.05
175	Mike Gminski	.10	.05
176	Tom Tolbert	.10	.05
177	Buck Williams	.30	.14
178	Mark Eaton	.10	.05
179	Danny Manning	.30	.14
180	Glen Rice	.75	.35
181	Sarunas Marciulionis	.10	.05
182	Danny Ferry	.10	.05
183	Chris Corchiani	.10	.05
184	Dan Majerle	.30	.14
185	Alvin Robertson	.10	.05
186	Vern Fleming	.10	.05
187	Kevin Lynch	.10	.05
188	John Williams	.10	.05
189	Checklist 1-100	.10	.05
190	Checklist 101-200	.10	.05
191	David Robinson MC	.60	.25
192	Larry Johnson MC	.60	.25
193	Derrick Coleman MC	.10	.05
194	Larry Bird MC	1.25	.55
195	Billy Owens MC	.10	.05
196	Dikembe Mutombo MC	.60	.25
197	Charles Barkley MC	.60	.25
198	Scottie Pippen MC	1.00	.45
199	Clyde Drexler MC	.60	.25
200	John Stockton MC	.60	.25
201	Shaquille O'Neal MC	3.00	1.35
202	Chris Mullin MC	.30	.14
203	Glen Rice MC	.60	.25
204	Isiah Thomas MC	.30	.14
205	Karl Malone MC	.60	.25
206	Christian Laettner MC	.75	.35
207	Patrick Ewing MC	.60	.25
208	Dominique Wilkins MC	.30	.14
209	Alonzo Mourning MC	1.00	.45
210	Michael Jordan MC	4.00	1.80
211	Tim Hardaway MC	1.00	.45
212	Rodney McCray	.10	.05
213	Larry Johnson	.75	.35
214	Charles Smith	.10	.05
215	Kevin Brooks	.10	.05
216	Kevin Johnson	.60	.25
217	Duane Cooper	.10	.05
218	Christian Laettner UER	1.50	.70
	(Missing '92 Draft Pick logo)		
219	Tim Perry	.10	.05
220	Hakeem Olajuwon	1.25	.55
221	Lee Mayberry	.10	.05
222	Mark Bryant	.10	.05
223	Robert Horry	1.00	.45
224	Tracy Murray UER	.30	.14
	(Missing '92 Draft Pick logo)		
225	Greg Grant	.10	.05
226	Rolando Blackman	.10	.05
227	James Edwards UER	.10	.05
	(Rookie Card is 1978-79, not 1980-81)		
228	Sean Green	.10	.05
229	Buck Johnson	.10	.05
230	Andrew Lang	.10	.05
231	Tracy Moore	.10	.05
232	Adam Keefe UER	.10	.05
	(Missing '92 Draft Pick logo)		
233	Tony Campbell	.10	.05
234	Rod Strickland	.60	.25
235	Terry Mills	.30	.14
236	Billy Owens	.30	.14
237	Bryant Stith UER	.30	.14
	(Missing '92 Draft Pick logo)		
238	Tony Bennett UER	.10	.05
	(Missing '92 Draft Pick logo)		
239	David Wood	.10	.05
240	Jay Humphries	.10	.05
241	Doc Rivers	.30	.14
242	Wayman Tisdale	.10	.05
243	Litterial Green	.10	.05
244	Jon Barry	.10	.05
245	Brad Daugherty	.10	.05
246	Nate McMillan	.10	.05
247	Shaquille O'Neal	12.00	5.50
248	Chris Smith	.10	.05
249	Duane Ferrell	.10	.05
250	Anthony Peeler	.30	.14
251	Gundars Vetra	.10	.05
252	Danny Ainge	.30	.14
253	Mitch Richmond	.60	.25
254	Malik Sealy	.30	.14
255	Brent Price	.30	.14
256	Xavier McDaniel	.10	.05
257	Bobby Phills	.60	.25
258	Donald Royal	.10	.05
259	Olden Polynice	.10	.05
260	D.Wilkins UER	.60	.25
	(Scoring 10,000th point, should be 20,000th)		
261	Larry Krystkowiak	.10	.05
262	Duane Causwell	.10	.05
263	Todd Day	.10	.05
264	Sam Mack	.10	.05
265	John Stockton	.60	.25
266	Eddie Lee Wilkins	.10	.05
267	Gerald Glass	.10	.05
268	Robert Pack	.10	.05
269	Gerald Wilkins	.10	.05
270	Reggie Lewis	.30	.14
271	Scott Brooks	.10	.05
272	Randy Woods UER	.10	.05
	(Missing '92 Draft Pick logo)		
273	Dikembe Mutombo	.60	.25
274	Kiki Vandeweghe	.10	.05
275	Rich King	.10	.05
276	Jeff Turner	.10	.05
277	Vinny Del Negro	.10	.05
278	Marlon Maxey	.10	.05
279	Elmore Spencer UER	.10	.05
	(Missing '92 Draft Pick logo)		
280	Cedric Ceballos	.30	.14
281	Alex Blackwell	.10	.05
282	Terry Davis	.10	.05
283	Morlon Wiley	.10	.05
284	Trent Tucker	.10	.05
285	Carl Herrera	.10	.05
286	Eric Anderson	.10	.05
287	Clyde Drexler	.75	.35
288	Tom Gugliotta	2.00	.90
289	Dale Ellis	.10	.05
290	Lance Blanks	.10	.05
291	Tom Hammonds	.10	.05
292	Eric Murdock	.10	.05
293	Walt Williams	.60	.25
294	Gerald Paddio	.10	.05
295	Brian Howard	.10	.05
296	Ken Williams	.10	.05
297	Alonzo Mourning	3.00	1.35
298	Larry Nance	.30	.14
299	Jeff Grayer	.10	.05
300	Dave Johnson	.10	.05
301	Bob McCann	.10	.05
302	Bart Kofoed	.10	.05
303	Anthony Cook	.10	.05
304	Radisav Curcic	.10	.05
305	John Crotty	.10	.05
306	Brad Sellers	.10	.05
307	Marcus Webb	.10	.05
308	Winston Garland	.10	.05
309	Walter Palmer	.10	.05
310	Rod Higgins	.10	.05
311	Travis Mays	.10	.05
312	Alex Stivrins	.10	.05
313	Greg Kite	.10	.05
314	Dennis Rodman	2.50	1.10
315	Mike Sanders	.10	.05
316	Ed Pinckney	.10	.05
317	Harold Miner	.30	.14
318	Pooh Richardson	.10	.05
319	Oliver Miller	.30	.14
320	Latrell Sprewell	2.00	.90
321	Anthony Pullard	.10	.05
322	Mark Randall	.10	.05
323	Jeff Hornacek	.30	.14
324	Rick Mahorn UER	.10	.05
	(Rookie Card is 1981-82, 1992-93)		
325	Sean Rooks	.10	.05
326	Paul Pressey	.10	.05
327	James Worthy	.60	.25
328	Matt Bullard	.10	.05
329	Reggie Smith	.10	.05
330	Don MacLean UER	.10	.05
	(Missing '92 Draft Pick logo)		

☐ 331	John Williams UER .... .10	.05
	(Rookie Card erroneously	
	shows Hot Rod)	
☐ 332	Frank Johnson.............10	.05
☐ 333	Hubert Davis UER ...... .30	.14
	(Missing '92 Draft	
	Pick logo)	
☐ 334	Lloyd Daniels..............10	.05
☐ 335	Steve Bardo................10	.05
☐ 336	Jeff Sanders...............10	.05
☐ 337	Tree Rollins.................10	.05
☐ 338	Micheal Williams........10	.05
☐ 339	Lorenzo Williams........10	.05
☐ 340	Harvey Grant..............10	.05
☐ 341	Avery Johnson...........10	.05
☐ 342	Bo Kimble...................10	.05
☐ 343	LaPhonso Ellis UER.. 1.00	.45
	(Missing '92 Draft	
	Pick logo)	
☐ 344	Mookie Blaylock .... .30	.14
☐ 345	Isaiah Morris UER ...... .10	.05
	(Missing '92 Draft	
	Pick logo)	
☐ 346	C.Weatherspoon .... .60	.25
☐ 347	Manute Bol 10	.05
☐ 348	Victor Alexander .... .10	.05
☐ 349	Corey Williams .... .10	.05
☐ 350	Byron Houston .... .10	.05
☐ 351	Stanley Roberts.........10	.05
☐ 352	Anthony Avent............10	.05
☐ 353	Vincent Askew...........10	.05
☐ 354	Herb Williams .... .10	.05
☐ 355	J.R. Reid 10	.05
☐ 356	Brad Lohaus 10	.05
☐ 357	Reggie Miller.............. .60	.25
☐ 358	Blue Edwards 10	.05
☐ 359	Tom Tolbert................10	.05
☐ 360	Charles Barkley 1.00	.45
☐ 361	David Robinson 1.00	.45
☐ 362	Dale Davis 10	.05
☐ 363	Robert Werdann UER .10	.05
	(Missing '92 Draft	
	Pick logo)	
☐ 364	Chuck Person 10	.05
☐ 365	Alaa Abdelnaby .... .10	.05
☐ 366	Dave Jamerson .... .10	.05
☐ 367	Scottie Pippen 2.00	.90
☐ 368	Mark Jackson .... .30	.14
☐ 369	Keith Askins 10	.05
☐ 370	Marty Conlon..............10	.05
☐ 371	Chucky Brown .... .10	.05
☐ 372	LaBradford Smith ...... .10	.05
☐ 373	Tim Kempton 10	.05
☐ 374	Sam Mitchell...............10	.05
☐ 375	John Salley 10	.05
☐ 376	Mario Elie .... .30	.14
☐ 377	Mark West...................10	.05
☐ 378	David Wingate 10	.05
☐ 379	Jaren Jackson .... .10	.05
☐ 380	Rumeal Robinson ...... .10	.05
☐ 381	Kennard Winchester .. .10	.05
☐ 382	Walter Bond 10	.05
☐ 383	Isaac Austin...............10	.05
☐ 384	Derrick Coleman .... .30	.14
☐ 385	Larry Smith.................10	.05
☐ 386	Joe Dumars................ .60	.25
☐ 387	Matt Geiger UER .... .30	.14
	(Missing '92 Draft	
	Pick logo)	
☐ 388	Stephen Howard .... .10	.05
☐ 389	William Bedford.........10	.05
☐ 390	Jayson Williams .... .30	.14
☐ 391	Kurt Rambis 10	.05
☐ 392	Keith Jennings...........10	.05
☐ 393	Steve Kerr UER .... .30	.14
	(The words key stat	
	are repeated on back)	
☐ 394	Larry Stewart..............10	.05
☐ 395	Danny Young..............10	.05
☐ 396	Doug Overton 10	.05
☐ 397	Mark Acres 10	.05
☐ 398	John Bagley.................10	.05
☐ 399	Checklist 201-300 ...... .10	.05
☐ 400	Checklist 301-400 ...... .10	.05

1992-93 Stadium Club Beam Team

Comprised of some of the NBA's biggest stars, "Beam Team" cards commemorate Topps' 1993 sponsorship of a six-minute NBA laser animation show called Beams Above the Rim. The show premiered at the 1993 NBA All-Star Game. Afterwards, the laser show embarked on a ten-city tour and was featured in either the pre-game or half-time events in ten NBA arenas. These cards were randomly inserted in second series 15-card packs at a rate of one in 36. The color action player photos on the fronts are bordered on two sides by an angled silver light beam border design with a light refracting pattern. The player's name appears on a white-outlined burnt orange bar superimposed over a basketball icon at the bottom. The backs present a color head shot and, on a basketball icon, career highlights.

	MINT	NRMT
COMPLETE SET (21)	250.00	110.00
COMMON CARD (1-21)	2.00	.90
SEMISTARS	3.00	1.35
UNLISTED STARS	6.00	2.70
SER.2 STATED ODDS 1:36		

			MINT	NRMT
☐ 1	Michael Jordan		70.00	32.00
☐ 2	Dominique Wilkins		6.00	2.70
☐ 3	Shawn Kemp		20.00	9.00
☐ 4	Clyde Drexler		8.00	3.60
☐ 5	Scottie Pippen		20.00	9.00
☐ 6	Chris Mullin		6.00	2.70
☐ 7	Reggie Miller..............		6.00	2.70
☐ 8	Glen Rice...................		6.00	3.60
☐ 9	Jeff Hornacek		3.00	1.35
☐ 10	Jeff Malone		2.00	.90
☐ 11	John Stockton		6.00	2.70
☐ 12	Kevin Johnson		6.00	2.70
☐ 13	Mark Price..................		2.00	.90
☐ 14	Tim Hardaway		10.00	4.50
☐ 15	Charles Barkley		10.00	4.50
☐ 16	Hakeem Olajuwon		12.00	5.50
☐ 17	Karl Malone...............		4.50	4.50
☐ 18	Patrick Ewing		6.00	2.70
☐ 19	Dennis Rodman..........		25.00	11.00
☐ 20	David Robinson		10.00	4.50
☐ 21	Shaquille O'Neal		70.00	32.00

1993-94 Stadium Club

The 1993-94 Stadium Club set consists of 360 standard-size cards issued in two series of 180 cards. Cards were issued in 12 and 20-card packs. There were 24 twelve-card packs per box. The full-bleed fronts feature glossy color action photos. The player's name is superimposed on the lower portion of the picture in white and gold foil lettering. The borderless backs are divided in half vertically with a torn effect. The left side sports a vertical player photo and on the right side, over a purple background, is biography and player's name and team. A brief section named "The Buzz" provides career highlights. A multi-colored box lists the 1992-93 statistics, career statistics and a Topps Skills Rating System that provides a score including player intimidation, mobility, shooting range and defense. Subsets featured are Triple Double (1-11, 101-111) and High Court (61-69, 170-178) and interspersed NBA Draft Picks. Card number 345 was never issued. Due to an error in numbering, both Toni Kukoc and Chris Corchiani are numbered 336. Corchiani is actually listed on the checklist card as number 345, thus we've listed him below in that order. Rookie Cards of note in this set include Vin Baker, Anfernee Hardaway, Allan Houston, Toni Kukoc, Jamal Mashburn, Nick Van Exel and Chris Webber.

	MINT	NRMT
COMPLETE SET (360)	40.00	18.00
COMPLETE SERIES 1 (180)	20.00	9.00

COMPLETE SERIES 2 (180) 20.00 9.00
COMMON CARD (1-180) ...... .10 .05
COMMON CARD (181-360) .. .05 .02
SEMISTARS SER.1 .... .20 .09
SEMISTARS SER.2 .... .15 .07
UNLISTED STARS SER.1 .. .40 .18
UNLISTED STARS SER.2 .. .30 .14
NUMBER 345 NEVER ISSUED
KUKOC AND CORCHIANI NUMBERED 336
COMP.FDI SER.(360) 1100.00 500.00
COMP.FDI SER.1 (180) 500.00 220.00
COMP.FDI SER.2 (180) 600.00 275.00
COMMON FDI (1-360) .... 2.00 .90
*STARS: 12.5X TO 25X HI COLUMN
*RCs: 10X TO 20X HI
SER.1/2 STATED ODDS 1:24

1	Michael Jordan TD	2.50	1.10
2	Kenny Anderson TD ...	.10	.05
3	Steve Smith TD	.20	.09
4	Kevin Gamble TD	.10	.05
5	Detlef Schrempf TD ..	.10	.05
6	Larry Johnson TD	.20	.09
7	Brad Daugherty TD ...	.10	.05
8	Rumeal Robinson TD ..	.10	.05
9	Micheal Williams TD .	.10	.05
10	David Robinson TD ...	.40	.18
11	Sam Perkins TD	.10	.05
12	Thurl Bailey	.10	.05
13	Sherman Douglas	.10	.05
14	Larry Stewart	.10	.05
15	Kevin Johnson	.20	.09
16	Bill Cartwright	.10	.05
17	Larry Nance	.20	.09
18	P.J. Brown	.10	.05
19	Tony Bennett	.10	.05
20	Robert Parish	.20	.09
21	David Benoit	.10	.05
22	Detlef Schrempf	.20	.09
23	Hubert Davis	.10	.05
24	Donald Hodge	.10	.05
25	Hersey Hawkins	.20	.09
26	Mark Jackson	.20	.09
27	Reggie Williams	.10	.05
28	Lionel Simmons	.10	.05
29	Ron Harper	.20	.09
30	Chris Mills	.60	.25
31	Danny Schayes	.10	.05
32	J.R. Reid	.10	.05
33	Willie Burton	.10	.05
34	Greg Anthony	.10	.05
35	Elden Campbell	.10	.05
36	Ervin Johnson	.20	.09
37	Scott Brooks	.10	.05
38	Johnny Newman	.10	.05
39	Rex Chapman	.10	.05
40	Chuck Person	.10	.05
41	John Williams	.10	.05
42	Anthony Bowie	.10	.05
43	Negele Knight	.10	.05
44	Tyrone Corbin	.10	.05
45	Jud Buechler	.10	.05
46	Adam Keefe	.10	.05
47	Glen Rice	.40	.18
48	Tracy Murray	.10	.05
49	Rick Mahorn	.10	.05
50	Vlade Divac	.20	.09
51	Eric Murdock	.10	.05
52	Isaiah Morris	.10	.05
53	Bobby Hurley	.20	.09
54	Mitch Richmond	.40	.18
55	Danny Ainge	.20	.09
56	Dikembe Mutombo	.40	.18
57	Jeff Hornacek	.20	.09
58	Tony Campbell	.10	.05
59	Vinny Del Negro	.10	.05
60	Xavier McDaniel HC ..	.10	.05
61	Scottie Pippen HC ...	.60	.25
62	Larry Nance HC	.10	.05
63	Dikembe Mutombo HC ..	.10	.05
64	Hakeem Olajuwon HC ..	.40	.18
65	Dominique Wilkins HC	.20	.09
66	C.Weatherspoon HC ...	.10	.05
67	Chris Morris HC	.10	.05
68	Patrick Ewing HC	.20	.09
69	Kevin Willis HC	.10	.05

70	Jon Barry	.10	.05
71	Jerry Reynolds	.10	.05
72	Sarunas Marciulionis.	.10	.05
73	Mark West	.10	.05
74	B.J. Armstrong	.10	.05
75	Greg Kite	.10	.05
76	LaSalle Thompson	.10	.05
77	Randy White	.10	.05
78	Alaa Abdelnaby	.10	.05
79	Kevin Brooks	.10	.05
80	Vern Fleming	.10	.05
81	Doc Rivers	.20	.09
82	Shawn Bradley	.50	.23
83	Wayman Tisdale	.10	.05
84	Olden Polynice	.10	.05
85	Michael Cage	.10	.05
86	Harold Miner	.10	.05
87	Doug Smith	.10	.05
88	Tom Gugliotta	.40	.18
89	Hakeem Olajuwon	.75	.35
90	Loy Vaught	.20	.09
91	James Worthy	.40	.18
92	John Paxson	.10	.05
93	Jon Koncak	.10	.05
94	Lee Mayberry	.10	.05
95	Clarence Weatherspoon	.10	.05
96	Mark Eaton	.10	.05
97	Rex Walters	.10	.05
98	Alvin Robertson	.10	.05
99	Dan Majerle	.20	.09
100	Shaquille O'Neal	1.50	.70
101	Derrick Coleman TD ..	.10	.05
102	Hersey Hawkins TD ...	.10	.05
103	Scottie Pippen TD ...	.60	.25
104	Scott Skiles TD	.10	.05
105	Rod Strickland TD ...	.10	.05
106	Pooh Richardson TD ..	.10	.05
107	Tom Gugliotta TD	.20	.09
108	Mark Jackson TD	.10	.05
109	Dikembe Mutombo TD ..	.10	.05
110	Charles Barkley TD ..	.40	.18
111	Otis Thorpe TD	.10	.05
112	Malik Sealy	.10	.05
113	Mark Macon	.10	.05
114	Dee Brown	.10	.05
115	Nate McMillan	.10	.05
116	John Starks	.20	.09
117	Clyde Drexler	.50	.23
118	Antoine Carr	.10	.05
119	Doug West	.10	.05
120	Victor Alexander	.10	.05
121	Kenny Gattison	.10	.05
122	Spud Webb	.20	.09
123	Rumeal Robinson	.10	.05
124	Tim Kempton	.10	.05
125	Karl Malone	.60	.25
126	Randy Woods	.10	.05
127	Calbert Cheaney	.40	.18
128	Johnny Dawkins	.10	.05
129	Dominique Wilkins ...	.40	.18
130	Horace Grant	.20	.09
131	Bill Laimbeer	.10	.05
132	Kenny Smith	.10	.05
133	Sedale Threatt	.10	.05
134	Brian Shaw	.10	.05
135	Dennis Scott	.20	.09
136	Mark Bryant	.10	.05
137	Xavier McDaniel	.10	.05
138	David Wood	.10	.05
139	Luther Wright	.10	.05
140	Lloyd Daniels	.10	.05
141	Marlon Maxey UER	.10	.05
	(Name spelled Maxley on the front)		
142	Pooh Richardson	.10	.05
143	Jeff Grayer	.10	.05
144	LaPhonso Ellis	.20	.09
145	Gerald Wilkins	.10	.05
146	Dell Curry	.10	.05
147	Duane Causwell	.10	.05
148	Tim Hardaway	.50	.23
149	Isiah Thomas	.40	.18
150	Doug Edwards	.10	.05
151	Anthony Peeler	.10	.05
152	Tate George	.10	.05
153	Terry Davis	.10	.05
154	Sam Perkins	.20	.09

155	John Salley	.10	.05
156	Vernon Maxwell	.10	.05
157	Anthony Avent	.10	.05
158	Clifford Robinson ...	.20	.09
159	Corie Blount	.10	.05
160	Gerald Paddio	.10	.05
161	Blair Rasmussen	.10	.05
162	Carl Herrera	.10	.05
163	Chris Smith	.10	.05
164	Pervis Ellison	.10	.05
165	Rod Strickland.......	.20	.09
166	Jeff Malone	.10	.05
167	Danny Ferry	.10	.05
168	Kevin Lynch	.10	.05
169	Michael Jordan	5.00	2.20
170	Derrick Coleman HC ..	.10	.05
171	Jerome Kersey HC	.10	.05
172	David Robinson HC ...	.40	.18
173	Shawn Kemp HC	.60	.25
174	Karl Malone HC	.40	.18
175	Shaquille O'Neal HC .	.75	.35
176	Alonzo Mourning HC ..	.40	.18
177	Charles Barkley HC ..	.40	.18
178	Larry Johnson HC	.20	.09
179	Checklist 1-90	.10	.05
180	Checklist 91-180	.10	.05
181	Michael Jordan FF ...	2.00	.90
182	Dominique Wilkins FF	.15	.07
183	Dennis Rodman FF	.60	.25
184	Scottie Pippen FF ...	.50	.23
185	Larry Johnson FF	.20	.09
186	Karl Malone FF	.20	.09
187	C.Weatherspoon FF ...	.05	.02
188	Charles Barkley FF ..	.30	.14
189	Patrick Ewing FF	.20	.09
190	Derrick Coleman FF ..	.05	.02
191	LaBradford Smith	.05	.02
192	Derek Harper	.15	.07
193	Ken Norman	.05	.02
194	Rodney Rogers	.05	.02
195	Chris Dudley	.05	.02
196	Gary Payton	.50	.23
197	Andrew Lang	.05	.02
198	Billy Owens	.05	.02
199	Bryon Russell	.30	.14
200	Patrick Ewing	.30	.14
201	Stacey King	.05	.02
202	Grant Long	.05	.02
203	Sean Elliott	.15	.07
204	Muggsy Bogues	.15	.07
205	Kevin Edwards	.05	.02
206	Dale Davis	.05	.02
207	Dale Ellis	.05	.02
208	Terrell Brandon	.30	.14
209	Kevin Gamble	.05	.02
210	Robert Horry	.15	.07
211	Moses Malone UER	.20	.09
	Birthdate on back is 1993		
212	Gary Grant	.05	.02
213	Bobby Hurley	.15	.07
214	Larry Krystkowiak ...	.05	.02
215	A.C. Green	.15	.07
216	Christian Laettner ..	.30	.14
217	Orlando Woolridge ...	.05	.02
218	Craig Ehlo	.05	.02
219	Terry Porter	.05	.02
220	Jamal Mashburn	.75	.35
221	Kevin Duckworth	.05	.02
222	Shawn Kemp	1.00	.45
223	Frank Brickowski	.05	.02
224	Chris Webber	2.00	.90
225	Charles Oakley	.15	.07
226	Jay Humphries	.05	.02
227	Steve Kerr	.15	.07
228	Tim Perry	.05	.02
229	Sleepy Floyd	.05	.02
230	Bimbo Coles	.05	.02
231	Eddie Johnson	.05	.02
232	Terry Mills	.05	.02
233	Danny Manning	.05	.02
234	Isaiah Rider	.40	.18
235	Darnell Mee	.05	.02
236	Haywoode Workman	.05	.02
237	Scott Skiles	.05	.02
238	Otis Thorpe	.15	.07
239	Mike Peplowski	.05	.02

☐ 240 Eric Leckner	.05	.02
☐ 241 Johnny Newman	.05	.02
☐ 242 Benoit Benjamin	.05	.02
☐ 243 Doug Christie	.05	.02
☐ 244 Acie Earl	.05	.02
☐ 245 Luc Longley	.15	.07
☐ 246 Tyrone Hill	.05	.02
☐ 247 Allan Houston	.60	.25
☐ 248 Joe Kleine	.05	.02
☐ 249 Mookie Blaylock	.15	.07
☐ 250 Anthony Bonner	.05	.02
☐ 251 Luther Wright	.05	.02
☐ 252 Todd Day	.05	.02
☐ 253 Kendall Gill	.15	.07
☐ 254 Mario Elie	.05	.02
☐ 255 Pete Myers UER	.05	.02
Card has born in 1993		
☐ 256 Jim Les	.05	.02
☐ 257 Stanley Roberts	.05	.02
☐ 258 Michael Adams	.05	.02
☐ 259 Hersey Hawkins	.15	.07
☐ 260 Shawn Bradley	.20	.09
☐ 261 Scott Haskin	.05	.02
☐ 262 Corie Blount	.05	.02
☐ 263 Charles Smith	.05	.02
☐ 264 Armon Gilliam	.05	.02
☐ 265 Jamal Mashburn NW	.30	.14
☐ 266 A.Hardaway NW	1.50	.70
☐ 267 Shawn Bradley NW	.20	.09
☐ 268 Chris Webber NW	.75	.35
☐ 269 Bobby Hurley NW	.15	.07
☐ 270 Isaiah Rider NW	.15	.07
☐ 271 Dino Radja NW	.15	.07
☐ 272 Chris Mills NW	.15	.07
☐ 273 Nick Van Exel NW	.40	.18
☐ 274 Lindsey Hunter NW	.20	.09
☐ 275 Toni Kukoc NW	.30	.14
☐ 276 Popeye Jones NW	.05	.02
☐ 277 Chris Mills	.20	.09
☐ 278 Ricky Pierce	.05	.02
☐ 279 Negele Knight	.05	.02
☐ 280 Kenny Walker	.05	.02
☐ 281 Nick Van Exel	1.00	.45
☐ 282 Derrick Coleman UER	.15	.07
(Career stats listed under '92-93)		
☐ 283 Popeye Jones	.05	.02
☐ 284 Derrick McKey	.05	.02
☐ 285 Rick Fox	.05	.02
☐ 286 Jerome Kersey	.05	.02
☐ 287 Steve Smith	.20	.09
☐ 288 Brian Williams	.05	.02
☐ 289 Chris Mullin	.30	.14
☐ 290 Terry Cummings	.05	.02
☐ 291 Donald Royal	.05	.02
☐ 292 Alonzo Mourning	.50	.23
☐ 293 Mike Brown	.05	.02
☐ 294 Latrell Sprewell	.30	.14
☐ 295 Oliver Miller	.05	.02
☐ 296 Terry Dehere	.05	.02
☐ 297 Detlef Schrempf	.15	.07
☐ 298 Sam Bowie UER	.05	.02
(Last name Bowe on front)		
☐ 299 Chris Morris	.05	.02
☐ 300 Scottie Pippen	1.00	.45
☐ 301 Warren Kidd	.05	.02
☐ 302 Don MacLean	.05	.02
☐ 303 Sean Rooks	.05	.02
☐ 304 Matt Geiger	.05	.02
☐ 305 Dennis Rodman	1.25	.55
☐ 306 Reggie Miller	.30	.14
☐ 307 Vin Baker	2.00	.90
☐ 308 Anfernee Hardaway	4.00	1.80
☐ 309 Lindsey Hunter	.30	.14
☐ 310 Stacey Augmon	.05	.02
☐ 311 Randy Brown	.05	.02
☐ 312 Anthony Mason	.15	.07
☐ 313 John Stockton	.30	.14
☐ 314 Sam Cassell	.75	.35
☐ 315 Buck Williams	.15	.07
☐ 316 Bryant Stith	.05	.02
☐ 317 Brad Daugherty	.05	.02
☐ 318 Dino Radja	.05	.02
☐ 319 Rony Seikaly	.05	.02
☐ 320 Charles Barkley	.50	.23
☐ 321 Avery Johnson	.05	.02
☐ 322 Mahmoud Abdul-Rauf	.05	.02

☐ 323 Larry Johnson	.30	.14
☐ 324 Micheal Williams	.05	.02
☐ 325 Mark Aguirre	.05	.02
☐ 326 Jim Jackson	.30	.14
☐ 327 Antonio Harvey	.05	.02
☐ 328 David Robinson	.50	.23
☐ 329 Calbert Cheaney	.20	.09
☐ 330 Kenny Anderson	.20	.09
☐ 331 Walt Williams	.20	.09
☐ 332 Kevin Willis	.05	.02
☐ 333 Nick Anderson	.15	.07
☐ 334 Rik Smits	.15	.07
☐ 335 Joe Dumars	.20	.09
☐ 336 Toni Kukoc	.75	.35
☐ 337 Harvey Grant	.05	.02
☐ 338 Tom Chambers	.05	.02
☐ 339 Blue Edwards	.05	.02
☐ 340 Mark Price	.05	.02
☐ 341 Ervin Johnson	.15	.07
☐ 342 Rolando Blackman	.05	.02
☐ 343 Scott Burrell	.30	.14
☐ 344 Gheorghe Muresan	.50	.23
☐ 345 C.Corchiani UER 336..	.05	.02
☐ 346 Richard Petruska	.05	.02
☐ 347 Dana Barros	.05	.02
☐ 348 Hakeem Olajuwon FF	.30	.14
☐ 349 Dee Brown FF	.05	.02
☐ 350 John Starks FF	.05	.02
☐ 351 Ron Harper FF	.05	.02
☐ 352 Chris Webber FF	.75	.35
☐ 353 Dan Majerle FF	.05	.02
☐ 354 Clyde Drexler FF	.20	.09
☐ 355 Shawn Kemp FF	.50	.23
☐ 356 David Robinson FF	.30	.14
☐ 357 Chris Morris FF	.05	.02
☐ 358 Shaquille O'Neal FF	.60	.25
☐ 359 Checklist	.05	.02
☐ 360 Checklist	.05	.02

the other. The cards are numbered on the back as "X of 27."

	MINT	NRMT
COMPLETE SET (27)	80.00	36.00
COMPLETE SERIES 1 (13)	30.00	13.50
COMPLETE SERIES 2 (14)	50.00	22.00
COMMON CARD (1-13)	.50	.23
COMMON CARD (14-27)	1.00	.45
SEMISTARS SER.1	1.00	.45
SEMISTARS SER.2	1.25	.55
UNLISTED STARS SER.1	1.25	.55
UNLISTED STARS SER.2	2.50	1.10
SER.1/2 STATED ODDS 1:24		

☐ 1 Shaquille O'Neal	6.00	2.70
☐ 2 Mark Price	.50	.23
☐ 3 Patrick Ewing	1.25	.55
☐ 4 Michael Jordan	20.00	9.00
☐ 5 Charles Barkley	2.00	.90
☐ 6 Reggie Miller	1.25	.55
☐ 7 Derrick Coleman	1.00	.45
☐ 8 Dominique Wilkins	1.25	.55
☐ 9 Karl Malone	2.00	.90
☐ 10 Alonzo Mourning	2.00	.90
☐ 11 Tim Hardaway	1.50	.70
☐ 12 Hakeem Olajuwon	2.50	1.10
☐ 13 David Robinson	2.00	.90
☐ 14 Dan Majerle	1.25	.55
☐ 15 Larry Johnson	2.50	1.10
☐ 16 LaPhonso Ellis	1.25	.55
☐ 17 Nick Van Exel	5.00	2.20
☐ 18 Scottie Pippen	8.00	3.60
☐ 19 John Stockton	2.50	1.10
☐ 20 Bobby Hurley	1.00	.45
☐ 21 Chris Webber	10.00	4.50
☐ 22 Jamal Mashburn	4.00	1.80
☐ 23 Anfernee Hardaway	25.00	11.00
☐ 24 Isaiah Rider	2.50	1.10
☐ 25 Ken Norman	1.00	.45
☐ 26 Danny Manning	1.00	.45
☐ 27 Calbert Cheaney	2.50	1.10

1993-94 Stadium Club Beam Team

KARL MALONE

Randomly inserted in first and second series 12-card and 20-card foil packs at a rate of one in 24, cards from this standard-size 27-card set features a selection of top NBA stars and rookies. Cards were issued in two series of 13 and 14, respectively. The design consists of borderless fronts with color player action photos set against game-crowd backgrounds. Silver metallic beams appear near the bottom above the player's name. The horizontal back carries a color action photo on one side, with player profile on

1993-94 Stadium Club Big Tips

Randomly inserted about one in every four packs, these 27 team logo cards measure the standard size. The horizontal card fronts are framed by a thin white line and carry the words "NBA Showdown '94," the NBA logo and the team name and logo within a team-colored stripe across the bottom. The back carries game hints for the Electronic Arts NBA Showdown '94 and a videogame offer. The logo cards are unnumbered and checklisted below in alphabetical team order.

	MINT	NRMT
COMPLETE SET (27)	5.00	2.20
COMMON CARD (1-27)	.25	.11
SER.2 STATED ODDS 1:6		

		MINT	NRMT
□ 1	Atlanta Hawks	.25	.11
□ 2	Boston Celtics	.25	.11
□ 3	Charlotte Hornets	.25	.11
□ 4	Chicago Bulls	.25	.11
□ 5	Cleveland Cavaliers	.25	.11
□ 6	Dallas Mavericks	.25	.11
□ 7	Denver Nuggets	.25	.11
□ 8	Detroit Pistons	.25	.11
□ 9	Golden State Warriors	.25	.11
□ 10	Houston Rockets	.25	.11
□ 11	Indiana Pacers	.25	.11
□ 12	Los Angeles Clippers	.25	.11
□ 13	Los Angeles Lakers	.25	.11
□ 14	Miami Heat	.25	.11
□ 15	Milwaukee Bucks	.25	.11
□ 16	Minnesota T'wolves	.25	.11
□ 17	New Jersey Nets	.25	.11
□ 18	New York Knicks	.25	.11
□ 19	Orlando Magic	.25	.11
□ 20	Philadelphia 76ers	.25	.11
□ 21	Phoenix Suns	.25	.11
□ 22	Portland Trail Blazers	.25	.11
□ 23	Sacramento Kings	.25	.11
□ 24	San Antonio Spurs	.25	.11
□ 25	Seattle Supersonics	.25	.11
□ 26	Utah Jazz	.25	.11
□ 27	Washington Bullets	.25	.11

1993-94 Stadium Club Frequent Flyer Upgrades

Cards from this 20-card standard size set are based upon the Frequent Flyer subsets in the basic 1993-94 Stadium Club issue. Upgrades are identical to the basic cards with the exception of a chromium like metallic gloss and Upgrade logo on front. Upgrades were available only through a mail offer based on Frequent Flyer Point cards which were randomly inserted at a rate of 1 in every 6 second series packs. Each of the 21 players featured in the Frequent Flyer subsets (except for Michael Jordan) had five different point cards (based upon point totals derived from actual games during the season) making for a total of 100 different point cards. Since none of the point cards feature player photos, none trade for a premium and are priced below as expired point cards. To obtain a Frequent Flyer Upgrade card, collectors had to accumulate 50 points or more of an individual player and redeem them by September 15, 1994.

	MINT	NRMT
COMPLETE SET (20)	75.00	34.00
COMMON CARD	1.00	.45
SEMISTARS	1.50	.70
UNLISTED STARS	4.00	1.80
ONE CARD BY MAIL PER 50 FF POINTS		
POINT CARDS: SER.2 STATED ODDS 1:6		

		MINT	NRMT
□ 182	Dominique Wilkins	4.00	1.80
□ 183	Dennis Rodman	15.00	6.75
□ 184	Scottie Pippen	12.00	5.50
□ 185	Larry Johnson	4.00	1.80
□ 186	Karl Malone	6.00	2.70
□ 187	C.Weatherspoon	1.00	.45
□ 188	Charles Barkley	6.00	2.70
□ 189	Patrick Ewing	4.00	1.80
□ 190	Derrick Coleman	1.50	.70
□ 348	Hakeem Olajuwon	8.00	3.60
□ 349	Dee Brown	1.00	.45
□ 350	John Starks	1.50	.70
□ 351	Ron Harper	1.50	.70
□ 352	Chris Webber	15.00	6.75
□ 353	Dan Majerle	1.50	.70
□ 354	Clyde Drexler	5.00	2.20
□ 355	Shawn Kemp	12.00	5.50
□ 356	David Robinson	6.00	2.70
□ 357	Chris Morris	1.00	.45
□ 358	Shaquille O'Neal	15.00	6.75
□ NNO	Expired Point Cards	.25	.11

1993-94 Stadium Club Rim Rockers

Randomly inserted in second series 12-card packs at a rate of one in 24, these six standard-size cards feature some of the NBA's top dunkers. Fronts contain color player action shots. The player's name appears near the bottom. His first name is printed in white lowercase lettering; his last is gold-foil stamped in uppercase lettering. The back carries another borderless color player action shot, but its right side is ghosted, blue-screened, and overprinted with career highlights in white lettering. The cards are numbered on the back as "X of 6."

	MINT	NRMT
COMPLETE SET (6)	6.00	2.70
COMMON CARD (1-6)	.25	.11
SEMISTARS	.40	.18
SER.2 STATED ODDS 1:24		

		MINT	NRMT
□ 1	Shaquille O'Neal	3.00	1.35
□ 2	Harold Miner	.25	.11
□ 3	Charles Barkley	1.25	.55
□ 4	Dominique Wilkins	.60	.25
□ 5	Shawn Kemp	2.50	1.10
□ 6	Robert Horry	.40	.18

1993-94 Stadium Club Super Teams

Randomly inserted in first series 12 and 20-card foil packs at a rate of one in 24, cards from this standard-size 27-card set feature borderless fronts with color team action photos. The team name appears in gold-foil lettering at the bottom. The back features the NBA Super Team Card rules. If the team shown on the card won its division, conference or league championship, the collector could have redeemed it for special prizes until Nov. 1, 1994. Atlanta, Houston, New York and Seattle were all winners. Their cards are currently in shorter supply than non-winner Super Team cards. The four winning teams are designated below with a "W". In addition, Conference, Division and Finals winner cards have "C", "D" and "F" designations.

1994-95 Stadium Club

The 362 standard size cards that comprise the 1994-95 Stadium Club set were issued in two separate series of 182 and 180 cards each. Cards were primarily distributed in 12-card packs, each with a suggested retail price of $2.00. Full-bleed fronts feature full-color action shots with player's name placed along the bottom in foil. Topical subsets featured are College Teammates (100-114), Draft Picks (172, 179-182), All-Import (201-205, 251-255), Back Court Tandem (226-230, 276-280, 326-330), and Faces of the Game (353-362). Other topical subsets, such as Thru the Glass as well as First and Second Round '94 Draft Picks, are scattered throughout the set. Autographed cards of Reggie Miller were randomly inserted one per box into special retail boxes. Rookie Cards of note include Grant Hill, Juwan Howard, Eddie Jones, Jason Kidd and Glenn Robinson.

	MINT	NRMT
COMPLETE SET (27)	15.00	6.75
COMMON CARD (1-27)	.40	.18
SER.1 STATED ODDS 1:24		
COMP.DW BAG HAWKS (11)	6.00	2.70
COMP.DW BAG KNICKS (11)	6.00	2.70
COMP.DW BAG ROCKETS (11)	10.00	4.50
COMP.DW BAG SONICS (11)	10.00	4.50
ONE BAG BY MAIL PER DIV.WIN.SUPER TM.		
COMP.MP BAG KNICKS (11)	10.00	4.50
COMP.MP BAG ROCKETS (11)	15.00	6.75
ONE BAG BY MAIL PER CON.WIN.SUP.TEAM		

		MINT	NRMT
☐ 1	Atlanta Hawks WD (Kevin Willis Dominique Wilkins)	.40	.18
☐ 2	Boston Celtics (Xavier McDaniel Robert Parish)	.40	.18
☐ 3	Charlotte Hornets (Larry Johnson Alonzo Mourning)	2.00	.90
☐ 4	Chicago Bulls (Horace Grant)	.40	.18
☐ 5	Cleveland Cavaliers (Brad Daugherty John Williams)	.40	.18
☐ 6	Dallas Mavericks (Group photo)	.40	.18
☐ 7	Denver Nuggets (Dikembe Mutombo Kevin Brooks)	.60	.25
☐ 8	Detroit Pistons (Group photo)	.40	.18
☐ 9	Golden State Warriors (Group photo)	.40	.18
☐ 10	Houston Rockets WCDF	6.00	2.70
☐ 11	Indiana Pacers (Group photo)	.40	.18
☐ 12	Los Angeles Clippers (Danny Manning Ron Harper)	.40	.18
☐ 13	Los Angeles Lakers (Group photo)	.40	.18
☐ 14	Miami Heat (John Salley Willie Burton)	.40	.18
☐ 15	Milwaukee Bucks (Group photo)	.40	.18
☐ 16	Minnesota T'wolves (Christian Laettner Felton Spencer)	.60	.25
☐ 17	New Jersey Nets (Derrick Coleman)	.40	.18
☐ 18	New York Knicks WCD (Patrick Ewing)	2.50	1.10
☐ 19	Orlando Magic (Shaquille O'Neal)	5.00	2.20
☐ 20	Philadelphia 76ers (Clarence Weatherspoon Jeff Hornacek)	.40	.18
☐ 21	Phoenix Suns (Charles Barkley Dan Majerle)	1.25	.55
☐ 22	Portland Trail Blazers (Buck Williams)	.40	.18
☐ 23	Sacramento Kings (Lionel Simmons)	.40	.18
☐ 24	San Antonio Spurs (David Robinson)	1.25	.55
☐ 25	Seattle Supersonics WD (Shawn Kemp)	4.00	1.80
☐ 26	Utah Jazz (Group photo)	.40	.18
☐ 27	Washington Bullets (Group photo)	.40	.18

		MINT	NRMT
COMPLETE SET (362)		40.00	18.00
COMPLETE SERIES 1 (182)		20.00	9.00
COMPLETE SERIES 2 (180)		20.00	9.00
COMMON CARD (1-362)		.10	.05
SEMISTARS		.15	.07
UNLISTED STARS		.40	.18
COMP.FDI SET (362)		900.00	400.00
COMP.FDI SER.1 (182)		600.00	275.00
COMP.FDI SER.2 (180)		300.00	135.00
COMMON FDI (1-362)		1.50	.70
*STARS: 12.5X TO 25X HI COLUMN			
*RCs: 7.5X TO 15X HI			
SER.1/2 STATED ODDS 1:24			
R.MILLER AU: ONE PER SPECIAL RETAIL BOX			

☐ 1	Patrick Ewing	.40	.18
☐ 2	Patrick Ewing TTG	.15	.07
☐ 3	Bimbo Coles	.10	.05
☐ 4	Elden Campbell	.15	.07
☐ 5	Brent Price	.10	.05
☐ 6	Hubert Davis	.10	.05
☐ 7	Donald Royal	.10	.05
☐ 8	Tim Perry	.10	.05
☐ 9	Chris Webber	1.00	.45
☐ 10	Chris Webber TTG	.50	.23
☐ 11	Brad Daugherty	.10	.05
☐ 12	P.J. Brown	.10	.05
☐ 13	Charles Barkley	.60	.25
☐ 14	Mario Elie	.10	.05
☐ 15	Tyrone Hill	.10	.05
☐ 16	Anfernee Hardaway	1.50	.70
☐ 17	Anfernee Hardaway TTG	.75	.35
☐ 18	Toni Kukoc	.40	.18
☐ 19	Chris Morris	.10	.05
☐ 20	Gerald Wilkins	.10	.05
☐ 21	David Benoit	.10	.05
☐ 22	Kevin Duckworth	.10	.05
☐ 23	Derrick Coleman	.15	.07
☐ 24	Adam Keefe	.10	.05
☐ 25	Marlon Maxey	.10	.05
☐ 26	Vern Fleming	.10	.05
☐ 27	Jeff Malone	.10	.05
☐ 28	Rodney Rogers	.10	.05
☐ 29	Terry Mills	.10	.05
☐ 30	Doug West	.10	.05
☐ 31	Doug West TTG	.10	.05
☐ 32	Shaquille O'Neal	1.50	.70
☐ 33	Scottie Pippen	1.25	.55
☐ 34	Lee Mayberry	.10	.05
☐ 35	Dale Ellis	.10	.05
☐ 36	Cedric Ceballos	.15	.07
☐ 37	Lionel Simmons	.10	.05
☐ 38	Kenny Gattison	.10	.05
☐ 39	Popeye Jones	.10	.05
☐ 40	Jerome Kersey	.10	.05
☐ 41	Jerome Kersey TTG	.10	.05
☐ 42	Larry Stewart	.10	.05
☐ 43	Rod Strickland	.15	.07
☐ 44	Chris Mills	.15	.07
☐ 45	Latrell Sprewell	.15	.07
☐ 46	Haywoode Workman	.10	.05
☐ 47	Charles Smith	.10	.05
☐ 48	Detlef Schrempf	.15	.07
☐ 49	Gary Grant	.10	.05
☐ 50	Gary Grant TTG	.10	.05
☐ 51	Tom Chambers	.10	.05
☐ 52	J.R. Reid	.10	.05
☐ 53	Mookie Blaylock	.15	.07
☐ 54	Mookie Blaylock TTG	.10	.05
☐ 55	Rony Seikaly	.10	.05
☐ 56	Isaiah Rider	.15	.07
☐ 57	Isaiah Rider TTG	.10	.05
☐ 58	Nick Anderson	.15	.07
☐ 59	Victor Alexander	.10	.05
☐ 60	Lucious Harris	.10	.05
☐ 61	Mark Macon	.10	.05
☐ 62	Otis Thorpe	.15	.07
☐ 63	Randy Woods	.10	.05
☐ 64	Clyde Drexler	.50	.23
☐ 65	Dikembe Mutombo	.40	.18
☐ 66	Todd Day	.10	.05
☐ 67	Greg Anthony	.10	.05
☐ 68	Sherman Douglas	.10	.05
☐ 69	Chris Mullin	.40	.18
☐ 70	Kevin Johnson	.15	.07
☐ 71	Kendall Gill	.15	.07
☐ 72	Dennis Rodman	1.50	.70
☐ 73	Dennis Rodman TTG	.75	.35
☐ 74	Jeff Turner	.10	.05
☐ 75	John Stockton	.40	.18
☐ 76	John Stockton TTG	.15	.07
☐ 77	Doug Edwards	.10	.05
☐ 78	Jim Jackson	.15	.07
☐ 79	Hakeem Olajuwon	.75	.35
☐ 80	Glen Rice	.40	.18
☐ 81	Christian Laettner	.15	.07
☐ 82	Terry Porter	.10	.05
☐ 83	Joe Dumars	.40	.18
☐ 84	David Wingate	.10	.05
☐ 85	B.J. Armstrong	.10	.05
☐ 86	Derrick McKey	.10	.05
☐ 87	Elmore Spencer	.10	.05
☐ 88	Walt Williams	.15	.07
☐ 89	Shawn Bradley	.15	.07
☐ 90	Acie Earl	.10	.05
☐ 91	Acie Earl TTG	.10	.05
☐ 92	Randy Brown	.10	.05
☐ 93	Grant Long	.10	.05
☐ 94	Terry Dehere	.10	.05

95	Spud Webb	.15	.07
96	Lindsey Hunter	.15	.07
97	Blair Rasmussen	.10	.05
98	Tim Hardaway	.50	.23
99	Kevin Edwards	.10	.05
100	Patrick Ewing CT	.15	.07
	Reggie Williams CT		
	Georgetown Hoyas		
101	Chuck Person CT	.40	.18
	Charles Barkley CT		
	Auburn Tigers		
102	M.Abdul-Rauf CT	.40	.18
	Shaquille O'Neal CT		
	LSU Tigers		
103	Rony Seikaly CT	.10	.05
	Derrick Coleman CT		
	Syracuse Orangemen		
104	Hakeem Olajuwon CT	.40	.18
	Clyde Drexler CT		
	Houston Cougars		
105	Chris Mullin CT	.15	.07
	Mark Jackson CT		
	St. John Red Storm		
106	Robert Horry CT	.15	.07
	Latrell Sprewell CT		
	Alabama Crimson Tide		
107	Pooh Richardson CT	.15	.07
	Reggie Miller CT		
	UCLA Bruins		
108	Dennis Scott CT	.15	.07
	Kenny Anderson CT		
	GA Tech Yellow Jackets		
109	Kendall Gill CT	.10	.05
	Ken Norman CT		
	Illinois Fightin' Illini		
110	Scott Skiles CT	.10	.05
	Kevin Willis CT		
	Michigan State Spartans		
111	Terry Mills CT	.15	.07
	Glen Rice CT		
	Michigan Wolverines		
112	Christian Laettner CT	.10	.05
	Bobby Hurley CT		
	Duke Blue Devils		
113	Stacey Augmon CT	.10	.05
	Larry Johnson CT		
	UNLV Runnin' Rebels		
114	Sam Perkins CT	.15	.07
	James Worthy CT		
	North Carolina Tar Heels		
115	Carl Herrera	.10	.05
116	Sam Bowie	.10	.05
117	Gary Payton	.60	.25
118	Danny Ainge	.15	.07
119	Danny Ainge TTG	.10	.05
120	Luc Longley	.10	.05
121	Antonio Davis	.10	.05
122	Terry Cummings	.10	.05
123	Terry Cummings TTG	.10	.05
124	Mark Price	.10	.05
125	Jamal Mashburn	.40	.18
126	Mahmoud Abdul-Rauf	.10	.05
127	Charles Oakley	.15	.07
128	Steve Smith	.15	.07
129	Vin Baker	1.00	.45
130	Robert Horry	.15	.07
131	Doug Christie	.10	.05
132	Wayman Tisdale	.10	.05
133	Wayman Tisdale TTG	.10	.05
134	Muggsy Bogues	.15	.07
135	Dino Radja	.10	.05
136	Jeff Hornacek	.15	.07
137	Gheorghe Muresan	.15	.07
138	Loy Vaught	.15	.07
139	Loy Vaught TTG	.10	.05
140	Benoit Benjamin	.10	.05
141	Johnny Dawkins	.10	.05
142	Allan Houston	.40	.18
143	Jon Barry	.10	.05
144	Reggie Miller	.40	.18
145	Kevin Willis	.10	.05
146	James Worthy	.40	.18
147	James Worthy TTG	.15	.07
148	Scott Burrell	.10	.05
149	Tom Gugliotta	.40	.18
150	LaPhonso Ellis	.15	.07
151	Doug Smith	.10	.05
152	A.C. Green	.15	.07
153	A.C. Green TTG	.10	.05
154	George Lynch	.10	.05
155	Sam Perkins	.15	.07
156	Corie Blount	.10	.05
157	Xavier McDaniel	.10	.05
158	Xavier McDaniel TTG	.10	.05
159	Eric Murdock	.10	.05
160	David Robinson	.60	.25
161	Karl Malone	.60	.25
162	Karl Malone TTG	.40	.18
163	C.Weatherspoon	.10	.05
164	Calbert Cheaney	.15	.07
165	Tom Hammonds	.10	.05
166	Tom Hammonds TTG	.10	.05
167	Alonzo Mourning	.50	.23
168	Clifford Robinson	.15	.07
169	Micheal Williams	.10	.05
170	Ervin Johnson	.10	.05
171	Mike Gminski	.10	.05
172	Jason Kidd	3.00	1.35
173	Anthony Bonner	.10	.05
174	Stacey King	.10	.05
175	Rex Chapman	.10	.05
176	Greg Graham	.10	.05
177	Stanley Roberts	.10	.05
178	Mitch Richmond	.40	.18
179	Eric Montross	.10	.05
180	Eddie Jones	3.00	1.35
181	Grant Hill	5.00	2.20
182	Donyell Marshall	.50	.23
183	Glenn Robinson	1.50	.70
184	Dominique Wilkins	.40	.18
185	Mark Price	.10	.05
186	Anthony Mason	.15	.07
187	Tyrone Corbin	.10	.05
188	Dale Davis	.10	.05
189	Nate McMillan	.10	.05
190	Jason Kidd	1.50	.70
191	John Salley	.10	.05
192	Keith Jennings	.10	.05
193	Mark Bryant	.10	.05
194	Sleepy Floyd	.10	.05
195	Grant Hill	2.50	1.10
196	Joe Kleine	.10	.05
197	Anthony Peeler	.10	.05
198	Malik Sealy	.10	.05
199	Kenny Walker	.10	.05
200	Donyell Marshall	.40	.18
201	Vlade Divac Al	.10	.05
202	Dino Radja Al	.10	.05
203	Carl Herrera Al	.10	.05
204	Olden Polynice Al	.10	.05
205	Patrick Ewing Al	.15	.07
206	Willie Anderson	.10	.05
207	Mitch Richmond	.40	.18
208	John Crotty	.10	.05
209	Tracy Murray	.10	.05
210	Juwan Howard	2.00	.90
211	Robert Parish	.15	.07
212	Steve Kerr	.15	.07
213	Anthony Bowie	.10	.05
214	Tim Breaux	.10	.05
215	Sharone Wright	.10	.05
216	Brian Williams	.10	.05
217	Rick Fox	.10	.05
218	Harold Miner	.10	.05
219	Duane Ferrell	.10	.05
220	Lamond Murray	.15	.07
221	Blue Edwards	.10	.05
222	Bill Cartwright	.10	.05
223	Sergei Bazarevich	.10	.05
224	Herb Williams	.10	.05
225	Brian Grant	.40	.18
	John Starks		
227	Rod Strickland BCT	.40	.18
	Clyde Drexler		
228	Kevin Johnson BCT	.10	.05
	Dan Majerle		
229	Lindsey Hunter BCT	.10	.05
	Joe Dumars		
230	Tim Hardaway BCT	.15	.07
	Latrell Sprewell		
231	Bill Wennington	.10	.05
232	Brian Shaw	.10	.05
233	Jamie Watson	.15	.07
234	Chris Whitney	.10	.05
235	Eric Montross	.10	.05
236	Kenny Smith	.10	.05
237	Andrew Lang	.10	.05
238	Lorenzo Williams	.10	.05
239	Dana Barros	.10	.05
240	Eddie Jones	1.50	.70
241	Harold Ellis	.10	.05
242	James Edwards	.10	.05
243	Don MacLean	.10	.05
244	Ed Pinckney	.10	.05
245	Carlos Rogers	.10	.05
246	Michael Adams	.10	.05
247	Rex Walters	.10	.05
248	John Starks	.15	.07
249	Terrell Brandon	.40	.18
250	Khalid Reeves	.10	.05
251	Dominique Wilkins Al	.15	.07
252	Toni Kukoc Al	.15	.07
253	Rick Fox Al	.10	.05
254	Detlef Schrempf Al	.10	.05
255	Rik Smits Al	.10	.05
256	Johnny Dawkins	.10	.05
257	Dan Majerle	.15	.07
258	Mike Brown	.10	.05
259	Byron Scott	.15	.07
260	Jalen Rose	.40	.18
261	Byron Houston	.10	.05
262	Frank Brickowski	.10	.05
263	Vernon Maxwell	.10	.05
264	Craig Ehlo	.10	.05
265	Yinka Dare	.10	.05
266	Dee Brown	.10	.05
267	Felton Spencer	.10	.05
268	Harvey Grant	.10	.05
269	Nick Van Exel	.40	.18
270	Bob Martin	.10	.05
271	Hersey Hawkins	.15	.07
272	Scott Williams	.10	.05
273	Sarunas Marciulionis	.10	.05
274	Kevin Gamble	.10	.05
275	Clifford Rozier	.10	.05
276	B.J. Armstrong BCT	.10	.05
	Ron Harper		
277	John Stockton BCT	.15	.07
	Jeff Hornacek		
278	Bobby Hurley BCT	.15	.07
	Mitch Richmond		
279	A.Hardaway BCT	.40	.18
	Dennis Scott		
280	Jason Kidd BCT	.40	.18
	Jim Jackson		
281	Ron Harper	.15	.07
282	Chuck Person	.10	.05
283	John Williams	.10	.05
284	Robert Pack	.10	.05
285	Aaron McKie	.10	.05
286	Chris Smith	.10	.05
287	Horace Grant	.15	.07
288	Oliver Miller	.10	.05
289	Derek Harper	.15	.07
290	Eric Mobley	.10	.05
291	Scott Skiles	.10	.05
292	Olden Polynice	.10	.05
293	Mark Jackson	.15	.07
294	Wayman Tisdale	.10	.05
295	Tony Dumas	.10	.05
296	Bryon Russell	.10	.05
297	Vlade Divac	.15	.07
298	David Wesley	.15	.07
299	Askia Jones	.10	.05
300	B.J. Tyler	.10	.05
301	Hakeem Olajuwon Al	.40	.18
302	Luc Longley Al	.10	.05
303	Rony Seikaly Al	.10	.05
304	S.Marciulionis Al	.10	.05
305	Dikembe Mutombo Al	.15	.07
306	Ken Norman	.10	.05
307	Dell Curry	.10	.05
308	Danny Ferry	.10	.05
309	Shawn Kemp	1.25	.55
310	Dickey Simpkins	.10	.05
311	Johnny Newman	.10	.05
312	Dwayne Schintzius	.10	.05

☐ 313 Sean Elliott	.15	.07
☐ 314 Sean Rooks	.10	.05
☐ 315 Bill Curley	.10	.05
☐ 316 Bryant Stith	.10	.05
☐ 317 Pooh Richardson	.10	.05
☐ 318 Jim McIlvaine	.10	.05
☐ 319 Dennis Scott	.15	.07
☐ 320 Wesley Person	.50	.23
☐ 321 Bobby Hurley	.10	.05
☐ 322 Armon Gilliam	.10	.05
☐ 323 Rik Smits	.15	.07
☐ 324 Tony Smith	.10	.05
☐ 325 Monty Williams	.10	.05
☐ 326 Gary Payton BCT	.40	.18
Kendall Gill		
☐ 327 Mookie Blaylock BCT	.10	.05
Stacey Augmon		
☐ 328 Mark Jackson BCT	.15	.07
Reggie Miller		
☐ 329 Sam Cassell BCT	.10	.05
Vernon Maxwell		
☐ 330 Harold Miner BCT	.10	.05
Khalid Reeves		
☐ 331 Vinny Del Negro	.10	.05
☐ 332 Billy Owens	.10	.05
☐ 333 Mark West	.10	.05
☐ 334 Matt Geiger	.10	.05
☐ 335 Greg Minor	.10	.05
☐ 336 Larry Johnson	.15	.07
☐ 337 Donald Hodge	.10	.05
☐ 338 Aaron Williams	.10	.05
☐ 339 Jay Humphries	.10	.05
☐ 340 Charlie Ward	.15	.07
☐ 341 Scott Brooks	.10	.05
☐ 342 Stacey Augmon	.10	.05
☐ 343 Will Perdue	.10	.05
☐ 344 Dale Ellis	.10	.05
☐ 345 Brooks Thompson	.10	.05
☐ 346 Manute Bol	.10	.05
☐ 347 Kenny Anderson	.15	.07
☐ 348 Willie Burton	.10	.05
☐ 349 Michael Cage	.10	.05
☐ 350 Danny Manning	.10	.05
☐ 351 Ricky Pierce	.10	.05
☐ 352 Sam Cassell	.40	.18
☐ 353 Reggie Miller FG	.15	.07
☐ 354 David Robinson FG	.40	.18
☐ 355 Shaquille O'Neal FG	.75	.35
☐ 356 Scottie Pippen FG	.60	.25
☐ 357 Alonzo Mourning FG	.10	.18
☐ 358 C.Weatherspoon FG	.10	.05
☐ 359 Derrick Coleman FG	.10	.00
☐ 360 Charles Barkley FG	.40	.18
☐ 361 Karl Malone FG	.40	.18
☐ 362 Chris Webber FG	.50	.23

1994-95 Stadium Club Beam Team

Randomly inserted at a rate of 1 in every 24 second series packs, this 27-card standard-size set features a star player from each

NBA team spotlit with lazer light foil. The borderless fronts feature a player photo with his name in the upper left corner and the words "Beam Team" in funky lettering on the bottom. The backs are split between a player photo and some notes. Vital statistics are in the lower left corner and the cards are numbered in the lower corner as "X" of 27. The set is sequenced in alphabetical order by team.

	MINT	NRMT
COMPLETE SET (27)	75.00	34.00
COMMON CARD (1-27)	1.00	.45
SEMISTARS	1.25	.55
UNLISTED STARS	3.00	1.35
SER.2 STATED ODDS 1:24		
☐ 1 Mookie Blaylock	1.25	.55
☐ 2 Dominique Wilkins	3.00	1.35
☐ 3 Alonzo Mourning	4.00	1.80
☐ 4 Toni Kukoc	3.00	1.35
☐ 5 Mark Price	1.00	.45
☐ 6 Jason Kidd	12.00	5.50
☐ 7 Jalen Rose	3.00	1.35
☐ 8 Grant Hill	20.00	9.00
☐ 9 Latrell Sprewell	1.25	.55
☐ 10 Hakeem Olajuwon	6.00	2.70
☐ 11 Reggie Miller	3.00	1.35
☐ 12 Lamond Murray	1.25	.55
☐ 13 George Lynch	1.00	.45
☐ 14 Khalid Reeves	1.00	.45
☐ 15 Glenn Robinson	6.00	2.70
☐ 16 Donyell Marshall	3.00	1.35
☐ 17 Derrick Coleman	1.25	.55
☐ 18 Patrick Ewing	3.00	1.35
☐ 19 Shaquille O'Neal	12.00	5.50
☐ 20 Clarence Weatherspoon	1.00	.45
☐ 21 Charles Barkley	5.00	2.20
☐ 22 Clifford Robinson	1.25	.55
☐ 23 Bobby Hurley	1.00	.45
☐ 24 David Robinson	5.00	2.20
☐ 25 Shawn Kemp	10.00	4.50
☐ 26 Karl Malone	5.00	2.20
☐ 27 Chris Webber	8.00	3.60

1994-95 Stadium Club Clear Cut

Randomly inserted in all first series packs at a rate of one in 12, cards from this 27-card acetate set spotlight one key player from each NBA team. The set has "see through" fronts

with some statistical information on the back. The player is identified on the right side of the card and the words "Clear Cut" are located in the bottom right. The set is sequenced in alphabetical order by team.

	MINT	NRMT
COMPLETE SET (27)	30.00	13.50
COMMON CARD (1-27)	.75	.35
SEMISTARS	1.25	.55
UNLISTED STARS	2.50	1.10
SER.1 STATED ODDS 1:12		
☐ 1 Stacey Augmon	.75	.35
☐ 2 Dino Radja	.75	.35
☐ 3 Alonzo Mourning	3.00	1.35
☐ 4 Scottie Pippen	8.00	3.60
☐ 5 Gerald Wilkins	.75	.35
☐ 6 Jamal Mashburn	2.50	1.10
☐ 7 Dikembe Mutombo	2.50	1.10
☐ 8 Lindsey Hunter	1.25	.55
☐ 9 Chris Mullin	2.50	1.10
☐ 10 Hakeem Olajuwon	5.00	2.20
☐ 11 Reggie Miller	2.50	1.10
☐ 12 Gary Grant	.75	.35
☐ 13 Doug Christie	.75	.35
☐ 14 Steve Smith	1.25	.55
☐ 15 Vin Baker	6.00	2.70
☐ 16 Christian Laettner	1.25	.55
☐ 17 Derrick Coleman	1.25	.55
☐ 18 Charles Oakley	1.25	.55
☐ 19 Dennis Scott	1.25	.55
☐ 20 Clarence Weatherspoon	.75	.35
☐ 21 Charles Barkley	4.00	1.80
☐ 22 Clifford Robinson	1.25	.55
☐ 23 Mitch Richmond	2.50	1.10
☐ 24 David Robinson	4.00	1.80
☐ 25 Shawn Kemp	8.00	3.60
☐ 26 Karl Malone	4.00	1.80
☐ 27 Don MacLean	.75	.35

1994-95 Stadium Club Dynasty and Destiny

This 20-card standard-size set was randomly inserted in first series foil packs at a rate of one in six and were also inserted one per first series rack pack. This set features a mixture of youthful phenoms paired up with a matching veteran star. The borderless fronts feature player photos, the player's name in the upper left corner and either the word "Destiny" or "Dynasty" in the lower right. The back has a player photo in a lower corner with a brief note and stats on the other side.

	MINT	NRMT
COMPLETE SET (20)	12.00	5.50
COMMON CARD (1A-20B)	.25	.11
SEMISTARS	.40	.18
UNLISTED STARS	.60	.25
SER.1 STATED ODDS 1:6		
ONE PER SER.1 RACK PACK		

☐ 1A Mark Price	.25	.11
☐ 1B Kenny Anderson	.40	.18
☐ 2A Karl Malone	1.00	.45
☐ 2B Derrick Coleman	.40	.18
☐ 3A John Stockton	.60	.25
☐ 3B Anfernee Hardaway	2.50	1.10
☐ 4A Mitch Richmond	.40	.18
☐ 4B Jim Jackson	.40	.18
☐ 5A James Worthy	.60	.25
☐ 5B Jamal Mashburn	.60	.25
☐ 6A Patrick Ewing	.60	.25
☐ 6B Alonzo Mourning	.75	.35
☐ 7A Hakeem Olajuwon	1.25	.55
☐ 7B Shaquille O'Neal	2.50	1.10
☐ 8A Clyde Drexler	.75	.35
☐ 8B Isaiah Rider	.40	.18
☐ 9A Scottie Pippen	2.00	.90
☐ 9B Latrell Sprewell	.40	.18
☐ 10A Charles Barkley	1.00	.45
☐ 10B Chris Webber	1.50	.70

1994-95 Stadium Club Rising Stars

Randomly inserted in all first series packs at a rate of one in 24, cards from this 10-card standard-size set feature a selection of young NBA stars. Card fronts feature full-color player action shots cut out against etched-foil backgrounds, with a prismatic galaxy design.

	MINT	NRMT
COMPLETE SET (12)	60.00	27.00
COMMON CARD (1-12)	1.00	.45
SEMISTARS	2.00	.90
UNLISTED STARS	5.00	2.20
SER.1 STATED ODDS 1:24		

☐ 1 Kenny Anderson	2.00	.90
☐ 2 Latrell Sprewell	2.00	.90
☐ 3 Jamal Mashburn	5.00	2.20

☐ 4 Alonzo Mourning	6.00	2.70
☐ 5 Shaquille O'Neal	20.00	9.00
☐ 6 LaPhonso Ellis	2.00	.90
☐ 7 Chris Webber	12.00	5.50
☐ 8 Isaiah Rider	2.00	.90
☐ 9 Dikembe Mutombo	5.00	2.20
☐ 10 Anfernee Hardaway	20.00	9.00
☐ 11 Antonio Davis	1.00	.45
☐ 12 Robert Horry	2.00	.90

1994-95 Stadium Club Super Skills

Randomly inserted at a rate of 1 in every 24 second series 12-card second series retail rack pack, and seeded one per second series retail rack pack, cards from this 25-card standard-size set feature Topps selection of the five top players at each position in the NBA. Card fronts feature a multi-hued rainbow foil background.

	MINT	NRMT
COMPLETE SET (25)	40.00	18.00
COMMON CARD (1-25)	.50	.23
SEMISTARS	1.00	.45
UNLISTED STARS	2.00	.90
SER.2 STATED ODDS 1:24		
ONE PER SER.2 RACK PACK		

☐ 1 Mark Price	.50	.23
☐ 2 Tim Hardaway	2.50	1.10
☐ 3 Kevin Johnson	1.00	.45
☐ 4 John Stockton	.50	.23
☐ 5 Mookie Blaylock	1.00	.45
☐ 6 Reggie Miller	2.00	.90
☐ 7 Jeff Hornacek	1.00	.45
☐ 8 Latrell Sprewell	1.00	.45
☐ 9 John Starks	1.00	.45
☐ 10 Nate McMillan	.50	.23
☐ 11 Chris Mullin	2.00	.90
☐ 12 Toni Kukoc	2.00	.90
☐ 13 Anthony Mason	1.00	.45
☐ 14 Robert Horry	1.00	.45
☐ 15 Scottie Pippen	6.00	2.70
☐ 16 Charles Barkley	3.00	1.35
☐ 17 Dennis Rodman	8.00	3.60
☐ 18 Karl Malone	3.00	1.35
☐ 19 Chris Webber	5.00	2.20
☐ 20 Charles Oakley	1.00	.45
☐ 21 Patrick Ewing	2.00	.90
☐ 22 Shaquille O'Neal	8.00	3.60
☐ 23 Dikembe Mutombo	2.00	.90
☐ 24 David Robinson	3.00	1.35
☐ 25 Hakeem Olajuwon	4.00	1.80

1994-95 Stadium Club Super Teams

Randomly inserted in all first series packs at a rate of one in 24, cards from this 27-card standard-size set feature an action shot or group photo from each team in the league. Teams that won either their Division, their Conference or the NBA Finals were redeemable for special team sets or other prizes. The expiration date for Super Team cards was December 31st, 1995. The five winning cards (Houston, Indiana, Orlando, Phoenix and San Antonio) carry "W" designations. In addition "C", "D" and "F" designations are used to denote conference, division and finals winners.

	MINT	NRMT
COMPLETE SET (27)	35.00	16.00
COMMON TEAM (1-27)	1.00	.45
SEMISTARS	1.50	.70
UNLISTED STARS	2.50	1.10
SER.1 STATED ODDS 1:24		
COMP.DW BAG MAGIC (11)	12.00	5.50
COMP.DW BAG PACERS (11)	3.00	1.35
COMP.DW BAG SPURS (11)	8.00	3.60
COMP.DW BAG SUNS (11)	6.00	2.70
ONE BAG BY MAIL PER DIV.WIN.SUPER		
TM.		
COMP.MP BAG MAGIC (11)	15.00	6.75
COMP.MP BAG ROCKETS (11)	8.00	3.60
ONE BAG BY MAIL PER		
CONF.WIN.SUP.TEAM		

☐ 1 Atlanta Hawks	1.00	.45
Kevin Willis		
☐ 2 Boston Celtics	1.00	.45
Group		
☐ 3 Charlotte Hornets	1.00	.45
Muggsy Bogues		
☐ 4 Chicago Bulls	1.00	.45
Group		
☐ 5 Cleveland Cavaliers	1.00	.45
Danny Ferry		
☐ 6 Dallas Mavericks	1.50	.70
Jim Jackson		
☐ 7 Denver Nuggets	1.00	.45
Rodney Rogers		
☐ 8 Detroit Pistons	1.50	.70
Joe Dumars		
☐ 9 Golden State Warriors	6.00	2.70
Chris Webber		

	MINT	NRMT
☐ 10 Houston Rockets WCF	12.00	5.50
Hakeem Olajuwon		
☐ 11 Indiana Pacers WD	1.00	.45
Rik Smits		
☐ 12 LA Clippers	1.00	.45
Group		
☐ 13 L.A. Lakers	2.50	1.10
Nick Van Exel		
☐ 14 Miami Heat	2.50	1.10
Glen Rice		
☐ 15 Milwaukee Bucks	6.00	2.70
Vin Baker		
☐ 16 Minnesota T'wolves..	1.50	.70
Christian Laettner		
☐ 17 New Jersey Nets	1.00	.45
Chris Morris		
☐ 18 New York Knicks	1.00	.45
Group		
☐ 19 Orlando Magic WCD ..	12.00	5.50
Shaquille O'Neal		
☐ 20 Philadelphia 76ers.....	1.00	.45
Dana Barros		
☐ 21 Phoenix Suns WD	5.00	2.20
Charles Barkley		
☐ 22 Portland Trail Blazers	1.00	.45
Group		
☐ 23 Sacramento Kings......	1.00	.45
Olden Polynice		
☐ 24 San Antonio Spurs WD	1.00	.45
Group		
☐ 25 Seattle Supersonics...	1.00	.45
Group		
☐ 26 Utah Jazz..................	2.50	1.10
John Stockton		
☐ 27 Washington Bullets	1.00	.45
Group		

1994-95
Stadium Club
Team of the Future

Randomly inserted at a rate of 1
in every 24 second series packs,
this 10-card standard-size set is
comprised of tomorrow's superstars. Card fronts feature color
player action shots against bril-
liant gold, etched-foil backgrounds.

	MINT	NRMT
COMPLETE SET (10)	40.00	18.00
COMMON CARD (1-10)	1.25	.55
SEMISTARS	2.00	.90
SER.2 STATED ODDS 1:24		
☐ 1 Anfernee Hardaway	8.00	3.60
☐ 2 Latrell Sprewell	1.25	.55
☐ 3 Grant Hill	12.00	5.50
☐ 4 Chris Webber	5.00	2.20
☐ 5 Shaquille O'Neal	8.00	3.60

	MINT	NRMT
☐ 6 Jason Kidd	8.00	3.60
☐ 7 Jim Jackson	1.25	.55
☐ 8 Jamal Mashburn	2.00	.90
☐ 9 Glenn Robinson	4.00	1.80
☐ 10 Alonzo Mourning	2.50	1.10

1995-96
Stadium Club

The 1995-96 Stadium Club basketball set was issued in two
series of 180 and 181 standard-
size cards, for a total of 361.
Cards were distributed in 13-
card regular packs at a suggested retail price of $2.50, and in
24-card jumbo packs. The packs
were distributed in 24-piece
boxes. Fronts are full-bleed full-
color action player shots. The
player's name appears in
etched foil against an exploding
star background and his team's
name is printed in gold foil at the
bottom. Backs feature a close-
up head shot and a full-color
action photo with a blue background. The player's name is
printed at the top as is his biography, player profile and '94-95
statistics. A category statistic
chart appears on the lower right
side of the chart. Second series
cards included these variations.
The "Rookie Cards" as well as
other subset cards were issued
in basic hobby and retail packs
with a silver prismatic foil. These
cards were also issued one per
special retail pack with a
gold/orange-type foil background. Subsets include 10
cards of players from the two
expansion teams (Vancouver
Grizzlies and Toronto Raptors),
29 "Extreme Corps" and six
"Trans-Action" cards. A parallel
version of every subset card
was inserted in rack and jumbo
packs. The parallel versions of
the subset cards feature silver
and blue diffraction foil around

the player's name and team
name. These foil variations are
priced at equal value.

	MINT	NRMT
COMPLETE SET (361)	50.00	22.00
COMPLETE SERIES 1 (180)	25.00	11.00
COMPLETE SERIES 2 (181)	25.00	11.00
COMMON CARD (1-361)	.15	.07
SEMISTARS	.20	.09
UNLISTED STARS	.40	.18
FOIL VARIATIONS: SAME PRICE		
☐ 1 Michael Jordan	5.00	2.20
☐ 2 Glenn Robinson	.50	.23
☐ 3 Jason Kidd	1.00	.45
☐ 4 Clyde Drexler	.50	.23
☐ 5 Horace Grant	.20	.09
☐ 6 Allan Houston	.20	.09
☐ 7 Xavier McDaniel	.15	.07
☐ 8 Jeff Hornacek	.20	.09
☐ 9 Vlade Divac	.20	.09
☐ 10 Juwan Howard	.60	.25
☐ 11 Keith Jennings EXP ...	.15	.07
☐ 12 Grant Long	.15	.07
☐ 13 Jalen Rose	.20	.09
☐ 14 Malik Sealy	.15	.07
☐ 15 Gary Payton	.60	.25
☐ 16 Danny Ferry	.15	.07
☐ 17 Glen Rice	.40	.18
☐ 18 Randy Brown	.15	.07
☐ 19 Greg Graham	.15	.07
☐ 20 Kenny Anderson UER ..	.20	.09
Name is spelled Kenney		
☐ 21 Aaron McKie	.15	.07
☐ 22 John Salley EXP	.15	.07
☐ 23 Darrin Hancock	.15	.07
☐ 24 Carlos Rogers	.15	.07
☐ 25 Vin Baker	.75	.35
☐ 26 Bill Wennington	.15	.07
☐ 27 Kenny Smith	.15	.07
☐ 28 Sherman Douglas	.15	.07
☐ 29 Terry Davis	.15	.07
☐ 30 Grant Hill	2.50	1.10
☐ 31 Reggie Miller	.40	.18
☐ 32 Anfernee Hardaway ...	1.50	.70
☐ 33 Patrick Ewing	.40	.18
☐ 34 Charles Barkley	.60	.25
☐ 35 Eddie Jones	1.00	.45
☐ 36 Kevin Duckworth	.15	.07
☐ 37 Tom Hammonds	.15	.07
☐ 38 Craig Ehlo	.15	.07
☐ 39 Micheal Williams	.15	.07
☐ 40 Alonzo Mourning	.40	.18
☐ 41 John Williams	.15	.07
☐ 42 Felton Spencer	.15	.07
☐ 43 Lamond Murray	.15	.07
☐ 44 Dontonio Wingfield EXP	.15	.07
☐ 45 Rik Smits	.20	.09
☐ 46 Donyell Marshall	.20	.09
☐ 47 Clarence Weatherspoon	.15	.07
☐ 48 Kevin Edwards	.15	.07
☐ 49 Charlie Ward	.15	.07
☐ 50 David Robinson	.60	.25
☐ 51 James Robinson	.15	.07
☐ 52 Bill Cartwright	.15	.07
☐ 53 Bobby Hurley	.15	.07
☐ 54 Kevin Gamble	.15	.07
☐ 55 B.J. Tyler EXP	.15	.07
☐ 56 Chris Smith	.15	.07
☐ 57 Wesley Person	.20	.09
☐ 58 Tim Breaux	.15	.07
☐ 59 Mitchell Butler	.15	.07
☐ 60 Toni Kukoc	.20	.09
☐ 61 Roy Tarpley	.15	.07
☐ 62 Todd Day	.15	.07
☐ 63 Anthony Peeler	.15	.07
☐ 64 Brian Williams	.15	.07
☐ 65 Muggsy Bogues	.20	.09
☐ 66 Jerome Kersey EXP ...	.15	.07
☐ 67 Eric Piatkowski	.15	.07
☐ 68 Tim Perry	.15	.07
☐ 69 Chris Gatling	.15	.07
☐ 70 Mark Price	.15	.07

71	Terry Mills	.15	.07
72	Anthony Avent	.15	.07
73	Matt Geiger	.15	.07
74	Walt Williams	.15	.07
75	Sean Elliott	.15	.07
76	Ken Norman	.15	.07
77	Kendall Gill TA	.15	.07
78	Byron Houston	.15	.07
79	Rick Fox	.15	.07
80	Derek Harper	.20	.09
81	Rod Strickland	.20	.09
82	Bryon Russell	.15	.07
83	Antonio Davis	.15	.07
84	Isaiah Rider	.20	.09
85	Kevin Johnson	.20	.09
86	Derrick Coleman	.20	.09
87	Doug Overton	.15	.07
88	Hersey Hawkins TA	.15	.07
89	Popeye Jones	.15	.07
90	Dickey Simpkins	.15	.07
91	Rodney Rogers TA	.15	.07
92	Rex Chapman TA	.15	.07
93	Spud Webb TA	.15	.07
94	Lee Mayberry	.15	.07
95	Cedric Ceballos	.15	.07
96	Tyrone Hill	.15	.07
97	Bill Curley	.15	.07
98	Jeff Turner	.15	.07
99	Tyrone Corbin TA	.15	.07
100	John Stockton	.40	.18
101	Mookie Blaylock EC	.20	.09
102	Dino Radja EC	.15	.07
103	Alonzo Mourning EC	.40	.18
104	Scottie Pippen EC	1.25	.55
105	Terrell Brandon EC	.15	.07
106	Jim Jackson EC	.20	.09
107	M.Abdul-Rauf EC	.15	.07
108	Grant Hill EC	2.50	1.10
109	Tim Hardaway EC	.40	.18
110	Hakeem Olajuwon EC	.75	.35
111	Rik Smits EC	.20	.09
112	Loy Vaught EC	.15	.07
113	Vlade Divac EC	.20	.09
114	Kevin Willis EC	.15	.07
115	Glenn Robinson EC	.50	.23
116	Christian Laettner EC	.20	.09
117	Derrick Coleman EC	.15	.07
118	Patrick Ewing EC	.40	.18
119	Shaquille O'Neal EC	1.50	.70
120	Dana Barros EC	.15	.07
121	Charles Barkley EC	.60	.25
122	Rod Strickland EC	.20	.09
123	Brian Grant EC	.15	.07
124	David Robinson EC	.60	.25
125	Shawn Kemp EC	1.25	.55
126	Oliver Miller EC	.15	.07
127	Karl Malone EC	.60	.25
128	Benoit Benjamin EC	.15	.07
129	Chris Webber EC	1.00	.45
130	Dan Majerle	.15	.07
131	Calbert Cheaney	.15	.07
132	Mark Jackson	.20	.09
133	Greg Anthony EXP	.15	.07
134	Scott Burrell	.15	.07
135	Detlef Schrempf	.20	.09
136	Marty Conlon	.15	.07
137	Rony Seikaly	.15	.07
138	Olden Polynice	.15	.07
139	Terry Cummings	.15	.07
140	Stacey Augmon	.15	.07
141	Bryant Stith	.15	.07
142	Sean Higgins	.15	.07
143	Antoine Carr	.15	.07
144	Blue Edwards EXP	.15	.07
145	A.C. Green	.20	.09
146	Bobby Phills	.15	.07
147	Terry Dehere	.15	.07
148	Sharone Wright	.15	.07
149	Nick Anderson	.15	.07
150	Jim Jackson	.20	.09
151	Eric Montross	.15	.07
152	Doug West	.15	.07
153	Charles Smith	.15	.07
154	Will Perdue	.15	.07
155	Gerald Wilkins EXP	.15	.07
156	Robert Horry	.15	.07
157	Robert Parish	.20	.09
158	Lindsey Hunter	.15	.07
159	Harvey Grant	.15	.07
160	Tim Hardaway	.50	.23
161	Sarunas Marciulionis	.15	.07
162	Khalid Reeves	.15	.07
163	Bo Outlaw	.15	.07
164	Dale Davis	.15	.07
165	Nick Van Exel	.40	.18
166	Byron Scott EXP	.15	.07
167	Steve Smith	.20	.09
168	Brian Grant	.20	.09
169	Avery Johnson	.15	.07
170	Dikembe Mutombo	.20	.09
171	Tom Gugliotta	.40	.18
172	Armon Gilliam	.15	.07
173	Shawn Bradley	.20	.09
174	Herb Williams	.15	.07
175	Dino Radja	.15	.07
176	Billy Owens	.15	.07
177	Kenny Gattison EXP	.15	.07
178	J.R. Reid	.15	.07
179	Otis Thorpe	.20	.09
180	Sam Cassell	.20	.09
181	Pooh Richardson	.15	.07
182	Johnny Newman	.15	.07
183	Dennis Scott	.15	.07
184	Will Perdue	.15	.07
185	Andrew Lang	.15	.07
186	Karl Malone	.60	.25
187	Buck Williams	.15	.07
188	P.J. Brown	.15	.07
189	Khalid Reeves	.15	.07
190	Kevin Willis	.15	.07
191	Robert Pack	.15	.07
192	Joe Dumars	.40	.18
193	Dan Majerle	.15	.07
194	Sam Perkins	.20	.09
195	John Williams	.15	.07
196	Reggie Williams	.15	.07
197	Greg Anthony	.15	.07
198	Steve Kerr	.20	.09
199	Richard Dumas	.15	.07
200	Dee Brown	.15	.07
201	Zan Tabak	.15	.07
202	David Wood	.15	.07
203	Duane Causwell	.15	.07
204	Sedale Threatt	.15	.07
205	Hubert Davis	.15	.07
206	Donald Hodge	.15	.07
207	Duane Ferrell	.15	.07
208	Sam Mitchell	.15	.07
209	Adam Keefe	.15	.07
210	Clifford Robinson	.15	.07
211	Rodney Rogers	.15	.07
212	Jayson Williams	.20	.09
213	Brian Shaw	.15	.07
214	Luc Longley	.20	.09
215	Don MacLean	.15	.07
216	Rex Chapman	.15	.07
217	Wayman Tisdale	.15	.07
218	Shawn Kemp	1.25	.55
219	Chris Webber	1.00	.45
220	Antonio Harvey	.15	.07
221	Sarunas Marciulionis	.15	.07
222	Jeff Malone	.15	.07
223	Chucky Brown	.15	.07
224	Greg Minor	.15	.07
225	Clifford Rozier	.15	.07
226	Derrick McKey	.15	.07
227	Tony Dumas	.15	.07
228	Oliver Miller	.15	.07
229	Charles Oakley	.15	.07
230	Fred Roberts	.15	.07
231	Glen Rice	.40	.18
232	Terry Porter	.15	.07
233	Mark Macon	.15	.07
234	Michael Cage	.15	.07
235	Eric Murdock	.15	.07
236	Vinny Del Negro	.15	.07
237	Spud Webb	.20	.09
238	Mario Elie	.15	.07
239	Blue Edwards	.15	.07
240	Dontonio Wingfield	.15	.07
241	Brooks Thompson	.15	.07
242	Alonzo Mourning	.40	.18
244	Dennis Rodman	2.50	1.10
245	Lorenzo Williams	.15	.07
246	Haywoode Workman	.15	.07
247	Loy Vaught	.15	.07
248	Vernon Maxwell	.15	.07
249	Lionel Simmons	.15	.07
250	Chris Childs	.15	.07
251	Mahmoud Abdul-Rauf	.15	.07
252	Vincent Askew	.15	.07
253	Chris Morris	.15	.07
254	Elliot Perry	.15	.07
255	Dell Curry	.15	.07
256	Dana Barros	.15	.07
257	Terrell Brandon	.40	.18
258	Monty Williams	.15	.07
259	Corie Blount	.15	.07
260	B.J. Armstrong	.15	.07
261	Jim McIlvaine	.15	.07
262	Otis Thorpe	.20	.09
263	Sean Rooks	.15	.07
264	Tony Massenburg	.15	.07
265	Steve Smith	.20	.09
266	Ron Harper	.20	.09
267	Dale Ellis	.15	.07
268	Clyde Drexler	.50	.23
269	Jamie Watson	.15	.07
270	Doc Rivers	.20	.09
271	Derrick Alston	.15	.07
272	Eric Mobley	.15	.07
273	Ricky Pierce	.15	.07
274	David Wesley	.15	.07
275	John Starks	.20	.09
276	Chris Mullin	.40	.18
277	Ervin Johnson	.15	.07
278	Jamal Mashburn	.20	.09
279	Joe Kleine	.15	.07
280	Mitch Richmond	.40	.18
281	Chris Mills	.15	.07
282	Bimbo Coles	.15	.07
283	Larry Johnson	.20	.09
284	Stanley Roberts	.15	.07
285	Rex Walters	.15	.07
286	Donald Royal	.15	.07
287	Benoit Benjamin	.15	.07
288	Chris Dudley	.15	.07
289	Elden Campbell	.20	.09
290	Mookie Blaylock	.20	.09
291	Hersey Hawkins	.20	.09
292	Anthony Mason	.20	.09
293	Latrell Sprewell	.20	.09
294	Harold Miner	.15	.07
295	Scott Williams	.15	.07
296	David Benoit	.15	.07
297	Christian Laettner	.20	.09
298	LaPhonso Ellis	.20	.09
299	Gheorghe Muresan	.15	.07
300	Kendall Gill	.20	.09
301	Eddie Johnson	.15	.07
302	Terry Cummings	.15	.07
303	Chuck Person	.15	.07
304	Michael Smith	.15	.07
305	Mark West	.15	.07
306	Willie Anderson	.15	.07
307	Pervis Ellison	.15	.07
308	Brian Williams	.15	.07
309	Danny Manning	.20	.09
310	Hakeem Olajuwon	.75	.35
311	Scottie Pippen	1.25	.55
312	Jon Koncak	.15	.07
313	Sasha Danilovic	.15	.07
314	Lucious Harris	.15	.07
315	Yinka Dare	.15	.07
316	Eric Williams	.20	.09
317	Gary Trent	.15	.07
318	Theo Ratliff	.40	.18
319	Lawrence Moten	.15	.07
320	Jerome Allen	.15	.07
321	Tyus Edney	.15	.07
322	Loren Meyer	.15	.07
323	Michael Finley	1.50	.70
324	Alan Henderson	.40	.18
325	Bob Sura	.20	.09
326	Joe Smith	1.50	.70
327	Damon Stoudamire	3.00	1.35
328	Sherrell Ford	.15	.07
329	Jerry Stackhouse	1.50	.70

| 243 | Alonzo Mourning | .40 | .18 |

☐ 330 George Zidek	.15	.07
☐ 331 Brent Barry	.40	.18
☐ 332 Shawn Respert	.15	.07
☐ 333 Rasheed Wallace	1.00	.45
☐ 334 Antonio McDyess	2.00	.90
☐ 335 David Vaughn	.15	.07
☐ 336 Cory Alexander	.15	.07
☐ 337 Jason Caffey	.40	.18
☐ 338 Frankie King	.15	.07
☐ 339 Travis Best	.20	.09
☐ 340 Greg Ostertag	.15	.07
☐ 341 Ed O'Bannon	.15	.07
☐ 342 Kurt Thomas	.20	.09
☐ 343 Kevin Garnett	5.00	2.20
☐ 344 Bryant Reeves	1.00	.45
☐ 345 Corliss Williamson	.50	.23
☐ 346 Cherokee Parks	.15	.07
☐ 347 Junior Burrough	.15	.07
☐ 348 Randolph Childress	.15	.07
☐ 349 Lou Roe	.15	.07
☐ 350 Mario Bennett	.15	.07
☐ 351 Dikembe Mutombo XP	.15	.07
☐ 352 Larry Johnson XP	.20	.09
☐ 353 Vlade Divac XP	.15	.07
☐ 354 Karl Malone XP	.60	.25
☐ 355 John Stockton XP	.40	.18
☐ 356 Alonzo Mourning TA	.20	.09
☐ 357 Glen Rice TA	.20	.09
☐ 358 Dan Majerle TA	.15	.07
☐ 359 John Williams TA	.15	.07
☐ 360 Mark Price TA	.15	.07
☐ 361 Magic Johnson	1.25	.55

1995-96 Stadium Club Beam Team

Randomly inserted in all first and second series packs, this 20-card standard-size set features Topps' annual selection of their Beam Team stars. First series cards were randomly seeded into one in every 18 hobby and retail packs. Second series cards were randomly seeded into one in every 36 hobby packs and one in every 72 retail packs. Card front design from first to second series is radically different. First series cards feature borderless fronts with full-color action player cutouts set against a dark background of laser beams. Second series cards feature very bright neon green, yellow and red die cut backgrounds set against a cut out action shot of the featured player.

	MINT	NRMT
COMPLETE SET (20)	80.00	36.00
COMPLETE SERIES 1 (10)	10.00	4.50
COMPLETE SERIES 2 (10)	70.00	32.00
COMMON CARD (BT1-BT10)	.75	.35
COMMON CARD (BT11-BT20)	2.00	.90
SEMISTARS SER.1	1.00	.45
SEMISTARS SER.2	2.50	1.10
UNLISTED STARS SER.1	1.50	.70
UNLISTED STARS SER.2	4.00	1.80
SER.1 STATED ODDS 1:18 HOB/RET, 1:9 JUM		
SER.2 STATED ODDS 1:36 HOB, 1:144 JUM		
SER.2 STATED ODDS 1:72 RETAIL		

		MINT	NRMT
☐ BT1	David Robinson	2.50	1.10
☐ BT2	Juwan Howard	2.50	1.10
☐ BT3	Mitch Richmond	1.50	.70
☐ BT4	Reggie Miller	1.50	.70
☐ BT5	Glenn Robinson	2.00	.90
☐ BT6	Shaquille O'Neal	6.00	2.70
☐ BT7	Shawn Kemp	5.00	2.20
☐ BT8	Karl Malone	2.50	1.10
☐ BT9	Jamal Mashburn	.75	.35
☐ BT10	Alonzo Mourning	1.50	.70
☐ BT11	Charles Barkley	6.00	2.70
☐ BT12	Hakeem Olajuwon	8.00	3.60
☐ BT13	Kenny Anderson	2.50	1.10
☐ BT14	Michael Jordan	50.00	22.00
☐ BT15	Dikembe Mutombo	2.50	1.10
☐ BT16	Rod Strickland	2.50	1.10
☐ BT17	Patrick Ewing	4.00	1.80
☐ BT18	Latrell Sprewell	2.50	1.10
☐ BT19	Grant Hill	25.00	11.00
☐ BT20	Cedric Ceballos	2.00	.90

1995-96 Stadium Club Draft Picks

Randomly inserted in series one packs, this set of 15 skip-numbered standard-size cards is numbered in the order of the 1995 NBA draft. Some draft picks are missing in the series one collection but those cards were not included in the second series. Full-bleed fronts picture the player in full-color action shots with the TSC logo at the top. "NBA Draft Pick" and the player's name are printed in red type at the bottom of the card.

Blue and white backs are numbered according to place in draft with the player's name is printed in lower case white type at the top. The white areas resemble torn, crumpled paper and contain the player's biography, college statistics and a player profile, which is printed vertically in black type on the lower right side of the back.

	MINT	NRMT
COMPLETE SET (15)	10.00	4.50
COMMON CARD	.15	.07
SEMISTARS	.25	.11
UNLISTED STARS	.40	.18
RANDOM INSERTS IN ALL SER.1 PACKS		
SKIP-NUMBERED SET		

		MINT	NRMT
☐ 2	Antonio McDyess	2.00	.90
☐ 3	Jerry Stackhouse	1.50	.70
☐ 4	Rasheed Wallace	1.00	.45
☐ 5	Kevin Garnett	5.00	2.20
☐ 6	Bryant Reeves	1.00	.45
☐ 8	Shawn Respert	.15	.07
☐ 9	Ed O'Bannon	.15	.07
☐ 11	Gary Trent	.15	.07
☐ 12	Cherokee Parks	.15	.07
☐ 15	Brent Barry	.40	.18
☐ 16	Alan Henderson	.40	.18
☐ 17	Bob Sura	.25	.11
☐ 18	Theo Ratliff	.40	.18
☐ 19	Randolph Childress	.15	.07
☐ 22	George Zidek	.15	.07

1995-96 Stadium Club Nemeses

Randomly inserted in series one packs at a rate of one in 18, this 10-card standard-size set portrays arch rivals on each side of the card. Both sides are silver and blue etched foil with alternating full-color action cutouts of the players. Both sides carry a smaller full-color shot of each player's nemesis looking on. Each side carries a highlight of a game when one player got the better of the other. The "Nemeses" logo appears at the top of each side in gold etched foil.

	MINT	NRMT
COMPLETE SET (10)	80.00	36.00
COMMON CARD (N1-N10)	1.00	.45
SEMISTARS	1.50	.70
UNLISTED STARS	2.50	1.10
SER.1 STATED ODDS 1:18 HOB/RET, 1:9 JUM		

		MINT	NRMT
☐ N1	Hakeem Olajuwon	8.00	3.60
	David Robinson		
☐ N2	Patrick Ewing	2.50	1.10
	Rik Smits		
☐ N3	John Stockton	2.50	1.10
	Kevin Johnson		
☐ N4	Shaquille O'Neal	12.00	5.50
	Alonzo Mourning		
☐ N5	Charles Barkley	8.00	3.60
	Karl Malone		
☐ N6	Scottie Pippen	20.00	9.00
	Grant Hill		
☐ N7	Anfernee Hardaway	12.00	5.50
	Kenny Anderson		
☐ N8	Reggie Miller	2.50	1.10
	John Starks		
☐ N9	Toni Kukoc	1.00	.45
	Dino Radja		
☐ N10	Michael Jordan	30.00	13.50
	Joe Dumars		

1995-96 Stadium Club Power Zone

Randomly inserted in first and second series packs, this set of twelve standard-size cards feature the men who drive to the basket with authority. First series cards were randomly seeded into one in every 36 hobby and retail packs. Second series cards were randomly seeded into one in every 48 hobby and retail packs. First and second series card design differ radically. The first series cards feature borderless fronts with full-color action player cutouts set against a silver diffracted foil background. Second series cards contain a foil-etched background.

	MINT	NRMT
COMPLETE SET (12)	65.00	29.00
COMPLETE SERIES 1 (6)	25.00	11.00
COMPLETE SERIES 2 (6)	40.00	18.00

	MINT	NRMT
COMMON CARD (PZ1-PZ6)	1.50	.70
COMMON CARD (PZ7-PZ12)	4.00	1.80
SEMISTARS SER.1	2.00	.90
UNLISTED STARS SER.1	3.00	1.35
SER.1 STATED ODDS 1:36 H/R, 1:18 JUM		
SER.2 STATED ODDS 1:48 HOB/JUM/RET		

		MINT	NRMT
☐ PZ1	Shaquille O'Neal	12.00	5.50
☐ PZ2	Charles Barkley	5.00	2.20
☐ PZ3	Patrick Ewing	3.00	1.35
☐ PZ4	Karl Malone	5.00	2.20
☐ PZ5	Larry Johnson	2.00	.90
☐ PZ6	Derrick Coleman	1.50	.70
☐ PZ7	Hakeem Olajuwon	8.00	3.60
☐ PZ8	David Robinson	6.00	2.70
☐ PZ9	Shawn Kemp	12.00	5.50
☐ PZ10	Dennis Rodman	20.00	9.00
☐ PZ11	Alonzo Mourning	4.00	1.80
☐ PZ12	Vin Baker	8.00	3.60

1995-96 Stadium Club Reign Men

Randomly inserted in second-series hobby and retail packs at a rate of one in 48, this 10-card set features the NBA's slam dunk kings. Card fronts have a foil-etched background with the card name "Reign Men" running vertically along the right side. Card backs are horizontal with a head shot of the player, biographical information and a brief commentary. The cards are numbered with an "RM" prefix.

	MINT	NRMT
COMPLETE SET (10)	90.00	40.00
COMMON CARD (RM1-RM10)	2.00	.90
SEMISTARS	2.50	1.10
SER.2 STATED ODDS 1:48 HOB, 1:96 JUM		
SER.2 STATED ODDS 1:24 RETAIL		

		MINT	NRMT
☐ RM1	Shawn Kemp	12.00	5.50
☐ RM2	Michael Jordan	50.00	22.00
☐ RM3	Larry Johnson	2.50	1.10
☐ RM4	Grant Hill	25.00	11.00
☐ RM5	Isaiah Rider	2.50	1.10
☐ RM6	Sean Elliott	2.00	.90
☐ RM7	Scottie Pippen	12.00	5.50
☐ RM8	Robert Horry	2.00	.90
☐ RM9	Kendall Gill	2.50	1.10
☐ RM10	Jerry Stackhouse	8.00	3.60

1995-96 Stadium Club Spike Says

Filmmaker Spike Lee picks his 10 favorite NBA players and tells us all about them in his inimitable style. Cards in this 10-piece set were randomly inserted at a rate of one in every 12 retail packs and one in every 24 hobby packs. Card fronts are full bleed action shots with the player's name and the set name in silver refractive foil. Spike Lee is also pictured on each card front in a small circle in the lower right. Card backs are horizontal with Spike Lee's commentary on the player. The cards are numbered with a "SS" prefix.

	MINT	NRMT
COMPLETE SET (10)	25.00	11.00
COMMON CARD (SS1-SS10)	.60	.25
SEMISTARS	.75	.35
UNLISTED STARS	1.25	.55
SER.2 STATED ODDS 1:24 HOB, 1:12 RET		

		MINT	NRMT
☐ SS1	Michael Jordan	15.00	6.75
☐ SS2	Alonzo Mourning	1.25	.55
☐ SS3	Reggie Miller	1.25	.55
☐ SS4	Patrick Ewing	1.25	.55
☐ SS5	Charles Barkley	2.00	.90
☐ SS6	Kenny Anderson	.75	.35
☐ SS7	Scottie Pippen	4.00	1.80
☐ SS8	Jerry Stackhouse	2.50	1.10
☐ SS9	Shaquille O'Neal	5.00	2.20
☐ SS10	John Starks	.60	.25

1995-96 Stadium Club Warp Speed

Randomly inserted in first and second series packs, this 12-card standard-size set features the players with the quickest first steps in the league. First series cards were randomly seeded in hobby and retail packs at a rate of one in 36. Second series cards were randomly seeded in

hobby and retail packs at a rate of one in 48. First and second series card designs differ radically. First series features full-bleed fronts, a full-color action player cutout with a trailing ghost image set against a silver foil "outer space" background with shiny silver flecks. The "Warp Speed" logo appears vertically on the left side and the player's name printed in red at the bottom. Second series cards feature cut out action shots of each player set against a silver foil, vortex background.

	MINT	NRMT
COMPLETE SET (12)	110.00	50.00
COMPLETE SERIES 1 (6)	80.00	36.00
COMPLETE SERIES 2 (6)	30.00	13.50
COMMON CARD (WS1-WS6)	2.50	1.10
COMMON CARD (WS7-WS12)	2.00	.90
SEMISTARS SER.1	5.00	2.20
SEMISTARS SER.2	4.00	1.80
SER.1 STATED ODDS 1:36 H/R, 1:36 JUM		
SER.2 STATED ODDS 1:48 H/R, 1:48 JUM		

		MINT	NRMT
☐ WS1	Michael Jordan	60.00	27.00
☐ WS2	Kevin Johnson	5.00	2.20
☐ WS3	Gary Payton	8.00	3.60
☐ WS4	Anfernee Hardaway	20.00	9.00
☐ WS5	Mookie Blaylock	2.50	1.10
☐ WS6	Tim Hardaway	6.00	2.70
☐ WS7	Scottie Pippen	12.00	5.50
☐ WS8	Jason Kidd	10.00	4.50
☐ WS9	Grant Hill	25.00	11.00
☐ WS10	Nick Van Exel	4.00	1.80
☐ WS11	Kenny Anderson	2.00	.90
☐ WS12	Latrell Sprewell	2.00	.90

1995-96 Stadium Club Wizards

Randomly inserted exclusively in series one hobby packs at a rate of one in 24, this 10-card standard-size set features the best ball handlers in the game. Borderless etched foil fronts feature the player in a full-color action cutout with the Blue etched foil "Wizard" logo at the top. The player's name is stamped in gold foil at the bottom.

	MINT	NRMT
COMPLETE SET (10)	50.00	22.00
COMMON CARD (W1-W10)	2.00	.90
SEMISTARS	3.00	1.35
UNLISTED STARS	5.00	2.20
SER.1 STATED ODDS 1:24 HOB, 1:9 JUM		

		MINT	NRMT
☐ W1	Nick Van Exel	5.00	2.20
☐ W2	Tim Hardaway	6.00	2.70
☐ W3	Mookie Blaylock	3.00	1.35
☐ W4	Gary Payton	8.00	3.60
☐ W5	Jason Kidd	12.00	5.50
☐ W6	Kenny Anderson	3.00	1.35
☐ W7	John Stockton	5.00	2.20
☐ W8	Kevin Johnson	3.00	1.35
☐ W9	Muggsy Bogues	2.00	.90
☐ W10	Anfernee Hardaway	20.00	9.00

1995-96 Stadium Club X-2

Randomly inserted exclusively in second series hobby packs at a rate of one in 24 and second series retail packs at one in 48, this 10-card set showcases elite players who averaged double-doubles last season. Card fronts have an etched "X" in the background with an action shot. Card backs contain the same background with biographical and statistical information.

	MINT	NRMT
COMPLETE SET (10)	25.00	11.00
COMMON CARD (X1-X10)	1.00	.45
SEMISTARS	1.50	.70
UNLISTED STARS	2.50	1.10

	SER.2 STATED ODDS 1:24 HOB, 1:96 JUM		
	SER.2 STATED ODDS 1:48 RETAIL		

		MINT	NRMT
☐ X1	Hakeem Olajuwon	5.00	2.20
☐ X2	Shaquille O'Neal	10.00	4.50
☐ X3	David Robinson	4.00	1.80
☐ X4	Patrick Ewing	2.50	1.10
☐ X5	Charles Barkley	4.00	1.80
☐ X6	Karl Malone	4.00	1.80
☐ X7	Derrick Coleman	1.00	.45
☐ X8	Shawn Kemp	6.00	2.70
☐ X9	Vin Baker	5.00	2.20
☐ X10	Vlade Divac	1.50	.70

1996-97 Stadium Club

The 180-card Stadium Club set features embossed, foil color action player photos printed on 20 pt. stock, making them noticeably sturdier than previous Stadium Club releases. The cards were released in two series, each containing 90 cards. Cards were distributed in eight-card packs with a suggested retail price of $2.50. The fronts feature full-color game action photography with the players name running vertically up the right side of the card in an embossed foil strip. No subsets or Rookie Cards were included in the first series set. Two Moments or Rookies insert cards were guaranteed to be in each first series pack.

	MINT	NRMT
COMPLETE SET (180)	25.00	11.00
COMPLETE SERIES 1 (90)	10.00	4.50
COMPLETE SERIES 2 (90)	15.00	6.75
COMMON CARD (1-180)	.15	.07
CL (NNO)	.05	.02
SEMISTARS	.20	.09
UNLISTED STARS	.40	.18
COMP.MATRIX SET (90)	250.00	110.00
COMMON MATRIX (1-90)	2.00	.90
*MATRIX STARS: 6X TO 12X HI COLUMN		
MAT: SER.1 STATED ODDS 1:12 H, 1:10 R		

		MINT	NRMT
☐ 1	Scottie Pippen	1.25	.55
☐ 2	Dale Davis	.15	.07
☐ 3	Horace Grant	.20	.09
☐ 4	Gheorghe Muresan	.15	.07
☐ 5	Elliot Perry	.15	.07
☐ 6	Carlos Rogers	.15	.07
☐ 7	Glenn Robinson	.40	.18
☐ 8	Avery Johnson	.15	.07

□ 9 Dee Brown	.15 .07
□ 10 Grant Hill	2.50 1.10
□ 11 Tyus Edney	.15 .07
□ 12 Patrick Ewing	.40 .18
□ 13 Jason Kidd	.75 .35
□ 14 Clifford Robinson	.15 .07
□ 15 Robert Horry	.20 .09
□ 16 Dell Curry	.15 .07
□ 17 Terry Porter	.15 .07
□ 18 Shaquille O'Neal	1.50 .70
□ 19 Bryant Stith	.15 .07
□ 20 Shawn Kemp	1.25 .55
□ 21 Kurt Thomas	.15 .07
□ 22 Pooh Richardson	.15 .07
□ 23 Bob Sura	.15 .07
□ 24 Olden Polynice	.15 .07
□ 25 Lawrence Moten	.15 .07
□ 26 Kendall Gill	.20 .09
□ 27 Cedric Ceballos	.15 .07
□ 28 Latrell Sprewell	.20 .09
□ 29 Christian Laettner	.20 .09
□ 30 Jamal Mashburn	.20 .09
□ 31 Jerry Stackhouse	.50 .23
□ 32 John Stockton	.40 .18
□ 33 Arvydas Sabonis	.20 .09
□ 34 Detlef Schrempf	.20 .09
□ 35 Toni Kukoc	.20 .09
□ 36 Sasha Danilovic	.15 .07
□ 37 Dana Barros	.15 .07
□ 38 Loy Vaught	.20 .09
□ 39 John Starks	.20 .09
□ 40 Marty Conlon	.15 .07
□ 41 Antonio McDyess	.60 .25
□ 42 Michael Finley	.50 .23
□ 43 Tom Gugliotta	.40 .18
□ 44 Terrell Brandon	.40 .18
□ 45 Derrick McKey	.15 .07
□ 46 Damon Stoudamire	1.00 .45
□ 47 Eden Campbell	.20 .09
□ 48 Luc Longley	.20 .09
□ 49 B.J. Armstrong	.15 .07
□ 50 Lindsey Hunter	.15 .07
□ 51 Glen Rice	.40 .18
□ 52 Shawn Respert	.15 .07
□ 53 Cory Alexander	.15 .07
□ 54 Tim Legler	.15 .07
□ 55 Bryant Reeves	.20 .09
□ 56 Anfernee Hardaway	1.50 .70
□ 57 Charles Barkley	.25 .25
□ 58 Mookie Blaylock	.20 .09
□ 59 Kevin Garnett	2.50 1.10
□ 60 Hersey Hawkins	.20 .09
□ 61 Ed O'Bannon	.15 .07
□ 62 George Zidek	.15 .07
□ 63 Mitch Richmond	.40 .18
□ 64 Derrick Coleman	.20 .09
□ 65 Chris Webber	1.00 .45
□ 66 Bobby Phills	.15 .07
□ 67 Rik Smits	.20 .09
□ 68 Jeff Hornacek	.20 .09
□ 69 Sam Cassell	.20 .09
□ 70 Gary Trent	.15 .07
□ 71 LaPhonso Ellis	.15 .07
□ 72 Oliver Miller	.15 .07
□ 73 Rex Chapman	.15 .07
□ 74 Jim Jackson	.20 .09
□ 75 Eric Williams	.15 .07
□ 76 Brent Barry	.15 .07
□ 77 Nick Anderson	.15 .07
□ 78 David Robinson	.60 .25
□ 79 Calbert Cheaney	.15 .07
□ 80 Joe Smith	.50 .23
□ 81 Steve Kerr	.15 .07
□ 82 Wayman Tisdale	.15 .07
□ 83 Steve Smith	.20 .09
□ 84 Clyde Drexler	.50 .23
□ 85 Theo Ratliff	.15 .07
□ 86 Charlie Ward	.15 .07
□ 87 Karl Malone	.25 .25
□ 88 Clarence Weatherspoon	.15 .07
□ 89 Greg Anthony	.15 .07
□ 90 Shawn Bradley	.15 .07
□ 91 Otis Thorpe	.20 .09
□ 92 Larry Johnson	.20 .09
□ 93 Sharone Wright	.15 .07
□ 94 Charles Barkley	.60 .25

□ 95 Wesley Person	.15 .07
□ 96 Dikembe Mutombo	.20 .09
□ 97 Eddie Jones	.75 .35
□ 98 Juwan Howard	.50 .23
□ 99 Grant Hill	2.50 1.10
□ 100 Chris Carr	.15 .07
□ 101 Michael Jordan	5.00 2.20
□ 102 Vincent Askew	.15 .07
□ 103 Gary Payton	.60 .25
□ 104 Chris Mills	.15 .07
□ 105 Reggie Miller	.40 .18
□ 106 Don MacLean	.15 .07
□ 107 John Stockton	.40 .18
□ 108 Mahmoud Abdul-Rauf	.15 .07
□ 109 P.J. Brown	.15 .07
□ 110 Kenny Anderson	.20 .09
□ 111 Mark Price	.15 .07
□ 112 Derek Harper	.15 .07
□ 113 Dino Radja	.15 .07
□ 114 Terry Dehere	.15 .07
□ 115 Mark Jackson	.15 .07
□ 116 Vin Baker	.75 .35
□ 117 Dennis Scott	.15 .07
□ 118 Sean Elliott	.15 .07
□ 119 Lee Mayberry	.15 .07
□ 120 Vlade Divac	.20 .09
□ 121 Joe Dumars	.40 .18
□ 122 Isaiah Rider	.20 .09
□ 123 Hakeem Olajuwon	.75 .35
□ 124 Robert Pack	.15 .07
□ 125 Jalen Rose	.15 .07
□ 126 Allan Houston	.20 .09
□ 127 Nate McMillan	.15 .07
□ 128 Rod Strickland	.20 .09
□ 129 Sean Rooks	.15 .07
□ 130 Dennis Rodman	1.50 .70
□ 131 Alonzo Mourning	.40 .18
□ 132 Danny Ferry	.15 .07
□ 133 Sam Cassell	.20 .09
□ 134 Brian Grant	.15 .07
□ 135 Karl Malone	.60 .25
□ 136 Chris Gatling	.15 .07
□ 137 Tom Gugliotta	.40 .18
□ 138 Hubert Davis	.15 .07
□ 139 Lucious Harris	.15 .07
□ 140 Rony Seikaly	.15 .07
□ 141 Alan Henderson	.15 .07
□ 142 Mario Elie	.15 .07
□ 143 Vinny Del Negro	.15 .07
□ 144 Harvey Grant	.15 .07
□ 145 Muggsy Bogues	.15 .07
□ 146 Rodney Rogers	.15 .07
□ 147 Kevin Johnson	.20 .09
□ 148 Anthony Peeler	.15 .07
□ 149 Jon Koncak	.15 .07
□ 150 Ricky Pierce	.15 .07
□ 151 Todd Day	.15 .07
□ 152 Tyrone Hill	.15 .07
□ 153 Nick Van Exel	.40 .18
□ 154 Rasheed Wallace	.20 .09
□ 155 Jayson Williams	.20 .09
□ 156 Sherman Douglas	.15 .07
□ 157 Bryon Russell	.15 .07
□ 158 Ron Harper	.20 .09
□ 159 Stacey Augmon	.15 .07
□ 160 Antonio Davis	.15 .07
□ 161 Tim Hardaway	.50 .23
□ 162 Charles Oakley	.15 .07
□ 163 Billy Owens	.15 .07
□ 164 Sam Perkins	.20 .09
□ 165 Chris Whitney	.15 .07
□ 166 Matt Geiger	.15 .07
□ 167 Andrew Lang	.15 .07
□ 168 Danny Manning	.20 .09
□ 169 Doug Christie	.15 .07
□ 170 George Lynch	.15 .07
□ 171 Malik Sealy	.15 .07
□ 172 Eric Montross	.15 .07
□ 173 Rick Fox	.15 .07
□ 174 Chris Mullin	.40 .18
□ 175 Ken Norman	.15 .07
□ 176 Sarunas Marciulionis	.15 .07
□ 177 Kevin Garnett	2.50 1.10
□ 178 Brian Shaw	.15 .07
□ 179 Will Perdue	.15 .07
□ 180 Scott Williams	.15 .07

1996-97 Stadium Club Class Acts

Randomly inserted in all series two packs at a rate of one in 24, this 20-card dual player set features players who were either college teammates or went to the same school. The cards incorporated the use of the Finest technology. Card backs were numbered with a "CA" prefix.

	MINT	NRMT
COMPLETE SET (10)	60.00	27.00
COMMON CARD (CA1-CA10)	3.00	1.35
SER.2 STATED ODDS 1:24 HOBBY/RETAIL		
COMP.REF.SET (10)	225.00	100.00
COMMON REF. (CA1-CA10)	10.00	4.50
*REF: 1.25X TO 3X HI COLUMN		
REF: SER.2 STATED ODDS 1:96 H/R		
COMP.ATO.REF.SET (10)	500.00	220.00
COMMON ATO. (CA1-CA10)	20.00	9.00
*ATO.REF: 2.5X TO 6X HI		
ATO.REF: SER.2 STATED ODDS 1:192 H/R		

□ CA1 Michael Jordan Jerry Stackhouse	20.00	9.00
□ CA2 Patrick Ewing Alonzo Mourning	3.00	1.35
□ CA3 Gary Payton Brent Barry	3.00	1.35
□ CA4 Chris Webber Juwan Howard	6.00	2.70
□ CA5 Christian Laettner Grant Hill	10.00	4.50
□ CA6 Shareef Abdur-Rahim Jason Kidd	10.00	4.50
□ CA7 Clyde Drexler Hakeem Olajuwon	5.00	2.20
□ CA8 Stephon Marbury Kenny Anderson	10.00	4.50
□ CA9 Anfernee Hardaway Lorenzen Wright	6.00	2.70
□ CA10 Allen Iverson Dikembe Mutombo	10.00	4.50

1996-97 Stadium Club Finest Reprints

Randomly inserted in series one packs at the rate of one in 24 hobby and one in 20 retail, this 25-card set features reprints of 25 of the 50 greatest NBA play-

ers as they appeared on their first Topps, Star Co., or Bowman cards. Cards utilize the Finest technology. The remaining 25 cards were issued in 1996-97 Topps series two.

	MINT	NRMT
COMPLETE SERIES 1 (25)	100.00	45.00
COMMON CARD (1-50)	3.00	1.35
COMP.REF.SER.1 (25)	350.00	160.00
SER.1 STATED ODDS 1:24 HOB, 1:20 RET		
COMMON REFRACTOR (1-50)	6.00	2.70

*REF: 1.5X TO 3X HI COLUMN
REF: SER.1 STATED ODDS 1:36 HOB, 1:80 RET
SKIP-NUMBERED SET
SERIES 2 SET LISTED UNDER TOPPS

		MINT	NRMT
☐ 2	Nate Archibald	3.00	1.35
☐ 4	Charles Barkley	8.00	3.60
☐ 5	Rick Barry	3.00	1.35
☐ 6	Elgin Baylor	3.00	1.35
☐ 7	Dave Bing	3.00	1.35
☐ 8	Larry Bird	15.00	6.75
	Julius Erving		
	Magic Johnson		
☐ 10	Bob Cousy	6.00	2.70
☐ 12	Billy Cunningham	3.00	1.35
☐ 13	Dave DeBusschere	3.00	1.35
☐ 15	Julius Erving	6.00	2.70
☐ 17	Walt Frazier	3.00	1.35
☐ 18	George Gervin	3.00	1.35
☐ 19	Hal Greer	3.00	1.35
☐ 24	Michael Jordan	40.00	18.00
☐ 26	Karl Malone	6.00	2.70
☐ 28	Pete Maravich	4.00	1.80
☐ 29	Kevin McHale	3.00	1.35
☐ 34	Robert Parish	3.00	1.35
☐ 35	Bob Pettit	3.00	1.35
☐ 36	Scottie Pippen	8.00	3.60
☐ 41	Dolph Schayes	3.00	1.35
☐ 44	Isiah Thomas	3.00	1.35
☐ 48	Jerry West	6.00	2.70
☐ 49	Lenny Wilkens UER	3.00	1.35
☐ 50	James Worthy	3.00	1.35

1996-97 Stadium Club Fusion

Randomly inserted in both series hobby packs at a rate of one in 24, this 32-card set features color player photos on fusion laser cut cards. Each card displays one player and fits together with another card creating a larger image. Only the cards displaying the correct

teammates can be "fused" together. Card backs are numbered with a "F" prefix.

	MINT	NRMT
COMPLETE SET (32)	170.00	75.00
COMPLETE SERIES 1 (16)	110.00	50.00
COMPLETE SERIES 2 (16)	60.00	27.00
COMMON CARD (F1-F32)	1.50	.70
SEMISTARS	2.50	1.10
UNLISTED STARS	4.00	1.80
SER.1/2 STATED ODDS 1:24 HOBBY		

		MINT	NRMT
☐ F1	Michael Jordan	50.00	22.00
☐ F2	Chris Webber	10.00	4.50
☐ F3	Glenn Robinson	4.00	1.80
☐ F4	Glen Rice	4.00	1.80
☐ F5	Gary Payton	6.00	2.70
☐ F6	Rik Smits	2.50	1.10
☐ F7	Grant Hill	25.00	11.00
☐ F8	Horace Grant	2.50	1.10
☐ F9	Scottie Pippen	15.00	6.75
☐ F10	Gheorghe Muresan	1.50	.70
☐ F11	Vin Baker	8.00	3.60
☐ F12	Dell Curry	1.50	.70
☐ F13	Shawn Kemp	12.00	5.50
☐ F14	Reggie Miller	4.00	1.80
☐ F15	Joe Dumars	4.00	1.80
☐ F16	Anfernee Hardaway	15.00	6.75
☐ F17	Charles Barkley	6.00	2.70
☐ F18	Juwan Howard	5.00	2.20
☐ F19	Patrick Ewing	4.00	1.80
☐ F20	John Stockton	4.00	1.80
☐ F21	David Robinson	6.00	2.70
☐ F22	Cedric Ceballos	1.50	.70
☐ F23	Alonzo Mourning	4.00	1.80
☐ F24	Mookie Blaylock	2.50	1.10
☐ F25	Clyde Drexler	5.00	2.20
☐ F26	Rod Strickland	2.50	1.10
☐ F27	Larry Johnson	2.50	1.10
☐ F28	Karl Malone	6.00	2.70
☐ F29	Sean Elliott	1.50	.70
☐ F30	Shaquille O'Neal	15.00	6.75
☐ F31	Tim Hardaway	5.00	2.20
☐ F32	Dikembe Mutombo	2.50	1.10

1996-97 Stadium Club Gallery Player's Private Issue

Randomly inserted at a rate of one in 96 series 2 hobby packs, this 18-card set completes the 1995-96 Topps Gallery Player's Private Issue set. Cards are identical to the 1995-96 release.

	MINT	NRMT
COMPLETE SET (18)	650.00	300.00
COMMON CARD (1-18)	8.00	3.60
SEMISTARS	10.00	4.50
UNLISTED STARS	15.00	6.75
SER.2 STATED ODDS 1:96 HOBBY		

		MINT	NRMT
☐ 1	Shaquille O'Neal	60.00	27.00
☐ 2	Shawn Kemp	50.00	22.00
☐ 3	Reggie Miller	15.00	6.75
☐ 4	Mitch Richmond	15.00	6.75
☐ 5	Grant Hill	100.00	45.00
☐ 6	Magic Johnson	40.00	18.00
☐ 7	Vin Baker	30.00	13.50
☐ 8	Charles Barkley	25.00	11.00
☐ 9	Hakeem Olajuwon	30.00	13.50
☐ 10	Michael Jordan	250.00	110.00
☐ 11	Patrick Ewing	15.00	6.75
☐ 12	David Robinson	25.00	11.00
☐ 13	Alonzo Mourning	15.00	6.75
☐ 14	Karl Malone	25.00	11.00
☐ 15	Chris Webber	40.00	18.00
☐ 16	Dikembe Mutombo	8.00	3.60
☐ 17	Larry Johnson	8.00	3.60
☐ 18	Jamal Mashburn	8.00	3.60

1996-97 Stadium Club Golden Moments

Five Golden Moment cards (GM1-M5) highlighted memorable events in the NBA from 1995 and 1996. These cards feature record-breaking occasions. The cards feature sturdy 20 pt. stock, actual event photography and were seeded at an approximate rate of one per first series pack.

	MINT	NRMT
COMPLETE SET (5)	5.00	2.20
COMMON CARD (GM1-GM5)	.15	.07

		MINT	NRMT
	SEMISTARS	.20	.09
	UNLISTED STARS	.40	.18
	RANDOM INSERTS IN ALL SER.1 PACKS		
□ GM1	Robert Parish	.20	.09
□ GM2	John Stockton	.40	.18
□ GM3	Michael Jordan	4.00	1.80
	Dennis Rodman		
□ GM4	Dennis Scott	.15	.07
□ GM5	Hakeem Olajuwon	.75	.35

1996-97 Stadium Club High Risers

Randomly inserted in second series packs at a rate of one in 36, this 15-card set features a combination of Power Matrix and embossed technologies. The set features some of the NBA's best players above the rim. Card backs carry a "HR" prefix.

		MINT	NRMT
	COMPLETE SET (15)	150.00	70.00
	COMMON CARD (HR1-HR15)	2.00	.90
	SER.2 STATED ODDS 1:36 HOBBY/RETAIL		
□ HR1	Scottie Pippen	12.00	5.50
□ HR2	Anfernee Hardaway	15.00	6.75
□ HR3	Vin Baker	8.00	3.60
□ HR4	Brent Barry	2.00	.90
□ HR5	Clyde Drexler	5.00	2.20
□ HR6	Kevin Garnett	25.00	11.00
□ HR7	Grant Hill	25.00	11.00
□ HR8	Michael Finley	5.00	2.20
□ HR9	Jerry Stackhouse	5.00	2.20
□ HR10	Isaiah Rider	2.00	.90
□ HR11	Shaquille O'Neal	15.00	6.75
□ HR12	Antonio McDyess	6.00	2.70
□ HR13	Shawn Kemp	12.00	5.50
□ HR14	Michael Jordan	50.00	22.00
□ HR15	Juwan Howard	5.00	2.20

1996-97 Stadium Club Mega Heroes

Randomly inserted in second series retail packs only at a rate of one in 20, this 9-card set features NBA players who have famous nicknames. Card fronts feature different themes depending on the player's partic-

ular nickname. Card backs carry a "MH" prefix.

		MINT	NRMT
	COMPLETE SET (9)	15.00	6.75
	COMMON CARD (MH1-MH9)	.75	.35
	SEMISTARS	1.50	.70
	SER.2 STATED ODDS 1:20 RETAIL		
□ MH1	Dennis Rodman	6.00	2.70
□ MH2	David Robinson	2.50	1.10
□ MH3	Karl Malone	2.50	1.10
□ MH4	Clyde Drexler	2.00	.90
□ MH5	Anfernee Hardaway	6.00	2.70
□ MH6	Hakeem Olajuwon	3.00	1.35
□ MH7	Charles Oakley	.75	.35
□ MH8	Joe Smith	2.00	.90
□ MH9	Glenn Robinson	1.50	.70

1996-97 Stadium Club Rookie Showcase

Randomly inserted in all series two packs at a rate of one in 12, this 25-card set features Topps first shot at holography. The cards focus on rookies and feature a "two-shot" hologram. Card backs carry a "RS" prefix.

		MINT	NRMT
	COMPLETE SET (25)	100.00	45.00
	COMMON CARD (RS1-RS25)	1.00	.45
	SEMISTARS	2.00	.90
	UNLISTED STARS	3.00	1.35
	SER.2 STATED ODDS 1:12 HOBBY/RETAIL		
□ RS1	Marcus Camby	4.00	1.80
□ RS2	Shareef Abdur-Rahim	10.00	4.50
□ RS3	Stephon Marbury	15.00	6.75
□ RS4	Ray Allen	5.00	2.20
□ RS5	Antoine Walker	15.00	6.75
□ RS6	Lorenzen Wright	3.00	1.35
□ RS7	Kerry Kittles	4.00	1.80
□ RS8	Samaki Walker	3.00	1.35
□ RS9	Erick Dampier	3.00	1.35
□ RS10	Todd Fuller	1.00	.45
□ RS11	Kobe Bryant	30.00	13.50
□ RS12	Steve Nash	3.00	1.35
□ RS13	Tony Delk	3.00	1.35
□ RS14	Jermaine O'Neal	3.00	1.35
□ RS15	John Wallace	3.00	1.35
□ RS16	Walter McCarty	2.00	.90
□ RS17	Dontae' Jones	1.00	.45
□ RS18	Roy Rogers	1.00	.45
□ RS19	Derek Fisher	3.00	1.35
□ RS20	Martin Muursepp	1.00	.45
□ RS21	Jerome Williams	2.00	.90
□ RS22	Brian Evans	1.00	.45
□ RS23	Priest Lauderdale	1.00	.45
□ RS24	Travis Knight	2.00	.90
□ RS25	Allen Iverson	15.00	6.75

1996-97 Stadium Club Rookies 1

This set of 25 standard-sized cards feature most of the top rookies selected in the first round of the 1996 NBA Draft. These cards were seeded at an approximate rate of one per first series pack. Cards are printed on sturdy 20 pt. stock and were the first cards released to picture the rookies in their pro uniforms. Card fronts feature full color, borderless photographs with the word "Rookie" running down the side of the card. A number of the top foreign draft picks were excluded from the set.

		MINT	NRMT
	COMPLETE SET (25)	20.00	9.00
	COMMON CARD (1-25)	.15	.07
	SEMISTARS	.20	.09
	UNLISTED STARS	.40	.18
	RANDOM INSERTS IN ALL SER.1 PACKS		
□ R1	Allen Iverson	4.00	1.80
□ R2	Marcus Camby	1.00	.45
□ R3	Shareef Abdur-Rahim	2.50	1.10
□ R4	Stephon Marbury	4.00	1.80
□ R5	Ray Allen	1.25	.55

	MINT	NRMT
☐ R6 Antoine Walker	4.00	1.80
☐ R7 Lorenzen Wright	.50	.23
☐ R8 Kerry Kittles	1.00	.45
☐ R9 Samaki Walker	.50	.23
☐ R10 Erick Dampier	.50	.23
☐ R11 Todd Fuller	.15	.07
☐ R12 Kobe Bryant	8.00	3.60
☐ R13 Steve Nash	.40	.18
☐ R14 Tony Delk	.50	.23
☐ R15 Jermaine O'Neal	.60	.25
☐ R16 John Wallace	.60	.25
☐ R17 Walter McCarty	.20	.09
☐ R18 Dontae Jones	.15	.07
☐ R19 Roy Rogers	.15	.07
☐ R20 Derek Fisher	.50	.23
☐ R21 Martin Muursepp	.15	.07
☐ R22 Jerome Williams	.20	.09
☐ R23 Brian Evans	.15	.07
☐ R24 Priest Lauderdale	.15	.07
☐ R25 Travis Knight	.20	.09

1996-97 Stadium Club Rookies 2

This set of 20 standard-sized cards feature most of the top rookies selected in the first round of the 1996 NBA Draft. These cards were seeded at an approximate rate of one per second series pack. Cards are printed on 20 pt. stock.

	MINT	NRMT
COMPLETE SET (20)	20.00	9.00
COMMON CARD (R1-R20)	.15	.07
SEMISTARS	.20	.09
UNLISTED STARS	.40	.18
RANDOM INSERTS IN ALL SER.2 PACKS		
☐ R1 Shareef Abdur-Rahim	2.50	1.10
☐ R2 Tony Delk	.50	.23
☐ R3 Priest Lauderdale	.15	.07
☐ R4 Roy Rogers	.15	.07
☐ R5 Lorenzen Wright	.50	.23
☐ R6 Stephon Marbury	4.00	1.80
☐ R7 Derek Fisher	.50	.23
☐ R8 John Wallace	.60	.25
☐ R9 Kobe Bryant	8.00	3.60
☐ R10 Kerry Kittles	1.00	.45
☐ R11 Antoine Walker	4.00	1.80
☐ R12 Steve Nash	.40	.18
☐ R13 Erick Dampier	.50	.23
☐ R14 Walter McCarty	.20	.09
☐ R15 Vitaly Potapenko	.20	.09
☐ R16 Allen Iverson	4.00	1.80
☐ R17 Marcus Camby	1.00	.45
☐ R18 Todd Fuller	.15	.07
☐ R19 Ray Allen	1.25	.55
☐ R20 Jermaine O'Neal	.60	.25

1996-97 Stadium Club Shining Moments

The fifteen Shining Moments cards showcase the slamming and jamming plays that made the '95-96 season memorable. The cards feature sturdy 20 pt. stock, actual event photography and were seeded at an approximate rate of one per first series pack.

	MINT	NRMT
COMPLETE SET (15)	10.00	4.50
COMMON CARD (SM1-SM15)	.15	.07
SEMISTARS	.20	.09
UNLISTED STARS	.40	.18
RANDOM INSERTS IN ALL SER.1 PACKS		
☐ SM1 Charles Barkley	.60	.25
☐ SM2 Michael Jordan	5.00	2.20
☐ SM3 Karl Malone	.60	.25
☐ SM4 Hakeem Olajuwon	.75	.35
☐ SM5 John Stockton	.40	.18
☐ SM6 Patrick Ewing	.40	.18
☐ SM7 Reggie Miller	.40	.18
☐ SM8 David Robinson	.60	.25
☐ SM9 Dennis Rodman	1.50	.70
☐ SM10 Damon Stoudamire	1.00	.45
☐ SM11 Brent Barry	.15	.07
☐ SM12 Tim Legler	.15	.07
☐ SM13 Jason Kidd	.75	.35
☐ SM14 Terrell Brandon	.40	.18
☐ SM15 Allen Iverson	4.00	1.80

1996-97 Stadium Club Special Forces

Randomly inserted in series one packs at a rate of one in 20, this 10-card retail only set features color action photos of supercharged stars printed with the Electra-Etch foil technology.

	MINT	NRMT
COMPLETE SET (10)	60.00	27.00
COMMON CARD (SF1-SF10)	2.50	1.10
SER.1 STATED ODDS 1:20 RETAIL		
☐ SF1 Anfernee Hardaway	8.00	3.60
☐ SF2 Grant Hill	12.00	5.50
☐ SF3 Shawn Kemp	6.00	2.70
☐ SF4 Michael Jordan	25.00	11.00
☐ SF5 Shaquille O'Neal	8.00	3.60
☐ SF6 Scottie Pippen	6.00	2.70
☐ SF7 Damon Stoudamire	5.00	2.20
☐ SF8 Jerry Stackhouse	2.50	1.10
☐ SF9 Gary Payton	3.00	1.35
☐ SF10 Dennis Rodman	8.00	3.60

1996-97 Stadium Club Top Crop

Randomly inserted in series one packs at a rate of one in 24, this 12-card set features color action player photos on double-sided Power Matrix cards with NBA All-Stars from both the East and the West Conferences pitted against each other. One side displays an all-star player from the Eastern Conference with the other side carrying the corresponding Western Conference all-star player.

	MINT	NRMT
COMPLETE SET (12)	60.00	27.00
COMMON CARD (TC1-TC12)	3.00	1.35
SER.1 STATED ODDS 1:24 HOB, 1:20 RET		
☐ TC1 Shaquille O'Neal	10.00	4.50
Hakeem Olajuwon		
☐ TC2 Alonzo Mourning	3.00	1.35
Dikembe Mutombo		
☐ TC3 Patrick Ewing	5.00	2.20
David Robinson		
☐ TC4 Grant Hill	12.00	5.50
Sean Elliott		
☐ TC5 Scottie Pippen	12.00	5.50

Shawn Kemp
- TC6 Vin Baker 6.00 2.70
  Karl Malone
- TC7 Juwan Howard 5.00 2.20
  Charles Barkley
- TC8 Glen Rice 5.00 2.20
  Clyde Drexler
- TC9 Michael Jordan 30.00 13.50
  Gary Payton
- TC10 Terrell Brandon 3.00 1.35
  John Stockton
- TC11 Reggie Miller 4.00 1.80
  Mitch Richmond
- TC12 Anfernee Hardaway 12.00 5.50
  Jason Kidd

1996-97 Stadium Club Welcome Additions

The 25 Welcome Addition cards showcase the new additions that NBA teams made in the off-season. The cards feature sturdy 20 pt. stock and were seeded at an approximate rate of one per second series pack.

	MINT	NRMT
COMPLETE SET (25)	3.00	1.35
COMMON CARD (WA1-WA25)	.15	.07
SEMISTARS	.20	.09
UNLISTED STARS	.40	.18
RANDOM INSERTS IN ALL SER.2 PACKS		

☐ WA1 Charles Barkley	.60	.25
☐ WA2 Armon Gilliam	.15	.07
☐ WA3 Larry Johnson	.20	.09
☐ WA4 Felton Spencer	.15	.07
☐ WA5 Isaiah Rider	.20	.09
☐ WA6 Kevin Willis	.15	.07
☐ WA7 Mahmoud Abdul-Rauf	.15	.07
☐ WA8 Chris Childs	.15	.07
☐ WA9 Robert Horry	.20	.09
☐ WA10 Dan Majerle	.20	.09
☐ WA11 Robert Pack	.15	.07
☐ WA12 Rod Strickland	.20	.09
☐ WA13 Tyrone Corbin	.15	.07
☐ WA14 Anthony Mason	.20	.09
☐ WA15 Derek Harper	.15	.07
☐ WA16 Kenny Anderson	.20	.09
☐ WA17 Hubert Davis	.15	.07
☐ WA18 Allan Houston	.20	.09
☐ WA19 Shaquille O'Neal	1.50	.70
☐ WA20 Brent Price	.15	.07
☐ WA21 Ervin Johnson	.15	.07
☐ WA22 Craig Ehlo	.15	.07
☐ WA23 Jalen Rose	.15	.07
☐ WA24 Oliver Miller	.15	.07
☐ WA25 Mark West	.15	.07

1997-98 Stadium Club

The 1997-98 Stadium Club first series was issued with a total of 120 cards and was distributed in 10-card packs for a suggested retail price of $3.00. The fronts feature full-bleed color action player photos embossed and printed on 20 pt. stock and containing a new holographic foil logo. The backs carry expanded career and previous season statistics, including the player's ranking among other players at the same position. The cards of series one are the odd numbered cards.

	MINT	NRMT
COMPLETE SET (240)	45.00	20.00
COMPLETE SERIES 1 (120)	25.00	11.00
COMPLETE SERIES 2 (120)	20.00	9.00
COMMON CARD (1-240)	.15	.07
SEMISTARS	.20	.09
UNLISTED STARS	.40	.18
COMP.FDI SET (240)	1800.00	800.00
COMP.FDI SER.1 (120)	1000.00	450.00
COMP.FDI SER.2 (120)	800.00	350.00
COMMON FDI (1-240)	2.00	.90
*FDI STARS: 15X TO 30X HI COLUMN		
*FDI RCs: 7.5X TO 15X HI		
FDI: SER.1/2 STATED ODDS 1:24 RET		
FDI: STATED PRINT RUN 200 SETS		

☐ 1 Scottie Pippen	1.25	.55
☐ 2 Bryon Russell	.15	.07
☐ 3 Muggsy Bogues	.15	.07
☐ 4 Gary Payton	.60	.25
☐ 5 Bulls - Team of the 90s	5.00	2.20
Ron Harper		
Michael Jordan		
Scottie Pippen		
Dennis Rodman		
☐ 6 Corliss Williamson	.20	.09
☐ 7 Samaki Walker	.15	.07
☐ 8 Allan Houston	.20	.09
☐ 9 Ray Allen	.50	.23
☐ 10 Nick Van Exel	.40	.18
☐ 11 Chris Mullin	.40	.18
☐ 12 Popeye Jones	.15	.07
☐ 13 Horace Grant	.20	.09
☐ 14 Rik Smits	.20	.09
☐ 15 Wayman Tisdale	.15	.07
☐ 16 Donny Marshall	.15	.07
☐ 17 Rod Strickland	.20	.09
☐ 18 Rod Strickland	.20	.09
☐ 19 Greg Anthony	.15	.07
☐ 20 Lindsey Hunter	.15	.07
☐ 21 Glen Rice	.40	.18

☐ 22 Anthony Goldwire	.15	.07
☐ 23 Mahmoud Abdul-Rauf	.15	.07
☐ 24 Sean Elliott	.15	.07
☐ 25 Cory Alexander	.15	.07
☐ 26 Tyrone Corbin	.15	.07
☐ 27 Sam Perkins	.20	.09
☐ 28 Brian Shaw	.15	.07
☐ 29 Doug Christie	.15	.07
☐ 30 Mark Jackson	.15	.07
☐ 31 Christian Laettner	.20	.09
☐ 32 Damon Stoudamire	.75	.35
☐ 33 Eric Williams	.15	.07
☐ 34 Glenn Robinson	.40	.18
☐ 35 Brooks Thompson	.15	.07
☐ 36 Derrick Coleman	.20	.09
☐ 37 Theo Ratliff	.15	.07
☐ 38 Ron Harper	.20	.09
☐ 39 Hakeem Olajuwon	.75	.35
☐ 40 Mitch Richmond	.40	.18
☐ 41 Reggie Miller	.40	.18
☐ 42 Reggie Miller	.40	.18
☐ 43 Shaquille O'Neal	1.50	.70
☐ 44 Zydrunas Ilgauskas	.20	.09
☐ 45 Jamal Mashburn	.20	.09
☐ 46 Isaiah Rider	.20	.09
☐ 47 Tom Gugliotta	.40	.18
☐ 48 Rex Chapman	.15	.07
☐ 49 Lorenzen Wright	.15	.07
☐ 50 Pooh Richardson	.15	.07
☐ 51 Armon Gilliam	.15	.07
☐ 52 Kevin Johnson	.20	.09
☐ 53 Kerry Kittles	.40	.18
☐ 54 Kerry Kittles	.40	.18
☐ 55 Charles Oakley	.15	.07
☐ 56 Dennis Rodman	1.50	.70
☐ 57 Greg Ostertag	.15	.07
☐ 58 Todd Fuller	.15	.07
☐ 59 Mark Davis	.15	.07
☐ 60 Erick Strickland	.20	.09
☐ 61 Clifford Robinson	.15	.07
☐ 62 Nate McMillan	.15	.07
☐ 63 Steve Kerr	.15	.07
☐ 64 Bob Sura	.15	.07
☐ 65 Danny Ferry	.15	.07
☐ 66 Loy Vaught	.20	.09
☐ 67 A.C. Green	.20	.09
☐ 68 John Stockton	.40	.18
☐ 69 Terry Mills	.15	.07
☐ 70 Voshon Lenard	.15	.07
☐ 71 Matt Maloney	.15	.07
☐ 72 Charlie Ward	.15	.07
☐ 73 Brent Barry	.15	.07
☐ 74 Chris Webber	1.00	.45
☐ 75 Stephon Marbury	2.00	.90
☐ 76 Bryant Stith	.15	.07
☐ 77 Shareef Abdur-Rahim	1.25	.55
☐ 78 Sean Rooks	.15	.07
☐ 79 Rony Seikaly	.15	.07
☐ 80 Brent Price	.15	.07
☐ 81 Wesley Person	.15	.07
☐ 82 Michael Smith	.15	.07
☐ 83 Gary Trent	.15	.07
☐ 84 Dan Majerle	.20	.09
☐ 85 Rex Walters	.15	.07
☐ 86 Clarence Weatherspoon	.15	.07
☐ 87 Patrick Ewing	.40	.18
☐ 88 B.J. Armstrong	.15	.07
☐ 89 Travis Best	.15	.07
☐ 90 Steve Smith	.20	.09
☐ 91 Vitaly Potapenko	.15	.07
☐ 92 Derek Strong	.15	.07
☐ 93 Michael Finley	.40	.18
☐ 94 Will Perdue	.15	.07
☐ 95 Antoine Walker	2.00	.90
☐ 96 Chuck Person	.15	.07
☐ 97 Mookie Blaylock	.20	.09
☐ 98 Eric Snow	.15	.07
☐ 99 Tony Delk	.15	.07
☐ 100 Mario Elie	.15	.07
☐ 101 Terrell Brandon	.40	.18
☐ 102 Shawn Bradley	.15	.07
☐ 103 Latrell Sprewell	.20	.09
☐ 104 Latrell Sprewell	.20	.09
☐ 105 Tim Hardaway	.50	.23
☐ 106 Terry Porter	.15	.07
☐ 107 Darrell Armstrong	.15	.07

☐ 108 Rasheed Wallace	.20	.09	☐ 194 Anfernee Hardaway ..	1.50	.70		
☐ 109 Vinny Del Negro	.15	.07	☐ 195 Harvey Grant	.15	.07		
☐ 110 Tracy Murray	.15	.07	☐ 196 Nick Anderson	.15	.07		
☐ 111 Lawrence Moten	.15	.07	☐ 197 Luc Longley	.20	.09		
☐ 112 Lamond Murray	.15	.07	☐ 198 Andrew Lang	.15	.07		
☐ 113 Juwan Howard	.40	.18	☐ 199 P.J. Brown	.15	.07		
☐ 114 Juwan Howard	.40	.18	☐ 200 Cedric Ceballos	.15	.07		
☐ 115 Karl Malone	.60	.25	☐ 201 Tim Duncan	5.00	2.20		
☐ 116 Aaron McKie	.15	.07	☐ 202 Ervin Johnson TRAN ..	.15	.07		
☐ 117 Shawn Respert	.15	.07	☐ 203 Keith Van Horn	4.00	1.80		
☐ 118 Michael Jordan	5.00	2.20	☐ 204 David Wesley TRAN ..	.15	.07		
☐ 119 Shawn Kemp	1.25	.55	☐ 205 Chauncey Billups ..	1.50	.70		
☐ 120 Arvydas Sabonis	.20	.09	☐ 206 Jim Jackson TRAN ..	.20	.09		
☐ 121 Tyus Edney	.15	.07	☐ 207 Antonio Daniels ..	1.00	.45		
☐ 122 Bryant Reeves	.20	.09	☐ 208 Travis Knight TRAN ..	.15	.07		
☐ 123 Jason Kidd	.75	.35	☐ 209 Tony Battie	.75	.35		
☐ 124 Dikembe Mutombo	.20	.09	☐ 210 Bobby Phills TRAN ..	.15	.07		
☐ 125 Allen Iverson	2.00	.90	☐ 211 Bobby Jackson	.75	.35		
☐ 126 Allen Iverson	2.00	.90	☐ 212 Otis Thorpe TRAN ..	.15	.07		
☐ 127 Larry Johnson	.20	.09	☐ 213 Tim Thomas	2.50	1.10		
☐ 128 Jerry Stackhouse	.40	.18	☐ 214 Chris Mullin TRAN ..	.20	.09		
☐ 129 Kendall Gill	.20	.09	☐ 215 Adonal Foyle	.50	.23		
☐ 130 Kendall Gill	.20	.09	☐ 216 Brian Williams TRAN ..	.15	.07		
☐ 131 Vin Baker	.75	.35	☐ 217 Tracy McGrady	2.50	1.10		
☐ 132 Joe Dumars	.40	.18	☐ 218 Tyus Edney TRAN ..	.15	.07		
☐ 133 Calbert Cheaney	.15	.07	☐ 219 Danny Fortson	.75	.35		
☐ 134 Alonzo Mourning	.40	.18	☐ 220 C.Robinson TRAN ..	.15	.07		
☐ 135 Isaac Austin	.15	.07	☐ 221 Olivier Saint-Jean	.60	.25		
☐ 136 Joe Smith	.40	.18	☐ 222 Vin Baker TRAN ..	.40	.18		
☐ 137 Elden Campbell	.20	.09	☐ 223 Austin Croshere	.50	.23		
☐ 138 Kevin Garnett	2.50	1.10	☐ 224 John Wallace TRAN ..	.15	.07		
☐ 139 Malik Sealy	.15	.07	☐ 225 Derek Anderson ..	1.25	.55		
☐ 140 John Starks	.20	.09	☐ 226 Kelvin Cato	.50	.23		
☐ 141 Clyde Drexler	.50	.23	☐ 227 Maurice Taylor ..	1.25	.55		
☐ 142 Matt Geiger	.15	.07	☐ 228 Scot Pollard	.15	.07		
☐ 143 Mark Price	.15	.07	☐ 229 John Thomas	.15	.07		
☐ 144 Buck Williams	.15	.07	☐ 230 Dean Garrett TRAN ..	.15	.07		
☐ 145 Grant Hill	2.50	1.10	☐ 231 Brevin Knight ..	1.25	.55		
☐ 146 Kobe Bryant	3.00	1.35	☐ 232 Ron Mercer	3.00	1.35		
☐ 147 Dale Ellis	.15	.07	☐ 233 Johnny Taylor	.15	.07		
☐ 148 Jason Caffey	.15	.07	☐ 234 A.McDyess TRAN ..	.40	.18		
☐ 149 Toni Kukoc	.20	.09	☐ 235 Ed Gray	.50	.23		
☐ 150 Avery Johnson	.15	.07	☐ 236 Terrell Brandon TRAN	.20	.09		
☐ 151 Alan Henderson	.15	.07	☐ 237 Anthony Parker	.15	.07		
☐ 152 Walt Williams	.15	.07	☐ 238 Shawn Kemp TRAN ..	.60	.25		
☐ 153 Greg Minor	.15	.07	☐ 239 Paul Grant	.15	.07		
☐ 154 Calbert Cheaney	.15	.07	☐ 240 Dennis Scott TRAN ..	.15	.07		
☐ 155 Vlade Divac	.20	.09					
☐ 156 Greg Foster	.15	.07					
☐ 157 LaPhonso Ellis	.15	.07					
☐ 158 Charles Barkley	.60	.25					
☐ 159 Antonio Davis	.15	.07					
☐ 160 Roy Rogers	.15	.07					
☐ 161 Robert Horry	.20	.09					
☐ 162 Sam Cassell	.20	.09					
☐ 163 Chris Carr	.15	.07					
☐ 164 Robert Pack	.15	.07					
☐ 165 Sam Cassell	.20	.09					
☐ 166 Rodney Rogers	.15	.07					
☐ 167 Chris Childs	.15	.07					
☐ 168 Shandon Anderson	.15	.07					
☐ 169 Kenny Anderson	.20	.09					
☐ 170 Anthony Mason	.20	.09					
☐ 171 Olden Polynice	.15	.07					
☐ 172 David Wingate	.15	.07					
☐ 173 David Robinson	.60	.25					
☐ 174 Billy Owens	.15	.07					
☐ 175 Detlef Schrempf	.20	.09					
☐ 176 Carlos Rogers	.15	.07					
☐ 177 Marcus Camby	.40	.18					
☐ 178 Dana Barros	.15	.07					
☐ 179 Shandon Anderson	.20	.09					
☐ 180 Jayson Williams	.20	.09					
☐ 181 Eldridge Recasner	.15	.07					
☐ 182 Doug West	.15	.07					
☐ 183 Kevin Willis	.15	.07					
☐ 184 Eddie Johnson	.15	.07					
☐ 185 Derek Fisher	.15	.07					
☐ 186 Eddie Jones	.75	.35					
☐ 187 Sherman Douglas	.15	.07					
☐ 188 Anthony Peeler	.15	.07					
☐ 189 Danny Manning	.20	.09					
☐ 190 Stacey Augmon	.15	.07					
☐ 191 Hersey Hawkins	.20	.09					
☐ 192 Micheal Williams	.15	.07					
☐ 193 Jeff Hornacek	.20	.09					

150. Card fronts differ by carrying a metal look.

	MINT	NRMT
COMMON CARD (1-240)	10.00	4.50
SEMISTARS	15.00	6.75
UNLISTED STARS	25.00	11.00
SER.1 STATED ODDS 1:86 HOBBY		
SER.2 STATED ODDS 1:69 HOBBY		
SHARED PRINT RUN 150 SERIAL #'d SETS		

☐ 1 Scottie Pippen	......	75.00	34.00
☐ 2 Bryon Russell	......	10.00	4.50
☐ 3 Muggsy Bogues	......	10.00	4.50
☐ 4 Gary Payton	......	40.00	18.00
☐ 5 Bulls - Team of the 90s		250.00	110.00
Ron Harper			
Michael Jordan			
Scottie Pippen			
Dennis Rodman			
☐ 6 Corliss Williamson	......	15.00	6.75
☐ 7 Samaki Walker	......	10.00	4.50
☐ 8 Allan Houston	......	15.00	6.75
☐ 9 Ray Allen	......	30.00	13.50
☐ 10 Nick Van Exel	......	25.00	11.00
☐ 11 Chris Mullin	......	25.00	11.00
☐ 12 Popeye Jones	......	10.00	4.50
☐ 13 Horace Grant	......	15.00	6.75
☐ 14 Rik Smits	......	15.00	6.75
☐ 15 Wayman Tisdale	......	10.00	4.50
☐ 16 Donny Marshall	......	10.00	4.50
☐ 17 Rod Strickland	......	15.00	6.75
☐ 18 Rod Strickland	......	10.00	4.50
☐ 19 Greg Anthony	......	10.00	4.50
☐ 20 Lindsey Hunter	......	10.00	4.50
☐ 21 Glen Rice	......	25.00	11.00
☐ 22 Anthony Goldwire	......	10.00	4.50
☐ 23 Mahmoud Abdul-Rauf		10.00	4.50
☐ 24 Sean Elliott	......	10.00	4.50
☐ 25 Cory Alexander	......	10.00	4.50
☐ 26 Tyrone Corbin	......	10.00	4.50
☐ 27 Sam Perkins	......	15.00	6.75
☐ 28 Brian Shaw	......	10.00	4.50
☐ 29 Doug Christie	......	10.00	4.50
☐ 30 Mark Jackson	......	10.00	4.50
☐ 31 Christian Laettner	......	15.00	6.75
☐ 32 Damon Stoudamire	......	50.00	22.00
☐ 33 Eric Williams	......	10.00	4.50
☐ 34 Glenn Robinson	......	25.00	11.00
☐ 35 Brooks Thompson	......	10.00	4.50
☐ 36 Derrick Coleman	......	15.00	6.75
☐ 37 Theo Ratliff	......	10.00	4.50
☐ 38 Ron Harper	......	15.00	6.75
☐ 39 Hakeem Olajuwon	......	50.00	22.00
☐ 40 Mitch Richmond	......	25.00	11.00
☐ 41 Reggie Miller	......	25.00	11.00
☐ 42 Reggie Miller	......	25.00	11.00
☐ 43 Shaquille O'Neal	......	100.00	45.00
☐ 44 Zydrunas Ilgauskas	..	15.00	6.75
☐ 45 Jamal Mashburn	......	15.00	6.75
☐ 46 Isaiah Rider	......	15.00	6.75
☐ 47 Tom Gugliotta	......	25.00	11.00
☐ 48 Rex Chapman	......	10.00	4.50
☐ 49 Lorenzen Wright	......	10.00	4.50
☐ 50 Pooh Richardson	......	10.00	4.50
☐ 51 Armon Gilliam	......	10.00	4.50
☐ 52 Kevin Johnson	......	15.00	6.75
☐ 53 Kerry Kittles	......	25.00	11.00
☐ 54 Kerry Kittles	......	25.00	11.00
☐ 55 Charles Oakley	......	10.00	4.50
☐ 56 Dennis Rodman	......	100.00	45.00
☐ 57 Greg Ostertag	......	10.00	4.50
☐ 58 Todd Fuller	......	10.00	4.50
☐ 59 Mark Davis	......	10.00	4.50
☐ 60 Erick Strickland	......	15.00	6.75
☐ 61 Clifford Robinson	......	10.00	4.50
☐ 62 Nate McMillan	......	10.00	4.50
☐ 63 Steve Kerr	......	10.00	4.50
☐ 64 Bob Sura	......	10.00	4.50
☐ 65 Danny Ferry	......	10.00	4.50
☐ 66 Loy Vaught	......	15.00	6.75
☐ 67 A.C. Green	......	15.00	6.75
☐ 68 John Stockton	......	25.00	11.00
☐ 69 Terry Mills	......	10.00	4.50
☐ 70 Voshon Lenard	......	10.00	4.50

1997-98 Stadium Club One Of A Kind

Randomly inserted in both series hobby only packs, with series one inserted at the rate of one in 86 and series two inserted at one in 69, this 240-card set parallels the base set. The cards are serially numbered to

#	Player	MINT	NRMT
71	Matt Maloney	10.00	4.50
72	Charlie Ward	10.00	4.50
73	Brent Barry	10.00	4.50
74	Chris Webber	60.00	27.00
75	Stephon Marbury	120.00	55.00
76	Bryant Stith	10.00	4.50
77	Shareef Abdur-Rahim	75.00	34.00
78	Sean Rooks	10.00	4.50
79	Rony Seikaly	10.00	4.50
80	Brent Price	10.00	4.50
81	Wesley Person	10.00	4.50
82	Michael Smith	10.00	4.50
83	Gary Trent	10.00	4.50
84	Dan Majerle	15.00	6.75
85	Rex Walters	10.00	4.50
86	Clarence Weatherspoon	10.00	4.50
87	Patrick Ewing	25.00	11.00
88	B.J. Armstrong	10.00	4.50
89	Travis Best	10.00	4.50
90	Steve Smith	15.00	6.75
91	Vitaly Potapenko	10.00	4.50
92	Dereck Strong	10.00	4.50
93	Michael Finley	25.00	11.00
94	Will Perdue	10.00	4.50
95	Antoine Walker	120.00	55.00
96	Chuck Person	10.00	4.50
97	Mookie Blaylock	15.00	6.75
98	Eric Snow	10.00	4.50
99	Tony Delk	10.00	4.50
100	Mario Elie	10.00	4.50
101	Terrell Brandon	25.00	11.00
102	Shawn Bradley	10.00	4.50
103	Latrell Sprewell	15.00	6.75
104	Latrell Sprewell	15.00	6.75
105	Tim Hardaway	30.00	13.50
106	Terry Porter	10.00	4.50
107	Darrell Armstrong	10.00	4.50
108	Rasheed Wallace	15.00	6.75
109	Vinny Del Negro	10.00	4.50
110	Tracy Murray	10.00	4.50
111	Lawrence Moten	10.00	4.50
112	Lamond Murray	10.00	4.50
113	Juwan Howard	25.00	11.00
114	Juwan Howard	25.00	11.00
115	Karl Malone	40.00	18.00
116	Aaron McKie	10.00	4.50
117	Shawn Respert	10.00	4.50
118	Michael Jordan	350.00	160.00
119	Shawn Kemp	75.00	34.00
120	Arvydas Sabonis	15.00	6.75
121	Tyus Edney	10.00	4.50
122	Bryant Reeves	15.00	6.75
123	Jason Kidd	50.00	22.00
124	Dikembe Mutombo	15.00	6.75
125	Allen Iverson	120.00	55.00
126	Allen Iverson	120.00	55.00
127	Larry Johnson	15.00	6.75
128	Jerry Stackhouse	25.00	11.00
129	Kendall Gill	15.00	6.75
130	Kendall Gill	15.00	6.75
131	Vin Baker	50.00	22.00
132	Joe Dumars	25.00	11.00
133	Calbert Cheaney	10.00	4.50
134	Alonzo Mourning	25.00	11.00
135	Isaac Austin	10.00	-4.50
136	Joe Smith	25.00	11.00
137	Elden Campbell	10.00	6.75
138	Kevin Garnett	150.00	70.00
139	Malik Sealy	10.00	4.50
140	John Starks	15.00	6.75
141	Clyde Drexler	30.00	13.50
142	Matt Geiger	10.00	4.50
143	Mark Price	10.00	4.50
144	Buck Williams	10.00	4.50
145	Grant Hill	150.00	70.00
146	Kobe Bryant	200.00	90.00
147	Dale Ellis	10.00	4.50
148	Jason Caffey	10.00	4.50
149	Toni Kukoc	15.00	6.75
150	Avery Johnson	10.00	4.50
151	Alan Henderson	10.00	4.50
152	Walt Williams	10.00	4.50
153	Greg Minor	10.00	4.50
154	Calbert Cheaney	10.00	4.50
155	Vlade Divac	15.00	6.75
156	Greg Foster	10.00	4.50
157	LaPhonso Ellis	10.00	4.50
158	Charles Barkley	40.00	18.00
159	Antonio Davis	10.00	4.50
160	Roy Rogers	10.00	4.50
161	Robert Horry	15.00	6.75
162	Sam Cassell	15.00	6.75
163	Chris Carr	10.00	4.50
164	Robert Pack	10.00	4.50
165	Sam Cassell	15.00	6.75
166	Rodney Rogers	10.00	4.50
167	Chris Childs	10.00	4.50
168	Shandon Anderson	10.00	4.50
169	Kenny Anderson	15.00	6.75
170	Anthony Mason	15.00	6.75
171	Olden Polynice	10.00	4.50
172	David Wingate	10.00	4.50
173	David Robinson	40.00	18.00
174	Billy Owens	10.00	4.50
175	Detlef Schrempf	15.00	6.75
176	Carlos Rogers	10.00	4.50
177	Marcus Camby	25.00	11.00
178	Dana Barros	10.00	4.50
179	Shandon Anderson	10.00	4.50
180	Jayson Williams	15.00	6.75
181	Eldridge Recasner	10.00	4.50
182	Doug West	10.00	4.50
183	Kevin Willis	10.00	4.50
184	Eddie Johnson	10.00	4.50
185	Derek Fisher	10.00	4.50
186	Eddie Jones	50.00	22.00
187	Sherman Douglas	10.00	4.50
188	Anthony Peeler	10.00	4.50
189	Danny Manning	15.00	6.75
190	Stacey Augmon	10.00	4.50
191	Hersey Hawkins	15.00	6.75
192	Micheal Williams	10.00	4.50
193	Jeff Hornacek	15.00	6.75
194	Anfernee Hardaway	100.00	45.00
195	Harvey Grant	10.00	4.50
196	Nick Anderson	10.00	4.50
197	Luc Longley	15.00	6.75
198	Andrew Lang	10.00	4.50
199	P.J. Brown	10.00	4.50
200	Cedric Ceballos	10.00	4.50
201	Tim Duncan	150.00	70.00
202	Ervin Johnson TRAN	10.00	4.50
203	Keith Van Horn	125.00	55.00
204	David Wesley TRAN	10.00	4.50
205	Chauncey Billups	50.00	22.00
206	Jim Jackson TRAN	15.00	6.75
207	Antonio Daniels	30.00	13.50
208	Travis Knight TRAN	10.00	4.50
209	Tony Battie	25.00	11.00
210	Bobby Phills TRAN	10.00	4.50
211	Bobby Jackson	25.00	11.00
212	Otis Thorpe TRAN	10.00	4.50
213	Tim Thomas	75.00	34.00
214	Chris Mullin TRAN	15.00	6.75
215	Adonal Foyle	25.00	11.00
216	Brian Williams TRAN	10.00	4.50
217	Tracy McGrady	75.00	34.00
218	Tyus Edney TRAN	10.00	4.50
219	Danny Fortson	25.00	11.00
220	C.Robinson TRAN	10.00	4.50
221	Olivier Saint-Jean	25.00	11.00
222	Vin Baker TRAN	25.00	11.00
223	Austin Croshere	25.00	11.00
224	John Wallace TRAN	10.00	4.50
225	Derek Anderson	40.00	18.00
226	Kelvin Cato	25.00	11.00
227	Maurice Taylor	40.00	18.00
228	Scot Pollard	10.00	4.50
229	John Thomas	10.00	4.50
230	Dean Garrett TRAN	10.00	4.50
231	Brevin Knight	40.00	18.00
232	Ron Mercer	90.00	40.00
233	Johnny Taylor	10.00	4.50
234	A.McDyess TRAN	25.00	11.00
235	Ed Gray	25.00	11.00
236	Terrell Brandon TRAN	15.00	6.75
237	Anthony Parker	10.00	4.50
238	Shawn Kemp TRAN	40.00	18.00
239	Paul Grant	10.00	4.50
240	Dennis Scott TRAN	10.00	4.50

1997-98 Stadium Club Bowman's Best Previews

Randomly inserted in packs at the rate of one in 24, this 10-card set is a sneak preview of the Bowman's Best series and features color action player photos with a section of a large gold basketball in the background. Card backs are numbered with a BBP prefix.

	MINT	NRMT
COMPLETE SET (20)	50.00	22.00
COMPLETE SERIES 1 (10)	35.00	16.00
COMPLETE SERIES 2 (10)	15.00	6.75
COMMON CARD (BBP1-20)	.75	.35
SEMISTARS	1.00	.45
UNLISTED STARS	1.50	.70
SER.1/2 STATED ODDS 1:24 HOB/RET		
COMP.REF.SET (20)	140.00	65.00
COMP.REF.SER.1 (10)	100.00	45.00
COMP.REF.SER.2 (10)	40.00	18.00
COMMON REF.	2.00	.90
*REF: 1.25X TO 3X HI COLUMN		
REF: SER.1/2 STATED ODDS 1:96 H/R		
COMP.ATO.REF.SET (20)	250.00	110.00
COMP.ATO.REF.SER.1 (10)	175.00	80.00
COMP.ATO.REF.SER.2 (10)	75.00	34.00
COMMON ATO.REF.	4.00	1.80
*ATO.REF: 2X TO 5X HI		
ATO.REF: SER.1/2 STATED ODDS 1:192 H/R		
BBP1 Allen Iverson	8.00	3.60
BBP2 Gary Payton	2.50	1.10
BBP3 Grant Hill	10.00	4.50
BBP4 Anfernee Hardaway	6.00	2.70
BBP5 Karl Malone	2.50	1.10
BBP6 Glen Rice	1.50	.70
BBP7 Antoine Walker	8.00	3.60
BBP8 Alonzo Mourning	1.50	.70
BBP9 Shareef Abdur-Rahim	5.00	2.20
BBP10 Shaquille O'Neal	6.00	2.70
BBP11 Maurice Taylor	2.50	1.10
BBP12 Chauncey Billups	3.00	1.35
BBP13 Paul Grant	.75	.35
BBP14 Tony Battie	1.50	.70
BBP15 Austin Croshere	1.00	.45
BBP16 Brevin Knight	2.50	1.10
BBP17 Bobby Jackson	1.50	.70
BBP18 Johnny Taylor	.75	.35
BBP19 Scot Pollard	.75	.35
BBP20 Tariq Abdul-Wahad	1.50	.70

1997-98 Stadium Club Co-Signers

Randomly inserted in both series, with series one inserted at one in 387 hobby and series two at one in 309 hobby, this 12-card set features a color action photo of a different player on each side of the card along with an authentic autograph of each player. Each of these double-sided cards are stamped with the Topps Certified Autograph issue stamp to ensure authenticity. The cards were inserted within three groups at different levels. Group "A", or cards CO1-CO4 were inserted at one in 15,483. Group "B", or cards CO5-CO8 were inserted at one in 5,161. Group "C", or cards CO9-CO12 were inserted at one in 430 packs. Card backs carry a CO prefix.

	MINT	NRMT
COMMON CARD (CO1-24) ..	80.00	36.00
SER.1 STATED ODDS 1:387 HOB		
SER.2 STATED ODDS 1:309 HOB		

		MINT	NRMT
☐ CO1	Karl Malone .... Kobe Bryant	1200.00	550.00
☐ CO2	Juwan Howard .... Hakeem Olajuwon	350.00	160.00
☐ CO3	John Starks .... Tim Hardaway	250.00	110.00
☐ CO4	Clyde Drexler ...... Kobe Bryant	400.00	180.00
☐ CO5	Kobe Bryant .... John Starks	450.00	200.00
☐ CO6	Hakeem Olajuwon Clyde Drexler	200.00	90.00
☐ CO7	Tim Hardaway...... Juwan Howard	150.00	70.00
☐ CO8	Joe Smith .... Karl Malone	125.00	55.00
☐ CO9	Juwan Howard .... Clyde Drexler	125.00	55.00
☐ CO10	Hakeem Olajuwon Tim Hardaway	125.00	55.00
☐ CO11	Joe Smith .... Kobe Bryant	225.00	100.00
☐ CO12	Karl Malone .... John Starks	80.00	36.00
☐ CO13	Dikembe Mutombo Chauncey Billups	200.00	90.00
☐ CO14	Keith Van Horn ... Chris Webber	600.00	275.00
☐ CO15	Karl Malone .... Kerry Kittles	300.00	135.00
☐ CO16	Ron Mercer........ Antoine Walker	600.00	275.00
☐ CO17	Chris Webber ..... Karl Malone	150.00	70.00
☐ CO18	Antoine Walker .. Dikembe Mutombo	125.00	55.00
☐ CO19	Kerry Kittles ...... Keith Van Horn	300.00	135.00
☐ CO20	Chauncey Billups Ron Mercer	250.00	110.00
☐ CO21	Antoine Walker .. Chauncey Billups	150.00	70.00
☐ CO22	Dikembe Mutombo Ron Mercer	80.00	36.00
☐ CO23	Keith Van Horn .. Karl Malone	250.00	110.00
☐ CO24	Chris Webber ..... Kerry Kittles	100.00	45.00

1997-98 Stadium Club Hardcourt Heroics

Randomly inserted in series one packs at the rate of one in 12, this 10-card set features color player images of some of the greatest NBA stars printed on a bright, colorful background with uniluster technology. Card backs are numbered with a H prefix.

	MINT	NRMT
COMPLETE SET (10)	40.00	18.00
COMMON CARD (H1-H10)..	1.25	.55
SER.1 STATED ODDS 1:12 HOB/RET		

		MINT	NRMT
☐ H1	Michael Jordan ...	15.00	6.75
☐ H2	Gary Payton	2.00	.90
☐ H3	Charles Barkley ..	2.00	.90
☐ H4	Mitch Richmond ..	1.25	.55
☐ H5	Shawn Kemp.......	4.00	1.80
☐ H6	Anfernee Hardaway ..	5.00	2.20
☐ H7	Vin Baker	2.50	1.10
☐ H8	Shaquille O'Neal .	5.00	2.20
☐ H9	Scottie Pippen....	4.00	1.80
☐ H10	Grant Hill..........	8.00	3.60

1997-98 Stadium Club Hardwood Hopefuls

Randomly inserted in series one packs at the rate of one in 36, this 10-card set features color action photos of the top 1997

NBA Draft Picks printed on rainbow foil cards. Card backs are numbered with a HH prefix.

	MINT	NRMT
COMPLETE SET (10)	80.00	36.00
COMMON CARD (HH1-HH10)	2.00	.90
SEMISTARS......................	2.50	1.10
UNLISTED STARS	4.00	1.80
SER.1 STATED ODDS 1:36 HOB/RET		

		MINT	NRMT
☐ HH1	Brevin Knight	6.00	2.70
☐ HH2	Adonal Foyle........	2.50	1.10
☐ HH3	Keith Van Horn	20.00	9.00
☐ HH4	Tim Duncan	25.00	11.00
☐ HH5	Danny Fortson	4.00	1.80
☐ HH6	Tracy McGrady.....	12.00	5.50
☐ HH7	Tony Battie	4.00	1.80
☐ HH8	Chauncey Billups ...	8.00	3.60
☐ HH9	Austin Croshere	2.00	.90
☐ HH10	Antonio Daniels	5.00	2.20

1997-98 Stadium Club Hoop Screams

Randomly inserted in series one packs at the rate of one in 12, this 10-card set features color action photos of players who display intensity around the rim by their game faces. Card backs are numbered with a HS prefix.

	MINT	NRMT
COMPLETE SET (10)	40.00	18.00
COMMON CARD (HS1-HS10)	.60	.25
SEMISTARS......................	.75	.35
UNLISTED STARS	1.25	.55
SER.1 STATED ODDS 1:12 HOB/RET		

		MINT	NRMT
☐ HS1	Shaquille O'Neal .	5.00	2.20
☐ HS2	Cedric Ceballos....	.60	.25

	MINT	NRMT
☐ HS3 Kevin Garnett	8.00	3.60
☐ HS4 Shawn Kemp	4.00	1.80
☐ HS5 Jerry Stackhouse	1.25	.55
☐ HS6 Grant Hill	8.00	3.60
☐ HS7 Patrick Ewing	1.25	.55
☐ HS8 Marcus Camby	1.25	.55
☐ HS9 Kobe Bryant	10.00	4.50
☐ HS10 Michael Jordan	15.00	6.75

1997-98 Stadium Club Never Compromise

Randomly inserted into series two packs at a rate of one in 36, this 20-card set focuses on players who never compromise in their game play. Card backs carry a "NC" prefix.

	MINT	NRMT
COMPLETE SET (20)	150.00	70.00
COMMON CARD (NC1-NC20)	1.50	.70
SEMISTARS	2.00	.90
UNLISTED STARS	3.00	1.35
SER.2 STATED ODDS 1:36 HOB/RET		

		MINT	NRMT
☐ NC1	Michael Jordan	40.00	18.00
☐ NC2	Karl Malone	5.00	2.20
☐ NC3	Hakeem Olajuwon	6.00	2.70
☐ NC4	Kevin Garnett	20.00	9.00
☐ NC5	Dikembe Mutombo	2.00	.90
☐ NC6	Gary Payton	5.00	2.20
☐ NC7	Grant Hill	20.00	9.00
☐ NC8	Charles Barkley	5.00	2.20
☐ NC9	Shaquille O'Neal	12.00	5.50
☐ NC10	Anfernee Hardaway	12.00	5.50
☐ NC11	Tim Duncan	20.00	9.00
☐ NC12	Keith Van Horn	15.00	6.75
☐ NC13	Tracy McGrady	10.00	4.50
☐ NC14	Tim Thomas	10.00	4.50
☐ NC15	Austin Croshere	1.50	.70
☐ NC16	Maurice Taylor	5.00	2.20
☐ NC17	Chauncey Billups	6.00	2.70
☐ NC18	Adonal Foyle	1.50	.70
☐ NC19	Tony Battie	3.00	1.35
☐ NC20	Bobby Jackson	3.00	1.35

1997-98 Stadium Club Royal Court

Randomly inserted into series two packs at a rate of one in 12, this 20-card set features the elite players in the NBA. The card fronts feature a Royal Court logo against a silver foil

background. Card backs carry a "RC" prefix.

	MINT	NRMT
COMPLETE SET (20)	80.00	36.00
COMMON CARD (RC1-RC20)	.75	.35
SEMISTARS	1.00	.45
UNLISTED STARS	1.50	.70
SER.2 STATED ODDS 1:12 HOB/RET		

		MINT	NRMT
☐ RC1	Scottie Pippen	5.00	2.20
☐ RC2	Karl Malone	2.50	1.10
☐ RC3	Gary Payton	2.50	1.10
☐ RC4	Kobe Bryant	12.00	5.50
☐ RC5	Antoine Walker	8.00	3.60
☐ RC6	Michael Jordan	20.00	9.00
☐ RC7	Shaquille O'Neal	6.00	2.70
☐ RC8	Dikembe Mutombo	1.00	.45
☐ RC9	Hakeem Olajuwon	3.00	1.35
☐ RC10	Grant Hill	10.00	4.50
☐ RC11	Tim Duncan	10.00	4.50
☐ RC12	Keith Van Horn	8.00	3.60
☐ RC13	Chauncey Billups	3.00	1.35
☐ RC14	Antonio Daniels	2.00	.90
☐ RC15	Tony Battie	1.50	.70
☐ RC16	Bobby Jackson	1.50	.70
☐ RC17	Tim Thomas	5.00	2.20
☐ RC18	Adonal Foyle	.75	.35
☐ RC19	Tracy McGrady	5.00	2.20
☐ RC20	Danny Fortson	1.50	.70

1997-98 Stadium Club Triumvirate

Randomly inserted in both series retail packs only at one in 48, these cards feature three NBA teammates that can be fused together. These laser cut cards use Luminous technology. Card backs are numbered with a "T" prefix.

	MINT	NRMT
COMPLETE SET (48)	500.00	220.00
COMPLETE SERIES 1 (24)	200.00	90.00
COMPLETE SERIES 2 (24)	300.00	135.00
COMMON CARD (T1A-T16C)	2.00	.90
SEMISTARS	3.00	1.35
UNLISTED STARS	5.00	2.20
SER.1/2 STATED ODDS 1:48 RETAIL		
COMP.LUM.SET (48)	1400.00	650.00
COMP.LUM.SER.1 (24)	600.00	275.00
COMP.LUM.SER.2 (24)	800.00	350.00
COMMON LUM. (T1A-T16C)	6.00	2.70
*LUM.CARDS: 1.5X TO 3X HI COLUMN		
LUM: SER.1/2 STATED ODDS 1:192 RET		
COMP.ILLUM.SET (48)	2600.00	1150.00
COMP.ILLUM.SER.1 (24)	1100.00	500.00
COMP.ILLUM.SER.2 (24)	1500.00	700.00
COMMON ILLUM. (T1A-T16C)	10.00	4.50
*ILLUM.CARDS: 2.5X TO 5X HI		
ILLUM: SER.1/2 STATED ODDS 1:384 RET		

		MINT	NRMT
☐ T1A	Scottie Pippen	15.00	6.75
☐ T1B	Michael Jordan	60.00	27.00
☐ T1C	Dennis Rodman	20.00	9.00
☐ T2A	Ray Allen	6.00	2.70
☐ T2B	Vin Baker	10.00	4.50
☐ T2C	Glenn Robinson	5.00	2.20
☐ T3A	Juwan Howard	5.00	2.20
☐ T3B	Chris Webber	12.00	5.50
☐ T3C	Rod Strickland	3.00	1.35
☐ T4A	Christian Laettner	3.00	1.35
☐ T4B	Dikembe Mutombo	3.00	1.35
☐ T4C	Steve Smith	3.00	1.35
☐ T5A	Tom Gugliotta	5.00	2.20
☐ T5B	Kevin Garnett	30.00	13.50
☐ T5C	Stephon Marbury	25.00	11.00
☐ T6A	Charles Barkley	8.00	3.60
☐ T6B	Hakeem Olajuwon	10.00	4.50
☐ T6C	Clyde Drexler	6.00	2.70
☐ T7A	John Stockton	5.00	2.20
☐ T7B	Karl Malone	8.00	3.60
☐ T7C	Bryon Russell	2.00	.90
☐ T8A	Larry Johnson	3.00	1.35
☐ T8B	Patrick Ewing	5.00	2.20
☐ T8C	Allan Houston	3.00	1.35
☐ T9A	Tim Hardaway	6.00	2.70
☐ T9B	Michael Jordan	60.00	27.00
☐ T9C	Anfernee Hardaway	20.00	9.00
☐ T10A	Glen Rice	5.00	2.20
☐ T10B	Scottie Pippen	15.00	6.75
☐ T10C	Grant Hill	30.00	13.50
☐ T11A	Dikembe Mutombo	3.00	1.35
☐ T11B	Patrick Ewing	5.00	2.20
☐ T11C	Alonzo Mourning	5.00	2.20
☐ T12A	Ron Mercer	20.00	9.00
☐ T12B	Keith Van Horn	25.00	11.00
☐ T12C	Tracy McGrady	15.00	6.75
☐ T13A	Gary Payton	8.00	3.60
☐ T13B	John Stockton	5.00	2.20
☐ T13C	Stephon Marbury	25.00	11.00
☐ T14A	Karl Malone	8.00	3.60
☐ T14B	Charles Barkley	8.00	3.60
☐ T14C	Kevin Garnett	30.00	13.50
☐ T15A	David Robinson	8.00	3.60
☐ T15B	Hakeem Olajuwon	10.00	4.50
☐ T15C	Shaquille O'Neal	20.00	9.00
☐ T16A	Antonio Daniels	6.00	2.70
☐ T16B	Tim Duncan	30.00	13.50
☐ T16C	Adonal Foyle	5.00	2.20

1983-84 Star

This set of 276 standard-size cards was issued in four series during the first six months of 1984. Several teams in the first series (1-100) are difficult to obtain due to extensive miscuts (all of which, according to the company, were destroyed) in the initial production process. The team sets were issued in

clear sealed bags. Many of the team bags were distributed to hobby dealers through a small group of Star Co. master distributors. According to Star Company's original sales materials and order forms, reportedly 5,000 team bags were printed for each team although quality control problems with the early sets apparently reduced that number considerably. The retail price per bag was $2.50 to $5 for most of the teams. Color borders around the fronts and color printing on the backs correspond to team colors. Cards are numbered according to team order: Philadelphia 76ers (1-12), Los Angeles Lakers (13-25), Boston Celtics (26-37), Milwaukee Bucks (38-48), Dallas Mavericks (49-60), New York Knicks (61-72), Houston Rockets (73-84), Detroit Pistons (85-96), Portland Trail Blazers (97-108), Phoenix Suns (109-120), San Diego Clippers (121-132), Utah Jazz (133-144), New Jersey Nets (145-156), Indiana Pacers (157-168), Chicago Bulls (169-180), Denver Nuggets (181-192), Seattle Supersonics (193-203), Washington Bullets (204-215), Kansas City Kings (216-227), Cleveland Cavaliers (228-240), San Antonio Spurs (241-251), Golden State Warriors (252-262), and Atlanta Hawks (264-275). Extended Rookie Cards include Mark Aguirre, Danny Ainge, Rolando Blackman, Tom Chambers, Clyde Drexler, Dale Ellis, Derek Harper, Larry Nance, Rickey Pierce, Isiah Thomas, Dominique Wilkins, Buck Williams and James Worthy. A promotional card of Sidney Moncrief was produced in limited quantities, but it was numbered 39 rather than 38 as it was in the regular set. There is typically a slight discount on sales of opened team bags.

	NRMT-MT	EXC
COMPLETE SET (275)	1800.00	800.00
COMP.76ERS (1-12)	100.00	45.00
COMP.LAKERS (13-25)	150.00	70.00
COMP.CELTICS (26-37)	500.00	220.00
COMP.BUCKS (38-48)	50.00	22.00
COMP.MAVS (49-60)	325.00	145.00
COMP.KNICKS (61-72)	25.00	11.00
COMP.ROCKETS (73-84) ..	20.00	9.00
COMP.PISTONS (85-96) ...	125.00	55.00
COMP.BLAZERS (97-108) .	225.00	100.00
COMP.SUNS (109-120)	40.00	18.00
COMP.CLIPPERS (121-132)	40.00	18.00
COMP.JAZZ (133-144)........	20.00	9.00
COMP.NETS (145-156)	20.00	9.00
COMP.PACERS (157-168) ..	18.00	8.00
COMP.BULLS (169-180)	25.00	11.00
COMP.NUGGETS (181-192)	20.00	9.00
COMP.SONICS (193-203) ..	35.00	16.00
COMP.BULLETS (204-215) .	25.00	11.00
COMP.KINGS (216-227)	20.00	9.00
COMP.CAVS (228-240)	18.00	8.00
COMP.SPURS (241-251)	25.00	11.00
COMP.WARRIORS (252-262)	20.00	9.00
COMP.HAWKS (263-275)	180.00	80.00
COMMON SP (1-25/38-48) ..	4.00	1.80
COMMON SP (26-37)...........	8.00	3.60
COMMON SP (49-60) !	18.00	8.00
COMMON CARD (61-275)	2.00	.90
SEMISTARS	4.00	1.80
UNLISTED STARS	8.00	3.60

ABOVE PRICES ARE FOR SEALED BAGS
*OPENED TEAM SETS: .75X to 1.0X
CONDITION SENSITIVE SET

☐ 1	Julius Erving SP	65.00	29.00
☐ 2	Maurice Cheeks SP	10.00	4.50
☐ 3	Franklin Edwards SP ..	4.00	1.80
☐ 4	Marc Iavaroni SP........	4.00	1.80
☐ 5	Clemon Johnson SP ...	4.00	1.80
☐ 6	Bobby Jones SP	10.00	4.50
☐ 7	Moses Malone SP	25.00	11.00
☐ 8	Leo Rautins SP	4.00	1.80
☐ 9	Clint Richardson SP	4.00	1.80
☐ 10	Sedale Threatt SP	12.00	5.50
☐ 11	Andrew Toney SP	10.00	4.50
☐ 12	Sam Williams SP.........	4.00	1.80
☐ 13	Magic Johnson SP	70.00	32.00
☐ 14	K.Abdul-Jabbar SP	40.00	18.00
☐ 15	Michael Cooper SP	10.00	4.50
☐ 16	Calvin Garrett SP	4.00	1.80
☐ 17	Mitch Kupchak SP	6.00	2.70
☐ 18	Bob McAdoo SP	10.00	4.50
☐ 19	Mike McGee SP	4.00	1.80
☐ 20	Swen Nater SP	6.00	2.70
☐ 21	Kurt Rambis SP	8.00	3.60
☐ 22	Byron Scott SP	25.00	11.00
☐ 23	Larry Spriggs SP	4.00	1.80
☐ 24	Jamaal Wilkes SP	8.00	3.60
☐ 25	James Worthy SP.........	45.00	20.00
☐ 26	Larry Bird SP	350.00	160.00
☐ 27	Danny Ainge SP	45.00	20.00
☐ 28	Quinn Buckner SP	10.00	4.50
☐ 29	M.L. Carr SP	10.00	4.50
☐ 30	Carlos Clark SP	8.00	3.60
☐ 31	Gerald Henderson SP ..	8.00	3.60
☐ 32	Dennis Johnson SP	18.00	8.00
☐ 33	Cedric Maxwell SP	8.00	3.60
☐ 34	Kevin McHale SP.........	55.00	25.00
☐ 35	Robert Parish SP	45.00	20.00
☐ 36	Scott Wedman SP	10.00	4.50
☐ 37	Greg Kite SP	8.00	3.60
☐ 38	Sidney Moncrief SP......	15.00	6.75
☐ 39A	Sidney Moncrief	30.00	13.50
	(Promotional card)		
☐ 39B	Nate Archibald SP......	15.00	6.75
☐ 40	Randy Breuer SP	4.00	1.80
☐ 41	Junior Bridgeman SP ..	5.00	2.20
☐ 42	Harvey Catchings SP ..	4.00	1.80
☐ 43	Kevin Grevey SP	4.00	1.80
☐ 44	Marques Johnson SP	10.00	4.50
☐ 45	Bob Lanier SP	20.00	9.00
☐ 46	Alton Lister SP	4.00	1.80
☐ 47	Paul Mokeski SP	4.00	1.80
☐ 48	Paul Pressey SP	5.00	2.20
☐ 49	Mark Aguirre SP	40.00	18.00
☐ 50	Rolando Blackman SP	40.00	18.00
☐ 51	Pat Cummings SP	18.00	8.00
☐ 52	Brad Davis SP	25.00	11.00
☐ 53	Dale Ellis SP	40.00	18.00
☐ 54	Bill Garnett SP	18.00	8.00
☐ 55	Derek Harper SP	60.00	27.00
☐ 56	Kurt Nimphius SP	18.00	8.00
☐ 57	Jim Spanarkel SP	18.00	8.00
☐ 58	Elston Turner SP	18.00	8.00
☐ 59	Jay Vincent SP	18.00	8.00
☐ 60	Mark West SP	20.00	9.00
☐ 61	Bernard King	8.00	3.60
☐ 62	Bill Cartwright	4.00	1.80
☐ 63	Len Elmore	3.00	1.35
☐ 64	Eric Fernsten	2.00	.90
☐ 65	Ernie Grunfeld	3.00	1.35
☐ 66	Louis Orr	2.00	.90
☐ 67	Leonard Robinson	2.00	.90
☐ 68	Rory Sparrow	2.00	.90
☐ 69	Trent Tucker	2.00	.90
☐ 70	Darrell Walker	3.00	1.35
☐ 71	Marvin Webster	3.00	1.35
☐ 72	Ray Williams	2.00	.90
☐ 73	Ralph Sampson	4.00	1.80
☐ 74	James Bailey	2.00	.90
☐ 75	Phil Ford	3.00	1.35
☐ 76	Elvin Hayes	10.00	4.50
☐ 77	Caldwell Jones	3.00	1.35
☐ 78	Major Jones	2.00	.90
☐ 79	Allen Leavell	2.00	.90
☐ 80	Lewis Lloyd	2.00	.90
☐ 81	Rodney McCray..........	2.00	.90
☐ 82	Robert Reid	2.00	.90
☐ 83	Terry Teagle	2.00	.90
☐ 84	Wally Walker	2.00	.90
☐ 85	Kelly Tripucka	3.00	1.35
☐ 86	Kent Benson	3.00	1.35
☐ 87	Earl Cureton	2.00	.90
☐ 88	Lionel Hollins	2.00	.90
☐ 89	Vinnie Johnson	3.00	1.35
☐ 90	Bill Laimbeer	4.00	1.80
☐ 91	Cliff Levingston	2.00	.90
☐ 92	John Long	2.00	.90
☐ 93	David Thirdkill	2.00	.90
☐ 94	Isiah Thomas.............	100.00	45.00
☐ 95	Ray Tolbert	2.00	.90
☐ 96	Terry Tyler	2.00	.90
☐ 97	Jim Paxson	3.00	1.35
☐ 98	Kenny Carr	2.00	.90
☐ 99	Wayne Cooper............	2.00	.90
☐ 100	Clyde Drexler	200.00	90.00
☐ 101	Jeff Lamp	2.00	.90
☐ 102	Lafayette Lever	3.00	1.35
☐ 103	Calvin Natt	2.00	.90
☐ 104	Audie Norris	2.00	.90
☐ 105	Tom Piotrowski	2.00	.90
☐ 106	Mychal Thompson......	3.00	1.35
☐ 107	Darnell Valentine	3.00	1.35
☐ 108	Pete Verhoeven	2.00	.90
☐ 109	Walter Davis	4.00	1.80
☐ 110	Alvan Adams	3.00	1.35
☐ 111	James Edwards	3.00	1.35
☐ 112	Rod Foster	2.00	.90
☐ 113	Maurice Lucas	3.00	1.35
☐ 114	Kyle Macy	3.00	1.35
☐ 115	Larry Nance..............	25.00	11.00
☐ 116	Charles Pittman	2.00	.90
☐ 117	Rick Robey	3.00	1.35
☐ 118	Mike Sanders	2.00	.90
☐ 119	Alvin Scott	2.00	.90
☐ 120	Paul Westphal	4.00	1.80
☐ 121	Bill Walton	18.00	8.00
☐ 122	Michael Brooks	2.00	.90
☐ 123	Terry Cummings	10.00	4.50
☐ 124	James Donaldson	2.00	1.35
☐ 125	Craig Hodges............	4.00	1.80
☐ 126	Greg Kelser	3.00	1.35
☐ 127	Hank McDowell	2.00	.90
☐ 128	Billy McKinney..........	2.00	.90
☐ 129	Norm Nixon..............	3.00	1.35

#	Player	NRMT-MT	EXC
130	Ricky Pierce UER (Misspelled Rickey on both sides)	10.00	4.50
131	Derek Smith	3.00	1.35
132	Jerome Whitehead	2.00	.90
133	Adrian Dantley	8.00	3.60
134	Mitchell Anderson	2.00	.90
135	Thurl Bailey	3.00	1.35
136	Tom Boswell	2.00	.90
137	John Drew	2.00	.90
138	Mark Eaton	4.00	1.80
139	Jerry Eaves	2.00	.90
140	Rickey Green	3.00	1.35
141	Darrell Griffith	3.00	1.35
142	Bobby Hansen	2.00	.90
143	Rich Kelley	2.00	.90
144	Jeff Wilkins	2.00	.90
145	Buck Williams	15.00	6.75
146	Otis Birdsong	3.00	1.35
147	Darwin Cook	2.00	.90
148	Darryl Dawkins	4.00	1.80
149	Mike Gminski	3.00	1.35
150	Reggie Johnson	2.00	.90
151	Albert King	2.00	.90
152	Mike O'Koren	3.00	1.35
153	Kelvin Ransey	2.00	.90
154	M.Ray Richardson	2.00	.90
155	Clarence Walker	2.00	.90
156	Bill Willoughby	3.00	1.35
157	Steve Stipanovich	3.00	1.35
158	Butch Carter	2.00	.90
159	Edwin Leroy Combs	2.00	.90
160	George L. Johnson	2.00	.90
161	Clark Kellogg	4.00	1.80
162	Sidney Lowe	3.00	1.35
163	Kevin McKenna	2.00	.90
164	Jerry Sichting	2.00	.90
165	Brook Steppe	2.00	.90
166	Jimmy Thomas	2.00	.90
167	Granville Waiters	2.00	.90
168	Herb Williams	3.00	1.35
169	Dave Corzine	3.00	1.35
170	Wallace Bryant	2.00	.90
171	Quintin Dailey	2.00	.90
172	Sidney Green	3.00	1.35
173	David Greenwood	3.00	1.35
174	Rod Higgins	2.00	.90
175	Clarence Johnson	2.00	.90
176	Ronnie Lester	2.00	.90
177	Jawann Oldham	2.00	.90
178	Ennis Whatley	3.00	1.35
179	Mitchell Wiggins	2.00	.90
180	Orlando Woolridge	4.00	1.80
181	Kiki Vandeweghe	4.00	1.80
182	Richard Anderson	2.00	.90
183	Howard Carter	2.00	.90
184	T.R. Dunn	2.00	.90
185	Keith Edmonson	2.00	.90
186	Alex English	8.00	3.60
187	Mike Evans	2.00	.90
188	Bill Hanzlik	2.00	.90
189	Dan Issel	10.00	4.50
190	Anthony Roberts	2.00	.90
191	Danny Schayes	3.00	1.35
192	Rob Williams	2.00	.90
193	Jack Sikma	3.00	1.35
194	Fred Brown	3.00	1.35
195	Tom Chambers	15.00	6.75
196	Steve Hawes	2.00	.90
197	Steve Hayes	2.00	.90
198	Reggie King	2.00	.90
199	Scooter McCray	3.00	1.35
200	Jon Sundvold	3.00	1.35
201	Danny Vranes	2.00	.90
202	Gus Williams	3.00	1.35
203	Al Wood	2.00	.90
204	Jeff Ruland	3.00	1.35
205	Greg Ballard	2.00	.90
206	Charles Davis	2.00	.90
207	Darren Daye	2.00	.90
208	Michael Gibson	2.00	.90
209	Frank Johnson	3.00	1.35
210	Joe Kopicki	2.00	.90
211	Rick Mahorn	3.00	1.35
212	Jeff Malone	10.00	4.50
213	Tom McMillen	3.00	1.35
214	Ricky Sobers	2.00	.90
215	Bryan Warrick	2.00	.90
216	Billy Knight	3.00	1.35
217	Don Buse	3.00	1.35
218	Larry Drew	3.00	1.35
219	Eddie Johnson	4.00	1.80
220	Joe Meriweather	2.00	.90
221	Larry Micheaux	2.00	.90
222	Ed Nealy	2.00	.90
223	Mark Olberding	2.00	.90
224	Dave Robisch	3.00	1.35
225	Reggie Theus	3.00	1.35
226	LaSalle Thompson	3.00	1.35
227	Mike Woodson	2.00	.90
228	World B. Free	3.00	1.35
229	John Bagley	2.00	.90
230	Jeff Cook	2.00	.90
231	Geoff Crompton	2.00	.90
232	John Garris	2.00	.90
233	Stewart Granger	2.00	.90
234	Roy Hinson	2.00	.90
235	Phil Hubbard	3.00	1.35
236	Geoff Huston	2.00	.90
237	Ben Poquette	2.00	.90
238	Cliff Robinson	2.00	.90
239	Lonnie Shelton	3.00	1.35
240	Paul Thompson	2.00	.90
241	George Gervin	15.00	6.75
242	Gene Banks	3.00	1.35
243	Ron Brewer	2.00	.90
244	Artis Gilmore	4.00	1.80
245	Edgar Jones	2.00	.90
246	John Lucas	4.00	1.80
247A	Mike Mitchell ERR.. (Photo actually Mark McNamara)	3.00	1.35
247B	Mike Mitchell COR	3.00	1.35
248A	Mark McNamara ERR (Photo actually Mike Mitchell)	3.00	1.35
248B	Mark McNamara COR	4.00	1.80
249	Johnny Moore	2.00	.90
250	John Paxson	10.00	4.50
251	Fred Roberts	2.00	.90
252	Joe Barry Carroll	3.00	1.35
253	Mike Bratz	2.00	.90
254	Don Collins	2.00	.90
255	Lester Conner	2.00	.90
256	Chris Engler	2.00	.90
257	Sleepy Floyd	4.00	1.80
258	Wallace Johnson	2.00	.90
259	Pace Mannion	2.00	.90
260	Purvis Short	2.00	.90
261	Larry Smith	3.00	1.35
262	Darren Tillis	2.00	.90
263	Dominique Wilkins	125.00	55.00
264	Rickey Brown	2.00	.90
265	Johnny Davis	2.00	.90
266	Mike Glenn	3.00	1.35
267	Scott Hastings	3.00	1.35
268	Eddie Johnson	2.00	.90
269	Mark Landsberger	2.00	.90
270	Billy Paultz	2.00	.90
271	Doc Rivers	12.00	5.50
272	Tree Rollins	3.00	1.35
273	Dan Roundfield	3.00	1.35
274	Sly Williams	2.00	.90
275	Randy Wittman	3.00	1.35

1984-85 Star

This set of 288 standard-size cards was issued in three series during the first five months of 1985 by Star Company. The set is comprised of team sets that were issued in clear sealed bags. Many of these team bags were distributed to hobby dealers through a small group of Star Company master distributors and retailed for $2.50-$5.

RALPH SAMPSON
Forward-Houston Rockets

According to Star Company's original sales materials and order forms, reportedly 3,000 team bags were printed for each team. The cards have a colored border around the fronts of the cards according to the team with corresponding color printing on the backs. Cards are organized numerically by team, i.e., Boston Celtics (1-12), Los Angeles Clippers (13-24), New York Knicks (25-37), Phoenix Suns (38-51), Indiana Pacers (52-63), San Antonio Spurs (64-75), Atlanta Hawks (76-87), New Jersey Nets (88-100), Chicago Bulls (101-112), Seattle Supersonics (113-124), Milwaukee Bucks (125-136), Denver Nuggets (137-148), Golden State Warriors (149-160), Portland Trail Blazers (161-171), Los Angeles Lakers (172-184), Washington Bullets (185-194), Philadelphia 76ers (201-212), Cleveland Cavaliers (213-224), Utah Jazz (225-236), Houston Rockets (237-249), Dallas Mavericks (250-260), Detroit Pistons (261-269) and Sacramento Kings (270-280). The set also features a special subset (195-200) honoring Gold Medal-winning players from the 1984 Olympic basketball competition as well as a subset of NBA specials (281-288). Michael Jordan's Extended Rookie Card appears in this set. Other Extended Rookie include Charles Barkley, Craig Ehlo, Hakeem Olajuwon, Alvin Robertson, Sam Perkins, John Stockton and Otis Thorpe. There is typically a slight discount on sales of opened team bags.

	NRMT-MT	EXC
COMPLETE SET (288)	5200.00	2300.00
COMP.CELTICS (1-12)	250.00	110.00
COMP.CLIPPERS (13-24)	20.00	9.00

COMP.KNICKS (25-37)	20.00	9.00
COMP.SUNS (38-51)	25.00	11.00
COMP.PACERS (52-63)	50.00	22.00
COMP.SPURS (64-75)	25.00	11.00
COMP.HAWKS (76-87)	80.00	36.00
COMP.NETS (88-100)	18.00	8.00
COMP.BULLS (101-112)	3100.00	1400.00
COMP.SONICS (113-124)	20.00	9.00
COMP.BUCKS (125-136)	18.00	8.00
COMP.NUGGETS (137-148)	20.00	9.00
COMP.WARRIORS (149-160)	18.00	8.00
COMP.BLAZERS (161-171)	110.00	50.00
COMP.LAKERS (172-184)	130.00	57.50
COMP.BULLETS (185-194)	18.00	8.00
COMP.SC (195-200/281-288)	900.00	400.00
COMP.76ERS (201-212)	275.00	125.00
COMP.CAVS (213-224)	18.00	8.00
COMP.JAZZ (225-236)	200.00	90.00
COMP.ROCKETS (237-249)	350.00	160.00
COMP.MAVS (250-260) !	40.00	18.00
COMP.PISTONS (261-269)	50.00	22.00
COMP.KINGS (270-280)	25.00	11.00
COMMON CARD (1-51/64-288)	2.00	.90
COMMON SP (52-63)	5.00	2.20
SEMISTARS	4.00	1.80
UNLISTED STARS	6.00	2.70

ABOVE PRICES ARE FOR SEALED BAGS
*OPENED TEAM SETS: .75X to 1.0X
CONDITION SENSITIVE SET
BEWARE JORDAN COUNTERFEITS

☐ 1	Larry Bird	175.00	80.00
☐ 2	Danny Ainge	12.00	5.50
☐ 3	Quinn Buckner	3.00	1.35
☐ 4	Rick Carlisle	2.00	.90
☐ 5	M.L. Carr	3.00	1.35
☐ 6	Dennis Johnson	4.00	1.80
☐ 7	Greg Kite	2.00	.90
☐ 8	Cedric Maxwell	3.00	1.35
☐ 9	Kevin McHale	15.00	6.75
☐ 10	Robert Parish	12.00	5.50
☐ 11	Scott Wedman	2.00	.90
☐ 12	Larry Bird	90.00	40.00
	1983-84 NBA MVP		
☐ 13	Marques Johnson	3.00	1.35
☐ 14	Junior Bridgeman	2.00	.90
☐ 15	Michael Cage	3.00	1.35
☐ 16	Harvey Catchings	2.00	.90
☐ 17	James Donaldson	2.00	.90
☐ 18	Lancaster Gordon	2.00	.90
☐ 19	Jay Murphy	2.00	.90
☐ 20	Norm Nixon	3.00	1.35
☐ 21	Derek Smith	2.00	.90
☐ 22	Bill Walton	15.00	6.75
☐ 23	Bryan Warrick	2.00	.90
☐ 24	Rory White	2.00	.90
☐ 25	Bernard King	6.00	2.70
☐ 26	James Bailey	2.00	.90
☐ 27	Ken Bannister	2.00	.90
☐ 28	Butch Carter	2.00	.90
☐ 29	Bill Cartwright	3.00	1.35
☐ 30	Pat Cummings	2.00	.90
☐ 31	Ernie Grunfeld	3.00	1.35
☐ 32	Louis Orr	2.00	.90
☐ 33	Leonard Robinson	3.00	1.35
☐ 34	Rory Sparrow	2.00	.90
☐ 35	Trent Tucker	2.00	.90
☐ 36	Darrell Walker	2.00	.90
☐ 37	Eddie Lee Wilkins	2.00	.90
☐ 38	Alvan Adams	3.00	1.35
☐ 39	Walter Davis	4.00	1.80
☐ 40	James Edwards	3.00	1.35
☐ 41	Rod Foster	2.00	.90
☐ 42	Michael Holton	2.00	.90
☐ 43	Jay Humphries	3.00	1.35
☐ 44	Charles Jones	2.00	.90
☐ 45	Maurice Lucas	3.00	1.35
☐ 46	Kyle Macy	3.00	1.35
☐ 47	Larry Nance	10.00	4.50
☐ 48	Charles Pittman	2.00	.90
☐ 49	Rick Robey	3.00	1.35
☐ 50	Mike Sanders	2.00	.90
☐ 51	Alvin Scott	2.00	.90
☐ 52	Clark Kellogg SP	6.00	2.70
☐ 53	Tony Brown SP	5.00	2.20
☐ 54	Devin Durrant SP	5.00	2.20
☐ 55	Vern Fleming SP	6.00	2.70
☐ 56	Bill Garnett	5.00	2.20
☐ 57	Stuart Gray SP UER	5.00	2.20
	(Photo actually Tony Brown)		
☐ 58	Jerry Sichting SP	5.00	2.20
☐ 59	Terence Stansbury SP	5.00	2.20
☐ 60	Steve Stipanovich SP	5.00	2.20
☐ 61	Jimmy Thomas SP	5.00	2.20
☐ 62	Granville Waiters SP	5.00	2.20
☐ 63	Herb Williams SP	5.00	2.20
☐ 64	Artis Gilmore	4.00	1.80
☐ 65	Gene Banks	2.00	.90
☐ 66	Ron Brewer	2.00	.90
☐ 67	George Gervin	15.00	6.75
☐ 68	Edgar Jones	2.00	.90
☐ 69	Ozell Jones	2.00	.90
☐ 70	Mark McNamara	2.00	.90
☐ 71	Mike Mitchell	2.00	.90
☐ 72	Johnny Moore	2.00	.90
☐ 73	John Paxson	3.00	1.35
☐ 74	Fred Roberts	2.00	.90
☐ 75	Alvin Robertson	4.00	1.80
☐ 76	Dominique Wilkins	50.00	22.00
☐ 77	Rickey Brown	2.00	.90
☐ 78	Antoine Carr	3.00	1.35
☐ 79	Mike Glenn	2.00	.90
☐ 80	Scott Hastings	2.00	.90
☐ 81	Eddie Johnson	2.00	.90
☐ 82	Cliff Levingston	2.00	.90
☐ 83	Leo Rautins	2.00	.90
☐ 84	Doc Rivers	3.00	1.35
☐ 85	Tree Rollins	3.00	1.35
☐ 86	Randy Wittman	2.00	.90
☐ 87	Sly Williams	2.00	.90
☐ 88	Darryl Dawkins	4.00	1.80
☐ 89	Otis Birdsong	3.00	1.35
☐ 90	Darwin Cook	2.00	.90
☐ 91	Mike Gminski	3.00	1.35
☐ 92	George L. Johnson	2.00	.90
☐ 93	Albert King	2.00	.90
☐ 94	Mike O'Koren	2.00	.90
☐ 95	Kelvin Ransey	2.00	.90
☐ 96	M.R. Richardson	2.00	.90
☐ 97	Wayne Sappleton	2.00	.90
☐ 98	Jeff Turner	2.00	.90
☐ 99	Buck Williams	4.00	1.80
☐ 100	Michael Wilson	2.00	.90
☐ 101	Michael Jordan	3000.00	1350.00
☐ 102	Dave Corzine	2.00	.90
☐ 103	Quintin Dailey	2.00	.90
☐ 104	Sidney Green	2.00	.90
☐ 105	David Greenwood	3.00	1.35
☐ 106	Rod Higgins	2.00	.90
☐ 107	Steve Johnson	2.00	.90
☐ 108	Caldwell Jones	3.00	1.35
☐ 109	Wes Matthews	2.00	.90
☐ 110	Jawann Oldham	2.00	.90
☐ 111	Ennis Whatley	2.00	.90
☐ 112	Orlando Woolridge	3.00	1.35
☐ 113	Tom Chambers	4.00	1.80
☐ 114	Cory Blackwell	2.00	.90
☐ 115	Frank Brickowski	3.00	1.35
☐ 116	Gerald Henderson	2.00	.90
☐ 117	Reggie King	2.00	.90
☐ 118	Tim McCormick	2.00	.90
☐ 119	John Schweitz	2.00	.90
☐ 120	Jack Sikma	3.00	1.35
☐ 121	Ricky Sobers	2.00	.90
☐ 122	Jon Sundvold	2.00	.90
☐ 123	Danny Vranes	2.00	.90
☐ 124	Al Wood	2.00	.90
☐ 125	Terry Cummings UER	4.00	1.80
	(Robert Cummings on card back)		
☐ 126	Randy Breuer	2.00	.90
☐ 127	Charles Davis	2.00	.90
☐ 128	Mike Dunleavy	3.00	1.35
☐ 129	Kenny Fields	2.00	.90
☐ 130	Kevin Grevey	3.00	1.35
☐ 131	Craig Hodges	2.00	.90
☐ 132	Alton Lister	2.00	.90
☐ 133	Larry Micheaux	2.00	.90
☐ 134	Paul Mokeski	2.00	.90
☐ 135	Sidney Moncrief	4.00	1.80
☐ 136	Paul Pressey	2.00	.90
☐ 137	Alex English	6.00	2.70
☐ 138	Wayne Cooper	2.00	.90
☐ 139	T.R. Dunn	2.00	.90
☐ 140	Mike Evans	2.00	.90
☐ 141	Bill Hanzlik	2.00	.90
☐ 142	Dan Issel	8.00	3.60
☐ 143	Joe Kopicki	2.00	.90
☐ 144	Lafayette Lever	3.00	1.35
☐ 145	Calvin Natt	2.00	.90
☐ 146	Danny Schayes	3.00	1.35
☐ 147	Elston Turner	2.00	.90
☐ 148	Willie White	2.00	.90
☐ 149	Purvis Short	2.00	.90
☐ 150	Chuck Aleksinas	2.00	.90
☐ 151	Mike Bratz	2.00	.90
☐ 152	Steve Burtt	2.00	.90
☐ 153	Lester Conner	2.00	.90
☐ 154	Sleepy Floyd	3.00	1.35
☐ 155	Mickey Johnson	2.00	.90
☐ 156	Gary Plummer	2.00	.90
☐ 157	Larry Smith	3.00	1.35
☐ 158	Peter Thibeaux	2.00	.90
☐ 159	Jerome Whitehead	2.00	.90
☐ 160	Othell Wilson	2.00	.90
☐ 161	Kiki Vandeweghe	3.00	1.35
☐ 162	Sam Bowie	4.00	1.80
☐ 163	Kenny Carr	2.00	.90
☐ 164	Steve Colter	2.00	.90
☐ 165	Clyde Drexler	100.00	45.00
☐ 166	Audie Norris	2.00	.90
☐ 167	Jim Paxson	3.00	1.35
☐ 168	Tom Scheffler	2.00	.90
☐ 169	Bernard Thompson	2.00	.90
☐ 170	Mychal Thompson	3.00	1.35
☐ 171	Darnell Valentine	2.00	.90
☐ 172	Magic Johnson	80.00	36.00
☐ 173	Kareem Abdul-Jabbar	40.00	18.00
☐ 174	Michael Cooper	3.00	1.35
☐ 175	Earl Jones	2.00	.90
☐ 176	Mitch Kupchak	2.00	.90
☐ 177	Ronnie Lester	2.00	.90
☐ 178	Bob McAdoo	4.00	1.80
☐ 179	Mike McGee	2.00	.90
☐ 180	Kurt Rambis	2.00	.90
☐ 181	Byron Scott	6.00	2.70
☐ 182	Larry Spriggs	2.00	.90
☐ 183	Jamaal Wilkes	3.00	1.35
☐ 184	James Worthy	12.00	5.50
☐ 185	Gus Williams	3.00	1.35
☐ 186	Greg Ballard	2.00	.90
☐ 187	Dudley Bradley	2.00	.90
☐ 188	Darren Daye	2.00	.90
☐ 189	Frank Johnson	2.00	.90
☐ 190	Charles Jones	2.00	.90
☐ 191	Rick Mahorn	2.00	.90
☐ 192	Jeff Malone	3.00	1.35
☐ 193	Tom McMillen	2.00	.90
☐ 194	Jeff Ruland	2.00	.90
☐ 195	Michael Jordan OLY	450.00	200.00
☐ 196	Vern Fleming OLY	3.00	1.35
☐ 197	Sam Perkins OLY	6.00	2.70
☐ 198	Alvin Robertson OLY	3.00	1.35
☐ 199	Jeff Turner OLY	2.00	.90
☐ 200	Leon Wood OLY	2.00	.90
☐ 201	Moses Malone	12.00	5.50
☐ 202	Charles Barkley	235.00	105.00
☐ 203	Maurice Cheeks	4.00	1.80
☐ 204	Julius Erving	40.00	18.00
☐ 205	Clemon Johnson	2.00	.90
☐ 206	George L. Johnson	2.00	.90
☐ 207	Bobby Jones	4.00	1.80
☐ 208	Clint Richardson	2.00	.90
☐ 209	Sedale Threatt	3.00	1.35
☐ 210	Andrew Toney	2.00	.90
☐ 211	Sam Williams	2.00	.90
☐ 212	Leon Wood	2.00	.90
☐ 213	Mel Turpin	2.00	.90
☐ 214	Ron Anderson	2.00	.90
☐ 215	John Bagley	2.00	.90
☐ 216	Johnny Davis	2.00	.90
☐ 217	World B. Free	3.00	1.35
☐ 218	Roy Hinson	2.00	.90
☐ 219	Phil Hubbard	2.00	.90
☐ 220	Edgar Jones	2.00	.90
☐ 221	Ben Poquette	2.00	.90
☐ 222	Lonnie Shelton	2.00	.90

☐ 223	Mark West	2.00	.90
☐ 224	Kevin Williams	2.00	.90
☐ 225	Mark Eaton	3.00	1.35
☐ 226	Mitchell Anderson	2.00	.90
☐ 227	Thurl Bailey	3.00	1.35
☐ 228	Adrian Dantley	6.00	2.70
☐ 229	Rickey Green	3.00	1.35
☐ 230	Darrell Griffith	3.00	1.35
☐ 231	Rich Kelley	2.00	.90
☐ 232	Pace Mannion	2.00	.90
☐ 233	Billy Paultz	3.00	1.35
☐ 234	Fred Roberts	2.00	.90
☐ 235	John Stockton	175.00	80.00
☐ 236	Jeff Wilkins	2.00	.90
☐ 237	Hakeem Olajuwon	325.00	145.00
☐ 238	Craig Ehlo	15.00	6.75
☐ 239	Lionel Hollins	2.00	.90
☐ 240	Allen Leavell	2.00	.90
☐ 241	Lewis Lloyd	2.00	.90
☐ 242	John Lucas	3.00	1.35
☐ 243	Rodney McCray	3.00	1.35
☐ 244	Hank McDowell	2.00	.90
☐ 245	Larry Micheaux	2.00	.90
☐ 246	Jim Peterson	2.00	.90
☐ 247	Robert Reid	2.00	.90
☐ 248	Ralph Sampson	3.00	1.35
☐ 249	Mitchell Wiggins	2.00	.90
☐ 250	Mark Aguirre	4.00	1.80
☐ 251	Rolando Blackman	3.00	1.35
☐ 252	Wallace Bryant	2.00	.90
☐ 253	Brad Davis	3.00	1.35
☐ 254	Dale Ellis	3.00	1.35
☐ 255	Derek Harper	8.00	3.60
☐ 256	Kurt Nimphius	2.00	.90
☐ 257	Sam Perkins	12.00	5.50
☐ 258	Charlie Sitton	2.00	.90
☐ 259	Tom Sluby	2.00	.90
☐ 260	Jay Vincent	2.00	.90
☐ 261	Isiah Thomas	35.00	16.00
☐ 262	Kent Benson	3.00	1.35
☐ 263	Earl Cureton	2.00	.90
☐ 264	Vinnie Johnson	3.00	1.35
☐ 265	Bill Laimbeer	4.00	1.80
☐ 266	John Long	2.00	.90
☐ 267	Dan Roundfield	3.00	1.35
☐ 268	Kelly Tripucka	3.00	1.35
☐ 269	Terry Tyler	2.00	.90
☐ 270	Reggie Theus	3.00	1.35
☐ 271	Don Buse	2.00	.90
☐ 272	Larry Drew	3.00	1.35
☐ 273	Eddie Johnson	2.00	.90
☐ 274	Billy Knight	3.00	1.35
☐ 275	Joe Meriwether	2.00	.90
☐ 276	Mark Olberding	2.00	.90
☐ 277	LaSalle Thompson	2.00	.90
☐ 278	Otis Thorpe	15.00	6.75
☐ 279	Pete Verhoeven	2.00	.90
☐ 280	Mike Woodson	2.00	.90
☐ 281	Julius Erving	20.00	9.00
☐ 282	Kareem Abdul-Jabbar	20.00	9.00
☐ 283	Dan Issel	6.00	2.70
☐ 284	Bernard King	3.00	1.35
☐ 285	Moses Malone	8.00	3.60
☐ 286	Mark Eaton	3.00	1.35
☐ 287	Isiah Thomas	15.00	6.75
☐ 288	Michael Jordan	450.00	200.00

1984-85 Star Court Kings 5x7

This over-sized 50-card set was issued as two series of 25. Cards measure approximately 5" by 7" and have a yellow (first series 1-25) or blue (second series 26-50) colored border around the fronts of the cards and blue and yellow printing on the backs. These large cards feature the Star '85 logo on the front. The set features early pro-

fessional cards of Charles Barkley, Michael Jordan and Hakeem Olajuwon.

	NRMT-MT	EXC
COMPLETE BAG SET (50)	450.00	200.00
COMP.BAG SER.1 (25)	110.00	50.00
COMP.BAG SER.2 (25)	350.00	160.00
COMMON CARD (1-25)	2.00	.90
COMMON CARD (26-50)	2.50	1.10
SEMISTARS	4.00	1.80
UNLISTED STARS	6.00	2.70
*OPENED TEAM SETS: .75X to 1.0X		

☐ 1	Kareem Abdul-Jabbar	20.00	9.00
☐ 2	Jeff Ruland	2.00	.90
☐ 3	Mark Aguirre	4.00	1.80
☐ 4	Julius Erving	20.00	9.00
☐ 5	Kelly Tripucka	2.00	.90
☐ 6	Buck Williams	2.00	.90
☐ 7	Sidney Moncrief	4.00	1.80
☐ 8	World B. Free	4.00	1.80
☐ 9	Bill Walton	6.00	2.70
☐ 10	Purvis Short	2.00	.90
☐ 11	Rickey Green	2.00	.90
☐ 12	Dominique Wilkins	12.00	5.50
☐ 13	Jim Paxson	2.00	.90
☐ 14	Ralph Sampson	4.00	1.80
☐ 15	Magic Johnson	30.00	13.50
☐ 16	Reggie Theus	4.00	1.80
☐ 17	Moses Malone	6.00	2.70
☐ 18	Larry Bird	50.00	22.00
☐ 19	Larry Nance	2.00	.90
☐ 20	Clark Kellogg	2.00	.90
☐ 21	Jack Sikma	4.00	1.80
☐ 22	Alex English	4.00	1.80
☐ 23	Bernard King	4.00	1.80
☐ 24	Dave Corzine	2.00	.90
☐ 25	George Gervin	6.00	2.70
☐ 26	Michael Jordan	275.00	125.00
☐ 27	Rolando Blackman	4.00	1.80
☐ 28	Dan Issel	6.00	2.70
☐ 29	Maurice Cheeks	4.00	1.80
☐ 30	Isiah Thomas	12.00	5.50
☐ 31	Robert Parish	6.00	2.70
☐ 32	Mark Eaton	4.00	1.80
☐ 33	Sam Perkins	2.50	1.10
☐ 34	Artis Gilmore	4.00	1.80
☐ 35	Andrew Toney	2.50	1.10
☐ 36	Adrian Dantley	4.00	1.80
☐ 37	Terry Cummings	4.00	1.80
☐ 38	Orlando Woolridge	2.50	1.10
☐ 39	Tom Chambers	4.00	1.80
☐ 40	Gus Williams	2.50	1.10
☐ 41	Charles Barkley	50.00	22.00
☐ 42	Kevin McHale	8.00	3.60
☐ 43	Otis Birdsong	2.50	1.10
☐ 44	Sam Bowie	2.50	1.10
☐ 45	Darrell Griffith	2.50	1.10
☐ 46	Kiki Vandeweghe	4.00	1.80
☐ 47	Hakeem Olajuwon	55.00	25.00
☐ 48	Marques Johnson	4.00	1.80
☐ 49	James Worthy	6.00	2.70
☐ 50	Mel Turpin	2.50	1.10

1985 Star Crunch'n'Munch All-Stars

The 1985 Star Crunch'n'Munch NBA All-Stars set is an 11-card standard-size set featuring the ten starting players in the 1985 NBA All-Star Game plus a checklist card. The set was produced for the Crunch 'n' Munch Food Company and was originally available to the hobby exclusively through Don Guilbert of Woonsocket, Rhode Island. The set's basic design is identical to those of the Star Company's regular NBA sets. The cards show a Star '85 logo in the upper right corner. The front borders are yellowish orange and the backs show each player's All-Star Game record.

	NRMT-MT	EXC
COMPLETE BAG SET (11)	500.00	220.00
COMMON CARD (1-11)	5.00	2.20
UNLISTED STARS	10.00	4.50
*OPENED SET: .75X to 1.0X		

☐ 1	Checklist Card	10.00	4.50
☐ 2	Larry Bird	100.00	45.00
☐ 3	Julius Erving	25.00	11.00
☐ 4	Michael Jordan	350.00	160.00
☐ 5	Moses Malone	10.00	4.50
☐ 6	Isiah Thomas	10.00	4.50
☐ 7	Kareem Abdul-Jabbar	25.00	11.00
☐ 8	Adrian Dantley	7.50	3.40
☐ 9	George Gervin	15.00	6.75
☐ 10	Magic Johnson	60.00	27.00
☐ 11	Ralph Sampson	5.00	2.20

1985 Star Gatorade Slam Dunk

This nine-card set was given to the people who attended the 1985 NBA All-Star Weekend Banquet at Indianapolis. Cards measure the standard size and have a green border around the fronts of the cards and green printing

on the backs. Cards feature the Star '85 and Gatorade logos on the fronts. Since Terence Stansbury was a late substitute in the Slam Dunk contest for Charles Barkley, both cards were produced, but the Barkley card was not released at that time. However, the Barkley card has since surfaced in the marketplace. The Barkley card is unnumbered and shows him dunking.

	NRMT-MT	EXC
COMPLETE BAG SET (9)	300.00	135.00
COMMON CARD (1-9)	3.00	1.35
SEMISTARS	5.00	2.20
*OPENED SET: .75X to 1.0X		

		NRMT-MT	EXC
☐ 1	Gatorade 2nd Annual Slam Dunk Championship (Checklist back)	6.00	2.70
☐ 2	Larry Nance	6.00	2.70
☐ 3	Terence Stansbury	3.00	1.35
☐ 4	Clyde Drexler	30.00	13.50
☐ 5	Julius Erving	25.00	11.00
☐ 6	Darrell Griffith	4.00	1.80
☐ 7	Michael Jordan	275.00	125.00
☐ 8	Dominique Wilkins	10.00	4.50
☐ 9	Orlando Woolridge	4.00	1.80
☐ NNO	Charles Barkley SP (Withdrawn)	80.00	36.00

1985 Star
Last 11 ROY's

The 1985 Star Rookies of the Year set is an 11-card standard-size set depicting each of the

NBA's ROY award winners from the 1974-75 through 1984-85 seasons. Michael Jordan's card only shows his collegiate statistics while all others provide NBA statistics up through the 1983-84 season. Cards of Darrell Griffith and Jamaal Wilkes show the Star '86 logo in the upper right corner while all others in the set show Star '85. The set's basic design is identical to those of the Star Company's regular NBA sets and the front borders are off-white. The set is sequenced in reverse chronological order according to when each player won the ROY.

	NRMT-MT	EXC
COMPLETE BAG SET (11)	300.00	135.00
COMMON CARD (1-11)	2.50	1.10
SEMISTARS	4.00	1.80
*OPENED SET: .75X to 1.0X		

		NRMT-MT	EXC
☐ 1	Michael Jordan	250.00	110.00
☐ 2	Ralph Sampson	2.50	1.10
☐ 3	Terry Cummings	2.50	1.10
☐ 4	Buck Williams	6.00	2.70
☐ 5	Darrell Griffith	2.50	1.10
☐ 6	Larry Bird	80.00	36.00
☐ 7	Phil Ford	4.00	1.80
☐ 8	Walter Davis	4.00	1.80
☐ 9	Adrian Dantley	6.00	2.70
☐ 10	Alvan Adams	4.00	1.80
☐ 11	Keith/Jamaal Wilkes	4.00	1.80

1985 Star
Lite All-Stars

This 13-card standard-size set was given to the people who attended the 1985 All-Star Weekend Banquet at Indianapolis. The set was issued in a clear, sealed plastic bag. Cards have a blue border around the fronts of the cards and blue printing on the backs. Cards feature the Star '85 and Lite Beer logos on the fronts. Players featured are the 1985 NBA All-Star starting line-ups and coaches.

	NRMT-MT	EXC
COMPLETE BAG SET (13)	350.00	160.00
COMMON CARD (1-13)	3.00	1.35
SEMISTARS	5.00	2.20
*OPENED SET: .75X to 1.0X		
BEWARE JORDAN COUNTERFEIT		

		NRMT-MT	EXC
☐ 1	1985 NBA All-Stars Starting Line-Ups	3.00	1.35
☐ 2	Larry Bird	90.00	40.00
☐ 3	Julius Erving	25.00	11.00
☐ 4	Michael Jordan	250.00	110.00
☐ 5	Moses Malone	8.00	3.60
☐ 6	Isiah Thomas	10.00	4.50
☐ 7	K.C. Jones CO	3.00	1.35
☐ 8	Kareem Abdul-Jabbar	25.00	11.00
☐ 9	Adrian Dantley	5.00	2.20
☐ 10	George Gervin	10.00	4.50
☐ 11	Magic Johnson	60.00	27.00
☐ 12	Ralph Sampson	3.00	1.35
☐ 13	Pat Riley CO	8.00	3.60

1985 Star
Slam Dunk Supers
5x7

This ten-card set uses actual photography from the 1985 Slam Dunk contest in Indianapolis held during the NBA All-Star Weekend. Cards measure approximately 5" by 7" and have a red border around the fronts of the cards and red printing on the backs. Cards feature Star '85 logo on the fronts. The set ordering for these numbered cards is alphabetical by subject's name.

	NRMT-MT	EXC
COMPLETE BAG SET (10)	275.00	125.00
COMMON CARD (1-10)	2.00	.90
*OPENED SET: .75X to 1.0X		

		NRMT-MT	EXC
☐ 1	Checklist Card (Group photo)	50.00	22.00
☐ 2	Clyde Drexler	30.00	13.50
☐ 3	Julius Erving	20.00	9.00
☐ 4	Darrell Griffith	3.00	1.35
☐ 5	Michael Jordan	250.00	110.00
☐ 6	Larry Nance	6.00	2.70
☐ 7	Terence Stansbury	2.00	.90
☐ 8	Dominique Wilkins	10.00	4.50
☐ 9	Orlando Woolridge	3.00	1.35
☐ 10	Dominique Wilkins (1985 Slam Dunk Champ)	8.00	3.60

1985 Star
Team Supers 5x7

This 40-card set is actually eight team sets of five each except for the Sixers having ten players included. Cards measure approximately 5" by 7" and have a colored border around the fronts of the cards according to the team with corresponding color printing on the backs. Cards feature Star '85 logo on the front. Cards are numbered below by assigning a team prefix based on the initials of the team, for example, BC for Boston Celtics.

	NRMT-MT	EXC
COMPLETE SET (40)	500.00	220.00
COMP.CELTICS (BC1-BC5)	70.00	32.00
COMP.BULLS (CB1-CB5)	260.00	115.00
COMP.PISTONS (DP1-DP5)	20.00	9.00
COMP.ROCKETS (HR1-HR5)	60.00	27.00
COMP.LAKERS (LA-LA5)	70.00	32.00
COMP.BUCKS (MB1-MB5)	12.00	5.50
COMP.76ERS (PS1-PS10)	80.00	36.00
COMMON CARD	2.00	.90
SEMISTARS	3.00	1.35
UNLISTED STARS	6.00	2.70
ABOVE PRICES ARE FOR SEALED BAGS		
*OPENED TEAM SETS: .75X to 1.0X		

		NRMT-MT	EXC
☐ BC1	Larry Bird	50.00	22.00
☐ BC2	Robert Parish	5.00	2.20
☐ BC3	Kevin McHale	7.00	3.10
☐ BC4	Dennis Johnson	3.00	1.35
☐ BC5	Danny Ainge	6.00	2.70
☐ CB1	Michael Jordan	250.00	110.00
☐ CB2	Orlando Woolridge	3.00	1.35
☐ CB3	Quintin Dailey	2.00	.90
☐ CB4	Dave Corzine	2.00	.90
☐ CB5	Steve Johnson	2.00	.90
☐ DP1	Isiah Thomas	6.00	2.70
☐ DP2	Kelly Tripucka	3.00	1.35
☐ DP3	Vinnie Johnson	3.00	1.35
☐ DP4	Bill Laimbeer	6.00	2.70
☐ DP5	John Long	2.00	.90
☐ HR1	Ralph Sampson	3.00	1.35
☐ HR2	Hakeem Olajuwon	50.00	22.00
☐ HR3	Lewis Lloyd	2.00	.90
☐ HR4	Rodney McCray	3.00	1.35
☐ HR5	Lionel Hollins	2.00	.90
☐ LA1	Kareem Abdul-Jabbar	20.00	9.00
☐ LA2	Magic Johnson	35.00	16.00
☐ LA3	James Worthy	6.00	2.70
☐ LA4	Byron Scott	3.00	1.35
☐ LA5	Bob McAdoo	3.00	1.35
☐ MB1	Terry Cummings	3.00	1.35

☐ MB2	Sidney Moncrief	3.00	1.35
☐ MB3	Paul Pressey	2.00	.90
☐ MB4	Mike Dunleavy	3.00	1.35
☐ MB5	Alton Lister	2.00	.90
☐ PS1	Julius Erving	20.00	9.00
☐ PS2	Maurice Cheeks	3.00	1.35
☐ PS3	Bobby Jones	3.00	1.35
☐ PS4	Clemon Johnson	2.00	.90
☐ PS5	Leon Wood	2.00	.90
☐ PS6	Moses Malone	6.00	2.70
☐ PS7	Andrew Toney	2.00	.90
☐ PS8	Charles Barkley	50.00	22.00
☐ PS9	Clint Richardson	2.00	.90
☐ PS10	Sedale Threatt	2.00	.90

1985-86 Star

This 172-card standard-size set was produced by the Star Company and features players in the NBA. Cards were released in two groups, 1-94 and 95-172. The team sets were issued in clear sealed bags. Many of these team bags were distributed to hobby dealers through a small group of Star Company master distributors. The original wholesale price per bag was $2-$3 for most of the teams. According to Star Company's original sales materials and order forms, reportedly 2,000 team bags were printed for each team and an additional 2,200 team sets were printed for the more popular teams of that time. Cards are numbered in team order and measure the standard 2 1/2" by 3 1/2". The team ordering is as follows, Philadelphia 76ers (1-9), Detroit Pistons (10-17), Houston Rockets (18-25), Los Angeles Lakers (26-33), Phoenix Suns (34-41), Atlanta Hawks (42-49), Denver Nuggets (50-57), New Jersey Nets (58-65), Seattle Supersonics (66-73), Sacramento Kings (74-80), Indiana Pacers (81-87), Los Angeles Clippers (88-94), Boston Celtics (95-102), Portland Trail Blazers (103-109), Washington Bullets (110-116), Chicago Bulls (117-123), Milwaukee Bucks (124-130), Golden State Warriors (131-136), Utah Jazz (137-144), San Antonio Spurs (145-151), Cleveland Cavaliers (152-158), Dallas Mavericks (159-165) and New York Knicks (166-172). Borders are colored according to team. Card backs are very similar to the other Star basketball sets except that the player statistics go up through the 1984-85 season. Extended Rookie Cards in this set include Patrick Ewing and Kevin Willis. There is typically a slight discount on sales of opened team bags. Cards of Celtics players (95-102) have either green or white borders. Many cards in this set (particularly 95-176) have been counterfeited and are prevalent on the market. Among those affected are the Ewing Extended Rookie Card (166) and Jordan (117). Both the Green and White Celtics are valued equally.

	NRMT-MT	EXC
COMPLETE SET (172)	1500.00	700.00
COMP.76ERS (1-9)	130.00	57.50
COMP.PISTONS (10-17)	40.00	18.00
COMP.ROCKETS (18-25)	160.00	70.00
COMP.LAKERS SP (26-33)	250.00	110.00
COMP.SUNS (34-41)	15.00	6.75
COMP.HAWKS (42-49)	60.00	27.00
COMP.NUGGETS (50-57)	15.00	6.75
COMP.NETS (58-65)	15.00	6.75
COMP.SONICS (66-73)	15.00	6.75
COMP.KINGS (74-80)	15.00	6.75
COMP.PACERS (81-87)	15.00	6.75
COMP.CLIPPERS (88-94)	15.00	6.75
COMP.CELTICS GR. (95-102)	70.00	32.00
COMP.CELTICS WH. (95-102)	120.00	55.00
COMP.BLAZERS (103-109)	80.00	36.00
COMP.BULLETS (110-116)	15.00	6.75
COMP.BULLS (117-123)	975.00	450.00
COMP.BUCKS (124-130)	15.00	6.75
COMP.WARRIORS (131-137)	15.00	6.75
COMP.JAZZ (138-144)	90.00	40.00
COMP.SPURS (145-151)	15.00	6.75
COMP.CAVS (152-158)	15.00	6.75
COMP.MAVS (159-165)	20.00	9.00
COMP.KNICKS (166-172)	175.00	80.00
COMMON CARD (1-25/34/172)	2.00	.90
COMMON SP (26-33)	4.00	1.80
SEMISTARS	4.00	1.80
UNLISTED STARS	6.00	2.70
ABOVE PRICES ARE FOR SEALED BAGS		
*OPENED TEAM SETS: .75X to 1.0X		
*GREEN/WHITE CELTICS: EQUAL VALUE		
CONDITION SENSITIVE SET		
BEWARE COUNTERFEITS ON 95-172		

☐ 1	Maurice Cheeks	4.00	1.80
☐ 2	Charles Barkley	90.00	40.00
☐ 3	Julius Erving	35.00	16.00
☐ 4	Clemon Johnson	2.00	.90
☐ 5	Bobby Jones	3.00	1.35
☐ 6	Moses Malone	10.00	4.50
☐ 7	Sedale Threatt	3.00	1.35
☐ 8	Andrew Toney	2.00	.90

☐ 9 Leon Wood	2.00	.90
☐ 10 Isiah Thomas UER	25.00	11.00
(No Pistons logo		
on card front)		
☐ 11 Kent Benson	2.00	.90
☐ 12 Earl Cureton	2.00	.90
☐ 13 Vinnie Johnson	3.00	1.35
☐ 14 Bill Laimbeer	4.00	1.80
☐ 15 John Long	2.00	.90
☐ 16 Rick Mahorn	2.00	.90
☐ 17 Kelly Tripucka	3.00	1.35
☐ 18 Hakeem Olajuwon	140.00	65.00
☐ 19 Allen Leavell	2.00	.90
☐ 20 Lewis Lloyd	2.00	.90
☐ 21 John Lucas	3.00	1.35
☐ 22 Rodney McCray	2.00	.90
☐ 23 Robert Reid	2.00	.90
☐ 24 Ralph Sampson	3.00	1.35
☐ 25 Mitchell Wiggins	2.00	.90
☐ 26 K.Abdul-Jabbar SP	50.00	22.00
☐ 27 Michael Cooper SP	8.00	3.60
☐ 28 Magic Johnson SP	120.00	55.00
☐ 29 Mitch Kupchak SP	4.00	1.80
☐ 30 Maurice Lucas SP	6.00	2.70
☐ 31 Kurt Rambis SP	6.00	2.70
☐ 32 Byron Scott SP	8.00	3.60
☐ 33 James Worthy SP	18.00	8.00
☐ 34 Larry Nance	8.00	3.60
☐ 35 Alvan Adams	3.00	1.35
☐ 36 Walter Davis	3.00	1.35
☐ 37 James Edwards	3.00	1.35
☐ 38 Jay Humphries	2.00	.90
☐ 39 Charles Pittman	2.00	.90
☐ 40 Rick Robey	2.00	.90
☐ 41 Mike Sanders	2.00	.90
☐ 42 Dominique Wilkins	25.00	11.00
☐ 43 Scott Hastings	2.00	.90
☐ 44 Eddie Johnson	2.00	.90
☐ 45 Cliff Levingston	2.00	.90
☐ 46 Tree Rollins	3.00	1.35
☐ 47 Doc Rivers UER	3.00	1.35
(Ray Williams is		
pictured on the front)		
☐ 48 Kevin Willis	18.00	8.00
☐ 49 Randy Wittman	2.00	.90
☐ 50 Alex English	4.00	1.80
☐ 51 Wayne Cooper	2.00	.90
☐ 52 T.R. Dunn	2.00	.90
☐ 53 Mike Evans	2.00	.90
☐ 54 Lafayette Lever	3.00	1.35
☐ 55 Calvin Natt	2.00	.90
☐ 56 Danny Schayes	3.00	1.35
☐ 57 Elston Turner	2.00	.90
☐ 58 Buck Williams	4.00	1.80
☐ 59 Otis Birdsong	3.00	1.35
☐ 60 Darwin Cook	2.00	.90
☐ 61 Darryl Dawkins	3.00	1.35
☐ 62 Mike Gminski	3.00	1.35
☐ 63 Mickey Johnson	2.00	.90
☐ 64 Mike O'Koren	3.00	1.35
☐ 65 Micheal R. Richardson	2.00	.90
☐ 66 Tom Chambers	4.00	1.80
☐ 67 Gerald Henderson	2.00	.90
☐ 68 Tim McCormick	2.00	.90
☐ 69 Jack Sikma	3.00	1.35
☐ 70 Ricky Sobers	2.00	.90
☐ 71 Danny Vranes	2.00	.90
☐ 72 Al Wood	2.00	.90
☐ 73 Danny Young	3.00	1.35
☐ 74 Reggie Theus	3.00	1.35
☐ 75 Larry Drew	2.00	.90
☐ 76 Eddie Johnson	3.00	1.35
☐ 77 Mark Olberding	2.00	.90
☐ 78 LaSalle Thompson	2.00	.90
☐ 79 Otis Thorpe	6.00	2.70
☐ 80 Mike Woodson	2.00	.90
☐ 81 Clark Kellogg	3.00	1.35
☐ 82 Quinn Buckner	3.00	1.35
☐ 83 Vern Fleming	3.00	1.35
☐ 84 Bill Garnett	2.00	.90
☐ 85 Terence Stansbury	2.00	.90
☐ 86 Steve Stipanovich	2.00	.90
☐ 87 Herb Williams	3.00	1.35
☐ 88 Marques Johnson	3.00	1.35
☐ 89 Michael Cage	2.00	.90

☐ 90 Franklin Edwards	2.00	.90
☐ 91 Cedric Maxwell	3.00	1.35
☐ 92 Derek Smith	2.00	.90
☐ 93 Rory White	2.00	.90
☐ 94 Jamaal Wilkes	3.00	1.35
☐ 95G Larry Bird Green	25.00	11.00
☐ 95W Larry Bird White	90.00	40.00
☐ 96 Danny Ainge	10.00	4.50
☐ 97 Dennis Johnson	4.00	1.80
☐ 98 Kevin McHale	12.00	5.50
☐ 99 Robert Parish	8.00	3.60
☐ 100 Jerry Sichting	2.00	.90
☐ 101 Bill Walton	12.00	5.50
☐ 102 Scott Wedman	2.00	.90
☐ 103 Kiki Vandeweghe	3.00	1.35
☐ 104 Sam Bowie	3.00	1.35
☐ 105 Kenny Carr	2.00	.90
☐ 106 Clyde Drexler	70.00	32.00
☐ 107 Jerome Kersey	3.00	1.35
☐ 108 Jim Paxson	2.00	.90
☐ 109 Mychal Thompson	3.00	1.35
☐ 110 Gus Williams	3.00	1.35
☐ 111 Darren Daye	3.00	1.35
☐ 112 Jeff Malone	3.00	1.35
☐ 113 Tom McMillen	3.00	1.35
☐ 114 Cliff Robinson	2.00	.90
☐ 115 Dan Roundfield	3.00	1.35
☐ 116 Jeff Ruland	2.00	.90
☐ 117 Michael Jordan	950.00	425.00
☐ 118 Gene Banks	2.00	.90
☐ 119 Dave Corzine	2.00	.90
☐ 120 Quintin Dailey	2.00	.90
☐ 121 George Gervin	12.00	5.50
☐ 122 Jawann Oldham	2.00	.90
☐ 123 Orlando Woolridge	3.00	1.35
☐ 124 Terry Cummings	3.00	1.35
☐ 125 Craig Hodges	2.00	.90
☐ 126 Alton Lister	2.00	.90
☐ 127 Paul Mokeski	2.00	.90
☐ 128 Sidney Moncrief	3.00	1.35
☐ 129 Ricky Pierce	3.00	1.35
☐ 130 Paul Pressey	2.00	.90
☐ 131 Purvis Short	2.00	.90
☐ 132 Joe Barry Carroll	3.00	1.35
☐ 133 Lester Conner	2.00	.90
☐ 134 Sleepy Floyd	3.00	1.35
☐ 135 Geoff Huston	2.00	.90
☐ 136 Larry Smith	2.00	.90
☐ 137 Jerome Whitehead	2.00	.90
☐ 138 Adrian Dantley	4.00	1.80
☐ 139 Mitchell Anderson	2.00	.90
☐ 140 Thurl Bailey	3.00	1.35
☐ 141 Mark Eaton	3.00	1.35
☐ 142 Rickey Green	3.00	1.35
☐ 143 Darrell Griffith	3.00	1.35
☐ 144 John Stockton	80.00	36.00
☐ 145 Artis Gilmore	4.00	1.80
☐ 146 Marc Iavaroni	2.00	.90
☐ 147 Steve Johnson	2.00	.90
☐ 148 Mike Mitchell	2.00	.90
☐ 149 Johnny Moore	2.00	.90
☐ 150 Alvin Robertson	3.00	1.35
☐ 151 Jon Sundvold	2.00	.90
☐ 152 World B. Free	3.00	1.35
☐ 153 John Bagley	2.00	.90
☐ 154 Johnny Davis	2.00	.90
☐ 155 Roy Hinson	2.00	.90
☐ 156 Phil Hubbard	2.00	.90
☐ 157 Ben Poquette	2.00	.90
☐ 158 Mel Turpin	2.00	.90
☐ 159 Rolando Blackman	3.00	1.35
☐ 160 Mark Aguirre	3.00	1.35
☐ 161 Brad Davis	2.00	.90
☐ 162 Dale Ellis	3.00	1.35
☐ 163 Derek Harper	6.00	2.70
☐ 164 Sam Perkins	4.00	1.80
☐ 165 Jay Vincent	2.00	.90
☐ 166 Patrick Ewing	160.00	70.00
☐ 167 Bill Cartwright	3.00	1.35
☐ 168 Pat Cummings	2.00	.90
☐ 169 Ernie Grunfeld	3.00	1.35
☐ 170 Rory Sparrow	2.00	.90
☐ 171 Trent Tucker	2.00	.90
☐ 172 Darrell Walker	2.00	.90

1985-86 Star All-Rookie Team

The 1985-86 Star NBA All-Rookie Team is an 11-card standard-size set that features 11 top rookies from the previous (1984-85) season. The set's basic design is identical to those of the Star Company's regular NBA sets. The front borders are red and the backs include each player's collegiate statistics. Alvin Robertson's card shows the Star '86 logo in the upper right corner. All others in the set show Star '85.

	NRMT-MT	EXC
COMPLETE BAG SET (11)	400.00	180.00
COMMON CARD (1-11)	4.00	1.80
*OPENED SET: .75X to 1.0X		
BEWARE JORDAN COUNTERFEIT		

☐ 1 Hakeem Olajuwon	70.00	32.00
☐ 2 Michael Jordan	300.00	135.00
☐ 3 Charles Barkley	40.00	18.00
☐ 4 Sam Bowie	7.50	3.40
☐ 5 Sam Perkins	7.50	3.40
☐ 6 Vern Fleming	4.00	1.80
☐ 7 Otis Thorpe	7.50	3.40
☐ 8 John Stockton	30.00	13.50
☐ 9 Kevin Willis	10.00	4.50
☐ 10 Tim McCormick	4.00	1.80
☐ 11 Alvin Robertson	4.00	1.80

1986 Star Best of the Best

The Star Company reportedly produced only 1,400 sets and planned to release them in

1986. However, they were not issued until as late as 1990. This set and the Magic Johnson set were printed on the same uncut sheet. No factory-sealed bags exist for this set due to the fact that the sets were cut from the sheets years after the original printing. It is understood that the uncut sheets were sold to hobbyists who cut the sheets and packaged sets to be sold into the hobby. The cards measure the standard size. The fronts feature color action photos with white inner borders and a blue card face. The player's name, position, and team name appear at the bottom. The set title "Best of the Best" appears in a white circle at the lower left corner. The backs are white with blue borders and contain biography and statistics. The cards are numbered and arranged in alphabetical order.

	NRMT-MT	EXC
COMPLETE SET (15)	250.00	110.00
COMMON CARD (1-15)	1.50	.70
SEMISTARS	2.00	.90

BEWARE JORDAN COUNTERFEIT

		NRMT-MT	EXC
☐ 1	Kareem Abdul-Jabbar	8.00	3.60
☐ 2	Charles Barkley	20.00	9.00
☐ 3	Larry Bird	40.00	18.00
☐ 4	Tom Chambers	1.50	.70
☐ 5	Terry Cummings	1.50	.70
☐ 6	Julius Erving	8.00	3.60
☐ 7	Patrick Ewing	12.00	5.50
☐ 8	Magic Johnson	25.00	11.00
☐ 9	Michael Jordan	125.00	55.00
☐ 10	Moses Malone	2.00	.90
☐ 11	Hakeem Olajuwon	25.00	11.00
☐ 12	John Stockton	15.00	6.75
☐ 13	Isiah Thomas	3.00	1.35
☐ 14	Dominique Wilkins	2.50	1.10
☐ 15	James Worthy	2.00	.90

1986 Star Best of the New/Old

The Star Company distributed these sets to dealers who purchased 1985-86 complete sets.

Dealers received one set for every five regular sets purchased. The cards measure the standard size. The cards are unnumbered and checklisted below in alphabetical order. The Best of the New are numbered 1-4 and the Best of the Old are numbered 5-8. The numbering is alphabetical within each group. Counterfeiting has been a problem with the Best of the New series.

	NRMT-MT	EXC
COMPLETE SET (8)	600.00	275.00
COMPLETE NEW SET (4)	200.00	90.00
COMPLETE OLD SET (4)	400.00	180.00
COMMON NEW CARD (1-4)	5.00	2.20
COMMON OLD CARD (5-8)	75.00	34.00

*BAGGED SETS: 1.0X to 1.5X
BEWARE COUNTERFEITS ON NEW

☐ 1	Patrick Ewing	15.00	6.75
☐ 2	Michael Jordan	150.00	70.00
☐ 3	Hakeem Olajuwon	30.00	13.50
☐ 4	Ralph Sampson	5.00	2.20
☐ 5	Kareem Abdul-Jabbar	140.00	65.00
☐ 6	Julius Erving	140.00	65.00
☐ 7	George Gervin	75.00	34.00
☐ 8	Bill Walton	75.00	34.00

1986 Star Court Kings

The 1986 Star Court Kings set contains 33 standard-size cards which feature many of the NBA's top players. The set's basic design is identical to those of the Star Company's regular NBA sets. The front borders are yellow, and the backs have career narrative summaries of each player but no statistics. The cards show a Star '86 logo in the upper right corner. The cards are numbered in the upper left corner of the reverse. The numbering is alphabetical by last name.

	NRMT-MT	EXC
COMPLETE BAG SET (33)	300.00	135.00
COMMON CARD (1-33)	1.50	.70
SEMISTARS	2.50	1.10
UNLISTED STARS	4.00	1.80

*OPENED SET: .75X to 1.0X
CONDITION SENSITIVE SET

☐ 1	Mark Aguirre	2.50	1.10
☐ 2	Kareem Abdul-Jabbar	12.00	5.50
☐ 3	Charles Barkley	25.00	11.00
☐ 4	Larry Bird	40.00	18.00
☐ 5	Rolando Blackman	1.50	1.10
☐ 6	Tom Chambers	2.50	1.10
☐ 7	Maurice Cheeks	2.50	1.10
☐ 8	Terry Cummings	2.50	1.10
☐ 9	Adrian Dantley	2.50	1.10
☐ 10	Darryl Dawkins	4.00	1.80
☐ 11	Mark Eaton	1.50	.70
☐ 12	Alex English	2.50	1.10
☐ 13	Julius Erving	12.00	5.50
☐ 14	Patrick Ewing	12.00	5.50
☐ 15	George Gervin	5.00	2.20
☐ 16	Darrell Griffith	1.50	.70
☐ 17	Magic Johnson	25.00	11.00
☐ 18	Michael Jordan	200.00	90.00
☐ 19	Clark Kellogg	2.50	1.10
☐ 20	Bernard King	2.50	1.10
☐ 21	Moses Malone	4.00	1.80
☐ 22	Kevin McHale	5.00	2.20
☐ 23	Sidney Moncrief	2.50	1.10
☐ 24	Larry Nance	4.00	1.80
☐ 25	Hakeem Olajuwon	25.00	11.00
☐ 26	Robert Parish	4.00	1.80
☐ 27	Ralph Sampson	1.50	.70
☐ 28	Isiah Thomas	5.00	2.20
☐ 29	Andrew Toney	1.50	.70
☐ 30	Kelly Tripucka	1.50	.70
☐ 31	Kiki Vandeweghe	1.50	.70
☐ 32	Dominique Wilkins	6.00	2.70
☐ 33	James Worthy	5.00	2.20

1957-58 Topps

The 1957-58 Topps basketball set of 80 cards was Topps' first basketball issue. Topps did not produce another basketball set until it released a test issue in 1968. A major set followed in 1969. Cards were issued in 5-cent packs (six cards per pack, 24 per box) and measure the standard size. A number of cards in the set were double printed (indicated by DP in checklist below). The set contains 49 double prints, 30 single prints and one quadruple print (No. 24 Bob Pettit). Card backs give statistical information from the 1956-57 NBA season. Bill Russell's Rookie Card is part of the set. Other Rookie Cards include Paul Arizin, Nat "Sweetwater" Clifton, Bob

Cousy, Cliff Hagan, Tom Heinsohn, Rod Hundley, Red Kerr, Clyde Lovellette, Pettit, Dolph Schayes, Bill Sharman and Jack Twyman. The set contains the only card of Maurice Stokes. Topps also produced a three-card advertising panel featuring the fronts of Walt Davis, Joe Graboski and Cousy with an advertisement for the upcoming Topps basketball set on the combined reverse.

	EX-MT	VG-E
COMPLETE SET (80)	5500.00	2500.00
COMMON NON-DP (1-80)	40.00	18.00
DP (9/11/14/20)	25.00	11.00
DP (31/38/46/47/52)	25.00	11.00
DP (55/57/64/65/68/79)	25.00	11.00
DP (6/7/8/18/21/25/34/66)	35.00	16.00

CONDITION SENSITIVE SET
CARDS PRICED IN EX-MT CONDITION

		EX-MT	VG-E
☐ 1	Nat Clifton DP	250.00	75.00
☐ 2	George Yardley DP	70.00	32.00
☐ 3	Neil Johnston DP	55.00	25.00
☐ 4	Carl Braun DP	50.00	22.00
☐ 5	Bill Sharman DP	175.00	80.00
☐ 6	George King DP	35.00	16.00
☐ 7	Kenny Sears DP	35.00	16.00
☐ 8	Dick Ricketts DP	35.00	16.00
☐ 9	Jack Nichols DP	25.00	11.00
☐ 10	Paul Arizin DP	110.00	50.00
☐ 11	Chuck Noble DP	25.00	11.00
☐ 12	Slater Martin DP	70.00	32.00
☐ 13	Dolph Schayes DP	140.00	65.00
☐ 14	Dick Atha DP	25.00	11.00
☐ 15	Frank Ramsey DP	90.00	40.00
☐ 16	Dick McGuire DP	55.00	25.00
☐ 17	Bob Cousy DP	500.00	220.00
☐ 18	Larry Foust DP	35.00	16.00
☐ 19	Tom Heinsohn DP	325.00	145.00
☐ 20	Bill Thieben DP	25.00	11.00
☐ 21	Don Meineke DP	35.00	16.00
☐ 22	Tom Marshall	40.00	18.00
☐ 23	Dick Garmaker	40.00	18.00
☐ 24	Bob Pettit DP	200.00	90.00
☐ 25	Jim Krebs DP	60.00	27.00
☐ 26	Gene Shue DP	35.00	16.00
☐ 27	Ed Macauley DP	70.00	32.00
☐ 28	Vern Mikkelsen	100.00	45.00
☐ 29	Willie Naulls	55.00	25.00
☐ 30	Walter Dukes DP	45.00	20.00
☐ 31	Dave Piontek DP	25.00	11.00
☐ 32	John Kerr	140.00	65.00
☐ 33	Larry Costello DP	50.00	22.00
☐ 34	W.Sauldsberry DP	35.00	16.00
☐ 35	Ray Felix	45.00	20.00
☐ 36	Ernie Beck	40.00	18.00
☐ 37	Cliff Hagan	135.00	60.00
☐ 38	Guy Sparrow DP	25.00	11.00
☐ 39	Jim Loscutoff	50.00	22.00
☐ 40	Arnie Risen DP	45.00	20.00
☐ 41	Joe Graboski	40.00	18.00
☐ 42	M.Stokes DP UER	140.00	65.00
	(Text refers to N.F.L. Record)		
☐ 43	Rod Hundley DP	140.00	65.00
☐ 44	Tom Gola DP	80.00	36.00
☐ 45	Med Park	45.00	20.00
☐ 46	Mel Hutchins DP	25.00	11.00
☐ 47	Larry Friend DP	25.00	11.00
☐ 48	L.Rosenbluth DP	55.00	25.00
☐ 49	Walt Davis	40.00	18.00
☐ 50	Richie Regan	45.00	20.00
☐ 51	Frank Selvy DP	50.00	22.00
☐ 52	Art Spoelstra DP	25.00	11.00
☐ 53	Bob Hopkins	45.00	20.00
☐ 54	Earl Lloyd	50.00	22.00
☐ 55	Phil Jordan DP	25.00	11.00

☐ 56	Bob Houbregs DP	40.00	18.00
☐ 57	Lou Tsioropoulos DP	25.00	11.00
☐ 58	Ed Conlin	45.00	20.00
☐ 59	Al Bianchi	75.00	34.00
☐ 60	George Dempsey	45.00	20.00
☐ 61	Chuck Share	40.00	18.00
☐ 62	Harry Gallatin DP	45.00	20.00
☐ 63	Bob Harrison	40.00	18.00
☐ 64	Bob Burrow DP	25.00	11.00
☐ 65	Win Wilfong DP	25.00	11.00
☐ 66	Jack McMahon DP	35.00	16.00
☐ 67	Jack George	40.00	18.00
☐ 68	Charlie Tyra DP	25.00	11.00
☐ 69	Ron Sobie	40.00	18.00
☐ 70	Jack Coleman	40.00	18.00
☐ 71	Jack Twyman DP	110.00	50.00
☐ 72	Paul Seymour	45.00	20.00
☐ 73	Jim Paxson DP	55.00	25.00
☐ 74	Bob Leonard	55.00	25.00
☐ 75	Andy Phillip	55.00	25.00
☐ 76	Joe Holup	40.00	18.00
☐ 77	Bill Russell	1800.00	800.00
☐ 78	Clyde Lovellette DP	120.00	55.00
☐ 79	Ed Fleming DP	25.00	11.00
☐ 80	Dick Schnittker	120.00	36.00

1969-70 Topps

BILL BRADLEY
forward

NEW YORK

The 1969-70 Topps set of 99 cards was Topps' first major basketball issue since 1957. Cards were issued in 10-cent packs (10 cards per pack, 24 packs per box) and measure 2 1/2" by 4 11/16". The set features the first card of Lew Alcindor (later Kareem Abdul-Jabbar). Other notable Rookie Cards in the set are Dave Bing, Bill Bradley, Billy Cunningham, Dave DeBusschere, Walt Frazier, John Havlicek, Connie Hawkins, Elvin Hayes, Jerry Lucas, Earl Monroe, Don Nelson, Willis Reed, Nate Thurmond and Wes Unseld. The set was printed on a sheet of 99 cards (nine rows of eleven across) with the checklist card occupying the lower right corner of the sheet. As a result, the checklist is prone to wear and very difficult to obtain in Near Mint or better condition.

	NRMT-MT	EXC
COMPLETE SET (99)	1600.00	700.00
COMMON CARD (1-99)	4.00	1.80
CL (99) !	325.00	145.00

SEMISTARS	6.00	2.70
UNLISTED STARS	8.00	3.60

CONDITION SENSITIVE SET
1969-70 THRU 1985-86 PRICED IN NM-MT

☐ 1	Wilt Chamberlain	180.00	55.00
☐ 2	Gail Goodrich	40.00	18.00
☐ 3	Cazzie Russell	15.00	6.75
☐ 4	Darrall Imhoff	5.00	2.20
☐ 5	Bailey Howell	7.00	3.10
☐ 6	Lucius Allen	7.00	3.10
☐ 7	Tom Boerwinkle	5.00	2.20
☐ 8	Jimmy Walker	8.00	3.60
☐ 9	John Block	5.00	2.20
☐ 10	Nate Thurmond	30.00	13.50
☐ 11	Gary Gregor	4.00	1.80
☐ 12	Gus Johnson	15.00	6.75
☐ 13	Luther Rackley	4.00	1.80
☐ 14	Jon McGlocklin	5.00	2.20
☐ 15	Connie Hawkins	50.00	22.00
☐ 16	Johnny Egan	4.00	1.80
☐ 17	Jim Washington	4.00	1.80
☐ 18	Dick Barnett	8.00	3.60
☐ 19	Tom Meschery	5.00	2.20
☐ 20	John Havlicek	160.00	70.00
☐ 21	Eddie Miles	4.00	1.80
☐ 22	Walt Wesley	5.00	2.20
☐ 23	Rick Adelman	8.00	3.60
☐ 24	Al Attles	5.00	2.20
☐ 25	Lew Alcindor	600.00	275.00
☐ 26	Jack Marin	8.00	3.60
☐ 27	Walt Hazzard	12.00	5.50
☐ 28	Connie Dierking	4.00	1.80
☐ 29	Keith Erickson	10.00	4.50
☐ 30	Bob Rule	10.00	4.50
☐ 31	Dick Van Arsdale	10.00	4.50
☐ 32	Archie Clark	12.00	5.50
☐ 33	Terry Dischinger	4.00	1.80
☐ 34	Henry Finkel	4.00	1.80
☐ 35	Elgin Baylor	50.00	22.00
☐ 36	Ron Williams	4.00	1.80
☐ 37	Loy Petersen	4.00	1.80
☐ 38	Guy Rodgers	5.00	2.20
☐ 39	Toby Kimball	4.00	1.80
☐ 40	Billy Cunningham	45.00	20.00
☐ 41	Joe Caldwell	5.00	2.20
☐ 42	Leroy Ellis	5.00	2.20
☐ 43	Bill Bradley	125.00	55.00
☐ 44	Len Wilkens UER	35.00	16.00
	(Misspelled Wilkins on card back)		
☐ 45	Jerry Lucas	30.00	13.50
☐ 46	Neal Walk	5.00	2.20
☐ 47	Emmette Bryant	5.00	2.20
☐ 48	Bob Kauffman	4.00	1.80
☐ 49	Mel Counts	5.00	2.20
☐ 50	Oscar Robertson	60.00	27.00
☐ 51	Jim Barnett	5.00	2.20
☐ 52	Don Smith	4.00	1.80
☐ 53	Jim Davis	4.00	1.80
☐ 54	Wally Jones	5.00	2.20
☐ 55	Dave Bing	40.00	18.00
☐ 56	Wes Unseld	40.00	18.00
☐ 57	Joe Ellis	4.00	1.80
☐ 58	John Tresvant	4.00	1.80
☐ 59	Larry Siegfried	5.00	2.20
☐ 60	Willis Reed	45.00	20.00
☐ 61	Paul Silas	15.00	6.75
☐ 62	Bob Weiss	8.00	3.60
☐ 63	Willie McCarter	4.00	1.80
☐ 64	Don Kojis	4.00	1.80
☐ 65	Lou Hudson	20.00	9.00
☐ 66	Jim King	4.00	1.80
☐ 67	Luke Jackson	5.00	2.20
☐ 68	Len Chappell	4.00	1.80
☐ 69	Ray Scott	4.00	1.80
☐ 70	Jeff Mullins	8.00	3.60
☐ 71	Howie Komives	4.00	1.80
☐ 72	Tom Sanders	10.00	4.50
☐ 73	Dick Snyder	4.00	1.80
☐ 74	Dave Stallworth	5.00	2.20
☐ 75	Elvin Hayes	60.00	27.00
☐ 76	Art Harris	4.00	1.80
☐ 77	Don Ohl	5.00	2.20
☐ 78	Bob Love	30.00	13.50
☐ 79	Tom Van Arsdale	10.00	4.50

	NRMT-MT	EXC
□ 80 Earl Monroe	45.00	20.00
□ 81 Greg Smith	4.00	1.80
□ 82 Don Nelson	35.00	16.00
□ 83 Happy Hairston	8.00	3.60
□ 84 Hal Greer	12.00	5.50
□ 85 Dave DeBusschere	45.00	20.00
□ 86 Bill Bridges	8.00	3.60
□ 87 Herm Gilliam	5.00	2.20
□ 88 Jim Fox	4.00	1.80
□ 89 Bob Boozer	5.00	2.20
□ 90 Jerry West	90.00	40.00
□ 91 Chet Walker	15.00	6.75
□ 92 Flynn Robinson	5.00	2.20
□ 93 Clyde Lee	4.00	1.80
□ 94 Kevin Loughery	10.00	4.50
□ 95 Walt Bellamy	10.00	4.50
□ 96 Art Williams	4.00	1.80
□ 97 Adrian Smith	5.00	2.20
□ 98 Walt Frazier	70.00	32.00
□ 99 Checklist 1-99	325.00	100.00

1970-71 Topps

The 1970-71 Topps basketball card set of 175 color cards continued the larger-size (2 1/2" by 4 11/16") format established the previous year. Cards were issued in 10-cent wax packs with 10 cards per pack and 24 packs per box. Cards numbered 106 to 115 contain the previous season's NBA first and second team All-Star selections. The first six cards in the set (1-6) feature the statistical league leaders from the previous season. The last eight cards in the set (168-175) summarize the results of the previous season's NBA championship playoff series won by the Knicks over the Lakers. The key Rookie Cards in this set are Pete Maravich, Calvin Murphy and Pat Riley. There are 22 short-printed cards in the first series which are marked SP in the checklist below.

	NRMT-MT	EXC
COMPLETE SET (175)	1100.00	500.00
COMMON CARD (1-110)	2.50	1.10
COMMON CARD (111-175)	3.00	1.35
SP (32/33/35/49/78/87)	5.00	2.20
SP (31/36/37/62/74/104)	8.00	3.60
CL (24) !	50.00	22.00
CL DP (101A/101B) !	30.00	13.50
LL (1-6)	5.00	2.20

AS (106-110)	8.00	3.60
AS (111-115)	4.00	1.80
PLAYOFFS (168-175)	5.00	2.20
SEMISTARS	4.00	1.80
UNLISTED STARS	6.00	2.70
CONDITION SENSITIVE SET		
□ 1 NBA Scoring Leaders	40.00	12.00
Lew Alcindor		
Jerry West		
Elvin Hayes		
□ 2 NBA Scoring SP	40.00	18.00
Average Leaders		
Jerry West		
Lew Alcindor		
Elvin Hayes		
□ 3 NBA FG Pct Leaders	5.00	2.20
Johnny Green		
Darrall Imhoff		
Lou Hudson		
□ 4 NBA FT Pct Leaders SP	10.00	4.50
Flynn Robinson		
Chet Walker		
Jeff Mullins		
□ 5 NBA Rebound Leaders	25.00	11.00
Elvin Hayes		
Wes Unseld		
Lew Alcindor		
□ 6 NBA Assist Leaders SP	12.00	5.50
Len Wilkens		
Walt Frazier		
Clem Haskins		
□ 7 Bill Bradley	40.00	18.00
□ 8 Ron Williams	2.50	1.10
□ 9 Otto Moore	2.50	1.10
□ 10 John Havlicek SP	80.00	36.00
□ 11 George Wilson	2.50	1.10
□ 12 John Trapp	2.50	1.10
□ 13 Pat Riley	60.00	27.00
□ 14 Jim Washington	2.50	1.10
□ 15 Bob Rule	4.00	1.80
□ 16 Bob Weiss	4.00	1.80
□ 17 Neil Johnson	2.50	1.10
□ 18 Walt Bellamy	7.00	3.10
□ 19 McCoy McLemore	2.50	1.10
□ 20 Earl Monroe	12.00	5.50
□ 21 Wally Anderzunas	2.50	1.10
□ 22 Guy Rodgers	4.00	1.80
□ 23 Rick Roberson	2.50	1.10
□ 24 Checklist 1-110	50.00	15.00
□ 25 Jimmy Walker	4.00	1.80
□ 26 Mike Riordan	5.00	2.20
□ 27 Henry Finkel	2.50	1.10
□ 28 Joe Ellis	2.50	1.10
□ 29 Mike Davis	2.50	1.10
□ 30 Lou Hudson	6.00	2.70
□ 31 Lucius Allen SP	7.00	3.10
□ 32 Toby Kimball SP	5.00	2.20
□ 33 Luke Jackson SP	5.00	2.20
□ 34 Johnny Egan	2.50	1.10
□ 35 Leroy Ellis SP	5.00	2.20
□ 36 Jack Marin SP	7.00	3.10
□ 37 Joe Caldwell SP	7.00	3.10
□ 38 Keith Erickson	4.00	1.80
□ 39 Don Smith	2.50	1.10
□ 40 Flynn Robinson	4.00	1.80
□ 41 Bob Boozer	2.50	1.10
□ 42 Howie Komives	2.50	1.10
□ 43 Dick Barnett	4.00	1.80
□ 44 Stu Lantz	2.50	1.10
□ 45 Dick Van Arsdale	6.00	2.70
□ 46 Jerry Lucas	8.00	3.60
□ 47 Don Chaney	8.00	3.60
□ 48 Ray Scott	2.50	1.10
□ 49 D.Cunningham SP	5.00	2.20
□ 50 Wilt Chamberlain	80.00	36.00
□ 51 Kevin Loughery	4.00	1.80
□ 52 Stan McKenzie	2.50	1.10
□ 53 Fred Foster	2.50	1.10
□ 54 Jim Davis	2.50	1.10
□ 55 Walt Wesley	2.50	1.10
□ 56 Bill Hewitt	2.50	1.10
□ 57 Darrall Imhoff	2.50	1.10
□ 58 John Block	2.50	1.10
□ 59 Al Attles SP	8.00	3.60
□ 60 Chet Walker	6.00	2.70

□ 61 Luther Rackley	2.50	1.10
□ 62 Jerry Chambers SP	6.00	2.70
□ 63 Bob Dandridge	8.00	3.60
□ 64 Dick Snyder	2.50	1.10
□ 65 Elgin Baylor	25.00	11.00
□ 66 Connie Dierking	2.50	1.10
□ 67 Steve Kuberski	2.50	1.10
□ 68 Tom Boerwinkle	2.50	1.10
□ 69 Paul Silas	6.00	2.70
□ 70 Elvin Hayes	25.00	11.00
□ 71 Bill Bridges	4.00	1.80
□ 72 Wes Unseld	12.00	5.50
□ 73 Herm Gilliam	2.50	1.10
□ 74 Bobby Smith SP	8.00	3.60
□ 75 Lew Alcindor	100.00	45.00
□ 76 Jeff Mullins	4.00	1.80
□ 77 Happy Hairston	4.00	1.80
□ 78 Dave Stallworth SP	5.00	2.20
□ 79 Fred Hetzel	2.50	1.10
□ 80 Len Wilkens SP	25.00	11.00
□ 81 Johnny Green	5.00	2.20
□ 82 Erwin Mueller	2.50	1.10
□ 83 Wally Jones	4.00	1.80
□ 84 Bob Love	8.00	3.60
□ 85 Dick Garrett	2.50	1.10
□ 86 Don Nelson SP	25.00	11.00
□ 87 Neal Walk SP	5.00	2.20
□ 88 Larry Siegfried	2.50	1.10
□ 89 Gary Gregor	2.50	1.10
□ 90 Nate Thurmond	8.00	3.60
□ 91 John Warren	2.50	1.10
□ 92 Gus Johnson	6.00	2.70
□ 93 Gail Goodrich	12.00	5.50
□ 94 Dorie Murrey	2.50	1.10
□ 95 Cazzie Russell SP	10.00	4.50
□ 96 Terry Dischinger	2.50	1.10
□ 97 Norm Van Lier SP	15.00	6.75
□ 98 Jim Fox	2.50	1.10
□ 99 Tom Meschery	2.50	1.10
□ 100 Oscar Robertson	35.00	16.00
□ 101A CL 111-175	30.00	9.00
(1970-71 in black)		
□ 101B CL 111-175	30.00	9.00
(1970-71 in white)		
□ 102 Rich Johnson	2.50	1.10
□ 103 Mel Counts	4.00	1.80
□ 104 Bill Hosket SP	6.00	2.70
□ 105 Archie Clark	4.00	1.80
□ 106 Walt Frazier AS	10.00	4.50
□ 107 Jerry West AS	30.00	13.50
□ 108 Bill Cunningham AS	10.00	4.50
□ 109 Connie Hawkins AS	8.00	3.60
□ 110 Willis Reed AS	8.00	3.60
□ 111 Nate Thurmond AS	5.00	2.20
□ 112 John Havlicek AS	25.00	11.00
□ 113 Elgin Baylor AS	18.00	8.00
□ 114 O.Robertson AS	20.00	9.00
□ 115 Lou Hudson AS	4.00	1.80
□ 116 Emmette Bryant	3.00	1.35
□ 117 Greg Howard	3.00	1.35
□ 118 Rick Adelman	4.50	2.00
□ 119 Barry Clemens	3.00	1.35
□ 120 Walt Frazier	25.00	11.00
□ 121 Jim Barnes	3.00	1.35
□ 122 Bernie Williams	3.00	1.35
□ 123 Pete Maravich	275.00	125.00
□ 124 Matt Guokas	8.00	3.60
□ 125 Dave Bing	12.00	5.50
□ 126 John Tresvant	3.00	1.35
□ 127 Shaler Halimon	3.00	1.35
□ 128 Don Ohl	3.00	1.35
□ 129 Fred Carter	5.00	2.20
□ 130 Connie Hawkins	15.00	6.75
□ 131 Jim King	3.00	1.35
□ 132 Ed Manning	3.00	1.35
□ 133 Adrian Smith	3.00	1.35
□ 134 Walt Hazzard	5.00	2.20
□ 135 Dave DeBusschere	12.00	5.50
□ 136 Don Kojis	3.00	1.35
□ 137 Calvin Murphy	30.00	13.50
□ 138 Nate Bowman	3.00	1.35
□ 139 Jon McGlocklin	4.50	2.00
□ 140 Billy Cunningham	15.00	6.75
□ 141 Willie McCarter	3.00	1.35
□ 142 Jim Barnett	3.00	1.35
□ 143 JoJo White	20.00	9.00

☐ 144 Clyde Lee	3.00	1.35
☐ 145 Tom Van Arsdale	6.00	2.70
☐ 146 Len Chappell	3.00	1.35
☐ 147 Lee Winfield	3.00	1.35
☐ 148 Jerry Sloan	20.00	9.00
☐ 149 Art Harris	3.00	1.35
☐ 150 Willis Reed	12.00	5.50
☐ 151 Art Williams	3.00	1.35
☐ 152 Don May	3.00	1.35
☐ 153 Loy Petersen	3.00	1.35
☐ 154 Dave Gambee	3.00	1.35
☐ 155 Hal Greer	6.00	2.70
☐ 156 Dave Newmark	3.00	1.35
☐ 157 Jimmy Collins	3.00	1.35
☐ 158 Bill Turner	3.00	1.35
☐ 159 Eddie Miles	3.00	1.35
☐ 160 Jerry West	50.00	22.00
☐ 161 Bob Quick	3.00	1.35
☐ 162 Fred Crawford	3.00	1.35
☐ 163 Tom Sanders	5.00	2.20
☐ 164 Dale Schlueter	3.00	1.35
☐ 165 Clem Haskins	12.00	5.50
☐ 166 Greg Smith	3.00	1.35
☐ 167 Rod Thorn	8.00	3.60
☐ 168 Willis Reed PO	8.00	3.60
☐ 169 Dick Garnett PO	5.00	2.20
☐ 170 D.DeBusschere PO	8.00	3.60
☐ 171 Jerry West PO	15.00	6.75
☐ 172 Bill Bradley PO	12.00	5.50
☐ 173 Wilt Chamberlain	18.00	8.00
☐ 174 Walt Frazier PO	10.00	4.50
☐ 175 Knicks Celebrate	20.00	6.00
(New York Knicks, World Champs)		

1971-72 Topps

LARRY BROWN
ROCKETS' GUARD

The 1971-72 Topps basketball set of 233 witnessed a return to the standard-sized card, i.e., 2 1/2" by 3 1/2". Cards were issued in 10-card, 10 cent packs with 24 packs per box. National Basketball Association players are depicted on cards 1 to 144 and American Basketball Association players are depicted on cards 145 to 233. The set was produced on two sheets. The second production sheet contained the ABA players (145-233) as well as 31 double-printed cards (NBA players) from the first sheet. These DP's are indicated in the checklist below. Subsets include NBA Playoffs (133-137), NBA Statistical Leaders (138-143) and ABA Statistical Leaders (146-151). The key Rookie Cards in this set are Nate Archibald, Rick Barry, Larry Brown, Dave Cowens, Spencer Haywood, Dan Issel, Bob Lanier, Rudy Tomjanovich and Doug Moe.

	NRMT-MT	EXC
COMPLETE SET (233)	750.00	350.00
COM. NBA CARD (1-144)	1.50	.70
COM. ABA CARD (145-233)	2.00	.90
NBA PLAYOFFS (133-137)	3.00	1.35
CL (144A/144B/145)	18.00	8.00
ABA LL (146-151)	4.00	1.80
NBA SEMISTARS	2.00	.90
ABA SEMISTARS	2.50	1.10
UNLISTED STARS	4.00	1.80

☐ 1 Oscar Robertson	40.00	12.00
☐ 2 Bill Bradley	25.00	11.00
☐ 3 Jim Fox	1.50	.70
☐ 4 John Johnson	2.00	.90
☐ 5 Luke Jackson	2.00	.90
☐ 6 Don May DP	1.50	.70
☐ 7 Kevin Loughery	2.00	.90
☐ 8 Terry Dischinger	1.50	.70
☐ 9 Neal Walk	2.00	.90
☐ 10 Elgin Baylor	25.00	11.00
☐ 11 Rick Adelman	2.00	.90
☐ 12 Clyde Lee	1.50	.70
☐ 13 Jerry Chambers	1.50	.70
☐ 14 Fred Carter	2.00	.90
☐ 15 Tom Boerwinkle DP	1.50	.70
☐ 16 John Block	1.50	.70
☐ 17 Dick Barnett	2.00	.90
☐ 18 Henry Finkel	1.50	.70
☐ 19 Norm Van Lier	4.00	1.80
☐ 20 Spencer Haywood	10.00	4.50
☐ 21 George Johnson	1.50	.70
☐ 22 Bobby Lewis	1.50	.70
☐ 23 Bill Hewitt	1.50	.70
☐ 24 Walt Hazzard DP	3.00	1.35
☐ 25 Happy Hairston	2.00	.90
☐ 26 George Wilson	1.50	.70
☐ 27 Lucius Allen	2.00	.90
☐ 28 Jim Washington	1.50	.70
☐ 29 Nate Archibald	25.00	11.00
☐ 30 Willis Reed	10.00	4.50
☐ 31 Erwin Mueller	1.50	.70
☐ 32 Art Harris	1.50	.70
☐ 33 Pete Cross	1.50	.70
☐ 34 Geoff Petrie	4.00	1.80
☐ 35 John Havlicek	30.00	13.50
☐ 36 Larry Siegfried	1.50	.70
☐ 37 John Tresvant DP	1.50	.70
☐ 38 Ron Williams	1.50	.70
☐ 39 Lamar Green DP	1.50	.70
☐ 40 Bob Rule DP	2.00	.90
☐ 41 Jim McMillian	2.00	.90
☐ 42 Wally Jones	2.00	.90
☐ 43 Bob Boozer	1.50	.70
☐ 44 Eddie Miles	1.50	.70
☐ 45 Bob Love DP	5.00	2.20
☐ 46 Claude English	1.50	.70
☐ 47 Dave Cowens	45.00	20.00
☐ 48 Emmette Bryant	1.50	.70
☐ 49 Dave Stallworth	2.00	.90
☐ 50 Jerry West	40.00	18.00
☐ 51 Joe Ellis	1.50	.70
☐ 52 Walt Wesley DP	1.50	.70
☐ 53 Howie Komives	1.50	.70
☐ 54 Paul Silas	4.00	1.80
☐ 55 Pete Maravich DP	50.00	22.00
☐ 56 Gary Gregor	1.50	.70
☐ 57 Sam Lacey	3.00	1.35
☐ 58 Calvin Murphy DP	6.00	2.70
☐ 59 Bob Dandridge	2.00	.90
☐ 60 Hal Greer	4.00	1.80
☐ 61 Keith Erickson	2.00	.90
☐ 62 Joe Cooke	1.50	.70
☐ 63 Bob Lanier	40.00	18.00
☐ 64 Don Kojis	1.50	.70
☐ 65 Walt Frazier	12.00	5.50
☐ 66 Chet Walker DP	3.00	1.35
☐ 67 Dick Garrett	1.50	.70

☐ 68 John Trapp	2.00	.90
☐ 69 JoJo White	6.00	2.70
☐ 70 Wilt Chamberlain	40.00	18.00
☐ 71 Dave Sorenson	1.50	.70
☐ 72 Jim King	1.50	.70
☐ 73 Cazzie Russell	4.00	1.80
☐ 74 Jon McGlocklin	2.00	.90
☐ 75 Tom Van Arsdale	2.00	.90
☐ 76 Dale Schlueter	1.50	.70
☐ 77 Gus Johnson DP	2.00	.90
☐ 78 Dave Bing	8.00	3.60
☐ 79 Billy Cunningham	10.00	4.50
☐ 80 Len Wilkens	10.00	4.50
☐ 81 Jerry Lucas DP	5.00	2.20
☐ 82 Don Chaney	2.00	.90
☐ 83 McCoy McLemore	1.50	.70
☐ 84 Bob Kauffman DP	1.50	.70
☐ 85 Dick Van Arsdale	2.00	.90
☐ 86 Johnny Green	2.00	.90
☐ 87 Jerry Sloan	5.00	2.20
☐ 88 Luther Rackley DP	1.50	.70
☐ 89 Shaler Halimon	1.50	.70
☐ 90 Jimmy Walker	2.00	.90
☐ 91 Rudy Tomjanovich	25.00	11.00
☐ 92 Levi Fontaine	1.50	.70
☐ 93 Bobby Smith	2.00	.90
☐ 94 Bob Arnzen	1.50	.70
☐ 95 Wes Unseld DP	6.00	2.70
☐ 96 Clem Haskins DP	3.00	1.35
☐ 97 Jim Davis	1.50	.70
☐ 98 Steve Kuberski	1.50	.70
☐ 99 Mike Davis DP	1.50	.70
☐ 100 Lew Alcindor	60.00	27.00
☐ 101 Willie McCarter	1.50	.70
☐ 102 Charlie Paulk	1.50	.70
☐ 103 Lee Winfield	1.50	.70
☐ 104 Jim Barnett	1.50	.70
☐ 105 Connie Hawkins DP	8.00	3.60
☐ 106 Archie Clark DP	2.00	.90
☐ 107 Dave DeBusschere	8.00	3.60
☐ 108 Stu Lantz DP	2.00	.90
☐ 109 Don Smith	1.50	.70
☐ 110 Lou Hudson	3.00	1.35
☐ 111 Leroy Ellis	1.50	.70
☐ 112 Jack Marin	2.00	.90
☐ 113 Matt Guokas	2.00	.90
☐ 114 Don Nelson	6.00	2.70
☐ 115 Jeff Mullins DP	2.00	.90
☐ 116 Walt Bellamy	4.00	1.80
☐ 117 Bob Quick	1.50	.70
☐ 118 John Warren	1.50	.70
☐ 119 Barry Clemens	1.50	.70
☐ 120 Elvin Hayes DP	10.00	4.50
☐ 121 Gail Goodrich	8.00	3.60
☐ 122 Ed Manning	2.00	.90
☐ 123 Herm Gilliam DP	1.50	.70
☐ 124 Dennis Awtrey	2.00	.90
☐ 125 John Hummer DP	1.50	.70
☐ 126 Mike Riordan	2.00	.90
☐ 127 Mel Counts	2.00	.90
☐ 128 Bob Weiss DP	1.50	.70
☐ 129 Greg Smith DP	1.50	.70
☐ 130 Earl Monroe	8.00	3.60
☐ 131 Nate Thurmond DP	4.00	1.80
☐ 132 Bill Bridges DP	2.00	.90
☐ 133 Lew Alcindor PO	12.00	5.50
☐ 134 NBA Playoffs G2 Bucks make it Two Straight	3.00	1.35
☐ 135 Bob Dandridge PO	3.00	1.35
☐ 136 Oscar Robertson PO	3.00	3.60
☐ 137 NBA Champs Oscar Bucks sweep Bullets	8.00	3.60
☐ 138 NBA Scoring Leaders Lew Alcindor Elvin Hayes John Havlicek	20.00	9.00
☐ 139 NBA Scoring Average Leaders Lew Alcindor John Havlicek Elvin Hayes	20.00	9.00
☐ 140 NBA FG Pct Leaders Johnny Green Lew Alcindor Wilt Chamberlain	18.00	8.00

		NRMT-MT	EXC
☐ 141	NBA FT Pct Leaders.. 5.00		2.20
	Chet Walker		
	Oscar Robertson		
	Ron Williams		
☐ 142	NBA Rebound Ldrs 25.00		11.00
	Wilt Chamberlain		
	Elvin Hayes		
	Lew Alcindor		
☐ 143	NBA Assist Leaders 12.00		5.50
	Norm Van Lier		
	Oscar Robertson		
	Jerry West		
☐ 144A	NBA Checklist 1-144 18.00		5.50
	(Copyright notation extends up to card 110)		
☐ 144B	NBA Checklist 1-144 18.00		5.50
	(Copyright notation extends up to card 108)		
☐ 145	ABA Checklist 145-233 18.00		5.50
☐ 146	ABA Scoring Leaders 8.00		3.60
	Dan Issel		
	John Brisker		
	Charlie Scott		
☐ 147	ABA Scoring Average 12.00		5.50
	Leaders		
	Dan Issel		
	Rick Barry		
	John Brisker		
☐ 148	ABA 2pt FG Pct Ldrs 4.00		1.80
	Zelmo Beaty		
	Bill Paultz		
	Roger Brown		
☐ 149	ABA FT Pct Ldrs ... 10.00		4.50
	Rick Barry		
	Darrell Carrier		
	Billy Keller		
☐ 150	ABA Rebound Ldrs .. 4.00		1.80
	Mel Daniels		
	Julius Keye		
	Mike Lewis		
☐ 151	ABA Assist Leaders.. 4.00		1.80
	Bill Melchionni		
	Mack Calvin		
	Charlie Scott		
☐ 152	Larry Brown 18.00		8.00
☐ 153	Bob Bedell 2.00		.90
☐ 154	Merv Jackson 2.00		.90
☐ 155	Joe Caldwell 2.50		1.10
☐ 156	Billy Paultz 5.00		2.20
☐ 157	Les Hunter 2.50		1.10
☐ 158	Charlie Williams 2.00		.90
☐ 159	Stew Johnson 2.00		.90
☐ 160	Mack Calvin 5.00		2.20
☐ 161	Don Sidle 2.00		.90
☐ 162	Mike Barrett 2.00		.90
☐ 163	Tom Workman 2.00		.90
☐ 164	Joe Hamilton 2.50		1.10
☐ 165	Zelmo Beaty 8.00		3.60
☐ 166	Dan Hester 2.00		.90
☐ 167	Bob Verga 2.00		.90
☐ 168	Wilbert Jones 2.00		.90
☐ 169	Skeeter Swift 2.00		.90
☐ 170	Rick Barry 45.00		20.00
☐ 171	Billy Keller 4.00		1.80
☐ 172	Ron Franz 2.00		.90
☐ 173	Roland Taylor 2.50		1.10
☐ 174	Julian Hammond 2.00		.90
☐ 175	Steve Jones 6.00		2.70
☐ 176	Gerald Govan 2.50		1.10
☐ 177	Darrell Carrier 2.50		1.10
☐ 178	Ron Boone 5.00		2.20
☐ 179	George Peeples 2.00		.90
☐ 180	John Brisker 2.50		1.10
☐ 181	Doug Moe 6.00		2.70
☐ 182	Ollie Taylor 2.00		.90
☐ 183	Bob Netolicky 2.50		1.10
☐ 184	Sam Robinson 2.00		.90
☐ 185	James Jones 2.50		1.10
☐ 186	Julius Keye 2.50		1.10
☐ 187	Wayne Hightower 2.00		.90
☐ 188	Warren Armstrong 2.50		1.10
☐ 189	Mike Lewis 2.00		.90
☐ 190	Charlie Scott 8.00		3.60
☐ 191	Jim Ard 2.00		.90
☐ 192	George Lehmann 2.00		.90
☐ 193	Ira Harge 2.00		.90
☐ 194	Willie Wise 5.00		2.20
☐ 195	Mel Daniels 8.00		3.60
☐ 196	Larry Cannon 2.00		.90
☐ 197	Jim Eakins 2.50		1.10
☐ 198	Rich Jones 2.50		1.10
☐ 199	Bill Melchionni 4.00		1.80
☐ 200	Dan Issel 35.00		16.00
☐ 201	George Stone 2.00		.90
☐ 202	George Thompson 2.00		.90
☐ 203	Craig Raymond 2.00		.90
☐ 204	Freddie Lewis 2.50		1.10
☐ 205	George Carter 2.50		1.10
☐ 206	Lonnie Wright 2.00		.90
☐ 207	Cincy Powell 2.50		1.10
☐ 208	Larry Miller 2.50		1.10
☐ 209	Sonny Dove 2.00		.90
☐ 210	Byron Beck 2.50		1.10
☐ 211	John Beasley 2.00		.90
☐ 212	Lee Davis 2.00		.90
☐ 213	Rick Mount 6.00		2.70
☐ 214	Walt Simon 2.00		.90
☐ 215	Glen Combs 2.00		.90
☐ 216	Neil Johnson 2.00		.90
☐ 217	Manny Leaks 2.00		.90
☐ 218	Chuck Williams 2.50		1.10
☐ 219	Warren Davis 2.00		.90
☐ 220	Donnie Freeman 2.50		1.10
☐ 221	Randy Mahaffey 2.00		.90
☐ 222	John Barnhill 2.00		.90
☐ 223	Al Cueto 2.00		.90
☐ 224	Louie Dampier 8.00		3.60
☐ 225	Roger Brown 5.00		2.20
☐ 226	Joe DePre 2.00		.90
☐ 227	Ray Scott 2.00		.90
☐ 228	Arvesta Kelly 2.00		.90
☐ 229	Vann Williford 2.00		.90
☐ 230	Larry Jones 2.50		1.10
☐ 231	Gene Moore 2.00		.90
☐ 232	Ralph Simpson 2.50		1.10
☐ 233	Red Robbins 5.00		1.50

1972-73 Topps

The 1972-73 Topps set of 264 standard size cards contains NBA players (1-176) and ABA players (177-264). Cards were issued in 10-card packs with 24 packs per box. All-Star selections are depicted for the NBA on cards 161-170 and for the ABA on cards 249-258. Subsets include NBA Playoffs (154-159), NBA Statistical Leaders (171-176), ABA Playoffs (241-247) and ABA Statistical Leaders (259-264). The key Rookie Card is Julius Erving. Other Rookie Cards include Artis Gilmore and Phil Jackson.

		NRMT-MT	EXC
	COMPLETE SET (264) 800.00		350.00
	COM. NBA CARD (1-176)	1.00	.45
	COM. ABA CARD (177-264)	1.50	.70
	NBA PLAYOFFS (154-159)..	2.50	1.10
	NBA AS (161-170)	2.00	.90
	ABA PLAYOFFS (241-247)..	2.50	1.10
	ABA AS (249-258)	2.00	.90
	ABA LL (259-264)	2.50	1.10
	CL (160/248)	16.00	7.25
	NBA SEMISTARS	1.50	.70
	ABA SEMISTARS	2.00	.90
	UNLISTED STARS	3.00	1.35
☐ 1	Wilt Chamberlain	50.00	15.00
☐ 2	Stan Love	1.00	.45
☐ 3	Geoff Petrie	1.50	.70
☐ 4	Curtis Perry	1.00	.45
☐ 5	Pete Maravich	50.00	22.00
☐ 6	Gus Johnson	1.50	.70
☐ 7	Dave Cowens	18.00	8.00
☐ 8	Randy Smith	4.00	1.80
☐ 9	Matt Guokas	1.00	.45
☐ 10	Spencer Haywood	4.00	1.80
☐ 11	Jerry Sloan	1.50	.70
☐ 12	Dave Sorenson	1.00	.45
☐ 13	Howie Komives	1.00	.45
☐ 14	Joe Ellis	1.00	.45
☐ 15	Jerry Lucas	4.00	1.80
☐ 16	Stu Lantz	1.50	.70
☐ 17	Bill Bridges	1.50	.70
☐ 18	Leroy Ellis	1.00	.45
☐ 19	Art Williams	1.00	.45
☐ 20	Sidney Wicks	8.00	3.60
☐ 21	Wes Unseld	6.00	2.70
☐ 22	Jim Washington	1.00	.45
☐ 23	Fred Hilton	1.00	.45
☐ 24	Curtis Rowe	1.50	.70
☐ 25	Oscar Robertson	18.00	8.00
☐ 26	Larry Steele	1.50	.70
☐ 27	Charlie Davis	1.00	.45
☐ 28	Nate Thurmond	4.00	1.80
☐ 29	Fred Carter	1.50	.70
☐ 30	Connie Hawkins	7.00	3.10
☐ 31	Calvin Murphy	5.00	2.20
☐ 32	Phil Jackson	40.00	18.00
☐ 33	Lee Winfield	1.00	.45
☐ 34	Jim Fox	1.00	.45
☐ 35	Dave Bing	6.00	2.70
☐ 36	Gary Gregor	1.00	.45
☐ 37	Mike Riordan	1.50	.70
☐ 38	George Trapp	1.00	.45
☐ 39	Mike Davis	1.00	.45
☐ 40	Bob Rule	1.50	.70
☐ 41	John Block	1.00	.45
☐ 42	Bob Dandridge	1.50	.70
☐ 43	John Johnson	1.50	.70
☐ 44	Rick Barry	15.00	6.75
☐ 45	JoJo White	3.00	1.35
☐ 46	Cliff Meely	1.00	.45
☐ 47	Charlie Scott	2.50	1.10
☐ 48	Johnny Green	1.50	.70
☐ 49	Pete Cross	1.00	.45
☐ 50	Gail Goodrich	6.00	2.70
☐ 51	Jim Davis	1.00	.45
☐ 52	Dick Barnett	1.50	.70
☐ 53	Bob Christian	1.00	.45
☐ 54	Jon McGlocklin	1.50	.70
☐ 55	Paul Silas	3.00	1.35
☐ 56	Hal Greer	3.00	1.35
☐ 57	Barry Clemens	1.00	.45
☐ 58	Nick Jones	1.00	.45
☐ 59	Cornell Warner	1.00	.45
☐ 60	Walt Frazier	10.00	4.50
☐ 61	Dorie Murrey	1.00	.45
☐ 62	Dick Cunningham	1.00	.45
☐ 63	Sam Lacey	1.50	.70
☐ 64	John Warren	1.00	.45
☐ 65	Tom Boerwinkle	1.00	.45
☐ 66	Fred Foster	1.00	.45
☐ 67	Mel Counts	1.00	.45
☐ 68	Toby Kimball	1.00	.45
☐ 69	Dale Schlueter	1.00	.45
☐ 70	Jack Marin	1.50	.70
☐ 71	Jim Barnett	1.00	.45
☐ 72	Clem Haskins	2.50	1.10

73	Earl Monroe	6.00	2.70
74	Tom Sanders	1.50	.70
75	Jerry West	25.00	11.00
76	Elmore Smith	1.00	.70
77	Don Adams	1.00	.45
78	Wally Jones	1.00	.70
79	Tom Van Arsdale	1.50	.70
80	Bob Lanier	10.00	4.50
81	Len Wilkens	8.00	3.60
82	Neal Walk	1.00	.70
83	Kevin Loughery	1.50	.70
84	Stan McKenzie	1.00	.45
85	Jeff Mullins	1.50	.70
86	Otto Moore	1.00	.45
87	John Tresvant	1.00	.45
88	Dean Meminger	1.00	.45
89	Jim McMillian	1.50	.70
90	Austin Carr	7.00	3.10
91	Clifford Ray	1.50	.70
92	Don Nelson	4.00	1.80
93	Mahdi Abdul-Rahman (formerly Walt Hazzard)	1.50	.70
94	Willie Norwood	1.00	.45
95	Dick Van Arsdale	1.50	.70
96	Don May	1.00	.45
97	Walt Bellamy	2.50	1.10
98	Garfield Heard	4.00	1.80
99	Dave Wohl	1.00	.45
100	k.Abdul-Jabbar	40.00	18.00
101	Ron Knight	1.00	.45
102	Phil Chenier	4.00	1.80
103	Rudy Tomjanovich	8.00	3.60
104	Flynn Robinson	1.00	.45
105	Dave DeBusschere	6.00	2.70
106	Dennis Layton	1.00	.45
107	Bill Hewitt	1.00	.45
108	Dick Garrett	1.00	.45
109	Walt Wesley	1.00	.45
110	John Havlicek	20.00	9.00
111	Norm Van Lier	1.50	.70
112	Cazzie Russell	2.50	1.10
113	Herm Gilliam	1.00	.45
114	Greg Smith	1.00	.45
115	Nate Archibald	6.00	2.70
116	Don Kojis	1.00	.45
117	Rick Adelman	1.50	.70
118	Luke Jackson	1.00	.45
119	Lamar Green	1.00	.45
120	Archie Clark	1.50	.70
121	Happy Hairston	1.50	.70
122	Bill Bradley	16.00	7.25
123	Ron Williams	1.00	.45
124	Jimmy Walker	1.50	.70
125	Bob Kauffman	1.00	.45
126	Rick Roberson	1.00	.70
127	Howard Porter	1.50	.70
128	Mike Newlin	1.50	.70
129	Willis Reed	7.00	3.10
130	Lou Hudson	2.50	1.10
131	Don Chaney	1.50	.70
132	Dave Stallworth	1.00	.45
133	Charlie Yelverton	1.00	.45
134	Ken Durrett	1.00	.45
135	John Brisker	1.50	.70
136	Dick Snyder	1.00	.45
137	Jim McDaniels	1.00	.45
138	Clyde Lee	1.00	.45
139	Dennis Awtrey UER (Misspelled Awtry on card front)	1.00	.45
140	Keith Erickson	1.50	.70
141	Bob Weiss	1.50	.70
142	Butch Beard	3.00	1.35
143	Terry Dischinger	1.00	.45
144	Pat Riley	18.00	8.00
145	Lucius Allen	1.50	.70
146	John Mengelt	1.00	.45
147	John Hummer	1.00	.45
148	Bob Love	4.00	1.80
149	Bobby Smith	1.50	.70
150	Elvin Hayes	10.00	4.50
151	Nate Williams	1.00	.45
152	Chet Walker	2.50	1.10
153	Steve Kuberski	1.00	.45
154	Earl Monroe PO	3.00	1.35
155	NBA Playoffs G2 / Lakers Come Back (under the basket)	2.50	1.10
156	NBA Playoffs G3 / Two in a Row (under the basket)	2.50	1.10
157	Leroy Ellis PO	2.50	1.10
158	Jerry West PO	8.00	3.60
159	Wilt Chamberlain PO	10.00	4.50
160	NBA Checklist 1-176 UER (135 Jim King)	16.00	4.80
161	John Havlicek AS	10.00	4.50
162	S.Haywood AS	2.00	.90
163	K.Abdul-Jabbar AS	25.00	11.00
164	Jerry West AS	15.00	6.75
165	Walt Frazier AS	5.00	2.20
166	Bob Love AS	2.00	.90
167	Billy Cunningham AS	4.00	1.80
168	Wilt Chamberlain AS	20.00	9.00
169	Nate Archibald AS	4.00	1.80
170	Archie Clark AS	2.00	.90
171	NBA Scoring Ldrs / Kareem Abdul-Jabbar / John Havlicek / Nate Archibald	14.00	6.25
172	NBA Scoring Average Leaders / Kareem Abdul-Jabbar / Nate Archibald / John Havlicek	14.00	6.25
173	NBA FG Pct Leaders / Wilt Chamberlain / Kareem Abdul-Jabbar / Walt Bellamy	15.00	6.75
174	NBA FT Pct Leaders / Jack Marin / Calvin Murphy / Gail Goodrich	3.00	1.35
175	NBA Rebound Leaders / Wilt Chamberlain / Kareem Abdul-Jabbar / Wes Unseld	15.00	6.75
176	NBA Assist Leaders / Len Wilkens / Jerry West / Nate Archibald	12.00	5.50
177	Roland Taylor	1.50	.70
178	Art Becker	1.50	.70
179	Mack Calvin	2.00	.90
180	Artis Gilmore	20.00	9.00
181	Collis Jones	1.50	.70
182	John Roche	2.00	.90
183	George McGinnis	14.00	6.25
184	Johnny Neumann	2.00	.90
185	Willie Wise	2.00	.90
186	Bernie Williams	1.50	.70
187	Byron Beck	2.00	.90
188	Larry Miller	2.00	.90
189	Cincy Powell	1.50	.70
190	Donnie Freeman	1.50	.70
191	John Baum	1.50	.70
192	Billy Keller	2.00	.90
193	Wilbert Jones	1.50	.70
194	Glen Combs	1.50	.70
195	Julius Erving (Forward on front, but Center on back)	300.00	135.00
196	Al Smith	1.50	.70
197	George Carter	1.50	.70
198	Louie Dampier	3.00	1.35
199	Rich Jones	1.50	.70
200	Mel Daniels	3.00	1.35
201	Gene Moore	1.50	.70
202	Randy Denton	1.50	.70
203	Larry Jones	1.50	.70
204	Jim Ligon	2.00	.90
205	Warren Jabali	2.00	.90
206	Joe Caldwell	2.00	.90
207	Darrell Carrier	2.00	.90
208	Gene Kennedy	1.50	.70
209	Ollie Taylor	1.50	.70
210	Roger Brown	2.00	.90
211	George Lehmann	1.50	.70
212	Red Robbins	2.00	.90
213	Jim Eakins	2.00	.90
214	Willie Long	1.50	.70
215	Billy Cunningham	8.00	3.60
216	Steve Jones	2.00	.90
217	Les Hunter	1.50	.70
218	Billy Paultz	2.00	.90
219	Freddie Lewis	2.00	.90
220	Zelmo Beaty	2.00	.90
221	George Thompson	1.50	.70
222	Neil Johnson	1.50	.70
223	Dave Robisch	2.00	.90
224	Walt Simon	1.50	.70
225	Bill Melchionni	2.00	.90
226	Wendell Ladner	2.00	.90
227	Joe Hamilton	1.50	.70
228	Bob Netolicky	2.00	.90
229	James Jones	2.00	.90
230	Dan Issel	10.00	4.50
231	Charlie Williams	1.50	.70
232	Willie Sojourner	1.50	.70
233	Merv Jackson	1.50	.70
234	Mike Lewis	1.50	.70
235	Ralph Simpson	2.00	.90
236	Darnell Hillman	2.00	.90
237	Rick Mount	3.00	1.35
238	Gerald Govan	1.50	.70
239	Ron Boone	2.00	.90
240	Tom Washington	1.50	.70
241	ABA Playoffs G1 / Pacers take lead (under the basket)	2.50	1.10
242	Rick Barry PO	5.00	2.20
243	George McGinnis PO	4.00	1.80
244	Rick Barry PO	5.00	2.20
245	Billy Keller PO	2.50	1.10
246	ABA Playoffs G6 / Tight Defense	2.50	1.10
247	ABA Champs: Pacers	3.00	1.35
248	ABA CL 177-264 UER (236 John Brisker)	16.00	4.80
249	Dan Issel AS	6.00	2.70
250	Rick Barry AS	8.00	3.60
251	Artis Gilmore AS	6.00	2.70
252	Donnie Freeman AS	2.00	.90
253	Bill Melchionni AS	2.00	.90
254	Willie Wise AS	2.50	1.10
255	Julius Erving AS	50.00	22.00
256	Zelmo Beaty AS	2.50	1.10
257	Ralph Simpson AS	2.50	1.10
258	Charlie Scott AS	2.50	1.10
259	ABA Scoring Average Leaders / Charlie Scott / Rick Barry / Dan Issel	8.00	3.60
260	ABA 2pt FG Pct. Leaders / Artis Gilmore / Tom Washington / Larry Jones	4.00	1.80
261	ABA 3pt FG Pct. Leaders / Glen Combs / Louie Dampier / Warren Jabali	2.50	1.10
262	ABA FT Pct Leaders / Rick Barry / Mack Calvin / Steve Jones	4.00	1.80
263	ABA Rebound Ldrs / Artis Gilmore / Julius Erving / Mel Daniels	20.00	9.00
264	ABA Assist Leaders / Bill Melchionni / Larry Brown / Louie Dampier	6.00	1.80

1973-74 Topps

The 1973-74 Topps set of 264 standard-size cards contains NBA players on cards numbered 1 to 176 and ABA players on cards numbered 177 to 264. Cards were issued in 10-card packs with 24 packs per box.

HOUSTON ROCKETS
CALVIN MURPHY

All-Star selections (first and second team) for both leagues are noted on the respective player's regular cards. Card backs are printed in red and green on gray card stock. The backs feature year-by-year ABA and NBA statistics. Subsets include NBA Playoffs (62-68), NBA League Leaders (153-158), ABA Playoffs (202-208) and ABA League Leaders (234-239). The only notable Rookie Cards in this set are Chris Ford, Bob McAdoo, and Paul Westphal.

	NRMT-MT	EXC
COMPLETE SET (264)	325.00	145.00
COM. NBA CARD (1-176)	.50	.23
COM. ABA CARD (177-264)	1.00	.45
NBA PLAYOFFS (62-68)	1.00	.45
CL (121/242)	12.00	5.50
ABA PLAYOFFS (202-208)	2.00	.90
ABA LL (234-239)	2.00	.90
NBA SEMISTARS	1.00	.45
ABA SEMISTARS	1.50	.70
UNLISTED STARS	3.00	1.35
CONDITION SENSITIVE SET		

☐ 1 Nate Archibald AS1	10.00	3.00
☐ 2 Steve Kuberski	.50	.23
☐ 3 John Mengelt	.50	.23
☐ 4 Jim McMillian	1.00	.45
☐ 5 Nate Thurmond	3.00	1.35
☐ 6 Dave Wohl	.50	.23
☐ 7 John Brisker	.50	.23
☐ 8 Charlie Davis	.50	.23
☐ 9 Lamar Green	.50	.23
☐ 10 Walt Frazier AS2	6.00	2.70
☐ 11 Bob Christian	.50	.23
☐ 12 Cornell Warner	.50	.23
☐ 13 Calvin Murphy	4.00	1.80
☐ 14 Dave Sorenson	.50	.23
☐ 15 Archie Clark	1.00	.45
☐ 16 Clifford Ray	1.00	.45
☐ 17 Terry Driscoll	.50	.23
☐ 18 Matt Guokas	1.00	.45
☐ 19 Elmore Smith	1.00	.45
☐ 20 John Havlicek AS1	15.00	6.75
☐ 21 Pat Riley	8.00	3.60
☐ 22 George Trapp	.50	.23
☐ 23 Ron Williams	.50	.23
☐ 24 Jim Fox	.50	.23
☐ 25 Dick Van Arsdale	1.00	.45
☐ 26 John Tresvant	.50	.23
☐ 27 Rick Adelman	1.00	.45
☐ 28 Eddie Mast	.50	.23
☐ 29 Jim Cleamons	1.00	.45
☐ 30 D.Busschere AS2	5.00	2.20
☐ 31 Norm Van Lier	1.00	.45
☐ 32 Stan McKenzie	.50	.23
☐ 33 Bob Dandridge	1.00	.45

☐ 34 Leroy Ellis	1.00	.45
☐ 35 Mike Riordan	1.00	.45
☐ 36 Fred Hilton	.50	.23
☐ 37 Toby Kimball	.50	.23
☐ 38 Jim Price	.50	.23
☐ 39 Willie Norwood	.50	.23
☐ 40 Dave Cowens AS2	10.00	4.50
☐ 41 Cazzie Russell	1.00	.45
☐ 42 Lee Winfield	.50	.23
☐ 43 Connie Hawkins	5.00	2.20
☐ 44 Mike Newlin	1.00	.45
☐ 45 Chet Walker	1.00	.45
☐ 46 Walt Bellamy	2.50	1.10
☐ 47 John Johnson	1.00	.45
☐ 48 Henry Bibby	5.00	2.20
☐ 49 Bobby Smith	1.00	.45
☐ 50 K.Abdul-Jabbar AS1	30.00	13.50
☐ 51 Mike Price	.50	.23
☐ 52 John Hummer	.50	.23
☐ 53 Kevin Porter	5.00	2.20
☐ 54 Nate Williams	.50	.23
☐ 55 Gail Goodrich	4.00	1.80
☐ 56 Fred Foster	.50	.23
☐ 57 Don Chaney	1.00	.45
☐ 58 Bud Stallworth	.50	.23
☐ 59 Clem Haskins	1.00	.45
☐ 60 Bob Love AS2	3.00	1.35
☐ 61 Jimmy Walker	1.00	.45
☐ 62 NBA Eastern Semis	1.00	.45
	Knicks shoot down		
	Bullets in 5		
☐ 63 NBA Eastern Semis	1.00	.45
	Celts ousts Hawks		
	2nd Straight Year		
☐ 64 Wilt Chamberlain PO	8.00	3.60
☐ 65 NBA Western Semis	1.00	.45
	Warriors over-		
	whelm Milwaukee		
☐ 66 Willis Reed PO	3.00	1.35
	Henry Finkel		
☐ 67 NBA Western Finals	1.00	.45
	Lakers Breeze Past		
	Golden State		
☐ 68 NBA Championship	4.00	1.80
	Knicks Do It,		
	Repeat '70 Miracle		
	(W.Frazier/Erickson)		
☐ 69 Larry Steele	1.00	.45
☐ 70 Oscar Robertson	12.00	5.50
☐ 71 Phil Jackson	12.00	5.50
☐ 72 John Wetzel	.50	.23
☐ 73 Steve Patterson	.50	.23
☐ 74 Manny Leaks	.50	.23
☐ 75 Jeff Mullins	1.00	.45
☐ 76 Stan Love	.50	.23
☐ 77 Dick Garrett	.50	.23
☐ 78 Don Nelson	3.00	1.35
☐ 79 Chris Ford	4.00	1.80
☐ 80 Wilt Chamberlain	25.00	11.00
☐ 81 Dennis Layton	.50	.23
☐ 82 Bill Bradley	10.00	4.50
☐ 83 Jerry Sloan	1.00	.45
☐ 84 Cliff Meely	.50	.23
☐ 85 Sam Lacey	.50	.23
☐ 86 Dick Snyder	.50	.23
☐ 87 Jim Washington	.50	.23
☐ 88 Lucius Allen	1.00	.45
☐ 89 LaRue Martin	.50	.23
☐ 90 Rick Barry	8.00	3.60
☐ 91 Fred Boyd	.50	.23
☐ 92 Barry Clemens	.50	.23
☐ 93 Dean Meminger	.50	.23
☐ 94 Henry Finkel	.50	.23
☐ 95 Elvin Hayes	6.00	2.70
☐ 96 Stu Lantz	1.00	.45
☐ 97 Bill Hewitt	.50	.23
☐ 98 Neal Walk	.50	.23
☐ 99 Garfield Heard	1.00	.45
☐ 100 Jerry West AS1	20.00	9.00
☐ 101 Otto Moore	.50	.23
☐ 102 Don Kojis	.50	.23
☐ 103 Fred Brown	6.00	2.70
☐ 104 Dwight Davis	.50	.23
☐ 105 Willis Reed	5.00	2.20
☐ 106 Herm Gilliam	.50	.23
☐ 107 Mickey Davis	.50	.23

☐ 108 Jim Barnett	.50	.23
☐ 109 Ollie Johnson	.50	.23
☐ 110 Bob Lanier	6.00	2.70
☐ 111 Fred Carter	1.00	.45
☐ 112 Paul Silas	1.00	.45
☐ 113 Phil Chenier	1.00	.45
☐ 114 Dennis Awtrey	.50	.23
☐ 115 Austin Carr	1.00	.45
☐ 116 Bob Kauffman	.50	.23
☐ 117 Keith Erickson	1.00	.45
☐ 118 Walt Wesley	.50	.23
☐ 119 Steve Bracey	.50	.23
☐ 120 S.Haywood AS1	2.50	1.10
☐ 121 NBA Checklist 1-176	12.00	3.60
☐ 122 Jack Marin	1.00	.45
☐ 123 Jon McGlocklin	.50	.23
☐ 124 Johnny Green	1.00	.45
☐ 125 Jerry Lucas	3.00	1.35
☐ 126 Paul Westphal	12.00	5.50
☐ 127 Curtis Rowe	1.00	.45
☐ 128 M.Abdul-Rahman	1.00	.45
	(formerly Walt Hazzard)		
☐ 129 Lloyd Neal	.50	.23
☐ 130 Pete Maravich AS1	35.00	16.00
☐ 131 Don May	.50	.23
☐ 132 Bob Weiss	1.00	.45
☐ 133 Dave Stallworth	.50	.23
☐ 134 Dick Cunningham	.50	.23
☐ 135 Bob McAdoo	25.00	11.00
☐ 136 Butch Beard	1.00	.45
☐ 137 Happy Hairston	1.00	.45
☐ 138 Bob Rule	1.00	.45
☐ 139 Don Adams	1.00	.45
☐ 140 Charlie Scott	1.00	.45
☐ 141 Ron Riley	.50	.23
☐ 142 Earl Monroe	4.00	1.80
☐ 143 Clyde Lee	.50	.23
☐ 144 Rick Roberson	.50	.23
☐ 145 Rudy Tomjanovich	6.00	2.70
	(Printed without		
	Houston on basket)		
☐ 146 Tom Van Arsdale	1.00	.45
☐ 147 Art Williams	.50	.23
☐ 148 Curtis Perry	.50	.23
☐ 149 Rich Rinaldi	.50	.23
☐ 150 Lou Hudson	1.00	.45
☐ 151 Mel Counts	.50	.23
☐ 152 Jim McDaniels	.50	.23
☐ 153 NBA Scoring Leaders	8.00	3.60
	Nate Archibald		
	Kareem Abdul-Jabbar		
	Spencer Haywood		
☐ 154 NBA Scoring Average	8.00	3.60
	Leaders		
	Nate Archibald		
	Kareem Abdul-Jabbar		
	Spencer Haywood		
☐ 155 NBA FG Pct Leaders	12.00	5.50
	Wilt Chamberlain		
	Matt Guokas		
	Kareem Abdul-Jabbar		
☐ 156 NBA FT Pct Leaders	4.00	1.80
	Rick Barry		
	Calvin Murphy		
	Mike Newlin		
☐ 157 NBA Rebound Leaders	8.00	3.60
	Wilt Chamberlain		
	Nate Thurmond		
	Dave Cowens		
☐ 158 NBA Assist Leaders	4.00	1.80
	Nate Archibald		
	Len Wilkens		
	Dave Bing		
☐ 159 Don Smith	.50	.23
☐ 160 Sidney Wicks	2.50	1.10
☐ 161 Howie Komives	.50	.23
☐ 162 John Gianelli	.50	.23
☐ 163 Jeff Halliburton	.50	.23
☐ 164 Kennedy McIntosh	.50	.23
☐ 165 Len Wilkens	6.00	2.70
☐ 166 Corky Calhoun	.50	.23
☐ 167 Howard Porter	1.00	.45
☐ 168 JoJo White	2.50	1.10
☐ 169 John Block	.50	.23
☐ 170 Dave Bing	4.00	1.80
☐ 171 Joe Ellis	.50	.23

☐ 172 Chuck Terry	.50	.23
☐ 173 Randy Smith	1.00	.45
☐ 174 Bill Bridges	1.00	.45
☐ 175 Geoff Petrie	1.00	.45
☐ 176 Wes Unseld	4.00	1.80
☐ 177 Skeeter Swift	1.00	.45
☐ 178 Jim Eakins	1.50	.70
☐ 179 Steve Jones	1.50	.70
☐ 180 G.McGinnis AS1	3.00	1.35
☐ 181 Al Smith	1.00	.45
☐ 182 Tom Washington	1.00	.45
☐ 183 Louie Dampier	1.50	.70
☐ 184 Simmie Hill	1.00	.45
☐ 185 George Thompson	1.00	.45
☐ 186 Cincy Powell	1.50	.70
☐ 187 Larry Jones	1.00	.45
☐ 188 Neil Johnson	1.00	.45
☐ 189 Tom Owens	1.00	.45
☐ 190 Ralph Simpson AS2	1.50	.70
☐ 191 George Carter	1.50	.70
☐ 192 Rick Mount	1.50	.70
☐ 193 Red Robbins	1.50	.70
☐ 194 George Lehmann	1.00	.45
☐ 195 Mel Daniels AS2	1.50	.70
☐ 196 Bob Warren	1.00	.45
☐ 197 Gene Kennedy	1.00	.45
☐ 198 Mike Barr	1.00	.45
☐ 199 Dave Robisch	1.00	.45
☐ 200 B.Cunningham AS1	5.00	2.20
☐ 201 John Roche	1.50	.70
☐ 202 ABA Western Semis	2.00	.90
Pacers Oust		
Injured Rockets		
☐ 203 ABA Western Semis	2.00	.90
Stars sweep Q's		
in Four Straight		
☐ 204 Dan Issel PO	2.00	.90
☐ 205 ABA Eastern Semis	2.00	.90
Cougars in strong		
finish over Nets		
☐ 206 ABA Western Finals	2.00	.90
Pacers nip bitter		
rival, Stars		
☐ 207 Artis Gilmore PO	3.00	1.35
☐ 208 George McGinnis PO	2.00	.90
☐ 209 Glen Combs	1.00	.45
☐ 210 Dan Issel AS2	6.00	2.70
☐ 211 Randy Denton	1.00	.45
☐ 212 Freddie Lewis	1.50	.70
☐ 213 Stew Johnson	1.00	.45
☐ 214 Roland Taylor	1.00	.45
☐ 215 Rich Jones	1.00	.45
☐ 216 Billy Paultz	1.50	.70
☐ 217 Ron Boone	1.50	.70
☐ 218 Walt Simon	1.00	.45
☐ 219 Mike Lewis	1.00	.45
☐ 220 Warren Jabali AS1	1.50	.70
☐ 221 Wilbert Jones	1.00	.45
☐ 222 Don Buse	1.50	.70
☐ 223 Gene Moore	1.00	.45
☐ 224 Joe Hamilton	1.50	.70
☐ 225 Zelmo Beaty	1.50	.70
☐ 226 Brian Taylor	1.50	.70
☐ 227 Julius Keye	1.00	.45
☐ 228 Mike Gale	1.00	.45
☐ 229 Warren Davis	1.00	.45
☐ 230 Mack Calvin AS2	1.50	.70
☐ 231 Roger Brown	1.50	.70
☐ 232 Chuck Williams	1.50	.70
☐ 233 Gerald Govan	1.50	.70
☐ 234 ABA Scoring Average	10.00	4.50
Leaders		
Julius Erving		
George McGinnis		
Dan Issel		
☐ 235 ABA 2 Pt. Pct.	2.50	1.10
Leaders		
Artis Gilmore		
Gene Kennedy		
Tom Owens		
☐ 236 ABA 3 Pt. Pct.	2.00	.90
Leaders		
Glen Combs		
Roger Brown		
Louie Dampier		
☐ 237 ABA F.T. Pct. Leaders	2.00	.90
Billy Keller		
Ron Boone		
Bob Warren		
☐ 238 ABA Rebound Ldrs	2.50	1.10
Artis Gilmore		
Mel Daniels		
Bill Paultz		
☐ 239 ABA Assist Leaders	2.00	.90
Bill Melchionni		
Chuck Williams		
Warren Jabali		
☐ 240 Julius Erving AS2	50.00	22.00
☐ 241 Jimmy O'Brien	1.00	.45
☐ 242 ABA CL 177-264	12.00	3.60
☐ 243 Johnny Neumann	1.00	.45
☐ 244 Darnell Hillman	1.50	.70
☐ 245 Willie Wise	1.50	.70
☐ 246 Collis Jones	1.00	.45
☐ 247 Ted McClain	1.00	.45
☐ 248 George Irvine	1.00	.45
☐ 249 Bill Melchionni	1.50	.70
☐ 250 Artis Gilmore AS1	6.00	2.70
☐ 251 Willie Long	1.00	.45
☐ 252 Larry Miller	1.00	.45
☐ 253 Lee Davis	1.00	.45
☐ 254 Donnie Freeman	1.50	.70
☐ 255 Joe Caldwell	1.50	.70
☐ 256 Bob Netolicky	1.50	.70
☐ 257 Bernie Williams	1.00	.45
☐ 258 Byron Beck	1.50	.70
☐ 259 Jim Chones	3.00	1.35
☐ 260 James Jones AS1	1.50	.70
☐ 261 Wendell Ladner	1.00	.45
☐ 262 Ollie Taylor	1.00	.45
☐ 263 Les Hunter	1.00	.45
☐ 264 Billy Keller	2.50	.75

1974-75 Topps

The 1974-75 Topps set of 264 standard-size cards contains NBA players on cards numbered 1 to 176 and ABA players on cards numbered 177 to 264. For the first time Team Leader (TL) cards are provided for each team. The cards were issued in 10-card packs with 24 packs per box. All-Star selections (first and second team) for both leagues are noted on the respective player's regular cards. The card backs are printed in blue and red on gray card stock. Subsets include NBA Team Leaders (81-98), NBA Statistical Leaders (144-149), NBA Playoffs (161-164), ABA Statistical Leaders (207-212), ABA Team Leaders (221-230) and ABA Playoffs (246-249). The key Rookie Cards in this set are Doug Collins, George Gervin and Bill Walton.

	NRMT-MT	EXC
COMPLETE SET (264)	325.00	145.00
COM. NBA CARD (1-176)	.50	.23
COM. ABA CARD (177-264)	1.00	.45
NBA TL (81-98)	1.00	.45
CL (141/203)	10.00	4.50
NBA LL (144-149)	1.00	.45
NBA PLAYOFFS (161-164)	1.00	.45
ABA LL (207-212)	2.00	.90
ABA TL (221-230)	2.00	.90
ABA PLAYOFFS (246-249)	2.00	.90
NBA SEMISTARS	1.00	.45
ABA SEMISTARS	1.50	.70
UNLISTED STARS	3.00	1.35

☐ 1 K.Abdul-Jabbar AS1	30.00	9.00
☐ 2 Don May	.50	.23
☐ 3 Bernie Fryer	.50	.23
☐ 4 Don Adams	.50	.23
☐ 5 Herm Gilliam	.50	.23
☐ 6 Jim Chones	1.00	.45
☐ 7 Rick Adelman	1.00	.45
☐ 8 Randy Smith	1.00	.45
☐ 9 Paul Silas	2.00	.90
☐ 10 Pete Maravich	25.00	11.00
☐ 11 Ron Behagen	.50	.23
☐ 12 Kevin Porter	1.00	.45
☐ 13 Bill Bridges	1.00	.45
(On back team shown as		
Los And., should		
be Los Ang.)		
☐ 14 Charles Johnson	.50	.23
☐ 15 Bob Love	1.00	.45
☐ 16 Henry Bibby	1.00	.45
☐ 17 Neal Walk	.50	.23
☐ 18 John Brisker	.50	.23
☐ 19 Lucius Allen	.50	.23
☐ 20 Tom Van Arsdale	1.00	.45
☐ 21 Larry Steele	.50	.23
☐ 22 Curtis Rowe	1.00	.45
☐ 23 Dean Meminger	.50	.23
☐ 24 Steve Patterson	.50	.23
☐ 25 Earl Monroe	3.00	1.35
☐ 26 Jack Marin	.50	.23
☐ 27 JoJo White	2.00	.90
☐ 28 Rudy Tomjanovich	6.00	2.70
☐ 29 Otto Moore	.50	.23
☐ 30 Elvin Hayes AS2	5.00	2.20
☐ 31 Pat Riley	3.00	3.60
☐ 32 Clyde Lee	.50	.23
☐ 33 Bob Weiss	.50	.23
☐ 34 Jim Fox	.50	.23
☐ 35 Charlie Scott	1.00	.45
☐ 36 Cliff Meely	.50	.23
☐ 37 Jon McGlocklin	.50	.23
☐ 38 Jim McMillian	1.00	.45
☐ 39 Bill Walton	60.00	27.00
☐ 40 Dave Bing AS2	3.00	1.35
☐ 41 Jim Washington	.50	.23
☐ 42 Jim Cleamons	1.00	.45
☐ 43 Mel Davis	.50	.23
☐ 44 Garfield Heard	1.00	.45
☐ 45 Jimmy Walker	1.00	.45
☐ 46 Don Nelson	1.00	.45
☐ 47 Jim Barnett	.50	.23
☐ 48 Manny Leaks	.50	.23
☐ 49 Elmore Smith	1.00	.45
☐ 50 Rick Barry AS1	6.00	2.70
☐ 51 Jerry Sloan	1.00	.45
☐ 52 John Hummer	1.00	.45
☐ 53 Keith Erickson	1.00	.45
☐ 54 George E. Johnson	.50	.23
☐ 55 Oscar Robertson	10.00	4.50
☐ 56 Steve Mix	1.00	.45
☐ 57 Rick Roberson	.50	.23
☐ 58 John Mengelt	1.00	.45
☐ 59 Dwight Jones	1.00	.45
☐ 60 Austin Carr	1.00	.45
☐ 61 Nick Weatherspoon	1.00	.45
☐ 62 Clem Haskins	1.00	.45

☐ 63	Don Kojis	.50	.23
☐ 64	Paul Westphal	4.00	1.80
☐ 65	Walt Bellamy	2.00	.90
☐ 66	John Johnson	1.00	.45
☐ 67	Butch Beard	1.00	.45
☐ 68	Happy Hairston	1.00	.45
☐ 69	Tom Boerwinkle	.50	.23
☐ 70	S.Haywood AS2	2.00	.90
☐ 71	Gary Melchionni	.50	.23
☐ 72	Ed Ratleff	1.00	.45
☐ 73	Mickey Davis	.50	.23
☐ 74	Dennis Awtrey	.50	.23
☐ 75	Fred Carter	1.00	.45
☐ 76	George Trapp	.50	.23
☐ 77	John Wetzel	.50	.23
☐ 78	Bobby Smith	1.00	.45
☐ 79	John Gianelli	.50	.23
☐ 80	Bob McAdoo AS2	6.00	2.70
☐ 81	Atlanta Hawks TL	6.00	2.70
	Pete Maravich		
	Lou Hudson		
	Walt Bellamy		
	Pete Maravich		
☐ 82	Boston Celtics TL	5.00	2.20
	John Havlicek		
	JoJo White		
	Dave Cowens		
	JoJo White		
☐ 83	Buffalo Braves TL	1.50	.70
	Bob McAdoo		
	Ernie DiGregorio		
	Bob McAdoo		
	Ernie DiGregorio		
☐ 84	Chicago Bulls TL	2.50	1.10
	Bob Love		
	Chet Walker		
	Clifford Ray		
	Norm Van Lier		
☐ 85	Cleveland Cavs TL	1.50	.70
	Austin Carr		
	Austin Carr		
	Dwight Davis		
	Len Wilkens		
☐ 86	Detroit Pistons TL	1.50	.70
	Bob Lanier		
	Stu Lantz		
	Bob Lanier		
	Dave Bing		
☐ 87	Golden State	2.50	1.10
	Warriors TL		
	Rick Barry		
	Rick Barry		
	Nate Thurmond		
	Rick Barry		
☐ 88	Houston Rockets TL ..	1.50	.70
	Rudy Tomjanovich		
	Calvin Murphy		
	Don Smith		
	Calvin Murphy		
☐ 89	Kansas City Omaha TL	1.00	.45
	Jimmy Walker		
	Jimmy Walker		
	Sam Lacey		
	Jimmy Walker		
☐ 90	Los Angeles Lakers TL	1.00	.45
	Gail Goodrich		
	Gail Goodrich		
	Happy Hairston		
	Gail Goodrich		
☐ 91	Milwaukee Bucks TL	12.00	5.50
	Kareem Abdul-Jabbar		
	Oscar Robertson		
	Kareem Abdul-Jabbar		
	Oscar Robertson		
☐ 92	New Orleans Jazz	1.00	.45
	Emblem; Expansion		
	Draft Picks on Back		
☐ 93	New York Knicks TL	5.00	2.20
	Walt Frazier		
	Bill Bradley		
	Dave DeBusschere		
	Walt Frazier		
☐ 94	Philadelphia 76ers TL	1.50	.70
	Fred Carter		
	Tom Van Arsdale		
	Leroy Ellis		
	Fred Carter		
☐ 95	Phoenix Suns TL	1.50	.70
	Charlie Scott		
	Dick Van Arsdale		
	Neal Walk		
	Neal Walk		
☐ 96	Portland Trail	1.50	.70
	Blazers TL		
	Geoff Petrie		
	Geoff Petrie		
	Rick Roberson		
	Sidney Wicks		
☐ 97	Seattle Supersonics TL	1.50	.70
	Spencer Haywood		
	Dick Snyder		
	Spencer Haywood		
	Fred Brown		
☐ 98	Capitol Bullets TL	1.50	.70
	Phil Chenier		
	Phil Chenier		
	Elvin Hayes		
	Kevin Porter		
☐ 99	Sam Lacey	.50	.23
☐ 100	John Havlicek AS1	10.00	4.50
☐ 101	Stu Lantz	1.00	.45
☐ 102	Mike Riordan	.50	.23
☐ 103	Larry Jones	.50	.23
☐ 104	Connie Hawkins	4.00	1.80
☐ 105	Nate Thurmond	2.00	.90
☐ 106	Dick Gibbs	.50	.23
☐ 107	Corky Calhoun	.50	.23
☐ 108	Dave Wohl	.50	.23
☐ 109	Cornell Warner	.50	.23
☐ 110	Geoff Petrie UER	1.00	.45
	(Misspelled Patrie		
	on card front)		
☐ 111	Leroy Ellis	1.00	.45
☐ 112	Chris Ford	1.00	.45
☐ 113	Bill Bradley	8.00	3.60
☐ 114	Clifford Ray	1.00	.45
☐ 115	Dick Snyder	.50	.23
☐ 116	Nate Williams	.50	.23
☐ 117	Matt Guokas	1.00	.45
☐ 118	Henry Finkel	.50	.23
☐ 119	Curtis Perry	.50	.23
☐ 120	Gail Goodrich AS1	3.00	1.35
☐ 121	Wes Unseld	3.00	1.35
☐ 122	Howard Porter	1.00	.45
☐ 123	Jeff Mullins	.50	.23
☐ 124	Mike Bantom	1.00	.45
☐ 125	Fred Brown	1.00	.45
☐ 126	Bob Dandridge	1.00	.45
☐ 127	Mike Newlin	1.00	.45
☐ 128	Greg Smith	.50	.23
☐ 129	Doug Collins	16.00	7.25
☐ 130	Lou Hudson	1.00	.45
☐ 131	Bob Lanier	5.00	2.20
☐ 132	Phil Jackson	8.00	3.60
☐ 133	Don Chaney	1.00	.45
☐ 134	Jim Brewer	1.00	.45
☐ 135	Ernie DiGregorio	2.50	1.10
☐ 136	Steve Kuberski	.50	.23
☐ 137	Jim Price	.50	.23
☐ 138	Mike D'Antoni	.50	.23
☐ 139	John Brown	.50	.23
☐ 140	Norm Van Lier AS2	1.00	.45
☐ 141	NBA Checklist 1-176	10.00	3.00
☐ 142	Don Slick Watts	1.00	.45
☐ 143	Walt Wesley	.50	.23
☐ 144	NBA Scoring Leaders	12.00	5.50
	Bob McAdoo		
	Kareem Abdul-Jabbar		
	Pete Maravich		
☐ 145	NBA Scoring	12.00	5.50
	Average Leaders		
	Bob McAdoo		
	Pete Maravich		
	Kareem Abdul-Jabbar		
☐ 146	NBA F.G. Pct. Leaders	10.00	4.50
	Bob McAdoo		
	Kareem Abdul-Jabbar		
	Rudy Tomjanovich		
☐ 147	NBA F.T. Pct. Leaders	1.00	.45
	Ernie DiGregorio		
	Rick Barry		
	Jeff Mullins		
☐ 148	NBA Rebound Leaders	4.00	1.80
	Elvin Hayes		
	Dave Cowens		
	Bob McAdoo		
☐ 149	NBA Assist Leaders..	1.00	.45
	Ernie DiGregorio		
	Calvin Murphy		
	Len Wilkens		
☐ 150	Walt Frazier AS1	5.00	2.20
☐ 151	Cazzie Russell	1.00	.45
☐ 152	Calvin Murphy	3.00	1.35
☐ 153	Bob Kauffman	.50	.23
☐ 154	Fred Boyd	.50	.23
☐ 155	Dave Cowens	6.00	2.70
☐ 156	Willie Norwood	.50	.23
☐ 157	Lee Winfield	.50	.23
☐ 158	Dwight Davis	.50	.23
☐ 159	George T. Johnson	.50	.23
☐ 160	Dick Van Arsdale	1.00	.45
☐ 161	NBA Eastern Semis ..	1.00	.45
	Celts over Braves		
	Knicks edge Bullets		
☐ 162	NBA Western Semis	1.00	.45
	Bucks over Lakers		
	Bulls edge Pistons		
☐ 163	NBA Div. Finals	1.00	.45
	Celts over Knicks		
	Bucks sweep Bulls		
☐ 164	NBA Championship	1.50	.70
	Celtics over Bucks		
☐ 165	Phil Chenier	1.00	.45
☐ 166	Kermit Washington ..	1.00	.45
☐ 167	Dale Schlueter	.50	.23
☐ 168	John Block	.50	.23
☐ 169	Don Smith	.50	.23
☐ 170	Nate Archibald	4.00	1.80
☐ 171	Chet Walker	1.00	.45
☐ 172	Archie Clark	1.00	.45
☐ 173	Kennedy McIntosh	.50	.23
☐ 174	George Thompson	.50	.23
☐ 175	Sidney Wicks	2.00	.90
☐ 176	Jerry West	20.00	9.00
☐ 177	Dwight Lamar	1.00	.45
☐ 178	George Carter	1.50	.70
☐ 179	Wil Robinson	1.00	.45
☐ 180	Artis Gilmore AS1	4.00	1.80
☐ 181	Brian Taylor	1.50	.70
☐ 182	Darnell Hillman	1.50	.70
☐ 183	Dave Robisch	1.50	.70
☐ 184	Gene Littles	1.50	.70
☐ 185	Willie Wise AS2	1.50	.70
☐ 186	James Silas	2.50	1.10
☐ 187	Caldwell Jones	3.00	1.35
☐ 188	Roland Taylor	1.00	.45
☐ 189	Randy Denton	1.00	.45
☐ 190	Dan Issel AS2	5.00	2.20
☐ 191	Mike Gale	1.00	.45
☐ 192	Mel Daniels	1.50	.70
☐ 193	Steve Jones	1.50	.70
☐ 194	Marv Roberts	1.00	.45
☐ 195	Ron Boone AS2	1.50	.70
☐ 196	George Gervin	60.00	27.00
☐ 197	Flynn Robinson	1.00	.45
☐ 198	Cincy Powell	1.50	.70
☐ 199	Glen Combs...	1.00	.45
☐ 200	J.Erving AS1 UER ..	45.00	20.00
	(Misspelled Irving		
	on card back)		
☐ 201	Billy Keller	1.50	.70
☐ 202	Willie Long	1.00	.45
☐ 203	ABA Checklist 177-264	10.00	3.00
☐ 204	Joe Caldwell	1.50	.70
☐ 205	Swen Nater AS2	1.50	.70
☐ 206	Rick Mount	1.50	.70
☐ 207	ABA Scoring	10.00	4.50
	Avg. Leaders		
	Julius Erving		
	George McGinnis		
	Dan Issel		
☐ 208	ABA Two-Point Field	2.00	.90
	Goal Percent Leaders		
	Swen Nater		
	James Jones		
	Tom Owens		
☐ 209	ABA Three-Point Field	2.00	.90
	Goal Percent Leaders		

Louie Dampier
Billy Keller
Roger Brown
□ 210 ABA Free Throw ...... 2.00 .90
   Percent Leaders
   James Jones
   Mack Calvin
   Ron Boone
□ 211 ABA Rebound Leaders 2.50 1.10
   Artis Gilmore
   George McGinnis
   Caldwell Jones
□ 212 ABA Assist Leaders .. 2.00 .90
   Al Smith
   Chuck Williams
   Louie Dampier
□ 213 Larry Miller .... 1.00 .45
□ 214 Stew Johnson .... 1.00 .45
□ 215 Larry Finch .... 1.50 .70
□ 216 Larry Kenon 3.00 1.35
□ 217 Joe Hamilton .... 1.50 .70
□ 218 Gerald Govan .... 1.50 .70
□ 219 Ralph Simpson .... 1.50 .70
□ 220 G.McGinnis AS1 .... 2.50 1.10
□ 221 Carolina Cougars TL 2.50 1.10
   Billy Cunningham
   Mack Calvin
   Tom Owens
   Joe Caldwell
□ 222 Denver Nuggets TL .. 2.50 1.10
   Ralph Simpson
   Byron Beck
   Dave Robisch
   Al Smith
□ 223 Indiana Pacers TL .. 2.50 1.10
   George McGinnis
   Billy Keller
   George McGinnis
   Freddie Lewis
□ 224 Kentucky Colonels TL 3.00 1.35
   Dan Issel
   Louie Dampier
   Artis Gilmore
   Louie Dampier
□ 225 Memphis Sounds TL 2.00 .90
   George Thompson
   Larry Finch
   Randy Denton
   George Thompson
□ 226 New York Nets TL .. 10.00 4.50
   Julius Erving
   John Roche
   Larry Kenon
   Julius Erving
□ 227 San Antonio Spurs TL 6.00 2.70
   George Gervin
   George Gervin
   Swen Nater
   George Silas
□ 228 San Diego Conq. TL 2.00 .90
   Dwight Lamar
   Stew Johnson
   Caldwell Jones
   Chuck Williams
□ 229 Utah Stars TL 2.50 1.10
   Willie Wise
   James Jones
   Gerald Govan
   James Jones
□ 230 Virginia Squires TL .. 2.00 .90
   George Carter
   George Irvine
   Jim Eakins
   Roland Taylor
□ 231 Bird Averitt .... 1.00 .45
□ 232 John Roche .... 1.00 .45
□ 233 George Irvine .... 1.00 .45
□ 234 John Williamson ...... 1.50 .70
□ 235 Billy Cunningham 4.00 1.80
□ 236 Jimmy O'Brien .... 1.00 .45
□ 237 Wilbert Jones .... 1.00 .45
□ 238 Johnny Neumann ..... 1.00 .45
□ 239 Al Smith .... 1.00 .45
□ 240 Roger Brown .... 1.50 .70
□ 241 Chuck Williams .... 1.50 .70
□ 242 Rich Jones .... 1.00 .45

□ 243 Dave Twardzik .... 1.50 .70
□ 244 Wendell Ladner .... 1.50 .70
□ 245 Mack Calvin AS1 ..... 1.50 .70
□ 246 ABA Eastern Semis . 2.00 .90
   Nets over Squires
   Colonels sweep Cougars
□ 247 ABA Western Semis .. 2.00 .90
   Stars over Conquistadors
   Pacers over Spurs
□ 248 ABA Div. Finals .... 2.00 .90
   Nets sweep Colonels
   Stars edge Pacers
□ 249 Julius Erving PO 12.00 5.50
□ 250 Wilt Chamberlain CO 25.00 11.00
□ 251 Ron Robinson .... 1.00 .45
□ 252 Zelmo Beaty .... 1.50 .70
□ 253 Donnie Freeman ...... 1.50 .70
□ 254 Mike Green .... 1.00 .45
□ 255 Louie Dampier AS2 .. 1.50 .70
□ 256 Tom Owens .... 1.00 .45
□ 257 George Karl 10.00 4.50
□ 258 Jim Eakins .... 1.50 .70
□ 259 Travis Grant .... 1.50 .70
□ 260 James Jones AS1 .... 1.50 .70
□ 261 Mike Jackson .... 1.00 .45
□ 262 Billy Paultz .... 1.50 .70
□ 263 Freddie Lewis .... 1.50 .70
□ 264 Byron Beck .... 2.00 .60
   (Back refers to ANA,
   should be ABA)

1975-76 Topps

The 1975-76 Topps basketball card set of 330 standard-size cards was the largest basketball set ever produced up to that time. Cards were issued in 10-card packs with 24 packs per box. NBA players are depicted on cards 1-220 and ABA players on cards 221-330. Team Leaders (TL) cards are 116-133 (NBA teams) and 278-287 (ABA). Other subsets include NBA Statistical Leaders (1-6), NBA Playoffs (188-189), NBA Team Checklists (203-220), ABA Statistical Leaders (221-226), ABA Playoffs (309-310) and ABA Team Checklists (321-330). All-Star selections (first and second team) for both leagues are noted on the respective player's regular cards. Card backs are printed in blue and green on gray card stock. The set is particularly hard to sort numerically, as the small card number on the back is printed in blue on a dark green background. The set was printed on three large sheets each containing 110 different cards. Investigation of the second (series) sheet reveals that 22 of the cards were double printed; they are marked DP in the checklist below. Rookie Cards in this set include Bobby Jones, Maurice Lucas, Moses Malone and Keith (Jamaal) Wilkes.

	NRMT-MT	EXC
COMPLETE SET (330)	450.00	200.00
COM. NBA CARD (1-220)	.75	.35
COM. ABA CARD (221-330)	1.50	.70
COMMON NBA TL (116-133)	1.50	.70
NBA LL (1-6)	1.50	.70
NBA TL (117/119/121)	3.00	1.35
NBA TL (122/128/133)	3.00	1.35
NBA PLAYOFFS (188-189)	1.50	.70
NBA TC (203-220)	1.50	.70
ABA LL (221-226)	2.00	.90
ABA TL (278-287)	2.00	.90
ABA PLAYOFFS (309-310)	2.00	.90
ABA TC (321-330)	2.00	.90
CL (61/181/257)	8.00	3.60
NBA SEMISTARS	.85	.55
ABA SEMISTARS	2.00	.90
UNLISTED STARS	3.00	1.35

□ 1 NBA Scoring Average 15.00 4.50
   Leaders
   Bob McAdoo
   Rick Barry
   Kareem Abdul-Jabbar
□ 2 NBA Field Goal 4.00 1.80
   Percentage Leaders
   Don Nelson
   Butch Beard
   Rudy Tomjanovich
□ 3 NBA Free Throw 5.00 2.20
   Percentage Leaders
   Rick Barry
   Calvin Murphy
   Bill Bradley
□ 4 NBA Rebounds Leaders 1.50 .70
   Wes Unseld
   Dave Cowens
   Sam Lacey
□ 5 NBA Assists Leaders 3.00 1.35
   Kevin Porter
   Dave Bing
   Nate Archibald
□ 6 NBA Steals Leaders 4.00 1.80
   Rick Barry
   Walt Frazier
   Larry Steele
□ 7 Tom Van Arsdale ...... 1.25 .55
□ 8 Paul Silas .... 1.25 .55
□ 9 Jerry Sloan .... 1.25 .55
□ 10 Bob McAdoo AS1 ...... 6.00 2.70
□ 11 Dwight Davis .... .75 .35
□ 12 John Mengelt .... .75 .35
□ 13 George Johnson .... .75 .35
□ 14 Ed Ratleff .... .75 .35
□ 15 Nate Archibald AS1 .. 4.00 1.80
□ 16 Elmore Smith .... .75 .35
□ 17 Bob Dandridge .... 1.25 .55
□ 18 Louie Nelson .... .75 .35
□ 19 Neal Walk .... .75 .35
□ 20 Billy Cunningham 4.00 1.80
□ 21 Gary Melchionni ...... .75 .35
□ 22 Barry Clemens .... .75 .35
□ 23 Jimmy Jones .... .75 .35
□ 24 Tom Burleson .... 1.25 .55
□ 25 Lou Hudson .... 1.25 .55
□ 26 Henry Finkel .... .75 .35

☐ 27	Jim McMillian	1.25	.55
☐ 28	Matt Guokas	1.25	.55
☐ 29	Fred Foster DP	.75	.35
☐ 30	Bob Lanier	5.00	2.20
☐ 31	Jimmy Walker	1.25	.55
☐ 32	Cliff Meely	.75	.35
☐ 33	Butch Beard	1.25	.55
☐ 34	Cazzie Russell	1.25	.55
☐ 35	Jon McGlocklin	.75	.35
☐ 36	Bernie Fryer	.75	.35
☐ 37	Bill Bradley	6.00	2.70
☐ 38	Fred Carter	1.25	.55
☐ 39	Dennis Awtrey DP	.75	.35
☐ 40	Sidney Wicks	1.25	.55
☐ 41	Fred Brown	1.25	.55
☐ 42	Rowland Garrett	.75	.35
☐ 43	Herm Gilliam	.75	.35
☐ 44	Don Nelson	1.25	.55
☐ 45	Ernie DiGregorio	1.25	.55
☐ 46	Jim Brewer	.75	.35
☐ 47	Chris Ford	1.25	.55
☐ 48	Nick Weatherspoon	.75	.35
☐ 49	Zaid Abdul-Aziz	.75	.35
	(formerly Don Smith)		
☐ 50	Keith Wilkes	10.00	4.50
☐ 51	Ollie Johnson DP	.75	.35
☐ 52	Lucius Allen	1.25	.55
☐ 53	Mickey Davis	.75	.35
☐ 54	Otto Moore	.75	.35
☐ 55	Walt Frazier AS1	5.00	2.20
☐ 56	Steve Mix	1.25	.55
☐ 57	Nate Hawthorne	.75	.35
☐ 58	Lloyd Neal	.75	.35
☐ 59	Don Slick Watts	1.25	.55
☐ 60	Elvin Hayes	5.00	2.20
☐ 61	Checklist 1-110	8.00	2.40
☐ 62	Mike Sojourner	.75	.35
☐ 63	Randy Smith	1.25	.55
☐ 64	John Block DP	.75	.35
☐ 65	Charlie Scott	1.25	.55
☐ 66	Jim Chones	1.25	.55
☐ 67	Rick Adelman	1.25	.55
☐ 68	Curtis Rowe	.75	.35
☐ 69	Derrek Dickey	1.25	.55
☐ 70	Rudy Tomjanovich	5.00	2.20
☐ 71	Pat Riley	6.00	2.70
☐ 72	Cornell Warner	.75	.35
☐ 73	Earl Monroe	3.00	1.35
☐ 74	Allan Bristow	3.00	1.35
☐ 75	Pete Maravich DP	25.00	11.00
☐ 76	Curtis Perry	.75	.35
☐ 77	Bill Walton	18.00	8.00
☐ 78	Leonard Gray	.75	.35
☐ 79	Kevin Porter	1.25	.55
☐ 80	John Havlicek AS2	10.00	4.50
☐ 81	Dwight Jones	.75	.35
☐ 82	Jack Marin	.75	.35
☐ 83	Dick Snyder	.75	.35
☐ 84	George Trapp	.75	.35
☐ 85	Nate Thurmond	2.50	1.10
☐ 86	Charles Johnson	.75	.35
☐ 87	Ron Riley	.75	.35
☐ 88	Stu Lantz	1.25	.55
☐ 89	Scott Wedman	1.25	.55
☐ 90	Kareem Abdul-Jabbar	25.00	11.00
☐ 91	Aaron James	.75	.35
☐ 92	Jim Barnett	.75	.35
☐ 93	Clyde Lee	.75	.35
☐ 94	Larry Steele	1.25	.55
☐ 95	Mike Riordan	.75	.35
☐ 96	Archie Clark	1.25	.55
☐ 97	Mike Bantom	.75	.35
☐ 98	Bob Kauffman	.75	.35
☐ 99	Kevin Stacom	.75	.35
☐ 100	Rick Barry AS1	6.00	2.70
☐ 101	Ken Charles	.75	.35
☐ 102	Tom Boerwinkle	.75	.35
☐ 103	Mike Newlin	1.25	.55
☐ 104	Leroy Ellis	1.25	.55
☐ 105	Austin Carr	1.25	.55
☐ 106	Ron Behagen	.75	.35
☐ 107	Jim Price	.75	.35
☐ 108	Bud Stallworth	.75	.35
☐ 109	Earl Williams	.75	.35
☐ 110	Gail Goodrich	3.00	1.35
☐ 111	Phil Jackson	7.00	3.10

☐ 112	Rod Derline	.75	.35
☐ 113	Keith Erickson	.75	.35
☐ 114	Phil Lumpkin	.75	.35
☐ 115	Wes Unseld	3.00	1.35
☐ 116	Atlanta Hawks TL	1.50	.70
	Lou Hudson		
	Lou Hudson		
	John Drew		
	Dean Meminger		
☐ 117	Boston Celtics TL	3.00	1.35
	Dave Cowens		
	Kevin Stacom		
	Paul Silas		
	JoJo White		
☐ 118	Buffalo Braves TL	2.00	.90
	Bob McAdoo		
	Jack Marin		
	Bob McAdoo		
	Randy Smith		
☐ 119	Chicago Bulls TL	2.50	1.10
	Bob Love		
	Chet Walker		
	Nate Thurmond		
	Norm Van Lier		
☐ 120	Cleveland Cavs TL	1.50	.70
	Bobby Smith		
	Dick Snyder		
	Jim Chones		
	Jim Cleamons		
☐ 121	Detroit Pistons TL	3.00	1.35
	Bob Lanier		
	John Mengelt		
	Bob Lanier		
	Dave Bing		
☐ 122	Golden State TL	3.00	1.35
	Rick Barry		
	Rick Barry		
	Clifford Ray		
	Rick Barry		
☐ 123	Houston Rockets TL	2.00	.90
	Rudy Tomjanovich		
	Calvin Murphy		
	Kevin Kunnert		
	Mike Newlin		
☐ 124	Kansas City Kings TL	2.00	.90
	Nate Archibald		
	Ollie Johnson		
	Sam Lacey UER		
	(Lacy on front)		
	Nate Archibald		
☐ 125	Los Angeles Lakers TL	1.50	.70
	Gail Goodrich		
	Cazzie Russell		
	Happy Hairston		
	Gail Goodrich		
☐ 126	Milwaukee Bucks TL	8.00	3.60
	Kareem Abdul-Jabbar		
	Mickey Davis		
	Kareem Abdul-Jabbar		
	Kareem Abdul-Jabbar		
☐ 127	New Orleans Jazz TL	10.00	4.50
	Pete Maravich		
	Stu Lantz		
	E.C. Coleman		
	Pete Maravich		
☐ 128	N.Y. Knicks TL DP	3.00	1.35
	Walt Frazier		
	Bill Bradley		
	John Gianelli		
	Walt Frazier		
☐ 129	Phila. 76ers TL DP	2.00	.90
	Fred Carter		
	Doug Collins		
	Billy Cunningham		
	Billy Cunningham		
☐ 130	Phoenix Suns TL DP	1.50	.70
	Charlie Scott		
	Keith Erickson		
	Curtis Perry		
	Dennis Awtrey		
☐ 131	Portland Blazers TL DP	1.50	.70
	Sidney Wicks		
	Geoff Petrie		
	Sidney Wicks		
	Geoff Petrie		
☐ 132	Seattle Sonics TL	2.00	.90

	Spencer Haywood		
	Archie Clark		
	Spencer Haywood		
	Don Watts		
☐ 133	Washington Bullets TL	3.00	1.35
	Elvin Hayes		
	Clem Haskins		
	Wes Unseld		
	Kevin Porter		
☐ 134	John Drew	1.25	.55
☐ 135	JoJo White AS2	2.00	.90
☐ 136	Garfield Heard	1.25	.55
☐ 137	Jim Cleamons	.75	.35
☐ 138	Howard Porter	1.25	.55
☐ 139	Phil Smith	1.25	.55
☐ 140	Bob Love	1.25	.55
☐ 141	John Gianelli DP	.75	.35
☐ 142	Larry McNeill	.75	.35
☐ 143	Brian Winters	3.00	1.35
☐ 144	George Thompson	.75	.35
☐ 145	Kevin Kunnert	.75	.35
☐ 146	Henry Bibby	1.25	.55
☐ 147	John Johnson	.75	.35
☐ 148	Doug Collins	4.00	1.80
☐ 149	John Brisker	.75	.35
☐ 150	Dick Van Arsdale	1.25	.55
☐ 151	Leonard Robinson	2.50	1.10
☐ 152	Dean Meminger	.75	.35
☐ 153	Phil Hankinson	.75	.35
☐ 154	Dale Schlueter	.75	.35
☐ 155	Norm Van Lier	1.25	.55
☐ 156	Campy Russell	3.00	1.35
☐ 157	Jeff Mullins	1.25	.55
☐ 158	Sam Lacey	.75	.35
☐ 159	Happy Hairston	1.25	.55
☐ 160	Dave Bing DP	2.50	1.10
☐ 161	Kevin Restani	.75	.35
☐ 162	Dave Wohl	.75	.35
☐ 163	E.C. Coleman	.75	.35
☐ 164	Jim Fox	.75	.35
☐ 165	Geoff Petrie	1.25	.55
☐ 166	H.Wingo DP UER	.75	.35
	(Misspelled Harthorne		
	on card front)		
☐ 167	Fred Boyd	.75	.35
☐ 168	Willie Norwood	.75	.35
☐ 169	Bob Wilson	.75	.35
☐ 170	Dave Cowens	6.00	2.70
☐ 171	Tom Henderson	.75	.35
☐ 172	Jim Washington	.75	.35
☐ 173	Clem Haskins	1.25	.55
☐ 174	Jim Davis	.75	.35
☐ 175	Bobby Smith DP	.75	.35
☐ 176	Mike D'Antoni	.75	.35
☐ 177	Zelmo Beaty	1.25	.55
☐ 178	Gary Brokaw	.75	.35
☐ 179	Mel Davis	.75	.35
☐ 180	Calvin Murphy	3.00	1.35
☐ 181	Checklist 111-220 DP	8.00	2.40
☐ 182	Nate Williams	.75	.35
☐ 183	LaRue Martin	.75	.35
☐ 184	George McGinnis	2.50	1.10
☐ 185	Clifford Ray	.75	.35
☐ 186	Paul Westphal	3.00	1.35
☐ 187	Talvin Skinner	.75	.35
☐ 188	NBA Playoff Semis DP	1.50	.70
	Warriors edge Bulls		
	Bullets over Celts		
☐ 189	Clifford Ray PO	1.50	.70
☐ 190	Phil Chenier AS2 DP	1.25	.55
☐ 191	John Brown	.75	.35
☐ 192	Lee Winfield	.75	.35
☐ 193	Steve Patterson	.75	.35
☐ 194	Charles Dudley	.75	.35
☐ 195	Connie Hawkins DP	3.00	1.35
☐ 196	Leon Benbow	.75	.35
☐ 197	Don Kojis	.75	.35
☐ 198	Ron Williams	.75	.35
☐ 199	Mel Counts	.75	.35
☐ 200	Spencer Haywood AS2	1.50	.70
☐ 201	Greg Jackson	.75	.35
☐ 202	Tom Kozelko DP	.75	.35
☐ 203	Atlanta Hawks	1.50	.70
	Checklist		
☐ 204	Boston Celtics	3.00	1.35
	Checklist		

☐ 205 Buffalo Braves 1.50	☐ 253 James Silas AS2 ..... 2.00	.90
Checklist .70	☐ 254 Moses Malone 40.00	18.00
☐ 206 Chicago Bulls 2.50	☐ 255 Willie Wise 2.00	.90
Checklist 1.10	☐ 256 Dwight Lamar 1.50	.70
☐ 207 Cleveland Cavs 1.50	☐ 257 Checklist 221-330 .... 8.00	2.40
Checklist .70	☐ 258 Byron Beck 2.00	.90
☐ 208 Detroit Pistons 1.50	☐ 259 Len Elmore 3.00	1.35
Checklist .70	☐ 260 Dan Issel 5.00	2.20
☐ 209 Golden State 1.50	☐ 261 Rick Mount 1.50	.70
Checklist .70	☐ 262 Billy Paultz 2.00	.90
☐ 210 Houston Rockets 1.50	☐ 263 Donnie Freeman 1.50	.70
Checklist .70	☐ 264 George Adams 1.50	.70
☐ 211 Kansas City Kings DP 1.50	☐ 265 Don Chaney 2.00	.90
Checklist .70	☐ 266 Randy Denton 1.50	.70
☐ 212 Los Angeles Lakers DP 1.50	☐ 267 Don Washington 1.50	.70
Checklist .70	☐ 268 Roland Taylor 1.50	.70
☐ 213 Milwaukee Bucks..... 1.50	☐ 269 Charlie Edge 1.50	.70
Checklist .70	☐ 270 Louie Dampier 2.00	.90
☐ 214 New Orleans Jazz ... 1.50	☐ 271 Collis Jones 1.50	.70
Checklist .70	☐ 272 Al Skinner 1.50	.70
☐ 215 New York Knicks 1.50	☐ 273 Coby Dietrick....... 1.50	.70
Checklist .70	☐ 274 Tim Bassett 1.50	.70
☐ 216 Philadelphia 76ers... 1.50	☐ 275 Freddie Lewis 2.00	.90
Checklist .70	☐ 276 Gerald Govan....... 1.50	.70
☐ 217 Phoenix Suns DP 1.50	☐ 277 Ron Thomas 1.50	.70
Checklist .70	☐ 278 Denver Nuggets TL .. 2.00	.90
☐ 218 Portland Blazers 1.50	Ralph Simpson	
Checklist .70	Mack Calvin	
☐ 219 Seattle Sonics DP .. 10.00	Mike Green	
Checklist 4.50	Mack Calvin	
☐ 220 Washington Bullets .. 1.50	☐ 279 Indiana Pacers TL .. 2.50	1.10
Checklist .70	George McGinnis	
☐ 221 ABA Scoring 8.00	Billy Keller	
Average Leaders 3.60	George McGinnis	
George McGinnis	George McGinnis	
Julius Erving	☐ 280 Kentucky Colonels TL 2.50	1.10
Ron Boone	Artis Gilmore	
☐ 222 ABA 2 Pt. Field Goal 8.00	Louie Dampier	
Percentage Leaders 3.60	Artis Gilmore	
Bobby Jones	Louie Dampier	
Artis Gilmore	☐ 281 Memphis Sounds TL 2.00	.90
Moses Malone	George Carter	
☐ 223 ABA 3 Pt. Field Goal 2.00	Larry Finch	
Percentage Leaders .90	Tom Owens	
Billy Shepherd	Chuck Williams	
Louie Dampier	☐ 282 New York Nets TL .. 10.00	4.50
Al Smith	Julius Erving	
☐ 224 ABA Free Throw 2.00	Julius Williamson	
Percentage Leaders .90	Julius Erving	
Mack Calvin	Julius Erving	
James Silas	☐ 283 St. Louis Spirits TL .. 2.50	1.10
Dave Robisch	Marvin Barnes	
☐ 225 ABA Rebounds Leaders 2.00	Freddie Lewis	
Swen Nater .90	Marvin Barnes	
Artis Gilmore	Freddie Lewis	
Marvin Barnes	☐ 284 San Antonio Spurs TL 5.00	2.20
☐ 226 ABA Assists Leaders 2.00	George Gervin	
Mack Calvin .90	James Silas	
Chuck Williams	Swen Nater	
George McGinnis	James Silas	
☐ 227 Mack Calvin AS1 ... 2.00	☐ 285 San Diego Sails TL .. 2.00	.90
☐ 228 Billy Knight AS1 ..... 3.00	Travis Grant	
☐ 229 Bird Averitt 1.50	Jimmy O'Brien	
☐ 230 George Carter 1.50	Caldwell Jones	
☐ 231 Swen Nater AS2 ..... 2.00	Jimmy O'Brien	
☐ 232 Steve Jones 2.00	☐ 286 Utah Stars TL 8.00	3.60
☐ 233 George Gervin 18.00	Ron Boone	
☐ 234 Lee Davis 1.50	Ron Boone	
☐ 235 Ron Boone AS1 ..... 2.00	Moses Malone	
☐ 236 Mike Jackson 1.50	Al Smith	
☐ 237 Kevin Joyce 1.50	☐ 287 Virginia Squires TL .. 2.00	.90
☐ 238 Marv Roberts 1.50	Willie Wise	
☐ 239 Tom Owens 1.50	Red Robbins	
☐ 240 Ralph Simpson 2.00	Dave Vaughn	
☐ 241 Gus Gerard 1.50	Dave Twardzik	
☐ 242 Brian Taylor AS2 .... 2.00	☐ 288 Claude Terry 1.50	.70
☐ 243 Rich Jones 1.50	☐ 289 Wilbert Jones 1.50	.70
☐ 244 John Roche 1.50	☐ 290 Darnell Hillman 2.00	.90
☐ 245 Travis Grant 2.00	☐ 291 Bill Melchionni 2.00	.90
☐ 246 Dave Twardzik 2.00	☐ 292 Mel Daniels 2.00	.90
☐ 247 Mike Green 1.50	☐ 293 Fly Williams 2.00	.90
☐ 248 Billy Keller 2.00	☐ 294 Larry Kenon 2.00	.90
☐ 249 Stew Johnson 1.50	☐ 295 Red Robbins 2.00	.90
☐ 250 Artis Gilmore AS1 ... 4.00	☐ 296 Warren Jabali 2.00	.90
☐ 251 John Williamson 2.00	☐ 297 Jim Eakins 2.00	.90
☐ 252 Marvin Barnes AS2 .. 4.00	☐ 298 Bobby Jones 12.00	5.50

☐ 299 Don Buse............ 2.00	.90
☐ 300 Julius Erving AS1 .. 45.00	20.00
☐ 301 Billy Shepherd...... 1.50	.70
☐ 302 Maurice Lucas...... 6.00	2.70
☐ 303 George Karl 5.00	2.20
☐ 304 Jim Bradley 1.50	.70
☐ 305 Caldwell Jones 2.00	.90
☐ 306 Al Smith 1.50	.70
☐ 307 Jan Van Breda Kolff.. 2.00	.90
☐ 308 Darrell Elston....... 1.50	.70
☐ 309 ABA Playoff Semifinals 2.00	.90
Colonels over Spirits;	
Pacers edge Nuggets	
☐ 310 Artis Gilmore PO 2.50	1.10
☐ 311 Ted McClain 1.50	.70
☐ 312 Willie Sojourner..... 1.50	.70
☐ 313 Bob Warren........ 1.50	.70
☐ 314 Bob Netolicky 2.00	.90
☐ 315 Chuck Williams 1.50	.70
☐ 316 Gene Kennedy 1.50	.70
☐ 317 Jimmy O'Brien 1.50	.70
☐ 318 Dave Robisch 1.50	.70
☐ 319 Wali Jones 1.50	.70
☐ 320 George Irvine....... 1.50	.70
☐ 321 Denver Nuggets..... 2.00	.90
Checklist	
☐ 322 Indiana Pacers....... 2.00	.90
Checklist	
☐ 323 Kentucky Colonels.... 2.00	.90
Checklist	
☐ 324 Memphis Sounds 2.00	.90
Checklist	
☐ 325 New York Nets 2.00	.90
Checklist	
☐ 326 St. Louis Spirits...... 2.00	.90
Checklist	
(Spirits of St. Louis	
on card back)	
☐ 327 San Antonio Spurs .. 2.00	.90
Checklist	
☐ 328 San Diego Sails 2.00	.90
Checklist	
☐ 329 Utah Stars 2.00	.90
Checklist	
☐ 330 Virginia Squires 4.00	1.20
Checklist	

1976-77 Topps

Perhaps the most popular set of the seventies, the 144-card 1976-77 Topps set witnessed a return to the larger-size at 3 1/8" by 5 1/4". The larger size and excellent photo quality are appealing to collectors. Also, because of the size, they are attractive to autograph collectors. Cards were issued in 10-card packs with 24 packs per box. The fronts have a large color photo with the team name vertical on the left border. The player's name and position are at the bottom. Backs have statistical and biographical data. Cards numbered 126-135 are the previous season's NBA All-Star selections. The cards were printed on two large sheets, each with eight rows and nine columns. The checklist card was located in the lower right corner of the second sheet. Card No. 1, Julius Erving, is rarely found centered. Rookie Cards include Alvan Adams, Lloyd Free, Gus Williams and David Thompson.

	NRMT-MT	EXC
COMPLETE SET (144)	375.00	170.00
COMMON CARD (1-144)	1.75	.80
AS (126-135)	2.00	.90
CL (48)	40.00	18.00
SEMISTARS	2.50	1.10
UNLISTED STARS	5.00	2.20
CONDITION SENSITIVE SET		

		NRMT-MT	EXC
☐ 1	Julius Erving	75.00	22.00
☐ 2	Dick Snyder	1.75	.80
☐ 3	Paul Silas	2.50	1.10
☐ 4	Keith Erickson	1.75	.80
☐ 5	Wes Unseld	4.00	1.80
☐ 6	Butch Beard	2.50	1.10
☐ 7	Lloyd Neal	1.75	.80
☐ 8	Tom Henderson	1.75	.80
☐ 9	Jim McMillian	2.50	1.10
☐ 10	Bob Lanier	6.00	2.70
☐ 11	Junior Bridgeman	2.50	1.10
☐ 12	Corky Calhoun	1.75	.80
☐ 13	Billy Keller	2.50	1.10
☐ 14	Mickey Johnson	1.75	.80
☐ 15	Fred Brown	2.50	1.10
☐ 16	Jamaal Wilkes	3.00	1.35
☐ 17	Louie Nelson	1.75	.80
☐ 18	Ed Ratleff	1.75	.80
☐ 19	Billy Paultz	2.50	1.10
☐ 20	Nate Archibald	5.00	2.20
☐ 21	Steve Mix	2.50	1.10
☐ 22	Ralph Simpson	1.75	.80
☐ 23	Campy Russell	2.50	1.10
☐ 24	Charlie Scott	2.50	1.10
☐ 25	Artis Gilmore	5.00	2.20
☐ 26	Dick Van Arsdale	2.50	1.10
☐ 27	Phil Chenier	2.50	1.10
☐ 28	Spencer Haywood	3.00	1.35
☐ 29	Chris Ford	2.50	1.10
☐ 30	Dave Cowens	10.00	4.50
☐ 31	Sidney Wicks	2.50	1.10
☐ 32	Jim Price	1.75	.80
☐ 33	Dwight Jones	1.75	.80
☐ 34	Lucius Allen	1.75	.80
☐ 35	Marvin Barnes	2.50	1.10
☐ 36	Henry Bibby	2.50	1.10
☐ 37	Joe Meriweather	1.75	.80
☐ 38	Doug Collins	6.00	2.70
☐ 39	Garfield Heard	2.50	1.10
☐ 40	Randy Smith	2.50	1.10
☐ 41	Tom Burleson	2.50	1.10
☐ 42	Dave Twardzik	2.50	1.10
☐ 43	Bill Bradley	12.00	5.50
☐ 44	Calvin Murphy	4.00	1.80
☐ 45	Bob Love	2.50	1.10
☐ 46	Brian Winters	2.50	1.10
☐ 47	Glenn McDonald	1.75	.80
☐ 48	Checklist 1-144	40.00	12.00
☐ 49	Brad Averitt	1.75	.80
☐ 50	Rick Barry	10.00	4.50
☐ 51	Ticky Burden	1.75	.80
☐ 52	Rich Jones	1.75	.80
☐ 53	Austin Carr	2.50	1.10
☐ 54	Steve Kuberski	1.75	.80
☐ 55	Paul Westphal	4.00	1.80
☐ 56	Mike Riordan	1.75	.80

		NRMT-MT	EXC
☐ 57	Bill Walton	25.00	11.00
☐ 58	Eric Money	1.75	.80
☐ 59	John Drew	2.50	1.10
☐ 60	Pete Maravich	45.00	20.00
☐ 61	John Shumate	2.50	1.10
☐ 62	Mack Calvin	2.50	1.10
☐ 63	Bruce Seals	1.75	.80
☐ 64	Walt Frazier	6.00	2.70
☐ 65	Elmore Smith	1.75	.80
☐ 66	Rudy Tomjanovich	6.00	2.70
☐ 67	Sam Lacey	1.75	.80
☐ 68	George Gervin	25.00	11.00
☐ 69	Gus Williams	5.00	2.20
☐ 70	George McGinnis	2.50	1.10
☐ 71	Len Elmore	1.75	.80
☐ 72	Jack Marin	1.75	.80
☐ 73	Brian Taylor	1.75	.80
☐ 74	Jim Brewer	1.75	.80
☐ 75	Alvan Adams	6.00	2.70
☐ 76	Dave Bing	4.00	1.80
☐ 77	Phil Jackson	10.00	4.50
☐ 78	Geoff Petrie	2.50	1.10
☐ 79	Mike Sojourner	1.75	.80
☐ 80	James Silas	2.50	1.10
☐ 81	Bob Dandridge	2.50	1.10
☐ 82	Ernie DiGregorio	2.50	1.10
☐ 83	Cazzie Russell	2.50	1.10
☐ 84	Kevin Porter	2.50	1.10
☐ 85	Tom Boerwinkle	1.75	.80
☐ 86	Darnell Hillman	2.50	1.10
☐ 87	Herm Gilliam	1.75	.80
☐ 88	Nate Williams	1.75	.80
☐ 89	Phil Smith	1.75	.80
☐ 90	John Havlicek	16.00	7.25
☐ 91	Kevin Kunnert	1.75	.80
☐ 92	Jimmy Walker	2.50	1.10
☐ 93	Billy Cunningham	5.00	2.20
☐ 94	Dan Issel	6.00	2.70
☐ 95	Ron Boone	2.50	1.10
☐ 96	Lou Hudson	2.50	1.10
☐ 97	Jim Chones	2.50	1.10
☐ 98	Earl Monroe	4.00	1.80
☐ 99	Tom Van Arsdale	2.50	1.10
☐ 100	K.Abdul-Jabbar	40.00	18.00
☐ 101	Moses Malone	18.00	8.00
☐ 102	Ricky Sobers	1.75	.80
☐ 103	Swen Nater	2.50	1.10
☐ 104	Leonard Robinson	2.50	1.10
☐ 105	Don Slick Watts	2.50	1.10
☐ 106	Otto Moore	1.75	.80
☐ 107	Maurice Lucas	2.50	1.10
☐ 108	Norm Van Lier	2.50	1.10
☐ 109	Clifford Ray	1.75	.80
☐ 110	David Thompson	40.00	18.00
☐ 111	Fred Carter	2.50	1.10
☐ 112	Caldwell Jones	2.50	1.10
☐ 113	John Williamson	2.50	1.10
☐ 114	Bobby Smith	2.50	1.10
☐ 115	JoJo White	2.50	1.10
☐ 116	Curtis Perry	1.75	.80
☐ 117	John Gianelli	1.75	.80
☐ 118	Curtis Rowe	1.75	.80
☐ 119	Lionel Hollins	2.50	1.10
☐ 120	Elvin Hayes	6.00	2.70
☐ 121	Ken Charles	1.75	.80
☐ 122	Dave Meyers	2.50	1.10
☐ 123	Jerry Sloan	2.50	1.10
☐ 124	Billy Knight	2.50	1.10
☐ 125	Gail Goodrich	2.50	1.10
☐ 126	K.Abdul-Jabbar AS	20.00	9.00
☐ 127	Julius Erving AS	25.00	11.00
☐ 128	George McGinnis AS	2.75	1.25
☐ 129	Nate Archibald AS	3.00	1.35
☐ 130	Pete Maravich AS	25.00	11.00
☐ 131	Dave Cowens AS	5.00	2.20
☐ 132	Rick Barry AS	5.00	2.20
☐ 133	Elvin Hayes AS	4.00	1.80
☐ 134	James Silas AS	2.00	.90
☐ 135	Randy Smith AS	2.00	.90
☐ 136	Leonard Gray	1.75	.80
☐ 137	Charles Johnson	1.75	.80
☐ 138	Ron Behagen	1.75	.80
☐ 139	Mike Newlin	2.50	1.10
☐ 140	Bob McAdoo	6.00	2.70
☐ 141	Mike Gale	1.75	.80
☐ 142	Scott Wedman	2.50	1.10
☐ 143	Lloyd Free	6.00	2.70
☐ 144	Bobby Jones	8.00	2.40

1977-78 Topps

The 1977-78 Topps basketball card set consists of 132 standard-size cards. Cards were issued in 10-card packs with 24 packs per box. Fronts feature team and player name at the bottom with the player's position in a basketball at bottom left of the photo. Card backs are printed in green and black on either white or gray card stock. The white card stock is considered more desirable by most collectors and may even be a little tougher to find. However, there is no difference in value for either card stock. Rookie Cards include Adrian Dantley, Darryl Dawkins, John Lucas, Tom McMillen and Robert Parish.

		NRMT-MT	EXC
COMPLETE SET (132)		90.00	40.00
COMMON CARD (1-132)		.30	.14
CL (29)		3.00	1.35
SEMISTARS		.75	.35
*GRAY AND WHITE BACKS: EQUAL VALUE			

		NRMT-MT	EXC
☐ 1	Kareem Abdul-Jabbar	15.00	4.50
☐ 2	Henry Bibby	.40	.18
☐ 3	Curtis Rowe	.30	.14
☐ 4	Norm Van Lier	.40	.18
☐ 5	Darnell Hillman	.40	.18
☐ 6	Earl Monroe	1.50	.70
☐ 7	Leonard Gray	.30	.14
☐ 8	Bird Averitt	.30	.14
☐ 9	Jim Brewer	.30	.14
☐ 10	Paul Westphal	1.00	.45
☐ 11	Bob Gross	.40	.18
☐ 12	Phil Smith	.30	.14
☐ 13	Dan Roundfield	.60	.25
☐ 14	Brian Taylor	.30	.14
☐ 15	Rudy Tomjanovich	2.00	.90
☐ 16	Kevin Porter	.40	.18
☐ 17	Scott Wedman	.40	.18
☐ 18	Lloyd Free	.60	.25
☐ 19	Tom Boswell	.30	.14
☐ 20	Pete Maravich	15.00	6.75
☐ 21	Cliff Pondexter	.30	.14
☐ 22	Bubbles Hawkins	.40	.18
☐ 23	Kevin Grevey	.60	.25
☐ 24	Ken Charles	.30	.14
☐ 25	Bob Dandridge	.40	.18
☐ 26	Lonnie Shelton	.30	.14
☐ 27	Don Chaney	.40	.18
☐ 28	Larry Kenon	.40	.18

No.	Player	NRMT-MT	EXC
29	Checklist 1-132	3.00	.90
30	Fred Brown	.40	.18
31	John Gianelli UER	.30	.14
	(Listed as Cavaliers, should be Buffalo Braves)		
32	Austin Carr	.40	.18
33	Jamaal Wilkes	.60	.25
34	Caldwell Jones	.40	.18
35	JoJo White	.60	.25
36	Scott May	.75	.35
37	Mike Newlin	.30	.14
38	Mel Davis	.30	.14
39	Lionel Hollins	.60	.25
40	Elvin Hayes	2.50	1.10
41	Dan Issel	2.00	.90
42	Ricky Sobers	.30	.14
43	Don Ford	.30	.14
44	John Williamson	.30	.14
45	Bob McAdoo	2.00	.90
46	Geoff Petrie	.40	.18
47	M.L. Carr	2.00	.90
48	Brian Winters	.60	.25
49	Sam Lacey	.30	.14
50	George McGinnis	.60	.25
51	Don Slick Watts	.40	.18
52	Sidney Wicks	.60	.25
53	Wilbur Holland	.30	.14
54	Tim Bassett	.30	.14
55	Phil Chenier	.40	.18
56	Adrian Dantley	8.00	3.60
57	Jim Chones	.30	.14
58	John Lucas	2.50	1.10
59	Cazzie Russell	.40	.18
60	David Thompson	5.00	2.20
61	Bob Lanier	2.00	.90
62	Dave Twardzik	.40	.18
63	Wilbert Jones	.30	.14
64	Clifford Ray	.30	.14
65	Doug Collins	1.50	.70
66	Tom McMillen	2.50	1.10
67	Rich Kelley	.30	.14
68	Mike Bantom	.30	.14
69	Tom Boerwinkle	.30	.14
70	John Havlicek	6.00	2.70
71	Marvin Webster	.40	.18
72	Curtis Perry	.30	.14
73	George Gervin	8.00	3.60
74	Leonard Robinson	.60	.25
75	Wes Unseld	1.50	.70
76	Dave Meyers	.40	.18
77	Gail Goodrich	.60	.25
78	Richard Washington	.60	.25
79	Mike Gale	.30	.14
80	Maurice Lucas	.60	.25
81	Harvey Catchings	.30	.14
82	Randy Smith	.30	.14
83	Campy Russell	.40	.18
84	Kevin Kunnert	.30	.14
85	Lou Hudson	.40	.18
86	Mickey Johnson	.30	.14
87	Lucius Allen	.30	.14
88	Spencer Haywood	1.00	.45
89	Gus Williams	.60	.25
90	Dave Cowens	3.00	1.35
91	Al Skinner	.30	.14
92	Swen Nater	.30	.14
93	Tom Henderson	.30	.14
94	Don Buse	.40	.18
95	Alvan Adams	.60	.25
96	Mack Calvin	.40	.18
97	Tom Burleson	.30	.14
98	John Drew	.40	.18
99	Mike Green	.30	.14
100	Julius Erving	15.00	6.75
101	John Mengelt	.40	.18
102	Howard Porter	.30	.14
103	Billy Paultz	.40	.18
104	John Shumate	.30	.18
105	Calvin Murphy	1.50	.70
106	Elmore Smith	.30	.14
107	Jim McMillian	.30	.14
108	Kevin Stacom	.30	.14
109	Jan Van Breda Kolff	.30	.14
110	Billy Knight	.40	.18
111	Robert Parish	30.00	13.50
112	Larry Wright	.30	.14
113	Bruce Seals	.30	.14
114	Junior Bridgeman	.40	.18
115	Artis Gilmore	1.50	.70
116	Steve Mix	.40	.18
117	Don Lee	.30	.14
118	Bobby Jones	.60	.25
119	Ron Boone	.40	.18
120	Bill Walton	8.00	3.60
121	Chris Ford	.40	.18
122	Earl Tatum	.30	.14
123	E.C. Coleman	.30	.14
124	Moses Malone	6.00	2.70
125	Charlie Scott	.40	.18
126	Bobby Smith	.30	.14
127	Nate Archibald	1.50	.70
128	Mitch Kupchak	.75	.35
129	Walt Frazier	2.50	1.10
130	Rick Barry	3.00	1.35
131	Ernie DiGregorio	.40	.18
132	Darryl Dawkins	12.00	3.60

1978-79 Topps

The 1978-79 Topps basketball card set contains 132 standard-size cards. Cards were issued in 10-card packs with 36 packs per box. Card fronts feature the player and team name down the left border and a small head shot inserted at bottom right. Card backs are printed in orange and brown on gray card stock. The key Rookie Cards in this set include Quinn Buckner, Walter Davis, James "Buddha" Edwards, Dennis Johnson, Marques Johnson, Bernard King, Norm Nixon and Jack Sikma.

	NRMT-MT	EXC
COMPLETE SET (132)	70.00	32.00
COMMON CARD (1-132)	.30	.14
CL (67)	2.00	.90
SEMISTARS	.75	.35

No.	Player	NRMT-MT	EXC
1	Bill Walton	10.00	3.00
2	Doug Collins	1.50	.70
3	Jamaal Wilkes	.75	.35
4	Wilbur Holland	.30	.14
5	Bob McAdoo	1.25	.55
6	Lucius Allen	.30	.14
7	Wes Unseld	1.25	.55
8	Dave Meyers	.50	.23
9	Austin Carr	.50	.23
10	Walter Davis	7.00	3.10
11	John Williamson	.30	.14
12	E.C. Coleman	.30	.14
13	Calvin Murphy	1.00	.45
14	Bobby Jones	.75	.35
15	Chris Ford	.50	.23
16	Kermit Washington	.50	.23
17	Butch Beard	.50	.23
18	Steve Mix	.30	.14
19	Marvin Webster	.50	.23
20	George Gervin	6.00	2.70
21	Steve Hawes	.30	.14
22	Johnny Davis	.30	.14
23	Swen Nater	.30	.14
24	Lou Hudson	.50	.23
25	Elvin Hayes	1.50	.70
26	Nate Archibald	1.00	.45
27	James Edwards	3.00	1.35
28	Howard Porter	.50	.23
29	Quinn Buckner	1.25	.55
30	Leonard Robinson	.50	.23
31	Jim Cleamons	.30	.14
32	Campy Russell	.50	.23
33	Phil Smith	.30	.14
34	Darryl Dawkins	2.00	.90
35	Don Buse	.50	.23
36	Mickey Johnson	.30	.14
37	Mike Gale	.30	.14
38	Moses Malone	4.00	1.80
39	Gus Williams	.75	.35
40	Dave Cowens	2.00	.90
41	Bobby Wilkerson	.50	.23
42	Wilbert Jones	.30	.14
43	Charlie Scott	.50	.23
44	John Drew	.50	.23
45	Earl Monroe	1.25	.55
46	John Shumate	.50	.23
47	Earl Tatum	.30	.14
48	Mitch Kupchak	.50	.23
49	Ron Boone	.50	.23
50	Maurice Lucas	.75	.35
51	Louie Dampier	.50	.23
52	Aaron James	.30	.14
53	John Mengelt	.30	.14
54	Garfield Heard	.30	.14
55	George Johnson	.30	.14
56	Junior Bridgeman	.30	.14
57	Elmore Smith	.30	.14
58	Rudy Tomjanovich	1.50	.70
59	Fred Brown	.50	.23
60	Rick Barry UER	2.00	.90
	(reversed negative)		
61	Dave Bing	1.25	.55
62	Anthony Roberts	.30	.14
63	Norm Nixon	2.00	.90
64	Leon Douglas	.30	.14
65	Henry Bibby	.50	.23
66	Lonnie Shelton	.30	.14
67	Checklist 1-132	2.00	.60
68	Tom Henderson	.30	.14
69	Dan Roundfield	.50	.23
70	Armond Hill	.50	.23
71	Larry Kenon	.50	.23
72	Billy Knight	.50	.23
73	Artis Gilmore	1.00	.45
74	Lionel Hollins	.50	.23
75	Bernard King	7.00	3.10
76	Brian Winters	.75	.35
77	Alvan Adams	.75	.35
78	Dennis Johnson	8.00	3.60
79	Scott Wedman	.30	.14
80	Pete Maravich	10.00	4.50
81	Dan Issel	1.50	.70
82	M.L. Carr	.75	.35
83	Walt Frazier	1.50	.70
84	Dwight Jones	.30	.14
85	JoJo White	.75	.35
86	Robert Parish	5.00	2.20
87	Charlie Criss	.50	.23
88	Jim McMillian	.50	.23
89	Chuck Williams	.30	.14
90	George McGinnis	.75	.35
91	Billy Paultz	.50	.23
92	Bob Dandridge	.50	.23
93	Ricky Sobers	.30	.14
94	Paul Silas	.50	.23
95	Gail Goodrich	.75	.35
96	Tim Bassett	.30	.14
97	Ron Lee	.30	.14
98	Bob Gross	.50	.23
99	Sam Lacey	.30	.14
100	David Thompson	3.00	1.35

(College North Carolina, should be NC State)

		NRMT	EXC
☐ 101	John Gianelli	.30	
☐ 102	Norm Van Lier	.50	.23
☐ 103	Caldwell Jones	.50	.23
☐ 104	Eric Money	.30	.14
☐ 105	Jim Chones	.50	.23
☐ 106	John Lucas	1.00	.45
☐ 107	Spencer Haywood	.75	.35
☐ 108	Eddie Johnson	.30	.14
☐ 109	Sidney Wicks	.75	.35
☐ 110	Kareem Abdul-Jabbar	8.00	3.60
☐ 111	Sonny Parker	.30	.14
☐ 112	Randy Smith	.30	.14
☐ 113	Kevin Grevey	.50	.23
☐ 114	Rich Kelley	.30	.14
☐ 115	Scott May	.50	.23
☐ 116	Lloyd Free	.75	.35
☐ 117	Jack Sikma	2.00	.90
☐ 118	Kevin Porter	.50	.23
☐ 119	Darnell Hillman	.50	.23
☐ 120	Paul Westphal	1.00	.45
☐ 121	Richard Washington	.30	.14
☐ 122	Dave Twardzik	.50	.23
☐ 123	Mike Bantom	.30	.14
☐ 124	Mike Newlin	.30	.14
☐ 125	Bob Lanier	1.50	.70
☐ 126	Marques Johnson	4.00	1.80
☐ 127	Foots Walker	.50	.23
☐ 128	Cedric Maxwell	1.25	.55
☐ 129	Ray Williams	.30	.14
☐ 130	Julius Erving	10.00	4.50
☐ 131	Clifford Ray	.30	.14
☐ 132	Adrian Dantley	3.00	.90

1979-80 Topps

The 1979-80 Topps basketball set contains 132 standard-size cards. Cards were issued in 12-card packs along with a stick of bubble gum. The player's name, team and position are at the bottom. The team name is wrapped around a basketball. Card backs are printed in red and black on gray card stock. All-Star selections are designated as AS1 for first team selections and AS2 for second team selections and are denoted on the front of the player's regular card. Notable Rookie Cards in this set include Alex English, Reggie Theus, and Mychal Thompson.

	NRMT-MT	EXC
COMPLETE SET (132)	70.00	32.00
COMMON CARD (1-132)	.30	.14
CL (101)	2.00	.90
SEMISTARS	.60	.25

☐ 1	George Gervin	6.00	2.70
☐ 2	Mitch Kupchak	.40	.18
☐ 3	Henry Bibby	.40	.18
☐ 4	Bob Gross	.40	.18
☐ 5	Dave Cowens	2.00	.90
☐ 6	Dennis Johnson	1.50	.70
☐ 7	Scott Wedman	.30	.14
☐ 8	Earl Monroe	1.25	.55
☐ 9	Mike Bantom	.30	.14
☐ 10	K.Abdul-Jabbar AS	8.00	3.60
☐ 11	JoJo White	.60	.25
☐ 12	Spencer Haywood	.60	.25
☐ 13	Kevin Porter	.40	.18
☐ 14	Bernard King	1.50	.70
☐ 15	Mike Newlin	.30	.14
☐ 16	Sidney Wicks	.60	.25
☐ 17	Dan Issel	1.25	.55
☐ 18	Tom Henderson	.30	.14
☐ 19	Jim Chones	.40	.18
☐ 20	Julius Erving	10.00	4.50
☐ 21	Brian Winters	.60	.25
☐ 22	Billy Paultz	.40	.18
☐ 23	Cedric Maxwell	.40	.18
☐ 24	Eddie Johnson	.30	.14
☐ 25	Artis Gilmore	.75	.35
☐ 26	Maurice Lucas	.60	.25
☐ 27	Gus Williams	.60	.25
☐ 28	Sam Lacey	.30	.14
☐ 29	Toby Knight	.30	.14
☐ 30	Paul Westphal AS1	.75	.35
☐ 31	Alex English	8.00	3.60
☐ 32	Gail Goodrich	.60	.25
☐ 33	Caldwell Jones	.40	.18
☐ 34	Kevin Grevey	.40	.18
☐ 35	Jamaal Wilkes	.60	.25
☐ 36	Sonny Parker	.30	.14
☐ 37	John Gianelli	.30	.14
☐ 38	John Long	.40	.18
☐ 39	George Johnson	.30	.14
☐ 40	Lloyd Free AS2	.60	.25
☐ 41	Rudy Tomjanovich	1.25	.55
☐ 42	Foots Walker	.40	.18
☐ 43	Dan Roundfield	.40	.18
☐ 44	Reggie Theus	3.00	1.35
☐ 45	Bill Walton	3.00	1.35
☐ 46	Fred Brown	.40	.18
☐ 47	Darnell Hillman	.40	.18
☐ 48	Ray Williams	.30	.14
☐ 49	Larry Kenon	.40	.18
☐ 50	David Thompson	2.00	.90
☐ 51	Billy Knight	.40	.18
☐ 52	Alvan Adams	.60	.25
☐ 53	Phil Smith	.30	.14
☐ 54	Adrian Dantley	1.25	.55
☐ 55	John Williamson	.30	.14
☐ 56	Campy Russell	.40	.18
☐ 57	Armond Hill	.40	.18
☐ 58	Bob Lanier	1.25	.55
☐ 59	Mickey Johnson	.30	.14
☐ 60	Pete Maravich	10.00	4.50
☐ 61	Nick Weatherspoon	.30	.14
☐ 62	Robert Reid	.60	.25
☐ 63	Mychal Thompson	1.50	.70
☐ 64	Doug Collins	1.00	.45
☐ 65	Wes Unseld	1.25	.55
☐ 66	Jack Sikma	.60	.25
☐ 67	Bobby Wilkerson	.30	.14
☐ 68	Bill Robinzine	.30	.14
☐ 69	Joe Meriweather	.30	.14
☐ 70	Marques Johnson AS1	.40	.18
☐ 71	Ricky Sobers	.30	.14
☐ 72	Clifford Ray	.30	.14
☐ 73	Tim Bassett	.30	.14
☐ 74	James Silas	.40	.18
☐ 75	Bob McAdoo	.75	.35
☐ 76	Austin Carr	.40	.18
☐ 77	Don Ford	.30	.14
☐ 78	Steve Hawes	.30	.14
☐ 79	Ron Brewer	.30	.14
☐ 80	Walter Davis	1.00	.45
☐ 81	Calvin Murphy	.75	.35
☐ 82	Tom Boswell	.30	.14
☐ 83	Lonnie Shelton	.30	.14
☐ 84	Terry Tyler	.30	.14
☐ 85	Randy Smith	.30	.14
☐ 86	Rich Kelley	.30	.14

☐ 87	Otis Birdsong	.40	.18
☐ 88	Marvin Webster	.30	.14
☐ 89	Eric Money	.30	.14
☐ 90	Elvin Hayes AS1	1.50	.70
☐ 91	Junior Bridgeman	.30	.14
☐ 92	Johnny Davis	.30	.14
☐ 93	Robert Parish	3.00	1.35
☐ 94	Eddie Jordan	.40	.18
☐ 95	Leonard Robinson	.40	.18
☐ 96	Rick Robey	.40	.18
☐ 97	Norm Nixon	.60	.25
☐ 98	Mark Olberding	.30	.14
☐ 99	Wilbur Holland	.30	.14
☐ 100	Moses Malone AS1	3.00	1.35
☐ 101	Checklist 1-132	2.00	.60
☐ 102	Tom Owens	.30	.14
☐ 103	Phil Chenier	.40	.18
☐ 104	John Johnson	.30	.14
☐ 105	Darryl Dawkins	1.00	.45
☐ 106	Charlie Scott	.40	.18
☐ 107	M.L. Carr	.60	.25
☐ 108	Phil Ford	2.50	1.10
☐ 109	Swen Nater	.30	.14
☐ 110	Nate Archibald	1.25	.55
☐ 111	Aaron James	.30	.14
☐ 112	Jim Cleamons	.30	.14
☐ 113	James Edwards	.60	.25
☐ 114	Don Buse	.40	.18
☐ 115	Steve Mix	.30	.14
☐ 116	Charles Johnson	.30	.14
☐ 117	Elmore Smith	.30	.14
☐ 118	John Drew	.30	.14
☐ 119	Lou Hudson	.40	.18
☐ 120	Rick Barry	2.00	.90
☐ 121	Kent Benson	.30	.14
☐ 122	Mike Gale	.30	.14
☐ 123	Jan Van Breda Kolff	.30	.14
☐ 124	Chris Ford	.40	.18
☐ 125	George McGinnis	.60	.25
☐ 126	Leon Douglas	.30	.14
☐ 127	John Lucas	.60	.25
☐ 128	Kermit Washington	.40	.18
☐ 129	Lionel Hollins	.40	.18
☐ 130	Bob Dandridge AS2	.40	.18
☐ 131	James McElroy	.30	.14
☐ 132	Bobby Jones	1.50	.70

1980-81 Topps

The 1980-81 Topps basketball card set contains 264 different individual players (1 1/6" by 2 1/2") on 176 different panels of three (2 1/2" by 3 1/2"). This set was issued in packs of eight cards with 36 packs per box. The cards come with three individual players per standard card. A perforation line segments each card into three players. In all, there are 176 different complete cards, however, the same player will be on more than one card. The variations stem from the fact that the cards in this set were printed on two separate sheets. In the checklist below, the first 88 cards comprise a complete set of all 264 players. The second 88 cards (89-176) provide a slight rearrangement of players within the card, but still contain the same 264 players. The cards are numbered within each series of 88 by any ordering of the left-hand player's number when the card is viewed from the back. In the checklist below, SD refers to a "Slam Dunk" star card. The letters AS in the checklist refer to an All-Star selection pictured on the front of the checklist card. There are a number of Team Leader (TL) cards which depict the team's leader in assists, scoring or rebounds. Prices given below are for complete panels, as that is the typical way these cards are collected. Cards which have been separated into the three parts are relatively valueless. The key card in this set features Larry Bird, Julius Erving and Magic Johnson. It the Rookie Card for Bird and Magic. In addition to Bird and Magic, other noteworthy players making their first card appearance in this set include Bill Cartwright, Maurice Cheeks, Michael Cooper, Sidney Moncrief and Tree Rollins. Other lesser-known players making their first card appearance include James Bailey, Greg Ballard, Dudley Bradley, Mike Bratz, Joe Bryant, Kenny Carr, Wayne Cooper, David Greenwood, Phil Hubbard, Geoff Huston, Abdul Jeelani, Greg Kelser, Reggie King, Tom LaGarde, Mark Landsberger, Allen Leavell, Calvin Natt, Roger Phegley, Ben Poquette, Micheal Ray Richardson, Cliff Robinson, Purvis Short, Jerome Whitehead, and Freeman Williams.

	NRMT-MT	EXC
COMPLETE SET (176)	525.00	240.00
COMMON PANEL (1-176)	.30	.14
SEMISTARS	.60	.25
UNLISTED STARS	1.00	.45
CONDITION SENSITIVE SET		

		NRMT-MT	EXC
☐ 1	3 Dan Roundfield AS	5.00	2.20
	181 Elvin Hayes		
	258 Ron Brewer SD		
☐ 2	7 Moses Malone AS	1.50	.70
	185 Steve Mix		
	92 Robert Parish TL		
☐ 3	12 Gus Williams AS........	.60	.25
	67 Geoff Huston		
	5 John Drew AS		
☐ 4	24 Steve Hawes...........	1.00	.45
	32 Nate Archibald TL		
	248 Elvin Hayes		
☐ 5	29 Dan Roundfield	.60	.25
	73 Dan Issel TL		
	152 Brian Winters		
☐ 6	34 Larry Bird	400.00	180.00
	174 Julius Erving TL		
	139 Magic Johnson		
☐ 7	36 Dave Cowens	1.00	.45
	186 Paul Westphal TL		
	142 Jamaal Wilkes		
☐ 8	38 Pete Maravich	6.00	2.70
	264 Lloyd Free SD		
	194 Dennis Johnson		
☐ 9	40 Rick Robey..............	.60	.25
	234 Ad.Dantley TL		
	26 Eddie Johnson		
☐ 10	47 Scott May	.30	.14
	196 K.Washington TL		
	177 Henry Bibby		
☐ 11	55 Don Ford	.30	.14
	145 Quinn Buckner TL		
	138 Brad Holland		
☐ 12	58 Campy Russell	.30	.14
	247 Kevin Grevey		
	52 Dave Robisch TL		
☐ 13	60 Foots Walker	.30	.14
	113 Mick.Johnson TL		
	130 Bill Robinzine		
☐ 14	61 Austin Carr	3.00	1.35
	8 Kareem Abdul-Jabbar AS		
	200 Calvin Natt		
☐ 15	63 Jim Cleamons	.30	.14
	256 Robert Reid SD		
	22 Charlie Criss		
☐ 16	69 Tom LaGarde	.30	.14
	215 Swen Nater TL		
	213 James Silas		
☐ 17	71 Jerome Whitehead	.60	.25
	259 Artis Gilmore SD		
	184 Caldwell Jones		
☐ 18	74 John Roche TL.........	.30	.14
	99 Clifford Ray		
	235 Ben Poquette TL		
☐ 19	75 Alex English	1.25	.55
	2 Marques Johnson AS		
	68 Jeff Judkins		
☐ 20	82 Terry Tyler...........	.30	.14
	21 Armond Hill TL		
	18 M.R. Richardson		
☐ 21	84 Kent Benson............	.60	.25
	212 John Shumate		
	229 Paul Westphal		
☐ 22	86 Phil Hubbard	1.50	.70
	93 Robert Parish TL		
	126 Tom Burleson		
☐ 23	88 John Long	3.00	1.35
	1 Julius Erving AS		
	49 Ricky Sobers		
☐ 24	90 Eric Money............	.30	.14
	57 Dave Robisch		
	254 Rick Robey SD		
☐ 25	95 Wayne Cooper	.30	.14
	226 John Johnson TL		
	45 David Greenwood		
☐ 26	97 Robert Parish	2.00	.90
	187 Leon.Robinson TL		
	46 Dwight Jones		
☐ 27	98 Sonny Parker	.30	.14
	197 Dave Twardzik TL		
	39 Cedric Maxwell		
☐ 28	105 Rick Barry	1.00	.45
	122 Otis Birdsong TL		
	48 John Mengelt		
☐ 29	106 Allen Leavell	.30	.14
	53 Foots Walker TL		
	223 Freeman Williams		
☐ 30	108 Calvin Murphy	.60	.25
	176 Maur.Cheeks TL		
	87 Greg Kelser		
☐ 31	110 Robert Reid	.60	.25
	243 Wes Unseld TL		
	50 Reggie Theus		
☐ 32	111 Rudy Tomjanovich .60		.25
	13 Eddie Johnson AS		
	179 Doug Collins		
☐ 33	112 Mickey Johnson TL .30		.14
	28 Wayne Rollins		
	15 M.R.Richardson AS		
☐ 34	115 Mike Bantom	.60	.25
	6 Adrian Dantley AS		
	227 James Bailey		
☐ 35	116 Dudley Bradley	.30	.14
	155 Eddie Jordan TL		
	239 Allan Bristow		
☐ 36	118 James Edwards	.30	.14
	153 Mike Newlin TL		
	182 Lionel Hollins		
☐ 37	119 Mickey Johnson	.30	.14
	154 Geo.Johnson TL		
	193 Leonard Robinson		
☐ 38	120 Billy Knight..........	.60	.25
	16 Paul Westphal AS		
	59 Randy Smith		
☐ 39	121 George McGinnis .. .60		.25
	83 Eric Money TL		
	65 Mike Bratz		
☐ 40	124 Phil Ford TL	.30	.14
	101 Phil Smith		
	224 Gus Williams TL		
☐ 41	127 Phil Ford..........	.30	.14
	19 John Drew TL		
	209 Larry Kenon		
☐ 42	131 Scott Wedman	.60	.25
	164 D.Cartwright TL		
	23 John Drew		
☐ 43	132 K.Abdul-Jabbar TL 3.00		1.35
	56 Mike Mitchell		
	81 Terry Tyler TL		
☐ 44	135 K.Abdul-Jabbar ... 5.00		2.20
	79 David Thompson		
	216 Brian Taylor TL		
☐ 45	137 Michael Cooper .. 2.00		.90
	103 Moses Malone TL		
	148 George Johnson		
☐ 46	140 Mark Landsberger 1.50		.70
	10 Bob Lanier AS		
	222 Bill Walton		
☐ 47	141 Norm Nixon	.60	.25
	123 Sam Lacey TL		
	54 Kenny Carr		
☐ 48	143 Marq.Johnson TL 15.00		6.75
	30 Larry Bird TL		
	232 Jack Sikma		
☐ 49	146 Junior Bridgeman 15.00		6.75
	31 Larry Bird TL		
	198 Ron Brewer		
☐ 50	147 Quinn Buckner 3.00		1.35
	133 K.Abdul-Jabbar TL		
	207 Mike Gale		
☐ 51	149 Marques Johnson 3.00		1.35
	262 Julius Erving SD		
	62 Abdul Jeelani		
☐ 52	151 Sidney Moncrief .. 3.00		1.35
	260 Lonnie Shelton SD		
	220 Paul Silas		
☐ 53	156 George Johnson......	.60	.25
	9 Bill Cartwright AS		
	199 Bob Gross		
☐ 54	158 Maurice Lucas	.60	.25
	261 James Edwards SD		
	157 Eddie Jordan		
☐ 55	159 Mike Newlin	.30	.14
	134 Norm Nixon TL		
	180 Darryl Dawkins		
☐ 56	160 Roger Phegley	.30	.14
	206 James Silas TL		
	91 Terry Tyler UER		
	(First name spelled Jams)		
☐ 57	161 Cliff Robinson	.30	.14
	51 Mike Mitchell TL		
	80 Bobby Wilkerson		
☐ 58	162 Jan V.Breda Kolff .. .60		.25
	204 George Gervin TL		
	117 Johnny Davis		
☐ 59	165 M.R.Richardson TL .30		.14
	214 Lloyd Free TL		

```
        44 Artis Gilmore
□ 60 166 Bill Cartwright ..... 1.50    .70
        244 Kevin Porter TL
        25 Armond Hill
□ 61 168 Toby Knight ........ .30      .14
        14 Lloyd Free AS
        240 Adrian Dantley
□ 62 169 Joe Meriweather .... .60      .25
        218 Lloyd Free
        42 D.Greenwood TL
□ 63 170 Earl Monroe ........ .60      .25
        27 James McElroy
        85 Leon Douglas
□ 64 172 Marvin Webster ..... .60      .25
        175 Caldwell Jones TL
        129 Sam Lacey
□ 65 173 Ray Williams ....... .30      .14
        94 John Lucas TL
        202 Dave Twardzik
□ 66 178 Maurice Cheeks 12.00         5.50
        18 Magic Johnson AS
        237 Ron Boone
□ 67 183 Bobby Jones ....... 1.00      .45
        37 Chris Ford
        66 Joe Hassett
□ 68 189 Alvan Adams ....... 1.00      .45
        163 B.Cartwright TL
        76 Dan Issel
□ 69 190 Don Buse .......... .60       .25
        242 Elvin Hayes TL
        35 M.L. Carr
□ 70 191 Walter Davis ...... 1.00      .45
        11 George.Gervin AS
        136 Jim Chones
□ 71 192 Rich Kelley ....... 1.00      .45
        102 Moses Malone TL
        64 Winford Boynes
□ 72 201 Tom Owens ......... .30       .14
        225 Jack Sikma TL
        100 Purvis Short
□ 73 208 George Gervin ..... 1.50      .70
        72 Dan Issel TL
        249 Mitch Kupchak
□ 74 217 Joe Bryant ........ 1.50      .70
        263 Bobby Jones SD
        107 Moses Malone
□ 75 219 Swen Nater ........ .60       .25
        17 Calvin Murphy AS
        70 Rich.Washington
□ 76 221 Brian Taylor ...... .30       .14
        253 John Shumate SD
        167 Larry Demic
□ 77 228 Fred Brown ........ .30       .14
        205 Larry Kenon TL
        203 Kerm Washington
□ 78 230 John Johnson ...... 1.00      .45
        4 Walter Davis AS
        33 Nate Archibald
□ 79 231 Lonnie Shelton .... .60       .25
        104 Allen Leavell TL
        96 John Lucas
□ 80 233 Gus Williams ...... .30       .14
        20 Dan Roundfield TL
        211 Kevin Restani
□ 81 236 Allan Bristow TL... .30       .14
        210 Mark Olberding
        255 James Bailey SD
□ 82 238 Tom Boswell ....... .60       .45
        109 Billy Paultz
        150 Bob Lanier
□ 83 241 Ben Poquette ...... 1.00      .45
        188 Paul Westphal TL
        77 Charlie Scott
□ 84 245 Greg Ballard ...... .30       .14
        43 Reggie Theus TL
        252 John Williamson
□ 85 246 Bob Dandridge ..... .60       .25
        41 Reggie Theus TL
        128 Reggie King
□ 86 250 Kevin Porter ...... .30       .14
        114 Johnny Davis TL
        125 Otis Birdsong
□ 87 251 Wes Unseld ........ .60       .25
        195 Tom Owens TL
        199 John Roche
□ 88 257 Elvin Hayes TL .... .60       .25

        144 Marq.Johnson TL
        89 Bob McAdoo
□ 89 3 Dan Roundfield ...... .60       .25
        218 Lloyd Free
        42 D.Greenwood TL
□ 90 7 Moses Malone ....... 1.00       .45
        247 Kevin Grevey
        52 Dave Robisch TL
□ 91 12 Gus Williams ...... .30        .14
        210 Mark Olberding
        255 James Bailey TL
□ 92 24 Steve Hawes ....... .30        .14
        226 John Johnson TL
        45 David Greenwood
□ 93 29 Dan Roundfield .... .30        .14
        113 Mick.Johnson TL
        130 Bill Robinzine
□ 94 34 Larry Bird ....... 40.00      18.00
        164 B.Cartwright TL
        23 John Drew
□ 95 36 Dave Cowens ...... 1.00        .45
        16 Paul Westphal AS
        59 Randy Smith
□ 96 38 Pete Maravich .... 5.00       2.20
        187 Leon.Robinson TL
        46 Dwight Jones
□ 97 40 Rick Robey ........ .60        .25
        37 Chris Ford
        66 Joe Hassett
□ 98 47 Scott May ........ 15.00      6.75
        30 Larry Bird TL
        232 Jack Sikma
□ 99 55 Dom Ford ......... 1.00        .45
        144 Marq.Johnson TL
        89 Bob McAdoo
□ 100 58 Campy Russell .... .60        .25
        21 Armond Hill TL
        171 M.R.Richardson
□ 101 60 Foots Walker ..... .30        .14
        122 Otis Birdsong TL
        48 John Mengelt
□ 102 61 Austin Carr ...... .30        .14
        56 Mike Mitchell
        81 Terry Tyler TL
□ 103 63 Jim Cleamons ..... .30        .14
        261 James Edwards SD
        157 Eddie Jordan
□ 104 69 Tom LaGarde ...... 1.00       .45
        109 Billy Paultz
        150 Bob Lanier
□ 105 71 Jerome Whitehead .60          .25
        17 Calvin Murphy AS
        70 Rich.Washington
□ 106 74 John Roche TL..... .30        .14
        28 Wayne Rollins
        15 M.R.Richardson AS
□ 107 75 Alex English ..... 1.50       .70
        102 Moses Malone TL
        64 Winford Boynes
□ 108 82 Terry Tyler TL.... .30        .14
        79 David Thompson
        216 Brian Taylor TL
□ 109 84 Kent Benson ...... .60        .25
        259 Artis Gilmore SD
        184 Caldwell Jones
□ 110 86 Phil Hubbard ..... .30        .14
        195 Tom Owens TL
        78 John Roche
□ 111 88 John Long ....... 10.00      4.50
        18 Magic Johnson AS
        237 Ron Boone
□ 112 90 Eric Money ....... .30        .14
        215 Swen Nater TL
        213 James Silas
□ 113 95 Wayne Cooper ..... .30        .14
        154 Geo.Johnson TL
        193 Leon.Robinson
□ 114 97 Robert Parish ... 2.00        .90
        103 Moses Malone TL
        148 George Johnson
□ 115 98 Sonny Parker ..... .60        .25
        94 John Lucas TL
        202 Dave Twardzik
□ 116 105 Rick Barry ...... 1.00       .45
        123 Sam Lacey TL
        54 Kenny Carr

□ 117 106 Allen Leavell ..... .30      .14
        197 Dave Twardzik TL
        39 Cedric Maxwell
□ 118 108 Calvin Murphy .... .60       .25
        51 Mike Mitchell TL
        80 Bobby Wilkerson
□ 119 110 Robert Reid ...... .60       .25
        153 Mike Newlin TL
        182 Lionel Hollins
□ 120 111 Rudy Tomjanovich 1.00        .45
        73 Dan Issel TL
        152 Brian Winters
□ 121 112 Mick.Johnson TL 1.00         .45
        264 Lloyd Free SD
        194 Dennis Johnson
□ 122 115 Mike Bantom ...... .60       .25
        204 George Gervin TL
        117 Johnny Davis
□ 123 116 Dudley Bradley.. 1.00        .45
        186 Paul Westphal TL
        142 Jamaal Wilkes
□ 124 118 James Edwards 1.25           .55
        32 Nate Archibald TL
        248 Elvin Hayes
□ 125 119 Mickey Johnson 1.00          .45
        72 Dan Issel TL
        249 Mitch Kupchak
□ 126 120 Billy Knight ...... .30      .14
        104 Allen Leavell TL
        96 John Lucas
□ 127 121 George McGinnis 1.50         .70
        10 Bob Lanier AS
        222 Bill Walton
□ 128 124 Phil Ford TL ..... .60       .25
        234 Adr.Dantley TL
        26 Eddie Johnson
□ 129 127 Phil Ford ......... .60      .25
        43 Reggie Theus TL
        252 John Williamson
□ 130 131 Scott Wedman ...... .30      .14
        244 Kevin Porter TL
        25 Armond Hill
□ 131 132 K.Abdul-Jabbar TL 4.00      1.80
        93 Robert Parish TL
        126 Tom Burleson
□ 132 135 K.Abdul-Jabbar .... 5.00    2.20
        253 John Shumate SD
        167 Larry Demic
□ 133 137 Michael Cooper ... 1.00      .45
        212 John Shumate
        229 Paul Westphal
□ 134 140 Mark Landsberger .60         .25
        214 Lloyd Free TL
        44 Artis Gilmore
□ 135 141 Norm Nixon ....... .60       .25
        242 Elvin Hayes TL
        35 M.L. Carr
□ 136 143 Marq.Johnson TL .30          .14
        57 Dave Robisch
        254 Rick Robey SD
□ 137 146 Junior Bridgeman 3.00       1.35
        1 Julius Erving AS
        49 Ricky Sobers
□ 138 147 Quinn Buckner .... .60       .25
        2 Marques Johnson AS
        68 Jeff Judkins
□ 139 149 Marques Johnson .30          .14
        83 Eric Money TL
        65 Mike Bratz
□ 140 151 Sidney Moncrief 4.00        1.80
        133 K.Abdul-Jabbar TL
        207 Mike Gale
□ 141 156 George Johnson.. .30         .14
        175 Caldw.Jones TL
        129 Sam Lacey
□ 142 158 Maurice Lucas .. 3.00       1.35
        262 Julius Erving SD
        42 Abdul Jeelani
□ 143 159 Mike Newlin ...... .60       .25
        243 Wes Unseld TL
        50 Reggie Theus
□ 144 160 Roger Phegley .... .30       .14
        145 Quinn Buckner TL
        138 Brad Holland
□ 145 161 Cliff Robinson .... .30      .14
        114 Johnny Davis TL
```

125 Otis Birdsong
□ 146 162 Jan V.Breda Kolff 35.00 16.00
174 Julius Erving TL
139 Magic Johnson
□ 147 165 M.R.Richardson TL 1.00 .45
185 Steve Mix
92 Robert Parish TL
□ 148 166 Bill Cartwright .. 1.00 .45
13 Eddie Johnson AS
179 Doug Collins
□ 149 168 Toby Knight .... .60 .25
188 Paul Westphal TL
77 Charlie Scott
□ 150 169 Joe Meriweather .. .30 .14
196 K.Washington TL
177 Henry Bibby
□ 151 170 Earl Monroe .... .30 .14
206 James Silas TL
91 Terry Tyler
□ 152 172 Marvin Webster .. .60 .25
155 Eddie Jordan TL
239 Allan Bristow
□ 153 173 Ray Williams ...... .30 .14
225 Jack Sikma TL
100 Purvis Short
□ 154 178 Maurice Cheeks 4.00 1.80
11 George Gervin AS
136 Jim Chones
□ 155 183 Bobby Jones ...... .60 .25
99 Clifford Ray
235 Ben Poquette TL
□ 156 189 Alvan Adams ...... .60 .25
14 Lloyd Free AS
240 Adrian Dantley
□ 157 190 Don Buse .... .60 .25
6 Adrian Dantley AS
227 James Bailey
□ 158 191 Walter Davis .... .60 .25
9 Bill Cartwright AS
199 Bob Gross
□ 159 192 Rich Kelley .... 1.50 .70
263 Bobby Jones SD
107 Moses Malone
□ 160 201 Tom Owens .... .60 .25
134 Norm Nixon TL
180 Darryl Dawkins
□ 161 208 George Gervin .. 1.50 .70
53 Foots Walker TL
223 Freeman Williams
□ 162 217 Joe Bryant 3.00 1.35
8 K.Abdul-Jabbar AS
200 Calvin Natt
□ 163 219 Swen Nater .... .30 .14
101 Phil Smith
224 Gus Williams TL
□ 164 221 Brian Taylor ...... .30 .14
256 Robert Reid SD
22 Charlie Criss
□ 165 228 Fred Brown....... 15.00 6.75
31 Larry Bird TL
198 Ron Brewer
□ 166 230 John Johnson .. 1.00 .45
163 B.Cartwright TL
76 Dan Issel
□ 167 231 Lonnie Shelton ... .30 .14
205 Larry Kenon TL
203 Kermit Washington
□ 168 233 Gus Williams ..... .60 .25
41 Reggie Theus TL
128 Reggie King
□ 169 236 Allan Bristow TL .. .30 .14
260 Lonnie Shelton SD
220 Paul Silas
□ 170 238 Tom Boswell ...... .30 .14
27 James McElroy
85 Leon Douglas
□ 171 241 Ben Poquette ... 1.00 .45
176 Maurice Cheeks TL
87 Greg Kelser
□ 172 245 Greg Ballard .... 1.00 .45
4 Walter Davis AS
33 Nate Archibald
□ 173 246 Bob Dandridge .... .30 .14
19 John Drew TL
209 Larry Kenon
□ 174 250 Kevin Porter .... .30 .14

20 Dan Roundfield TL
211 Kevin Restani
□ 175 251 Wes Unseld ...... 1.00 .45
67 Geoff Huston
5 John Drew AS
□ 176 257 Elvin Hayes SD .. 5.00 2.20
181 Julius Erving
258 Ron Brewer SD

1981-82 Topps

The 1981-82 Topps basketball card set contains a total of 198 standard-size cards that were issued in 13-card, 30-cent wax packs with 36 packs per box. These cards are numbered depending upon the regional distribution used in the issue. A 66-card national set was issued to all parts of the country, however, subsets of 44 cards each were issued in the East, Midwest and West. The national set is easier to acquire than any of the regional issues. Card numbers over 66 are prefaced on the card by the region in which they were distributed, e.g., East 96. The cards feature the Topps logo in the frame line and a quarter-round sunburst in the lower left-hand corner which lists the name, position and team of the player depicted. Cards 44-66 are Team Leader (TL) cards picturing each team's statistical leaders. The back, printed in orange and brown on gray stock, features standard Topps biographical data and career statistics. There are a number of Super Action (SA) cards in the set. Rookie Cards include Joe Barry Carroll, Mike Dunleavy, Mike Gminski, Darrell Griffith, Ernie Grunfeld, Vinnie Johnson, Bill Laimbeer, Rick Mahorn, Kevin McHale, Jim Paxson and Larry Smith. The card numbering sequence is alphabetical within team within each series. This was Topps'

last basketball card issue until 1992.

	NRMT-MT	EXC
COMPLETE SET (198)	80.00	36.00
COMMON CARD (1-66)	.10	.05
COMMON CARD (E67-E110)	.15	.07
COMMON CARD (MW67-110)	.15	.07
COMMON CARD (W67-W110)	.15	.07
TL (44-66)	.15	.07
CL (E93B/MW76/W97)	1.00	.45
CL ERR (E93A)	2.00	.90
SEMISTARS	.25	.11

ALL CARDS 1-66 ARE DP
CONDITION SENSITIVE SET

□ 1 John Drew............ .20 .09
□ 2 Dan Roundfield ..... .20 .09
□ 3 Nate Archibald...... .60 .25
□ 4 Larry Bird 22.00 10.00
□ 5 Cedric Maxwell ..... .20 .09
□ 6 Robert Parish ...... 1.50 .70
□ 7 Artis Gilmore .... .60 .25
□ 8 Ricky Sobers .... .10 .05
□ 9 Mike Mitchell .... .20 .09
□ 10 Tom LaGarde........ .10 .05
□ 11 Dan Issel .... .75 .35
□ 12 David Thompson ... .75 .35
□ 13 Lloyd Free .... .25 .11
□ 14 Moses Malone ...... 1.50 .70
□ 15 Calvin Murphy...... .25 .11
□ 16 Johnny Davis .... .10 .05
□ 17 Otis Birdsong ...... .25 .11
□ 18 Phil Ford .... .20 .09
□ 19 Scott Wedman....... .10 .05
□ 20 Kareem Abdul-Jabbar 4.00 1.80
□ 21 Magic Johnson 16.00 7.25
□ 22 Norm Nixon.......... .25 .11
□ 23 Jamaal Wilkes ...... .25 .11
□ 24 Marques Johnson ... .25 .11
□ 25 Bob Lanier .... .75 .35
□ 26 Bill Cartwright ..... .50 .23
□ 27 Michael Ray Richardson .20 .09
□ 28 Ray Williams .... .20 .09
□ 29 Darryl Dawkins ..... .25 .11
□ 30 Julius Erving 4.00 1.80
□ 31 Lionel Hollins ...... .10 .05
□ 32 Bobby Jones .... .25 .11
□ 33 Walter Davis .... .50 .23
□ 34 Dennis Johnson .... .50 .23
□ 35 Leonard Robinson .. .25 .11
□ 36 Mychal Thompson... .25 .11
□ 37 George Gervin ..... 2.00 .90
□ 38 Swen Nater .... .10 .05
□ 39 Jack Sikma .... .25 .11
□ 40 Adrian Dantley ..... .60 .25
□ 41 Darrell Griffith .... 1.00 .45
□ 42 Elvin Hayes .... .75 .35
□ 43 Fred Brown .... .25 .11
□ 44 Atlanta Hawks TL .. .15 .07
     John Drew
     Dan Roundfield
     Eddie Johnson
□ 45 Boston Celtics TL .. 2.00 .90
     Larry Bird
     Larry Bird
     Nate Archibald
□ 46 Chicago Bulls TL ... .25 .11
     Reggie Theus
     Artis Gilmore
     Reggie Theus
□ 47 Cleveland Cavs TL .. .15 .07
     Mike Mitchell
     Kenny Carr
     Mike Bratz
□ 48 Dallas Mavericks TL .15 .07
     Jim Spanarkel
     Tom LaGarde
     Brad Davis
□ 49 Denver Nuggets TL .. .25 .11
     David Thompson
     Dan Issel
     Kenny Higgs
□ 50 Detroit Pistons TL .. .15 .07
     John Long

Phil Hubbard				
Ron Lee				
□ 51 Golden State TL	.25	.11		
Lloyd Free				
Larry Smith				
John Lucas				
□ 52 Houston Rockets TL	.40	.18		
Moses Malone				
Moses Malone				
Allen Leavell				
□ 53 Indiana Pacers TL	.25	.11		
Billy Knight				
James Edwards				
Johnny Davis				
□ 54 Kansas City Kings TL	.15	.07		
Otis Birdsong				
Reggie King				
Phil Ford				
□ 55 Los Angeles Lakers TL	1.25	.55		
Kareem Abdul-Jabbar				
Kareem Abdul-Jabbar				
Norm Nixon				
□ 56 Milwaukee Bucks TL	.25	.11		
Marques Johnson				
Mickey Johnson				
Quinn Buckner				
□ 57 New Jersey Nets TL	.15	.07		
Mike Newlin				
Maurice Lucas				
Mike Newlin				
□ 58 New York Knicks TL	.25	.11		
Bill Cartwright				
Bill Cartwright				
M.R. Richardson				
□ 59 Philadelphia 76ers TL	1.25	.55		
Julius Erving				
Caldwell Jones				
Maurice Cheeks				
□ 60 Phoenix Suns TL	.25	.11		
Truck Robinson				
Truck Robinson				
Alvan Adams				
□ 61 Portland Blazers TL	.15	.07		
Jim Paxson				
Mychal Thompson				
Kermit Washington				
Kelvin Ransey				
□ 62 San Antonio Spurs TL	.25	.11		
George Gervin				
Dave Corzine				
Johnny Moore				
□ 63 San Diego Clippers TL	.15	.07		
Freeman Williams				
Swen Nater				
Brian Taylor				
□ 64 Seattle Sonics TL	.25	.11		
Jack Sikma				
Jack Sikma				
Vinnie Johnson				
□ 65 Utah Jazz TL	.25	.11		
Adrian Dantley				
Ben Poquette				
Allan Bristow				
□ 66 Washington Bullets TL	.25	.11		
Elvin Hayes				
Elvin Hayes				
Kevin Porter				
□ E67 Charlie Criss	.25	.11		
□ E68 Eddie Johnson	.15	.07		
□ E69 Wes Matthews	.15	.07		
□ E70 Tom McMillen	.40	.18		
□ E71 Tree Rollins	.40	.18		
□ E72 M.L. Carr	.25	.11		
□ E73 Chris Ford	.25	.11		
□ E74 Gerald Henderson	.40	.18		
□ E75 Kevin McHale	20.00	9.00		
□ E76 Rick Robey	.25	.11		
□ E77 Darwin Cook	.15	.07		
□ E78 Mike Gminski	.75	.35		
□ E79 Maurice Lucas	.25	.11		
□ E80 Mike Newlin	.15	.07		
□ E81 Mike O'Koren	.25	.11		
□ E82 Steve Hawes	.15	.07		
□ E83 Foots Walker	.25	.11		
□ E84 Campy Russell	.25	.11		
□ E85 DeWayne Scales	.15	.07		

□ E86 Randy Smith	.25	.11
□ E87 Marvin Webster	.25	.11
□ E88 Sly Williams	.15	.07
□ E89 Mike Woodson	.25	.11
□ E90 Maurice Cheeks	1.50	.70
□ E91 Caldwell Jones	.25	.11
□ E92 Steve Mix	.25	.11
□ E93A Checklist 1-110 ERR	2.00	.60
(WEST above card number)		
□ E93B Checklist 1-110 COR	1.00	.30
□ E94 Greg Ballard	.15	.07
□ E95 Don Collins	.15	.07
□ E96 Kevin Grevey	.25	.11
□ E97 Mitch Kupchak	.25	.11
□ E98 Rick Mahorn	.75	.35
□ E99 Kevin Porter	.25	.11
□ E100 Nate Archibald SA	.25	.11
□ E101 Larry Bird SA	12.00	5.50
□ E102 Bill Cartwright SA	.15	.07
□ E103 Darryl Dawkins SA	.25	.11
□ E104 Julius Erving SA	2.00	.90
□ E105 Kevin Porter SA	.25	.11
□ E106 Bobby Jones SA	.25	.11
□ E107 Cedric Maxwell SA	.25	.11
□ E108 Robert Parish SA	1.00	.45
□ E109 M.R.Richardson SA	.25	.11
□ E110 Dan Roundfield SA	.25	.11
□ W67 T.R. Dunn	.15	.07
□ W68 Alex English	1.50	.70
□ W69 Billy McKinney	.25	.11
□ W70 Dave Robisch	.25	.11
□ W71 Joe Barry Carroll	.40	.18
□ W72 Bernard King	1.00	.45
□ W73 Sonny Parker	.15	.07
□ W74 Purvis Short	.25	.11
□ W75 Larry Smith	.40	.18
□ W76 Jim Chones	.25	.11
□ W77 Michael Cooper	.75	.35
□ W78 Mark Landsberger	.15	.07
□ W79 Alvan Adams	.25	.11
□ W80 Jeff Cook	.15	.07
□ W81 Rich Kelley	.15	.07
□ W82 Kyle Macy	.40	.18
□ W83 Billy Ray Bates	.40	.18
□ W84 Bob Gross	.25	.11
□ W85 Calvin Natt	.25	.11
□ W86 Lonnie Shelton	.25	.11
□ W87 Jim Paxson	.75	.35
□ W88 Kelvin Ransey	.15	.07
□ W89 Kermit Washington	.15	.07
□ W90 Henry Bibby	.25	.11
□ W91 Michael Brooks	.15	.07
□ W92 Joe Bryant	.15	.07
□ W93 Phil Smith	.15	.07
□ W94 Brian Taylor	.15	.07
□ W95 Freeman Williams	.25	.11
□ W96 James Bailey	.15	.07
□ W97 Checklist 1-110	1.00	.30
□ W98 John Johnson	.15	.07
□ W99 Vinnie Johnson	1.50	.70
□ W100 Wally Walker	.25	.11
□ W101 Paul Westphal	.25	.11
□ W102 Allan Bristow	.15	.07
□ W103 Wayne Cooper	.15	.07
□ W104 Carl Nicks	.15	.07
□ W105 Ben Poquette	.15	.07
□ W106 K.Abdul-Jabbar SA	2.00	.90
□ W107 Dan Issel SA	.50	.23
□ W108 Dennis Johnson SA	.25	.11
□ W109 Jack Sikma SA	8.00	3.60
□ W110 Jack Sikma SA	.25	.11
□ MW67 David Greenwood	.25	.11
□ MW68 Dwight Jones	.15	.07
□ MW69 Reggie Theus	.25	.11
□ MW70 Bobby Wilkerson	.15	.07
□ MW71 Mike Bratz	.15	.07
□ MW72 Kenny Carr	.15	.07
□ MW73 Geoff Huston	.15	.07
□ MW74 Bill Laimbeer	3.00	1.35
□ MW75 Roger Phegley	.15	.07
□ MW76 Checklist 1-110	1.00	.30
□ MW77 Abdul Jeelani	.15	.07
□ MW78 Bill Robinzine	.15	.07
□ MW79 Jim Spanarkel	.15	.07
□ MW80 Kent Benson	.25	.11
□ MW81 Keith Herron	.15	.07

□ MW82 Phil Hubbard	.15	.07
□ MW83 John Long	.15	.07
□ MW84 Terry Tyler	.15	.07
□ MW85 Mike Dunleavy	.75	.35
□ MW86 Tom Henderson	.15	.07
□ MW87 Billy Paultz	.25	.11
□ MW88 Robert Reid	.15	.07
□ MW89 Mike Bantom	.15	.07
□ MW90 James Edwards	.25	.11
□ MW91 Billy Knight	.25	.11
□ MW92 George McGinnis	.25	.11
□ MW93 Louis Orr	.15	.07
□ MW94 Ernie Grunfeld	.40	.18
□ MW95 Reggie King	.25	.11
□ MW96 Sam Lacey	.15	.07
□ MW97 Junior Bridgeman	.25	.11
□ MW98 Mickey Johnson	.25	.11
□ MW99 Sidney Moncrief	.75	.35
□ MW100 Brian Winters	.25	.11
□ MW101 Dave Corzine	.15	.07
□ MW102 Paul Griffin	.15	.07
□ MW103 Johnny Moore	.25	.11
□ MW104 Mark Olberding	.15	.07
□ MW105 James Silas	.25	.11
□ MW106 George Gervin SA	.75	.35
□ MW107 Artis Gilmore SA	.25	.11
□ MW108 M.Johnson SA	.25	.11
□ MW109 Bob Lanier SA	.50	.23
□ MW110 Moses Malone SA	1.00	.45

1992-93 Topps

The complete 1992-93 Topps basketball set consists of 396 standard-size cards, issued in two 198-card series. Cards were issued in 15-card wrap packs (suggested retail 79 cents, 36 packs per box), 18-card mini-jumbo packs, 45-card retail packs and 41-card magazine jumbo packs. In addition, factory sets were also released. On a white card face, the fronts display color action player photos framed by two-color border stripes. The player's name and team name appear in two different colored bars across the bottom of the picture. In addition to a color close-up photo, the horizontal backs have biography on a light blue panel as well as statistics and brief player profile on a yellow panel. Most Rookie Cards have the a gold-foil "92 Draft Pix" emblem on their card fronts. Topical subsets included are Highlight (2-4), All-Star (100-

126), 50 Point Club (199-215), and 20 Assist Club (216-224). Rookie Cards of note include Tom Gugliotta, Robert Horry, Christian Laettner, Alonzo Mourning, Shaquille O'Neal, Latrell Sprewell and Clarence Weatherspoon.

	MINT	NRMT
COMPLETE SET (396)	12.00	5.50
COMPLETE FACT. SET (408)	15.00	6.75
COMPLETE SERIES 1 (198)	4.00	1.80
COMPLETE SERIES 2 (198)	8.00	3.60
COMMON CARD (1-396)	.05	.02
SEMISTARS	.08	.04
UNLISTED STARS	.15	
COMPLETE GOLD SET (396)	60.00	27.00
COMP.GOLD FACT. SET (403)	75.00	34.00
COMP.GOLD SERIES 1 (198)	20.00	9.00
COMP.GOLD SERIES 2 (198)	40.00	18.00
COMM.GOLD CARD (1G-396G)	.10	.05
CL REPLACE (197G-198G)	.50	.23
CL REPLACE (395G-396G)	.50	.23

*GOLD STARS: 2.5X TO 5X HI COLUMN
*GOLD RCs: 1.5X TO 3X HI
ONE GOLD PER PACK
TWELVE GOLD PER FACTORY SET

- [ ] 1 Larry Bird .60 .25
- [ ] 2 Magic Johnson HL .25 .11
  Earvin's Magical Moment 2/9/92
- [ ] 3 Michael Jordan HL 1.00 .45
  Michael Lights It Up 6/3/92
- [ ] 4 David Robinson HL .15 .07
  Admiral Ranks High In Five 4/19/92
- [ ] 5 Johnny Newman .05 .02
- [ ] 6 Mike Iuzzolino .05 .02
- [ ] 7 Ken Norman .05 .02
- [ ] 8 Chris Jackson .05 .02
- [ ] 9 Duane Ferrell .05 .02
- [ ] 10 Sean Elliott .08 .04
- [ ] 11 Bernard King .05 .02
- [ ] 12 Armon Gilliam .05 .02
- [ ] 13 Reggie Williams .05 .02
- [ ] 14 Steve Kerr .08 .04
- [ ] 15 Anthony Bowie .05 .02
- [ ] 16 Alton Lister .05 .02
- [ ] 17 Dee Brown .05 .02
- [ ] 18 Tom Chambers .05 .02
- [ ] 19 Otis Thorpe .08 .04
- [ ] 20 Karl Malone .25 .11
- [ ] 21 Kenny Gattison .05 .02
- [ ] 22 Lionel Simmons UER .05 .02
  (Misspelled Lionell on card front)
- [ ] 23 Vern Fleming .05 .02
- [ ] 24 John Paxson .08 .04
- [ ] 25 Mitch Richmond .15 .07
- [ ] 26 Danny Schayes .05 .02
- [ ] 27 Derrick McKey .05 .02
- [ ] 28 Mark Randall .05 .02
- [ ] 29 Bill Laimbeer .08 .04
- [ ] 30 Chris Morris .05 .02
- [ ] 31 Alec Kessler .05 .02
- [ ] 32 Vlade Divac .08 .04
- [ ] 33 Rick Fox .08 .04
- [ ] 34 Charles Shackleford .05 .02
- [ ] 35 Dominique Wilkins .15 .07
- [ ] 36 Sleepy Floyd .05 .02
- [ ] 37 Doug West .05 .02
- [ ] 38 Pete Chilcutt .05 .02
- [ ] 39 Orlando Woolridge .05 .02
- [ ] 40 Eric Leckner .05 .02
- [ ] 41 Joe Kleine .05 .02
- [ ] 42 Scott Skiles .05 .02
- [ ] 43 Jerrod Mustaf .05 .02
- [ ] 44 John Starks .08 .04
- [ ] 45 Sedale Threatt .05 .02
- [ ] 46 Doug Smith .05 .02
- [ ] 47 Byron Scott .08 .04
- [ ] 48 Willie Anderson .05 .02
- [ ] 49 David Benoit .05 .02
- [ ] 50 Scott Hastings .05 .02
- [ ] 51 Terry Porter .05 .02
- [ ] 52 Sidney Green .05 .02
- [ ] 53 Danny Young .05 .02
- [ ] 54 Magic Johnson .50 .23
- [ ] 55 Brian Williams .08 .04
- [ ] 56 Randy Wittman .05 .02
- [ ] 57 Kevin McHale .15 .07
- [ ] 58 Dana Barros .05 .02
- [ ] 59 Thurl Bailey .05 .02
- [ ] 60 Kevin Duckworth .05 .02
- [ ] 61 John Williams .05 .02
- [ ] 62 Willie Burton .05 .02
- [ ] 63 Spud Webb .08 .04
- [ ] 64 Detlef Schrempf .08 .04
- [ ] 65 Sherman Douglas .05 .02
- [ ] 66 Patrick Ewing .15 .07
- [ ] 67 Michael Adams .05 .02
- [ ] 68 Vernon Maxwell .05 .02
- [ ] 69 Terrell Brandon .25 .11
- [ ] 70 Terry Catledge .05 .02
- [ ] 71 Mark Eaton .05 .02
- [ ] 72 Tony Smith .05 .02
- [ ] 73 B.J. Armstrong .05 .02
- [ ] 74 Moses Malone .15 .07
- [ ] 75 Anthony Bonner .05 .02
- [ ] 76 George McCloud .05 .02
- [ ] 77 Glen Rice .20 .09
- [ ] 78 Jon Koncak .05 .02
- [ ] 79 Michael Cage .05 .02
- [ ] 80 Ron Harper .08 .04
- [ ] 81 Tom Tolbert .05 .02
- [ ] 82 Brad Sellers .05 .02
- [ ] 83 Winston Garland .05 .02
- [ ] 84 Negele Knight .05 .02
- [ ] 85 Ricky Pierce .05 .02
- [ ] 86 Mark Aguirre .05 .02
- [ ] 87 Ron Anderson .05 .02
- [ ] 88 Loy Vaught .08 .04
- [ ] 89 Luc Longley .05 .02
- [ ] 90 Jerry Reynolds .05 .02
- [ ] 91 Terry Cummings .08 .04
- [ ] 92 Rony Seikaly .05 .02
- [ ] 93 Derek Harper .08 .04
- [ ] 94 Clifford Robinson .08 .04
- [ ] 95 Kenny Anderson .15 .07
- [ ] 96 Chris Gatling .05 .02
- [ ] 97 Stacey Augmon .08 .04
- [ ] 98 Chris Corchiani .05 .02
- [ ] 99 Pervis Ellison .05 .02
- [ ] 100 Larry Bird AS .30 .14
- [ ] 101 John Stockton AS UER .15 .07
  (Listed as Center on card back)
- [ ] 102 Clyde Drexler AS .15 .07
- [ ] 103 Scottie Pippen AS .25 .11
- [ ] 104 Reggie Lewis AS .05 .02
- [ ] 105 Hakeem Olajuwon AS .15 .07
- [ ] 106 David Robinson AS .15 .07
- [ ] 107 Charles Barkley AS .15 .07
- [ ] 108 James Worthy AS .08 .04
- [ ] 109 Kevin Willis AS .05 .02
- [ ] 110 D.Mutombo AS .15 .07
- [ ] 111 Joe Dumars AS .08 .04
- [ ] 112 Jeff Hornacek AS UER .05 .02
  (5 or 7 shots should be 6 or 7 shots)
- [ ] 113 Mark Price AS .05 .02
- [ ] 114 Michael Adams AS .05 .02
- [ ] 115 Michael Jordan AS 1.00 .45
- [ ] 116 Brad Daugherty AS .05 .02
- [ ] 117 Dennis Rodman AS .30 .14
- [ ] 118 Isiah Thomas AS .08 .04
- [ ] 119 Tim Hardaway AS .15 .07
- [ ] 120 Patrick Ewing AS .15 .07
- [ ] 121 Patrick Ewing AS .15 .07
- [ ] 122 Dan Majerle AS .05 .02
- [ ] 123 Karl Malone AS .15 .07
- [ ] 124 Otis Thorpe AS .05 .02
- [ ] 125 Dominique Wilkins AS .08 .04
- [ ] 126 Magic Johnson AS .25 .11
- [ ] 127 Charles Oakley .05 .02
- [ ] 128 Robert Pack .05 .02
- [ ] 129 Billy Owens .08 .04
- [ ] 130 Jeff Malone .05 .02
- [ ] 131 Danny Ferry .05 .02
- [ ] 132 Sam Bowie .05 .02
- [ ] 133 Avery Johnson .05 .02
- [ ] 134 Jayson Williams .08 .04
- [ ] 135 Fred Roberts .05 .02
- [ ] 136 Greg Sutton .05 .02
- [ ] 137 Dennis Rodman .60 .25
- [ ] 138 John Williams .05 .02
- [ ] 139 Greg Dreiling .05 .02
- [ ] 140 Rik Smits .08 .04
- [ ] 141 Michael Jordan 2.00 .90
- [ ] 142 Nick Anderson .05 .02
- [ ] 143 Jerome Kersey .05 .02
- [ ] 144 Fat Lever .05 .02
- [ ] 145 Tyrone Corbin .05 .02
- [ ] 146 Robert Parish .08 .04
- [ ] 147 Steve Smith .15 .07
- [ ] 148 Chris Dudley .05 .02
- [ ] 149 Antoine Carr .05 .02
- [ ] 150 Eldon Campbell .08 .04
- [ ] 151 Randy White .05 .02
- [ ] 152 Felton Spencer .05 .02
- [ ] 153 Cedric Ceballos .08 .04
- [ ] 154 Mark Macon .05 .02
- [ ] 155 Jack Haley .05 .02
- [ ] 156 Bimbo Coles .05 .02
- [ ] 157 A.J. English .05 .02
- [ ] 158 Kendall Gill .08 .04
- [ ] 159 A.C. Green .05 .02
- [ ] 160 Mark West .05 .02
- [ ] 161 Benoit Benjamin .05 .02
- [ ] 162 Tyrone Hill .05 .02
- [ ] 163 Larry Nance .05 .02
- [ ] 164 Gary Grant .05 .02
- [ ] 165 Bill Cartwright .05 .02
- [ ] 166 Greg Anthony .05 .02
- [ ] 167 Jim Les .05 .02
- [ ] 168 Johnny Dawkins .05 .02
- [ ] 169 Alvin Robertson .05 .02
- [ ] 170 Kenny Smith .05 .02
- [ ] 171 Gerald Glass .05 .02
- [ ] 172 Harvey Grant .05 .02
- [ ] 173 Paul Graham .05 .02
- [ ] 174 Sam Perkins .08 .04
- [ ] 175 Manute Bol .05 .02
- [ ] 176 Muggsy Bogues .08 .04
- [ ] 177 Mike Brown .05 .02
- [ ] 178 Donald Hodge .05 .02
- [ ] 179 Dave Jamerson .05 .02
- [ ] 180 Mookie Blaylock .08 .04
- [ ] 181 Randy Brown .05 .02
- [ ] 182 Todd Lichti .05 .02
- [ ] 183 Kevin Gamble .05 .02
- [ ] 184 Gary Payton .30 .14
- [ ] 185 Brian Shaw .05 .02
- [ ] 186 Grant Long .05 .02
- [ ] 187 Frank Brickowski .05 .02
- [ ] 188 Tim Hardaway .25 .11
- [ ] 189 Danny Manning .10 .04
- [ ] 190 Kevin Johnson .15 .07
- [ ] 191 Craig Ehlo .05 .02
- [ ] 192 Dennis Scott .08 .04
- [ ] 193 Reggie Miller .15 .07
- [ ] 194 Darrell Walker .05 .02
- [ ] 195 Anthony Mason .15 .07
- [ ] 196 Buck Williams .05 .02
- [ ] 197 Checklist 1-99 .05 .02
- [ ] 198 Checklist 100-198 .05 .02
- [ ] 199 Karl Malone 50P .15 .07
- [ ] 200 Dominique Wilkins 50P .08 .04
- [ ] 201 Tom Chambers 50P .05 .02
- [ ] 202 Bernard King 50P .05 .02
- [ ] 203 Kiki Vandeweghe 50P .05 .02
- [ ] 204 Dale Ellis 50P .05 .02
- [ ] 205 Michael Jordan 50P 1.00 .45
- [ ] 206 Michael Adams 50P .05 .02
- [ ] 207 Charles Smith 50P .05 .02
- [ ] 208 Moses Malone 50P .08 .04
- [ ] 209 Terry Cummings 50P .05 .02
- [ ] 210 Vernon Maxwell 50P .05 .02
- [ ] 211 Patrick Ewing 50P .15 .07
- [ ] 212 Clyde Drexler 50P .15 .07
- [ ] 213 Kevin McHale 50P .08 .04
- [ ] 214 Hakeem Olajuwon 50P .15 .07

☐ 215 Reggie Miller 50P	.15	.07
☐ 216 Gary Grant 20A	.05	.02
☐ 217 Doc Rivers 20A	.05	.02
☐ 218 Mark Price 20A	.05	.02
☐ 219 Isiah Thomas 20A	.08	.04
☐ 220 Nate McMillan 20A	.05	.02
☐ 221 Fat Lever 20A	.05	.02
☐ 222 Kevin Johnson 20A	.08	.04
☐ 223 John Stockton 20A	.15	.07
☐ 224 Scott Skiles 20A	.05	.02
☐ 225 Kevin Brooks	.05	.02
☐ 226 Bobby Phills	.15	.07
☐ 227 Oliver Miller	.05	.02
☐ 228 John Williams	.05	.02
☐ 229 Brad Lohaus	.05	.02
☐ 230 Derrick Coleman	.08	.04
☐ 231 Ed Pinckney	.05	.02
☐ 232 Trent Tucker	.05	.02
☐ 233 Lance Blanks	.05	.02
☐ 234 Drazen Petrovic	.05	.02
☐ 235 Mark Bryant	.05	.02
☐ 236 Lloyd Daniels	.05	.02
☐ 237 Dale Davis	.05	.02
☐ 238 Jayson Williams	.05	.04
☐ 239 Mike Sanders	.05	.02
☐ 240 Mike Gminski	.05	.02
☐ 241 William Bedford	.05	.02
☐ 242 Dell Curry	.05	.02
☐ 243 Gerald Paddio	.05	.02
☐ 244 Chris Smith	.05	.02
☐ 245 Jud Buechler	.05	.02
☐ 246 Walter Palmer	.05	.02
☐ 247 Larry Krystkowiak	.05	.02
☐ 248 Marcus Liberty	.05	.02
☐ 249 Sam Mitchell	.05	.02
☐ 250 Kiki Vandeweghe	.05	.02
☐ 251 Vincent Askew	.05	.02
☐ 252 Travis Mays	.05	.02
☐ 253 Charles Smith	.05	.02
☐ 254 John Bagley	.05	.02
☐ 255 James Worthy	.15	.07
☐ 256 Paul Pressey P/CO	.05	.02
☐ 257 Rumeal Robinson	.05	.02
☐ 258 Tom Gugliotta	.50	.23
☐ 259 Eric Anderson	.05	.02
☐ 260 Hersey Hawkins	.08	.04
☐ 261 Terry Davis	.05	.02
☐ 262 Rex Chapman	.05	.02
☐ 263 Chucky Brown	.05	.02
☐ 264 Danny Young	.05	.02
☐ 265 Olden Polynice	.05	.02
☐ 266 Kevin Willis	.05	.02
☐ 267 Shawn Kemp	.60	.25
☐ 268 Mookie Blaylock	.08	.04
☐ 269 Malik Sealy	.08	.04
☐ 270 Charles Barkley	.25	.11
☐ 271 Corey Williams	.05	.02
☐ 272 Stephen Howard	.05	.02
(See also card 286)		
☐ 273 Keith Askins	.05	.02
☐ 274 Matt Bullard	.05	.02
☐ 275 John Battle	.05	.02
☐ 276 Andrew Lang	.05	.02
☐ 277 David Robinson	.25	.11
☐ 278 Harold Miner	.08	.04
☐ 279 Tracy Murray	.05	.02
☐ 280 Pooh Richardson	.05	.02
☐ 281 Dikembe Mutombo	.15	.07
☐ 282 Wayman Tisdale	.05	.02
☐ 283 Larry Johnson	.20	.09
☐ 284 Todd Day	.05	.02
☐ 285 Stanley Roberts	.05	.02
☐ 286 Randy Woods UER	.05	.02
(Card misnumbered 272; run be run should be run the show)		
☐ 287 Avery Johnson	.05	.02
☐ 288 Anthony Peeler	.08	.04
☐ 289 Mario Elie	.05	.02
☐ 290 Doc Rivers	.08	.04
☐ 291 Blue Edwards	.05	.02
☐ 292 Sean Rooks	.05	.02
☐ 293 Xavier McDaniel	.05	.02
☐ 294 C.Weatherspoon	.15	.07
☐ 295 Morlon Wiley	.05	.02
☐ 296 LaBradford Smith	.05	

☐ 297 Reggie Lewis	.08	.04
☐ 298 Chris Mullin	.15	.07
☐ 299 Litterial Green	.05	.02
☐ 300 Elmore Spencer	.05	.02
☐ 301 John Stockton	.15	.07
☐ 302 Walt Williams	.15	.07
☐ 303 Anthony Pullard	.05	.02
☐ 304 Gundars Vetra	.05	.02
☐ 305 LaSalle Thompson	.05	.02
☐ 306 Nate McMillan	.05	.02
☐ 307 Steve Bardo	.05	.02
☐ 308 Robert Horry	.25	.11
☐ 309 Scott Williams	.05	.02
☐ 310 Bo Kimble	.05	.02
☐ 311 Tree Rollins	.05	.02
☐ 312 Tim Perry	.05	.02
☐ 313 Isaac Austin	.08	.04
☐ 314 Tate George	.05	.02
☐ 315 Kevin Lynch	.05	.02
☐ 316 Victor Alexander	.05	.02
☐ 317 Doug Overton	.05	.02
☐ 318 Tom Hammonds	.05	.02
☐ 319 LaPhonso Ellis	.25	.11
☐ 320 Scott Brooks	.05	.02
☐ 321 Anthony Avent UER	.05	.02
(Front photo actually Blue Edwards)		
☐ 322 Matt Geiger	.08	.04
☐ 323 Duane Causwell	.05	.02
☐ 324 Horace Grant	.08	.04
☐ 325 Mark Jackson	.08	.04
☐ 326 Dan Majerle	.08	.04
☐ 327 Chuck Person	.05	.02
☐ 328 Buck Johnson	.05	.02
☐ 329 Duane Cooper	.05	.02
☐ 330 Rod Strickland	.15	.07
☐ 331 Isiah Thomas	.15	.07
☐ 332 Greg Kite	.05	.02
(See also card 387)		
☐ 333 Don MacLean	.05	.02
☐ 334 Christian Laettner	.40	.18
☐ 335 John Crotty	.05	.02
☐ 336 Tracy Moore	.05	.02
☐ 337 Hakeem Olajuwon	.30	.14
☐ 338 Byron Houston	.05	.02
☐ 339 Walter Bond	.05	.02
☐ 340 Brent Price	.08	.04
☐ 341 Bryant Stith	.08	.04
☐ 342 Will Perdue	.05	.02
☐ 343 Jeff Hornacek	.08	.04
☐ 344 Adam Keefe	.05	.02
☐ 345 Rafael Addison	.05	.02
☐ 346 Marlon Maxey	.05	.02
☐ 347 Joe Dumars	.15	.07
☐ 348 Jon Barry	.05	.02
☐ 349 Marty Conlon	.05	.02
☐ 350 Alaa Abdelnaby	.05	.02
☐ 351 Micheal Williams	.05	.02
☐ 352 Brad Daugherty	.05	.02
☐ 353 Tony Bennett	.05	.02
☐ 354 Clyde Drexler	.20	.09
☐ 355 Rolando Blackman	.05	.02
☐ 356 Tom Tolbert	.05	.02
☐ 357 Sarunas Marciulionis	.05	.02
☐ 358 Jaren Jackson	.05	.02
☐ 359 Stacey King	.05	.02
☐ 360 Danny Ainge	.08	.04
☐ 361 Dale Ellis	.05	.02
☐ 362 Shaquille O'Neal	3.00	1.35
☐ 363 Bob McCann	.05	.02
☐ 364 Reggie Smith	.05	.02
☐ 365 Vinny Del Negro	.05	.02
☐ 366 Robert Pack	.05	.02
☐ 367 David Wood	.05	.02
☐ 368 Rodney McCray	.05	.02
☐ 369 Terry Mills	.08	.04
☐ 370 Eric Murdock UER	.05	.02
(Jazz on back spelled Jass)		
☐ 371 Alex Blackwell	.05	.02
☐ 372 Jay Humphries	.05	.02
☐ 373 Eddie Lee Wilkins	.05	.02
☐ 374 James Edwards	.05	.02
☐ 375 Tim Kempton	.05	.02
☐ 376 J.R. Reid	.05	.02
☐ 377 Sam Mack	.05	.02
☐ 378 Donald Royal	.05	.02

☐ 379 Mark Price	.05	.02
☐ 380 Mark Acres	.05	.02
☐ 381 Hubert Davis	.08	.04
☐ 382 Dave Johnson	.05	.02
☐ 383 John Salley	.05	.02
☐ 384 Eddie Johnson	.05	.02
☐ 385 Brian Howard	.05	.02
☐ 386 Isaiah Morris	.05	.02
☐ 387 Frank Johnson	.05	.02
(Card misnumbered 332)		
☐ 388 Rick Mahorn	.05	.02
☐ 389 Scottie Pippen	.50	.23
☐ 390 Lee Mayberry	.05	.02
☐ 391 Tony Campbell	.05	.02
☐ 392 Latrell Sprewell	.50	.23
☐ 393 Alonzo Mourning	.75	.35
☐ 394 Robert Werdann	.05	.02
☐ 395 Checklist 199-297 UER	.05	.02
(286 Kennard Winchester; should be Randy Woods)		
☐ 396 Checklist 298-396	.05	.02

1992-93 Topps Beam Team

Comprised of some of the NBA's biggest stars, the Topps Beam Team set contains seven standard size cards. Inserted in 15-card second series packs at a ratio of one in 18, these special "Topps Beam Team" bonus cards commemorate Topps' 1993 sponsorship of a six-minute NBA laser animation show. Called Beams Above the Rim, the show premiered at the NBA All-Star Game on Feb. 21. Afterwards, the laser show embarked on a ten-city tour and was featured in either the pre-game or half-time events in ten NBA arenas. Three players are featured on each Topps Beam Team card. The horizontal fronts display three color action player photos on a dark blue background with a grid of brightly colored light beams. The set title "Beam Team" appears in pastel green block lettering across the top. The backs carry three light blue panels, with a close-up color photo, biography, and player profile on each panel.

	MINT	NRMT
COMPLETE SET (7)	10.00	4.50
COMMON TRIO (1-7)	.75	.35
SER.2 STATED ODDS 1:18		
COMP.GOLD BEAM TEAM (7)	25.00	11.00
*GOLD: 1.5X TO 3X HI COLUMN		
ONE GOLD BT SET PER GOLD FACTORY SET		

☐ 1 Reggie Miller	1.00	.45
Charles Barkley		
Clyde Drexler		
☐ 2 Patrick Ewing	.75	.35
Tim Hardaway		
Jeff Hornacek		
☐ 3 Kevin Johnson	5.00	2.20
Michael Jordan		
Dennis Rodman		
☐ 4 Dominique Wilkins	.75	.35
John Stockton		
Karl Malone		
☐ 5 Hakeem Olajuwon	1.50	.70
Mark Price		
Shawn Kemp		
☐ 6 Scottie Pippen	1.00	.45
David Robinson		
Jeff Malone		
☐ 7 Chris Mullin	3.00	1.35
Shaquille O'Neal		
Glen Rice		

1993-94 Topps

The complete 1993-94 Topps basketball set consists of 396 standard-size cards issued in two 198-card series. Cards were issued in 12, 15 and 29-card packs. Factory sets contain 410 cards including 10 Gold, three Black Gold and one Finest Redemption card. The Finest Redemption card enabled a collector to mail away for two random Finest cards. The redemption deadline was July 31, 1994. The white bordered fronts display team color action player photos with a team color coded inner border. The player's name is printed in white script in the lower left corner with the team name appearing on a team color coded bar at the very bottom. The horizontal backs carry a close-up player photo on the right with complete NBA statistics, biography, and career highlights on the left on a beige panel. Subsets featured are

Highlights (1-5), 50 Point Club (50, 57, 64), Topps All-Star 1st Team (100-104), Topps All-Star 2nd Team (115-119), Topps All-Star 3rd Team (130-134), Topps All-Rookie 1st Team (150-154), Topps All-Rookie 2nd Team (175-179), Future Playoff MVP's (199-209) and Future Scoring Leaders (384-394). Rookie Cards of note in this set include Vin Baker, Anfernee Hardaway, Allan Houston, Jamal Mashburn, Nick Van Exel and Chris Webber.

	MINT	NRMT
COMPLETE SET (396)	20.00	9.00
COMPLETE FACT.SET (410)	25.00	11.00
COMPLETE SERIES 1 (198)	10.00	4.50
COMPLETE SERIES 2 (198)	10.00	4.50
COMMON CARD (1-396)	.05	.02
SEMISTARS	.10	.05
UNLISTED STARS	.25	.11
COMP.GOLD SET (396)	70.00	32.00
COMP.GOLD SER.1 (198)	30.00	13.50
COMP.GOLD SER.2 (198)	40.00	18.00
COMMON GOLD (1G-396G)	.10	.05
CL REPLACE (197G/198G)	.50	.23
CL REPLACE (395G/396G)	.50	.23
*GOLD STARS: 2X TO 4X HI COLUMN		
*GOLD RCs: 1.25X TO 2.5X HI		
ONE GOLD PER PACK		
TEN GOLD PER FACTORY SET		

☐ 1	Charles Barkley HL	.25	.11
☐ 2	Hakeem Olajuwon HL	.25	.11
☐ 3	Shaquille O'Neal HL	.50	.23
☐ 4	Chris Jackson HL	.05	.02
☐ 5	Clifford Robinson HL	.05	.02
☐ 6	Donald Hodge	.05	.02
☐ 7	Victor Alexander	.05	.02
☐ 8	Chris Morris	.05	.02
☐ 9	Muggsy Bogues	.10	.05
☐ 10	Steve Smith UER	.05	.02
	(Listed with Kings in '90-91;		
	was not in NBA that year)		
☐ 11	Dave Johnson	.05	.02
☐ 12	Tom Gugliotta	.25	.11
☐ 13	Doug Edwards	.05	.02
☐ 14	Vlade Divac	.10	.05
☐ 15	Corie Blount	.05	.02
☐ 16	Derek Harper	.10	.05
☐ 17	Matt Bullard	.05	.02
☐ 18	Terry Catledge	.05	.02
☐ 19	Mark Eaton	.05	.02
☐ 20	Mark Jackson	.10	.05
☐ 21	Terry Mills	.05	.02
☐ 22	Johnny Dawkins	.05	.02
☐ 23	Michael Jordan UER	3.00	1.35
	(Listed as a forward with birthdate		
	of 1968; he is a guard with		
	bithdate of 1963)		
☐ 24	Rick Fox UER	.05	.02
	(Listed with Kings in '91-92)		
☐ 25	Charles Oakley	.10	.05
☐ 26	Derrick McKey	.05	.02
☐ 27	Christian Laettner	.25	.11
☐ 28	Todd Day	.05	.02
☐ 29	Danny Ferry	.05	.02
☐ 30	Kevin Johnson	.10	.05
☐ 31	Vinny Del Negro	.05	.02
☐ 32	Kevin Brooks	.05	.02
☐ 33	Pete Chilcutt	.05	.02
☐ 34	Larry Stewart	.05	.02
☐ 35	Dave Jamerson	.05	.02
☐ 36	Sidney Green	.05	.02
☐ 37	J.R. Reid	.05	.02
☐ 38	Jim Jackson	.25	.11
☐ 39	Micheal Williams UER	.05	.02
	(350.2 minutes per game)		
☐ 40	Rex Walters	.05	.02
☐ 41	Shawn Bradley	.30	.14
☐ 42	Jon Koncak	.05	.02
☐ 43	Byron Houston	.05	.02
☐ 44	Brian Shaw	.05	.02
☐ 45	Bill Cartwright	.05	.02
☐ 46	Jerome Kersey	.05	.02
☐ 47	Danny Schayes	.05	.02
☐ 48	Olden Polynice	.05	.02
☐ 49	Anthony Peeler	.05	.02
☐ 50	Nick Anderson 50	.05	.02
☐ 51	David Benoit	.05	.02
☐ 52	David Robinson	.25	.11
☐ 53	Greg Kite	.05	.02
☐ 54	Gerald Paddio	.05	.02
☐ 55	Don MacLean	.05	.02
☐ 56	Randy Woods	.05	.02
☐ 57	Reggie Miller 50	.10	.05
☐ 58	Kevin Gamble	.05	.02
☐ 59	Sean Green	.05	.02
☐ 60	Jeff Hornacek	.05	.02
☐ 61	John Starks	.10	.05
☐ 62	Gerald Wilkins	.05	.02
☐ 63	Jim Les	.05	.02
☐ 64	Michael Jordan 50	1.50	.70
☐ 65	Alvin Robertson	.05	.02
☐ 66	Tim Kempton	.05	.02
☐ 67	Bryant Stith	.05	.02
☐ 68	Jeff Turner	.05	.02
☐ 69	Malik Sealy	.05	.02
☐ 70	Dell Curry	.05	.02
☐ 71	Brent Price	.05	.02
☐ 72	Kevin Lynch	.05	.02
☐ 73	Bimbo Coles	.05	.02
☐ 74	Larry Nance	.10	.05
☐ 75	Luther Wright	.05	.02
☐ 76	Willie Anderson	.05	.02
☐ 77	Dennis Rodman	1.00	.45
☐ 78	Anthony Mason	.10	.05
☐ 79	Chris Gatling	.05	.02
☐ 80	Antoine Carr	.05	.02
☐ 81	Kevin Willis	.05	.02
☐ 82	Thurl Bailey	.05	.02
☐ 83	Reggie Williams	.05	.02
☐ 84	Rod Strickland	.10	.05
☐ 85	Rolando Blackman	.05	.02
☐ 86	Bobby Hurley	.10	.05
☐ 87	Jeff Malone	.05	.02
☐ 88	James Worthy	.25	.11
☐ 89	Alaa Abdelnaby	.05	.02
☐ 90	Duane Ferrell	.05	.02
☐ 91	Anthony Avent	.05	.02
☐ 92	Scottie Pippen	.75	.35
☐ 93	Ricky Pierce	.05	.02
☐ 94	P.J. Brown	.05	.02
☐ 95	Jeff Grayer	.05	.02
☐ 96	Jerrod Mustaf	.05	.02
☐ 97	Elmore Spencer	.05	.02
☐ 98	Walt Williams	.10	.05
☐ 99	Otis Thorpe	.10	.05
☐ 100	Patrick Ewing AS	.10	.05
☐ 101	Michael Jordan AS	1.50	.70
☐ 102	John Stockton AS	.10	.05
☐ 103	Dominique Wilkins AS	.10	.05
☐ 104	Charles Barkley AS	.25	.11
☐ 105	Lee Mayberry	.05	.02
☐ 106	James Edwards	.05	.02
☐ 107	Scott Brooks	.05	.02
☐ 108	John Battle	.05	.02
☐ 109	Kenny Gattison	.05	.02
☐ 110	Pooh Richardson	.05	.02
☐ 111	Rony Seikaly	.05	.02
☐ 112	Mahmoud Abdul-Rauf	.05	.02
☐ 113	Nick Anderson	.10	.05
☐ 114	Gundars Vetra	.05	.02
☐ 115	Joe Dumars AS	.10	.05
☐ 116	Hakeem Olajuwon AS	.25	.11
☐ 117	Scottie Pippen AS	.40	.18
☐ 118	Mark Price AS	.05	.02
☐ 119	Karl Malone AS	.25	.11
☐ 120	Michael Cage	.05	.02
☐ 121	Ed Pinckney	.05	.02
☐ 122	Jay Humphries	.05	.02
☐ 123	Dale Davis	.05	.02
☐ 124	Sean Rooks	.05	.02
☐ 125	Mookie Blaylock	.10	.05

126	Buck Williams	.10	.05
127	John Williams	.05	.02
128	Stacey King	.05	.02
129	Tim Perry	.05	.02
130	Tim Hardaway AS	.25	.11
131	Larry Johnson AS	.10	.05
132	Detlef Schrempf AS	.05	.02
133	Reggie Miller AS	.10	.05
134	Shaquille O'Neal	.50	.23
135	Dale Ellis	.05	.02
136	Duane Causwell	.05	.02
137	Rumeal Robinson	.05	.02
138	Billy Owens	.05	.02
139	Malcolm Mackey	.05	.02
140	Vernon Maxwell	.05	.02
141	LaPhonso Ellis	.10	.05
142	Robert Parish	.10	.05
143	LaBradford Smith	.05	.02
144	Charles Smith	.05	.02
145	Terry Porter	.05	.02
146	Elden Campbell	.10	.05
147	Bill Laimbeer	.05	.02
148	Chris Mills	.40	.18
149	Brad Lohaus	.05	.02
150	Jimmy Jackson ART	.10	.05
151	Tom Gugliotta ART	.10	.05
152	Shaquille O'Neal ART	.50	.23
153	Latrell Sprewell ART	.25	.11
154	Walt Williams ART	.05	.02
155	Gary Payton	.40	.18
156	Orlando Woolridge	.05	.02
157	Adam Keefe	.05	.02
158	Calbert Cheaney	.25	.11
159	Rick Mahorn	.05	.02
160	Robert Horry	.10	.05
161	John Salley	.05	.02
162	Sam Mitchell	.05	.02
163	Stanley Roberts	.05	.02
164	C.Weatherspoon	.05	.02
165	Anthony Bowie	.05	.02
166	Derrick Coleman	.10	.05
167	Negele Knight	.05	.02
168	Marlon Maxey	.05	.02
169	Spud Webb UER	.10	.05

(Listed as center instead of guard)

170	Alonzo Mourning	.40	.18
171	Ervin Johnson	.10	.05
172	Sedale Threatt	.05	.02
173	Mark Macon	.05	.02
174	B.J. Armstrong	.05	.02
175	Harold Miner ART	.05	.02
176	Anthony Peeler ART	.05	.02
177	Alonzo Mourning ART	.25	.11
178	Christian Laettner ART	.10	.05
179	C.Weatherspoon ART	.05	.02
180	Dee Brown	.05	.02
181	Shaquille O'Neal	1.00	.45
182	Loy Vaught	.05	.02
183	Terrell Brandon	.25	.11
184	Lionel Simmons	.05	.02
185	Mark Aguirre	.05	.02
186	Danny Ainge	.10	.05
187	Reggie Miller	.25	.11
188	Terry Davis	.05	.02
189	Mark Bryant	.05	.02
190	Tyrone Corbin	.05	.02
191	Chris Mullin	.25	.11
192	Johnny Newman	.05	.02
193	Doug West	.05	.02
194	Keith Askins	.05	.02
195	Bo Kimble	.05	.02
196	Sean Elliott	.10	.05
197	Checklist 1-99 UER	.05	.02

(No. 18 listed as Terry Mills instead of Terry Cummings and No. 23 listed as Sam Mitchell instead of Michael Jordan)

198	Checklist 100-198	.05	.02
199	Michael Jordan FPM	1.50	.70
200	Patrick Ewing FPM	.10	.05
201	John Stockton FPM	.10	.05
202	Shawn Kemp FPM	.40	.18
203	Mark Price FPM	.05	.02
204	Charles Barkley FPM	.25	.11
205	Hakeem Olajuwon FPM	.25	.11
206	Clyde Drexler FPM	.25	.11
207	Kevin Johnson FPM	.05	.02
208	John Starks FPM	.05	.02
209	Chris Mullin FPM	.05	.02
210	Doc Rivers	.10	.05
211	Kenny Walker	.05	.02
212	Doug Christie	.05	.02
213	James Robinson	.05	.02
214	Larry Krystkowiak	.05	.02
215	Manute Bol	.05	.02
216	Carl Herrera	.05	.02
217	Paul Graham	.05	.02
218	Jud Buechler	.05	.02
219	Mike Brown	.05	.02
220	Tom Chambers	.05	.02
221	Kendall Gill	.10	.05
222	Kenny Anderson	.10	.05
223	Larry Johnson	.25	.11
224	Chris Webber	1.50	.70
225	Randy White	.05	.02
226	Rik Smits	.10	.05
227	A.C. Green	.10	.05
228	David Robinson	.40	.18
229	Sean Elliott	.10	.05
230	Gary Grant	.05	.02
231	Dana Barros	.05	.02
232	Bobby Hurley	.10	.05
233	Blue Edwards	.05	.02
234	Tom Hammonds	.05	.02
235	Pete Myers UER	.05	.02

Card says born in 1993

236	Acie Earl	.05	.02
237	Tony Smith	.05	.02
238	Bill Wennington	.05	.02
239	Andrew Lang	.05	.02
240	Ervin Johnson	.10	.05
241	Byron Scott	.10	.05
242	Eddie Johnson	.05	.02
243	Anthony Bonner	.05	.02
244	Luther Wright	.05	.02
245	LaSalle Thompson	.05	.02
246	Harold Miner	.05	.02
247	Chris Smith	.05	.02
248	John Williams	.05	.02
249	Clyde Drexler	.30	.14
250	Calbert Cheaney	.25	.11
251	Avery Johnson	.05	.02
252	Steve Kerr	.05	.02
253	Warren Kidd	.05	.02
254	Wayman Tisdale	.05	.02
255	Bob Martin	.05	.02
256	Popeye Jones	.05	.02
257	Jimmy Oliver	.05	.02
258	Kevin Edwards	.05	.02
259	Dan Majerle	.10	.05
260	Jon Barry	.05	.02
261	Allan Houston	.50	.23
262	Dikembe Mutombo	.25	.11
263	Sleepy Floyd	.05	.02
264	George Lynch	.05	.02
265	Stacey Augmon UER	.05	.02

(Listed with Heat in stats)

266	Hakeem Olajuwon	.50	.23
267	Scott Skiles	.05	.02
268	Detlef Schrempf	.10	.05
269	Brian Davis	.05	.02
270	Tracy Murray	.05	.02
271	Gheorghe Muresan	.30	.14
272	Terry Dehere	.05	.02
273	Terry Cummings	.05	.02
274	Keith Jennings	.05	.02
275	Tyrone Hill	.05	.02
276	Harvey Hawkins	.10	.05
277	Grant Long	.05	.02
278	Herb Williams	.05	.02
279	Karl Malone	.40	.18
280	Mitch Richmond	.25	.11
281	Derek Strong	.05	.02
282	Dino Radja	.10	.05
283	Jack Haley	.05	.02
284	Derek Harper	.10	.05
285	Dwayne Schintzius	.05	.02
286	Michael Curry	.05	.02
287	Rodney Rogers	.05	.02
288	Horace Grant	.10	.05
289	Oliver Miller	.05	.02
290	Luc Longley	.10	.05
291	Walter Bond	.05	.02
292	Dominique Wilkins	.25	.11
293	Vern Fleming	.05	.02
294	Mark Price	.05	.02
295	Mark Aguirre	.05	.02
296	Shawn Kemp	.75	.35
297	Pervis Ellison	.05	.02
298	Josh Grant	.05	.02
299	Scott Burrell	.25	.11
300	Patrick Ewing	.25	.11
301	Sam Cassell	.60	.25
302	Nick Van Exel	.75	.35
303	Clifford Robinson	.10	.05
304	Frank Johnson	.05	.02
305	Matt Geiger	.05	.02
306	Vin Baker	1.50	.70
307	Benoit Benjamin	.05	.02
308	Shawn Bradley	.25	.11
309	Chris Whitney	.05	.02
310	Eric Riley	.05	.02
311	Isiah Thomas	.25	.11
312	Jamal Mashburn	.60	.25
313	Xavier McDaniel	.05	.02
314	Mike Peplowski	.05	.02
315	Darnell Mee	.05	.02
316	Toni Kukoc	.60	.25
317	Felton Spencer	.05	.02
318	Sam Bowie	.05	.02
319	Mario Elie	.05	.02
320	Tim Hardaway	.30	.14
321	Ken Norman	.05	.02
322	Isaiah Rider	.30	.14
323	Rex Chapman	.05	.02
324	Dennis Rodman	1.00	.45
325	Derrick McKey	.05	.02
326	Corie Blount	.05	.02
327	Fat Lever	.05	.02
328	Ron Harper	.10	.05
329	Eric Anderson	.05	.02
330	Armon Gilliam	.05	.02
331	Lindsey Hunter	.25	.11
332	Eric Leckner	.05	.02
333	Chris Corchiani	.05	.02
334	Anfernee Hardaway	3.00	1.35
335	Randy Brown	.05	.02
336	Sam Perkins	.10	.05
337	Glen Rice	.25	.11
338	Orlando Woolridge	.05	.02
339	Mike Gminski	.05	.02
340	Latrell Sprewell	.25	.11
341	Harvey Grant	.05	.02
342	Doug Smith	.05	.02
343	Kevin Duckworth	.05	.02
344	Cedric Ceballos	.10	.05
345	Chuck Person	.05	.02
346	Scott Haskin	.05	.02
347	Frank Brickowski	.05	.02
348	Scott Williams	.05	.02
349	Brad Daugherty	.05	.02
350	Willie Burton	.05	.02
351	Joe Dumars	.25	.11
352	Craig Ehlo	.05	.02
353	Lucious Harris	.05	.02
354	Danny Manning	.05	.02
355	Litterial Green	.05	.02
356	John Stockton	.25	.11
357	Nate McMillan	.05	.02
358	Greg Graham	.05	.02
359	Rex Walters	.05	.02
360	Lloyd Daniels	.05	.02
361	Antonio Harvey	.05	.02
362	Brian Williams	.05	.02
363	LeRon Ellis	.05	.02
364	Chris Dudley	.05	.02
365	Hubert Davis	.05	.02
366	Evers Burns	.05	.02
367	Sherman Douglas	.05	.02
368	Sarunas Marciulionis	.05	.02
369	Tom Tolbert	.05	.02
370	Robert Pack	.05	.02
371	Michael Adams	.05	.02
372	Negele Knight	.05	.02
373	Charles Barkley	.40	.18
374	Bryon Russell	.25	.11
375	Greg Anthony	.05	.02
376	Ken Williams	.05	.02

			MINT	NRMT
☐ 377	John Paxson	.05		.02
☐ 378	Corey Gaines	.05		.02
☐ 379	Eric Murdock	.05		.02
☐ 380	Kevin Thompson	.05		.02
☐ 381	Moses Malone	.25		.11
☐ 382	Kenny Smith	.05		.02
☐ 383	Dennis Scott	.10		.05
☐ 384	Michael Jordan FSL	1.50		.70
☐ 385	Hakeem Olajuwon FSL	.25		.11
☐ 386	Shaquille O'Neal FSL	.50		.23
☐ 387	David Robinson FSL	.25		.11
☐ 388	Derrick Coleman FSL	.05		.02
☐ 389	Karl Malone FSL	.25		.11
☐ 390	Patrick Ewing FSL	.10		.05
☐ 391	Scottie Pippen FSL	.40		.18
☐ 392	Dominique Wilkins FSL	.10		.05
☐ 393	Charles Barkley FSL	.25		.11
☐ 394	Larry Johnson FSL	.10		.05
☐ 395	Checklist	.05		.02
☐ 396	Checklist	.05		.02
☐ NNO	Expired Finest Redemption Card	1.00		.45

1993-94 Topps Black Gold

Randomly inserted in first and second series packs and three per factory set, this 25-card standard size set features the top five draft picks each year from 1989-1993. Thirteen cards were inserts in series one and 12 in series two. They were inserted at a rate of one in 72 for 12-card packs and one in 18 for 29-card packs. Winner A cards, redeemable for a series 1 set, were randomly inserted into 1 in every 144 series 1 packs. Winner B cards, redeemable for a series 2 set, were randomly inserted into 1 in every 144 series 2 packs. The A/B Winner card (randomly inserted into 1 in every 288 series 2 packs only) was redeemable for a complete set. Each white-bordered front displays a color action player shot with the background tinted in black. Gold prismatic wavy stripes appear above and below the photo with the player's name reversed out of the black bar near the bottom. The white-bordered horizontal backs carry a close-up color cutout on a black background with white concentric stripes. The player's name appears in gold-foil lettering on a wood textured bar with the team name directly to the right in black lettering. Player statistics appear below in an orange background.

	MINT	NRMT
COMPLETE SET (25)	25.00	11.00
COMPLETE SERIES 1 (13)	5.00	2.20
COMPLETE SERIES 2 (12)	20.00	9.00
COMMON CARD (1-25)	.25	.11
SEMISTARS	.60	.25
UNLISTED STARS	1.00	.45
SER.1/2 STATED ODDS 1:72 HOB/RET		
SER.1/2 STATED ODDS 1:18 JUM/RACK		
THREE PER FACTORY SET		

			MINT	NRMT
☐ 1	Sean Elliott		.60	.25
☐ 2	Dennis Scott		.25	.11
☐ 3	Kenny Anderson		.60	.25
☐ 4	Alonzo Mourning		1.50	.70
☐ 5	Glen Rice		1.00	.45
☐ 6	Billy Owens		.25	.11
☐ 7	Jim Jackson		1.00	.45
☐ 8	Derrick Coleman		.60	.25
☐ 9	Larry Johnson		1.00	.45
☐ 10	Gary Payton		2.00	.90
☐ 11	Christian Laettner		1.00	.45
☐ 12	Dikembe Mutombo		1.00	.45
☐ 13	Mahmoud Abdul-Rauf		.25	.11
☐ 14	Isaiah Rider		1.00	.45
☐ 15	Steve Smith		1.00	.45
☐ 16	LaPhonso Ellis		.60	.25
☐ 17	Danny Ferry		.25	.11
☐ 18	Shaquille O'Neal		4.00	1.80
☐ 19	Anfernee Hardaway		12.00	5.50
☐ 20	J.R. Reid		.25	.11
☐ 21	Shawn Bradley		.60	.25
☐ 22	Pervis Ellison		.25	.11
☐ 23	Chris Webber		5.00	2.20
☐ 24	Jamal Mashburn		2.00	.90
☐ 25	Kendall Gill		.60	.25
☐ A	Expired Winner A		.75	.35
☐ B	Expired Winner B		.75	.35
☐ AX	Redeemed Winner A		.25	.11
☐ BX	Redeemed Winner B		.25	.11
☐ AB	Expired Winner A/B		1.00	.45

1994-95 Topps

The 396 standard-size cards that comprise the 1994-95 Topps set were issued in two separate series of 198 cards each. Cards were distributed primarily in 12-card packs that carried a suggested retail price of $1.00 each. Fronts feature full-color action photos framed by a jagged white border. Player's name and team are placed in gold foil along the bottom. The following subsets are included in this set: Eastern All-Star (1-13), Paint Patrol (100-109), and Western All-Star (183-195). In addition, various "From the Roof" subsets cards are intermingled within the set. Rookie Cards of note in this set include Grant Hill, Juwan Howard, Eddie Jones, Jason Kidd and Glenn Robinson.

	MINT	NRMT
COMPLETE SET (396)	25.00	11.00
COMPLETE SERIES 1 (198)	10.00	4.50
COMPLETE SERIES 2 (198)	15.00	6.75
COMMON CARD (1-396)	.05	.02
SEMISTARS	.10	.05
UNLISTED STARS	.25	.11
COMP.SPECT.SET (396)	300.00	135.00
COMP.SPECT.SER 1 (198)	125.00	55.00
COMP.SPECT.SER 2 (198)	175.00	80.00
COMMON SPECT. (1-396)	.25	.11
CL REPLACEMENT (197-198)	.50	.23
*SPECT.STARS: 5X TO 10X HI COLUMN		
*SPECT.RCs: 4X TO 8X HI		
SER.1/2 STATED ODDS 1:4		

			MINT	NRMT
☐ 1	Patrick Ewing AS		.10	.05
☐ 2	Mookie Blaylock AS		.05	.02
☐ 3	Charles Oakley AS		.05	.02
☐ 4	Mark Price AS		.05	.02
☐ 5	John Starks AS		.05	.02
☐ 6	Dominique Wilkins AS		.10	.05
☐ 7	Horace Grant AS		.05	.02
☐ 8	Alonzo Mourning AS		.25	.11
☐ 9	B.J. Armstrong AS		.05	.02
☐ 10	Kenny Anderson AS		.05	.02
☐ 11	Scottie Pippen AS		.40	.18
☐ 12	Derrick Coleman AS		.05	.02
☐ 13	Shaquille O'Neal AS		.50	.23
☐ 14	A.Hardaway SPEC		.50	.23
☐ 15	Isaiah Rider SPEC		.05	.02
☐ 16	John Williams		.05	.02
☐ 17	Todd Day		.05	.02
☐ 18	Dale Davis		.05	.02
☐ 19	Sean Rooks		.05	.02
☐ 20	George Lynch		.05	.02
☐ 21	Mitchell Butler		.05	.02
☐ 22	Stacey King		.05	.02
☐ 23	Sherman Douglas		.05	.02
☐ 24	Derrick McKey		.05	.02
☐ 25	Joe Dumars		.25	.11
☐ 26	Scott Brooks		.05	.02
☐ 27	C.Weatherspoon		.05	.02
☐ 28	Jayson Williams		.10	.05
☐ 29	Scottie Pippen		.75	.35
☐ 30	John Starks		.10	.05
☐ 31	Robert Pack		.05	.02
☐ 32	Donald Royal		.05	.02
☐ 33	Haywoode Workman		.05	.02
☐ 34	Greg Graham		.05	.02
☐ 35	Terry Cummings		.05	.02
☐ 36	Andrew Lang		.05	.02
☐ 37	Jason Kidd		2.00	.90
☐ 38	Terry Mills		.05	.02
☐ 39	Alonzo Mourning		.30	.14
☐ 40	Shawn Kemp		.75	.35
☐ 41	Kevin Willis FTR		.05	.02
☐ 42	Kevin Willis		.05	.02
☐ 43	Armon Gilliam		.05	.02
☐ 44	Bobby Hurley		.05	.02
☐ 45	Jerome Kersey		.05	.02
☐ 46	Xavier McDaniel		.05	.02
☐ 47	Chris Webber		.60	.25
☐ 48	Chris Webber FTR		.30	.14
☐ 49	Jeff Malone		.05	.02
☐ 50	D.Mutombo SPEC		.10	.05

51	Dan Majerle SPEC	.05	.02
52	Dee Brown SPEC	.05	.02
53	John Stockton SPEC	.10	.05
54	Dennis Rodman SPEC	.50	.23
55	Eric Murdock SPEC	.05	.02
56	Glen Rice	.25	.11
57	Glen Rice FTR	.10	.05
58	Dino Radja	.05	.02
59	Billy Owens	.05	.02
60	Doc Rivers	.10	.05
61	Don MacLean	.05	.02
62	Lindsey Hunter	.10	.05
63	Sam Cassell	.25	.11
64	James Worthy	.25	.11
65	Christian Laettner	.10	.05
66	Wesley Person	.30	.14
67	Rich King	.05	.02
68	Jon Koncak	.05	.02
69	Muggsy Bogues	.10	.05
70	Jamal Mashburn	.25	.11
71	Gary Grant	.05	.02
72	Eric Murdock	.05	.02
73	Scott Burrell	.05	.02
74	Scott Burrell FTR	.05	.02
75	Anfernee Hardaway	1.00	.45
76	A.Hardaway FTR	.50	.23
77	Yinka Dare	.05	.02
78	Anthony Avent	.05	.02
79	Jon Barry	.05	.02
80	Rodney Rogers	.05	.02
81	Chris Mills	.10	.05
82	Antonio Davis	.05	.02
83	Steve Smith	.10	.05
84	Buck Williams	.10	.05
85	Spud Webb	.10	.05
86	Stacey Augmon	.05	.02
87	Allan Houston	.25	.11
88	Will Perdue	.05	.02
89	Chris Gatling	.05	.02
90	Danny Ainge	.10	.05
91	Rick Mahorn	.05	.02
92	Elmore Spencer	.05	.02
93	Vin Baker	.60	.25
94	Rex Chapman	.05	.02
95	Dale Ellis	.05	.02
96	Doug Smith	.05	.02
97	Tim Perry	.05	.02
98	Toni Kukoc	.25	.11
99	Terry Dehere	.05	.02
100	Shaquille O'Neal PP	.50	.23
101	Shawn Kemp PP	.40	.18
102	Hakeem Olajuwon PP	.25	.11
103	Derrick Coleman PP	.05	.02
104	Alonzo Mourning PP	.25	.11
105	D.Mutombo PP	.10	.05
106	Chris Webber PP	.30	.14
107	Dennis Rodman PP	.50	.23
108	David Robinson PP	.25	.11
109	Charles Barkley PP	.25	.11
110	Brad Daugherty	.05	.02
111	Derek Harper	.10	.05
112	Detlef Schrempf	.10	.05
113	Harvey Grant	.05	.02
114	Vlade Divac	.10	.05
115	Isaiah Rider	.25	.11
116	Mitch Richmond	.25	.11
117	Tom Chambers	.05	.02
118	Kenny Gattison	.05	.02
119	Kenny Gattison FTR	.05	.02
120	Vernon Maxwell	.05	.02
121	Reggie Williams	.05	.02
122	Chris Mullin	.25	.11
123	Harold Miner	.05	.02
124	Harold Miner FTR	.05	.02
125	Calbert Cheaney	.10	.05
126	Randy Woods	.05	.02
127	Mike Gminski	.05	.02
128	Willie Anderson	.05	.02
129	Mark Macon	.05	.02
130	Avery Johnson	.05	.02
131	Bimbo Coles	.05	.02
132	Kenny Smith	.05	.02
133	Dennis Scott	.05	.02
134	Lionel Simmons	.05	.02
135	Nate McMillan	.05	.02
136	Eric Montross	.05	.02
137	Sedale Threatt	.05	.02
138	Kenny Anderson	.10	.05
139	Micheal Williams	.05	.02
140	Grant Long	.05	.02
141	Grant Long FTR	.05	.02
142	Tyrone Corbin	.05	.02
143	Craig Ehlo	.05	.02
144	Gerald Wilkins	.05	.02
145	LaPhonso Ellis	.10	.05
146	Reggie Miller	.25	.11
147	Tracy Murray	.05	.02
148	Victor Alexander	.05	.02
149	Victor Alexander FTR	.05	.02
150	Clifford Robinson	.10	.05
151	Anthony Mason FTR	.05	.02
152	Anthony Mason	.05	.02
153	Jim Jackson	.25	.11
154	Jeff Hornacek	.10	.05
155	Nick Anderson	.05	.02
156	Mike Brown	.05	.02
157	Kevin Johnson	.10	.05
158	John Paxson	.05	.02
159	Loy Vaught	.05	.02
160	Carl Herrera	.05	.02
161	Shawn Bradley	.10	.05
162	Hubert Davis	.05	.02
163	David Benoit	.05	.02
164	Dell Curry	.05	.02
165	Dee Brown	.05	.02
166	LaSalle Thompson	.05	.02
167	Eddie Jones	2.00	.90
168	Walt Williams	.05	.02
169	A.C. Green	.10	.05
170	Kendall Gill	.10	.05
171	Kendall Gill FTR	.05	.02
172	Danny Ferry	.05	.02
173	Bryant Stith	.05	.02
174	John Salley	.05	.02
175	Cedric Ceballos	.10	.05
176	Derrick Coleman	.10	.05
177	Tony Bennett	.05	.02
178	Kevin Duckworth	.05	.02
179	Jay Humphries	.05	.02
180	Sean Elliott	.10	.05
181	Sam Perkins	.10	.05
182	Luc Longley	.05	.02
183	Mitch Richmond AS	.10	.05
184	Clyde Drexler AS	.25	.11
185	Karl Malone AS	.25	.11
186	Shawn Kemp AS	.40	.18
187	Hakeem Olajuwon AS	.25	.11
188	Danny Manning AS	.05	.02
189	Kevin Johnson AS	.10	.05
190	John Stockton AS	.10	.05
191	Latrell Sprewell AS	.05	.02
192	Gary Payton AS	.25	.11
193	Clifford Robinson AS	.05	.02
194	David Robinson AS	.25	.11
195	Charles Barkley AS	.25	.11
196	Mark Price SPEC	.05	.02
197	Checklist 1-99	.05	.02
198	Checklist 100-198	.05	.02
199	Patrick Ewing	.25	.11
200	Patrick Ewing FTR	.10	.05
201	Tracy Murray PP	.05	.02
202	Craig Ehlo PP	.05	.02
203	Nick Anderson PP	.05	.02
204	John Starks PP	.05	.02
205	Rex Chapman PP	.05	.02
206	Hersey Hawkins PP	.05	.02
207	Glen Rice PP	.10	.05
208	Jeff Malone PP	.05	.02
209	Dan Majerle PP	.05	.02
210	Chris Mullin PP	.10	.05
211	Grant Hill	3.00	1.35
212	Bobby Phills	.05	.02
213	Dennis Rodman	1.00	.45
214	Doug West	.05	.02
215	Harold Ellis	.05	.02
216	Kevin Edwards	.05	.02
217	Lorenzo Williams	.05	.02
218	Rick Fox	.05	.02
219	Mookie Blaylock	.10	.05
220	Mookie Blaylock FTR	.05	.02
221	John Williams	.05	.02
222	Keith Jennings	.05	.02
223	Nick Van Exel	.25	.11
224	Gary Payton	.40	.18
225	John Stockton	.25	.11
226	Ron Harper	.10	.05
227	Monty Williams	.05	.02
228	Marty Conlon	.05	.02
229	Hersey Hawkins	.10	.05
230	Rik Smits	.10	.05
231	James Robinson	.05	.02
232	Malik Sealy	.05	.02
233	Sergei Bazarevich	.05	.02
234	Brad Lohaus	.05	.02
235	Olden Polynice	.05	.02
236	Brian Williams	.05	.02
237	Tyrone Hill	.05	.02
238	Jim McIlvaine	.05	.02
239	Latrell Sprewell	.10	.05
240	Latrell Sprewell FTR	.05	.05
241	Popeye Jones	.05	.02
242	Scott Williams	.05	.02
243	Eddie Jones	1.00	.45
244	Moses Malone	.25	.11
245	B.J. Armstrong	.05	.02
246	Jim Les	.05	.02
247	Greg Grant	.05	.02
248	Lee Mayberry	.05	.02
249	Mark Jackson	.10	.05
250	Larry Johnson	.10	.05
251	Terrell Brandon	.25	.11
252	Ledell Eackles	.05	.02
253	Yinka Dare	.05	.02
254	Dontonio Wingfield	.05	.02
255	Clyde Drexler	.30	.14
256	Andres Guibert	.05	.02
257	Gheorghe Muresan	.10	.05
258	Tom Hammonds	.05	.02
259	Charles Barkley	.40	.18
260	Charles Barkley FTR	.25	.11
261	Acie Earl	.05	.02
262	Lamond Murray	.10	.05
263	Dana Barros	.05	.02
264	Greg Anthony	.05	.02
265	Dan Majerle	.10	.05
266	Zan Tabak	.05	.02
267	Ricky Pierce	.05	.02
268	Eric Leckner	.05	.02
269	Duane Ferrell	.05	.02
270	Mark Price	.05	.02
271	Anthony Peeler	.05	.02
272	Adam Keefe	.05	.02
273	Rex Walters	.05	.02
274	Scott Skiles	.05	.02
275	Glenn Robinson	1.00	.45
276	Tony Dumas	.05	.02
277	Elliot Perry	.05	.02
278	Charles Outlaw	.05	.02
279	Karl Malone	.40	.18
280	Karl Malone FTR	.25	.11
281	Herb Williams	.05	.02
282	Vincent Askew	.05	.02
283	Askia Jones	.05	.02
284	Shawn Bradley	.10	.05
285	Tim Hardaway	.30	.14
286	Mark West	.05	.02
287	Chuck Person	.05	.02
288	James Edwards	.05	.02
289	Antonio Lang	.05	.02
290	Dominique Wilkins	.25	.11
291	Khalid Reeves	.05	.02
292	Jamie Watson	.10	.05
293	Darnell Mee	.05	.02
294	Brian Grant	.25	.11
295	Hakeem Olajuwon	.50	.23
296	Dickey Simpkins	.05	.02
297	Tyrone Corbin	.05	.02
298	David Wingate	.05	.02
299	Shaquille O'Neal	1.00	.45
300	Shaquille O'Neal FTR	.50	.23
301	B.J. Armstrong PP	.05	.02
302	Mitch Richmond PP	.10	.05
303	Jim Jackson PP	.05	.05
304	Jeff Hornacek PP	.05	.05
305	Mark Price PP	.05	.05
306	Kendall Gill PP	.05	.02
307	Dale Ellis PP	.05	.02
308	Vernon Maxwell PP	.05	.02

☐ 309 Joe Dumars PP	.10	.05
☐ 310 Reggie Miller PP	.05	.05
☐ 311 Geert Hammink	.05	.02
☐ 312 Charles Smith	.05	.02
☐ 313 Bill Cartwright	.05	.02
☐ 314 Aaron McKie	.05	.02
☐ 315 Tom Gugliotta	.25	.11
☐ 316 P.J. Brown	.05	.02
☐ 317 David Wesley	.10	.05
☐ 318 Felton Spencer	.05	.02
☐ 319 Robert Horry	.10	.05
☐ 320 Robert Horry FR	.05	.02
☐ 321 Larry Krystkowiak	.05	.02
☐ 322 Eric Piatkowski	.05	.02
☐ 323 Anthony Bonner	.05	.02
☐ 324 Keith Askins	.05	.02
☐ 325 Mahmoud Abdul-Rauf	.05	.02
☐ 326 Darrin Hancock	.05	.02
☐ 327 Vern Fleming	.05	.02
☐ 328 Wayman Tisdale	.05	.02
☐ 329 Sam Bowie	.05	.02
☐ 330 Billy Owens	.05	.02
☐ 331 Donald Hodge	.05	.02
☐ 332 Derrick Alston	.05	.02
☐ 333 Doug Edwards	.05	.02
☐ 334 Johnny Newman	.05	.02
☐ 335 Otis Thorpe	.10	.05
☐ 336 Bill Curley	.05	.02
☐ 337 Michael Cage	.05	.02
☐ 338 Chris Smith	.05	.02
☐ 339 D.Mutombo	.25	.11
☐ 340 D.Mutombo FTR	.10	.05
☐ 341 Duane Causwell	.05	.02
☐ 342 Sean Higgins	.05	.02
☐ 343 Steve Kerr	.10	.05
☐ 344 Eric Montross	.05	.02
☐ 345 Charles Oakley	.10	.05
☐ 346 Brooks Thompson	.05	.02
☐ 347 Rony Seikaly	.05	.02
☐ 348 Chris Dudley	.05	.02
☐ 349 Sharone Wright	.05	.02
☐ 350 Sarunas Marciulionis	.05	.02
☐ 351 Anthony Miller	.05	.02
☐ 352 Pooh Richardson	.05	.02
☐ 353 Byron Scott	.10	.05
☐ 354 Michael Adams	.05	.02
☐ 355 Ken Norman	.05	.02
☐ 356 Clifford Rozier	.05	.02
☐ 357 Tim Breaux	.05	.02
☐ 358 Derek Strong	.05	.02
☐ 359 David Robinson	.40	.18
☐ 360 David Robinson FR	.25	.11
☐ 361 Benoit Benjamin	.05	.02
☐ 362 Terry Porter	.05	.02
☐ 363 Ervin Johnson	.05	.02
☐ 364 Alaa Abdelnaby	.05	.02
☐ 365 Robert Parish	.05	.02
☐ 366 Mario Elie	.05	.02
☐ 367 Antonio Harvey	.05	.02
☐ 368 Charlie Ward	.10	.05
☐ 369 Kevin Gamble	.05	.02
☐ 370 Rod Strickland	.10	.05
☐ 371 Jason Kidd	1.00	.45
☐ 372 Oliver Miller	.05	.02
☐ 373 Eric Mobley	.05	.02
☐ 374 Brian Shaw	.05	.02
☐ 375 Horace Grant	.10	.05
☐ 376 Corie Blount	.05	.02
☐ 377 Sam Mitchell	.05	.02
☐ 378 Jalen Rose	.25	.11
☐ 379 Elden Campbell	.10	.05
☐ 380 Elden Campbell FTR	.05	.02
☐ 381 Donyell Marshall	.30	.14
☐ 382 Frank Brickowski	.05	.02
☐ 383 B.J. Tyler	.05	.02
☐ 384 Bryon Russell	.10	.05
☐ 385 Danny Manning	.05	.02
☐ 386 Manute Bol	.05	.02
☐ 387 Brent Price	.05	.02
☐ 388 J.R. Reid	.05	.02
☐ 389 Byron Houston	.05	.02
☐ 390 Blue Edwards	.05	.02
☐ 391 Adrian Caldwell	.05	.02
☐ 392 Wesley Person	.25	.11
☐ 393 Juwan Howard	1.25	.55
☐ 394 Chris Morris	.05	.02

☐ 395 Checklist 199-296	.05	.02
☐ 396 Checklist 297-396	.05	.02

1994-95 Topps Franchise/Futures

Randomly inserted into all second series packs at a rate of one in 18, cards from this 20-card set feature a selection of promising youngsters coupled with established stars from the same team. Card fronts feature full-color action shots surrounded by a white border.

	MINT	NRMT
COMPLETE SET (20)	60.00	27.00
COMMON CARD (1-20)	1.00	.45
SEMISTARS	1.50	.70
UNLISTED STARS	3.00	1.35
SER.2 STATED ODDS 1:18		
☐ 1 Mookie Blaylock	1.50	.70
☐ 2 Stacey Augmon	1.00	.45
☐ 3 Dominique Wilkins	3.00	1.35
☐ 4 Eric Montross	1.00	.45
☐ 5 Dikembe Mutombo	3.00	1.35
☐ 6 Jalen Rose	3.00	1.35
☐ 7 Joe Dumars	3.00	1.35
☐ 8 Grant Hill	20.00	9.00
☐ 9 Chris Mullin	3.00	1.35
☐ 10 Latrell Sprewell	1.50	.70
☐ 11 Glen Rice	3.00	1.35
☐ 12 Khalid Reeves	1.00	.45
☐ 13 Derrick Coleman	1.50	.70
☐ 14 Yinka Dare	1.00	.45
☐ 15 Patrick Ewing	3.00	1.35
☐ 16 Monty Williams	1.00	.45
☐ 17 Shaquille O'Neal	12.00	5.50
☐ 18 Anfernee Hardaway	12.00	5.50
☐ 19 Charles Barkley	5.00	2.20
☐ 20 Wesley Person	3.00	1.35

1994-95 Topps Own the Game

Randomly inserted in all first series packs (12-card packs one in 18, jumbo packs one in 9), cards from this 50-card standard-size unnumbered set featured nine top players in five different statistical categories (Super Passers, Super Rebounders, Super Scorers, Super Stealers and Super Swatters) in addition to five

Field Cards. If the player pictured on the card (Field Card represented all other players in the league) led the league in that respective category, it became redeemable for a special 10-card Own the Game redemption set for that category.

	MINT	NRMT
COMPLETE SET (50)	25.00	11.00
COMMON CARD (1-50)	.15	.07
SEMISTARS	.30	.14
UNLISTED STARS	.60	.25
SER.1 STATED ODDS 1:18		
COMP.EXCHANGE SET (10)	10.00	4.50
*EXCHANGE CARDS: 1X HI COLUMN		
ONE EXCHANGE SET PER 'W' CARD BY MAIL		
NNO CARDS LISTED ALPHABETICALLY		
☐ 1 Kenny Anderson PASS	.30	.14
☐ 2 Charles Barkley SCORE	1.00	.45
☐ 3 Mookie Blaylock PASS	.30	.14
☐ 4 Mookie Blaylock STEAL	.30	.14
☐ 5 Muggsy Bogues PASS	.30	.14
☐ 6 Shawn Bradley SWAT	.15	.07
☐ 7 Derrick Coleman REB	.30	.14
☐ 8 Sherman Douglas PASS	.15	.07
☐ 9 Patrick Ewing REB	.60	.25
☐ 10 Patrick Ewing SCORE	.60	.25
☐ 11 Patrick Ewing SWAT	.60	.25
☐ 12 Tom Gugliotta STEAL	.60	.25
☐ 13 A.Hardaway PASS	2.50	1.10
☐ 14 Mark Jackson PASS	.30	.14
☐ 15 Kevin Johnson PASS	.30	.14
☐ 16 Karl Malone REB	1.00	.45
☐ 17 Karl Malone SCORE	1.00	.45
☐ 18 Nate McMillan STEAL	.15	.07
☐ 19 Oliver Miller SWAT	.15	.07
☐ 20 Alonzo Mourning SWAT	.75	.35
☐ 21 Eric Murdock STEAL	.15	.07
☐ 22 D.Mutombo REB	.60	.25
☐ 23 D.Mutombo SWAT W	.60	.25
☐ 24 Charles Oakley REB	.15	.07
☐ 25 H.Olajuwon REB	1.25	.55
☐ 26 H.Olajuwon SCORE	1.25	.55
☐ 27 H.Olajuwon SWAT	1.25	.55
☐ 28 Shaquille O'Neal REB	2.50	1.10
☐ 29 S.O'Neal SCORE W	3.00	1.35
☐ 30 Shaquille O'Neal SWAT	2.50	1.10
☐ 31 Gary Payton STEAL	1.00	.45
☐ 32 Scottie Pippen SCORE	2.00	.90
☐ 33 S.Pippen STEAL W	2.50	1.10
☐ 34 Mark Price PASS	.15	.07
☐ 35 Mitch Richmond SCORE	.60	.25
☐ 36 D.Robinson SCORE	1.00	.45
☐ 37 David Robinson SWAT	1.00	.45
☐ 38 D.Rodman REB W	3.00	1.35
☐ 39 Latrell Sprewell STEAL	.15	.07
☐ 40 John Stockton PASS W	.75	.35
☐ 41 John Stockton STEAL	.60	.25
☐ 42 Rod Strickland PASS	.30	.14
☐ 43 Chris Webber SWAT	1.50	.70
☐ 44 Kevin Willis REB	.15	.07

	MINT	NRMT
☐ 45 D.Wilkins SCORE	.60	.25
☐ 46 Passers Field Card	.15	.07
☐ 47 Rebounders Field Card	.15	.07
☐ 48 Scorers Field Card	.15	.07
☐ 49 Stealers Field Card	.15	.07
☐ 50 Swatters Field Card	.15	.07

1994-95 Topps Super Sophomores

Randomly inserted into all second series packs at a rate of one in 36, cards from this 10-card standard-size set spotlight a selection of young phenoms in their second NBA season. Fronts feature full-color player action shots cut out against silver-foil backgrounds.

	MINT	NRMT
COMPLETE SET (10)	50.00	22.00
COMMON CARD (1-10)	1.50	.70
SEMISTARS	2.50	1.10
UNLISTED STARS	5.00	2.20
SER.2 STATED ODDS 1:36		

	MINT	NRMT
☐ 1 Chris Webber	12.00	5.50
☐ 2 Anfernee Hardaway	20.00	9.00
☐ 3 Vin Baker	12.00	5.50
☐ 4 Sam Cassell	5.00	2.20
☐ 5 Jamal Mashburn	5.00	2.20
☐ 6 Isaiah Rider	2.50	1.10
☐ 7 Chris Mills	2.50	1.10
☐ 8 Antonio Davis	1.50	.70
☐ 9 Nick Van Exel	5.00	2.20
☐ 10 Lindsey Hunter	2.50	1.10

1995-96 Topps

The 1995-96 Topps Basketball set was issued in two separate series of 181 and 110 standard-size cards for a total of 291.

Both first and second series cards were issued in 12-card hobby and retail packs (SRP $1.29). The white bordered fronts have a full-color action photo with the player's name in gold set against a black shadow. Horizontal backs have color head-shots with statistics and information. Subsets include Active Leaders (1-5), Scoring Leaders (6-10), Rebound Leaders (11-15), Assist Leaders (16-20), Steal Leaders (21-25) and Block Leaders (26-30). Rookie Cards of note in this set include Michael Finley, Kevin Garnett, Antonio McDyess, Joe Smith, Jerry Stackhouse and Damon Stoudamire.

	MINT	NRMT
COMPLETE SET (291)	30.00	13.50
COMPLETE SERIES 1 (181)	15.00	6.75
COMPLETE SERIES 2 (110)	15.00	6.75
COMMON CARD (1-291)	.10	.05
SEMISTARS	.15	.07
UNLISTED STARS	.25	.11

	MINT	NRMT
☐ 1 Michael Jordan AL	1.50	.70
☐ 2 Dennis Rodman AL	.50	.23
☐ 3 John Stockton AL	.15	.07
☐ 4 Michael Jordan AL	1.50	.70
☐ 5 David Robinson AL	.25	.11
☐ 6 Shaquille O'Neal LL	.50	.23
☐ 7 Hakeem Olajuwon LL	.25	.11
☐ 8 David Robinson LL	.25	.11
☐ 9 Karl Malone LL	.25	.11
☐ 10 Jamal Mashburn LL	.10	.05
☐ 11 Dennis Rodman LL	.50	.23
☐ 12 Dikembe Mutombo LL	.10	.05
☐ 13 Shaquille O'Neal LL	.50	.23
☐ 14 Patrick Ewing LL	.15	.07
☐ 15 Tyrone Hill LL	.10	.05
☐ 16 John Stockton LL	.15	.07
☐ 17 Kenny Anderson LL	.10	.05
☐ 18 Tim Hardaway LL	.25	.11
☐ 19 Rod Strickland LL	.10	.05
☐ 20 Muggsy Bogues LL	.10	.05
☐ 21 Scottie Pippen LL	.40	.18
☐ 22 Mookie Blaylock LL	.10	.05
☐ 23 Gary Payton LL	.25	.11
☐ 24 John Stockton LL	.15	.07
☐ 25 Nate McMillan LL	.10	.05
☐ 26 Dikembe Mutombo LL	.10	.05
☐ 27 Hakeem Olajuwon LL	.25	.11
☐ 28 Shawn Bradley LL	.10	.05
☐ 29 David Robinson LL	.25	.11
☐ 30 Alonzo Mourning LL	.15	.07
☐ 31 Reggie Miller	.25	.11
☐ 32 Karl Malone	.40	.18
☐ 33 Grant Hill	1.50	.70
☐ 34 Charles Barkley	.40	.18
☐ 35 Cedric Ceballos	.10	.05
☐ 36 Gheorghe Muresan	.10	.05
☐ 37 Doug West	.10	.05
☐ 38 Tony Dumas	.10	.05
☐ 39 Kenny Gattison	.10	.05
☐ 40 Chris Mullin	.25	.11
☐ 41 Pervis Ellison	.10	.05
☐ 42 Vinny Del Negro	.10	.05
☐ 43 Mario Elie	.10	.05
☐ 44 Todd Day	.10	.05
☐ 45 Scottie Pippen	.75	.35
☐ 46 Buck Williams	.10	.05
☐ 47 P.J. Brown	.10	.05
☐ 48 Bimbo Coles	.10	.05
☐ 49 Terrell Brandon	.25	.11
☐ 50 Charles Oakley	.10	.05

	MINT	NRMT
☐ 51 Sam Perkins	.15	.07
☐ 52 Dale Ellis	.10	.05
☐ 53 Andrew Lang	.10	.05
☐ 54 Harold Ellis	.10	.05
☐ 55 C.Weatherspoon	.10	.05
☐ 56 Bill Curley	.10	.05
☐ 57 Robert Parish	.15	.07
☐ 58 David Benoit	.10	.05
☐ 59 Anthony Avent	.10	.05
☐ 60 Jamal Mashburn	.15	.07
☐ 61 Duane Ferrell	.10	.05
☐ 62 Elden Campbell	.15	.07
☐ 63 Rex Chapman	.10	.05
☐ 64 Wesley Person	.15	.07
☐ 65 Mitch Richmond	.25	.11
☐ 66 Micheal Williams	.10	.05
☐ 67 Clifford Rozier	.10	.05
☐ 68 Eric Montross	.10	.05
☐ 69 Dennis Rodman	1.00	.45
☐ 70 Vin Baker	.50	.23
☐ 71 Tyrone Hill	.10	.05
☐ 72 Tyrone Corbin	.10	.05
☐ 73 Chris Dudley	.10	.05
☐ 74 Nate McMillan	.10	.05
☐ 75 Kenny Anderson	.15	.07
☐ 76 Monty Williams	.10	.05
☐ 77 Kenny Smith	.10	.05
☐ 78 Rodney Rogers	.10	.05
☐ 79 Corie Blount	.10	.05
☐ 80 Glen Rice	.25	.11
☐ 81 Walt Williams	.10	.05
☐ 82 Scott Williams	.10	.05
☐ 83 Michael Adams	.10	.05
☐ 84 Terry Mills	.10	.05
☐ 85 Horace Grant	.15	.07
☐ 86 Chuck Person	.10	.05
☐ 87 Adam Keefe	.10	.05
☐ 88 Scott Brooks	.10	.05
☐ 89 George Lynch	.10	.05
☐ 90 Kevin Johnson	.15	.07
☐ 91 Armon Gilliam	.10	.05
☐ 92 Greg Minor	.10	.05
☐ 93 Derrick McKey	.10	.05
☐ 94 Victor Alexander	.10	.05
☐ 95 B.J. Armstrong	.10	.05
☐ 96 Terry Dehere	.10	.05
☐ 97 Christian Laettner	.15	.07
☐ 98 Hubert Davis	.10	.05
☐ 99 Aaron McKie	.10	.05
☐ 100 Hakeem Olajuwon	.50	.23
☐ 101 Michael Cage	.10	.05
☐ 102 Grant Long	.10	.05
☐ 103 Calbert Cheaney	.10	.05
☐ 104 Olden Polynice	.10	.05
☐ 105 Sharone Wright	.10	.05
☐ 106 Lee Mayberry	.10	.05
☐ 107 Robert Pack	.10	.05
☐ 108 Loy Vaught	.10	.05
☐ 109 Khalid Reeves	.10	.05
☐ 110 Shawn Kemp	.75	.35
☐ 111 Lindsey Hunter	.10	.05
☐ 112 Dell Curry	.10	.05
☐ 113 Dan Majerle	.15	.07
☐ 114 Bryon Russell	.10	.05
☐ 115 John Starks	.15	.07
☐ 116 Roy Tarpley	.10	.05
☐ 117 Dale Davis	.10	.05
☐ 118 Nick Anderson	.10	.05
☐ 119 Rex Walters	.10	.05
☐ 120 Dominique Wilkins	.25	.11
☐ 121 Sam Cassell	.15	.07
☐ 122 Sean Elliott	.10	.05
☐ 123 B.J. Tyler	.10	.05
☐ 124 Eric Mobley	.10	.05
☐ 125 Toni Kukoc	.15	.07
☐ 126 Poon Richardson	.10	.05
☐ 127 Isaiah Rider	.15	.07
☐ 128 Steve Smith	.15	.07
☐ 129 Chris Mills	.10	.05
☐ 130 Detlef Schrempf	.15	.07
☐ 131 Donyell Marshall	.15	.07
☐ 132 Eddie Jones	.60	.25
☐ 133 Otis Thorpe	.15	.07
☐ 134 Lionel Simmons	.10	.05
☐ 135 Jeff Hornacek	.15	.07
☐ 136 Jalen Rose	.15	.07

□ 137 Kevin Willis	.10	.05
□ 138 Don MacLean	.10	.05
□ 139 Dee Brown	.10	.05
□ 140 Glenn Robinson	.30	.14
□ 141 Joe Kleine	.10	.05
□ 142 Ron Harper	.15	.07
□ 143 Antonio Davis	.10	.05
□ 144 Jeff Malone	.10	.05
□ 145 Joe Dumars	.25	.11
□ 146 Jason Kidd	.60	.25
□ 147 J.R. Reid	.10	.05
□ 148 Lamond Murray	.10	.05
□ 149 Derrick Coleman	.15	.07
□ 150 Alonzo Mourning	.25	.11
□ 151 Clifford Robinson	.10	.05
□ 152 Kendall Gill	.15	.07
□ 153 Doug Christie	.10	.05
□ 154 Stacey Augmon	.10	.05
□ 155 Anfernee Hardaway ..	1.00	.45
□ 156 Mahmoud Abdul-Rauf	.10	.05
□ 157 Latrell Sprewell	.15	.07
□ 158 Mark Price	.10	.05
□ 159 Brian Grant	.15	.07
□ 160 Clyde Drexler	.30	.14
□ 161 Juwan Howard	.40	.18
□ 162 Tom Gugliotta	.25	.11
□ 163 Nick Van Exel	.25	.11
□ 164 Billy Owens	.10	.05
□ 165 Brooks Thompson	.10	.05
□ 166 Acie Earl	.10	.05
□ 167 Ed Pinckney	.10	.05
□ 168 Oliver Miller	.10	.05
□ 169 John Salley	.10	.05
□ 170 Jerome Kersey	.10	.05
□ 171 Willie Anderson	.10	.05
□ 172 Keith Jennings	.10	.05
□ 173 Doug Smith	.10	.05
□ 174 Gerald Wilkins	.10	.05
□ 175 Byron Scott	.10·	
□ 176 Benoit Benjamin	.10	.05
□ 177 Blue Edwards	.10	.05
□ 178 Greg Anthony	.10	.05
□ 179 Trevor Ruffin	.10	.05
□ 180 Kenny Gattison	.10	.05
□ 181 Checklist 1-181	.10	.05
□ 182 Cherokee Parks	.10	.05
□ 183 Kurt Thomas	.15	.07
□ 184 Ervin Johnson	.10	.05
□ 185 Chucky Brown	.10	.05
□ 186 Luc Longley	.15	.07
□ 187 Anthony Miller	.10	.05
□ 188 Ed O'Bannon	.10	.05
□ 189 Bobby Hurley	.10	.05
□ 190 Dikembe Mutombo	.15	.07
□ 191 Robert Horry	.10	.05
□ 192 George Zidek	.10	.05
□ 193 Rasheed Wallace	.60	.25
□ 194 Marty Conlon	.10	.05
□ 195 A.C. Green	.15	.07
□ 196 Mike Brown	.10	.05
□ 197 Oliver Miller	.10	.05
□ 198 Charles Smith	.10	.05
□ 199 Eric Williams	.15	.07
□ 200 Rik Smits	.15	.07
□ 201 Donald Royal	.10	.05
□ 202 Bryant Reeves	.60	.25
□ 203 Danny Ferry	.10	.05
□ 204 Brian Williams	.10	.05
□ 205 Joe Smith	1.00	.45
□ 206 Gary Trent	.10	.05
□ 207 Greg Ostertag	.10	.05
□ 208 Ken Norman	.10	.05
□ 209 Avery Johnson	.10	.05
□ 210 Theo Ratliff UER	.25	.11
Card has no draft pick logo		
□ 211 Corie Blount	.10	.05
□ 212 Hersey Hawkins	.15	.07
□ 213 Loren Meyer	.10	.05
□ 214 Mario Bennett	.10	.05
□ 215 Randolph Childress	.10	.07
□ 216 Spud Webb	.15	.07
□ 217 Popeye Jones	.10	.05
□ 218 Shawn Respert	.10	.05
□ 219 Malik Sealy	.10	.05
□ 220 Dino Radja	.10	.05
□ 221 James Robinson	.10	.05
□ 222 David Vaughn	.10	.05
□ 223 Michael Smith	.10	.05
□ 224 Jamie Watson	.10	.05
□ 225 LaPhonso Ellis	.15	.07
□ 226 Kevin Gamble	.10	.05
□ 227 Dennis Rodman	1.50	.70
□ 228 B.J. Armstrong	.10	.05
□ 229 Jerry Stackhouse	1.00	.45
□ 230 Muggsy Bogues	.15	.07
□ 231 Lawrence Moten	.10	.05
□ 232 Cory Alexander	.10	.05
□ 233 Carlos Rogers	.10	.05
□ 234 Tyus Edney	.10	.05
□ 235 Doc Rivers	.15	.07
□ 236 Antonio Harvey	.10	.05
□ 237 Kevin Garnett	3.00	1.35
□ 238 Derek Harper	.15	.07
□ 239 Kevin Edwards	.10	.05
□ 240 Chris Smith	.10	.05
□ 241 Haywoode Workman	.10	.05
□ 242 Bobby Phills	.10	.05
□ 243 Sherrell Ford	.10	.05
□ 244 Corliss Williamson	.30	.14
□ 245 Shawn Bradley	.15	.07
□ 246 Jason Caffey	.25	.11
□ 247 Bryant Stith	.10	.05
□ 248 Mark West	.10	.05
□ 249 Dennis Scott	.10	.05
□ 250 Jim Jackson	.15	.07
□ 251 Travis Best	.15	.07
□ 252 Sean Rooks	.10	.05
□ 253 Yinka Dare	.10	.05
□ 254 Felton Spencer	.10	.05
□ 255 Vlade Divac	.15	.07
□ 256 Michael Finley	1.00	.45
□ 257 Damon Stoudamire .	2.00	.90
□ 258 Mark Bryant	.10	.05
□ 259 Brent Barry	.25	.11
□ 260 Rony Seikaly	.10	.05
□ 261 Alan Henderson	.25	.11
□ 262 Kendall Gill	.15	.07
□ 263 Rex Chapman	.10	.05
□ 264 Eric Murdock	.10	.05
□ 265 Rodney Rogers	.10	.05
□ 266 Greg Graham	.10	.05
□ 267 Jayson Williams	.15	.07
□ 268 Antonio McDyess	1.25	.55
□ 269 Sedale Threatt	.10	.05
□ 270 Danny Manning	.15	.07
□ 271 Pete Chilcutt	.10	.05
□ 272 Bob Sura	.15	.07
□ 273 Dana Barros	.10	.05
□ 274 Allan Houston	.15	.07
□ 275 Tracy Murray	.10	.05
□ 276 Anthony Mason	.15	.07
□ 277 Michael Jordan	3.00	1.35
□ 278 Patrick Ewing	.25	.11
□ 279 Shaquille O'Neal	1.00	.45
□ 280 Larry Johnson	.15	.07
□ 281 Mark Jackson	.10	.05
□ 282 Chris Webber	.60	.25
□ 283 David Robinson	.40	.18
□ 284 John Stockton	.25	.11
□ 285 Mookie Blaylock	.15	.07
□ 286 Mark Price	.10	.05
□ 287 Tim Hardaway	.30	.14
□ 288 Rod Strickland	.10	.05
□ 289 Sherman Douglas	.10	.05
□ 290 Gary Payton	.40	.18
□ 291 Checklist (182-291)	.10	.05

one in 18). These cards feature all foil silver bordered fronts with a full-color action shot of the featured rookie. The first series exchange cards each featured a large number on the card front representing the player that was chosen at that slot in the 1995 NBA draft. Collectors had to then mail the card in to Topps to receive their player card. The redemption deadline for these cards was April 1, 1996.

	MINT	NRMT
COMPLETE SET (29)	100.00	45.00
COMMON CARD (1-29)	1.50	.70
SEMISTARS	2.50	1.10
UNLISTED STARS	4.00	1.80
ONE CARD PER EXCHANGE CARD BY MAIL		
EXCH.CARDS: SER.1 STATED ODDS 1:18		
□ 1 Joe Smith	8.00	3.60
□ 2 Antonio McDyess	10.00	4.50
□ 3 Jerry Stackhouse	8.00	3.60
□ 4 Rasheed Wallace	5.00	2.20
□ 5 Kevin Garnett	30.00	13.50
□ 6 Bryant Reeves	5.00	2.20
□ 7 Damon Stoudamire	15.00	6.75
□ 8 Shawn Respert	1.50	.70
□ 9 Ed O'Bannon	1.50	.70
□ 10 Kurt Thomas	2.50	1.10
□ 11 Gary Trent	1.50	.70
□ 12 Cherokee Parks	1.50	.70
□ 13 Corliss Williamson	4.00	1.80
□ 14 Eric Williams	2.50	1.10
□ 15 Brent Barry	4.00	1.80
□ 16 Alan Henderson	4.00	1.80
□ 17 Bob Sura	2.50	1.10
□ 18 Theo Ratliff	4.00	1.80
□ 19 Randolph Childress	1.50	.70
□ 20 Jason Caffey	4.00	1.80
□ 21 Michael Finley	8.00	3.60
□ 22 George Zidek	1.50	.70
□ 23 Travis Best	2.50	1.10
□ 24 Loren Meyer	1.50	.70
□ 25 David Vaughn	1.50	.70
□ 26 Sherrell Ford	1.50	.70
□ 27 Mario Bennett	1.50	.70
□ 28 Greg Ostertag	1.50	.70
□ 29 Cory Alexander	1.50	.70
□ NNO Expired Trade Cards..	.50	.23

1995-96 Topps Draft Redemption

These 29 draft pick cards (covering the entire first round of the 1995 NBA draft) were available exclusively by redeeming one of the Topps Draft Redemption insert cards (randomly inserted in series one packs at a rate of

1995-96 Topps Mystery Finest

Randomly inserted into all second series packs at a rate of one in 36, cards from this 22-card standard-size insert set

spotlight a selection of top forwards and guards in the league. Each Mystery Finest card was inserted into packs with a black plastic coating on front. Hence, the "mystery" was to peel off the coating to see whether one had a basic card or a parallel refractor. Card fronts feature a silver foil border and a player action photo cut out against a galaxy design background. These cards are often found poorly centered.

full-color player cutout set against a mine shaft background. The player's team name is printed in silver across the top and his name is stamped in gold foil across the bottom. Horizontal backs have a full-color player head shot on the left third of the card with his name, biography and details of his draft and school information on the right. Pieces of gold serve as a background for the back. These cards are numbered with a "PFG" prefix.

two regular cards in every they came in. Full-bleed fronts carry a full-color action player cutout set against diffraction foil background with the player's name stamped in gold foil across the top. The Power Boosters logo appears at the bottom of the card with the individual's category listed above the logo. Borderless backs are one-color background with a full-color player head shot boxed on the right. Player name, team name, profile and biography appear on the back.

	MINT	NRMT
COMPLETE SET (22)	120.00	55.00
COMMON CARD (M1-M22)	2.00	.90
SEMISTARS	2.50	1.10
UNLISTED STARS	4.00	1.80
SER.2 STATED ODDS 1:36 HOBBY/RETAIL		
COMP.REF.SET (22)	800.00	350.00
COMMON REF. (M1-M22)	12.00	5.50
*REFRACTORS: 3X TO 6X HI COLUMN		
SER.2 STATED ODDS 1:36 HOB, 1:216 RET		
CONDITION SENSITIVE SET		

		MINT	NRMT
☐	M1 Michael Jordan	50.00	22.00
☐	M2 A.Hardaway	15.00	6.75
☐	M3 Clyde Drexler	5.00	2.20
☐	M4 Mark Price	2.00	.90
☐	M5 Steve Smith	2.50	1.10
☐	M6 Jim Jackson	2.50	1.10
☐	M7 Nick Anderson	2.00	.90
☐	M8 Kenny Anderson	2.50	1.10
☐	M9 Mookie Blaylock	2.50	1.10
☐	M10 Jason Kidd	10.00	4.50
☐	M11 Tim Hardaway	5.00	2.20
☐	M12 Kevin Johnson	2.50	1.10
☐	M13 Gary Payton	6.00	2.70
☐	M14 John Stockton	4.00	1.80
☐	M15 Rod Strickland	2.50	1.10
☐	M16 Jamal Mashburn	2.50	1.10
☐	M17 Danny Manning	2.50	1.10
☐	M18 Billy Owens	2.00	.90
☐	M19 Grant Hill	25.00	11.00
☐	M20 Scottie Pippen	12.00	5.50
☐	M21 Isaiah Rider	2.50	1.10
☐	M22 Latrell Sprewell	2.50	1.10

1995-96 Topps Pan For Gold

Randomly inserted in first series retail packs only at a rate of one in eight, this 15-card standard-size set chronicles the play of NBA stars who came from small colleges and were drafted late. White-bordered fronts feature a

	MINT	NRMT
COMPLETE SET (15)	40.00	18.00
COMMON CARD (1-15)	1.00	.45
SEMISTARS	2.50	1.10
UNLISTED STARS	4.00	1.80
SER.1 STATED ODDS 1:4 JUM, 1:8 RET		
PFG PREFIX ON CARD NUMBERS		

		MINT	NRMT
☐	1 Vin Baker	8.00	3.60
☐	2 John Stockton	4.00	1.80
☐	3 Dan Majerle	1.00	.45
☐	4 Joe Dumars	4.00	1.80
☐	5 Rik Smits	2.50	1.10
☐	6 Tim Hardaway	5.00	2.20
☐	7 Charles Oakley	1.00	.45
☐	8 Cedric Ceballos	1.00	.45
☐	9 Karl Malone	6.00	2.70
☐	10 Scottie Pippen	12.00	5.50
☐	11 David Robinson	6.00	2.70
☐	12 Gary Payton	6.00	2.70
☐	13 Mitch Richmond	4.00	1.80
☐	14 Antonio Davis	1.00	.45
☐	15 Dennis Rodman	15.00	6.75

1995-96 Topps Power Boosters

This 45-card insert standard-size set is printed on 28-point stock and features the leaders in points, rebounds, assists, steals and blocks paralleling the regular issue subset cards. The first 30 cards in the set (1-30) were seeded into first series packs at a rate of 1 in 36. The last 15 cards in the set (276-290) were seeded into second series packs also at a rate of one in 36. A Power Boosters card replaced

	MINT	NRMT
COMPLETE SET (45)	280.00	125.00
COMPLETE SERIES 1 (30)	200.00	90.00
COMPLETE SERIES 2 (15)	80.00	36.00
COMMON CARD (1-30)	1.50	.70
COMMON CARD (276-290)	1.25	.55
SEMISTARS SER.1	2.50	1.10
SEMISTARS SER.2	2.00	.90
UNLISTED STARS SER.1	4.00	1.80
UNLISTED STARS SER.2	3.00	1.35
SER.1/2 STATED ODDS 1:36 HOBBY/RETAIL		

		MINT	NRMT
☐	1 Michael Jordan	50.00	22.00
☐	2 Dennis Rodman	15.00	6.75
☐	3 John Stockton	4.00	1.80
☐	4 Michael Jordan	50.00	22.00
☐	5 David Robinson	6.00	2.70
☐	6 Shaquille O'Neal	15.00	6.75
☐	7 Hakeem Olajuwon	8.00	3.60
☐	8 David Robinson	6.00	2.70
☐	9 Karl Malone	6.00	2.70
☐	10 Jamal Mashburn	2.50	1.10
☐	11 Dennis Rodman	15.00	6.75
☐	12 Dikembe Mutombo	2.50	1.10
☐	13 Shaquille O'Neal	15.00	6.75
☐	14 Patrick Ewing	4.00	1.80
☐	15 Tyrone Hill	1.50	.70
☐	16 John Stockton	4.00	1.80
☐	17 Kenny Anderson	2.50	1.10
☐	18 Tim Hardaway	5.00	2.20
☐	19 Rod Strickland	2.50	1.10
☐	20 Muggsy Bogues	1.50	.70
☐	21 Scottie Pippen	12.00	5.50
☐	22 Mookie Blaylock	2.50	1.10
☐	23 Gary Payton	6.00	2.70
☐	24 John Stockton	4.00	1.80
☐	25 Nate McMillan	1.50	.70
☐	26 Dikembe Mutombo	2.50	1.10
☐	27 Hakeem Olajuwon	8.00	3.60
☐	28 Shawn Bradley	1.50	.70
☐	29 David Robinson	6.00	2.70
☐	30 Alonzo Mourning	4.00	1.80
☐	276 Anthony Mason	1.25	.55
☐	277 Michael Jordan	40.00	18.00
☐	278 Patrick Ewing	3.00	1.35

		MINT	NRMT
☐ 279	Shaquille O'Neal	12.00	5.50
☐ 280	Larry Johnson	2.00	.90
☐ 281	Mark Jackson	1.25	.55
☐ 282	Chris Webber	8.00	3.60
☐ 283	David Robinson	5.00	2.20
☐ 284	John Stockton	3.00	1.35
☐ 285	Mookie Blaylock	2.00	.90
☐ 286	Mark Price	1.25	.55
☐ 287	Tim Hardaway	4.00	1.80
☐ 288	Rod Strickland	2.00	.90
☐ 289	Sherman Douglas	1.25	.55
☐ 290	Gary Payton	5.00	2.20

1995-96 Topps Rattle and Roll

Randomly inserted in second series retail packs only at a rate of one in 12, this 10-card set takes aim at the power mongers of the NBA. Fronts are bordered in silver foil with a blue and red silver swirl pattern for a background. A full-color player cutout appears on the front with his name printed in a copper foil at the bottom. White-bordered backs contain a player head shot and his name printed underneath in red type. The blue and red swirl pattern continues and the player's biography and profile are printed in white type.

	MINT	NRMT
COMPLETE SET (10)	20.00	9.00
COMMON CARD (R1-R10)	.75	.35
SEMISTARS	1.00	.45
SER.2 STATED ODDS 1:12 RETAIL		

		MINT	NRMT
☐ R1	Juwan Howard	2.50	1.10
☐ R2	Glenn Robinson	2.00	.90
☐ R3	Grant Hill	10.00	4.50
☐ R4	Sharone Wright	.75	.35
☐ R5	Brian Grant	1.00	.45
☐ R6	Antonio McDyess	4.00	1.80
☐ R7	Bryant Reeves	2.00	.90
☐ R8	Gary Trent	.75	.35
☐ R9	Jerry Stackhouse	3.00	1.35
☐ R10	Joe Smith	3.00	1.35

1995-96 Topps Show Stoppers

Cards in this set of ten were randomly issued in first series hobby packs only at a rate of one in 24 and feature the top

players of the NBA. Fronts are white bordered with silver foil and a full-color player action cutout. The player's name is printed in gold foil at the bottom. Backs have a player head shot with a spotlight description, a game high feature and a show stopper highlight.

	MINT	NRMT
COMPLETE SET (10)	90.00	40.00
COMMON CARD (1-10)	3.00	1.35
SER.1 STATED ODDS 1:24 HOBBY		

		MINT	NRMT
☐ SS1	Michael Jordan	40.00	18.00
☐ SS2	Grant Hill	20.00	9.00
☐ SS3	Glenn Robinson	4.00	1.80
☐ SS4	A.Hardaway	12.00	5.50
☐ SS5	Charles Barkley	5.00	2.20
☐ SS6	Patrick Ewing	3.00	1.35
☐ SS7	Shaquille O'Neal	12.00	5.50
☐ SS8	Jason Kidd	8.00	3.60
☐ SS9	Glen Rice	3.00	1.35
☐ SS10	Karl Malone	5.00	2.20

1995-96 Topps Spark Plugs

Randomly inserted in all second series retail packs at a rate of one in 8, cards from this 10-card chase set highlight NBA scorers on full-foil fronts. Silver foil serves as a border and a blue and silver foil are background for a full-color action player cutout. A spark plug with sparks flying out and the player's name are printed in silver foil. Horizontal backs are white bor-

dered with a full-color action shot on one side and a player biography and '94-95 season highlights on the other.

	MINT	NRMT
COMPLETE SET (10)	30.00	13.50
COMMON CARD (SP1-SP10)	1.25	.55
SER.2 STATED ODDS 1:8 HOBBY/RETAIL		

		MINT	NRMT
☐ SP1	Shaquille O'Neal	5.00	2.20
☐ SP2	Michael Jordan	15.00	6.75
☐ SP3	Reggie Miller	1.25	.55
☐ SP4	Anfernee Hardaway	5.00	2.20
☐ SP5	John Stockton	1.25	.55
☐ SP6	David Robinson	2.00	.90
☐ SP7	Hakeem Olajuwon	2.50	1.10
☐ SP8	Tim Hardaway	1.50	.70
☐ SP9	Grant Hill	8.00	3.60
☐ SP10	Scottie Pippen	4.00	1.80

1995-96 Topps Sudden Impact

Sudden Impact is a hobby-exclusive insert set of ten rookies that were expected to make a significant impact on their teams. The horizontally designed "all foil" cards were randomly inserted at a rate of 1 in 72 second series hobby packs. The cards are numbered on the back with an "S" prefix.

	MINT	NRMT
COMPLETE SET (10)	80.00	36.00
COMMON CARD (S1-S10)	3.00	1.35
SEMISTARS	4.00	1.80
SER.2 STATED ODDS 1:72 HOBBY		

		MINT	NRMT
☐ S1	Damon Stoudamire	25.00	11.00
☐ S2	Cherokee Parks	3.00	1.35
☐ S3	Kurt Thomas	4.00	1.80
☐ S4	Gary Trent	3.00	1.35
☐ S5	Bryant Reeves	8.00	3.60
☐ S6	Ed O'Bannon	3.00	1.35
☐ S7	Shawn Respert	3.00	1.35
☐ S8	Antonio McDyess	15.00	6.75
☐ S9	Joe Smith	12.00	5.50
☐ S10	Jerry Stackhouse	12.00	5.50

1995-96 Topps Top Flight

Cards in this 20-piece set feature the high flyers of the NBA and were inserted one per retail

pack. The white bordered fronts have a full-color player action cutout set against a background with two fighter jets. The player's name is printed in gold foil near the bottom above a gold foil swooshing jet whose vapor spells out "Top Flight." Backs have a full-color head shot inset within a sky background of a jet in flight. A biography and special abilities box appear on the back.

"WK" and continue with a basketball court background. A full-color player head shot appears inside the key of the court and his name appears underneath the photo in red print on a blue banner. Career stats, biography and a trivia question appear on the lower half and the answer to the question on the preceding card appears at the bottom.

$1.29. The white-bordered fronts have a full-color action photo with the player's name in gold set against the trail of a moving basketball. Horizontal backs have color head shots with career statistics and information. The checklist card (#111) actually looks more like a premium Finest brand card than a Topps issue. Because it was so much tougher than a normal checklist, it is not considered part of the series one set. Rookie cards include Kobe Bryant, Marcus Camby, Allen Iverson, Stephon Marbury, Shareef Abdur-Rahim and Antoine Walker, among others. Several cards including Shawn Kemp and Damon Stoudamire were used for promotional purposes. The card numbers are identical to the regular issue, but on the front of the card, the Topps logo and the team logo are switched. In addition, Topps released factory sets for both the hobby and retail markets. Each set contained the full 221-card set, 2 of the Season's Best inserts, 1 card from the NBA at 50 parallel and 2 of the Pro File inserts. The hobby factory set also contained one of the 10 autographed cards originally released in the 1996 Topps NBA Stars Reprint Autograph set.

	MINT	NRMT
COMPLETE SET (20)	70.00	32.00
COMMON CARD (TF1-TF20)	1.00	.45
SEMISTARS	1.50	.70
UNLISTED STARS	2.50	1.10
ONE PER SPECIAL SER.1 RETAIL PACK		

		MINT	NRMT
☐ TF1	Michael Jordan	30.00	13.50
☐ TF2	Isaiah Rider	1.50	.70
☐ TF3	Harold Miner	1.00	.45
☐ TF4	Dominique Wilkins	2.50	1.10
☐ TF5	Clyde Drexler	3.00	1.35
☐ TF6	Scottie Pippen	8.00	3.60
☐ TF7	Shawn Kemp	8.00	3.60
☐ TF8	Chris Webber	6.00	2.70
☐ TF9	A.Hardaway	10.00	4.50
☐ TF10	Grant Hill	15.00	6.75
☐ TF11	Kevin Johnson	1.50	.70
☐ TF12	John Starks	1.50	.70
☐ TF13	Dan Majerle	1.00	.45
☐ TF14	Latrell Sprewell	1.50	.70
☐ TF15	Dee Brown	1.00	.45
☐ TF16	Stacey Augmon	1.00	.45
☐ TF17	David Benoit	1.00	.45
☐ TF18	Sean Elliott	1.00	.45
☐ TF19	Cedric Ceballos	1.00	.45
☐ TF20	Robert Horry	1.00	.45

1995-96 Topps Whiz Kids

Randomly inserted in all first series packs at a rate of one in 24, this set of 12 standard-size cards highlights the young power of the NBA. Etched silver foil fronts have a basketball court background and a full-color player action cutout. "Whiz Kids" is spelled out in children's letter blocks on the top. The players name is printed in red at the bottom. Borderless backs are numbered with the prefix

	MINT	NRMT
COMPLETE SET (12)	50.00	22.00
COMMON CARD (WK1-WK12)	1.00	.45
SEMISTARS	2.00	.90
UNLISTED STARS	3.00	1.35
SER.1 STATED ODDS 1:24 HOBBY/RETAIL		

		MINT	NRMT
☐ WK1	Grant Hill	20.00	9.00
☐ WK2	Nick Van Exel	3.00	1.35
☐ WK3	Juwan Howard	5.00	2.20
☐ WK4	Chris Webber	8.00	3.60
☐ WK5	Brian Grant	1.00	.45
☐ WK6	Glenn Robinson	4.00	1.80
☐ WK7	Donyell Marshall	2.00	.90
☐ WK8	Jason Kidd	8.00	3.60
☐ WK9	A.Hardaway	12.00	5.50
☐ WK10	Jamal Mashburn	2.00	.90
☐ WK11	Vin Baker	6.00	2.70
☐ WK12	Eddie Jones	8.00	3.60

1996-97 Topps

The 1996-97 Topps basketball set was issued in two series totaling 222 standard-size cards, although the checklist card from series one (#111) is not considered part of the basic set. Both series cards were issued in 11-card hobby and retail packs carrying a suggested retail price of

	MINT	NRMT
COMPLETE SET (221)	25.00	11.00
COMP.FACT.HOB.SET (227)	35.00	16.00
COMPLETE SERIES 1 (110)	12.00	5.50
COMPLETE SERIES 2 (111)	15.00	6.75
COMMON CARD (1-221)	.10	.05
CL (111) SP	2.50	1.10
SEMISTARS	.15	.07
UNLISTED STARS	.25	.11
SERIES 1 CL NOT CONSIDERED PART OF SET		
COMP.NBA 50 SET (220)	200.00	90.00
COMP.NBA 50 SER.1 (110)	70.00	32.00
COMP.NBA 50 SER.2 (110)	130.00	57.50
COMMON NBA 50 (1-220)	.25	.11
*NBA 50 STARS: 3X TO 6X HI COLUMN		
*NBA 50 RCs: 2.5X TO 5X HI		
NBA 50: SER.1/2 STATED ODDS 1:3 H/R		
NBA 50: ONE CARD PER FACTORY SET		

		MINT	NRMT
☐ 1	Patrick Ewing	.25	.11
☐ 2	Christian Laettner	.15	.07
☐ 3	Mahmoud Abdul-Rauf	.10	.05
☐ 4	Chris Webber	.60	.25
☐ 5	Jason Kidd	.50	.23
☐ 6	Clifford Rozier	.10	.05
☐ 7	Elden Campbell	.15	.07
☐ 8	Chuck Person	.10	.05
☐ 9	Jeff Hornacek	.15	.07
☐ 10	Rik Smits	.15	.07
☐ 11	Kurt Thomas	.10	.05
☐ 12	Rod Strickland	.15	.07
☐ 13	Kendall Gill	.15	.07
☐ 14	Brian Williams	.10	.05
☐ 15	Tom Gugliotta	.25	.11

□ 16 Ron Harper	.15	.07
□ 17 Eric Williams	.10	.05
□ 18 A.C. Green	.15	.07
□ 19 Scott Williams	.10	.05
□ 20 Damon Stoudamire	.60	.25
□ 21 Bryant Reeves	.15	.07
□ 22 Bob Sura	.10	.05
□ 23 Mitch Richmond	.25	.11
□ 24 Larry Johnson	.15	.07
□ 25 Vin Baker	.50	.23
□ 26 Mark Bryant	.10	.05
□ 27 Horace Grant	.15	.07
□ 28 Allan Houston	.15	.07
□ 29 Sam Perkins	.15	.07
□ 30 Antonio McDyess	.40	.18
□ 31 Rasheed Wallace	.15	.07
□ 32 Malik Sealy	.10	.05
□ 33 Scottie Pippen	.75	.35
□ 34 Charles Barkley	.40	.18
□ 35 Hakeem Olajuwon	.50	.23
□ 36 John Starks	.15	.07
□ 37 Byron Scott	.15	.07
□ 38 Arvydas Sabonis	.15	.07
□ 39 Vlade Divac	.15	.07
□ 40 Joe Dumars	.25	.11
□ 41 Danny Ferry	.10	.05
□ 42 Jerry Stackhouse	.30	.14
□ 43 B.J. Armstrong	.10	.05
□ 44 Shawn Bradley	.10	.05
□ 45 Kevin Garnett	1.50	.70
□ 46 Dee Brown	.10	.05
□ 47 Michael Smith	.10	.05
□ 48 Doug Christie	.10	.05
□ 49 Mark Jackson	.10	.05
□ 50 Shawn Kemp	.75	.35
□ 51 Sasha Danilovic	.10	.05
□ 52 Nick Anderson	.10	.05
□ 53 Matt Geiger	.10	.05
□ 54 Charles Smith	.10	.05
□ 55 Mookie Blaylock	.15	.07
□ 56 Johnny Newman	.10	.05
□ 57 George McCloud	.10	.05
□ 58 Greg Ostertag	.10	.05
□ 59 Reggie Williams	.10	.05
□ 60 Brent Barry	.10	.05
□ 61 Doug West	.10	.05
□ 62 Donald Royal	.10	.05
□ 63 Randy Brown	.10	.05
□ 64 Vincent Askew	.10	.05
□ 65 John Stockton	.25	.11
□ 66 Joe Kleine	.10	.05
□ 67 Keith Askins	.10	.05
□ 68 Bobby Phills	.10	.05
□ 69 Chris Mullin	.25	.11
□ 70 Nick Van Exel	.25	.11
□ 71 Rick Fox	.10	.05
□ 72 Chicago Bulls - 72 Wins	1.50	.70
□ 73 Shawn Respert	.10	.05
□ 74 Hubert Davis	.10	.05
□ 75 Jim Jackson	.15	.07
□ 76 Olden Polynice	.10	.05
□ 77 Gheorghe Muresan	.10	.05
□ 78 Theo Ratliff	.10	.05
□ 79 Khalid Reeves	.10	.05
□ 80 David Robinson	.40	.18
□ 81 Lawrence Moten	.10	.05
□ 82 Sam Cassell	.15	.07
□ 83 George Zidek	.10	.05
□ 84 Sharone Wright	.10	.05
□ 85 C.Weatherspoon	.10	.05
□ 86 Alan Henderson	.10	.05
□ 87 Chris Dudley	.10	.05
□ 88 Ed O'Bannon	.15	.07
□ 89 Calbert Cheaney	.10	.05
□ 90 Cedric Ceballos	.10	.05
□ 91 Michael Cage	.10	.05
□ 92 Ervin Johnson	.10	.05
□ 93 Gary Trent	.10	.05
□ 94 Sherman Douglas	.10	.05
□ 95 Joe Smith	.30	.14
□ 96 Dale Davis	.10	.05
□ 97 Tony Dumas	.10	.05
□ 98 Muggsy Bogues	.15	.07
□ 99 Toni Kukoc	.15	.07
□ 100 Grant Hill	1.50	.70
□ 101 Michael Finley	.30	.14

□ 102 Isaiah Rider	.15	.07
□ 103 Bryant Stith	.10	.05
□ 104 Pooh Richardson	.10	.05
□ 105 Karl Malone	.40	.18
□ 106 Brian Grant	.10	.05
□ 107 Sean Elliott	.10	.05
□ 108 Charles Oakley	.10	.05
□ 109 Pervis Ellison	.10	.05
□ 110 A.Hardaway	1.00	.45
□ 111 Checklist	2.50	1.10
□ 112 Dikembe Mutombo	.15	.07
□ 113 Alonzo Mourning	.25	.11
□ 114 Hubert Davis	.10	.05
□ 115 Rony Seikaly	.10	.05
□ 116 Danny Manning	.15	.07
□ 117 Donyell Marshall	.10	.05
□ 118 Gerald Wilkins	.10	.05
□ 119 Ervin Johnson	.10	.05
□ 120 Jalen Rose	.10	.05
□ 121 Dino Radja	.10	.05
□ 122 Glenn Robinson	.25	.11
□ 123 John Stockton	.25	.11
□ 124 Matt Maloney	.40	.18
□ 125 Clifford Robinson	.10	.05
□ 126 Steve Kerr	.10	.05
□ 127 Nate McMillan	.10	.05
□ 128 S.Abdur-Rahim	1.50	.70
□ 129 Loy Vaught	.15	.07
□ 130 Anthony Mason	.15	.07
□ 131 Kevin Garnett	1.50	.70
□ 132 Roy Rogers	.10	.05
□ 133 Erick Dampier	.30	.14
□ 134 Tyus Edney	.10	.05
□ 135 Chris Mills	.10	.05
□ 136 Cory Alexander	.10	.05
□ 137 Juwan Howard	.30	.14
□ 138 Kobe Bryant	5.00	2.20
□ 139 Michael Jordan	3.00	1.35
□ 140 Jayson Williams	.15	.07
□ 141 Rod Strickland	.10	.05
□ 142 Lorenzen Wright	.30	.14
□ 143 Will Perdue	.10	.05
□ 144 Derek Harper	.10	.05
□ 145 Billy Owens	.10	.05
□ 146 Antoine Walker	2.50	1.10
□ 147 P.J. Brown	.10	.05
□ 148 Terrell Brandon	.25	.11
□ 149 Larry Johnson	.15	.07
□ 150 Steve Smith	.15	.07
□ 151 Eddie Jones	.50	.23
□ 152 Detlef Schrempf	.15	.07
□ 153 Dale Ellis	.10	.05
□ 154 Isaiah Rider	.15	.07
□ 155 Tony Delk	.30	.14
□ 156 Adrian Caldwell	.10	.05
□ 157 Jamal Mashburn	.15	.07
□ 158 Dennis Scott	.10	.05
□ 159 Dana Barros	.10	.05
□ 160 Martin Muursepp	.10	.05
□ 161 Marcus Camby	.60	.25
□ 162 Jerome Williams	.15	.07
□ 163 Wesley Person	.10	.05
□ 164 Luc Longley	.15	.07
□ 165 Charlie Ward	.10	.05
□ 166 Mark Jackson	.10	.05
□ 167 Derrick Coleman	.15	.07
□ 168 Dell Curry	.10	.05
□ 169 Armon Gilliam	.10	.05
□ 170 Vlade Divac	.15	.07
□ 171 Allen Iverson	2.50	1.10
□ 172 Vitaly Potapenko	.15	.07
□ 173 Jon Koncak	.10	.05
□ 174 Lindsey Hunter	.10	.05
□ 175 Kevin Johnson	.15	.07
□ 176 Dennis Rodman	1.00	.45
□ 177 Stephon Marbury	2.50	1.10
□ 178 Karl Malone	.40	.18
□ 179 Charles Barkley	.40	.18
□ 180 Popeye Jones	.10	.05
□ 181 Samaki Walker	.30	.14
□ 182 Steve Nash	.10	.05
□ 183 Latrell Sprewell	.15	.07
□ 184 Kenny Anderson	.15	.07
□ 185 Tyrone Hill	.10	.05
□ 186 Robert Pack	.10	.05
□ 187 Greg Anthony	.10	.05

□ 188 Derrick McKey	.10	.05
□ 189 John Wallace	.40	.18
□ 190 Bryon Russell	.10	.05
□ 191 Jermaine O'Neal	.40	.18
□ 192 Clyde Drexler	.30	.14
□ 193 Mahmoud Abdul-Rauf	.10	.05
□ 194 Eric Montross	.10	.05
□ 195 Allan Houston	.15	.07
□ 196 Harvey Grant	.10	.05
□ 197 Rodney Rogers	.10	.05
□ 198 Kerry Kittles	.60	.25
□ 199 Grant Hill	1.50	.70
□ 200 Lionel Simmons	.10	.05
□ 201 Reggie Miller	.25	.11
□ 202 Avery Johnson	.10	.05
□ 203 LaPhonso Ellis	.10	.05
□ 204 Brian Shaw	.10	.05
□ 205 Priest Lauderdale	.10	.05
□ 206 Derek Fisher	.30	.14
□ 207 Terry Porter	.10	.05
□ 208 Todd Fuller	.10	.05
□ 209 Hersey Hawkins	.15	.07
□ 210 Tim Legler	.10	.05
□ 211 Terry Dehere	.10	.05
□ 212 Gary Payton	.40	.18
□ 213 Joe Dumars	.25	.11
□ 214 Don MacLean	.10	.05
□ 215 Greg Minor	.10	.05
□ 216 Tim Hardaway	.30	.14
□ 217 Ray Allen	.75	.35
□ 218 Mario Elie	.10	.05
□ 219 Brooks Thompson	.10	.05
□ 220 Shaquille O'Neal	1.00	.45

1996-97 Topps Draft Redemption

These trade cards were randomly inserted in first series packs at a rate of one in 18. Each trade card has a number printed on front that corresponds to each draft position of the first round of the 1996 NBA draft. Collectors that exchanged their trade card would then receive an exchange card picturing the player selected at that spot in the draft. The Draft Redemption trade deadline was April 1, 1997.

	MINT	NRMT
COMPLETE SET (27)	120.00	55.00
COMMON CARD (1-27)	2.00	.90
SEMISTARS	2.50	1.10
UNLISTED STARS	4.00	1.80
ONE CARD PER EXCHANGE CARD BY MAIL		
EXCH.CARDS: SER.1 STATED ODDS 1:18		
H/R		

		MINT	NRMT
☐ 1	Allen Iverson	20.00	9.00
☐ 2	Marcus Camby	5.00	2.20
☐ 3	S.Abdur-Rahim	12.00	5.50
☐ 4	Stephon Marbury	20.00	9.00
☐ 5	Ray Allen	6.00	2.70
☐ 6	Antoine Walker	20.00	9.00
☐ 7	Lorenzen Wright	4.00	1.80
☐ 8	Kerry Kittles	5.00	2.20
☐ 9	Samaki Walker	4.00	1.80
☐ 10	Erick Dampier	3.00	1.35
☐ 11	Todd Fuller	2.00	.90
☐ 12	Vitaly Potapenko	2.50	1.10
☐ 13	Kobe Bryant	40.00	18.00
☐ 14	Predrag Stojakovic	2.00	.90
☐ 15	Steve Nash	4.00	1.80
☐ 16	Tony Delk	4.00	1.80
☐ 17	Jermaine O'Neal	4.00	1.80
☐ 18	John Wallace	4.00	1.80
☐ 19	Walter McCarty	2.50	1.10
☐ 20	Zydrunas Ilgauskas	4.00	1.80
☐ 21	Dontae' Jones	3.00	1.35
☐ 22	Roy Rogers	2.00	.90
☐ 23	Efthimis Retzias	2.00	.90
☐ 24	Derek Fisher	3.00	1.35
☐ 25	Martin Muursepp	2.00	.90
☐ 26	Jerome Williams	2.50	1.10
☐ 27	Brian Evans	2.00	.90
☐ 28	Priest Lauderdale	2.00	.90
☐ 29	Travis Knight	2.50	1.10
☐ NNO	Expired Trade Cards	.50*	.23

1996-97 Topps Finest Reprints

Randomly inserted in series two packs at the rate of one in 36, this 25-card set features reprints of 25 of the 50 greatest NBA players as they appeared on their first Topps, Star Co., or Bowman cards. Cards utilize the Finest technology. The first 25 cards were issued in 1996-97 Stadium Club series one. Card values below refer to unpeeled cards. Peeled cards generally trade for ten to twenty-five percent less.

	MINT	NRMT
COMPLETE SERIES 2 (25)	150.00	70.00
COMMON CARD (1-50)	4.00	1.80
SER.2 STATED ODDS 1:36 HOBBY/RETAIL		
COMP.REF.SER.2 (25)	450.00	200.00
COMMON REFRACTOR (1-50)	8.00	3.60
*REF: 1.5X TO 3X HI COLUMN		
REF: SER.2 STATED ODDS 1:144 HOB/RET		
SKIP-NUMBERED SET		
SER.1 SET LISTED UNDER STADIUM CLUB		

		MINT	NRMT
☐ 1	Lew Alcindor	12.00	5.50
☐ 3	Paul Arizin	4.00	1.80

		MINT	NRMT
☐ 9	Wilt Chamberlain	12.00	5.50
☐ 11	Dave Cowens	4.00	1.80
☐ 14	Clyde Drexler	10.00	4.50
☐ 16	Patrick Ewing	8.00	3.60
☐ 20	John Havlicek	10.00	4.50
☐ 21	Elvin Hayes	4.00	1.80
☐ 22	Larry Bird	15.00	6.75
	Julius Erving		
	Magic Johnson		
☐ 23	Sam Jones	4.00	1.80
☐ 25	Jerry Lucas	4.00	1.80
☐ 27	Moses Malone	4.00	1.80
☐ 30	George Mikan	10.00	4.50
☐ 31	Earl Monroe	8.00	3.60
☐ 32	Shaquille O'Neal	10.00	4.50
☐ 33	Hakeem Olajuwon	10.00	4.50
☐ 37	Willis Reed	4.00	1.80
☐ 38	Oscar Robertson	8.00	3.60
☐ 39	David Robinson	8.00	3.60
☐ 40	Bill Russell	12.00	5.50
☐ 42	Bill Sharman	4.00	1.80
☐ 43	John Stockton	8.00	3.60
☐ 45	Nate Thurmond	4.00	1.80
☐ 46	Wes Unseld	4.00	1.80
☐ 47	Bill Walton	4.00	1.80

1996-97 Topps Hobby Masters

Randomly inserted exclusively into both series hobby packs at a rate of one in every 36, these inserts feature a selection of twenty top NBA stars as determined by Topps hobby dealer network. In addition to player selection, the dealers also determined the rate of insertion. Each card features 28 point full diffraction foil stock. Due to the thickness, a Hobby Masters insert replaced two regular issue cards within the packs they were seeded into. The card backs are numbered with an "HM" prefix. The cards are numbered 11-30 due to the fact that they are part of a cross-sport (football, baseball and basketball) insert program by Topps.

	MINT	NRMT
COMPLETE SET (20)	160.00	70.00
COMPLETE SERIES 1 (10)	100.00	45.00
COMPLETE SERIES 2 (10)	60.00	27.00
COMMON CARD (HM11-HM30)	3.00	1.35
SEMISTARS	5.00	2.20
SER.1/2 STATED ODDS 1:36 HOBBY		

		MINT	NRMT
☐ HM11	Shaquille O'Neal	20.00	9.00
☐ HM12	Jerry Stackhouse	6.00	2.70
☐ HM13	Dennis Rodman	20.00	9.00
☐ HM14	Joe Smith	6.00	2.70
☐ HM15	D.Stoudamire	12.00	5.50
☐ HM16	Gary Payton	8.00	3.60
☐ HM17	Mitch Richmond	5.00	2.20
☐ HM18	Reggie Miller	5.00	2.20
☐ HM19	Chris Webber	12.00	5.50
☐ HM20	Vin Baker	10.00	4.50
☐ HM21	Grant Hill	30.00	13.50
☐ HM22	Scottie Pippen	15.00	6.75
☐ HM23	Karl Malone	8.00	3.60
☐ HM24	Patrick Ewing	5.00	2.20
☐ HM25	Shawn Kemp	15.00	6.75
☐ HM26	A.Hardaway	20.00	9.00
☐ HM27	Charles Barkley	8.00	3.60
☐ HM28	Jason Kidd	10.00	4.50
☐ HM29	Hakeem Olajuwon	10.00	4.50
☐ HM30	Larry Johnson	3.00	1.35

1996-97 Topps Holding Court

Cards in this set of fifteen were randomly inserted in series one hobby and retail packs at a rate of one in 36 and feature the undeniable members of the NBA royalty, crowned "kings of the court" due to their impact on the game. Each card is printed utilizing Topps' exclusive Finest technology. Card backs are numbered with an "HC" prefix. Prices below refer to unpeeled cards. Peeled cards generally trade for ten to twenty-five percent less.

	MINT	NRMT
COMPLETE SET (15)	100.00	45.00
COMMON CARD (HC1-HC15)	1.50	.70
SEMISTARS	2.00	.90
UNLISTED STARS	3.00	1.35
SER.1 STATED ODDS 1:36 H/R, 1:24 JUM		
COMP.REF.SET (15)	200.00	90.00
COMMON REF. (HC1-HC15)	3.00	1.35
*REF: 1X TO 2X HI COLUMN		
REF: SER.1 STATED ODDS 1:108 H/R, 1:72 J		

		MINT	NRMT
☐ HC1	Larry Johnson	2.00	.90
☐ HC2	Michael Jordan	40.00	18.00
☐ HC3	Cedric Ceballos	1.50	.70
☐ HC4	Grant Hill	20.00	9.00
☐ HC5	A.Hardaway	12.00	5.50
☐ HC6	Reggie Miller	3.00	1.35
☐ HC7	Glenn Robinson	3.00	1.35
☐ HC8	Patrick Ewing	3.00	1.35
☐ HC9	Chris Webber	8.00	3.60
☐ HC10	Shaquille O'Neal	12.00	5.50

☐ HC11 John Stockton	3.00	1.35
☐ HC12 Mitch Richmond	3.00	1.35
☐ HC13 David Robinson	5.00	2.20
☐ HC14 Gary Payton	5.00	2.20
☐ HC15 Karl Malone	5.00	2.20

	MINT	NRMT
☐ M20 Joe Smith	5.00	2.20
☐ M21 Charles Barkley	6.00	2.70
☐ M22 Reggie Miller	4.00	1.80

1996-97 Topps Mystery Finest

Randomly inserted in all second series packs at a rate of one 36, this 22-card set featues some of the top players from each division. Cards were issued with an opaque protector to keep the player a mystery until peeled. Card backs carry a "M" prefix.

	MINT	NRMT
COMPLETE SET (22)	150.00	70.00
COMMON CARD (M1-M22)	2.00	.90
SEMISTARS	2.50	1.10
UNLISTED STARS	4.00	1.80
SER.2 STATED ODDS 1:36 HOBBY/RETAIL		
COMP.MYS.BDLS.SET (22)	275.00	125.00
COMMON BDLS. (M1-22)	3.00	1.35
*BORDERLESS: .75X TO 1.5X HI COLUMN		
BDLS: SER.2 STATED ODDS 1:72 HOB/RET		
COMP.MYS.BDLS.REF.SET	800.00	350.00
COMMON BDLS.REF. (M1-22)	8.00	3.60
*BDLS.REF: 2X TO 4X HI		
BDLS.REF: SER.2 STATED ODDS 1:216 H/R		
COMP.DW BDRD.ATLANTIC (5)	15.00	6.75
COMP.DW BDRD.CENTRAL (6)	20.00	9.00
COMP.DW BDRD.MIDWEST (6)	15.00	6.75
COMP.DW BDRD.PACIFIC (5)	15.00	6.75
*SUP.TM.CARDS: .1X TO 2X HI		
ONE DW SET BY MAIL PER DW SUPER TM.		
COMP.CON.BDLS.EAST (11)	40.00	18.00
COMP.CON.BDLS.WEST (11)	25.00	11.00
*SUP.TM.CARDS: .1X TO 2X HI		
ONE CON.SET BY MAIL PER		
CON.WIN.SUP.TM.		
☐ M1 Scottie Pippen	12.00	5.50
☐ M2 Jason Kidd	8.00	3.60
☐ M3 A.Hardaway	15.00	6.75
☐ M4 Gary Payton	6.00	2.70
☐ M5 Juwan Howard	5.00	2.20
☐ M6 Sean Elliott	2.00	.90
☐ M7 Dennis Rodman	15.00	6.75
☐ M8 Shawn Kemp	12.00	5.50
☐ M9 David Robinson	6.00	2.70
☐ M10 Alonzo Mourning	4.00	1.80
☐ M11 D.Mutombo	2.50	1.10
☐ M12 Shaquille O'Neal	15.00	6.75
☐ M13 Clyde Drexler	5.00	2.20
☐ M14 Michael Jordan	50.00	22.00
☐ M15 D.Stoudamire	10.00	4.50
☐ M16 Mitch Richmond	4.00	1.80
☐ M17 Patrick Ewing	4.00	1.80
☐ M18 Vin Baker	8.00	3.60
☐ M19 Hakeem Olajuwon	8.00	3.60

1996-97 Topps Mystery Finest Bordered Refractors

Randomly inserted exclusively into second series jumbo packs at a rate of one in 66 packs, these cards parallel the more common Mystery Finest inserts. The refractive sheen on the front of these cards differentiates them. Card backs carry a "M" prefix.

	MINT	NRMT
COMPLETE SET (22)	1000.00	450.00
COMMON CARD (M1-M22)	10.00	4.50
SEMISTARS	12.00	5.50
UNLISTED STARS	20.00	9.00
SER.2 STATED ODDS 1:36 HOBBY JUMBO		
COMP.SUP.TM.FIN.SET (22)	150.00	70.00
*SUP.TM.CARDS: .1X TO .15X HI COLUMN		
ONE BDRD.REF.ST.SET BY MAIL PER		
BULLS		
ONE BDRD.REF.ST.SET BY MAIL PER		
SPURS		
☐ M1 Scottie Pippen	60.00	27.00
☐ M2 Jason Kidd	40.00	18.00
☐ M3 A.Hardaway	80.00	36.00
☐ M4 Gary Payton	30.00	13.50
☐ M5 Juwan Howard	30.00	13.50
☐ M6 Sean Elliott	10.00	4.50
☐ M7 Dennis Rodman	80.00	36.00
☐ M8 Shawn Kemp	60.00	27.00
☐ M9 David Robinson	30.00	13.50
☐ M10 Alonzo Mourning	20.00	9.00
☐ M11 D.Mutombo	12.00	5.50
☐ M12 Shaquille O'Neal	80.00	36.00
☐ M13 Clyde Drexler	25.00	11.00
☐ M14 Michael Jordan	300.00	135.00
☐ M15 D.Stoudamire	50.00	22.00
☐ M16 Mitch Richmond	20.00	9.00
☐ M17 Patrick Ewing	20.00	9.00
☐ M18 Vin Baker	40.00	18.00
☐ M19 Hakeem Olajuwon	40.00	18.00
☐ M20 Joe Smith	25.00	11.00
☐ M21 Charles Barkley	30.00	13.50
☐ M22 Reggie Miller	20.00	9.00

1996-97 Topps Pro Files

Cards in this set of twenty were randomly issued in both series hobby and retail packs at a rate of one in 12. Topps' basketball spokesperson David Robinson was handed the assignment of writing all of the card backs for this insert set. "The Admiral" came through with flying colors as he gets up close and peronal with ten of the NBA's top stars. Card fronts contain a prismatic foil background with an action shot of the player and a head

shot of David Robinson in the bottom left corner. Card backs are numbered with a "PF" prefix. In addition, two of these cards were inserted into Factory sets.

	MINT	NRMT
COMPLETE SET (20)	30.00	13.50
COMPLETE SERIES 1 (10)	20.00	9.00
COMPLETE SERIES 2 (10)	12.00	5.50
COMMON CARD (PF1-PF20)	.40	.18
SEMISTARS	.75	.35
SER.1/2 STATED ODDS 1:12 H/R, 1:6 JUM		
TWO PER FACTORY SET		
☐ PF1 Grant Hill	5.00	2.20
☐ PF2 Shawn Kemp	2.50	1.10
☐ PF3 Michael Jordan	10.00	4.50
☐ PF4 Vin Baker	1.50	.70
☐ PF5 Chris Webber	2.00	.90
☐ PF6 Joe Smith	1.00	.45
☐ PF7 Shaquille O'Neal	3.00	1.35
☐ PF8 Patrick Ewing	.75	.35
☐ PF9 Scottie Pippen	2.50	1.10
☐ PF10 D.Stoudamire	2.00	.90
☐ PF11 A.Hardaway	3.00	1.35
☐ PF12 Juwan Howard	1.00	.45
☐ PF13 D.Mutombo	.40	.18
☐ PF14 Dennis Rodman	3.00	1.35
☐ PF15 Kevin Garnett	5.00	2.20
☐ PF16 Jerry Stackhouse	1.00	.45
☐ PF17 Alonzo Mourning	.75	.35
☐ PF18 Karl Malone	1.25	.55
☐ PF19 Hakeem Olajuwon	1.50	.70
☐ PF20 Gary Payton	1.25	.55

1996-97 Topps Season's Best

Cards in this set of 25 were randomly issued in first series hobby and retail packs at a rate of one in eight and feature five players who have excelled in the *five key statistical categories of the game: Points - En Fuego; Rebounds - Board Members; Steals - Sticky Fingers; Assists - Dish Men and Blocks - Swat Team. Card fronts feature a prismatic background with the statistical theme title located around the action shot. Card backs are numbered with a "Season's Best" prefix. In addition, two of these cards were inserted in the Factory sets.*

	MINT	NRMT
COMPLETE SET (25)	50.00	22.00
COMMON CARD (SB1-SB25)	.40	.18
SEMISTARS	.75	.35
UNLISTED STARS	1.25	.55
SER.1 STATED ODDS 1:8 HOB/RET, 1:4 JUM TWO PER FACTORY SET		

		MINT	NRMT
☐	SB1 Michael Jordan	15.00	6.75
☐	SB2 Hakeem Olajuwon	2.50	1.10
☐	SB3 Shaquille O'Neal	5.00	2.20
☐	SB4 Karl Malone	2.00	.90
☐	SB5 David Robinson	2.00	.90
☐	SB6 Dennis Rodman	5.00	2.20
☐	SB7 David Robinson	2.00	.90
☐	SB8 D.Mutombo	.75	.35
☐	SB9 Charles Barkley	2.00	.90
☐	SB10 Shawn Kemp	4.00	1.80
☐	SB11 John Stockton	1.25	.55
☐	SB12 Jason Kidd	2.50	1.10
☐	SB13 Avery Johnson	.40	.18
☐	SB14 Rod Strickland	.75	.35
☐	SB15 D.Stoudamire	3.00	1.35
☐	SB16 Gary Payton	2.00	.90
☐	SB17 Mookie Blaylock	.75	.35
☐	SB18 Michael Jordan	15.00	6.75
☐	SB19 Jason Kidd	2.50	1.10
☐	SB20 Alvin Robertson	.40	.18
☐	SB21 D.Mutombo	.75	.35
☐	SB22 Shawn Bradley	.40	.18
☐	SB23 David Robinson	2.00	.90
☐	SB24 Hakeem Olajuwon	1.25	.55
☐	SB25 Alonzo Mourning	1.25	.55

1996-97 Topps Super Teams

After a one-year hiatus, Topps decided to transfer this insert set concept from their Stadium Club brand which had featured interactive Super Team inserts in 1993-94 and 1994-95. Cards from this set of 29 were randomly issued in first series hobby and retail packs at a rate of one

in 36 and featured an action shot or group photo from each team in the league. Cards that feature teams that won either their division, their conference or the NBA finals or was the team selected to have the first draft pick in the 1997 NBA Draft are redeemable for various special Mystery Finest cards. The expiration date for Super Team cards is December 31, 1997.

	MINT	NRMT
COMPLETE SET (29)	80.00	36.00
COMMON CARD (ST1-ST29)	2.00	.90
SER.1 STATED ODDS 1:36 HOBBY/RETAIL RED.SETS LISTED UNDER MYSTERY FINEST		

		MINT	NRMT
☐	ST1 Atlanta Hawks	2.00	.90
	Stacy Augmon		
	Grant Long		
	Ken Norman		
☐	ST2 Boston Celtics	2.00	.90
	Dino Radja		
	Dana Barros		
	Eric Williams		
☐	ST3 Charlotte Hornets	2.00	.90
	Robert Parish		
	Glen Rice		
	Kenny Anderson		
	Larry Johnson		
	Dell Curry		
	Muggsy Bogues		
☐	ST4 Chicago Bulls	25.00	11.00
	Michael Jordan		
	Scottie Pippen		
	Dennis Rodman		
	Luc Longley		
	Ron Harper		
☐	ST5 Cleveland Cavaliers	2.00	.90
	Bob Sura		
	Dan Majerle		
	Donny Marshall		
☐	ST6 Dallas Mavericks	2.00	.90
	Jason Kidd		
	Jamal Mashburn		
	Jim Jackson		
	Popeye Jones		
☐	ST7 Denver Nuggets	2.00	.90
	Dikembe Mutombo		
	Bryant Stith		
	Don MacLean		
☐	ST8 Detroit Pistons	2.50	1.10
	Mark West		
	Theo Ratliff		
	Lindsey Hunter		
	Joe Dumars		
	Terry Cummings		
	Grant Hill		
	Lou Roe		
☐	ST9 Golden State Warriors	2.00	.90
	B.J. Armstrong		
	Latrell Sprewell		
	Joe Smith		
☐	ST10 Houston Rockets	3.00	1.35
	Hakeem Olajuwon		
	Robert Horry		
	Chucky Brown		
	Eldridge Recasner		
	Clyde Drexler		
☐	ST11 Indiana Pacers	2.00	.90
	Rik Smits		
	Reggie Miller		
	Dale Davis		
	Mark Jackson		
☐	ST12 Los Angeles Clippers	2.00	.90
	Malik Sealy		
	Terry Dehere		
☐	ST13 Los Angeles Lakers	4.00	1.80
	Elden Campbell		

		MINT	NRMT
	Sedale Threatt		
	Vlade Divac		
	Anthony Peeler		
	Eddie Jones		
	Derek Strong		
	Frankie King		
☐	ST14 Miami Heat	4.00	1.80
	Voshon Lenard		
	Alonzo Mourning		
	Rex Chapman		
	Keith Askins		
	Dan Schayes		
	Jeff Malone		
	Tony Smith		
☐	ST15 Milwaukee Bucks	2.00	.90
	Glenn Robinson		
	Vin Baker		
	Benoit Benjamin		
	Lee Mayberry		
	Johnny Newman		
☐	ST16 Minnesota T'wolves	2.00	.90
	Doug West		
	Tom Gugliotta		
	Kevin Garnett		
	Sam Mitchell		
☐	ST17 New Jersey Nets	2.00	.90
	P.J. Brown		
	Armon Gilliam		
	Ed O'Bannon		
	Chris Childs		
	Vern Fleming		
☐	ST18 New York Knicks	2.50	1.10
	J.R. Reid		
	Anthony Mason		
	Hubert Davis		
☐	ST19 Orlando Magic	2.00	.90
	Anfernee Hardaway		
	Shaquille O'Neal		
	Dennis Scott		
☐	ST20 Philadelphia 76ers	2.00	.90
	Trevor Ruffin		
	Derrick Alston		
	LaSalle Thompson		
☐	ST21 Phoenix Suns	2.00	.90
	Joe Kleine		
	Charles Barkley		
	Wayman Tisdale		
	Michael Finley		
	Elliot Perry		
☐	ST22 Portland Trail Blazers	2.00	.90
	Arvydas Sabonis		
	Chris Dudley		
	Clifford Robinson		
	James Robinson		
	Gary Trent		
	Aaron McKie		
☐	ST23 Sacramento Kings	2.00	.90
	Bobby Hurley		
	Sarunas Marciulionis		
	Mitch Richmond		
	Olden Polynice		
	Brian Grant		
☐	ST24 San Antonio Spurs	10.00	4.50
	Vinny Del Negro		
	David Robinson		
	Doc Rivers		
	Dell Demps		
☐	ST25 Seattle Supersonics	4.00	1.80
	Ervin Johnson		
	Gary Payton		
	Shawn Kemp		
☐	ST26 Toronto Raptors	2.00	.90
	Acie Earl		
	Carlos Rogers		
	Alvin Robertson		
	B.J. Tyler		
☐	ST27 Utah Jazz	5.00	2.20
	John Stockton		
	Karl Malone		
	David Benoit		
	Felton Spencer		
☐	ST28 Vancouver Grizzlies	2.00	.90
	Eric Murdock		
	Eric Mobley		
	Lawrence Moten		
	Blue Edwards		

Doug Edwards
Ashraf Amaya
Liternil Green
ST29 Washington Bullets 2.00 .90
Juwan Howard
Gheorghe Muresan
Chris Webber
Ledell Eackles

1996-97 Topps Youthquake

Randomly inserted into second series retail packs only at a rate of one in 36, this 15-card set features some of the NBA's top young stars. Cards are printed on wood. Card backs carry a "YQ" prefix.

	MINT	NRMT
COMPLETE SET (15)	110.00	50.00
COMMON CARD (YQ1-YQ15)	1.50	.70
SEMISTARS	2.50	1.10
UNLISTED STARS	4.00	1.80
SER.2 STATED ODDS 1:36 RETAIL		

□ YQ1 Allen Iverson	20.00	9.00
□ YQ2 Samaki Walker	4.00	1.80
□ YQ3 Stephon Marbury	20.00	9.00
□ YQ4 D.Stoudamire	10.00	4.50
□ YQ5 John Wallace	4.00	1.80
□ YQ6 Michael Finley	4.00	1.80
□ YQ7 Marcus Camby	5.00	2.20
□ YQ8 Kerry Kittles	5.00	2.20
□ YQ9 Ray Allen	6.00	2.70
□ YQ10 Jerry Stackhouse	5.00	2.20
□ YQ11 S.Abdur-Rahim	12.00	5.50
□ YQ12 Antonio McDyess	6.00	2.70
□ YQ13 Joe Smith	5.00	2.20
□ YQ14 Brent Barry	1.50	.70
□ YQ15 Kobe Bryant	40.00	18.00

1997-98 Topps

The 1997-98 release from Topps contained 220 basic cards, with each series containing 110. The cards were distributed in 11-card packs with a suggested retail price of $1.29. The set features color player photos printed on 16 pt. card

stock with foil stamping and spot UV-Coating.

	MINT	NRMT
COMPLETE SET (220)	30.00	13.50
COMPLETE SERIES 1 (110)	10.00	4.50
COMPLETE SERIES 2 (110)	20.00	9.00
COMMON CARD (1-220)	.10	.05
SEMISTARS	.15	.07
UNLISTED STARS	.25	.11
COMP.MINT SET (220)	200.00	90.00
COMP.MINT SER.1 (110)	80.00	36.00
COMP.MINT SER.2 (110)	120.00	55.00
COMMON MINT (1-220)	.50	.23
*MINT STARS: 2X TO 5X HI COLUMN		
*MINT RCs: 2X TO 4X HI		
MINT: SER.1 STATED ODDS 1:6 HOB/RET		
MINT: SER.2 STATED ODDS 1:9 HOB/RET		

□ 1 Scottie Pippen	.75	.35
□ 2 Nate McMillan	.10	.05
□ 3 Byron Scott	.15	.07
□ 4 Mark Davis	.10	.05
□ 5 Rod Strickland	.25	.11
□ 6 Brian Grant	.10	.05
□ 7 Damon Stoudamire	.50	.23
□ 8 John Stockton	.25	.11
□ 9 Grant Long	.10	.05
□ 10 Darrell Armstrong	.10	.05
□ 11 Anthony Mason	.15	.07
□ 12 Travis Best	.10	.05
□ 13 Stephon Marbury	1.25	.55
□ 14 Jamal Mashburn	.15	.07
□ 15 Detlef Schrempf	.15	.07
□ 16 Terrell Brandon	.25	.11
□ 17 Charles Barkley	.40	.18
□ 18 Vin Baker	.50	.23
□ 19 Gary Trent	.10	.05
□ 20 Vinny Del Negro	.10	.05
□ 21 Todd Day	.10	.05
□ 22 Malik Sealy	.10	.05
□ 23 Wesley Person	.10	.05
□ 24 Reggie Miller	.25	.11
□ 25 Dan Majerle	.15	.07
□ 26 Todd Fuller	.10	.05
□ 27 Juwan Howard	.25	.11
□ 28 C.Weatherspoon	.10	.05
□ 29 Grant Hill	1.50	.70
□ 30 John Williams	.15	.07
□ 31 Ken Norman	.10	.05
□ 32 Patrick Ewing	.25	.11
□ 33 Bryon Russell	.10	.05
□ 34 Tony Smith	.10	.05
□ 35 Andrew Lang	.10	.05
□ 36 Rony Seikaly	.10	.05
□ 37 Billy Owens	.10	.05
□ 38 Dino Radja	.10	.05
□ 39 Chris Gatling	.10	.05
□ 40 Dale Davis	.10	.05
□ 41 Arvydas Sabonis	.15	.07
□ 42 Chris Mills	.10	.05
□ 43 A.C. Green	.15	.07
□ 44 Tyrone Hill	.10	.05
□ 45 Tracy Murray	.10	.05
□ 46 David Robinson	.40	.18
□ 47 Lee Mayberry	.10	.05

□ 48 Jayson Williams	.15	.07
□ 49 Jason Kidd	.50	.23
□ 50 Bryant Stith	.10	.05
□ 51 Latrell Sprewell	.15	.07
□ 52 Brent Barry	.10	.05
□ 53 Henry James	.10	.05
□ 54 Allen Iverson	1.25	.55
□ 55 Shandon Anderson	.10	.05
□ 56 Mitch Richmond	.25	.11
□ 57 Allan Houston	.15	.07
□ 58 Ron Harper	.15	.07
□ 59 Gheorghe Muresan	.10	.05
□ 60 Vincent Askew	.10	.05
□ 61 Ray Allen	.30	.14
□ 62 Kenny Anderson	.15	.07
□ 63 Dikembe Mutombo	.15	.07
□ 64 Sam Perkins	.15	.07
□ 65 Walt Williams	.10	.05
□ 66 Chris Carr	.10	.05
□ 67 Vlade Divac	.15	.07
□ 68 LaPhonso Ellis	.10	.05
□ 69 B.J. Armstrong	.10	.05
□ 70 Jim Jackson	.15	.07
□ 71 Clyde Drexler	.30	.14
□ 72 Lindsey Hunter	.10	.05
□ 73 Sasha Danilovic	.10	.05
□ 74 Elden Campbell	.10	.05
□ 75 Robert Pack	.10	.05
□ 76 Dennis Scott	.10	.05
□ 77 Will Perdue	.10	.05
□ 78 Anthony Peeler	.10	.05
□ 79 Steve Smith	.25	.11
□ 80 Steve Kerr	.10	.05
□ 81 Buck Williams	.10	.05
□ 82 Terry Mills	.10	.05
□ 83 Michael Smith	.10	.05
□ 84 Adam Keefe	.10	.05
□ 85 Kevin Willis	.10	.05
□ 86 David Wesley	.10	.05
□ 87 Muggsy Bogues	.15	.07
□ 88 Bimbo Coles	.10	.05
□ 89 Tom Gugliotta	.25	.11
□ 90 Jermaine O'Neal	.15	.07
□ 91 Cedric Ceballos	.10	.05
□ 92 Shawn Kemp	.75	.35
□ 93 Horace Grant	.15	.07
□ 94 S.Abdur-Rahim	.75	.35
□ 95 Robert Horry	.10	.05
□ 96 Vitaly Potapenko	.10	.05
□ 97 Pooh Richardson	.10	.05
□ 98 Doug Christie	.10	.05
□ 99 Voshon Lenard	.10	.05
□ 100 Dominique Wilkins	.25	.11
□ 101 Alonzo Mourning	.25	.11
□ 102 Sam Cassell	.15	.07
□ 103 Sherman Douglas	.10	.05
□ 104 Shawn Bradley	.10	.05
□ 105 Mark Jackson	.10	.05
□ 106 Dennis Rodman	1.00	.45
□ 107 Charles Oakley	.10	.05
□ 108 Matt Maloney	.10	.05
□ 109 Shaquille O'Neal	1.00	.45
□ 110 Checklist	.10	.05
□ 111 Antonio McDyess	.30	.14
□ 112 Bob Sura	.10	.05
□ 113 Terrell Brandon	.25	.11
□ 114 Tim Thomas	1.50	.70
□ 115 Tim Duncan	3.00	1.35
□ 116 Antonio Daniels	.60	.25
□ 117 Bryant Reeves	.15	.07
□ 118 Keith Van Horn	2.50	1.10
□ 119 Loy Vaught	.15	.07
□ 120 Rasheed Wallace	.25	.11
□ 121 Bobby Jackson	.50	.23
□ 122 Kevin Johnson	.15	.07
□ 123 Michael Jordan	3.00	1.35
□ 124 Ron Mercer	2.00	.90
□ 125 Tracy McGrady	1.50	.70
□ 126 Antoine Walker	1.25	.55
□ 127 Carlos Rogers	.10	.05
□ 128 Isaac Austin	.10	.05
□ 129 Mookie Blaylock	.15	.07
□ 130 Rodrick Rhodes	.30	.14
□ 131 Dennis Scott	.10	.05
□ 132 Chris Mullin	.25	.11

☐ 133 P.J. Brown	.10	.05
☐ 134 Rex Chapman	.10	.05
☐ 135 Sean Elliott	.10	.05
☐ 136 Alan Henderson	.10	.05
☐ 137 Austin Croshere	.30	.14
☐ 138 Nick Van Exel	.25	.11
☐ 139 Derek Strong	.10	.05
☐ 140 Glenn Robinson	.25	.11
☐ 141 Avery Johnson	.10	.05
☐ 142 Calbert Cheaney	.10	.05
☐ 143 Mahmoud Abdul-Rauf	.10	.05
☐ 144 Stojko Vrankovic	.10	.05
☐ 145 Chris Childs	.10	.05
☐ 146 Danny Manning	.15	.07
☐ 147 Jeff Hornacek	.15	.07
☐ 148 Kevin Garnett	1.50	.70
☐ 149 Joe Dumars	.25	.11
☐ 150 Johnny Taylor	.10	.05
☐ 151 Mark Price	.10	.05
☐ 152 Toni Kukoc	.15	.07
☐ 153 Erick Dampier	.10	.05
☐ 154 Lorenzen Wright	.10	.05
☐ 155 Matt Geiger	.10	.05
☐ 156 Tim Hardaway	.30	.14
☐ 157 Charles Smith	.10	.05
☐ 158 Hersey Hawkins	.15	.07
☐ 159 Michael Finley	.25	.11
☐ 160 Tyus Edney	.10	.05
☐ 161 Christian Laettner	.15	.07
☐ 162 Doug West	.10	.05
☐ 163 Jim Jackson	.15	.07
☐ 164 Larry Johnson	.15	.07
☐ 165 Vin Baker	.50	.23
☐ 166 Karl Malone	.40	.18
☐ 167 Kevin Cato	.30	.14
☐ 168 Luc Longley	.10	.05
☐ 169 Dale Davis	.10	.05
☐ 170 Joe Smith	.25	.11
☐ 171 Kobe Bryant	2.00	.90
☐ 172 Scot Pollard	.10	.05
☐ 173 Derek Anderson	.75	.35
☐ 174 Erick Strickland	.10	.07
☐ 175 Olden Polynice	.10	.05
☐ 176 Chris Whitney	.10	.05
☐ 177 Anthony Parker	.10	.05
☐ 178 Armon Gilliam	.10	.05
☐ 179 Gary Payton	.40	.18
☐ 180 Glen Rice	.25	.11
☐ 181 Chauncey Billups	1.00	.45
☐ 182 Derek Fisher	.10	.05
☐ 183 John Starks	.15	.07
☐ 184 Mario Elie	.10	.05
☐ 185 Chris Webber	.60	.25
☐ 186 Shawn Kemp	.75	.35
☐ 187 Greg Ostertag	.10	.05
☐ 188 Olivier Saint-Jean	.40	.18
☐ 189 Eric Snow	.10	.05
☐ 190 Isaiah Rider	.15	.07
☐ 191 Paul Grant	.10	.05
☐ 192 Samaki Walker	.10	.05
☐ 193 Cory Alexander	.10	.05
☐ 194 Eddie Jones	.50	.23
☐ 195 John Thomas	.10	.05
☐ 196 Otis Thorpe	.15	.07
☐ 197 Rod Strickland	.10	.05
☐ 198 David Wesley	.10	.05
☐ 199 Jacque Vaughn	.40	.18
☐ 200 Rik Smits	.15	.07
☐ 201 Brevin Knight	.75	.35
☐ 202 Clifford Robinson	.10	.05
☐ 203 Hakeem Olajuwon	.50	.23
☐ 204 Jerry Stackhouse	.25	.11
☐ 205 Tyrone Hill	.10	.05
☐ 206 Kendall Gill	.15	.07
☐ 207 Marcus Camby	.25	.11
☐ 208 Tony Battie	.50	.23
☐ 209 Brent Price	.10	.05
☐ 210 Danny Fortson	.50	.23
☐ 211 Jerome Williams	.10	.05
☐ 212 Maurice Taylor	.75	.35
☐ 213 Brian Williams	.10	.05
☐ 214 Keith Booth	.10	.05
☐ 215 Nick Anderson	.10	.05
☐ 216 Travis Knight	.10	.05
☐ 217 Adonal Foyle	.30	.14
☐ 218 Anfernee Hardaway	1.00	.45

☐ 219 Kerry Kittles	.25	.11
☐ 220 Checklist	.10	.05

1997-98 Topps Autographs

Randomly inserted in first series hobby packs at a rate of one in 212, this eight-card set features autographs from some of the NBA's top players. The Hakeem Olajuwon card was available as both a redemption and an actual autograph from packs.

	MINT	NRMT
COMPLETE SET (8)	350.00	160.00
COMMON CARD (1-8)	30.00	13.50
SER.1 STATED ODDS 1:212 HOBBY		
☐ 1 John Starks	30.00	13.50
☐ 2 Juwan Howard	50.00	22.00
☐ 3 Mitch Richmond	40.00	18.00
☐ 4 Hakeem Olajuwon	60.00	27.00
☐ 5 Glenn Robinson	40.00	18.00
☐ 6 Steve Smith	30.00	13.50
☐ 7 Antoine Walker	80.00	36.00
☐ 8 Clyde Drexler	60.00	27.00

1997-98 Topps Bound for Glory

Randomly inserted in series one hobby packs only at a rate of one in 36, this 15-card set is printed on rainbow foilboard stock and features some of the NBA's top players. Card backs carry a "BG" prefix.

	MINT	NRMT
COMPLETE SET (15)	80.00	36.00
COMMON CARD (BG1-BG15)	1.25	.55
SEMISTARS		1.50	.70
UNLISTED STARS		2.50	1.10
SER.1 STATED ODDS 1:36 HOBBY		
☐ BG1 Robert Parish	1.25	.55
☐ BG2 Grant Hill	15.00	6.75
☐ BG3 Chris Mullin	1.25	.55
☐ BG4 Hakeem Olajuwon	5.00	2.20
☐ BG5 Dennis Rodman	10.00	4.50
☐ BG6 Patrick Ewing	2.50	1.10
☐ BG7 Karl Malone	4.00	1.80
☐ BG8 Charles Barkley	4.00	1.80
☐ BG9 David Robinson	4.00	1.80
☐ BG10 Michael Jordan	30.00	13.50
☐ BG11 Dominique Wilkins	2.50	1.10
☐ BG12 Shaquille O'Neal	10.00	4.50
☐ BG13 Clyde Drexler	3.00	1.35
☐ BG14 John Stockton	2.50	1.10
☐ BG15 Scottie Pippen	8.00	3.60

1997-98 Topps Clutch Time

Randomly inserted into series two hobby packs only at a rate of one in 36, this 20-card set focuses on players who can get it done in the clutch. Card fronts feature a foil background with "Clutch Time" written across the top of the card as if it was a scoreboard. Card backs contain a "CT" prefix.

	MINT	NRMT
COMPLETE SET (20)	100.00	45.00
COMMON CARD (CT1-CT20)	1.25	.55
SEMISTARS		1.50	.70
UNLISTED STARS		2.50	1.10
SER.2 STATED ODDS 1:36 HOBBY		
☐ CT1 Michael Jordan	30.00	13.50
☐ CT2 Christian Laettner	1.25	.55
☐ CT3 Patrick Ewing	2.50	1.10
☐ CT4 Glen Rice	2.50	1.10
☐ CT5 Stephon Marbury	12.00	5.50
☐ CT6 Tim Hardaway	3.00	1.35
☐ CT7 Reggie Miller	2.50	1.10
☐ CT8 Gary Payton	4.00	1.80
☐ CT9 Charles Barkley	4.00	1.80
☐ CT10 Grant Hill	15.00	6.75
☐ CT11 Karl Malone	4.00	1.80
☐ CT12 D.Mutombo	1.25	.55
☐ CT13 Hakeem Olajuwon	5.00	2.20
☐ CT14 Shawn Kemp	8.00	3.60
☐ CT15 John Stockton	2.50	1.10
☐ CT16 A.Hardaway	10.00	4.50
☐ CT17 Glenn Robinson	2.50	1.10
☐ CT18 Chris Webber	6.00	2.70

	MINT	NRMT
☐ CT19 Allen Iverson	12.00	5.50
☐ CT20 Scottie Pippen	8.00	3.60

1997-98 Topps Destiny

Randomly inserted into retail packs only at a rate of one in 18, this 15-card set focuses on players who are destined to become NBA legends. Card fronts feature a full shot of the player surrounded by an embossed circle with the card theme "Destiny" also embossed across the top. Card backs carry a "D" prefix.

	MINT	NRMT
COMPLETE SET (15)	80.00	36.00
COMMON CARD (D1-D15)	1.50	.70
SER.2 STATED ODDS 1:18 RETAIL		
☐ D1 Grant Hill	10.00	4.50
☐ D2 Kevin Garnett	10.00	4.50
☐ D3 Vin Baker	3.00	1.35
☐ D4 Antoine Walker	8.00	3.60
☐ D5 Kobe Bryant	12.00	5.50
☐ D6 Tracy McGrady	5.00	2.20
☐ D7 Keith Van Horn	8.00	3.60
☐ D8 Tim Duncan	10.00	4.50
☐ D9 Eddie Jones	3.00	1.35
☐ D10 Stephon Marbury	8.00	3.60
☐ D11 Marcus Camby	1.50	.70
☐ D12 Antonio McDyess	2.00	.90
☐ D13 S.Abdur-Rahim	5.00	2.20
☐ D14 Allen Iverson	8.00	3.60
☐ D15 Shaquille O'Neal	6.00	2.70

1997-98 Topps Draft Redemption

Randomly inserted into series one hobby packs at a rate of 1:12 and retail packs at a rate of 1:18, this 29-card set features trade cards for the first 29 picks of the 1997 NBA Draft. Each redemption card had a number corresponding to each draft position of the first round, and could be exchanged for a special card of the player taken in that draft position once they signed their NBA Contract. The

expiration date for the cards was April 1, 1998

	MINT	NRMT
COMPLETE SET (29)	100.00	45.00
COMMON CARD (1-29)	1.50	.70
SEMISTARS	2.00	.90
UNLISTED STARS	3.00	1.35
*TRADE CARDS: 25X 1X .5X HI COLUMN		
SER.1 STATED ODDS 1:12 HOB, 1:18 RET		
☐ 1 Tim Duncan	20.00	9.00
☐ 2 Keith Van Horn	15.00	6.75
☐ 3 Chauncey Billups	6.00	2.70
☐ 4 Antonio Daniels	4.00	1.80
☐ 5 Tony Battie	3.00	1.35
☐ 6 Ron Mercer	12.00	5.50
☐ 7 Tim Thomas	10.00	4.50
☐ 8 Adonal Foyle	3.00	1.35
☐ 9 Tracy McGrady	10.00	4.50
☐ 10 Danny Fortson	3.00	1.35
☐ 11 Olivier Saint-Jean	3.00	1.35
☐ 12 Austin Croshere	2.00	.90
☐ 13 Derek Anderson	5.00	2.20
☐ 14 Maurice Taylor	5.00	2.20
☐ 15 Kelvin Cato	3.00	1.35
☐ 16 Brevin Knight	5.00	2.20
☐ 17 Johnny Taylor	1.50	.70
☐ 18 Chris Anstey	3.00	1.35
☐ 19 Scot Pollard	1.50	.70
☐ 20 Paul Grant	1.50	.70
☐ 21 Anthony Parker	1.50	.70
☐ 22 Ed Gray	3.00	1.35
☐ 23 Bobby Jackson	3.00	1.35
☐ 24 Rodrick Rhodes	3.00	1.35
☐ 25 John Thomas	1.50	.70
☐ 26 Charles Smith	1.50	.70
☐ 27 Jacque Vaughn	3.00	1.35
☐ 28 Keith Booth	1.50	.70
☐ 29 Serge Zwikker	1.50	.70

1997-98 Topps Fantastic 15

Randomly inserted in series one retail packs at a rate of one in

36, this 15-card set showcases up-and-comoing greats on holographic cards. Card backs carry a "F" prefix.

	MINT	NRMT
COMPLETE SET (15)	110.00	50.00
COMMON CARD (F1-F15)	1.50	.70
SEMISTARS	2.00	.90
UNLISTED STARS	3.00	1.35
SER.1 STATED ODDS 1:36 RETAIL		
☐ F1 Antoine Walker	15.00	6.75
☐ F2 Damon Stoudamire	6.00	2.70
☐ F3 Brent Barry	1.50	.70
☐ F4 Michael Finley	3.00	1.35
☐ F5 Ray Allen	4.00	1.80
☐ F6 Allen Iverson	15.00	6.75
☐ F7 Stephon Marbury	15.00	6.75
☐ F8 Kerry Kittles	3.00	1.35
☐ F9 John Wallace	2.00	.90
☐ F10 Kevin Garnett	20.00	9.00
☐ F11 Jerry Stackhouse	3.00	1.35
☐ F12 Kobe Bryant	25.00	11.00
☐ F13 Marcus Camby	3.00	1.35
☐ F14 Joe Smith	3.00	1.35
☐ F15 S.Abdur-Rahim	10.00	4.50

1997-98 Topps Generations

Randomly inserted into series two packs at a rate of one in 36, this 30-card set features the best rookies from each draft class. The cards are die cut and finished in the Finest technology. Card backs are numbered with a "G" prefix.

	MINT	NRMT
COMPLETE SET (30)	300.00	135.00
COMMON CARD (G1-G30)	2.00	.90
SEMISTARS	2.50	1.10
UNLISTED STARS	4.00	1.80
SER.2 STATED ODDS 1:36 HOBBY/RETAIL		
COMP.REF.SET (30)	1000.00	450.00
COMMON REF. (G1-G30)	6.00	2.70
*REF: 1.5X TO 3X HI COLUMN		
REF: SER.2 STATED ODDS 1:144 HOB/RET		
☐ G1 Clyde Drexler	5.00	2.20
☐ G2 Michael Jordan	50.00	22.00
☐ G3 Charles Barkley	6.00	2.70
☐ G4 Hakeem Olajuwon	8.00	3.60
☐ G5 John Stockton	4.00	1.80
☐ G6 Patrick Ewing	4.00	1.80
☐ G7 Karl Malone	6.00	2.70
☐ G8 Dennis Rodman	15.00	6.75
☐ G9 Scottie Pippen	12.00	5.50
☐ G10 David Robinson	6.00	2.70
☐ G11 Mitch Richmond	4.00	1.80

		MINT	NRMT
☐ G12	Glen Rice	4.00	1.80
☐ G13	Shawn Kemp	12.00	5.50
☐ G14	Gary Payton	6.00	2.70
☐ G15	D.Mutombo	2.00	.90
☐ G16	Steve Smith	2.00	.90
☐ G17	Christian Laettner	2.00	.90
☐ G18	Shaquille O'Neal	15.00	6.75
☐ G19	Alonzo Mourning	4.00	1.80
☐ G20	Tom Gugliotta	4.00	1.80
☐ G21	A.Hardaway	15.00	6.75
☐ G22	Grant Hill	25.00	11.00
☐ G23	Kevin Garnett	25.00	11.00
☐ G24	Kobe Bryant	30.00	13.50
☐ G25	Stephon Marbury	20.00	9.00
☐ G26	Antoine Walker	20.00	9.00
☐ G27	S.Abdur-Rahim	12.00	5.50
☐ G28	Tim Duncan	25.00	11.00
☐ G29	Keith Van Horn	20.00	9.00
☐ G30	Tracy McGrady	12.00	5.50

1997-98 Topps Inside Stuff

Randomly inserted into series two packs at a rate of one in 36, this 10-card set features some of the best plays from the 1997 NBA Playoffs. Card fronts have a foil background and card backs carry an "IS" prefix.

		MINT	NRMT
COMPLETE SET (10)		50.00	22.00
COMMON CARD (IS1-IS10)		.75	.35
SEMISTARS		1.00	.45
UNLISTED STARS		1.50	.70
SER.2 STATED ODDS 1:36 HOBBY/RETAIL			

		MINT	NRMT
☐ IS1	Michael Jordan	20.00	9.00
☐ IS2	Eddie Johnson	.75	.35
☐ IS3	John Stockton	1.50	.70
☐ IS4	Patrick Ewing	1.50	.70
☐ IS5	Shaquille O'Neal	6.00	2.70
☐ IS6	Rex Chapman	.75	.35
☐ IS7	Shawn Kemp	5.00	2.20
☐ IS8	Scottie Pippen	5.00	2.20
☐ IS9	Kobe Bryant	12.00	5.50
☐ IS10	A.Hardaway	6.00	2.70

1997-98 Topps New School

Randomly inserted in series two hobby packs at a rate of one in 36 and series two retail packs at one in 18, this 15-card set focuses on the key rookies from the 1997 class. Card fronts feature the theme "New School" in a banner and the front is sprinkled

in glitter. Card backs contain a "NS" prefix.

	MINT	NRMT
COMPLETE SET (15)	80.00	36.00
COMMON CARD (NS1-NS15)	1.50	.70
SEMISTARS	2.00	.90
UNLISTED STARS	3.00	1.35
SER.2 STATED ODDS 1:36 HOBBY/RETAIL		

		MINT	NRMT
☐ NS1	Austin Croshere	2.00	.90
☐ NS2	Antonio Daniels	4.00	1.80
☐ NS3	Tim Thomas	10.00	4.50
☐ NS4	Keith Van Horn	15.00	6.75
☐ NS5	Bobby Jackson	3.00	1.35
☐ NS6	Derek Anderson	5.00	2.20
☐ NS7	Adonal Foyle	2.00	.90
☐ NS8	Johnny Taylor	1.50	.70
☐ NS9	Jacque Vaughn	2.00	.90
☐ NS10	Chauncey Billups	6.00	2.70
☐ NS11	Brevin Knight	5.00	2.20
☐ NS12	Tracy McGrady	10.00	4.50
☐ NS13	Tony Battie	3.00	1.35
☐ NS14	Scot Pollard	1.50	.70
☐ NS15	Tim Duncan	20.00	9.00

1997-98 Topps Rock Stars

Randomly inserted in series one packs at a rate of one in 36, this 20-card set features a die-cut borderless Finest design. Card backs carry a "RS" prefix.

	MINT	NRMT
COMPLETE SET (20)	175.00	80.00
COMMON CARD (RS1-RS20)	1.50	.70
SEMISTARS	2.00	.90
UNLISTED STARS	3.00	1.35
SER.1 STATED ODDS 1:36 HOBBY/RETAIL		
COMP.REF.SET (20)	550.00	250.00
COMMON REF (RS1-RS20)	5.00	2.20
*REF: 1.25X TO 3X HI COLUMN		
REF: SER.1 STATED ODDS 1:144 H/R		

		MINT	NRMT
☐ RS1	Michael Jordan	40.00	18.00
☐ RS2	Jerry Stackhouse	3.00	1.35
☐ RS3	Chris Webber	8.00	3.60
☐ RS4	Charles Barkley	5.00	2.20
☐ RS5	Dennis Rodman	12.00	5.50
☐ RS6	A.Hardaway	12.00	5.50
☐ RS7	Juwan Howard	3.00	1.35
☐ RS8	Tim Hardaway	4.00	1.80
☐ RS9	Gary Payton	5.00	2.20
☐ RS10	D.Mutombo	1.50	.70
☐ RS11	Tom Gugliotta	2.00	.90
☐ RS12	Kevin Garnett	20.00	9.00
☐ RS13	Shaquille O'Neal	12.00	5.50
☐ RS14	Hakeem Olajuwon	6.00	2.70
☐ RS15	Grant Hill	20.00	9.00
☐ RS16	Karl Malone	5.00	2.20
☐ RS17	D.Stoudamire	6.00	2.70
☐ RS18	Shawn Kemp	10.00	4.50
☐ RS19	Alonzo Mourning	3.00	1.35
☐ RS20	Scottie Pippen	10.00	4.50

1997-98 Topps Season's Best

Randomly inserted in series one packs at a rate of one in 16, this 30-card set showcases 25 superstars who have dominated the game in different statistical categories, and five rookies from the 1996 class featured on borderless prismatic illusion foilboard. The groupings used were Key Masters, Power Core, Shooting Stars, Frontcourt Finesse, Pressure Points and Hot Shots. Card backs carry a "SB" prefix.

	MINT	NRMT
COMPLETE SET (30)	80.00	36.00
COMMON CARD (SB1-SB30)	.75	.35
SEMISTARS	1.00	.45
UNLISTED STARS	1.50	.70
SER.1 STATED ODDS 1:16 HOBBY/RETAIL		

		MINT	NRMT
☐ SB1	Gary Payton	2.50	1.10
☐ SB2	Kevin Johnson	.75	.35
☐ SB3	Tim Hardaway	2.00	.90
☐ SB4	John Stockton	1.50	.70
☐ SB5	D.Stoudamire	3.00	1.35
☐ SB6	Michael Jordan	20.00	9.00
☐ SB7	Mitch Richmond	1.50	.70
☐ SB8	Latrell Sprewell	1.00	.45
☐ SB9	Reggie Miller	1.50	.70
☐ SB10	Clyde Drexler	2.00	.90
☐ SB11	Grant Hill	10.00	4.50
☐ SB12	Scottie Pippen	5.00	2.20
☐ SB13	Kendall Gill	.75	.35
☐ SB14	Glen Rice	1.50	.70
☐ SB15	LaPhonso Ellis	.75	.35
☐ SB16	Karl Malone	2.50	1.10

		MINT	NRMT
□ SB17	Charles Barkley	2.50	1.10
□ SB18	Vin Baker	3.00	1.35
□ SB19	Chris Webber	4.00	1.80
□ SB20	Tom Gugliotta	.75	.35
□ SB21	Shaquille O'Neal	6.00	2.70
□ SB22	Patrick Ewing	1.50	.70
□ SB23	Hakeem Olajuwon	3.00	1.35
□ SB24	Alonzo Mourning	1.50	.70
□ SB25	D.Mutombo	.75	.35
□ SB26	Allen Iverson	8.00	3.60
□ SB27	Antoine Walker	8.00	3.60
□ SB28	S.Abdur-Rahim	5.00	2.20
□ SB29	Stephon Marbury	8.00	3.60
□ SB30	Kerry Kittles	1.50	.70

1997-98 Topps Topps 40

Randomly inserted in both series packs at a rate of one in 12, this set of 40 cards was divided up among both series one and two packs and features 40 of the top players in the NBA as voted by NBA players, coaches and writers. The cards are printed on foil-stamped mirrorrboard cards. Card backs carry a "T40" prefix.

		MINT	NRMT
COMPLETE SET (40)		80.00	36.00
COMPLETE SERIES 1 (20)		40.00	18.00
COMPLETE SERIES 2 (20)		40.00	18.00
COMMON CARD (T1-T40)		.75	.35
SEMISTARS		1.00	.45
UNLISTED STARS		1.50	.70
BOTH SERIES STATED ODDS 1:12 H/R			
T40 PREFIX ON CARD NUMBERS			
□ T1	Glen Rice	1.50	.70
□ T2	Patrick Ewing	1.50	.70
□ T3	Terrell Brandon	.75	.35
□ T4	Jerry Stackhouse	1.50	.70
□ T5	Michael Jordan	20.00	9.00
□ T6	Christian Laettner	.75	.35
□ T7	Latrell Sprewell	1.00	.45
□ T8	Reggie Miller	1.50	.70
□ T9	Gary Payton	2.50	1.10
□ T10	Detlef Schrempf	.75	.35
□ T11	Kevin Garnett	10.00	4.50
□ T12	Eddie Jones	3.00	1.35
□ T13	Clyde Drexler	2.00	.90
□ T14	Anfernee Hardaway	6.00	2.70
□ T15	Chris Webber	4.00	1.80
□ T16	Jayson Williams	.75	.35
□ T17	Joe Smith	1.50	.70
□ T18	Karl Malone	2.50	1.10
□ T19	Tim Hardaway	2.00	.90
□ T20	Vin Baker	3.00	1.35

		MINT	NRMT
□ T21	Tom Gugliotta	1.50	.70
□ T22	Allen Iverson	8.00	3.60
□ T23	David Robinson	2.50	1.10
□ T24	D.Mutombo	1.00	.45
□ T25	John Stockton	1.50	.70
□ T26	Charles Barkley	2.50	1.10
□ T27	Mitch Richmond	1.50	.70
□ T28	Damon Stoudamire	3.00	1.35
□ T29	Anthony Mason	1.00	.45
□ T30	Shaquille O'Neal	6.00	2.70
□ T31	Glenn Robinson	1.50	.70
□ T32	Juwan Howard	1.50	.70
□ T33	Shawn Kemp	5.00	2.20
□ T34	Dennis Rodman	6.00	2.70
□ T35	Grant Hill	10.00	4.50
□ T36	Kevin Johnson	1.00	.45
□ T37	Alonzo Mourning	1.50	.70
□ T38	Hakeem Olajuwon	3.00	1.35
□ T39	Joe Dumars	1.50	.70
□ T40	Scottie Pippen	5.00	2.20

1998-99 Topps

The first series of Topps was issued as a 110 card set in 11-card packs with a suggested retail price of $1.29. Each card was produced on a super gloss coated 16-point stock with foil-stamping.

		MINT	NRMT
COMPLETE SERIES 1 (110)		10.00	4.50
COMMON CARD (1-110)		.10	.05
SEMISTARS		.15	.07
□ 1	Scottie Pippen	.75	.35
□ 2	S.Abdur-Rahim	.60	.25
□ 3	Rod Strickland	.15	.07
□ 4	Keith Van Horn	1.25	.55
□ 5	Ray Allen	.25	.11
□ 6	Chris Mullin	.15	.07
□ 7	Anthony Parker	.10	.05
□ 8	Lindsey Hunter	.10	.05
□ 9	Mario Elie	.10	.05
□ 10	Jerry Stackhouse	.20	.09
□ 11	Eldridge Recasner	.10	.05
□ 12	Jeff Hornacek	.15	.07
□ 13	Chris Webber	.60	.25
□ 14	Lee Mayberry	.10	.05
□ 15	Erick Strickland	.10	.05
□ 16	Arvydas Sabonis	.15	.07
□ 17	Tim Thomas	.75	.35
□ 18	Luc Longley	.15	.07
□ 19	Detlef Schrempf	.15	.07
□ 20	Alonzo Mourning	.25	.11
□ 21	Adonal Foyle	.10	.05
□ 22	Tony Battie	.20	.09
□ 23	Robert Horry	.15	.07
□ 24	Derek Harper	.10	.05
□ 25	Jamal Mashburn	.15	.07
□ 26	Elliot Perry	.10	.05

		MINT	NRMT
□ 27	Jalen Rose	.10	.05
□ 28	Joe Smith	.20	.09
□ 29	Henry James	.10	.05
□ 30	Travis Knight	.10	.05
□ 31	Tom Gugliotta	.15	.07
□ 32	Chris Anstey	.10	.05
□ 33	Antonio Daniels	.25	.11
□ 34	Elden Campbell	.15	.07
□ 35	Charlie Ward	.10	.05
□ 36	Eddie Johnson	.10	.05
□ 37	John Wallace	.15	.07
□ 38	Antonio Davis	.10	.05
□ 39	Antoine Walker	1.00	.45
□ 40	Patrick Ewing	.25	.11
□ 41	Doug Christie	.10	.05
□ 42	Andrew Lang	.10	.05
□ 43	Joe Dumars	.15	.07
□ 44	Jaren Jackson	.10	.05
□ 45	Loy Vaught	.15	.07
□ 46	Allan Houston	.15	.07
□ 47	Mark Jackson	.10	.05
□ 48	Tracy Murray	.10	.05
□ 49	Tim Duncan	1.50	.70
□ 50	Micheal Williams	.10	.05
□ 51	Steve Nash	.15	.07
□ 52	Matt Maloney	.15	.07
□ 53	Sam Cassell	.15	.07
□ 54	Voshon Lenard	.10	.05
□ 55	Dikembe Mutombo	.15	.07
□ 56	Malik Sealy	.10	.05
□ 57	Dell Curry	.10	.05
□ 58	Stephon Marbury	1.00	.45
□ 59	Tariq Abdul-Wahad	.15	.07
□ 60	Isaiah Rider	.15	.07
□ 61	Kelvin Cato	.10	.05
□ 62	LaPhonso Ellis	.10	.05
□ 63	Jim Jackson	.15	.07
□ 64	Greg Ostertag	.10	.05
□ 65	Glenn Robinson	.20	.09
□ 66	Chris Carr	.10	.05
□ 67	Marcus Camby	.20	.09
□ 68	Kobe Bryant	2.00	.90
□ 69	Bobby Jackson	.20	.09
□ 70	B.J. Armstrong	.10	.05
□ 71	Alan Henderson	.10	.05
□ 72	Terry Davis	.10	.05
□ 73	John Stockton	.25	.11
□ 74	Lamond Murray	.10	.05
□ 75	Mark Price	.10	.05
□ 76	Rex Chapman	.10	.05
□ 77	Michael Jordan	3.00	1.35
□ 78	Terry Cummings	.10	.05
□ 79	Dan Majerle	.15	.07
□ 80	Charles Outlaw	.10	.05
□ 81	Michael Finley	.20	.09
□ 82	Vin Baker	.50	.23
□ 83	Clifford Robinson	.10	.05
□ 84	Greg Anthony	.10	.05
□ 85	Brevin Knight	.30	.14
□ 86	Jacque Vaughn	.10	.05
□ 87	Bobby Phills	.10	.05
□ 88	Sherman Douglas	.10	.05
□ 89	Kevin Johnson	.15	.07
□ 90	Mahmoud Abdul-Rauf..	.10	.05
□ 91	Lorenzen Wright	.10	.05
□ 92	Eric Williams	.10	.05
□ 93	Will Perdue	.10	.05
□ 94	Charles Barkley	.40	.18
□ 95	Kendall Gill	.10	.05
□ 96	Wesley Person	.10	.05
□ 97	Buck Williams	.10	.05
□ 98	Erick Dampier	.10	.05
□ 99	Nate McMillan	.10	.05
□ 100	Sean Elliott	.10	.05
□ 101	Rasheed Wallace	.15	.07
□ 102	Zydrunas Ilgauskas	.15	.07
□ 103	Eddie Jones	.50	.23
□ 104	Ron Mercer	1.00	.45
□ 105	Horace Grant	.10	.05
□ 106	Corliss Williamson	.15	.07
□ 107	Anthony Mason	.10	.05
□ 108	Mookie Blaylock	.15	.07
□ 109	Dennis Rodman	1.00	.45
□ 110	Checklist	.10	.05

1998-99 Topps Apparitions

·Randomly inserted in series one retail packs only at a rate of one in 36, this 15-card set features players whose moves defy the mind's eye. The cards feature micro-dyna etch technology. Card backs are numbered with an "A" prefix.

		MINT	NRMT
COMPLETE SET (15)		125.00	55.00
COMMON CARD (A1-A15)		1.50	.70
SER.1 STATED ODDS 1:36 RETAIL			

		MINT	NRMT
☐ A1	Kobe Bryant	20.00	9.00
☐ A2	Stephon Marbury	12.00	5.50
☐ A3	Brent Barry	1.50	.70
☐ A4	Karl Malone	4.00	1.80
☐ A5	Shaquille O'Neal	10.00	4.50
☐ A6	Chris Webber	6.00	2.70
☐ A7	Shawn Kemp	8.00	3.60
☐ A8	Hakeem Olajuwon	5.00	2.20
☐ A9	Anfernee Hardaway	10.00	4.50
☐ A10	Michael Finley	2.00	.90
☐ A11	Keith Van Horn	12.00	5.50
☐ A12	Kevin Garnett	15.00	6.75
☐ A13	Vin Baker	5.00	2.20
☐ A14	Tim Duncan	15.00	6.75
☐ A15	Michael Jordan	30.00	13.50

1998-99 Topps Autographs

Randomly inserted in series one hobby packs at a rate of one in 329, this 8-card set features certified autographs of some of the top players in the NBA. Each card features a "Topps Certified

Autograph Issue" stamp on the front. Card backs feature an "AG" prefix.

		MINT	NRMT
COMPLETE SET (8)		500.00	220.00
COMMON CARD (AG1-AG8)		30.00	13.50
SER.1 STATED ODDS 1:320 HOBBY			

		MINT	NRMT
☐ AG1	Joe Smith	40.00	18.00
☐ AG2	Kobe Bryant	150.00	70.00
☐ AG3	Stephon Marbury	80.00	36.00
☐ AG4	D.Mutombo	30.00	13.50
☐ AG5	S.Abdur-Rahim	70.00	32.00
☐ AG6	Eddie Jones	70.00	32.00
☐ AG7	Keith Van Horn	100.00	45.00
☐ AG8	Glen Rice	40.00	18.00

1998-99 Topps Cornerstones

Randomly inserted in series one hobby packs only at a rate of one in 36, this 15-card set features players that teams would love to build entire teams around. The cards feature uniluster technology. Card backs feature a "C" prefix.

		MINT	NRMT
COMPLETE SET (15)		100.00	45.00
COMMON CARD (C1-C15)		1.50	.70
SER.1 STATED ODDS 1:36 HOBBY			

		MINT	NRMT
☐ C1	Keith Van Horn	10.00	4.50
☐ C2	Kevin Garnett	12.00	5.50
☐ C3	S.Abdur-Rahim	5.00	2.20
☐ C4	Antoine Walker	8.00	3.60
☐ C5	Allen Iverson	8.00	3.60
☐ C6	Grant Hill	12.00	5.50
☐ C7	Marcus Camby	1.50	.70
☐ C8	Stephon Marbury	8.00	3.60
☐ C9	Kobe Bryant	15.00	6.75
☐ C10	Bobby Jackson	1.50	.70
☐ C11	Kerry Kittles	1.50	.70
☐ C12	Ron Mercer	8.00	3.60
☐ C13	Eddie Jones	4.00	1.80
☐ C14	Tim Thomas	6.00	2.70
☐ C15	Tim Duncan	12.00	5.50

1998-99 Topps Draft Redemption

Randomly inserted in series one packs at a rate of one in 18, this 29-card set features a redemp-

tion for the players drafted in the first round of the 1998 NBA Draft. Each card number contained a number corresponding to each draft position, and could be redeemed for a special card of that particular player selected. Cards had to be redeemed before April 1, 1999.

		MINT	NRMT
COMPLETE SET (29)		125.00	55.00
COMMON CARD (1-29)		1.50	.70
SER.1 STATED ODDS 1:18 HOB/RET			
EXPIRATION: 4/1/99			

		MINT	NRMT
☐ 1	M.Olowokandi Trade	20.00	9.00
☐ 2	Mike Bibby Trade	15.00	6.75
☐ 3	Raef LaFrentz Trade	10.00	4.50
☐ 4	Antawn Jamison Trade	15.00	6.75
☐ 5	Vince Carter Trade	10.00	4.50
☐ 6	Robert Traylor Trade	10.00	4.50
☐ 7	Jason Williams Trade	6.00	2.70
☐ 8	Larry Hughes Trade	8.00	3.60
☐ 9	Dirk Nowitzki Trade	5.00	2.20
☐ 10	Paul Pierce Trade	8.00	3.60
☐ 11	Bonzi Wells Trade	5.00	2.20
☐ 12	Michael Doleac Trade	3.00	1.35
☐ 13	Keon Clark Trade	3.00	1.35
☐ 14	M.Dickerson Trade	5.00	2.20
☐ 15	Matt Harpring Trade	2.50	1.10
☐ 16	Bryce Drew Trade	2.50	1.10
☐ 17	R.Nesterovic Trade	1.50	.70
☐ 18	M.Turkcan Trade	1.50	.70
☐ 19	Pat Garrity Trade	1.50	.70
☐ 20	R.McLeod Trade	2.50	1.10
☐ 21	Ricky Davis Trade	4.00	1.80
☐ 22	Brian Skinner Trade	3.00	1.35
☐ 23	Tyronn Lue Trade	1.50	.70
☐ 24	Felipe Lopez Trade	2.50	1.10
☐ 25	Al Harrington Trade	4.00	1.80
☐ 26	Sam Jacobson Trade	1.50	.70
☐ 27	Vladimir Stepania Trade	1.50	.70
☐ 28	Corey Benjamin Trade	3.00	1.35
☐ 29	Nazr Mohammed Trade	4.00	1.80

1998-99 Topps Emissaries

Randomly inserted in series one packs at a rate of one in 24, this 20-card set features players who have represented their country in tough international competition. The cards are produced with mirrorboard technology. Card backs are labeled with an "E" prefix.

EMISSARIES

SCOTTIE PIPPEN

	MINT	NRMT
COMPLETE SET (20)	50.00	22.00
COMMON CARD (E1-E20)	1.00	.45
SER.1 STATED ODDS 1:24 HOB/RET		

			MINT	NRMT
☐	E1	Scottie Pippen	6.00	2.70
☐	E2	Karl Malone	3.00	1.35
☐	E3	Chris Webber	5.00	2.20
☐	E4	Anfernee Hardaway	8.00	3.60
☐	E5	Detlef Schrempf	1.00	.45
☐	E6	Mitch Richmond	2.00	.90
☐	E7	Vlade Divac	1.00	.45
☐	E8	Shaquille O'Neal	8.00	3.60
☐	E9	Luc Longley	1.00	.45
☐	E10	Grant Hill	12.00	5.50
☐	E11	Christian Laettner	1.00	.45
☐	E12	Gary Payton	3.00	1.35
☐	E13	Patrick Ewing	2.00	.90
☐	E14	Shawn Kemp	6.00	2.70
☐	E15	Toni Kukoc	1.00	.45
☐	E16	David Robinson	3.00	1.35
☐	E17	Hakeem Olajuwon	4.00	1.80
☐	E18	Charles Barkley	3.00	1.35
☐	E19	John Stockton	2.00	.90
☐	E20	Arvydas Sabonis	1.00	.45

1998-99 Topps Roundball Royalty

Roundball Royalty

Randomly inserted in series one packs at a rate of one in 36, this 20-card set features the best in the NBA on Finest technology. Card backs are numbered with a "R" prefix.

			MINT	NRMT
COMPLETE SET (20)			150.00	70.00
COMMON CARD (R1-R20)			2.00	.90
SER.1 STATED ODDS 1:36 HOB/RET				

☐	R1	Michael Jordan	40.00	18.00
☐	R2	Kevin Garnett	20.00	9.00
☐	R3	David Robinson	5.00	2.20
☐	R4	Allen Iverson	12.00	5.50
☐	R5	Hakeem Olajuwon	6.00	2.70

☐	R6	Anfernee Hardaway	12.00	5.50
☐	R7	Gary Payton	5.00	2.20
☐	R8	Scottie Pippen	10.00	4.50
☐	R9	Shaquille O'Neal	12.00	5.50
☐	R10	Mitch Richmond	3.00	1.35
☐	R11	John Stockton	3.00	1.35
☐	R12	Grant Hill	20.00	9.00
☐	R13	Charles Barkley	5.00	2.20
☐	R14	Dikembe Mutombo	2.00	.90
☐	R15	Karl Malone	5.00	2.20
☐	R16	Shawn Kemp	10.00	4.50
☐	R17	Patrick Ewing	3.00	1.35
☐	R18	Kobe Bryant	25.00	11.00
☐	R19	Terrell Brandon	2.50	1.10
☐	R20	Vin Baker	6.00	2.70

1998-99 Topps Roundball Royalty Refractors

Randomly inserted in series one packs at a rate of one in 144, this 20-card set parallels the basic Roundball Royalty insert, but utilizes the "classic" Refractor technology. Card backs are numbered with a "R" prefix.

			MINT	NRMT
COMPLETE SET (20)			450.00	200.00
COMMON CARD (R1-R20)			5.00	2.20
SER.1 STATED ODDS 1:144 HOB/RET				

☐	R1	Michael Jordan	100.00	45.00
☐	R2	Kevin Garnett	50.00	22.00
☐	R3	David Robinson	12.00	5.50
☐	R4	Allen Iverson	30.00	13.50
☐	R5	Hakeem Olajuwon	15.00	6.75
☐	R6	Anfernee Hardaway	30.00	13.50
☐	R7	Gary Payton	12.00	5.50
☐	R8	Scottie Pippen	25.00	11.00
☐	R9	Shaquille O'Neal	30.00	13.50
☐	R10	Mitch Richmond	8.00	3.60
☐	R11	John Stockton	8.00	3.60
☐	R12	Grant Hill	50.00	22.00
☐	R13	Charles Barkley	12.00	5.50
☐	R14	Dikembe Mutombo	5.00	2.20
☐	R15	Karl Malone	12.00	5.50
☐	R16	Shawn Kemp	25.00	11.00
☐	R17	Patrick Ewing	8.00	3.60
☐	R18	Kobe Bryant	60.00	27.00
☐	R19	Terrell Brandon	6.00	2.70
☐	R20	Vin Baker	15.00	6.75

1998-99 Topps Season's Best

ROCK MEN

CHRIS WEBBER

Randomly inserted in series one packs at a rate of one in 12, this 30-card set features 25 of the top players by position and five of the top rookies from 1997-98. This set is also broken into six themes: Postmen, Rockmen, Bombardiers, Navigators, Soarers and Newcomers. Card backs are numbered with a "SB" prefix.

	MINT	NRMT
COMPLETE SET (30)	100.00	45.00
COMMON CARD (SB1-SB30)	1.00	.45
SER.1 STATED ODDS 1:12 HOB/RET		

☐	SB1	Rod Strickland	1.00	.45
☐	SB2	Gary Payton	2.50	1.10
☐	SB3	Tim Hardaway	2.00	.90
☐	SB4	Stephon Marbury	6.00	2.70
☐	SB5	Sam Cassell	1.00	.45
☐	SB6	Michael Jordan	20.00	9.00
☐	SB7	Mitch Richmond	1.50	.70
☐	SB8	Steve Smith	1.00	.45
☐	SB9	Ray Allen	1.50	.70
☐	SB10	Isaiah Rider	1.00	.45
☐	SB11	Grant Hill	10.00	4.50
☐	SB12	Kevin Garnett	10.00	4.50
☐	SB13	S.Abdur-Rahim	4.00	1.80
☐	SB14	Glenn Robinson	1.25	.55
☐	SB15	Michael Finley	1.25	.55
☐	SB16	Karl Malone	2.50	1.10
☐	SB17	Tim Duncan	10.00	4.50
☐	SB18	Antoine Walker	6.00	2.70
☐	SB19	Chris Webber	4.00	1.80
☐	SB20	Vin Baker	3.00	1.35
☐	SB21	Shaquille O'Neal	6.00	2.70
☐	SB22	David Robinson	2.50	1.10
☐	SB23	Alonzo Mourning	1.50	.70
☐	SB24	D.Mutombo	1.00	.45
☐	SB25	Hakeem Olajuwon	3.00	1.35
☐	SB26	Tim Duncan	10.00	4.50
☐	SB27	Keith Van Horn	8.00	3.60
☐	SB28	Zydrunas Ilgauskas	1.00	.45
☐	SB29	Brevin Knight	2.00	.90
☐	SB30	Bobby Jackson	1.25	.55

1996-97 Topps Chrome

The debut 1996-97 Topps Chrome basketball set was issued in one series totaling 220 standard-size cards. The card design is very similar to the 1996-97 Topps issue, but utilizes a Chrome background and silver borders. This product was produced for retail outlets exclusively, but was carried in many hobby stores. The cards were *issued in 4-card packs carrying a suggested retail price of $2.99. Rookie cards include Shareef Abdur-Rahim, Kobe Bryant, Marcus Camby, Allen Iverson, Stephon Marbury and Antoine Walker, among others. The set is condition sensitive.*

	MINT	NRMT
COMPLETE SET (220)	700.00	325.00
COMMON CARD (1-220)	.40	.18
SEMISTARS	.50	.23
UNLISTED STARS	.75	.35
CONDITION SENSITIVE SET		
BEWARE KOBE COUNTERFEITS		

No	Player	MINT	NRMT
1	Patrick Ewing	.75	.35
2	Christian Laettner	.50	.23
3	Mahmoud Abdul-Rauf	.40	.18
4	Chris Webber	2.00	.90
5	Jason Kidd	1.50	.70
6	Clifford Rozier	.40	.18
7	Elden Campbell	.50	.23
8	Chuck Person	.40	.18
9	Jeff Hornacek	.50	.23
10	Rik Smits	.50	.23
11	Kurt Thomas	.40	.18
12	Rod Strickland	.50	.23
13	Kendall Gill	.50	.23
14	Brian Williams	.40	.18
15	Tom Gugliotta	.75	.35
16	Ron Harper	.50	.23
17	Eric Williams	.40	.18
18	A.C. Green	.50	.23
19	Scott Williams	.40	.18
20	Damon Stoudamire	2.00	.90
21	Bryant Reeves	.50	.23
22	Bob Sura	.40	.18
23	Mitch Richmond	.75	.35
24	Larry Johnson	.50	.23
25	Vin Baker	1.50	.70
26	Mark Bryant	.40	.18
27	Horace Grant	.50	.23
28	Allan Houston	.50	.23
29	Sam Perkins	.50	.23
30	Antonio McDyess	1.25	.55
31	Rasheed Wallace	.50	.23
32	Malik Sealy	.40	.18
33	Scottie Pippen	2.50	1.10
34	Charles Barkley	1.25	.55
35	Hakeem Olajuwon	1.50	.70
36	John Starks	.50	.23
37	Byron Scott	.50	.23
38	Arvydas Sabonis	.50	.23
39	Vlade Divac	.50	.23
40	Joe Dumars	.75	.35
41	Danny Ferry	.40	.18
42	Jerry Stackhouse	1.00	.45
43	B.J. Armstrong	.40	.18
44	Shawn Bradley	.40	.18
45	Kevin Garnett	6.00	2.70
46	Dee Brown	.40	.18
47	Michael Smith	.40	.18
48	Doug Christie	.40	.18
49	Mark Jackson	.40	.18
50	Shawn Kemp	2.50	1.10
51	Sasha Danilovic	.40	.18
52	Nick Anderson	.40	.18
53	Matt Geiger	.40	.18
54	Charles Smith	.40	.18
55	Mookie Blaylock	.50	.23
56	Johnny Newman	.40	.18
57	George McCloud	.40	.18
58	Greg Ostertag	.40	.18
59	Reggie Williams	.40	.18
60	Brent Barry	.40	.18
61	Doug West	.40	.18
62	Donald Royal	.40	.18
63	Randy Brown	.40	.18
64	Vincent Askew	.40	.18
65	John Stockton	.75	.35
66	Joe Kleine	.40	.18
67	Keith Askins	.40	.18
68	Bobby Phills	.40	.18
69	Chris Mullin	.75	.35
70	Nick Van Exel	.75	.35
71	Rick Fox	.40	.18
72	Chicago Bulls	6.00	2.70
73	Shawn Respert	.40	.18
74	Hubert Davis	.40	.18
75	Jim Jackson	.50	.23
76	Olden Polynice	.40	.18
77	Gheorghe Muresan	.40	.18
78	Theo Ratliff	.40	.18
79	Khalid Reeves	.40	.18
80	David Robinson	1.25	.55
81	Lawrence Moten	.40	.18
82	Sam Cassell	.50	.23
83	George Zidek	.40	.18
84	Sharone Wright	.40	.18
85	C.Weatherspoon	.40	.18
86	Alan Henderson	.40	.18
87	Chris Dudley	.40	.18
88	Ed O'Bannon	.40	.18
89	Calbert Cheaney	.40	.18
90	Cedric Ceballos	.40	.18
91	Michael Cage	.40	.18
92	Ervin Johnson	.40	.18
93	Gary Trent	.40	.18
94	Sherman Douglas	.40	.18
95	Joe Smith	1.00	.45
96	Dale Davis	.40	.18
97	Tony Dumas	.40	.18
98	Muggsy Bogues	.40	.18
99	Toni Kukoc	.50	.23
100	Grant Hill	6.00	2.70
101	Michael Finley	1.00	.45
102	Isaiah Rider	.50	.23
103	Bryant Stith	.40	.18
104	Pooh Richardson	.40	.18
105	Karl Malone	1.25	.55
106	Brian Grant	.40	.18
107	Sean Elliott	.40	.18
108	Charles Oakley	.40	.18
109	Pervis Ellison	.40	.18
110	Anfernee Hardaway	3.00	1.35
111	Checklist (1-220)	.40	.18
112	Dikembe Mutombo	.50	.23
113	Alonzo Mourning	.75	.35
114	Hubert Davis	.40	.18
115	Rony Seikaly	.40	.18
116	Danny Manning	.50	.23
117	Donyell Marshall	.40	.18
118	Gerald Wilkins	.40	.18
119	Ervin Johnson	.40	.18
120	Jalen Rose	.50	.23
121	Dino Radja	.40	.18
122	Glenn Robinson	.75	.35
123	John Stockton	.75	.35
124	Matt Maloney	8.00	3.60
125	Clifford Robinson	.40	.18
126	Steve Kerr	.40	.18
127	Nate McMillan	.40	.18
128	S.Abdur-Rahim	60.00	27.00
129	Loy Vaught	.40	.18
130	Anthony Mason	.50	.23
131	Kevin Garnett	6.00	2.70
132	Roy Rogers	2.50	1.10
133	Erick Dampier	10.00	4.50
134	Tyus Edney	.40	.18
135	Chris Mills	.40	.18
136	Cory Alexander	.40	.18
137	Juwan Howard	1.00	.45
138	Kobe Bryant	250.00	110.00
139	Michael Jordan	40.00	18.00
140	Jayson Williams	.50	.23
141	Rod Strickland	.50	.23
142	Lorenzen Wright	10.00	4.50
143	Will Perdue	.40	.18
144	Derek Harper	.40	.18
145	Billy Owens	.40	.18
146	Antoine Walker	90.00	40.00
147	P.J. Brown	.40	.18
148	Terrell Brandon	.75	.35
149	Larry Johnson	.50	.23
150	Steve Smith	.50	.23
151	Eddie Jones	1.50	.70
152	Detlef Schrempf	.50	.23
153	Dale Ellis	.40	.18
154	Isaiah Rider	.50	.23
155	Tony Delk	8.00	3.60
156	Adrian Caldwell	.40	.18
157	Jamal Mashburn	.50	.23
158	Dennis Scott	.40	.18
159	Dana Barros	.40	.18
160	Martin Muursepp	1.00	.45
161	Marcus Camby	15.00	6.75
162	Jerome Williams	3.00	1.35
163	Wesley Person	.40	.18
164	Luc Longley	.50	.23
165	Charlie Ward	.40	.18
166	Mark Jackson	.40	.18
167	Derrick Coleman	.50	.23
168	Dell Curry	.40	.18
169	Armon Gilliam	.40	.18
170	Vlade Divac	.50	.23
171	Allen Iverson	60.00	27.00
172	Vitaly Potapenko	2.00	.90
173	Jon Koncak	.40	.18
174	Lindsey Hunter	.40	.18
175	Kevin Johnson	.50	.23
176	Dennis Rodman	3.00	1.35
177	Stephon Marbury	60.00	27.00
178	Karl Malone	1.25	.55
179	Charles Barkley	1.25	.55
180	Popeye Jones	.40	.18
181	Samaki Walker	8.00	3.60
182	Steve Nash	20.00	9.00
183	Latrell Sprewell	.50	.23
184	Kenny Anderson	.50	.23
185	Tyrone Hill	.40	.18
186	Robert Pack	.40	.18
187	Greg Anthony	.40	.18
188	Derrick McKey	.40	.18
189	John Wallace	10.00	4.50
190	Bryon Russell	.40	.18
191	Jermaine O'Neal	15.00	6.75
192	Clyde Drexler	1.00	.45
193	Mahmoud Abdul-Rauf	.40	.18
194	Eric Montross	.40	.18
195	Allan Houston	.50	.23
196	Harvey Grant	.40	.18
197	Rodney Rogers	.40	.18
198	Kerry Kittles	25.00	11.00
199	Grant Hill	6.00	2.70
200	Lionel Simmons	.40	.18
201	Reggie Miller	.75	.35
202	Avery Johnson	.40	.18
203	LaPhonso Ellis	.40	.18
204	Brian Shaw	.40	.18
205	Priest Lauderdale	1.00	.45
206	Derek Fisher	10.00	4.50
207	Terry Porter	.40	.18
208	Todd Fuller	1.00	.45
209	Hersey Hawkins	.50	.23
210	Tim Legler	.40	.18
211	Terry Dehere	.40	.18
212	Gary Payton	1.25	.55
213	Joe Dumars	.75	.35
214	Don MacLean	.40	.18
215	Greg Minor	.40	.18
216	Tim Hardaway	1.00	.45
217	Ray Allen	40.00	18.00
218	Mario Elie	.40	.18
219	Brooks Thompson	.40	.18
220	Shaquille O'Neal	3.00	1.35

1996-97 Topps Chrome Refractors

Randomly inserted into packs at a rate of one in 12, this 220-card set parallels the basic set but utilizes the Refractor technology. Card backs carry a "R" prefix. One card that does not is #72. The set is condition sensitive.

	MINT	NRMT
COMPLETE SET (220)	5500.00	2500.00
COMMON CARD (1-220)	10.00	4.50
SEMISTARS	12.00	5.50
CONDITION SENSITIVE SET		
STATED ODDS 1:12		

		MINT	NRMT
☐ 1	Patrick Ewing	20.00	9.00
☐ 2	Christian Laettner	12.00	5.50
☐ 3	Mahmoud Abdul-Rauf	10.00	4.50
☐ 4	Chris Webber	50.00	22.00
☐ 5	Jason Kidd	60.00	27.00
☐ 6	Clifford Rozier	10.00	4.50
☐ 7	Elden Campbell	12.00	5.50
☐ 8	Chuck Person	10.00	4.50
☐ 9	Jeff Hornacek	12.00	5.50
☐ 10	Rik Smits	12.00	5.50
☐ 11	Kurt Thomas	10.00	4.50
☐ 12	Rod Strickland	12.00	5.50
☐ 13	Kendall Gill	12.00	5.50
☐ 14	Brian Williams	10.00	4.50
☐ 15	Tom Gugliotta	15.00	6.75
☐ 16	Ron Harper	12.00	5.50
☐ 17	Eric Williams	10.00	4.50
☐ 18	A.C. Green	12.00	5.50
☐ 19	Scott Williams	10.00	4.50
☐ 20	Damon Stoudamire	50.00	22.00
☐ 21	Bryant Reeves	12.00	5.50
☐ 22	Bob Sura	10.00	4.50
☐ 23	Mitch Richmond	30.00	13.50
☐ 24	Larry Johnson	12.00	5.50
☐ 25	Vin Baker	40.00	18.00
☐ 26	Mark Bryant	10.00	4.50
☐ 27	Horace Grant	12.00	5.50
☐ 28	Allan Houston	12.00	5.50
☐ 29	Sam Perkins	12.00	5.50
☐ 30	Antonio McDyess	30.00	13.50
☐ 31	Rasheed Wallace	12.00	5.50
☐ 32	Malik Sealy	10.00	4.50
☐ 33	Scottie Pippen	70.00	32.00
☐ 34	Charles Barkley	35.00	16.00
☐ 35	Hakeem Olajuwon	40.00	18.00
☐ 36	John Starks	12.00	5.50
☐ 37	Byron Scott	12.00	5.50
☐ 38	Arvydas Sabonis	12.00	5.50
☐ 39	Vlade Divac	12.00	5.50
☐ 40	Joe Dumars	15.00	6.75
☐ 41	Danny Ferry	10.00	4.50
☐ 42	Jerry Stackhouse	25.00	11.00
☐ 43	B.J. Armstrong	10.00	4.50
☐ 44	Shawn Bradley	10.00	4.50
☐ 45	Kevin Garnett	125.00	55.00
☐ 46	Dee Brown	10.00	4.50
☐ 47	Michael Smith	10.00	4.50
☐ 48	Doug Christie	10.00	4.50
☐ 49	Mark Jackson	10.00	4.50
☐ 50	Shawn Kemp	60.00	27.00
☐ 51	Sasha Danilovic	10.00	4.50
☐ 52	Nick Anderson	10.00	4.50
☐ 53	Matt Geiger	10.00	4.50
☐ 54	Charles Smith	10.00	4.50
☐ 55	Mookie Blaylock	12.00	5.50
☐ 56	Johnny Newman	10.00	4.50
☐ 57	George McCloud	10.00	4.50
☐ 58	Greg Ostertag	10.00	4.50
☐ 59	Reggie Williams	10.00	4.50
☐ 60	Brent Barry	10.00	4.50
☐ 61	Doug West	10.00	4.50
☐ 62	Donald Royal	10.00	4.50
☐ 63	Randy Brown	10.00	4.50
☐ 64	Vincent Askew	10.00	4.50
☐ 65	John Stockton	25.00	11.00
☐ 66	Joe Kleine	10.00	4.50
☐ 67	Keith Askins	10.00	4.50
☐ 68	Bobby Phills	10.00	4.50
☐ 69	Chris Mullin	15.00	6.75
☐ 70	Nick Van Exel	15.00	6.75
☐ 71	Rick Fox	10.00	4.50
☐ 72	Chicago Bulls	150.00	70.00
☐ 73	Shawn Respert	10.00	4.50
☐ 74	Hubert Davis	10.00	4.50
☐ 75	Jim Jackson	12.00	5.50
☐ 76	Olden Polynice	10.00	4.50
☐ 77	Gheorghe Muresan	10.00	4.50
☐ 78	Theo Ratliff	10.00	4.50
☐ 79	Khalid Reeves	10.00	4.50
☐ 80	David Robinson	30.00	13.50
☐ 81	Lawrence Moten	10.00	4.50
☐ 82	Sam Cassell	12.00	5.50
☐ 83	George Zidek	10.00	4.50
☐ 84	Sharone Wright	10.00	4.50
☐ 85	C.Weatherspoon	10.00	4.50
☐ 86	Alan Henderson	10.00	4.50
☐ 87	Chris Dudley	10.00	4.50
☐ 88	Ed O'Bannon	10.00	4.50
☐ 89	Calbert Cheaney	10.00	4.50
☐ 90	Cedric Ceballos	10.00	4.50
☐ 91	Michael Cage	10.00	4.50
☐ 92	Ervin Johnson	10.00	4.50
☐ 93	Gary Trent	10.00	4.50
☐ 94	Sherman Douglas	10.00	4.50
☐ 95	Joe Smith	25.00	11.00
☐ 96	Dale Davis	10.00	4.50
☐ 97	Tony Dumas	10.00	4.50
☐ 98	Muggsy Bogues	10.00	4.50
☐ 99	Toni Kukoc	20.00	9.00
☐ 100	Grant Hill	125.00	55.00
☐ 101	Michael Finley	25.00	11.00
☐ 102	Isaiah Rider	12.00	5.50
☐ 103	Bryant Stith	10.00	4.50
☐ 104	Pooh Richardson	10.00	4.50
☐ 105	Karl Malone	35.00	16.00
☐ 106	Brian Grant	10.00	4.50
☐ 107	Sean Elliott	10.00	4.50
☐ 108	Charles Oakley	10.00	4.50
☐ 109	Pervis Ellison	10.00	4.50
☐ 110	A.Hardaway	100.00	45.00
☐ 111	Checklist	10.00	4.50
☐ 112	D.Mutombo	12.00	5.50
☐ 113	Alonzo Mourning	25.00	11.00
☐ 114	Hubert Davis	10.00	4.50
☐ 115	Rony Seikaly	10.00	4.50
☐ 116	Danny Manning	12.00	5.50
☐ 117	Donyell Marshall	10.00	4.50
☐ 118	Gerald Wilkins	10.00	4.50
☐ 119	Ervin Johnson	10.00	4.50
☐ 120	Jalen Rose	10.00	4.50
☐ 121	Dino Radja	10.00	4.50
☐ 122	Glenn Robinson	20.00	9.00
☐ 123	John Stockton	25.00	11.00
☐ 124	Matt Maloney	25.00	11.00
☐ 125	Clifford Robinson	10.00	4.50
☐ 126	Steve Kerr	10.00	4.50
☐ 127	Nate McMillan	10.00	4.50
☐ 128	S.Abdur-Rahim	200.00	90.00
☐ 129	Loy Vaught	12.00	5.50
☐ 130	Anthony Mason	12.00	5.50
☐ 131	Kevin Garnett	125.00	55.00
☐ 132	Roy Rogers	10.00	4.50
☐ 133	Erick Dampier	30.00	13.50
☐ 134	Tyus Edney	10.00	4.50
☐ 135	Chris Mills	10.00	4.50
☐ 136	Cory Alexander	10.00	4.50
☐ 137	Juwan Howard	25.00	11.00
☐ 138	Kobe Bryant	800.00	350.00
☐ 139	Michael Jordan	400.00	180.00
☐ 140	Jayson Williams	12.00	5.50
☐ 141	Rod Strickland	12.00	5.50
☐ 142	Lorenzen Wright	40.00	18.00
☐ 143	Will Perdue	10.00	4.50
☐ 144	Derek Harper	10.00	4.50
☐ 145	Billy Owens	10.00	4.50
☐ 146	Antoine Walker	350.00	160.00
☐ 147	P.J. Brown	10.00	4.50
☐ 148	Terrell Brandon	20.00	9.00
☐ 149	Larry Johnson	12.00	5.50
☐ 150	Steve Smith	12.00	5.50
☐ 151	Eddie Jones	50.00	22.00
☐ 152	Detlef Schrempf	12.00	5.50
☐ 153	Dale Ellis	10.00	4.50
☐ 154	Isaiah Rider	12.00	5.50
☐ 155	Tony Delk	30.00	13.50
☐ 156	Adrian Caldwell	10.00	4.50
☐ 157	Jamal Mashburn	12.00	5.50
☐ 158	Dennis Scott	10.00	4.50
☐ 159	Dana Barros	10.00	4.50
☐ 160	Martin Muursepp	10.00	4.50
☐ 161	Marcus Camby	75.00	34.00
☐ 162	Jerome Williams	15.00	6.75
☐ 163	Wesley Person	10.00	4.50
☐ 164	Luc Longley	12.00	5.50
☐ 165	Charlie Ward	10.00	4.50
☐ 166	Mark Jackson	10.00	4.50
☐ 167	Derrick Coleman	12.00	5.50
☐ 168	Dell Curry	10.00	4.50
☐ 169	Armon Gilliam	10.00	4.50
☐ 170	Vlade Divac	12.00	5.50
☐ 171	Allen Iverson	250.00	110.00
☐ 172	Vitaly Potapenko	12.00	5.50
☐ 173	Jon Koncak	10.00	4.50
☐ 174	Lindsey Hunter	10.00	4.50
☐ 175	Kevin Johnson	12.00	5.50
☐ 176	Dennis Rodman	90.00	40.00
☐ 177	Stephon Marbury	250.00	110.00
☐ 178	Karl Malone	35.00	16.00
☐ 179	Charles Barkley	35.00	16.00
☐ 180	Popeye Jones	10.00	4.50
☐ 181	Samaki Walker	25.00	11.00
☐ 182	Steve Nash	60.00	27.00
☐ 183	Latrell Sprewell	15.00	6.75
☐ 184	Kenny Anderson	12.00	5.50
☐ 185	Tyrone Hill	10.00	4.50
☐ 186	Robert Pack	10.00	4.50
☐ 187	Greg Anthony	10.00	4.50
☐ 188	Derrick McKey	10.00	4.50
☐ 189	John Wallace	50.00	22.00
☐ 190	Bryon Russell	10.00	4.50
☐ 191	Jermaine O'Neal	60.00	27.00
☐ 192	Clyde Drexler	25.00	11.00
☐ 193	Mahmoud Abdul-Rauf	10.00	4.50
☐ 194	Eric Montross	10.00	4.50
☐ 195	Allan Houston	12.00	5.50
☐ 196	Harvey Grant	10.00	4.50
☐ 197	Rodney Rogers	10.00	4.50
☐ 198	Kerry Kittles	80.00	36.00
☐ 199	Grant Hill	125.00	55.00
☐ 200	Lionel Simmons	10.00	4.50
☐ 201	Reggie Miller	20.00	9.00
☐ 202	Avery Johnson	10.00	4.50
☐ 203	LaPhonso Ellis	10.00	4.50
☐ 204	Brian Shaw	10.00	4.50
☐ 205	Priest Lauderdale	10.00	4.50
☐ 206	Derek Fisher	40.00	18.00
☐ 207	Terry Porter	10.00	4.50
☐ 208	Todd Fuller	10.00	4.50
☐ 209	Hersey Hawkins	12.00	5.50
☐ 210	Tim Legler	10.00	4.50
☐ 211	Terry Dehere	10.00	4.50
☐ 212	Gary Payton	35.00	16.00
☐ 213	Joe Dumars	15.00	6.75
☐ 214	Don MacLean	10.00	4.50
☐ 215	Greg Minor	10.00	4.50
☐ 216	Tim Hardaway	30.00	13.50
☐ 217	Ray Allen	150.00	70.00
☐ 218	Mario Elie	10.00	4.50
☐ 219	Brooks Thompson	10.00	4.50
☐ 220	Shaquille O'Neal	100.00	45.00

1996-97 Topps Chrome Pro Files

Randomly inserted into packs at a rate of one in 8, this 20-card set parallels the Pro Files insert set from the regular 1996-97

Topps issue, but with a Chrome background. Card backs carry a "PF" prefix.

	MINT	NRMT
COMPLETE SET (20)	50.00	22.00
COMMON CARD (PF1-PF20)	.75	.35
SEMISTARS	1.25	.55
STATED ODDS 1:8		

		MINT	NRMT
☐ PF1	Grant Hill	8.00	3.60
☐ PF2	Shawn Kemp	4.00	1.80
☐ PF3	Michael Jordan	15.00	6.75
☐ PF4	Vin Baker	2.50	1.10
☐ PF5	Chris Webber	3.00	1.35
☐ PF6	Joe Smith	1.50	.70
☐ PF7	Shaquille O'Neal	5.00	2.20
☐ PF8	Patrick Ewing	1.25	.55
☐ PF9	Scottie Pippen	4.00	1.80
☐ PF10	D.Stoudamire	3.00	1.35
☐ PF11	A.Hardaway	5.00	2.20
☐ PF12	Juwan Howard	1.50	.70
☐ PF13	D.Mutombo	.75	.35
☐ PF14	Dennis Rodman	5.00	2.20
☐ PF15	Kevin Garnett	8.00	3.60
☐ PF16	Jerry Stackhouse	1.50	.70
☐ PF17	Alonzo Mourning	1.25	.55
☐ PF18	Karl Malone	2.00	.90
☐ PF19	Hakeem Olajuwon	2.50	1.10
☐ PF20	Gary Payton	2.00	.90

1996-97
Topps Chrome
Season's Best

Randomly inserted into packs at a rate of one in 6, this 25-card set parallels the Season's Best insert set from the regular 1996-97 Topps issue, but with a Chrome background. Card backs carry a "SB" prefix.

	MINT	NRMT
COMPLETE SET (25)	50.00	22.00
COMMON CARD (SB1-SB25)	.40	.18
SEMISTARS	.75	.35
UNLISTED STARS	1.25	.55

		MINT	NRMT
☐ SB1	Michael Jordan	15.00	6.75
☐ SB2	Hakeem Olajuwon	2.50	1.10
☐ SB3	Shaquille O'Neal	5.00	2.20
☐ SB4	Karl Malone	2.00	.90
☐ SB5	David Robinson	2.00	.90
☐ SB6	Dennis Rodman	5.00	2.20
☐ SB7	David Robinson	2.00	.90
☐ SB8	Dikembe Mutombo	.75	.35
☐ SB9	Charles Barkley	2.00	.90
☐ SB10	Shawn Kemp	4.00	1.80
☐ SB11	John Stockton	1.25	.55
☐ SB12	Jason Kidd	2.50	1.10
☐ SB13	Avery Johnson	.40	.18
☐ SB14	Rod Strickland	.75	.35
☐ SB15	D.Stoudamire	3.00	1.35
☐ SB16	Gary Payton	2.00	.90
☐ SB17	Mookie Blaylock	.75	.35
☐ SB18	Michael Jordan	15.00	6.75
☐ SB19	Jason Kidd	2.50	1.10
☐ SB20	Alvin Robertson	.40	.18
☐ SB21	Dikembe Mutombo	.75	.35
☐ SB22	Shawn Bradley	.40	.18
☐ SB23	David Robinson	2.00	.90
☐ SB24	Hakeem Olajuwon	2.50	1.10
☐ SB25	Alonzo Mourning	1.25	.55

1996-97
Topps Chrome
Youthquake

Randomly inserted into packs at a rate of one in 12, this 15-card set parallels the Youthquake insert set from the regular 1996-97 Topps issue, but with a Chrome background. Card backs carry a "YQ" prefix.

	MINT	NRMT
COMPLETE SET (15)	90.00	40.00
COMMON CARD (YQ1-YQ15)	1.25	.55
SEMISTARS	2.00	.90
UNLISTED STARS	3.00	1.35
STATED ODDS 1:12		

		MINT	NRMT
☐ YQ1	Allen Iverson	15.00	6.75
☐ YQ2	Samaki Walker	3.00	1.35
☐ YQ3	Stephon Marbury	15.00	6.75
☐ YQ4	D.Stoudamire	8.00	3.60
☐ YQ5	John Wallace	3.00	1.35
☐ YQ6	Michael Finley	4.00	1.80
☐ YQ7	Marcus Camby	4.00	1.80
☐ YQ8	Kerry Kittles	4.00	1.80
☐ YQ9	Ray Allen	5.00	2.20
☐ YQ10	Jerry Stackhouse	4.00	1.80
☐ YQ11	S.Abdur-Rahim	10.00	4.50
☐ YQ12	Antonio McDyess	5.00	2.20
☐ YQ13	Joe Smith	4.00	1.80
☐ YQ14	Brent Barry	1.25	.55
☐ YQ15	Kobe Bryant	50.00	22.00

1997-98 Topps
Chrome

The 1997-98 Topps Chrome set was issued in one series totalling 220 cards. The cards are a semi-parallel of the regular Topps set - utilizing the same photography, but released in separate packaging at a sug-

gested retail price of $3 per pack.

	MINT	NRMT
COMPLETE SET (220)	350.00	160.00
COMMON CARD (1-220)	.40	.18
SEMISTARS	.50	.23
UNLISTED STARS	1.00	.45

		MINT	NRMT
☐ 1	Scottie Pippen	3.00	1.35
☐ 2	Nate McMillan	.40	.18
☐ 3	Byron Scott	.40	.18
☐ 4	Mark Davis	.40	.18
☐ 5	Rod Strickland	.50	.23
☐ 6	Brian Grant	.40	.18
☐ 7	Damon Stoudamire	2.00	.90
☐ 8	John Stockton	1.00	.45
☐ 9	Grant Long	.40	.18
☐ 10	Darrell Armstrong	.40	.18
☐ 11	Anthony Mason	.50	.23
☐ 12	Travis Best	.40	.18
☐ 13	Stephon Marbury	5.00	2.20
☐ 14	Jamal Mashburn	.50	.23
☐ 15	Detlef Schrempf	.50	.23
☐ 16	Terrell Brandon	1.00	.45
☐ 17	Charles Barkley	1.50	.70
☐ 18	Vin Baker	2.00	.90
☐ 19	Gary Trent	.40	.18
☐ 20	Vinny Del Negro	.40	.18
☐ 21	Todd Day	.40	.18
☐ 22	Malik Sealy	.40	.18
☐ 23	Wesley Person	.40	.18
☐ 24	Reggie Miller	1.00	.45
☐ 25	Dan Majerle	.50	.23
☐ 26	Todd Fuller	.40	.18
☐ 27	Juwan Howard	1.00	.45
☐ 28	C.Weatherspoon	.40	.18
☐ 29	Grant Hill	6.00	2.70
☐ 30	John Williams	.40	.18
☐ 31	Ken Norman	.40	.18
☐ 32	Patrick Ewing	1.00	.45
☐ 33	Bryon Russell	.40	.18
☐ 34	Tony Smith	.40	.18
☐ 35	Andrew Lang	.40	.18
☐ 36	Rony Seikaly	.40	.18
☐ 37	Billy Owens	.40	.18
☐ 38	Dino Radja	.40	.18
☐ 39	Chris Gatling	.40	.18
☐ 40	Dale Davis	.40	.18
☐ 41	Arvydas Sabonis	.50	.23
☐ 42	Chris Mills	.40	.18
☐ 43	A.C. Green	.50	.23
☐ 44	Tyrone Hill	.40	.18
☐ 45	Tracy Murray	.40	.18
☐ 46	David Robinson	1.50	.70
☐ 47	Lee Mayberry	.40	.18
☐ 48	Jayson Williams	.50	.23
☐ 49	Jason Kidd	2.00	.90
☐ 50	Bryant Stith	.40	.18
☐ 51	Checklist	6.00	2.70
	Bulls - Team of the 90s		
	Michael Jordan		
	Scottie Pippen		
	Dennis Rodman		
	Ron Harper		
☐ 52	Brent Barry	.40	.18

☐ 53	Henry James	.40	.18
☐ 54	Allen Iverson	5.00	2.20
☐ 55	Shandon Anderson	.40	.18
☐ 56	Mitch Richmond	1.00	.45
☐ 57	Allan Houston	.50	.23
☐ 58	Ron Harper	.50	.23
☐ 59	Gheorghe Muresan	.40	.18
☐ 60	Vincent Askew	.40	.18
☐ 61	Ray Allen	1.25	.55
☐ 62	Kenny Anderson	.50	.23
☐ 63	Dikembe Mutombo	.50	.23
☐ 64	Sam Perkins	.50	.23
☐ 65	Walt Williams	.40	.18
☐ 66	Chris Carr	.40	.18
☐ 67	Vlade Divac	.50	.23
☐ 68	LaPhonso Ellis	.40	.18
☐ 69	B.J. Armstrong	.40	.18
☐ 70	Jim Jackson	.50	.23
☐ 71	Clyde Drexler	1.25	.55
☐ 72	Lindsey Hunter	.40	.18
☐ 73	Sasha Danilovic	.40	.18
☐ 74	Elden Campbell	.50	.23
☐ 75	Robert Pack	.40	.18
☐ 76	Dennis Scott	.40	.18
☐ 77	Will Perdue	.40	.18
☐ 78	Anthony Peeler	.40	.18
☐ 79	Steve Smith	.50	.23
☐ 80	Steve Kerr	.40	.18
☐ 81	Buck Williams	.40	.18
☐ 82	Terry Mills	.40	.18
☐ 83	Michael Smith	.40	.18
☐ 84	Adam Keefe	.40	.18
☐ 85	Kevin Willis	.40	.18
☐ 86	David Wesley	.40	.18
☐ 87	Muggsy Bogues	.40	.18
☐ 88	Bimbo Coles	.40	.18
☐ 89	Tom Gugliotta	1.00	.45
☐ 90	Jermaine O'Neal	.50	.23
☐ 91	Cedric Ceballos	.40	.18
☐ 92	Shawn Kemp	3.00	1.35
☐ 93	Horace Grant	.50	.23
☐ 94	Shareef Abdur-Rahim	3.00	1.35
☐ 95	Robert Horry	.50	.23
☐ 96	Vitaly Potapenko	.40	.18
☐ 97	Pooh Richardson	.40	.18
☐ 98	Doug Christie	.40	.18
☐ 99	Voshon Lenard	.40	.18
☐ 100	Dominique Wilkins	1.00	.45
☐ 101	Alonzo Mourning	1.00	.45
☐ 102	Sam Cassell	.50	.23
☐ 103	Sherman Douglas	.40	.18
☐ 104	Shawn Bradley	.40	.18
☐ 105	Mark Jackson	.40	.18
☐ 106	Dennis Rodman	4.00	1.80
☐ 107	Charles Oakley	.40	.18
☐ 108	Matt Maloney	.40	.18
☐ 109	Shaquille O'Neal	4.00	1.80
☐ 110	Checklist	1.00	.45
	Karl Malone MVP		
☐ 111	Antonio McDyess	1.25	.55
☐ 112	Bob Sura	.40	.18
☐ 113	Terrell Brandon	1.00	.45
☐ 114	Tim Thomas	25.00	11.00
☐ 115	Tim Duncan	110.00	50.00
☐ 116	Antonio Daniels	10.00	4.50
☐ 117	Bryant Reeves	.50	.23
☐ 118	Keith Van Horn	50.00	22.00
☐ 119	Loy Vaught	.50	.23
☐ 120	Rasheed Wallace	.50	.23
☐ 121	Bobby Jackson	3.60	3.60
☐ 122	Kevin Johnson	.50	.23
☐ 123	Michael Jordan	20.00	9.00
☐ 124	Ron Mercer	30.00	13.50
☐ 125	Tracy McGrady	20.00	9.00
☐ 126	Antoine Walker	5.00	2.20
☐ 127	Carlos Rogers	.40	.18
☐ 128	Isaac Austin	.40	.18
☐ 129	Mookie Blaylock	.50	.23
☐ 130	Rodrick Rhodes	3.00	1.35
☐ 131	Dennis Scott	.40	.18
☐ 132	Chris Mullin	1.00	.45
☐ 133	P.J. Brown	.40	.18
☐ 134	Rex Chapman	.40	.18
☐ 135	Sean Elliott	.40	.18
☐ 136	Alan Henderson	.40	.18
☐ 137	Austin Croshere	2.50	1.10

☐ 138	Nick Van Exel	1.00	.45
☐ 139	Derek Strong	.40	.18
☐ 140	Glenn Robinson	1.00	.45
☐ 141	Avery Johnson	.40	.18
☐ 142	Calbert Cheaney	.40	.18
☐ 143	Mahmoud Abdul-Rauf	.40	.18
☐ 144	Stojko Vrankovic	.40	.18
☐ 145	Chris Childs	.40	.18
☐ 146	Danny Manning	.50	.23
☐ 147	Jeff Hornacek	.50	.23
☐ 148	Kevin Garnett	6.00	2.70
☐ 149	Joe Dumars	1.00	.45
☐ 150	Johnny Taylor	2.00	.90
☐ 151	Mark Price	.40	.18
☐ 152	Toni Kukoc	.50	.23
☐ 153	Erick Dampier	.40	.18
☐ 154	Lorenzen Wright	.40	.18
☐ 155	Matt Geiger	.40	.18
☐ 156	Tim Hardaway	1.25	.55
☐ 157	Charles Smith	2.00	.90
☐ 158	Hersey Hawkins	.50	.23
☐ 159	Michael Finley	1.00	.45
☐ 160	Tyus Edney	.40	.18
☐ 161	Christian Laettner	.50	.23
☐ 162	Doug West	.40	.18
☐ 163	Jim Jackson	.50	.23
☐ 164	Larry Johnson	.50	.23
☐ 165	Vin Baker	2.00	.90
☐ 166	Karl Malone	1.50	.70
☐ 167	Kelvin Cato	2.50	1.10
☐ 168	Luc Longley	.50	.23
☐ 169	Dale Davis	.40	.18
☐ 170	Joe Smith	1.00	.45
☐ 171	Kobe Bryant	15.00	6.75
☐ 172	Scot Pollard	2.00	.90
☐ 173	Derek Anderson	12.00	5.50
☐ 174	Erick Strickland	2.00	.90
☐ 175	Olden Polynice	.40	.18
☐ 176	Chris Whitney	.40	.18
☐ 177	Anthony Parker	2.00	.90
☐ 178	Armon Gilliam	.40	.18
☐ 179	Gary Payton	1.50	.70
☐ 180	Glen Rice	1.00	.45
☐ 181	Chauncey Billups	12.00	5.50
☐ 182	Derek Fisher	.40	.18
☐ 183	John Starks	.50	.23
☐ 184	Mario Elie	.40	.18
☐ 185	Chris Webber	2.50	1.10
☐ 186	Shawn Kemp	3.00	1.35
☐ 187	Greg Ostertag	.40	.18
☐ 188	Olivier Saint-Jean	5.00	2.20
☐ 189	Eric Snow	.40	.18
☐ 190	Isaiah Rider	.50	.23
☐ 191	Paul Grant	2.00	.90
☐ 192	Samaki Walker	.40	.18
☐ 193	Cory Alexander	.40	.18
☐ 194	Eddie Jones	2.00	.90
☐ 195	John Thomas	2.00	.90
☐ 196	Otis Thorpe	.50	.23
☐ 197	Rod Strickland	.50	.23
☐ 198	David Wesley	.40	.18
☐ 199	Jacque Vaughn	6.00	2.70
☐ 200	Rik Smits	.50	.23
☐ 201	Brevin Knight	12.00	5.50
☐ 202	Clifford Robinson	.40	.18
☐ 203	Hakeem Olajuwon	2.00	.90
☐ 204	Jerry Stackhouse	1.00	.45
☐ 205	Tyrone Hill	.40	.18
☐ 206	Kendall Gill	.50	.23
☐ 207	Marcus Camby	1.00	.45
☐ 208	Tony Battie	8.00	3.60
☐ 209	Brent Price	.40	.18
☐ 210	Danny Fortson	8.00	3.60
☐ 211	Jerome Williams	.40	.18
☐ 212	Maurice Taylor	12.00	5.50
☐ 213	Brian Williams	.40	.18
☐ 214	Keith Booth	2.00	.90
☐ 215	Nick Anderson	.40	.18
☐ 216	Travis Knight	.40	.18
☐ 217	Adonal Foyle	2.50	1.10
☐ 218	Anfernee Hardaway	4.00	1.80
☐ 219	Kerry Kittles	1.00	.45
☐ 220	Checklist	.40	.18
	Dikembe Mutombo		
	Defensive POY		

1997-98
Topps Chrome
Refractors

Randomly inserted into packs at one in 12, this 220-card set parallels the basic set utilizing the "classic" Refractor technology.

	MINT	NRMT
COMPLETE SET (220)	3500.00	1600.00
COMMON CARD (1-220)	4.00	1.80
SEMISTARS	6.00	2.70
STATED ODDS 1:12		

☐ 1	Scottie Pippen	40.00	18.00
☐ 2	Nate McMillan	4.00	1.80
☐ 3	Byron Scott	4.00	1.80
☐ 4	Mark Davis	4.00	1.80
☐ 5	Rod Strickland	6.00	2.70
☐ 6	Brian Grant	4.00	1.80
☐ 7	Damon Stoudamire	25.00	11.00
☐ 8	John Stockton	12.00	5.50
☐ 9	Grant Long	4.00	1.80
☐ 10	Darrell Armstrong	4.00	1.80
☐ 11	Anthony Mason	6.00	2.70
☐ 12	Travis Best	4.00	1.80
☐ 13	Stephon Marbury	60.00	27.00
☐ 14	Jamal Mashburn	6.00	2.70
☐ 15	Detlef Schrempf	6.00	2.70
☐ 16	Terrell Brandon	10.00	4.50
☐ 17	Charles Barkley	20.00	9.00
☐ 18	Vin Baker	25.00	11.00
☐ 19	Gary Trent	4.00	1.80
☐ 20	Vinny Del Negro	4.00	1.80
☐ 21	Todd Day	4.00	1.80
☐ 22	Malik Sealy	4.00	1.80
☐ 23	Wesley Person	4.00	1.80
☐ 24	Reggie Miller	12.00	5.50
☐ 25	Dan Majerle	6.00	2.70
☐ 26	Todd Fuller	4.00	1.80
☐ 27	Juwan Howard	12.00	5.50
☐ 28	C.Weatherspoon	4.00	1.80
☐ 29	Grant Hill	80.00	36.00
☐ 30	John Williams	4.00	1.80
☐ 31	Ken Norman	4.00	1.80
☐ 32	Patrick Ewing	12.00	5.50
☐ 33	Bryon Russell	4.00	1.80
☐ 34	Tony Smith	4.00	1.80
☐ 35	Andrew Lang	4.00	1.80
☐ 36	Rony Seikaly	4.00	1.80
☐ 37	Billy Owens	4.00	1.80
☐ 38	Dino Radja	4.00	1.80
☐ 39	Chris Gatling	4.00	1.80
☐ 40	Dale Davis	4.00	1.80
☐ 41	Arvydas Sabonis	6.00	2.70
☐ 42	Chris Mills	4.00	1.80
☐ 43	A.C. Green	6.00	2.70
☐ 44	Tyrone Hill	4.00	1.80
☐ 45	Tracy Murray	4.00	1.80
☐ 46	David Robinson	20.00	9.00
☐ 47	Lee Mayberry	4.00	1.80
☐ 48	Jayson Williams	6.00	2.70
☐ 49	Jason Kidd	25.00	11.00

☐ 50	Bryant Stith	4.00	1.80
☐ 51	Checklist	100.00	45.00
	Bulls - Team of the 90s		
	Michael Jordan		
	Scottie Pippen		
	Dennis Rodman		
	Ron Harper		
☐ 52	Brent Barry	4.00	1.80
☐ 53	Henry James	4.00	1.80
☐ 54	Allen Iverson	50.00	22.00
☐ 55	Shandon Anderson	4.00	1.80
☐ 56	Mitch Richmond	12.00	5.50
☐ 57	Allan Houston	6.00	2.70
☐ 58	Ron Harper	6.00	2.70
☐ 59	Gheorghe Muresan	4.00	1.80
☐ 60	Vincent Askew	4.00	1.80
☐ 61	Ray Allen	15.00	6.75
☐ 62	Kenny Anderson	6.00	2.70
☐ 63	Dikembe Mutombo	6.00	2.70
☐ 64	Sam Perkins	6.00	2.70
☐ 65	Walt Williams	4.00	1.80
☐ 66	Chris Carr	4.00	1.80
☐ 67	Vlade Divac	6.00	2.70
☐ 68	LaPhonso Ellis	4.00	1.80
☐ 69	B.J. Armstrong	4.00	1.80
☐ 70	Jim Jackson	4.00	1.80
☐ 71	Clyde Drexler	15.00	6.75
☐ 72	Lindsey Hunter	4.00	1.80
☐ 73	Sasha Danilovic	4.00	1.80
☐ 74	Elden Campbell	6.00	2.70
☐ 75	Robert Pack	4.00	1.80
☐ 76	Dennis Scott	4.00	1.80
☐ 77	Will Perdue	4.00	1.80
☐ 78	Anthony Peeler	4.00	1.80
☐ 79	Steve Smith	6.00	2.70
☐ 80	Steve Kerr	4.00	1.80
☐ 81	Buck Williams	4.00	1.80
☐ 82	Terry Mills	4.00	1.80
☐ 83	Michael Smith	4.00	1.80
☐ 84	Adam Keefe	4.00	1.80
☐ 85	Kevin Willis	4.00	1.80
☐ 86	David Wesley	4.00	1.80
☐ 87	Muggsy Bogues	4.00	1.80
☐ 88	Bimbo Coles	4.00	1.80
☐ 89	Tom Gugliotta	12.00	5.50
☐ 90	Jermaine O'Neal	6.00	2.70
☐ 91	Cedric Ceballos	4.00	1.80
☐ 92	Shawn Kemp	40.00	18.00
☐ 93	Horace Grant	6.00	2.70
☐ 94	S.Abdur-Rahim	40.00	18.00
☐ 95	Robert Horry	6.00	2.70
☐ 96	Vitaly Potapenko	4.00	1.80
☐ 97	Pooh Richardson	4.00	1.80
☐ 98	Doug Christie	4.00	1.80
☐ 99	Vinnie Lenard	4.00	1.80
☐ 100	Dominique Wilkins	12.00	5.50
☐ 101	Alonzo Mourning	12.00	5.50
☐ 102	Sam Cassell	6.00	2.70
☐ 103	Sherman Douglas	4.00	1.80
☐ 104	Shawn Bradley	4.00	1.80
☐ 105	Mark Jackson	4.00	1.80
☐ 106	Dennis Rodman	50.00	22.00
☐ 107	Charles Oakley	4.00	1.80
☐ 108	Matt Maloney	4.00	1.80
☐ 109	Shaquille O'Neal	50.00	22.00
☐ 110	Checklist	12.00	5.50
	Karl Malone MVP		
☐ 111	Antonio McDyess	15.00	6.75
☐ 112	Bob Sura	4.00	1.80
☐ 113	Terrell Brandon	10.00	4.50
☐ 114	Tim Thomas	100.00	45.00
☐ 115	Tim Duncan	400.00	180.00
☐ 116	Antonio Daniels	40.00	18.00
☐ 117	Bryant Reeves	6.00	2.70
☐ 118	Keith Van Horn	250.00	110.00
☐ 119	Loy Vaught	6.00	2.70
☐ 120	Rasheed Wallace	6.00	2.70
☐ 121	Bobby Jackson	40.00	18.00
☐ 122	Kevin Johnson	6.00	2.70
☐ 123	Michael Jordan	300.00	135.00
☐ 124	Ron Mercer	150.00	70.00
☐ 125	Tracy McGrady	100.00	45.00
☐ 126	Antoine Walker	60.00	27.00
☐ 127	Carlos Rogers	4.00	1.80
☐ 128	Isaac Austin	4.00	1.80
☐ 129	Mookie Blaylock	6.00	2.70

☐ 130	Rodrick Rhodes	15.00	6.75
☐ 131	Dennis Scott	4.00	1.80
☐ 132	Chris Mullin	12.00	5.50
☐ 133	P.J. Brown	4.00	1.80
☐ 134	Rex Chapman	4.00	1.80
☐ 135	Sean Elliott	4.00	1.80
☐ 136	Alan Henderson	4.00	1.80
☐ 137	Austin Croshere	15.00	6.75
☐ 138	Nick Van Exel	10.00	4.50
☐ 139	Derek Strong	4.00	1.80
☐ 140	Glenn Robinson	10.00	4.50
☐ 141	Avery Johnson	4.00	1.80
☐ 142	Calbert Cheaney	4.00	1.80
☐ 143	Mahmoud Abdul-Rauf	4.00	1.80
☐ 144	Stojko Vrankovic	4.00	1.80
☐ 145	Chris Childs	4.00	1.80
☐ 146	Danny Manning	6.00	2.70
☐ 147	Jeff Hornacek	6.00	2.70
☐ 148	Kevin Garnett	80.00	36.00
☐ 149	Joe Dumars	12.00	5.50
☐ 150	Johnny Taylor	12.00	5.50
☐ 151	Mark Price	4.00	1.80
☐ 152	Toni Kukoc	6.00	2.70
☐ 153	Erick Dampier	4.00	1.80
☐ 154	Lorenzen Wright	4.00	1.80
☐ 155	Matt Geiger	4.00	1.80
☐ 156	Tim Hardaway	15.00	6.75
☐ 157	Charles Smith	12.00	5.50
☐ 158	Hersey Hawkins	6.00	2.70
☐ 159	Michael Finley	12.00	5.50
☐ 160	Tyus Edney	4.00	1.80
☐ 161	Christian Laettner	6.00	2.70
☐ 162	Doug West	4.00	1.80
☐ 163	Jim Jackson	6.00	2.70
☐ 164	Larry Johnson	6.00	2.70
☐ 165	Vin Baker	25.00	11.00
☐ 166	Karl Malone	20.00	9.00
☐ 167	Kelvin Cato	15.00	6.75
☐ 168	Luc Longley	6.00	2.70
☐ 169	Dale Davis	4.00	1.80
☐ 170	Joe Smith	12.00	5.50
☐ 171	Kobe Bryant	150.00	70.00
☐ 172	Scot Pollard	12.00	5.50
☐ 173	Derek Anderson	60.00	27.00
☐ 174	Erick Strickland	12.00	5.50
☐ 175	Olden Polynice	4.00	1.80
☐ 176	Chris Whitney	4.00	1.80
☐ 177	Anthony Parker	12.00	5.50
☐ 178	Armon Gilliam	4.00	1.80
☐ 179	Gary Payton	20.00	9.00
☐ 180	Glen Rice	12.00	5.50
☐ 181	Chauncey Billups	70.00	32.00
☐ 182	Derek Fisher	4.00	1.80
☐ 183	John Starks	6.00	2.70
☐ 184	Mario Elie	4.00	1.80
☐ 185	Chris Webber	30.00	13.50
☐ 186	Shawn Kemp	40.00	18.00
☐ 187	Greg Ostertag	4.00	1.80
☐ 188	Olivier Saint-Jean	20.00	9.00
☐ 189	Eric Snow	4.00	1.80
☐ 190	Isaiah Rider	6.00	2.70
☐ 191	Paul Grant	12.00	5.50
☐ 192	Samaki Walker	4.00	1.80
☐ 193	Cory Alexander	4.00	1.80
☐ 194	Eddie Jones	25.00	11.00
☐ 195	John Thomas	12.00	5.50
☐ 196	Otis Thorpe	6.00	2.70
☐ 197	Rod Strickland	6.00	2.70
☐ 198	David Wesley	4.00	1.80
☐ 199	Jacque Vaughn	20.00	9.00
☐ 200	Rik Smits	6.00	2.70
☐ 201	Brevin Knight	60.00	27.00
☐ 202	Clifford Robinson	4.00	1.80
☐ 203	Hakeem Olajuwon	25.00	11.00
☐ 204	Jerry Stackhouse	12.00	5.50
☐ 205	Tyrone Hill	4.00	1.80
☐ 206	Kendall Gill	6.00	2.70
☐ 207	Marcus Camby	12.00	5.50
☐ 208	Tony Battie	40.00	18.00
☐ 209	Brent Price	4.00	1.80
☐ 210	Danny Fortson	40.00	18.00
☐ 211	Jerome Williams	4.00	1.80
☐ 212	Maurice Taylor	60.00	27.00
☐ 213	Brian Williams	4.00	1.80
☐ 214	Keith Booth	12.00	5.50
☐ 215	Nick Anderson	4.00	1.80

☐ 216	Travis Knight	4.00	1.80
☐ 217	Adonal Foyle	15.00	6.75
☐ 218	A.Hardaway	50.00	22.00
☐ 219	Kerry Kittles	12.00	5.50
☐ 220	Checklist	4.00	1.80
	Dikembe Mutombo		
	Defensive POY		

1997-98 Topps Chrome Destiny

Randomly inserted into packs at a rate of one in 12, this 15-card set is a parallel of the regular Topps Destiny utilizing the Chrome technology. Card backs are numbered with a "D" prefix.

	MINT	NRMT
COMPLETE SET (15)	80.00	36.00
COMMON CARD (D1-D15)	1.50	.70
STATED ODDS 1:12		
COMP.REF.SET (15)	250.00	110.00
COMMON REF. (D1-D15)	4.00	1.80
*REF: 1X TO 2.5X HI COLUMN		
REF: STATED ODDS 1:48		

☐ D1	Grant Hill	10.00	4.50
☐ D2	Kevin Garnett	10.00	4.50
☐ D3	Vin Baker	3.00	1.35
☐ D4	Antoine Walker	8.00	3.60
☐ D5	Kobe Bryant	12.00	5.50
☐ D6	Tracy McGrady	8.00	3.60
☐ D7	Keith Van Horn	12.00	5.50
☐ D8	Tim Duncan	15.00	6.75
☐ D9	Eddie Jones	3.00	1.35
☐ D10	Stephon Marbury	8.00	3.60
☐ D11	Marcus Camby	1.50	.70
☐ D12	Antonio McDyess	2.00	.90
☐ D13	S.Abdur-Rahim	5.00	2.20
☐ D14	Allen Iverson	8.00	3.60
☐ D15	Shaquille O'Neal	6.00	2.70

1997-98 Topps Chrome Season's Best

Randomly inserted into packs at a rate of one in 8, this 29-card set is a parallel of the regular Topps Season's Best set utilizing the Chrome technology. The only card not available is SB8, which was not produced. Card backs are numbered with a "SB" prefix.

	MINT	NRMT
COMPLETE SET (29)	60.00	27.00
COMMON CARD (SB1-SB30)	.60	.25
SEMISTARS	.75	.35
UNLISTED STARS	1.25	.55
STATED ODDS 1:8		
COMP.REF.SET (29)	200.00	90.00
COMMON REF. (SB1-SB30)	2.00	.90
*REF: 1.25X TO 3X HI COLUMN		
REF: STATED ODDS 1:24		
CARD S88 DOES NOT EXIST		

☐ SB1 Gary Payton	2.00	.90
☐ SB2 Kevin Johnson	.75	.35
☐ SB3 Tim Hardaway	1.50	.70
☐ SB4 John Stockton	1.25	.55
☐ SB5 Damon Stoudamire	2.50	1.10
☐ SB6 Michael Jordan	15.00	6.75
☐ SB7 Mitch Richmond	1.25	.55
☐ SB9 Reggie Miller	1.25	.55
☐ SB10 Clyde Drexler	1.50	.70
☐ SB11 Grant Hill	8.00	3.60
☐ SB12 Scottie Pippen	4.00	1.80
☐ SB13 Kendall Gill	.75	.35
☐ SB14 Glen Rice	1.25	.55
☐ SB15 LaPhonso Ellis	.60	.25
☐ SB16 Karl Malone	2.00	.90
☐ SB17 Charles Barkley	2.00	.90
☐ SB18 Vin Baker	2.50	1.10
☐ SB19 Chris Webber	3.00	1.35
☐ SB20 Tom Gugliotta	1.25	.55
☐ SB21 Shaquille O'Neal	5.00	2.20
☐ SB22 Patrick Ewing	1.25	.55
☐ SB23 Hakeem Olajuwon	2.50	1.10
☐ SB24 Alonzo Mourning	1.25	.55
☐ SB25 D.Mutombo	.75	.35
☐ SB26 Allen Iverson	6.00	2.70
☐ SB27 Antoine Walker	6.00	2.70
☐ SB28 S.Abdur-Rahim	4.00	1.80
☐ SB29 Stephon Marbury	6.00	2.70
☐ SB30 Kerry Kittles	1.25	.55

1997-98 Topps Chrome Topps 40

Randomly inserted into packs at a rate of one in 6, this 39-card set is a parallel of the regular Topps 40 set utilizing the Chrome technology. Card T-40 7 was not produced. Card backs are numbered with a "T40" prefix.

	MINT	NRMT
COMPLETE SET (39)	80.00	36.00
COMMON CARD (T1-T40)	.60	.35
SEMISTARS	.75	.35
UNLISTED STARS	1.25	.55
STATED ODDS 1:6		
COMP.REF.SET (39)	250.00	110.00

COMMON REF. (T1-T40)	2.00	.90
*REF: 1.25X TO 3X HI COLUMN		
REF: STATED ODDS 1:18		
T-40 PREFIX ON CARD NUMBERS		
CARD T-40 7 DOES NOT EXIST		

☐ T1 Glen Rice	1.25	.55
☐ T2 Patrick Ewing	1.25	.55
☐ T3 Terrell Brandon	1.25	.55
☐ T4 Jerry Stackhouse	1.25	.55
☐ T5 Michael Jordan	15.00	6.75
☐ T6 Christian Laettner	.75	.35
☐ T7 Reggie Miller	1.25	.55
☐ T8 Reggie Miller	1.25	.55
☐ T9 Gary Payton	2.00	.90
☐ T10 Detlef Schrempf	1.00	.45
☐ T11 Kevin Garnett	8.00	3.60
☐ T12 Eddie Jones	2.50	1.10
☐ T13 Clyde Drexler	1.50	.70
☐ T14 Anfernee Hardaway	5.00	2.20
☐ T15 Chris Webber	3.00	1.35
☐ T16 Jayson Williams	.75	.35
☐ T17 Joe Smith	1.25	.55
☐ T18 Karl Malone	2.00	.90
☐ T19 Tim Hardaway	1.50	.70
☐ T20 Vin Baker	2.50	1.10
☐ T21 Tom Gugliotta	1.25	.55
☐ T22 Allen Iverson	6.00	2.70
☐ T23 David Robinson	2.00	.90
☐ T24 D.Mutombo	.75	.35
☐ T25 John Stockton	1.25	.55
☐ T26 Charles Barkley	2.00	.90
☐ T27 Mitch Richmond	1.25	.55
☐ T28 Damon Stoudamire	2.50	1.10
☐ T29 Anthony Mason	.75	.35
☐ T30 Shaquille O'Neal	5.00	2.20
☐ T31 Glenn Robinson	1.25	.55
☐ T32 Juwan Howard	1.25	.55
☐ T33 Shawn Kemp	4.00	1.80
☐ T34 Dennis Rodman	5.00	2.20
☐ T35 Grant Hill	8.00	3.60
☐ T36 Kevin Johnson	.60	.25
☐ T37 Alonzo Mourning	1.25	.55
☐ T38 Hakeem Olajuwon	2.50	1.10
☐ T39 Joe Dumars	1.25	.55
☐ T40 Scottie Pippen	4.00	1.80

1995-96 Topps Gallery

The 1995-96 Topps Gallery set was issued in one series of 144 cards. The 8-card packs, offered exclusively to hobby outlets, retailed for $3.00 each. The set features the topical subsets: The Masters (1-18), The Modernists (19-36), New Editions (37-84) and The Classics (85-144). Each card is printed on 24-point stock, covered with an exclusive high-gloss film and etch stamped with one or more foils.

Rookie Cards of note in this set include Michael Finley, Kevin Garnett, Antonio McDyess, Jerry Stackhouse and Damon Stoudamire.

	MINT	NRMT
COMPLETE SET (144)	30.00	13.50
COMMON CARD (1-144)	.15	.07
SEMISTARS	.20	.09
UNLISTED STARS	.40	.18
COMP.PPI SET (126)	1300.00	575.00
COMMON PPI (19-144)	5.00	2.20
*PPI STARS: 25X TO 50X HI COLUMN		
*PPI RCs: 10X TO 20X HI		
PPI: STATED ODDS 1:12		
1-18 ISSUED IN 96/7 ST.CLUB 2		
HOB.PACKS		

☐ 1 Shaquille O'Neal	1.50	.70
☐ 2 Shawn Kemp	1.25	.55
☐ 3 Reggie Miller	.40	.18
☐ 4 Mitch Richmond	.40	.18
☐ 5 Grant Hill	2.50	1.10
☐ 6 Magic Johnson	1.25	.55
☐ 7 Vin Baker	.75	.35
☐ 8 Charles Barkley	.60	.25
☐ 9 Hakeem Olajuwon	.75	.35
☐ 10 Michael Jordan	6.00	2.70
☐ 11 Patrick Ewing	.40	.18
☐ 12 David Robinson	.60	.25
☐ 13 Alonzo Mourning	.40	.18
☐ 14 Karl Malone	.60	.25
☐ 15 Chris Webber	1.00	.45
☐ 16 Dikembe Mutombo	.20	.09
☐ 17 Larry Johnson	.20	.09
☐ 18 Jamal Mashburn	.20	.09
☐ 19 Anfernee Hardaway	1.50	.70
☐ 20 Bryant Stith	.15	.07
☐ 21 Juwan Howard	.60	.25
☐ 22 Jason Kidd	1.00	.45
☐ 23 Sharone Wright	.15	.07
☐ 24 Tom Gugliotta	.40	.18
☐ 25 Eric Montross	.15	.07
☐ 26 Allan Houston	.20	.09
☐ 27 Antonio Davis	.15	.07
☐ 28 Brian Grant	.20	.09
☐ 29 Terrell Brandon	.40	.18
☐ 30 Eddie Jones	1.00	.45
☐ 31 James Robinson	.15	.07
☐ 32 Wesley Person	.20	.09
☐ 33 Glenn Robinson	.50	.23
☐ 34 Donyell Marshall	.20	.09
☐ 35 Sam Cassell	.25	.11
☐ 36 Lamond Murray	.15	.07
☐ 37 Damon Stoudamire	3.00	1.35
☐ 38 Tyus Edney	.15	.07
☐ 39 Jerry Stackhouse	1.50	.70
☐ 40 Arvydas Sabonis	.75	.35
☐ 41 Kevin Garnett	5.00	2.20
☐ 42 Brent Barry	.40	.18
☐ 43 Alan Henderson	.40	.18
☐ 44 Bryant Reeves	1.00	.45
☐ 45 Shawn Respert	.15	.07
☐ 46 Michael Finley	1.50	.70

☐ 47 Gary Trent	.15	.07
☐ 48 Antonio McDyess	2.00	.90
☐ 49 George Zidek	.15	.07
☐ 50 Joe Smith	1.50	.70
☐ 51 Ed O'Bannon	.15	.07
☐ 52 Rasheed Wallace	1.00	.45
☐ 53 Eric Williams	.20	.09
☐ 54 Kurt Thomas	.20	.09
☐ 55 Mookie Blaylock	.20	.09
☐ 56 Robert Pack	.15	.07
☐ 57 Dana Barros	.15	.07
☐ 58 Eric Murdock	.15	.07
☐ 59 Glen Rice	.40	.18
☐ 60 John Stockton	.40	.18
☐ 61 Scottie Pippen	1.25	.55
☐ 62 Oliver Miller	.15	.07
☐ 63 Tyrone Hill	.15	.07
☐ 64 Gary Payton	.60	.25
☐ 65 Jim Jackson	.20	.09
☐ 66 Avery Johnson	.15	.07
☐ 67 Mahmoud Abdul-Rauf	.15	.07
☐ 68 Olden Polynice	.15	.07
☐ 69 Joe Dumars	.40	.18
☐ 70 Rod Strickland	.20	.09
☐ 71 Chris Mullin	.40	.18
☐ 72 Kevin Johnson	.20	.09
☐ 73 Derrick Coleman	.20	.09
☐ 74 Clyde Drexler	.50	.23
☐ 75 Dale Davis	.15	.07
☐ 76 Horace Grant	.20	.09
☐ 77 Loy Vaught	.15	.07
☐ 78 Armon Gilliam	.15	.07
☐ 79 Nick Van Exel	.40	.18
☐ 80 Charles Oakley	.15	.07
☐ 81 Kevin Willis	.15	.07
☐ 82 Sherman Douglas	.15	.07
☐ 83 Isaiah Rider	.20	.09
☐ 84 Steve Smith	.20	.09
☐ 85 Dee Brown	.15	.07
☐ 86 Dell Curry	.15	.07
☐ 87 Calbert Cheaney	.15	.07
☐ 88 Greg Anthony	.15	.07
☐ 89 Jeff Hornacek	.20	.09
☐ 90 Dennis Rodman	2.00	.90
☐ 91 Willie Anderson	.15	.07
☐ 92 Chris Mills	.15	.07
☐ 93 Hersey Hawkins	.20	.09
☐ 94 Popeye Jones	.15	.07
☐ 95 Chuck Person	.15	.07
☐ 96 Reggie Williams	.15	.07
☐ 97 A.C. Green	.20	.09
☐ 98 Otis Thorpe	.20	.09
☐ 99 Walt Williams	.15	.07
☐ 100 Latrell Sprewell	.20	.09
☐ 101 Buck Williams	.15	.07
☐ 102 Robert Horry	.15	.07
☐ 103 C.Weatherspoon	.15	.07
☐ 104 Dennis Scott	.15	.07
☐ 105 Rik Smits	.20	.09
☐ 106 Jayson Williams	.15	.09
☐ 107 Pooh Richardson	.15	.07
☐ 108 Anthony Mason	.20	.09
☐ 109 Cedric Ceballos	.15	.07
☐ 110 Billy Owens	.15	.07
☐ 111 Johnny Newman	.15	.07
☐ 112 Christian Laettner	.20	.09
☐ 113 Stacey Augmon	.15	.07
☐ 114 Chris Morris	.15	.07
☐ 115 Detlef Schrempf	.20	.09
☐ 116 Dino Radja	.15	.07
☐ 117 Sean Elliott	.15	.07
☐ 118 Muggsy Bogues	.20	.09
☐ 119 Toni Kukoc	.20	.09
☐ 120 Clifford Robinson	.15	.07
☐ 121 Bobby Hurley	.15	.07
☐ 122 Lorenzo Williams	.15	.07
☐ 123 Wayman Tisdale	.15	.07
☐ 124 Bobby Phills	.15	.07
☐ 125 Nick Anderson	.15	.07
☐ 126 LaPhonso Ellis	.20	.09
☐ 127 Scott Williams	.15	.07
☐ 128 Mark West	.15	.07
☐ 129 P.J. Brown	.15	.07
☐ 130 Tim Hardaway	.50	.23
☐ 131 Derek Harper	.20	.09
☐ 132 Mario Elie	.15	.07

☐ 133 Benoit Benjamin	.15	.07
☐ 134 Terry Porter	.15	.07
☐ 135 Derrick McKey	.15	.07
☐ 136 Bimbo Coles	.15	.07
☐ 137 John Salley	.15	.07
☐ 138 Malik Sealy	.15	.07
☐ 139 Byron Scott	.15	.07
☐ 140 Vlade Divac	.20	.09
☐ 141 Mark Price	.15	.07
☐ 142 Rony Seikaly	.15	.07
☐ 143 Mark Jackson	.20	.09
☐ 144 John Starks	.20	.09

1995-96 Topps Gallery Expressionists

Randomly inserted into 1 in every 24 packs, these inserts feature a collection of fifteen NBA team leaders. Each card attempts to capture the intensity and spirit of the featured player incorporating an embossed, textured, brush stroke effect.

	MINT	NRMT
COMPLETE SET (15)	110.00	50.00
COMMON CARD (EX1-EX15)	1.00	.45
SEMISTARS	2.00	.90
UNLISTED STARS	3.00	1.35
STATED ODDS 1:24		
☐ EX1 Shawn Kemp	10.00	4.50
☐ EX2 Michael Jordan	50.00	22.00
☐ EX3 Reggie Miller	3.00	1.35
☐ EX4 Kevin Willis	1.00	.45
☐ EX5 Jason Kidd	8.00	3.60
☐ EX6 Larry Johnson	2.00	.90
☐ EX7 Patrick Ewing	3.00	1.35
☐ EX8 Rasheed Wallace	4.00	1.80
☐ EX9 Karl Malone	5.00	2.20
☐ EX10 Shaquille O'Neal	12.00	5.50
☐ EX11 Joe Smith	6.00	2.70
☐ EX12 Jerry Stackhouse	6.00	2.70
☐ EX13 Glen Rice	3.00	1.35
☐ EX14 Clyde Drexler	4.00	1.80
☐ EX15 Grant Hill	20.00	9.00

1995-96 Topps Gallery Photo Gallery

Randomly inserted into 1 in every 30 packs, this seventeen card set features a selection of

premium quality photographs, chronicling classic moments from some of the NBA's biggest stars. Each card is custom-designed to compliment the photography. Multiple foils were also used on each card.

	MINT	NRMT
COMPLETE SET (17)	150.00	70.00
COMMON CARD (PG1-PG17)	2.50	1.10
SEMISTARS	3.00	1.35
STATED ODDS 1:30		
☐ PG1 Vin Baker	10.00	4.50
☐ PG2 Brian Grant	3.00	1.35
☐ PG3 George Zidek	2.50	1.10
☐ PG4 Hakeem Olajuwon	10.00	4.50
☐ PG5 Stacey Augmon	2.50	1.10
☐ PG6 Oliver Miller	2.50	1.10
☐ PG7 Kenny Gattison	2.50	1.10
☐ PG8 D.Mutombo	3.00	1.35
☐ PG9 Rony Seikaly	2.50	1.10
☐ PG10 Tom Gugliotta	3.00	1.35
☐ PG11 Scottie Pippen	15.00	6.75
☐ PG12 David Robinson	8.00	3.60
☐ PG13 A.Hardaway	20.00	9.00
☐ PG14 Dennis Rodman	20.00	9.00
☐ PG15 Kevin Garnett	30.00	13.50
☐ PG16 D.Stoudamire	20.00	9.00
☐ PG17 Charles Barkley	8.00	3.60

1996 Topps Stars

This set was created to commemorate the NBA's announcement of their top 50 players of all time. The set contained 150-cards and was issued in 8-card packs that carried a suggested retail price of $3.00. Each player had three cards - a Golden

Season card highlighting their best year and two versions of a Commemorative card, in which the card fronts were the same but one had an all-text back and the other featured all the career statistics showing how each player is among the NBA's top 50. Each player has three different cards, but only one card is priced below. All cards carry the same value. All the cards were full-bleed, double-foil stamped and printed on 20-point stock.

	MINT	NRMT
COMPLETE SET (150)	30.00	13.50
COMMON CARD (1-150)	.10	.05
CL (NNO)	.05	.02
SEMISTARS	.15	.07
UNLISTED STARS	.25	.11

*FINEST: 4X TO 8X HI COLUMN
FINEST: STATED ODDS 1:6
*FIN.REF: 15X TO 30X HI COLUMN
FIN.REF: STATED ODDS 1:20 HOB, 1:24 RET
*ATO.REF: 40X TO 80X HI COLUMN
ATO.REF: STATED ODDS 1:96
EACH PLAYER HAS THREE DIFF.CARDS
PRICES BELOW ARE FOR INDIVIDUAL CARDS

☐ 1 Kareem Abdul-Jabbar	.50	.23
☐ 2 Nate Archibald	.15	.07
☐ 3 Paul Arizin	.10	.05
☐ 4 Charles Barkley	.40	.18
☐ 5 Rick Barry	.25	.11
☐ 6 Elgin Baylor	.10	.05
☐ 7 Dave Bing	.10	.05
☐ 8 Larry Bird	1.00	.45
☐ 9 Wilt Chamberlain	.40	.45
☐ 10 Bob Cousy	.40	.18
☐ 11 Dave Cowens	.10	.05
☐ 12 Billy Cunningham	.10	.05
☐ 13 Dave DeBusschere	.10	.05
☐ 14 Clyde Drexler	.30	.14
☐ 16 Julius Erving	.60	.25
☐ 16 Patrick Ewing	.25	.11
☐ 17 Walt Frazier	.15	.07
☐ 18 George Gervin	.25	.11
☐ 19 Hal Greer	.10	.05
☐ 20 John Havlicek	.40	.18
☐ 21 Elvin Hayes	.25	.11
☐ 22 Magic Johnson	.75	.35
☐ 23 Sam Jones	.10	.05
☐ 24 Michael Jordan	3.00	1.35
☐ 25 Jerry Lucas	.10	.05
☐ 26 Karl Malone	.40	.18
☐ 27 Moses Malone	.25	.11
☐ 28 Pete Maravich	.50	.23
☐ 29 Kevin McHale	.15	.07
☐ 30 George Mikan	.75	.35
☐ 31 Earl Monroe	.25	.11
☐ 32 Shaquille O'Neal	1.00	.45
☐ 33 Hakeem Olajuwon	.50	.23
☐ 34 Robert Parish	.15	.07
☐ 35 Bob Pettit	.10	.05
☐ 36 Scottie Pippen	.60	.25
☐ 37 Willis Reed	.10	.05
☐ 38 Oscar Robertson	.50	.23
☐ 39 David Robinson	.30	.14
☐ 40 Bill Russell	1.00	.45
☐ 41 Dolph Schayes	.15	.07
☐ 42 Bill Sharman	.10	.05
☐ 43 John Stockton	.25	.11
☐ 44 Isiah Thomas	.25	.11
☐ 45 Nate Thurmond	.10	.05
☐ 46 Wes Unseld	.10	.05
☐ 47 Bill Walton	.25	.11
☐ 48 Jerry West	.75	.35
☐ 49 Lenny Wilkens	.15	.07
☐ 50 James Worthy	.25	.11

1996 Topps Stars Imagine

Randomly inserted into all packs at a rate of one in 18, this 25-card dual player set uses computer imagery to pit two players from different eras against one another. Card backs carry an "I" prefix.

	MINT	NRMT
COMPLETE SET (25)	125.00	55.00
COMMON PAIR (1-25)	3.00	1.35
STATED ODDS 1:18		

☐ I1 Shaquille O'Neal	12.00	5.50
Wilt Chamberlain		
☐ I2 David Robinson	5.00	2.20
Dave Cowens		
☐ I3 Kareem Abdul-Jabbar	10.00	4.50
Bill Russell		
☐ I4 Scottie Pippen	10.00	4.50
Julius Erving		
☐ I5 Hakeem Olajuwon	6.00	2.70
Elvin Hayes		
☐ I6 Michael Jordan	30.00	13.50
Oscar Robertson		
☐ I7 Clyde Drexler	5.00	2.20
Earl Monroe		
☐ I8 Magic Johnson	10.00	4.50
Jerry West		
☐ I9 Larry Bird	8.00	3.60
Rick Barry		
☐ I10 Kevin McHale	3.00	1.35
Dave DeBusschere		
☐ I11 Moses Malone	3.00	1.35
Jerry Lucas		
☐ I12 Robert Parish	3.00	1.35
Nate Thurmond		
☐ I13 Pete Maravich	5.00	2.20
Sam Jones		
☐ I14 John Stockton	6.00	2.70
Bob Cousy		
☐ I15 Isiah Thomas	3.00	1.35
Bill Sharman		
☐ I16 Karl Malone	6.00	2.70
Bob Pettit		
☐ I17 Bill Walton	6.00	2.70
George Mikan		
☐ I18 Patrick Ewing	4.00	1.80
Willis Reed		
☐ I19 Billy Cunningham	3.00	1.35
James Worthy		
☐ I20 George Gervin	3.00	1.35
Hal Greer		
☐ I21 Wes Unseld	3.00	1.35
Dolph Schayes		
☐ I22 Nate Archibald	3.00	1.35
Lenny Wilkens		
☐ I23 Walt Frazier	3.00	1.35
Paul Arizin		
☐ I24 Charles Barkley	6.00	2.70
Elgin Baylor		
☐ I25 Dave Bing	6.00	2.70
John Havlicek		

1996 Topps Stars Reprints

Randomly inserted into hobby packs at a rate of one in 9 and retail at one in 6, this 50-card set features reprints of each player's first Topps, Bowman or Star Company cards.

	MINT	NRMT
COMPLETE SET (50)	300.00	135.00
COMMON CARD (1-50)	2.00	.90
SEMISTARS	3.00	1.35
UNLISTED STARS	4.00	1.80
STATED ODDS 1:9 HOBBY, 1:6 RETAIL		

☐ 1 Lew Alcindor	12.00	5.50
☐ 2 Nate Archibald	3.00	1.35
☐ 3 Paul Arizin	2.00	.90
☐ 4 Charles Barkley	10.00	4.50
☐ 5 Rick Barry	3.00	1.35
☐ 6 Elgin Baylor	2.00	.90
☐ 7 Dave Bing	2.00	.90
☐ 8 Larry Bird	25.00	11.00
Julius Erving		
Magic Johnson		
☐ 9 Wilt Chamberlain	12.00	5.50
☐ 10 Bob Cousy	8.00	3.60
☐ 11 Dave Cowens	2.00	.90
☐ 12 Billy Cunningham	2.00	.90
☐ 13 Dave DeBusschere	2.00	.90
☐ 14 Clyde Drexler	6.00	2.70
☐ 15 Julius Erving	12.00	5.50
☐ 16 Patrick Ewing	6.00	2.70
☐ 17 Walt Frazier	3.00	1.35
☐ 18 George Gervin	3.00	1.35
☐ 19 Hal Greer	2.00	.90
☐ 20 John Havlicek	8.00	3.60
☐ 21 Elvin Hayes	3.00	1.35
☐ 22 Larry Bird	25.00	11.00
Julius Erving		
Magic Johnson		
☐ 23 Sam Jones	2.00	.90
☐ 24 Michael Jordan	40.00	18.00
☐ 25 Jerry Lucas	2.00	.90
☐ 26 Karl Malone	6.00	2.70
☐ 27 Moses Malone	4.00	1.80
☐ 28 Pete Maravich	8.00	3.60
☐ 29 Kevin McHale	3.00	1.35
☐ 30 George Mikan	8.00	3.60
☐ 31 Earl Monroe	2.00	.90
☐ 32 Shaquille O'Neal	8.00	3.60
☐ 33 Hakeem Olajuwon	10.00	4.50
☐ 34 Robert Parish	3.00	1.35
☐ 35 Bob Pettit	2.00	.90
☐ 36 Scottie Pippen	10.00	4.50
☐ 37 Willis Reed	2.00	.90
☐ 38 Oscar Robertson	8.00	3.60
☐ 39 David Robinson	6.00	2.70
☐ 40 Bill Russell	12.00	5.50

			MINT	NRMT
☐ 41	Dolph Schayes	3.00		1.35
☐ 42	Bill Sharman	2.00		.90
☐ 43	John Stockton	6.00		2.70
☐ 44	Isiah Thomas	4.00		1.80
☐ 45	Nate Thurmond	2.00		.90
☐ 46	Wes Unseld	2.00		.90
☐ 47	Bill Walton	3.00		1.35
☐ 48	Jerry West	10.00		4.50
☐ 49	Len Wilkens UER	2.00		.90
☐ 50	James Worthy	4.00		1.80

1996 Topps Stars Reprint Autographs

Inserted one per retail box, 10 of the 50 players from the Topps NBA Stars signed their reprint cards. Each card has a gold seal of authenticity and is signed on the front of the card in black ink. The set is skip-numbered. In addition, one of the ten cards were inserted into 1996-97 Topps Factory Hobby sets.

	MINT	NRMT
COMPLETE SET (10)	200.00	90.00
COMMON CARD	15.00	6.75

SKIP-NUMBERED SET
ONE PER SPECIAL RETAIL BOX
ONE PER 96/7 TOPPS FACT.HOB.SET

☐ 2	Nate Archibald	20.00	9.00
☐ 5	Rick Barry	25.00	11.00
☐ 17	Walt Frazier	25.00	11.00
☐ 18	George Gervin	25.00	11.00
☐ 21	Elvin Hayes	25.00	11.00
☐ 23	Sam Jones	15.00	6.75
☐ 30	George Mikan	80.00	36.00
☐ 31	Earl Monroe	20.00	9.00
☐ 37	Willis Reed	20.00	9.00
☐ 47	Bill Walton	25.00	11.00

1992-93 Ultra

The complete premier 1992-93 Ultra basketball set (made by Fleer) consists of 375 standard-size cards. The set was released in two series of 200 and 175 cards, respectively. Both series packs contained 14 cards each with 36 packs to a box. Suggested retail pack price was $1.79. The glossy color action player photos on the fronts are full-bleed except at the bottom where a diagonal

gold-foil stripe edges a pale green variegated border. The player's name and team appear on two team color-coded bars that overlay the bottom border. The horizontal backs display action and close-up cut-out player photos against a basketball court background. The team logo and biographical information appear in a pale green bar like that on the front that edges the right side, while the player's name and statistics are given in bars running across the card bottom. The cards are numbered on the back and grouped alphabetically within team order. The first series closes with an NBA Draft Picks subset (193-198) and both series close with checklists (199-200/373-375). The second series contains more than 40 rookies, 30 trade cards, free agent signings, and other veterans omitted from the first series. The second series opens with an NBA Jam Session (201-220) subset. Three players from this Jam Session subset, Duane Causwell, Pervis Ellison, and Stacey Augmon, autographed a total of more than 2,500 cards that were randomly inserted in second series foil packs. These cards were embossed with Fleer logos for authenticity. On each series two pack, a mail-in offer provided the opportunity to acquire two more exclusive Jam Session cards, showing all 20 players in the set, for ten wrappers and $1.00 for postage and handling. According to Fleer, they anticipated about 100,000 requests. Key Rookie Cards include Tom Gugliotta, Robert Horry, Christian Laettner, Alonzo Mourning, Shaquille O'Neal, Latrell Sprewell and Clarence Weatherspoon.

		MINT	NRMT
COMPLETE SET (375)		30.00	13.50
COMPLETE SERIES 1 (200)		15.00	6.75
COMPLETE SERIES 2 (175)		15.00	6.75
COMMON CARD (1-200)		.10	.05
COMMON CARD (201-375)		.05	.02
SEMISTARS SER.1		.25	.11
SEMISTARS SER.2		.15	.07
UNLISTED STARS SER.1		.50	.23
UNLISTED STARS SER.2		.30	.14

☐ 1	Stacey Augmon	.25	.11
☐ 2	Duane Ferrell	.10	.05
☐ 3	Paul Graham	.10	.05
☐ 4	Blair Rasmussen	.10	.05
☐ 5	Rumeal Robinson	.10	.05
☐ 6	Dominique Wilkins	.50	.23
☐ 7	Kevin Willis	.10	.05
☐ 8	John Bagley	.10	.05
☐ 9	Dee Brown	.10	.05
☐ 10	Rick Fox	.25	.11
☐ 11	Kevin Gamble	.10	.05
☐ 12	Joe Kleine	.10	.05
☐ 13	Reggie Lewis	.25	.11
☐ 14	Kevin McHale	.50	.23
☐ 15	Robert Parish	.25	.11
☐ 16	Ed Pinckney	.10	.05
☐ 17	Muggsy Bogues	.25	.11
☐ 18	Dell Curry	.10	.05
☐ 19	Kenny Gattison	.10	.05
☐ 20	Kendall Gill	.25	.11
☐ 21	Larry Johnson	.60	.25
☐ 22	Johnny Newman	.10	.05
☐ 23	J.R. Reid	.10	.05
☐ 24	B.J. Armstrong	.10	.05
☐ 25	Bill Cartwright	.10	.05
☐ 26	Horace Grant	.25	.11
☐ 27	Michael Jordan	6.00	2.70
☐ 28	Stacey King	.10	.05
☐ 29	John Paxson	.25	.11
☐ 30	Will Perdue	.10	.05
☐ 31	Scottie Pippen	1.50	.70
☐ 32	Scott Williams	.10	.05
☐ 33	John Battle	.10	.05
☐ 34	Terrell Brandon	.75	.35
☐ 35	Brad Daugherty	.10	.05
☐ 36	Craig Ehlo	.10	.05
☐ 37	Larry Nance	.25	.11
☐ 38	Mark Price	.10	.05
☐ 39	Mike Sanders	.10	.05
☐ 40	John Williams	.10	.05
☐ 41	Terry Davis	.10	.05
☐ 42	Derek Harper	.25	.11
☐ 43	Donald Hodge	.10	.05
☐ 44	Mike Iuzzolino	.10	.05
☐ 45	Fat Lever	.10	.05
☐ 46	Doug Smith	.10	.05
☐ 47	Randy White	.10	.05
☐ 48	Winston Garland	.10	.05
☐ 49	Chris Jackson	.10	.05
☐ 50	Marcus Liberty	.10	.05
☐ 51	Todd Lichti	.10	.05
☐ 52	Mark Macon	.10	.05
☐ 53	Dikembe Mutombo	.50	.23
☐ 54	Reggie Williams	.10	.05
☐ 55	Mark Aguirre	.10	.05
☐ 56	Joe Dumars	.50	.23
☐ 57	Bill Laimbeer	.25	.11
☐ 58	Dennis Rodman	2.00	.90
☐ 59	Isiah Thomas	.50	.23
☐ 60	Darrell Walker	.10	.05
☐ 61	Orlando Woolridge	.10	.05
☐ 62	Victor Alexander	.10	.05
☐ 63	Chris Gatling	.10	.05
☐ 64	Tim Hardaway	.75	.35
☐ 65	Tyrone Hill	.10	.05
☐ 66	Sarunas Marciulionis	.10	.05
☐ 67	Chris Mullin	.50	.23
☐ 68	Billy Owens	.25	.11
☐ 69	Sleepy Floyd	.10	.05
☐ 70	Avery Johnson	.10	.05
☐ 71	Vernon Maxwell	.10	.05
☐ 72	Hakeem Olajuwon	1.00	.45
☐ 73	Kenny Smith	.10	.05
☐ 74	Otis Thorpe	.25	.11
☐ 75	Dale Davis	.10	.05

#	Name		
76	Vern Fleming	.10	.05
77	George McCloud	.10	.05
78	Reggie Miller	.50	.23
79	Detlef Schrempf	.25	.11
80	Rik Smits	.25	.11
81	LaSalle Thompson	.10	.05
82	Gary Grant	.10	.05
83	Ron Harper	.25	.11
84	Mark Jackson	.10	.05
85	Danny Manning	.25	.11
86	Ken Norman	.10	.05
87	Stanley Roberts	.10	.05
88	Loy Vaught	.25	.11
89	Elden Campbell	.25	.11
90	Vlade Divac	.25	.11
91	A.C. Green	.25	.11
92	Sam Perkins	.25	.11
93	Byron Scott	.25	.11
94	Tony Smith	.10	.05
95	Sedale Threatt	.10	.05
96	James Worthy	.50	.23
97	Willie Burton	.10	.05
98	Bimbo Coles	.10	.05
99	Kevin Edwards	.10	.05
100	Grant Long	.10	.05
101	Glen Rice	.60	.25
102	Rony Seikaly	.10	.05
103	Brian Shaw	.10	.05
104	Steve Smith	.50	.23
105	Frank Brickowski	.10	.05
106	Moses Malone	.50	.23
107	Fred Roberts	.10	.05
108	Alvin Robertson	.10	.05
109	Thurl Bailey	.10	.05
110	Gerald Glass	.10	.05
111	Luc Longley	.10	.05
112	Felton Spencer	.10	.05
113	Doug West	.10	.05
114	Kenny Anderson	.50	.23
115	Mookie Blaylock	.25	.11
116	Sam Bowie	.10	.05
117	Derrick Coleman	.25	.11
118	Chris Dudley	.10	.05
119	Chris Morris	.10	.05
120	Drazen Petrovic	.10	.05
121	Greg Anthony	.10	.05
122	Patrick Ewing	.50	.23
123	Anthony Mason	.25	.11
124	Charles Oakley	.25	.11
125	Doc Rivers	.10	.05
126	Charles Smith	.10	.05
127	John Starks	.25	.11
128	Nick Anderson	.25	.11
129	Anthony Bowie	.10	.05
130	Terry Catledge	.10	.05
131	Jerry Reynolds	.10	.05
132	Dennis Scott	.10	.05
133	Scott Skiles	.10	.05
134	Brian Williams	.25	.11
135	Ron Anderson	.10	.05
136	Manute Bol	.10	.05
137	Johnny Dawkins	.10	.05
138	Armon Gilliam	.10	.05
139	Hersey Hawkins	.25	.11
140	Jeff Ruland	.10	.05
141	Charles Shackleford	.10	.05
142	Cedric Ceballos	.25	.11
143	Tom Chambers	.10	.05
144	Kevin Johnson	.50	.23
145	Negele Knight	.10	.05
146	Dan Majerle	.25	.11
147	Mark West	.10	.05
148	Mark Bryant	.10	.05
149	Clyde Drexler	.60	.25
150	Kevin Duckworth	.10	.05
151	Jerome Kersey	.10	.05
152	Robert Pack	.10	.05
153	Terry Porter	.10	.05
154	Clifford Robinson	.25	.11
155	Buck Williams	.25	.11
156	Anthony Bonner	.10	.05
157	Duane Causwell	.10	.05
158	Mitch Richmond	.50	.23
159	Lionel Simmons	.10	.05
160	Wayman Tisdale	.10	.05
161	Spud Webb	.25	.11
162	Willie Anderson	.10	.05
163	Antoine Carr	.10	.05
164	Terry Cummings	.25	.11
165	Sean Elliott	.25	.11
166	Sidney Green	.10	.05
167	David Robinson	.75	.35
168	Dana Barros	.10	.05
169	Benoit Benjamin	.10	.05
170	Michael Cage	.10	.05
171	Eddie Johnson	.10	.05
172	Shawn Kemp	2.00	.90
173	Derrick McKey	.10	.05
174	Nate McMillan	.10	.05
175	Gary Payton	1.00	.45
176	Ricky Pierce	.10	.05
177	David Benoit	.10	.05
178	Mike Brown	.10	.05
179	Tyrone Corbin	.10	.05
180	Mark Eaton	.10	.05
181	Jeff Malone	.10	.05
182	Karl Malone	.75	.35
183	John Stockton	.50	.23
184	Michael Adams	.10	.05
185	Ledell Eackles	.10	.05
186	Pervis Ellison	.10	.05
187	A.J. English	.10	.05
188	Harvey Grant	.10	.05
189	Buck Johnson	.10	.05
190	LaBradford Smith	.10	.05
191	Larry Stewart	.10	.05
192	David Wingate	.10	.05
193	Alonzo Mourning	2.50	1.10
194	Adam Keefe	.10	.05
195	Robert Horry	.25	.11
196	Anthony Peeler	.25	.11
197	Tracy Murray	.25	.11
198	Dave Johnson	.10	.05
199	Checklist 1-104	.10	.05
200	Checklist 105-200	.10	.05
201	David Robinson JS	.30	.14
202	D.Mutombo JS	.30	.14
203	Otis Thorpe JS	.05	.02
204	Hakeem Olajuwon JS	.30	.14
205	Shawn Kemp JS	.60	.25
206	Charles Barkley JS	.30	.14
207	Pervis Ellison JS	.05	.02
208	Chris Morris JS	.05	.02
209	Brad Daugherty JS	.05	.02
210	Derrick Coleman JS	.05	.02
211	Tim Perry JS	.05	.02
212	Duane Causwell JS	.05	.02
213	Scottie Pippen JS	.50	.23
214	Robert Parish JS	.05	.02
215	Stacey Augmon JS	.05	.02
216	Michael Jordan JS	2.00	.90
217	Karl Malone JS	.30	.14
218	John Williams JS	.05	.02
219	Horace Grant JS	.05	.02
220	Orlando Woolridge JS	.05	.02
221	Mookie Blaylock	.15	.07
222	Greg Foster	.05	.02
223	Steve Henson	.05	.02
224	Adam Keefe	.05	.02
225	Jon Koncak	.05	.02
226	Travis Mays	.05	.02
227	Alaa Abdelnaby	.05	.02
228	Sherman Douglas	.05	.02
229	Xavier McDaniel	.05	.02
230	Marcus Webb	.05	.02
231	Tony Bennett	.05	.02
232	Mike Gminski	.05	.02
233	Kevin Lynch	.05	.02
234	Alonzo Mourning	.75	.35
235	David Wingate	.05	.02
236	Rodney McCray	.05	.02
237	Trent Tucker	.05	.02
238	Corey Williams	.05	.02
239	Danny Ferry	.05	.02
240	Jay Guidinger	.05	.02
241	Jerome Lane	.05	.02
242	Bobby Phills	.30	.14
243	Gerald Wilkins	.05	.02
244	Walter Bond	.05	.02
245	Dexter Cambridge	.05	.02
246	Radisav Curcic UER	.05	.02
	(Misspelled Radislav		
	on card front)		
247	Brian Howard	.05	.02
248	Tracy Moore	.05	.02
249	Sean Rooks	.05	.02
250	Kevin Brooks	.05	.02
251	LaPhonso Ellis	.50	.23
252	Scott Hastings	.05	.02
253	Robert Pack	.05	.02
254	Gary Plummer	.05	.02
255	Bryant Stith	.15	.07
256	Robert Werdann	.05	.02
257	Gerald Glass	.05	.02
258	Terry Mills	.15	.07
259	Olden Polynice	.05	.02
260	Danny Young	.05	.02
261	Jud Buechler	.05	.02
262	Jeff Grayer	.05	.02
263	Bryon Houston	.05	.02
264	Keith Jennings	.05	.02
265	Ed Nealy	.05	.02
266	Latrell Sprewell	1.00	.45
267	Scott Brooks	.05	.02
268	Matt Bullard	.05	.02
269	Winston Garland	.05	.02
270	Carl Herrera	.05	.02
271	Robert Horry	.30	.14
272	Tree Rollins	.05	.02
273	Greg Dreiling	.05	.02
274	Sean Green	.05	.02
275	Sam Mitchell	.05	.02
276	Pooh Richardson	.05	.02
277	Malik Sealy	.15	.07
278	Kenny Williams	.05	.02
279	Mark Jackson	.15	.07
280	Stanley Roberts	.05	.02
281	Elmore Spencer	.05	.02
282	Kiki Vandeweghe	.05	.02
283	John S. Williams	.05	.02
284	Randy Woods	.05	.02
285	Alex Blackwell	.05	.02
286	Duane Cooper	.05	.02
287	James Edwards	.05	.02
288	Jack Haley	.05	.02
289	Anthony Peeler	.15	.07
290	Keith Askins	.05	.02
291	Matt Geiger	.15	.07
292	Alec Kessler	.05	.02
293	Harold Miner	.15	.07
294	John Salley	.05	.02
295	Anthony Avent	.05	.02
296	Jon Barry	.05	.02
297	Todd Day	.15	.07
298	Blue Edwards	.05	.02
299	Brad Lohaus	.05	.02
300	Lee Mayberry	.05	.02
301	Eric Murdock	.05	.02
302	Dan Schayes	.05	.02
303	Lance Blanks	.05	.02
304	Christian Laettner	.75	.35
305	Marlon Maxey	.05	.02
306	Bob McCann	.05	.02
307	Chuck Person	.05	.02
308	Brad Sellers	.05	.02
309	Chris Smith	.05	.02
310	Gundars Vetra	.05	.02
311	Micheal Williams	.05	.02
312	Rafael Addison	.05	.02
313	Chucky Brown	.05	.02
314	Maurice Cheeks	.05	.02
315	Tate George	.05	.02
316	Rick Mahorn	.05	.02
317	Rumeal Robinson	.05	.02
318	Eric Anderson	.05	.02
319	Rolando Blackman	.05	.02
320	Tony Campbell	.05	.02
321	Hubert Davis	.15	.07
322	Doc Rivers	.15	.07
323	Charles Smith	.05	.02
324	Herb Williams	.05	.02
325	Litterial Green	.05	.02
326	Steve Kerr	.15	.07
327	Greg Kite	.05	.02
328	Shaquille O'Neal	5.00	2.20
329	Tom Tolbert	.05	.02
330	Jeff Turner	.05	.02
331	Greg Grant	.05	.02

	MINT	NRMT
☐ 332 Jeff Hornacek	.15	.07
☐ 333 Andrew Lang	.05	.02
☐ 334 Tim Perry	.05	.02
☐ 335 C.Weatherspoon	.30	.14
☐ 336 Danny Ainge	.15	.07
☐ 337 Charles Barkley	.50	.23
☐ 338 Richard Dumas	.05	.02
☐ 339 Frank Johnson	.05	.02
☐ 340 Tim Kempton	.05	.02
☐ 341 Oliver Miller	.15	.07
☐ 342 Jerrod Mustaf	.05	.02
☐ 343 Mario Elie	.15	.07
☐ 344 Dave Johnson	.05	.02
☐ 345 Tracy Murray	.15	.07
☐ 346 Rod Strickland	.15	.07
☐ 347 Randy Brown	.05	.02
☐ 348 Pete Chilcutt	.05	.02
☐ 349 Marty Conlon	.05	.02
☐ 350 Jim Les	.05	.02
☐ 351 Kurt Rambis	.05	.02
☐ 352 Walt Williams	.30	.14
☐ 353 Lloyd Daniels	.05	.02
☐ 354 Vinny Del Negro	.05	.02
☐ 355 Dale Ellis	.05	.02
☐ 356 Avery Johnson	.05	.02
☐ 357 Sam Mack	.05	.02
☐ 358 J.R. Reid	.05	.02
☐ 359 David Wood	.05	.02
☐ 360 Vincent Askew	.05	.02
☐ 361 Isaac Austin	.15	.07
☐ 362 John Crotty	.05	.02
☐ 363 Stephen Howard	.05	.02
☐ 364 Jay Humphries	.05	.02
☐ 365 Larry Krystkowiak	.05	.02
☐ 366 Rex Chapman	.05	.02
☐ 367 Tom Gugliotta	1.00	.45
☐ 368 Buck Johnson	.05	.02
☐ 369 Charles Jones	.05	.02
☐ 370 Don MacLean	.05	.02
☐ 371 Doug Overton	.05	.02
☐ 372 Brent Price	.15	.07
☐ 373 Checklist 201-266	.05	.02
☐ 374 Checklist 267-330	.05	.02
☐ 375 Checklist 331-375	.05	.02
☐ JS207 Pervis Ellison AU	20.00	9.00
(Certified Autograph)		
☐ JS212 Duane Causwell AU	15.00	6.75
(Certified Autograph)		
☐ JS215 Stacey Augmon AU	30.00	13.50
(Certified Autograph)		
☐ NNO JS Rank 1-10	2.50	1.10
David Robinson		
Dikembe Mutombo		
Otis Thorpe		
Hakeem Olajuwon		
Shawn Kemp		
Charles Barkley		
Pervis Ellison		
Chris Morris		
Brad Daugherty		
Derrick Coleman		
☐ NNO JS Rank 11-20	2.50	1.10
Tim Perry		
Duane Causwell		
Scottie Pippen		
Robert Parish		
Stacey Augmon		
Michael Jordan		
Karl Malone		
John Williams		
Horace Grant		
Orlando Woolridge		

1992-93 Ultra All-NBA

This set features 15 standard-size cards, one for each All-NBA first, second, and third-team player. The cards were randomly inserted into approximately one out of every 14 first series

foil packs. The fronts feature color action player photos which are full-bleed except at the bottom, where a gold foil stripe separates a marbleized diagonal bottom border. A crest showing which All-NBA team the player was on overlaps the border and picture. The player's name is gold-foil stamped at the bottom. The horizontal backs carry a cut-out player close-up and career highlights on a marbleized background.

	MINT	NRMT
COMPLETE SET (15)	40.00	18.00
COMMON CARD (1-15)	.40	.18
SEMISTARS	.75	.35
UNLISTED STARS	2.00	.90
SER.1 STATED ODDS 1:14		
☐ 1 Karl Malone	3.00	1.35
☐ 2 Chris Mullin	2.00	.90
☐ 3 David Robinson	3.00	1.35
☐ 4 Michael Jordan	25.00	11.00
☐ 5 Clyde Drexler	2.50	1.10
☐ 6 Scottie Pippen	6.00	2.70
☐ 7 Charles Barkley	3.00	1.35
☐ 8 Patrick Ewing	2.00	.90
☐ 9 Tim Hardaway	3.00	1.35
☐ 10 John Stockton	2.00	.90
☐ 11 Dennis Rodman	8.00	3.60
☐ 12 Kevin Willis	.75	.35
☐ 13 Brad Daugherty	.40	.18
☐ 14 Mark Price	.40	.18
☐ 15 Kevin Johnson	2.00	.90

1992-93 Ultra All-Rookies

Randomly inserted in second series foil packs at a reported

rate of approximately one card per nine packs, this ten-card standard-size set focuses on the 1992-93 class of outstanding rookies. A color action shot on the front has been cut out and superimposed on grid of identical close-up shots of the player, which resemble the effect produced by a wall of TV sets displaying the same image. The "All-Rookie" logo and the player's name are gold-foil stamped across the bottom of the picture. On the backs, a wheat-colored panel carrying a player profile overlays a second full-bleed color action photo. The set is sequenced in alphabetical order.

	MINT	NRMT
COMPLETE SET (10)	20.00	9.00
COMMON CARD (1-10)	.25	.11
SEMISTARS	.75	.35
UNLISTED STARS	1.25	.55
SER.2 STATED ODDS 1:13		
☐ 1 LaPhonso Ellis	1.25	.55
☐ 2 Tom Gugliotta	2.50	1.10
☐ 3 Robert Horry	1.25	.55
☐ 4 Christian Laettner	2.00	.90
☐ 5 Harold Miner	.25	.11
☐ 6 Alonzo Mourning	4.00	1.80
☐ 7 Shaquille O'Neal	12.00	5.50
☐ 8 Latrell Sprewell	2.50	1.10
☐ 9 C.Weatherspoon	.75	.35
☐ 10 Walt Williams	.75	.35

1992-93 Ultra Award Winners

This five-card standard-size Ultra Award Winners insert set spotlights the 1991-92 MVP, Rookie of the Year, Defensive Player of the Year, top "6th Man" and Most Improved Player. These cards were randomly inserted into first series packs at a rate of one card in every 42 packs according to information printed on the wrappers. Card fronts feature an action photo with the player's name and Award Winners logo at the bottom. Backs have career highlights and a photo.

	MINT	NRMT
COMPLETE SET (5)	25.00	11.00
COMMON CARD (1-5)	1.00	.45
SEMISTARS	1.25	.55
UNLISTED STARS	1.50	.70
SER.1 STATED ODDS 1:42		
☐ 1 Michael Jordan	25.00	11.00
☐ 2 David Robinson	3.00	1.35
☐ 3 Larry Johnson	1.50	.70
☐ 4 Detlef Schrempf	1.25	.55
☐ 5 Pervis Ellison	1.00	.45

1992-93 Ultra Scottie Pippen

This 12-card standard-size "Career Highlights" set chronicles Scottie Pippen's rise to NBA stardom. The cards were inserted at a rate of one card per 21 first series packs according to information printed on the wrappers. Pippen autographed more than 2,000 of these cards for random insertion in first series packs. These autograph cards have embossed Fleer logos for authenticity. Through a special mail-in offer only, two additional Pippen cards were made available to collectors who sent in ten wrappers and $1.00 for postage and handling. On the front, the cards feature color action player photos with brownish-green marbleized borders. The player's name and the words "Career Highlights" are stamped in gold foil below the picture. On the same marbleized background, the backs carry a color head shot as well as biography and career summary.

	MINT	NRMT
COMPLETE SET (10)	15.00	6.75
COMMON PIPPEN (1-10)	1.50	.70
SER.1 STATED ODDS 1:21		
PIPPEN AU: SER.1 STATED ODDS 1:9,000		
COMMON SEND-OFF (11-12) 1.50		.70
TWO CARDS PER 10 SER.1 WRAPPERS		

☐ 1 Scottie Pippen	1.50		.70
(Dribbling, right index finger pointing down)			
☐ 2 Scottie Pippen	1.50		
(Dribbling, Magnavox ad in background)			
☐ 3 Scottie Pippen	1.50		.70
(Preparing to dunk)			
☐ 4 Scottie Pippen	1.50		.70
(Dribbling, defender's hand reaching in)			
☐ 5 Scottie Pippen	1.50		.70
(In air, ball in both hands, vs. Bucks)			
☐ 6 Scottie Pippen	1.50		.70
(Driving toward basket, vs. Nuggets)			
☐ 7 Scottie Pippen	1.50		.70
(Shooting over McDaniel of the Knicks)			
☐ 8 Scottie Pippen	1.50		.70
(Dribbling, Laker cheerleader in background)			
☐ 9 Scottie Pippen	1.50		.70
(Defending against McDaniel of the Knicks)			
☐ 10 Scottie Pippen	1.50		.70
(Driving toward basket, vs. Nets)			
☐ 11 Scottie Pippen	1.50		.70
(Defended by Rodman; ball in left hand)			
☐ 12 Scottie Pippen	1.50		.70
(Dunking over Nugget player)			
☐ AU Scottie Pippen	250.00		110.00
(Certified autograph)			

1992-93 Ultra Playmakers

Randomly inserted in second series foil packs at a reported rate of one card per 13 packs, this ten-card standard-size set features the NBA's top point guards. The glossy color action photos on the fronts are full-bleed except at the bottom where a lavender stripe edges the picture. The "Playmaker" logo and the player's name are gold-foil stamped across the bottom of the picture. On the backs, a wheat-colored panel carrying a player profile overlays a second full-bleed color action photo. The cards are numbered in the lower left corner of the panel.

	MINT	NRMT
COMPLETE SET (10)	4.00	1.80
COMMON CARD (1-10)	.25	.11
SEMISTARS	.50	.23
UNLISTED STARS	1.50	.70
SER.2 STATED ODDS 1:13		
☐ 1 Kenny Anderson	1.50	.70
☐ 2 Muggsy Bogues	.50	.23
☐ 3 Tim Hardaway	2.50	1.10
☐ 4 Mark Jackson	.50	.23
☐ 5 Kevin Johnson	1.50	.70
☐ 6 Mark Price	.25	.11
☐ 7 Terry Porter	.25	.11
☐ 8 Scott Skiles	.25	.11
☐ 9 John Stockton	1.50	.70
☐ 10 Isiah Thomas	1.50	.70

1992-93 Ultra Rejectors

Randomly inserted in second series foil packs at a reported rate of one in 26, this five-card standard-size set showcases defensive big men who are aptly dubbed "Rejectors." The glossy color action photos on the fronts are full-bleed except at the bottom where a gold stripe edges the picture. The player's name and the "Rejector" logo are gold-foil stamped across the bottom of the picture. On a black panel inside gold borders, the horizontal backs carry text describing the player's defensive accomplishments and a color close-up photo. The set is sequenced in alphabetical order.

	MINT	NRMT
COMPLETE SET (5)	12.00	5.50
COMMON CARD (1-5)	.50	.23
SER.2 STATED ODDS 1:26		
☐ 1 Alonzo Mourning	2.50	1.10
☐ 2 Dikembe Mutombo	.50	.23
☐ 3 Hakeem Olajuwon	1.50	.70
☐ 4 Shaquille O'Neal	8.00	3.60
☐ 5 David Robinson	1.25	.55

1993-94 Ultra

The complete 1993-94 Ultra basketball set consists of 375 standard-size cards that were issued in series of 200 and 175

respectively. Cards were issued in 14 and 19-card packs. There are 36 packs per box. The glossy color action player photos on the fronts are full-bleed except at the bottom. The bottom of the front consists of player name, team name and a peach colored border. The horizontal backs feature a player photos against a basketball court background. The team logo and biographical information appear a pale peach bar, while the player's name and statistics are printed in team color-coded bars running across the card bottom. The cards are alphabetically arranged by team and are numbered alphabetically within team order. A USA Basketball subset contains cards 361-372. Ten second series wrappers and $1.50 could be redeemed for USA cards of Reggie Miller (M1), Shaquille O'Neal (M2) and a team photo (M3). The offer was good through June 10, 1994. These cards are not considered part of the basic set. Rookie Cards of note in this set include Vin Baker, Anfernee Hardaway, Allan Houston, Toni Kukoc, Jamal Mashburn, Nick Van Exel and Chris Webber.

	MINT	NRMT
COMPLETE SET (375)	30.00	13.50
COMPLETE SERIES 1 (200)	15.00	6.75
COMPLETE SERIES 2 (175)	15.00	6.75
COMMON CARD (1-375)	.05	.02
SEMISTARS	.15	.07
UNLISTED STARS	.30	.14

☐ 1 Stacey Augmon	.05	.02
☐ 2 Mookie Blaylock	.15	.07
☐ 3 Doug Edwards	.05	.02
☐ 4 Duane Ferrell	.05	.02
☐ 5 Paul Graham	.05	.02
☐ 6 Adam Keefe	.05	.02
☐ 7 Dominique Wilkins	.30	.14
☐ 8 Kevin Willis	.05	.02
☐ 9 Alaa Abdelnaby	.05	.02
☐ 10 Dee Brown	.05	.02
☐ 11 Sherman Douglas	.05	.02
☐ 12 Rick Fox	.05	.02
☐ 13 Kevin Gamble	.05	.02
☐ 14 Xavier McDaniel	.05	.02
☐ 15 Robert Parish	.15	.07
☐ 16 Muggsy Bogues	.15	.07
☐ 17 Scott Burrell	.30	.14
☐ 18 Dell Curry	.05	.02
☐ 19 Kenny Gattison	.05	.02
☐ 20 Hersey Hawkins	.15	.07
☐ 21 Eddie Johnson	.05	.02
☐ 22 Larry Johnson	.30	.14
☐ 23 Alonzo Mourning	.50	.23
☐ 24 Johnny Newman	.05	.02
☐ 25 David Wingate	.05	.02
☐ 26 B.J. Armstrong	.05	.02
☐ 27 Corie Blount	.05	.02
☐ 28 Bill Cartwright	.05	.02
☐ 29 Horace Grant	.15	.07
☐ 30 Michael Jordan	4.00	1.80
☐ 31 Stacey King	.05	.02
☐ 32 John Paxson	.05	.02
☐ 33 Will Perdue	.05	.02
☐ 34 Scottie Pippen	1.00	.45
☐ 35 Terrell Brandon	.30	.14
☐ 36 Brad Daugherty	.05	.02
☐ 37 Danny Ferry	.05	.02
☐ 38 Chris Mills	.50	.23
☐ 39 Larry Nance	.15	.07
☐ 40 Mark Price	.15	.07
☐ 41 Gerald Wilkins	.05	.02
☐ 42 John Williams	.05	.02
☐ 43 Terry Davis	.05	.02
☐ 44 Derek Harper	.15	.07
☐ 45 Donald Hodge	.05	.02
☐ 46 Jim Jackson	.30	.14
☐ 47 Sean Rooks	.05	.02
☐ 48 Doug Smith	.05	.02
☐ 49 Mahmoud Abdul-Rauf	.05	.02
☐ 50 LaPhonso Ellis	.15	.07
☐ 51 Mark Macon	.05	.02
☐ 52 D.Mutombo	.30	.14
☐ 53 Bryant Stith	.05	.02
☐ 54 Reggie Williams	.05	.02
☐ 55 Mark Aguirre	.05	.02
☐ 56 Joe Dumars	.30	.14
☐ 57 Bill Laimbeer	.05	.02
☐ 58 Terry Mills	.05	.02
☐ 59 Olden Polynice	.05	.02
☐ 60 Alvin Robertson	.05	.02
☐ 61 Sean Elliott	.15	.07
☐ 62 Isiah Thomas	.30	.14
☐ 63 Victor Alexander	.05	.02
☐ 64 Chris Gatling	.05	.02
☐ 65 Tim Hardaway	.40	.18
☐ 66 Byron Houston	.05	.02
☐ 67 Sarunas Marciulionis	.05	.02
☐ 68 Chris Mullin	.30	.14
☐ 69 Billy Owens	.05	.02
☐ 70 Latrell Sprewell	.30	.14
☐ 71 Matt Bullard	.05	.02
☐ 72 Sam Cassell	.75	.35
☐ 73 Carl Herrera	.05	.02
☐ 74 Robert Horry	.15	.07
☐ 75 Vernon Maxwell	.05	.02
☐ 76 Hakeem Olajuwon	.60	.25
☐ 77 Kenny Smith	.05	.02
☐ 78 Otis Thorpe	.15	.07
☐ 79 Dale Davis	.05	.02
☐ 80 Vern Fleming	.05	.02
☐ 81 Reggie Miller	.30	.14
☐ 82 Sam Mitchell	.05	.02
☐ 83 Pooh Richardson	.05	.02
☐ 84 Detlef Schrempf	.15	.07
☐ 85 Rik Smits	.15	.07
☐ 86 Ron Harper	.15	.07
☐ 87 Mark Jackson	.15	.07
☐ 88 Danny Manning	.15	.07
☐ 89 Stanley Roberts	.05	.02
☐ 90 Loy Vaught	.15	.07
☐ 91 John Williams	.05	.02
☐ 92 Sam Bowie	.05	.02
☐ 93 Doug Christie	.15	.07
☐ 94 Vlade Divac	.15	.07
☐ 95 George Lynch	.05	.02
☐ 96 Anthony Peeler	.05	.02
☐ 97 James Worthy	.30	.14
☐ 98 Bimbo Coles	.05	.02
☐ 99 Grant Long	.05	.02
☐ 100 Harold Miner	.05	.02
☐ 101 Glen Rice	.30	.14
☐ 102 Rony Seikaly	.05	.02
☐ 103 Brian Shaw	.05	.02
☐ 104 Steve Smith	.15	.07
☐ 105 Anthony Avent	.05	.02
☐ 106 Vin Baker	2.00	.90
☐ 107 Frank Brickowski	.05	.02
☐ 108 Todd Day	.05	.02
☐ 109 Blue Edwards	.05	.02
☐ 110 Lee Mayberry	.05	.02
☐ 111 Eric Murdock	.05	.02
☐ 112 Orlando Woolridge	.05	.02
☐ 113 Thurl Bailey	.05	.02
☐ 114 Christian Laettner	.30	.14
☐ 115 Chuck Person	.05	.02
☐ 116 Doug West	.05	.02
☐ 117 Micheal Williams	.05	.02
☐ 118 Kenny Anderson	.15	.07
☐ 119 Derrick Coleman	.15	.07
☐ 120 Rick Mahorn	.05	.02
☐ 121 Chris Morris	.05	.02
☐ 122 Rumeal Robinson	.05	.02
☐ 123 Rex Walters	.05	.02
☐ 124 Greg Anthony	.05	.02
☐ 125 Rolando Blackman	.05	.02
☐ 126 Hubert Davis	.05	.02
☐ 127 Patrick Ewing	.30	.14
☐ 128 Anthony Mason	.15	.07
☐ 129 Charles Oakley	.15	.07
☐ 130 Doc Rivers	.05	.02
☐ 131 Charles Smith	.05	.02
☐ 132 John Starks	.15	.07
☐ 133 Nick Anderson	.15	.07
☐ 134 Anthony Bowie	.05	.02
☐ 135 Shaquille O'Neal	1.25	.55
☐ 136 Dennis Scott	.15	.07
☐ 137 Scott Skiles	.05	.02
☐ 138 Jeff Turner	.05	.02
☐ 139 Shawn Bradley	.40	.18
☐ 140 Johnny Dawkins	.05	.02
☐ 141 Jeff Hornacek	.15	.07
☐ 142 Tim Perry	.05	.02
☐ 143 C.Weatherspoon	.05	.02
☐ 144 Danny Ainge	.15	.07
☐ 145 Charles Barkley	.50	.23
☐ 146 Cedric Ceballos	.05	.02
☐ 147 Kevin Johnson	.15	.07
☐ 148 Negele Knight	.05	.02
☐ 149 Malcolm Mackey	.05	.02
☐ 150 Dan Majerle	.15	.07
☐ 151 Oliver Miller	.05	.02
☐ 152 Mark West	.05	.02
☐ 153 Mark Bryant	.05	.02
☐ 154 Clyde Drexler	.40	.18
☐ 155 Jerome Kersey	.05	.02
☐ 156 Terry Porter	.05	.02
☐ 157 Clifford Robinson	.15	.07
☐ 158 Rod Strickland	.15	.07
☐ 159 Buck Williams	.15	.07
☐ 160 Duane Causwell	.05	.02
☐ 161 Bobby Hurley	.15	.07
☐ 162 Mitch Richmond	.30	.14
☐ 163 Lionel Simmons	.05	.02
☐ 164 Wayman Tisdale	.05	.02
☐ 165 Spud Webb	.15	.07
☐ 166 Walt Williams	.15	.07
☐ 167 Willie Anderson	.05	.02
☐ 168 Antoine Carr	.05	.02
☐ 169 Lloyd Daniels	.05	.02
☐ 170 Dennis Rodman	1.25	.55
☐ 171 Dale Ellis	.05	.02
☐ 172 Avery Johnson	.05	.02
☐ 173 J.R. Reid	.05	.02
☐ 174 David Robinson	.50	.23
☐ 175 Michael Cage	.05	.02
☐ 176 Kendall Gill	.15	.07
☐ 177 Ervin Johnson	.15	.07
☐ 178 Shawn Kemp	1.00	.45
☐ 179 Derrick McKey	.05	.02
☐ 180 Nate McMillan	.05	.02
☐ 181 Gary Payton	.50	.23
☐ 182 Sam Perkins	.15	.07
☐ 183 Ricky Pierce	.05	.02

☐ 184 David Benoit	.05	.02
☐ 185 Tyrone Corbin	.05	.02
☐ 186 Mark Eaton	.05	.02
☐ 187 Jay Humphries	.05	.02
☐ 188 Jeff Malone	.05	.02
☐ 189 Karl Malone	.50	.23
☐ 190 John Stockton	.30	.14
☐ 191 Luther Wright	.05	.02
☐ 192 Michael Adams	.05	.02
☐ 193 Calbert Cheaney	.30	.14
☐ 194 Pervis Ellison	.05	.02
☐ 195 Tom Gugliotta	.30	.14
☐ 196 Buck Johnson	.05	.02
☐ 197 LaBradford Smith	.05	.02
☐ 198 Larry Stewart	.05	.02
☐ 199 Checklist	.05	.02
☐ 200 Checklist	.05	.02
☐ 201 Doug Edwards	.05	.02
☐ 202 Craig Ehlo	.05	.02
☐ 203 Jon Koncak	.05	.02
☐ 204 Andrew Lang	.05	.02
☐ 205 Ennis Whatley	.05	.02
☐ 206 Chris Corchiani	.05	.02
☐ 207 Acie Earl	.05	.02
☐ 208 Jimmy Oliver	.05	.02
☐ 209 Ed Pinckney	.05	.02
☐ 210 Dino Radja	.15	.07
☐ 211 Matt Wenstrom	.05	.02
☐ 212 Tony Bennett	.05	.02
☐ 213 Scott Burrell	.30	.14
☐ 214 LeRon Ellis	.05	.02
☐ 215 Hersey Hawkins	.15	.07
☐ 216 Eddie Johnson	.05	.02
☐ 217 Rumeal Robinson	.05	.02
☐ 218 Corie Blount	.05	.02
☐ 219 Dave Johnson	.15	.07
☐ 220 Steve Kerr	.15	.07
☐ 221 Toni Kukoc	.75	.35
☐ 222 Pete Myers	.05	.02
☐ 223 Bill Wennington	.05	.02
☐ 224 Scott Williams	.05	.02
☐ 225 John Battle	.05	.02
☐ 226 Tyrone Hill	.05	.02
☐ 227 Gerald Madkins	.05	.02
☐ 228 Chris Mills	.30	.14
☐ 229 Bobby Phills	.05	.02
☐ 230 Greg Dreiling	.05	.02
☐ 231 Lucious Harris	.05	.02
☐ 232 Popeye Jones	.05	.02
☐ 233 Tim Legler	.05	.02
☐ 234 Fat Lever	.05	.02
☐ 235 Jamal Mashburn	.75	.35
☐ 236 Tom Hammonds	.05	.02
☐ 237 Darnell Mee	.05	.02
☐ 238 Robert Pack	.05	.02
☐ 239 Rodney Rogers	.05	.02
☐ 240 Brian Williams	.05	.02
☐ 241 Greg Anderson	.05	.02
☐ 242 Sean Elliott	.15	.07
☐ 243 Allan Houston	.60	.25
☐ 244 Lindsey Hunter	.30	.14
☐ 245 Mark Macon	.05	.02
☐ 246 David Wood	.05	.02
☐ 247 Jud Buechler	.05	.02
☐ 248 Josh Grant	.05	.02
☐ 249 Jeff Grayer	.05	.02
☐ 250 Keith Jennings	.05	.02
☐ 251 Avery Johnson	.05	.02
☐ 252 Chris Webber	2.00	.90
☐ 253 Scott Brooks	.05	.02
☐ 254 Sam Cassell	.30	.14
☐ 255 Mario Elie	.05	.02
☐ 256 Richard Petruska	.05	.02
☐ 257 Eric Riley	.05	.02
☐ 258 Antonio Davis	.15	.07
☐ 259 Scott Haskin	.05	.02
☐ 260 Derrick McKey	.05	.02
☐ 261 Byron Scott	.15	.07
☐ 262 Malik Sealy	.05	.02
☐ 263 Kenny Williams	.05	.02
☐ 264 Haywoode Workman	.05	.02
☐ 265 Mark Aguirre	.05	.02
☐ 266 Terry Dehere	.05	.02
☐ 267 Harold Ellis	.05	.02
☐ 268 Gary Grant	.05	.02
☐ 269 Bob Martin	.05	.02

☐ 270 Elmore Spencer	.05	.02
☐ 271 Tom Tolbert	.05	.02
☐ 272 Sam Bowie	.05	.02
☐ 273 Elden Campbell	.15	.07
☐ 274 Antonio Harvey	.05	.02
☐ 275 George Lynch	.05	.02
☐ 276 Tony Smith	.05	.02
☐ 277 Sedale Threatt	.05	.02
☐ 278 Nick Van Exel	1.00	.45
☐ 279 Willie Burton	.05	.02
☐ 280 Matt Geiger	.05	.02
☐ 281 John Salley	.05	.02
☐ 282 Vin Baker	1.00	.45
☐ 283 Jon Barry	.05	.02
☐ 284 Brad Lohaus	.05	.02
☐ 285 Ken Norman	.05	.02
☐ 286 Derek Strong	.05	.02
☐ 287 Mike Brown	.05	.02
☐ 288 Brian Davis	.05	.02
☐ 289 Tellis Frank	.05	.02
☐ 290 Luc Longley	.15	.07
☐ 291 Marlon Maxey	.05	.02
☐ 292 Isaiah Rider	.40	.18
☐ 293 Chris Smith	.05	.02
☐ 294 P.J. Brown	.05	.02
☐ 295 Kevin Edwards	.05	.02
☐ 296 Armon Gilliam	.05	.02
☐ 297 Johnny Newman	.05	.02
☐ 298 Rex Walters	.05	.02
☐ 299 David Wesley	.30	.14
☐ 300 Jayson Williams	.15	.07
☐ 301 Anthony Bonner	.05	.02
☐ 302 Derek Harper	.15	.07
☐ 303 Herb Williams	.05	.02
☐ 304 Litterial Green	.05	.02
☐ 305 Anfernee Hardaway	4.00	1.80
☐ 306 Greg Kite	.05	.02
☐ 307 Larry Krystkowiak	.05	.02
☐ 308 Keith Tower	.05	.02
☐ 309 Dana Barros	.05	.02
☐ 310 Shawn Bradley	.30	.14
☐ 311 Greg Graham	.05	.02
☐ 312 Sean Green	.05	.02
☐ 313 Warren Kidd	.05	.02
☐ 314 Eric Leckner	.05	.02
☐ 315 Moses Malone	.30	.14
☐ 316 Orlando Woolridge	.05	.02
☐ 317 Duane Cooper	.05	.02
☐ 318 Joe Courtney	.05	.02
☐ 319 A.C. Green	.15	.07
☐ 320 Frank Johnson	.05	.02
☐ 321 Joe Kleine	.05	.02
☐ 322 Chris Dudley	.05	.02
☐ 323 Harvey Grant	.05	.02
☐ 324 Jaren Jackson	.05	.02
☐ 325 Tracy Murray	.05	.02
☐ 326 James Robinson	.05	.02
☐ 327 Reggie Smith	.05	.02
☐ 328 Kevin Thompson	.05	.02
☐ 329 Randy Brown	.05	.02
☐ 330 Evers Burns	.05	.02
☐ 331 Pete Chilcutt	.05	.02
☐ 332 Bobby Hurley	.15	.07
☐ 333 Mike Peplowski	.05	.02
☐ 334 LaBradford Smith	.05	.02
☐ 335 Trevor Wilson	.05	.02
☐ 336 Terry Cummings	.05	.02
☐ 337 Vinny Del Negro	.05	.02
☐ 338 Sleepy Floyd	.05	.02
☐ 339 Negele Knight	.05	.02
☐ 340 Dennis Rodman	1.25	.55
☐ 341 Chris Whitney	.05	.02
☐ 342 Vincent Askew	.05	.02
☐ 343 Kendall Gill	.15	.07
☐ 344 Ervin Johnson	.15	.07
☐ 345 Chris King	.05	.02
☐ 346 Detlef Schrempf	.15	.07
☐ 347 Walter Bond	.05	.02
☐ 348 Tom Chambers	.05	.02
☐ 349 John Crotty	.05	.02
☐ 350 Bryon Russell	.30	.14
☐ 351 Felton Spencer	.05	.02
☐ 352 Mitchell Butler	.05	.02
☐ 353 Rex Chapman	.05	.02
☐ 354 Calbert Cheaney	.30	.14
☐ 355 Kevin Duckworth	.05	.02

☐ 356 Don MacLean	.05	.02
☐ 357 Gheorghe Muresan	.40	.18
☐ 358 Doug Overton	.05	.02
☐ 359 Brent Price	.05	.02
☐ 360 Kenny Walker	.05	.02
☐ 361 Derrick Coleman USA	.05	.02
☐ 362 Joe Dumars USA	.15	.07
☐ 363 Tim Hardaway USA	.30	.14
☐ 364 Larry Johnson USA	.15	.07
☐ 365 Shawn Kemp USA	.50	.23
☐ 366 Dan Majerle USA	.05	.02
☐ 367 Alonzo Mourning USA	.30	.14
☐ 368 Mark Price USA	.05	.02
☐ 369 Steve Smith USA	.15	.07
☐ 370 Isiah Thomas USA	.15	.07
☐ 371 D.Wilkins USA	.15	.07
☐ 372 Don Nelson	.15	.07
Don Chaney		
☐ 373 Jamal Mashburn CL	.30	.14
☐ 374 Checklist	.05	.02
☐ 375 Checklist	.05	.02
☐ M1 Reggie Miller USA	.75	.35
☐ M2 Shaquille O'Neal USA	5.00	2.20
☐ M3 Team Checklist USA	2.00	.90

1993-94 Ultra All-Defensive

Randomly inserted in 1 of 24 first series 19-card jumbo packs, this standard-size ten-card set features members of the first (1-5) and second (6-10) All-NBA defensive teams. The design features a borderless front and color player action cutout set against a background of an enlarged and ghosted version of the same photo. The player's name appears in gold-foil lettering at the bottom. The back features a color player photo at the lower left, along with his career highlights set against the same ghosted photo background. The cards are numbered on the back as "X of 10."

	MINT	NRMT
COMPLETE SET (10)	150.00	70.00
COMMON CARD (1-10)	2.50	1.10
SEMISTARS	4.00	1.80
SER.1 STATED ODDS 1:24 JUMBO		

☐ 1 Joe Dumars	4.00	1.80
☐ 2 Michael Jordan	100.00	45.00
☐ 3 Hakeem Olajuwon	15.00	6.75
☐ 4 Scottie Pippen	25.00	11.00

	MINT	NRMT
☐ 5 Dennis Rodman	30.00	13.50
☐ 6 Horace Grant	4.00	1.80
☐ 7 Dan Majerle	4.00	1.80
☐ 8 Larry Nance	2.50	1.10
☐ 9 David Robinson	12.00	5.50
☐ 10 John Starks	4.00	1.80

1993-94 Ultra All-NBA

Randomly inserted in 14-card first series packs at a rate of approximately one in 16, this 14-card standard-size set features one card for each All-NBA first (1-5), second (6-10) and third (11-14) team player from the 1992-93 season. Drazen Petrovic was named to the third team. Due to his death following the '92-93 season, a card was not produced. The fronts display full-bleed glossy color action photos with a series of three smaller photos along the left side. The player's name appears in gold-foil lettering at the lower right. The back carries a hardwood floor-design background with three small photos along the left side that progressively zoom in on the player. Career highlights appear alongside. The cards are numbered on the back as "X of 14."

	MINT	NRMT
COMPLETE SET (14)	50.00	22.00
COMMON CARD (1-14)	1.00	.45
SEMISTARS	1.50	.70
UNLISTED STARS	2.50	1.10
SER.1 STATED ODDS 1:16		
☐ 1 Charles Barkley	4.00	1.80
☐ 2 Michael Jordan	30.00	13.50
☐ 3 Karl Malone	4.00	1.80
☐ 4 Hakeem Olajuwon	5.00	2.20
☐ 5 Mark Price	1.00	.45
☐ 6 Joe Dumars	2.50	1.10
☐ 7 Patrick Ewing	2.50	1.10
☐ 8 Larry Johnson	2.50	1.10
☐ 9 John Stockton	2.50	1.10
☐ 10 Dominique Wilkins	2.50	1.10
☐ 11 Derrick Coleman	1.50	.70
☐ 12 Tim Hardaway	3.00	1.35
☐ 13 Scottie Pippen	8.00	3.60
☐ 14 David Robinson	4.00	1.80

1993-94 Ultra All-Rookie Series

Randomly inserted in 14-card second series packs at an approximate rate of one in seven, this 15-card standard-size set features some of the NBA's top draft picks of 1993-94. Each borderless front features a color action photo. The player's name appears in silver foil near the bottom. The horizontal borderless back carries a color player action shot on one side and career highlights on the other. The cards are numbered on the back as "X of 15" and are sequenced in alphabetical order.

	MINT	NRMT
COMPLETE SET (15)	40.00	18.00
COMMON CARD (1-15)	.75	.35
SEMISTARS	1.00	.45
UNLISTED STARS	2.00	.90
SER.2 STATED ODDS 1:7		
☐ 1 Vin Baker	8.00	3.60
☐ 2 Shawn Bradley	2.00	.90
☐ 3 Calbert Cheaney	2.00	.90
☐ 4 Anfernee Hardaway	20.00	9.00
☐ 5 Lindsey Hunter	2.00	.90
☐ 6 Bobby Hurley	.75	.35
☐ 7 Popeye Jones	.75	.35
☐ 8 Toni Kukoc	3.00	1.35
☐ 9 Jamal Mashburn	3.00	1.35
☐ 10 Chris Mills	2.00	.90
☐ 11 Dino Radja	1.00	.45
☐ 12 Isaiah Rider	2.00	.90
☐ 13 Rodney Rogers	.75	.35
☐ 14 Nick Van Exel	4.00	1.80
☐ 15 Chris Webber	8.00	3.60

1993-94 Ultra All-Rookie Team

Randomly inserted in series one 14-card packs at an approximate rate of one in 24, this five-card standard-size set features the NBA's 1992-93 All-Rookie Team. Fronts feature borderless fronts with color player action cutouts breaking out of hardwood floor backgrounds. The player's name appears in gold-

foil lettering at the bottom. The horizontal borderless back carries a color player cutout and career highlights on a hardwood floor background. The cards are numbered on the back as "X of 5" and are sequenced in alphabetical order.

	MINT	NRMT
COMPLETE SET (5)	10.00	4.50
COMMON CARD (1-5)	.50	.23
SEMISTARS	1.25	.55
UNLISTED STARS	1.50	.70
SER.1 STATED ODDS 1:24		
☐ 1 LaPhonso Ellis	.50	.23
☐ 2 Tom Gugliotta	1.50	.70
(with Michael Jordan)		
☐ 3 Christian Laettner	1.25	.55
☐ 4 Alonzo Mourning	2.50	1.10
☐ 5 Shaquille O'Neal	8.00	3.60

1993-94 Ultra Award Winners

Randomly inserted in first series 19-card jumbo packs at a rate of one in 36, this five-card standard-size set features NBA award winners from the 1992-93 season. Borderless fronts feature color player action cutouts on metallic backgrounds. The player's name appears in silver-foil lettering at the bottom. The back carries a color player close-up and career highlights. The cards are numbered on the back as "X of 5." and are sequenced in alphabetical order.

	MINT	NRMT
COMPLETE SET (5)	20.00	9.00
COMMON CARD (1-5)	1.00	.45
SEMISTARS	1.50	.70
SER.1 STATED ODDS 1:36 JUMBO		
☐ 1 Mahmoud Abdul-Rauf..	1.00	.45
☐ 2 Charles Barkley	4.00	1.80
☐ 3 Hakeem Olajuwon	5.00	2.20
☐ 4 Shaquille O'Neal	10.00	4.50
☐ 5 Clifford Robinson	1.50	.70

1993-94 Ultra Famous Nicknames

Randomly inserted into 14-card second series packs at a rate of one in five, this 15-card standard-size set features popular nicknames of today's stars. Borderless fronts feature color action cutouts on hardwood-floor and basket-net backgrounds. The player's nickname appears in silver-foil lettering on the right. The borderless back carries a color player photo on one side. On the other, the shot's game background blends into a hardwood-floor background for the player's name in vertical silver-foil lettering and his career highlights. The cards are numbered on the back as "X of 15" and are sequenced in alphabetical order.

	MINT	NRMT
COMPLETE SET (15)	60.00	27.00
COMMON CARD (1-15)	.50	.23
SEMISTARS	1.00	.45
UNLISTED STARS	2.00	.90
SER.2 STATED ODDS 1:5		
☐ 1 Charles Barkley	3.00	1.35
Sir Charles		
☐ 2 Tyrone Bogues	1.00	.45
Muggsy		
☐ 3 Derrick Coleman	1.00	.45
D.C.		
☐ 4 Clyde Drexler	2.50	1.10
The Glide		
☐ 5 Anfernee Hardaway	20.00	9.00
Penny		
☐ 6 Larry Johnson	2.00	.90
L.J.		
☐ 7 Michael Jordan	25.00	11.00
Air		

	MINT	NRMT
☐ 8 Toni Kukoc	3.00	1.35
The Pink Panther		
☐ 9 Karl Malone	3.00	1.35
The Mailman		
☐ 10 Harold Miner	.50	.23
Baby Jordan		
☐ 11 Alonzo Mourning	3.00	1.35
Zo		
☐ 12 Hakeem Olajuwon	4.00	1.80
The Dream		
☐ 13 Shaquille O'Neal	8.00	3.60
Shaq		
☐ 14 David Robinson	3.00	1.35
The Admiral		
☐ 15 Dominique Wilkins	2.00	.90
Human Highlight Film		

1993-94 Ultra Inside/Outside

Randomly inserted in 14-card second series packs, this 10-card standard-size set features on each borderless front a color player action cutout over a shot of a comet like basketball going through the basket, all on a black background. The player's name appears in gold foil near the bottom. This design, but with a different action cutout, is mirrored somewhat on the borderless back, which also carries to the left of the player photo his career highlights within a ghosted box framed by a purple line. The cards are numbered on the back as "X of 10" and are sequenced in alphabetical order.

	MINT	NRMT
COMPLETE SET (10)	12.00	5.50
COMMON CARD (1-10)	.25	.11
SEMISTARS	.40	.18
UNLISTED STARS	.60	.25
RANDOM INSERTS IN ALL SER.2 PACKS		
☐ 1 Patrick Ewing	.60	.25
☐ 2 Jim Jackson	.60	.25
☐ 3 Larry Johnson	.60	.25
☐ 4 Michael Jordan	8.00	3.60
☐ 5 Dan Majerle	.40	.18
☐ 6 Hakeem Olajuwon	1.25	.55
☐ 7 Scottie Pippen	2.00	.90
☐ 8 Latrell Sprewell	.60	.25
☐ 9 John Starks	.40	.18
☐ 10 Walt Williams	.25	.11

1993-94 Ultra Jam City

Randomly inserted in 19-card second series jumbo packs at a rate of one in 37, this 9-card standard-size set features borderless fronts with color player action cutouts on black and purple metallic cityscape backgrounds. The player's name appears in gold foil in a lower corner. The borderless back carries a color player action cutout on a non-metallic cityscape background otherwise similar to the front. The player's name and career highlights appear in a ghosted box to the left of the photo. The cards are numbered on the back as "X of 10" and are sequenced in alphabetical order.

	MINT	NRMT
COMPLETE SET (9)	60.00	27.00
COMMON CARD (1-9)	1.25	.55
SEMISTARS	2.00	.90
UNLISTED STARS	5.00	2.20
SER.2 STATED ODDS 1:37 JUMBO		
☐ 1 Charles Barkley	8.00	3.60
☐ 2 Derrick Coleman	2.00	.90
☐ 3 Clyde Drexler	6.00	2.70
☐ 4 Patrick Ewing	5.00	2.20
☐ 5 Shawn Kemp	15.00	6.75
☐ 6 Harold Miner	1.25	.55
☐ 7 Shaquille O'Neal	20.00	9.00
☐ 8 David Robinson	8.00	3.60
☐ 9 Dominique Wilkins	5.00	2.20

1993-94 Ultra Karl Malone

This ten-card standard-size set of Career Highlights spotlights Utah Jazz forward Karl Malone. The cards were randomly inserted in 14-card first series packs at a rate of approximately one in 16. The full-bleed color fronts have purple tinted ghosted backgrounds with Malone por-

trayed in normal color action and posed photos. Across the bottom edge is a marbleized border with the subset title "Career Highlights", above the lower border is a silver and black box containing Malone's name. The backs carry information about Malone within a purple tinted ghosted box that is superimposed over a color photo. More than 2,000 autographed cards were randomly inserted in packs. These card have embossed Fleer logos for authenticity. An additional two cards (Nos.11 and 12) were available through a mail-in offer. Prior to June 10, 1994, collectors had to send 10 first series Ultra wrappers and $1.50 to receive the cards. The set is considered complete without these cards.

	MINT	NRMT
COMPLETE SET (10)	10.00	4.50
COMMON MALONE (1-10)	1.25	.55
SER.1 STATED ODDS 1:16		
COMMON SEND-OFF (11-12)	2.00	.90
TWO CARDS PER 10 SER.1 WRAPPERS		
□ 1 Karl Malone Power Rig	1.25	.55
□ 2 Karl Malone Summerfield	1.25	.55
□ 3 Karl Malone Mailman-Born	1.25	.55
□ 4 Karl Malone Luck of the Draw	1.25	.55
□ 5 Karl Malone Double-Double	1.25	.55
□ 6 Karl Malone Dynamic Duo	1.25	.55
□ 7 Karl Malone Mt. Malone	1.25	.55
□ 8 Karl Malone Salt Lake Slammer	1.25	.55
□ 9 Karl Malone Overhead Delivery	1.25	.55
□ 10 Karl Malone Truckin'	1.25	.55
□ 11 Karl Malone Role Player	2.00	.90
□ 12 Karl Malone Rigged	2.00	.90
□ AU Karl Malone Certified Autograph	125.00	55.00

1993-94 Ultra Power In The Key

Randomly inserted in 14-card second series packs at a rate of one in 37, this nine-card standard-size features some of the NBA's top power players. Card fronts feature borderless color player action cutouts on multicolored metallic court illustration backgrounds. The player's name appears in gold-foil lettering at the lower right. The borderless horizontal back carries on its right side a color player close-up on a nonmetallic background otherwise similar to the front. The player's name and career highlights appear in a ghosted box to the left of the photo. The cards are numbered on the back as "X of 9" and are sequenced in alphabetical order.

	MINT	NRMT
COMPLETE SET (9)	80.00	36.00
COMMON CARD (1-9)	1.00	.45
SEMISTARS	2.50	1.10
SER.2 STATED ODDS 1:37 HOBBY		
□ 1 Larry Johnson	2.50	1.10
□ 2 Michael Jordan	40.00	18.00
□ 3 Karl Malone	5.00	2.20
□ 4 Oliver Miller	1.00	.45
□ 5 Alonzo Mourning	5.00	2.20
□ 6 Hakeem Olajuwon	6.00	2.70
□ 7 Shaquille O'Neal	12.00	5.50
□ 8 Otis Thorpe	2.50	1.10
□ 9 Chris Webber	12.00	5.50

1993-94 Ultra Rebound Kings

Randomly inserted in 14-card second series packs at a rate of one in four, this 10-card standard-size set features some of the NBA's top rebounders. Borderless fronts feature color player action shots on backgrounds that blend from the actual action background at the bottom to a ghosted and color-screened player close-up at the

top. The player's name appears vertically in gold foil on one side. The borderless horizontal back carries a color player cutout on one side and the player's name in gold foil and career highlights on the other, all on a ghosted and color-screened background. The cards are numbered on the back as "X of 10" and are sequenced in alphabetical order.

	MINT	NRMT
COMPLETE SET (10)	10.00	4.50
COMMON CARD (1-10)	.25	.11
SEMISTARS	.40	.18
SER.2 STATED ODDS 1:4		
□ 1 Charles Barkley	1.00	.45
□ 2 Derrick Coleman	.40	.18
□ 3 Shawn Kemp	2.00	.90
□ 4 Karl Malone	1.00	.45
□ 5 Alonzo Mourning	1.00	.45
□ 6 Dikembe Mutombo	.40	.18
□ 7 Charles Oakley	.25	.11
□ 8 Hakeem Olajuwon	1.25	.55
□ 9 Shaquille O'Neal	2.50	1.10
□ 10 Dennis Rodman	2.50	1.10

1993-94 Ultra Scoring Kings

Randomly inserted in first series hobby packs at a rate of one in 36, this 10-card standard-size set features some of the NBA's top scorers. Card fronts feature color player action cutouts on borderless metallic backgrounds highlighted by lightning filaments. The player's name appears in silver-foil lettering in a lower corner. The horizontal back carries a color player close-up on the right, with the player's name appearing in silver-foil lettering at the upper left, followed below by career highlights, all on a dark borderless background again highlighted by lightning filaments. The cards are numbered on the back as "X of 10" and are sequenced in alphabetical order.

	MINT	NRMT
COMPLETE SET (10)	150.00	70.00
COMMON CARD (1-10)	2.50	1.10
SEMISTARS	4.00	1.80
UNLISTED STARS	6.00	2.70
SER.1 STATED ODDS 1:36 HOBBY		

□ 1	Charles Barkley	10.00	4.50
□ 2	Joe Dumars	4.00	1.80
□ 3	Patrick Ewing	6.00	2.70
□ 4	Larry Johnson	2.50	1.10
□ 5	Michael Jordan	80.00	36.00
□ 6	Karl Malone	10.00	4.50
□ 7	Alonzo Mourning	10.00	4.50
□ 8	Shaquille O'Neal	25.00	11.00
□ 9	David Robinson	10.00	4.50
□ 10	Dominique Wilkins	4.00	1.80

1994-95 Ultra

The 350 standard-size cards comprising the 1994-95 Ultra set were issued in two separate series of 200 and 150 cards each. Cards were distributed in 14-card ($1.99) and 17-card ($2.69) retail packs. Borderless fronts feature color player action shots. The player's name, team name, and position appear in vertical silver-foil lettering in an upper corner. The borderless back carries multiple player images, with the player's name and team logo appearing in gold foil, followed by biography and statistics near the bottom. The cards are numbered on the back and grouped alphabetically within team order. Unlike previous years, there are no subset cards in this set. Rookie Cards of note include Grant Hill, Juwan Howard, Jason Kidd, Eddie Jones, and Glenn Robinson. There is an insert in every pack. Every 72nd pack is a Hot Pack that contains inserts only.

	MINT	NRMT
COMPLETE SET (350)	35.00	16.00
COMPLETE SERIES 1 (200)	20.00	9.00
COMPLETE SERIES 2 (150)	15.00	6.75
COMMON CARD (1-350)	.10	.05
SEMISTARS	.15	.07
UNLISTED STARS	.40	.18

□ 1	Stacey Augmon	.10	.05
□ 2	Mookie Blaylock	.15	.07
□ 3	Craig Ehlo	.10	.05
□ 4	Adam Keefe	.10	.05
□ 5	Andrew Lang	.10	.05
□ 6	Ken Norman	.10	.05
□ 7	Kevin Willis	.10	.05
□ 8	Dee Brown	.10	.05
□ 9	Sherman Douglas	.10	.05
□ 10	Acie Earl	.10	.05
□ 11	Pervis Ellison	.10	.05
□ 12	Rick Fox	.10	.05
□ 13	Xavier McDaniel	.10	.05
□ 14	Eric Montross	.10	.05
□ 15	Dino Radja	.10	.05
□ 16	Dominique Wilkins	.40	.18
□ 17	Michael Adams	.10	.05
□ 18	Muggsy Bogues	.15	.07
□ 19	Dell Curry	.10	.05
□ 20	Kenny Gattison	.10	.05
□ 21	Hersey Hawkins	.15	.07
□ 22	Larry Johnson	.15	.07
□ 23	Alonzo Mourning	.50	.23
□ 24	Robert Parish	.15	.07
□ 25	B.J. Armstrong	.10	.05
□ 26	Steve Kerr	.15	.07
□ 27	Toni Kukoc	.40	.18
□ 28	Luc Longley	.15	.07
□ 29	Pete Myers	.10	.05
□ 30	Will Perdue	.10	.05
□ 31	Scottie Pippen	1.25	.55
□ 32	Terrell Brandon	.40	.18
□ 33	Brad Daugherty	.10	.05
□ 34	Tyrone Hill	.10	.05
□ 35	Chris Mills	.15	.07
□ 36	Bobby Phills	.10	.05
□ 37	Mark Price	.15	.07
□ 38	Gerald Wilkins	.10	.05
□ 39	John Williams	.10	.05
□ 40	Terry Davis	.10	.05
□ 41	Jim Jackson	.15	.07
□ 42	Popeye Jones	.10	.05
□ 43	Jason Kidd	3.00	1.35
□ 44	Jamal Mashburn	.40	.18
□ 45	Sean Rooks	.10	.05
□ 46	Doug Smith	.10	.05
□ 47	Mahmoud Abdul-Rauf	.10	.05
□ 48	LaPhonso Ellis	.15	.07
□ 49	Dikembe Mutombo	.40	.18
□ 50	Robert Pack	.10	.05
□ 51	Rodney Rogers	.10	.05
□ 52	Bryant Stith	.10	.05
□ 53	Brian Williams	.10	.05
□ 54	Reggie Williams	.10	.05
□ 55	Greg Anderson	.10	.05
□ 56	Joe Dumars	.40	.18
□ 57	Allan Houston	.40	.18
□ 58	Lindsey Hunter	.15	.07
□ 59	Terry Mills	.10	.05
□ 60	Tim Hardaway	.50	.23
□ 61	Chris Mullin	.40	.18
□ 62	Billy Owens	.10	.05
□ 63	Latrell Sprewell	.15	.07
□ 64	Chris Webber	1.00	.45
□ 65	Sam Cassell	.40	.18
□ 66	Carl Herrera	.10	.05
□ 67	Robert Horry	.15	.07
□ 68	Vernon Maxwell	.10	.05
□ 69	Hakeem Olajuwon	.75	.35
□ 70	Kenny Smith	.10	.05
□ 71	Otis Thorpe	.15	.07
□ 72	Antonio Davis	.10	.05
□ 73	Dale Davis	.10	.05
□ 74	Mark Jackson	.15	.07
□ 75	Derrick McKey	.10	.05
□ 76	Reggie Miller	.40	.18
□ 77	Byron Scott	.15	.07
□ 78	Rik Smits	.15	.07
□ 79	Haywoode Workman	.10	.05
□ 80	Gary Grant	.10	.05
□ 81	Ron Harper	.15	.07
□ 82	Elmore Spencer	.10	.05
□ 83	Loy Vaught	.15	.07
□ 84	Elden Campbell	.10	.05
□ 85	Doug Christie	.10	.05
□ 86	Vlade Divac	.15	.07
□ 87	Eddie Jones	3.00	1.35
□ 88	George Lynch	.10	.05
□ 89	Anthony Peeler	.10	.05
□ 90	Sedale Threatt	.10	.05
□ 91	Nick Van Exel	.40	.18
□ 92	James Worthy	.40	.18
□ 93	Bimbo Coles	.10	.05
□ 94	Matt Geiger	.10	.05
□ 95	Grant Long	.10	.05
□ 96	Harold Miner	.10	.05
□ 97	Glen Rice	.40	.18
□ 98	John Salley	.10	.05
□ 99	Rony Seikaly	.10	.05
□ 100	Brian Shaw	.10	.05
□ 101	Steve Smith	.15	.07
□ 102	Vin Baker	1.00	.45
□ 103	Jon Barry	.10	.05
□ 104	Todd Day	.10	.05
□ 105	Lee Mayberry	.10	.05
□ 106	Eric Murdock	.10	.05
□ 107	Thurl Bailey	.10	.05
□ 108	Stacey King	.10	.05
□ 109	Christian Laettner	.15	.07
□ 110	Isaiah Rider	.15	.07
□ 111	Chris Smith	.10	.05
□ 112	Doug West	.10	.05
□ 113	Micheal Williams	.10	.05
□ 114	Kenny Anderson	.15	.07
□ 115	Benoit Benjamin	.10	.05
□ 116	P.J. Brown	.10	.05
□ 117	Derrick Coleman	.15	.07
□ 118	Yinka Dare	.10	.05
□ 119	Kevin Edwards	.10	.05
□ 120	Armon Gilliam	.10	.05
□ 121	Chris Morris	.10	.05
□ 122	Greg Anthony	.10	.05
□ 123	Anthony Bonner	.10	.05
□ 124	Hubert Davis	.10	.05
□ 125	Patrick Ewing	.40	.18
□ 126	Derek Harper	.15	.07
□ 127	Anthony Mason	.15	.07
□ 128	Charles Oakley	.15	.07
□ 129	Doc Rivers	.10	.05
□ 130	John Starks	.15	.07
□ 131	Nick Anderson	.10	.05
□ 132	Anthony Avent	.10	.05
□ 133	Anthony Bowie	.10	.05
□ 134	Anfernee Hardaway	1.50	.70
□ 135	Shaquille O'Neal	1.50	.70
□ 136	Dennis Scott	.15	.07
□ 137	Jeff Turner	.10	.05
□ 138	Dana Barros	.10	.05
□ 139	Shawn Bradley	.15	.07
□ 140	Greg Graham	.10	.05
□ 141	Jeff Malone	.10	.05
□ 142	Tim Perry	.10	.05
□ 143	C.Weatherspoon	.10	.05
□ 144	Scott Williams	.10	.05
□ 145	Danny Ainge	.15	.07
□ 146	Charles Barkley	.60	.25
□ 147	Cedric Ceballos	.15	.07
□ 148	A.C. Green	.15	.07
□ 149	Frank Johnson	.10	.05
□ 150	Kevin Johnson	.15	.07
□ 151	Dan Majerle	.15	.07
□ 152	Oliver Miller	.10	.05
□ 153	Wesley Person	.50	.23
□ 154	Mark Bryant	.10	.05
□ 155	Clyde Drexler	.50	.23

□			
□ 156 Harvey Grant	.10	.05
□ 157 Jerome Kersey	.10	.05
□ 158 Tracy Murray	.10	.05
□ 159 Terry Porter	.10	.05
□ 160 Clifford Robinson	.15	.07
□ 161 James Robinson	.10	.05
□ 162 Rod Strickland	.15	.07
□ 163 Buck Williams	.10	.05
□ 164 Duane Causwell	.10	.05
□ 165 Olden Polynice	.10	.05
□ 166 Mitch Richmond	.40	.18
□ 167 Lionel Simmons	.10	.05
□ 168 Walt Williams	.10	.05
□ 169 Willie Anderson	.10	.05
□ 170 Terry Cummings	.10	.05
□ 171 Sean Elliott	.15	.07
□ 172 Avery Johnson	.10	.05
□ 173 J.R. Reid	.10	.05
□ 174 David Robinson	.60	.25
□ 175 Dennis Rodman	1.50	.70
□ 176 Kendall Gill	.15	.07
□ 177 Shawn Kemp	1.25	.55
□ 178 Nate McMillan	.10	.05
□ 179 Gary Payton	.60	.25
□ 180 Sam Perkins	.15	.07
□ 181 Detlef Schrempf	.15	.07
□ 182 David Benoit	.10	.05
□ 183 Tyrone Corbin	.10	.05
□ 184 Jeff Hornacek	.15	.07
□ 185 Jay Humphries	.10	.05
□ 186 Karl Malone	.60	.25
□ 187 Bryon Russell	.15	.07
□ 188 Felton Spencer	.10	.05
□ 189 John Stockton	.40	.18
□ 190 Mitchell Butler	.10	.05
□ 191 Rex Chapman	.10	.05
□ 192 Calbert Cheaney	.15	.07
□ 193 Kevin Duckworth	.10	.05
□ 194 Tom Gugliotta	.40	.18
□ 195 Don MacLean	.10	.05
□ 196 Gheorghe Muresan	.15	.07
□ 197 Scott Skiles	.10	.05
□ 198 Checklist	.10	.05
□ 199 Checklist	.10	.05
□ 200 Checklist	.10	.05
□ 201 Tyrone Corbin	.10	.05
□ 202 Doug Edwards	.10	.05
□ 203 Jim Les	.10	.05
□ 204 Grant Long	.10	.05
□ 205 Ken Norman	.10	.05
□ 206 Steve Smith	.15	.07
□ 207 Blue Edwards	.10	.05
□ 208 Greg Minor	.10	.05
□ 209 Eric Montross	.10	.05
□ 210 Derek Strong	.10	.05
□ 211 David Wesley	.15	.07
□ 212 Tony Bennett	.10	.05
□ 213 Scott Burrell	.10	.05
□ 214 Darrin Hancock	.10	.05
□ 215 Greg Sutton	.10	.05
□ 216 Corie Blount	.10	.05
□ 217 Jud Buechler	.10	.05
□ 218 Ron Harper	.15	.07
□ 219 Larry Krystkowiak	.10	.05
□ 220 Dickey Simpkins	.10	.05
□ 221 Bill Wennington	.10	.05
□ 222 Michael Cage	.10	.05
□ 223 Tony Campbell	.10	.05
□ 224 Steve Colter	.10	.05
□ 225 Greg Dreiling	.10	.05
□ 226 Danny Ferry	.10	.05
□ 227 Tony Dumas	.10	.05
□ 228 Lucious Harris	.10	.05
□ 229 Donald Hodge	.10	.05
□ 230 Jason Kidd	1.50	.70
□ 231 Lorenzo Williams	.10	.05
□ 232 Dale Ellis	.10	.05
□ 233 Tom Hammonds	.10	.05
□ 234 Jalen Rose	.40	.18
□ 235 Reggie Slater	.10	.05
□ 236 Rafael Addison	.10	.05
□ 237 Bill Curley	.15	.07
□ 238 Johnny Dawkins	.10	.05
□ 239 Grant Hill	5.00	2.20
□ 240 Eric Leckner	.10	.05
□ 241 Mark Macon	.10	.05
□ 242 Oliver Miller	.10	.05
□ 243 Mark West	.10	.05
□ 244 Victor Alexander	.10	.05
□ 245 Chris Gatling	.10	.05
□ 246 Tom Gugliotta	.40	.18
□ 247 Keith Jennings	.10	.05
□ 248 Ricky Pierce	.10	.05
□ 249 Carlos Rogers	.10	.05
□ 250 Clifford Rozier	.10	.05
□ 251 Rony Seikaly	.10	.05
□ 252 David Wood	.10	.05
□ 253 Tim Breaux	.10	.05
□ 254 Scott Brooks	.10	.05
□ 255 Zan Tabak	.10	.05
□ 256 Duane Ferrell	.10	.05
□ 257 Mark Jackson	.15	.07
□ 258 Sam Mitchell	.10	.05
□ 259 John Williams	.10	.05
□ 260 Terry Dehere	.10	.05
□ 261 Harold Ellis	.10	.05
□ 262 Matt Fish	.10	.05
□ 263 Tony Massenburg	.10	.05
□ 264 Lamond Murray	.15	.07
□ 265 Charles Outlaw	.10	.05
□ 266 Eric Piatkowski	.10	.05
□ 267 Pooh Richardson	.10	.05
□ 268 Malik Sealy	.10	.05
□ 269 Randy Woods	.10	.05
□ 270 Sam Bowie	.10	.05
□ 271 Cedric Ceballos	.15	.07
□ 272 Antonio Harvey	.10	.05
□ 273 Eddie Jones	1.50	.70
□ 274 Anthony Miller	.10	.05
□ 275 Tony Smith	.10	.05
□ 276 Ledell Eackles	.10	.05
□ 277 Kevin Gamble	.10	.05
□ 278 Brad Lohaus	.10	.05
□ 279 Billy Owens	.10	.05
□ 280 Khalid Reeves	.10	.05
□ 281 Kevin Willis	.10	.05
□ 282 Marty Conlon	.10	.05
□ 283 Alton Lister	.10	.05
□ 284 Eric Mobley	.10	.05
□ 285 Johnny Newman	.10	.05
□ 286 Ed Pinckney	.10	.05
□ 287 Glenn Robinson	1.50	.70
□ 288 Howard Eisley	.10	.05
□ 289 Winston Garland	.10	.05
□ 290 Andres Guibert	.10	.05
□ 291 Donyell Marshall	.50	.23
□ 292 Sean Rooks	.10	.05
□ 293 Yinka Dare	.10	.05
□ 294 Sleepy Floyd	.10	.05
□ 295 Sean Higgins	.10	.05
□ 296 Rex Walters	.10	.05
□ 297 Jayson Williams	.15	.07
□ 298 Charles Smith	.10	.05
□ 299 Charlie Ward	.15	.07
□ 300 Herb Williams	.10	.05
□ 301 Monty Williams	.10	.05
□ 302 Horace Grant	.15	.07
□ 303 Geert Hammink	.10	.05
□ 304 Tree Rollins	.10	.05
□ 305 Donald Royal	.10	.05
□ 306 Brian Shaw	.10	.05
□ 307 Brooks Thompson	.10	.05
□ 308 Derrick Alston	.10	.05
□ 309 Willie Burton	.10	.05
□ 310 Jaren Jackson	.10	.05
□ 311 B.J. Tyler	.10	.05
□ 312 Scott Williams	.10	.05
□ 313 Sharone Wright	.10	.05
□ 314 Joe Kleine	.10	.05
□ 315 Danny Manning	.15	.07
□ 316 Elliot Perry	.10	.05
□ 317 Wesley Person	.40	.18
□ 318 Trevor Ruffin	.10	.05
□ 319 Dan Schayes	.10	.05
□ 320 Wayman Tisdale	.10	.05
□ 321 Chris Dudley	.10	.05
□ 322 James Edwards	.10	.05
□ 323 Alaa Abdelnaby	.10	.05
□ 324 Randy Brown	.10	.05
□ 325 Brian Grant	.40	.18
□ 326 Bobby Hurley	.10	.05
□ 327 Michael Smith	.15	.07
□ 328 Henry Turner	.10	.05
□ 329 Trevor Wilson	.10	.05
□ 330 Vinny Del Negro	.10	.05
□ 331 Moses Malone	.40	.18
□ 332 Julius Nwosu	.10	.05
□ 333 Chuck Person	.10	.05
□ 334 Chris Whitney	.10	.05
□ 335 Vincent Askew	.10	.05
□ 336 Bill Cartwright	.10	.05
□ 337 Ervin Johnson	.10	.05
□ 338 Sarunas Marciulionis	.10	.05
□ 339 Antoine Carr	.10	.05
□ 340 Tom Chambers	.10	.05
□ 341 John Crotty	.10	.05
□ 342 Jamie Watson	.15	.07
□ 343 Juwan Howard	2.00	.90
□ 344 Jim McIlvaine	.10	.05
□ 345 Doug Overton	.10	.05
□ 346 Scott Skiles	.10	.05
□ 347 Anthony Tucker	.10	.05
□ 348 Chris Webber	1.00	.45
□ 349 Checklist	.10	.05
□ 350 Checklist	.10	.05

1994-95 Ultra All-NBA

Randomly inserted into approximately one in every three first series packs, cards from this 15-card standard-size set feature members of the All-NBA first (1-5), second (6-10), and third (11-15) teams. The fronts are laid out horizontally and have a color action photo and three photos that look like they were taken in a room with a black light. On the right side is the player's first name in white behind his last name in the color of his team. At the bottom in gold-foil are the words "ALL-NBA" and the corresponding team he made. On the backs are a color photo in front of the same photo with the black light look. Their is also player information and the cards are numbered "X of 15."

	MINT	NRMT
COMPLETE SET (15)	15.00	6.75
COMMON CARD (1-15)	.40	.18
SEMISTARS	.60	.25
UNLISTED STARS	1.00	.45
SER.1 STATED ODDS 1:3 HOBBY/RETAIL		

□ 1 Karl Malone	1.50	.70
□ 2 Hakeem Olajuwon	2.00	.90

		MINT	NRMT
☐ 3	Scottie Pippen	3.00	1.35
☐ 4	Latrell Sprewell	.60	.25
☐ 5	John Stockton	1.00	.45
☐ 6	Charles Barkley	1.50	.70
☐ 7	Kevin Johnson	.60	.25
☐ 8	Shawn Kemp	3.00	1.35
☐ 9	Mitch Richmond	1.00	.45
☐ 10	David Robinson	1.50	.70
☐ 11	Derrick Coleman	.60	.25
☐ 12	Shaquille O'Neal	4.00	1.80
☐ 13	Gary Payton	1.50	.70
☐ 14	Mark Price	.40	.18
☐ 15	Dominique Wilkins	1.00	.45

1994-95 Ultra All-Rookie Team

Randomly inserted exclusively into first series jumbo packs at a rate of one in 36, cards from this 10-card standard-size set feature some of the top rookies from the 1993-94 season. Fronts feature a full-color action shot aside a bold, gold-foil All-Rookie logo with the player's name.

		MINT	NRMT
COMPLETE SET (10)		125.00	55.00
COMMON CARD (1-10)		2.50	1.10
SEMISTARS		5.00	2.20
UNLISTED STARS		12.00	5.50
SER.1 STATED ODDS 1:36 JUMBO			
☐ 1	Vin Baker	30.00	13.50
☐ 2	Anfernee Hardaway	50.00	22.00
☐ 3	Jamal Mashburn	12.00	5.50
☐ 4	Isaiah Rider	5.00	2.20
☐ 5	Chris Webber	30.00	13.50
☐ 6	Shawn Bradley	5.00	2.20
☐ 7	Lindsey Hunter	5.00	2.20
☐ 8	Toni Kukoc	12.00	5.50
☐ 9	Dino Radja	2.50	1.10
☐ 10	Nick Van Exel	12.00	5.50

1994-95 Ultra All-Rookies

Randomly inserted at a rate of one in every five second series packs, this 15-card standard-size set captures the best first-year players from the 1994-95 season. The fronts saw a full-color photo with a hardwood floor background. The words "All-Rookie" and the player's name are on the left side in

gold-foil. The backs a full-color photo with his name and a hardwood floor in the background. There is also player information and the cards are numbered "X of 15." The set is sequenced in alphabetical order.

		MINT	NRMT
COMPLETE SET (15)		25.00	11.00
COMMON CARD (1-15)		.40	.18
SEMISTARS		.75	.35
SER.2 STATED ODDS 1:5 HOBBY/RETAIL			
☐ 1	Brian Grant	.75	.35
☐ 2	Grant Hill	10.00	4.50
☐ 3	Juwan Howard	4.00	1.80
☐ 4	Eddie Jones	6.00	2.70
☐ 5	Jason Kidd	6.00	2.70
☐ 6	Donyell Marshall	.75	.35
☐ 7	Eric Montross	.40	.18
☐ 8	Lamond Murray	.40	.18
☐ 9	Wesley Person	.75	.35
☐ 10	Khalid Reeves	.40	.18
☐ 11	Glenn Robinson	3.00	1.35
☐ 12	Carlos Rogers	.40	.18
☐ 13	Jalen Rose	.75	.35
☐ 14	B.J. Tyler	.40	.18
☐ 15	Sharone Wright	.40	.18

1994-95 Ultra Award Winners

Randomly inserted into approximately one in every four first series packs, cards from this four-card standard-size set feature players who won individual awards during the 1993-94 season. The fronts are laid out horizontally and have a color-action photo with the backgrounds having a black and white head

shot with horizontal white lines across the card. At on of the bottom corners are the words "NBA Award Winner" with a basketball in gold-foil. The backs have a color photo from the chest up with a similar background to the front. There is also player information and the cards are numbered "X of 4." The set is sequenced in alphabetical order.

		MINT	NRMT
COMPLETE SET (4)		4.00	1.80
COMMON CARD (1-4)		.25	.11
SER.1 STATED ODDS 1:4 HOBBY/RETAIL			
☐ 1	Dell Curry	.25	.11
☐ 2	Don MacLean	.25	.11
☐ 3	Hakeem Olajuwon	2.00	.90
☐ 4	Chris Webber	2.50	1.10

1994-95 Ultra Defensive Gems

Randomly inserted at a rate of one in every 37 second-series packs, this 6-card standard-size set focuses on six NBA stars who play standout defense. The borderless fronts feature 100% etched-foil backgrounds. The player's name is located at the bottom while the words "Defensive Gems" surrounding a diamond are in the lower right. The backs are split between another player photo and some information about the player's defensive prowess. The cards are numbered in the lower left as "X" of 6. The set is sequenced in alphabetical order.

		MINT	NRMT
COMPLETE SET (6)		40.00	18.00
COMMON CARD (1-6)		2.00	.90
SER.2 STATED ODDS 1:37 HOBBY/RETAIL			
☐ 1	Mookie Blaylock	2.00	.90
☐ 2	Hakeem Olajuwon	10.00	4.50
☐ 3	Gary Payton	8.00	3.60
☐ 4	Scottie Pippen	15.00	6.75
☐ 5	David Robinson	8.00	3.60
☐ 6	Latrell Sprewell	2.00	.90

1994-95 Ultra Double Trouble

Randomly inserted into approximately one in every five first series packs, cards from this 10-card standard-size set feature a selection of multi-skilled NBA stars. The fronts feature two photos of the player in a split player design. The words "Double Trouble" and player's name are printed in silver foil on the bottom. The borderless backs are split between an explanation of the the player's skills as well as a photo. The cards are numbered "X" of 10 in the lower left corner. The set is sequenced in alphabetical order.

	MINT	NRMT
COMPLETE SET (10)	10.00	4.50
COMMON CARD (1-10)	.40	.18
SEMISTARS	.60	.25
UNLISTED STARS	1.00	.45
SER.1 STATED ODDS 1:5 HOBBY/RETAIL		
□ 1 Derrick Coleman	.40	.18
□ 2 Patrick Ewing	1.00	.45
□ 3 Anfernee Hardaway	4.00	1.80
□ 4 Jamal Mashburn	.60	.25
□ 5 Reggie Miller	1.00	.45
□ 6 Alonzo Mourning	1.25	.55
□ 7 Scottie Pippen	3.00	1.35
□ 8 David Robinson	1.50	.70
□ 9 Latrell Sprewell	.40	.18
□ 10 John Stockton	1.00	.45

1994-95 Ultra Inside/Outside

Randomly inserted exclusively into one in every seven second series hobby packs, cards from this 10-card standard-size set focus on players who can score from anywhere on the court. The borderless fronts feature dual player photos against a gray background. The player's name is in the lower left corner while the words "Inside/Outside" are in the lower right corner. The backs describe the player's

shooting ability and have a small photo as well. The cards are numbered in the lower right as "X" of 10. The set is sequenced in alphabetical order.

	MINT	NRMT
COMPLETE SET (10)	10.00	4.50
COMMON CARD (1-10)	.25	.11
SEMISTARS	.50	.23
UNLISTED STARS	1.25	.55
SER.2 STATED ODDS 1:7 HOBBY		
□ 1 Sam Cassell	1.25	.55
□ 2 Cedric Ceballos	.50	.23
□ 3 Calbert Cheaney	.25	.11
□ 4 Anfernee Hardaway	5.00	2.20
□ 5 Jim Jackson	.50	.23
□ 6 Dan Majerle	.50	.23
□ 7 Robert Pack	.25	.11
□ 8 Scottie Pippen	4.00	1.80
□ 9 Mitch Richmond	1.25	.55
□ 10 Latrell Sprewell	.50	.23

1994-95 Ultra Jam City

Randomly inserted exclusively into one in every seven second series jumbo packs, cards from this 10-card standard size set spotlight ten well known dunkers. The borderless fronts feature color player action cutouts on a multi colored metallic cityscape background. The words "Jam City" and the player's name are printed in gold foil on the bottom of the card. The back features another cutout photo against a different skyscraper background with the

player's name in the middle in gold foil. A brief blurb about the player is inset at the bottom. The cards are numbered "X" of 10 in the bottom right. The set is sequenced in alphabetical order.

	MINT	NRMT
COMPLETE SET (10)	50.00	22.00
COMMON CARD (1-10)	1.50	.70
SEMISTARS	2.00	.90
UNLISTED STARS	4.00	1.80
SER.2 STATED ODDS 1:7 JUMBO		
□ 1 Vin Baker	10.00	4.50
□ 2 Grant Hill	25.00	11.00
□ 3 Robert Horry	1.50	.70
□ 4 Shawn Kemp	12.00	5.50
□ 5 Jamal Mashburn	2.00	.90
□ 6 Alonzo Mourning	5.00	2.20
□ 7 Dikembe Mutombo	4.00	1.80
□ 8 Shaquille O'Neal	15.00	6.75
□ 9 Glenn Robinson	8.00	3.60
□ 10 Dominique Wilkins	4.00	1.80

1994-95 Ultra Power

Randomly inserted in all first series packs at an approximate rate of one in three, cards from this 10-card standard-size set feature a selection of the NBA's most powerful stars. This set features color player action cutouts set on a colorful and sparkly starburst background design. The player's name appears in vertical gold lettering in a lower corner. The colorful starburst design continues on the borderless horizontal back, which carries a color player head shot on one side, and career highlights on the other. The cards are numbered on the back as "X of 10." The set is sequenced in alphabetical order.

	MINT	NRMT
COMPLETE SET (10)	10.00	4.50
COMMON CARD (1-10)	.25	.11
SEMISTARS	.50	.23
SER.1 STATED ODDS 1:3 HOBBY/RETAIL		
□ 1 Charles Barkley	1.25	.55
□ 2 Derrick Coleman	.50	.23
□ 3 Larry Johnson	.50	.23

		MINT	NRMT
☐ 4	Shawn Kemp	2.50	1.10
☐ 5	Karl Malone	1.25	.55
☐ 6	Dikembe Mutombo	.50	.23
☐ 7	Charles Oakley	.25	.11
☐ 8	Shaquille O'Neal	3.00	1.35
☐ 9	Dennis Rodman	3.00	1.35
☐ 10	Chris Webber	2.00	.90

1994-95 Ultra Power In The Key

Randomly inserted exclusively into one in every seven second series retail packs, cards from this 10-card standard-size set feature ten players who are effective playing near the basket. The front feature a player cutout against a multicolored basketball court design. The words "Power in the Key" are on either side, with the player's name directly underneath those words. The backs contain biographical information along with an inset photo of the player. The cards are numbered in the lower right as "X" of 10. The set is sequenced in alphabetical order.

		MINT	NRMT
COMPLETE SET (10)		25.00	11.00
COMMON CARD (1-10)		.50	.23
SEMISTARS		1.00	.45
UNLISTED STARS		2.00	.90
SER.2 STATED ODDS 1:7 RETAIL			
☐ 1	Charles Barkley	3.00	1.35
☐ 2	Patrick Ewing	2.00	.90
☐ 3	Horace Grant	1.00	.45
☐ 4	Larry Johnson	1.00	.45
☐ 5	Karl Malone	3.00	1.35
☐ 6	Hakeem Olajuwon	4.00	1.80
☐ 7	Shaquille O'Neal	8.00	3.60
☐ 8	David Robinson	3.00	1.35
☐ 9	Chris Webber	5.00	2.20
☐ 10	Kevin Willis	.50	.23

1994-95 Ultra Rebound Kings

Randomly inserted at a rate of one in every two second-series packs, cards from this 10-card standard-size set focus on league's top rebounders. The fronts have a color-action photo

and a color picture of his head at the bottom along with a gold-foil crown. The words "Rebound King" are at the top and side with rebound behind king at the top and vice-versa on the side, each card uses different colors for the words. The backs have a color photo with his name in gold-foil and information on why he is a top rebounder. The cards are numbered "X" of 10." The set is sequenced in alphabetical order.

		MINT	NRMT
COMPLETE SET (10)		4.00	1.80
COMMON CARD (1-10)		.15	.07
SEMISTARS		.25	.11
SER.2 STATED ODDS 1:2 HOBBY/RETAIL			
☐ 1	Derrick Coleman	.25	.11
☐ 2	A.C. Green	.15	.07
☐ 3	Alonzo Mourning	.50	.23
☐ 4	Dikembe Mutombo	.25	.11
☐ 5	Charles Oakley	.15	.07
☐ 6	Hakeem Olajuwon	.75	.35
☐ 7	Shaquille O'Neal	1.50	.70
☐ 8	David Robinson	.60	.25
☐ 9	Chris Webber	1.00	.45
☐ 10	Kevin Willis	.15	.07

1994-95 Ultra Scoring Kings

Randomly inserted exclusively into one in every 37 first series hobby packs, cards from this 10-card standard-size set feature a selection of perennial NBA scoring leaders. Fronts feature full-

color player action shots cut out against 100% etched-foil backgrounds. The set is sequenced in alphabetical order.

		MINT	NRMT
COMPLETE SET (10)		80.00	36.00
COMMON CARD (1-10)		3.00	1.35
SEMISTARS		6.00	2.70
SER.1 STATED ODDS 1:37 HOBBY			
☐ 1	Charles Barkley	10.00	4.50
☐ 2	Patrick Ewing	6.00	2.70
☐ 3	Karl Malone	10.00	4.50
☐ 4	Hakeem Olajuwon	12.00	5.50
☐ 5	Shaquille O'Neal	25.00	11.00
☐ 6	Scottie Pippen	20.00	9.00
☐ 7	Mitch Richmond	6.00	2.70
☐ 8	David Robinson	10.00	4.50
☐ 9	Latrell Sprewell	3.00	1.35
☐ 10	Dominique Wilkins	3.00	1.35

1995-96 Ultra

The 1995-96 Ultra set was issued in two series of 200 and 150 for a total of 350 standard-size cards. They were issued in 12-card hobby and retail packs (SRP $2.49) in addition to 17-card pre-priced packs (SRP $2.99). Each 12-card pack contains two insert cards and one in every 72 packs contains nothing but insert cards (referred to as a "Hot Pack"). Fleer upgraded the stock of the 1995-96 cards by making them 40% thicker than the previous year's Ultra release. The fronts have a full-color action photo with the player's name and team at the bottom in gold-foil. The backs have two-color photos and one full black-and-white with statistics at the bottom. The basic issue cards are grouped alphabetically within teams and checklisted below alphabetically according to city. Subsets featured are Rookies (263-298) and Encore (299-348). Rookie Cards of note in this set include Michael Finley, Kevin Garnett, Antonio McDyess, Joe Smith, Jerry

Stackhouse and Damon Stoudamire.

	MINT	NRMT
COMPLETE SET (350)	40.00	18.00
COMPLETE SERIES 1 (200)	20.00	9.00
COMPLETE SERIES 2 (150)	20.00	9.00
COMMON CARD (1-350)	.15	.07
SEMISTARS	.20	.09
UNLISTED STARS	.40	.18
COMP.G.MED.SET (200)	125.00	55.00
COMMON G.MED (1-200)	.30	.14

*G.MED.STARS: 3X TO 6X HI COLUMN
ONE GOLD MED.IN EVERY SER.1 PACK

#	Player	MINT	NRMT
1	Stacey Augmon	.15	.07
2	Mookie Blaylock	.20	.09
3	Craig Ehlo	.15	.07
4	Andrew Lang	.15	.07
5	Grant Long	.15	.07
6	Ken Norman	.15	.07
7	Steve Smith	.20	.09
8	Spud Webb	.20	.09
9	Dee Brown	.15	.07
10	Sherman Douglas	.15	.07
11	Pervis Ellison	.15	.07
12	Rick Fox	.15	.07
13	Eric Montross	.15	.07
14	Dino Radja	.15	.07
15	David Wesley	.15	.07
16	Dominique Wilkins	.40	.18
17	Muggsy Bogues	.20	.09
18	Scott Burrell	.15	.07
19	Dell Curry	.15	.07
20	Kendall Gill	.20	.09
21	Larry Johnson	.20	.09
22	Alonzo Mourning	.40	.18
23	Robert Parish	.20	.09
24	Ron Harper	.20	.09
25	Michael Jordan	5.00	2.20
26	Toni Kukoc	.20	.09
27	Will Perdue	.15	.07
28	Scottie Pippen	1.25	.55
29	Terrell Brandon	.40	.18
30	Michael Cage	.15	.07
31	Tyrone Hill	.15	.07
32	Chris Mills	.15	.07
33	Bobby Phills	.15	.07
34	Mark Price	.15	.07
35	John Williams	.15	.07
36	Lucious Harris	.15	.07
37	Jim Jackson	.20	.09
38	Popeye Jones	.15	.07
39	Jason Kidd	1.00	.45
40	Jamal Mashburn	.20	.09
41	George McCloud	.15	.07
42	Roy Tarpley	.15	.07
43	Lorenzo Williams	.15	.07
44	Mahmoud Abdul-Rauf	.15	.07
45	Dikembe Mutombo	.20	.09
46	Robert Pack	.15	.07
47	Jalen Rose	.20	.09
48	Bryant Stith	.15	.07
49	Brian Williams	.15	.07
50	Reggie Williams	.15	.07
51	Joe Dumars	.40	.18
52	Grant Hill	2.50	1.10
53	Allan Houston	.20	.09
54	Lindsey Hunter	.15	.07
55	Terry Mills	.15	.07
56	Mark West	.15	.07
57	Chris Gatling	.15	.07
58	Tim Hardaway	.50	.23
59	Donyell Marshall	.20	.09
60	Chris Mullin	.40	.18
61	Carlos Rogers	.15	.07
62	Clifford Rozier	.15	.07
63	Rony Seikaly	.15	.07
64	Latrell Sprewell	.20	.09
65	Sam Cassell	.20	.09
66	Clyde Drexler	.50	.23
67	Mario Elie	.15	.07
68	Carl Herrera	.15	.07
69	Robert Horry	.15	.07
70	Hakeem Olajuwon	.75	.35
71	Kenny Smith	.15	.07
72	Antonio Davis	.15	.07
73	Dale Davis	.15	.07
74	Mark Jackson	.20	.09
75	Derrick McKey	.15	.07
76	Reggie Miller	.40	.18
77	Rik Smits	.20	.09
78	Terry Dehere	.15	.07
79	Lamond Murray	.15	.07
80	Charles Outlaw	.15	.07
81	Pooh Richardson	.15	.07
82	Rodney Rogers	.15	.07
83	Malik Sealy	.15	.07
84	Loy Vaught	.15	.07
85	Sam Bowie	.15	.07
86	Elden Campbell	.20	.09
87	Cedric Ceballos	.15	.07
88	Vlade Divac	.20	.09
89	Eddie Jones	1.00	.45
90	Anthony Peeler	.15	.07
91	Sedale Threatt	.15	.07
92	Nick Van Exel	.40	.18
93	Rex Chapman	.15	.07
94	Bimbo Coles	.15	.07
95	Matt Geiger	.15	.07
96	Billy Owens	.15	.07
97	Khalid Reeves	.15	.07
98	Glen Rice	.40	.18
99	Kevin Willis	.15	.07
100	Vin Baker	.75	.35
101	Marty Conlon	.15	.07
102	Todd Day	.15	.07
103	Eric Murdock	.15	.07
104	Glenn Robinson	.50	.23
105	Winston Garland	.15	.07
106	Tom Gugliotta	.40	.18
107	Christian Laettner	.20	.09
108	Isaiah Rider	.20	.09
109	Sean Rooks	.15	.07
110	Doug West	.15	.07
111	Kenny Anderson	.20	.09
112	P.J. Brown	.15	.07
113	Derrick Coleman	.20	.09
114	Armon Gilliam	.15	.07
115	Chris Morris	.15	.07
116	Anthony Bonner	.15	.07
117	Patrick Ewing	.40	.18
118	Derek Harper	.15	.07
119	Anthony Mason	.20	.09
120	Charles Oakley	.15	.07
121	Charles Smith	.15	.07
122	John Starks	.20	.09
123	Nick Anderson	.15	.07
124	Horace Grant	.20	.09
125	Anfernee Hardaway	1.50	.70
126	Shaquille O'Neal	1.50	.70
127	Donald Royal	.15	.07
128	Dennis Scott	.15	.07
129	Brian Shaw	.15	.07
130	Derrick Alston	.15	.07
131	Dana Barros	.15	.07
132	Shawn Bradley	.20	.09
133	Willie Burton	.15	.07
134	Jeff Malone	.15	.07
135	C.Weatherspoon	.15	.07
136	Scott Williams	.15	.07
137	Sharone Wright	.15	.07
138	Danny Ainge	.20	.09
139	Charles Barkley	.60	.25
140	A.C. Green	.20	.09
141	Kevin Johnson	.20	.09
142	Dan Majerle	.15	.07
143	Danny Manning	.20	.09
144	Elliot Perry	.15	.07
145	Wesley Person	.20	.09
146	Wayman Tisdale	.15	.07
147	Chris Dudley	.15	.07
148	Harvey Grant	.15	.07
149	Aaron McKie	.15	.07
150	Terry Porter	.15	.07
151	Clifford Robinson	.15	.07
152	Rod Strickland	.20	.09
153	Otis Thorpe	.20	.09
154	Buck Williams	.15	.07
155	Brian Grant	.20	.09
156	Bobby Hurley	.15	.07
157	Olden Polynice	.15	.07
158	Mitch Richmond	.40	.18
159	Michael Smith	.15	.07
160	Walt Williams	.15	.07
161	Vinny Del Negro	.15	.07
162	Sean Elliott	.15	.07
163	Avery Johnson	.15	.07
164	Chuck Person	.15	.07
165	J.R. Reid	.15	.07
166	Doc Rivers	.20	.09
167	David Robinson	.60	.25
168	Dennis Rodman	1.50	.70
169	Vincent Askew	.15	.07
170	Hersey Hawkins	.20	.09
171	Shawn Kemp	1.25	.55
172	Sarunas Marciulionis	.15	.07
173	Nate McMillan	.15	.07
174	Gary Payton	.60	.25
175	Sam Perkins	.20	.09
176	Detlef Schrempf	.20	.09
177	B.J. Armstrong	.15	.07
178	Jerome Kersey	.15	.07
179	Tony Massenburg	.15	.07
180	Oliver Miller	.15	.07
181	John Salley	.15	.07
182	David Benoit	.15	.07
183	Antoine Carr	.15	.07
184	Jeff Hornacek	.20	.09
185	Karl Malone	.60	.25
186	Felton Spencer	.15	.07
187	John Stockton	.40	.18
188	Greg Anthony	.15	.07
189	Benoit Benjamin	.15	.07
190	Byron Scott	.15	.07
191	Calbert Cheaney	.15	.07
192	Juwan Howard	.60	.25
193	Don MacLean	.15	.07
194	Gheorghe Muresan	.15	.07
195	Doug Overton	.15	.07
196	Scott Skiles	.15	.07
197	Chris Webber	1.00	.45
198	Checklist (1-94)	.15	.07
199	Checklist (95-190)	.15	.07
200	Checklist (191-200)	.15	.07
201	Stacey Augmon	.15	.07
202	Mookie Blaylock	.20	.09
203	Grant Long	.15	.07
204	Steve Smith	.20	.09
205	Dana Barros	.15	.07
206	Kendall Gill	.20	.09
207	Khalid Reeves	.15	.07
208	Glen Rice	.40	.18
209	Luc Longley	.20	.09
210	Dennis Rodman	2.50	1.10
211	Dan Majerle	.15	.07
212	Tony Dumas	.15	.07
213	Elmore Spencer	.15	.07
214	Otis Thorpe	.20	.09
215	B.J. Armstrong	.15	.07
216	Sam Cassell	.20	.09
217	Clyde Drexler	.50	.23
218	Robert Horry	.15	.07
219	Hakeem Olajuwon	.75	.35
220	Eddie Johnson	.15	.07
221	Ricky Pierce	.15	.07
222	Eric Piatkowski	.15	.07
223	Rodney Rogers	.15	.07
224	Brian Williams	.15	.07
225	George Lynch	.15	.07
226	Alonzo Mourning	.40	.18
227	Benoit Benjamin	.15	.07
228	Terry Porter	.15	.07
229	Shawn Bradley	.20	.09
230	Kevin Edwards	.15	.07
231	Jayson Williams	.20	.09
232	Charlie Ward	.15	.07
233	Jon Koncak	.15	.07
234	Derrick Coleman	.20	.09
235	Richard Dumas	.15	.07
236	Vernon Maxwell	.15	.07
237	John Williams	.15	.07
238	Dontonio Wingfield	.15	.07
239	Tyrone Corbin	.15	.07
240	Will Perdue	.15	.07
241	Shawn Kemp	1.25	.55
242	Gary Payton	.60	.25

□			
243	Sam Perkins	.20	.09
244	Detlef Schrempf	.20	.09
245	Chris Morris	.15	.07
246	Robert Pack	.15	.07
247	Willie Anderson EXP	.15	.07
248	Oliver Miller EXP	.15	.07
249	Tracy Murray EXP	.15	.07
250	Alvin Robertson EXP	.15	.07
251	Carlos Rogers EXP	.15	.07
252	John Salley EXP	.15	.07
253	D.Stoudamire EXP	1.25	.55
254	Zan Tabak EXP	.15	.07
255	Greg Anthony EXP	.15	.07
256	Blue Edwards EXP	.15	.07
257	Kenny Gattison EXP	.15	.07
258	Chris King EXP	.15	.07
259	Lawrence Moten EXP	.15	.07
260	Eric Murdock EXP	.15	.07
261	Bryant Reeves EXP	.40	.18
262	Byron Scott EXP	.15	.07
263	Cory Alexander	.15	.07
264	Brent Barry	.40	.18
265	Mario Bennett	.15	.07
266	Travis Best	.20	.09
267	Junior Burrough	.15	.07
268	Jason Caffey	.40	.18
269	Randolph Childress	.15	.07
270	Sasha Danilovic	.15	.07
271	Tyus Edney	.15	.07
272	Michael Finley	1.50	.70
273	Sherrell Ford	.15	.07
274	Kevin Garnett	5.00	2.20
275	Alan Henderson	.40	.18
276	Donny Marshall	.15	.07
277	Antonio McDyess	2.00	.90
278	Loren Meyer	.15	.07
279	Lawrence Moten	.15	.07
280	Ed O'Bannon	.15	.07
281	Greg Ostertag	.15	.07
282	Cherokee Parks	.15	.07
283	Theo Ratliff	.40	.18
284	Bryant Reeves	1.00	.45
285	Shawn Respert	.15	.07
286	Lou Roe	.15	.07
287	Arvydas Sabonis	.75	.35
288	Joe Smith	1.50	.70
289	Jerry Stackhouse	1.50	.70
290	Damon Stoudamire	3.00	1.35
291	Bob Sura	.20	.09
292	Kurt Thomas	.20	.09
293	Gary Trent	.15	.07
294	David Vaughn	.15	.07
295	Rasheed Wallace	1.00	.45
296	Eric Williams	.20	.09
297	Corliss Williamson	.50	.23
298	George Zidek	.15	.07
299	M.Abdul-Rauf ENC	.15	.07
300	Kenny Anderson ENC	.15	.07
301	Vin Baker ENC	.40	.18
302	Charles Barkley ENC	.40	.18
303	Mookie Blaylock ENC	.15	.07
304	Cedric Ceballos ENC	.15	.07
305	Vlade Divac ENC	.15	.07
306	Clyde Drexler ENC	.40	.18
307	Joe Dumars ENC	.20	.09
308	Sean Elliott ENC	.15	.07
309	Patrick Ewing ENC	.20	.09
310	A.Hardaway ENC	.75	.35
311	Tim Hardaway ENC	.40	.18
312	Grant Hill ENC	1.25	.55
313	Tyrone Hill ENC	.15	.07
314	Robert Horry ENC	.15	.07
315	Juwan Howard ENC	.40	.18
316	Jim Jackson ENC	.15	.07
317	Kevin Johnson ENC	.15	.07
318	Larry Johnson ENC	.15	.07
319	Eddie Jones ENC	.50	.23
320	Shawn Kemp ENC	.60	.25
321	Jason Kidd ENC	.50	.23
322	Christian Laettner ENC	.15	.07
323	Karl Malone ENC	.40	.18
324	Jamal Mashburn ENC	.15	.07
325	Reggie Miller ENC	.20	.09
326	Alonzo Mourning ENC	.20	.09
327	D.Mutombo ENC	.15	.07
328	Hakeem Olajuwon ENC	.40	.18
329	Gary Payton ENC	.40	.18
330	Scottie Pippen ENC	.60	.25
331	Dino Radja ENC	.15	.07
332	Glen Rice ENC	.20	.09
333	Mitch Richmond ENC	.20	.09
334	Clifford Robinson ENC	.15	.07
335	David Robinson ENC	.40	.18
336	Glenn Robinson ENC	.40	.18
337	Dennis Rodman ENC	1.25	.55
338	Carlos Rogers ENC	.15	.07
339	Detlef Schrempf ENC	.15	.07
340	Byron Scott ENC	.15	.07
341	Rik Smits ENC	.15	.07
342	Latrell Sprewell ENC	.15	.07
343	John Stockton ENC	.20	.09
344	Nick Van Exel ENC	.20	.09
345	Loy Vaught ENC	.15	.07
346	C.Weatherspoon ENC	.15	.07
347	Chris Webber ENC	.50	.23
348	Kevin Willis ENC	.15	.07
349	Checklist (201-298)	.15	.07
350	CL (299-350/inserts)	.15	.07

1995-96 Ultra All-NBA

Randomly inserted in all series one packs at a rate of one in five, this 15-card set features the league's best and is divided into three standard-size sets of five (first, second and third team NBA All-Stars). Borderless fronts picture the player in a full-color action cutout with a black and gold metallic streak background. The "All NBA" box is printed in reverse-type metallic foil on the bottom left with the player's name printed in gold foil across the bottom right. Full-bleed backs continue with the black and gold metallic streaks and another full-color action player cutout. A screened box highlights the player's accomplishments and includes his name in gold foil.

		MINT	NRMT
	COMPLETE SET (15)	20.00	9.00
	COMMON CARD (1-15)	.40	.18
	SEMISTARS	.60	.25
	UNLISTED STARS	1.00	.45
	SER.1 STATED ODDS 1:5 RETAIL		
	*GOLD MEDALLION: 1.5X TO 3X HI CLMN		
	GOLD: SER.1 STATED ODDS 1:50 HOB/RET		

□			
1	Anfernee Hardaway	4.00	1.80
2	Karl Malone	1.50	.70
3	Scottie Pippen	3.00	1.35
4	David Robinson	1.50	.70
5	John Stockton	1.00	.45
6	Charles Barkley	1.50	.70
7	Shawn Kemp	3.00	1.35
8	Shaquille O'Neal	4.00	1.80
9	Gary Payton	1.50	.70
10	Mitch Richmond	1.00	.45
11	Clyde Drexler	1.25	.55
12	Reggie Miller	1.00	.45
13	Hakeem Olajuwon	2.00	.90
14	Dennis Rodman	4.00	1.80
15	Detlef Schrempf	.40	.18

1995-96 Ultra All-Rookie Team

Randomly inserted in first series retail cello packs at a rate of one in seven, this 10-card set is divided into first team rookies (1-5) and second team rookies (6-10). Borderless fronts feature a full-color action player cutout set against a dark background with multicolored basketballs. All-Rookie team and the player's name are printed in gold foil across the bottom. Borderless backs continue with the multicolored basketball backgrounds and a full-color cutout of the player. A tan-screened box profiles the player and his name is printed in gold foil script across the top of the screen.

		MINT	NRMT
	COMPLETE SET (10)	35.00	16.00
	COMMON CARD (1-10)	1.00	.45
	SEMISTARS	2.00	.90
	SER.1 STATED ODDS 1:7 RETAIL		
	*GOLD MEDALLION: 1.5X TO 3X HI COLUMN		
	GOLD: SER.1 STATED ODDS 1:70 RETAIL		

□			
1	Brian Grant	2.00	.90
2	Grant Hill	20.00	9.00
3	Eddie Jones	8.00	3.60
4	Jason Kidd	8.00	3.60
5	Glenn Robinson	4.00	1.80
6	Juwan Howard	5.00	2.20
7	Donyell Marshall	1.00	.45
	Sharone Wright		
8	Eric Montross	1.00	.45
9	Wesley Person	2.00	.90
10	Jalen Rose	2.00	.90

1995-96 Ultra All-Rookies

Randomly inserted in all second series packs at a rate of one in 30, this set of 10 standard-size cards focuses on the play of the hot rookies of the '95 draft. Borderless fronts have a team color spectrum background with a full-color action cutout. The player's name and position are printed in gold foil near the bottom and "All Rookies" appears at the top. Backs have another full-color action cutout set against a color spectrum background. A screened box holds the player's name and a player profile. Card #'s 4 and 8 (McDyess and Stoudamire) were featured on an unperforated promo sheet of Ultra cards saluting card stores across America. The sheets were distributed to shop owners nationwide. Unfortunately, some unscrupulous parties cut up a number of the sheets and distributed the cut cards into the hobby market under false pretenses. The cut up cards are identical to the real inserts, thus supply has been altered and we've applied a "DP" designation to signify a double-print on this card.

	MINT	NRMT
COMPLETE SET (10)	50.00	22.00
COMMON CARD (1-10)	1.50	.70
SEMISTARS	2.50	1.10
SER.2 STATED ODDS 1:30 HOBBY/RETAIL		

☐ 1	Tyus Edney	1.50	.70
☐ 2	Michael Finley	8.00	3.60
☐ 3	Kevin Garnett	25.00	11.00
☐ 4	Antonio McDyess DP	5.00	2.20
☐ 5	Ed O'Bannon	1.50	.70
☐ 6	Joe Smith	8.00	3.60
☐ 7	Jerry Stackhouse	8.00	3.60
☐ 8	D.Stoudamire DP	8.00	3.60
☐ 9	Rasheed Wallace	4.00	1.80
☐ 10	Eric Williams	2.50	1.10

1995-96 Ultra Double Trouble

Randomly inserted in all first series packs at a rate of one in five, this 10-card standard-size set celebrates the players who perform well in more than one category. Full-bleed fronts feature a full-color action player cutout and a one-color action shot that serves as a background. "Double Trouble" is repeatedly printed in the background with a shadow effect. The player's name and "Double Trouble" are printed in alternating black and gold foil at the bottom. Another full-color action cutout appears on the back against the repeating "Double Trouble" colored background. A light screened box appears on the back with the player's abilities and accomplishments printed in black type. The player's name is printed in gold foil above the screened box. The set is sequenced in alphabetical order.

	MINT	NRMT
COMPLETE SET (10)	15.00	6.75
COMMON CARD (1-10)	.60	.25
SER.1 STATED ODDS 1:5 HOBBY/RETAIL		
*GOLD MEDALLION: 1.5X TO 3X HI COLUMN		
GOLD: SER.1 STATED ODDS 1:50 HOB/RET		

☐ 1	Charles Barkley	1.00	.45
☐ 2	Anfernee Hardaway	2.50	1.10
☐ 3	Michael Jordan	8.00	3.60
☐ 4	Alonzo Mourning	.50	.23
☐ 5	Hakeem Olajuwon	1.25	.55
☐ 6	Shaquille O'Neal	2.50	1.10
☐ 7	Gary Payton	1.00	.45
☐ 8	Scottie Pippen	2.00	.90
☐ 9	David Robinson	1.00	.45
☐ 10	John Stockton	.50	.23

1995-96 Ultra Fabulous Fifties

Randomly inserted in first series hobby packs at a rate of one in

12, this seven-card standard-size set spotlights players who scored 50 or more points in a 94/95 NBA single game. The horizontal fronts feature a full-color action player cutout set against a two-color background with basketball nets and "Fabulous 50's" printed in alternating red boxes. Player's name and "Fabulous 50's" are printed in silver foil across the bottom left. A one-color picture of a basketball net serves as a backdrop on the back with the player's name and team printed in silver foil on the top. A full-color action cutout appears with a story of how and when the player reached his 50-point scoring mark. The set is sequenced in alphabetical order.

	MINT	NRMT
COMPLETE SET (7)	18.00	8.00
COMMON CARD (1-7)	.50	.23
SEMISTARS	.75	.35
UNLISTED STARS	1.25	.55
SER.1 STATED ODDS 1:12 HOBBY		
*GOLD MEDALLION: 1.5X TO 3X HI COLUMN		
GOLD: SER.1 STATED ODDS 1:120 HOBBY		

☐ 1	Dana Barros	.50	.23
☐ 2	Willie Burton	.50	.23
☐ 3	Cedric Ceballos	.50	.23
☐ 4	Jim Jackson	.75	.35
☐ 5	Michael Jordan	15.00	6.75
☐ 6	Jamal Mashburn	.75	.35
☐ 7	Glen Rice	1.25	.55

1995-96 Ultra Jam City

Randomly inserted exclusively in second series retail packs at a rate of one in 12, cards from this 12-card standard-size set focus on the NBA's most powerful dunkers. Borderless fronts have full-color action cutouts set against a one-color etched foil background. "Jam City" is printed in gold foil vertically along one side and the player's name

is printed in silver foil vertically. Borderless backs feature a full-color player cutout with a halo effect set against a skyline background and a player profile. The set is sequenced in alphabetical order.

	MINT	NRMT
COMPLETE SET (12)	80.00	36.00
COMMON CARD (1-12)	1.00	.45
SEMISTARS	1.50	.70
UNLISTED STARS	2.50	1.10
SER.2 STATED ODDS 1:12 RETAIL
COMP.HOT PACK SET (12)	25.00	11.00
HP CARDS: 33% VALUE OF LISTED CARDS
HP: SER.2 STATED ODDS 1:72 RETAIL

☐ 1	Grant Hill	15.00	6.75
☐ 2	Robert Horry	1.00	.45
☐ 3	Michael Jordan	30.00	13.50
☐ 4	Shawn Kemp	8.00	3.60
☐ 5	Jamal Mashburn	1.50	.70
☐ 6	Antonio McDyess	6.00	2.70
☐ 7	Alonzo Mourning	2.50	1.10
☐ 8	Hakeem Olajuwon	5.00	2.20
☐ 9	Shaquille O'Neal	10.00	4.50
☐ 10	David Robinson	4.00	1.80
☐ 11	Joe Smith	5.00	2.20
☐ 12	Jerry Stackhouse	5.00	2.20

1995-96 Ultra Power

Randomly inserted in all first series packs at a rate of one in four, this 10-card standard-size set features the big rebounders and strong inside men of the NBA. A multicolored kaleidoscopic front serves as a background for a full-color action shot. The "Ultra Power" logo

and player's name are stamped at the bottom left in gold foil. Backs continue with the kaleidoscopic background and another full-color action cutout. A screened box holds the player's name in gold foil along with a synopsis of the player's abilities and accomplishments. Gold Medallion editions were seeded in packs at 10 percent the rate of regular cards. Backs are identical to regular inserts.

	MINT	NRMT
COMPLETE SET (10)	8.00	3.60
COMMON CARD (1-10)	.30	.14
SEMISTARS	.40	.18
UNLISTED STARS	.60	.25
SER.1 STATED ODDS 1:4 HOBBY/RETAIL
*GOLD MEDALLION: 1.5X TO 3X HI CLMN
GOLD: SER.1 STATED ODDS 1:40 HOB/RET

☐ 1	Charles Barkley	1.00	.45
☐ 2	Patrick Ewing	.60	.25
☐ 3	Larry Johnson	.40	.18
☐ 4	Shawn Kemp	2.00	.90
☐ 5	Karl Malone	1.00	.45
☐ 6	Alonzo Mourning	.60	.25
☐ 7	Dikembe Mutombo	.40	.18
☐ 8	Hakeem Olajuwon	1.25	.55
☐ 9	Shaquille O'Neal	2.50	1.10
☐ 10	David Robinson	1.00	.45

1995-96 Ultra Rising Stars

Randomly inserted in all first series packs at a rate of one in 37, this nine-card standard-size set features promising youngsters of the NBA. Etched foil fronts feature multicolored basketballs and a full-color action cutout. The "Rising Star" logo and player's name are printed in silver foil on the fronts. Backs include a screened player information box and a full-color action cutout set against a multicolored basketball background. The set is sequenced in alphabetical order.

	MINT	NRMT
COMPLETE SET (9)	100.00	45.00
COMMON CARD (1-9)	3.00	1.35

| SEMISTARS | 5.00 | 2.20 |
| SER.1 STATED ODDS 1:37 HOBBY/RETAIL |
| *GOLD MEDALLION: 2X TO 4X HI COLUMN |
| GOLD: SER.1 STATED ODDS 1:370 HOB/RET |

☐ 1	Vin Baker	10.00	4.50
☐ 2	Anfernee Hardaway	20.00	9.00
☐ 3	Grant Hill	30.00	13.50
☐ 4	Jason Kidd	12.00	5.50
☐ 5	Jamal Mashburn	3.00	1.35
☐ 6	Shaquille O'Neal	20.00	9.00
☐ 7	Glenn Robinson	6.00	2.70
☐ 8	Nick Van Exel	5.00	2.20
☐ 9	Chris Webber	12.00	5.50

1995-96 Ultra Scoring Kings

Randomly inserted at a rate of one in 24 hobby boxes only, this 12-card standard-size set spotlights the number crunchers of the NBA. Borderless fronts have full color player action shots and are stamped with gold foil. Backs have another full-color action shot and include a player profile. The set is sequenced in alphabetical order.

	MINT	NRMT
COMPLETE SET (12)	125.00	55.00
COMMON CARD (1-12)	2.00	.90
SEMISTARS	2.50	1.10
UNLISTED STARS	4.00	1.80
SER.2 STATED ODDS 1:24 HOBBY
COMP.HOT PACK SET (12)	30.00	13.50
HP CARDS: 25% VALUE OF LISTED CARDS
HP: SER.2 STATED ODDS 1:72 HOBBY

☐ 1	Patrick Ewing	4.00	1.80
☐ 2	Grant Hill	25.00	11.00
☐ 3	Jim Jackson	2.00	.90
☐ 4	Michael Jordan	50.00	22.00
☐ 5	Karl Malone	6.00	2.70
☐ 6	Reggie Miller	4.00	1.80
☐ 7	Hakeem Olajuwon	8.00	3.60
☐ 8	Shaquille O'Neal	15.00	6.75
☐ 9	Scottie Pippen	12.00	5.50
☐ 10	David Robinson	6.00	2.70
☐ 11	Glenn Robinson	5.00	2.20
☐ 12	Jerry Stackhouse	8.00	3.60

1995-96 Ultra USA Basketball

Randomly inserted into all second series packs at a rate of one in 54, cards from this 10-card standard-size set capture

the first 10 members named to the USA Olympic team in their new red, white and blue jerseys. Borderless fronts feature the player in full-color action set against an American flag backdrop. The player's name, position and the USA basketball logo are stamped in gold foil at the bottom. Backs have a full-color action shot on one side and a player profile set against a red and white stripe background with blue stars on the other side. The set is sequenced in alphabetical order.

	MINT	NRMT
COMPLETE SET (10)	180.00	80.00
COMMON CARD (1-10)	8.00	3.60
SER.2 STATED ODDS 1:54 HOBBY/RETAIL		

		MINT	NRMT
☐ 1	Anfernee Hardaway	30.00	13.50
☐ 2	Grant Hill	50.00	22.00
☐ 3	Karl Malone	12.00	5.50
☐ 4	Reggie Miller	8.00	3.60
☐ 5	Hakeem Olajuwon	15.00	6.75
☐ 6	Shaquille O'Neal	30.00	13.50
☐ 7	Scottie Pippen	25.00	11.00
☐ 8	David Robinson	12.00	5.50
☐ 9	Glenn Robinson	10.00	4.50
☐ 10	John Stockton	8.00	3.60

1996-97 Ultra

The 300-card Ultra set from Fleer/SkyBox was issued in two series in 12-card packs with a suggested retail price of $2.49. Each basic player card front features full-bleed photography with the player's name written in

script at the bottom of the card in silver holofoil, with the team name printed on the "tail" of the script. Card backs contain two photos of the player with biographical information and career statistics. Subsets include On the Block, Ultra Effort, Maximum Effort, Rookie Encore, Step It Up and Play of the Game. Rookie cards include Shareef Abdur-Rahim, Ray Allen, Kobe Bryant, Marcus Camby, Allen Iverson, Stephon Marbury and Antoine Walker, among others. A Jerry Stackhouse promo was released before the cards went live. It looks exactly like the regular issue card except it does not bear a card number. It is listed below at the end of the set.

	MINT	NRMT
COMPLETE SET (300)	40.00	18.00
COMPLETE SERIES 1 (150)	25.00	11.00
COMPLETE SERIES 2 (150)	15.00	6.75
COMMON CARD (1-300)	.15	.07
SEMISTARS	.20	
UNLISTED STARS	.40	.18
COMP.GOLD SET (296)	700.00	325.00
COMP.GOLD SER.1 (148)	600.00	275.00
COMP.GOLD SER.2 (148)	120.00	55.00
COMMON GOLD (G1-G123)	2.00	.90
COMMON GOLD (124-148)	2.00	.90
COMMON GOLD (G151-G298)	.30	.14
*SER.1 GOLD STARS: 6X TO 12X HI COL.		
*SER.1 GOLD RCs: 5X TO 10X HI		
*SER.2 GOLD STARS: 1.25X TO 3X HI		
*SER.2 GOLD RCs: 1X TO 2.5X HI		
GOLD: SER.1 STATED ODDS 1:12 H/R		
GOLD: ONE PER SER.2 PACK		
SER.1 GOLD SUB.CARDS HAVE NO "G" PREFIX		
COMP.GOLD PLAT.SET (296)	8000.00	3600.00
COMP.PLAT.SER.1 (148)	5000.00	2200.00
COMP.PLAT.SER.2 (148)	3000.00	1350.00
COMMON PLATINUM	10.00	4.50
*PLAT.STARS: 40X TO 80X HI COLUMN		
*PLAT.RCs: 20X TO 40X HI		
PLAT: SER.1 STATED ODDS 1:180 H/R		
PLAT: SER.2 STATED ODDS 1:100 H/R		
PLAT: STATED PRT.RUN LESS THAN 250 SETS		
SER.1 PLAT.SUB.CARDS HAVE NO "P" PREFIX		

☐ 1	Mookie Blaylock	.20	.09
☐ 2	Alan Henderson	.15	.07
☐ 3	Christian Laettner	.20	.09
☐ 4	Dikembe Mutombo	.20	.09
☐ 5	Steve Smith	.20	.09
☐ 6	Dana Barros	.15	.07
☐ 7	Rick Fox	.15	.07
☐ 8	Dino Radja	.15	.07
☐ 9	Antoine Walker	4.00	1.80
☐ 10	Eric Williams	.15	.07
☐ 11	Dell Curry	.15	.07
☐ 12	Tony Delk	.50	.23
☐ 13	Matt Geiger	.15	.07
☐ 14	Glen Rice	.40	.18
☐ 15	Ron Harper	.20	.09
☐ 16	Michael Jordan	5.00	2.20
☐ 17	Toni Kukoc	.20	.09
☐ 18	Scottie Pippen	1.25	.55
☐ 19	Dennis Rodman	1.50	.70
☐ 20	Terrell Brandon	.40	.18
☐ 21	Chris Mills	.15	.07
☐ 22	Bobby Phills	.15	.07
☐ 23	Bob Sura	.15	.07

☐ 24	Jim Jackson	.20	.09
☐ 25	Jason Kidd	.75	.35
☐ 26	Jamal Mashburn	.20	.09
☐ 27	George McCloud	.15	.07
☐ 28	Samaki Walker	.50	.23
☐ 29	LaPhonso Ellis	.15	.07
☐ 30	Antonio McDyess	.60	.25
☐ 31	Bryant Stith	.15	.07
☐ 32	Joe Dumars	.40	.18
☐ 33	Grant Hill	2.50	1.10
☐ 34	Theo Ratliff	.15	.07
☐ 35	Otis Thorpe	.20	.09
☐ 36	Chris Mullin	.40	.18
☐ 37	Joe Smith	.50	.23
☐ 38	Latrell Sprewell	.20	.09
☐ 39	Charles Barkley	.60	.25
☐ 40	Clyde Drexler	.50	.23
☐ 41	Mario Elie	.15	.07
☐ 42	Hakeem Olajuwon	.75	.35
☐ 43	Erick Dampier	.50	.23
☐ 44	Dale Davis	.15	.07
☐ 45	Derrick McKey	.15	.07
☐ 46	Reggie Miller	.40	.18
☐ 47	Rik Smits	.20	.09
☐ 48	Brent Barry	.15	.07
☐ 49	Malik Sealy	.15	.07
☐ 50	Loy Vaught	.20	.09
☐ 51	Lorenzen Wright	.50	.23
☐ 52	Kobe Bryant	8.00	3.60
☐ 53	Cedric Ceballos	.15	.07
☐ 54	Eddie Jones	.75	.35
☐ 55	Shaquille O'Neal	1.50	.70
☐ 56	Nick Van Exel	.40	.18
☐ 57	Tim Hardaway	.50	.23
☐ 58	Alonzo Mourning	.40	.18
☐ 59	Kurt Thomas	.15	.07
☐ 60	Ray Allen	1.25	.55
☐ 61	Vin Baker	.75	.35
☐ 62	Sherman Douglas	.15	.07
☐ 63	Glenn Robinson	.40	.18
☐ 64	Kevin Garnett	2.50	1.10
☐ 65	Tom Gugliotta	.40	.18
☐ 66	Stephon Marbury	4.00	1.80
☐ 67	Doug West	.15	.07
☐ 68	Shawn Bradley	.15	.07
☐ 69	Kendall Gill	.20	.09
☐ 70	Kerry Kittles	1.00	.45
☐ 71	Ed O'Bannon	.15	.07
☐ 72	Patrick Ewing	.40	.18
☐ 73	Larry Johnson	.20	.09
☐ 74	Charles Oakley	.15	.07
☐ 75	John Starks	.20	.09
☐ 76	John Wallace	.60	.25
☐ 77	Nick Anderson	.15	.07
☐ 78	Horace Grant	.20	.09
☐ 79	Anfernee Hardaway	1.50	.70
☐ 80	Dennis Scott	.15	.07
☐ 81	Derrick Coleman	.20	.09
☐ 82	Allen Iverson	4.00	1.80
☐ 83	Jerry Stackhouse	.50	.23
☐ 84	C.Weatherspoon	.15	.07
☐ 85	Michael Finley	.50	.23
☐ 86	Kevin Johnson	.20	.09
☐ 87	Steve Nash	.60	.25
☐ 88	Wesley Person	.15	.07
☐ 89	Jermaine O'Neal	.60	.25
☐ 90	Clifford Robinson	.15	.07
☐ 91	Arvydas Sabonis	.20	.09
☐ 92	Gary Trent	.15	.07
☐ 93	Tyus Edney	.15	.07
☐ 94	Brian Grant	.15	.07
☐ 95	Olden Polynice	.15	.07
☐ 96	Mitch Richmond	.40	.18
☐ 97	Corliss Williamson	.20	.09
☐ 98	Vinny Del Negro	.15	.07
☐ 99	Sean Elliott	.15	.07
☐ 100	Avery Johnson	.15	.07
☐ 101	David Robinson	.60	.25
☐ 102	Hersey Hawkins	.20	.09
☐ 103	Shawn Kemp	1.25	.55
☐ 104	Gary Payton	.60	.25
☐ 105	Sam Perkins	.20	.09
☐ 106	Detlef Schrempf	.20	.09
☐ 107	Marcus Camby	1.00	.45
☐ 108	Doug Christie	.15	.07
☐ 109	Damon Stoudamire	1.00	.45

110	Sharone Wright	.15	.07
111	Jeff Hornacek	.20	.09
112	Karl Malone	.60	.25
113	Chris Morris	.15	.07
114	Bryon Russell	.15	.07
115	John Stockton	.40	.18
116	S.Abdur-Rahim	2.50	1.10
117	Greg Anthony	.15	.07
118	Blue Edwards	.15	.07
119	Bryant Reeves	.20	.09
120	Calbert Cheaney	.15	.07
121	Juwan Howard	.50	.23
122	Gheorghe Muresan	.15	.07
123	Chris Webber	1.00	.45
124	Vin Baker OTB	.40	.18
125	Charles Barkley OTB	.40	.18
126	Kevin Garnett OTB	1.25	.55
127	Juwan Howard OTB	.40	.18
128	Larry Johnson OTB	.15	.07
129	Shawn Kemp OTB	.60	.25
130	Karl Malone OTB	.40	.18
131	Anthony Mason OTB	.15	.07
132	Antonio McDyess OTB	.40	.18
133	Alonzo Mourning OTB	.20	.09
134	Hakeem Olajuwon OTB	.40	.18
135	Shaquille O'Neal OTB	.75	.35
136	David Robinson OTB	.40	.18
137	Dennis Rodman OTB	.75	.35
138	Joe Smith OTB	.40	.18
139	Mookie Blaylock UE	.15	.07
140	Terrell Brandon UE	.20	.09
141	A.Hardaway UE	.75	.35
142	Grant Hill UE	1.25	.55
143	Michael Jordan UE	2.50	1.10
144	Jason Kidd UE	.40	.18
145	Gary Payton UE	.40	.18
146	Jerry Stackhouse UE	.40	.18
147	D.Stoudamire UE	.50	.23
148	Hakeem Olajuwon	.40	.18
	David Robinson		
	Robert Horry		
	Oliver Miller		
	C.Weatherspoon		
149	Checklist	.15	.07
150	Checklist	.15	.07
151	Tyrone Corbin	.15	.07
152	Priest Lauderdale	.15	.07
153	Dikembe Mutombo	.20	.09
154	Eldridge Recasner	.15	.07
155	Todd Day	.15	.07
156	Greg Minor	.15	.07
157	David Wesley	.15	.07
158	Vlade Divac	.20	.09
159	Anthony Mason	.20	.09
160	Malik Rose	.15	.07
161	Jason Caffey	.15	.07
162	Steve Kerr	.15	.07
163	Luc Longley	.20	.09
164	Danny Ferry	.15	.07
165	Tyrone Hill	.15	.07
166	Vitaly Potapenko	.20	.09
167	Sam Cassell	.20	.09
168	Michael Finley	.50	.23
169	Chris Gatling	.15	.07
170	A.C. Green	.20	.09
171	Oliver Miller	.15	.07
172	Eric Montross	.15	.07
173	Dale Ellis	.15	.07
174	Mark Jackson	.15	.07
175	Ervin Johnson	.15	.07
176	Sarunas Marciulionis	.15	.07
177	Stacey Augmon	.15	.07
178	Joe Dumars	.40	.18
179	Grant Hill	2.50	1.10
180	Lindsey Hunter	.15	.07
181	Grant Long	.15	.07
182	Terry Mills	.15	.07
183	Otis Thorpe	.15	.07
184	Jerome Williams	.20	.09
185	Todd Fuller	.15	.07
186	Ray Owes	.15	.07
187	Mark Price	.15	.07
188	Felton Spencer	.15	.07
189	Charles Barkley	.60	.25
190	Emanual Davis	.15	.07
191	Othella Harrington	.20	.09
192	Matt Maloney	.60	.25
193	Brent Price	.15	.07
194	Kevin Willis	.15	.07
195	Travis Best	.15	.07
196	Antonio Davis	.15	.07
197	Jalen Rose	.15	.07
198	Pooh Richardson	.15	.07
199	Stanley Roberts	.15	.07
200	Rodney Rogers	.15	.07
201	Elden Campbell	.20	.09
202	Derek Fisher	.50	.23
203	Travis Knight	.20	.09
204	Shaquille O'Neal	1.50	.70
205	Byron Scott	.20	.09
206	Sasha Danilovic	.15	.07
207	Dan Majerle	.20	.09
208	Martin Muursepp	.15	.07
209	Armon Gilliam	.15	.07
210	Andrew Lang	.15	.07
211	Johnny Newman	.15	.07
212	Kevin Garnett	2.50	1.10
213	Tom Gugliotta	.40	.18
214	Shane Heal	.15	.07
215	Stojko Vrankovic	.15	.07
216	Robert Pack	.15	.07
217	Khalid Reeves	.15	.07
218	Jayson Williams	.20	.09
219	Chris Childs	.15	.07
220	Allan Houston	.20	.09
221	Larry Johnson	.20	.09
222	Walter McCarty	.15	.07
223	Charlie Ward	.15	.07
224	Brian Evans	.15	.07
225	Amal McCaskill	.15	.07
226	Rony Seikaly	.15	.07
227	Gerald Wilkins	.15	.07
228	Mark Davis	.15	.07
229	Lucious Harris	.15	.07
230	Don MacLean	.15	.07
231	Cedric Ceballos	.15	.07
232	Rex Chapman	.15	.07
233	Jason Kidd	.75	.35
234	Danny Manning	.20	.09
235	Kenny Anderson	.20	.09
236	Aaron McKie	.15	.07
237	Isaiah Rider	.20	.09
238	Rasheed Wallace	.20	.09
239	Mahmoud Abdul-Rauf	.15	.07
240	Billy Owens	.15	.07
241	Michael Smith	.15	.07
242	Vernon Maxwell	.15	.07
243	Charles Smith	.15	.07
244	Dominique Wilkins	.40	.18
245	Craig Ehlo	.15	.07
246	Jim McIlvaine	.15	.07
247	Nate McMillan	.15	.07
248	Hubert Davis	.15	.07
249	Carlos Rogers	.15	.07
250	Zan Tabak	.15	.07
251	Walt Williams	.15	.07
252	Jeff Hornacek	.20	.09
253	Karl Malone	.60	.25
254	Greg Ostertag	.15	.07
255	Bryon Russell	.15	.07
256	John Stockton	.40	.18
257	George Lynch	.15	.07
258	Lawrence Moten	.15	.07
259	Anthony Peeler	.15	.07
260	Roy Rogers	.15	.07
261	Tracy Murray	.15	.07
262	Rod Strickland	.20	.09
263	Ben Wallace	.15	.07
264	S.Abdur-Rahim RE	1.25	.55
265	Ray Allen RE	.60	.25
266	Kobe Bryant RE	4.00	1.80
267	Marcus Camby RE	.50	.23
268	Erick Dampier RE	.40	.18
269	Tony Delk RE	.40	.18
270	Allen Iverson RE	2.00	.90
271	Kerry Kittles RE	.50	.23
272	Stephon Marbury RE	2.00	.90
273	Steve Nash RE	.40	.18
274	Jermaine O'Neal RE	.40	.18
275	Antoine Walker RE	2.00	.90
276	Samaki Walker RE	.40	.18
277	John Wallace RE	.40	.18
278	Lorenzen Wright RE	.40	.18
279	A.Hardaway SU	.75	.35
280	Michael Jordan SU	2.50	1.10
281	Jason Kidd SU	.40	.18
282	Hakeem Olajuwon SU	.40	.18
283	Gary Payton SU	.40	.18
284	Mitch Richmond SU	.20	.09
285	David Robinson SU	.40	.18
286	John Stockton SU	.20	.09
287	D.Stoudamire SU	.50	.23
288	Chris Webber SU	.50	.23
289	Clyde Drexler PG	.40	.18
290	Kevin Garnett PG	1.25	.55
291	Grant Hill PG	1.25	.55
292	Shawn Kemp PG	.60	.25
293	Karl Malone PG	.40	.18
294	Antonio McDyess PG	.20	.09
295	Alonzo Mourning PG	.20	.09
296	Shaquille O'Neal PG	.75	.35
297	Scottie Pippen PG	.60	.25
298	Jerry Stackhouse PG	.40	.18
299	Checklist (151-263)	.15	.07
300	CL (264-300/inserts)	.15	.07
NNO	J.Stackhouse Promo	3.00	1.35

1996-97 Ultra All-Rookies

Randomly inserted in series two packs at a rate of one in 4, this 15-card set focuses on some of the top players from the 1996-97 rookie class. The cards feature gold foil-stamping, glossy UV coating and embossing of the spotlight in the background.

	MINT	NRMT
COMPLETE SET (15)	50.00	22.00
COMMON CARD (1-15)	1.00	.45
SEMISTARS	1.25	.55
UNLISTED STARS	2.00	.90
SER.2 STATED ODDS 1:4 HOBBY/RETAIL		

1	Shareef Abdur-Rahim	6.00	2.70
2	Ray Allen	3.00	1.35
3	Kobe Bryant	20.00	9.00
4	Marcus Camby	2.50	1.10
5	Tony Delk	2.00	.90
6	Derek Fisher	2.00	.90
7	Allen Iverson	10.00	4.50
8	Kerry Kittles	2.50	1.10
9	Matt Maloney	1.00	.90
10	Stephon Marbury	10.00	4.50
11	Vitaly Potapenko	1.00	.45
12	Roy Rogers	1.00	.45
13	Antoine Walker	10.00	4.50
14	Samaki Walker	2.00	.90
15	John Wallace	2.00	.90

1996-97 Ultra Board Game

Randomly inserted in series two packs at a rate of one in 9, this 20-card set features some of the top rebounders in the NBA featured against a "checkerboard" pattern on the front of the cards.

	MINT	NRMT
COMPLETE SET (20)	60.00	27.00
COMMON CARD (1-20)	.75	.35
SEMISTARS	1.00	.45
UNLISTED STARS	1.50	.70
SER.2 STATED ODDS 1:9 HOBBY/RETAIL		

		MINT	NRMT
☐ 1	Vin Baker	3.00	1.35
☐ 2	Charles Barkley	2.50	1.10
☐ 3	Dale Davis	.75	.35
☐ 4	Clyde Drexler	2.00	.90
☐ 5	Patrick Ewing	1.50	.70
☐ 6	Grant Hill	10.00	4.50
☐ 7	Michael Jordan	20.00	9.00
☐ 8	Shawn Kemp	5.00	2.20
☐ 9	Jason Kidd	3.00	1.35
☐ 10	Karl Malone	2.50	1.10
☐ 11	Alonzo Mourning	1.50	.70
☐ 12	Dikembe Mutombo	1.00	.45
☐ 13	Hakeem Olajuwon	3.00	1.35
☐ 14	Shaquille O'Neal	6.00	2.70
☐ 15	Scottie Pippen	5.00	2.20
☐ 16	David Robinson	2.50	1.10
☐ 17	Dennis Rodman	6.00	2.70
☐ 18	Loy Vaught	1.00	.45
☐ 19	Chris Webber	4.00	1.80
☐ 20	Jayson Williams	1.00	.45

1996-97 Ultra Court Masters

This 15-card set was randomly inserted into series one retail packs only at a rate of one in

180. *The cards are made with a plastic stock and features members of the 1st, 2nd and 3rd 1995-96 All-NBA teams.*

	MINT	NRMT
COMPLETE SET (15)	500.00	220.00
COMMON CARD (1-15)	12.00	5.50
SER.1 STATED ODDS 1:180 RETAIL		

		MINT	NRMT
☐ 1	Anfernee Hardaway	50.00	22.00
☐ 2	Michael Jordan	150.00	70.00
☐ 3	Karl Malone	20.00	9.00
☐ 4	Scottie Pippen	40.00	18.00
☐ 5	David Robinson	20.00	9.00
☐ 6	Grant Hill	80.00	36.00
☐ 7	Shawn Kemp	40.00	18.00
☐ 8	Hakeem Olajuwon	25.00	11.00
☐ 9	Gary Payton	20.00	9.00
☐ 10	John Stockton	12.00	5.50
☐ 11	Charles Barkley	20.00	9.00
☐ 12	Juwan Howard	15.00	6.75
☐ 13	Reggie Miller	12.00	5.50
☐ 14	Shaquille O'Neal	50.00	22.00
☐ 15	Mitch Richmond	12.00	5.50

1996-97 Ultra Decade of Excellence

Randomly inserted in both series packs at a rate of one in 100, this 20-card set salutes twenty of the players who were included in the 1986-87 Fleer set. Each card features the 1986-87 design, with gold-foil trim and the words "Ultra Decade 1986-1996" in gold foil. Card backs are numbered with a "U" prefix.

	MINT	NRMT
COMPLETE SET (20)	80.00	36.00
COMPLETE SERIES 1 (10)	50.00	22.00
COMPLETE SERIES 2 (10)	30.00	13.50
COMMON CARD (U1-U20)	2.50	1.10
SEMISTARS	5.00	2.20
SER.1/2 STATED ODDS 1:100 HOBBY/RETAIL		

		MINT	NRMT
☐ U1	Clyde Drexler	4.00	1.80
☐ U2	Joe Dumars	2.50	1.10
☐ U3	Derek Harper	2.50	1.10
☐ U4	Michael Jordan	40.00	18.00
☐ U5	Karl Malone	5.00	2.20
☐ U6	Chris Mullin	2.50	1.10
☐ U7	Charles Oakley	2.50	1.10
☐ U8	Sam Perkins	2.50	1.10
☐ U9	Ricky Pierce	2.50	1.10
☐ U10	Buck Williams	2.50	1.10
☐ U11	Charles Barkley	8.00	3.60
☐ U12	Patrick Ewing	5.00	2.20
☐ U13	Eddie Johnson	2.50	1.10
☐ U14	Hakeem Olajuwon	10.00	4.50
☐ U15	Robert Parish	2.50	1.10
☐ U16	Byron Scott	2.50	1.10
☐ U17	Wayman Tisdale	2.50	1.10
☐ U18	Gerald Wilkins	2.50	1.10
☐ U19	Herb Williams	2.50	1.10
☐ U20	Kevin Willis	2.50	1.10

1996-97 Ultra Fresh Faces

Randomly inserted in series one packs at a rate of one in 72, this 9-card set focuses on top players from the 1996 NBA Draft. Each card is die cut featuring an action photo of the player printed against a backdrop of a die cut team jersey. The design was submitted by Shinto Imai, who submitted the winning entry in the 1995-96 Fleer "Design Your Own NBA Card" contest.

	MINT	NRMT
COMPLETE SET (9)	110.00	50.00
COMMON CARD (1-9)	4.00	1.80
SER.1 STATED ODDS 1:72 HOBBY/RETAIL		

		MINT	NRMT
☐ 1	Shareef Abdur-Rahim	15.00	6.75
☐ 2	Ray Allen	8.00	3.60
☐ 3	Kobe Bryant	50.00	22.00
☐ 4	Marcus Camby	6.00	2.70
☐ 5	Allen Iverson	25.00	11.00
☐ 6	Kerry Kittles	6.00	2.70
☐ 7	Stephon Marbury	25.00	11.00
☐ 8	Steve Nash	4.00	1.80
☐ 9	Antoine Walker	25.00	11.00

1996-97 Ultra Full Court Trap

Randomly inserted in series one packs at a rate of one in 15, this 10-card set showcases the players selected to the NBA 1st and 2nd All-Defensive Teams. Card fronts have a foil-etched colored background.

	MINT	NRMT
COMPLETE SET (10)	30.00	13.50
COMMON CARD (1-10)	1.00	.45
SER.1 STATED ODDS 1:15 HOBBY/RETAIL		

COMP. GOLD SET (10) 200.00   90.00
COMMON GOLD (1-10) 6.00   2.70
*GOLD STARS: 3X TO 6X HI COLUMN
GOLD: SER.1 STATED ODDS 1:180 HOB/RET

		MINT	NRMT
☐ 1	Michael Jordan	20.00	9.00
☐ 2	Gary Payton	2.50	1.10
☐ 3	Scottie Pippen	5.00	2.20
☐ 4	David Robinson	2.50	1.10
☐ 5	Dennis Rodman	6.00	2.70
☐ 6	Mookie Blaylock	1.00	.45
☐ 7	Horace Grant	1.00	.45
☐ 8	Derrick McKey	1.00	.45
☐ 9	Hakeem Olajuwon	3.00	1.35
☐ 10	Bobby Phills	1.00	.45

1996-97 Ultra Give and Take

Randomly inserted in series two retail packs only at a rate of one in 18, this 10-card set focuses on players who can not only dish out the assist, but make the key steals. The cards have a full foil background that is divided into a gold and silver tone split equally from top to bottom.

		MINT	NRMT
COMPLETE SET (10)		55.00	25.00
COMMON CARD (1-10)		1.50	.70
SEMISTARS		2.00	.90
SER.2 STATED ODDS 1:18 RETAIL			

		MINT	NRMT
☐ 1	Mookie Blaylock	1.50	.70
☐ 2	Anfernee Hardaway	8.00	3.60
☐ 3	Tim Hardaway	2.50	1.10
☐ 4	Allen Iverson	10.00	4.50
☐ 5	Michael Jordan	30.00	13.50
☐ 6	Jason Kidd	4.00	1.80
☐ 7	Gary Payton	3.00	1.35
☐ 8	Scottie Pippen	6.00	2.70
☐ 9	John Stockton	2.00	.90
☐ 10	Damon Stoudamire	5.00	2.20

1996-97 Ultra Rising Stars

Randomly inserted in series one hobby packs only at a rate of one in 180, this 10-card set focuses on young stars and rookies. Each card front features a full photo shot of the player against a matted background.

		MINT	NRMT
COMPLETE SET (10)		100.00	45.00
COMMON CARD (1-10)		5.00	2.20
SER.1 STATED ODDS 1:180 HOBBY			

		MINT	NRMT
☐ 1	Shareef Abdur-Rahim	12.00	5.50
☐ 2	Kobe Bryant	40.00	18.00
☐ 3	Anfernee Hardaway	15.00	6.75
☐ 4	Grant Hill	25.00	11.00
☐ 5	Juwan Howard	5.00	2.20
☐ 6	Allen Iverson	20.00	9.00
☐ 7	Jason Kidd	8.00	3.60
☐ 8	Stephon Marbury	20.00	9.00
☐ 9	Joe Smith	5.00	2.20
☐ 10	Damon Stoudamire	10.00	4.50

1996-97 Ultra Rookie Flashback

Randomly inserted in series one packs at a rate of one in 45, this 11-card set features the members of the 1995-96 NBA All-Rookie Team, printed against an etched-foil design.

		MINT	NRMT
COMPLETE SET (11)		50.00	22.00
COMMON CARD (1-11)		2.00	.90
SEMISTARS		2.50	1.10
UNLISTED STARS		4.00	1.80
SER.1 STATED ODDS 1:45 HOBBY/RETAIL			

☐ 1	Michael Finley	5.00	2.20
☐ 2	Antonio McDyess	6.00	2.70
☐ 3	Arvydas Sabonis	2.50	1.10
☐ 4	Joe Smith	5.00	2.20
☐ 5	Jerry Stackhouse	5.00	2.20
☐ 6	Damon Stoudamire	10.00	4.50
☐ 7	Brent Barry	2.00	.90
☐ 8	Tyus Edney	2.00	.90
☐ 9	Kevin Garnett	25.00	11.00
☐ 10	Bryant Reeves	2.50	1.10
☐ 11	Rasheed Wallace	2.50	1.10

1996-97 Ultra Scoring Kings

Randomly inserted in series two hobby packs only at a rate of one in 24, this 29-card set returns for the fourth straight year focusing on some of the NBA's top scorers. The cards feature a metallic ink background.

		MINT	NRMT
COMPLETE SET (29)		250.00	110.00
COMMON CARD (1-29)		2.50	1.10
SEMISTARS		3.00	1.35
UNLISTED STARS		5.00	2.20
SER.2 STATED ODDS 1:24 HOBBY			
COMP. PLUS SET (29)		650.00	300.00
COMMON PLUS (1-29)		6.00	2.70
*PLUS STARS: 1.25X TO 2.5X HI COLUMN			
PLUS: SER.2 STATED ODDS 1:96 HOBBY			

☐ 1	Steve Smith	3.00	1.35
☐ 2	Dino Radja	2.50	1.10
☐ 3	Glen Rice	5.00	2.20
☐ 4	Michael Jordan	60.00	27.00
☐ 5	Terrell Brandon	5.00	2.20
☐ 6	Jim Jackson	3.00	1.35
☐ 7	Antonio McDyess	8.00	3.60
☐ 8	Grant Hill	30.00	13.50
☐ 9	Latrell Sprewell	3.00	1.35
☐ 10	Hakeem Olajuwon	10.00	4.50
☐ 11	Reggie Miller	5.00	2.20
☐ 12	Loy Vaught	3.00	1.35
☐ 13	Shaquille O'Neal	20.00	9.00
☐ 14	Alonzo Mourning	5.00	2.20
☐ 15	Vin Baker	10.00	4.50
☐ 16	Tom Gugliotta	5.00	2.20
☐ 17	Kendall Gill	3.00	1.35
☐ 18	Patrick Ewing	5.00	2.20
☐ 19	A.Hardaway	20.00	9.00
☐ 20	Allen Iverson	25.00	11.00
☐ 21	Danny Manning	3.00	1.35
☐ 22	Kenny Anderson	3.00	1.35
☐ 23	Mitch Richmond	5.00	2.20
☐ 24	David Robinson	8.00	3.60
☐ 25	Shawn Kemp	15.00	6.75
☐ 26	Damon Stoudamire	12.00	5.50
☐ 27	Karl Malone	8.00	3.60

□ 28 S.Abdur-Rahim 15.00 6.75
□ 29 Chris Webber 12.00 5.50

1996-97 Ultra Starring Role

Randomly inserted in series two packs at a rate of one in 288, this 10-card set focuses on players who are spotlighted on their teams. The card design is plastic with silver foil.

	MINT	NRMT
COMPLETE SET (10)	500.00	220.00
COMMON CARD (1-10)	20.00	9.00
SER.2 STATED ODDS 1:288 HOBBY/RETAIL		

□ 1 Kevin Garnett	80.00	36.00
□ 2 A.Hardaway	50.00	22.00
□ 3 Grant Hill	80.00	36.00
□ 4 Michael Jordan	150.00	70.00
□ 5 Shawn Kemp	40.00	18.00
□ 6 Karl Malone	20.00	9.00
□ 7 Hakeem Olajuwon	25.00	11.00
□ 8 Shaquille O'Neal	50.00	22.00
□ 9 David Robinson	20.00	9.00
□ 10 Damon Stoudamire	30.00	13.50

1997-98 Ultra

The 1997-98 Ultra set, produced by Fleer/SkyBox, was issued in two series with the first containing 150 cards and the second 125 and were packaged in 10-card packs that carried a suggested retail price of $2.49. The first series feature most of the 1997-98 rookie class including Derek Anderson, Tony Battie, Chauncey Billups, Antonio Daniels, Tim Duncan, Brevin Knight, Ron Mercer, Tim Thomas and Keith Van Horn. Those cards were seeded in packs at a rate of one in four. The second series featured the subset "98 Greats" and were inserted at a rate of one in four. A Jerry Stackhouse promo card was also issued. Since that card shares the same number as the regular Stackhouse in the base set (#105), we have made it a "NNO" and listed it at the bottom of the set.

	MINT	NRMT
COMPLETE SET (275)	250.00	110.00
COMPLETE SERIES 1 (150)	200.00	90.00
COMPLETE SERIES 2 (125)	50.00	22.00
COMMON CARD (1-148)	.15	.07
SEMISTARS	.20	.09
COMMON CARD (149-275)	.15	.07
UNLISTED STARS	.40	.18
SER.1 ROOKIE SUBSET ODDS 1:4 H/R		
'98 GREATS SUBSET ODDS 1:4 H/R		
COMP.GOLD SET (275)	250.00	110.00
COMP.GOLD SER.1 (148)	150.00	70.00
COMP.GOLD SER.2 (123)	100.00	45.00
COMMON GOLD	.40	.18

*SER.1 GOLD STARS: 1.25X TO 2.5X HI COL.
*SER.1 GOLD RCs: .25X TO .5X HI
*SER.2 GOLD STARS/RC's: 1.25X TO 2.5X HI
*SER.2 GOLD '98 GRE: .75X TO 1.25X HI
GOLD: ONE PER SER.1/2 HOBBY PACK
SUBSETS ARE NOT SP'S IN PARALLEL SET

□ 1 Kobe Bryant	3.00	1.35
□ 2 Charles Barkley	.60	.25
□ 3 Joe Dumars	.40	.18
□ 4 Wesley Person	.15	.07
□ 5 Walt Williams	.15	.07
□ 6 Vlade Divac	.20	.09
□ 7 Mookie Blaylock	.20	.09
□ 8 Jason Kidd	.75	.35
□ 9 Ron Harper	.20	.09
□ 10 Sherman Douglas	.15	.07
□ 11 Cedric Ceballos	.15	.07
□ 12 Karl Malone	.60	.25
□ 13 Antonio McDyess	.50	.23
□ 14 Steve Kerr	.15	.07
□ 15 Matt Maloney	.15	.07
□ 16 Glenn Robinson	.40	.18
□ 17 Rony Seikaly	.15	.07
□ 18 Derrick Coleman	.20	.09
□ 19 Jermaine O'Neal	.20	.09
□ 20 Scott Burrell	.15	.07
□ 21 Glen Rice	.40	.18
□ 22 Dale Ellis	.15	.07
□ 23 Michael Jordan	5.00	2.20
□ 24 Anfernee Hardaway	1.50	.70
□ 25 Bryon Russell	.15	.07
□ 26 Toni Kukoc	.20	.09
□ 27 Theo Ratliff	.15	.07
□ 28 Tom Gugliotta	.40	.18
□ 29 Dennis Rodman	1.50	.70
□ 30 John Stockton	.40	.18
□ 31 Priest Lauderdale	.15	.07
□ 32 Luc Longley	.20	.09
□ 33 Grant Hill	2.50	1.10
□ 34 Antonio Davis	.15	.07
□ 35 Eddie Jones	.75	.35
□ 36 Nick Anderson	.15	.07
□ 37 Shareef Abdur-Rahim	1.25	.55
□ 38 Stephon Marbury	2.00	.90
□ 39 Todd Day	.15	.07
□ 40 Tim Hardaway	.50	.23
□ 41 Larry Johnson	.20	.09
□ 42 Sam Perkins	.20	.09

□ 43 Dikembe Mutombo	.20	.09
□ 44 Charles Outlaw	.15	.07
□ 45 Mitch Richmond	.40	.18
□ 46 Bryant Reeves	.20	.09
□ 47 P.J. Brown	.15	.07
□ 48 Steve Smith	.20	.09
□ 49 Martin Muursepp	.15	.07
□ 50 Jamal Mashburn	.20	.09
□ 51 Kendall Gill	.20	.09
□ 52 Vinny Del Negro	.15	.07
□ 53 Roy Rogers	.15	.07
□ 54 Khalid Reeves	.15	.07
□ 55 Scottie Pippen	1.25	.55
□ 56 Joe Smith	.40	.18
□ 57 Mark Jackson	.15	.07
□ 58 Voshon Lenard	.15	.07
□ 59 Dan Majerle	.20	.09
□ 60 Alonzo Mourning	.40	.18
□ 61 Kerry Kittles	.40	.18
□ 62 Chris Childs	.15	.07
□ 63 Patrick Ewing	.40	.18
□ 64 Allan Houston	.20	.09
□ 65 Marcus Camby	.40	.18
□ 66 Christian Laettner	.20	.09
□ 67 Loy Vaught	.20	.09
□ 68 Jayson Williams	.20	.09
□ 69 Avery Johnson	.15	.07
□ 70 Damon Stoudamire	.75	.35
□ 71 Kevin Johnson	.20	.09
□ 72 Gheorghe Muresan	.15	.07
□ 73 Reggie Miller	.40	.18
□ 74 John Wallace	.20	.09
□ 75 Terrell Brandon	.40	.18
□ 76 Dale Davis	.15	.07
□ 77 Latrell Sprewell	.20	.09
□ 78 Lorenzen Wright	.15	.07
□ 79 Rod Strickland	.15	.07
□ 80 Kenny Anderson	.20	.09
□ 81 Anthony Mason	.20	.09
□ 82 Hakeem Olajuwon	.75	.35
□ 83 Kevin Garnett	2.50	1.10
□ 84 Isaiah Rider	.20	.09
□ 85 Mark Price	.15	.07
□ 86 Shawn Bradley	.15	.07
□ 87 Vin Baker	.75	.35
□ 88 Steve Nash	.20	.09
□ 89 Jeff Hornacek	.15	.07
□ 90 Tony Delk	.15	.07
□ 91 Horace Grant	.20	.09
□ 92 Othella Harrington	.15	.07
□ 93 Arvydas Sabonis	.20	.09
□ 94 Antoine Walker	2.00	.90
□ 95 Todd Fuller	.15	.07
□ 96 John Starks	.15	.07
□ 97 Olden Polynice	.15	.07
□ 98 Sean Elliott	.15	.07
□ 99 Travis Best	.15	.07
□ 100 Chris Gatling	.15	.07
□ 101 Derek Harper	.15	.07
□ 102 LaPhonso Ellis	.15	.07
□ 103 Dean Garrett	.15	.07
□ 104 Hersey Hawkins	.20	.09
□ 105 Jerry Stackhouse	.40	.18
□ 106 Ray Allen	.50	.23
□ 107 Allen Iverson	2.00	.90
□ 108 Chris Webber	1.00	.45
□ 109 Robert Pack	.15	.07
□ 110 Gary Payton	.60	.25
□ 111 Mario Elie	.15	.07
□ 112 Dell Curry	.15	.07
□ 113 Lindsey Hunter	.15	.07
□ 114 Robert Horry	.20	.09
□ 115 David Robinson	.60	.25
□ 116 Kevin Willis	.15	.07
□ 117 Tyrone Hill	.15	.07
□ 118 Vitaly Potapenko	.15	.07
□ 119 Clyde Drexler	.50	.23
□ 120 Derek Fisher	.20	.09
□ 121 Detlef Schrempf	.20	.09
□ 122 Gary Trent	.15	.07
□ 123 Danny Ferry	.15	.07
□ 124 Derek Anderson	10.00	4.50
□ 125 Chris Anstey	3.00	1.35
□ 126 Tony Battie	4.00	1.80
□ 127 Chauncey Billups	10.00	4.50
□ 128 Kelvin Cato	2.50	1.10

☐ 129 Austin Croshere	2.50	1.10
☐ 130 Antonio Daniels	6.00	2.70
☐ 131 Tim Duncan	60.00	27.00
☐ 132 Danny Fortson	4.00	1.80
☐ 133 Adonal Foyle	2.50	1.10
☐ 134 Paul Grant	1.50	.70
☐ 135 Ed Gray	2.50	1.10
☐ 136 Bobby Jackson	6.00	2.70
☐ 137 Brevin Knight	10.00	4.50
☐ 138 Tracy McGrady	15.00	6.75
☐ 139 Ron Mercer	25.00	11.00
☐ 140 Anthony Parker	1.50	.70
☐ 141 Scot Pollard	1.50	.70
☐ 142 Rodrick Rhodes	2.50	1.10
☐ 143 Olivier Saint-Jean	3.00	1.35
☐ 144 Maurice Taylor	10.00	4.50
☐ 145 Johnny Taylor	1.50	.70
☐ 146 Tim Thomas	20.00	9.00
☐ 147 Keith Van Horn	35.00	16.00
☐ 148 Jacque Vaughn	2.50	1.10
☐ 149 Checklist	.15	.07
☐ 150 Checklist	.15	.07
☐ 151 Scott Burrell	.15	.07
☐ 152 Brian Williams	.15	.07
☐ 153 Terry Mills	.15	.07
☐ 154 Jim Jackson	.20	.09
☐ 155 Michael Finley	.40	.18
☐ 156 Jeff Nordgaard	.15	.07
☐ 157 Carl Herrera	.15	.07
☐ 158 Otis Thorpe	.20	.09
☐ 159 Wesley Person	.15	.07
☐ 160 Tyrone Hill	.15	.07
☐ 161 Charles O'Bannon	.15	.07
☐ 162 Greg Anthony	.15	.07
☐ 163 Rusty LaRue	.15	.07
☐ 164 David Wesley	.15	.07
☐ 165 Chris Garner	.15	.07
☐ 166 George McCloud	.15	.07
☐ 167 Mark Price	.15	.07
☐ 168 God Shammgod	.15	.07
☐ 169 Isaac Austin	.15	.07
☐ 170 Alan Henderson	.15	.07
☐ 171 Eric Washington	.40	.18
☐ 172 Darrell Armstrong	.15	.07
☐ 173 Calbert Cheaney	.15	.07
☐ 174 Cedric Henderson	.50	.23
☐ 175 Bryant Stith	.15	.07
☐ 176 Sean Rooks	.15	.07
☐ 177 Chris Mills	.15	.07
☐ 178 Eldridge Recasner	.15	.07
☐ 179 Priest Lauderdale	.15	.07
☐ 180 Rick Fox	.15	.07
☐ 181 Keith Closs	.15	.07
☐ 182 Chris Dudley	.15	.07
☐ 183 L.Funderburke	.40	.18
☐ 184 Michael Stewart	.40	.18
☐ 185 Alvin Williams	.50	.23
☐ 186 Adam Keefe	.15	.07
☐ 187 Chauncey Billups	.75	.35
☐ 188 Jon Barry	.15	.07
☐ 189 Bobby Jackson	.40	.18
☐ 190 Sam Cassell	.20	.09
☐ 191 Dee Brown	.15	.07
☐ 192 Travis Knight	.15	.07
☐ 193 Dean Garrett	.15	.07
☐ 194 David Benoit	.15	.07
☐ 195 Chris Morris	.15	.07
☐ 196 Bubba Wells	.15	.07
☐ 197 James Robinson	.15	.07
☐ 198 Anthony Johnson	.15	.07
☐ 199 Dennis Scott	.15	.07
☐ 200 DeJunn Wheat	.15	.07
☐ 201 Rodney Rogers	.15	.07
☐ 202 Tariq Abdul-Wahad	.40	.18
☐ 203 Cherokee Parks	.15	.07
☐ 204 Jacque Vaughn	.40	.18
☐ 205 Cory Alexander	.15	.07
☐ 206 Kevin Ollie	.15	.07
☐ 207 George Lynch	.15	.07
☐ 208 Lamond Murray	.15	.07
☐ 209 Jud Buechler	.15	.07
☐ 210 Erick Dampier	.15	.07
☐ 211 Malcolm Huckaby	.15	.07
☐ 212 Chris Webber	1.00	.45
☐ 213 Chris Crawford	.15	.07
☐ 214 J.R. Reid	.15	.07

☐ 215 Eddie Johnson	.15	.07
☐ 216 Nick Van Exel	.40	.18
☐ 217 Antonio McDyess	.50	.23
☐ 218 David Wingate	.15	.07
☐ 219 Malik Sealy	.15	.07
☐ 220 Charles Outlaw	.15	.07
☐ 221 Serge Zwikker	.15	.07
☐ 222 Bobby Phills	.15	.07
☐ 223 Shea Seals	.15	.07
☐ 224 Clifford Robinson	.15	.07
☐ 225 Zydrunas Ilgauskas	.20	.09
☐ 226 John Thomas	.15	.07
☐ 227 Rik Smits	.20	.09
☐ 228 Rasheed Wallace	.20	.09
☐ 229 John Wallace	.20	.09
☐ 230 Bob Sura	.15	.07
☐ 231 Ervin Johnson	.15	.07
☐ 232 Keith Booth	.15	.07
☐ 233 Chuck Person	.15	.07
☐ 234 Brian Shaw	.15	.07
☐ 235 Todd Day	.15	.07
☐ 236 C.Weatherspoon	.15	.07
☐ 237 Charlie Ward	.15	.07
☐ 238 Rod Strickland	.20	.09
☐ 239 Shawn Kemp	1.25	.55
☐ 240 Terrell Brandon	.40	.18
☐ 241 Corey Beck	.15	.07
☐ 242 Vin Baker	.75	.35
☐ 243 Fred Hoiberg	.15	.07
☐ 244 Chris Mullin	.40	.18
☐ 245 Brian Grant	.15	.07
☐ 246 Derek Anderson	.60	.25
☐ 247 Zan Tabak	.15	.07
☐ 248 Charles Smith	.15	.07
☐ 249 S.Abdur-Rahim GRE	2.50	1.10
☐ 250 Ray Allen GRE	1.00	.45
☐ 251 Charles Barkley GRE	1.25	.55
☐ 252 Kobe Bryant GRE	6.00	2.70
☐ 253 Marcus Camby GRE	.75	.35
☐ 254 Kevin Garnett GRE	5.00	2.20
☐ 255 A.Hardaway GRE	3.00	1.35
☐ 256 Grant Hill GRE	5.00	2.20
☐ 257 Juwan Howard GRE	.75	.35
☐ 258 Allen Iverson GRE	4.00	1.80
☐ 259 M.Jordan GRE	10.00	4.50
☐ 260 Shawn Kemp GRE	2.50	1.10
☐ 261 Kerry Kittles GRE	.75	.35
☐ 262 Karl Malone GRE	1.25	.55
☐ 263 S.Marbury GRE	4.00	1.80
☐ 264 H.Olajuwon GRE	1.50	.70
☐ 265 Shaquille O'Neal GRE	3.00	1.35
☐ 266 Gary Payton GRE	1.25	.55
☐ 267 Scottie Pippen GRE	2.50	1.10
☐ 268 D.Robinson GRE	1.25	.55
☐ 269 D.Rodman GRE	3.00	1.35
☐ 270 Joe Smith GRE	.75	.35
☐ 271 J.Stackhouse GRE	.75	.35
☐ 272 D.Stoudamire GRE	1.50	.70
☐ 273 Antoine Walker GRE	4.00	1.80
☐ 274 Checklist	.15	.07
☐ 275 Checklist	.15	.07
☐ NNO J.Stackhouse Promo	2.00	.90

1997-98 Ultra Platinum Medallion

Randomly inserted into both series hobby packs, this 271-card set parallels the basic set. Each card is serial numbered on the back to 150 sets. The last ten sets were available via redemption cards randomly inserted into packs. Each card was good for a complete Platinum Medallion set.

	MINT	NRMT
COMMON CARD	20.00	9.00
SEMISTARS	25.00	11.00
RANDOM INSERTS SER.1/2 HOBBY PACKS		
STATED PRINT RUN 100 SERIAL #'d SETS		
☐ 1 Kobe Bryant	400.00	180.00
☐ 2 Charles Barkley	60.00	27.00
☐ 3 Joe Dumars	30.00	13.50
☐ 4 Wesley Person	20.00	9.00
☐ 5 Walt Williams	20.00	9.00
☐ 6 Vlade Divac	25.00	11.00
☐ 7 Mookie Blaylock	25.00	11.00
☐ 8 Jason Kidd	80.00	36.00
☐ 9 Ron Harper	25.00	11.00
☐ 10 Sherman Douglas	20.00	9.00
☐ 11 Cedric Ceballos	20.00	9.00
☐ 12 Karl Malone	60.00	27.00
☐ 13 Antonio McDyess	50.00	22.00
☐ 14 Steve Kerr	20.00	9.00
☐ 15 Matt Maloney	20.00	9.00
☐ 16 Glenn Robinson	30.00	13.50
☐ 17 Rony Seikaly	20.00	9.00
☐ 18 Derrick Coleman	25.00	11.00
☐ 19 Jermaine O'Neal	25.00	11.00
☐ 20 Scott Burrell	20.00	9.00
☐ 21 Glen Rice	40.00	18.00
☐ 22 Dale Ellis	20.00	9.00
☐ 23 Michael Jordan	750.00	350.00
☐ 24 A.Hardaway	200.00	90.00
☐ 25 Bryon Russell	20.00	9.00
☐ 26 Toni Kukoc	25.00	11.00
☐ 27 Theo Ratliff	20.00	9.00
☐ 28 Tom Gugliotta	30.00	13.50
☐ 29 Dennis Rodman	150.00	70.00
☐ 30 John Stockton	40.00	18.00
☐ 31 Priest Lauderdale	20.00	9.00
☐ 32 Luc Longley	25.00	11.00
☐ 33 Grant Hill	250.00	110.00
☐ 34 Antonio Davis	20.00	9.00
☐ 35 Eddie Jones	80.00	36.00
☐ 36 Nick Anderson	20.00	9.00
☐ 37 S.Abdur-Rahim	125.00	55.00
☐ 38 Stephon Marbury	200.00	90.00
☐ 39 Todd Day	20.00	9.00
☐ 40 Tim Hardaway	50.00	22.00
☐ 41 Larry Johnson	25.00	11.00
☐ 42 Sam Perkins	25.00	11.00
☐ 43 Dikembe Mutombo	25.00	11.00
☐ 44 Charles Outlaw	20.00	9.00
☐ 45 Mitch Richmond	40.00	18.00
☐ 46 Bryant Reeves	25.00	11.00
☐ 47 P.J. Brown	20.00	9.00
☐ 48 Steve Smith	25.00	11.00
☐ 49 Martin Muursepp	20.00	9.00
☐ 50 Jamal Mashburn	25.00	11.00
☐ 51 Kendall Gill	25.00	11.00
☐ 52 Vinny Del Negro	20.00	9.00
☐ 53 Roy Rogers	20.00	9.00
☐ 54 Khalid Reeves	20.00	9.00
☐ 55 Scottie Pippen	125.00	55.00
☐ 56 Joe Smith	40.00	18.00
☐ 57 Mark Jackson	20.00	9.00
☐ 58 Voshon Lenard	20.00	9.00
☐ 59 Dan Majerle	25.00	11.00
☐ 60 Alonzo Mourning	40.00	18.00
☐ 61 Kerry Kittles	40.00	18.00
☐ 62 Chris Childs	20.00	9.00

#	Player	MINT	NRMT
☐ 63	Patrick Ewing	40.00	18.00
☐ 64	Allan Houston	25.00	11.00
☐ 65	Marcus Camby	40.00	18.00
☐ 66	Christian Laettner	25.00	11.00
☐ 67	Loy Vaught	25.00	11.00
☐ 68	Jayson Williams	25.00	11.00
☐ 69	Avery Johnson	20.00	9.00
☐ 70	Damon Stoudamire	80.00	36.00
☐ 71	Kevin Johnson	25.00	11.00
☐ 72	Gheorghe Muresan	20.00	9.00
☐ 73	Reggie Miller	40.00	18.00
☐ 74	John Wallace	25.00	11.00
☐ 75	Terrell Brandon	30.00	13.50
☐ 76	Dale Davis	20.00	9.00
☐ 77	Latrell Sprewell	25.00	11.00
☐ 78	Lorenzen Wright	20.00	9.00
☐ 79	Rod Strickland	25.00	11.00
☐ 80	Kenny Anderson	25.00	11.00
☐ 81	Anthony Mason	25.00	11.00
☐ 82	Hakeem Olajuwon	80.00	36.00
☐ 83	Kevin Garnett	250.00	110.00
☐ 84	Isaiah Rider	25.00	11.00
☐ 85	Mark Price	20.00	9.00
☐ 86	Shawn Bradley	20.00	9.00
☐ 87	Vin Baker	80.00	36.00
☐ 88	Steve Nash	25.00	11.00
☐ 89	Jeff Hornacek	25.00	11.00
☐ 90	Tony Delk	20.00	9.00
☐ 91	Horace Grant	25.00	11.00
☐ 92	Othella Harrington	20.00	9.00
☐ 93	Arvydas Sabonis	25.00	11.00
☐ 94	Antoine Walker	200.00	90.00
☐ 95	Todd Fuller	20.00	9.00
☐ 96	John Starks	25.00	11.00
☐ 97	Olden Polynice	20.00	9.00
☐ 98	Sean Elliott	20.00	9.00
☐ 99	Travis Best	20.00	9.00
☐ 100	Chris Gatling	20.00	9.00
☐ 101	Derek Harper	20.00	9.00
☐ 102	LaPhonso Ellis	20.00	9.00
☐ 103	Dean Garrett	20.00	9.00
☐ 104	Hersey Hawkins	25.00	11.00
☐ 105	Jerry Stackhouse	40.00	18.00
☐ 106	Ray Allen	50.00	22.00
☐ 107	Allen Iverson	200.00	90.00
☐ 108	Chris Webber	100.00	45.00
☐ 109	Robert Pack	20.00	9.00
☐ 110	Gary Payton	60.00	27.00
☐ 111	Mario Elie	20.00	9.00
☐ 112	Dell Curry	20.00	9.00
☐ 113	Lindsey Hunter	20.00	9.00
☐ 114	Robert Horry	25.00	11.00
☐ 115	David Robinson	60.00	27.00
☐ 116	Kevin Willis	20.00	9.00
☐ 117	Tyrone Hill	20.00	9.00
☐ 118	Vitaly Potapenko	20.00	9.00
☐ 119	Clyde Drexler	50.00	22.00
☐ 120	Derek Fisher	20.00	9.00
☐ 121	Detlef Schrempf	25.00	11.00
☐ 122	Gary Trent	20.00	9.00
☐ 123	Danny Ferry	20.00	9.00
☐ 124	Derek Anderson	60.00	27.00
☐ 125	Chris Anstey	30.00	13.50
☐ 126	Tony Battie	40.00	18.00
☐ 127	Chauncey Billups	80.00	36.00
☐ 128	Kelvin Cato	30.00	13.50
☐ 129	Austin Croshere	30.00	13.50
☐ 130	Antonio Daniels	50.00	22.00
☐ 131	Tim Duncan	250.00	110.00
☐ 132	Danny Fortson	40.00	18.00
☐ 133	Adonal Foyle	30.00	13.50
☐ 134	Paul Grant	20.00	9.00
☐ 135	Ed Gray	30.00	13.50
☐ 136	Bobby Jackson	40.00	18.00
☐ 137	Brevin Knight	60.00	27.00
☐ 138	Tracy McGrady	125.00	55.00
☐ 139	Ron Mercer	150.00	70.00
☐ 140	Anthony Parker	20.00	9.00
☐ 141	Scot Pollard	20.00	9.00
☐ 142	Rodrick Rhodes	30.00	13.50
☐ 143	Olivier Saint-Jean	30.00	13.50
☐ 144	Maurice Taylor	60.00	27.00
☐ 145	Johnny Taylor	20.00	9.00
☐ 146	Tim Thomas	125.00	55.00
☐ 147	Keith Van Horn	200.00	90.00
☐ 148	Jacque Vaughn	30.00	13.50
☐ 151	Scott Burrell	20.00	9.00
☐ 152	Brian Williams	20.00	9.00
☐ 153	Terry Mills	20.00	9.00
☐ 154	Jim Jackson	25.00	11.00
☐ 155	Michael Finley	40.00	18.00
☐ 156	Jeff Nordgaard	20.00	9.00
☐ 157	Carl Herrera	20.00	9.00
☐ 158	Otis Thorpe	25.00	11.00
☐ 159	Wesley Person	20.00	9.00
☐ 160	Tyrone Hill	20.00	9.00
☐ 161	Charles O'Bannon	20.00	9.00
☐ 162	Greg Anthony	20.00	9.00
☐ 163	Rusty LaRue	20.00	9.00
☐ 164	David Wesley	20.00	9.00
☐ 165	Chris Garner	20.00	9.00
☐ 166	George McCloud	20.00	9.00
☐ 167	Mark Price	20.00	9.00
☐ 168	God Shammgod	20.00	9.00
☐ 169	Isaac Austin	20.00	9.00
☐ 170	Alan Henderson	20.00	9.00
☐ 171	Eric Washington	30.00	13.50
☐ 172	Darrell Armstrong	20.00	9.00
☐ 173	Calbert Cheaney	20.00	9.00
☐ 174	Cedric Henderson	30.00	13.50
☐ 175	Bryant Stith	20.00	9.00
☐ 176	Sean Rooks	20.00	9.00
☐ 177	Chris Mills	20.00	9.00
☐ 178	Eldridge Recasner	20.00	9.00
☐ 179	Priest Lauderdale	20.00	9.00
☐ 180	Rick Fox	20.00	9.00
☐ 181	Keith Closs	20.00	9.00
☐ 182	Chris Dudley	20.00	9.00
☐ 183	L.Funderburke	30.00	13.50
☐ 184	Michael Stewart	30.00	13.50
☐ 185	Alvin Williams	30.00	13.50
☐ 186	Adam Keefe	20.00	9.00
☐ 187	Chauncey Billups	60.00	27.00
☐ 188	Jon Barry	20.00	9.00
☐ 189	Bobby Jackson	30.00	13.50
☐ 190	Sam Cassell	25.00	11.00
☐ 191	Dee Brown	20.00	9.00
☐ 192	Travis Knight	20.00	9.00
☐ 193	Dean Garrett	20.00	9.00
☐ 194	David Benoit	20.00	9.00
☐ 195	Chris Morris	20.00	9.00
☐ 196	Bubba Wells	20.00	9.00
☐ 197	James Robinson	20.00	9.00
☐ 198	Anthony Johnson	20.00	9.00
☐ 199	Dennis Scott	20.00	9.00
☐ 200	DeJuan Wheat	20.00	9.00
☐ 201	Rodney Rogers	20.00	9.00
☐ 202	Tariq Abdul-Wahad	30.00	13.50
☐ 203	Cherokee Parks	20.00	9.00
☐ 204	Jacque Vaughn	30.00	13.50
☐ 205	Cory Alexander	20.00	9.00
☐ 206	Kevin Ollie	20.00	9.00
☐ 207	George Lynch	20.00	9.00
☐ 208	Lamond Murray	20.00	9.00
☐ 209	Jud Buechler	20.00	9.00
☐ 210	Erick Dampier	20.00	9.00
☐ 211	Malcolm Huckaby	20.00	9.00
☐ 212	Chris Webber	100.00	45.00
☐ 213	Chris Crawford	20.00	9.00
☐ 214	J.R. Reid	20.00	9.00
☐ 215	Eddie Johnson	20.00	9.00
☐ 216	Nick Van Exel	30.00	13.50
☐ 217	Antonio McDyess	50.00	22.00
☐ 218	David Wingate	20.00	9.00
☐ 219	Malik Sealy	20.00	9.00
☐ 220	Charles Outlaw	20.00	9.00
☐ 221	Serge Zwikker	20.00	9.00
☐ 222	Bobby Phills	20.00	9.00
☐ 223	Shea Seals	20.00	9.00
☐ 224	Clifford Robinson	20.00	9.00
☐ 225	Zydrunas Ilgauskas	25.00	11.00
☐ 226	John Thomas	20.00	9.00
☐ 227	Rik Smits	25.00	11.00
☐ 228	Rasheed Wallace	25.00	11.00
☐ 229	John Wallace	25.00	11.00
☐ 230	Bob Sura	20.00	9.00
☐ 231	Erin Johnson	20.00	9.00
☐ 232	Keith Booth	20.00	9.00
☐ 233	Chuck Person	20.00	9.00
☐ 234	Brian Shaw	20.00	9.00
☐ 235	Todd Day	20.00	9.00
☐ 236	C.Weatherspoon	20.00	9.00
☐ 237	Charlie Ward	20.00	9.00
☐ 238	Rod Strickland	25.00	11.00
☐ 239	Shawn Kemp	125.00	55.00
☐ 240	Terrell Brandon	30.00	13.50
☐ 241	Corey Beck	20.00	9.00
☐ 242	Vin Baker	80.00	36.00
☐ 243	Fred Hoiberg	20.00	9.00
☐ 244	Chris Mullin	30.00	13.50
☐ 245	Brian Grant	20.00	9.00
☐ 246	Derek Anderson	50.00	22.00
☐ 247	Zan Tabak	20.00	9.00
☐ 248	Charles Smith	20.00	9.00
☐ 249	S.Abdur-Rahim GRE	100.00	45.00
☐ 250	Ray Allen GRE	40.00	18.00
☐ 251	C.Barkley GRE	50.00	22.00
☐ 252	Kobe Bryant GRE	300.00	135.00
☐ 253	M.Camby GRE	30.00	13.50
☐ 254	K.Garnett GRE	200.00	90.00
☐ 255	A.Hardaway GRE	150.00	70.00
☐ 256	Grant Hill GRE	200.00	90.00
☐ 257	J.Howard GRE	30.00	13.50
☐ 258	A.Iverson GRE	150.00	70.00
☐ 259	M.Jordan GRE	600.00	275.00
☐ 260	Shawn Kemp GRE	100.00	45.00
☐ 261	Kerry Kittles GRE	30.00	13.50
☐ 262	Karl Malone GRE	50.00	22.00
☐ 263	S.Marbury GRE	150.00	70.00
☐ 264	H.Olajuwon GRE	60.00	27.00
☐ 265	S.O'Neal GRE	125.00	55.00
☐ 266	Gary Payton GRE	50.00	22.00
☐ 267	S.Pippen GRE	100.00	45.00
☐ 268	D.Robinson GRE	50.00	22.00
☐ 269	D.Rodman GRE	125.00	55.00
☐ 270	Joe Smith GRE	30.00	13.50
☐ 271	J.Stackhouse GRE	30.00	13.50
☐ 272	D.Stoudamire GRE	60.00	27.00
☐ 273	A.Walker GRE	150.00	70.00

1997-98 Ultra All-Rookies

Randomly inserted into series two packs at one in four, this 15-card set features the top players from the 1997 Draft. Card backs carry an "AR" prefix.

	MINT	NRMT
COMPLETE SET (15)	30.00	13.50
COMMON CARD (AR1-AR15)	.75	.35
UNLISTED STARS	1.25	.55
SER.2 STATED ODDS 1:4 HOB/RET		
☐ AR1 Tim Duncan	8.00	3.60
☐ AR2 Tony Battie	1.25	.55
☐ AR3 Keith Van Horn	6.00	2.70
☐ AR4 Antonio Daniels	1.50	.70
☐ AR5 Chauncey Billups	2.50	1.10
☐ AR6 Ron Mercer	5.00	2.20
☐ AR7 Tracy McGrady	4.00	1.80
☐ AR8 Danny Fortson	1.25	.55
☐ AR9 Brevin Knight	2.00	.90
☐ AR10 Derek Anderson	2.00	.90
☐ AR11 Cedric Henderson	.75	.35

			MINT	NRMT
☐	AR12	Jacque Vaughn	1.25	.55
☐	AR13	Tim Thomas	4.00	1.80
☐	AR14	Austin Croshere	1.25	.55
☐	AR15	Kelvin Cato	1.25	.55

1997-98 Ultra Big Shots

Randomly inserted into series one packs at a rate of one in four, this 15-card set focuses on some of the best clutch shots from the 1996-97 season.

			MINT	NRMT
	COMPLETE SET (15)		20.00	9.00
	COMMON CARD (1-15)		.60	.25
	SER.1 STATED ODDS 1:4 HOB/RET			
☐	1	Michael Jordan	8.00	3.60
☐	2	Allen Iverson	3.00	1.35
☐	3	Shaquille O'Neal	2.50	1.10
☐	4	Anfernee Hardaway	2.50	1.10
☐	5	Dennis Rodman	2.50	1.10
☐	6	Grant Hill	4.00	1.80
☐	7	Juwan Howard	.60	.25
☐	8	David Robinson	1.00	.45
☐	9	Gary Payton	1.00	.45
☐	10	Joe Smith	.60	.25
☐	11	Charles Barkley	1.00	.45
☐	12	Terrell Brandon	.60	.25
☐	13	John Stockton	.60	.25
☐	14	Mitch Richmond	.60	.25
☐	15	Vin Baker	1.25	.55

1997-98 Ultra Court Masters

Randomly inserted into series two packs at one in 144, this 20-card set features double images of players who have mastered the game. Each player is shown

in both his home and away uniform. The background of the card fronts mimic a hardwood court. Card backs carry a "CM" prefix.

			MINT	NRMT
	COMPLETE SET (20)		600.00	275.00
	COMMON CARD (CM1-CM20)	8.00		3.60
	SER.2 STATED ODDS 1:144 HOB/RET			
☐	CM1	Michael Jordan	100.00	45.00
☐	CM2	Allen Iverson	40.00	18.00
☐	CM3	Kobe Bryant	60.00	27.00
☐	CM4	Shaquille O'Neal	30.00	13.50
☐	CM5	Stephon Marbury	40.00	18.00
☐	CM6	Shawn Kemp	25.00	11.00
☐	CM7	A.Hardaway	30.00	13.50
☐	CM8	Kevin Garnett	50.00	22.00
☐	CM9	S.Abdur-Rahim	25.00	11.00
☐	CM10	Dennis Rodman	30.00	13.50
☐	CM11	Grant Hill	50.00	22.00
☐	CM12	Kerry Kittles	8.00	3.60
☐	CM13	Antoine Walker	40.00	18.00
☐	CM14	Scottie Pippen	25.00	11.00
☐	CM15	D.Stoudamire	15.00	6.75
☐	CM16	Marcus Camby	8.00	3.60
☐	CM17	Hakeem Olajuwon	15.00	6.75
☐	CM18	Tim Duncan	50.00	22.00
☐	CM19	Keith Van Horn	40.00	18.00
☐	CM20	Chauncey Billups	15.00	6.75

1997-98 Ultra Heir to the Throne

Randomly inserted in series one packs at a rate of one in 18, this 15-card set focuses on some of the best rookies from the 1997-98 class. The cards feature each rookie sitting in a chair that is made up of basketballs.

			MINT	NRMT
	COMPLETE SET (15)		90.00	40.00
	COMMON CARD (1-15)		1.50	.70
	SEMISTARS		2.00	.90
	UNLISTED STARS		3.00	1.35
	SER.1 STATED ODDS 1:18 HOB/RET			
☐	1	Derek Anderson	5.00	2.20
☐	2	Tony Battie	3.00	1.35
☐	3	Chauncey Billups	6.00	2.70
☐	4	Kelvin Cato	1.50	.70
☐	5	Austin Croshere	1.50	.70
☐	6	Antonio Daniels	4.00	1.80
☐	7	Tim Duncan	20.00	9.00
☐	8	Danny Fortson	3.00	1.35
☐	9	Jacque Vaughn	2.00	.90
☐	10	Tracy McGrady	10.00	4.50
☐	11	Ron Mercer	12.00	5.50
☐	12	Olivier Saint-Jean	2.00	.90

			MINT	NRMT
☐	13	Maurice Taylor	5.00	2.20
☐	14	Tim Thomas	10.00	4.50
☐	15	Keith Van Horn	15.00	6.75

1997-98 Ultra Inside/Outside

Randomly inserted in series one packs at a rate of one in six, this 15-card set focuses on players who can get the job done with both their inside and outside games.

			MINT	NRMT
	COMPLETE SET (15)		10.00	4.50
	COMMON CARD (1-15)		.60	.25
	SER.1 STATED ODDS 1:6 HOB/RET			
☐	1	Shareef Abdur-Rahim	2.00	.90
☐	2	Juwan Howard	.60	.25
☐	3	David Robinson	1.00	.45
☐	4	Joe Smith	.60	.25
☐	5	Charles Barkley	1.00	.45
☐	6	Tom Gugliotta	.60	.25
☐	7	Glenn Robinson	.60	.25
☐	8	Patrick Ewing	.60	.25
☐	9	Chris Webber	1.50	.70
☐	10	Glen Rice	.60	.25
☐	11	Shawn Kemp	2.00	.90
☐	12	Antonio McDyess	.75	.35
☐	13	Clyde Drexler	.75	.35
☐	14	Eddie Jones	1.25	.55
☐	15	Jason Kidd	1.25	.55

1997-98 Ultra Jam City

Randomly inserted in series one packs at a rate of one in eight, this 18-card set features some of the NBA's high flying players.

	MINT	NRMT
COMPLETE SET (18)	40.00	18.00
COMMON CARD (1-18)	.50	.23
SEMISTARS	.60	.25
UNLISTED STARS	1.00	.45
SER.1 STATED ODDS 1:8 HOB/RET		

		MINT	NRMT
☐ 1	Kevin Garnett	6.00	2.70
☐ 2	Antoine Walker	5.00	2.20
☐ 3	Scottie Pippen	3.00	1.35
☐ 4	Shawn Kemp	3.00	1.35
☐ 5	Hakeem Olajuwon	2.00	.90
☐ 6	Jerry Stackhouse	1.00	.45
☐ 7	Karl Malone	1.50	.70
☐ 8	Shaquille O'Neal	4.00	1.80
☐ 9	John Wallace	.50	.23
☐ 10	Marcus Camby	1.00	.45
☐ 11	Juwan Howard	1.00	.45
☐ 12	David Robinson	1.50	.70
☐ 13	Gary Payton	1.50	.70
☐ 14	Dennis Rodman	4.00	1.80
☐ 15	Joe Smith	1.00	.45
☐ 16	Charles Barkley	1.50	.70
☐ 17	Terrell Brandon	1.00	.45
☐ 18	Kobe Bryant	8.00	3.60

1997-98 Ultra Neat Feats

Randomly inserted into series two packs at one in eight, this 18-card set focuses on player's career highlights. The card fronts features UV coated player photos on a matte finish background. Card backs are numbered with a "NF" prefix.

	MINT	NRMT
COMPLETE SET (18)	15.00	6.75
COMMON CARD (NF1-NF18)	.50	.23
SEMISTARS	.60	.25
UNLISTED STARS	1.00	.45
SER.2 STATED ODDS 1:8 HOB/RET		

		MINT	NRMT
☐ NF1	Michael Finley	1.00	.45
☐ NF2	Jason Kidd	2.00	.90
☐ NF3	Rasheed Wallace	.50	.23
☐ NF4	Shaquille O'Neal	4.00	1.80
☐ NF5	Tom Gugliotta	1.00	.45
☐ NF6	Marcus Camby	1.00	.45
☐ NF7	Jerry Stackhouse	1.00	.45
☐ NF8	John Wallace	.50	.23
☐ NF9	Juwan Howard	1.00	.45
☐ NF10	David Robinson	1.50	.70
☐ NF11	Gary Payton	1.50	.70
☐ NF12	Joe Smith	1.00	.45
☐ NF13	Charles Barkley	1.50	.70
☐ NF14	Terrell Brandon	1.00	.45
☐ NF15	John Stockton	1.00	.45
☐ NF16	Vin Baker	2.00	.90
☐ NF17	Antonio McDyess	1.25	.55
☐ NF18	Antonio Daniels	1.25	.55

1997-98 Ultra Quick Picks

Randomly inserted in series one packs at a rate of one in eight, this 12-card set focuses on the young defensive wizards of the NBA.

	MINT	NRMT
COMPLETE SET (12)	8.00	3.60
COMMON CARD (1-12)	.30	.14
SEMISTARS	.40	.18
UNLISTED STARS	.60	.25
SER.1 STATED ODDS 1:8 HOB/RET		

		MINT	NRMT
☐ 1	Stephon Marbury	3.00	1.35
☐ 2	Ray Allen	.75	.35
☐ 3	Damon Stoudamire	1.25	.55
☐ 4	Kerry Kittles	.60	.25
☐ 5	Gary Payton	1.00	.45
☐ 6	Terrell Brandon	.60	.25
☐ 7	John Stockton	.60	.25
☐ 8	Mookie Blaylock	.30	.14
☐ 9	Eddie Jones	1.25	.55
☐ 10	Nick Van Exel	.60	.25
☐ 11	Kenny Anderson	.40	.18
☐ 12	Tim Hardaway	.75	.35

1997-98 Ultra Rim Rocker

Randomly inserted into series two packs at one in eight, this 12-card set features color photos of some of the best dunkers in the game printed on custom die-cut silver holofoil cards. Card backs are numbered with a "RR" prefix.

	MINT	NRMT
COMPLETE SET (12)	8.00	3.60
COMMON CARD (RR1-RR12)	.60	.25
SER.2 STATED ODDS 1:8 HOB/RET		

		MINT	NRMT
☐ RR1	Ron Mercer	2.50	1.10
☐ RR2	Juwan Howard	.60	.25
☐ RR3	David Robinson	1.00	.45
☐ RR4	Gary Payton	1.00	.45
☐ RR5	Joe Smith	.60	.25
☐ RR6	Charles Barkley	1.00	.45
☐ RR7	Terrell Brandon	.60	.25
☐ RR8	John Stockton	.60	.25
☐ RR9	Adonal Foyle	.60	.25
☐ RR10	Tim Thomas	2.00	.90
☐ RR11	Tony Battie	.60	.25
☐ RR12	Antonio McDyess	1.25	.55

1997-98 Ultra Star Power

Randomly inserted into series two packs at one in four, this 20-card set chronicles the path of some notable NBA players. These cards in particular focus on early to mid-career highlights. Card backs carry a "SP" prefix.

	MINT	NRMT
COMPLETE SET (20)	40.00	18.00
COMMON CARD (SP1-SP20)	.60	.25
SER.2 STATED ODDS 1:4 HOB/RET		
COMP.PLUS SET (20)	225.00	100.00
COMMON PLUS	3.00	1.35
*PLUS: 2X TO 5X HI COLUMN		
PLUS: SER.2 STATED ODDS 1:36 H/R		
COMP.SUPREME SET (20)	1300.00	575.00
COMMON SUPREME	15.00	6.75
*SUPREME: 15X TO 30X HI		
SUPREME: SER.2 STATED ODDS 1:288 H/R		

		MINT	NRMT
☐ SP1	Michael Jordan	8.00	3.60
☐ SP2	Allen Iverson	3.00	1.35
☐ SP3	Kobe Bryant	5.00	2.20
☐ SP4	Shaquille O'Neal	2.50	1.10
☐ SP5	Stephon Marbury	3.00	1.35
☐ SP6	Shawn Kemp	2.00	.90
☐ SP7	Anfernee Hardaway	2.50	1.10
☐ SP8	Kevin Garnett	4.00	1.80
☐ SP9	S.Abdur-Rahim	2.00	.90
☐ SP10	Dennis Rodman	2.50	1.10
☐ SP11	Grant Hill	4.00	1.80
☐ SP12	Gary Payton	1.00	.45
☐ SP13	Antoine Walker	3.00	1.35
☐ SP14	Scottie Pippen	2.00	.90
☐ SP15	D.Stoudamire	1.25	.55
☐ SP16	Marcus Camby	.60	.25
☐ SP17	Hakeem Olajuwon	1.25	.55
☐ SP18	Tim Duncan	4.00	1.80
☐ SP19	Keith Van Horn	3.00	1.35
☐ SP20	Jerry Stackhouse	.60	.25

1997-98 Ultra Stars

Randomly inserted in series one packs at a rate of one in 288, this 20-card set features some of the NBA's top stars. Ten percent of the print run was done in gold foil as opposed to the more common silver foil.

	MINT	NRMT
COMPLETE SET (20)	600.00	275.00
COMMON CARD (1-20)	5.00	2.20
UNLISTED STARS	8.00	3.60
SER.1 STATED ODDS 1:144 HOB/RET		
*GOLD: 2X TO 4X HI COLUMN		
GOLD: RANDOM INSERTS IN PACKS		
TEN PERCENT OF PRINT RUN IS GOLD		

		MINT	NRMT
☐ 1	Michael Jordan	100.00	45.00
☐ 2	Allen Iverson	40.00	18.00
☐ 3	Kobe Bryant	60.00	27.00
☐ 4	Shaquille O'Neal	30.00	13.50
☐ 5	Stephon Marbury	40.00	18.00
☐ 6	Marcus Camby	8.00	3.60
☐ 7	Anfernee Hardaway	30.00	13.50
☐ 8	Kevin Garnett	50.00	22.00
☐ 9	Shareef Abdur-Rahim	25.00	11.00
☐ 10	Dennis Rodman	30.00	13.50
☐ 11	Ray Allen	10.00	4.50
☐ 12	Grant Hill	50.00	22.00
☐ 13	Kerry Kittles	8.00	3.60
☐ 14	Antoine Walker	40.00	18.00
☐ 15	Scottie Pippen	25.00	11.00
☐ 16	Damon Stoudamire	15.00	6.75
☐ 17	Shawn Kemp	25.00	11.00
☐ 18	Hakeem Olajuwon	15.00	6.75
☐ 19	Jerry Stackhouse	8.00	3.60
☐ 20	John Wallace	5.00	2.20

1997-98 Ultra Sweet Deal

Randomly inserted into series two packs at one in six, this 12-card set gives insight to some of the best players in the game. Card backs carry a "SD" prefix.

	MINT	NRMT
COMPLETE SET (12)	8.00	3.60
COMMON CARD (SD1-SD12)	.30	.14
SEMISTARS	.40	.18
UNLISTED STARS	.60	.25
SER.2 STATED ODDS 1:6 HOB/RET		

		MINT	NRMT
☐ SD1	Ray Allen	.75	.35
☐ SD2	Chauncey Billups	1.25	.55
☐ SD3	Ron Mercer	2.50	1.10
☐ SD4	Hakeem Olajuwon	1.25	.55
☐ SD5	Jerry Stackhouse	.60	.25
☐ SD6	John Wallace	.30	.14
☐ SD7	Juwan Howard	.60	.25
☐ SD8	David Robinson	1.00	.45
☐ SD9	Bobby Jackson	.60	.25
☐ SD10	Joe Smith	.60	.25
☐ SD11	Charles Barkley	1.00	.45
☐ SD12	Terrell Brandon	.60	.25

1997-98 Ultra Ultrabilities

Randomly inserted in series one packs at a rate of one in four, this 20-card set features NBA players that have many different abilities.

	MINT	NRMT
COMPLETE SET (20)	40.00	18.00
COMMON CARD (1-20)	.60	.25
SER.1 STATED ODDS 1:4 HOB/RET		
COMP.ALL-STAR SET (20)	200.00	90.00
COMMON ALL-STAR	3.00	1.35
*ALL-STAR: 2X TO 5X HI COLUMN		
ALL-STAR: SER.1 STATED ODDS 1:36 H/R		
COMP.SUPER SET (20)	1100.00	500.00
COMMON SUPERSTAR	15.00	6.75
*SUPERSTAR: 15X TO 30X HI		
SUPERSTAR: SER.1 STATED ODDS 1:288 H/R		

		MINT	NRMT
☐ 1	Michael Jordan	8.00	3.60
☐ 2	Allen Iverson	3.00	1.35
☐ 3	Kobe Bryant	5.00	2.20
☐ 4	Shaquille O'Neal	2.50	1.10
☐ 5	Stephon Marbury	3.00	1.35
☐ 6	Gary Payton	1.00	.45
☐ 7	Anfernee Hardaway	2.50	1.10
☐ 8	Kevin Garnett	4.00	1.80
☐ 9	Scottie Pippen	2.00	.90
☐ 10	Grant Hill	4.00	1.80
☐ 11	Marcus Camby	.60	.25
☐ 12	Ray Allen	.75	.35
☐ 13	Kerry Kittles	.60	.25
☐ 14	Antoine Walker	3.00	1.35
☐ 15	Shareef Abdur-Rahim	2.00	.90
☐ 16	Damon Stoudamire	1.25	.55
☐ 17	Shawn Kemp	2.00	.90
☐ 18	Hakeem Olajuwon	1.25	.55
☐ 19	Jerry Stackhouse	.60	.25
☐ 20	Juwan Howard	.60	.25

1997-98 Ultra View to a Thrill

Randomly inserted into series two packs at one in 18, this 15-card set features colorful profiles of players that make the game a thrill to watch. Card backs carry a "VT" prefix.

	MINT	NRMT
COMPLETE SET (15)	90.00	40.00
COMMON CARD (VT1-VT15)	1.50	.70
SER.2 STATED ODDS 1:18 HOB/RET		

		MINT	NRMT
☐ VT1	Michael Jordan	20.00	9.00
☐ VT2	Allen Iverson	8.00	3.60
☐ VT3	Kobe Bryant	12.00	5.50
☐ VT4	Tracy McGrady	5.00	2.20
☐ VT5	Stephon Marbury	8.00	3.60
☐ VT6	Shawn Kemp	5.00	2.20
☐ VT7	A.Hardaway	6.00	2.70
☐ VT8	Kevin Garnett	10.00	4.50
☐ VT9	S.Abdur-Rahim	5.00	2.20
☐ VT10	Dennis Rodman	6.00	2.70
☐ VT11	Grant Hill	10.00	4.50
☐ VT12	Kerry Kittles	1.50	.70
☐ VT13	Antoine Walker	8.00	3.60
☐ VT14	Scottie Pippen	5.00	2.20
☐ VT15	D.Stoudamire	3.00	1.35

1991-92 Upper Deck

The 1991-92 set marks Upper Deck's debut in the basketball card industry. The set contains

500 standard-size cards. The set was released in two series of 400 and 100 cards, respectively. High series cards are in relatively shorter supply because high series packs contained a mix of both high and low series cards. High series lockers contained seven 12-card packs of cards 1-500 and a special "Rookie Standouts" card. Both low and high series were offered in a 500-card factory set. The fronts feature glossy color player photos, bordered below and on the right by a hardwood basketball floor design. The player's name appears beneath the picture, while the team name is printed vertically alongside the picture. The backs display a second color player photo as well as biographical and statistical information. Special subsets featured include Draft Choices (1-21), Classic Confrontations (30-34), All-Rookie Team (35-39), All-Stars (49-72), and Team Checklists (73-99). The fronts feature glossy color player photos, bordered below and on the right by a hardwood basketball floor design. The player's name appears beneath the picture, while the team name is printed vertically alongside the picture. The backs display a second color player photo as well as biographical and statistical information. In addition to rookie and traded players, the high series includes the following topical subsets; Top Prospects (438-448), All-Star Skills (476-484), capturing players who participated in the slam dunk competition as well as the three-point shootout winner, Eastern All-Star Team (449, 451-462), and Western All-Star Team (450, 463-475). Rookie Cards of note include Kenny Anderson, Stacey Augmon, Terrell Brandon, Larry Johnson, Anthony Mason, Dikembe Mutombo, Steve Smith, and John Starks.

	MINT	NRMT
COMPLETE SET (500)	20.00	9.00
COMPLETE FACT.SET (500)	20.00	9.00
COMPLETE SERIES 1 (400)	12.00	5.50
COMPLETE SERIES 2 (100)	8.00	3.60
COMMON CARD (1-400)	.05	.02
COMMON CARD (401-500)	.10	.05
SEMISTARS SER.1	.10	.05
SEMISTARS SER.2	.25	.11
UNLISTED STARS SER.1	.25	.11
UNLISTED STARS SER.2	.50	.23

☐ 1 Stacey Augmon CL	.05	.02
Rodney Monroe		
☐ 2 Larry Johnson UER	1.00	.45
(Career FG Percentage is .643 not .648)		
☐ 3 Dikembe Mutombo	.75	.35
☐ 4 Steve Smith	.60	.25
☐ 5 Stacey Augmon	.25	.11
☐ 6 Terrell Brandon	1.25	.55
☐ 7 Greg Anthony	.25	.11
☐ 8 Rich King	.05	.02
☐ 9 Chris Gatling	.25	.11
☐ 10 Victor Alexander	.05	.02
☐ 11 John Turner	.05	.02
☐ 12 Eric Murdock	.05	.02
☐ 13 Mark Randall	.05	.02
☐ 14 Rodney Monroe	.05	.02
☐ 15 Myron Brown	.05	.02
☐ 16 Mike Iuzzolino	.05	.02
☐ 17 Chris Corchiani	.05	.02
☐ 18 Elliot Perry	.25	.11
☐ 19 Jimmy Oliver	.05	.02
☐ 20 Doug Overton	.05	.02
☐ 21 Steve Hood UER	.05	.02
(Card has NBA record, but he's a rookie)		
☐ 22 Michael Jordan	.75	.35
Stay In School		
☐ 23 Kevin Johnson	.10	.05
Stay In School		
☐ 24 Kurk Lee	.05	.02
☐ 25 Sean Higgins	.05	.02
☐ 26 Morlon Wiley	.05	.02
☐ 27 Derek Smith	.05	.02
☐ 28 Kenny Payne	.05	.02
☐ 29 Magic Johnson	.40	.18
Assist Record		
☐ 30 Larry Bird CC	.25	.11
and Chuck Person		
☐ 31 Karl Malone CC	.25	.11
and Charles Barkley		
☐ 32 Kevin Johnson CC	.10	.05
and John Stockton		
☐ 33 Hakeem Olajuwon CC	.25	.11
and Patrick Ewing		
☐ 34 Magic Johnson CC	1.00	.45
and Michael Jordan		
☐ 35 Derrick Coleman ART	.05	.02
☐ 36 Lionel Simmons ART	.05	.02
☐ 37 Dee Brown ART	.05	.02
☐ 38 Dennis Scott ART	.05	.02
☐ 39 Kendall Gill ART	.05	.02
☐ 40 Winston Garland	.05	.02
☐ 41 Danny Young	.05	.02
☐ 42 Rick Mahorn	.05	.02
☐ 43 Michael Adams	.05	.02
☐ 44 Michael Jordan	3.00	1.35
☐ 45 Magic Johnson	.75	.35
☐ 46 Doc Rivers	.10	.05
☐ 47 Moses Malone	.25	.11
☐ 48 Michael Jordan AS CL	1.50	.70
☐ 49 James Worthy AS	.10	.05
☐ 50 Tim Hardaway AS	.25	.11
☐ 51 Karl Malone AS	.25	.11
☐ 52 John Stockton AS	.25	.11
☐ 53 Clyde Drexler AS	.25	.11
☐ 54 Terry Porter AS	.05	.02
☐ 55 Kevin Duckworth AS	.05	.02
☐ 56 Tom Chambers AS	.05	.02
☐ 57 Magic Johnson AS	.40	.18
☐ 58 David Robinson AS	.25	.11
☐ 59 Kevin Johnson AS	.10	.05
☐ 60 Chris Mullin AS	.10	.05
☐ 61 Joe Dumars AS	.10	.05
☐ 62 Kevin McHale AS	.05	.02
☐ 63 Brad Daugherty AS	.05	.02
☐ 64 Alvin Robertson AS	.05	.02
☐ 65 Bernard King AS	.05	.02
☐ 66 Dominique Wilkins AS	.10	.05
☐ 67 Ricky Pierce AS	.05	.02
☐ 68 Patrick Ewing AS	.25	.11
☐ 69 Michael Jordan AS	1.50	.70
☐ 70 Charles Barkley AS	.25	.11
☐ 71 Hersey Hawkins AS	.05	.02
☐ 72 Robert Parish AS	.05	.02
☐ 73 Alvin Robertson TC	.05	.02
☐ 74 Bernard King TC	.05	.02
☐ 75 Michael Jordan TC	1.50	.70
☐ 76 Brad Daugherty TC	.05	.02
☐ 77 Larry Bird TC	.50	.23
☐ 78 Ron Harper TC	.05	.02
☐ 79 Dominique Wilkins TC	.10	.05
☐ 80 Rony Seikaly TC	.05	.02
☐ 81 Rex Chapman TC	.05	.02
☐ 82 Mark Eaton TC	.05	.02
☐ 83 Lionel Simmons TC	.05	.02
☐ 84 Gerald Wilkins TC	.05	.02
☐ 85 James Worthy TC	.10	.05
☐ 86 Scott Skiles TC	.05	.02
☐ 87 Rolando Blackman TC	.05	.02
☐ 88 Derrick Coleman TC	.05	.02
☐ 89 Chris Jackson TC	.05	.02
☐ 90 Reggie Miller TC	.25	.11
☐ 91 Isiah Thomas TC	.10	.05
☐ 92 Hakeem Olajuwon TC	.25	.11
☐ 93 Hersey Hawkins TC	.05	.02
☐ 94 David Robinson TC	.25	.11
☐ 95 Tom Chambers TC	.05	.02
☐ 96 Shawn Kemp TC	.60	.25
☐ 97 Pooh Richardson TC	.05	.02
☐ 98 Clyde Drexler TC	.25	.11
☐ 99 Chris Mullin TC	.10	.05
☐ 100 Checklist 1-100	.05	.02
☐ 101 John Shasky	.05	.02
☐ 102 Dana Barros	.05	.02
☐ 103 Stojko Vrankovic	.05	.02
☐ 104 Larry Drew	.05	.02
☐ 105 Randy White	.05	.02
☐ 106 Dave Corzine	.05	.02
☐ 107 Joe Kleine	.05	.02
☐ 108 Lance Blanks	.05	.02
☐ 109 Rodney McCray	.05	.02
☐ 110 Sedale Threatt	.05	.02
☐ 111 Ken Norman	.05	.02
☐ 112 Rickey Green	.05	.02
☐ 113 Andy Toolson	.05	.02
☐ 114 Bo Kimble	.05	.02
☐ 115 Mark West	.05	.02
☐ 116 Mark Eaton	.05	.02
☐ 117 John Paxson	.10	.05
☐ 118 Mike Brown	.05	.02
☐ 119 Brian Oliver	.05	.02
☐ 120 Will Perdue	.05	.02
☐ 121 Michael Smith	.05	.02
☐ 122 Sherman Douglas	.05	.02
☐ 123 Reggie Lewis	.10	.05
☐ 124 James Donaldson	.05	.02
☐ 125 Scottie Pippen	.75	.35
☐ 126 Elden Campbell	.10	.05
☐ 127 Michael Cage	.05	.02
☐ 128 Tony Smith	.05	.02
☐ 129 Ed Pinckney	.05	.02
☐ 130 Keith Askins	.05	.02
☐ 131 Darrell Griffith	.05	.02
☐ 132 Vinnie Johnson	.05	.02
☐ 133 Ron Harper	.10	.05
☐ 134 Andre Turner	.05	.02
☐ 135 Jeff Hornacek	.10	.05
☐ 136 John Stockton	.25	.11
☐ 137 Derek Harper	.10	.05
☐ 138 Loy Vaught	.10	.05
☐ 139 Thurl Bailey	.05	.02
☐ 140 Olden Polynice	.05	.02
☐ 141 Kevin Edwards	.05	.02
☐ 142 Byron Scott	.10	.05
☐ 143 Dee Brown	.05	.02
☐ 144 Sam Perkins	.10	.05
☐ 145 Rony Seikaly	.05	.02
☐ 146 James Worthy	.25	.11
☐ 147 Glen Rice	.40	.18
☐ 148 Craig Hodges	.05	.02
☐ 149 Bimbo Coles	.05	.02
☐ 150 Mychal Thompson	.05	.02
☐ 151 Xavier McDaniel	.05	.02
☐ 152 Roy Tarpley	.05	.02
☐ 153 Gary Payton	.60	.25
☐ 154 Rolando Blackman	.05	.02
☐ 155 Hersey Hawkins	.10	.05
☐ 156 Ricky Pierce	.05	.02
☐ 157 Fat Lever	.05	.02
☐ 158 Andrew Lang	.05	.02
☐ 159 Benoit Benjamin	.05	.02

☐ 416	James Edwards	.10	.05
☐ 417	Jerrod Mustaf	.10	.05
☐ 418	Thurl Bailey	.10	.05
☐ 419	Spud Webb	.25	.11
☐ 420	Doc Rivers	.10	.05
☐ 421	Sean Green	.10	.05
☐ 422	Walter Davis	.10	.05
☐ 423	Terry Davis	.10	.05
☐ 424	John Battle	.10	.05
☐ 425	Vinnie Johnson	.10	.05
☐ 426	Sherman Douglas	.10	.05
☐ 427	Kevin Brooks	.10	.05
☐ 428	Greg Sutton	.10	.05
☐ 429	Rafael Addison	.10	.05
☐ 430	Anthony Mason	1.00	.45
☐ 431	Paul Graham	.10	.05
☐ 432	Anthony Frederick	.10	.05
☐ 433	Dennis Hopson	.10	.05
☐ 434	Rory Sparrow	.10	.05
☐ 435	Michael Adams	.10	.05
☐ 436	Kevin Lynch	.10	.05
☐ 437	Randy Brown	.10	.05
☐ 438	Larry Johnson CL	.50	.23
	Billy Owens		
☐ 439	Stacey Augmon TP	.50	.23
☐ 440	Larry Stewart TP	.10	.05
☐ 441	Terrell Brandon TP	.50	.23
☐ 442	Billy Owens TP	.50	.23
☐ 443	Rick Fox TP	.50	.23
☐ 444	Kenny Anderson TP	1.00	.45
☐ 445	Larry Johnson TP	.50	.23
☐ 446	D.Mutombo TP	.50	.23
☐ 447	Steve Smith TP	.50	.23
☐ 448	Greg Anthony TP	.25	.11
☐ 449	East All-Star	.25	.11
	Checklist		
☐ 450	West All-Star	.25	.11
	Checklist		
☐ 451	Isiah Thomas AS	.30	.14
	(Magic Johnson		
	also shown)		
☐ 452	Michael Jordan AS	3.00	1.35
☐ 453	Scottie Pippen AS	.75	.35
☐ 454	Charles Barkley AS	.50	.23
☐ 455	Patrick Ewing AS	.25	.11
☐ 456	Michael Adams AS	.10	.05
☐ 457	Dennis Rodman AS	1.00	.45
☐ 458	Reggie Lewis AS	.10	.05
☐ 459	Joe Dumars AS	.25	.11
☐ 460	Mark Price AS	.10	.05
☐ 461	Brad Daugherty AS	.10	.05
☐ 462	Kevin Willis AS	.10	.05
☐ 463	Clyde Drexler AS	.30	.14
☐ 464	Magic Johnson AS	.75	.35
☐ 465	Chris Mullin AS	.25	.11
☐ 466	Karl Malone AS	.50	.23
☐ 467	David Robinson AS	.50	.23
☐ 468	Tim Hardaway AS	.30	.14
☐ 469	Jeff Hornacek AS	.10	.05
☐ 470	John Stockton AS	.25	.11
☐ 471	D.Mutombo AS UER	.50	.23
	(Drafted in 1992,		
	should be 1991)		
☐ 472	Hakeem Olajuwon AS	.50	.23
☐ 473	James Worthy AS	.25	.11
☐ 474	Otis Thorpe AS	.10	.05
☐ 475	Dan Majerle AS	.10	.05
☐ 476	Cedric Ceballos CL	.25	.11
	All-Star Skills		
☐ 477	Nick Anderson SD	.10	.05
☐ 478	Stacey Augmon SD	.50	.23
☐ 479	Cedric Ceballos SD	.25	.11
☐ 480	Larry Johnson SD	.50	.23
☐ 481	Shawn Kemp SD	1.25	.55
☐ 482	John Starks SD	.50	.23
☐ 483	Doug West SD	.10	.05
☐ 484	Craig Hodges	.10	.05
	Long Distance Shoot Out		
☐ 485	LaBradford Smith	.10	.05
☐ 486	Winston Garland	.10	.05
☐ 487	David Benoit	.25	.11
☐ 488	John Bagley	.10	.05
☐ 489	Mark Macon	.10	.05
☐ 490	Mitch Richmond	.60	.25
☐ 491	Luc Longley	.60	.25
☐ 492	Sedale Threatt	.10	.05

☐ 493	Doug Smith	.10	.05
☐ 494	Travis Mays	.10	.05
☐ 495	Xavier McDaniel	.10	.05
☐ 496	Brian Shaw	.10	.05
☐ 497	Stanley Roberts	.10	.05
☐ 498	Blair Rasmussen	.10	.05
☐ 499	Brian Williams	.50	.23
☐ 500	Checklist Card	.10	.05

1991-92 Upper Deck Award Winner Holograms

These holograms feature NBA statistical leaders in nine different categories. The first six holograms were random inserts in 1991-92 Upper Deck low series foil and jumbo packs, while the last three were inserted in high series foil and jumbo packs. The standard-size holograms have the player's name and award received in the lower right corner on the front. The back has a color player photo and a summary of the player's performance. The cards are numbered on the back with an "AW" prefix before the number.

		MINT	NRMT
	COMPLETE SET (9)	25.00	11.00
	COMMON CARD (AW1-AW9)	.40	.18
	SEMISTARS	.60	.25
	UNLISTED STARS	1.00	.45
	RANDOM INSERTS IN BOTH SERIES PACKS		
☐ AW1	Michael Jordan	12.00	5.50
	Scoring Leader		
☐ AW2	Alvin Robertson	.40	.18
	Steals Leader		
☐ AW3	John Stockton	1.00	.45
	Assists Leader		
☐ AW4	Michael Jordan	12.00	5.50
	MVP		
☐ AW5	Detlef Schrempf	.60	.25
	Sixth Man		
☐ AW6	David Robinson	2.00	.90
	Rebounds Leader		
☐ AW7	Derrick Coleman	.40	.18
	Rookie of the Year		
☐ AW8	Hakeem Olajuwon	2.00	.90
	Blocked Shots Leader		
☐ AW9	Dennis Rodman	4.00	1.80
	Defensive POY		

1991-92 Upper Deck Rookie Standouts

Inserted one per jumbo and locker pack in both the low and high series, fronts of this standard-size 40-card set feature color action player photos, bordered on the right and below by a hardwood basketball court and with the "'91-92 Rookie Standouts" emblem in the lower right corner. The back features a second color player photo and player profile.

		MINT	NRMT
	COMPLETE SET (40)	15.00	6.75
	COMPLETE SERIES 1 (20)	5.00	2.20
	COMPLETE SERIES 2 (20)	10.00	4.50
	COMMON CARD (R1-R40)	.25	.11
	SEMISTARS	.40	.18
	UNLISTED STARS	.60	.25
	ONE PER LO OR HI JUMBO OR LOCKER PACK		
☐ R1	Gary Payton	2.50	1.10
☐ R2	Dennis Scott	.40	.18
☐ R3	Kendall Gill	.60	.25
☐ R4	Felton Spencer	.25	.11
☐ R5	Bo Kimble	.25	.11
☐ R6	Willie Burton	.25	.11
☐ R7	Tyrone Hill	.40	.18
☐ R8	Loy Vaught	.60	.25
☐ R9	Travis Mays	.25	.11
☐ R10	Derrick Coleman	.60	.25
☐ R11	Duane Causwell	.25	.11
☐ R12	Dee Brown	.25	.11
☐ R13	Gerald Glass	.25	.11
☐ R14	Jayson Williams	.60	.25
☐ R15	Elden Campbell	.40	.18
☐ R16	Negele Knight	.25	.11
☐ R17	Chris Jackson	.25	.11
☐ R18	Danny Ferry	.25	.11
☐ R19	Tony Smith	.25	.11
☐ R20	Cedric Ceballos	.60	.25
☐ R21	Victor Alexander	.25	.11
☐ R22	Terrell Brandon	3.00	1.35
☐ R23	Rick Fox	.25	.11
☐ R24	Stacey Augmon	.60	.25
☐ R25	Mark Macon	.25	.11
☐ R26	Larry Johnson	2.50	1.10
☐ R27	Paul Graham	.25	.11
☐ R28	Stanley Roberts UER	.25	.11
	(Not the Magic's 1st pick in 1991)		
☐ R29	D.Mutombo	2.00	.90
☐ R30	Robert Pack	.25	.11
☐ R31	Doug Smith	.25	.11
☐ R32	Steve Smith	1.50	.70
☐ R33	Billy Owens	.60	.25

		MINT	NRMT
☐ R34	David Benoit	.40	.18
☐ R35	Brian Williams	.60	.25
☐ R36	Kenny Anderson	1.25	.55
☐ R37	Greg Anthony	.60	.25
☐ R38	Dale Davis	.60	.25
☐ R39	Larry Stewart	.25	.11
☐ R40	Mike Iuzzolino	.25	.11

1991-92 Upper Deck Jerry West Heroes

This ten-card insert set was randomly inserted in Upper Deck's high series basketball foil packs. Also included in the packs were 2,500 checklist cards autographed by West. The fronts of the standard-size cards capture memorable moments from his college and professional career. The player photos are cut out and superimposed over a jump ball circle on a hardwood basketball floor design. The card backs present commentary.

	MINT	NRMT
COMPLETE SET (10)	6.00	2.70
COMMON WEST (1-9)	1.00	.45
WEST HEROES HEADER (NNO)	1.50	.70
RANDOM INSERTS IN HI SERIES PACKS		

		MINT	NRMT
☐ 1	Jerry West	1.00	.45
	1959 NCAA Tournament MVP		
☐ 2	Jerry West	1.00	.45
	1960 U.S. Team		
☐ 3	Jerry West	1.00	.45
	1968-69 NBA Playoff MVP		
☐ 4	Jerry West	1.00	.45
	1969-70 NBA Scoring Leader		
☐ 5	Jerry West	1.00	.45
	1972 NBA World Championship		
☐ 6	Jerry West	1.00	.45
	1973-74 25,000 Points		
☐ 7	Jerry West	1.00	.45
	1979 Basketball Hall of Fame		
☐ 8	Jerry West	1.00	.45
	1982 to the present Front Office Success		
☐ 9	Jerry West	1.00	.45
	Portrait Card		
☐ AU	Jerry West AU/2500	150.00	70.00
	(Certified autograph)		
☐ NNO	Jerry West Cover/Title Card	1.50	.70

1992-93 Upper Deck

The complete 1992-93 Upper Deck basketball set consists of 510 standard-size cards issued in two series of 310 and 200 cards, respectively. High series cards are slightly tougher to find (compared to the low numbers) because high series packs contained a mix of high and low series cards. For both series, cards were issued in 15-card hobby and retail foil packs, 27-card locker packs and 27-card jumbo packs. No factory sets were produced by Upper Deck for this issue. Both series were also distributed through 27-card Locker packs. Card number 1A (available only in low series packs) is a "Trade Upper Deck" card that the collector could trade to Upper Deck for a Shaquille O'Neal mail-away trade card beginning on Jan. 1, 1993. The offer expired June 30, 1993. The fronts feature color action player photos with white borders. The team name is gold-foil stamped across the top of the picture. The border design at the bottom consists of a team colored stripe that shades from one team color to the other with diagonal stripes within the larger stripe that add texture. The entire design is edged in gold foil. The right end is off-set slightly by the Upper Deck logo. The backs show an action player photo that runs down the left side of the card. The right side displays statistics printed on a ghosted NBA logo. Topical subsets featured include NBA Draft (2-21), Team Checklists (35-61), and Scoring Threats (62-66). The set also includes two art cards (67-68) and one Stay in School card (69). Second series subsets featured are Team Fact Cards (350-376), NBA East All-Star Game (421-433), NBA West All-Star Game (434-445), In Your Face (446-454), Top Prospects (455-482), NBA Game Faces (483-497), Scoring Threats (498-505), and Fanimation (506-510). The cards are numbered on the back. Rookie Cards of note include Doug Christie (second series SP), Tom Gugliotta, Jim Jackson (second series SP), Christian Laettner, Alonzo Mourning, Shaquille O'Neal (second series SP), Latrell Sprewell and Clarence Weatherspoon. A card commemorating the retirement of Larry Bird and Magic Johnson (SP1) and the 20,000th point scored by Dominique Wilkins and Michael Jordan (SP2) were first and second series inserts, respectively. There were inserted at a rate of one in 72 packs. The basic card numbers of Jordan (23), Magic (32) and Bird (33) represent their uniform numbers.

	MINT	NRMT
COMPLETE SET (514)	50.00	22.00
COMPLETE LO SERIES (311)	20.00	9.00
COMPLETE HI SERIES (203)	30.00	13.50
COMMON CARD (1-510)	.05	.02
ERR (100A)	1.00	.45
ERR (110A)	4.00	1.80
SEMISTARS	.15	.07
UNLISTED STARS	.30	.14
LO SERIES SET INCLUDES 1AX/1B/32A/33A		
HI SERIES SET INCLUDES 1/32/33		
SP1: SER.1 STATED ODDS 1:72		
SP2: SER.2 STATED ODDS 1:72		

		MINT	NRMT
☐ 1	Shaquille O'Neal SP	15.00	6.75
	NBA First Draft Pick		
☐ 1A	1992 NBA Draft Trade Card SP	.30	.14
☐ 1B	Shaquille O'Neal TRADE	5.00	2.20
☐ 1AX	1992 NBA Draft Trade Card (Stamped)	.30	.14
☐ 2	Alonzo Mourning	1.50	.70
☐ 3	Christian Laettner	.75	.35
☐ 4	LaPhonso Ellis	.50	.23
☐ 5	C.Weatherspoon	.30	.14
☐ 6	Adam Keefe	.05	.02
☐ 7	Robert Horry	.50	.23
☐ 8	Harold Miner	.15	.07
☐ 9	Bryant Stith	.15	.07
☐ 10	Malik Sealy	.15	.07
☐ 11	Anthony Peeler	.15	.07
☐ 12	Randy Woods	.05	.02
☐ 13	Tracy Murray	.15	.07
☐ 14	Tom Gugliotta	1.00	.45
☐ 15	Hubert Davis	.15	.07
☐ 16	Don MacLean	.05	.02
☐ 17	Lee Mayberry	.05	.02
☐ 18	Corey Williams	.05	.02
☐ 19	Sean Rooks	.05	.02
☐ 20	Todd Day	.05	.02
☐ 21	Bryant Stith CL	.30	.14
	LaPhonso Ellis		
☐ 22	Jeff Hornacek	.15	.07
☐ 23	Michael Jordan	4.00	1.80

☐ 24	John Salley	.05	.02
☐ 25	Andre Turner	.05	.02
☐ 26	Charles Barkley	.50	.23
☐ 27	Anthony Frederick	.05	.02
☐ 28	Mario Elie	.15	.07
☐ 29	Olden Polynice	.05	.02
☐ 30	Rodney Monroe	.05	.02
☐ 31	Tim Perry	.05	.02
☐ 32	Doug Christie SP	.50	.23
☐ 32A	Magic Johnson SP	2.00	.90
☐ 33	Jim Jackson SP	2.50	1.10
☐ 33A	Larry Bird SP	2.50	1.10
☐ 34	Randy White	.05	.02
☐ 35	Frank Brickowski TC	.05	.02
☐ 36	Michael Adams TC	.05	.02
☐ 37	Scottie Pippen TC	.50	.23
☐ 38	Mark Price TC	.05	.02
☐ 39	Robert Parish TC	.05	.02
☐ 40	Danny Manning TC	.05	.02
☐ 41	Kevin Willis TC	.05	.02
☐ 42	Glen Rice TC	.15	.07
☐ 43	Kendall Gill TC	.05	.02
☐ 44	Karl Malone TC	.30	.14
☐ 45	Mitch Richmond TC	.30	.14
☐ 46	Patrick Ewing TC	.30	.14
☐ 47	Sam Perkins TC	.05	.02
☐ 48	Dennis Scott TC	.05	.02
☐ 49	Derek Harper TC	.05	.02
☐ 50	Drazen Petrovic TC	.05	.02
☐ 51	Reggie Williams TC	.05	.02
☐ 52	Rik Smits TC	.15	.07
☐ 53	Joe Dumars TC	.15	.07
☐ 54	Otis Thorpe TC	.05	.02
☐ 55	Johnny Dawkins TC	.05	.02
☐ 56	Sean Elliott TC	.05	.02
☐ 57	Kevin Johnson TC	.15	.07
☐ 58	Ricky Pierce TC	.05	.02
☐ 59	Doug West TC	.05	.02
☐ 60	Terry Porter TC	.05	.02
☐ 61	Tim Hardaway TC	.30	.14
☐ 62	Michael Jordan ST / Scottie Pippen	1.00	.45
☐ 63	Kendall Gill ST / Larry Johnson	.30	.14
☐ 64	Tom Chambers ST / Kevin Johnson	.15	.07
☐ 65	Tim Hardaway ST / Chris Mullin	.15	.07
☐ 66	Karl Malone ST / John Stockton	.30	.14
☐ 67	Michael Jordan MVP	2.00	.90
☐ 68	Stacey Augmon / Six Million Point Man	.05	.02
☐ 69	Bob Lanier / Stay in School	.15	.07
☐ 70	Alaa Abdelnaby	.05	.02
☐ 71	Andrew Lang	.05	.02
☐ 72	Larry Krystkowiak	.05	.02
☐ 73	Gerald Wilkins	.05	.02
☐ 74	Rod Strickland	.30	.14
☐ 75	Danny Ainge	.15	.07
☐ 76	Chris Corchiani	.05	.02
☐ 77	Jeff Grayer	.05	.02
☐ 78	Eric Murdock	.05	.02
☐ 79	Rex Chapman	.05	.02
☐ 80	LaBradford Smith	.05	.02
☐ 81	Jay Humphries	.05	.02
☐ 82	David Robinson	.50	.23
☐ 83	William Bedford	.05	.02
☐ 84	James Edwards	.05	.02
☐ 85	Dan Schayes	.05	.02
☐ 86	Lloyd Daniels	.05	.02
☐ 87	Blue Edwards	.05	.02
☐ 88	Dale Ellis	.05	.02
☐ 89	Rolando Blackman	.05	.02
☐ 90	Michael Jordan CL	.25	.11
☐ 91	Rik Smits	.15	.07
☐ 92	Terry Davis	.05	.02
☐ 93	Bill Cartwright	.05	.02
☐ 94	Avery Johnson	.05	.02
☐ 95	Michael Williams	.05	.02
☐ 96	Spud Webb	.15	.07
☐ 97	Benoit Benjamin	.05	.02
☐ 98	Derek Harper	.15	.07
☐ 99	Matt Bullard	.05	.02
☐ 100A	Tyrone Corbin ERR	1.00	.45
	(Heat on front)		
☐ 100B	Tyrone Corbin COR	.05	.02
☐ 101	Doc Rivers	.15	.07
☐ 102	Tony Smith	.05	.02
☐ 103	Doug West	.05	.02
☐ 104	Kevin Duckworth	.05	.02
☐ 105	Luc Longley	.15	.07
☐ 106	Antoine Carr	.05	.02
☐ 107	Clifford Robinson	.15	.07
☐ 108	Grant Long	.05	.02
☐ 109	Terry Porter	.05	.02
☐ 110A	Steve Smith ERR	4.00	1.80
	(Jazz on front)		
☐ 110B	Steve Smith COR	.30	.14
☐ 111	Brian Williams	.15	.07
☐ 112	Karl Malone	.50	.23
☐ 113	Reggie Williams	.05	.02
☐ 114	Tom Chambers	.05	.02
☐ 115	Winston Garland	.05	.02
☐ 116	John Stockton	.30	.14
☐ 117	Chris Jackson	.05	.02
☐ 118	Mike Brown	.05	.02
☐ 119	Kevin Johnson	.30	.14
☐ 120	Reggie Lewis	.15	.07
☐ 121	Bimbo Coles	.05	.02
☐ 122	Drazen Petrovic	.05	.02
☐ 123	Reggie Miller	.30	.14
☐ 124	Derrick Coleman	.15	.07
☐ 125	Chuck Person	.05	.02
☐ 126	Glen Rice	.40	.18
☐ 127	Kenny Anderson	.30	.14
☐ 128	Willie Burton	.05	.02
☐ 129	Chris Morris	.05	.02
☐ 130	Patrick Ewing	.30	.14
☐ 131	Sean Elliott	.15	.07
☐ 132	Clyde Drexler	.40	.18
☐ 133	Scottie Pippen	1.00	.45
☐ 134	Pooh Richardson	.05	.02
☐ 135	Horace Grant	.05	.02
☐ 136	Hakeem Olajuwon	.60	.25
☐ 137	John Paxson	.15	.07
☐ 138	Kendall Gill	.15	.07
☐ 139	Michael Adams	.05	.02
☐ 140	Otis Thorpe	.15	.07
☐ 141	Dennis Scott	.05	.02
☐ 142	Stacey Augmon	.15	.07
☐ 143	Robert Pack	.05	.02
☐ 144	Kevin Willis	.05	.02
☐ 145	Jerome Kersey	.05	.02
☐ 146	Paul Graham	.05	.02
☐ 147	Stanley Roberts	.05	.02
☐ 148	Dominique Wilkins	.30	.14
☐ 149	Scott Skiles	.05	.02
☐ 150	Rumeal Robinson	.05	.02
☐ 151	Mookie Blaylock	.15	.07
☐ 152	Elden Campbell	.15	.07
☐ 153	Chris Dudley	.05	.02
☐ 154	Sedale Threatt	.05	.02
☐ 155	Tate George	.05	.02
☐ 156	James Worthy	.30	.14
☐ 157	B.J. Armstrong	.05	.02
☐ 158	Gary Payton	.60	.25
☐ 159	Ledell Eackles	.05	.02
☐ 160	Sam Perkins	.05	.02
☐ 161	Nick Anderson	.15	.07
☐ 162	Mitch Richmond	.30	.14
☐ 163	Buck Williams	.15	.07
☐ 164	Blair Rasmussen	.05	.02
☐ 165	Vern Fleming	.05	.02
☐ 166	Duane Ferrell	.05	.02
☐ 167	George McCloud	.15	.07
☐ 168	Terry Cummings	.15	.07
☐ 169	Detlef Schrempf	.15	.07
☐ 170	Willie Anderson	.05	.02
☐ 171	Scott Williams	.05	.02
☐ 172	Vernon Maxwell	.05	.02
☐ 173	Todd Lichti	.05	.02
☐ 174	David Benoit	.05	.02
☐ 175	Marcus Liberty	.05	.02
☐ 176	Kenny Smith	.05	.02
☐ 177	Dan Majerle	.15	.07
☐ 178	Jeff Malone	.05	.02
☐ 179	Robert Parish	.15	.07
☐ 180	Mark Eaton	.05	.02
☐ 181	Rony Seikaly	.05	.02
☐ 182	Tony Campbell	.05	.02
☐ 183	Kevin McHale	.30	.14
☐ 184	Thurl Bailey	.05	.02
☐ 185	Kevin Edwards	.05	.02
☐ 186	Gerald Glass	.05	.02
☐ 187	Hersey Hawkins	.15	.07
☐ 188	Sam Mitchell	.05	.02
☐ 189	Brian Shaw	.05	.02
☐ 190	Felton Spencer	.05	.02
☐ 191	Mark Macon	.05	.02
☐ 192	Jerry Reynolds	.05	.02
☐ 193	Dale Davis	.05	.02
☐ 194	Sleepy Floyd	.05	.02
☐ 195	A.C. Green	.15	.07
☐ 196	Terry Catledge	.05	.02
☐ 197	Byron Scott	.15	.07
☐ 198	Sam Bowie	.05	.02
☐ 199	Vlade Divac	.15	.07
☐ 200	Michael Jordan CL	.25	.11
☐ 201	Brad Lohaus	.05	.02
☐ 202	Johnny Newman	.05	.02
☐ 203	Gary Grant	.05	.02
☐ 204	Sidney Green	.05	.02
☐ 205	Frank Brickowski	.05	.02
☐ 206	Anthony Bowie	.05	.02
☐ 207	Duane Causwell	.05	.02
☐ 208	A.J. English	.05	.02
☐ 209	Mark Aguirre	.05	.02
☐ 210	Jon Koncak	.05	.02
☐ 211	Kevin Gamble	.05	.02
☐ 212	Craig Ehlo	.05	.02
☐ 213	Herb Williams	.15	.07
☐ 214	Cedric Ceballos	.15	.07
☐ 215	Mark Jackson	.15	.07
☐ 216	John Bagley	.05	.02
☐ 217	Ron Anderson	.05	.02
☐ 218	John Battle	.05	.02
☐ 219	Kevin Lynch	.05	.02
☐ 220	Donald Hodge	.05	.02
☐ 221	Chris Gatling	.05	.02
☐ 222	Muggsy Bogues	.15	.07
☐ 223	Bill Laimbeer	.15	.07
☐ 224	Anthony Bonner	.05	.02
☐ 225	Fred Roberts	.05	.02
☐ 226	Larry Stewart	.05	.02
☐ 227	Darrell Walker	.05	.02
☐ 228	Larry Smith	.05	.02
☐ 229	Billy Owens	.15	.07
☐ 230	Vinnie Johnson	.05	.02
☐ 231	Johnny Dawkins	.05	.02
☐ 232	Rick Fox	.15	.07
☐ 233	Travis Mays	.05	.02
☐ 234	Mark Price	.30	.14
☐ 235	Derrick McKey	.05	.02
☐ 236	Greg Anthony	.05	.02
☐ 237	Doug Smith	.05	.02
☐ 238	Alec Kessler	.05	.02
☐ 239	Anthony Mason	.30	.14
☐ 240	Shawn Kemp	1.25	.55
☐ 241	Jim Les	.05	.02
☐ 242	Dennis Rodman	1.25	.55
☐ 243	Lionel Simmons	.05	.02
☐ 244	Pervis Ellison	.05	.02
☐ 245	Terrell Brandon	.50	.23
☐ 246	Mark Bryant	.05	.02
☐ 247	Brad Daugherty	.15	.07
☐ 248	Scott Brooks	.05	.02
☐ 249	Sarunas Marciulionis	.05	.02
☐ 250	Danny Ferry	.05	.02
☐ 251	Loy Vaught	.15	.07
☐ 252	Dee Brown	.05	.02
☐ 253	Alvin Robertson	.05	.02
☐ 254	Charles Smith	.05	.02
☐ 255	Dikembe Mutombo	.30	.14
☐ 256	Greg Kite	.05	.02
☐ 257	Ed Pinckney	.05	.02
☐ 258	Ron Harper	.15	.07
☐ 259	Elliot Perry	.05	.02
☐ 260	Rafael Addison	.05	.02
☐ 261	Tim Hardaway	.50	.23
☐ 262	Randy Brown	.05	.02
☐ 263	Isiah Thomas	.30	.14
☐ 264	Victor Alexander	.05	.02
☐ 265	Wayman Tisdale	.05	.02
☐ 266	Harvey Grant	.05	.02
☐ 267	Mike Iuzzolino	.05	.02
☐ 268	Joe Dumars	.30	.14

269	Xavier McDaniel	.05	.02
270	Jeff Sanders	.05	.02
271	Danny Manning	.15	.07
272	Jayson Williams	.15	.07
273	Ricky Pierce	.05	.02
274	Will Perdue	.05	.02
275	Dana Barros	.05	.02
276	Randy Breuer	.05	.02
277	Manute Bol	.05	.02
278	Negele Knight	.05	.02
279	Rodney McCray	.05	.02
280	Greg Sutton	.05	.02
281	Larry Nance	.05	.02
282	John Starks	.15	.07
283	Pete Chilcutt	.05	.02
284	Kenny Gattison	.05	.02
285	Stacey King	.05	.02
286	Bernard King	.05	.02
287	Larry Johnson	.40	.18
288	John Williams	.05	.02
289	Dell Curry	.05	.02
290	Orlando Woolridge	.05	.02
291	Nate McMillan	.05	.02
292	Terry Mills	.15	.07
293	Sherman Douglas	.05	.02
294	Charles Shackleford	.05	.02
295	Ken Norman	.05	.02
296	LaSalle Thompson	.05	.02
297	Chris Mullin	.30	.14
298	Eddie Johnson	.05	.02
299	Armon Gilliam	.05	.02
300	Michael Cage	.05	.02
301	Moses Malone	.30	.14
302	Charles Oakley	.15	.07
303	David Wingate	.05	.02
304	Steve Kerr	.15	.07
305	Tyrone Hill	.05	.02
306	Mark West	.05	.02
307	Fat Lever	.05	.02
308	J.R. Reid	.05	.02
309	Ed Nealy	.05	.02
310	Michael Jordan CL	.25	.11
311	Alaa Abdelnaby	.05	.02
312	Stacey Augmon	.15	.07
313	Anthony Avent	.05	.02
314	Walter Bond	.05	.02
315	Byron Houston	.05	.02
316	Rick Mahorn	.05	.02
317	Sam Mitchell	.05	.02
318	Mookie Blaylock	.15	.07
319	Lance Blanks	.05	.02
320	John Williams	.05	.02
321	Rolando Blackman	.05	.02
322	Danny Ainge	.15	.07
323	Gerald Glass	.05	.02
324	Robert Pack	.05	.02
325	Oliver Miller	.15	.07
326	Charles Smith	.05	.02
327	Duane Ferrell	.05	.02
328	Pooh Richardson	.05	.02
329	Scott Brooks	.05	.02
330	Walt Williams	.30	.14
331	Andrew Lang	.05	.02
332	Eric Murdock	.05	.02
333	Vinny Del Negro	.05	.02
334	Charles Barkley	.50	.23
335	James Edwards	.05	.02
336	Xavier McDaniel	.05	.02
337	Paul Graham	.05	.02
338	David Wingate	.05	.02
339	Richard Dumas	.05	.02
340	Jay Humphries	.05	.02
341	Mark Jackson	.15	.07
342	John Salley	.05	.02
343	Jon Koncak	.05	.02
344	Rodney McCray	.05	.02
345	Chuck Person	.05	.02
346	Mario Elie	.15	.07
347	Frank Johnson	.05	.02
348	Rumeal Robinson	.05	.02
349	Terry Mills	.15	.07
350	Kevin Willis TFC	.05	.02
351	Dee Brown TFC	.05	.02
352	Muggsy Bogues TFC	.05	.02
353	B.J. Armstrong TFC	.05	.02
354	Larry Nance TFC	.05	.02
355	Doug Smith TFC	.05	.02
356	Robert Pack TFC	.05	.02
357	Joe Dumars TFC	.15	.07
358	S.Marciulionis TFC	.05	.02
359	Kenny Smith TFC	.05	.02
360	Pooh Richardson TFC	.05	.02
361	Mark Jackson TFC	.05	.02
362	Sedale Threatt TFC	.05	.02
363	Grant Long TFC	.05	.02
364	Eric Murdock TFC	.05	.02
365	Doug West TFC	.05	.02
366	Kenny Anderson TFC	.15	.07
367	Anthony Mason TFC	.05	.02
368	Nick Anderson TFC	.05	.02
369	Jeff Hornacek TFC	.05	.02
370	Dan Majerle TFC	.05	.02
371	Clifford Robinson TFC	.05	.02
372	Lionel Simmons TFC	.05	.02
373	Dale Ellis TFC	.05	.02
374	Gary Payton TFC	.30	.14
375	David Benoit TFC	.05	.02
376	Harvey Grant TFC	.05	.02
377	Buck Johnson	.05	.02
378	Brian Howard	.05	.02
379	Travis Mays	.05	.02
380	Jud Buechler	.05	.02
381	Matt Geiger	.15	.07
382	Bob McCann	.05	.02
383	Cedric Ceballos	.15	.07
384	Rod Strickland	.30	.14
385	Kiki Vandeweghe	.05	.02
386	Latrell Sprewell	1.00	.45
387	Larry Krystkowiak	.05	.02
388	Dale Ellis	.05	.02
389	Trent Tucker	.05	.02
390	Negele Knight	.05	.02
391	Stanley Roberts	.05	.02
392	Tony Campbell	.05	.02
393	Tim Perry	.05	.02
394	Doug Overton	.05	.02
395	Dan Majerle	.15	.07
396	Duane Cooper	.05	.02
397	Kevin Willis	.05	.02
398	Micheal Williams	.05	.02
399	Avery Johnson	.05	.02
400	Dominique Wilkins	.30	.14
401	Chris Smith	.05	.02
402	Blair Rasmussen	.05	.02
403	Jeff Hornacek	.15	.07
404	Blue Edwards	.05	.02
405	Olden Polynice	.05	.02
406	Jeff Grayer	.05	.02
407	Tony Bennett	.05	.02
408	Don MacLean	.05	.02
409	Tom Chambers	.05	.02
410	Keith Jennings	.05	.02
411	Gerald Wilkins	.05	.02
412	Kennard Winchester	.05	.02
413	Doc Rivers	.15	.07
414	Brent Price	.15	.07
415	Mark West	.05	.02
416	J.R. Reid	.05	.02
417	Jon Barry	.05	.02
418	Kevin Johnson	.30	.14
419	Michael Jordan CL	.25	.11
420	Michael Jordan CL	.25	.11
421	Brad Daugherty CL ... Mark Price Larry Nance	.05	.02
422	Scottie Pippen AS	.50	.23
423	Larry Johnson AS	.30	.14
424	Shaquille O'Neal AS ..	1.50	.70
425	Michael Jordan AS ..	2.00	.90
426	Isiah Thomas AS	.15	.07
427	Brad Daugherty AS	.05	.02
428	Joe Dumars AS	.15	.07
429	Patrick Ewing AS	.30	.14
430	Larry Nance AS	.05	.02
431	Mark Price AS	.05	.02
432	Detlef Schrempf AS	.05	.02
433	Dominique Wilkins AS	.15	.07
434	Karl Malone AS	.30	.14
435	Charles Barkley AS	.30	.14
436	David Robinson AS	.30	.14
437	John Stockton AS	.30	.14
438	Clyde Drexler AS	.30	.14
439	Sean Elliott AS	.05	.02
440	Tim Hardaway AS	.30	.14
441	Shawn Kemp AS	.60	.25
442	Dan Majerle AS	.05	.02
443	Danny Manning AS	.05	.02
444	Hakeem Olajuwon AS	.30	.14
445	Terry Porter AS	.05	.02
446	Harold Miner FACE	.15	.07
447	David Benoit FACE	.05	.02
448	Cedric Ceballos FACE	.05	.02
449	Chris Jackson FACE	.05	.02
450	Tim Perry FACE	.05	.02
451	Kenny Smith FACE	.05	.02
452	C.Weatherspoon FACE	.30	.14
453A	Michael Jordan .... FACE ERR (Slam Dunk Champ in 1985 and 1990)	20.00	9.00
453B	Michael Jordan .. FACE COR (Slam Dunk Champ in 1987 and 1988)	2.00	.90
454A	Dominique Wilkins FACE ERR (Slam Dunk Champ in 1987 and 1988)	2.00	.90
454B	Dominique Wilkins .. FACE COR (Slam Dunk Champ in 1985 and 1990)	.30	.14
455	Anthony Peeler Duane Cooper CL	.05	.02
456	Adam Keefe TP	.05	.02
457	Alonzo Mourning TP	.50	.23
458	Jim Jackson TP	.50	.23
459	Sean Rooks TP	.05	.02
460	LaPhonso Ellis TP	.15	.07
461	Bryant Stith TP	.05	.02
462	Byron Houston TP	.05	.02
463	Latrell Sprewell TP	.30	.14
464	Robert Horry TP	.30	.14
465	Malik Sealy TP	.05	.02
466	Doug Christie TP	.30	.14
467	Duane Cooper TP	.05	.02
468	Anthony Peeler TP	.05	.02
469	Harold Miner TP	.05	.02
470	Todd Day TP	.05	.02
471	Lee Mayberry TP	.05	.02
472	Christian Laettner TP	.30	.14
473	Hubert Davis TP	.05	.02
474	Shaquille O'Neal TP ..	1.50	.70
475	C.Weatherspoon TP	.30	.14
476	Richard Dumas TP	.05	.02
477	Oliver Miller TP	.05	.02
478	Tracy Murray TP	.05	.02
479	Walt Williams TP	.30	.14
480	Lloyd Daniels TP	.05	.02
481	Tom Gugliotta TP	.30	.14
482	Brent Price TP	.05	.02
483	Mark Aguirre GF	.05	.02
484	Frank Brickowski GF	.05	.02
485	Derrick Coleman GF	.30	.14
486	Clyde Drexler GF	.30	.14
487	Harvey Grant GF	.05	.02
488	Michael Jordan GF ..	2.00	.90
489	Karl Malone GF	.30	.14
490	Xavier McDaniel GF	.05	.02
491	Drazen Petrovic GF	.05	.02
492	John Starks GF	.05	.02
493	Robert Parish GF	.15	.07
494	Christian Laettner GF	.40	.18
495	Ron Harper GF	.05	.02
496	David Robinson GF	.30	.14
497	John Salley GF	.05	.02
498	Brad Daugherty ST Mark Price	.05	.02
499	D.Mutombo ST Chris Jackson	.15	.07
500	Isiah Thomas ST Joe Dumars	.30	.14
501	Hakeem Olajuwon Otis Thorpe ST	.30	.14
502	Derrick Coleman ST Drazen Petrovic	.15	.07
503	Terry Porter ST Clyde Drexler	.30	.14
504	Lionel Simmons ST Mitch Richmond	.15	.07
505	David Robinson ST	.30	.14

		MINT	NRMT
	Sean Elliott		
☐ 506	Michael Jordan FAN	2.00	.90
☐ 507	Larry Bird FAN	.60	.25
☐ 508	Karl Malone FAN	.30	.14
☐ 509	D.Mutombo FAN	.30	.14
☐ 510	Larry Bird FAN	1.00	.45
	Michael Jordan		
☐ SP1	Larry Bird	3.00	1.35
	Magic Johnson		
	Retirement		
☐ SP2	20,000 Points	8.00	3.60
	Dominique Wilkins		
	Nov. 6, 1992		
	Michael Jordan		
	Jan. 8, 1993		

☐ AD5	Kenny Anderson	.75	.35
☐ AD6	Brad Daugherty	.25	.11
☐ AD7	Dominique Wilkins	.75	.35
☐ AD8	Larry Johnson	.40	.18
☐ AD9	Michael Jordan	10.00	4.50
☐ AD10	Mark Price	.25	.11
☐ AD11	David Robinson	1.25	.55
☐ AD12	Karl Malone	1.25	.55
☐ AD13	Sean Elliott	.40	.18
☐ AD14	John Stockton	.75	.35
☐ AD15	Derek Harper	.40	.18
☐ AD16	Kevin Duckworth	.25	.11
☐ AD17	Chris Mullin	.75	.35
☐ AD18	Charles Barkley	1.25	.55
☐ AD19	Tim Hardaway	1.25	.55
☐ AD20	Clyde Drexler	1.00	.45

1992-93 Upper Deck All-Division

Inserted one per second series red or gray jumbo pack, this 20-card standard-size set consists of Upper Deck's selection of the top five players in each of the NBA's four divisions. There is a special logo representing each division. The cards are arranged according to division as follows: Atlantic (1-5), Central (6-10), Midwest (11-15), and Pacific (16-20). The cards are numbered with an "AD" prefix. The fronts feature full-bleed, color, action player photos. A black and team color-coded bar outlined with gold foil carries the player's name and position. These cards can be distinguished by an All-Division Team icon in the lower left corner above the player's name. The backs display career highlights against a light blue panel. A U.S. map shows the player's division.

	MINT	NRMT
COMPLETE SET (20)	20.00	9.00
COMMON CARD (AD1-AD20)	.25	.11
SEMISTARS	.40	.18
UNLISTED STARS	.75	.35
ONE PER HI SERIES JUMBO PACK		
☐ AD1 Shaquille O'Neal	8.00	3.60
☐ AD2 Derrick Coleman	.40	.18
☐ AD3 Glen Rice	1.00	.45
☐ AD4 Reggie Lewis		.18

1992-93 Upper Deck All-NBA

This ten-card standard-size set featuring the 1991-92 All-NBA team was issued one per 27-card low series Locker pack. Each plastic locker box contained four specially wrapped. The fronts feature full-bleed color action player photos with black bottom borders. The player's name is foil-stamped in the border, and the words "All-NBA Team" are foil-stamped at the top. Gold and silver foil stamping are used to designate the First (1-5) and Second Teams (6-10) respectively. The backs carry a close-up player photo and career summary. The cards are numbered on the back with an "AN" prefix.

	MINT	NRMT
COMPLETE SET (10)	50.00	22.00
COMMON CARD (AN1-AN10)	2.50	1.10
ONE PER LO SERIES LOCKER PACK		
CONDITION SENSITIVE SET		
☐ AN1 Michael Jordan	30.00	13.50
☐ AN2 Clyde Drexler	3.00	1.35
☐ AN3 David Robinson	4.00	1.80
☐ AN4 Karl Malone	4.00	1.80
☐ AN5 Chris Mullin	2.50	1.10
☐ AN6 John Stockton	2.50	1.10
☐ AN7 Tim Hardaway	4.00	1.80
☐ AN8 Patrick Ewing	2.50	1.10
☐ AN9 Scottie Pippen	8.00	3.60
☐ AN10 Charles Barkley	4.00	1.80

1992-93 Upper Deck All-Rookies

Randomly inserted in low series 15-card retail foil packs at a reported rate of one card for every twelve packs, this ten-card standard-size insert set features the top first-year players of the 1991-92 season. Card numbers 1-5 present the first team and card numbers 6-10 the second team. The cards are numbered with an "AR" prefix. The fronts feature full-bleed, color, action player photos. A gold and red bottom border design carries the player's name, position, the number team (first or second), and an NBA All-Rookie Team icon. The backs carry player profiles.

	MINT	NRMT
COMPLETE SET (10)	10.00	4.50
COMMON CARD (AR1-AR10)	.50	.23
SEMISTARS	.75	.35
UNLISTED STARS	2.00	.90
LO SERIES STATED ODDS 1:12 RETAIL		
☐ AR1 Larry Johnson	2.50	1.10
☐ AR2 D.Mutombo	2.00	.90
☐ AR3 Billy Owens	.75	.35
☐ AR4 Steve Smith	2.00	.90
☐ AR5 Stacey Augmon	.75	.35
☐ AR6 Rick Fox	.75	.35
☐ AR7 Terrell Brandon	3.00	1.35
☐ AR8 Larry Stewart	.50	.23
☐ AR9 Stanley Roberts	.50	.23
☐ AR10 Mark Macon	.50	.23

1992-93 Upper Deck Award Winner Holograms

The 1992-93 Upper Deck Award Winner Holograms set features nine holograms depicting league leaders in various statistical categories. The set also honors 1991-92 award winners such as top Sixth Man, Rookie of the

Year, Defensive Player of the Year and Most Valuable Player. Card numbers 1-6 were randomly inserted in all forms of low series packs while card numbers 7-9 were included in all forms of high series packs. The card numbers have an "AW" prefix. The fronts feature holographic cut-out images of the player against a game-action photo of the player. The player's name and award are displayed at the bottom. The cards carry vertical, color player photos. A light blue plaque-style panel contains information about the player and the award won.

with the Boston Celtics. The color action player photos on the fronts are bordered on the left and bottom by black borders that carry the card subtitle and "Basketball Heroes, Larry Bird" respectively. On a background shading from white to green, brief summaries of Bird's career are presented on a center panel. The cards are numbered on the back in continuation of the Upper Deck Basketball Heroes.

depict Wilt from college, to the Globetrotter's to pro basketball. Information on the back corresponds to the portion of his career that is represented on front. The set is numbered in continuation of Upper Deck's Hero series.

	MINT	NRMT
COMPLETE SET (10)	5.00	2.20
COMMON CHAMBER. (10-18)	.50	.23
CHAMBERLAIN HEADER (NNO)	1.00	.45
LO SERIES STATED ODDS 1:9		

		MINT	NRMT
□ 10	Wilt Chamberlain	.50	.23
	1956-58 College Star		
□ 11	Wilt Chamberlain	.50	.23
	1958-59 Harlem Globetrotter		
□ 12	Wilt Chamberlain	.50	.23
	1960 NBA ROY		
□ 13	Wilt Chamberlain	.50	.23
	1962 100-Point Game		
□ 14	Wilt Chamberlain	.50	.23
	1960-68 Four-time NBA MVP		
□ 15	Wilt Chamberlain	.50	.23
	1960-66 Seven consecutive scoring titles		
□ 16	Wilt Chamberlain	.50	.23
	1971-72 30,000-Point Plateau		
□ 17	Wilt Chamberlain	.50	.23
	1978 Basketball HOF		
□ 18	Wilt Chamberlain	.50	.23
	Basketball Heroes CL		
□ NNO	Basketball Heroes ..	1.00	.45
	(Header card)		

	MINT	NRMT
COMPLETE SET (10)	10.00	4.50
COMMON BIRD (19-27)	1.00	.45
BIRD HEADER (NNO)	2.00	.90
HI SERIES STATED ODDS 1:9		

		MINT	NRMT
□ 19	Larry Bird	1.00	.45
	1979 College Player of the Year		
□ 20	Larry Bird	1.00	.45
	1979-80 Rookie of the Year		
□ 21	Larry Bird	1.00	.45
	1980-92 12-Time NBA All-Star		
□ 22	Larry Bird	1.00	.45
	1981-86 Three NBA Championships		
□ 23	Larry Bird	1.00	.45
	1984-86 3-Time NBA MVP		
□ 24	Larry Bird	1.00	.45
	1986-88 3-Point King		
□ 25	Larry Bird	1.00	.45
	1990 20,000 Points		
□ 26	Larry Bird	1.00	.45
	Larry Legend		
□ 27	Larry Bird	1.00	.45
	(Portrait by Alan Studt)		
□ NNO	Larry Bird	2.00	.90
	Title/Header Card		

	MINT	NRMT
COMPLETE SET (9)	30.00	13.50
COMPLETE LO SERIES (6)	15.00	6.75
COMPLETE HI SERIES (3)	15.00	6.75
COMMON CARD (AW1-AW9)	.50	.23
SEMISTARS	.75	.35
UNLISTED STARS	1.00	.45
LO/HI SERIES STATED ODDS 1:18 HOB/RET		

		MINT	NRMT
□ AW1	Michael Jordan	15.00	6.75
	Scoring		
□ AW2	John Stockton	1.00	.45
	Steals		
□ AW3	Dennis Rodman	4.00	1.80
	Rebounds		
□ AW4	Detlef Schrempf	.50	.23
	Sixth Man		
□ AW5	Larry Johnson	.75	.35
	Rookie of the Year		
□ AW6	David Robinson	1.50	.70
	Blocked Shots		
□ AW7	David Robinson	1.50	.70
	Def. Player of Year		
□ AW8	John Stockton	1.00	.45
	Assists		
□ AW9	Michael Jordan	15.00	6.75
	Most Valuable Player		

1992-93 Upper Deck Larry Bird Heroes

Randomly inserted into all forms of high series packs, this ten-card standard-size set chronicles the career of Larry Bird from his college days at Indiana State University to pro stardom

1992-93 Upper Deck Wilt Chamberlain Heroes

Randomly inserted in all types of low series packs, this ten-card standard-size set honors Wilt Chamberlain by highlighting various points in his career. Circular photos on the fronts

1992-93 Upper Deck 15000 Point Club

Randomly inserted in 15-card high series hobby packs at a

reported rate of one card per nine packs, this 20-card standard-size set spotlights then-active NBA players who had scored more than 15,000 points in their career. The fronts feature full-bleed color action player photos accented at the top and bottom by team color-coded stripes carrying the phrase "15,000 Point Club" and the player's name respectively. A gold 15,000-Point club logo at the lower left corner carries the season the player joined this elite club. The backs display a small player photo and year-by-year scoring totals. The cards are numbered with an "PC" prefix.

	MINT	NRMT
COMPLETE SET (20)	50.00	22.00
COMMON CARD (PC1-PC20)	1.00	.45
SEMISTARS	1.50	.70
UNLISTED STARS	2.50	1.10
HI SERIES STATED ODDS 1:9 HOBBY		

		MINT	NRMT
☐ PC1	Dominique Wilkins ..	2.50	1.10
☐ PC2	Kevin McHale	2.50	1.10
☐ PC3	Robert Parish	1.50	.70
☐ PC4	Michael Jordan	30.00	13.50
☐ PC5	Isiah Thomas	2.50	1.10
☐ PC6	Mark Aguirre	1.00	.45
☐ PC7	Kiki Vandeweghe	1.00	.45
☐ PC8	James Worthy	2.50	1.10
☐ PC9	Rolando Blackman	1.00	.45
☐ PC10	Moses Malone	2.50	1.10
☐ PC11	Charles Barkley	4.00	1.80
☐ PC12	Tom Chambers	1.00	.45
☐ PC13	Clyde Drexler	3.00	1.35
☐ PC14	Terry Cummings	1.50	.70
☐ PC15	Eddie Johnson	1.00	.45
☐ PC16	Karl Malone	4.00	1.80
☐ PC17	Bernard King	1.00	.45
☐ PC18	Larry Nance	1.50	.70
☐ PC19	Jeff Malone	1.00	.45
☐ PC20	Hakeem Olajuwon	5.00	2.20

1992-93 Upper Deck Foreign Exchange

Inserted one card per pack in second series 4-pack locker boxes, this ten-card standard-size set showcases foreign born

players who are stars in the NBA. Each card uses the colors of the flag from the player's homeland as well as a "Foreign Exchange" logo. The cards are numbered with an "FE" prefix. The fronts carry full-bleed, color, action player photos. The player's name, position, and place of birth appear in border stripes at the bottom. The backs display either an action or close-up player photo on a pale beige panel along with a player profile. A small representation of the player's home flag appears at the lower right corner of the picture. The set is sequenced in alphabetical order.

	MINT	NRMT
COMPLETE SET (10)	20.00	9.00
COMMON CARD (FE1-FE10)	1.00	.45
SEMISTARS	2.50	1.10
UNLISTED STARS	4.00	1.80
ONE PER HI SERIES LOCKER PACK		

		MINT	NRMT
☐ FE1	Manute Bol	1.00	.45
☐ FE2	Vlade Divac	2.50	1.10
☐ FE3	Patrick Ewing	4.00	1.80
☐ FE4	Sarunas Marciulionis	1.00	.45
☐ FE5	D.Mutombo	4.00	1.80
☐ FE6	Hakeem Olajuwon	8.00	3.60
☐ FE7	Drazen Petrovic	1.00	.45
☐ FE8	Detlef Schrempf	2.50	1.10
☐ FE9	Rik Smits	2.50	1.10
☐ FE10	Dominique Wilkins	4.00	1.80

1992-93 Upper Deck Rookie Standouts

Randomly inserted in high series retail and high series red jumbo packs at a reported rate of one card per nine packs, this 20-card standard-size set honors top rookies who made the most impact during the 1992-93 NBA season. The cards are numbered on the back with an "RS" prefix. The fronts feature full-bleed, color, action player photos. The player's name and

position appear in a teal stripe across the bottom. A "Rookie Standouts" icon overlaps the stripe and the picture at the lower right corner. The backs have a vertical action photo and career highlights within a gold box. A red banner over a gold basketball icon accent the top of the box.

	MINT	NRMT
COMPLETE SET (20)	25.00	11.00
COMMON CARD (RS1-RS20)	.25	.11
SEMISTARS	.75	.35
UNLISTED STARS	1.25	.55
HI SERIES STATED ODDS 1:9 RET/JUM		

		MINT	NRMT
☐ RS1	Adam Keefe	.25	.11
☐ RS2	Alonzo Mourning	4.00	1.80
☐ RS3	Sean Rooks	.25	.11
☐ RS4	LaPhonso Ellis	.75	.35
☐ RS5	Latrell Sprewell	2.50	1.10
☐ RS6	Robert Horry	1.25	.55
☐ RS7	Malik Sealy	.75	.35
☐ RS8	Anthony Peeler	.75	.35
☐ RS9	Harold Miner	.75	.35
☐ RS10	Anthony Avent	.25	.11
☐ RS11	Todd Day	.25	.11
☐ RS12	Lee Mayberry	.25	.11
☐ RS13	Christian Laettner ..	2.00	.90
☐ RS14	Hubert Davis	.75	.35
☐ RS15	Shaquille O'Neal ..	12.00	5.50
☐ RS16	C.Weatherspoon ...	.75	.35
☐ RS17	Richard Dumas	.25	.11
☐ RS18	Walt Williams	.75	.35
☐ RS19	Lloyd Daniels	.25	.11
☐ RS20	Tom Gugliotta	2.50	1.10

1992-93 Upper Deck Team MVPs

This 28-card standard-size set honors a top player from each NBA team. One "Team MVP" card was inserted into each 1992-93 Upper Deck low series 27-card jumbo pack. Card fronts feature a photo that takes up most of the front. The only other feature on front is the player's name within a bottom border. Backs contain a photo with highlights. These cards are numbered on the back with a "TM" prefix.

	MINT	NRMT
COMPLETE SET (28)	60.00	27.00
COMMON CARD (TM1-TM28)	.50	.23
SEMISTARS	1.25	.55
UNLISTED STARS	2.00	.90
ONE PER LO SERIES JUMBO PACK		

			MINT	NRMT
☐	TM1	Michael Jordan CL	25.00	11.00
☐	TM2	Dominique Wilkins	2.00	.90
☐	TM3	Reggie Lewis	1.25	.55
☐	TM4	Kendall Gill	1.25	.55
☐	TM5	Michael Jordan	25.00	11.00
☐	TM6	Brad Daugherty	.50	.23
☐	TM7	Derek Harper	1.25	.55
☐	TM8	D.Mutombo	2.00	.90
☐	TM9	Isiah Thomas	2.00	.90
☐	TM10	Chris Mullin	2.00	.90
☐	TM11	Hakeem Olajuwon	4.00	1.80
☐	TM12	Reggie Miller	2.00	.90
☐	TM13	Ron Harper	1.25	.55
☐	TM14	James Worthy	2.00	.90
☐	TM15	Rony Seikaly	.50	.23
☐	TM16	Alvin Robertson	.50	.23
☐	TM17	Pooh Richardson	.50	.23
☐	TM18	Derrick Coleman	1.25	.55
☐	TM19	Patrick Ewing	2.00	.90
☐	TM20	Scott Skiles	.50	.23
☐	TM21	Hersey Hawkins	1.25	.55
☐	TM22	Kevin Johnson	2.00	.90
☐	TM23	Clyde Drexler	2.50	1.10
☐	TM24	Mitch Richmond	2.00	.90
☐	TM25	David Robinson	3.00	1.35
☐	TM26	Ricky Pierce	.50	.23
☐	TM27	John Stockton	2.00	.90
☐	TM28	Pervis Ellison	.50	.23

1992-93 Upper Deck Jerry West Selects

Randomly inserted in 15-card low series hobby packs at a reported rate of one card per nine packs, this 20-card standard-size set pays tribute to Jerry West's selection of NBA players who are the most dominant (or projected to be) in ten different basketball skills. The cards feature color action player photos bordered on the right edge by a white stripe containing the player's name. Two stripes border the bottom of the cards, a black stripe containing a gold foil facsimile autograph of Jerry West and the word "Select," and a gradated team-colored stripe. This second stripe contains the player's specific achievement. The backs show a smaller color action shot of the player above a pale gray panel containing comments by West. The right edge of the card has a 1/2" white border containing the player's name. A small cut-out action image of Jerry West appears in the lower right corner. Card numbers 1-10 feature his present selections for best in ten different categories while card numbers 11-20 are his future selections. The cards are numbered on the back with a "JW" prefix. The set includes four cards of Michael Jordan.

	MINT	NRMT
COMPLETE SET (20)	80.00	36.00
COMMON CARD (JW1-JW20)	.60	.25
SEMISTARS	1.00	.45
UNLISTED STARS	1.50	.70
LO SERIES STATED ODDS 1:9 HOBBY		

			MINT	NRMT
☐	JW1	Michael Jordan Best Shooter	20.00	9.00
☐	JW2	Dennis Rodman Best Rebounder	8.00	3.60
☐	JW3	David Robinson Best Shot Blocker	3.00	1.35
☐	JW4	Michael Jordan Best Defender	20.00	9.00
☐	JW5	Magic Johnson Best Point Guard	3.00	1.35
☐	JW6	Detlef Schrempf Best Sixth Man	.60	.25
☐	JW7	Magic Johnson Most Inspirational Player	3.00	1.35
☐	JW8	Michael Jordan Best All-Around Player	20.00	9.00
☐	JW9	Michael Jordan Best Clutch Player	20.00	9.00
☐	JW10	Magic Johnson Best Court Leader	3.00	1.35
☐	JW11	Glen Rice Best Shooter	2.50	1.10
☐	JW12	D.Mutombo Best Rebounder	1.50	.70
☐	JW13	D.Mutombo Best Shot Blocker	1.50	.70
☐	JW14	Stacey Augmon Best Defender	1.00	.45
☐	JW15	Tim Hardaway Best Point Guard	2.50	1.10
☐	JW16	Shawn Kemp Best Sixth Man	8.00	3.60
☐	JW17	Danny Manning Most Inspirational Player	1.00	.45
☐	JW18	Michael Jordan Best All-Around Player	1.00	.45
☐	JW19	Reggie Lewis Best Clutch Player	1.00	.45
☐	JW20	Tim Hardaway Best Court Leader	2.50	1.10

1993-94 Upper Deck

This 510-card standard-size UV-coated set was issued in two series of 255. The cards were issued in 12-card hobby and retail packs (36 per box), 22-

card green and blue retail jumbo packs (first series only), 22-card red and purple retail jumbo packs (second series only) and 22-card hobby locker packs for both series. Card fronts feature glossy color player action photos on the fronts. The left and bottom borders (team colors) contain the team and player's name respectively. The backs feature another color action player photo at the top. At bottom, player stats are shaded in team colors. Topical subsets featured are the following: Season Leaders (166-177), NBA Playoffs Highlights (178-197), NBA Finals Highlights (198-209), Schedules (210-236), Signature Moves (237-251), Executive Board (421-435), Breakaway Threats (436-455), Game Images (456-465), Skylights (467-480), Top Prospects (482-497) and McDonald's Open (498-507). The cards are numbered on the back. The SP3 card was inserted randomly in all forms of first series packaging with the SP4 in the second series. Both cards were inserted at a rate of 1 in 72 packs. Rookie Cards of note include Vin Baker, Anfernee Hardaway, Allan Houston, Toni Kukoc, Jamal Mashburn, Nick Van Exel and Chris Webber.

	MINT	NRMT
COMPLETE SET (510)	30.00	13.50
COMPLETE SERIES 1 (255)	15.00	6.75
COMPLETE SERIES 2 (255)	15.00	6.75
COMMON CARD (1-510)	.05	.02
SEMISTARS	.15	.07
UNLISTED STARS	.30	.14
SP3: SER.1 STATED ODDS 1:72		
SP4: SER.2 STATED ODDS 1:72		

			MINT	NRMT
☐	1	Muggsy Bogues	.15	.07
☐	2	Kenny Anderson	.15	.07
☐	3	Dell Curry	.05	.02
☐	4	Charles Smith	.05	.02
☐	5	Chuck Person	.05	.02
☐	6	Chucky Brown	.05	.02
☐	7	Kevin Johnson	.15	.07

8	Winston Garland	.05	.02
9	John Salley	.05	.02
10	Dale Ellis	.05	.02
11	Otis Thorpe	.15	.07
12	John Stockton	.30	.14
13	Kendall Gill	.15	.07
14	Randy White	.05	.02
15	Mark Jackson	.15	.07
16	Vlade Divac	.15	.07
17	Scott Skiles	.05	.02
18	Xavier McDaniel	.05	.02
19	Jeff Hornacek	.15	.07
20	Stanley Roberts	.05	.02
21	Harold Miner	.05	.02
22	Terrell Brandon	.30	.14
23	Michael Jordan	4.00	1.80
24	Jim Jackson	.30	.14
25	Keith Askins	.05	.02
26	Corey Williams	.05	.02
27	David Benoit	.05	.02
28	Charles Oakley	.15	.07
29	Michael Adams	.05	.02
30	C.Weatherspoon	.05	.02
31	Jon Koncak	.05	.02
32	Gerald Wilkins	.05	.02
33	Anthony Bowie	.05	.02
34	Willie Burton	.05	.02
35	Stacey Augmon	.05	.02
36	Doc Rivers	.15	.07
37	Luc Longley	.15	.07
38	Dee Brown	.05	.02
39	Litterial Green	.05	.02
40	Dan Majerle	.15	.07
41	Doug West	.05	.02
42	Joe Dumars	.30	.14
43	Dennis Scott	.05	.02
44	Mahmoud Abdul-Rauf	.05	.02
45	Mark Eaton	.05	.02
46	Danny Ferry	.05	.02
47	Kenny Smith	.05	.02
48	Ron Harper	.15	.07
49	Adam Keefe	.05	.02
50	David Robinson	.50	.23
51	John Starks	.15	.07
52	Jeff Malone	.05	.02
53	Vern Fleming	.05	.02
54	Olden Polynice	.05	.02
55	D.Mutombo	.30	.14
56	Chris Morris	.05	.02
57	Paul Graham	.05	.02
58	Richard Dumas	.05	.02
59	J.R. Reid	.05	.02
60	Brad Daugherty	.05	.02
61	Blue Edwards	.05	.02
62	Mark Macon	.05	.02
63	Latrell Sprewell	.30	.14
64	Mitch Richmond	.30	.14
65	David Wingate	.05	.02
66	LaSalle Thompson	.05	.02
67	Sedale Threatt	.05	.02
68	Larry Krystkowiak	.05	.02
69	John Paxson	.05	.02
70	Frank Brickowski	.05	.02
71	Duane Causwell	.05	.02
72	Fred Roberts	.05	.02
73	Rod Strickland	.15	.07
74	Willie Anderson	.05	.02
75	Thurl Bailey	.05	.02
76	Ricky Pierce	.05	.02
77	Todd Day	.05	.02
78	Hot Rod Williams	.05	.02
79	Danny Ainge	.15	.07
80	Mark West	.05	.02
81	Marcus Liberty	.05	.02
82	Keith Jennings	.05	.02
83	Derrick Coleman	.15	.07
84	Larry Stewart	.05	.02
85	Tracy Murray	.05	.02
86	Robert Horry	.15	.07
87	Derek Harper	.15	.07
88	Scott Hastings	.05	.02
89	Sam Perkins	.15	.07
90	Clyde Drexler	.40	.18
91	Brent Price	.05	.02
92	Chris Mullin	.30	.14
93	Rafael Addison	.05	.02
94	Tyrone Corbin	.05	.02
95	Sarunas Marciulionis	.05	.02
96	Antoine Carr	.05	.02
97	Tony Bennett	.05	.02
98	Sam Mitchell	.05	.02
99	Lionel Simmons	.05	.02
100	Tim Perry	.05	.02
101	Horace Grant	.15	.07
102	Tom Hammonds	.05	.02
103	Walter Bond	.05	.02
104	Detlef Schrempf	.15	.07
105	Terry Porter	.05	.02
106	Dan Schayes	.05	.02
107	Rumeal Robinson	.05	.02
108	Gerald Glass	.05	.02
109	Mike Gminski	.05	.02
110	Terry Mills	.15	.07
111	Loy Vaught	.15	.07
112	Jim Les	.05	.02
113	Byron Houston	.05	.02
114	Randy Brown	.05	.02
115	Anthony Avent	.05	.02
116	Donald Hodge	.05	.02
117	Kevin Willis	.05	.02
118	Robert Pack	.05	.02
119	Dale Davis	.05	.02
120	Grant Long	.05	.02
121	Anthony Bonner	.05	.02
122	Chris Smith	.05	.02
123	Elden Campbell	.15	.07
124	Clifford Robinson	.15	.07
125	Sherman Douglas	.05	.02
126	Alvin Robertson	.05	.02
127	Rolando Blackman	.05	.02
128	Malik Sealy	.05	.02
129	Ed Pinckney	.05	.02
130	Anthony Peeler	.05	.02
131	Scott McKey	.05	.02
132	Rik Smits	.15	.07
133	Derrick McKey	.05	.02
134	Alaa Abdelnaby	.05	.02
135	Rex Chapman	.05	.02
136	Tony Campbell	.05	.02
137	John Williams	.05	.02
138	Vincent Askew	.05	.02
139	LaBradford Smith	.05	.02
140	Vinny Del Negro	.05	.02
141	Darrell Walker	.05	.02
142	James Worthy	.30	.14
143	Jeff Turner	.05	.02
144	Duane Ferrell	.05	.02
145	Larry Smith	.05	.02
146	Eddie Johnson	.05	.02
147	Chris Gatling	.05	.02
148	Buck Williams	.15	.07
149	Donald Royal	.05	.02
150	Dino Radja	.15	.07
151	Johnny Dawkins	.05	.02
152	Tim Legler	.05	.02
153	Bill Laimbeer	.05	.02
154	Glen Rice	.30	.14
155	Bill Cartwright	.05	.02
156	Luther Wright	.05	.02
157	Rex Walters	.05	.02
158	Doug Edwards	.05	.02
159	George Lynch	.05	.02
160	Chris Mills	.50	.23
161	Sam Cassell	.75	.35
162	Nick Van Exel	1.00	.45
163	Shawn Bradley	.40	.18
164	Calbert Cheaney	.30	.14
165	Corie Blount	.05	.02
166	Michael Jordan SL — Scoring	2.00	.90
167	Dennis Rodman SL — Rebounds	.60	.25
168	John Stockton SL — Assists	.15	.07
169	B.J. Armstrong SL — 3-pt. field goals	.05	.02
170	Hakeem Olajuwon SL — Blocked shots	.30	.14
171	Michael Jordan SL — Steals	2.00	.90
172	Cedric Ceballos SL — Field goal percentage	.05	.02
173	Mark Price SL — Free-throw percentage	.05	.02
174	Charles Barkley SL — MVP	.30	.14
175	Clifford Robinson SL — Sixth man	.05	.02
176	Hakeem Olajuwon SL — Defensive player	.30	.14
177	Shaquille O'Neal SL — ROY	.60	.25
178	Reggie Miller — Charles Oakley PO	.15	.07
179	Rick Fox — Kenny Gattison PO	.05	.02
180	Michael Jordan — Stackey Augmon PO	1.00	.45
181	Brad Daugherty PO	.05	.02
182	Oliver Miller — Byron Scott PO	.05	.02
183	David Robinson — Sean Elliott PO	.30	.14
184	Kenny Smith — Mark Jackson PO	.05	.02
185	Eddie Johnson	.05	.02
186	Anthony Mason — Patrick Ewing A Mourning PO	.30	.14
187	Michael Jordan — Gerald Wilkins PO	1.00	.45
188	Oliver Miller PO	.05	.02
189	Sam Perkins — Hakeem Olajuwon PO	.30	.14
190	Bill Cartwright PO	.05	.02
191	Kevin Johnson PO	.15	.07
192	Dan Majerle PO	.05	.02
193	Michael Jordan PO	2.00	.90
194	Larry Johnson — Muggsy Bogues PO	.15	.07
195	Reggie Miller PO	.15	.07
196	John Starks — Scottie Pippen PO	.30	.14
197	Charles Barkley PO	.30	.14
198	Michael Jordan FIN	2.00	.90
199	Scottie Pippen FIN	.50	.23
200	Kevin Johnson FIN	.05	.02
201	Michael Jordan FIN	2.00	.90
202	Richard Dumas FIN	.05	.02
203	Horace Grant FIN	.05	.02
204	Michael Jordan FIN — 1993 Finals MVP	2.00	.90
205	Scottie Pippen FIN — Charles Barkley	.30	.14
206	John Paxson FIN — Hits 3 for title	.05	.02
207	B.J. Armstrong FIN — Finals records	.05	.02
208	1992-93 Bulls FIN — Road to 1993 Finals	.05	.02
209	1992-93 Suns FIN — Road to 1993 Finals	.05	.02
210	Atlanta Hawks Sked — Kevin Willis	.05	.02
211	Boston Celtics Sked — Brian Shaw	.05	.02
212	Charlotte Hornets Sked — Michael Jordan	.05	.02
213	Chicago Bulls Sked — Michael Jordan	1.00	.45
214	Cleveland Cavaliers Sked (Mark Price)	.05	.02
215	Dallas Mavericks Sked (Jim Jackson Sean Rooks)	.05	.02
216	Denver Nuggets Sked — Dikembe Mutumbo	.15	.07
217	Detroit Pistons Sked — Isiah Thomas Bill Laimbeer Terry Mills	.15	.07
218	Golden State Warriors Sked	.05	.02
219	Houston Rockets Sked (Hakeem Olajuwon)	.30	.14
220	Indiana Pacers Sked — Rik Smits Detlef Schrempf	.05	.02
221	L.A. Clippers Sked	.05	.02

	Ron Harper		
	Danny Manning		
	Mark Jackson		
☐ 222	L.A. Lakers Sked	.05	.02
☐ 223	Miami Heat Sked	.15	.07
	Steve Smith		
	Harold Miner		
	Rony Seikaly		
☐ 224	Milwaukee Bucks Sked	.05	.02
☐ 225	Minnesota T'wolves Sked	.05	.02
☐ 226	New Jersey Nets Sked	.05	.02
	Kenny Anderson		
☐ 227	New York Knicks Sked	.05	.02
	Rolando Blackmon		
☐ 228	Orlando Magic Sked	.40	.18
	(Shaquille O'Neal)		
☐ 229	Philadelphia 76ers Sked	.05	.02
	Hersey Hawkins		
	Jeff Hornacek		
☐ 230	Phoenix Suns Sked	.30	.14
	(Charles Barkley)		
☐ 231	Portland Trail Blazers Sked	.05	.02
	Buck Williams		
	Jerome Kersey		
	Terry Porter		
☐ 232	Sacramento Kings	.05	.02
☐ 233	San Antonio Spurs	.30	.14
	David Robinson		
	Avery Johnson		
	Sean Elliott		
☐ 234	Seattle Supersonics	.15	.07
	Gary Payton		
	Shawn Kemp		
☐ 235	Utah Jazz Sked	.05	.02
☐ 236	Washington Bullets Sked	.15	.07
	Tom Gugliotta		
	Michael Adams		
☐ 237	Michael Jordan SM	2.00	.90
☐ 238	Clyde Drexler SM	.30	.14
☐ 239	Tim Hardaway SM	.30	.14
☐ 240	Dominique Wilkins SM	.15	.07
☐ 241	Brad Daugherty SM	.05	.02
☐ 242	Chris Mullin SM	.05	.02
☐ 243	Kenny Anderson SM	.05	.02
☐ 244	Patrick Ewing SM	.15	.07
☐ 245	Isiah Thomas SM	.15	.07
☐ 246	D.Mutombo SM	.05	.02
☐ 247	Danny Manning SM	.05	.02
☐ 248	David Robinson SM	.30	.14
☐ 249	Karl Malone SM	.30	.14
☐ 250	James Worthy SM	.15	.07
☐ 251	Shawn Kemp SM	.50	.23
☐ 252	Checklist 1-64	.05	.02
☐ 253	Checklist 65-128	.05	.02
☐ 254	Checklist 129-192	.05	.02
☐ 255	Checklist 193-255	.05	.02
☐ 256	Patrick Ewing	.30	.14
☐ 257	B.J. Armstrong	.05	.02
☐ 258	Oliver Miller	.05	.02
☐ 259	Jud Buechler	.05	.02
☐ 260	Pooh Richardson	.05	.02
☐ 261	Victor Alexander	.05	.02
☐ 262	Kevin Gamble	.05	.02
☐ 263	Doug Smith	.05	.02
☐ 264	Isiah Thomas	.30	.14
☐ 265	Doug Christie	.05	.02
☐ 266	Mark Bryant	.05	.02
☐ 267	Lloyd Daniels	.05	.02
☐ 268	Micheal Williams	.05	.02
☐ 269	Nick Anderson	.15	.07
☐ 270	Tom Gugliotta	.30	.14
☐ 271	Kenny Gattison	.05	.02
☐ 272	Vernon Maxwell	.05	.02
☐ 273	Terry Cummings	.05	.02
☐ 274	Karl Malone	.50	.23
☐ 275	Rick Fox	.05	.02
☐ 276	Matt Bullard	.05	.02
☐ 277	Johnny Newman	.05	.02
☐ 278	Mark Price	.05	.02
☐ 279	Mookie Blaylock	.15	.07
☐ 280	Charles Barkley	.50	.23
☐ 281	Larry Nance	.15	.07
☐ 282	Walt Williams	.15	.07
☐ 283	Brian Shaw	.05	.02
☐ 284	Robert Parish	.15	.07
☐ 285	Pervis Ellison	.05	.02
☐ 286	Spud Webb	.15	.07
☐ 287	Hakeem Olajuwon	.60	.25
☐ 288	Jerome Kersey	.05	.02
☐ 289	Carl Herrera	.05	.02
☐ 290	Dominique Wilkins	.30	.14
☐ 291	Billy Owens	.05	.02
☐ 292	Greg Anthony	.05	.02
☐ 293	Nate McMillan	.05	.02
☐ 294	Christian Laettner	.30	.14
☐ 295	Gary Payton	.50	.23
☐ 296	Steve Smith	.15	.07
☐ 297	Anthony Mason	.15	.07
☐ 298	Sean Rooks	.05	.02
☐ 299	Toni Kukoc	.75	.35
☐ 300	Shaquille O'Neal	1.25	.55
☐ 301	Jay Humphries	.05	.02
☐ 302	Sleepy Floyd	.05	.02
☐ 303	Bimbo Coles	.05	.02
☐ 304	John Battle	.05	.02
☐ 305	Shawn Kemp	1.00	.45
☐ 306	Scott Williams	.05	.02
☐ 307	Wayman Tisdale	.05	.02
☐ 308	Rony Seikaly	.05	.02
☐ 309	Reggie Miller	.30	.14
☐ 310	Scottie Pippen	1.00	.45
☐ 311	Chris Webber	2.00	.90
☐ 312	Trevor Wilson	.05	.02
☐ 313	Derek Strong	.05	.02
☐ 314	Bobby Hurley	.15	.07
☐ 315	Herb Williams	.05	.02
☐ 316	Rex Walters	.05	.02
☐ 317	Doug Edwards	.05	.02
☐ 318	Ken Williams	.05	.02
☐ 319	Jon Barry	.05	.02
☐ 320	Joe Courtney	.05	.02
☐ 321	Ervin Johnson	.15	.07
☐ 322	Sam Cassell	.30	.14
☐ 323	Tim Hardaway	.40	.18
☐ 324	Ed Stokes	.05	.02
☐ 325	Steve Kerr	.15	.07
☐ 326	Doug Overton	.05	.02
☐ 327	Reggie Williams	.05	.02
☐ 328	Avery Johnson	.05	.02
☐ 329	Stacey King	.05	.02
☐ 330	Vin Baker	2.00	.90
☐ 331	Greg Kite	.05	.02
☐ 332	Michael Cage	.05	.02
☐ 333	Alonzo Mourning	.50	.23
☐ 334	Acie Earl	.05	.02
☐ 335	Terry Dehere	.05	.02
☐ 336	Negele Knight	.05	.02
☐ 337	Gerald Madkins	.05	.02
☐ 338	Lindsey Hunter	.30	.14
☐ 339	Luther Wright	.05	.02
☐ 340	Mike Peplowski	.05	.02
☐ 341	Gerald Paddio	.05	.02
☐ 342	Danny Manning	.05	.02
☐ 343	Chris Mills	.30	.14
☐ 344	Kevin Lynch	.05	.02
☐ 345	Shawn Bradley	.30	.14
☐ 346	Evers Burns	.05	.02
☐ 347	Rodney Rogers	.05	.02
☐ 348	Cedric Ceballos	.15	.07
☐ 349	Warren Kidd	.05	.02
☐ 350	Darnell Mee	.05	.02
☐ 351	Matt Geiger	.05	.02
☐ 352	Jamal Mashburn	.75	.35
☐ 353	Antonio Davis	.15	.07
☐ 354	Calbert Cheaney	.30	.14
☐ 355	George Lynch	.05	.02
☐ 356	Derrick McKey	.05	.02
☐ 357	Jerry Reynolds	.05	.02
☐ 358	Don MacLean	.05	.02
☐ 359	Scott Haskin	.05	.02
☐ 360	Malcolm Mackey	.05	.02
☐ 361	Isaiah Rider	.40	.18
☐ 362	Detlef Schrempf	.15	.07
☐ 363	Josh Grant	.05	.02
☐ 364	Richard Petruska	.05	.02
☐ 365	Larry Johnson	.30	.14
☐ 366	Felton Spencer	.05	.02
☐ 367	Ken Norman	.05	.02
☐ 368	Anthony Cook	.05	.02
☐ 369	James Robinson	.05	.02
☐ 370	Kevin Duckworth	.05	.02
☐ 371	Chris Whitney	.05	.02
☐ 372	Moses Malone	.30	.14
☐ 373	Nick Van Exel	.50	.23
☐ 374	Scott Burrell	.30	.14
☐ 375	Harvey Grant	.05	.02
☐ 376	Benoit Benjamin	.05	.02
☐ 377	Henry James	.05	.02
☐ 378	Craig Ehlo	.05	.02
☐ 379	Ennis Whatley	.05	.02
☐ 380	Sean Green	.05	.02
☐ 381	Eric Murdock	.05	.02
☐ 382	A.Hardaway	4.00	1.80
☐ 383	Gheorghe Muresan	.40	.18
☐ 384	Kendall Gill	.15	.07
☐ 385	David Wood	.05	.02
☐ 386	Mario Elie	.05	.02
☐ 387	Chris Corchiani	.05	.02
☐ 388	Greg Graham	.05	.02
☐ 389	Hersey Hawkins	.15	.07
☐ 390	Mark Aguirre	.05	.02
☐ 391	LaPhonso Ellis	.15	.07
☐ 392	Anthony Bonner	.05	.02
☐ 393	Lucious Harris	.05	.02
☐ 394	Andrew Lang	.05	.02
☐ 395	Chris Dudley	.05	.02
☐ 396	Dennis Rodman	1.25	.55
☐ 397	Larry Krystkowiak	.05	.02
☐ 398	A.C. Green	.15	.07
☐ 399	Eddie Johnson	.05	.02
☐ 400	Kevin Edwards	.05	.02
☐ 401	Tyrone Hill	.05	.02
☐ 402	Greg Anderson	.05	.02
☐ 403	P.J. Brown	.05	.02
☐ 404	Dana Barros	.05	.02
☐ 405	Allan Houston	.60	.25
☐ 406	Mike Brown	.05	.02
☐ 407	Lee Mayberry	.05	.02
☐ 408	Fat Lever	.05	.02
☐ 409	Tony Smith	.05	.02
☐ 410	Tom Chambers	.05	.02
☐ 411	Manute Bol	.05	.02
☐ 412	Joe Kleine	.05	.02
☐ 413	Bryant Stith	.05	.02
☐ 414	Eric Riley	.05	.02
☐ 415	Jo Jo English	.05	.02
☐ 416	Sean Elliott	.15	.07
☐ 417	Sam Bowie	.05	.02
☐ 418	Armon Gilliam	.05	.02
☐ 419	Brian Williams	.05	.02
☐ 420	Popeye Jones	.05	.02
☐ 421	Dennis Rodman EB	.60	.25
☐ 422	Karl Malone EB	.30	.14
☐ 423	Tom Gugliotta EB	.15	.07
☐ 424	Kevin Willis EB	.05	.02
☐ 425	Hakeem Olajuwon EB	.30	.14
☐ 426	Charles Oakley EB	.05	.02
☐ 427	C.Weatherspoon EB	.05	.02
☐ 428	Derrick Coleman EB	.05	.02
☐ 429	Buck Williams EB	.05	.02
☐ 430	Christian Laettner EB	.15	.07
☐ 431	D.Mutombo EB	.05	.02
☐ 432	Rony Seikaly EB	.05	.02
☐ 433	Brad Daugherty EB	.05	.02
☐ 434	Horace Grant EB	.05	.02
☐ 435	Larry Johnson EB	.15	.07
☐ 436	Dee Brown BT	.05	.02
☐ 437	Muggsy Bogues BT	.05	.02
☐ 438	Michael Jordan BT	2.00	.90
☐ 439	Tim Hardaway BT	.30	.14
☐ 440	Micheal Williams BT	.05	.02
☐ 441	Gary Payton BT	.30	.14
☐ 442	Mookie Blaylock BT	.05	.02
☐ 443	Doc Rivers BT	.05	.02
☐ 444	Kenny Smith BT	.05	.02
☐ 445	John Stockton BT	.15	.07
☐ 446	Alvin Robertson BT	.05	.02
☐ 447	Mark Jackson BT	.05	.02
☐ 448	Kenny Anderson BT	.05	.02
☐ 449	Scottie Pippen BT	.50	.23
☐ 450	Isiah Thomas BT	.15	.07
☐ 451	Mark Price BT	.05	.02
☐ 452	Latrell Sprewell BT	.30	.14
☐ 453	Sedale Threatt BT	.05	.02

☐	454	Nick Anderson BT .05	.02
☐	455	Rod Strickland BT .05	.02
☐	456	Oliver Miller GI .05	.02
☐	457	James Worthy .05	.02
		Vlade Divac GI	
☐	458	Robert Horry GI .05	.02
☐	459	Rockets GI .05	.02
☐	460	Sean Rooks .05	.02
		Jim Jackson	
		Tim Legler GI	
☐	461	Mitch Richmond GI .15	.07
☐	462	Chris Morris GI .05	.02
☐	463	Mark Jackson .05	.02
		Gary Grant GI	
☐	464	David Robinson GI .30	.14
☐	465	Danny Ainge GI .05	.02
☐	466	Michael Jordan SL .. 2.00	.90
☐	467	Dominique Wilkins SL .15	.07
☐	468	Alonzo Mourning SL .. .30	.14
☐	469	Shaquille O'Neal SL.. .60	.25
☐	470	Tim Hardaway SL .30	.14
☐	471	Patrick Ewing SL .15	.07
☐	472	Kevin Johnson SL .05	.02
☐	473	Clyde Drexler SL .30	.14
☐	474	David Robinson SL .30	.14
☐	475	Shawn Kemp SL .50	.23
☐	476	Dee Brown SL .05	.02
☐	477	Jim Jackson SL .15	.07
☐	478	John Stockton SL .15	.07
☐	479	Robert Horry SL .05	.02
☐	480	Glen Rice SL .15	.07
☐	481	M.Williams SIS .05	.02
☐	482	George Lynch .05	.02
		Terry Dehere CL	
☐	483	Chris Webber TP .75	.35
☐	484	A.Hardaway TP .. 1.50	.70
☐	485	Shawn Bradley TP .15	.07
☐	486	Jamal Mashburn TP .30	.14
☐	487	Calbert Cheaney TP .15	.07
☐	488	Isaiah Rider TP .15	.07
☐	489	Bobby Hurley TP .05	.02
☐	490	Vin Baker TP .75	.35
☐	491	Rodney Rogers TP .05	.02
☐	492	Lindsey Hunter TP .15	.07
☐	493	Allan Houston TP .30	.14
☐	494	Terry Dehere TP .05	.02
☐	495	George Lynch TP .05	.02
☐	496	Toni Kukoc TP .30	.14
☐	497	Nick Van Exel TP .40	.18
☐	498	Charles Barkley MO .30	.14
☐	499	A.C. Green MO .05	.02
☐	500	Dan Majerle MO .05	.02
☐	501	Jerrod Mustaf MO .05	.02
☐	502	Kevin Johnson MO .05	.02
☐	503	Negele Knight MO .05	.02
☐	504	Danny Ainge MO .05	.02
☐	505	Oliver Miller MO .05	.02
☐	506	Joe Courtney MO .05	.02
☐	507	Checklist .05	.02
☐	508	Checklist .05	.02
☐	509	Checklist .05	.02
☐	510	Checklist .05	.02
☐	SP3	Michael Jordan .. 8.00	3.60
		Wilt Chamberlain	
☐	SP4	Chicago Bulls' Third 8.00	3.60
		NBA Championship	

1993-94 Upper Deck All-NBA

Inserted one per blue and green first series retail 22-card jumbo packs, this 15-card standard-size set spotlights All-NBA first, second and third teams. The cards feature a borderless front with a color action photo set against a game-crowd background. The player's name

appears in a red vertical stripe along the right side. The All NBA Team appears in a blue vertical stripe along the right side. The back features a color action photo along the left side with player's statistics along the right side.

	MINT	NRMT
COMPLETE SET (15)	15.00	6.75
COMMON CARD (AN1-AN15)	.25	.11
SEMISTARS	.40	.18
UNLISTED STARS	.60	.25

ONE PER SER.1 RETAIL/GREEN JUMBO PACK

☐	AN1	Charles Barkley 1.00	.45
☐	AN2	Karl Malone 1.00	.45
☐	AN3	Hakeem Olajuwon 1.25	.55
☐	AN4	Michael Jordan 8.00	3.60
☐	AN5	Mark Price .25	.11
☐	AN6	Dominique Wilkins .60	.25
☐	AN7	Larry Johnson .60	.25
☐	AN8	Patrick Ewing .60	.25
☐	AN9	John Stockton .60	.25
☐	AN10	Joe Dumars .60	.25
☐	AN11	Scottie Pippen 2.00	.90
☐	AN12	Derrick Coleman .40	.18
☐	AN13	David Robinson 1.00	.45
☐	AN14	Tim Hardaway .75	.35
☐	AN15	Michael Jordan CL 4.00	1.80

1993-94 Upper Deck All-Rookies

Randomly inserted in first series 12-card retail packs at a rate of one in 30, this 10-card standard-size set features the NBA All-Rookie first (1-5) and second (6-10) teams from 1992-93. The

cards feature color game-action player photos on their fronts. They are borderless, except at the top, where a red stripe edges the cards of the first team and a blue one edges those of the second. The player's name appears in white lettering within a red or blue stripe near the bottom. The back carries a color player action photo on the left and career highlights on the right.

	MINT	NRMT
COMPLETE SET (10)	15.00	6.75
COMMON CARD (AR1-AR10)	.50	.23
SEMISTARS	1.00	.45
UNLISTED STARS	2.00	.90

SER. 1 STATED ODDS 1:30 RETAIL

☐	AR1	Shaquille O'Neal 8.00	3.60
☐	AR2	Alonzo Mourning 3.00	1.35
☐	AR3	Christian Laettner 2.00	.90
☐	AR4	Tom Gugliotta 2.00	.90
☐	AR5	LaPhonso Ellis 1.00	.45
☐	AR6	Walt Williams 1.00	.45
☐	AR7	Robert Horry 1.00	.45
☐	AR8	Latrell Sprewell 2.00	.90
☐	AR9	C.Weatherspoon .50	.23
☐	AR10	Richard Dumas .50	.23

1993-94 Upper Deck Flight Team

Michael Jordan selected the league's best dunkers for this 20-card insert set. The cards are randomly inserted in first series 12-card hobby packs at a rate of one in 30. The standard-size cards feature on their fronts full-bleed color action player photos. The words "Michael Jordan's Flight Team" appear in ghosted block lettering over the background. The player's name is gold-foil stamped at the bottom, with the Flight Team insignia displayed immediately above carrying his team's city name and the his uniform number. On a background consisting of blue sky and clouds, the back carries a color player action cutout and an evaluative quote by Jordan. The set is sequenced in alphabetical order.

	MINT	NRMT
COMPLETE SET (20)	90.00	40.00
COMMON CARD (FT1-FT20)	1.50	.70
SEMISTARS	3.00	1.35
UNLISTED STARS	6.00	2.70
SER.1 STATED ODDS 1:30 HOBBY		

		MINT	NRMT
☐ FT1	Stacey Augmon	1.50	.70
☐ FT2	Charles Barkley	10.00	4.50
☐ FT3	David Benoit	1.50	.70
☐ FT4	Dee Brown	1.50	.70
☐ FT5	Cedric Ceballos	3.00	1.35
☐ FT6	Derrick Coleman	3.00	1.35
☐ FT7	Clyde Drexler	8.00	3.60
☐ FT8	Sean Elliott	3.00	1.35
☐ FT9	LaPhonso Ellis	3.00	1.35
☐ FT10	Kendall Gill	3.00	1.35
☐ FT11	Larry Johnson	6.00	2.70
☐ FT12	Shawn Kemp	20.00	9.00
☐ FT13	Karl Malone	10.00	4.50
☐ FT14	Harold Miner	1.50	.70
☐ FT15	Alonzo Mourning	10.00	4.50
☐ FT16	Shaquille O'Neal	25.00	11.00
☐ FT17	Scottie Pippen	20.00	9.00
☐ FT18	C.Weatherspoon	1.50	.70
☐ FT19	Spud Webb	3.00	1.35
☐ FT20	Dominique Wilkins	6.00	2.70

1993-94 Upper Deck Future Heroes

Inserted one per first series locker pack, this set continues Upper Deck's year-by-year basketball Heroes program. Unlike previous sets devoted to individual players, the 1993-94 set features a selection of young phenoms destined to be stars. This 10-card standard-size set features color player action shots on its fronts. The photos are bordered on the left and bottom by gray and team color-coded stripes. The player's name and position appear in white lettering in the color-coded stripe at the bottom. An embossed silver-foil basketball appears at the lower left. The white back carries the

player's career highlights. The set is numbered in continuation of Upper Deck's Hero Series and is sequenced in alphabetical order.

	MINT	NRMT
COMPLETE SET (10)	25.00	11.00
COMMON CARD (28-36)	1.00	.45
CL HEADER (NNO)	1.00	.45
SEMISTARS	1.50	.70
UNLISTED STARS	2.50	1.10
ONE PER SER.1 LOCKER PACK		

		MINT	NRMT
☐ 28	Derrick Coleman	1.50	.70
☐ 29	LaPhonso Ellis	1.50	.70
☐ 30	Jim Jackson	2.50	1.10
☐ 31	Larry Johnson	2.50	1.10
☐ 32	Shawn Kemp	8.00	3.60
☐ 33	Christian Laettner	2.50	1.10
☐ 34	Alonzo Mourning	4.00	1.80
☐ 35	Shaquille O'Neal	10.00	4.50
☐ 36	Walt Williams	1.50	.70
☐ NNO	LaPhonso Ellis CL	1.00	.45
	Christian Laettner		

1993-94 Upper Deck Locker Talk

Inserted one per Series II locker pack, this 15-card standard-size set features color player action photos on their fronts. The player's name appears in white lettering within the gold stripe that edges the left side. A personal player quote appears in white lettering within the photo's "torn" lower right corner. The back carries the same quote at the upper right, within a shot of a locker that has a print of the front's action shot taped to the door. Another player photo and more personal player quotes round out the back.

	MINT	NRMT
COMPLETE SET (15)	70.00	32.00
COMMON CARD (LT1-LT15)	1.00	.45
SEMISTARS	1.50	.70
UNLISTED STARS	3.00	1.35
ONE PER SER.2 LOCKER PACK		
CONDITION SENSITIVE SET		

		MINT	NRMT
☐ LT1	Michael Jordan	40.00	18.00
☐ LT2	Stacey Augmon	1.00	.45
☐ LT3	Shaquille O'Neal	12.00	5.50
☐ LT4	Alonzo Mourning	5.00	2.20
☐ LT5	Harold Miner	1.00	.45
☐ LT6	C.Weatherspoon	1.00	.45
☐ LT7	Derrick Coleman	1.50	.70
☐ LT8	Charles Barkley	5.00	2.20
☐ LT9	David Robinson	5.00	2.20
☐ LT10	Chuck Person	1.00	.45
☐ LT11	Karl Malone	5.00	2.20
☐ LT12	Muggsy Bogues	1.50	.70
☐ LT13	Latrell Sprewell	3.00	1.35
☐ LT14	John Starks	1.50	.70
☐ LT15	Jim Jackson	3.00	1.35

1993-94 Upper Deck Mr. June

Randomly inserted in series two 12-card hobby packs at a rate of one in 30, this 10-card standard-size set focuses on Michael Jordan's performance while leading his team to three consecutive NBA Championships. The front features a color action shot of Michael Jordan with his name, accomplishment, and year thereof printed in the team-colored (Chicago Bulls) stripe at bottom. The back features a color action photo at the upper right with a description of his accomplishments printed alongside and below.

	MINT	NRMT
COMPLETE SET (10)	180.00	80.00
COMMON JORDAN (1-10)	20.00	9.00
SER.2 STATED ODDS 1:30 HOBBY		

		MINT	NRMT
☐ MJ1	Michael Jordan Jordan's a Steal	20.00	9.00
☐ MJ2	Michael Jordan M.J.'s High Five	20.00	9.00
☐ MJ3	Michael Jordan 1991 NBA Finals MVP	20.00	9.00
☐ MJ4	Michael Jordan 35 Points in One Half	20.00	9.00
☐ MJ5	Michael Jordan Three-Points King	20.00	9.00
☐ MJ6	Michael Jordan Back-To-Back Finals MVP	20.00	9.00
☐ MJ7	Michael Jordan 55-Point Game	20.00	9.00

□ MJ8	Michael Jordan.......... 20.00	9.00
	Record Scoring Average	
□ MJ9	Michael Jordan.......... 20.00	9.00
	Jordan's Three-Peat	
□ MJ10	Checklist............. 20.00	9.00

1993-94 Upper Deck Rookie Exchange

This 10-card standard-size set features the top ten players from the 1993 NBA Draft. The set could only be obtained by mail in exchange for the Silver Trade card that was randomly inserted in first series 12-card packs at a rate of one in 72. The Silver Exchange expiration date was 12/31/93. The borderless front features a color player action photo with the his name printed in white lettering within a red stripe near the bottom. The word "Exchange" runs vertically along the left side in silver-foil lettering. The white and gray back carries a color player photo at the upper left and career highlights and statistics alongside and below. The set is sequenced in draft order.

	MINT	NRMT
COMPLETE SILVER SET (10)	8.00	3.60
COMMON SILVER (RE1-RE10)	.15	.07
SEMISTARS	.30	.14
UNLISTED STARS	.50	.23
COMPLETE GOLD SET (10)	15.00	6.75
*GOLD CARDS: 1X TO 2X HI COLUMN		
ONE SET PER EXCHANGE CARD BY MAIL		
SIL.EXCH: SER.1 STATED ODDS 1:72		
GOLD EXCH: SER.1 STATED ODDS 1:288		

□ RE1	Chris Webber...........	2.00	.90
□ RE2	Shawn Bradley..........	.50	.23
□ RE3	A.Hardaway.............	5.00	2.20
□ RE4	Jamal Mashburn.........	.75	.35
□ RE5	Isaiah Rider...........	.50	.23
□ RE6	Calbert Cheaney........	.50	.23
□ RE7	Bobby Hurley...........	.30	.14
□ RE8	Vin Baker..............	2.00	.90
□ RE9	Rodney Rogers..........	.15	.07
□ RE10	Lindsey Hunter........	.50	.23
□ TC2	Redmd Silver Trade	.25	.11
□ TC2	Unred Silver Trade	.10	.05

1993-94 Upper Deck Rookie Standouts

Randomly inserted at a rate of one in 30 second series 12-card retail packs and inserted one per second series 22-card purple jumbo pack, this 20-card standard-size set showcases top rookies of the 1993-94 NBA season. The borderless front features a color player action photo with his name printed in a gold-foil banner beneath the silver-foil set logo in a lower corner. The gray back carries a color player photo on one side and career highlights on the other.

	MINT	NRMT
COMPLETE SET (20)	40.00	18.00
COMMON CARD (RS1-RS20)	.50	.23
SEMISTARS	1.00	.45
UNLISTED STARS	2.00	.90
SER.2 STATED ODDS 1:30 RETAIL		
ONE PER SER.2 PURPLE JUMBO PACK		

□ RS1	Chris Webber...........	8.00	3.60
□ RS2	Bobby Hurley...........	1.00	.45
□ RS3	Isaiah Rider...........	2.00	.90
□ RS4	Terry Dehere...........	.50	.23
□ RS5	Toni Kukoc.............	3.00	1.35
□ RS6	Shawn Bradley..........	2.00	.90
□ RS7	Allan Houston..........	2.50	1.10
□ RS8	Chris Mills............	2.00	.90
□ RS9	Jamal Mashburn.........	3.00	1.35
□ RS10	Acie Earl.............	.50	.23
□ RS11	George Lynch..........	.50	.23
□ RS12	Scott Burrell.........	2.00	.90
□ RS13	Calbert Cheaney.......	2.00	.90
□ RS14	Lindsey Hunter........	2.00	.90
□ RS15	Nick Van Exel.........	4.00	1.80
□ RS16	Rex Walters...........	.50	.23
□ RS17	A.Hardaway............	20.00	9.00
□ RS18	Sam Cassell...........	3.00	1.35
□ RS19	Vin Baker.............	8.00	3.60
□ RS20	Rodney Rogers.........	.50	.23

1993-94 Upper Deck Team MVPs

Cards from this 27-card standard-size set were issued one per second series red and pur-ple 22-card jumbo packs. The set highlights one key "Team MVP" from each of the 27 NBA teams. The white and prismatic team-colored foil-bordered front features a color player action shot, with the player's name printed vertically in the foil border at the upper right. The horizontal back is bordered in white and a team color and carries a color action shot on the left with career highlights appearing in a gray panel alongside on the right. The set is sequenced in team alphabetical order.

	MINT	NRMT
COMPLETE SET (27)	20.00	9.00
COMMON CARD (TM1-TM27)	.25	.11
SEMISTARS	.40	.18
UNLISTED STARS	.75	.35
ONE PER SER.2 RETAIL/PURPLE JUM.PACK		

□ TM1	Dominique Wilkins.....	.75	.35
□ TM2	Robert Parish.........	.40	.18
□ TM3	Larry Johnson.........	.75	.35
□ TM4	Scottie Pippen........	2.50	1.10
□ TM5	Mark Price............	.25	.11
□ TM6	Jim Jackson...........	.75	.35
□ TM7	Mahmoud Abdul-Rauf	.25	.11
□ TM8	Joe Dumars............	.75	.35
□ TM9	Chris Mullin..........	.75	.35
□ TM10	Hakeem Olajuwon......	1.50	.70
□ TM11	Reggie Miller........	.75	.35
□ TM12	Danny Manning........	.25	.11
□ TM13	James Worthy.........	.75	.35
□ TM14	Glen Rice............	.75	.35
□ TM15	Blue Edwards.........	.25	.11
□ TM16	Christian Laettner...	.75	.35
□ TM17	Derrick Coleman......	.40	.18
□ TM18	Patrick Ewing........	.75	.35
□ TM19	Shaquille O'Neal.....	3.00	1.35
□ TM20	C.Weatherspoon.......	.25	.11
□ TM21	Charles Barkley......	1.25	.55
□ TM22	Clyde Drexler........	1.00	.45
□ TM23	Mitch Richmond.......	.75	.35
□ TM24	David Robinson.......	1.25	.55
□ TM25	Shawn Kemp...........	2.50	1.10
□ TM26	John Stockton........	.75	.35
□ TM27	Tom Gugliotta........	.75	.35

1993-94 Upper Deck Triple Double

This 10-card standard-size set features the NBA leaders in

triple-doubles from the 1992-93 season. Cards were randomly inserted at a rate of 1 in 20 first series 12-card hobby and retail packs, 1 in 20 first series 22-card blue jumbo packs, one per first series 22-card green jumbo pack and approximately 1 in every 11 first series 22-card locker packs. The standard-size horizontal hologram cards feature one color player action cutout and two hologram action shots on their fronts. Each of the three images show the player performing three different skills (scoring, rebounding, passing or blocking) necessary to achieve a triple-double. The words "Triple Double" appear vertically on the left. The player's name appears at the upper right of the hologram. The horizontal back displays another color player action shot on the right, with a story of the player's triple-double feat on the right. The player's name appears in a team-colored bar at the bottom.

	MINT	NRMT
COMPLETE SET (10)	20.00	9.00
COMMON CARD (TD1-TD10)	.40	.18
SEMISTARS	.75	.35
UNLISTED STARS	1.25	.55
SER.1 STATED ODDS 1:20		
ONE PER SER.1 GREEN JUMBO PACK		

		MINT	NRMT
□ TD1	Charles Barkley	2.00	.90
□ TD2	Michael Jordan	15.00	6.75
□ TD3	Scottie Pippen	4.00	1.80
□ TD4	Detlef Schrempf	.75	.35
□ TD5	Mark Jackson	.75	.35
□ TD6	Kenny Anderson	.75	.35
□ TD7	Larry Johnson	1.25	.55
□ TD8	D.Mutombo	.75	.35
□ TD9	Rumeal Robinson	.40	.18
□ TD10	Micheal Williams	.40	.18

1994-95 Upper Deck

The 1994-95 Upper Deck basketball set consists of 360 standard-size cards, released in two

separate 180-card series. Cards were primarily distributed in 12-card packs, each of which carried a suggested retail price of $1.99. Fronts feature full-color action photos with player's name and team running in color-coded bars along the side. Topical subsets featured are All-Rookie Team (1-10), All-NBA (11-25), USA Basketball (167-180), Draft Analysis (181-198), and Then and Now (352-360). Rookie Cards of note include Grant Hill, Juwan Howard, Eddie Jones, Jason Kidd and Glenn Robinson.

	MINT	NRMT
COMPLETE SET (360)	45.00	20.00
COMPLETE SERIES 1 (180)	25.00	11.00
COMPLETE SERIES 2 (180)	20.00	9.00
COMMON CARD (1-360)	.10	.05
SEMISTARS	.15	.07
UNLISTED STARS	.40	.18

		MINT	NRMT
□ 1	Chris Webber ART	.50	.23
□ 2	A.Hardaway ART	.75	.35
□ 3	Vin Baker ART	.50	.23
□ 4	Jamal Mashburn ART	.15	.07
□ 5	Isaiah Rider ART	.10	.05
□ 6	Dino Radja ART	.10	.05
□ 7	Nick Van Exel ART	.15	.07
□ 8	Shawn Bradley ART	.10	.05
□ 9	Toni Kukoc ART	.15	.07
□ 10	Lindsey Hunter ART	.10	.05
□ 11	Scottie Pippen AN	.60	.25
□ 12	Karl Malone AN	.40	.18
□ 13	Hakeem Olajuwon AN	.40	.18
□ 14	John Stockton AN	.15	.07
□ 15	Latrell Sprewell AN	.10	.05
□ 16	Shawn Kemp AN	.60	.25
□ 17	Charles Barkley AN	.40	.18
□ 18	David Robinson AN	.40	.18
□ 19	Mitch Richmond AN	.15	.07
□ 20	Dominique Wilkins AN	.10	.05
□ 21	Derrick Coleman AN	.10	.05
□ 22	Dominique Wilkins AN	.15	.07
□ 23	Shaquille O'Neal AN	.75	.35
□ 24	Mark Price AN	.10	.05
□ 25	Gary Payton AN	.40	.18
□ 26	Dan Majerle	.15	.07
□ 27	Vernon Maxwell	.10	.05
□ 28	Matt Geiger	.10	.05
□ 29	Jeff Turner	.10	.05
□ 30	Vinny Del Negro	.10	.05
□ 31	B.J. Armstrong	.10	.05
□ 32	Chris Gatling	.10	.05
□ 33	Tony Smith	.10	.05
□ 34	Doug West	.10	.05
□ 35	Clyde Drexler	.50	.23
□ 36	Keith Jennings	.10	.05

		MINT	NRMT
□ 37	Steve Smith	.15	.07
□ 38	Kendall Gill	.15	.07
□ 39	Bob Martin	.10	.05
□ 40	Calbert Cheaney	.15	.07
□ 41	Terrell Brandon	.40	.18
□ 42	Pete Chilcutt	.10	.05
□ 43	Avery Johnson	.10	.05
□ 44	Tom Gugliotta	.40	.18
□ 45	LaBradford Smith	.10	.05
□ 46	Sedale Threatt	.10	.05
□ 47	Chris Smith	.10	.05
□ 48	Kevin Edwards	.10	.05
□ 49	Lucious Harris	.10	.05
□ 50	Tim Perry	.10	.05
□ 51	Lloyd Daniels	.10	.05
□ 52	Dee Brown	.10	.05
□ 53	Sean Elliott	.15	.07
□ 54	Tim Hardaway	.50	.23
□ 55	Christian Laettner	.15	.07
□ 56	Charles Outlaw	.10	.05
□ 57	Kevin Johnson	.15	.07
□ 58	Duane Ferrell	.10	.05
□ 59	Jo Jo English	.10	.05
□ 60	Stanley Roberts	.10	.05
□ 61	Kevin Willis	.10	.05
□ 62	Dana Barros	.10	.05
□ 63	Gheorghe Muresan	.15	.07
□ 64	Vern Fleming	.10	.05
□ 65	Anthony Peeler	.10	.05
□ 66	Negele Knight	.10	.05
□ 67	Harold Ellis	.10	.05
□ 68	Vincent Askew	.10	.05
□ 69	Ennis Whatley	.10	.05
□ 70	Elden Campbell	.15	.07
□ 71	Sherman Douglas	.10	.05
□ 72	Luc Longley	.15	.07
□ 73	Lorenzo Williams	.10	.05
□ 74	Jay Humphries	.10	.05
□ 75	Chris King	.10	.05
□ 76	Tyrone Corbin	.10	.05
□ 77	Bobby Hurley	.10	.05
□ 78	Dell Curry	.10	.05
□ 79	Dino Radja	.10	.05
□ 80	A.C. Green	.15	.07
□ 81	Craig Ehlo	.10	.05
□ 82	Gary Payton	.60	.25
□ 83	Sleepy Floyd	.10	.05
□ 84	Rodney Rogers	.10	.05
□ 85	Brian Shaw	.10	.05
□ 86	Kevin Gamble	.10	.05
□ 87	John Stockton	.40	.18
□ 88	Hersey Hawkins	.15	.07
□ 89	Johnny Newman	.10	.05
□ 90	Larry Johnson	.15	.07
□ 91	Robert Pack	.10	.05
□ 92	Willie Burton	.10	.05
□ 93	Bobby Phills	.10	.05
□ 94	David Benoit	.10	.05
□ 95	Harold Miner	.10	.05
□ 96	David Robinson	.60	.25
□ 97	Nate McMillan	.10	.05
□ 98	Chris Mills	.15	.07
□ 99	Hubert Davis	.10	.05
□ 100	Shaquille O'Neal	1.50	.70
□ 101	Loy Vaught	.15	.07
□ 102	Kenny Smith	.10	.05
□ 103	Terry Dehere	.10	.05
□ 104	Carl Herrera	.10	.05
□ 105	LaPhonso Ellis	.10	.05
□ 106	Armon Gilliam	.10	.05
□ 107	Greg Graham	.10	.05
□ 108	Eric Murdock	.10	.05
□ 109	Ron Harper	.15	.07
□ 110	Andrew Lang	.10	.05
□ 111	Johnny Dawkins	.10	.05
□ 112	David Wingate	.10	.05
□ 113	Tom Hammonds	.10	.05
□ 114	Brad Daugherty	.15	.07
□ 115	Charles Smith	.10	.05
□ 116	Dale Ellis	.10	.05
□ 117	Bryant Stith	.10	.05
□ 118	Lindsey Hunter	.15	.07
□ 119	Patrick Ewing	.40	.18
□ 120	Kenny Anderson	.15	.07
□ 121	Charles Barkley	.60	.25
□ 122	Harvey Grant	.10	.05

☐ 123	Anthony Bowie	.10	.05
☐ 124	Shawn Kemp	1.25	.55
☐ 125	Lee Mayberry	.10	.05
☐ 126	Reggie Miller	.40	.18
☐ 127	Scottie Pippen	1.25	.55
☐ 128	Spud Webb	.15	.07
☐ 129	Antonio Davis	.10	.05
☐ 130	Greg Anderson	.10	.05
☐ 131	Jim Jackson	.15	.07
☐ 132	D.Mutombo	.40	.18
☐ 133	Terry Porter	.10	.05
☐ 134	Mario Elie	.10	.05
☐ 135	Vlade Divac	.15	.07
☐ 136	Robert Horry	.15	.07
☐ 137	Popeye Jones	.10	.05
☐ 138	Brad Lohaus	.10	.05
☐ 139	Anthony Bonner	.10	.05
☐ 140	Doug Christie	.10	.05
☐ 141	Rony Seikaly	.10	.05
☐ 142	Allan Houston	.40	.18
☐ 143	Tyrone Hill	.10	.05
☐ 144	Latrell Sprewell	.15	.07
☐ 145	Andres Guibert	.10	.05
☐ 146	Dominique Wilkins	.40	.18
☐ 147	Jon Barry	.10	.05
☐ 148	Tracy Murray	.10	.05
☐ 149	Mike Peplowski	.10	.05
☐ 150	Mike Brown	.10	.05
☐ 151	Cedric Ceballos	.15	.07
☐ 152	Stacey King	.10	.05
☐ 153	Trevor Wilson	.10	.05
☐ 154	Anthony Avent	.10	.05
☐ 155	Horace Grant	.15	.07
☐ 156	Bill Curley	.10	.05
☐ 157	Grant Hill	5.00	2.20
☐ 158	Charlie Ward	.15	.07
☐ 159	Jalen Rose	.40	.18
☐ 160	Jason Kidd	3.00	1.35
☐ 161	Yinka Dare	.10	.05
☐ 162	Eric Montross	.10	.05
☐ 163	Donyell Marshall	.50	.23
☐ 164	Tony Dumas	.10	.05
☐ 165	Wesley Person	.50	.23
☐ 166	Eddie Jones	3.00	1.35
☐ 167	Tim Hardaway USA	.40	.18
☐ 168	Isiah Thomas USA	.15	.07
☐ 169	Joe Dumars USA	.15	.07
☐ 170	Mark Price USA	.10	.05
☐ 171	Derrick Coleman USA	.10	.05
☐ 172	Shawn Kemp USA	.60	.25
☐ 173	Steve Smith USA	.10	.05
☐ 174	Dan Majerle USA	.10	.05
☐ 175	Reggie Miller USA	.15	.07
☐ 176	Kevin Johnson USA	.10	.05
☐ 177	D.Wilkins USA	.15	.07
☐ 178	Shaquille O'Neal USA	.75	.35
☐ 179	Alonzo Mourning USA	.40	.18
☐ 180	Larry Johnson USA	.10	.05
☐ 181	Brian Grant DA	.15	.07
☐ 182	Darrin Hancock DA	.10	.05
☐ 183	Grant Hill DA	2.00	.90
☐ 184	Jalen Rose DA	.15	.07
☐ 185	Lamond Murray DA	.10	.05
☐ 186	Jason Kidd DA	1.25	.55
☐ 187	Donyell Marshall DA	.15	.07
☐ 188	Eddie Jones DA	1.25	.55
☐ 189	Eric Montross DA	.10	.05
☐ 190	Khalid Reeves DA	.10	.05
☐ 191	Sharone Wright DA	.10	.05
☐ 192	Wesley Person DA	.15	.07
☐ 193	Glenn Robinson DA	.60	.25
☐ 194	Carlos Rogers DA	.10	.05
☐ 195	Aaron McKie DA	.10	.05
☐ 196	Juwan Howard DA	.75	.35
☐ 197	Charlie Ward DA	.10	.05
☐ 198	Brooks Thompson DA	.10	.05
☐ 199	Tony Massenburg	.10	.05
☐ 200	James Robinson	.10	.05
☐ 201	Dickey Simpkins	.10	.05
☐ 202	Johnny Dawkins	.10	.05
☐ 203	Joe Kleine	.10	.05
☐ 204	Bill Wennington	.10	.05
☐ 205	Sean Higgins	.10	.05
☐ 206	Larry Krystkowiak	.10	.05
☐ 207	Winston Garland	.10	.05
☐ 208	Muggsy Bogues	.15	.07
☐ 209	Charles Oakley	.15	.07
☐ 210	Vin Baker	1.00	.45
☐ 211	Malik Sealy	.10	.05
☐ 212	Willie Anderson	.10	.05
☐ 213	Dale Davis	.10	.05
☐ 214	Grant Long	.10	.05
☐ 215	Danny Ainge	.15	.07
☐ 216	Toni Kukoc	.40	.18
☐ 217	Doug Smith	.10	.05
☐ 218	Danny Manning	.10	.05
☐ 219	Otis Thorpe	.15	.07
☐ 220	Mark Price	.10	.05
☐ 221	Victor Alexander	.10	.05
☐ 222	Brent Price	.10	.05
☐ 223	Howard Eisley	.10	.05
☐ 224	Chris Mullin	.40	.18
☐ 225	Nick Van Exel	.40	.18
☐ 226	Xavier McDaniel	.10	.05
☐ 227	Khalid Reeves	.10	.05
☐ 228	A.Hardaway	1.50	.70
☐ 229	B.J. Tyler	.10	.05
☐ 230	Elmore Spencer	.10	.05
☐ 231	Rick Fox	.10	.05
☐ 232	Alonzo Mourning	.50	.23
☐ 233	Hakeem Olajuwon	.75	.35
☐ 234	Blue Edwards	.10	.05
☐ 235	P.J. Brown	.10	.05
☐ 236	Ron Harper	.15	.07
☐ 237	Isaiah Rider	.15	.07
☐ 238	Eric Mobley	.10	.05
☐ 239	Brian Williams	.10	.05
☐ 240	Eric Piatkowski	.10	.05
☐ 241	Karl Malone	.60	.25
☐ 242	Wayman Tisdale	.10	.05
☐ 243	Sarunas Marciulionis	.10	.05
☐ 244	Sean Rooks	.10	.05
☐ 245	Ricky Pierce	.10	.05
☐ 246	Don MacLean	.10	.05
☐ 247	Aaron McKie	.10	.05
☐ 248	Kenny Gattison	.10	.05
☐ 249	Derek Harper	.15	.07
☐ 250	Michael Smith	.15	.07
☐ 251	John Williams	.10	.05
☐ 252	Pooh Richardson	.10	.05
☐ 253	Sergei Bazarevich	.10	.05
☐ 254	Brian Grant	.40	.18
☐ 255	Ed Pinckney	.10	.05
☐ 256	Ken Norman	.10	.05
☐ 257	Marty Conlon	.10	.05
☐ 258	Matt Fish	.10	.05
☐ 259	Darrin Hancock	.10	.05
☐ 260	Mahmoud Abdul-Rauf	.10	.05
☐ 261	Roy Tarpley	.10	.05
☐ 262	Chris Morris	.10	.05
☐ 263	Sharone Wright	.10	.05
☐ 264	Jamal Mashburn	.40	.18
☐ 265	John Starks	.15	.07
☐ 266	Rod Strickland	.10	.05
☐ 267	Adam Keefe	.10	.05
☐ 268	Scott Burrell	.10	.05
☐ 269	Eric Riley	.10	.05
☐ 270	Sam Perkins	.15	.07
☐ 271	Stacey Augmon	.10	.05
☐ 272	Kevin Willis	.10	.05
☐ 273	Lamond Murray	.15	.07
☐ 274	Derrick Coleman	.15	.07
☐ 275	Scott Skiles	.10	.05
☐ 276	Buck Williams	.10	.05
☐ 277	Sam Cassell	.40	.18
☐ 278	Rik Smits	.15	.07
☐ 279	Dennis Rodman	1.50	.70
☐ 280	Olden Polynice	.10	.05
☐ 281	Glenn Robinson	1.50	.70
☐ 282	C.Weatherspoon	.10	.05
☐ 283	Monty Williams	.10	.05
☐ 284	Terry Mills	.10	.05
☐ 285	Oliver Miller	.10	.05
☐ 286	Dennis Scott	.15	.07
☐ 287	Micheal Williams	.10	.05
☐ 288	Moses Malone	.40	.18
☐ 289	Donald Royal	.10	.05
☐ 290	Mark Jackson	.15	.07
☐ 291	Walt Williams	.10	.05
☐ 292	Bimbo Coles	.10	.05
☐ 293	Derrick Alston	.10	.05
☐ 294	Scott Williams	.10	.05
☐ 295	Acie Earl	.10	.05
☐ 296	Jeff Hornacek	.15	.07
☐ 297	Kevin Duckworth	.10	.05
☐ 298	Dontonio Wingfield	.10	.05
☐ 299	Danny Ferry	.10	.05
☐ 300	Mark West	.10	.05
☐ 301	Jayson Williams	.15	.07
☐ 302	David Wesley	.10	.05
☐ 303	Jim McIlvaine	.10	.05
☐ 304	Michael Adams	.10	.05
☐ 305	Greg Minor	.10	.05
☐ 306	Jeff Malone	.10	.05
☐ 307	Pervis Ellison	.10	.05
☐ 308	Clifford Rozier	.10	.05
☐ 309	Billy Owens	.10	.05
☐ 310	Duane Causwell	.10	.05
☐ 311	Rex Chapman	.10	.05
☐ 312	Detlef Schrempf	.15	.07
☐ 313	Mitch Richmond	.40	.18
☐ 314	Carlos Rogers	.10	.05
☐ 315	Byron Scott	.15	.07
☐ 316	Dwayne Morton	.10	.05
☐ 317	Bill Cartwright	.10	.05
☐ 318	J.R. Reid	.10	.05
☐ 319	Derrick McKey	.10	.05
☐ 320	Jamie Watson	.10	.05
☐ 321	Mookie Blaylock	.15	.07
☐ 322	Chris Webber	1.00	.45
☐ 323	Joe Dumars	.40	.18
☐ 324	Shawn Bradley	.15	.07
☐ 325	Chuck Person	.10	.05
☐ 326	Haywoode Workman	.10	.05
☐ 327	Benoit Benjamin	.10	.05
☐ 328	Will Perdue	.10	.05
☐ 329	Sam Mitchell	.10	.05
☐ 330	George Lynch	.10	.05
☐ 331	Juwan Howard	2.00	.90
☐ 332	Robert Parish	.15	.07
☐ 333	Glen Rice	.40	.18
☐ 334	Michael Cage	.10	.05
☐ 335	Brooks Thompson	.10	.05
☐ 336	Rony Seikaly	.10	.05
☐ 337	Steve Kerr	.15	.07
☐ 338	Anthony Miller	.10	.05
☐ 339	Nick Anderson	.15	.07
☐ 340	Clifford Robinson	.15	.07
☐ 341	Todd Day	.10	.05
☐ 342	Jon Koncak	.10	.05
☐ 343	Felton Spencer	.10	.05
☐ 344	Willie Burton	.10	.05
☐ 345	Ledell Eackles	.10	.05
☐ 346	Anthony Mason	.15	.07
☐ 347	Derek Strong	.10	.05
☐ 348	Reggie Williams	.10	.05
☐ 349	Johnny Newman	.10	.05
☐ 350	Terry Cummings	.10	.05
☐ 351	Anthony Tucker	.10	.05
☐ 352	Junior Bridgeman TN	.10	.05
☐ 353	Jerry West TN	.40	.18
☐ 354	Harvey Catchings TN	.10	.05
☐ 355	John Lucas TN	.15	.07
☐ 356	Bill Bradley TN	.15	.07
☐ 357	Bill Walton TN	.15	.07
☐ 358	Don Nelson TN	.15	.07
☐ 359	Michael Jordan TN	2.50	1.10
☐ 360	T.(Satch) Sanders TN	.10	.05

1994-95 Upper Deck Draft Trade

This set was available exclusively by redeeming the Upper Deck Draft Trade card before the June 30th, 1995 deadline. Draft Trade cards were randomly seeded into one in every 240 first series Upper Deck packs. The first ten players selected in the 1994 NBA Draft are featured

within this set. The fronts feature the words NBA Draft Lottery Picks 1994 on the top of the card with the player vertically identified on the front left. The NBA draft logo is in the lower left corner. All of this surrounds a player cutout photo against a shaded background. The backs contain player information as well as a player photo. The cards are numbered with a "D" prefix in the upper left corner.

	MINT	NRMT
COMPLETE SET (10)	25.00	11.00
COMMON CARD (D1-D10)	.40	.18
SEMISTARS	.75	.35

ONE SET PER DRAFT TRADE CARD BY MAIL
TRADE: SER.1 STATED ODDS 1:240

□ D1 Glenn Robinson	3.00	1.35
□ D2 Jason Kidd	6.00	2.70
□ D3 Grant Hill	10.00	4.50
□ D4 Donyell Marshall	.75	.35
□ D5 Juwan Howard	4.00	1.80
□ D6 Sharone Wright	.40	.18
□ D7 Lamond Murray	.40	.18
□ D8 Brian Grant	.75	.35
□ D9 Eric Montross	.40	.18
□ D10 Eddie Jones	6.00	2.70
□ NNO Draft Trade Card	1.00	.45

1994-95 Upper Deck Jordan He's Back Reprints

The nine standard-size cards were reissued to celebrate the return of Michael Jordan. These cards parallel earlier Upper Deck Michael Jordan cards, the difference being that each is stamped with a foil "He's Back" logo on front. The cards were distributed one per second series rack pack. Jumbo versions of these cards were also released. They are priced in the header.

	MINT	NRMT
COMPLETE SET (9)	12.00	5.50
COMMON CARD (1-9)	1.50	.70

ONE PER SER.2 RETAIL RACK PACK

□ 23 Michael Jordan	1.50	.70
(92-93 Upper Deck)		
□ 23 Michael Jordan	1.50	.70
(93-94 Upper Deck)		
□ 41 Michael Jordan	1.50	.70
(94-95 SP Championship)		
□ 44 Michael Jordan	1.50	.70
(91-92 Upper Deck)		
□ 204 Michael Jordan	1.50	.70
(93-94 Upper Deck)		
□ 237 Michael Jordan	1.50	.70
(93-94 Upper Deck)		
□ 402 Michael Jordan	1.50	.70
(94-95 Collector's Choice)		
□ 425 Michael Jordan	1.50	.70
(92-93 Upper Deck)		
□ 453 Michael Jordan	1.50	.70
(92-93 Upper Deck)		
□ J1 Michael Jordan	5.00	2.20
(Team logo upper left)		
□ J2 Michael Jordan	5.00	2.20
(Team logo lower left)		
□ J3 Michael Jordan	5.00	2.20
(Team logo upper right)		

1994-95 Upper Deck Jordan Heroes

Randomly inserted in 12-card first series hobby and retail packs at a rate of one in 30, these 10 (nine numbered cards and one unnumbered header card) standard-size cards spotlight Michael Jordan's outstanding career. The fronts feature color action shots of Jordan from different stages in his career. His name appears in gold-foil lettering in the bottom margin and also as a facsimile autograph in gold foil in the upper margin. The card's subtitle appears in vertical gold-foil lettering in the left margin. The right side is full-bleed. The back carries a color action shot of Jordan on a ghosted background. A small color action shot appears at the lower left. Career highlights appear in a colored panel set off to one side. The cards are numbered on the back 37-45, a continuation of previous Heroes sets which included Jerry West, Wilt Chamberlain, Larry Bird, and Future Heroes. A 3" by 5" jumbo version of the entire set was also issued one card per blister pack sold at retail outlets. These cards are valued at approximately 50% of the values of the standard-size cards.

	MINT	NRMT
COMPLETE SET (10)	80.00	36.00
COMM JORDAN (37-45/HDR)	10.00	4.50

SER.1 STATED ODDS 1:30 HOB/RET

□ 37 Michael Jordan	10.00	4.50
1985 NBA Rookie of the Year		
□ 38 Michael Jordan	10.00	4.50
1986 63-Point Game		
□ 39 Michael Jordan	10.00	4.50
1987-88 Air Raid		
□ 40 Michael Jordan	10.00	4.50
1988		
□ 41 Michael Jordan	10.00	4.50
1985-93 9-Time NBA All-Star		
□ 42 Michael Jordan	10.00	4.50
1984		
□ 43 Michael Jordan	10.00	4.50
1991-93 MJo's Highlight Zone		
□ 44 Michael Jordan	10.00	4.50
1984-93 Rare Air		
□ 45 Checklist	10.00	4.50
□ NNO Header Card	10.00	4.50

1994-95 Upper Deck Predictor Award Winners

Randomly inserted exclusively into one in every 25 first and second series hobby packs, cards from this 40-card standard-size set are subdivided into

All-Star MVP (H1-H10), Defensive Player of the Year (H11-H20), MVP (H21-H30) and ROY (H31-H40) subsets. If the featured player placed first or second in his respective category, the card is redeemable before the June 30th, 1995 deadline for a special Predictors exchange set (of which mailing was delayed until late October, 1995). Winner cards have been designated below with a "W1" (good for a 20-card exchange set) or "W2" (good for a 10-card exchange set) listing. The fronts feature the player photo for most of the card. The award that the card is good for is vertically on the left side of the card. The player's name, team and position is in the lower right corner and is printed in white. The backs of the card contain contest information. The cards are numbered with an "H" prefix.

	MINT	NRMT
COMPLETE SET (40)	125.00	55.00
COMPLETE SERIES 1 (20)	50.00	22.00
COMPLETE SERIES 2 (20)	75.00	34.00
COMMON AS MVP (H1-H10)	.75	.35
COMMON DEF POY (H11-H20)	.75	.35
COMMON MVP (H21-H30)	.75	.35
COMMON ROY (H31-H40)	.75	.35
SEMISTARS	1.25	.55
UNLISTED STARS	2.00	.90
SER.1 STATED ODDS 1:25 HOBBY		
SER.2 STATED ODDS 1:30 HOBBY		
COMP.AS MVP RED.SET (10)	15.00	6.75
COMP.DEF.POY RED.SET (10)	10.00	4.50
COMP.MVP RED.SET (10)	15.00	6.75
COMP.ROY RED.SET (10)	15.00	6.75
*AW EXCHANGE CARDS: 50% OF HI CLMN		
TWO EXCH.SETS PER 'W1' CARD BY MAIL		
ONE EXCH.SET PER 'W2' CARD BY MAIL		

			MINT	NRMT
☐	H1	Charles Barkley	3.00	1.35
☐	H2	Hakeem Olajuwon	4.00	1.80
☐	H3	Shaquille O'Neal	8.00	3.60
☐	H4	Scottie Pippen	6.00	2.70
☐	H5	David Robinson	3.00	1.35
☐	H6	Shawn Kemp W2	6.00	2.70
☐	H7	Alonzo Mourning	2.50	1.10
☐	H8	Larry Johnson	1.25	.55
☐	H9	Patrick Ewing	2.00	.90
☐	H10	AS-MVP WC W1	.75	.35
☐	H11	Hakeem Olajuwon	4.00	1.80
☐	H12	D.Mutombo W1	2.00	.90
☐	H13	Nate McMillan	.75	.35
☐	H14	Dennis Rodman	8.00	3.60
☐	H15	Alonzo Mourning	2.50	1.10
☐	H16	Patrick Ewing	2.00	.90
☐	H17	Charles Barkley	3.00	1.35
☐	H18	David Robinson	3.00	1.35
☐	H19	John Stockton	2.00	.90
☐	H20	DEF-POY WC W2	.75	.35
☐	H21	Shaquille O'Neal W2	8.00	3.60
☐	H22	Hakeem Olajuwon	4.00	1.80
☐	H23	David Robinson W1	3.00	1.35
☐	H24	Scottie Pippen	6.00	2.70
☐	H25	Alonzo Mourning	2.50	1.10
☐	H26	Shawn Kemp	6.00	2.70
☐	H27	Charles Barkley	3.00	1.35
☐	H28	Patrick Ewing	2.00	.90
☐	H29	Larry Johnson	1.25	.55
☐	H30	MVP Wild Card	.75	.35
☐	H31	Jason Kidd W1	8.00	3.60
☐	H32	Grant Hill W1	12.00	5.50
☐	H33	Glenn Robinson	4.00	1.80
☐	H34	Eddie Jones	8.00	3.60
☐	H35	Donyell Marshall	2.00	.90
☐	H36	Eric Montross	.75	.35
☐	H37	Sharone Wright	.75	.35
☐	H38	Juwan Howard	5.00	2.20
☐	H39	Carlos Rogers	.75	.35
☐	H40	ROY Wild Card W1	.75	.35

1994-95 Upper Deck Predictor League Leaders

Randomly inserted exclusively into one in every 25 first and second series retail packs, cards from this 40-card standard-size set are subdivided into Scoring (R1-R10), Assists (R11-R20), Rebounds (R21-R30) and Blocks (R31-R40) subsets. If the featured player placed first or second in his respective category, the card was redeemable before the June 30th, 1995 deadline for a special Predictors exchange set (of which mailing was delayed until late October, 1995). Winner cards have been designated below with a "W1" (good for a 20-card exchange set) or "W2" (good for a 10-card exchange set) listing.

	MINT	NRMT
COMPLETE SET (40)	100.00	45.00
COMPLETE SERIES 1 (20)	50.00	22.00
COMPLETE SERIES 2 (20)	50.00	22.00
COMMON SCORERS (R1-R10)	.75	.35
COMMON ASSISTS (R11-R20)	.75	.35
COMMON REB. (R21-R30)	.75	.35
COMMON BLOCKS (R31-R40)	.75	.35
SEMISTARS	1.25	.55
UNLISTED STARS	2.00	.90
SER.1 STATED ODDS 1:25 RETAIL		
SER.2 STATED ODDS 1:30 RETAIL		
COMP.SCORE.RED.SET (10)	12.00	5.50
COMP.AST.RED.SET (10)	6.00	2.70
COMP.REB.RED.SET (10)	10.00	4.50
COMP.BLK.RED.SET (10)	12.00	5.50
*LL EXCHANGE CARDS: 50% OF HI CLMN		
TWO EXCH.SETS PER 'W1' CARD BY MAIL		
ONE EXCH.SET PER 'W2' CARD BY MAIL		

			MINT	NRMT
☐	R1	David Robinson	3.00	1.35
☐	R2	Shaquille O'Neal W1	8.00	3.60
☐	R3	Hakeem Olajuwon W2	4.00	1.80
☐	R4	Scottie Pippen	6.00	2.70
☐	R5	Chris Webber	5.00	2.20
☐	R6	Karl Malone	3.00	1.35
☐	R7	Patrick Ewing	2.00	.90
☐	R8	Mitch Richmond	2.00	.90
☐	R9	Charles Barkley	3.00	1.35
☐	R10	Scorers Wild Card	.75	.35
☐	R11	John Stockton W1	2.00	.90
☐	R12	Mookie Blaylock	1.25	.55
☐	R13	Kenny Anderson W2	1.25	.55
☐	R14	Kevin Johnson	1.25	.55
☐	R15	Muggsy Bogues	1.25	.55
☐	R16	Tim Hardaway	2.50	1.10
☐	R17	A.Hardaway	8.00	3.60
☐	R18	Rod Strickland	1.25	.55
☐	R19	Sherman Douglas	.75	.35
☐	R20	Assists Wild Card	.75	.35
☐	R21	Shaquille O'Neal	8.00	3.60
☐	R22	Hakeem Olajuwon	4.00	1.80
☐	R23	Dennis Rodman W1	8.00	3.60
☐	R24	D.Mutombo W2	2.00	.90
☐	R25	Karl Malone	3.00	1.35
☐	R26	Kevin Willis	.75	.35
☐	R27	Chris Webber	5.00	2.20
☐	R28	Alonzo Mourning	2.50	1.10
☐	R29	Derrick Coleman	1.25	.55
☐	R30	Rebounds Wild Card	.75	.35
☐	R31	D.Mutombo W1	2.00	.90
☐	R32	Hakeem Olajuwon W2	4.00	1.80
☐	R33	David Robinson	3.00	1.35
☐	R34	Shawn Bradley	1.25	.55
☐	R35	Shaquille O'Neal	8.00	3.60
☐	R36	Patrick Ewing	2.00	.90
☐	R37	Alonzo Mourning	2.50	1.10
☐	R38	Shawn Kemp	6.00	2.70
☐	R39	Derrick Coleman	1.25	.55
☐	R40	Blocks Wild Card	.75	.35

1994-95 Upper Deck Rookie Standouts

Randomly inserted into one in every 30 second series packs, cards from this 20-card standard size set feature a selection of the top rookies from the 1994-95 season. The borderless fronts feature a color photo in the middle. The words "Rookie Standouts" are in gold foil in the bottom left corner. The hard to read player's names are in the upper left corner. The backs have player information and are numbered with a RS prefix in the upper left corner. The set is sequenced in 1994 NBA draft order.

	MINT	NRMT
COMPLETE SET (20)	80.00	36.00
COMMON CARD (RS1-RS20)	1.00	.45
SEMISTARS	2.50	1.10
SER.2 STATED ODDS 1:30 HOBBY/RETAIL		

		MINT	NRMT
☐ RS1	Glenn Robinson	10.00	4.50
☐ RS2	Jason Kidd	20.00	9.00
☐ RS3	Grant Hill	30.00	13.50
☐ RS4	Donyell Marshall	2.50	1.10
☐ RS5	Juwan Howard	12.00	5.50
☐ RS6	Sharone Wright	1.00	.45
☐ RS7	Lamond Murray	1.00	.45
☐ RS8	Brian Grant	2.50	1.10
☐ RS9	Eric Montross	1.00	.45
☐ RS10	Eddie Jones	20.00	9.00
☐ RS11	Carlos Rogers	1.00	.45
☐ RS12	Khalid Reeves	1.00	.45
☐ RS13	Jalen Rose	2.50	1.10
☐ RS14	Michael Smith	1.00	.45
☐ RS15	Eric Piatkowski	1.00	.45
☐ RS16	Clifford Rozier	1.00	.45
☐ RS17	Aaron McKie	1.00	.45
☐ RS18	Eric Mobley	1.00	.45
☐ RS19	Bill Curley	1.00	.45
☐ RS20	Wesley Person	2.50	1.10

1994-95 Upper Deck Slam Dunk Stars

Randomly inserted into one in every 30 second series packs, cards from this 20-card standard-size set feature Upper Deck spokesperson Shawn Kemp's selections of the top dunkers. The fronts feature the words "Kemp Slam Dunk Stars" as well as a sculpture of Kemp in gold foil on the left. The rest of the card is dedicated to a photo of the player dunking. The back has Kemp's opinion of each player. There is also a small inset photo of Kemp as well as a cutout of the featured player. The set is sequenced in alphabetical order.

	MINT	NRMT
COMPLETE SET (20)	120.00	55.00
COMMON CARD (S1-S20)	1.50	.70
SEMISTARS	3.00	1.35
UNLISTED STARS	6.00	2.70

SER.2 STATED ODDS 1:30 HOBBY/RETAIL

		MINT	NRMT
☐ S1	Vin Baker	15.00	6.75
☐ S2	Charles Barkley	10.00	4.50
☐ S3	Derrick Coleman	3.00	1.35
☐ S4	Clyde Drexler	8.00	3.60
☐ S5	LaPhonso Ellis	3.00	1.35
☐ S6	Larry Johnson	3.00	1.35
☐ S7	Shawn Kemp	20.00	9.00
☐ S8	Donyell Marshall	6.00	2.70
☐ S9	Jamal Mashburn	6.00	2.70
☐ S10	Gheorghe Muresan	1.50	.70
☐ S11	Alonzo Mourning	8.00	3.60
☐ S12	Shaquille O'Neal	25.00	11.00
☐ S13	Hakeem Olajuwon	12.00	5.50
☐ S14	Scottie Pippen	20.00	9.00
☐ S15	Isaiah Rider	3.00	1.35
☐ S16	David Robinson	10.00	4.50
☐ S17	M.Weatherspoon	1.50	.70
☐ S18	Chris Webber	15.00	6.75
☐ S19	Dominique Wilkins	6.00	2.70
☐ S20	Rik Smits	3.00	1.35

1994-95 Upper Deck Special Edition

Inserted one per pack into both first and second series 12-card packs and four per second series rack pack, cards from this 180-card standard-size set (issued in two separate 90-card series) are comprised of a wide selection of the top stars and prospects in the NBA. Fronts feature full-color player action shots against silver-foil backgrounds. The players are categorized by team name as follows: Atlanta Hawks (1-3, 91, 93-94), Boston Celtics (4-6, 95-97), Charlotte Hornets (5-7, 98-100), Chicago Bulls (10-12, 101-103), Cleveland Cavaliers (13-15, 104-106), Dallas Mavericks (16-19, 107-109, 116), Denver Nuggets (20-23, 110-112), Detroit Pistons (24-26, 113-115), Golden State Warriors (27-30, 117-121), Houston Rockets (31-34, 122-124), Indiana Pacers (35-37, 125-127), Los Angeles Clippers (38-40, 128-130, 134), Los Angeles Lakers (41-44, 131-133), Miami Heat (45-48, 135-137), Milwaukee Bucks (49-51, 138-140), Minnesota Timberwolves (52-54, 141-143), New Jersey Nets (55-57, 144-146), New York Knicks (58-62, 148-150), Orlando Magic (63-65, 151-154), Philadelphia 76ers (66-68, 147, 155-157), Phoenix Suns (69-71, 158-161), Portland Trail Blazers (72-74, 162-164), Sacramento Kings (75-77, 165-167, 174), San Antonio Spurs (78-81, 168-170), Seattle Supersonics (82-84, 171-173), Utah Jazz (85-87, 175-177), Washington Bullets (88-90, 92, 178-180). Cards are numbered with an SE prefix on back.

	MINT	NRMT
COMPLETE SET (180)	50.00	22.00
COMPLETE SERIES 1 (90)	15.00	6.75
COMPLETE SERIES 2 (90)	35.00	16.00
COMMON CARD (1-180)	.15	.07
SEMISTARS	.40	.18
UNLISTED STARS	.75	.35
ONE PER PACK		
COMP.GOLD SET (180)	500.00	220.00
COMP.GOLD SER.1 (90)	150.00	70.00
COMP.GOLD SER.2 (90)	350.00	160.00
COMM GOLD (SE1-SE180)	1.00	.45
*GOLD STARS: 4X TO 8X HI COLUMN		
*GOLD RCs: 3X TO 5X HI COLUMN		
GOLD: SER.1/2 STATED ODDS 1:35 HOB/RET		
SE PREFIX ON CARD NUMBERS		

		MINT	NRMT
☐ 1	Stacey Augmon	.15	.07
☐ 2	Kevin Willis	.15	.07
☐ 3	Mookie Blaylock	.40	.18
☐ 4	Rick Fox	.15	.07
☐ 5	Xavier McDaniel	.15	.07
☐ 6	Dee Brown	.15	.07
☐ 7	Muggsy Bogues	.40	.18
☐ 8	Kenny Gattison	.15	.07
☐ 9	Alonzo Mourning	1.00	.45
☐ 10	B.J. Armstrong	.15	.07
☐ 11	Bill Cartwright	.15	.07
☐ 12	Toni Kukoc	.75	.35
☐ 13	Mark Price	.15	.07
☐ 14	Gerald Wilkins	.15	.07
☐ 15	John Williams	.15	.07
☐ 16	Jamal Mashburn	.75	.35
☐ 17	Sean Rooks	.15	.07
☐ 18	Doug Smith	.15	.07
☐ 19	Jim Jackson	.40	.18
☐ 20	Mahmoud Abdul-Rauf	.15	.07
☐ 21	Rodney Rogers	.15	.07
☐ 22	Reggie Williams	.15	.07
☐ 23	LaPhonso Ellis	.40	.18
☐ 24	Allan Houston	.75	.35
☐ 25	Terry Mills	.15	.07
☐ 26	Joe Dumars	.75	.35
☐ 27	Chris Mullin	.40	.18
☐ 28	Billy Owens	.15	.07
☐ 29	Latrell Sprewell	.40	.18
☐ 30	Chris Webber	2.00	.90
☐ 31	Sam Cassell	.75	.35
☐ 32	Vernon Maxwell	.15	.07
☐ 33	Hakeem Olajuwon	1.50	.70
☐ 34	Otis Thorpe	.40	.18
☐ 35	Rik Smits	.40	.18
☐ 36	Derrick McKey	.15	.07
☐ 37	Haywoode Workman	.15	.07
☐ 38	Charles Outlaw	.15	.07
☐ 39	Elmore Spencer	.15	.07

40 Loy Vaught	.40	.18
41 George Lynch	.15	.07
42 Nick Van Exel	.75	.35
43 James Worthy	.75	.35
44 Elden Campbell	.40	.18
45 Grant Long	.15	.07
46 Harold Miner	.15	.07
47 Glen Rice	.75	.35
48 Steve Smith	.40	.18
49 Todd Day	.15	.07
50 Eric Murdock	.15	.07
51 Vin Baker	2.00	.90
52 Christian Laettner	.40	.18
53 Isaiah Rider	.40	.18
54 Micheal Williams	.15	.07
55 Benoit Benjamin	.15	.07
56 Derrick Coleman	.40	.18
57 Chris Morris	.15	.07
58 Charles Smith	.15	.07
59 Greg Anthony	.15	.07
60 Doc Rivers	.40	.18
61 Derek Harper	.40	.18
62 John Starks	.40	.18
63 Anfernee Hardaway	3.00	1.35
64 Dennis Scott	.15	.07
65 Nick Anderson	.40	.18
66 Shawn Bradley	.40	.18
67 M.Weatherspoon	.15	.07
68 Jeff Malone	.15	.07
69 Cedric Ceballos	.40	.18
70 Kevin Johnson	.40	.18
71 Oliver Miller	.15	.07
72 Clifford Robinson	.40	.18
73 Rod Strickland	.40	.18
74 Buck Williams	.40	.18
75 Mitch Richmond	.75	.35
76 Walt Williams	.15	.07
77 Lionel Simmons	.15	.07
78 Willie Anderson	.15	.07
79 Terry Cummings	.15	.07
80 J.R. Reid	.15	.07
81 Dennis Rodman	3.00	1.35
82 Kendall Gill	.40	.18
83 Sam Perkins	.40	.18
84 Detlef Schrempf	.40	.18
85 Jeff Hornacek	.40	.18
86 Karl Malone	1.25	.55
87 Felton Spencer	.15	.07
88 Calbert Cheaney	.40	.18
89 Calbert Cheaney	.40	.18
90 Brent Price	.15	.07
91 Tyrone Corbin	.15	.07
92 Rex Chapman	.15	.07
93 Ken Norman	.15	.07
94 Steve Smith	.40	.18
95 Eric Montross	.15	.07
96 Dino Radja	.15	.07
97 Dominique Wilkins	.75	.35
98 Scott Burrell	.15	.07
99 Hersey Hawkins	.40	.18
100 Larry Johnson	.40	.18
101 Ron Harper	.40	.18
102 Scottie Pippen	2.50	1.10
103 Dickey Simpkins	.15	.07
104 Tyrone Hill	.15	.07
105 Chris Mills	.40	.18
106 Bobby Phills	.15	.07
107 Lorenzo Williams	.15	.07
108 Popeye Jones	.15	.07
109 Jason Kidd	5.00	2.20
110 Dikembe Mutombo	.75	.35
111 Robert Pack	.15	.07
112 Jalen Rose	.75	.35
113 Bill Curley	.15	.07
114 Grant Hill	8.00	3.60
115 Lindsey Hunter	.40	.18
116 Roy Tarpley	.15	.07
117 Tim Hardaway	1.00	.45
118 Ricky Pierce	.15	.07
119 Carlos Rogers	.15	.07
120 Clifford Rozier	.15	.07
121 Rony Seikaly	.15	.07
122 Mario Elie	.15	.07
123 Robert Horry	.40	.18
124 Kenny Smith	.15	.07
125 Antonio Davis	.15	.07
126 Dale Davis	.15	.07
127 Reggie Miller	.75	.35
128 Lamond Murray	.40	.18
129 Eric Piatkowski	.15	.07
130 Pooh Richardson	.15	.07
131 Cedric Ceballos	.40	.18
132 Vlade Divac	.40	.18
133 Eddie Jones	5.00	2.20
134 Mark Jackson	.40	.18
135 Matt Geiger	.15	.07
136 Khalid Reeves	.15	.07
137 Kevin Willis	.15	.07
138 Lee Mayberry	.15	.07
139 Eric Mobley	.15	.07
140 Glenn Robinson	2.50	1.10
141 Doug West	.15	.07
142 Donyell Marshall	.75	.35
143 Chris Smith	.15	.07
144 Kenny Anderson	.40	.18
145 Chris Morris	.15	.07
146 Armon Gilliam	.15	.07
147 Dana Barros	.40	.18
148 Patrick Ewing	.75	.35
149 Charles Oakley	.40	.18
150 Charlie Ward	.40	.18
151 Horace Grant	.40	.18
152 Shaquille O'Neal	3.00	1.35
153 Brian Shaw	.15	.07
154 Brooks Thompson	.15	.07
155 B.J. Tyler	.15	.07
156 Scott Williams	.15	.07
157 Sharone Wright	.15	.07
158 Charles Barkley	1.25	.55
159 Dan Majerle	.40	.18
160 Danny Manning	.15	.07
161 Wesley Person	.75	.35
162 Clyde Drexler	1.00	.45
163 Harvey Grant	.15	.07
164 Terry Porter	.15	.07
165 Brian Grant	.75	.35
166 Bobby Hurley	.15	.07
167 Olden Polynice	.15	.07
168 Sean Elliott	.40	.18
169 Chuck Person	.15	.07
170 David Robinson	1.25	.55
171 Shawn Kemp	2.50	1.10
172 Nate McMillan	.15	.07
173 Gary Payton	1.25	.55
174 Michael Smith	.40	.18
175 David Benoit	.15	.07
176 Jay Humphries	.15	.07
177 John Stockton	.75	.35
178 Juwan Howard	3.00	1.35
179 Chris Webber	2.00	.90
180 Scott Skiles	.15	.07

1995-96 Upper Deck

series of 180 cards each, for a total of 360 cards. Twelve-card packs carried a suggested retail price of $1.99. The fronts are borderless full-color player action shots with the player's name printed in gold foil at the bottom. The backs feature another player color action shot with a graph of the player's career stats. The player's name and biography are printed vertically on the left side of the back in white type. The set features the following topical subsets: The Rookie Years (136-154), All-Rookie team (155-165), All NBA Team (166-180), USAI '96 (316-325), Images of '95 (326-335), Major Attractions (336-346) and Slams and Jams (347-360). Rookie Cards of note include Michael Finley, Kevin Garnett, Antonio McDyess, Jerry Stackhouse and Damon Stoudamire.

The 1995-96 Upper Deck set was issued in two separate

	MINT	NRMT
COMPLETE SET (360)	50.00	22.00
COMPLETE SERIES 1 (180)	20.00	9.00
COMPLETE SERIES 2 (180)	30.00	13.50
COMMON CARD (1-360)	.15	.07
SEMISTARS	.20	.09
UNLISTED STARS	.40	.18
COMP.ELEC.SET (360)	100.00	45.00
COMP.ELEC.SER.1 (180)	50.00	22.00
COMP.ELEC.SER.2 (180)	50.00	22.00
COMMON ELEC. (1-360)	.30	.14
*ELEC.STARS: 1.25X TO 2.5X HI COLUMN		
*ELEC.RCs: 1X TO 2X HI		
ONE ELEC.COURT PER RETAIL PACK		
COMP.ELE.GLD.SET (360)	1200.00	550.00
COMP.ELE.GLD.SER.1 (180)	600.00	275.00
COMP.ELE.GLD.SER.2 (180)	600.00	275.00
COMMON GOLD (1-360)	2.00	.90
*GOLD STARS: 12.5X TO 25X HI COLUMN		
*GOLD RCs: 7.5X TO 15X HI		
GOLD: SER.1/2 STATED ODDS 1:35 RETAIL		

1 Eddie Jones	1.00	.45
2 Hubert Davis	.15	.07
3 Latrell Sprewell	.20	.09
4 Stacey Augmon	.15	.07
5 Mario Elie	.15	.07
6 Tyrone Hill	.15	.07
7 Dikembe Mutombo	.20	.09
8 Antonio Davis	.15	.07
9 Horace Grant	.20	.09
10 Ken Norman	.15	.07
11 Aaron McKie	.15	.07
12 Vinny Del Negro	.15	.07
13 Glenn Robinson	.50	.23
14 Allan Houston	.20	.09
15 Bryon Russell	.15	.07
16 Tony Dumas	.15	.07
17 Gary Payton	.60	.25
18 Rik Smits	.20	.09
19 Dino Radja	.15	.07
20 Robert Pack	.15	.07
21 Calbert Cheaney	.15	.07
22 C.Weatherspoon	.15	.07
23 Michael Jordan	5.00	2.20
24 Felton Spencer	.15	.07
25 J.R. Reid	.15	.07
26 Cedric Ceballos	.15	.07
27 Dan Majerle	.15	.07
28 Donald Hodge	.15	.07
29 Nate McMillan	.15	.07

30	Bimbo Coles	.15	.07
31	Mitch Richmond	.40	.18
32	Scott Brooks	.15	.07
33	Patrick Ewing	.40	.18
34	Carl Herrera	.15	.07
35	Rick Fox	.15	.07
36	James Robinson	.15	.07
37	Donald Royal	.15	.07
38	Joe Dumars	.40	.18
39	Rony Seikaly	.15	.07
40	Dennis Rodman	1.50	.70
41	Muggsy Bogues	.20	.09
42	Gheorghe Muresan	.15	.07
43	Ervin Johnson	.15	.07
44	Todd Day	.15	.07
45	Rex Walters	.15	.07
46	Terrell Brandon	.40	.18
47	Wesley Person	.20	.09
48	Terry Dehere	.15	.07
49	Steve Smith	.20	.09
50	Brian Grant	.20	.09
51	Eric Piatkowski	.15	.07
52	Lindsey Hunter	.15	.07
53	Chris Webber	1.00	.45
54	Antoine Carr	.15	.07
55	Chris Dudley	.15	.07
56	Clyde Drexler	.50	.23
57	P.J. Brown	.15	.07
58	Kevin Willis	.15	.07
59	Jeff Turner	.15	.07
60	Sean Elliott	.20	.09
61	Kevin Johnson	.20	.09
62	Scott Skiles	.15	.07
63	Charles Smith	.15	.07
64	Derrick McKey	.15	.07
65	Danny Ferry	.15	.07
66	Detlef Schrempf	.20	.09
67	Shawn Bradley	.20	.09
68	Isaiah Rider	.20	.09
69	Karl Malone	.60	.25
70	Will Perdue	.15	.07
71	Terry Mills	.15	.07
72	Glen Rice	.40	.18
73	Tim Breaux	.15	.07
74	Malik Sealy	.15	.07
75	Walt Williams	.15	.07
76	Bobby Phills	.15	.07
77	Anthony Avent	.15	.07
78	Jamal Mashburn UER	.20	.09
	Career FG percentage is wrong		
79	Vlade Divac	.20	.09
80	Reggie Williams	.15	.07
81	Xavier McDaniel	.15	.07
82	Avery Johnson	.15	.07
83	Derek Harper	.20	.09
84	Don MacLean	.15	.07
85	Tom Gugliotta	.40	.18
86	Craig Ehlo	.15	.07
87	Robert Horry	.15	.07
88	Kevin Edwards	.15	.07
89	Chuck Person	.15	.07
90	Sharone Wright	.15	.07
91	Steve Kerr	.20	.09
92	Marty Conlon	.15	.07
93	Jalen Rose	.20	.09
94	Bryant Reeves	1.00	.45
95	Shaquille O'Neal	1.50	.70
96	David Wesley	.15	.07
97	Chris Mills	.15	.07
98	Rod Strickland	.20	.09
99	Pooh Richardson	.15	.07
100	Sam Perkins	.15	.07
101	Dell Curry	.15	.07
102	David Benoit	.15	.07
103	Christian Laettner	.20	.09
104	Duane Causwell	.15	.07
105	Jason Kidd	1.00	.45
106	Mark West	.15	.07
107	Lee Mayberry	.15	.07
108	John Salley	.15	.07
109	Jeff Malone	.15	.07
110	George Zidek	.15	.07
111	Kenny Smith	.15	.07
112	George Lynch	.15	.07
113	Toni Kukoc	.20	.09
114	A.C. Green	.20	.09
115	Kenny Anderson	.20	.09
116	Robert Parish	.20	.09
117	Chris Mullin	.40	.18
118	Loy Vaught	.15	.07
119	Olden Polynice	.15	.07
120	Clifford Robinson	.15	.07
121	Eric Mobley	.15	.07
122	Doug West	.15	.07
123	Sam Cassell	.20	.09
124	Nick Anderson	.15	.07
125	Matt Geiger	.15	.07
126	Elden Campbell	.20	.09
127	Alonzo Mourning	.40	.18
128	Bryant Stith	.15	.07
129	Mark Jackson	.20	.09
130	Cherokee Parks	.15	.07
131	Shawn Respert	.15	.07
132	Alan Henderson	.40	.18
133	Jerry Stackhouse	1.50	.70
134	Rasheed Wallace	1.00	.45
135	Antonio McDyess	2.00	.90
136	Charles Barkley ROO	.40	.18
137	M.Jordan ROO	2.50	1.10
138	H.Olajuwon ROO	.40	.18
139	Joe Dumars ROO	.40	.18
140	Patrick Ewing ROO	.20	.09
141	A.C. Green ROO	.20	.09
142	Karl Malone ROO	.40	.18
143	Detlef Schrempf ROO	.15	.07
144	Chuck Person ROO	.15	.07
145	Muggsy Bogues ROO	.15	.07
146	Horace Grant ROO	.15	.07
147	Mark Jackson ROO	.15	.07
148	Kevin Johnson ROO	.15	.07
149	Mitch Richmond ROO	.20	.09
150	Rik Smits ROO	.15	.07
151	Nick Anderson ROO	.15	.07
152	Tim Hardaway ROO	.40	.18
153	Shawn Kemp ROO	.60	.25
154	David Robinson ROO	.40	.18
155	Jason Kidd ART	.50	.23
156	Grant Hill ART	1.25	.55
157	Glenn Robinson ART	.40	.18
158	Eddie Jones ART	.50	.23
159	Brian Grant ART	.15	.07
160	Juwan Howard ART	.40	.18
161	Eric Montross ART	.15	.07
162	Wesley Person ART	.15	.07
163	Jalen Rose ART	.15	.07
164	Donnell Marshall ART	.15	.07
165	Sharone Wright ART	.15	.07
166	Karl Malone AN	.40	.18
167	Scottie Pippen AN	.60	.25
168	David Robinson AN	.40	.18
169	John Stockton AN	.20	.09
170	A.Hardaway AN	.75	.35
171	Charles Barkley AN	.40	.18
172	Shawn Kemp AN	.60	.25
173	Shaquille O'Neal AN	.75	.35
174	Gary Payton AN	.40	.18
175	Mitch Richmond AN	.20	.09
176	Dennis Rodman AN	.75	.35
177	Detlef Schrempf AN	.15	.07
178	Hakeem Olajuwon AN	.40	.18
179	Reggie Miller AN	.20	.09
180	Clyde Drexler AN	.40	.18
181	Hakeem Olajuwon	.75	.35
182	Vin Baker	.75	.35
183	Jeff Hornacek	.20	.09
184	Popeye Jones	.15	.07
185	Sedale Threatt	.15	.07
186	Scottie Pippen	1.25	.55
187	Terry Porter	.15	.07
188	Dan Majerle	.15	.07
189	Clifford Rozier	.15	.07
190	Greg Minor	.15	.07
191	Dennis Scott	.15	.07
192	Hersey Hawkins	.20	.09
193	Chris Gatling	.15	.07
194	Charles Oakley	.15	.07
195	Dale Davis	.15	.07
196	Robert Pack	.15	.07
197	Lamond Murray	.15	.07
198	Mookie Blaylock	.20	.09
199	Dickey Simpkins	.15	.07
200	Kevin Gamble	.15	.07
201	Lorenzo Williams	.15	.07
202	Scott Burrell	.15	.07
203	Armon Gilliam	.15	.07
204	Doc Rivers	.20	.09
205	Blue Edwards	.15	.07
206	Billy Owens	.15	.07
207	Juwan Howard	.60	.25
208	Harvey Grant	.15	.07
209	Richard Dumas	.15	.07
210	Anthony Peeler	.15	.07
211	Matt Geiger	.15	.07
212	Lucious Harris	.15	.07
213	Grant Long	.15	.07
214	Sasha Danilovic	.15	.07
215	Chris Morris	.15	.07
216	Donyell Marshall	.20	.09
217	Alonzo Mourning	.40	.18
218	John Stockton	.40	.18
219	Khalid Reeves	.15	.07
220	M.Abdul-Raf	.15	.07
221	Sean Rooks	.15	.07
222	Shawn Kemp	1.25	.55
223	John Williams	.15	.07
224	Dee Brown	.15	.07
225	Jim Jackson	.20	.09
226	Harold Miner	.15	.07
227	B.J. Armstrong	.15	.07
228	Elliot Perry	.15	.07
229	Anthony Miller	.15	.07
230	Donny Marshall	.15	.07
231	Tyrone Corbin	.15	.07
232	Anthony Mason	.20	.09
233	Grant Hill	2.50	1.10
234	Buck Williams	.15	.07
235	Brian Shaw	.15	.07
236	Dale Ellis	.15	.07
237	Magic Johnson	1.25	.55
238	Eric Montross	.15	.07
239	Rex Chapman	.15	.07
240	Otis Thorpe	.15	.07
241	Tracy Murray	.15	.07
242	Sarunas Marciulionis	.15	.07
243	Luc Longley	.20	.09
244	Elmore Spencer	.15	.07
245	Terry Cummings	.15	.07
246	Sam Mitchell	.15	.07
247	Terrence Rencher	.15	.07
248	Byron Houston	.15	.07
249	Pervis Ellison	.15	.07
250	Carlos Rogers	.15	.07
251	Kendall Gill	.20	.09
252	Sherrell Ford	.15	.07
253	Michael Finley	1.50	.70
254	Kurt Thomas	.20	.09
255	Joe Smith	1.50	.70
256	Bobby Hurley	.15	.07
257	Greg Anthony	.15	.07
258	Willie Anderson	.15	.07
259	Theo Ratliff	.40	.18
260	Duane Ferrell	.15	.07
261	Antonio Harvey	.15	.07
262	Gary Grant	.15	.07
263	Brian Williams	.15	.07
264	Danny Manning	.20	.09
265	Micheal Williams	.15	.07
266	Dennis Rodman	2.50	1.10
267	Arvydas Sabonis	.75	.35
268	Don MacLean	.15	.07
269	Keith Askins	.15	.07
270	Reggie Miller	.40	.18
271	Ed Pinckney	.15	.07
272	Bob Sura	.20	.09
273	Kevin Garnett	5.00	2.20
274	Byron Scott	.15	.07
275	Mario Bennett	.15	.07
276	Junior Burrough	.15	.07
277	A.Hardaway	1.50	.70
278	George McCloud	.15	.07
279	Loren Meyer	.15	.07
280	Ed O'Bannon	.15	.07
281	Lawrence Moten	.15	.07
282	Dana Barros	.15	.07
283	Damon Stoudamire	3.00	1.35
284	Eric Williams	.20	.09
285	Wayman Tisdale	.15	.07
286	Rodney Rogers	.15	.07

☐ 287	Sherman Douglas	.15	.07
☐ 288	Greg Ostertag	.15	.07
☐ 289	Alvin Robertson	.15	.07
☐ 290	Tim Legler	.15	.07
☐ 291	Zan Tabak	.15	.07
☐ 292	Gary Trent	.15	.07
☐ 293	Haywoode Workman	.15	.07
☐ 294	Charles Barkley	.60	.25
☐ 295	Derrick Coleman	.20	.09
☐ 296	Ricky Pierce	.15	.07
☐ 297	Benoit Benjamin	.15	.07
☐ 298	Larry Johnson	.20	.09
☐ 299	Travis Best	.20	.09
☐ 300	Jason Caffey	.40	.18
☐ 301	Cory Alexander	.15	.07
☐ 302	Nick Van Exel	.40	.18
☐ 303	Corliss Williamson	.50	.23
☐ 304	Eric Murdock	.15	.07
☐ 305	Tyus Edney	.15	.07
☐ 306	Lou Roe	.15	.07
☐ 307	John Salley	.15	.07
☐ 308	Spud Webb	.20	.09
☐ 309	Brent Barry	.40	.18
☐ 310	David Robinson	.60	.25
☐ 311	Glen Rice	.18	.18
☐ 312	Chris King	.15	.07
☐ 313	David Vaughn	.15	.07
☐ 314	Kenny Gattison	.15	.07
☐ 315	Randolph Childress	.15	.07
☐ 316	A.Hardaway USA	.75	.35
☐ 317	Grant Hill USA	1.25	.55
☐ 318	Karl Malone USA	.40	.18
☐ 319	Reggie Miller USA	.40	.09
☐ 320	H.Olajuwon USA	.40	.18
☐ 321	Shaquille O'Neal USA	.75	.35
☐ 322	Scottie Pippen USA	.60	.25
☐ 323	David Robinson USA	.40	.18
☐ 324	Glenn Robinson USA	.40	.18
☐ 325	John Stockton USA	.20	.09
☐ 326	Cedric Ceballos I95	.15	.07
☐ 327	Shaquille O'Neal I95	.75	.35
☐ 328	Glenn Robinson I95	.40	.18
☐ 329	Shawn Kemp I95	.60	.25
☐ 330	Nick Anderson I95	.15	.07
☐ 331	Shawn Bradley I95	.15	.07
☐ 332	Horace Grant I95 Brooks Thompson	.20	.09
☐ 333	Robert Horry I95	.15	.07
☐ 334	NBA Expansion I95 Grizzlies/Raptors	.15	.07
☐ 335	Michael Jordan I95	2.50	1.10
☐ 336	Nick Van Exel Dyan Cannon MA	.20	.09
☐ 337	Michael Jordan David Hanson MA	1.25	.55
☐ 338	Scottie Pippen Jenna Von Oy MA	.40	.18
☐ 339	Michael Jordan Charlie Sheen MA	1.25	.55
☐ 340	Jason Kidd Christopher "Kid" Reid MA	.40	.18
☐ 341	Michael Jordan Queen Latifah MA	1.25	.55
☐ 342	Charles Barkley Don Johnson MA	.40	.18
☐ 343	Hakeem Olajuwon Corbin Bernsen MA	.40	.18
☐ 344	Ahmad Rashad MA	.15	.07
☐ 345	Willow Bay MA	.15	.07
☐ 346	Gary Payton Mark Curry MA	.40	.18
☐ 347	Horace Grant SJ	.15	.07
☐ 348	Juwan Howard SJ	.40	.18
☐ 349	David Robinson SJ	.40	.18
☐ 350	Reggie Miller SJ	.20	.09
☐ 351	Brian Grant SJ	.15	.07
☐ 352	Michael Jordan SJ	2.50	1.10
☐ 353	Cedric Ceballos SJ	.15	.07
☐ 354	Blue Edwards SJ	.15	.07
☐ 355	Acie Earl SJ	.15	.07
☐ 356	Dennis Rodman SJ	1.25	.55
☐ 357	Shawn Kemp SJ	.60	.25
☐ 358	Jerry Stackhouse SJ	.60	.25
☐ 359	Jamal Mashburn SJ	.15	.07
☐ 360	Antonio McDyess SJ	.75	.35

1995-96 Upper Deck All-Star Class

Randomly inserted in first series packs at a rate of one in 17, this 25-card standard-size set high lights the play of the NBA's best in the 1995 All Star Game. Borderless foil fronts feature the player in full-color action and include the Upper Deck logo stamped in blue foil in the upper right. "1995 NBA All Star Class" is printed in blue foil and centered at the bottom. On either side of the logo are gold pyramids which feature the player's name, team and position printed in black type. Blue backs have a copper bordered posed player shot with game highlights. The Phoenix All Star Weekend logo is printed at the top of the picture and the player's name, team and position are printed over the logo.

	MINT	NRMT
COMPLETE SET (25)	150.00	70.00
COMMON CARD (AS1-AS25)	2.00	.90
SEMISTARS	3.00	1.35
UNLISTED STARS	5.00	2.20
SER.1 STATED ODDS 1:17 HOBBY/RETAIL		

		MINT	NRMT
☐ AS1	A.Hardaway	20.00	9.00
☐ AS2	Reggie Miller	5.00	2.20
☐ AS3	Grant Hill	30.00	13.50
☐ AS4	Scottie Pippen	15.00	6.75
☐ AS5	Shaquille O'Neal	20.00	9.00
☐ AS6	Larry Johnson	3.00	1.35
☐ AS7	Dana Barros	2.00	.90
☐ AS8	Vin Baker	10.00	4.50
☐ AS9	Alonzo Mourning	5.00	2.20
☐ AS10	Joe Dumars	5.00	2.20
☐ AS11	Patrick Ewing	5.00	2.20
☐ AS12	Tyrone Hill	2.00	.90
☐ AS13	Latrell Sprewell	3.00	1.35
☐ AS14	Dan Majerle	2.00	.90
☐ AS15	Shawn Kemp	15.00	6.75
☐ AS16	Karl Malone	8.00	3.60
☐ AS17	Hakeem Olajuwon	10.00	4.50
☐ AS18	Gary Payton	8.00	3.60
☐ AS19	Mitch Richmond	5.00	2.20
☐ AS20	David Robinson	8.00	3.60
☐ AS21	Detlef Schrempf	3.00	1.35
☐ AS22	Cedric Ceballos	2.00	.90
☐ AS23	John Stockton	5.00	2.20
☐ AS24	D.Mutombo	3.00	1.35
☐ AS25	Charles Barkley	8.00	3.60

1995-96 Upper Deck Jordan Collection

Upper Deck spokesperson and NBA legend Michael Jordan is featured on these eight, multi-series insert cards. Cards JC5-JC8 were randomly inserted into one in every 29 first series packs. Cards JC13-JC16 were randomly inserted one in every 29 second series packs. The eight cards actually represent two segments of a twenty-four card set issued in six different series across all of Upper Deck's 1995-96 products (except SPx). Full-bleed, silver-foil fronts feature Jordan in full color in both posed and action shots. Backs feature Jordan in a spectacular action shot with alternating boxes of separated colors. A "Jordan Collection" box appears at the mid-left of the card with an explanation of the award that was featured on the front.

	MINT	NRMT
COMPLETE SET (24)	120.00	55.00
COMP.COLC SER.1 (4)	10.00	4.50
COMP.UD SER.1 (4)	30.00	13.50
COMP.COLC SER.2 (4)	10.00	4.50
COMP.UD SER.2 (4)	30.00	13.50
COMP.SP SET (4)	40.00	18.00
COMP.SPC SET (4)	40.00	18.00
COMMON COLC 1 (JC1-JC4)	3.00	1.35
COMMON UD 1 (JC5-JC8)	10.00	4.50
COMMON COLC 2 (JC9-JC12)	3.00	1.35
COMMON UD 2 (JC13-JC16)	10.00	4.50
COMMON SP (JC17-JC20)	12.00	5.50
COMMON SPC (JC21-JC24)	12.00	5.50
SER.1/2 COLC STATED ODDS 1:11 HOB/RET		
SER.1/2 UD STATED ODDS 1:29 HOB/RET		
SP/SPC STATED ODDS 1:29		
FOUR COLC PER COLC FACTORY SET		

		MINT	NRMT
☐ JC5	Michael Jordan Slam Dunk Champion 1987	10.00	4.50
☐ JC6	Michael Jordan Slam Dunk Champion 1988	10.00	4.50
☐ JC7	Michael Jordan	10.00	4.50

Rising To The Occasion		4.50
☐ JO8 Michael Jordan 10.00		
Walking On Air		

1995-96 Upper Deck Predictor MVP

Randomly inserted exclusively into second series retail packs at a rate of one in 30, this 10-card standard-size set features five Michael Jordan cards, four top NBA stars and a Long Shot card (representing all other NBA players). In addition, Upper Deck offered dealers a 5-card Predictor pack with the purchase of one case (20 boxes) of second series product. Dealers were given all 20 second series Predictor cards (retail MVP and hobby Scoring) with the purchase of two cases. Black and red basketball court fronts frame a full-color action player cutout. A black border surrounds the player's name, team and the month of the predicted award, all of which are stamped in gold foil. The outer border of the front is a black marble texture. Numbered backs are printed on white, have the prefix "R" and explain the rules of the game. Those holding a winning Predictor cards redeemed the cards through a mail-in offer for a full set of the Predictor MVP cards. The expiration date to redeem winning cards was July 8, 1996.

	MINT	NRMT
COMPLETE SET (10)	50.00	22.00
COMMON CARD (R1-R10)......	.75	.35
SER.2 STATED ODDS 1:30 RETAIL		
COMP.MVP RED.SET (10) ..	15.00	6.75
*MVP RED.CARDS: 50% OF HI COLUMN		
ONE RED.SET PER 'W' CARD BY MAIL		

☐ R1 Michael Jordan	8.00	3.60
MVP W		
☐ R2 Michael Jordan	8.00	3.60
All-NBA W		
☐ R3 Michael Jordan	8.00	3.60
Defensive POY L		
☐ R4 Michael Jordan	8.00	3.60
All-Defensive W		
☐ R5 Michael Jordan	8.00	3.60
Finals MVP W		
☐ R6 Hakeem Olajuwon L ..	2.50	1.10
☐ R7 Charles Barkley L	2.00	.90
☐ R8 Karl Malone L	2.00	.90
☐ R9 A.Hardaway L	5.00	2.20
☐ R10 Long Shot Card L	.75	.35

1995-96 Upper Deck Predictor Player of the Month

Randomly inserted exclusively into first series retail packs at a rate of one in 30, this 10-card standard-size set features five Michael Jordan cards, four top NBA stars and a Long Shot card (representing all other NBA players). In addition, Upper Deck offered dealers a 5-card Predictor pack with the purchase of one case (20 boxes) of first series product. Dealers were given all 20 first series Predictor cards (retail Player of the Month and hobby Player of the Week) with the purchase of two cases. Each card lists months that the featured player might win Player of the Month honors. Black and red basketball court fronts frame a full-color action player cutout. A black border surrounds the player's name, team and the month of the predicted award, all of which are stamped in gold foil. The outer border of the front is a black marble texture. Numbered backs are printed on white, have the prefix "R" and explain the rules of the game. Those holding a winning Predictor card redeemed the cards through a mail-in offer for a full set of the Predictor Player of the Month

cards. The expiration date to redeem winning cards was July 1, 1996.

	MINT	NRMT
COMPLETE SET (10)	40.00	18.00
COMMON CARD (R1-R10) ..	.75	.35
SEMISTARS	1.25	.55
SER.1 STATED ODDS 1:30 RETAIL		
COMP.POM RED.SET (10) ..	15.00	6.75
*POM RED.CARDS: 50% OF HI COLUMN		
ONE RED.SET PER 'W' CARD BY MAIL		

☐ R1 Michael Jordan	8.00	3.60
Nov./Dec. L		
☐ R2 Michael Jordan	8.00	3.60
Jan. W		
☐ R3 Michael Jordan	8.00	3.60
Feb. L		
☐ R4 Michael Jordan	8.00	3.60
Mar. L		
☐ R5 Michael Jordan	8.00	3.60
Apr. L		
☐ R6 Jamal Mashburn L	1.25	.55
☐ R7 David Robinson W	2.00	.90
☐ R8 Latrell Sprewell L	1.25	.55
☐ R9 Chris Webber L	3.00	1.35
☐ R10 Long Shot Card W	.75	.35

1995-96 Upper Deck Predictor Player of the Week

Randomly inserted exclusively into first series hobby packs at a rate of one in 30, this 10-card standard-sized set features five Michael Jordan cards, four top NBA stars and a Long Shot card (representing all other NBA players). In addition, Upper Deck offered dealers a 5-card Predictor pack with the purchase of one case (20 boxes) of first series product. Dealers were given all 20 first series Predictor cards (retail Player of the Month and hobby Player of the Week) with the purchase of two cases. Each card lists weeks that the featured player might win Player of the Week honors. The fronts feature the player in a full color cutout set against a red court background and a black border surrounding the red. The player's name, team name and predictor category are printed in gold foil. Card edges are trimmed with a black marble texture. Those holding a winning Predictor card redeemed the cards through a mail-in offer for a full set of the Predictor Player of the Week cards. The expiration date to redeem winning cards was July 1, 1996.

	MINT	NRMT
COMPLETE SET (10)	50.00	22.00
COMMON CARD (H1-H10)	.75	.35
SER.1 STATED ODDS 1:30 HOBBY		
COMP.POW RED.SET (10)	15.00	6.75
*POW RED.CARDS: 50% OF HI COLUMN		
ONE RED.SET PER "W" CARD BY MAIL		
□ H1 Michael Jordan Nov./Dec. W	8.00	3.60
□ H2 Michael Jordan Jan. W	8.00	3.60
□ H3 Michael Jordan Feb. L	8.00	3.60
□ H4 Michael Jordan Mar. L	8.00	3.60
□ H5 Michael Jordan Apr. L	8.00	3.60
□ H6 A.Hardaway W	5.00	2.20
□ H7 Hakeem Olajuwon W	2.50	1.10
□ H8 Scottie Pippen W	4.00	1.80
□ H9 Glenn Robinson L	1.50	.70
□ H10 Long Shot Card W	.75	.35

1995-96
Upper Deck
Predictor Scoring

Randomly inserted in second series hobby packs at a rate of one in 30, cards from this 10-card insert set feature five Michael Jordan cards, four top NBA stars and a Long Shot card (representing all other NBA players). In addition, Upper Deck offered dealers a 5-card Predictor pack with the purchase of one case (20 boxes) of second series product. Dealers were given all 20 second series Predictor cards (retail MVP and hobby Scoring) with the pur-

chase of two cases. Card fronts feature the player in a full color cutout set against a red court background and a black border surrounding the red. The player's name, team name and predictor category are printed in gold foil. Card edges are trimmed with a black marble texture. If the player pictured won the NBA scoring title, the card was redeemable for a special version of the hobby Predictor Scoring set. The expiration date to redeem winning cards was July 8, 1996.

	MINT	NRMT
COMPLETE SET (10)	50.00	22.00
COMMON CARD (H1-H10)	.75	.35
SER.2 STATED ODDS 1:30 HOBBY		
COMP.SCORE.RED.SET (10)	15.00	6.75
*SCORE.RED.CARDS: 50% OF HI COLUMN		
ONE RED.SET PER "W" CARD BY MAIL		
□ H1 Michael Jordan Scoring W	8.00	3.60
□ H2 Michael Jordan Assists L	8.00	3.60
□ H3 Michael Jordan Steals L	8.00	3.60
□ H4 Michael Jordan 3-pt. L	8.00	3.60
□ H5 Michael Jordan Playoff W	8.00	3.60
□ H6 David Robinson L	2.00	.90
□ H7 Scottie Pippen L	4.00	1.80
□ H8 Jerry Stackhouse L	2.50	1.10
□ H9 Glenn Robinson L	1.50	.70
□ H10 Long Shot Card L	.75	.35

1995-96
Upper Deck
Special Edition

These 180 standard-size cards were inserted at a rate of one per hobby pack only and were printed on a silver foil front. The cards were issued in two separate series of 90 (1-90 in first series packs and 91-180 in second series packs). Only the top veterans and rookies were selected for inclusion in this set. The player is featured in an action shot but only he is singled out

for color. The rest of the shot is faded out to black and white. The player's name is stamped in silver foil at the bottom and the Special Edition logo is stamped in silver foil at the top right. "SE" is stamped in silver foil and runs vertically down the left side of the front. Backs are printed on a white and gray background and include a player biography, career statistics and player highlights. A color player action shot appears on the upper left side and includes the card number.

	MINT	NRMT
COMPLETE SET (180)	90.00	40.00
COMPLETE SERIES 1 (90)	30.00	13.50
COMPLETE SERIES 2 (90)	60.00	27.00
COMMON CARD (1-180)	.25	.11
SEMISTARS SER.1	.75	.35
SEMISTARS SER.2	.60	.25
UNLISTED STARS SER.1	1.25	.55
UNLISTED STARS SER.2	1.00	.45
ONE PER BOTH SERIES HOBBY PACK		
COMP.GOLD SET (180)	600.00	275.00
COMP.GOLD SER.1 (90)	200.00	90.00
COMP.GOLD SER.2 (90)	400.00	180.00
COMMON GOLD (SE1-SE180)	1.50	.70
*GOLD STARS: 4X TO 8X HI COLUMN		
*GOLD RCs: 2.5X TO 5X HI		
GOLD: SER.1/2 STATED ODDS 1:35 HOBBY		
SE PREFIX ON CARD NUMBERS		
□ 1 Mookie Blaylock	.75	.35
□ 2 Tryone Corbin	.25	.11
□ 3 Grant Long	.25	.11
□ 4 Dee Brown	.25	.11
□ 5 Sherman Douglas	.25	.11
□ 6 Eric Montross	.25	.11
□ 7 Scott Burrell	.25	.11
□ 8 Dell Curry	.25	.11
□ 9 Larry Johnson	.75	.35
□ 10 Will Perdue	.25	.11
□ 11 Scottie Pippen	4.00	1.80
□ 12 Dickey Simpkins	.25	.11
□ 13 Michael Cage	.25	.11
□ 14 Mark Price	.25	.11
□ 15 John Williams	.25	.11
□ 16 Lucious Harris	.25	.11
□ 17 Jim Jackson	.75	.35
□ 18 Popeye Jones	.25	.11
□ 19 Mahmoud Abdul-Rauf	.25	.11
□ 20 LaPhonso Ellis	.75	.35
□ 21 Robert Pack	.25	.11
□ 22 Bill Curley	.25	.11
□ 23 Grant Hill	8.00	3.60
□ 24 Allan Houston	.75	.35
□ 25 Chris Gatling	.25	.11
□ 26 Tim Hardaway	1.50	.70
□ 27 Donyell Marshall	.75	.35
□ 28 Clifford Rozier	.25	.11
□ 29 Mario Elie	.25	.11
□ 30 Robert Horry	.25	.11
□ 31 Hakeem Olajuwon	2.50	1.10
□ 32 Kenny Smith	.25	.11
□ 33 Dale Davis	.25	.11
□ 34 Duane Ferrell	.25	.11
□ 35 Derrick McKey	.25	.11
□ 36 Reggie Miller	1.25	.55
□ 37 Lamond Murray	.25	.11
□ 38 Charles Outlaw	.25	.11
□ 39 Eric Piatkowski	.25	.11
□ 40 Anthony Peeler	.25	.11
□ 41 Sedale Threatt	.25	.11
□ 42 Nick Van Exel	1.25	.55
□ 43 Kevin Gamble	.25	.11
□ 44 Matt Geiger	.25	.11
□ 45 Billy Owens	.25	.11
□ 46 Khalid Reeves	.25	.11

□	#	Name		
□	47	Vin Baker	2.50	1.10
□	48	Lee Mayberry	.25	.11
□	49	Eric Murdock	.25	.11
□	50	Christian Laettner	.75	.35
□	51	Sean Rooks	.25	.11
□	52	Doug West	.25	.11
□	53	P.J. Brown	.25	.11
□	54	Derrick Coleman	.75	.35
□	55	Armon Gilliam	.25	.11
□	56	Hubert Davis	.25	.11
□	57	Charles Oakley	.25	.11
□	58	John Starks	.75	.35
□	59	Monty Williams	.25	.11
□	60	Anfernee Hardaway	5.00	2.20
□	61	Donald Royal	.25	.11
□	62	Dennis Scott	.25	.11
□	63	Jeff Turner	.25	.11
□	64	C.Weatherspoon	.25	.11
□	65	Jeff Malone	.25	.11
□	66	Scott Williams	.25	.11
□	67	A.C. Green	.75	.35
□	68	Kevin Johnson	.75	.35
□	69	Elliot Perry	.25	.11
□	70	Wesley Person	.75	.35
□	71	Harvey Grant	.25	.11
□	72	Aaron McKie	.25	.11
□	73	Rod Strickland	.75	.35
□	74	Buck Williams	.25	.11
□	75	Randy Brown	.25	.11
□	76	Bobby Hurley	.25	.11
□	77	Lionel Simmons	.25	.11
□	78	Terry Cummings	.25	.11
□	79	Vinny Del Negro	.25	.11
□	80	Avery Johnson	.25	.11
□	81	David Robinson	2.00	.90
□	82	Vincent Askew	.25	.11
□	83	Shawn Kemp	4.00	1.80
□	84	Nate McMillan	.25	.11
□	85	David Benoit	.25	.11
□	86	Jeff Hornacek	.75	.35
□	87	John Stockton	1.25	.55
□	88	Juwan Howard	2.00	.90
□	89	Gheorghe Muresan	.25	.11
□	90	Doug Overton	.25	.11
□	91	Stacey Augmon	.25	.11
□	92	Alan Henderson	1.00	.45
□	93	Steve Smith	.60	.25
□	94	Rick Fox	.25	.11
□	95	Dino Radja	.25	.11
□	96	Eric Williams	.60	.25
□	97	Muggsy Bogues	.60	.25
□	98	Kendall Gill	.25	.11
□	99	Glen Rice	1.00	.45
□	100	Michael Jordan	12.00	5.50
□	101	Toni Kukoc	.60	.25
□	102	Dennis Rodman	6.00	2.70
□	103	Terrell Brandon	.75	.45
□	104	Tyrone Hill	.25	.11
□	105	Dan Majerle	.25	.11
□	106	Jason Kidd	2.50	1.10
□	107	Jamal Mashburn	.60	.25
□	108	Cherokee Parks	.25	.11
□	109	Antonio McDyess	4.00	1.80
□	110	D.Mutombo	.60	.25
□	111	Reggie Williams	.25	.11
□	112	Joe Dumars	1.00	.45
□	113	Lindsey Hunter	.25	.11
□	114	Otis Thorpe	.60	.25
□	115	Chris Mullin	1.00	.45
□	116	Joe Smith	3.00	1.35
□	117	Latrell Sprewell	.60	.25
□	118	Chucky Brown	.25	.11
□	119	Sam Cassell	.60	.25
□	120	Clyde Drexler	1.25	.55
□	121	Travis Best	.25	.11
□	122	Mark Jackson	.60	.25
□	123	Rik Smits	.60	.25
□	124	Brent Barry	1.00	.45
□	125	Rodney Rogers	.25	.11
□	126	Loy Vaught	.25	.11
□	127	Cedric Ceballos	.25	.11
□	128	Magic Johnson	3.00	1.35
□	129	Eddie Jones	2.50	1.10
□	130	Alonzo Mourning	1.00	.45
□	131	Kurt Thomas	.60	.25
□	132	Kevin Willis	.25	.11
□	133	Sherman Douglas	.25	.11
□	134	Shawn Respert	.25	.11
□	135	Glenn Robinson	1.25	.55
□	136	Kevin Garnett	10.00	4.50
□	137	Tom Gugliotta	1.00	.45
□	138	Isaiah Rider	.60	.25
□	139	Kenny Anderson	.60	.25
□	140	Ed O'Bannon	.25	.11
□	141	Jayson Williams	.60	.25
□	142	Patrick Ewing	1.00	.45
□	143	Derek Harper	.60	.25
□	144	Charles Smith	.25	.11
□	145	Nick Anderson	.25	.11
□	146	Horace Grant	.60	.25
□	147	Shaquille O'Neal	4.00	1.80
□	148	Vernon Maxwell	.25	.11
□	149	Jerry Stackhouse	3.00	1.35
□	150	Sharone Wright	.25	.11
□	151	Charles Barkley	1.50	.70
□	152	Michael Finley	3.00	1.35
□	153	Danny Manning	.60	.25
□	154	John Williams	.25	.11
□	155	Clifford Robinson	.25	.11
□	156	Arvydas Sabonis	1.50	.70
□	157	Gary Trent	.25	.11
□	158	Brian Grant	.60	.25
□	159	Mitch Richmond	1.00	.45
□	160	Corliss Williamson	.25	.11
□	161	Sean Elliott	.25	.11
□	162	Will Perdue	.25	.11
□	163	Doc Rivers	.60	.25
□	164	Gary Payton	1.50	.70
□	165	Sam Perkins	.60	.25
□	166	Detlef Schrempf	.60	.25
□	167	Tracy Murray	.25	.11
□	168	Ed Pinckney	.25	.11
□	169	Carlos Rogers	.25	.11
□	170	D.Stoudamire	6.00	2.70
□	171	Karl Malone	1.50	.70
□	172	Chris Morris	.25	.11
□	173	Greg Ostertag	.25	.11
□	174	Greg Anthony	.25	.11
□	175	Lawrence Moten	.25	.11
□	176	Bryant Reeves	2.00	.90
□	177	Byron Scott	.25	.11
□	178	Calbert Cheaney	.25	.11
□	179	Rasheed Wallace	2.00	.90
□	180	Chris Webber	2.50	1.10

1996-97 Upper Deck

This 360-card Upper Deck set was distributed in two series with packs of 12 cards each at the suggested retail price of $2.49. The fronts feature color action player photos with the date stamped in foil indicating the actual game of the photo featured on each card. The backs carry player information. Rookies from both series include Kobe Bryant, Marcus Camby, Allen Iverson, Stephon Marbury, Shareef Abdur-Rahim and Antoine Walker, among others. Randomly inserted in packs at the rate of one in three were "Meet the Stars" trivia game cards which gave the collector a chance to answer questions for prizes including a chance to meet a star player. Inserted one in 56 packs were instant win cards which entitled the holder to prizes without answering questions. One in seven series one packs contained "NBA Pick Up Game" cards which featured stickers representing players' jersey numbers in which the collector affixed to a "3-in-a-Row" game board and sent in for a chance to win a trip to All-Star Weekend. Series two packs also contained autographs of the following players: Anfernee Hardaway, Shawn Kemp, Antonio McDyess and Damon Stoudamire. Each of these cards were hand numbered and limited to 500. The backs of these cards contained a congratulatory message from Brian Burr.

		MINT	NRMT
COMPLETE SET (360)		45.00	20.00
COMPLETE SERIES 1 (180)		25.00	11.00
COMPLETE SERIES 2 (180)		20.00	9.00
COMMON CARD (1-360)		.15	.07
SEMISTARS		.20	.09
UNLISTED STARS		.40	.18
AUTOGRAPHS NUMBERED TO 500			
AU: RANDOM INSERTS IN SER.2 PACKS			

□	#	Name		
□	1	Mookie Blaylock	.20	.09
□	2	Alan Henderson	.15	.07
□	3	Christian Laettner	.20	.09
□	4	Ken Norman	.15	.07
□	5	Dee Brown	.15	.07
□	6	Todd Day	.15	.07
□	7	Rick Fox	.15	.07
□	8	Dino Radja	.15	.07
□	9	Dana Barros	.15	.07
□	10	Eric Williams	.15	.07
□	11	Scott Burrell	.15	.07
□	12	Dell Curry	.15	.07
□	13	Matt Geiger	.15	.07
□	14	Glen Rice	.40	.18
□	15	Ron Harper	.20	.09
□	16	Michael Jordan	5.00	2.20
□	17	Luc Longley	.20	.09
□	18	Toni Kukoc	.20	.09
□	19	Dennis Rodman	1.50	.70
□	20	Danny Ferry	.15	.07
□	21	Tyrone Hill	.15	.07
□	22	Bobby Phills	.15	.07
□	23	Bob Sura	.15	.07
□	24	Tony Dumas	.15	.07
□	25	George McCloud	.15	.07
□	26	Jim Jackson	.20	.09
□	27	Jamal Mashburn	.20	.09
□	28	Loren Meyer	.15	.07
□	29	Dale Ellis	.15	.07
□	30	LaPhonso Ellis	.15	.07
□	31	Tom Hammonds	.15	.07
□	32	Antonio McDyess	.60	.25
□	33	Joe Dumars	.40	.18

□ 34	Grant Hill	2.50	1.10
□ 35	Lindsey Hunter	.15	.07
□ 36	Terry Mills	.15	.07
□ 37	Theo Ratliff	.15	.07
□ 38	B.J. Armstrong	.15	.07
□ 39	Donyell Marshall	.15	.07
□ 40	Chris Mullin	.40	.18
□ 41	Rony Seikaly	.15	.07
□ 42	Joe Smith	.50	.23
□ 43	Sam Cassell	.20	.09
□ 44	Clyde Drexler	.50	.23
□ 45	Mario Elie	.15	.07
□ 46	Robert Horry	.20	.09
□ 47	Travis Best	.15	.07
□ 48	Antonio Davis	.15	.07
□ 49	Dale Davis	.15	.07
□ 50	Eddie Johnson	.15	.07
□ 51	Derrick McKey	.15	.07
□ 52	Reggie Miller	.40	.18
□ 53	Brent Barry	.15	.07
□ 54	Lamond Murray	.15	.07
□ 55	Eric Piatkowski	.15	.07
□ 56	Rodney Rogers	.15	.07
□ 57	Loy Vaught	.20	.09
□ 58	Kobe Bryant	8.00	3.60
□ 59	Eddie Jones	.75	.35
□ 60	Elden Campbell	.20	.09
□ 61	Shaquille O'Neal	1.50	.70
□ 62	Nick Van Exel	.40	.18
□ 63	Keith Askins	.15	.07
□ 64	Rex Chapman	.15	.07
□ 65	Sasha Danilovic	.15	.07
□ 66	Alonzo Mourning	.40	.18
□ 67	Kurt Thomas	.15	.07
□ 68	Tim Hardaway	.50	.23
□ 69	Ray Allen	1.25	.55
□ 70	Johnny Newman	.15	.07
□ 71	Shawn Respert	.15	.07
□ 72	Glenn Robinson	.40	.18
□ 73	Tom Gugliotta	.40	.18
□ 74	Stephon Marbury	4.00	1.80
□ 75	Terry Porter	.15	.07
□ 76	Doug West	.15	.07
□ 77	Shawn Bradley	.15	.07
□ 78	Kevin Edwards	.15	.07
□ 79	Vern Fleming	.15	.07
□ 80	Ed O'Bannon	.15	.07
□ 81	Jayson Williams	.20	.09
□ 82	John Starks	.20	.09
□ 83	Patrick Ewing	.40	.18
□ 84	Charlie Ward	.15	.07
□ 85	Nick Anderson	.15	.07
□ 86	Anfernee Hardaway	1.50	.70
□ 87	Jon Koncak	.15	.07
□ 88	Donald Royal	.15	.07
□ 89	Brian Shaw	.15	.07
□ 90	Derrick Coleman	.20	.09
□ 91	Allen Iverson	4.00	1.80
□ 92	Jerry Stackhouse	.50	.23
□ 93	C.Weatherspoon	.15	.07
□ 94	Charles Barkley	.60	.25
□ 95	Kevin Johnson	.20	.09
□ 96	Danny Manning	.20	.09
□ 97	Elliot Perry	.15	.07
□ 98	Wayman Tisdale	.15	.07
□ 99	Randolph Childress	.15	.07
□ 100	Aaron McKie	.15	.07
□ 101	Arvydas Sabonis	.20	.09
□ 102	Gary Trent	.15	.07
□ 103	Chris Dudley	.15	.07
□ 104	Tyus Edney	.15	.07
□ 105	Brian Grant	.15	.07
□ 106	Bobby Hurley	.15	.07
□ 107	Olden Polynice	.15	.07
□ 108	Corliss Williamson	.20	.09
□ 109	Vinny Del Negro	.15	.07
□ 110	Avery Johnson	.15	.07
□ 111	Will Perdue	.15	.07
□ 112	David Robinson	.60	.25
□ 113	Hersey Hawkins	.20	.09
□ 114	Shawn Kemp	1.25	.55
□ 115	Nate McMillan	.15	.07
□ 116	Detlef Schrempf	.20	.09
□ 117	Gary Payton	.60	.25
□ 118	Marcus Camby	1.00	.45
□ 119	Zan Tabak	.15	.07

□ 120	Damon Stoudamire ..	1.00	.45
□ 121	Carlos Rogers	.15	.07
□ 122	Sharone Wright	.15	.07
□ 123	Antoine Carr	.15	.07
□ 124	Jeff Hornacek	.20	.09
□ 125	Adam Keefe	.15	.07
□ 126	Chris Morris	.15	.07
□ 127	John Stockton	.40	.18
□ 128	Blue Edwards	.15	.07
□ 129	S.Abdur-Rahim	2.50	1.10
□ 130	Bryant Reeves	.20	.09
□ 131	Roy Rogers	.15	.07
□ 132	Calbert Cheaney	.15	.07
□ 133	Tim Legler	.15	.07
□ 134	Gheorghe Muresan	.15	.07
□ 135	Chris Webber	1.00	.45
□ 136	D.Mutombo	.40	.18

Mookie Blaylock
Steve Smith
Christian Laettner
Alan Henderson
BW - Atlanta Hawks

□ 137	Dana Barros	.15	.07

Dino Radja
Eric Williams
Dee Brown
Pervis Ellison
BW - Boston Celtics

□ 138	Glen Rice	.40	.18

Matt Geiger
Vlade Divac
Scott Burrell
George Zidek
BW - Charlotte Hornets

□ 139	Michael Jordan	2.00	.90

Scottie Pippen
Dennis Rodman
Toni Kukoc
Ron Harper
BW - Chicago Bulls

□ 140	Terrell Brandon	.20	.09

Danny Ferry
Tyrone Hill
Bobby Phills
Bobby Sura
BW - Cleveland Cavaliers

□ 141	Jason Kidd	.20	.09

Jamal Mashburn
Jim Jackson
Tony Dumas
Loren Meyer
BW - Dallas Mavericks

□ 142	LaPhonso Ellis	.15	.07

Antonio McDyess
Mark Jackson
Dale Ellis
Bryant Stith
BW - Denver Nuggets

□ 143	Joe Dumars	.75	.35

Grant Hill
Stacey Augmon
Lindsey Hunter
Theo Ratliff
BW - Detroit Pistons

□ 144	Joe Smith	.40	.18

Latrell Sprewell
Chris Mullin
Rony Seikaly
BJ Armstrong
BW - Golden State Warriors

□ 145	Hakeem Olajuwon	.40	.18

Clyde Drexler
Charles Barkley
Brent Price
Mario Elie
BW - Houston Rockets

□ 146	Reggie Miller	.20	.09

Travis Best
Rik Smits
Dale Davis
Antonio Davis
BW - Indiana Pacers

□ 147	Brent Barry	.15	.07

Lamond Murray
Rodney Rogers
Terry Dehere

Eric Piatkowski
BW - Los Angeles Clippers

□ 148	Shaquille O'Neal	2.00	.90

Eddie Jones
Kobe Bryant
Cedric Ceballos
Nick Van Exel
BW - Los Angeles Lakers

□ 149	Alonzo Mourning	.40	.18

Tim Hardaway
Sasha Danilovic
Kurt Thomas
Keith Askins
BW - Miami Heat

□ 150	Vin Baker	.40	.18

Glenn Robinson
Sherman Douglas
Shawn Respert
Johnnie Newman
BW - Milwaukee Bucks

□ 151	Kevin Garnett	1.00	.45

Tom Gugliotta
Cherokee Parks
Terry Porter
Doug West
BW - Minnesota Timberwolves

□ 152	Shawn Bradley	.20	.09

Kendall Gill
Ed O'Bannon
Jayson Williams
Robert Pack
BW - New Jersey Nets

□ 153	Patrick Ewing	.40	.18

Allan Houston
Larry Johnson
Charles Oakley
John Starks
BW - New York Knicks

□ 154	Anfernee Hardaway	.60	.25

Dennis Scott
Horace Grant
Nick Anderson
Brian Shaw
BW - Orlando Magic

□ 155	Jerry Stackhouse	.20	.09

C.Weatherspoon
Derrick Coleman
Scott Williams
Rex Walters
BW - Philadelphia 76'ers

□ 156	Kevin Johnson	.15	.07

Danny Manning
Michael Finley
Wesley Person
AC Green
BW - Phoenix Suns

□ 157	Clifford Robinson	.20	.09

Isaiah Rider
Arvydas Sabonis
Rasheed Wallace
Kenny Anderson
BW - Portland Trail Blazers

□ 158	Mitch Richmond	.20	.09

Brian Grant
Billy Owens
Tyus Edney
Michael Smith
BW - Sacramento Kings

□ 159	David Robinson	.40	.18

Sean Elliott
Avery Johnson
Vinny Del Negro
Chuck Person
BW - San Antonio Spurs

□ 160	Shawn Kemp	.50	.23

Gary Payton
Detlef Schrempf
Hersey Hawkins
Sam Perkins
BW - Seattle Supersonics

□ 161	Damon Stoudamire	.40	.18

Zan Tabak
Sharone Wright
Doug Christie
Carlos Rogers
BW - Toronto Raptors

☐ 162	John Stockton	.40	.18
	Karl Malone		
	Jeff Hornacek		
	Bryon Russell		
	Antoine Carr		
	BW - Utah Jazz		
☐ 163	Bryant Reeves	.60	.25
	Shareef Abdur-Rahim		
	Greg Anthony		
	Blue Edwards		
	Lawrence Moten		
	BW - Vancouver Grizzlies		
☐ 164	Juwan Howard	.50	.23
	Gheorge Muresan		
	Chris Webber		
	Calbert Cheaney		
	Tim Legler		
	BW - Washington Bullets		
☐ 165	Michael Jordan GP	2.50	1.10
☐ 166	Corliss Williamson GP	.15	.07
☐ 167	Dell Curry GP	.15	.07
☐ 168	John Starks GP	.15	.07
☐ 169	Dennis Rodman GP	.75	.35
☐ 170	Chris Webber	.40	.18
	Latrell Sprewell		
☐ 171	Cedric Ceballos GP	.15	.07
☐ 172	Theo Ratliff GP	.15	.07
☐ 173	A.Hardaway GP	.75	.35
☐ 174	Grant Hill GP	1.25	.55
☐ 175	Alonzo Mourning GP	.20	.09
☐ 176	Shawn Kemp GP	.60	.25
☐ 177	Jason Kidd GP	.40	.18
☐ 178	Avery Johnson GP	.15	.07
☐ 179	Gary Payton GP	.40	.18
☐ 180	Checklist	.15	.07
☐ 181	Priest Lauderdale	.15	.07
☐ 182	D.Mutombo	.20	.09
☐ 183	Eldridge Recasner	.15	.07
☐ 184	Steve Smith	.20	.09
☐ 185	Pervis Ellison	.15	.07
☐ 186	Greg Minor	.15	.07
☐ 187	Antoine Walker	4.00	1.80
☐ 188	David Wesley	.15	.07
☐ 189	Muggsy Bogues	.15	.07
☐ 190	Tony Delk	.50	.23
☐ 191	Vlade Divac	.20	.09
☐ 192	Anthony Mason	.20	.09
☐ 193	George Zidek	.15	.07
☐ 194	Jason Caffey	.15	.07
☐ 195	Steve Kerr	.15	.07
☐ 196	Robert Parish	.20	.09
☐ 197	Scottie Pippen	1.25	.55
☐ 198	Terrell Brandon	.40	.18
☐ 199	Antonio Lang	.15	.07
☐ 200	Chris Mills	.15	.07
☐ 201	Vitaly Potapenko	.20	.09
☐ 202	Mark West	.15	.07
☐ 203	Chris Gatling	.15	.07
☐ 204	Derek Harper	.15	.07
☐ 205	Sam Cassell	.20	.09
☐ 206	Eric Montross	.15	.07
☐ 207	Samaki Walker	.50	.23
☐ 208	Mark Jackson	.15	.07
☐ 209	Ervin Johnson	.15	.07
☐ 210	Sarunas Marciulionis	.15	.07
☐ 211	Ricky Pierce	.15	.07
☐ 212	Bryant Stith	.15	.07
☐ 213	Stacey Augmon	.15	.07
☐ 214	Grant Long	.15	.07
☐ 215	Rick Mahorn	.15	.07
☐ 216	Otis Thorpe	.20	.09
☐ 217	Jerome Williams	.20	.09
☐ 218	Bimbo Coles	.15	.07
☐ 219	Todd Fuller	.15	.07
☐ 220	Mark Price	.15	.07
☐ 221	Felton Spencer	.15	.07
☐ 222	Latrell Sprewell	.20	.09
☐ 223	Charles Barkley	.60	.25
☐ 224	Othella Harrington	.20	.09
☐ 225	Hakeem Olajuwon	.75	.35
☐ 226	Matt Maloney	.60	.25
☐ 227	Kevin Willis	.15	.07
☐ 228	Erick Dampier	.50	.23
☐ 229	Duane Ferrell	.15	.07
☐ 230	Jalen Rose	.15	.07
☐ 231	Rik Smits	.20	.09

☐ 232	Terry Dehere	.15	.07
☐ 233	Charles Outlaw	.15	.07
☐ 234	Pooh Richardson	.15	.07
☐ 235	Malik Sealy	.15	.07
☐ 236	Lorenzen Wright	.50	.23
☐ 237	Cedric Ceballos	.15	.07
☐ 238	Derek Fisher	.50	.23
☐ 239	Travis Knight	.20	.09
☐ 240	Sean Rooks	.15	.07
☐ 241	Byron Scott	.20	.09
☐ 242	P.J. Brown	.15	.07
☐ 243	Voshon Lenard	.20	.09
☐ 244	Dan Majerle	.20	.09
☐ 245	Martin Muursepp	.15	.07
☐ 246	Gary Grant	.15	.07
☐ 247	Vin Baker	.75	.35
☐ 248	Armon Gilliam	.15	.07
☐ 249	Andrew Lang	.15	.07
☐ 250	Elliot Perry	.15	.07
☐ 251	Kevin Garnett	2.50	1.10
☐ 252	Shane Heal	.15	.07
☐ 253	Cherokee Parks	.15	.07
☐ 254	Stojko Vrankovic	.15	.07
☐ 255	Kendall Gill	.20	.09
☐ 256	Kerry Kittles	1.00	.45
☐ 257	Xavier McDaniel	.15	.07
☐ 258	Robert Pack	.15	.07
☐ 259	Chris Childs	.15	.07
☐ 260	Allan Houston	.20	.09
☐ 261	Larry Johnson	.20	.09
☐ 262	Dontae' Jones	.15	.07
☐ 263	Walter McCarty	.20	.09
☐ 264	Charles Oakley	.15	.07
☐ 265	John Wallace	.60	.25
☐ 266	Buck Williams	.15	.07
☐ 267	Brian Evans	.15	.07
☐ 268	Horace Grant	.20	.09
☐ 269	Dennis Scott	.15	.07
☐ 270	Rony Seikaly	.15	.07
☐ 271	David Vaughn	.15	.07
☐ 272	Michael Cage	.15	.07
☐ 273	Lucious Harris	.15	.07
☐ 274	Don MacLean	.15	.07
☐ 275	Mark Davis	.15	.07
☐ 276	Jason Kidd	.75	.35
☐ 277	Michael Finley	.50	.23
☐ 278	A.C. Green	.20	.09
☐ 279	Robert Horry	.20	.09
☐ 280	Steve Nash	.60	.25
☐ 281	Wesley Person	.15	.07
☐ 282	Kenny Anderson	.20	.09
☐ 283	Aleksandar Djordjevic	.15	.07
☐ 284	Jermaine O'Neal	.60	.25
☐ 285	Isaiah Rider	.20	.09
☐ 286	Clifford Robinson	.15	.07
☐ 287	Rasheed Wallace	.20	.09
☐ 288	Mahmoud Abdul-Rauf	.15	.07
☐ 289	Billy Owens	.15	.07
☐ 290	Mitch Richmond	.40	.18
☐ 291	Michael Smith	.15	.07
☐ 292	Cory Alexander	.15	.07
☐ 293	Sean Elliott	.20	.09
☐ 294	Vernon Maxwell	.15	.07
☐ 295	Dominique Wilkins	.40	.18
☐ 296	Craig Ehlo	.15	.07
☐ 297	Jim McIlvaine	.15	.07
☐ 298	Sam Perkins	.20	.09
☐ 299	Steve Scheffler	.15	.07
☐ 300	Hubert Davis	.15	.07
☐ 301	Popeye Jones	.15	.07
☐ 302	Donald Whiteside	.15	.07
☐ 303	Walt Williams	.15	.07
☐ 304	Karl Malone	.60	.25
☐ 305	Greg Ostertag	.15	.07
☐ 306	Bryon Russell	.15	.07
☐ 307	Jamie Watson	.15	.07
☐ 308	Greg Anthony	.15	.07
☐ 309	George Lynch	.15	.07
☐ 310	Lawrence Moten	.15	.07
☐ 311	Anthony Peeler	.15	.07
☐ 312	Juwan Howard	.50	.23
☐ 313	Tracy Murray	.15	.07
☐ 314	Rod Strickland	.20	.09
☐ 315	Harvey Grant	.15	.07
☐ 316	Charles Barkley DN	.40	.18
☐ 317	Clyde Drexler DN	.40	.18

☐ 318	D.Mutombo DN	.15	.07
☐ 319	Larry Johnson DN	.15	.07
☐ 320	Shaquille O'Neal DN	.75	.35
☐ 321	Mookie Blaylock DN	.15	.07
☐ 322	Tim Hardaway DN	.40	.18
☐ 323	Dennis Rodman DN	.75	.35
☐ 324	Dan Majerle DN	.15	.07
☐ 325	Stacey Augmon DN	.15	.07
☐ 326	Anthony Mason DN	.15	.07
☐ 327	Kenny Anderson DN	.20	.09
☐ 328	M.Abdul-Rauf DN	.15	.07
☐ 329	Chris Webber DN	.50	.23
☐ 330	Dominique Wilkins DN	.15	.07
☐ 331	D.Mutombo WD	.15	.07
☐ 332	Dana Barros WD	.15	.07
☐ 333	Glen Rice WD	.20	.09
☐ 334	Dennis Rodman WD	.75	.35
☐ 335	Terrell Brandon WD	.20	.09
☐ 336	Jason Kidd WD	.40	.18
☐ 337	Antonio McDyess WD	.40	.18
☐ 338	Grant Hill WD	1.25	.55
☐ 339	Joe Smith WD	.40	.18
☐ 340	Charles Barkley WD	.20	.09
☐ 341	Reggie Miller WD	.20	.09
☐ 342	Brent Barry WD	.15	.07
☐ 343	Shaquille O'Neal WD	.75	.35
☐ 344	Alonzo Mourning WD	.20	.09
☐ 345	Glenn Robinson WD	.20	.09
☐ 346	S.Marbury WD	2.00	.90
☐ 347	Kerry Kittles WD	.50	.23
☐ 348	Patrick Ewing WD	.20	.09
☐ 349	A.Hardaway WD	.75	.35
☐ 350	Allen Iverson WD	2.00	.90
☐ 351	Danny Manning WD	.15	.07
☐ 352	Arvydas Sabonis WD	.15	.07
☐ 353	Mitch Richmond WD	.20	.09
☐ 354	David Robinson WD	.40	.18
☐ 355	Shawn Kemp WD	.60	.25
☐ 356	Marcus Camby WD	.50	.23
☐ 357	Karl Malone WD	.40	.18
☐ 358	S.Abdur-Rahim WD	1.25	.55
☐ 359	G.Muresan WD	.15	.07
☐ 360	Checklist	.15	.07
	181-360		
☐ A1	A.Hardaway	250.00	110.00
	Certified Autograph		
☐ A2	Shawn Kemp	175.00	80.00
	Certified Autograph		
☐ A3	Antonio McDyess	125.00	55.00
	Certified Autograph		
☐ A4	D.Stoudamire	125.00	55.00
	Certified Autograph		

1996-97 Upper Deck Fast Break Connections

Randomly inserted in series one packs at a rate of one in eight, this set features color photos of 30 players. Each card features three different players from the same team on special die-cut designs that are combined into one over-sized card. Each card is numbered with a "FB" prefix.

	MINT	NRMT
COMPLETE SET (30)	80.00	36.00
COMMON CARD (FB1-FB30)	1.00	.45
SEMISTARS	1.50	.70
UNLISTED STARS	2.50	1.10
SER.1 STATED ODDS 1:8		
☐ FB1 Jim Jackson	1.50	.70
☐ FB2 Jason Kidd	5.00	2.20
☐ FB3 Jamal Mashburn	1.50	.70
☐ FB4 Mario Elie	1.00	.45
☐ FB5 Hakeem Olajuwon	5.00	2.20
☐ FB6 Clyde Drexler	3.00	1.35
☐ FB7 Cedric Ceballos	1.00	.45
☐ FB8 Nick Van Exel	2.50	1.10
☐ FB9 Eddie Jones	5.00	2.20
☐ FB10 Danny Manning	1.50	.70
☐ FB11 Michael Finley	3.00	1.35
☐ FB12 Kevin Johnson	1.50	.70
☐ FB13 Tyus Edney	1.00	.45
☐ FB14 Brian Grant	1.00	.45
☐ FB15 Mitch Richmond	2.50	1.10
☐ FB16 Sean Elliott	1.00	.45
☐ FB17 David Robinson	4.00	1.80
☐ FB18 Avery Johnson	1.00	.45
☐ FB19 Shawn Kemp	8.00	3.60
☐ FB20 Gary Payton	4.00	1.80
☐ FB21 Detlef Schrempf	1.50	.70
☐ FB22 Scottie Pippen	8.00	3.60
☐ FB23 Michael Jordan	30.00	13.50
☐ FB24 Toni Kukoc	1.50	.70
☐ FB25 Sherman Douglas	1.00	.45
☐ FB26 Glenn Robinson	2.50	1.10
☐ FB27 Vin Baker	5.00	2.20
☐ FB28 Jeff Hornacek	1.50	.70
☐ FB29 John Stockton	2.50	1.10
☐ FB30 Karl Malone	4.00	1.80

1996-97 Upper Deck Generation Excitement

Randomly inserted in series one packs at a rate of one in 33, this 30-card set features some of the biggest young stars of the 1990's who willl take the game into the next century. The fronts display color action player images on a background with a head photo of the player on a unique die cut card. Each card is numbered with a "G" prefix.

	MINT	NRMT
COMPLETE SET (20)	150.00	70.00
COMMON CARD (G1-G20)	2.50	1.10
SEMISTARS	5.00	2.20
SER.1 STATED ODDS 1:33		
☐ G1 Steve Smith	5.00	2.20
☐ G2 Eric Williams	2.50	1.10
☐ G3 Jason Kidd	10.00	4.50
☐ G4 Antonio McDyess	8.00	3.60
☐ G5 Grant Hill	30.00	13.50
☐ G6 Joe Smith	6.00	2.70
☐ G7 Brent Barry	2.50	1.10
☐ G8 Eddie Jones	10.00	4.50
☐ G9 Vin Baker	10.00	4.50
☐ G10 Kevin Garnett	30.00	13.50
☐ G11 Ed O'Bannon	2.50	1.10
☐ G12 A.Hardaway	20.00	9.00
☐ G13 Jerry Stackhouse	6.00	2.70
☐ G14 Michael Finley	6.00	2.70
☐ G15 Gary Trent	2.50	1.10
☐ G16 Tyus Edney	2.50	1.10
☐ G17 Sean Elliott	2.50	1.10
☐ G18 Shawn Kemp	15.00	6.75
☐ G19 D.Stoudamire	12.00	5.50
☐ G20 Gheorghe Muresan	2.50	1.10

1996-97 Upper Deck Jordan Greater Heights

Randomly inserted in series one packs at a rate of one in 71, this 10-card set features highlights of Michael Jordan's many trips to the basket. Each card focuses on an area of the game including shooting, dunking, rebounding and defense. Each card is numbered with a "GH" prefix.

	MINT	NRMT
COMPLETE SET (10)	200.00	90.00
COMM JORDAN (GH1-GH10)	25.00	11.00
SER.1 STATED ODDS 1:66 HOB/RET		
☐ GH1 Michael Jordan	25.00	11.00
Dunking		
☐ GH2 Michael Jordan	25.00	11.00
Shooting		
☐ GH3 Michael Jordan	25.00	11.00
Rebounding		
☐ GH4 Michael Jordan	25.00	11.00
Defending		
☐ GH5 Michael Jordan	25.00	11.00
Breakaways		
☐ GH6 Michael Jordan	25.00	11.00
Put backs		
☐ GH7 Michael Jordan	25.00	11.00
Passing		

	MINT	NRMT
☐ GH8 Michael Jordan	25.00	11.00
Mid-air magic		
☐ GH9 Michael Jordan	25.00	11.00
Excitement		
☐ GH10 Michael Jordan	25.00	11.00
The Future		

1996-97 Upper Deck Jordan's Viewpoints

Randomly inserted in series two packs at a rate of one in 34, this 10-card die cut set focuses on Michael Jordan's preparation for a full game. Some of the card themes include practice, talking to the media and winning. Each card is numbered with a "VP" prefix.

	MINT	NRMT
COMPLETE SET (10)	125.00	55.00
COMM JORDAN (VP1-VP10)	15.00	6.75
SER.2 STATED ODDS 1:34 HOB/RET		
☐ VP1 Michael Jordan	15.00	6.75
MJ on practice		
☐ VP2 Michael Jordan	15.00	6.75
MJ on entering the arena		
☐ VP3 Michael Jordan	15.00	6.75
MJ on shooting		
☐ VP4 Michael Jordan	15.00	6.75
MJ on pressure		
☐ VP5 Michael Jordan	15.00	6.75
MJ on free throws		
☐ VP6 Michael Jordan	15.00	6.75
MJ on halftime		
☐ VP7 Michael Jordan	15.00	6.75
MJ on shooting three-pointers		
☐ VP8 Michael Jordan	15.00	6.75
MJ on playing defense		
☐ VP9 Michael Jordan	15.00	6.75
MJ on talking to the media		
☐ VP10 Michael Jordan	15.00	6.75
MJ on winning		

1996-97 Upper Deck Predictor Scoring 1

Randomly inserted in series one packs at a rate of one in 23, this 30-card set featured interactive cards based on the above-average game output of 30 players

	MINT	NRMT
COMPLETE SET (20)	50.00	22.00
COMMON CARD (R1-R20)	.60	.25
SEMISTARS	1.25	.55
UNLISTED STARS	2.00	.90
SER.2 STATED ODDS 1:4 HOB/RET, 1:2 JUM		

		MINT	NRMT
☐ R1	Allen Iverson	10.00	4.50
☐ R2	John Wallace	2.00	.90
☐ R3	Kerry Kittles	2.50	1.10
☐ R4	Roy Rogers	.60	.25
☐ R5	Marcus Camby	2.50	1.10
☐ R6	Antoine Walker	10.00	4.50
☐ R7	Ray Allen	3.00	1.35
☐ R8	Samaki Walker	2.00	.90
☐ R9	Walter McCarty	1.25	.55
☐ R10	Kobe Bryant	20.00	9.00
☐ R11	S.Abdur-Rahim	6.00	2.70
☐ R12	Dontae' Jones	.60	.25
☐ R13	Todd Fuller	.60	.25
☐ R14	Lorenzen Wright	2.00	.90
☐ R15	Stephon Marbury	10.00	4.50
☐ R16	Vitaly Potapenko	1.25	.55
☐ R17	Tony Delk	2.00	.90
☐ R18	Steve Nash	2.00	.90
☐ R19	Jermaine O'Neal	2.00	.90
☐ R20	Erick Dampier	2.00	.90

in the scoring category. If the player reached the performance goal printed on the front of the card, the card could be traded for a SP-quality replacement. Each card is numbered with a "P" prefix.

	MINT	NRMT
COMPLETE SET (20)	60.00	27.00
COMMON CARD (P1-P20)	1.00	.45
SEMISTARS	1.25	.55
UNLISTED STARS	2.00	.90
SER.1 STATED ODDS 1:23		
*TV CEL RED.CARDS: 1X TO 2X HI COL.		

		MINT	NRMT
☐ P1	M.Blaylock 30 PTS. W	1.25	.55
☐ P2	D.Radja 35 PTS. L	1.00	.45
☐ P3	M.Jordan 35 PTS. W	25.00	11.00
☐ P4	T.Brandon 35 PTS. L	2.00	.90
☐ P5	J.Kidd 30 PTS. W	4.00	1.80
☐ P6	J.Dumars 25 PTS. W	2.00	.90
☐ P7	J.Smith 35 PTS. W	2.50	1.10
☐ P8	H.Olajuwon 35 PTS. W	4.00	1.80
☐ P9	R.Smits 35 PTS. W	1.25	.55
☐ P10	B.Barry 25 PTS. L	1.00	.45
☐ P11	K.Thomas 25 PTS. L	1.00	.45
☐ P12	A.Hardaway 35 PTS. W	8.00	3.60
☐ P13	C.Weatherspoon35PTS.L	1.00	.45
☐ P14	C.Robinson 35 PTS. L	1.25	.55
☐ P15	M.Richmond 35PTS.W	2.00	.90
☐ P16	D.Robinson 35 PTS. L	3.00	1.35
☐ P17	S.Kemp 35 PTS. L	6.00	2.70
☐ P18	D.Stoudamire 35 PTS. W	5.00	2.20
☐ P19	K.Malone 35 PTS. W	3.00	1.35
☐ P20	B.Reeves 30 PTS. W	1.25	.55

	MINT	NRMT
COMPLETE SET (20)	90.00	40.00
COMMON CARD (P1-P20)	1.00	.45
SEMISTARS	1.25	.55
UNLISTED STARS	2.00	.90
SER.2 STATED ODDS 1:23		
*TV CEL RED.CARDS: 1X TO 2X HI COL.		

		MINT	NRMT
☐ P1	Glen Rice 35 PTS. W	2.00	.90
☐ P2	M.Jordan 35 PTS. W	25.00	11.00
☐ P3	J.Mashburn 30 PTS. L	1.25	.55
☐ P4	A.McDyess 30 PTS. W	3.00	1.35
☐ P5	C.Barkley 35 PTS. W	3.00	1.35
☐ P6	Reggie Miller 35 PTS. W	2.00	.90
☐ P7	S.O'Neal 35 PTS. W	8.00	3.60
☐ P8	A.Mourning 35 PTS. W	4.00	1.80
☐ P9	Vin Baker 30 PTS. W	4.00	1.80
☐ P10	K.Garnett 30 PTS. W	12.00	5.50
☐ P11	K.Kittles 25 PTS. W	2.50	1.10
☐ P12	P.Ewing 30 PTS. W	2.00	.90
☐ P13	A.Hardaway 35 PTS. W	8.00	3.60
☐ P14	A.Iverson 35 PTS. W	10.00	4.50
☐ P15	R.Horry 30 PTS. L	1.25	.55
☐ P16	S.Kemp 35 PTS. L	6.00	2.70
☐ P17	M.Camby 25 PTS. W	2.50	1.10
☐ P18	J.Stockton 25 PTS. W	2.00	.90
☐ P19	S.Abdur-Rahim25PTS.W	6.00	2.70
☐ P20	J.Howard 30 PTS. W	2.50	1.10

1996-97 Upper Deck Predictor Scoring 2

Randomly inserted in series two packs at a rate of one in 23, this 20-card set featured interactive cards based on the above-average game output of 30 players in the scoring category. If the player reached the performance goal printed on the front of the card, the card could be traded for a SP-quality replacement. Each card is numbered with a "P" prefix.

1996-97 Upper Deck Rookie Exclusives

Randomly inserted in series two packs at a rate of one in 4, this 20-card set focuses on the 1996-97 rookie class and features quotes from selected NBA stars on each rookie. Card fronts have a basketball textured background. Each card is numbered with a "R" prefix.

1996-97 Upper Deck Rookie of the Year Collection

Randomly inserted in series two packs at a rate of one in 138, this 14-card set spotlight current NBA players who have been named NBA Rookie of the Year. Each card is die cut and features a shot of the player in a rectangle in the middle of the card. Card backs are numbered with a "RC" prefix.

	MINT	NRMT
COMPLETE SET (14)	200.00	90.00
COMMON CARD (RC1-RC14)	3.00	1.35
SEMISTARS	4.00	1.80
UNLISTED STARS	6.00	2.70
SER.2 STATED ODDS 1:138		

		MINT	NRMT
☐ RC1	D.Stoudamire	15.00	6.75
☐ RC2	Grant Hill	40.00	18.00
☐ RC3	Jason Kidd	12.00	5.50
☐ RC4	Chris Webber	15.00	6.75
☐ RC5	Shaquille O'Neal	30.00	13.50
☐ RC6	Larry Johnson	4.00	1.80
☐ RC7	Derrick Coleman	4.00	1.80
☐ RC8	David Robinson	10.00	4.50

RC9 Mitch Richmond	6.00	2.70
RC10 Mark Jackson	3.00	1.35
RC11 Chuck Person	3.00	1.35
RC12 Patrick Ewing	6.00	2.70
RC13 Michael Jordan	100.00	45.00
RC14 Buck Williams	3.00	1.35

1996-97 Upper Deck Smooth Grooves

Randomly inserted in series two packs at a rate of one in 72, the 15-card set focuses on players whose slick moves were reminiscent of the great players of the 60's and 70's. Card fronts are full-bleed and feature a shot of the player "swirled" in the background. Card backs are numbered with a "SG" prefix.

	MINT	NRMT
COMPLETE SET (15)	300.00	135.00
COMMON CARD (SG1-SG15)	6.00	2.70
SER.2 STATED ODDS 1:72		

SG1 Dennis Rodman	25.00	11.00
SG2 Jason Kidd	12.00	5.50
SG3 Grant Hill	40.00	18.00
SG4 D.Stoudamire	15.00	6.75
SG5 Shaquille O'Neal	25.00	11.00
SG6 Clyde Drexler	8.00	3.60
SG7 S.Abdur-Rahim	20.00	9.00
SG8 Michael Jordan	80.00	36.00
SG9 Alonzo Mourning	6.00	2.70
SG10 Allen Iverson	30.00	13.50
SG11 Vin Baker	12.00	5.50
SG12 Kevin Garnett	40.00	18.00
SG13 A.Hardaway	25.00	11.00
SG14 Jerry Stackhouse	8.00	3.60
SG15 Shawn Kemp	20.00	9.00

1997-98 Upper Deck

The 1997-98 Upper Deck set was issued in two series totaling 360 cards and was distributed in 12-card packs with a suggested retail price of $2.49. The fronts feature color action player pho-

tos while the backs carry player information. The set contains the topical subsets: Jams '97 (136-164), Court Perspectives (165-179), Overtime (316-330) and Defining Moments (331-359).

	MINT	NRMT
COMPLETE SET (360)	50.00	22.00
COMPLETE SERIES 1 (180)	25.00	11.00
COMPLETE SERIES 2 (180)	25.00	11.00
COMMON CARD (1-360)	.15	.07
SEMISTARS	.20	.09
UNLISTED STARS	.40	.18
MJ BLACK POWER AUDIO 1:23 HOBBY		
MJ RED POWER AUDIO 1:72 HOBBY		
MJ WHITE POWER AUDIO: 1 OF 1		

1 Steve Smith	.20	.09
2 Christian Laettner	.20	.09
3 Alan Henderson	.15	.07
4 Dikembe Mutombo	.20	.09
5 Dana Barros	.15	.07
6 Antoine Walker	2.00	.90
7 Dee Brown	.15	.07
8 Eric Williams	.15	.07
9 Muggsy Bogues	.15	.07
10 Dell Curry	.15	.07
11 Vlade Divac	.20	.09
12 Anthony Mason	.20	.09
13 Glen Rice	.40	.18
14 Jason Caffey	.15	.07
15 Steve Kerr	.15	.07
16 Toni Kukoc	.20	.09
17 Luc Longley	.15	.07
18 Michael Jordan	5.00	2.20
19 Terrell Brandon	.40	.18
20 Danny Ferry	.15	.07
21 Tyrone Hill	.15	.07
22 Derek Anderson	1.25	.55
23 Bob Sura	.15	.07
24 Eric Williams	.15	.07
25 Michael Finley	.40	.18
26 Ed O'Bannon	.15	.07
27 Robert Pack	.15	.07
28 Samaki Walker	.15	.07
29 LaPhonso Ellis	.15	.07
30 Tony Battie	.75	.35
31 Antonio McDyess	.50	.23
32 Bryant Stith	.15	.07
33 Randolph Childress	.15	.07
34 Grant Hill	2.50	1.10
35 Lindsey Hunter	.15	.07
36 Grant Long	.15	.07
37 Theo Ratliff	.15	.07
38 B.J. Armstrong	.15	.07
39 Adonal Foyle RC	.50	.23
40 Mark Price	.15	.07
41 Felton Spencer	.15	.07
42 Latrell Sprewell	.20	.09
43 Clyde Drexler	.50	.23
44 Mario Elie	.15	.07
45 Hakeem Olajuwon	.75	.35
46 Brent Price	.15	.07

47 Kevin Willis	.15	.07
48 Erick Dampier	.15	.07
49 Antonio Davis	.15	.07
50 Dale Davis	.15	.07
51 Mark Jackson	.15	.07
52 Rik Smits	.20	.09
53 Brent Barry	.15	.07
54 Lamond Murray	.15	.07
55 Eric Piatkowski	.15	.07
56 Loy Vaught	.20	.09
57 Lorenzen Wright	.15	.07
58 Kobe Bryant	3.00	1.35
59 Elden Campbell	.20	.09
60 Derek Fisher	.15	.07
61 Eddie Jones	.75	.35
62 Nick Van Exel	.40	.18
63 Keith Askins	.15	.07
64 Isaac Austin	.15	.07
65 P.J. Brown	.15	.07
66 Tim Hardaway	.50	.23
67 Alonzo Mourning	.40	.18
68 Ray Allen	.50	.23
69 Vin Baker	.75	.35
70 Sherman Douglas	.15	.07
71 Armon Gilliam	.15	.07
72 Elliot Perry	.15	.07
73 Chris Carr	.15	.07
74 Tom Gugliotta	.40	.18
75 Kevin Garnett	2.50	1.10
76 Doug West	.15	.07
77 Keith Van Horn	4.00	1.80
78 Chris Gatling	.15	.07
79 Kendall Gill	.20	.09
80 Kerry Kittles	.40	.18
81 Jayson Williams	.20	.09
82 Chris Childs	.15	.07
83 Allan Houston	.20	.09
84 Larry Johnson	.20	.09
85 Charles Oakley	.15	.07
86 John Starks	.20	.09
87 Horace Grant	.20	.09
88 Anfernee Hardaway	1.50	.70
89 Dennis Scott	.15	.07
90 Rony Seikaly	.15	.07
91 Brian Shaw	.15	.07
92 Derrick Coleman	.20	.09
93 Allen Iverson	2.00	.90
94 Tim Thomas	2.50	1.10
95 Scott Williams	.15	.07
96 Cedric Ceballos	.15	.07
97 Kevin Johnson	.20	.09
98 Loren Meyer	.15	.07
99 Steve Nash	.20	.09
100 Wesley Person	.15	.07
101 Kenny Anderson	.20	.09
102 Jermaine O'Neal	.20	.09
103 Isaiah Rider	.20	.09
104 Arvydas Sabonis	.20	.09
105 Gary Trent	.15	.07
106 Mahmoud Abdul-Rauf	.15	.07
107 Billy Owens	.15	.07
108 Olden Polynice	.15	.07
109 Mitch Richmond	.40	.18
110 Michael Smith	.15	.07
111 Cory Alexander	.15	.07
112 Vinny Del Negro	.15	.07
113 Carl Herrera	.15	.07
114 Tim Duncan	5.00	2.20
115 Hersey Hawkins	.20	.09
116 Shawn Kemp	1.25	.55
117 Nate McMillan	.15	.07
118 Sam Perkins	.20	.09
119 Detlef Schrempf	.20	.09
120 Doug Christie	.15	.07
121 Popeye Jones	.15	.07
122 Carlos Rogers	.15	.07
123 Damon Stoudamire	.75	.35
124 Adam Keefe	.15	.07
125 Chris Morris	.15	.07
126 Greg Ostertag	.15	.07
127 John Stockton	.40	.18
128 S.Abdur-Rahim	1.25	.55
129 George Lynch	.15	.07
130 Lee Mayberry	.15	.07
131 Anthony Peeler	.15	.07
132 Calbert Cheaney	.15	.07

133	Tracy Murray	.15	.07
134	Rod Strickland	.20	.09
135	Chris Webber	1.00	.45
136	C.Laettner JAM	.20	.09
137	Eric Williams JAM	.15	.07
138	Vlade Divac JAM	.15	.07
139	Michael Jordan JAM	2.50	1.10
140	Tyrone Hill JAM	.15	.07
141	Michael Finley JAM	.20	.09
142	Tom Hammonds JAM	.15	.07
143	Theo Ratliff JAM	.15	.07
144	Latrell Sprewell JAM	.15	.07
145	Hakeem Olajuwon JAM	.40	.18
146	Reggie Miller JAM	.20	.09
147	Rodney Rogers JAM	.15	.07
148	Eddie Jones JAM	.40	.18
149	Jamal Mashburn JAM	.20	.09
150	Glenn Robinson JAM	.20	.09
151	Chris Carr JAM	.15	.07
152	Kendall Gill JAM	.15	.07
153	John Starks JAM	.20	.09
154	A.Hardaway JAM	.75	.35
155	D.Coleman JAM	.20	.09
156	Cedric Ceballos JAM	.15	.07
157	R.Wallace JAM	.15	.07
158	C.Williamson JAM	.20	.09
159	Sean Elliott JAM	.15	.07
160	Shawn Kemp JAM	.60	.25
161	Doug Christie JAM	.15	.07
162	Karl Malone JAM	.40	.18
163	Bryant Reeves JAM	.15	.07
164	G.Muresan JAM	.15	.07
165	Michael Jordan CP	2.50	1.10
166	D.Mutombo CP	.20	.09
167	Glen Rice CP	.20	.09
168	Mitch Richmond CP	.20	.09
169	Juwan Howard CP	.20	.09
170	Clyde Drexler CP	.40	.18
171	Terrell Brandon CP	.20	.09
172	Jerry Stackhouse CP	.20	.09
173	D.Stoudamire CP	.40	.18
174	Jayson Williams CP	.15	.07
175	P.J. Brown CP	.15	.07
176	A.Hardaway CP	.75	.35
177	Vin Baker CP	.40	.18
178	LaPhonso Ellis CP	.15	.07
179	Shawn Kemp CP	.60	.25
180	Checklist	.15	.07
181	Mookie Blaylock	.20	.09
182	Tyrone Corbin	.15	.07
183	Chucky Brown	.15	.07
184	Ed Gray	.50	.23
185	Chauncey Billups	1.50	.70
186	Tyus Edney	.15	.07
187	Travis Knight	.15	.07
188	Ron Mercer	3.00	1.35
189	Walter McCarty	.15	.07
190	B.J. Armstrong	.15	.07
191	Matt Geiger	.15	.07
192	Bobby Phills	.15	.07
193	David Wesley	.15	.07
194	Keith Booth	.15	.07
195	Randy Brown	.15	.07
196	Ron Harper	.20	.09
197	Scottie Pippen	1.25	.55
198	Dennis Rodman	1.50	.70
199	Zydrunas Ilgauskas	.20	.09
200	Brevin Knight	1.25	.55
201	Shawn Kemp	1.25	.55
202	Vitaly Potapenko	.15	.07
203	Wesley Person	.15	.07
204	Erick Strickland	.20	.09
205	A.C. Green	.20	.09
206	Khalid Reeves	.15	.07
207	Hubert Davis	.15	.07
208	Dennis Scott	.15	.07
209	Danny Fortson	.75	.35
210	Bobby Jackson	.75	.35
211	Eric Williams	.15	.07
212	Dean Garrett	.15	.07
213	Priest Lauderdale	.15	.07
214	Joe Dumars	.40	.18
215	Aaron McKie	.15	.07
216	Scot Pollard	.15	.07
217	Brian Williams	.15	.07
218	Malik Sealy	.15	.07
219	Duane Ferrell	.15	.07
220	Erick Dampier	.15	.07
221	Todd Fuller	.15	.07
222	Donyell Marshall	.15	.07
223	Joe Smith	.40	.18
224	Charles Barkley	.60	.25
225	Matt Bullard	.15	.07
226	Othella Harrington	.15	.07
227	Rodrick Rhodes	.50	.23
228	Eddie Johnson	.15	.07
229	Matt Maloney	.15	.07
230	Travis Best	.15	.07
231	Reggie Miller	.40	.18
232	Chris Mullin	.40	.18
233	Fred Hoiberg	.15	.07
234	Austin Croshere	.50	.23
235	Keith Closs	.15	.07
236	Darrick Martin	.15	.07
237	Pooh Richardson	.15	.07
238	Rodney Rogers	.15	.07
239	Maurice Taylor	1.25	.55
240	Robert Horry	.20	.09
241	Rick Fox	.15	.07
242	Shaquille O'Neal	1.50	.70
243	Corie Blount	.15	.07
244	Charles Smith	.15	.07
245	Voshon Lenard	.15	.07
246	Eric Murdock	.15	.07
247	Dan Majerle	.20	.09
248	Terry Mills	.15	.07
249	Terrell Brandon	.40	.18
250	Tyrone Hill	.15	.07
251	Ervin Johnson	.15	.07
252	Glenn Robinson	.40	.18
253	Terry Porter	.15	.07
254	Paul Grant	.15	.07
255	Stephon Marbury	2.00	.90
256	Sam Mitchell	.15	.07
257	Cherokee Parks	.15	.07
258	Sam Cassell	.20	.09
259	David Benoit	.15	.07
260	Kevin Edwards	.15	.07
261	Don MacLean	.15	.07
262	Patrick Ewing	.40	.18
263	Herb Williams	.15	.07
264	John Starks	.20	.09
265	Chris Mills	.15	.07
266	Chris Dudley	.15	.07
267	Darrell Armstrong	.15	.07
268	Nick Anderson	.15	.07
269	Derek Harper	.15	.07
270	Johnny Taylor	.15	.07
271	Mark Price	.15	.07
272	C.Weatherspoon	.15	.07
273	Jerry Stackhouse	.40	.18
274	Eric Montross	.15	.07
275	Anthony Parker	.15	.07
276	Antonio McDyess	.40	.23
277	Clifford Robinson	.15	.07
278	Jason Kidd	.75	.35
279	Danny Manning	.20	.09
280	Rex Chapman	.15	.07
281	Stacey Augmon	.15	.07
282	Kelvin Cato	.50	.23
283	Brian Grant	.20	.09
284	Rasheed Wallace	.20	.09
285	I.Funderburke	.40	.18
286	Anthony Johnson	.15	.07
287	Tariq Abdul-Wahad	.60	.25
288	Corliss Williamson	.20	.09
289	Sean Elliott	.15	.07
290	Avery Johnson	.15	.07
291	David Robinson	.60	.25
292	Will Perdue	.15	.07
293	Greg Anthony	.15	.07
294	Jim McIlvaine	.15	.07
295	Dale Ellis	.15	.07
296	Gary Payton	.60	.25
297	Aaron Williams	.15	.07
298	Marcus Camby	.40	.18
299	John Wallace	.20	.09
300	Tracy McGrady	2.50	1.10
301	Walt Williams	.15	.07
302	Shandon Anderson	.15	.07
303	Antoine Carr	.15	.07
304	Jeff Hornacek	.20	.09
305	Karl Malone	.60	.25
306	Bryon Russell	.15	.07
307	Jacque Vaughn	.60	.25
308	Antonio Daniels	1.00	.45
309	Blue Edwards	.15	.07
310	Bryant Reeves	.20	.09
311	Otis Thorpe	.20	.09
312	Harvey Grant	.15	.07
313	Terry Davis	.15	.07
314	Juwan Howard	.40	.18
315	Gheorghe Muresan	.15	.07
316	Michael Jordan OT	2.50	1.10
317	Allen Iverson OT	1.00	.45
318	Karl Malone OT	.40	.18
319	Glen Rice OT	.20	.09
320	D.Mutombo OT	.15	.07
321	Grant Hill OT	1.25	.55
322	H.Olajuwon OT	.40	.18
323	S.Marbury OT	1.00	.45
324	A.Hardaway OT	.75	.35
325	Eddie Jones OT	.40	.18
326	Mitch Richmond OT	.20	.09
327	Kevin Johnson OT	.15	.07
328	Kevin Garnett OT	1.25	.55
329	S.Abdur-Rahim OT	.60	.25
330	D.Stoudamire OT	.40	.18
331	Atlanta Hawks DM	.15	.07
	Dikembe Mutombo		
	Christian Laettner		
	Mookie Blaylock		
	Steve Smith		
332	Boston Celtics DM	.40	.18
	Antoine Walker		
	Ron Mercer		
	Chauncey Billups		
	Dana Barros		
333	Charlotte Hornets DM	.20	.09
	Glen Rice		
	Larry Johnson		
	Alonzo Mourning		
	Vlade Divac		
	Anthony Mason		
334	Chicago Bulls DM	1.00	.45
	Michael Jordan		
	Scottie Pippen		
	Dennis Rodman		
	Toni Kukoc		
335	Cleve. Cavaliers DM	.40	.18
	Shawn Kemp		
	Brevin Knight		
	Terrell Brandon		
	Mark Price		
336	Dallas Mavericks DM	.15	.07
	A.C. Green		
	Michael Finley		
	Derek Harper		
	Detlef Schrempf		
337	Denver Nuggets DM	.40	.18
	Bobby Jackson		
	Tony Battie		
	Dikembe Mutombo		
	LaPhonso Ellis		
338	Detroit Pistons DM	.50	.23
	Joe Dumars		
	Grant Hill		
	Dennis Rodman		
	Lindsey Hunter		
339	Gldn. St. Warriors DM	.40	.18
	Joe Smith		
	Chris Mullin		
	Chris Webber		
	Tim Hardaway		
340	Houston Rockets DM	.40	.18
	Hakeem Olajuwon		
	Charles Barkley		
	Clyde Drexler		
	Sam Cassell		
	Otis Thorpe		
341	Indiana Pacers DM	.20	.09
	Chris Mullin		
	Reggie Miller		
	Antonio Davis		
	Dale Davis		
	Rik Smits		
342	L.A. Clippers DM	.15	.07
	Brent Barry		

Loy Vaught
Danny Manning
Ron Harper
☐ 343 L.A. Lakers DM .... .60 .25
  Shaquille O'Neal
  Kobe Bryant
  Eddie Jones
  Nick Van Exel
☐ 344 Miami Heat DM .... .40 .18
  Tim Hardaway
  Alonzo Mourning
  P.J. Brown
  Rony Seikaly
  Glen Rice
☐ 345 Milwaukee Bucks DM .20 .09
  Terrell Brandon
  Glenn Robinson
  Vin Baker
  Terry Cummings
☐ 346 Minn. T'wolves DM .... .50 .23
  Kevin Garnett
  Stephon Marbury
  Tom Gugliotta
  Sam Mitchell
  Isaiah Rider
☐ 347 New Jersey Nets DM .. .40 .18
  Keith Van Horn
  Jayson Williams
  Buck Williams
  Kenny Anderson
☐ 348 New York Knicks DM.. .20 .09
  Patrick Ewing
  Larry Johnson
  John Starks
  Charles Oakley
☐ 349 Orlando Magic DM ..... .40 .18
  Anfernee Hardaway
  Rony Seikaly
  Shaquille O'Neal
  Nick Anderson
☐ 350 Philadelphia 76ers DM .40 .18
  Allen Iverson
  Jerry Stackhouse
  Charles Barkley
  Clarence Weatherspoon
☐ 351 Phoenix Suns DM ...... .40 .18
  Antonio McDyess
  Jason Kidd
  Charles Barkley
  Kevin Johnson
☐ 352 Portland TrBlazers DM .15 .07
  Kenny Anderson
  Isaiah Rider
  Clyde Drexler
  Terry Porter
☐ 353 Sacramento Kings DM .20 .09
  Mitch Richmond
  Corliss Williamson
  Lionel Simmons
  Billy Owens
☐ 354 San Antonio Spurs DM .50 .23
  Tim Duncan
  David Robinson
  Sean Elliott
  Dennis Rodman
☐ 355 Seattle Sonics DM...... .40 .18
  Gary Payton
  Vin Baker
  Nate McMillan
  Shawn Kemp
☐ 356 Toronto Raptors DM .. .40 .18
  Damon Stoudamire
  Tracy McGrady
  Marcus Camby
  Walt Williams
☐ 357 Utah Jazz DM .... .09
  John Stockton
  Karl Malone
  Jeff Hornacek
☐ 358 Vanc'vr Grizzlies DM .. .15 .07
  Bryant Reeves
  Shareef Abdur-Rahim
  Antonio Daniels
  Greg Anthony
☐ 359 WA Wizards DM .... .40 .18
  Chris Webber

Juwan Howard
Gheorghe Muresan
Rod Strickland
☐ 360 Checklist .... .15 .07
☐ NNO M.Jordan Black Audio 12.00 5.50
☐ NNO M.Jordan Red Audio 30.00 13.50

1997-98 Upper Deck Game Dated Memorable Moments

Randomly inserted in series one packs at the rate of one in 1,500, this 30-card set features color photos of memorable moments of the NBA season printed on stunning Light F/X cards. The date of the game and the significance of the moment is found in a bar at the bottom.

	MINT	NRMT
COMPLETE SET (30)	1600.00	700.00
COMMON CARD..................	15.00	6.75
SEMISTARS........................	20.00	9.00
UNLISTED STARS	30.00	13.50
SKIP NUMBERED SET		
SER.1 STATED ODDS 1:1500		
☐ 4 D.Mutombo	20.00	9.00
☐ 6 Antoine Walker	150.00	70.00
☐ 13 Glen Rice.................	30.00	13.50
☐ 18 Michael Jordan	500.00	220.00
☐ 23 Bob Sura.................	15.00	6.75
☐ 25 Michael Finley	30.00	13.50
☐ 31 Antonio McDyess	40.00	18.00
☐ 34 Grant Hill.................	200.00	90.00
☐ 42 Latrell Sprewell	20.00	9.00
☐ 43 Clyde Drexler...........	40.00	18.00
☐ 45 Hakeem Olajuwon	60.00	27.00
☐ 49 Antonio Davis	15.00	6.75
☐ 56 Loy Vaught..............	20.00	9.00
☐ 61 Eddie Jones.............	60.00	27.00
☐ 66 Tim Hardaway..........	40.00	18.00
☐ 69 Vin Baker................	60.00	27.00
☐ 75 Kevin Garnett...........	200.00	90.00
☐ 79 Kendall Gill	20.00	9.00
☐ 83 Allan Houston	20.00	9.00
☐ 88 A.Hardaway.............	150.00	70.00
☐ 93 Allen Iverson	150.00	70.00
☐ 97 Kevin Johnson..........	20.00	9.00
☐ 103 Isaiah Rider............	20.00	9.00
☐ 109 Mitch Richmond	30.00	13.50
☐ 112 Vinny Del Negro	15.00	6.75
☐ 116 Shawn Kemp..........	100.00	45.00
☐ 123 D.Stoudamire	60.00	27.00
☐ 127 John Stockton.........	30.00	13.50

☐ 128 S.Abdur-Rahim 100.00 45.00
☐ 135 Chris Webber 80.00 36.00

1997-98 Upper Deck AIRlines

Randomly inserted in series two packs at a rate of one in 230 packs, this 12-card die cut set chronicles each year in Michael Jordan's career. Card backs are numbered with an "AL" prefix.

	MINT	NRMT
COMPLETE SET (12)	900.00	400.00
COMMON JORDAN (AL1-AL12)	80.00	36.00
SER.2 STATED ODDS 1:230 HOB/RET		
☐ AL1 Michael Jordan	80.00	36.00
☐ AL2 Michael Jordan	80.00	36.00
☐ AL3 Michael Jordan	80.00	36.00
☐ AL4 Michael Jordan	80.00	36.00
☐ AL5 Michael Jordan	80.00	36.00
☐ AL6 Michael Jordan	80.00	36.00
☐ AL7 Michael Jordan	80.00	36.00
☐ AL8 Michael Jordan	80.00	36.00
☐ AL9 Michael Jordan	80.00	36.00
☐ AL10 Michael Jordan	80.00	36.00
☐ AL11 Michael Jordan	80.00	36.00
☐ AL12 Michael Jordan	80.00	36.00

1997-98 Upper Deck Diamond Dimensions

Randomly inserted in first series packs, this 30-card parallel of the High Dimension set features color images of the most versatile players of the NBA printed on die cut cards. Only 100 of each card was produced and are sequentially numbered.

	MINT	NRMT
COMMON CARD (D1-D30)..	20.00	9.00
SEMISTARS	30.00	13.50
STATED PRINT RUN 100 SERIAL #'d SETS		
RANDOM INSERTS IN SER.1 PACKS		
☐ D1 A.Hardaway..............	250.00	110.00
☐ D2 Gary Payton.............	80.00	36.00
☐ D3 Marcus Camby	50.00	22.00
☐ D4 Charles Barkley.........	80.00	36.00
☐ D5 Jason Kidd	100.00	45.00
☐ D6 Alonzo Mourning	50.00	22.00

☐ D7	Kenny Anderson	30.00	13.50
☐ D8	Kobe Bryant	400.00	180.00
☐ D9	Dennis Rodman	200.00	90.00
☐ D10	Kerry Kittles	50.00	22.00
☐ D11	D.Mutombo	30.00	13.50
☐ D12	Shaquille O'Neal	200.00	90.00
☐ D13	Glenn Robinson	40.00	18.00
☐ D14	Tony Delk	20.00	9.00
☐ D15	Larry Johnson	30.00	13.50
☐ D16	Brent Barry	20.00	9.00
☐ D17	Scottie Pippen	150.00	70.00
☐ D18	S.Abdur-Rahim	150.00	70.00
☐ D19	Sean Elliott	20.00	9.00
☐ D20	D.Stoudamire	100.00	45.00
☐ D21	Kevin Garnett	300.00	135.00
☐ D22	Bob Sura	20.00	9.00
☐ D23	Michael Jordan	750.00	350.00
☐ D24	Latrell Sprewell	30.00	13.50
☐ D25	Karl Malone	80.00	36.00
☐ D26	Antonio McDyess	60.00	27.00
☐ D27	Allen Iverson	250.00	110.00
☐ D28	Dale Davis	20.00	9.00
☐ D29	Antoine Walker	250.00	110.00
☐ D30	Chris Webber	125.00	55.00

1997-98
Upper Deck
Game Jerseys

Randomly inserted in both series packs at the rate of one in 2,500, this 22-card set features color player images on a jersey print background with an actual piece of an NBA game worn jersey embedded in the card. Series two packs also contained a special Michael Jordan autographed Game Jersey, which was hand-numbered to 23.

		MINT	NRMT
COMPL. SET (22)		8800.00	4000.00
COMPL. SERIES 1 (12)		3800.00	1700.00
COMPL. SERIES 2 (10)		5000.00	2200.00
COMM CARD (GJ1-GJ22)		175.00	80.00
SER.1/2 STATED ODDS 1:2500			
JORDAN AU #'d TO 23			
JORDAN AU NOT IN SET PRICE			
JORDAN AU: RANDOM INS.IN SER.2 HOB			

☐ GJ1	Charles Barkley	350.00	160.00
☐ GJ2	Clyde Drexler	275.00	125.00
☐ GJ3	Kevin Garnett	600.00	275.00
☐ GJ4	A.Hardaway	500.00	220.00
	Home Jersey		
☐ GJ5	Grant Hill	600.00	275.00
	Home Jersey		
☐ GJ6	Allen Iverson	400.00	180.00
☐ GJ7	Kerry Kittles	200.00	90.00
☐ GJ8	Toni Kukoc	250.00	110.00
☐ GJ9	Reggie Miller	275.00	125.00

☐ GJ10	H.Olajuwon	250.00	110.00
☐ GJ11	Glen Rice	225.00	100.00
☐ GJ12	David Robinson	250.00	110.00
☐ GJ13	M.Jordan	2500.00	1100.00
☐ GJ13S	M.Jordan	12000.00	5400.00
	Autographed Game Jersey		
☐ GJ14	Alonzo Mourning	250.00	110.00
☐ GJ15	Tim Hardaway	275.00	125.00
☐ GJ16	Marcus Camby	175.00	80.00
☐ GJ17	Antoine Walker	500.00	220.00
☐ GJ18	Kevin Johnson	175.00	80.00
☐ GJ19	Glenn Robinson	200.00	90.00
☐ GJ20	Patrick Ewing	250.00	110.00
☐ GJ21	A.Hardaway	500.00	220.00
	Away Jersey		
☐ GJ22	Grant Hill	600.00	275.00
	Away Jersey		

1997-98
Upper Deck
Great Eight

Randomly inserted into series two packs, this 8-card set features eight of the best veterans in the NBA. The card backs are serially numbered to 800 and carry a "G" prefix.

		MINT	NRMT
COMPLETE SET (8)		300.00	135.00
COMMON CARD (G1-G8)		10.00	4.50
UNLISTED STARS		15.00	6.75
STATED PRINT RUN 800 SERIAL #'d SETS			
RANDOM INSERTS IN SER.2 PACKS			

☐ G1	Charles Barkley	25.00	11.00
☐ G2	Clyde Drexler	20.00	9.00
☐ G3	Joe Dumars	10.00	4.50
☐ G4	Patrick Ewing	15.00	6.75
☐ G5	Michael Jordan	200.00	90.00
☐ G6	Karl Malone	25.00	11.00
☐ G7	Hakeem Olajuwon	30.00	13.50
☐ G8	John Stockton	15.00	6.75

1997-98
Upper Deck
High Dimensions

Randomly inserted in series one packs, this 30-card set is parallel to the Diamond Dimensions insert set. Only 2,000 of each card was produced and are sequentially numbered.

	MINT	NRMT
COMPLETE SET (30)	500.00	220.00

COMMON CARD (D1-D30)		3.00	1.35
SEMISTARS		5.00	2.20
UNLISTED STARS		8.00	3.60
STATED PRINT RUN 2000 SERIAL #'d SETS			
RANDOM INSERTS IN SER.1 PACKS			

☐ D1	A.Hardaway	30.00	13.50
☐ D2	Gary Payton	12.00	5.50
☐ D3	Marcus Camby	8.00	3.60
☐ D4	Charles Barkley	12.00	5.50
☐ D5	Jason Kidd	15.00	6.75
☐ D6	Alonzo Mourning	8.00	3.60
☐ D7	Kenny Anderson	5.00	2.20
☐ D8	Kobe Bryant	75.00	34.00
☐ D9	Dennis Rodman	30.00	13.50
☐ D10	Kerry Kittles	8.00	3.60
☐ D11	D.Mutombo	5.00	2.20
☐ D12	Shaquille O'Neal	30.00	13.50
☐ D13	Glenn Robinson	8.00	3.60
☐ D14	Tony Delk	3.00	1.35
☐ D15	Larry Johnson	5.00	2.20
☐ D16	Brent Barry	3.00	1.35
☐ D17	Scottie Pippen	25.00	11.00
☐ D18	S.Abdur-Rahim	25.00	11.00
☐ D19	Sean Elliott	3.00	1.35
☐ D20	D.Stoudamire	15.00	6.75
☐ D21	Kevin Garnett	50.00	22.00
☐ D22	Bob Sura	3.00	1.35
☐ D23	Michael Jordan	100.00	45.00
☐ D24	Latrell Sprewell	5.00	2.20
☐ D25	Karl Malone	12.00	5.50
☐ D26	Antonio McDyess	10.00	4.50
☐ D27	Allen Iverson	50.00	22.00
☐ D28	Dale Davis	3.00	1.35
☐ D29	Antoine Walker	40.00	18.00
☐ D30	Chris Webber	20.00	9.00

1997-98
Upper Deck
Jordan Air Time

Randomly inserted in series one packs at the rate of one in 12, this 10-card set features color action photos of Michael Jordan printed on double-front style cards. The set is comprised of three different fronts, or "Departures," and three different backs, or "Arrivals." The first nine cards combine to create a Jordan "Flight" to the basket. The tenth card features front and back photos and is tougher to find than the first nine, thus commanding a premium.

	MINT	NRMT
COMPLETE SET (10)	140.00	65.00
COMMON JORDAN (AT1-AT9)	10.00	4.50
COMMON JORDAN (AT10)	80.00	36.00
SER.1 STATED ODDS 1:12		

☐ AT1 Michael Jordan	10.00	4.50
☐ AT2 Michael Jordan	10.00	4.50
☐ AT3 Michael Jordan	10.00	4.50
☐ AT4 Michael Jordan	10.00	4.50
☐ AT5 Michael Jordan	10.00	4.50
☐ AT6 Michael Jordan	10.00	4.50
☐ AT7 Michael Jordan	10.00	4.50
☐ AT8 Michael Jordan	10.00	4.50
☐ AT9 Michael Jordan	10.00	4.50
☐ AT10 Michael Jordan	80.00	36.00

1997-98 Upper Deck Records Collection

Randomly inserted into series two packs at a rate of one in 23, this 30-card set features a special look at the outstanding achievements of great NBA performers. The card fronts are similar to a record with a black etched background. Card backs carry a "RC" prefix.

	MINT	NRMT
COMPLETE SET (30)	150.00	70.00
COMMON CARD (RC1-RC30)	1.50	.70
SEMISTARS	2.00	.90
UNLISTED STARS	3.00	1.35
SER.2 STATED ODDS 1:23		

☐ RC1 D.Mutombo	2.00	.90
☐ RC2 Dana Barros	1.50	.70
☐ RC3 Glen Rice	3.00	1.35
☐ RC4 Dennis Rodman	12.00	5.50
☐ RC5 Shawn Kemp	10.00	4.50
☐ RC6 A.C. Green	2.00	.90
☐ RC7 LaPhonso Ellis	1.50	.70
☐ RC8 Grant Hill	20.00	9.00

☐ RC9 Joe Smith	3.00	1.35
☐ RC10 Charles Barkley	5.00	2.20
☐ RC11 Reggie Miller	3.00	1.35
☐ RC12 Loy Vaught	2.00	.90
☐ RC13 Shaquille O'Neal	12.00	5.50
☐ RC14 Tim Hardaway	4.00	1.80
☐ RC15 Glenn Robinson	3.00	1.35
☐ RC16 Stephon Marbury	15.00	6.75
☐ RC17 Sam Cassell	2.00	.90
☐ RC18 Patrick Ewing	3.00	1.35
☐ RC19 A.Hardaway	12.00	5.50
☐ RC20 Allen Iverson	15.00	6.75
☐ RC21 Kevin Johnson	2.00	.90
☐ RC22 Kenny Anderson	2.00	.90
☐ RC23 Mitch Richmond	3.00	1.35
☐ RC24 David Robinson	5.00	2.20
☐ RC25 Gary Payton	5.00	2.20
☐ RC26 D.Stoudamire	6.00	2.70
☐ RC27 John Stockton	3.00	1.35
☐ RC28 Bryant Reeves	2.00	.90
☐ RC29 Chris Webber	8.00	3.60
☐ RC30 Michael Jordan	40.00	18.00

1997-98 Upper Deck Rookie Discovery 1

Randomly inserted into packs at a rate of one in four, this 15-card set focuses on the 1997 Rookie Class, and their thoughts and secrets on the game. Card backs are numbered with a "R" prefix.

	MINT	NRMT
COMPLETE SET (15)	30.00	13.50
COMMON CARD (R1-R15)	.60	.25
SEMISTARS	.75	.35
UNLISTED STARS	1.25	.55
SER.2 STATED ODDS 1:4		
COMP.RD2 SET (15)	300.00	135.00
COMMON RD2 (D1-D15)	5.00	2.20
*RD2: 3X TO 8X HI COLUMN		
RD2: SER.2 STATED ODDS 1:108		

☐ R1 Tim Duncan	8.00	3.60
☐ R2 Keith Van Horn	6.00	2.70
☐ R3 Chauncey Billups	2.50	1.10
☐ R4 Antonio Daniels	1.50	.70
☐ R5 Tony Battie	1.25	.55
☐ R6 Ron Mercer	5.00	2.20
☐ R7 Tim Thomas	4.00	1.80
☐ R8 Adonal Foyle	.75	.35
☐ R9 Tracy McGrady	4.00	1.80
☐ R10 Danny Fortson	1.25	.55
☐ R11 Tariq Abdul-Wahad	.75	.35
☐ R12 Austin Croshere	.60	.25
☐ R13 Derek Anderson	2.00	.90
☐ R14 Maurice Taylor	2.00	.90
☐ R15 Kelvin Cato	.60	.25

1997-98 Upper Deck Teammates

Randomly inserted in series one packs at the rate of one in four, this 60-card set features color action photos of players who are the top tandems for each team in the league printed in die-cut, embossed cards.. When the teammates are placed together, the cards spell out the team name.

	MINT	NRMT
COMPLETE SET (60)	80.00	36.00
COMMON CARD (T1-T60)	.50	.23
SEMISTARS	.60	.25
UNLISTED STARS	1.00	.45
SER.1 STATED ODDS 1:4		

☐ T1 Mookie Blaylock	.60	.25
☐ T2 Steve Smith	.60	.25
☐ T3 Antoine Walker	5.00	2.20
☐ T4 Dana Barros	.50	.23
☐ T5 Anthony Mason	.60	.25
☐ T6 Glen Rice	1.00	.45
☐ T7 Michael Jordan	12.00	5.50
☐ T8 Scottie Pippen	3.00	1.35
☐ T9 Terrell Brandon	1.00	.45
☐ T10 Tyrone Hill	.50	.23
☐ T11 Shawn Bradley	.50	.23
☐ T12 Robert Pack	.50	.23
☐ T13 LaPhonso Ellis	.50	.23
☐ T14 Antonio McDyess	1.25	.55
☐ T15 Grant Hill	6.00	2.70
☐ T16 Lindsey Hunter	.50	.23
☐ T17 Latrell Sprewell	1.00	.45
☐ T18 Joe Smith	1.00	.45
☐ T19 Hakeem Olajuwon	2.00	.90
☐ T20 Charles Barkley	1.50	.70
☐ T21 Mark Jackson	.50	.23
☐ T22 Reggie Miller	1.00	.45
☐ T23 Brent Barry	.50	.23
☐ T24 Loy Vaught	.60	.25
☐ T25 Shaquille O'Neal	4.00	1.80
☐ T26 Nick Van Exel	1.00	.45
☐ T27 Tim Hardaway	1.25	.55
☐ T28 Alonzo Mourning	1.00	.45
☐ T29 Vin Baker	2.00	.90
☐ T30 Glenn Robinson	1.00	.45
☐ T31 Kevin Garnett	6.00	2.70
☐ T32 Stephon Marbury	5.00	2.20
☐ T33 Kendall Gill	.60	.25
☐ T34 Kerry Kittles	1.00	.45
☐ T35 Patrick Ewing	1.00	.45
☐ T36 John Starks	.60	.25
☐ T37 Horace Grant	.60	.25
☐ T38 A.Hardaway	4.00	1.80
☐ T39 Allen Iverson	5.00	2.20
☐ T40 Jerry Stackhouse	1.00	.45

☐ T41	Jason Kidd	2.00	.90
☐ T42	Kevin Johnson	.60	.25
☐ T43	Kenny Anderson	.60	.25
☐ T44	Isaiah Rider	.60	.25
☐ T45	Billy Owens	.50	.23
☐ T46	Mitch Richmond	1.00	.45
☐ T47	Sean Elliott	.50	.23
☐ T48	David Robinson	1.50	.70
☐ T49	Gary Payton	1.50	.70
☐ T50	Shawn Kemp	3.00	1.35
☐ T51	Marcus Camby	1.00	.45
☐ T52	Damon Stoudamire	2.00	.90
☐ T53	John Stockton	1.00	.45
☐ T54	Karl Malone	1.50	.70
☐ T55	S.Abdur-Rahim	3.00	1.35
☐ T56	Bryant Reeves	.60	.25
☐ T57	Juwan Howard	1.00	.45
☐ T58	Chris Webber	2.50	1.10
☐ T59	Michael Jordan	12.00	5.50
☐ T60	A.Hardaway	4.00	1.80

1997-98 Upper Deck Ultimates

Randomly inserted in series one packs at the rate of one in 23, this 30-card set features color action player images on Light F/X cards with some of the player's abilities printed across the background.

		MINT	NRMT
COMPLETE SET (30)		100.00	45.00
COMMON CARD (U1-U30)		1.50	.70
SEMISTARS		2.00	.90
UNLISTED STARS		3.00	1.35
SER.1 STATED ODDS 1:23			

☐ U1	Michael Jordan	40.00	18.00
☐ U2	Grant Hill	20.00	9.00
☐ U3	Charles Barkley	5.00	2.20
☐ U4	Tom Gugliotta	3.00	1.35
☐ U5	Dennis Rodman	12.00	5.50
☐ U6	Reggie Miller	3.00	1.35
☐ U7	Jason Kidd	6.00	2.70
☐ U8	Loy Vaught	2.00	.90
☐ U9	Mookie Blaylock	2.00	.90
☐ U10	Tim Hardaway	4.00	1.80
☐ U11	Juwan Howard	3.00	1.35
☐ U12	Shawn Kemp	10.00	4.50
☐ U13	Mitch Richmond	3.00	1.35
☐ U14	Patrick Ewing	3.00	1.35
☐ U15	Marcus Camby	3.00	1.35
☐ U16	Bryant Stith	1.50	.70
☐ U17	Bryant Reeves	2.00	.90
☐ U18	Joe Smith	3.00	1.35
☐ U19	Jerry Stackhouse	3.00	1.35
☐ U20	Arvydas Sabonis	2.00	.90

☐ U21	John Stockton	3.00	1.35
☐ U22	Eddie Jones	6.00	2.70
☐ U23	A.Hardaway	12.00	5.50
☐ U24	Ray Allen	4.00	1.80
☐ U25	Terrell Brandon	3.00	1.35
☐ U26	David Robinson	5.00	2.20
☐ U27	Antonio Mason	2.00	.90
☐ U28	Robert Pack	1.50	.70
☐ U29	Dana Barros	1.50	.70
☐ U30	Kendall Gill	2.00	.90

1997-98 Upper Deck Diamond Vision

This 29-card set features color action player photos taken from actual NBA game footage using the latest cutting-edge technology. The set was distributed in one-card packs with a suggested retail price of $7.99.

		MINT	NRMT
COMPLETE SET (29)		125.00	55.00
COMMON CARD (1-29)		1.00	.45
SEMISTARS		1.50	.70
UNLISTED STARS		2.50	1.10
COMP.SIG.MOVES 1 (29)		275.00	125.00
COMMON SIG.MOVES (1-29)		2.00	.90
*SIG.MOVES: 1X TO 2X HI COLUMN			
SIG.MOVES: SER.1 STATED ODDS 1:3			
R1: SER.1 STATED ODDS 1:500			

☐ 1	D.Mutombo	1.50	.70
☐ 2	Dana Barros	1.00	.45
☐ 3	Glen Rice	2.50	1.10
☐ 4	Michael Jordan	30.00	13.50
☐ 5	Terrell Brandon	2.50	1.10
☐ 6	Michael Finley	2.50	1.10
☐ 7	Antonio McDyess	3.00	1.35
☐ 8	Grant Hill	15.00	6.75
☐ 9	Latrell Sprewell	1.50	.70
☐ 10	Hakeem Olajuwon	5.00	2.20
☐ 11	Reggie Miller	2.50	1.10
☐ 12	Loy Vaught	1.50	.70
☐ 13	Shaquille O'Neal	10.00	4.50
☐ 14	Alonzo Mourning	2.50	1.10
☐ 15	Vin Baker	5.00	2.20
☐ 16	Kevin Garnett	15.00	6.75
☐ 17	Kerry Kittles	2.50	1.10
☐ 18	Patrick Ewing	2.50	1.10
☐ 19	A.Hardaway	10.00	4.50
☐ 20	Allen Iverson	12.00	5.50
☐ 21	Jason Kidd	5.00	2.20
☐ 22	Isaiah Rider	1.50	.70
☐ 23	Mitch Richmond	2.50	1.10
☐ 24	David Robinson	4.00	1.80
☐ 25	Gary Payton	4.00	1.80
☐ 26	Damon Stoudamire	5.00	2.20
☐ 27	Karl Malone	4.00	1.80
☐ 28	S.Abdur-Rahim	8.00	3.60
☐ 29	Chris Webber	6.00	2.70

1997-98 Upper Deck Diamond Vision Dunk Vision

Randomly inserted in packs at the rate of one in 40, this six-card set features borderless color action game photos of spectacular dunks of NBA superstars.

		MINT	NRMT
COMPLETE SET (6)		300.00	135.00
COMMON CARD (D1-D6)		20.00	9.00
SER.1: STATED ODDS 1:40			

☐ D1	Michael Jordan	125.00	55.00
☐ D2	A.Hardaway	40.00	18.00
☐ D3	Shaquille O'Neal	40.00	18.00
☐ D4	Grant Hill	60.00	27.00
☐ D5	Kevin Garnett	60.00	27.00
☐ D6	Hakeem Olajuwon	20.00	9.00

1998 Upper Deck Hardcourt

The 1998 Upper Deck Hardcourt hobby-only set was issued in one series totalling 90 cards. The 4-card packs retail for $5.99 each. The cards feature 32-point stock with a "wood" designed background. The set contains the topical subset: Rookie Experience (71-90). A bonus Michael Jordan card was also included in packs (#23a) at a reported rate of one in every two boxes. Also included, was a 5" by 7" Michael Jordan jumbo card. It was included one per box.

	MINT	NRMT
COMPLETE SET (90)	75.00	34.00
COMMON CARD (1-90)	.40	.18
SEMISTARS	.60	.25

JORDAN SPEC. INSERTED EVERY TWO BOXES
JORDAN SPEC. NOT IN SET PRICE
ONE JORDAN JUMBO PER BOX

COMP.HOME CT.ADV(90)	350.00	160.00
COMMON HOME CT.ADV	1.25	.55

*HOME CT.ADV: 1.25X TO 3X HI COLUMN
HOME CT.ADV: STATED ODDS 1:4

□ 1 Kobe Bryant	8.00	3.60
□ 2 Donyell Marshall	.60	.25
□ 3 Bryant Reeves	.60	.25
□ 4 Keith Van Horn	5.00	2.20
□ 5 David Robinson	1.50	.70
□ 6 Nick Anderson	.40	.18
□ 7 Nick Van Exel	.75	.35
□ 8 David Wesley	.40	.18
□ 9 Alonzo Mourning	1.00	.45
□ 10 Shawn Kemp	3.00	1.35
□ 11 Maurice Taylor	1.25	.55
□ 12 Kenny Anderson	.60	.25
□ 13 Jason Kidd	2.00	.90
□ 14 Marcus Camby	.75	.35
□ 15 Tim Hardaway	1.25	.55
□ 16 Damon Stoudamire	1.50	.70
□ 17 Detlef Schrempf	.60	.25
□ 18 D.Mutombo	.60	.25
□ 19 Charles Barkley	1.50	.70
□ 20 Ray Allen	1.00	.45
□ 21 Ron Mercer	4.00	1.80
□ 22 Shawn Bradley	.40	.18
□ 23 Michael Jordan	12.00	5.50
□ 23A Michael Jordan Spec.	20.00	9.00
□ 24 Antonio McDyess	1.00	.45
□ 25 Stephon Marbury	4.00	1.80
□ 26 Rik Smits	.60	.25
□ 27 Michael Stewart	.60	.25
□ 28 Steve Smith	.60	.25
□ 29 Glenn Robinson	.75	.35
□ 30 Chris Webber	2.50	1.10
□ 31 Antoine Walker	4.00	1.80
□ 32 Eddie Jones	2.00	.90
□ 33 Mitch Richmond	1.00	.45
□ 34 Kevin Garnett	6.00	2.70
□ 35 Grant Hill	6.00	2.70
□ 36 John Stockton	1.00	.45
□ 37 Allan Houston	.60	.25
□ 38 Bobby Jackson	.75	.35
□ 39 Sam Cassell	.60	.25
□ 40 Allen Iverson	4.00	1.80
□ 41 LaPhonso Ellis	.40	.18
□ 42 Lorenzen Wright	.40	.18
□ 43 Gary Payton	1.50	.70
□ 44 Patrick Ewing	1.00	.45
□ 45 Scottie Pippen	3.00	1.35
□ 46 Hakeem Olajuwon	2.00	.90
□ 47 Glen Rice	1.00	.45
□ 48 Antonio Daniels	1.00	.45
□ 49 Jayson Williams	.60	.25
□ 50 Juwan Howard	1.00	.45
□ 51 Reggie Miller	1.00	.45
□ 52 Joe Smith	.75	.35
□ 53 Shaquille O'Neal	4.00	1.80
□ 54 Dennis Rodman	4.00	1.80
□ 55 Vin Baker	2.00	.90
□ 56 Rod Strickland	.60	.25
□ 57 A.Hardaway	4.00	1.80
□ 58 Zydrunas Ilgauskas	.60	.25
□ 59 Chris Mullin	.75	.35
□ 60 Rasheed Wallace	.60	.25
□ 61 Shareef Abdur-Rahim	2.50	1.10
□ 62 Tom Gugliotta	.75	.35
□ 63 Tim Duncan	6.00	2.70
□ 64 Michael Finley	.75	.35
□ 65 Jim Jackson	.60	.25
□ 66 Chauncey Billups	1.50	.70
□ 67 Jerry Stackhouse	.75	.35
□ 68 Jeff Hornacek	.60	.25
□ 69 Clyde Drexler	1.25	.55
□ 70 Karl Malone	1.50	.70
□ 71 Tim Duncan RE	3.00	1.35
□ 72 Keith Van Horn RE	2.50	1.10
□ 73 Chauncey Billups RE	.75	.35
□ 74 Antonio Daniels RE	.75	.35
□ 75 Tony Battie RE	.75	.35
□ 76 Ron Mercer RE	2.00	.90
□ 77 Tim Thomas RE	3.00	1.35
□ 78 Tracy McGrady RE	3.00	1.35
□ 79 Danny Fortson RE	.75	.35
□ 80 Derek Anderson RE	1.25	.55
□ 81 Maurice Taylor RE	.75	.35
□ 82 Kelvin Cato RE	.40	.18
□ 83 Brevin Knight RE	1.25	.55
□ 84 Bobby Jackson RE	.75	.35
□ 85 Rodrick Rhodes RE	.40	.18
□ 86 Anthony Johnson RE	.40	.18
□ 87 Cedric Henderson RE	.40	.18
□ 88 Chris Anstey RE	.40	.18
□ 89 Michael Stewart RE	.40	.18
□ 90 Zydrunas Ilgauskas RE	.40	.18
□ NNO M.Jordan Jumbo	10.00	4.50

1998 Upper Deck Hardcourt Home Court Advantage Plus

Randomly inserted in packs, this 90-card set parallels the basic set. The front features gold foil writing across the card front with the cards printed on wood paper stock. The cards are also serially numbered to 500 on the card back.

	MINT	NRMT
COMMON CARD (1-90)	6.00	2.70
SEMISTARS	10.00	4.50

RANDOM INSERTS IN PACKS
STATED PRINT RUN 500 SERIAL #'d SETS

□ 1 Kobe Bryant	125.00	55.00
□ 2 Donyell Marshall	6.00	2.70
□ 3 Bryant Reeves	10.00	4.50
□ 4 Keith Van Horn	80.00	36.00
□ 5 David Robinson	25.00	11.00
□ 6 Nick Anderson	6.00	2.70
□ 7 Nick Van Exel	12.00	5.50
□ 8 David Wesley	6.00	2.70
□ 9 Alonzo Mourning	15.00	6.75
□ 10 Shawn Kemp	50.00	22.00
□ 11 Maurice Taylor	20.00	9.00
□ 12 Kenny Anderson	10.00	4.50
□ 13 Jason Kidd	30.00	13.50
□ 14 Marcus Camby	12.00	5.50
□ 15 Tim Hardaway	20.00	9.00
□ 16 Damon Stoudamire	25.00	11.00
□ 17 Detlef Schrempf	10.00	4.50
□ 18 D.Mutombo	10.00	4.50
□ 19 Charles Barkley	25.00	11.00
□ 20 Ray Allen	15.00	6.75
□ 21 Ron Mercer	60.00	27.00
□ 22 Shawn Bradley	6.00	2.70
□ 23 Michael Jordan	200.00	90.00
□ 24 Antonio McDyess	15.00	6.75
□ 25 Stephon Marbury	60.00	27.00
□ 26 Rik Smits	10.00	4.50
□ 27 Michael Stewart	10.00	4.50
□ 28 Steve Smith	10.00	4.50
□ 29 Glenn Robinson	12.00	5.50
□ 30 Chris Webber	40.00	18.00
□ 31 Antoine Walker	60.00	27.00
□ 32 Eddie Jones	30.00	13.50
□ 33 Mitch Richmond	15.00	6.75
□ 34 Kevin Garnett	100.00	45.00
□ 35 Grant Hill	100.00	45.00
□ 36 John Stockton	15.00	6.75
□ 37 Allan Houston	10.00	4.50
□ 38 Bobby Jackson	12.00	5.50
□ 39 Sam Cassell	10.00	4.50
□ 40 Allen Iverson	60.00	27.00
□ 41 LaPhonso Ellis	6.00	2.70
□ 42 Lorenzen Wright	6.00	2.70
□ 43 Gary Payton	25.00	11.00
□ 44 Patrick Ewing	15.00	6.75
□ 45 Scottie Pippen	50.00	22.00
□ 46 Hakeem Olajuwon	30.00	13.50
□ 47 Glen Rice	15.00	6.75
□ 48 Antonio Daniels	15.00	6.75
□ 49 Jayson Williams	10.00	4.50
□ 50 Juwan Howard	15.00	6.75
□ 51 Reggie Miller	15.00	6.75
□ 52 Joe Smith	12.00	5.50
□ 53 Shaquille O'Neal	60.00	27.00
□ 54 Dennis Rodman	60.00	27.00
□ 55 Vin Baker	30.00	13.50
□ 56 Rod Strickland	10.00	4.50
□ 57 A.Hardaway	60.00	27.00
□ 58 Zydrunas Ilgauskas	10.00	4.50
□ 59 Chris Mullin	12.00	5.50
□ 60 Rasheed Wallace	10.00	4.50
□ 61 S.Abdur-Rahim	40.00	18.00
□ 62 Tom Gugliotta	12.00	5.50
□ 63 Tim.Duncan	100.00	45.00
□ 64 Michael Finley	12.00	5.50
□ 65 Jim Jackson	10.00	4.50
□ 66 Chauncey Billups	25.00	11.00
□ 67 Jerry Stackhouse	12.00	5.50
□ 68 Jeff Hornacek	10.00	4.50
□ 69 Clyde Drexler	20.00	9.00
□ 70 Karl Malone	25.00	11.00
□ 71 Tim Duncan RE	50.00	22.00
□ 72 Keith Van Horn RE	40.00	18.00
□ 73 Chauncey Billups RE	12.00	5.50
□ 74 Antonio Daniels RE	12.00	5.50
□ 75 Tony Battie RE	12.00	5.50
□ 76 Ron Mercer RE	30.00	13.50
□ 77 Tim Thomas RE	50.00	22.00
□ 78 Tracy McGrady RE	50.00	22.00
□ 79 Danny Fortson RE	12.00	5.50
□ 80 Derek Anderson RE	20.00	9.00
□ 81 Maurice Taylor RE	12.00	5.50
□ 82 Kelvin Cato RE	6.00	2.70
□ 83 Brevin Knight RE	20.00	9.00
□ 84 Bobby Jackson RE	12.00	5.50
□ 85 Rodrick Rhodes RE	6.00	2.70
□ 86 Anthony Johnson RE	6.00	2.70
□ 87 Cedric Henderson RE	6.00	2.70
□ 88 Chris Anstey RE	6.00	2.70
□ 89 Michael Stewart RE	6.00	2.70
□ 90 Z.Ilgauskas RE	6.00	2.70

1998 Upper Deck Hardcourt High Court

Randomly inserted into packs, this 30-card set features some

		MINT	NRMT
	Michael Jordan		
□ J30	Michael Jordan	80.00	36.00
	Michael Jordan		

1998 Upper Deck Hardcourt Jordan Holding Court Bronze

Randomly inserted into packs, this 30-card set features a duel-player, double-wood card. The cards feature 40-point stock. Each card features Michael Jordan on one side and one of 29 other NBA superstars on the other. The set features the title of the set and the Upper Deck logo in bronze foil. The cards are serially numbered to 230.

of the high-flying performers in the NBA. The cards are produced on wood paper stock with a silver logo titled "High Court" in the lower left corner. The cards are serially numbered to 1300 in gold foil on the card front.

title of the set and the Upper Deck logo in red foil. The cards are serially numbered to 2300.

	MINT	NRMT
COMPLETE SET (30)	450.00	200.00
COMMON CARD (J1-J30) ...	2.50	1.10
STATED ODDS 2300 SERIAL #'d SETS		

	MINT	NRMT
COMPLETE SET (30)	500.00	220.00
COMMON CARD (H1-H30) ...	3.00	1.35
RANDOM INSERTS IN PACKS		
STATED PRINT RUN 1300 SERIAL #'d SETS		

		MINT	NRMT
□ H1	D.Mutombo..............	5.00	2.20
□ H2	Ron Mercer..............	30.00	13.50
□ H3	Glen Rice	8.00	3.60
□ H4	Scottie Pippen.........	25.00	11.00
□ H5	Shawn Kemp............	25.00	11.00
□ H6	Michael Finley	6.00	2.70
□ H7	LaPhonso Ellis	3.00	1.35
□ H8	Grant Hill.................	50.00	22.00
□ H9	Erick Dampier	3.00	1.35
□ H10	Hakeem Olajuwon ...	15.00	6.75
□ H11	Chris Mullin	5.00	2.20
□ H12	Lamond Murray	3.00	1.35
□ H13	Kobe Bryant	60.00	27.00
□ H14	Tim Hardaway	10.00	4.50
□ H15	Ray Allen.................	8.00	3.60
□ H16	Stephon Marbury	30.00	13.50
□ H17	Keith Van Horn	40.00	18.00
□ H18	Allan Houston	5.00	2.20
□ H19	A.Hardaway..............	30.00	13.50
□ H20	Allen Iverson	30.00	13.50
□ H21	Antonio McDyess	8.00	3.60
□ H22	Rasheed Wallace......	5.00	2.20
□ H23	Mitch Richmond	8.00	3.60
□ H24	Tim Duncan..............	50.00	22.00
□ H25	Gary Payton	12.00	5.50
□ H26	Chauncey Billups ...	12.00	5.50
□ H27	John Stockton..........	8.00	3.60
□ H28	S.Abdur-Rahim........	20.00	9.00
□ H29	Juwan Howard	8.00	3.60
□ H30	Michael Jordan	100.00	45.00

1998 Upper Deck Hardcourt Jordan Holding Court Red

Randomly inserted into packs, this 30-card set features a duel-player, double-wood card. The cards feature 40-point stock. Each card features Michael Jordan on one side and one of 29 other NBA superstars on the other. The base set features the

		MINT	NRMT
□ J1	Steve Smith..............	4.00	1.80
	Michael Jordan		
□ J2	Antoine Walker	25.00	11.00
	Michael Jordan		
□ J3	Glen Rice	6.00	2.70
	Michael Jordan		
□ J4	Scottie Pippen.........	20.00	9.00
	Michael Jordan		
□ J5	Shawn Kemp............	20.00	9.00
	Michael Jordan		
□ J6	Michael Finley	5.00	2.20
	Michael Jordan		
□ J7	Bobby Jackson	5.00	2.20
	Michael Jordan		
□ J8	Grant Hill.................	40.00	18.00
	Michael Jordan		
□ J9	Jim Jackson	4.00	1.80
	Michael Jordan		
□ J10	Charles Barkley	10.00	4.50
	Michael Jordan		
□ J11	Reggie Miller	6.00	2.70
	Michael Jordan		
□ J12	Lorenzen Wright	2.50	1.10
	Michael Jordan		
□ J13	Kobe Bryant	50.00	22.00
	Michael Jordan		
□ J14	Tim Hardaway	8.00	3.60
	Michael Jordan		
□ J15	Glenn Robinson	5.00	2.20
	Michael Jordan		
□ J16	Kevin Garnett..........	40.00	18.00
	Michael Jordan		
□ J17	Keith Van Horn	30.00	13.50
	Michael Jordan		
□ J18	Patrick Ewing..........	6.00	2.70
	Michael Jordan		
□ J19	A.Hardaway..............	25.00	11.00
	Michael Jordan		
□ J20	Allen Iverson	25.00	11.00
	Michael Jordan		
□ J21	Jason Kidd	12.00	5.50
	Michael Jordan		
□ J22	D.Stoudamire	10.00	4.50
	Michael Jordan		
□ J23	Mitch Richmond	6.00	2.70
	Michael Jordan		
□ J24	Tim Duncan..............	40.00	18.00
	Michael Jordan		
□ J25	Gary Payton	10.00	4.50
	Michael Jordan		
□ J26	Chauncey Billups ...	10.00	4.50
	Michael Jordan		
□ J27	Karl Malone	10.00	4.50
	Michael Jordan		
□ J28	S.Abdur-Rahim........	15.00	6.75
	Michael Jordan		
□ J29	Chris Webber...........	15.00	6.75

	MINT	NRMT
COMMON CARD (J1-J30) ...	10.00	4.50
RANDOM INSERTS IN PACKS		
STATED PRINT RUN 230 SERIAL #'d SETS		

		MINT	NRMT
□ J1	Steve Smith..............	10.00	4.50
	Michael Jordan		
□ J2	Antoine Walker	100.00	45.00
	Michael Jordan		
□ J3	Glen Rice	25.00	11.00
	Michael Jordan		
□ J4	Scottie Pippen.........	75.00	34.00
	Michael Jordan		
□ J5	Shawn Kemp............	75.00	34.00
	Michael Jordan		
□ J6	Michael Finley	20.00	9.00
	Michael Jordan		
□ J7	Bobby Jackson	20.00	9.00
	Michael Jordan		
□ J8	Grant Hill.................	150.00	70.00
	Michael Jordan		
□ J9	Jim Jackson	10.00	4.50
	Michael Jordan		
□ J10	Charles Barkley	40.00	18.00
	Michael Jordan		
□ J11	Reggie Miller	25.00	11.00
	Michael Jordan		
□ J12	Lorenzen Wright	10.00	4.50
	Michael Jordan		
□ J13	Kobe Bryant	200.00	90.00
	Michael Jordan		
□ J14	Tim Hardaway	30.00	13.50
	Michael Jordan		
□ J15	Glenn Robinson	20.00	9.00
	Michael Jordan		
□ J16	Kevin Garnett..........	150.00	70.00
	Michael Jordan		
□ J17	Keith Van Horn	120.00	55.00
	Michael Jordan		
□ J18	Patrick Ewing..........	25.00	11.00
	Michael Jordan		
□ J19	A.Hardaway..............	100.00	45.00
	Michael Jordan		
□ J20	Allen Iverson	100.00	45.00
	Michael Jordan		
□ J21	Jason Kidd	50.00	22.00
	Michael Jordan		
□ J22	D.Stoudamire	40.00	18.00
	Michael Jordan		
□ J23	Mitch Richmond	25.00	11.00
	Michael Jordan		
□ J24	Tim Duncan..............	150.00	70.00
	Michael Jordan		
□ J25	Gary Payton	40.00	18.00
	Michael Jordan		
□ J26	Chauncey Billups ...	40.00	18.00
	Michael Jordan		

		MINT	NRMT
☐ J27	Karl Malone	40.00	18.00
	Michael Jordan		
☐ J28	S.Abdur-Rahim	60.00	27.00
	Michael Jordan		
☐ J29	Chris Webber	60.00	27.00
	Michael Jordan		
☐ J30	Michael Jordan	350.00	160.00
	Michael Jordan		

1993-94 Upper Deck SE

This 225-card standard-size set was distributed in 12-card hobby East, hobby West, retail and 10-card magazine retail packs. There are 36 packs per box. Card fronts feature color player action shots that are borderless, except on the left, where a strip carries the player's name in gold foil along with his position and a vertically distorted black-and-white version of the action shot. The player's team name appears in vertical gold-foil lettering near the right edge. The back carries a color player action photo, with his name, position, and brief biography appearing in stripes across the top. Statistics and career highlights are displayed horizontally in a ghosted panel on the left. The set closes with the following topical subsets: NBA All-Star Weekend Highlights (181-198) and Team Headlines (199-225). Two Michael Jordan insert cards are a Kilroy card (JK1) and a retirement tribute card (MJR1). These were inserted at a rate of 1 in 72 packs. Rookie Cards of note in this set include Vin Baker, Anfernee Hardaway, Jamal Mashburn, Nick Van Exel and Chris Webber.

	MINT	NRMT
COMPLETE SET (225)	15.00	6.75
COMMON CARD (1-225)	.05	.02
SEMISTARS	.15	.07
UNLISTED STARS	.30	.14
COMP.ELEC.CT.SET (225)	60.00	27.00
COMMON EC CARD (1-225)	.15	.07

*EC STARS: 1.25X TO 2.5X HI COLUMN
*EC RCs: 1X TO 2X HI
ONE ELECTRIC COURT PER PACK

		MINT	NRMT
COMP.ELEC.GLD.SET (225)		500.00	220.00
COMMON GOLD (1-225)		1.50	.70

*GOLD STARS: 12.5X TO 25X HI COLUMN
*GOLD RCs: 10X TO 20X HI
GOLD: STATED ODDS 1:36 HOB/RET
JK1/MJR1: STATED ODDS 1:72

☐ 1	Scottie Pippen	1.00	.45
☐ 2	Todd Day	.05	.02
☐ 3	Detlef Schrempf	.15	.07
☐ 4	Chris Webber	2.00	.90
☐ 5	Michael Adams	.05	.02
☐ 6	Loy Vaught	.15	.07
☐ 7	Doug West	.05	.02
☐ 8	A.C. Green	.15	.07
☐ 9	Anthony Mason	.15	.07
☐ 10	Clyde Drexler	.40	.18
☐ 11	Popeye Jones	.05	.02
☐ 12	Vlade Divac	.15	.07
☐ 13	Armon Gilliam	.05	.02
☐ 14	Hersey Hawkins	.15	.07
☐ 15	Dennis Scott	.15	.07
☐ 16	Bimbo Coles	.05	.02
☐ 17	Blue Edwards	.05	.02
☐ 18	Negele Knight	.05	.02
☐ 19	Dale Davis	.05	.02
☐ 20	Isiah Thomas	.30	.14
☐ 21	Latrell Sprewell	.30	.14
☐ 22	Kenny Smith	.05	.02
☐ 23	Bryant Stith	.05	.02
☐ 24	Terry Porter	.05	.02
☐ 25	Spud Webb	.15	.07
☐ 26	John Battle	.05	.02
☐ 27	Jeff Malone	.05	.02
☐ 28	Olden Polynice	.05	.02
☐ 29	Kevin Willis	.05	.02
☐ 30	Robert Parish	.15	.07
☐ 31	Kevin Johnson	.15	.07
☐ 32	Shaquille O'Neal	1.25	.55
☐ 33	Willie Anderson	.05	.02
☐ 34	Micheal Williams	.05	.02
☐ 35	Steve Smith	.15	.07
☐ 36	Rik Smits	.15	.07
☐ 37	Pete Myers	.05	.02
☐ 38	Oliver Miller	.05	.02
☐ 39	Eddie Johnson	.05	.02
☐ 40	Calbert Cheaney	.30	.14
☐ 41	Vernon Maxwell	.05	.02
☐ 42	James Worthy	.30	.14
☐ 43	Dino Radja	.15	.07
☐ 44	Derrick Coleman	.15	.07
☐ 45	Reggie Williams	.05	.02
☐ 46	Dale Ellis	.05	.02
☐ 47	Clifford Robinson	.15	.07
☐ 48	Doug Christie	.05	.02
☐ 49	Ricky Pierce	.05	.02
☐ 50	Sean Elliott	.15	.07
☐ 51	Anfernee Hardaway	4.00	1.80
☐ 52	Dana Barros	.05	.02
☐ 53	Reggie Miller	.30	.14
☐ 54	Brian Williams	.05	.02
☐ 55	Otis Thorpe	.15	.07
☐ 56	Jerome Kersey	.05	.02
☐ 57	Larry Johnson	.30	.14
☐ 58	Rex Chapman	.05	.02
☐ 59	Kevin Edwards	.05	.02
☐ 60	Nate McMillan	.05	.02
☐ 61	Chris Mullin	.30	.14
☐ 62	Bill Cartwright	.05	.02
☐ 63	Dennis Rodman	1.25	.55
☐ 64	Pooh Richardson	.05	.02
☐ 65	Tyrone Hill	.05	.02
☐ 66	Scott Brooks	.05	.02
☐ 67	Brad Daugherty	.05	.02
☐ 68	Joe Dumars	.30	.14
☐ 69	Vin Baker	2.00	.90
☐ 70	Rod Strickland	.15	.07
☐ 71	Tom Chambers	.05	.02
☐ 72	Charles Oakley	.15	.07
☐ 73	Craig Ehlo	.05	.02
☐ 74	LaPhonso Ellis	.15	.07
☐ 75	Kevin Gamble	.05	.02
☐ 76	Shawn Bradley	.40	.18
☐ 77	Kendall Gill	.15	.07
☐ 78	Hakeem Olajuwon	.60	.25
☐ 79	Nick Anderson	.15	.07
☐ 80	Anthony Peeler	.05	.02
☐ 81	Wayman Tisdale	.05	.02
☐ 82	Danny Manning	.05	.02
☐ 83	John Starks	.15	.07
☐ 84	Jeff Hornacek	.15	.07
☐ 85	Victor Alexander	.05	.02
☐ 86	Mitch Richmond	.30	.14
☐ 87	Mookie Blaylock	.15	.07
☐ 88	Harvey Grant	.05	.02
☐ 89	Doug Smith	.05	.02
☐ 90	John Stockton	.30	.14
☐ 91	Charles Barkley	.50	.23
☐ 92	Gerald Wilkins	.05	.02
☐ 93	Mario Elie	.05	.02
☐ 94	Ken Norman	.05	.02
☐ 95	B.J. Armstrong	.05	.02
☐ 96	John Williams	.05	.02
☐ 97	Rony Seikaly	.05	.02
☐ 98	Sean Rooks	.05	.02
☐ 99	Shawn Kemp	1.00	.45
☐ 100	Danny Ainge	.15	.07
☐ 101	Terry Mills	.05	.02
☐ 102	Doc Rivers	.15	.07
☐ 103	Chuck Person	.05	.02
☐ 104	Sam Cassell	.75	.35
☐ 105	Kevin Duckworth	.05	.02
☐ 106	Dan Majerle	.15	.07
☐ 107	Mark Jackson	.15	.07
☐ 108	Steve Kerr	.15	.07
☐ 109	Sam Perkins	.15	.07
☐ 110	C.Weatherspoon	.05	.02
☐ 111	Felton Spencer	.05	.02
☐ 112	Greg Anthony	.05	.02
☐ 113	Pete Chilcutt	.05	.02
☐ 114	Malik Sealy	.05	.02
☐ 115	Horace Grant	.15	.07
☐ 116	Chris Morris	.05	.02
☐ 117	Xavier McDaniel	.05	.02
☐ 118	Lionel Simmons	.05	.02
☐ 119	Dell Curry	.05	.02
☐ 120	Moses Malone	.30	.14
☐ 121	Lindsey Hunter	.30	.14
☐ 122	Buck Williams	.15	.07
☐ 123	Mahmoud Abdul-Rauf	.05	.02
☐ 124	Rumeal Robinson	.05	.02
☐ 125	Chris Mills	.50	.23
☐ 126	Scott Skiles	.05	.02
☐ 127	Derrick McKey	.05	.02
☐ 128	Avery Johnson	.05	.02
☐ 129	Harold Miner	.05	.02
☐ 130	Frank Brickowski	.05	.02
☐ 131	Gary Payton	.50	.23
☐ 132	Don MacLean	.05	.02
☐ 133	Thurl Bailey	.05	.02
☐ 134	Nick Van Exel	1.00	.45
☐ 135	Matt Geiger	.05	.02
☐ 136	Stacey Augmon	.05	.02
☐ 137	Sedale Threatt	.05	.02
☐ 138	Patrick Ewing	.30	.14
☐ 139	Tyrone Corbin	.05	.02
☐ 140	Jim Jackson	.30	.14
☐ 141	Christian Laettner	.30	.14
☐ 142	Robert Horry	.15	.07
☐ 143	J.R. Reid	.05	.02
☐ 144	Eric Murdock	.05	.02
☐ 145	Alonzo Mourning	.50	.23
☐ 146	Sherman Douglas	.05	.02
☐ 147	Tom Gugliotta	.30	.14
☐ 148	Glen Rice	.30	.14
☐ 149	Mark Price	.15	.07
☐ 150	D.Mutombo	.30	.14
☐ 151	Derek Harper	.15	.07
☐ 152	Karl Malone	.50	.23
☐ 153	Byron Scott	.15	.07
☐ 154	Reggie Jordan	.05	.02
☐ 155	Dominique Wilkins	.30	.14
☐ 156	Bobby Hurley	.15	.07
☐ 157	Ron Harper	.15	.07
☐ 158	Bryon Russell	.30	.14
☐ 159	Frank Johnson	.05	.02
☐ 160	Toni Kukoc	.75	.35
☐ 161	Lloyd Daniels	.05	.02
☐ 162	Jeff Turner	.05	.02

☐ 163 Muggsy Bogues	.15	.07
☐ 164 Chris Gatling	.05	.02
☐ 165 Kenny Anderson	.15	.07
☐ 166 Elmore Spencer	.05	.02
☐ 167 Jamal Mashburn	.75	.35
☐ 168 Tim Perry	.05	.02
☐ 169 Antonio Davis	.15	.07
☐ 170 Isaiah Rider	.40	.18
☐ 171 Dee Brown	.05	.02
☐ 172 Walt Williams	.15	.07
☐ 173 Elden Campbell	.15	.07
☐ 174 Benoit Benjamin	.05	.02
☐ 175 Billy Owens	.05	.02
☐ 176 Andrew Lang	.05	.02
☐ 177 David Robinson	.50	.23
☐ 178 Checklist 1	.05	.02
☐ 179 Checklist 2	.05	.02
☐ 180 Checklist 3	.05	.02
☐ 181 Shawn Bradley AS	.15	.07
☐ 182 Calbert Cheaney AS	.15	.07
☐ 183 Toni Kukoc AS	.30	.14
☐ 184 Popeye Jones AS	.05	.02
☐ 185 Lindsey Hunter AS	.15	.07
☐ 186 Chris Webber AS	.75	.35
☐ 187 Bryon Russell AS	.15	.07
☐ 188 A.Hardaway AS	1.50	.70
☐ 189 Nick Van Exel AS	.40	.18
☐ 190 P.J. Brown AS	.05	.02
☐ 191 Isaiah Rider AS	.15	.07
☐ 192 Chris Mills AS	.15	.07
☐ 193 Antonio Davis AS	.15	.07
☐ 194 Jamal Mashburn AS	.30	.14
☐ 195 Dino Radja AS	.05	.02
☐ 196 Sam Cassell AS	.30	.14
☐ 197 Isaiah Rider ASW	.15	.07
☐ 198 Mark Price ASW	.05	.02
☐ 199 Stacey Augmon TH	.05	.02
☐ 200 Celtics Team TH	.05	.02
☐ 201 Eddie Johnson TH	.05	.02
☐ 202 Scottie Pippen TH	.50	.23
☐ 203 Brad Daugherty TH	.05	.02
☐ 204 Jamal Mashburn TH	.30	.14
☐ 205 D.Mutombo TH	.05	.02
(Oliver Miller on defense)		
☐ 206 Lindsey Hunter TH	.15	.07
☐ 207 Chris Webber TH	.50	.23
☐ 208 Rockets Team TH	.05	.02
☐ 209 Derrick McKey TH	.05	.02
☐ 210 Danny Manning TH	.05	.02
☐ 211 Doug Christie HDL	.05	.02
☐ 212 Glen Rice TH	.15	.07
☐ 213 Todd Day TH	.05	.02
Ken Norman TH		
Vin Baker TH		
Jon Barry TH		
☐ 214 Isaiah Rider TH	.15	.07
☐ 215 Kenny Anderson TH	.05	.02
☐ 216 Patrick Ewing TH	.15	.07
☐ 217 A.Hardaway TH	1.00	.45
☐ 218 Moses Malone TH	.05	.02
☐ 219 Kevin Johnson TH	.05	.02
☐ 220 Clifford Robinson TH	.05	.02
☐ 221 Wayman Tisdale TH	.05	.02
☐ 222 David Robinson TH	.30	.14
☐ 223 Sonics Team TH	.05	.02
☐ 224 John Stockton TH	.15	.07
☐ 225 Don MacLean TH	.05	.02
☐ JK1 Johnny Kilroy	5.00	2.20
(Michael Jordan)		
☐ MJR1 Michael Jordan	10.00	4.50
Retirement Card		

1993-94 Upper Deck SE Behind the Glass

Randomly inserted in 12-card retail packs at a rate of one in 30, cards from this 15-card standard-size set capture some of the NBA's best dunkers from the unique camera angle behind the backboard glass. A gold-foil "Behind the Glass Trade Card" was randomly inserted in hobby packs at a rate of one in 360. The collector could redeem the card for the complete 15-card "Behind the Glass" set. The redemption deadline was August 31, 1994. The borderless front features a color player action shot on a gold metallic finish. The player's name and position appear vertically along the right side. The back features a color player action shot on the right side with career highlights appearing alongside on the left.

	MINT	NRMT
COMPLETE SET (15)	40.00	18.00
COMMON CARD (G1-G15)	.60	.25
SEMISTARS	1.00	.45
UNLISTED STARS	1.50	.70
STATED ODDS 1:30 RETAIL		
ONE SET PER BHG TRADE CARD BY MAIL		
BHG TRADE: STATED ODDS 1:360 HOBBY		

☐ G1 Shawn Kemp	5.00	2.20
☐ G2 Patrick Ewing	1.50	.70
☐ G3 D.Mutombo	1.00	.45
☐ G4 Charles Barkley	2.50	1.10
☐ G5 Hakeem Olajuwon	3.00	1.35
☐ G6 Larry Johnson	1.50	.70
☐ G7 Chris Webber	6.00	2.70
☐ G8 John Starks	1.00	.45
☐ G9 Kevin Willis	.60	.25
☐ G10 Scottie Pippen	5.00	2.20
☐ G11 Michael Jordan	20.00	9.00
☐ G12 Alonzo Mourning	2.50	1.10
☐ G13 Shaquille O'Neal	6.00	2.70
☐ G14 Shawn Bradley	1.50	.70
☐ G15 Ron Harper	1.00	.45
☐ NNO Behind the Glass	1.50	.70
Trade Card		
☐ NNO Redmd BHG Trade	.25	.11

1993-94 Upper Deck SE Die Cut All-Stars

In these two 15-card insert standard-size sets, Upper Deck saluted a selection of current and potential future all-stars. The cards were available in East hobby and West hobby packs at a rate of one in 30 packs. Hobby dealers in the East received cases containing players from the Eastern conference, while hobby dealers in the West received cases containing players from the Western conference. These die-cut cards were inserted in hobby packs only. This unique card design features a partial gold-foil border at the top only. Centered is a color player action photo. The player's name and team appear in red vertical lettering along the left side. The back features brief statistics. Each set is sequenced in alphabetical team order.

	MINT	NRMT
COMPLETE SET (30)	550.00	250.00
COMP.EAST SET (15)	300.00	135.00
COMP.WEST SET (15)	250.00	110.00
COMMON EAST (E1-E15)	4.00	1.80
COMMON WEST (W1-W15)	4.00	1.80
SEMISTARS	8.00	3.60
UNLISTED STARS	12.00	5.50
STATED ODDS 1:30 HOBBY		

☐ E1 Dominique Wilkins	12.00	5.50
☐ E2 Alonzo Mourning	20.00	9.00
☐ E3 B.J. Armstrong	4.00	1.80
☐ E4 Scottie Pippen	40.00	18.00
☐ E5 Mark Price	4.00	1.80
☐ E6 Isiah Thomas	12.00	5.50
☐ E7 Harold Miner	4.00	1.80
☐ E8 Vin Baker	50.00	22.00
☐ E9 Kenny Anderson	8.00	3.60
☐ E10 Derrick Coleman	8.00	3.60
☐ E11 Patrick Ewing	12.00	5.50
☐ E12 A.Hardaway	80.00	36.00
☐ E13 Shaquille O'Neal	50.00	22.00
☐ E14 Shawn Bradley	12.00	5.50
☐ E15 Calbert Cheaney	12.00	5.50
☐ W1 Jim Jackson	12.00	5.50
☐ W2 Jamal Mashburn	25.00	11.00
☐ W3 D.Mutombo	12.00	5.50
☐ W4 Latrell Sprewell	12.00	5.50
☐ W5 Chris Webber	50.00	22.00
☐ W6 Hakeem Olajuwon	25.00	11.00
☐ W7 Danny Manning	4.00	1.80
☐ W8 Nick Van Exel	30.00	13.50
☐ W9 Isaiah Rider	12.00	5.50
☐ W10 Charles Barkley	20.00	9.00
☐ W11 Clyde Drexler	15.00	6.75
☐ W12 Mitch Richmond	12.00	5.50
☐ W13 David Robinson	20.00	9.00
☐ W14 Shawn Kemp	40.00	18.00
☐ W15 Karl Malone	20.00	9.00

1993-94 Upper Deck SE USA Trade

This 24-card standard-size set was only available by exchanging the Upper Deck SE USA Trade card (random insert at one in 360 packs) before August 31, 1994. The set previewed the USA Basketball set that was released in the summer of 1994. The cards depict the 12 players selected by USA Basketball for "Dream Team II" plus Tim Hardaway, who was originally selected to the team was unable to participate due to injury, and 11 from the original Dream Team. Each card features a borderless color player action shot on its front. The player's name and position appear in white lettering within red and blue stripes near the bottom. The words "Exchange Set" in vertical gold-foil lettering and the gold-foil Upper Deck logo appear at the upper left. On a background of the American flag, the back carries a posed color shot of the player in his USA uniform and career highlights. The cards are numbered on the back with a "USA" prefix.

	MINT	NRMT
COMPLETE SET (24)	40.00	18.00
COMMON CARD (1-24)	.50	.23
SEMISTARS	1.00	.45
UNLISTED STARS	1.50	.70
ONE SET PER USA TRADE CARD BY MAIL		
TRADE CARD: STATED ODDS 1:360		
HOB/RET		
USA PREFIX ON CARD NUMBER		

		MINT	NRMT
☐ 1	Charles Barkley	2.50	1.10
☐ 2	Larry Bird	6.00	2.70
☐ 3	Clyde Drexler	2.00	.90
☐ 4	Patrick Ewing	1.50	.70
☐ 5	Michael Jordan	20.00	9.00
☐ 6	Christian Laettner	1.50	.70
☐ 7	Karl Malone	2.50	1.10
☐ 8	Chris Mullin	1.50	.70
☐ 9	Scottie Pippen	5.00	2.20
☐ 10	David Robinson	2.50	1.10
☐ 11	John Stockton	1.50	.70
☐ 12	Dominique Wilkins	1.50	.70
☐ 13	Isiah Thomas	1.50	.70
☐ 14	Dan Majerle	1.00	.45
☐ 15	Steve Smith	1.00	.45
☐ 16	Alonzo Mourning	2.50	1.10
☐ 17	Shawn Kemp	5.00	2.20
☐ 18	Larry Johnson	1.50	.70
☐ 19	Tim Hardaway	2.00	.90
☐ 20	Joe Dumars	1.50	.70
☐ 21	Mark Price	.50	.23
☐ 22	Derrick Coleman	1.00	.45
☐ 23	Reggie Miller	1.50	.70
☐ 24	Shaquille O'Neal	6.00	2.70
☐ NNO	Exp. USA Trade Card	1.50	.70
☐ NNO	Red. USA Trade Card	.25	.11

1998-99 Upper Deck UD Choice Preview

The 1998-99 Upper Deck UD Choice Preview set was issued in one series totalling 55 cards. The set is skip-numbered and features the word "Preview" in gold foil letters across the front of the card. The set previews the upcoming 1998-99 Upper Deck UD Choice release.

	MINT	NRMT
COMPLETE SET (55)	8.00	3.60
COMMON CARD (1-153)	.05	.02
SEMISTARS	.10	.05
SET IS SKIP-NUMBERED		

		MINT	NRMT
☐ 1	Dikembe Mutombo	.10	.05
☐ 3	Mookie Blaylock	.10	.05
☐ 7	Ron Mercer	.60	.25
☐ 9	Walter McCarty	.05	.02
☐ 13	Anthony Mason	.10	.05
☐ 14	Glen Rice	.15	.07
☐ 18	Toni Kukoc	.15	.07
☐ 23	Michael Jordan	2.00	.90
☐ 26	Zydrunas Ilgauskas	.10	.05
☐ 27	Cedric Henderson	.05	.02
☐ 29	Michael Finley	.15	.07
☐ 32	Hubert Davis	.05	.02
☐ 34	Bobby Jackson	.15	.07
☐ 37	Danny Fortson	.15	.07
☐ 41	Grant Hill	1.00	.45
☐ 43	Jerome Williams	.05	.02
☐ 45	Erick Dampier	.05	.02
☐ 48	Donyell Marshall	.05	.02
☐ 50	Charles Barkley	.25	.11
☐ 51	Hakeem Olajuwon	.30	.14
☐ 58	Reggie Miller	.15	.07
☐ 60	Chris Mullin	.10	.05
☐ 64	Eric Piatkowski	.05	.02
☐ 65	Maurice Taylor	.20	.09
☐ 68	Shaquille O'Neal	.60	.25
☐ 69	Kobe Bryant	1.25	.55
☐ 74	Alonzo Mourning	.15	.07
☐ 75	Tim Hardaway	.20	.09
☐ 79	Ray Allen	.15	.07
☐ 80	Terrell Brandon	.15	.07
☐ 84	Stephon Marbury	.60	.25
☐ 85	Kevin Garnett	1.00	.45
☐ 89	Keith Van Horn	.75	.35
☐ 90	Sam Cassell	.10	.05
☐ 95	Patrick Ewing	.15	.07
☐ 97	John Starks	.10	.05
☐ 100	A.Hardaway	.60	.25
☐ 101	Nick Anderson	.05	.02
☐ 105	Allen Iverson	.60	.25
☐ 110	Jason Kidd	.30	.14
☐ 117	Isaiah Rider	.10	.05
☐ 118	Rasheed Wallace	.10	.05
☐ 121	Corliss Williamson	.10	.05
☐ 123	Billy Owens	.05	.02
☐ 126	Tim Duncan	1.00	.45
☐ 127	Sean Elliott	.05	.02
☐ 131	Vin Baker	.30	.14
☐ 135	Gary Payton	.25	.11
☐ 137	Chauncey Billups	.25	.11
☐ 142	John Stockton	.15	.07
☐ 143	Karl Malone	.25	.11
☐ 148	Bryant Reeves	.10	.05
☐ 149	Shareef Abdur-Rahim	.40	.18
☐ 152	Harvey Grant	.05	.02
☐ 153	Juwan Howard	.15	.07

1998-99 Upper Deck UD Choice

The 1998-99 Upper Deck UD Choice Series One was issued with a total of 200 cards. Each pack contained 12 cards with a suggested retail price of $1.29.

	MINT	NRMT
COMPLETE SERIES 1 (200)	15.00	6.75
COMMON CARD (1-200)	.05	.02
SEMISTARS	.10	.05
COMP.RESERVE SER.1 (200)	100.00	45.00
COMMON RESERVE (1-200)	.25	.11
*RESERVE STARS: 2X TO 5X HI COLUMN		
RESERVE: SER.1 STATED ODDS 1:6 H/R		

		MINT	NRMT
☐ 1	Dikembe Mutombo	.10	.02
☐ 2	Alan Henderson	.05	.02
☐ 3	Mookie Blaylock	.10	.05
☐ 4	Ed Gray	.05	.02
☐ 5	Eldridge Recasner	.05	.02
☐ 6	Kenny Anderson	.10	.05
☐ 7	Ron Mercer	.75	.35
☐ 8	Dana Barros	.10	.05
☐ 9	Walter McCarty	.05	.02
☐ 10	Travis Knight	.05	.02
☐ 11	Andrew DeClercq	.05	.02
☐ 12	David Wesley	.05	.02
☐ 13	Anthony Mason	.10	.05
☐ 14	Glen Rice	.20	.09
☐ 15	J.R. Reid	.05	.02

□ 16 Bobby Phills	.05	.02
□ 17 Dell Curry	.05	.02
□ 18 Toni Kukoc	.10	.05
□ 19 Randy Brown	.05	.02
□ 20 Ron Harper	.05	.02
□ 21 Keith Booth	.05	.02
□ 22 Scott Burrell	.05	.02
□ 23 Michael Jordan	2.50	1.10
□ 24 Derek Anderson	.25	.11
□ 25 Brevin Knight	.25	.11
□ 26 Zydrunas Ilgauskas	.10	.05
□ 27 Cedric Henderson	.10	.05
□ 28 Vitaly Potapenko	.05	.02
□ 29 Michael Finley	.15	.07
□ 30 Erick Strickland	.05	.02
□ 31 Shawn Bradley	.05	.02
□ 32 Hubert Davis	.05	.02
□ 33 Khalid Reeves	.05	.02
□ 34 Bobby Jackson	.15	.07
□ 35 Tony Battie	.15	.07
□ 36 Bryant Stith	.05	.02
□ 37 Danny Fortson	.15	.07
□ 38 Dean Garrett	.05	.02
□ 39 Eric Williams	.05	.02
□ 40 Brian Williams	.05	.02
□ 41 Grant Hill	1.25	.55
□ 42 Lindsey Hunter	.05	.02
□ 43 Jerome Williams	.05	.02
□ 44 Eric Montross	.05	.02
□ 45 Erick Dampier	.05	.02
□ 46 Muggsy Bogues	.05	.02
□ 47 Tony Delk	.05	.02
□ 48 Donyell Marshall	.10	.05
□ 49 Bimbo Coles	.05	.02
□ 50 Charles Barkley	.30	.14
□ 51 Hakeem Olajuwon	.40	.18
□ 52 Brent Price	.05	.02
□ 53 Mario Elie	.05	.02
□ 54 Rodrick Rhodes	.10	.05
□ 55 Kevin Willis	.05	.02
□ 56 Reggie Miller	.20	.09
□ 57 Jalen Rose	.05	.02
□ 58 Mark Jackson	.05	.02
□ 59 Dale Davis	.05	.02
□ 60 Chris Mullin	.12	.05
□ 61 Derrick McKey	.05	.02
□ 62 Lorenzen Wright	.05	.02
□ 63 Rodney Rogers	.05	.02
□ 64 Eric Piatkowski	.05	.02
□ 65 Maurice Taylor	.25	.11
□ 66 Isaac Austin	.05	.02
□ 67 Corie Blount	.05	.02
□ 68 Shaquille O'Neal	.75	.35
□ 69 Kobe Bryant	1.50	.70
□ 70 Robert Horry	.10	.05
□ 71 Sean Rooks	.05	.02
□ 72 Derek Fisher	.05	.02
□ 73 P.J. Brown	.05	.02
□ 74 Alonzo Mourning	.20	.09
□ 75 Tim Hardaway	.25	.11
□ 76 Voshon Lenard	.05	.02
□ 77 Dan Majerle	.05	.02
□ 78 Ervin Johnson	.05	.02
□ 79 Ray Allen	.20	.09
□ 80 Terrell Brandon	.15	.07
□ 81 Tyrone Hill	.05	.02
□ 82 Elliot Perry	.05	.02
□ 83 Anthony Peeler	.05	.02
□ 84 Stephon Marbury	.75	.35
□ 85 Kevin Garnett	1.25	.55
□ 86 Paul Grant	.05	.02
□ 87 Chris Carr	.05	.02
□ 88 Micheal Williams UER	.05	.02
spelled Michael		
□ 89 Keith Van Horn	1.00	.45
□ 90 Sam Cassell	.05	.02
□ 91 Kendall Gill	.10	.05
□ 92 Chris Gatling	.05	.02
□ 93 Kerry Kittles	.15	.07
□ 94 Allan Houston	.10	.05
□ 95 Patrick Ewing UER	.20	.09
back Ewing Ewing		
□ 96 Charles Oakley	.05	.02
□ 97 John Starks	.05	.02
□ 98 Charlie Ward	.05	.02
□ 99 Chris Mills	.05	.02

□ 100 Anfernee Hardaway	.75	.35
□ 101 Nick Anderson	.05	.02
□ 102 Mark Price	.05	.02
□ 103 Horace Grant	.10	.05
□ 104 David Benoit	.05	.02
□ 105 Allen Iverson	.75	.35
□ 106 Joe Smith	.15	.07
□ 107 Tim Thomas	.60	.25
□ 108 Brian Shaw	.05	.02
□ 109 Aaron McKie	.05	.02
□ 110 Jason Kidd	.40	.18
□ 111 Danny Manning	.05	.02
□ 112 Steve Nash	.10	.05
□ 113 Rex Chapman	.05	.02
□ 114 Dennis Scott	.05	.02
□ 115 Antonio McDyess	.20	.09
□ 116 Damon Stoudamire	.30	.14
□ 117 Isaiah Rider	.05	.02
□ 118 Rasheed Wallace	.10	.05
□ 119 Kelvin Cato	.05	.02
□ 120 Jermaine O'Neal	.10	.05
□ 121 Corliss Williamson	.10	.05
□ 122 Olden Polynice	.05	.02
□ 123 Billy Owens	.05	.02
□ 124 L.Funderburke	.05	.02
□ 125 Anthony Johnson	.05	.02
□ 126 Tim Duncan	1.25	.55
□ 127 Sean Elliott	.05	.02
□ 128 Avery Johnson	.05	.02
□ 129 Vinny Del Negro	.05	.02
□ 130 Monty Williams	.05	.02
□ 131 Vin Baker	.40	.18
□ 132 Hersey Hawkins	.05	.02
□ 133 Nate McMillan	.05	.02
□ 134 Detlef Schrempf	.10	.05
□ 135 Gary Payton	.30	.14
□ 136 Jim McIlvaine	.05	.02
□ 137 Chauncey Billups	.30	.14
□ 138 Doug Christie	.05	.02
□ 139 John Wallace	.10	.05
□ 140 Tracy McGrady	.60	.25
□ 141 Dee Brown	.05	.02
□ 142 John Stockton	.20	.09
□ 143 Karl Malone	.30	.14
□ 144 Shandon Anderson	.05	.02
□ 145 Jacque Vaughn	.10	.05
□ 146 Bryon Russell	.05	.02
□ 147 Lee Mayberry	.05	.02
□ 148 Bryant Reeves	.10	.05
□ 149 Shareef Abdur-Rahim	.50	.23
□ 150 Michael Smith	.05	.02
□ 151 Pete Chilcutt	.05	.02
□ 152 Harvey Grant	.05	.02
□ 153 Juwan Howard	.20	.09
□ 154 Calbert Cheaney	.05	.02
□ 155 Tracy Murray	.05	.02
□ 156 D.Mutombo FS	.05	.02
□ 157 Antoine Walker FS	.40	.18
□ 158 Glen Rice FS	.10	.05
□ 159 Michael Jordan FS	1.25	.55
□ 160 Wesley Person FS	.05	.02
□ 161 Shawn Bradley FS	.05	.02
□ 162 Dean Garrett FS	.05	.02
□ 163 Jerry Stackhouse FS	.12	.05
□ 164 Donyell Marshall FS	.05	.02
□ 165 Hakeem Olajuwon FS	.20	.09
□ 166 Chris Mullin FS	.10	.05
□ 167 Isaac Austin FS	.05	.02
□ 168 Shaquille O'Neal FS	.40	.18
□ 169 Tim Hardaway FS	.12	.05
□ 170 Glenn Robinson FS	.10	.05
□ 171 Kevin Garnett FS	.60	.25
□ 172 Keith Van Horn FS	.50	.23
□ 173 Larry Johnson FS	.05	.02
□ 174 Horace Grant FS	.05	.02
□ 175 Derrick Coleman FS	.05	.02
□ 176 Steve Nash FS	.05	.02
□ 177 A.Sabonis FS UER	.05	.02
spelled Arvadas		
□ 178 Corliss Williamson FS	.05	.02
□ 179 David Robinson FS	.15	.07
□ 180 Vin Baker FS	.20	.09
□ 181 Marcus Camby FS	.10	.05
□ 182 John Stockton FS	.10	.05
□ 183 Antonio Daniels FS	.12	.05
□ 184 Rod Strickland FS	.05	.02

□ 185 Michael Jordan FS	1.25	.55
□ 186 Kobe Bryant YIR	.75	.35
□ 187 Clyde Drexler YIR	.12	.05
□ 188 Gary Payton YIR	.15	.07
□ 189 Michael Jordan YIR	1.25	.55
□ 190 David Robinson	.60	.25
Tim Duncan YIR		
□ 191 Attend. Record YIR	.05	.02
□ 192 Karl Malone YIR	.15	.07
□ 193 D.Mutombo YIR	.05	.02
□ 194 New Jersey Nets YIR	.40	.18
Keith Van Horn		
Kerry Kittles		
Jayson Williams		
Kendall Gill		
Sam Cassell		
□ 195 Ray Allen YIR	.10	.05
□ 196 Michael Jordan YIR	1.25	.55
□ 197 L.A. Lakers YIR	.75	.35
Kobe Bryant		
Eddie Jones		
Shaquille O'Neal		
Nick Van Exel		
□ 198 Michael Jordan YIR	1.25	.55
□ 199 Michael Jordan CL	.60	.25
□ 200 Michael Jordan CL	.60	.25

1998-99 Upper Deck UD Choice Premium Choice Reserve

Randomly inserted in series one packs, this 200-card set parallels the basic set. The card fronts feature a foil-treatment to differentiate the cards. They are also serially numbered to 100 on the back.

	MINT	NRMT
COMMON CARD (1-200)	10.00	4.50
SEMISTARS	15.00	6.75
RANDOM INSERTS IN SER.1 HOB/RET		
STATED PRINT RUN 100 SERIAL #'d SETS		

		MINT	NRMT
□ 1 Dikembe Mutombo	15.00	6.75
□ 2 Alan Henderson	10.00	4.50
□ 3 Mookie Blaylock	15.00	6.75
□ 4 Ed Gray	15.00	6.75
□ 5 Eldridge Recasner	10.00	4.50
□ 6 Kenny Anderson	15.00	6.75
□ 7 Ron Mercer	100.00	45.00
□ 8 Dana Barros	15.00	6.75
□ 9 Walter McCarty	10.00	4.50
□ 10 Travis Knight	10.00	4.50
□ 11 Andrew DeClercq	10.00	4.50
□ 12 David Wesley	10.00	4.50
□ 13 Anthony Mason	15.00	6.75
□ 14 Glen Rice	25.00	11.00
□ 15 J.R. Reid	10.00	4.50
□ 16 Bobby Phills	10.00	4.50

17	Dell Curry	10.00	4.50
18	Toni Kukoc	15.00	6.75
19	Randy Brown	10.00	4.50
20	Ron Harper	10.00	4.50
21	Keith Booth	10.00	4.50
22	Scott Burrell	10.00	4.50
23	Michael Jordan	300.00	135.00
24	Derek Anderson	30.00	13.50
25	Brevin Knight	30.00	13.50
26	Zydrunas Ilgauskas	15.00	6.75
27	Cedric Henderson	15.00	6.75
28	Vitaly Potapenko	10.00	4.50
29	Michael Finley	20.00	9.00
30	Erick Strickland	10.00	4.50
31	Shawn Bradley	10.00	4.50
32	Hubert Davis	10.00	4.50
33	Khalid Reeves	10.00	4.50
34	Bobby Jackson	20.00	9.00
35	Tony Battie	20.00	9.00
36	Bryant Stith	10.00	4.50
37	Danny Fortson	20.00	9.00
38	Dean Garrett	10.00	4.50
39	Eric Williams	10.00	4.50
40	Brian Williams	10.00	4.50
41	Grant Hill	150.00	70.00
42	Lindsey Hunter	10.00	4.50
43	Jerome Williams	10.00	4.50
44	Eric Montross	10.00	4.50
45	Erick Dampier	10.00	4.50
46	Muggsy Bogues	10.00	4.50
47	Tony Delk	10.00	4.50
48	Donyell Marshall	15.00	6.75
49	Bimbo Coles	10.00	4.50
50	Charles Barkley	40.00	18.00
51	Hakeem Olajuwon	50.00	22.00
52	Brent Price	10.00	4.50
53	Mario Elie	10.00	4.50
54	Rodrick Rhodes	15.00	6.75
55	Kevin Willis	10.00	4.50
56	Reggie Miller	25.00	11.00
57	Jalen Rose	10.00	4.50
58	Mark Jackson	10.00	4.50
59	Dale Davis	10.00	4.50
60	Chris Mullin	20.00	9.00
61	Derrick McKey	10.00	4.50
62	Lorenzen Wright	10.00	4.50
63	Rodney Rogers	10.00	4.50
64	Eric Piatkowski	10.00	4.50
65	Maurice Taylor	30.00	13.50
66	Isaac Austin	10.00	4.50
67	Corie Blount	10.00	4.50
68	Shaquille O'Neal	100.00	45.00
69	Kobe Bryant	200.00	90.00
70	Robert Horry	15.00	6.75
71	Sean Rooks	10.00	4.50
72	Derek Fisher	15.00	6.75
73	P.J. Brown	10.00	4.50
74	Alonzo Mourning	25.00	11.00
75	Tim Hardaway	30.00	13.50
76	Voshon Lenard	10.00	4.50
77	Dan Majerle	15.00	6.75
78	Ervin Johnson	10.00	4.50
79	Ray Allen	25.00	11.00
80	Terrell Brandon	20.00	9.00
81	Tyrone Hill	10.00	4.50
82	Elliot Perry	10.00	4.50
83	Anthony Peeler	10.00	4.50
84	Stephon Marbury	100.00	45.00
85	Kevin Garnett	150.00	70.00
86	Paul Grant	10.00	4.50
87	Chris Carr	10.00	4.50
88	Micheal Williams UER spelled Michael	10.00	4.50
89	Keith Van Horn	125.00	55.00
90	Sam Cassell	15.00	6.75
91	Kendall Gill	15.00	6.75
92	Chris Gatling	10.00	4.50
93	Kerry Kittles	20.00	9.00
94	Allan Houston	15.00	6.75
95	Patrick Ewing UER back Ewing Ewing	25.00	11.00
96	Charles Oakley	10.00	4.50
97	John Starks	15.00	6.75
98	Charlie Ward	10.00	4.50
99	Chris Mills	10.00	4.50
100	A.Hardaway	100.00	45.00
101	Nick Anderson	10.00	4.50
102	Mark Price	10.00	4.50
103	Horace Grant	15.00	6.75
104	David Benoit	10.00	4.50
105	Allen Iverson	100.00	45.00
106	Joe Smith	20.00	9.00
107	Tim Thomas	80.00	36.00
108	Brian Shaw	10.00	4.50
109	Aaron McKie	10.00	4.50
110	Jason Kidd	50.00	22.00
111	Danny Manning	15.00	6.75
112	Steve Nash	15.00	6.75
113	Rex Chapman	10.00	4.50
114	Dennis Scott	10.00	4.50
115	Antonio McDyess	25.00	11.00
116	D.Stoudamire	40.00	18.00
117	Isaiah Rider	15.00	6.75
118	Rasheed Wallace	15.00	6.75
119	Kelvin Cato	15.00	6.75
120	Jermaine O'Neal	15.00	6.75
121	Corliss Williamson	10.00	4.50
122	Olden Polynice	10.00	4.50
123	Billy Owens	10.00	4.50
124	Lawrence Funderburke	10.00	4.50
125	Anthony Johnson	10.00	4.50
126	Tim Duncan	150.00	70.00
127	Sean Elliott	10.00	4.50
128	Avery Johnson	10.00	4.50
129	Vinny Del Negro	10.00	4.50
130	Monty Williams	10.00	4.50
131	Vin Baker	50.00	22.00
132	Hersey Hawkins	15.00	6.75
133	Nate McMillan	10.00	4.50
134	Detlef Schrempf	15.00	6.75
135	Gary Payton	50.00	22.00
136	Jim McIlvaine	10.00	4.50
137	Chauncey Billups	50.00	22.00
138	Doug Christie	10.00	4.50
139	John Wallace	10.00	4.50
140	Tracy McGrady	80.00	36.00
141	Dee Brown	10.00	4.50
142	John Stockton	25.00	11.00
143	Karl Malone	40.00	18.00
144	Shandon Anderson	10.00	4.50
145	Jacque Vaughn	15.00	6.75
146	Bryon Russell	10.00	4.50
147	Lee Mayberry	10.00	4.50
148	Bryant Reeves	15.00	6.75
149	S.Abdur-Rahim	60.00	27.00
150	Michael Smith	10.00	4.50
151	Pete Chilcutt	10.00	4.50
152	Harvey Grant	10.00	4.50
153	Juwan Howard	25.00	11.00
154	Calbert Cheaney	10.00	4.50
155	Tracy Murray	10.00	4.50
156	D.Mutombo FS	10.00	4.50
157	Antoine Walker FS	50.00	22.00
158	Glen Rice FS	15.00	6.75
159	Michael Jordan FS	150.00	70.00
160	Wesley Person FS	10.00	4.50
161	Shawn Bradley FS	10.00	4.50
162	Dean Garrett FS	10.00	4.50
163	Jerry Stackhouse FS	20.00	9.00
164	Donyell Marshall FS	10.00	4.50
165	Hakeem Olajuwon FS	25.00	11.00
166	Chris Mullin FS	15.00	6.75
167	Isaac Austin FS	10.00	4.50
168	Shaquille O'Neal FS	50.00	22.00
169	Tim Hardaway FS	20.00	9.00
170	Glenn Robinson FS	15.00	6.75
171	Kevin Garnett FS	80.00	36.00
172	Keith Van Horn FS	60.00	27.00
173	Larry Johnson FS	10.00	4.50
174	Horace Grant FS	10.00	4.50
175	Derrick Coleman FS	10.00	4.50
176	Steve Nash FS	10.00	4.50
177	Arvydas Sabonis FS UER spelled Arvadas	10.00	4.50
178	Corliss Williamson FS	10.00	4.50
179	David Robinson FS	20.00	9.00
180	Vin Baker FS	25.00	11.00
181	Marcus Camby FS	15.00	6.75
182	John Stockton FS	15.00	6.75
183	Antonio Daniels FS	20.00	9.00
184	Rod Strickland FS	10.00	4.50
185	Michael Jordan FS	150.00	70.00
186	Kobe Bryant FS	100.00	45.00
187	Clyde Drexler YIR	20.00	9.00
188	Gary Payton YIR	20.00	9.00
189	Michael Jordan YIR	150.00	70.00
190	David Robinson Tim Duncan YIR	80.00	36.00
191	Attendance Record YIR	10.00	4.50
192	Karl Malone YIR	20.00	9.00
193	D.Mutombo YIR	10.00	4.50
194	New Jersey Nets YIR Keith Van Horn Kerry Kittles Jayson Williams Kendall Gill Sam Cassell	60.00	27.00
195	Ray Allen YIR	15.00	6.75
196	Michael Jordan YIR	150.00	70.00
197	Los Angeles Lakers YIR Kobe Bryant Eddie Jones Shaquille O'Neal Nick Van Exel	100.00	45.00
198	Michael Jordan YIR	150.00	70.00
199	Michael Jordan CL	80.00	36.00
200	Michael Jordan CL	80.00	36.00

1998-99 Upper Deck UD Choice Mini Bobbing Heads

Randomly inserted into series one packs at a rate of one in four, this 30-card set features cards that can be popped-up and displayed similar to a "bobbing" head.

	MINT	NRMT
COMPLETE SET (30)	10.00	4.50
COMMON CARD (1-30)	.10	.05
SER.1 STATED ODDS 1:4 HOB/RET		

1	Dikembe Mutombo	.15	.07
2	Antoine Walker	1.00	.45
3	Anthony Mason	.15	.07
4	Toni Kukoc	.15	.07
5	Shawn Kemp	.75	.35
6	Shawn Bradley	.10	.05
7	Danny Fortson	.20	.09
8	Brian Williams	.10	.05
9	Muggsy Bogues	.10	.05
10	Charles Barkley	.40	.18
11	Mark Jackson	.10	.05
12	Rodney Rogers	.10	.05
13	Kobe Bryant	2.00	.90
14	Tim Hardaway	.30	.14
15	Ray Allen	.25	.11
16	Kevin Garnett	1.50	.70
17	Sam Cassell	.15	.07

		MINT	NRMT
☐ 18	John Starks	.15	.07
☐ 19	Anfernee Hardaway	1.00	.45
☐ 20	Allen Iverson	1.00	.45
☐ 21	Danny Manning	.15	.07
☐ 22	Rasheed Wallace	.15	.07
☐ 23	Chris Webber	.60	.18
☐ 24	David Robinson	.40	.18
☐ 25	Gary Payton	.40	.18
☐ 26	Marcus Camby	.20	.09
☐ 27	John Stockton	.25	.11
☐ 28	Bryant Reeves	.15	.07
☐ 29	Juwan Howard	.25	.11
☐ 30	Michael Jordan	3.00	1.35

		MINT	NRMT
☐ SQ18	Patrick Ewing	.30	.14
☐ SQ19	A.Hardaway	1.25	.55
☐ SQ20	Allen Iverson	1.25	.55
☐ SQ21	Jason Kidd	.60	.25
☐ SQ22	Damon Stoudamire	.50	.23
☐ SQ23	Corliss Williamson	.20	.09
☐ SQ24	Tim Duncan	2.00	.90
☐ SQ25	Gary Payton	.50	.23
☐ SQ26	Chauncey Billups	.20	.09
☐ SQ27	Karl Malone	.50	.23
☐ SQ28	S.Abdur-Rahim	.75	.35
☐ SQ29	Juwan Howard	.30	.14
☐ SQ30	Michael Jordan	4.00	1.80

☐ SQ25	Gary Payton	30.00	13.50
☐ SQ26	Chauncey Billups	30.00	13.50
☐ SQ27	Karl Malone	30.00	13.50
☐ SQ28	S.Abdur-Rahim..	50.00	22.00
☐ SQ29	Juwan Howard	20.00	9.00
☐ SQ30	Michael Jordan..	250.00	110.00

1996-97 Upper Deck UD3

1998-99 Upper Deck UD Choice StarQuest Blue

1998-99 Upper Deck UD Choice StarQuest Gold

Randomly inserted into series one packs at a rate of one per pack, this 30-card set features some of the best players in the NBA. The card front features blue borders with a photo of the player in the middle. The card backs feature one star to denote the first tier of the insert. Card backs are also numbered with a "SQ" prefix.

Randomly inserted into series one packs, this 30-card set features some of the best players in the NBA. The card front features gold borders with a photo of the player in the middle. The card backs feature four stars to denote the final tier of the insert and are serially numbered out of 100. Card backs are also numbered with a "SQ" prefix.

The 1996-97 Upper Deck UD3 set was issued in one series totalling 60 cards. The set breaks down into three different technologies: Light F/X, Cel Chrome and Electric Wood-Cel. The Hardwood prospect cards (1-20) use the Wood-Cel technology, the NBA StarFocus cards (21-40) use the Cel Chrome technology and the Aerial Artists (41-60) use the Light F/X technology. Cards were issued in 3-card packs at a suggested retail price of $3.99.

	MINT	NRMT
COMPLETE SET (30)	15.00	6.75
COMMON CARD (SQ1-SQ30)	.15	.07
COMP.GREEN SER.1 (30)	50.00	22.00
COMM GREEN (SQ1-SQ30)	.50	.23
*GREEN STARS: 1.25X TO 3X HI COLUMN		
GREEN: SER.1 STATED ODDS 1:8 H/R		
COMP.RED SER.1 (30)......	150.00	70.00
COMMON RED (SQ1-SQ30)..	1.25	.55
*RED STARS: 4X TO 8X HI COLUMN		
RED: SER.1 STATED ODDS 1:23 H/R		
☐ SQ1 Steve Smith	.20	.09
☐ SQ2 Kenny Anderson	.20	.09
☐ SQ3 Glen Rice	.30	.14
☐ SQ4 Toni Kukoc	.20	.09
☐ SQ5 Shawn Kemp	1.00	.45
☐ SQ6 Michael Finley	.25	.11
☐ SQ7 Bobby Jackson	.25	.11
☐ SQ8 Grant Hill	2.00	.90
☐ SQ9 Donyell Marshall	.15	.07
☐ SQ10 Hakeem Olajuwon	.60	.25
☐ SQ11 Reggie Miller	.30	.14
☐ SQ12 Maurice Taylor	.40	.18
☐ SQ13 Kobe Bryant	2.50	1.10
☐ SQ14 Alonzo Mourning	.30	.14
☐ SQ15 Terrell Brandon	.15	.07
☐ SQ16 Stephon Marbury ..	1.25	.55
☐ SQ17 Keith Van Horn	1.50	.70

	MINT	NRMT
COMM CARD (SQ1-SQ30)	8.00	3.60
SEMISTARS	12.00	5.50
RANDOM INSERTS IN SER.1 HOB/RET		
STATED PRINT RUN 100 SERIAL #'d SETS		
☐ SQ1 Steve Smith	12.00	5.50
☐ SQ2 Kenny Anderson	12.00	5.50
☐ SQ3 Glen Rice	20.00	9.00
☐ SQ4 Toni Kukoc	12.00	5.50
☐ SQ5 Shawn Kemp	60.00	27.00
☐ SQ6 Michael Finley	15.00	6.75
☐ SQ7 Bobby Jackson	15.00	6.75
☐ SQ8 Grant Hill	125.00	55.00
☐ SQ9 Donyell Marshall	12.00	5.50
☐ SQ10 H.Olajuwon	40.00	18.00
☐ SQ11 Reggie Miller	20.00	9.00
☐ SQ12 Maurice Taylor	25.00	11.00
☐ SQ13 Kobe Bryant	150.00	70.00
☐ SQ14 Alonzo Mourning	20.00	9.00
☐ SQ15 Terrell Brandon	15.00	6.75
☐ SQ16 S.Marbury	80.00	36.00
☐ SQ17 Keith Van Horn	100.00	45.00
☐ SQ18 Patrick Ewing	20.00	9.00
☐ SQ19 A.Hardaway	80.00	36.00
☐ SQ20 Allen Iverson	80.00	36.00
☐ SQ21 Jason Kidd	40.00	18.00
☐ SQ22 D.Stoudamire	30.00	13.50
☐ SQ23 C.Williamson	12.00	5.50
☐ SQ24 Tim Duncan	125.00	55.00

	MINT	NRMT
COMPLETE SET (60)	50.00	22.00
COMMON CARD (1-20)	.15	.07
COMMON CARD (21-40)	.30	.14
COMMON CARD (41-60)	.20	.09
SEMISTARS 1-20	.20	.09
SEMISTARS 21-40	.40	.18
SEMISTARS 41-60	.25	.11
UNLISTED STARS 1-20	.40	.18
UNLISTED STARS 21-40	.75	.35
UNLISTED STARS 41-60	.50	.23
☐ 1 Kerry Kittles	1.00	.45
☐ 2 Stephon Marbury	4.00	1.80
☐ 3 Jermaine O'Neal	.60	.25
☐ 4 Shareef Abdur-Rahim	2.50	1.10
☐ 5 Ray Allen	1.25	.55
☐ 6 Antoine Walker	4.00	1.80
☐ 7 Erick Dampier	.50	.23
☐ 8 Walter McCarty	.20	.09
☐ 9 Todd Fuller	.15	.07
☐ 10 Tony Delk	.50	.23
☐ 11 Marcus Camby	1.00	.45
☐ 12 John Wallace	.60	.25
☐ 13 Vitaly Potapenko	.20	.09
☐ 14 Allen Iverson	4.00	1.80
☐ 15 Steve Nash	.60	.25
☐ 16 Derek Fisher	.50	.23
☐ 17 Samaki Walker	.50	.23
☐ 18 Roy Rogers	.15	.07
☐ 19 Kobe Bryant..	8.00	3.60
☐ 20 Lorenzen Wright	.50	.23
☐ 21 Kevin Garnett	5.00	2.20
☐ 22 Hakeem Olajuwon	1.50	.70

		MINT	NRMT
☐ 23	Michael Jordan	10.00	4.50
☐ 24	John Stockton	.75	.35
☐ 25	Terrell Brandon	.75	.35
☐ 26	Damon Stoudamire	2.00	.90
☐ 27	Charles Barkley	1.25	.55
☐ 28	Dikembe Mutombo	.40	.18
☐ 29	Gary Payton	1.25	.55
☐ 30	Patrick Ewing	.75	.35
☐ 31	Dennis Rodman	3.00	1.35
☐ 32	Joe Smith	1.00	.45
☐ 33	Grant Hill	5.00	2.20
☐ 34	Shaquille O'Neal	3.00	1.35
☐ 35	Kevin Johnson	.30	.14
☐ 36	David Robinson	1.25	.55
☐ 37	Juwan Howard	1.00	.45
☐ 38	Mitch Richmond	.75	.35
☐ 39	Alonzo Mourning	.75	.35
☐ 40	Reggie Miller	.75	.35
☐ 41	Shawn Kemp	1.50	.70
☐ 42	Scottie Pippen	1.50	.70
☐ 43	Kobe Bryant	10.00	4.50
☐ 44	Anfernee Hardaway	2.00	.90
☐ 45	Brent Barry	.20	.09
☐ 46	Glenn Robinson	.50	.23
☐ 47	Karl Malone	.75	.35
☐ 48	Chris Webber	1.25	.55
☐ 49	Danny Manning	.25	.11
☐ 50	Antonio McDyess	.75	.35
☐ 51	Dominique Wilkins	.50	.23
☐ 52	Vin Baker	1.00	.45
☐ 53	Isaiah Rider	.25	.11
☐ 54	Eddie Jones	1.00	.45
☐ 55	Glen Rice	.50	.23
☐ 56	Larry Johnson	.25	.11
☐ 57	Latrell Sprewell	.25	.11
☐ 58	Sean Elliott	.20	.09
☐ 59	Clyde Drexler	.50	.25
☐ 60	Jerry Stackhouse	.60	.25

1996-97 Upper Deck UD3 Court Commemorative Autograph Exchange

Randomly inserted in packs at a rate of one in 1500, this four-card set features autographed cards of the Upper Deck spokesmen.

	MINT	NRMT
COMPLETE SET (4)	2700.00	1200.00
COMMON CARD (C1-C4)	120.00	55.00
STATED ODDS 1:1500		
☐ C1 Michael Jordan AU	2500.00	1100.00
☐ C2 D.Stoudamire AU	100.00	45.00
☐ C3 A.Hardaway AU	350.00	160.00
☐ C4 Shawn Kemp AU	250.00	110.00

1996-97 Upper Deck UD3 Superstar Spotlight

Randomly inserted in packs at a rate of one in 144, this 10-card set utilizes Cel-Chrome technology and focuses on NBA All-Stars.

	MINT	NRMT
COMPLETE SET (10)	250.00	110.00
COMMON CARD (S1-S10)	8.00	3.60
STATED ODDS 1:144		
☐ S1 Shaquille O'Neal	30.00	13.50
☐ S2 Alonzo Mourning	8.00	3.60
☐ S3 A.Hardaway	30.00	13.50
☐ S4 Karl Malone	12.00	5.50
☐ S5 Michael Jordan	100.00	45.00
☐ S6 Hakeem Olajuwon	15.00	6.75
☐ S7 Shawn Kemp	25.00	11.00
☐ S8 Allen Iverson	40.00	18.00
☐ S9 Dennis Rodman	30.00	13.50
☐ S10 Charles Barkley	12.00	5.50

1996-97 Upper Deck UD3 The Winning Edge

Randomly inserted in packs at a rate of one in 11, this 20-card set utilizes the Light F/X technology, and each card focuses on a specific trait that makes these players a success in the NBA.

	MINT	NRMT
COMPLETE SET (20)	100.00	45.00
COMMON CARD (W1-W20)	1.25	.55

		MINT	NRMT
SEMISTARS		1.50	.70
UNLISTED STARS		2.50	1.10
STATED ODDS 1:11			
☐ W1	Michael Jordan	30.00	13.50
☐ W2	Charles Barkley	4.00	1.80
☐ W3	Reggie Miller	2.50	1.10
☐ W4	Grant Hill	15.00	6.75
☐ W5	Larry Johnson	1.50	.70
☐ W6	Hakeem Olajuwon	5.00	2.20
☐ W7	A.Hardaway	10.00	4.50
☐ W8	Shaquille O'Neal	10.00	4.50
☐ W9	Vin Baker	5.00	2.20
☐ W10	Kevin Garnett	15.00	6.75
☐ W11	Juwan Howard	3.00	1.35
☐ W12	John Stockton	2.50	1.10
☐ W13	Mookie Blaylock	1.25	.55
☐ W14	Shawn Kemp	8.00	3.60
☐ W15	David Robinson	4.00	1.80
☐ W16	Kevin Johnson	1.50	.70
☐ W17	Joe Dumars	2.50	1.10
☐ W18	Marcus Camby	3.00	1.35
☐ W19	Clyde Drexler	3.00	1.35
☐ W20	Chris Webber	6.00	2.70

1997-98 Upper Deck UD3

Released in three-card packs that carried a suggested retail price of $3.99, this 60 card set is broken up into three different "subset" themes. The first 20 cards are Jam Masters, the next 20 are All-Stars and the final 20 are The Big Picture. A Michael Jordan promo card was also released with the word "Sample" in white letters on the card front. Since the card is numbered the same as the basic Jordan card (#45), the promo is listed as a "NNO" at the end of the set.

	MINT	NRMT
COMPLETE SET (60)	50.00	22.00
COMMON CARD (1-40)	.15	.07
COMMON CARD (41-60)	.25	.11
SEMISTARS 1-40	.20	.09
SEMISTARS 41-60	.40	.18
UNLISTED STARS 1-40	.40	.18
UNLISTED STARS 41-60	.60	.25
MJ3-1 STATED ODDS 1:45		
MJ3-2 STATED ODDS 1:119		
MJ3-3 STATED ODDS 1:167		
☐ 1 A.Hardaway JM	1.50	.70
☐ 2 Alonzo Mourning JM	.40	.18
☐ 3 Grant Hill JM	2.50	1.10
☐ 4 Kerry Kittles JM	.40	.18
☐ 5 Latrell Sprewell JM	.20	.09

☐ 6 Rasheed Wallace JM	.20	.09
☐ 7 Jerry Stackhouse JM	.40	.18
☐ 8 Glen Rice JM	.40	.18
☐ 9 Marcus Camby JM	.40	.18
☐ 10 Scottie Pippen JM	1.25	.55
☐ 11 Patrick Ewing JM	.40	.18
☐ 12 Michael Finley JM	.40	.18
☐ 13 Karl Malone JM	.60	.25
☐ 14 Antonio McDyess JM	.50	.23
☐ 15 Michael Jordan JM	5.00	2.20
☐ 16 Clyde Drexler JM	.50	.23
☐ 17 Brent Barry JM	.15	.07
☐ 18 Glenn Robinson JM	.40	.18
☐ 19 Kobe Bryant JM	3.00	1.35
☐ 20 Reggie Miller JM	.40	.18
☐ 21 John Stockton AS	.40	.18
☐ 22 Gary Payton AS	.60	.25
☐ 23 Michael Jordan AS	5.00	2.20
☐ 24 Vin Baker AS	.75	.35
☐ 25 Karl Malone AS	.60	.25
☐ 26 Juwan Howard AS	.40	.18
☐ 27 Charles Barkley AS	.60	.25
☐ 28 Jason Kidd AS	.75	.35
☐ 29 Joe Dumars AS	.40	.18
☐ 30 A.Hardaway AS	1.50	.70
☐ 31 Mitch Richmond AS	.40	.18
☐ 32 Alonzo Mourning AS	.40	.18
☐ 33 Grant Hill AS	2.50	1.10
☐ 34 Shaquille O'Neal AS	1.50	.70
☐ 35 Scottie Pippen AS	1.25	.55
☐ 36 Reggie Miller AS	.40	.18
☐ 37 Hakeem Olajuwon AS	.75	.35
☐ 38 Tim Hardaway AS	.50	.23
☐ 39 David Robinson AS	.60	.25
☐ 40 Shawn Kemp AS	1.25	.55
☐ 41 Allen Iverson BP	3.00	1.35
☐ 42 Stephon Marbury BP	3.00	1.35
☐ 43 Dennis Rodman BP	2.50	1.10
☐ 44 Terrell Brandon BP	.60	.25
☐ 45 Michael Jordan BP	8.00	3.60
☐ 46 Kerry Kittles BP	.60	.25
☐ 47 Hakeem Olajuwon BP	1.25	.55
☐ 48 Loy Vaught BP	.40	.18
☐ 49 Antoine Walker BP	3.00	1.35
☐ 50 Gary Payton BP	1.00	.45
☐ 51 Kevin Johnson BP	.40	.18
☐ 52 Kevin Garnett BP	4.00	1.80
☐ 53 S.Abdur-Rahim BP	2.00	.90
☐ 54 Larry Johnson BP	.40	.18
☐ 55 D.Mutombo BP	.25	.11
☐ 56 Chris Webber BP	1.50	.70
☐ 57 Joe Smith BP	.60	.25
☐ 58 Kendall Gill BP	.40	.18
☐ 59 Kenny Anderson BP	.40	.18
☐ 60 D.Stoudamire BP	1.25	.55
☐ NNO M.Jordan Promo	10.00	4.50

1997-98 Upper Deck UD3 Awesome Action

Randomly inserted in packs at one in 11, this 20-card set features great action shots of the NBA's best. Card backs carry an "A" prefix.

	MINT	NRMT
COMPLETE SET (20)	225.00	100.00
COMMON CARD (A1-A20)	2.00	.90
SEMISTARS	2.50	1.10
UNLISTED STARS	4.00	1.80
STATED ODDS 1:11		
☐ A1 Michael Jordan	50.00	22.00
☐ A2 Nick Van Exel	4.00	1.80
☐ A3 Jerry Stackhouse	4.00	1.80
☐ A4 Shawn Kemp	12.00	5.50
☐ A5 Hakeem Olajuwon	8.00	3.60
☐ A6 Grant Hill	25.00	11.00
☐ A7 Scottie Pippen	12.00	5.50
☐ A8 Alonzo Mourning	4.00	1.80
☐ A9 D.Stoudamire	8.00	3.60
☐ A10 Kevin Garnett	25.00	11.00
☐ A11 A.Hardaway	15.00	6.75
☐ A12 S.Abdur-Rahim	12.00	5.50
☐ A13 Allen Iverson	20.00	9.00
☐ A14 Dennis Rodman	15.00	6.75
☐ A15 Shaquille O'Neal	15.00	6.75
☐ A16 Jason Kidd	8.00	3.60
☐ A17 Gary Payton	6.00	2.70
☐ A18 D.Mutombo	2.00	.90
☐ A19 Karl Malone	6.00	2.70
☐ A20 Stephon Marbury	20.00	9.00

1997-98 Upper Deck UD3 Rookie Portfolio

Randomly inserted into packs at one in 144, this 10-card set features a still shot of some of the top rookies from the 1997 class. The cards feature a portrait front against a see-through back. Card backs carry a "R" prefix.

	MINT	NRMT
COMPLETE SET (10)	225.00	100.00
COMMON CARD (R1-R10)	6.00	2.70
UNLISTED STARS	10.00	4.50
STATED ODDS 1:144		
☐ R1 Tim Duncan	60.00	27.00
☐ R2 Keith Van Horn	50.00	22.00

	MINT	NRMT
☐ R3 Chauncey Billups	20.00	9.00
☐ R4 Antonio Daniels	12.00	5.50
☐ R5 Tony Battie	10.00	4.50
☐ R6 Ron Mercer	40.00	18.00
☐ R7 Tim Thomas	30.00	13.50
☐ R8 Adonal Foyle	6.00	2.70
☐ R9 Tracy McGrady	30.00	13.50
☐ R10 Danny Fortson	10.00	4.50

1997-98 Upper Deck UD3 Season Ticket Autographs

Randomly inserted in packs at a rate of one in 1,800, this 4-card set features autographs against a facsimile ticket stub. Card backs carry a congratulatory message from Upper Deck.

	MINT	NRMT
COMPLETE SET (4)	3000.00	1350.00
COMMON CARD	150.00	70.00
STATED ODDS 1:1,800		
☐ AH A.Hardaway	400.00	180.00
☐ JH Juwan Howard	150.00	70.00
☐ MJ Michael Jordan	2500.00	1100.00
☐ TH Tim Hardaway	150.00	70.00

Acknowledgments

A great deal of diligence, hard work, and dedicated effort went into this year's volume. The high standards to which we hold ourselves, however, could not have been met without the expert input and generous amount of time contributed by many people. Our sincere thanks are extended to each and every one of you.

Each year we refine the process of developing the most accurate and up-to-date information for this book. I believe this year's Price Guide is our best yet. Thanks again to all of the contributors nationwide (listed below) as well as our staff here in Dallas.

Those who have worked closely with us on this and many other books, have again proven themselves invaluable in every aspect of producing this book: Rich Altman, Randy Archer, Mike Aronstein, Jerry Bell, Chris Benjamin, Mike Blaisdell, Bill Bossert (Mid-Atlantic Coin Exchange), Classic (Ken Goldin and Mark Pokedoff), Todd Crosner (California Sportscard Exchange), Bud Darland, Bill and Diane Dodge, Rick Donohoo, Willie Erving, Fleer/SkyBox International (Doug Drotman and Ted Taylor), Gervise Ford, Steve Freedman, Larry and Jeff Fritsch, Jim Galusha, Dick Gariepy, Dick Gilkeson, Mike and Howard Gordon, Sally Grace, Oscar Garcia, George Grauer, John Greenwald, Wayne Grove, Jess Guffey, Bill Haber, George Henn, Mike Hersh, John Inouye, Edward J. Kabala, Judy and Norman Kay, Lew Lipset, Dave Lucey, Paul Marchant, Brian Marcy (Scottsdale Baseball Cards), Dr. John McCue, Mike Mosier (Columbia City Collectibles Co.), Clark Muldavin, B.A. Murry, Pacific Trading Cards (Mike Cramer and Bob Wilke), Steven Panet, Earl N. Petersen (U.S.A. Coins), J.C (Boo) Phillips, Pinnacle (Laurie Goldberg), Jack Pollard, Jonathan Pullano, Tom Reid, Henry M. Reizes, Gavin Riley, Alan Rosen (Mr. Mint), Rotman Productions, John Rumierz, San Diego Sport Collectibles (Bill Goepner and Nacho Arredondo), Kevin Savage (Sports Gallery), Mike Schechter (MSA), Dan Sherlock, Bill Shonscheck, Glen J. Sidler, John Spalding, Spanky's, Nigel Spill (Oldies and Goodies), Sports Collectors Store (Pat Quinn and Don Steinbach), Frank Steele, Murvin Sterling, Dan Stickney, Steve Taft, Ed Taylor, Lee Temanson, Topps (Marty Appel, Sy Berger and Melissa Rosen), Upper Deck (Rich Bradley), Bill Vizas, Bill Wesslund (Portland Sports Card Co.), Jim Woods, Kit Young, Robert Zanze, and Bill Zimpleman.

Many other individuals have provided price input, illustrative material, checklist verifications, errata, and/or background information. At the risk of inadvertently overlooking or omitting these many contributors, we should like to personally thank Joseph A. Abram, Jerry Adamic, Tom Akins, Anthony Amada Jr., Dennis Anderson, Ellis Anmuth, Toni Axtell, Darryl B. Baker, Earle Baldwin, Baseball Cards Plus, Baseball Hobby News (Frank and Vivian Barning), William E. Baxendale, Bay State Cards (Lenny DeAngelico), John Beaman, Glen Beram (Lakeside National Cards, Inc.), Philip Berg, Carl Bergstrom, Beulah Sports, Brian Bigelow (Candl), Walter Bird, Theodore Bodnar, Keith and Ryan Bonner, Gary Boyd, Dan Brandenburg, Briggs Sportscards, Fritz Brogan, Douglas J. Brown (Doug's Dugout), George and Donald Brown, Jason Brown, Dan Bruner (The Card King), Bob Bubnick, Buckhead Baseball Cards (Marc Spector), Terry L. Bunt, Virgil Burns, California Card Co., David Cadelina, Mark Cantin, Danny Cariseo, Cee Tim's Cards, N. Garrett Chan (The Greatest Moment), Dwight Chapin, Philip L. Chapman, Manfred Chiu, Judy Chung (The Sportsman's Gallery), Michael Chung, Shane Cohen (Grand Slam), Barry Colla, Collectors Edge, Matt Collett, Jose E. Conde, H. William Cook, Joe Court, Steve Crane, Rob Croft, Robert Curtis, Herb Dallas Jr., David Diehl, Byron Dittamore, Bill Dodson, Cliff

400 / Acknowledgments

Dolgins, Discount Dorothy, Robin Doty, Eagle Collectibles, Ed Emmitt, Mark Enger, Tom England, Michael Estreicher, Karen Eudaley, Gary Farbstein, L.V. Fischer (The Collectors Den), G.E. Forst, Steve Foster, Mark Franke, Doug French, Rob Gagnon, Steve Galletta, Tony Galovich, Ron Gerencher, Michael R. Gionet, Steve Gold (AU Sports), Jeff Goldstein, Mark Goodman, Arthur Goyette, Gary W. Graber (Minden Games), David Grauf (Cards for the Connoisseur), Don Guilbert, Hall's Nostalgia, Monty Hamilton, Wynn Hansen, Lenny Helicher, Bill Henderson, Jerry and Etta Hersh, Clay Hill, Alisa Hills, H.L.T. and T. Sports (Harold and Todd Nelkin), Will Ho, Russell Hoffman, Home Plate of Provo (Ken Edick), Chris Hooper, James R. Hopper III, Keith Hora, Gene Horvath, Steve Johnson, Barbara-Lee Jordan, James Jordan (Squeeze Play), Jay and Mary Kasper, Alan Kaye, Koinz and Kardz, George Koziol, Roger Krafve, Thomas Kunnecke, Tim Landis, William Langley, Ted Larkins (The Card Clubhouse), Dan Lavin, John Law, Stephen M. Lawson, Henry Lee, Irv Lerner, Howie Levy, Scott Lewandowski, Kendall Loyd (Orlando Sportscards South), Brian Luther, Jim Macie, Ben Macre, Jack Maiden, Larry Marks, Robert Matonis, Jack Mayes, Mike McDonald (Sports Page), Brad McNail (ACCI Sports Cards), James McNaughton, Patrick Menasche, Blake Meyer, Deron Milligan, Pat Mills, Ronald Moermond, J.L. Montgomery Inc. (Colorado Cards), William Moorhead, Joe Morano, Michael Moretto, Brian Morris, John G. Most, Jeff Mowers, Randy Munn, Michael J. Nadeau, Dr. Richard Neel, Robert Neff, No Gum Just Cards, Lon J. Normandin, Efrain Ochoa, John O'Hara, G. Michael Oyster, Russ Palmer, Ed Parkin (Home Front), Clay Pasternack, Bill Pekarik (Pastime Hobbies), Daren Pelletier, Richard Pellizzer, G.N. Perkins (Illini Sportscards), Michael Petruso, Tom Pfirrmann, Wesley Philpott, Roger Porter, Adam Price, Lee Prince (Time Out Sports Shop), Randy Ramuglia, Richard H. Ranck, Phil Regli, David Renshaw, Rocky Mountain Sports Cards, Chuck Roethel, Terry Sack, Joe Sak, Dale A. Sakamoto, Jennifer Salems, Garret Salomon, Ron Sanders, Ray Sandlin, Bob Santos, Guy Scebat, Nathan Schank, Jason Schubert, Sebring Sports, Steven Senft, Rob Shilt, Greg Sholes (Hall of Fame Sportscards), Ryan Shrimplin, Darrin Silverman, Tom Skinner, Ron Smith, Steve Smith (Sports Memories, Inc.), David Snider, Bob Snyder, Carl Specht, Sports Legends, Paul M. Stefani, Allen Stengel (Perfect Image), Cary Stephenson, Arnold Stern, Jason Stern, Rao Tadikonda, George Tahinos, Mark Tanaka (Front Row), Chad Taniguchi, Chris Tateosian, Paul S. Taylor, Steve Taylor, Harold Teller, Nick Teresi, Bud Tompkins (Minnesota Connection), Felix F. Torres (Ponce Card & Memorabilia), Huy Tran, Jeffrey K. Tsai, Peter Tsang, Carlo Tulloch, University Trading Cards (Mike Livingston), Mark Velger (Trade Mark SportsCards), Steve Verkman (Baseball Cards & Sports Memorabilia), Adam Wandy, Howard Weissman, Adam B. Weldaz, Richard West, Paul Wetterau, Brian Wilkie, Ali Raza Williams, Al Wong, Jeff Williams, Mark Williams, Opry Winston, Matt Winters, John L. Witcher, Mike Woods (The Dugout), World Series Cards (Neil Armstrong), Scot York, Zards Cards, Dean Zindler, and Adam Zuwerink.

Every year we make active solicitations for expert input. We are particularly appreciative of the help (however extensive or cursory) provided for this volume. We receive many inquiries, comments and questions regarding material within this book. In fact, each and every one is read and digested. Time constraints, however, prevent us from personally replying. But keep sharing your knowledge. Your letters and input are part of the "big picture" of hobby information we can pass along to readers of our books and magazines. Even though we cannot respond to each letter, you are making significant contributions to the hobby through your interest and comments.

The effort to continually refine and improve this book also involves a growing number of people and types of expertise on our home team. Our company boasts a substantial Collectibles Data Publishing team, which strengthens our ability to provide comprehensive analysis of the marketplace. Collectibles Data Publishing capably handled numerous technical details and provided able assistance in the preparation of this edition.

Our basketball analysts played a major part in compiling this year's book, travelling thousands of miles during the past year to attend sports card shows and visit card shops around the United States and Canada. The Beckett basketball specialists are Steven Judd, Lon Levitan, and Rob Springs (Price Guide Editor). Their baseline analysis and careful proofreading were key contributions to the accuracy of this book.

Rob Springs' coordination of input as Beckett Basketball Monthly Price Guide Editor helped immeasurably, as did Lon Levitan's never-ending information gathering efforts. Pat Blandford, Steven Judd and Rich Klein also contributed many hours of painstaking analysis in the specialist roles.

The effort was led by the Vice President of Beckett Interactive Mark Harwell and Dan Hitt, the manager of Collectibles Data Publishing. They were ably assisted by the rest of the Price Guide analysts: Mark Anderson, Wayne Grove, Doug Kale, Grant Sandground and Bill Sutherland. Also contributing to Collectibles Data Publishing functions were Jeany Finch, Beverly Mills and Gabriel Rangel.

The price gathering and analytical talents of this fine group of hobbyists have helped make our Beckett team stronger, while making this guide and its companion monthly Price Guide more widely recognized as the hobby's most reliable and relied upon sources of pricing information.

The IS (Information Services) department, ably headed by Airey Baringer, played a critical role in technology. Assisting the IS role are Dana Alecknavage and Eric Best who spent countless hours programming, testing, and implementing it to simplify the handling of thousands of prices that must be checked and updated for each edition.

In the Production Department, Paul Kerutis and Patty Burrell were responsible for the typesetting and for the card photos you see throughout the book.

In the years since this guide debuted, Beckett Publications has grown beyond any rational expectation. A great many talented and hard working individuals have been instrumental in this growth and success. Our whole team is to be congratulated for what we together have accomplished.

Our Beckett Publications team is led by President Jeff Amano, Vice Presidents Claire Backus and Joe Galindo, Directors Jeff Anthony, C.R.Conant, Beth Harwell and Margaret Steele. They are ably assisted by Pete Adauto, Dana Alecknavage, John Ayres, Joel Brown, Kaye Ball, Airey Baringer, Therese Bellar, Julie Binion, Amy Brougher, Bob Brown, Angie Calandro, Allen Christopherson, Randall Calvert, Cara Carmichael, Susan Catka, Albert Chavez, Marty Click, Amy Durett, Von Daniel, Aaron Derr, Ryan Duckworth, Mitchell Dyson, Eric Evans, Kandace Elmore, Craig Ferris, Gean Paul Figari, Carol Fowler,Laura Garbeff, Mary Gonzalez-Davis, Rosanna Gonzalez-Oleachea, Jeff Greer, Robert Gregory, Jenifer Grellhesl, Julie Grove, Barry Hacker, Tracy Hackler, Patti Harris, Mark Hartley, Joanna Hayden, Chris Hellem, Pepper Hastings, Bob Johnson, Jamie Joyce, Doug Kale, Kevin King, Justin Kanoya, Eddie Kelly, Gayle Klancnik, Rudy J. Klancnik, Tom Layberger, Jane Ann Layton, Benedito Leme, Lori Lindsey, Stanley Lira, Louis Marroquin, John Marshall, Mike McAllister, Teri McGahey, Matt McGuire, Omar Mediano, Sherry Monday, Mila Morante, Daniel Moscoso Jr., Allan Muir, Hugh Murphy,

Shawn Murphy, Mike Obert, Stacy Olivieri, Andrea Paul, Clark Palomino, Mike Pagel, Wendy Pallugna, Missy Patrello, Laura Patterson, Mike Payne, Tim Polzer, Bob Richardson, Lisa Runyon, Wade Rugenstein, Christine Seibert, Brett Setter, Len Shelton, Dave Sliepka, Judi Smalling, Quentin Smith, Sheri Smith, Jeff Stanton, Marcia Stoesz, Mark Stokes, Dawn Sturgeon, Margie Swoyer, Tina Tackett, Doree Tate, Jim Tereschuk, Jim Thompson, Susan Thompson, Doug Williams, Michelle Wilson, Steve Wilson, Ed Wornson, David Yandry, Bryan Winstead, Jay Zwerner and Mark Zeske. The whole Beckett Publications team has my thanks for jobs well done. Thank you, everyone.

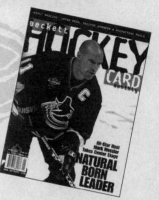

TIME OUT!

What do baseball, football and basketball have in common?—Dr. James Beckett, the leading authority on sports card values! All three price guides contain:

- All of the major series, including Topps
- Current market values
- Valuable tips on buying, selling, and finding cards
- Helpful two-price grading system

THESE BOOKS CAN'T BE BEAT!
House of Collectibles
Serving Collectors for More Than Thirty-Five Years

NOTES

NOTES

NOTES

NOTES

NOTES